A Historical Companion to Postcolonial Literatures in English

Outlining the historical contexts of postcolonial literatures, the *Companion* provides an important key to understanding complex contemporary debates about race, colonialism and neo-colonialism, politics, economics, culture and language. Its coverage of events, figures and movements along with political, social, and economic developments makes this indispensable reading for students, teachers and general readers alike.

Prem Poddar is Associate Professor in Postcolonial Studies at Aarhus University, Denmark. He is the author of *Violent Civilities: English, India, Culture* (Aarhus University Press, 2003) and editor of *Translating Nations* (Aarhus University Press, 2000) as well as of articles and book chapters in the area of postcolonial studies. His *Postkoloniale Perspektiver: Immigration, Identitet, Historie* (in Danish) is in press with Modtryk Forlaget.

David Johnson is Senior Lecturer in the Department of Literature at The Open University. He is the author of *Shakespeare and South Africa* (Clarendon Press, 1996), with Richard Danson Brown, of *Shakespeare 1609: Cymbeline and the Sonnets* (Macmillan, 2000) and, with Steve Pete and Max Du Plessis, of *Jurisprudence: A South African Perspective* (Butterworths, 2001). He is the editor, with Richard Danson Brown, of *A Shakespeare Reader: Sources and Criticism* (Macmillan, 2000).

Advisory Editors

Stephen Alomes	Shamil Jeppie
Karin Barber	Michelle Keown
Shirley Chew	Susan Knutson
Mahesh Daga	Shirley Lim
David Day	Geoff Nash
Denise DeCaries Narain	Bill Nasson
Justin Edwards	Susheila Nasta
Laura Fair	Benita Parry
Robert Fraser	David Richards
Bill Freund	Minoli Salgado
Katie Gramich	Mimi Sheller
Suman Gupta	Kelwyn Sole
Abdulrazak Gurnah	Dennis Walder

A Historical Companion to Postcolonial Literatures in English

Edited by Prem Poddar and David Johnson

Edinburgh University Press

Edinburgh University Press Ltd
22 George Square, Edinburgh

First published in hardback by Edinburgh Univerity Press in 2005

Typeset in 10/12 Goudy
by Servis Filmsetting Ltd, Stockport, Cheshire, and
printed and bound in Great Britain by
CPI Antony Rowe, Chippenham, Wiltshire

A CIP record for this book is available from the British Library

ISBN 978 0 7486 3602 0 (paperback)

Contents

Preface   vi
Acknowledgements   viii
Chronology   ix
List of Entries   xxii
Maps   xxviii

The Companion   1

Contributors   545
Index of Literary Works   549
Subject Index   571

Preface

The injunction 'always historicise' reverberates like a mantra in postcolonial literary criticism. For a variety of reasons, it is an injunction that all too often remains a gesture, with postcolonial histories relegated to peremptory footnotes. The ambition of this *Companion* is to provide detail of the many histories of colonialism and neo-colonialism, and to encourage critical reflection on the relation between postcolonial literary works and their historical contexts. To this end, we have assembled just over 220 entries written by 166 postcolonial scholars that survey major events, ideas, movements, and figures that constitute the historical contexts of postcolonial literatures.

The *Companion* focuses principally on the histories of postcolonial literatures in the Anglophone world – Africa (East, Southern and West), Australia, Canada, the Caribbean, the Middle East, New Zealand, the Pacific, South Asia, and South-east Asia. For each of these parts of the former British Empire, in addition to entries on specific events, there are long survey entries on their respective historiographies and women's histories. There are also long entries discussing the literatures and histories of those further areas that have claimed the title 'postcolonial', notably Britain, East Asia, Ireland, Latin America and the United States. The entries cover the period after the end of colonial rule, but as many postcolonial literary works revisit the pre-colonial and colonial periods, the *Companion* includes many entries on these earlier periods too. Certain events that fall outside the Anglophone world, but which have had an impact on postcolonial literatures in English, are also included. A supplementary volume to this *Companion* on the postcolonial literatures of Continental Europe is underway, and will elaborate these events in much more detail. We remain conscious that much of Britain's postcolonial history has inevitably been left out, but believe that within the constraints of one volume, the vast complexity of this history is conveyed.

Each entry provides a summary of the historical event/ idea/ movement/ figure, as well as bibliographies of postcolonial literary works and histories for further reading. The *Companion* is extensively cross-referenced and indexed. All related entries are cross-referenced, and there are two indexes at the back: the first index lists all the literary works mentioned in the *Companion*, and the second is a general index of names and subjects.

What the *Companion* demonstrates vividly is the variety of historical experiences under colonialism and neo-colonialism. While certain imperial patterns of economic, political and cultural domination might have been imposed in broadly similar fashion, local conditions have guaranteed very different outcomes. These differences continue to mark contemporary postcolonial writing, as common critical terms assume different shades of meaning in the different post-colonies. Does 'subaltern agency' mean the same thing in Canada as it does in West Africa or South-east Asia? What are the connotations of the term 'settler' in the Middle East, East Africa and New Zealand? Does 'hybrid identity' mean the same thing in the Caribbean as it does in Britain or the United States? Does 'nation-as-imagined-community' have the same resonance in Pakistan as Nigeria or the Pacific? Does reclaiming pre-colonial cultures mean the same thing in Australia and India? Do 'revisionist historians' in Ireland and Southern Africa share the same politics? Crucially, who arbitrates or ultimately determines the meanings of these contested terms? These are all difficult questions, and to answer them we need to proceed beyond abstract ideas of The Postcolonial Condition, and examine in turn the particularities of each postcolonial context and its histories. This *Companion* is not, however, an attempt to establish History as the master discourse against which Literature must be measured; there are clearly as many competing historical accounts as there are different literary representations of post-colonial societies. We have, however, given significantly more weight to those histories of colonialism and neo-colonialism that refuse the dominant myths of the British Empire and its aftermath. Our hope ultimately is that by studying the literatures and histories of post-colonial societies in critical juxtaposition, this *Companion* might inform and invigorate contemporary debates about globalisation and neo-colonialism; gender inequality; racism and nationalism; and ethnic, cultural and religious conflict.

Prem Poddar and David Johnson

Acknowledgements

Our first debt is to Jackie Jones at Edinburgh University Press, who contracted the *Companion*, and has supported us along the way with great patience, enthusiasm, and unstinting professionalism. Carol McDonald at Edinburgh University Press has displayed similar qualities in her editorial duties, and her hard work on much of the invisible labour is much appreciated. Nicola Wood and James Dale were conscientious and understanding in their great efforts with the copy-editing. Secondly, we are immensely grateful to our 166 contributors, who have embraced the ambition and spirit of the project, and produced excellent work to tight deadlines. We were especially pleased to have recruited contributors from such a wide range of institutions across the postcolonial world. The *Companion* as a result represents a fair snapshot of what postcolonial studies means for historians, critics and writers around the world. The third group to thank are our advisory editors, who helped to assemble the list of entries, track down contributors, and check the final submitted entries. We are particularly in debt to those advisory editors who helped with regions and histories way beyond our own areas of research. Our respective colleagues, too, have helped the project immensely. In Aarhus, Cheralyn Mealor's assistance with the early stages of editing was invaluable, and Heidi Bojsen's help with the Chronology rescued us when yet another deadline loomed. Colleagues at the Open University – Robert Fraser, Katie Gramich, Suman Gupta, Stephanie Jones, Susheila Nasta, David Richards and Dennis Walder – also had their patience tested way beyond reasonable limits with endless queries. Finally, there are many others who have given their time and consideration to our efforts, and to them our very sincere thanks: Rehnuma Ahmed, Emma Barker, Amanda Hammar, Isabel Hofmeyr, Tabish Khair, Lars Jensen, Susan Knutson, Rajesh Mohey, Rob Morrell, Rajeev Patke, Anmole Prasad, Dominic Rainsford, Lance van Sittert, Andrew Watt, and Jenny Yamamoto.

Chronology

1497	During a voyage underwritten by Bristol merchants, John Cabot (Giovanni Caboto) claims Cape Breton Island or Newfoundland or Labrador for Henry VII of England (24 June).
1553	Earliest regular English voyages to Guinea in West Africa begin.
1564	John Hawkins begins slaving voyages.
1576	Frobisher's first expedition to Newfoundland.
1577–80	Francis Drake circumnavigates the globe.
1584	Walter Raleigh's expedition to Guiana.
1585	Francis Drake's expedition to the West Indies.
1587	Chartered English trade voyage to Senegambia region of West Africa.
1600	English East India Company Charter.
1616	Dirk Hartog makes first recorded European landing on Australian continent, in Western Australia.
1627	Barbados colony established.
1637	Pequot War ('Puritan' massacre of the Pequots in New England).
1641	English slave trade to Barbados begins.
1658	First slaves imported to Cape.
1661	James Fort (Gambia) founded.
	Barbados' slave and servant codes passed.
1667	The result of Canada's first census lists 3,215 non-native inhabitants.
1672	Royal Africa Company chartered.
1690	English settlement at Calcutta established.
1692	Slave revolt in Barbados.
1698	End of Royal African Company's monopoly, and slave trade officially opened to private traders.
1713	Treaty of Utrecht: in the Caribbean, Britain gains all of St Kitts and Asiento grant to import slaves into Spanish America; in Canada, Britain gains Hudson Bay, Newfoundland and Acadia (Cape Breton Island).
1730–9	First war against Jamaican Maroons.

1744   British take French ships. Start of hostilities in South Asia.

1749   Settlement established in Halifax, Nova Scotia.

1750   Company of Merchants takes over administration of African forts protecting the slave trade.

1755   'Neutral' French settlers expelled from Nova Scotia, and Britain scatters the Nova Scotia Acadians throughout other North American colonies.

1756   Nawab of Bengal captures Calcutta and the deaths in the 'Black Hole' follow.

1757   Clive recovers Calcutta and defeats Nawab at Battle of Plassey.

1759   Anglo-Cherokee War in North America.

1760   Tacky's slave rebellion in Jamaica.

            Amherst captures Montreal and New France surrenders.

1763   End of the Seven Years War between England and France. At the Treaty of Paris, Britain is 'ceded' islands in West Indies and Senegal, as well as France's North American possessions to Britain. A royal proclamation imposes British institutions on Quebec.

1767   First Mysore War (1767–9) in India.

1769   James Cook charts coast of New Zealand.

1770   Cook lands in Botany Bay, later names and takes possession of New South Wales for Britain.

1772   Somerset case in England interpreted as conferring freedom on slaves upon landing in England.

1775   Start of British war with Marathas in western India.

            American Revolution (ends 1783).

1780   Second Mysore War (1780–4) in India.

1783   Peace of Versailles: Britain recognises US independence, loses Tobago and Senegal.

1784   New colony of New Brunswick established.

1786   First British settlement on Malay coast at Penang.

1787   Settlement established with freed slaves in Freetown, Sierra Leone.

1788   Trial of Warren Hastings on charges of corrupt administration in India (1788–95).

            Captain Arthur Phillip arrives with first fleet and establishes Port Jackson penal settlement in New South Wales and later at Norfolk, Australia.

1790   Third Mysore War (1790–2) in India.

1791   Canada Act establishes colonies of Upper and Lower Canada.

1793	Mackenzie reaches the Pacific at Dean Channel.
1795	War against Maroons in Jamaica.
	Dutch surrender Ceylon to the British.
	The British replace the Dutch at the Cape Colony.
1798	In Santo Domingo, slave leader Toussaint L'Ouverture defeats General Maitland.
	Rebellion of United Irishmen led by Wolfe Tone defeated in Ireland.
1799	Death of Tipu and part of Mysore brought under British rule.
1801	British troops occupy Egypt.
1802	Peace of Amiens: Britain returns certain colonies (including the Cape) to the Dutch.
1804	Following the war of independence (1802–3), Dessaline declares Santo Domingo independent under the name of Haiti.
1806	British reoccupy the Cape Colony.
1807	British abolition of the Atlantic slave trade.
	Sierra Leone and Gambia become British Crown colonies.
1811	British occupy Java.
1812	The USA starts a war with Britain in Canada. The USA repelled, and war ends in 1814.
1813	East India Company Charter Act opens India trade and eases restrictions on missionaries' access to India.
1815	Defeat of Napoleon at Waterloo, and at the Vienna Settlement, British rule of Mauritius, Cape Colony, Tobago, St Lucia and Guiana confirmed. The Dutch reclaim Ceylon, Java, and other territories they had lost to France.
1816	Barbados slave rebellion. Imperial government recommends Slave Registration Act.
	Britain return Java to the Dutch.
1819	East India Company establishes a settlement in Singapore.
1821	North-West Company ends Montreal fur trade. The Hudson's Bay Company and the North West Company amalgamate, creating unemployment for a substantial proportion of their Métis workforce.
1824	First Anglo-Burmese War (1824–6).
	First Anglo-Asante War.
1826	First British settlements established in Western Australia.
1829	Entire Australian continent declared British.

1833	Legislation passed for the emancipation of slaves in British colonies on 1 August 1834, with full emancipation to follow after a lengthy apprenticeship, on 31 July 1838.
1834	Daniel O'Connell tries unsuccessfully to have Ireland's union with Great Britain repealed.
1835	T. B. Macaulay's Minute on Education in India.
1836	South Australia established as a colony of free settlers.
	Afrikaner migration northwards from British rule in the Cape in 'The Great Trek'.
1837	Report of the Select Committee on Aborigines. Aborigines' Protection Society formed.
	Revolts in Lower and Upper Canada.
1838	First Afghan War (1838–42).
	First indentured labourers from India arrive in the Caribbean.
1839	First Opium War between Britain and China (1839–42).
1840	First signing of the Treaty of Waitangi in New Zealand.
	Lower and Upper Canada united by an Act of Parliament.
1841	British sovereignty over Hong Kong proclaimed.
1843	British annexation of Natal.
	Maori revolts against the British in New Zealand.
1845	First British-Sikh War in India (1845–6). British forces defeat the Sikhs.
1846	Theophilus Shepstone introduces segregated administration for Africans in Natal (the template for indirect rule).
	Repeal of the Corn Laws ends protectionism. Beginning of free trade.
	Beginning of potato famine in Ireland.
1848	Second British-Sikh War (1848–9), which ends in defeat for the Sikhs, and annexation of the Punjab by the British.
1852	Second Anglo-Burmese War (1852–3) leads to annexation of Lower Burma.
1854–6	Crimean War.
	Eureka Stockade, the unsuccessful miners' rebellion in Ballarat, Australia.
1856	Xhosa cattle-killing (1856–7) on eastern Cape Colony frontier.
	Britain begins war with Persia (1856–7).
	Outbreak of the Anglo-Chinese War (1856–8).
	Race riots in British Guiana.

1857	Outbreak of the Great Indian Rebellion (Indian Mutiny) (1857–8).
	First Indian Universities founded.
1858	Government of India Act abolishes the East India Company. Straits Settlements transferred from East India Company to the new India Office.
	Chinese immigrants from California arrive in British Columbia, attracted by the Fraser River Gold Rush.
	British campaign against tribes on north-west India frontier.
1860	Introduction of Indian indentured labourers to Natal (ends 1911).
	Second Maori War (1860–70).
1862	Amalgamation of Lower Burma, Arakan, and Tenasserim.
1865	Morant Bay rebellion in Jamaica.
1867	British North America Act establishes the Dominion of Canada.
1868	British forces invade Abyssinia.
1871	Britain annexes diamond-rich Griqualand West.
1873	Anglo-Asante War begins (1873–4).
	Famine in Bengal
1874	British annexation of Fiji.
1877	British annexation of Transvaal, South Africa.
1879	Anglo-Zulu War, British defeated at Isandhlwana, but achieve victory at Ulundi.
	British invasion of Afghanistan (1879–80).
1880	First South African (Anglo-Boer) War, with British defeat at Majuba Hill in February 1881.
	Bushranger Ned Kelly captured and hanged in Melbourne, Australia.
1882	British forces invade and occupy Cairo.
1883	Britain evacuates Sudan because of nationalist uprising led by the Mahdi.
	Formation of National Association for Promoting State-Directed Emigration and Colonisation.
1885	Formation of the Indian National Congress.
	Berlin Africa Conference (1884–5).
	British protectorates declared over Niger River region, Bechuanaland and Southern New Guinea.
	Suppression of Riel's rebellion in north-west Canada.
	Invasion of Upper Burma, followed by annexation in 1886.

1886	Transvaal gold rush and foundation of Johannesburg.
	Anglo-German agreement on spheres of influence in East Africa.
1888	Sikkim War.
1892	First sitting of the Maori Parliament.
1894	Uganda becomes a British protectorate.
1896	Chimurenga uprising (1896–7) against British in Rhodesia put down.
1898	Spanish-American War.
	Kitchener defeats Mahdist forces in the Sudan at the Battle of Omdurman.
1899	South African War (Anglo-Boer War) (1899–1902).
1900	British invasion and annexation of Asante (Gold Coast).
	Violent suppression of the Boxer Rebellion after 56-day siege.
	Asante rebels attack Britain's Kumasi fort in the Gold Coast.
	Colonial Office takes over administrative responsibility for Nigeria, and conquest of Northern Nigeria concluded with Kano and Sokoto taken in 1903.
	Annexation of Cook Islands by New Zealand.
1901	British concentration camps for Boer women and children in South Africa.
	Australian Immigration Restriction Act legislates a whites-only immigration policy.
	Britain annexes the Asante kingdom as part of the Gold Coast.
1902	Canada, Australia and New Zealand announce tariff preferences on British goods.
1904	Colonial Office takes over administration in Nyasaland, Uganda, East Africa protectorate, and Somaliland.
1905	British partition of Bengal, resistance by Indian National Congress.
	British Parliament passes Aliens' Act.
1906	All-India Muslim League established.
	British troops put down protests by Tiv people against Muslim Hausa rule in northern Nigeria.
	Zulu rebellion (Bambatha's rebellion) repressed.
1907	Colonial Conferences become institutionalised as Imperial Conferences: favour promotion of Empire settlement over foreign emigration.
1910	Canadian Immigration Act.
	Northern Nigeria Land and Native Rights Proclamation.
	Union of South Africa, Louis Botha the first prime minister.

1912   Foundation of South African Native National Congress, subsequently known as the African National Congress (ANC).

1913   South Africa Native Land Act. Language tests prescribed for immigrants to South Africa.

1914   Egypt declared a British protectorate and Khedive Abbas II deposed.

1915   Uprising led by John Chilembwe in Nyasaland put down.

          British conquest of Mesopotamia (Iraq).

1916   Home Rule Leagues established in India. Lucknow Pact between Muslim League and Indian National Congress.

          Female suffrage is first granted in Canada (Manitoba).

          Republicans revolt against British rule in Ireland's Easter Rising.

1917   Balfour Declaration promises British support of 'National Home for Jews' in Palestine.

          After pressure from Indian nationalists, indentured labour in the West Indies is banned by the Colonial Office (system carries on to 1921).

1919   Creation of overseas settlement schemes.

          Gandhi leads first all-India *satyagraha* against the Rowlatt Act.

          British troops kill 379 when they open fire on a peaceful demonstration, in Jallianwalla Bagh (Amritsar) massacre.

          Ceylon National Congress established.

          Riots in Jamaica, British Honduras, and Trinidad.

1920   Britain receives Mandate for Palestine and Iraq.

          Formation of National Congress of British West Africa.

1925   Dominions Office set up in Britain, and Imperial Conference in 1926 defines dominion status.

1928   Introduction of Crown colony government in British Guiana.

          The Supreme Court of Canada rules that the BNA Act does not define women as 'persons' and they are therefore not eligible to hold public office (overruled in 1929).

1929   'Women's war' anti-tax protests in south-east Nigeria.

1930   Gandhi leads Salt March, major civil disobedience campaign. Conference on India in London and brief truce in 1931.

          Hsaya San rebellion in Burma (1930–2).

1932   Indian National Congress banned and Gandhi arrested. Protest campaign resumed in 1932, and then suspended again in 1934.

1935	Government of India Act provides for provincial self-government, separates Burma from India.
1937	Aden becomes a British Crown colony.
	Cocoa farmers in Gold Coast and Nigeria launch trade boycott (1937–8).
1938	Aborigines' Progressive Association declares 26 January a 'day of mourning'.
1939	Viceroy declares India at war without consulting Indian leaders.
	Construction of Burma Road.
1940	Idola Saint-Jean with other feminists succeed in obtaining the vote for Québecois women.
	Britain authorises the transfer of Arab land to Jews in Palestine.
1941	Civil disobedience campaign protesting against the war in India.
1942	'Quit India' movement, Gandhi and Congress leaders jailed. Defection of 55,000 Indian soldiers from the Indian Army in support of Subhas Chandra Bose, who seeks links with the Japanese.
	Fall of Singapore and collapse of British Empire in the Far East.
1943	Famine in Bengal (1943–4) and an estimated three million starve to death.
1944	Bretton Woods Conference establishes World Bank and International Monetary Fund.
1945	United Nations Organisation established.
1946	Philippines achieve independence.
1947	Britain announces withdrawal from Palestine, United Nations Special Committee on Palestine (UNSCOP) proposes partition.
	Partition and independence of India and Pakistan. Fighting between India and Pakistan over Kashmir (1947–9).
	Burmese independence leader U Aung San assassinated shortly before Burma becomes a republic outside the British Commonwealth.
	European migration programme begins in Australia.
1948	Assassination of Gandhi.
	Burma gains independence and leaves the Commonwealth.
	Nationalist Party wins elections in South Africa.
	Riots in Accra, Gold Coast.
	British withdrawal from Palestine, State of Israel proclaimed, first Arab-Israeli War.
	Ceylon achieves independence (renamed Sri Lanka 1972).

Malayan communist rebels partially repressed by the British Army. Twelve-year war begins.

1949   Indonesia achieves independence, with Sukarno as first president.

Republic declared in Ireland.

1950   Establishment of Congress of Peoples Against Imperialism.

Colombo Conference of Commonwealth ministers leads to Colombo Plan for economic development in South and South-east Asia (1951–77).

1951   Pakistani Prime Minister Liaquat Ali Khan assassinated, Pakistan enters period of civil disorder.

Muhammed Mussadegh becomes prime minister of Iran and questions Britain's oil interests.

1952   Mau Mau rebellion in Kenya begins, and a state of emergency declared (1957–9). Repressive measures adopted, including forced resettlement. Estimates of up to 150,000 Kenyans killed.

Kwame Nkrumah becomes prime minister in Gold Coast.

Muhammad Neguib and Gamal Abdel Nasser seize power in Egypt, and a year later proclaim a republic.

Eritrea incorporated into Ethiopia as British troops leave.

1953   Creation of Central African Federation combining Northern and Southern Rhodesia and Nyasaland.

In Guyana, Cheddi Jagan's People's Progressive Party wins elections on a socialist, anti-colonial platform; Britain sends troops, suspends the constitution, and jails Jagan for six months.

1954   Nigerian constitution creates federal structure uniting northern, eastern and western Nigeria, along with the UN Trust Territory of the Cameroons and the federal territory of Lagos.

Algerian war of independence begins (1954–62).

1955   Bandung Conference inaugurates Non-Aligned Movement committed to protecting the interests of developing countries during the Cold War.

Congress of the People in Kliptown, South Africa, organised by the ANC, adopts the Freedom Charter.

Sudan wins independence from Britain and Egypt.

1956   Nasser nationalises Suez Canal Company, which precipitates the Suez Crisis.

In South Africa, 'coloureds' removed from Cape voters' roll. Women lead mass anti-pass law demonstrations.

1957   Gold Coast achieves independence as Ghana, but remains within Commonwealth.

Malaya achieves independence, with Abdul Rahman as first premier.

1958   West Indies Federation established.

All-Africa Conference in Ghana, seeking to co-ordinate anti-colonial movements in Africa.

1959   Singapore achieves internal self-government under Chief Minister Lee Kuan Yew.

Cuban revolution under the leadership of Fidel Castro.

Anti-British riots in Nyasaland and Northern Rhodesia, and leaders including Hastings Banda and Kenneth Kaunda arrested.

1960   Nigeria achieves independence from Britain, as do a number of other European colonies: French Congo, the Belgian Congo, Chad, Central African Republic, Togo, and Madagascar.

Sharpeville Massacre in South Africa, and the banning of ANC, Communist Party and PAC.

Canadian Bill of Rights approved. Native people win the right to vote in federal elections.

1961   South Africa leaves the Commonwealth to become the Republic of South Africa.

Sierra Leone, Tanganyika and Zanzibar achieve independence.

1962   Uganda, Trinidad and Tobago, and Jamaica become independent within the Commonwealth.

Algeria War ends and Algeria achieves independence.

Commonwealth Settlement Act and Commonwealth Immigrants Act.

Indo-Chinese War over border dispute.

Canada revokes ethnic discrimination in immigration legislation.

1963   Formation of the Organisation of African Unity.

Kenya achieves independence, and a year later becomes a republic under Jomo Kenyatta.

Singapore becomes independent as part of the Federation of Malaysia.

1964   Nyasaland (as Malawi), Northern Rhodesia (as Zambia) and Malta achieve independence.

Tanganyika and Zanzibar amalgamate to become Tanzania.

The Palestinian Liberation Organisation is formed.

Nelson Mandela and a number of other ANC leaders receive life sentences for treason.

1965   Singapore secedes from the Federation of Malaysia.

Gambia achieves independence.

Unilateral Declaration of Independence (UDI) by minority white government in Rhodesia.

Cook Islands achieve self-government in association with New Zealand.

Second Indo-Pakistan War over Kashmir (1965–6).

With US and British support, Suharto seizes power in Indonesia on the pretext of stemming communism, killing 700,000 and imprisoning 200,000 in the process.

1966   British Guiana (as Guyana), Barbados, Basutoland (as Lesotho) and Bechuanaland (as Botswana) achieve independence.

Military coup in Nigeria.

Nkrumah overthrown in Ghana.

1967   Ibo leader Odumegwu Oukwu declares the Republic of Biafra independent. Federal troops invade Biafra and reincorporate Biafra into Nigeria (1967–70).

After a referendum, Aboriginal Australians win full citizenship, but not land rights.

1968   Nauru, Mauritius and Swaziland achieve independence.

British decide to withdraw militarily from 'East of Suez'.

Kenya withdraws trading licences from Asians, leading to a mass exodus.

Commonwealth Immigration Act in Britain imposes immigration quotas.

1970   Independence of Fiji and Tonga. They join Commonwealth along with Western Samoa.

Gambia becomes an independent state within the Commonwealth.

1971   Civil war in Pakistan as Bangladesh (East Pakistan) declares independence from West Pakistan. West Pakistan troops attack Dacca, killing thousands and producing two million refugees who are decimated by cholera epidemic. India intervenes by invading Bangladesh, (the third Indo-Pakistan War), and helps East Pakistan become the independent state of Bangladesh.

In Uganda, Idi Amin overthrows Milton Obote and bans all political opposition.

1972   Aborigines in Australia set up 'tent embassy' at Parliament House, Canberra.

Bloody Sunday in Ireland when British paratroopers kill thirteen nationalist marchers on a civil rights march in Derry.

In Uganda, Amin expels 50,000 Asians.

In Australia, Whitlam's Labour government scraps the White Australia immigration policy.

1973   The Bahamas achieve independence.

            Yom Kippur War as Syria and Egypt attack Israel. Israel regains the Golan
            Heights.

1974   Grenada achieves independence.

            FRELIMO in Mozambique ends Portuguese colonial rule and assumes power.

            Niue achieves self-government in association with New Zealand.

1975   Independence for Angola and Guinea-Bissau (from Portugal), and Papua
            New Guinea (from Australia).

            Waitangi Tribunal created in New Zealand to address Maori concerns.

            Indonesian troops invade East Timor as it is about to achieve independence
            from Portugal.

1976   Student-led revolt in Soweto, South Africa against compulsory tuition in
            Afrikaans.

            Seychelles achieve independence.

1978   Tuvalu (Ellice Islands) and the Solomon Islands achieve independence.

1979   Revolution in Iran, the Shah is forced into exile, and Ayatollah Khomeini
            takes over control of the armed forces.

            Kiribati (Gilbert Islands), St Lucia, St Vincent and the Grenadines achieve
            independence.

1980   Rhodesia achieves majority rule as the independent state of Zimbabwe under
            Robert Mugabe's ZANU Party.

            Tanzanian forces invade Uganda and overthrow dictator Idi Amin, and
            Milton Obote takes control again.

            Vanuatu (New Hebrides) achieves independence.

1981   Belize (formerly British Honduras) and Antigua-Barbuda achieve indepen-
            dence.

            US-backed contras begin covert intervention in Nicaragua.

1983   USA invades Grenada.

1984   Brunei achieves independence.

1988   Bicentenary celebration in Australia accompanied by strong Aboriginal
            protests.

            Palestinian *intifada* rebellion begins on the West Bank and Gaza.

1989   USA invades Panama.

1990   In South Africa, leaders and members of anti-apartheid parties, including
            Nelson Mandela of the ANC, are set free, and negotiations towards ending
            apartheid set in motion.

Namibia achieves independence; SWAPO, led by Sam Nujoma, takes power.

1991   Elections in Zambia see Frederick Chiluba defeat Kaunda after twenty-seven years in power.

First Gulf War, precipitated by Iraq's invasion of Kuwait.

Indonesian forces kill thousands of East Timorese demonstrators.

1992   Aboriginal land rights recognised in the Mabo case in Australia.

1993   Banda voted out of power in Malawi.

1994   In South Africa, ANC win the first democratic elections, and Mandela becomes president.

Rwandan genocide in which approximately 900,000 Tutsi are killed by Hutu militias.

1997   Hong Kong handed over by British to China after ninety-nine year lease.

1998   Canadian federal government issues formal apology to native peoples for past injustices.

USA launches missile attack on pharmaceutical factory in Sudan.

1999   In November 1999, 70,000 anti-globalisation activists protest against the neo-liberal economic polices of the G8 and the World Trade Organisation in Seattle.

2001   Following the attack on the World Trade Center on 11 September, the US president George W. Bush declares an international war on terror, and invades Afghanistan.

Australia refuses to receive 433 asylum-seekers picked up from a sinking ship by the Norwegian vessel MV *Tampa*.

2003   A US-led coalition army bypasses UN Security Council resolutions and invades Iraq (second Gulf War).

Entries

Algerian War of Independence
Amin, Idi
Anglicisation
Anglo-Boer War
Anglo-Burmese Wars
Anglo-Zulu War
Anti-colonialism and Resistance: Caribbean
Anti-colonialism and Resistance: East Africa
Anti-colonialism and Resistance: South Asia
Anti-colonialism and Resistance: Southern Africa
Anti-colonialism and Resistance: West Africa
Anti-globalisation Movements
Anti-war Movements: Australia
Apartheid and Segregation
Asante Wars
Asian Expulsions: East Africa
Asianisation: Australia
Aung San Suu Kyi

'Back-to Africa' Movement
Balfour Declaration
Banda, Ngwazi Hastings Kamazu
Bangladesh: 1971
Battle of the Plains of Abraham
Bengal Famine
Berlin Conference
Biafran War
Big Bear
Black Britain
Black Consciousness: Southern Africa
Black Hole
Boat People
Border Disputes: South Asia
Botany Bay Convicts
Britain's Postwar Foreign Policy
British Imperialism
Bumiputra

Cabral, Amílcar
Castes: South Asia

Cattle-Killing
Chauri Chaura Incident
Chimurengas
Chinese Gold-diggers
Colonial Cultural Cringe: Australia
Coloured: Southern Africa
Commonwealth
Communism: South Asia
Communism: South-east Asia
Creolisation
Cromer, Lord
Cuban Revolution

Decolonisation
Detention Centres: Australia
Diaspora: Caribbean
Diaspora: Pacific
Diaspora: South Asia
Dutch East India Company (VOC)

East Asia
East India Company
East Timor
Emergency: India
English in India: Eighteenth and Nineteenth Centuries
Engmalchin
European Exploration and Settlement: Australia, New Zealand, Pacific
European Exploration and Settlement: Canada

Fanon, Frantz
Free Trade
Frontier Wars: Southern Africa

Garvey, Marcus Mosiah
Genocide: Canada
Genocide: Rwanda
Governors-General and Viceroys

Haitian Revolution
Hill Stations
Historiography: Australia
Historiography: British Empire
Historiography: Canada
Historiography: Caribbean
Historiography: East Africa
Historiography: Middle East
Historiography: South Asia
Historiography: South-east Asia

Historiography: Southern Africa
Historiography: West Africa
HIV/AIDS
Hong Kong Handover
Hudson's Bay Company

Indentured Labour: Caribbean
Indian National Army
Indians: Southern Africa
Indigo Rebellion
Indirect Rule
International Monetary Fund
Inuit
Iranian Revolution
Ireland
Islam

Jallianwala Bagh Massacre
James, C. L. R.
Japanese Internment: Canada
Japanese Occupation: South-east Asia
Jinnah, Mohammed Ali
JVP Insurrection

Kala Pani
Kama Sutra
Kashmir Dispute
Kaunda, Kenneth David
Kelly, Ned
Kemalism
Kenya African National Union
Khama, Seretse

Labour Histories: Southern Africa
Land: Australia
Land: Canada
Land: South Asia
Land: Southern Africa
Languages and Ethnicities: South Asia
Languages and Ethnicities: West Africa
Latin America
Lee Kuan Yew
Levant Company
Liberalism: Southern Africa

Maaori
Maghrebine Resistance: Algeria
Maghrebine Resistance: Morocco and Tunisia

Mahdism
Marcos, Ferdinand and Imelda
Merdeka
Mfecane
Migrancy: Southern Africa
Military Dictatorships: South Asia
Mineral Revolution: Southern Africa
Missionaries: Southern Africa
Morant Bay Uprising
Multiculturalism: Australia
Multiculturalism: Canada
Multinationals
Music: Caribbean
Music: East Africa
Music: West Africa
Mutinies in India

Nasser, Abdel Gamal
Nationalism(s): Arab
Nationalism(s): Canada
Nationalism(s): Southern Africa
Native Reservations
Naxalites
Negritude
Nehru, Jawaharlal
Nkrumah, Kwame
Nyerere, Julius and Ujamaa

Oil: Middle East
Ottoman Empire

Pacific Sub-imperialism
Pacific Way
Pakeha
Pakistan's Subaltern Struggles
Palestinian Political Movements
Pan-Africanism
Partition
Post-apartheid
Pre-colonial Histories: Australia
Pre-colonial Histories: Caribbean
Pre-colonial Histories: East Africa
Pre-colonial Histories: South Asia
Pre-colonial Histories: Southern Africa
Pre-colonial Histories: West Africa
Progressive Writers' Movement

Quebec Independence Movement

Racial Discrimination Act: Australia
Raj
Rebellions: Australia
Refugees
Religions: East Africa
Religions: South Asia
Religions: Southern Africa
Religions: West Africa
Riel's Métis Rebellion
Rodney, Walter
Rushdie Affair

San
Secessionism: South Asia
Senghor, Léopold Sédar
Sinhala Only Bill
Slave Trade: East Africa
Slavery: Caribbean
Slavery: Southern Africa
Slavery: West Africa
Spanish-American War
Sri Lankan Civil War
Stolen Generations
Straits Settlements
Sudanese Civil War
Suez Crisis

Terrorism: South Asia
Thomasites
Tourism: Caribbean

Underground Railroad: Canada
United Nations
United States of America
Universities: East Africa
Universities: West Africa
Urabi Revolt

Vietnam War

Wabenzi
Waitangi Treaty
War of 1812
West Indies Federation
White Australia Policy
Williams, Eric
Women's Histories: Australia, New Zealand, and the Pacific
Women's Histories: Canada

Women's Histories: Caribbean
Women's Histories: East Africa
Women's Histories: Middle East
Women's Histories: South Asia
Women's Histories: South-east Asia
Women's Histories: Southern Africa
Women's Histories: West Africa
World Bank
World Wars I and II: African Soldiers
World Wars I and II: Anzac
World Wars I and II: South African Soldiers
World Wars I and II: South Asian Soldiers

Years of Terror
Yellow Peril

Zionism

Maps

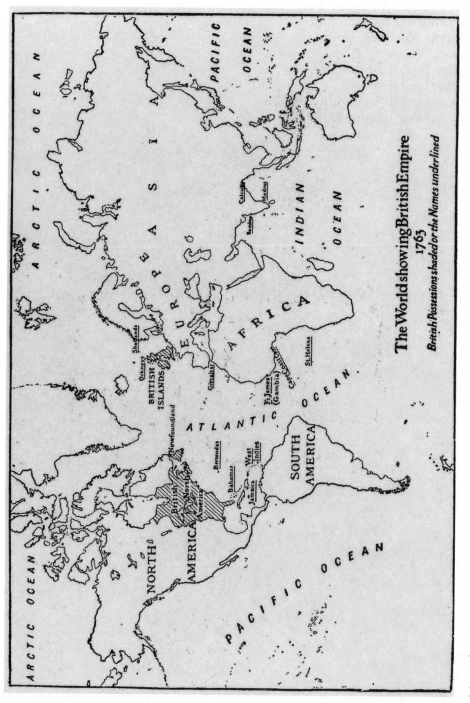

Map 1 from *Historical Atlas of the British Empire*, London: Macmillan and Co., 1924, p. 9.
Reproduced by permission of the British Library, Maps 27.b.39.

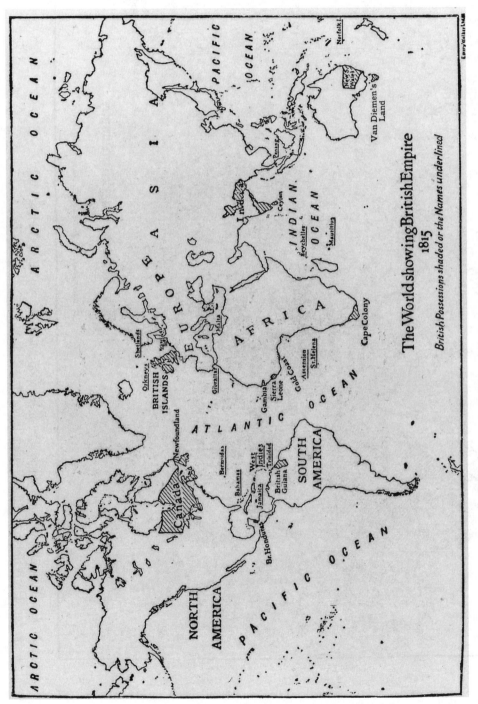

The World showing British Empire
1815
British Possessions shaded or the Names underlined

Map 2 from *Historical Atlas of the British Empire*, London: Macmillan and Co., 1924, p. 11.
Reproduced by permission of the British Library, Maps 27.b.39.

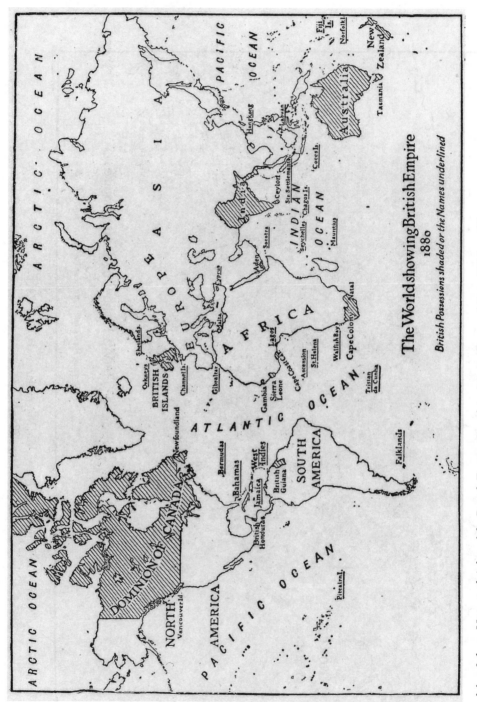

Map 3 from *Historical Atlas of the British Empire*, London: Macmillan and Co., 1924, p. 13.
Reproduced by permission of the British Library, Maps 27.b.39.

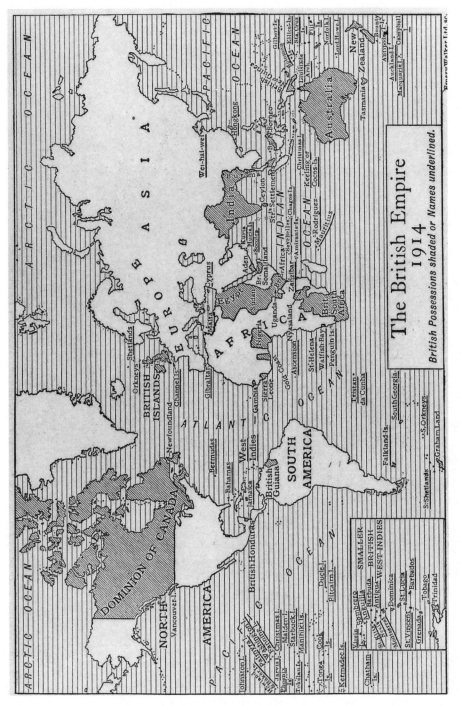

Map 4 from *Historical Atlas of the British Empire*, London: Macmillan and Co., 1924, p. 17.
Reproduced by permission of the British Library, Maps 27.b.39.

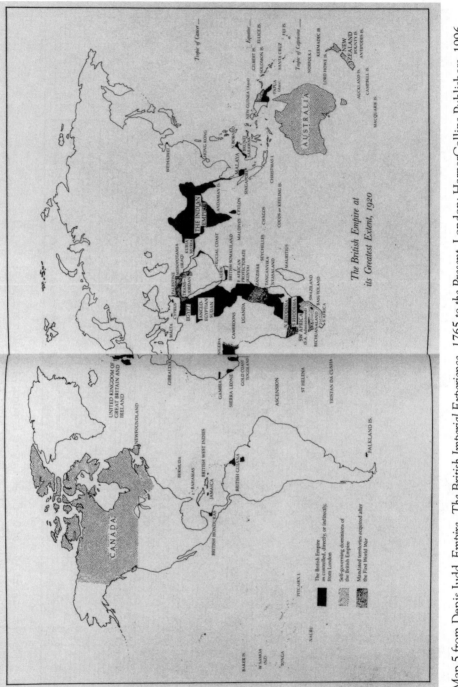

Map 5 from Denis Judd, *Empire. The British Imperial Experience, 1765 to the Present*, London: HarperCollins Publishers, 1996, pp. xviii–xix. Reproduced by permission of the British Library, YC.1997.114.

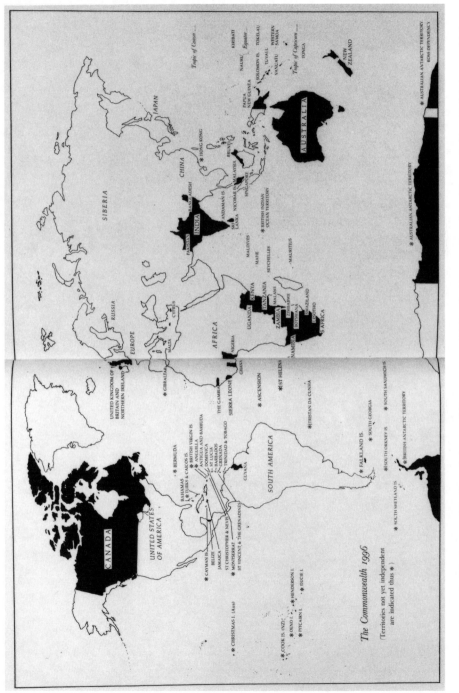

Map 6 from Denis Judd, *Empire. The British Imperial Experience, 1765 to the Present*, London: HarperCollins Publishers, 1996, pp. xx–xxi. Reproduced by permission of the British Library, YC.1997.114.

The Companion

A

Algerian War of Independence

Ostensibly the armed struggle by Muslim Algerians against the French army and French colonial power for independence, it assumed a variety of meanings because the dimensions of the struggle transcended the boundaries of the colony, resulting in unforeseen consequences. It was a brutal war on both sides. The French government sought by any means to retain its hold on Algeria, whilst the creation of the Front de Libération Nationale and its declaration of war split the nationalist movement, leading to an internal power struggle that resulted in the assassination of some of its leading figures including Abane Ramdane, the organiser, with Belkacem Krim, of the 1956 Congress of Soummam. The later division between the fighters on the ground in Algeria and the exiled leadership would provoke further assassinations and the 1965 coup d'état by the former commander-in-chief of the Armée de Libération Nationale, Houari Boumedienne. The tactics used by the French army, particularly the question of whether it used torture and the policy of forced resettlement (*regroupement*) continue to resonate, as for example, in the torture accusations made in 2000 by the former FLN militant Louisette Ighilahriz.

At a political level in France, the debate over the war and *Algérie française* destroyed the Fourth Republic and brought the return to power of Charles de Gaulle and a new, Fifth Republic. It also repatriated to France some one million *colons*, plus approximately half a million each of Algerian Jews and Algerian Muslims (*harki*). The resettlement of the *colons* in Corsica laid the foundations for the Corsican nationalist movement and their settlement in the southern French cities helped to provide a base for the growth of Jean-Marie Le Pen's National Front. Although the expatriated Algerian Jews settled into French society, the *harki*, viewed as traitors by the new Algerian government, and ambivalently by the French authorities, suffered an ostracisation that still leaves them amongst the poorest of France's immigrant communities. The open avowal of socialist principles by many of the leaders of the Algerian National Liberation Front, and the post-independence seizure of *colon* property by former farm labourers, saw European radicals looking to Algeria as a potential alternative model of the socialist utopia. The adoption of economic policies that appeared to reflect this commitment to socialism also helped to advance this image, which the events of the 1990s have finally unravelled.

Kay Adamson

Literary Works

Djebar, Assia [1985] (1993), *Fantasia. An Algerian Cavalcade*, London: Heinemann.
Feraoun, Mouloud [1962] (2000), *Journal 1955–1962: Reflections on the French-Algerian War*, Lincoln, NE: University of Nebraska Press.

Histories

Adamson, Kay (1998), *Algeria: A Study in Competing Ideologies*, London: Cassell.
Ageron, Ch-R. (1991), *Modern Algeria – A History from 1830 to the Present*, trans. and ed. Michael Brett, London: Hurst and Company.
Bennoune, M. (1988), *The Making of Contemporary Algeria, 1830–1987*, Cambridge: Cambridge University Press.
Horne, Alistair [1977] (1987), *A Savage War of Peace: Algeria, 1954–1962*, London: Macmillan.
Ottaway, David and Marina (1970), *Algeria: The Politics of a Socialist Revolution*, Berkeley and Los Angeles: University of California Press.

See also: **Historiography: Middle East; Maghrebine Resistance: Algeria**.

Amin, Idi

Idi Amin (c. 1925–2003) was president of Uganda in the 1970s. Barely educated, in 1946 he joined the King's African Rifles (KAR), and served in Burma, Somalia, Kenya – where he helped the British colonial forces quell the Mau Mau rebellion – and Uganda. After Uganda's independence, Prime Minister (later President) Milton Obote appointed Amin First Lieutenant of the Ugandan army. Obote then sent him for further military training in Britain, upon completion of which he promoted him to the rank of colonel, then major-general, and in 1966 made him Chief-of-Staff of the Ugandan army and air force. In 1970, Obote, sensing potential threat to his rule by Amin, who had begun using suspect means to consolidate his position within the army, stripped him of most of his powers. But Amin moved fast and overthrew Obote in a military coup, assuming the presidency on 25 January 1971.

Amin's ascent to power was initially received with enthusiasm both within and outside Uganda. He looked determined to reverse Obote's increasingly unpopular policies. The freeing of political prisoners and the dismantling of the Ugandan secret police seemed to confirm these expectations. But a merciless military dictatorship was in the making. Amin unleashed terror on individuals and whole ethnic groups, particularly Lango and Acholi, for their real or perceived support for Obote. Obsessively, he focused on dealing with what he saw as disloyalty to him or subversion of his rule, resorting to abduction, torture and murder. He is responsible for the elimination of some 400,000 lives.

Amin gained notoriety as the world learned of his execution of the Anglican Archbishop of Uganda, Janani Luwum, the chief justice, the vice-chancellor of Makerere College, the governor of the Bank of Uganda, and several ministers. However, international opinion against Amin was slow in forming. In 1972, Amin announced the expulsion from the country of some 50,000 Ugandan Asians. He described this act as 'economic war' on a foreign group that sought to dominate Uganda's trade and manufacturing sectors, and to occupy the civil service. Given only three months to leave, the expellees practically abandoned their businesses, which were handed over to Amin's supporters only to be run down. Severing diplomatic relations with Britain, Amin moved to 'nationalise' some British-owned businesses too. Paradoxically, in 1975, Amin became head of the Organisation of African Unity.

In October 1978, Amin invaded Tanzania in an attempt to annex its northern province, Kagera. The Tanzanian army repulsed the aggressors, and President Nyerere subsequently assisted the Uganda National Liberation Front (UNLF) to overthrow Amin. His regime fell on 13 April 1979. Obote then returned to power. By that time, enormous damage had been done. Uganda's economy was totally disorganised, with inflation exceeding 1,000 per cent. The profanation of human life and the all-pervasive corruption brought about a crisis in moral consciousness; hence, Amin's widespread designation as the 'Butcher of Uganda'. Immediately after his ousting, Amin fled into exile to Saudi Arabia, where he remained until his death.

Emilia Ilieva and Lennox Odiemo-Munra

Literary Works

Gakwandi, Arthur (1997), *Kosiya Kifefe*, Nairobi: East African Educational Publishers.
Ibingira, Grace (1980), *Bitter Harvest*, Nairobi: East Africa Publishing House.
Isegawa, Moses (2000), *Abyssinian Chronicles*, London: Picador.
Konrad, James (1977), *Target Amin*, London: Sphere Books.
Magala-Nyago (1985), *The Rape of the Pearl*, London: Macmillan.
Mukulu, Alex (1993), *Thirty Years of Bananas*, Kampala: Oxford University Press.
Nagenda, John (1986), *The Seasons of Thomas Tebo*, London: Heinemann.
Nazareth, Peter (1972), *In a Brown Mantle*, Nairobi: Kenya Literature Bureau.
Nazareth, Peter (1991), *The General is Up*, Toronto: TSAR Publications.
Okurut, Mary Karooro (1998), *The Invisible Weevil*, Kampala: Femrite Publications Limited.
Osinya, Alumidi (1977), *The Amazing Saga of Field Marshal Abdulla Salim Fisi (Or How the Hyena Got His!)*, Nairobi: Job Publications and Transafrica Books.
p'Chong, Cliff-Lubwa (1977), *Words of my Groaning*, Nairobi: Kenya Literature Bureau.
Ruganda, John (1980), *Floods*, Nairobi: East African Educational Publishers.
Watkins, Leslie (1976); (1977), *The Killing of Idi Amin*, London: Everest Books; New York: Avon.
Zake, S. Joshua L. (1980), *Truckful of Gold*, Chicago: Regenery Gateway Inc.

Histories

Avirgan, Tony and Martha Honey (1982), *War in Uganda: The Legacy of Idi Amin*, Westport, CT: Lawrence Hill; London: Zed Press.
Gingyera, A. G. G. (1994), 'The Militarization of Politics in the African State: The Case of Uganda', in Walter A. Oyugi (ed.), *Politics and Administration in East Africa*, Nairobi: East African Educational Publishers, pp. 215–44.
Hansen, Bernt Holger and Michael Twaddle (eds) (1988), *Uganda Now: Between Decay and Development*, London: James Currey.
Karugire, S. R. (1980), *A Political History of Uganda*, Nairobi; London: Heinemann.
Kasozi, A. B. K. (1994), *The Social Origins of Violence in Uganda, 1964–85*, Montreal: McGill-Queen's University Press.
Kyemba, Henry (1997), *A State of Blood: The Inside Story of Idi Amin, 1977*, foreword Godfrey Lule, Kampala: Fountain.

Mamdani, M. (1983), *Imperialism and Fascism in Uganda*, Nairobi: Heinemann.

Mazrui A. (1975), *Soldiers and Kinsmen in Uganda: The Making of a Military Ethnocracy*, Beverly Hills: Sage.

Mudoola, Dan M. (1993), *Religion, Ethnicity and Politics in Uganda*, Kampala: Fountain.

Museveni, Yoweri K. (1992), *What is Africa's Problem?*, foreword Julius K. Nyerere, Kampala: NRM Publications.

Omara-Otunnu A. (1987), *Politics and the Military in Uganda, 1890–1985*, London: Macmillan.

Omara-Otunnu A. (1998), 'The Currency of Militarism in Uganda', in Eboe Hutchful and Abdoulaye Bathily (eds), *The Military and Militarism in Uganda*, Dakar: CODESRIA, pp. 399–428.

Okoth, Godfrey P. (1995), 'Uganda's Foreign Policy towards the USA', in Macharia Munene, J. D. Olewe Nyunya and Korwa Adar (eds), *The United States and Africa from Independence to the End of the Cold War*, Nairobi: East African Educational Publishers, pp. 105–25.

See also: **Asian Expulsions: East Africa**.

Anglicisation

Anglicisation must not be understood simply as an inevitable long-term result or by-product of British colonial power, but as a primary strategy of domination employed to maintain and expand control. Military force was not the most efficacious means of maintaining order in the colonies: policies that promoted Anglicisation and the moulding of colonial subjects into the willing servants of Empire consolidated British power and reduced the threat of insurgency. The establishment of British colonial rule, with its administrative, legal and bureaucratic apparatus and disciplinary institutions (churches, schools, and so on), facilitated the process of Anglicisation and its devastating effects on the cultures of indigenous populations. Education played a crucial role in this process and, as in other areas of colonial governance, the rhetoric of the 'civilising mission' sought to legitimise this enterprise.

In British India, as Viswanathan (1989) explains, the origins of colonial education lay in attempts to compensate for the behaviour of the colonisers themselves and ward off insurrection, rather than any beneficent desire to 'enlighten' and improve the morals of the colonised. Debates raged over educational policy between the Orientalists, who promoted native languages and literature, and the Anglicists who, fearing the corrupting influence of native culture, advocated sole instruction in Western knowledge.

In 1835, English finally became the official language of instruction in India and the study of English literature was established on the curriculum – long before it was in England. Viswanathan argues that this literary education, which disseminated the belief in English cultural, intellectual and moral supremacy, assuaged missionaries' demands for religious instruction and, through its representation of the coloniser, masked the reality of colonial subjugation. Anglicisation was successful in producing sympathetic indigenous elites in many colonies. Colonial mimicry, however, also revealed the limits of the discourses of civility, as 'to be Anglicized is *emphatically* not to be English' (Bhabha 1995, p. 87).

Policies of Anglicisation have long been the site of conflict and resistance, not only from colonised indigenous populations but also, for example, the Afrikaner and francophone communities of South Africa and Canada. Anti-colonial and nationalist movements brought calls for the rejection of English language and culture and the 'rediscovery' of pre-colonial identities, but also led, in many cases, to the affirmation and celebration of creol-isation – new hybrid linguistic and cultural forms. Whilst policies of Anglicisation were aimed at 'civilising' native populations, English culture, religion and language were in fact transformed by colonised peoples as they were adapted – to varying degrees – to indigenous practices and traditions. Today, this colonial legacy is witnessed by the global popularity (and commercial success) of products and people seen to represent 'Englishness'. However, cosmopolitan, hybrid influences, intensified by postcolonial migrancy, continue to shape British as well as global culture, now influenced to a far greater extent by forces from the other side of the Atlantic.

Cheralyn Mealor

Literary Works

Achebe, Chinua [1958] (1986), *Things Fall Apart*, Oxford: Heinemann.
Kunzru, Hari (2003), *The Impressionist*, London: Penguin Books.
Naipaul, V. S. [1967] (2002), *The Mimic Men*, London: Picador.
Rushdie, Salman [1988] (1992), *The Satanic Verses*, Dover, DE: The Consortium, Inc.
Salih, Tayeb (1970), *Season of Migration to the North*, trans. D. Johnson-Davies, London: Heinemann.

Histories

Bhabha, Homi K. (1995), *The Location of Culture*, London and New York: Routledge.
Fanon, Frantz [1952] (1993), *Black Skin, White Masks*, trans. Charles Lam Markmann, London: Pluto Press.
Ngugi wa Thiong'o (1986), *Decolonising the Mind: The Politics of Language in African Literature*, London: James Currey.
Poddar, Prem (2002), *Violent Civilities: English, India, Culture*, Aarhus: Aarhus University Press.
Viswanathan, Gauri (1989), *Masks of Conquest: Literary Study and British Rule in India*, New York: Columbia University Press.

See also: **Anglo-Boer War; Universities: East Africa; Universities: West Africa**.

Anglo-Boer War

More commonly known now as the South African War, the origins of the war lay in Britain's late nineteenth-century empire-building in Southern Africa. In complete control of the important Cape Colony since 1815, the British were confident of their regional hegemony. Starting in 1834, disaffected Boer pastoralists were even allowed to slip colonial control and trek north to establish their own independent white republics of the Orange Free State and the South Africa Republic (Transvaal). These ramshackle agrarian territories were mostly left to go their own way, as Britain banked on evolution-ary commercial growth to bind together a divided settler minority under imperial author-ity. Instead, the discovery of the world's largest single supply of gold in the Transvaal in 1886 produced a crisis. Economic power suddenly shifted to a republic opposed to British imperial designs. Moreover, by the 1890s, British mining capitalists were complaining that the Boer state was too inefficient to meet their industrial needs.

British economic and strategic needs now required the removal of the Transvaal regime. High-handed imperial demands and a botched 1895 coup, the Jameson Raid, brought dip-lomatic breakdown in October 1899. Supported by its sister republic, the Transvaal declared war to defend its independence. Anticipating an easy victory, Britain instead experienced a costly war. Imperial armies suffered defeats and reverses in 1899 and 1900, followed by nearly two years of frustrating rural guerrilla warfare.

To crush resistance to imperial occupation, the British Commander-in-Chief, Lord Kitchener, intensified a scorched earth strategy, destroying crops and cattle, and inciner-ating farms. In a further measure to isolate guerrillas from resources, displaced Boer civil-ians and African peasants were expelled from the land and pushed into badly-run concentration camps. High mortality rates there, deepening hostilities from pro-British blacks, and rising Boer collaboration with the enemy eventually forced surviving die-hards to surrender and accept peace in May 1902. Independence was ended but post-war recon-struction terms were both generous and conciliatory, for Britain needed a strong and com-pliant settler order. A war that had threatened the existence of an anti-imperialist Afrikanerdom had also ensured its survival. In a conflict which sucked in many thousands of blacks as well as whites, Britain had to mobilise 450,000 troops to defeat 88,000 Boer commandos. Some 22,000 imperial soldiers and 7,000 Boer combatants were killed, while almost 50,000 Boer and African civilians died in camps. Cultivated public memory of the trauma of this major colonial war became inscribed within Afrikaner nationalist culture, fertilising its political growth through post-war decades.

                                                                                                              Bill Nasson

Literary Works

Blackburn, Douglas (1903), *A Burgher Quixote*, Edinburgh: Blackwood and Sons.
Joubert, Elsa (2001), *Isobelle's Journey*, Johannesburg: Jonathan Ball.
Le Roux, Etienne (1976), *Magersfontein, O Magersfontein*, Harmondsworth: Penguin.
Van Der Merwe, Chris N. and Michael Rice (eds) (1999), *A Century of Anglo-Boer War Stories*, Johannesburg: Jonathan Ball.

Histories

Cuthbertson, Greg, Albert Grundlingh and Mary-Lynn Suttie (eds) (2002), *Writing a Wider War: Rethinking Gender, Race, and Identity in the South African War, 1899–1902*, Athens, OH: Ohio University Press.
Gooch, John (ed.) (2000), *The Boer War: Direction, Experience and Image*, London: Frank Cass.
Judd, Denis and Keith Surridge (2002), *The Boer War*, London: John Murray.
Nasson, Bill (1999), *The South African War 1899–1902*, London: Arnold.

Omissi, David and Andrew Thompson (eds) (2002), *The Impact of the South African War*, London: Palgrave.

See also: **British Imperialism; Nationalism(s): Southern Africa**.

Anglo-Burmese Wars

The Anglo-Burmese Wars began in 1824 with minor skirmishes between the British and Burmese, and ended in 1886 with the complete annexation of Burma, then known as the Kingdom of Ava, by Great Britain. Beginning in the late eighteenth century, Burma began to expand westward towards India, annexing Arakan in 1785. In the period immediately preceding the first Anglo-Burmese War, Burma invaded Manipur and Assam and threatened Cachar, Jaintia, and Bhutan, territories bordering British India. A series of clashes between Burmese and British forces ensued, leading the British to declare war in March 1824. Although the Burmese made some initial gains, the British soon took Rangoon by sea and advanced north towards Mandalay, reaching Pagan in 1826. The war ended only when Burma ceded Manipur and Arakan to Great Britain, as well as Tennasserim, a coastal territory bordering Siam. Burma was also required to pay a large indemnity and accommodate British merchants and colonial representatives.

The second Anglo-Burmese War began in 1851 after the British blockaded Burma's ports in response to a dispute between the governor of Rangoon and British merchants. The British demanded reimbursement for military costs, and before Burma could respond to the ultimatum, the British attacked Rangoon and other coastal cities. British forces quickly occupied Lower Burma, taking Pegu in November 1852. King Pagan was deposed, and peace was established in 1853 as the new king, Mindon, accepted British control of Lower Burma, depriving the kingdom of its remaining seaports and the agriculturally-rich Irawaddy delta.

The third Anglo-Burmese War resulted from a number of factors, including the British desire to control Upper Burma economically and their fears that the kingdom would ally itself to France, which was then consolidating its control of South-east Asia. In October 1885, the British demanded control of Burma's foreign policy, and less than one month later they invaded, quickly taking Mandalay. In early 1886, Great Britain formally annexed Burma, incorporating it into British India.

Although resistance to British control continued into the twentieth century, British colonial policies quickly transformed Burma economically and socially as rice production was maximised and foreign labour was imported. British rule temporarily ended in 1942 after the Japanese, assisted by Burmese insurgents, invaded Burma. Although the British resumed control of the country immediately following World War II, Burma regained its independence in 1948 and refused to join the British Commonwealth.

Tom Henthorne

Literary Works

Fielding-Hall, Henry (1900), *Burmese Palace Tales*, London: Harper and Brothers.
Ghosh, Amitav (2000), *The Glass Palace*, London: HarperCollins.
Ma Ma Lay (1991), *Not out of Hate*, trans. Margaret Aung-Thwin, Athens, OH: Ohio University Center for International Studies.

Histories

Blackburn, Terence (2000), *The British Humiliation of Burma*, Bangkok: Orchid Press.
Ghosh, Parimal (2000), *Brave Men of the Hills: Resistance and Rebellion in Burma, 1825–1932*, Honolulu: University of Hawaii Press.
Mg Htin Aung (1965), *The Stricken Peacock: Ango-Burmese Relations, 1752–1948*, The Hague: Marinus Nijhoff.
Thant Myint-U (2001), *The Making of Modern Burma*, London: Cambridge University Press.

See also: **Aung San Suu Kyi**; **Britain's Postwar Foreign Policy**; **Commonwealth**; **Historiography: South-east Asia**.

Anglo-Zulu War

The Zulu kingdom was situated in south-east Africa in the region bounded by the Thukela and Phongolo rivers. It was founded in the first quarter of the nineteenth century by Shaka kaSenzangakhona who incorporated a number of surrounding peoples into the political structure of the kingdom. A key factor in this process was the drafting of all the kingdom's men into a single military system of formidable reputation. In the central decades of the nineteenth century the Zulu kings successfully defended their autonomy from the growing colonial and Afrikaner settler states on their borders. But, in the late 1870s, an attempt by the British government to facilitate the creation of a modernising centralised state in South Africa brought the polities seen as obstacles to such a move under imperial threat. At the end of 1878 the Zulu king Cetshwayo kaMpande (1873–9) was presented with an ultimatum demanding that he disband the Zulu military system. When he failed to accede to this and other demands the British army, supported by colonial troops, invaded the kingdom.

The campaign opened with a disaster for the invading force. On 22 January 1879 a British column was attacked by the Zulu army at Isandlwana and well over a thousand of the invading force were killed. That evening at Rorke's Drift a detachment of Zulu was driven off by defenders who were to receive eleven Victoria Crosses amongst them – the highest in any engagement in British military history. Despite such attempts to enhance the invading force's reputation it only suffered further when a Zulu ambush attacked a reconnaissance patrol and killed the son of Napoleon III. It was after this that Benjamin Disraeli is supposed to have said, 'A remarkable people the Zulu, they convert our bishops [a reference to John Colenso, the Bishop of Natal, who was alleged to have been led to heretical views by a Zulu convert], defeat our generals, and put an end to a great European dynasty.' The invasion culminated with the battle at Ulundi on 4 July 1879, but the Zulu victory at Isandlwana had done irreparable damage both to the reputation of the Conservative government and to the expansionist policy which had led to the war. On the other hand the reputation the Zulu gained for military prowess has characterised, and distorted, representations of the Zulu ever since. The name Zulu became identified with a reckless, African courage which drove to victory line upon line of men armed only with spears over the disciplined volley-firing of white men using the most technologically-advanced weaponry. The Anglo-Zulu War remains a ubiquitous feature of British popular culture, largely due to the fact that H. Rider Haggard was a young, minor official peripherally associated with these events which he drew on as material for some of his most successful and widely-read novels.

Jeff Guy

Literary Works

Dhlomo, H. I. E. [1935] (1985), *Cetshwayo* and *Battle of Isandlwana*, in T. Couzens and N. Visser (eds), *The Collected Works of H. I. E. Dhlomo*, Johannesburg: Ravan Press.
Filter, H. and S. Bourquin (eds) (1986), *Paulina Dlamini. Servant of Two Kings*, Durban and Pietermaritzburg: University of Natal Press.
McCord, Margaret (1995), *The Calling of Katie Makanya*, Cape Town and Johannesburg: David Philip.
Sher, Anthony (1988), *Middlepost*, London: Chatto and Windus.

Histories

Guy, J. (1979), *The Destruction of the Zulu Kingdom*, London: Longman.
Guy, J. (1998), 'Battling with Banality', *Journal of Natal and Zulu History* 18, pp. 156–93.
McClintock, A. (1995), *Imperial Leather: Race, Gender, and Sexuality in a Colonial Context*, London and New York: Routledge.
Peterson, B. (2000), *Monarchs, Missionaries and Intellectuals. African Theatre and the Unmaking of Colonial Marginality*, Johannesburg: Witwatersrand University Press.

See also: **British Imperialism**.

Anti-Colonialism and Resistance: Caribbean

Anti-colonialism is the struggle waged by the colonised against the theory and practice of colonisation. The Caribbean was not so much colonised, but rather created by colonialism. Whereas in other parts of the world native peoples were conquered, ruled and dominated by the British, in the Caribbean it was different in that the destruction of the majority of indigenous peoples forced the European invaders to repopulate the territories with other peoples. Hence millions of enslaved Africans were forcibly removed from their continent, and brought to work on Caribbean plantations.

The process of colonisation was therefore distinctive in the Caribbean, but as in other colonies the first anti-colonial struggles in the region were waged by the indigenous peoples: the Caribs (Kalinago, Calipuna, Ciboney peoples) and the Arawaks (Taíno people). Among the Amerindian resistance leaders were the Taíno chief, Hatuey (d. 1512), and Kalinago chief, Joseph Chatoyer (d. 1795). Hatuey is considered as the first martyr in the Cuban independence struggles. He led a guerrilla war in Cuba in the early sixteenth century against the Spanish invaders, and the Spanish tied him to a stake and burnt him alive. Chatoyer led the Black Carib resistance against British colonialism in St Vincent and the Grenadines, and like Hatuey was killed defending Amerindian sovereignty. Chatoyer was declared the first national hero of St Vincent and the Grenadines in 2002.

Anti-colonial writers have argued that colonialism precipitated the destruction of whole Caribbean societies, as well as the enslavement, dislocation and disenfranchisement of African societies. It was the exploitive nature of colonialism that engendered anti-colonial struggles. On this basis, slave resistance can be construed as a form of anti-colonial struggle. For close to 200 years enslaved Africans fought against the system of slavery by both violent and non-violent means. Slave uprisings occurred with increasing frequency and intensity from the second half of the eighteenth century: Tacky's Revolt in Jamaica (1760–1); the protracted struggle (1791–1804) in Santo Domingo led by Toussant L'Ouverture (d. 1803), which cost France 60,000 lives and culminated in the first black republic (renamed Haiti) in the western hemisphere; Bussa's Rebellion in Barbados in 1816; the Demerara Rebellion in British Guiana in 1823; and the 'Baptist War' in Jamaica in 1831. Apart from the successful uprising in Haiti, these rebellions were put down ruthlessly. Nonetheless they contributed fundamentally, together with the anti-slavery campaigns in Europe, to the ultimate abolition of the slave trade in 1807, and to the emancipation of all 750,000 slaves in British colonies on 31 July 1834.

There was still strong anti-colonial sentiment in the Caribbean after the formal end of slavery, as freed slaves were denied the franchise, and power remained in the hands of the white minority. Economic and social conditions for freed slaves were extremely difficult, and the arrival of indentured labour from India from 1838 onwards in increasing numbers (250,000 to British Guiana, 150,000 to Trinidad, and 36,000 to Jamaica) exacerbated unemployment and under-employment among ex-slaves and their offspring. Riots and protests against these harsh conditions proliferated: in 1844 in Dominica; in 1848 in Jamaica; again in 1859 in Jamaica; in 1862 in St Vincent; and in 1876 in Tobago and Barbados. The most important moment of protest was in Jamaica in the Morant Bay Uprising of 1856, when Governor Edward John Eyre (1815–1901) suppressed the rebellion with great cruelty, ordering the execution of George William Gordon (1818–65), Paul Bogle (1825–65), and 400 other rebels during a month of martial law. Eyre was recalled to England, and governance through Jamaica's House of Assembly was replaced by Crown Colony rule. This dispensation, which was enforced piecemeal throughout the British Caribbean following the Morant Bay Uprising, denied meaningful political representation to black Caribbeans, and swiftly became the focus of anti-colonial anger. In its most moderate form, this anger took the form of appeals to reinstitute representative government as a preliminary stage towards self-government. These arguments were made predominantly by political leaders drawn from the middle class, and from the 1870s onwards they won modest concessions. In 1884, for example, the Legislative Council in Jamaica admitted elected members with limited jurisdiction, and in 1891 the constitution of British Guiana made similar provisions.

The final quarter of the nineteenth century saw the economies of the West Indies experience a prolonged depression, with sugar prices on the world market collapsing, and the other Caribbean export crops incapable of making up the deficit. The repercussions for the agricultural working classes were devastating, with reduced wages, greater unemployment, malnutrition and disease. Again, anger about economic and social difficulties were expressed in violent riots across the Caribbean: in 1895 in Grenada; in 1891 in St Vincent; in 1893 in Dominica; in 1896 in British Guiana; in 1902 in Jamaica; and in 1905 again in British Guiana. This period also saw the tentative emergence of the first trade unions, like the Artisans' Union in Jamaica (formed in 1898), but these lost impetus and trade unionism only picked up momentum again after World War I. Also of significance in sustaining anti-colonial sentiment were the writings and speeches of anti-racist intellectuals like J. J. Thomas (1840–89) from Trinidad, the author of *Froudacity* (1888).

In the first two decades of the twentieth century, there were at least four political movements that contained significant strands of anti-colonial ideology. The first was the Caribbean League, which was formed in 1918 by soldiers in the British West Indies Regiment in reaction to racial discrimination experienced during World War I. The soldiers' grievances had led in 1918 to mutiny at Taranto, Italy, and in the immediate postwar years, returning soldiers participated in riots and protests in British Honduras and Trinidad. The second movement was the resurgence of trade unionism in response to war-time poverty, with strikes in 1917 and 1918 in British Guiana, St Lucia, St Kitts and Jamaica; and following legislation legalising trade unions, the formation of the Jamaican Federation of Labour, the British Guiana Labour Union, and the Trinidad Workingmen's Association, all in 1919. Thirdly, Marcus Garvey (1887–1940) founded the Universal Negro Improvement Association in 1912 in Jamaica, and through the organisation's newspaper *Negro World* promoted ideas of race pride and black nationalism. Finally, there were ongoing demands for constitutional reform led by middle-class politicians like George Augustus McIntosh (1886–1963) in St Vincent and the Grenadines, who believed that political change, including ultimately decolonisation, could best be achieved gradually through resolutions and petitions.

In the wake of the Depression, there was a wave of unrest in the British Caribbean, particularly in the years 1935 to 1939. According to Ralph Gonsalves (2002), 'The working people, the peasants, had taken to the streets in anti-colonial revolt, seeking to fashion their own destiny.' Perry Mars has argued that these protests, which began in St Kitts in January 1935, introduced 'a peculiar anti-colonialist brand of Caribbean radicalism' (Mars 1998, p. 44). Major worker protests followed throughout the British West Indies: in Trinidad's oilfields in March 1935; in British Guiana's sugar estates in September 1935; in St Vincent in October 1935; in the coal mines of St Lucia in December 1935; in Trinidad and Barbados in June 1937; in Jamaica in May/June 1938; and again in British Guiana in February 1939. The unrests threw up labour and political organisations, which were closely related. According to Mars, these:

> developed a typically anti-colonialist ideology combined with black consciousness as evidenced in the vigorous opposition to the Italian colonialist conquest of Abyssinia, and in some of the advocacy of prominent labour leaders of the time, such as Butler in Trinidad, H. N. Critchlow in Guyana and Clement Payne in Barbados. (Mars 1998, p. 47)

The 1930s and 1940s also saw the emergence of a number of prominent anti-colonial Caribbean intellectuals, many of whom played major roles in global anti-colonial movements. They included: the Jamaican-born Rastafari preacher Claudius Henry (1903–?), C. L. R. James (1901–89), George Padmore (1902–59), Eric Williams (1911–81), W. Adolphe Roberts (1886–1962), and later, George Lamming (1927–) and Walter Rodney (1942–80). Anti-colonial struggles in the British West Indies also drew strength from Caribbean intellectuals from the other islands, like Aimé Césaire (1913–), Léon Gontran Damas (1912–78), Nicolas Guillén (1902–89), and at a later stage, Frantz Fanon (1925–61) and Edouard Glissant (1928–). Writers from the USA like Langston Hughes (1902–67) and from Africa – notably Léopold Sédar Senghor (1906–2001) and Kwame Nkrumah (1909–72) – also inspired Caribbean struggles in their writings, with varieties of Negritude and Pan-African thought heavily informing Caribbean anti-colonial discourse.

The activism and protests of the late 1930s led the British colonial authorities to consider seriously the possibility of self-government for the Caribbean colonies, and incremental reforms followed: the extension of the franchise, universal adult suffrage, greater representation in the legislatures, and ultimately majority rule. Universal suffrage, for example, was introduced in Jamaica in 1944, in Trinidad and Tobago in 1945, in Barbados in 1950, the Leeward and Windward Isles in 1951, British Guiana in 1953, and in British Honduras in 1954. Throughout this period, anti-colonial politicians in the British Caribbean were tracked by British intelligence department MI5, which was alarmed by their growing links between the embryonic US civil rights movement and with black anti-colonial politicians in West Africa. The process of conceding political power was accordingly carefully regulated, and Britain's economic interests were always protected. This was clear in British Guiana (post-independence Guyana), where 133 days after the left-wing candidate Dr Cheddi Jagan (1918–97) had been democratically elected, British troops landed in Georgetown, suspended the constitution, and engineered the installation of the pro-British Forbes Burnham (1923–85).

In the 1950s, Britain was committed to a process of decolonisation, and the prevailing idea was for the British West Indies to move to political independence through a federation. The British were more willing to grant independence to a federation than to individual colonies, and anti-colonial writers and activists like James, Williams and Roberts articulated the view that the Caribbean was one region that had unity within its diversity. A British West Indian federation was eventually formed in 1958 but broke up in 1962. Following the break-up of the federation, political independence was 'returned' to various territories in the region. In 1962, Jamaica and Trinidad and Tobago became the first British Caribbean territories to become independent. British Guiana (now called Guyana) and Barbados followed in 1966. From the 1970s onwards more islands were given independence: the Bahamas in 1973, Grenada in 1974, Dominica in 1978, St Lucia, and St Vincent and the Grenadines in 1979, Antigua in 1980, Belize in 1981, and St Kitts and Nevis in 1983. However, not all British Caribbean territories have been decolonised, as some territories have opted to remain as colonies: the British Virgin Islands, Anguilla, Montserrat, Turks and Caicos and the Cayman Islands.

Anti-colonial struggles continued in some post-independence British Caribbean states. According to Bennett, 'Jamaica in 1968 and Trinidad in 1970 experienced social disturbances that took on a seemingly revolutionary character' (Bennett 1989, p. 129). In these territories, and elsewhere in the region, there were individuals as well as organisations calling for the severing of all colonial ties, the redistribution of wealth, and an end to colonial habits of dress and cuisine. At the vanguard of these demands were intellectuals and university students who saw independence as a failure since it had not brought meaningful changes or benefits to the masses. Unrest and protests were the result of this dissatisfaction. The New World Group (of intellectuals), for example, felt that decolonisation had simply led to, in the words of Bennett, 'another phase of colonialism' (Bennett 1989, p. 129).

The post-independence anti-colonial struggle was carried on largely by the Caribbean left, which were fairly consistent with a 'common advocacy of the anti-colonialist perspectives' (Mars 1998, p. 9). The Caribbean left drew from the success of liberation movements in Africa like FRELIMO (Frente de Liberaçao de Moçambique) in Mozambique. A political party in St Vincent and the Grenadines even coined a name, YULIMO, to reflect this inspiration. YULIMO emerged in the early 1970s, a period of growing radicalism in the Caribbean, with the burgeoning of black nationalism, black power, and the spread of Marxism-Leninism and Rastafarianism. YULIMO encompassed all these ideas into a political movement which was anti-imperialist and anti-colonial, and focused not only on Britain and its neo-colonial legacy, but also on the rest of Western Europe and the USA.

Cleve Scott

Literary Works

Césaire, Aimé [1956] (1995), *Notebook of a Return to my Native Land*, trans. M. Rosello with A. Pritchard, Newcastle: Bloodaxe.
Cliff, Michelle [1984] (1995), *Abeng*, New York: Plume-Penguin.
Collins, Merle (1987), *Angel*, London: Women's Press.
Edgell, Zee (1991), *In Times Like These*, Portsmouth, NH: Heinemann.
Glissant, Edouard (1992), *The Indies*, trans. D. O'Neill, Toronto: Editions du Gref.
James, C. L. R. (1963), *Beyond a Boundary*, London: Hutchinson.
Kincaid, Jamaica (1985), *Annie John*, London: Picador.
Lamming, George (1953), *In the Castle of my Skin*, London: Michael Joseph.
Lamming, George (1960), *The Pleasures of Exile*, London: Michael Joseph.
Reid, Vic (1949), *New Day*, New York: A. A. Knopf.

Histories

Beckles, Hilary (1982), 'The 200 Years War: Slave Resistance in the British West Indies: An Overview of the Historiography', *Jamaican Historical Review* 13, pp. 1–10.
Bennett, Herman L. (1989), 'The Challenge to the Post-Colonial State: A Case Study of the February Revolution in Trinidad', in Franklin W. Knight and Colin A. Palmer (eds), *The Modern Caribbean*, Chapel Hill, NC: University of North Carolina Press, pp. 129–46.
Bogues, Anthony (2003), *Black Heretics, Black Prophets, Radical Political Intellectuals*, New York and London: Routledge.
Craton, Michael (1982), *Testing the Chains: Resistance to Slavery in the British West Indies*, Ithaca, NY: Cornell University Press.
Creighton, Al (2003), 'George Lamming: 'An Outstanding Caribbean Literary Icon', *Arts on Sunday by Stabroek News*, 22 June.
Cross, Malcolm and Gad Heuman (eds) (1988), *Labour in the Caribbean: From Emancipation to Independence*, London: Macmillan.
Gonsalves, Ralph (2002), 'The Economics and Political Challenges Facing the Caribbean Labour Movement Today', address to the 63rd Annual Conference of Delegates, 26 July. Available at http://www.owtu.org/AC%20'02.htm, 27 Jan. 2004.
Hector, L. T. (1997), 'Now and Then There is an Oasis in this Desert of Glitz and Greed', *Fan the Flame*, 5 Mar. Available at http://www.candw.ag/~jardinea/ffhtm/ff990305.htm
Hoogbergen, Wim (ed.) (1995), *Born out of Resistance: On Caribbean Cultural Creativity*, Utrecht: ISOR Publications.
Mars, Perry (1998), *Ideology and Change: The Transformation of the Caribbean Left*, Barbados: University of West Indies Press.
Olwig, Karen Fog (ed.) (1995), *Small Islands, Large Questions: Society, Culture and Resistance in the Post-Emancipation Caribbean*, London: Frank Cass.

Richardson, David (ed.) (1985), *Abolition and its Aftermath: The Historical Context, 1790–1916*, London: Frank Cass.

Wright: Franklin W. (1990), *The Caribbean: Genesis of a Fragmented Nationalism*, Oxford: Oxford University Press.

See also: **Fanon, Frantz; Garvey, Marcus Mosiah; James, C. L. R.; Morant Bay Uprising; Rodney, Walter; Slavery: Caribbean; West Indies Federation; Williams, Eric.**

Anti-colonialism and Resistance: East Africa

Anti-colonial movements in East Africa, as in the rest of Africa, have tended to fall within two main categories: that is resistance movements based on religious faiths as a binding and protective institution on the one hand, and outright militant and violent resistance against colonial rule on the other. Although East African anti-colonial struggle was marked by a number of anti-colonial faith movements and violent uprisings, two stand out not just in the manner in which they have become central to our understanding of those motive forces that undergirded the anti-colonial struggle, but also in the way in which their iconographies have become so central in the literary imagination of the sub-continent. These two movements are the Maji Maji Uprising of 1904 to 1905 against the Germans in the then Southern Tanganyika, and the Mau Mau War against the British colonial forces from 1952 to 1956. How Mau Mau in particular is remembered has continued to dominate not just the thrust of Kenya's colonial historiography, but also the literary imagination of both settler writers and non-settler writers alike.

Looking first at the former, Maji Maji was one of the early resistance movements based on religious faiths that put up the fiercest anti-colonial struggles on the sub-continent. Maji Maji, derived from the Swahili word *maji*, meaning water, was a protest against the way the Germans ruled over Tanganyika. The main causes of the uprising involved heavy taxation, the imposition of a cash crop economy, specifically the growing of cotton in village plots owned by the local inhabitants, and the brutal beatings and inhuman treatment that the labourers received from the German agents notoriously called *akidas* (a Swahili word for overseers).

The Maji Maji rebellion was inspired by a prophet whose name was Kinjekitile, who lived at Ngarambe near the Rufiji River in southern Tanganyika. Local myth has it that Kinjekitile began his prophecy by sliding into a pool in the river some time in 1904. People tried to pull him out, but it was impossible. He disappeared into the water, and re-emerged the following morning unhurt and with his clothes dry. His message was simple: the Africans were one people and needed to unite against German brutality. He promised that he would fortify them with his medicine, *maji*, which was stronger than the German weapons. The Maji was the water from the river which people would drink and pour over their heads for protection against the enemy. It was also handed out in small bamboo shoots to be hung around the neck. His teaching spread around the Rufiji River and across the country. He warned that the time for war against the Germans had come, and that he was there to provide the leadership and protection. Pilgrims began to flock to Ngarambe in 1905 and Kinjekitile sent people out to train others. At last various groups were beginning to rally around the Maji, but they were restless, and wanted to start fighting because for the first time the Maji had brought them together to protest about their grievances and also guaranteed them protection.

The fighting began in July 1905. News of it spread rapidly along the Rufiji Valley, and was carried further by prophets called *hongo*, the messengers. The *hongo* carried the Maji which they gave to the people, promising them unity and protection against German weapons. They also promised to rid the world of witchcraft and European rule. In August 1905, the Maji Maji fighters scored great victories, but failed to overpower the Germans. The Germans resorted to withholding food and burning the villages which did not surrender. Although the peasants of Rufiji were defeated, the Maji Maji Uprising inspired nationalist struggles that followed, and it has remained a major icon of the anti-colonial struggle, and a symbol around which much of Tanzania's imagined nation has been constructed.

The significance of Maji Maji Uprising and the Maji myth lies in the way in which the *maji* ritual had become an instrument for truth-claiming, a vehicle for constituting knowledge and empowerment among the marginalised. Denied access to the centres of economic and political power in a colonial situation, the fragmented colonised community reconstituted itself by recourse to myth-making. The common aspiration of a reunited African community free from German oppression was formulated.

In the late 1960s, post-independence Tanzania was confronted with problems of unity and nation-building, and in 1967, Tanzanians came up with the Arusha Declaration, whose broad aims included directing cultural activity in line with their socialist goals. Creating 'a national culture' was one of the most challenging issues in Tanzania at the time, and nation-building (*kujenga nchi*) became the rallying word. Tanzanian writer Ebrahim Hussein's play *Kinjeketile* (first published and performed in 1969) drew its inspiration from the Maji Maji Uprising, and expressed the spirit of *kujenga*, the social unity which was the bedrock of the uprising. In the play, the eponymous hero Kinjeketile helps release the dormant energies of the people through the myth of the Maji, but lacks the ability to harness the energy and direct the action, although he can see the inevitable disaster. The discourse is constituted from a common cultural metaphor – a spiritual experience which relies on the peoples' known history – but Hussein secularises the myth by insisting that it has to be grounded on practical realities. Symbolism embedded in ritual but without rational discourse may play an emotional role in nation-building by rallying people, but Hussein's play makes the further point that ritual should go beyond symbolic gesture and encompass practical political strategies.

The second major anti-colonial movement in East Africa was the Kenyan Ithaka na Wiyathi (Land Freedom Army), which is more commonly known as the Mau Mau movement. The roots of the movement lie in the immediate post-World War II period, but it was only after the declaration of a state of emergency in 1952 that the use of violence was advocated in the anti-colonial struggle. The organisation was linked to the other political movements such as the Kikuyu Central Association (KCA) and the Kikuyu African Union (KAU) that preceded it. In terms of the Mau Mau oaths which defined the membership of the movement, it is difficult to separate Mau Mau from the KAU and particularly the KCA. Oathing had played an extremely important role in pre-colonial Gikuyu society and was, as Jomo Kenyatta writes in *Facing Mount Kenya*, the most important instrument of control in traditional Kikuyu court procedures. In its political aims, there were no essential differences between the movements because they all wanted land and freedom, and shared other demands and grievances expressed by the accepted political leaders.

Mau Mau in the rural areas was nourished by intense agricultural discontent, while its counterpart in the European-dominated urban areas was greatly fostered by the rapidly deteriorating social conditions especially in the post-war years. Mau Mau as a whole was, in this respect, largely the response of the landless in the Kikuyu reserves, the disinherited squatters in the White Highlands, and the Kikuyu urban lumpenproletariat. The vital role played by Nairobi militants in the development of the movement in the Kikuyu reserves in particular and in Kenya as a whole is now well established (see Furedi 1989, Spencer 1985 and Kaggia 1975). In the main, they all accepted the leadership of Kenyatta and regarded him as the true articulator of their grievances and hopes.

When the British governor declared a state of emergency on 20 October 1952, he authorised at the same time the detention of 183 leading Africans in what was known as Operation Jock Scott. His declaration coincided with the eviction of the squatters from the farmlands of the White Highlands. These events precipitated the transition to violent anti-colonial struggle, which took the form of guerrilla warfare in the forest regions. Although the Mau Mau was effectively defeated militarily by 1956, it had compelled the British to accept that the only possible future for Kenya was majority rule for Africans.

In spite of Mau Mau's image as one of the most influential anti-colonial movements on the continent, its status as a nationalist movement has been contested ever since by historians and fiction-writers, as well as by settler and Kenyan nationalist writers. While some have questioned Mau Mau's importance in the winning of independence or called for historical amnesia in the name of national unity, others have sought to project it as the moment of revolutionary heroism and the peak of Kenyan nationalism. Remembering Mau Mau in post-colonial Kenya has involved struggle over its uses, its relevance and place in Kenyan history. As Atieno Odhiambo writes, 'Mau Mau has been the conjuncture around which Kenya's pasts and Kenya's possible futures have been debated, contested and fought over' (Odhiambo 1991, p. 300). The result is a body of texts which draws attention to the relationship between history and literature.

As Maughan Brown has noted, the writing on Mau Mau has been produced by three clearly distinguishable groups of authors. The colonial settler writers such as Elspeth Huxley (1954) and Robert Ruark (1955), who set out to discredit the Mau Mau war by giving it a negative representation, are quite close to the British colonialist official version of the war. Then we have the autobiographical narratives of the former Mau Mau fighters, written after independence, which draw attention to the nature of the war in the forest, and are characterised by bitterness at the failure of the Kenyan government to reward and acknowledge them (Kaggia 1975; Barnett and Njama 1966). The third group of writers consists of those who sought to preserve the Mau Mau memory that the postcolonial leadership under Kenyatta had attempted to erase. Meja Mwangi, Godwin Wachira, Charles Mangua, Kenneth Watene, and almost all the works of Kenya's foremost writer, Ngugi wa Thiong'o, set out to provide a major contrast to the colonial settler fiction in the heroic manner in which they depict the forest fighters. The Kenyan writers have invariably shown that, in spite of the fact that the Mau Mau was defeated militarily, they won the moral battle with great courage.

Of these writers, Ngugi wa Thiong'o's works stand out in the manner in which the Mau Mau war is so central to their motivation and construction of meaning. For Ngugi, the memory of Mau Mau has always involved a meditation on the past through the filter-screen of the present. One detects in Ngugi's narratives some compelling urges in the post-Mau Mau space, the post-independence nation-state, that constantly call for new ways of reading the Mau Mau past. In his writings set before and during the emergency, Ngugi sets out to celebrate the ideal nation that was authorised by pre-independence nationalism. In Ngugi's works set in the post-independence period, he recuperates the war and turns it into a major icon around which the conflictual national identities have to be reconstituted. If the nationalist leadership wants to hijack the memory of Mau Mau to buttress their interests, Ngugi now insists that this has to be challenged by restoring Mau Mau to its historic role. His endorsement of Mau Mau violence marks a major shift from the earlier work in which violence is associated with self-seekers. In his later fiction Ngugi seeks to depict the Mau Mau phenomenon as a point at which the schismatic segments of Kenyan history are summoned and ordered to a coherent centre.

James Ogude

Literary Works

Hussein, Ebrahim (1970), *Kinjeketile*, Dar es Salaam: Oxford University Press.

Huxley, Elspeth (1954), *A Thing to Love*, London: Chatto and Windus.

Kaggia, Bildad (1975), *Roots of Freedom, 1921–1963. The Autobiography of Bildad Kaggia*, Nairobi: East Africa Publishing House.

Maughan-Brown, David (1985), *Land, Freedom and Fiction: History and Ideology in Kenya*, London: Zed Press.

Mwangi, Meja (1973), *Kill Me Quick*, London: Heinemann.

Mwangi, Meja (1974), *Carcase for Hounds*, London: Heinemann.

Mwangi, Meja (1975), *Taste of Death*, Nairobi: East Africa Publishing House.

Mwangi, Meja (1976), *Going Down River Road*, London: Heinemann.

Ngugi wa Thiong'o (1964), *Weep Not, Child*, London: Heinemann.

Ngugi wa Thiong'o (1965), *The River Between*, London: Heinemann.

Ngugi wa Thiong'o (1967), *A Grain of Wheat*, London: Heinemann.

Ngugi wa Thiong'o (1977), *Petals of Blood*, London: Heinemann.

Ngugi wa Thiong'o (1987), *Matigari*, London: Heinemann.

Ngugi wa Thiong'o and Micere Mugo (1976), *The Trial of Dedan Kimathi*, Nairobi: Heinemann.

Ruark, Robert (1955), *Something of Value*, London: Hamish Hamilton.

Ruark, Robert (1962), *Uhuru*, London: Hamish Hamilton.

Spencer, John (1985), *The Kenya African Union*, London: KPI.

Wachanga, H. K. (1975), *The Swords of Kirinyaga*, ed. R. Whittier, Nairobi: East Africa Publishing House.

Wachira, G. (1968), *Ordeal in the Forest*, Nairobi: East Africa Publishing House.

Waciuma, Charity (1969), *Daughter of Mumbi*, Nairobi: East Africa Publishing House.

Wamweya, J. (1971), *Freedom Fighter*, Nairobi: East Africa Publishing House.

Watene, Kenneth (1974), *Dedan Kimathi*, Nairobi: Transafrica.

Histories

Barnett, Donald L. and Karari Njama (1966), *Mau Mau from Within: Autobiography and Analysis of Kenya's Peasant Revolt*, New York: Modern Reader Paperbacks.

Buijtenhuijs, Robert (1973), *Mau Mau Twenty Years After: The Myth and the Survivors*, The Hague: Mouton.

Edgerton, Robert (1989), *Mau Mau: An African Crucible*, New York: Free Press.

Furedi, Frank (1989), *The Mau Mau War in Perspective*, London: James Currey.

Gwasa, G. C. K. (1967), *Records of Maji Maji Uprising*, Nairobi: East Africa Publishing House.

Kanogo, M. J. Thabitha (1987), *Squatters and the Roots of the Mau Mau 1905–63*, London: Heinemann.

Kariuki, Josiah Mwangi (1963), *Mau Mau Detainee*, Nairobi: Oxford University Press.

Kenyatta, Jomo (1968), *Suffering Without Bitterness*, Nairobi: East Africa Publishing House.

Kenyatta, Jomo (1979), *Facing Mount Kenya*, London: Heinemann.

Kershaw, Greet (1997), *Mau Mau from Below*, Oxford: James Currey.

Kinyatti, Maina wa (1977), 'Mau Mau: The Peak of African Nationalism in Kenya', *Kenya Historical Review* 5: 2, pp. 287–391.

Kinyatti, Maina wa (1980), *Thunder from the Mountains: Mau Mau Patriotic Songs*, London: Zed Press.

Kinyatti, Maina wa (1987), *Kenya's Freedom Struggle: The Dedan Kimathi Papers*, London: Zed Press.

Kinyatti, Maina wa (2000), *Mau Mau: A Revolution Betrayed*, Nairobi: East African Educational Publishers.

Lonsdale, John (1990), 'Mau Maus of the Mind: Making Mau Mau and Remaking Kenya', *Journal of African History* 31, pp. 393–421.

Maloba, O. Wunyabari (1993), *Mau Mau and Kenya: An Analysis of a Peasant Revolt*, Bloomington, IN: Indiana University Press.

Mazrui, Ali and M. T. Alamin (1995), *Swahili State and Society: The Political Economy of an African Language*, London: James Currey.

Odhiambo, E. S. Atieno (1991), 'The Production of History in Kenya: The Mau Mau Debate', *Canadian Journal of African Studies* 25: 2, pp. 300–7.

Odhiambo, E. S. Atieno and John Lonsdale (2003), *Mau Mau and Nationhood*, Oxford: James Currey.

Ogot, B. A. (1972), 'Revolt of the Elders: An Anatomy of the Loyalist Crowd in the Mau Mau Uprising 1952–1956', in B. A. Ogot (ed.), *Politics and Nationalism in Colonial Kenya*, Nairobi: East Africa Publishing House, pp. 134–48.

Ogude, J. A., (1991), '"The Truths of the Nation" and the Changing Image of Mau Mau in Kenyan Literature', in E. S. Atieno Odhiambo and John Lonsdale (eds), *Mau Mau and Nationhood*, London: James Currey.

Roseberg, G. Carl and John Nottingham (1966), *The Myth of Mau Mau: Nationalism in Kenya*, London: Oxford University Press.

Tamarkin, M. (1976), 'Mau Mau in Nakuru', *Journal of African History* 17: 1, pp. 119–34.

See also: **Historiography: East Africa; Kenya African National Union; Religions: East Africa.**

Anti-colonialism and Resistance: South Asia

The anti-colonial struggle against the British Empire in India was the product of various, often contradictory, social forces, ideas and tactics. Indians with opposing interests – capitalists and workers, landowners and peasants – did unite to fight the British, but also clashed over the movement's directions and ultimate aims. We are left, therefore, with a contradictory legacy: the tremendous heroism of the ordinary people who overthrew an empire, but also the tragedy of communal violence, partition, and continuing social inequality.

Resistance to colonialism after the 1857 revolt was fragmented and sporadic. The British had consolidated alliances with an old elite of landlords and princes; an emerging new group of English-educated civil servants and professionals was tied to the colonial structure. The peasant and tribal rebellions that did occur confronted their local oppressors, not the colonial state – even when they saw 'the foreigner' as part of the problem – and the fledgling urban classes were far from any nationalist consciousness. The Indian National Congress, formed in 1885 by new elites tiring of racist restrictions to their advancement, confined its activities to petitioning the government. Despite some limited agitational politics in the 1890s, it was only with the partition of the Bengal presidency in 1905 that the possibilities of mass action became apparent.

The Swadeshi movement of 1905 to 1908 began as a local initiative against the partition, but soon progressed to question the entire colonial edifice. Activists boycotted British goods and schools while developing plans for economic self-reliance and national education. The British responded with repression, but ultimately withdrew partition in 1911. Despite the victory of the Swadeshi movement, colonial strategies of divide-and-rule met with some success, especially in terms of Hindu–Muslim relations. Communal riots and religion-based mobilisations existed alongside instances of united, Hindu–Muslim opposition to partition. British claims that a divided East Bengal would benefit Muslims was convincing to some Muslim elites, who were under-represented in the class of English-educated men that constituted the Congress Party's initial base. Under these circumstances, and with the support of the colonial government, the Muslim League was founded in 1906. Muhammad Ali Jinnah, a Bombay lawyer and Congress Party member who would become the leader of independent Pakistan, joined the league in 1913.

World War I and its aftermath sparked political and economic changes that led to the expansion of anti-colonial struggle. To finance the war, British exploitation of the Indian economy via taxation intensified, increasing unrest and lending support to nationalist theories of the 'drain of wealth' from India to Britain. Further, although the state had traditionally not supported industrialisation in the colony, preferring India to be a market for British goods, the war forced the government to give some measure of support to Indian industry. In terms of political activity, home rule leagues formed across India from 1916 to 1918 under the leadership of Annie Besant and Bal Gangadhar Tilak, using political education to inspire new layers of activists to fight for Indian self-government. Although far from home rule demands, some limited expansion of 'responsible' government through the Montagu-Chelmsford reforms in 1919 also shaped the context for mass-based political activity.

It was at this juncture that Mohandas K. Gandhi became the leader of Congress and reorganised the party into a vehicle for mass struggle. Gandhi, a London-trained lawyer from Gujarat, first achieved celebrity in South Africa, where he led movements against the government's racist policies towards the Indian immigrant community. In these struggles, Gandhi developed the methods of *satyagraha*, emphasising the peaceful violation of specific laws by disciplined groups of activists, that he would use in India after his return in 1914. His insistence on mass *satyagraha* offered an alternative to existing forms of anti-colonial resistance, which had been polarised between individual acts of revolutionary terrorism on the one hand, and the constitutional agitation of the Congress Party on the other.

Some historians have argued that it is this vision of *satyagraha* – as a mass movement controlled from above by Congress leadership – that explains Gandhi's ability to unite various classes and social groups in struggle. Gandhi's emphasis on non-violence and cross-class co-operation, they suggest, gave confidence to landlords and capitalists to support anti-colonial resistance (e.g. Sarkar 2002). Other research has demonstrated the importance of rumours within a predominantly illiterate society, suggesting that people in struggle attached their own, often millenarian, meanings to the figure of Gandhi (Amin 1988). Indeed, we may trace a constant tension between Gandhi's attempts to discipline the masses into *satyagraha* and the pressures from below that strained Congress demands.

Gandhi's earliest activism in India, supporting indigo cultivators in Champaran, peasants in Kheda, and industrial workers in Ahmedabad, began a process of linking local actions to a broader nationalist movement. Gandhian methods of struggle emerged on the national level in the 'Rowlatt' *satyagraha* of 1919 and the Non-Co-operation Movement of 1921 to 1922. The anti-Rowlatt agitations for civil rights faced heavy British repression, culminating in the infamous Jallianwalah Bagh massacre of hundreds in Punjab. But the Non-Co-operation movement soon followed; with a clearer political orientation than the Swadeshi movement, Indians again organised mass boycotts of British institutions and goods and wore hand-woven cloth to symbolise economic and political self-sufficiency.

The Non-Co-operation movement drew its strength from and inspired other contemporary struggles. It represented a highpoint of Hindu–Muslim political unity by linking with the anti-British implications of the Khilafat movement, which had been building among Indian Muslims since the defeat of the Turkish Caliphate in World War I. Peasant movements forged crucial connections between nationalism and grassroots agitation. The strike wave of 1919 to 1921, forced by the shrinking of wartime demand, also fuelled the radical drift. However, as the anti-colonial movement proceeded with unprecedented intensity, activism adopted non-Gandhian tactics and threatened to move beyond Congress' control. Gandhi and Congress acted decisively to maintain their leadership, severing their links to anti-landlord agitations in Avadh and Malabar, and even calling off the Non-Co-operation movement itself when protesters attacked and killed policemen in the town of Chauri Chaura. Despite Congress' restraining attempts, however, the radicalisation and mass character of the 1920s' movements actually propelled anti-colonialism forward. In 1929, under pressure from labour militants, the Congress Party called for *purna swaraj* ('complete independence'), setting the stage for another upsurge when the Great Depression struck.

During the Depression, rural India suffered from a sharp decline in agricultural prices and urban areas faced high unemployment and low wages. These economic dislocations forced the colonial government to set up some protective tariffs for India-based industry; the Indian economy thus continued its transformation from being directly manipulated by Britain to being indirectly controlled by British capitalists collaborating with Indian capitalists in joint ventures. Nevertheless, even this could not soften the brunt of a colonial economy in depression. In the face of economic crisis, Congress mobilised masses of people into action through the Civil Disobedience campaigns of the 1930s.

The Civil Disobedience of 1930 to 1931 provides a sense of the movement's complex dynamics. It was launched by Gandhi's dramatic 287-mile march to the Gujarat seashore to make salt in defiance of the British tax on this basic commodity. The salt march electrified the nation by deftly tying the material needs of ordinary people to the political struggle for independence and self-reliance. Congress sanctioned the mass, illegal manufacture of salt, the boycott of foreign cloth and liquor, and the initiation of no-revenue campaigns.

The movement soon threatened the boundaries established by Congress, but Gandhi refused to call it off even when faced with such non-Gandhian struggles as the takeover of the Chittagong armoury, shootings of British officials in Bengal, militant forest *satyagrahas* by tribals against bans on tree-cutting, and an uprising in Peshawar in which Hindu soldiers refused to fire on the Muslim protestors. Overall, participation was even more widespread than in the Non-Co-operation struggle, and included unprecedented numbers of women, who were both mobilised by Congress and organised independently. However, Muslim participation was lower in comparison to 1921 and 1922. Sometimes alienated by the Hindu idioms of struggle ('cow protection' demands, for example), Muslims were also disproportionately represented among the small urban traders who stood to lose from the boycott of British goods.

The frequent and extended disruption of trade finally frightened moderate Indian merchants, who lobbied Congress for an end to the upsurge. By March 1931, the Gandhi-Irwin Pact was signed, securing the release of Civil Disobedience prisoners but pulling back from the demand for *purna swaraj*. Radicalised Indians were bitterly disappointed by the pact, including left-leaning Congress leaders like Jawaharlal Nehru, the future prime minister of independent India. Meanwhile, the results of the Congress' rightward drift were felt at the Second Round Table Conference in London. Having accommodated to Hindu communalism, the party weakened its claim to represent all Indians; organisations of Muslims, Sikhs, Christians, and Dalits ('untouchables'), drawing support from the British, continued their campaign for separate electorates under plans for 'responsible' government. The severe repression that followed the Round Table forced Congress itself to call for a new round of Civil Disobedience in 1932. Thus what historian Bipan Chandra has called the 'Pressure–Compromise–Pressure' pattern (Chandra 1981, p. 162) repeated itself through the 1930s: the nation moved ever closer to independence through mass struggle, but also moved away from the radical changes and communal unity required to bring more fundamental liberation.

World War II again heightened tensions between Indians and their British rulers. Price increases and shortages of rice and salt produced rampant profiteering that went virtually unchecked by the British government. Meanwhile, military recruitment and the Japanese march across South-east Asia brought the war ever closer to home for many Indians. The tragedy of the man-made Bengal famine sharply demonstrated the toll taken by British rule on Indian society.

In his declaration of war against Germany in August 1939, the British viceroy consulted no Indian leaders; Congress ministries that had been in power since 1937 resigned in protest. Congress leaders demanded freedom as a necessary pre-condition for participating in the war, but negotiations with the British, culminating in the Cripps Mission in 1942, were not successful. From this point onwards, nationalist support for the British war effort was out of the question – despite the strong anti-fascist traditions in Congress.

On 8 August 1942, the Congress issued its 'Quit India' resolution, summoning Indians to non-violent mass struggle. Anticipating the arrest of Congress leaders, the resolution called upon 'every Indian who desires freedom and strives for it [to] be his own guide' (cited in Chandra 1988, p. 469). The next morning most of the Congress leadership, including Gandhi and Nehru, were indeed arrested. Far from halting the movement, the arrests brought a new level of local activists to the forefront. The result was a powerful anti-colonial upsurge that frequently invoked the name of Gandhi, but over which Gandhi himself had little control.

In the days following the Quit India resolution, urban areas witnessed strikes, demonstrations, and clashes with the police and army. While posing a real challenge to colonial rule, the militancy of August 1942 was quickly crushed by the massive force of the wartime British military. From then on, new centres of struggle developed in the countryside, where the peasant leadership sought to destroy the infrastructure of British authority. In Midnapur (Bengal), Talcher (Orissa), and Satara (Maharashtra), the people created 'national governments' to take over the functions of the colonial state. Although this resistance continued until 1944, the threat to British rule was largely contained by the end of 1942.

Quit India successfully mobilised broad layers of Indian society in anti-colonial struggle, but uneven participation in the movement makes apparent its limitations. For example, the low level of Muslim participation speaks to the Congress Party's weakening influence among this population. Dalits, many of whom were among the poorest of the poor, hesitated to join a movement that was dominated by richer peasants. Overall, even in areas where rural resistance became peasant rebellion, popular mobilisation did not lead to social radicalism; peasant–landlord relations were relatively unquestioned and land was not redistributed. Class contradictions were relatively muted in urban areas as well, where nationalist strikes received some support from Indian factory owners and labour militancy was subsumed under calls for national unity.

Although Quit India was the last Congress-led struggle before independence, the colonial government faced significant resistance again in 1946, when a strike of 20,000 sailors on seventy-eight ships in the Royal Indian Navy drew support from students and workers across the country. Mutinous ships hoisted Congress, Muslim League, and Communist Party flags on their masts to show unity, but the strike was defeated when Congress and Muslim League leaders – showing unity of a different sort – ordered the sailors to surrender to British troops.

By the mid-1940s, the anti-colonial struggle had raised the economic and political costs of empire to an unsustainable level. However, critical questions about the timing and nature of Indian independence were still open for debate. The Muslim League's claim to be the sole representative of Muslims in India, implausible in 1937 when it lost many reserved Muslim seats in elections, had gained credibility during the war, in part through British support. In 1940, the league adopted a demand for a separate Muslim state of Pakistan; meanwhile, Hindu communalist groups continued their efforts to paint all India with a Hindu brush. Congress, unable to unite Hindus, Muslims and Sikhs in common anti-colonial struggle on the eve of the British departure, could not provide an effective counterweight to separatist demands. Instead, the partition of the subcontinent produced two independent nations, India and Pakistan, on 15 August 1947. In 1971, East Pakistan broke away from the west to form Bangladesh.

Sri Lanka's path to independence from Britain in 1948 can be linked to that of India and Pakistan in several ways. On one level, patterns of Sri Lankan resistance were structured by the general material and ideological conditions of colonial South Asia. Colonial exploitation of the economy and the land (highlighted during the world wars and the Depression), the cultural impact of English and Christian education, and undemocratic restrictions in government and employment spurred nationalist and anti-colonial consciousness among various sections of the populace. Further, Sri Lanka (called Ceylon until 1972) had to grapple with the classic problems of anti-colonial nationalism: the gap between the Westernised elite and the majority of the people; the inherent tensions of cross-class alliances; the urban/rural divide; and the clash of ethnic/regional/religious identities.

More specifically, from the early twentieth century onwards, events in the subcontinent had both direct and indirect implications for Sri Lankan politics. As in the Indian case, the early decades of the century witnessed the emergence of diverse forms of political expression, ranging from Sinhala-Buddhist revivalism, as expressed in the temperance movements of 1903 to 1905 and 1911 to 1914, and the creation of the Ceylon National Congress in 1919, to rising class consciousness in urban areas, leading to the general strike of 1923. However, whereas some left-leaning labour leaders such as A. E. Goonesinha drew inspiration from the mass actions and boycotts of the Indian anti-colonial struggle, mainstream Sri Lankan nationalism as embodied by the Ceylon National Congress did not develop a mass base or an agitational politics. Wedded to the 'constitutionalist' tactics that had been thoroughly rejected by the Indian National Congress by the 1920s, various leaders of the Ceylon National Congress – from P. Arunachalam to D. S. Senanayake – looked to gradual reform in co-operation with the colonial government. As a result, instead of the 'Pressure–Compromise–Pressure' dynamic that characterised Indian politics from the 1920s to the 1940s, the same period in Sri Lanka witnessed the inauguration of administrative reforms from above. Ironically, as exemplified by the Donoughmore Commission's recommendation for universal suffrage and rejection of communal electorates in 1927, Sri Lankan reforms sometimes went beyond their Indian counterparts.

The implications of the nationalists' non-confrontational, 'constitutionalist' outlook became apparent in the communalisation of Sri Lankan politics through the 1930s and 1940s. During this period, although the Ceylon National Congress attempted to build a more cohesive political and economic programme, it ultimately did not articulate a secular-nationalist vision that might bridge the growing divide between the Sinhala Buddhist majority and the Tamil Hindu–Muslim minority. Communalist organisations formed and flourished: S. W. R. D. Bandaranaike's Sinhala Maha Sabha (1937), the Ceylon Indian Congress (1939), and the All-Ceylon Tamil Congress (1944). The Ceylon National Congress retained an ambivalent relationship to communalism: by the early 1940s, joint membership with both Congress and communal organisations was specifically banned, but the Sinhala Maha Sabha remained within Congress and gained influence.

As independence approached, any political formation challenging the 'constitutionalist' strategy or the logic of mass-based, Sinhala nationalism had been marginalised – a process avidly encouraged by British officials. Left-wing parties like the Lanka Sama Samaj Party, though leading important strikes and local struggles through the 1930s and 1940s, had a small base and could not organise an ideological alternative to Sinhala communalism; in the postcolonial period, they actually capitulated to it. Tamil nationalist leaders like G. G. Ponnambalam now became more isolationist, either casting their lot with the British as sole protectors of minority rights, only to be sorely disappointed, or retreating into the closed universe of Tamil communalism. Meanwhile, in sharp contrast to the Indian nationalists at this time, Sri Lankan leaders continued their moderate course, committing themselves to and reaping benefits from the British effort in World War II, and finally – via the Soulbury Commission of 1944 – gaining dominion status in 1948.

In this context, the relatively peaceful nature of the 'transfer of power' in Sri Lanka compared to that in India and Pakistan served as a smokescreen for the actual weakness of that transformation in terms of secularism and democracy, one that was to be viciously revealed in the communal violence of the postcolonial period.

Developed in the context of colonial educational institutions and the British introduction of print capitalism, modern South Asian literatures were integrally linked to the colonial experience. These literatures, especially in prose, drew from various reform and nationalist movements; their growth was both the vehicle for, and the beneficiary of, an explosion of ideas about culture, society, and identity in the context of colonial rule. The uneven content of the anti-colonial struggle, consequently, was reflected in their pages.

Prior to the rise of mass struggle in the Indian subcontinent, texts like Gopal Hari

Deshmukh's *Satapatra* series (Marathi, 1848–50), called for national uplift but did not oppose colonialism; later, Bankim Chandra Chatterjee's *Anand Math* (Bengali, 1882) raised nationalist consciousness, but with a distinctly anti-Muslim note. Piyadasa Sirisena's poetry asserted traditional Sinhalese values against an encroaching Westernisation. New ideas about gender were central to early-twentieth-century writing in South Asia: Rokeya Sakhawat Hossain's *Sultana's Dream* (English, 1905), envisioned a new society free from gender oppression.

However, literary texts written around anti-colonial struggles explored various aspects of the movements and their impact on consciousness. In one of Kumaran Asan's poems (Malayalam, 1908), the poet complains to 'Mother India' about her children's blindness towards caste oppression. Rabindranath Tagore addressed the Swadeshi movement's backward ideas about gender and society in *Ghare-Baire* (Bengali, 1914). English-language novelists of the 1930s explored village life and its links to colonialism and nationalism from different perspectives, as in J. Vijayatunga's *Grass for My Feet* (Sri Lanka, 1933), Mulk Raj Anand's *Untouchable* (India, 1935), and Raja Rao's *Kanthapura* (India, 1938). Martin Wickramasinghe's nationalist novels and literary criticism of the 1940s were central to the development of modern Sinhalese literature. Faiz Ahmad Faiz's poem, 'Dawn of Freedom' (Urdu, 1947) sharply criticised politicians and communalists immediately after the devastation of partition, using imagery directly referring to Nehru's 'Tryst with Destiny' speech on the eve of independence.

Pre-1947 literatures helped consolidate debate about the nation and the formation of a national consciousness as ideas crackled across regional and linguistic boundaries. Postcolonial literature, more generally, has repeatedly turned to the colonial experience and the anti-colonial movements, as the social, political, and cultural dynamics of that era continue to impact on the present. Nayantara Sahgal's *Rich Like Us* (1988), Rohinton Mistry's *A Fine Balance* (1996), and A. Sivanandan's *When Memory Dies* (1997) have employed a more realist mode in documenting the growth and aftermath of nationalism in India and Sri Lanka – with a specific attention to its impact on the lower classes that hearkens back to the writings of the early postcolonial period. Representing the nation through a more postmodernist aesthetic, Salman Rushdie's *Midnight's Children* (1980), Amitav Ghosh's *The Shadow Lines* (1988), Arundhati Roy's *The God of Small Things* (1997), Kamila Shamsie's *Salt and Saffron* (2000) and Shyam Selvadurai's *Cinnamon Gardens* (1999) have highlighted the issues of transnational, sexual, and/or gendered identities.

Pranav Jani and Mytheli Sreenivas

Literary Works

Bhattacharya, Bhabhani (1966), *Shadow from Ladakh*, New York: Crown Publishers.
Desai, Anita [1980] (1982), *Clear Light of Day*, London: Penguin Books.
Ghosh, Amitav (1988), *The Shadow Lines*, Delhi: Ravi Dayal.
Hasan, Mushirul (ed.) (1995), *India Partitioned: The Other Face of Freedom*, New Delhi: Lotus Collection.
Hossain, Attia (1961), *Sunlight on a Broken Column*, London: Chatto and Windus.
Khan, Uzma Aslam (2003), *Trespassing*, New Delhi: Penguin India.
Markandaya, Kamala (1969), *The Coffer Dams*, New York: John Day.
Mistry, Rohinton [1995] (1996), *A Fine Balance*, New York: Knopf.
Mukaddam, Sharf (1982), *When Freedom Came*, New Delhi: Vikas.

Nahal, Chaman (1975), *Azadi*, Boston: Houghton Mifflin.

Narayan, R. K. [1955] (1997), *Waiting for the Mahatma*, Mysore: Indian Thought Publications.

Roy, Arundhati, (1997), *The God of Small Things*, New Delhi: Indialink.

Rushdie, Salman (1980), *Midnight's Children*, New York: Knopf.

Rushdie, Salman [1983] (1997), *Shame*, New York: Henry Holt and Company.

Rushdie, Salman and Elizabeth West (eds) (1997), *Mirrorwork: Fifty Years of Indian Writing, 1947–1997*, New York: Vintage.

Sahgal, Nayantara [1985] (1988), *Rich Like Us*, New York: New Directions.

Selvadurai, Shyam (1999), *Cinnamon Gardens*, New York: Hyperion.

Shamsie, Kamila (2000), *Salt and Saffron*, New York: Bloomsbury.

Shamsie, Muneeza (ed.) (1997), *A Dragonfly in the Sun: An Anthology of Pakistani Writing in English*, Oxford: Oxford University Press.

Sidhwa, Bapsi (1991), *Cracking India*, Minneapolis: Milkweed Editions.

Singh, Khushwant (1956), *Train to Pakistan*, New York: Grove Press.

Sivanandan, A. (1997), *When Memory Dies*, London: Arcadia Books.

Tharoor, Shashi (1989), *The Great Indian Novel*, New York: Arcade.

Vijayatunga, J. [1933] (1953), *Grass for My Feet*, London: Edward Arnold.

Histories

Amin, Shahid (1988), 'Gandhi as Mahatma', in Ranajit Guha and Gayatri Spivak (eds), *Selected Subaltern Studies*, Oxford: Oxford University Press, pp. 288–342.

Amin, Shahid (1995), *Event, Metaphor, Memory: Chauri Chaura, 1922–1992*, Berkeley: University of California Press.

Baker, Christopher J. and David Washbrook (1975), *South India: Political Institutions and Political Change 1880–1940*, Delhi: Macmillan.

Brown, Judith M. (1972), *Gandhi's Rise to Power: Indian Politics, 1915–1922*, Cambridge: Cambridge University Press.

Chandra, Bipan [1979] (1981), *Nationalism and Colonialism in Modern India*, Hyderabad: Orient Longman.

Chandra, Bipan, Mridula Mukherjee, Aditya Mukherjee, K. N. Panikkar and Sucheta Mahajan (1988), *India's Struggle for Independence*, New Delhi: Viking.

Chatterjee, Partha (1986), *Nationalist Thought and the Colonial World: A Derivative Discourse?*, Delhi: Oxford University Press.

De Silva, K. M. (1981), *A History of Sri Lanka*, London: C. Hurst and Company.

Epstein, S. J. M. (1988), *The Earthy Soil: Bombay Peasants and the Indian Nationalist Movement, 1919–1947*, New Delhi: Oxford University Press.

Guha, Ranajit (1988), 'On Some Aspects of the Historiography of Colonial India', in Ranajit Guha and Gayatri Spivak (eds), *Selected Subaltern Studies*, Oxford: Oxford University Press, pp. 37–44.

Hardiman, David (1981), *Peasant Nationalists of Gujarat: Kheda District, 1917–1934*, New Delhi: Oxford University Press.

Hardiman, David (1987), *The Coming of the Devi: Adivasi Assertion in Western India*, New Delhi: Oxford University Press.

Jalal, Ayesha (1985), *The Sole Spokesman: Jinnah, the Muslim League and the Demand for Pakistan*, Cambridge: Cambridge University Press.

Minault, Gail (2000), *The Khilafat Movement: Religious Symbolism and Political Mobilisation in India*, 2nd edn, New Delhi: Oxford University Press.

Pandey, Gyanendra (ed.) (1988), *The Indian Nation in 1942*, Calcutta: K. P. Bagchi.

Pouchepadass, Jacques (1999), *Champaran and Gandhi: Planters, Peasants, and Gandhian Politics*, trans. James Walker, New Delhi: Oxford University Press.

Russell, Jane (1982), *Communal Politics under the Donoughmore Constitution, 1931–1947*, Dehiwala: Tisara Prakaskayo.

Sarkar, Sumit (2002), *Modern India: 1885–1947*, 8th edn, Delhi: Macmillan.

Wilson, A. Jeyaratnam (1999), *Sri Lankan Tamil Nationalism: Its Origins and Development in the Nineteenth and Twentieth Centuries*, Vancouver: University of British Columbia Press.

See also: **Bengal Famine; Chauri-Chaura Incident; Communism: South Asia; Indian National Army; Indigo Rebellion; Jallianwalah Bagh Massacre; Jinnah, Mohammed Ali; Mutinies in India; Nehru, Jawaharlal; Partition; World Wars I and II: South Asian Soldiers; Years of Terror.**

Anti-colonialism and Resistance: Southern Africa

By 1960 colonialism was coming to an end across much of Africa, a result of the weakened position of European empires after World War II coupled with the upsurge of anti-colonial resistance. But Southern African settler societies resisted the movement to end white domination; the following years saw an intensification of white minority rule in the region and, accordingly, of black resistance.

The year 1948 had already seen the hardening of racial domination in South Africa, following the National Party's electoral victory and its implementation of apartheid, the policy of entrenched white supremacy in all spheres of South African society. The Cold War was sweeping across the world, and apartheid was rationalised by the need to fight communism; the Suppression of Communism Act was passed in 1950, and over the decade the state clamped down on peaceful protest. On 21 March 1960 South African police at Sharpeville massacred sixty-nine unarmed black demonstrators who were protesting against the country's notorious pass laws. This brutal response to a peaceful demonstration was an exemplar for other white minority regimes in Southern Africa: in June 1960 police in Mozambique massacred demonstrators at Mueda, killing up to 600.

But resistance could not be quashed. The next year, the revolt of Luanda in February 1961 inaugurated a brutal fifteen-year guerrilla struggle in Angola. Armed struggle began in South Africa in December 1961, in Mozambique in 1964, in Namibia in 1966 and in Rhodesia (now Zimbabwe) in 1972. These political struggles, which spawned vibrant cultures of resistance, rapidly became intertwined with Cold War political ambitions, as the United States, the Soviet Union and China jostled for influence in the region.

South Africa's liberation movement was the oldest. The African National Congress (ANC), founded in 1912, had a long history of peaceful protest, but across the liberation movement, the Sharpeville massacre signalled the failure of purely non-violent means. The ANC and the South African Communist Party (SACP) formed Umkhonto we Sizwe (Spear of the Nation) (MK) in 1961, launching a sabotage campaign that December; the Pan Africanist Congress (PAC) formed Poqo (We Stand Alone), which began its fight in 1962. The arrest of MK leaders in 1962 and 1963, of PAC leaders in April–June 1963 and of other activists over the next year ended this first stage of armed protest. But with overt political dissent inside South Africa silenced, the exiled ANC, PAC and, later, the much smaller Unity Movement of South Africa (UMSA), continued their efforts at armed struggle (see Lodge 1983).

In the Portuguese colonies of Angola and Mozambique, liberation movements developed in reaction to the intensification of racism spurred by waves of immigration, a process forcefully depicted by Pepetela's novel *Yaka* (1996), which spans several generations of a white family in Benguela, Angola. Portugal's authoritarian regime prevented criticism and reform; as censorship grew, political dissent was expressed through poetry and, when published poetry was banned, through oral culture. The Movimento Popular da Libertação de Angola (People's Movement for the Liberation of Angola – MPLA), based in and around Luanda, was formed in December 1956, many of its leaders influenced by Portuguese Marxists. After Luanda erupted in February 1961, the MPLA began organising a guerrilla struggle, supported by the Soviet Union. Its leaders were concerned to promote political education and to democratise the struggle, and the long guerrilla war radicalised sections of the population. Nonetheless, internecine rivalries kept the MPLA fragmented and frequently ineffective. The northern-based Frente Nacional para a Libertação de Angola (National Front for the Liberation of Angola – FNLA), supported by the Chinese, and the União Nacional para a Independência Total de Angola (National Union for the Total Independence of Angola – UNITA), based in the southern highlands and supported by the United States and South Africa, were founded as rivals to the MPLA (see Davidson 1972; Birmingham 1992).

By contrast, the Mozambican liberation movement achieved greater organisational unity and cohesion. In 1962 exiles formed the Frente de Libertação de Moçambique (Mozambique Liberation Front – FRELIMO) in neighbouring Tanzania. Two years later, in September 1964, FRELIMO launched its armed struggle in Cabo Delgado Province. The next decade saw victories and defeats for both sides. Forced by setbacks to rethink its approach to popular mobilisation, including that of women, FRELIMO had regionalised success in the north, where it gained peasant support through education and development projects (Birmingham 1992; Isaacman and Isaacman 1983).

South of Angola, appeals to the United Nations for assistance against South Africa's illegal occupation of Namibia received sympathy but had little practical effect. The South West African National Union (SWANU) was formed in 1959; the South West African People's Organisation (SWAPO) was launched the next year. Both parties had strong regional and ethnic bases, with SWAPO's support mainly from the Ovambo in the north. By 1966 SWAPO guerrillas were attacking South African forces, inspiring widespread support.

The transition from white minority rule had a different dynamic in Southern Africa's British colonies. The break-up of the Federation of Rhodesia and Nyasaland led to the independence of Zambia and Malawi in 1964. Lesotho and Botswana became independent in 1966, and Swaziland in 1968. But Britain refused to grant independence to Rhodesia without its commitment to majority rule. In retaliation, Ian Smith announced a unilateral declaration of independence under white minority rule on 11 November 1965. Black opposition had developed slowly since the 1950s and had faced repeated bannings. The Zimbabwe African People's Union (ZAPU) was formed in 1961, but in 1963 Robert Mugabe broke away and founded the Zimbabwe African National Union (ZANU), a split that largely followed ethnic lines (see Herbst 1990).

In South Africa, the 1960s had been the decade of 'grand apartheid', characterised by bannings, by increased repression and by the massive resettlement of Africans into *bantustans* or so-called 'black homelands'. But the temporary political quiescence that ensued ended with the strike wave of 1973 and the rise of the black consciousness movement. Influenced by black theology, by Paulo Freire's ideas on the pedagogy of liberation, by the American Black Power movement and by student protests overseas, black consciousness activists launched themselves into community and educational projects. Keenly aware of broader regional developments, they organised Viva FRELIMO rallies in support of the Mozambican struggle. They also engaged in trade union work, and their activities, together with those of white student radicals, strengthened the rapidly developing labour movement. Several years later, on 16 June 1976, school children in Soweto began a protest against the forced impo-sition of the Afrikaans language as a medium of instruction, signalling the significance of language as a symbol of both oppression and resistance in South Africa. This protest, the backdrop of Sipho Sepamla's (1981) novel, *A Ride on the Whirlwind*, became a year-long uprising that transformed politics in the country. In the ensuing state crackdown, many young people fled the country. The ANC's well-established networks and superior resources, compared to the PAC or the UMSA, inevitably brought it many new recruits from the most recent wave of exiles.

The intensity of events generated great cultural creativity. Nadine Gordimer's *Burger's Daughter* (1979) concerns the white communist left and the struggle of white radicals to find a role for themselves faced with the challenges posed by the black consciousness move-ment. It stands in counterpoint to Mandla Langa's *Tenderness of Blood* (1987), which depicts the black radical world from student life at Fort Hare, to exile, armed struggle and imprisonment. The novel's theme is betrayal. It addresses a paradox very germane to South Africa in that era: that those whose political courage earned them mythical status might lack emotional courage in personal relationships. The two novels suggest that, despite their commitment to a common struggle, black and white radicals lived in separate worlds that only occasionally intersected.

Guerrilla war dragged on in the Portuguese colonies. A military coup in Portugal on 25 April 1974 changed the course of the liberation struggles. In Mozambique, FRELIMO had achieved some striking success, controlling the north and parts of the central region, although the cities and coastal areas remained under Portuguese control. But military success in settler zones led to a ceasefire in September and independence under FRELIMO's rule in June 1975. By contrast, the struggle in oil-rich Angola was complicated by super-power rivalries. Pepetela's novel *Mayombe* (1996), set in Angola's Cabinda province around 1970–1, addresses the themes of tribalism, racism and sexual politics amongst a group of MPLA guerrillas, while depicting their commitment to political education. But the MPLA continued to be racked by internal dissension; and when the Portuguese coup occurred the internally-divided Angolan nationalists and the colonial forces were at a mil-itary stalemate. Thus, when Angola became independent in November 1975, it lacked a unified government. The MPLA established the People's Republic of Angola with a government in Luanda, while the FNLA and UNITA proclaimed the Democratic People's Republic of Angola, headquartered in Huambo. By January/February 1976, the MPLA had gained military dominance with the help of Cuban troops and Soviet arms, and South African troops withdrew into Namibia. In the USA, domestic political pressure led to the passage in 1976 of the Clark Amendment, which prevented further covert American aid to the FNLA and UNITA. The MPLA became recognised as the official government.

The independence of Angola and Mozambique facilitated diplomatic activity by the presidents of Angola, Mozambique, Tanzania and Zambia to resolve the struggle in Rhodesia, which had escalated in 1972. Mozambique's independence had allowed ZANU to open a base and infiltrate guerrillas into Rhodesia; however, neither ZANU nor ZAPU were as successful as FRELIMO had been. In the late 1970s ZANU and ZAPU formed a Patriotic Front (PF), an alliance of convenience. Following a ceasefire and a settlement negotiated at Lancaster House in London in late 1979, Zimbabwe became independent. ZANU (PF) won an overwhelming electoral victory the following year (Herbst 1990; Kriger 2003). The hidden side of the eulogised independence struggle was laid bare in a number of 'Chimurenga' novels, notably Chenjerai Hove's (1990) novel *Bones*.

The independence of Angola, Mozambique and Zimbabwe failed to bring peace to the region. The late 1970s and 1980s saw numerous advances of South African forces, with Western collusion, into the surrounding countries. In 1971 the International Court of Justice had ruled South Africa's occupation of Namibia illegal, but the apartheid regime refused to withdraw. South Africa gave some support to Zimbabwe dissidents, but it was more concerned about the radical leftist governments in Angola and Mozambique. The intensification of Soviet and American Cold War rivalries in the early 1980s exacerbated and prolonged the civil wars in those countries, traumatising the populations. While Mozambique's FRELIMO government lost control of major areas of the country to South African-backed Mozambique National Resistance (RENAMO) forces, Angola was devastated by continued incursions of South African troops in support of UNITA and FNLA forces, and the MPLA appealed to Cuba for troops to defend the government. The United States government repealed the Clark Amendment in 1985, paving the way for American military support to the rebel forces (Birmingham 1992; Urdang 1989; and Turshen and Twagiramariya 1998).

The destabilisation campaign also hurt the South African liberation struggle. In 1984 Mozambique signed the Nkomati Accord with South Africa. Ostensibly prohibiting guerrilla incursions from either country, in practice South Africa continued supporting RENAMO, while ANC and MK forces lost their access to Mozambique. Moreover, the conditions of exile stifled democracy within the ANC, and paranoia flourished in the guerrilla camps. The 1984 mutiny of ANC soldiers at its Quatro detention camp in Angola, evoked by Zoë Wicomb in *David's Story* (2001), was a telling example: soldiers protesting against the lack of democracy and against being caught up in the Angolan civil war rather than being repatriated to fight in their own country were cruelly suppressed by their leadership. Its buildings 'spoke of the battles that had been fought, the walls of barracks and the administration block pockmarked by bullets, much like the walls of firing squads' (Langa 1996, p. 79). The South African government continued its military aggression, with a raid on Gaborone, Botswana on 14 June 1985 and an apparent role in the military coup that overthrew the Lesotho prime minister, Chief Leabua Jonathan, in January 1986 (Bell 2001).

The mid-1980s saw a remarkable upsurge in popular protest in South Africa, culminating in the launch of two major trade union federations, the Congress of South African Trade Unions and the National Council of Trade Unions, and the 1985 Vaal Uprising. The United Democratic Front emerged as the largest umbrella organisation within the liberation movement, giving its weight to the exiled ANC. With the ANC 'effectively driven out of the neighbouring states' (Bell 2001), by 1987 behind the scenes talks were taking place between South African government and business representatives, on the one side, and the ANC, on the other.

In Angola, the battle of Cuito Cuanavale, fought in 1987 and 1988 with the support of Cuban troops, led to a decisive MPLA victory against both its domestic rivals and South African forces, who pulled out in May 1988. A peace accord was signed by all parties in

December 1988, although fighting between the MPLA and UNITA continued after the ceasefire signed in May 1991. The withdrawal of Cuban troops from Angola was linked to the acceptance of Namibian independence. Namibian elections took place in November 1989; with SWAPO victorious, independence was declared on 21 March 1990. In Mozambique, similar efforts to resolve the civil war were proceeding. FRELIMO and RENAMO signed a peace accord in 1992, and FRELIMO won multiparty elections held in Mozambique in 1994 (see Davidson 1994; Birmingham 1992; and Bell 2001).

The winding down of the Cold War meant that supporters of apartheid could no longer point to the spectre of a communist threat in Southern Africa. In February 1990 the ANC, PAC, SACP and thirty-three other organisations were unbanned, followed by the release of Nelson Mandela and other political prisoners. After several years of stop and start and sometimes contested negotiations, the first democratic elections took place in April 1994. The transition was accompanied by claims that popular participation had been sidelined to the benefit of black and white political elites. Political violence was as characteristic of apartheid's final years as was the desire for a negotiated settlement, as Sindiwe Magona's novel *Mother to Mother* poignantly illustrates. The Truth and Reconciliation Commission, set up to deal with apartheid's human rights violations and to promote national reconciliation, provoked intense criticism from diverse perspectives. The outpourings of stories at its sessions, heretofore suppressed due to trauma, fears of retaliation or the pressures of secrecy, challenged the teleological tales of good and evil that dominated the liberation struggles across the region, a challenge also seen in post-apartheid literature. 'I no longer know which story I am trying to write,' confessed one of Zoë Wicomb's characters. 'Who could keep going in a straight line with so many stories, like feral siblings, separated and each running wild, chasing each other's tales?' (Wicomb 2001, p. 201).

Allison Drew

Literary Works

Gordimer, Nadine (1979), *Burger's Daughter*, London: Penguin.

Hove, Chenjerai [1988] (1990), *Bones*, Oxford and Portsmouth, NH: Heinemann.

Langa, Mandla (1987), *Tenderness of Blood*, Harare: Zimbabwe Publishing House.

Langa, Mandla (1996), *The Naked Song and Other Stories*, Cape Town and Johannesburg: David Philip.

Magona, Sindiwe (1998), *Mother to Mother*, Boston, MA: Beacon Press.

Pepetela [Artur Carlos Maurício Pestana] [1980] (1996), *Mayombe*, trans. M. Wolfers, Oxford and Portsmouth, NH: Heinemann.

Pepetela [Artur Carlos Maurício Pestana] [1984] (1996), *Yaka*, trans. M. Holness, Oxford and Portsmouth, NH: Heinemann.

Sepamla, Sipho (1981), *A Ride on the Whirlwind*, Oxford and Portsmouth, NH: Heinemann.

Wicomb, Zoë (2001), *David's Story*, New York: Feminist Press.

Histories

Bell, Terry, with Dumisa Buhle Ntsebeza (2001), *Unfinished Business: South Africa, Apartheid and Truth*, Observatory, Cape Town: Red Works.

Birmingham, David (1992), *Frontline Nationalism in Angola and Mozambique*, London: James Currey; and Trenton, NJ: Africa World Press.

Davidson, Basil (1972), *In the Eye of the Storm: Angola's People*, London: Longman.

Davidson, Basil (1994), *Modern Africa: A Social and Political History*, 3rd edn, London and New York: Longman.

Drew, Allison (ed. and intro.) (1997), *South Africa's Radical Tradition. A Documentary History*, 2 vols, Cape Town: Buchu Books, Mayibuye Press, University of Cape Town Press.

Herbst, Jeffrey (1990), *State Politics in Zimbabwe*, Berkeley, Los Angeles and Oxford: University of California Press.

Isaacman, Allen and Barbara Isaacman (1983), *Mozambique: From Colonialism to Revolution, 1900–1982*, Boulder, CO, Westview; Aldershot: Gower.

Kriger, Norma J. (2003), *Guerrilla Veterans in Post-war Zimbabwe: Symbolic and Violent Politics, 1980–1987*, Cambridge: Cambridge University Press.

Lodge, Tom (1983), *Black Politics in South Africa since 1945*, London and New York: Longman.

Turshen, Meredith and Clotilde Twagiramariya (eds) (1998), *What Women Do in Wartime: Gender and Conflict in Africa*, London and New York: Zed Press.

Urdang, Stephanie (1989), *And Still they Dance: Women, War and the Struggle for Change in Mozambique*, London: Earthscan.

See also: **Apartheid and Segregation; Black Consciousness: Southern Africa; Chimurengas; Nationalism(s): Southern Africa**.

Anti-colonialism and Resistance: West Africa

Colonialism, as the thesis, by its very nature produced its anti-thesis, resistance and anti-colonial movements. Often resistance in the form of strikes, riots and demonstrations developed into fully-fledged rebellions, and more often than not, these acts of resistance took the colonial authorities by surprise. To take but a few examples: the 1898 military uprising led by Bai Bureh (d. 1908) in Sierra Leone saw the out-numbered but tactically inventive African guerrillas hold out for over ten months, and inflict significant losses on the British; in the case of the 'Aba Women's War' in south-eastern Nigeria in 1929, not only did the events take the colonial authorities unaware, but no European understood the exact significance of the war attire of the women, as they went about attacking the symbols of colonial rule; again in Sierra Leone the 1955 general strike and the 1956 tax revolts also wrong-footed the colonial authorities and provided effective anti-colonial resistance.

The four West African territories under British colonial rule were consolidated after military expeditions in the final quarter of the nineteenth century, and in 1900 consisted of Nigeria with a population of fifteen million, Gold Coast (Ghana after independence) with 2 million, Sierra Leone with 1 million, and the Gambia with 100,000 subjects. However, because colonialism did not assume a monolithic form even within the British Empire, the nature, form and extent of anti-colonial resistance varied in the different regions, and it is accordingly impossible to provide neat generalisations. The consequences of resisting British encroachments also had different outcomes for Africans. Under certain circumstances, protracted conflict may indeed have helped to increase African bargaining power under colonial rule, as in the case of the Emirates in Northern Nigeria, whose military resistance helped to forge 'special relations' with the British administration. Resistance and collaboration therefore frequently went hand-in-hand. Furthermore, resistance to European occupation did not by definition mean reluctance to modernise, as many traditional rulers utilised opportunities provided by colonial institutions and markets to privilege themselves and their siblings. In rejecting the resistance/collaboration binary, Terence Ranger observes that:

> Resistance on the part of an African people did not necessarily imply a romantic, reactionary rejection of 'modernity', though a lengthy war might of course occasion repudiation of European influence. Similarly, non-resistance, in the sense of abstaining from armed struggle, did not always imply readiness to modernise. (Ranger 1969, p. 305)

For Britain, the range of African responses to colonial rule had an important influence on political debates and policies, and violent acts of anti-colonial resistance in particular challenged all easy generalisations about the readiness of Africans to accept colonial rule.

Colonial rule in Africa took one of two forms: direct rule (French, Belgian and Portuguese); and indirect rule (British). The latter was worked out by Theophilus Shepstone in Natal in the nineteenth century, and elaborated in great detail subsequently by Lord Frederick Lugard in West Africa. Indirect rule is explained by Lord Malcolm Hailey in the *African Survey* of 1939 as 'the system by which the tutelary power recognizes existing African societies and assists them to adapt themselves to the functions of local government' (Hailey 1939, p. 143). Further, indirect rule accepted the 'prevailing indigenous administrative or authority units as the basis of colonial administration' (Cartey and Kilson 1970, p. 74). By contrast, direct rule ignored or negated African traditional authority structures, which were quickly replaced by imported structures from the metropolis. According to Mamdani, direct rule also:

> involved a comprehensive sway of market institutions: the appropriation of land, the destruction of communal autonomy, and the defeat and dispersal of tribal populations . . . [triggering off] the reintegration and domination of the natives in the institutional context of semiservile and semicapitalist agrarian relations. (Mamdani 1996, p. 17)

For the vast majority of Africans who were excluded from rights of citizenship, 'direct rule signified an unmediated – centralised – despotism' (Mamdani 1996, p.17). In reality, colonial rule was based on a hybrid form of both systems, and this was particularly true by the 1920s . However, one fundamental difference between the two systems was the higher ratio of colonial officials to African population, under direct rule. This relatively greater concentration of colonial administrators, Cartey and Kilson argue, made direct rule a 'more repressive' form of colonial administration. In general, the greater the European presence, particularly in terms of land appropriated from Africans, the greater the political awareness and the intensity of anti-colonial struggles.

Cartey and Kilson have also observed that European administrators did not have a monopoly of repression, as from the nineteenth century onwards African chiefs under indirect rule exercised power in a rather heavy-handed and corrupt manner – what Mamdani has called 'decentralised despotism' (Mamdani 1996, p. 17). Their power combined the autonomy to govern their subjects and the support of the colonial government. These two normative forms of colonial governance impacted on the nature of resistance and the type of anti-colonial movement that emerged in each territory. The contradictory position of the African chiefs as the gatekeeper of tradition and now endowed with modern authority gave rise to anti-chief agitations, as well as the emergence of militant popular groups, whose aim was to put an end to repression within the Native Administration system. As the number of educated young people increased, the challenge to what was seen as the authoritarian style of the chiefs became widespread and intensified in colonies such as Ghana and Sierra Leone. The situation was exacerbated by the support and many privileges which chiefs and their hangers-on enjoyed under colonial rule. Writing about the Native Administration system in the Gold Coast, Kofi Busia (1951) drew attention to the protection accorded by the colonial government to the chiefs in Agona, Ejisu, Akropong, Ahinkuro and Nsuatre in the face of rebellions by their subjects. Busia argued that under British rule, the struggle between commoners and traditional rulers became more acute, as the latter were dependent on the colonial government's support for the chiefs. The contest between youth and traditional authority soon metamorphosed into anti-colonial struggles, in which youth took centre stage.

After World War I, there were no large-scale, military anti-colonial uprisings like those in nineteenth-century West Africa (most importantly, the Asante Wars 1873–4 and 1891–8), and in other parts of Africa over the same period: the Chimurenga in Rhodesia (1896–7), the Herero Revolt in German South-West Africa (1905–6), or the Bambatha Rebellion in Natal (1906). There were nonetheless a number of significant moments of resistance. These can be loosely grouped under four headings: protests with direct economic causes; protests led by the educated African elites; rebellions cast in religious terms; and the rise of Pan-Africanism and Negritude. First, to summarise the economically motivated protests: in 1919, there were riots against inflation in Sierra Leone; in the early 1920s, substantial numbers of workers were unionised for the first time in the Gold Coast; in 1929, Igbo women in eastern Nigeria attacked the canteens of the British-owned monopolies in the 'Women's War'; and in 1930 and again in 1938, there were dramatic and extensive cocoa boycotts in the Gold Coast. Second, African elite protest in the inter-war years built on the work of the Aborigines' Rights Protection Society (ARPS – formed in 1897) in the Gold Coast, which had petitioned on issues like improved education promotion within the civil service. The ARPS was succeeded after the war by the pan-territorial National Congress of British West Africa (NCBWC) and Herbert Macauley's (d. 1949) Nigerian National Democratic Party (NNDP – formed in 1923), whose political energies were for the most part directed to single issues, as in the protracted opposition in Lagos to the rising water rate. Third, there were a number of rebellions against British rule that assumed a specifically religious character (see Tordoff 2002). This was true of the 1931 rebellion in northern Sierra Leone led by Haidara Kontorfilli (c. 1890–1931), a Marabout from the Senegalese Mouride who claimed to have the 'name of God with him' (see Crowder 1981). Other examples include the igniting of latent Mahdist beliefs in the Sudan, and the rise of independent Church movements as an avenue for expressing African dissent. Toyin Falola (2001) has drawn attention to the fact that in West Africa from the 1920s, members of the elite utilised the church, media, lectures and social activities to circulate anti-colonial ideas.

The fourth group of significant anti-colonial movements of this period included pan-territorial initiatives like Pan-Africanism, Negritude, and US and Caribbean anti-racism. Pan-Africanism was anglophone Africa's response to colonial rule, and emphasised the need for continental unity as a prerequisite for Africa to assume its rightful place in the world. Ackah explains that:

> in essence Pan-Africanism is a movement by Africans for an African response to European
> ideas of superiority and acts of imperialism . . . Pan Africanism because it has no single founder,

or particular set of political tenets almost defies definition . . . It is the diversity and the
attempts to bring some coherence to it which is ultimately the reality of Pan-Africanism.
(Ackah 1999, pp. 12–13)

The movement embraced not just continental Africans such as Kwame Nkrumah
(1909–72), Jomo Kenyatta (1889–1978), I. T. A Wallace Johnson (1894–1965), and
Nnamdi Azikiwe (1904–96), but also diasporic Africans such as the Caribbean intellectuals George Padmore (1902–59) and Marcus Garvey (1887–1940), and the American W.
E. Du Bois (1868–1963). It was a movement with a diversity of aims: Garvey's commercial
Ethiopianism, Padmore's non-conformist communism, Du Bois' perception of Africa for
Africans, and Nkrumah's belief in continental unity to include the colonised islands adja-
cent to the continent. The major francophone anti-colonial ideology was Negritude,
which like Pan-Africanism celebrated the culture of Blackness. The main intellectuals in
this movement were the Senegalese poet and statesman, Leopold Senghor (1906–2001),
and Martinique's poet and politician, Aimé Césaire (1913–). The rationale for Negritude
was to reappropriate African culture, which had been derided and ignored by both direct
rule and the *evoule* system of cultural assimilation.

World War II exposed the realities of African poverty to Europe, and Britain's response
in the immediate aftermath of the war was to undertake what historians have described as
'a second colonial occupation' (see Freund 1984, p. 195). This involved increased investment in infrastructure, education, and greater capital penetration via the introduction of
secondary industries and expanded cash crop agriculture. Britain's reinvigorated economic
ambitions in the region coincided with a dramatic escalation in anti-colonial sentiment,
which in West Africa assumed a radical nationalist aspect.

In general, the anti-colonial movements started quite modestly, but very quickly mush-
roomed and transformed themselves from congresses and youth movements into parties
with national appeal. The Gold Coast established itself as the paradigmatic case. Nkrumah
returned to the Gold Coast in 1947 amid riots and unrest: in 1948, one demonstration by
ex-servicemen in Accra precipitated the looting of foreign companies and led to twenty-
nine deaths; in the countryside, there were widespread protests by cocoa farmers against
the state's policy on swollen-shoot disease; and in January 1950, a general strike temporarily disabled the economy. Nkrumah formed the Convention People Party (CPP) in 1949
as a political means for expressing the popular anger of the moment. He was imprisoned in
1950 for promoting political sedition, but released two years later when the strength of his
support became clear to the authorities. Despite opposition to Nkrumah in Asante, in 1956
he won 72 of 104 seats to become prime minister, and in 1957 the Gold Coast achieved
independence and changed its name to Ghana. Nkrumah's importance for African anti-
colonial resistance if anything increased after independence, as he made Ghana a haven
for anti-colonial movements throughout Africa. Of the many national liberation movements which benefited from Nkrumah's patronage, one West African instance deserves
mention: in Guinea Bissau, the small Portuguese enclave in West Africa, the Partido
Africano para a Independencia da Guine e Cabo Verde (PAIGC) under the leadership of
Amilcar Cabral (1924–73) waged a highly successful guerrilla war against Portuguese colonialism, and in 1963 gained control of more than half of the country.

In Nigeria, deep divisions between the country's different regions complicated the
momentum towards independence. The National Council of Nigeria and the Cameroons
(NCNC), formed in 1944 by Macauley and Azikiwe, was the first major postwar party, and
it resembled Nkrumah's CPP in many respects. Its leadership was predominantly drawn

from the eastern Nigerian Igbo elite, and its small radical faction (known as 'Zikists') was purged from the party by about 1950. In the west, a significant majority of the Yoruba elite rejected the NCNC, and in 1951 formed the Action Group under the leadership of Obafemi Awolowo. In the north, two parties emerged: the Northern People's Congress (NPC) under Ahmadu Bello, and the more radical Northern Elements Progressive Union (NEPU). Both were centrally concerned to resist southern domination of Nigerian politics. All these parties agitated in their regions and (where they could) nationally, for an end to colonial rule. Their efforts culminated in 1959, when elections with 'universal' suffrage were held (women did not have the vote in the north), and the results saw Northern People's Congress (NPC) win the most seats, followed by NCNC. In a coalition government, Abubakar Tafawa Balewa (1912–66) of the NPC became the first prime minister, and a year later Nigeria achieved independence with Azikiwe appointed the first governor-general.

In Sierra Leone, the People's Party was founded in 1951, and they assumed political power in 1961 under Milton Margai (1895–1964) with decolonisation, although the credibility of the elections was damaged by the fact that the main opposition leader, the trade unionist Siaka Stevens (1905–88), was in prison during the voting. In Gambia, the main political party was the Protectorate Progressive Party (PPP) led by Dauda Jawara (1924–), and it assumed power after independence in 1965.

Falola makes the point that 'in the greater part of British West Africa, colonial rule lasted scarcely sixty years. It ended calmly: the transfer of power had been effected by the same constitutional process as in the Dominions of white settlement' (Falola 1999, p. 528). Anti-colonial struggles had forced the British to 'scramble out of Africa' (Freund 1984, p. 213) far sooner than they would have liked, but in the postcolonial period many of the economic causes of anti-colonial sentiment remain in place.

Alfred Zack-Williams

Literary Works

Achebe, Chinua [1958] (1986), *Things Fall Apart*, Oxford: Heinemann.
Achebe, Chinua (1960), *No Longer at Ease*, Oxford: Heinemann.
Achebe, Chinua (1977), *Arrow of God*, Oxford: Heinemann.
Armah, Ayi Kwei [1968] (1988), *The Beautiful Ones Are Not Yet Born*, Oxford: Heinemann.
Armah, Ayi Kwei (1972), *Why Are We So Blest?* Oxford: Heinemann.
Nwongo, D. I. (ed.) (1986), *West African Verse*, London: Longman.
Ousmane, Sembene [1960] (1970), *God's Bits of Wood*, trans. F. Price, Oxford: Heinemann.

Histories

Ackah, W. B. (1999), *Pan-Africanism: Exploring Contradictions, Politics, Identity and the Development of Africa and the African Diaspora*, Aldershot: Ashgate.
Busia, K. A. (1951), *Positions of the Chief in the Modern Political System of Ashanti*, London: Oxford University Press.
Cartey, W. and M. Kilson (eds) (1970), *The African Reader: Colonial Africa*, New York: Vintage Books.
Crowder, M. (1981), *West Africa under Colonial Rule*, London: Hutchinson.

Falola, T. (1999), 'West Africa', in J. M. Brown and W. R. Louis (eds), *The Oxford History of the British Empire Volume 4: The Twentieth Century*, Oxford: Oxford University Press, pp. 515–29.

Falola, T. (2001), *Nationalism and African Intellectuals*, Rochester, NY: University of Rochester Press.

Freund, Bill (1984), *The Making of Contemporary Africa*, Basingstoke: Macmillan.

Gann, L. H. and P. Duignan (eds) (1969), *Colonialism in Africa, 1870–1960 Volume 1: The History and Politics of Colonialism 1870–1914*, Cambridge: Cambridge University Press.

Hailey, William Malcolm (1938), *An African Survey*, London: Oxford University Press.

Hargreaves, J. D. (1988), *Decolonisation in Africa*, London: Longman.

Mamdani, M. (1996), *Citizens and Subjects: Contemporary Africa and the Legacy of Late Colonialism*, London: James Currey.

Perham, M. (1970), 'The Aba Market Women's Riot in Nigeria, 1929', in W. T. Cartey and M. Kilson (eds), *The Africa Reader: Colonial Africa*, New York: Vintage Books, pp. 163–9.

Phillips, A. (1989), *The Enigma of Colonialism: British Policy in West Africa*, London: James Currey.

Ranger, T. O. (1969), 'African Reactions to the Imposition of Colonial Rule in East and Central Africa', in L. H. Gann and P. Duignan (eds), *Colonialism in Africa 1870–1914*, Cambridge: Cambridge University Press, pp. 293–324.

Reader, J. (1998), *Africa: A Biography of the Continent*, London: Penguin Books.

Tordoff, W. (2002), *Government and Politics in Africa*, Basingstoke: Palgrave.

See also: **Asante Wars; Cabral, Amílcar; Indirect Rule; Nkrumah, Kwame; Pan-Africanism; Religions: West Africa; Senghor, Léopold Sédar.**

Anti-globalisation Movements

'Turtles love Teamsters' was the unlikely chant of welcome as the main US trade union section joined the protest of 70,000 in Seattle in November 1999 against the neo-liberal policies being promoted by the World Trade Organisation. The voices of the Green, jump-suited warriors for the planet were simultaneously an exuberance and a challenge. The response was even more remarkable. 'Teamsters love Turtles!' came the retort from the assembled chapters of hardhats of one of the largest of the US trade union movement's constituencies. An improbable unity had been initiated. It was between a core of the organised, industrial working class of the developed world, and those campaigning against environmental despoliation, against the economic ravages of neo-liberalism in the under-developed world, and thus against the policies of the IMF, the World Bank and the World Trade Organisation. It was a protest against the poverty and inequality perceived to be caused by the intensifying global reach of capital and the market (see Danaher and Burbach 2000; Danaher 2001; Went 2000; and Stiglitz 2002). It was also a potential unity between traditional parties and groups of the left, and new single issue, or more limited, campaigns. This was as unexpected as it was new. The question was whether it would be tempered in the experience of future struggles, or be torn asunder by the re-emergence of conflicting sectional interests.

The demonstration in Seattle paralysed the scheduled meetings of the assembled dignitaries, and led to the partial abandonment of the proceedings. It also raised awareness about the existence of a movement against neo-liberalism. Across the globe, in both developed and underdeveloped societies, images of armour-clad 'Robocop' riot police, wielding CS gas guns and stun grenades, confronting protesters armed with whistles and banners, transformed perceptions. The dominant view, propagated in news and current affairs, and in much of the academy, and reflected in the style and subject matter and foci of the products of mass culture, was no longer tenable. This view held that, with the collapse of Stalinism and social democracy in the 1980s and 1990s, there was no feasible alternative to liberal capitalism as a social and economic system, and no viable alternative to free market, neo-liberal policies not only in trade and commerce nationally and internationally, but equally in education, healthcare, welfare, sanitation, and development (see Giddens 1998). Here was evidence that this view was not being passively received and accepted. Here, too, was evidence, in the violent reaction against the protest, that governments and their representatives harboured a deep unease that their citizenries would not heed the message. It was as if the images of Seattle under siege announced a new war between the powerful and the marginalised, between the rich and the poor, between the beneficiaries of a liberal economic order and its casualties. In the years that immediately followed Seattle, this movement not only proved its resilience but gradually cohered around the slogans that expressed the common interests uniting the oppressed in rich and poor countries: 'Our world is not for sale!', 'Another world is possible!', and 'You are G8; we are 6 billion!'.

From these beginnings, the movement grew in strength and sophistication. The protests traversed the globe and all five continents. In January 2000, 250,000 protested in Vienna against neo-Nazism, and 40,000 against the IMF in Quito, Ecuador; in April, 30,000 against the IMF/World Bank meeting in Washington; in May, a strike of 80,000 against the IMF in Argentina; in June, 5,000 in Windsor, Ontario, against the Organisation of American States, 60,000 against McDonald's in Millau, France, and 20,000 against the Republican Convention in Philadelphia; in July, 10,000 in Okinawa against the G8 and the continued US occupation of the island; in August, 20,000 in Los Angeles against the Democratic Convention; in September, 20,000 against the Asia-Pacific Summit of the World Economic Forum in Melbourne, 20,000 against the IMF/World Bank in Prague, and 100,000 in Sao Paulo against the IMF/World Bank plan; in November, 10,000 against the Asia-Europe Summit in Seoul, South Korea, and 6,000 against the Climate Change Summit in The Hague; and in December, with the backing of most European trade unions, 100,000 against the EU Enlargement Conference in Nice, France. In January 2001, 5,000 against the World Economic Forum in Davos, Switzerland; in April, 80,000 protested in Quebec against the Free Trade Area of the Americas; in May, across the globe, May Day was reclaimed for the movement as a day of resistance and celebration; and in June, 20,000 protested against the EU summit in Gothenburg, Sweden. In July, there were three days of protest by 300,000 against the G8 summit in Genoa, Italy.

Even the attack on the Twin Towers, the Pentagon and the White House, on 11 September 2001, which many pundits thought might derail the movement, had little long-term effect as the invitation to guilt by false association was refused. Similarly, the challenge posed for the movement by the small confrontationist minority of autonomists in the Black Bloc was overcome. Attempts to marginalise the appeal of the movement by using a small minority to label the whole as destructive and irrational failed to convince either potential activists or public opinion (Neale 2002). The protests were loosely organised by a variety of nationally based coalitions. These co-ordinated arrangements using e-mail and internet sites as well as more traditional methods of meetings and word of mouth.

As the movement developed over the first years of the twenty-first century, the key characteristics of Seattle were repeated. On the one hand, there was no single, identifiable leadership of the movement, or control of the protest. This produced a powerful, vibrant and creative coalition. On the other hand, there was the developing, if occasionally suspicious, unity between the traditional organisations of the oppressed, the trade unions, and the new constituencies concerned with a variety of overlapping and often intersecting issues. Amongst these issues were concerns with ecology and the politics of sustainable development, with poverty, underdevelopment and famine, with asylum, refugee rights and migration, with racism and xenophobia, and with the oppression of women, of nations and of sub-national minorities. There was also concern with the erosion of cultural differences in literature, entertainment, education and culinary traditions by an anodyne yet hypocritical, corporate cosmopolitanism. The commodities of this inclusivist imposture (typified by the Nike logo, by Starbucks coffee houses, by the Coca-Cola script, and by the ubiquitous McDonald's fast food outlets) were presented in the sub-text of their commercials as expressions of enlightened humanism and belonging. They were, however, dependent for their production on sweated labour, and were designed for a deracinated, clientelist minority in the underdeveloped regions, and for an increasingly deculturated, populist majority in the rich countries (see Klein 2002, Bové and Dufour 2002; Jameson and Miyoshi 1998).

The increasing size and resonance of these protests, and the resilience of the somewhat inchoate movement of which they were the visible expression, evoked increasing security concerns, and a recognition from neo-liberal agencies and governments that a repetition of the shock and paralysis induced in Seattle could not be tolerated. The resiting of the gatherings to venues more inaccessible to protesters, or more easily defendable against popular siege, reinforced the image of the meetings, however, as cabals of a disdainful economic elite. The intensification and increasing muscularity of policing (culminating in the police murder by shooting of a young protester in Genoa) reinforced the image of neo-liberalism as an embattled project increasingly distant and dismissive of popular concerns, and defended by its champions with violence when and wherever necessary.

These negative protests against neo-liberalism were rapidly supplemented by a second novel phenomenon in the political arena. Commencing in Porto Allegre, Brazil, in 2001, with 1,000 delegates from 100 countries; and then replicated in a variety of European countries (in Florence in 2002; in Paris in 2003); and then with 100,000 participants, and 20,700 delegates representing 156 countries in Porto Allegre again in 2003; and thence to Cairo in 2003; and to Mumbai in India in 2004, were the series of 'Social Forums'. At these, militants, activists, political groups, journalists and intellectuals congregated. They gathered to consider not simply the effects of the protests but also the content of a positive agenda for the movement (see George et al. 2001). No barrier of distance, language, culture or political tradition was allowed to prevent the dialogue, despite the absence of elaborate transport, accommodation, finance or simultaneous translation services. Thousands travelled both within and between continents to participate.

The movement is not, however, seamless. It is divided politically by some key differences both in the analysis of the current conjuncture, and in the strategic orientation that should be adopted. Consequently, it is divided over its own self-perception: is it anti-neo-liberal, or anti-imperialist, or anti-capitalist? For Susan George et al. (2001) and Bernard Cassen (2003), the purpose seems primarily to bring pressure to bear on existing governments to alter their policy mix, and return to a more socially sensitive, Keynesian or structuralist interventionism. In this sense these figures might, for convenience, be taken as representative of a 'reformist' wing. For Michael Hardt and Tony Negri (2000), the task is rather to recognise the transformed nature of the world – a now 'deterritorialised' empire. Theirs is a world in which the role and power of nation states are being progressively displaced by the interests and influences of corporations. It is a world in which everyone is implicated to some degree in responsibility for oppression and exploitation, eliminating the possibility of a standpoint outside the system. It is one in which resistance emerges from the variety of (sometimes contradictory) interests that constitute individuals, and which periodically mobilises those individuals into unstable and shifting constituencies of opposition (see Aronowitz, Burrow and Gautney 2003, and Roy 2003). For Alex Callinicos (2001), on the other hand, neo-liberal policies are the current expression of the interests of capital in the variety of its forms and locations. The consequences of these policies, in the form of debt, poverty, oppressions and war, do have a unifying source, however complexly articulated. For him, the objective class divisions of the system, which persist through serial transformations of their detail, do provide the necessary terrain from which analysis and critique can be mounted. This wing argues that the movement is both anti-capitalist and *a fortiori* anti-imperialist (see Rees 2001).

Identifying the causes of this unprecedented development requires attention to the two decades preceding the Seattle protest. The renewed confidence of dominant classes in the 1980s and 1990s, first in the developed countries, and then progressively in Asia, Africa and Latin America, represented by the abandonment of Keynesianism and developmentalism in favour of market liberalism, set the context. The exhaustion of the social democratic project, and the collapse of reform-minded parties into compromises with neo-liberalism, created a vacuum of resistance in the developed countries. The implosion of the Stalinist regimes in Eastern Europe and the Soviet Union eliminated the external constraint on aggressive neo-liberalism in the West but simultaneously dissolved the strategic detour for resistance offered by Stalinist parties and politics in poor countries. Arguably, this set the stage for a resistance that was as unavoidable as it was necessary and hence had no choice but to reinvent itself.

The potential consequences of this movement, in both its positive and its protest guises, can scarcely be overestimated. The recognition and declaration of, if not common problems, then at least problems with a set of common causes for a large segment of humanity, could effect a seismic shift in the contours of identity, and hence in the location and nature of 'otherness'. In such a world, who are my friends and who are my enemies? Do I identify myself by the ascribed or imposed commonalities in the accident of nationality or citizenship? Alternatively, do I construct my identity by reference to the objective circumstances of my social position and economic situation, or perhaps by the elective affinity of political aspiration? In the past, and since their cogent expression in the mid-nineteenth century, most notably by Marx, such questions, if posed at all, confronted only a minority of humanity, and usually only abstractly. Since Seattle, they are taking concrete form, and challenging millions in all continents.

To date there has been little imaginative fiction that directly engages with the historical events associated with the anti-globalisation/anti-capitalist events of the last few years. One text of note, however, is the recent novel by British writer and political comedian, Rob Newman. *The Fountain at the Centre of the World* (2003) is set in Mexico, Costa Rica and North America. It charts the story of a Mexican political dissident, Chano Salgado, who is persuaded to blow up a toxic waste plant in north-east Mexico. His long-lost brother, Evan Hatch, a British PR executive, is dying of 'chagas', a disease endemic to Latin America, and together with Salgado's son they end up involved in the Seattle demonstrations. The novel, engaging with anti-free-trade activism in Mexico, explores the relationship between political violence and economic inequality against the backdrop of anti-globalisation activism and resistance.

In considering the relationship between anti-globalisation and postcolonialism, arguably, the vast majority of postcolonial literature critically engages with the cultural, political and economic transformations associated with contemporary globalisation. In this sense, it would be impossible to cite them all here. Recently, the debate over the reach of the 'postcolonial' as a conceptual container has been extended by an emerging definition, 'global fiction'. Writers cited as producing global fiction include Salman Rushdie, Nadine Gordimer, Derek Walcott, V. S. Naipaul, Zadie Smith, Hanan al Shayhk, and Arundhati Roy. Alex Garland's popular novel *The Beach* could also be put into this category as a work that offers a dystopic vision of the search for an exotic and pristine paradise that fuels global tourism. As with the enduring controversy over the postcolonial, though, this new literary category is open for contestation. Alongside the problems associated with the global access to fiction, one might ask whether this category 'postcolonial' should embrace texts that celebrate hybridity and the syncreticism of cultures or whether it should be marked by an emphasis on the damage caused by globalisation.

Arundhati Roy's Booker Prize-winning novel *The God of Small Things* (1997) might be termed a 'global', postcolonial and anti-globalisation novel. While it focuses on the private space of the family romance in Kerala, it explicitly engages with some of the issues that have also focused the wider anti-globalisation movement. The book is interwoven with observations about trans-corporate environmental destruction, American cultural imperialism, the desensitisation and alienation associated with global media networks, and the exploitation of migrant labour. Roy has elsewhere lent her active support to the anti-globalisation movement by campaigning, amongst other issues, against nuclear weapons, the Narmada Dam project in India, and for international equal rights. She has recently published a collection of her political and activist speeches and essays, *The Ordinary Person's Guide to the Empire* (2003).

The link between postcolonial literature and the critical engagement with the causes and effects of globalisation is incontestable, and to separate the categories is to deny the historical continuity and implicit relationship between them. The works cited below constitute only a few examples of the most sustained imaginative attempts to reflect on the effects of globalisation in ways that link them to the spirit of anti-globalisation.

Tom Hickey and Anita Rupprecht

Literary Works

Achebe, Chinua (1988), *Anthills of the Savannah*, London: Heinemann.
Al Shaykh, Hanan (1995), *Beirut Blues*, New York: Anchor Books.
Devi, Mahasweta (1995), *Imaginary Maps*, London: Routledge.
Danticat, Edwidge (1995), *Breath, Eyes, Memory*, London: Abacus.
El Saadawi, Nawal (1997), *Women at Point Zero*, London: Zed Books.
Fuentes, Carlos (1994), *The Orange Tree*, trans. A. MacAdam, London: Deutsch.
Garland, Alex (1996), *The Beach*, London: Viking.
Grace, Patricia (1997), *Potiki*, London: Women's Press.
Kincaid, Jamaica (1988), *A Small Place*, New York: Farrar, Straus and Giroux.
Kincaid, Jamaica (1990), *Lucy*, New York: Farrar, Straus and Giroux.

Mo, Timothy (1999), *Renegade or Halo²*, London: Paddleless Press.
Mudrooroo (1991), *Master of the Ghost Dreaming*, Sydney: Angus and Robertson.
Newman, Rob (2003), *The Fountain at the Centre of the World*, London: Verso.
Omowale, David (2002), *A Season of Waiting*, Nairobi: Kenyan East African Educational Publications.
Ondaatje, Michael (1987), *In the Skin of a Lion*, London: Picador.
Ondaatje, Michael (2000), *Anil's Ghost*, London: Bloomsbury Publishing.
Padmanabhan, Manjula (1997), *Harvest*, Delhi: Kali for Women.
Roy, Arundhati (1997), *The God of Small Things*, London: Flamingo.
Silko, Leslie Marmon (1991), *The Almanac of the Dead*, London: Penguin.

Histories

Aronowitz, S., C. W. Burrow and H. Gautney (eds) (2003), *Implicating Empire: Globalisation and Resistance in the c.21st World Disorder*, New York: Perseus.
Achcar, G. (2002), *The Clash of Barbarisms: September 11 and the Making of the New World Disorder*, New York: Monthly Review.
Bircham, Emma and John Charlton (eds), (2001), *Anti-Capitalism: A Guide to the Movement*, London: Bookmarks.
Bové, J. and F. Dufour (2002), *The World is Not For Sale: Farmers against Junk Food*, London: Verso.
Callinicos, A. (2001), *Against the Third Way: An Anti-capitalist Critique*, Cambridge: Polity.
Callinicos, A. (2003), *An Anti-Capitalist Manifesto*, Cambridge: Polity.
Cassen, B. (2003), 'On the Attack', *New Left Review* 19, pp. 41–60.
Danaher, K. (ed.) (2001), *Democratising the Global Economy: The Battle Against the World Bank and the IMF*, Monroe, ME: Common Courage.
Danaher, K. and R. Burbach (eds) (2000), *Globalise This! The Battle Against the World Trade organisation and Corporate Rule*, Monroe, ME and Philadelphia: Common Courage.
Farah, Reza (ed.) (2003), *Anti-Imperialism: A Guide for the Movement*, London: Bookmarks.
Feffer, J. (ed.) (2002), *Living in Hope. People Challenging Globalization*, London: Zed Books.
Giddens, A. (1998), *The Third Way: The Renewal of Social Democracy*, Cambridge: Polity.
Hardt, M. and T. Negri (2000), *Empire*, Cambridge, MA: Harvard University Press.
Jameson, F. and M. Miyoshi (eds) (1998), *The Cultures of Globalisation*, Durham, NC: Duke University Press.
Hopkins, A. G. (ed.) (2002), *Globalization in World History*, New York: Norton.
Klein, N. (2000), *No Logo*, London: Flamingo.
Klein, N. (2002), *Fences and Windows: Dispatches from the Front Line of the Globalisation Debate*, London: Flamingo.
Madely, John (2003), *A People's World: Alternatives to Economic Globalization*, London: Zed Books.
Neale, J. (2002), *You are G8, We are 6 Billion: The Truth Behind the Genoa Protests*, London: Vision.
Rees, J. (2001), 'Anti-Capitalism, Reformism and Imperialism', *International Socialism Journal*, Spring Issue, 90, pp. 3–40.
Roy, A. (2003), *The Ordinary Person's Guide to the Empire*, London: Flamingo.

Stiglitz, J. (2002), *Globalisation and its Discontents*, London: Penguin.
Went, R. (2000), *Globalisation: Neoliberal Challenge, Radical Response*, London: Pluto.

See also: **Free Trade; International Monetary Fund; United States of America; World Bank.**

Anti-war Movements: Australia

Although World War I saw Australians rush to join Britain's side, the war also saw a popular anti-war movement gradually develop and divide the nation. While pacifists and a few labour activists, including future prime minister John Curtin, had opposed the war from the beginning, it was the Labor government's attempt to introduce conscription, along with the mounting death toll, that saw a mass movement arise to oppose the war. Huge open-air meetings were held in the capital cities, as well as in town halls across the country, as the issue of conscription was passionately argued. With much of the labour movement and the Catholic Church opposing it, the campaign succeeded in defeating the two conscription referenda that were called in 1916 and 1917.

Whereas World War I had gradually lost popular support, the much longer World War II gained support as it widened to involve the Soviet Union. As a result, there was no anti-war movement of any consequence, not even when John Curtin decreed in late 1942 that the conscripted militia would have to fight outside Australian territory. Although it caused outrage among some Labor MPs, most notably Arthur Calwell, there was little public protest. This was partly due to the area in which they would have to fight being restricted to the south-west Pacific where Japanese forces still posed a threat to Australia.

Calwell was Labor leader when conscription was reintroduced by the conservative government in 1964 against the background of the growing conflict in Vietnam and tension with Indonesia. Although it cost Labor popular support, Calwell maintained his principled opposition to conscription when the first draftees were sent off in 1966 to Vietnam. The twin issues of conscription and Vietnam provoked a massive anti-war movement that organised street marches and meetings across Australia. Acts of civil disobedience became commonplace, with thousands of young men refusing to register for conscription and others claiming exemption based on conscientious objection. Several of the draft resisters were jailed for two years. As the war bogged down, and its obscenities were revealed, public support gradually swung behind the anti-war movement, with hundreds of thousands blocking city streets in Moratorium demonstrations in May 1970. The movement helped to inspire a generation of community activists with the methods of direct action. Many returned to the streets in 2003 when the prospect of Australian involvement in the Iraq war saw even greater crowds protesting than during the Vietnam Moratorium.

David Day

Literary Works

Cass, Shirley, Ros Cheney, David Malouf and Michael Wilding (eds) (1971), *We Took their Orders and are Dead: An Anti-War Anthology*, Sydney: Ure Smith.
Hutchinson, Garrie (1999), *Not Going to Vietnam: Journeys through Two Wars*, Sydney: Hodder Headline.

Lindsay, Jack (1985), *The Blood Vote*, Brisbane: University of Queensland Press.
Prichard, Katharine (1948), *Golden Miles*, Sydney: Jonathan Cape.

Histories

Cain, Frank (1993), *The Wobblies at War*, Melbourne: Spectrum.
Cochrane, Peter (2001), *Australians at War*, Sydney: ABC Books.
Edwards, Peter (1997), *A Nation at War*, Sydney: Allen and Unwin.
Main, J. M. (1970), *Conscription: The Australian Debate, 1901–1970*, Melbourne: Cassell.

See also: **Vietnam War; World Wars I and II: Anzac.**

Apartheid and Segregation

Although segregation and apartheid only came to be systematically codified in the twentieth century, they need to be positioned in the long and complex history of white supremacism in South Africa.

The origins of segregation have been the source of much historiographical dispute. Liberal historians writing in the early and mid-twentieth century ascribed legally entrenched racial discrimination to the frontier prejudices of nineteenth-century Afrikaners. Their accounts ignored the fact that British settlers and administrators themselves evinced racist attitudes, and that the colonial project was infused with pseudo-scientific social-Darwinist notions of racial superiority. Indeed, in the nineteenth century, the two Boer republics – the Transvaal and the Orange Free State – were less economically and territorially segregated than British Natal and the Eastern Cape.

The liberal emphasis on psychological factors was challenged in the 1970s and 1980s by Marxist scholars who argued that segregation was the product of the mineral revolution; in particular, capitalist reliance on cheap migrant labour. However, the Marxist account failed to address the pre-industrial antecedents of segregation. Perceptions of racial superiority and patterns of racial differentiation were key features of Cape slave society between 1658 and 1834, and persisted and intensified even after emancipation. In Natal, too, structured segregation took root in a form of indirect rule called the 'Shepstone system' in the mid-nineteenth century (see Welsh 1971). Sir Theophilus Shepstone, who took charge of 'native affairs' in the colony in 1846, set aside land unclaimed by white farmers as 'locations' for Africans, where they could cultivate under the supervision of chiefs and headmen whose authority was regulated under 'native law' by resident magistrates and administrators. The locations were introduced with a view to protecting white settlers from competition, and were policed by a strict system of curfews and pass laws – both of which became important features of 'native policy' after 1910.

Several key components of the Union's 'native policy' were formulated during the post-Anglo-Boer War reconstruction period. As Cell (1982) has shown, in many ways the South African Native Affairs Commission (SANAC), which sat between 1903 and 1905, provided a blueprint for segregationist legislation enacted between the 1910s and 1930s. The commission recommended the creation of separate urban 'native locations' (which were seen as temporary repositories for labourers who would eventually return to the reserves), the use of pass laws as a means of influx control, and racially differentiated wage levels.

Although many of these recommendations were informed by existing practices in different parts of the country, this was the first time that they were combined into an overarching national framework.

Many of SANAC's recommendations were subsequently legally entrenched under the successive South African Party governments of Louis Botha and Jan Smuts. The Mines and Works Act (1911) enforced the colour bar by reserving a wide range of skilled jobs for white workers. The Natives Land Act (1913) segregated land ownership, and gave Africans ownership rights in just over 7 per cent of the land area of South Africa. The Native Affairs Act (1920) provided for a nation-wide system of government-appointed tribal councils which were modelled on the Glen Grey Act of 1894, and which effectively denied Africans political representation in government. The Natives (Urban Areas) Act (1923) imposed residential segregation in the towns, and provided for a much stricter administration of pass laws.

The Pact government, which came into power under the ministry of General J. B. M. Hertzog, bolstered and extended these measures. The Mines and Works Amendment Act (1926) empowered the government to enforce the colour bar in private industry, and established racially differentiated wage rates in accordance with a 'civilised labour policy'. The Native Administration Act (1927) appointed the governor-general the 'Paramount Chief' of all Africans, and invested in him the power to appoint chiefs and headmen, as well as to define tribal boundaries and move tribes from one area to another. The Act consciously sought to foster tribalism, thus foreshadowing the homelands policy of the apartheid regime. And further attempts to stimulate tribalism came in the form of Hertzog's efforts to disenfranchise detribalised African property owners in the Cape. In 1926 he tabled a series of Bills in parliament which, among other things, aimed to remove individual African voters from the electoral roll, and instead provide them with representation by seven white MPs elected by chiefs and headmen. Hertzog's Bills were only approved in 1936, three years after his National Party had allied (and later fused) with Smuts' South African Party to form the United Party government. (Under the Union constitution any changes to the franchise required a two-thirds majority in parliament). The Representation of Natives Act was thus passed in 1936, while 'compensation' for the disenfranchisement of Cape Africans came in the form of the Native Trust and Land Act (1936) which extended the land area of the reserves to 14 per cent of the country.

During the inter-war years, then, a barrage of segregationist legislation effectively disbarred Africans from participation in political and civic life, and entrenched racial distinctions socially, culturally and economically. While segregation needs to be situated within the long history of white supremacism in South Africa, and while segregationist systems and practices pre-dated the twentieth century, there can be little doubt that twentieth-century segregation was its own historically specific phenomenon; a product of the industrial revolution. However, that is not to endorse the revisionist consensus of the 1970s and 1980s that segregation was designed to entrench the cheap labour policies first developed in the mines of Kimberley and the Witwatersrand in the 1870s and 1880s.

Segregation was not merely the rationalisation of capitalist class interests in an industrialising society. It was a flexible and protean ideology whose ideologues, as Dubow (1987, 1989) has shown, were as interested in cheap black migrant labour as in maintaining social control over the workforce. The drive to implement mechanisms of social control in the 1920s took place against the backdrop of increased worker militancy, rural rebellion, the growing power of the Industrial and Commercial Workers' Union, and millenarianism. In the 1930s, segregationist discourse came to employ the language of cultural rather than racial difference. A new socio-anthropological notion of culture freed from the evolution-ary constraints of biological determinism and universalist humanism came to be seized upon by South African segregationists (many of them liberals) seeking a middle way between assimilation and repression of the 'Native'. Notions of 'cultural adaptation' were popularised in government circles, and came to be enthusiastically embraced by Hertzog as a further legitimation of segregationist ideology.

The passage of Hertzog's Bills through parliament galvanised black opposition to segregation. The 1940s ushered in a period of popular protest coupled with a growing radicalisation of resistance movements, as World War II reshaped the socio-economic politics of the Union. The wartime imperative for greater production led to rapid industrialisation and increased African urbanisation, which in turn catapulted segregation into crisis. Economic integration was leading to social integration between the races, and in 1942 Smuts told the South African Institute of Race Relations that segregation had 'fallen on evil days' (Rich 1984, p. 74). That same year the Smit Report on the social, health and economic conditions of urbanised blacks recommended the administrative recognition of African trade unions and the abolition of pass laws. The pro-democratic climate induced by the fight against fascism also acted as a fillip to anti-segregationist movements.

The forces of Afrikaner nationalism, meanwhile, were mobilising and coalescing around D. F. Malan's 'purified' National Party (see O'Meara 1983). In the immediate aftermath of the war Malan stressed the need for a firmer, more coherent 'Native policy', and appointed a team headed by Paul Sauer to formulate various proposals. The Sauer Report recommended consolidation of the reserves, strenuous controls over African urban settlement, segregated amenities for coloureds and Indians, and the abolition of white representatives of Africans in parliament. This set of recommendations, styled as apartheid, was perceived to be much more uncompromising than those devised by the Smuts-appointed Fagan Commission, which described complete segregation as 'totally impracticable', and recommended easing influx control measures.

As Posel has shown (1987, 1991), apartheid in the 1940s was not a cohesive policy, but it did provide a rallying point for an intra-ethnic cross-class Afrikaner alliance which was agreed upon the need to bolster the mechanisms of white supremacy. The 1948 election was close fought, and Malan's Nationalists won with only a narrow majority. Nevertheless, the National Party remained in power from 1948 until the 1990s, during which time apartheid was systematically entrenched, challenged, and eventually dismantled.

During the 1950s apartheid laws were codified with a relentless zeal. The prohibition of 'mixed marriages' (1949) and the Immorality Act (1950) prohibited inter-racial sexual contact and marriage. The Population Registration Act (1950) provided for racial classification into four categories: white, coloured, 'Asiatic' (Indian), and 'Native' (later 'Bantu', or African). The Group Areas Act (1950) gave the state increased powers to enforce residential segregation, including recourse to 'forced removals', which also underpinned the Natives Resettlement Act (1954). The Reservation of Separate Amenities Act (1953) imposed social segregation in all public amenities such as cinemas, restaurants, sports facilities and transport. Educational apartheid was enforced in the schools by the Bantu Education Act (1953) which brought all African schools under the control of the Department of Native Affairs (thus phasing out mission education), and which imposed a curriculum aimed at education for servitude. The system whereby Indians were represented by whites in parliament (which had been introduced in 1946) was scrapped, while the Bantu Authorities Act (1951) replaced the Natives Representative Council with a system of government-approved chiefs in the reserves. No provision was made for the representation of urban Africans. The only remaining 'non-white' representation in parliament, that of Cape coloureds, was removed in 1956 when they were placed on a separate roll and restricted to electing four white representatives to parliament.

After the consolidation and extension of segregationist legislation in the 1950s, the 1960s saw a move to 'grand apartheid', characterised by a much broader scheme of social and political engineering pioneered by Hendrik Verwoerd, and known as 'separate development'. This entailed the large-scale relocation of Africans into reserves or 'Bantustans', which in effect were ethnic homelands, in which 'retribalised' Africans could enjoy political rights. The aim of this was to dissipate the forces of African nationalism and to create a completely white South Africa in which Africans had no claim to citizenship. However, in light of changing socio-economic circumstances, the Bantustan model began to break down from the late 1970s, and the government was forced to experiment with a number of reforms against a backdrop of intensified resistance. The ensuing cycle of rebellion and repression, thrust into the international spotlight by the events in Soweto on 16 June 1976, continued throughout the 1980s, as a combination of popular dissent led by the United Democratic Front, worker and trade union activism, the defeat of the South African army by MPLA and Cuban forces in Angola, and international pressure in the form of economic sanctions, edged the National Party in the direction of negotiation and change. The economic logic of apartheid collapsed with the repeal of the pass laws in 1986; and with the release of political prisoners in February 1990, the path was irreversibly set for the formal demise of apartheid with the first democratic elections in April 1994.

The output of literary works inspired by segregation and apartheid is immense. What follows is therefore but a small selection of writers and literary works that engage with segregation and apartheid. For the 1920s and 1930s, the major works by black writers were Sol Plaatje's *Mhudi* (1930) and Herbert Dhlomo's *An African Tragedy* (1929), and the range of white literary responses can be gauged by contrasting the racist novels of Sarah Gertrude Millin (*God's Stepchildren* (1924)) with more liberal works by William Scully (*Daniel Venanda* (1923), William Plomer (*Turbott Wolfe* (1925), and Ethelreda Lewis (*Wild Deer* (1933)). In the first two decades after 1948, the most interesting literary works to explore the human dimensions of apartheid included the short stories by the writers associated with *Drum* magazine like Can Themba, Casey Motsisi and Nat Nakasa, as well as the autobiographies of Peter Abrahams (*Tell Freedom* (1954)), Es'kia Mphahlele (*Down Second Avenue* (1959)) and Bloke Modisane (*Blame Me on History* (1963)). White writers of this period who questioned apartheid dogma in their literary work included Alan Paton (*Cry, the Beloved Country* (1948)), Nadine Gordimer (*The Lying Days* (1953) and *A World of Strangers* (1958)) and Dan Jacobson (*A Dance in the Sun* (1955)). The 1960s has often been called South Africa's 'silent decade' as a culture of censorship was imposed by the apartheid regime, but nonetheless significant literary works continued to be written: Alex La Guma's novels (*In the Fog of the Season's End* (1972), Athol Fugard's plays (*The Blood Knot* (1961), *Hello and Goodbye* (1965)), the poetry of Dennis Brutus, and the dissident Afrikaner novels of 'Die Sestigers' (Etienne Leroux's *Sewe Dae by die Silbersteins/ Seven Days at the Silbersteins* (1962), Andre Brink's *Kennis van die Aand/ Looking on Darkness* (1974) and the poetry of Ingrid Jonker and Breyten Breytenbach). The 1970s saw the rise of the black consciousness movement, whose literary practitioners like Mongane Serote, Mbuyiseni Mtshali, Sipho Sepamla and others produced vibrant poetry, as well as novels (Serote's *To Every Birth its Blood* (1981) and Sepamla's *A Ride on the Whirlwind* (1981)) and plays (Zakes Mda's *We Shall Sing for the Fatherland* (1979) and *The Hill* (1980)). Wessel Ebersohn's novel *Store up the Anger* (1980) depicted the police brutality of the decade, and established writers like Gordimer and Fugard continued to produce important works. New voices in the 1980s who attracted critical praise for their literary engagements with the history and politics of apartheid included: Njabulo Ndebele (*Fools and Other Stories* (1983)), J. M. Coetzee (*Life and Times of Michael K* (1983)), Breyten Breytenbach (*The True Confessions of an Albino Terrorist* (1984)), Karel Schoeman (*Another Country* (1984), translated into English in 1991), Ellen Kuzwayo (*Call Me Woman* (1985)), the worker poets Alfred Qabula and Mi Hlatswayo of Kwazulu Natal (in Ari Sitas' *Black Mamba Rising* (1986)), and Zoë Wicomb (*You Can't Get Lost in Cape Town* (1987)).

For further detail on the literature of segregation and apartheid, see Chapman's overview *Southern African Literatures* (2003) and Trump's critical collection (1990), and for drama specifically, see Kruger (1999) and Orkin (1991).

Michael Cardo

Literary Works

Abrahams, Peter (1954), *Tell Freedom*, London: Faber and Faber.

Breytenbach, Breyten (1984), *The True Confessions of an Albino Terrorist*, London: Faber and Faber.

Brink, André [1974] (1993), *Looking on Darkness*, London: Minerva.

Chapman, Michael (ed.) (1989), *The Drum Decade*, Pietermaritzburg: University of Natal Press.

Chapman, Michael and Achmat Dangor (eds) (1982), *Voices from Within: Black Poetry from Southern Africa*, Johannesburg: A. D. Donker.

Coetzee, J. M. (1983), *Life and Times of Michael K*, London: Secker.

Dhlomo, H. I. E. (1985), *Collected Works, H. I. E. Dhlomo*, Couzens, Tim and Nick Visser (eds) Johannesburg: Ravan Press.

Ebersohn, Wessel (1980), *Store up the Anger*, Johannesburg: Ravan Press.

Fugard, Athol (2000), *Port Elizabeth Plays*, ed. D. Walder, Oxford: Oxford University Press.

Gordimer, Nadine [1953] (1983), *The Lying Days*, London: Virago.

Gordimer, Nadine (1958), *World of Strangers*, London: Victor Gollancz.

Jacobson, Dan (1956), *Dance in the Sun*, London: Weidenfeld and Nicolson.

Kuzwayo, Ellen (1985), *Call Me Woman*, London: Women's Press.

La Guma, Alex (1972), *In the Fog of the Season's End*, London: Heinemann.

Le Roux, Etienne [1962] (1964), *Seven Days at the Silbersteins*, trans. C. Eglington, Johannesburg: Central News Agency.

Lewis, Ethelreda [1933] (1984), *Wild Deer*, Cape Town: David Philip.

Mda, Zakes (1990), *The Plays of Zakes Mda*, Johannesburg: Ravan Press.

Millin, Sarah Gertrude (1924), *God's Step-Children*, London: Constable and Company.

Modisane, William 'Bloke' (1963), *Blame Me on History*, London: Thames and Hudson.

Mphahlele, Es'kia (1959), *Down Second Avenue*, London: Faber and Faber.

Ndebele, Njabulo (1983), *Fools and Other Stories*, Johannesburg: Ravan Press.

Paton, Alan [1948] (1958), *Cry, the Beloved Country*, Harmondsworth: Penguin.

Plaatje, Sol [1930] (1978), *Mhudi: An Epic of South African Native Life a Hundred Years Ago*, London: Heinemann.

Plomer, William [1925] (1985), *Turbott Wolfe*, Oxford: Oxford University Press.

Schoeman, Karel [1984] (1991), *Another Country*, trans. D. Schalkwyk, London: Sinclair-Stevenson.

Scully, William (1923), *Daniel Venanda*, Cape Town: Juta and Co.

Sepamla, Sipho (1981), *A Ride on the Whirlwind*, Johannesburg: A. D. Donker.

Serote, Mongane (1981), *To Every Birth its Blood*, Johannesburg: Ravan Press.
Sitas, Ari (ed.) (1986), *Black Mamba Rising. South African Worker Poets in Struggle*, Durban: Worker Resistance and Culture Publications.
Wicomb, Zoë (1985), *You Can't Get Lost in Cape Town*, London: Virago.

Histories

Cell, John (1982), *The Highest Stage of White Supremacy: The Origins of Segregation in South Africa and the American South*, Cambridge: Cambridge University Press.
Chapman, Michael [1996] (2003), *Southern African Literatures*, 2nd edn, Pietermaritzburg: University of Natal Press.
Dubow, Saul (1987), 'Race, Civilisation and Culture: The Elaboration of Segregationist Discourse in the Inter-War Years', in S. Marks and S. Trapido (eds), *The Politics of Race, Class and Nationalism in Twentieth-Century South Africa*, London: Longman, pp. 71–94.
Dubow, Saul (1989), *Racial Segregation and the Origins of Apartheid in South Africa, 1919–1936*, London: Macmillan.
Kruger, Loren (1999), *The Drama of South Africa: Plays, Pageants and Publics since 1910*, London and New York: Routledge.
O'Meara, Dan (1983), *Volkskapitalisme: Class, Capital and Ideology in the Development of Afrikaner Nationalism, 1934–1948*, Cambridge: Cambridge University Press.
Orkin, Martin (1991), *Drama and the South African State*, Manchester: Manchester University Press.
Posel, Deborah (1987), 'The Meaning of Apartheid before 1948: Conflicting Interests and Forces within the Afrikaner Nationalist Alliance', *Journal of Southern African Studies* 14, pp. 123–39.
Posel, Deborah (1991), *The Making of Apartheid, 1948–1961: Conflict and Compromise*, Oxford: Clarendon Press.
Rich, Paul (1984), *White Power and the Liberal Conscience: Racial Segregation and South African Liberalism, 1921–1960*, Johannesburg: Ravan Press.
Trump, Martin (ed.) (1990), *Rendering Things Visible: A Survey of South African Literary Culture of the 1970s and the 1980s*, Johannesburg: Ravan Press.
Welsh, David (1971), *The Roots of Segregation: Native Policy in Colonial Natal, 1845–1910*, Cape Town: Oxford University Press.

See also: **Anti-colonialism and Resistance: Southern Africa; Black Consciousness: Southern Africa; Nationalism(s): Southern Africa; Post-apartheid.**

Asante Wars

The Asante Wars were a series of campaigns, raids, clashes and pitched battles fought between on the one side the kingdom of Asante, and on the other, a loosely connected group of independent Akan states and the British. The wars continued intermittently between 1824 and 1900 with major battles in 1824, 1826, 1863, 1874 and 1900. These conflicts took place roughly in the area of present-day Ghana. The Asante kingdom was a centralised state with an effectively organised administration, a standing army and near absolute power vested in the hands of the Asantehene.

The area of the Asante kingdom with the capital of Kumasi was situated inland, whilst the Akan states occupied the coast line and parts of southern Ghana. This meant that the Akan states barred the Asantes from access to the coast, which was a major obstacle to trade. The relative geographical positions of the two areas made it almost inevitable that the Asantes would want to invade the Fante states. In 1807 they did just that, and in the same year the British abolished the slave trade. The Fante were too weak and disunited to resist, and the Asante occupied the area until 1823 when the Fante revolted, spurred on by the British. The British supported the Fante states against the Asantes for two main reasons, to stop the Asantes' continuation of the slave trade and to further their own expansionist interests. The Fante states were weak and easy to play against each other as opposed to the strong centralised Asante kingdom.

The first armed clash occurred in 1824. An Asante army of 10,000 defeated a small British contingent, killing the governor, Sir Charles MacCarthy. The situation festered, and in 1826 the Asante suffered a serious defeat mainly due to the British use of superior weaponry (Congreve rockets). In the ensuing peace treaty, the Maclean treaty of 1831, the Asante renounced all rights to the Akan kingdoms south of the River Pra.

Hostilities resumed in 1863. The occasion was a British refusal to hand over two Asante fugitives, but the cause was the same mistrust and clash of expansionist and trade interests which had spurred the previous outbreaks. The Asante defeated the allied forces and then withdrew across the Pra. The British were set to march on Kumasi, but had to fall back, defeated by sickness and rain, causing them to consider seriously complete withdrawal from the Gold Coast. Despite this they bought the slave fort Elmina from the Dutch in 1871. The Asantes had an old claim to the fort, and war erupted again. A crushing defeat in 1873 caused the British to send for reinforcements from home, and in 1874 the British army marched into Kumasi and sacked the town. The Asante empire was destroyed, and five months later the British declared the area a formal British Protectorate.

In 1896 Joseph Chamberlain exiled Prempeh, the Asantehene, and in 1900 the governor demanded that the Asante hand over the Golden Stool. These humiliations sparked an Asante war of independence which ended with the annexation of the Asante confederacy to the British Crown in 1901.

Kirsten Holst Petersen

Literary Works

Armah, Ayi Kwei (1979), *The Healers*, London: Heinemann Educational.
Henty, G. A. (1884), *By Sheer Pluck: A Tale of the Ashanti Wars*, London: Blackie.

Histories

Boahen, Adu (1986–7), 'Politics in Ghana, 1800–1874' in A. F. J. Ajaji and Michael Crowder (eds), *History of West Africa*, 2 vols, London: Longman.
Coombs, D. (1963), *The Gold Coast, Britain and the Netherlands, 1850–74*, London: Oxford University Press.
Edgerton, Robert B. (1995), *The Fall of the Asante Empire. The Hundred-year War for Africa's Gold Coast*, New York and London: The Free Press.
Reindorf, Carl Christian [1889] (1966), *The History of the Gold Coast and Asante* Accra: Ghana University Press.

See also: **Anti-colonialism and Resistance: West Africa.**

Asian Expulsions (East Africa)

A sea-faring people of the north-west coast of India were possibly conducting trade with East African coastal markets as early as 3000 BC. In the following centuries administrative and trading communities became established on Zanzibar and the coasts of present-day Kenya and Tanzania. With the establishment of British rule over Kenya and Uganda in the nineteenth century, Asians were encouraged to form trading posts further inland. Between 1896 and 1922, labourers and skilled workers from India were indentured to build the railway from Mombasa to Uganda – a project partly funded by Asian businessmen.

With the independence of Tanganyika in 1961, Uganda in 1962, and Kenya and Zanzibar in 1963, the official rhetoric surrounding the Asian communities of East Africa changed. Valued by the colonial rulers as entrepreneurs – expanding the market for British goods – the African governments perceived and portrayed them as exploiters who lacked commitment to the new nations. In 1967, Jomo Kenyatta's administration passed laws that obstructed the Asians' ability to conduct business and become citizens. The resulting exodus of Kenyan Asians to Britain prompted the notorious 1968 Commonwealth Immigrants Act (UK), which curtailed the right of people without a British parent or grandparent to claim a passport. Many of these 'airport people', former British subjects, were denied entry into Britain, and forced to seek refuge in Canada, India and elsewhere.

Following the Kenyan example, Milton Obote of Uganda passed restrictive laws in 1969. When Idi Amin overthrew Obote's corrupt regime in a military coup on January 1971, many Asians – along with other Ugandans – were relieved. However, in December 1971 Amin called a conference of Asian leaders at which he blamed their communities for failing to integrate. In August 1972, Amin – claiming God had told him to turn Uganda into a black man's country – expelled all non-citizen Asians from Uganda. Following further decrees, over 40,000 Asians were forced to leave the country within three months, the majority settling in the United Kingdom and Canada. Amin's brutal rule ended in 1979, when Tanzanian forces combined with Ugandan exiles to bring Obote back to power. In 1986, Yoweri Museveni took power and invited Asian expellees to return and reclaim their property.

                                                                                                Stephanie Jones

Literary Works

Alibhai-Brown, Yasmin (1995), *No Place Like Home*, London: Virago Press.
Dawood, Yusuf K. (2000), *Return to Paradise*, Nairobi: East African Educational Publishers.
Markham, E. A. and Arnold Kingston (eds) (1973), *Merely a Matter of Colour: The Uganda Asian Anthology*, London: Q Books.
Mississippi Masala (1992), screenplay by Sooni Taraponevalla. Dir. Mira Nair.
Mukta, Parita (2002), *Shards of Memory: Woven Lives in Four Generations*, London: Weidenfeld and Nicolson.
Naipaul, Shiva (1979), *North of South: An African Journey*, Harmondsworth: Penguin.
Nazareth, Peter (1972), *In a Brown Mantle*, Nairobi: East African Literature Bureau.
Nazareth, Peter (1991), *The General is Up*, Toronto: TSAR Publications.
Patel, Kirit (1979), *In Search of Tomorrow*, Bognor Regis: New Horizon.
Siddiqi, Jameela (2001), *The Feast of the Nine Virgins*, London: Bogle L'Ouverture.

Tejani, Bahadur (1971), *Day after Tomorrow*, Nairobi: East African Literature Review.
Vassanji, M. G. (1991), *Uhuru Street*, African Writers Series. Oxford: Heinemann.

Histories

Gregory, Robert (1993), *Quest for Equality, Asian Politics in East Africa, 1900–1967*, Hyderabad: Orient Longman.
Mamdani, Mahmood (1973), *From Citizen to Refugee: Uganda Asians come to Britain*, London: Frances Pinter.
Twaddle, Michael (ed.) (1975), *Expulsion of a Minority: Essays on Ugandan Asians*, London: published for Institute of Commonwealth Studies by The Athlone Press.

See also: **Amin, Idi; Nyerere, Julius and Ujamaa**.

Asianisation: Australia

In the early 1980s, the concept of an 'Asian Turn' was introduced on the Australian political agenda in a belated reflection of the country's increasing multiculturalism and economic and cultural orientation towards Asia. The British and later American withdrawal from South-east Asia, together with the rise of the 'tiger' economies of South-east Asia, compelled Australia to come to terms with its geopolitical position on the Asian-Pacific Rim. Labor prime minister Paul Keating (1991–6) was heavily engaged in this process which sought to move the Australian self-perception away from the traditional British(-Irish) settler culture's monopoly on national identity to a more cosmopolitan outlook. In historical terms, it marked a dramatic break from Australia's historic fears of 'Asian hordes' casting their hungry eyes on the 'empty continent'.

The 'Asian Turn' has been criticised for being driven too much by economics while failing to protect poorly-organised workers from the competition posed by cheaper Asian imports. It also provoked a critical reaction from those opposed to the concurrent increase in Asian immigration. Together, these developments gave rise to Pauline Hanson's One Nation party, which appealed to working-class and lower middle-class voters, particularly in rural and outer-urban areas, who felt threatened by the tightening of the welfare system and suffered from the policies of economic rationalism. The party espoused an extreme British(-Irish) settler-derived nationalistic anti-Aboriginal and anti-Asian platform.

While One Nation has ceased to be an influential party, and was never very strong outside Queensland, its policies have been taken over by John Howard's Liberal and National Party government which has pursued since 1996 a neo-colonial foreign policy against its Pacific neighbouring countries and an anti-refugee policy that has generated much international criticism.

While John Howard managed to retard the progress of 'Asian Turn', and shift Australia's focus back towards Britain and the United States, the logic of Australia's geopolitical position, its economic interests and the changing composition of its population, have ensured that Howard cannot completely repudiate the policies of Paul Keating. The future will likely see the country's geography gradually become more important than its history as a British colony.

Lars Jensen

Literary Works

Castro, Brian (1983), *Birds of Passage*, Sydney: Allen and Unwin.
Khan, Adib (1994), *Seasonal Adjustments*, Sydney: Allen and Unwin.
Koch, Christopher (1982), *The Year of Living Dangerously*, Ringwood: Penguin.
Lazaroo, Simone (1994), *The World Waiting to be Made*, Fremantle: Fremantle Arts Centre
    Press.
Miller, Alex (1992), *The Ancestor Game*, Ringwood: Penguin.

Histories

Broinowski, Alison (1992), *The Yellow Lady: Australian Impressions of Asia*, Melbourne:
    Oxford University Press.
Dever, Maryanne (ed.) (1997), *Australia and Asia: Cultural Transactions*, Honolulu:
    University of Hawaii Press.
Rolls, Eric (1992), *Sojourners: The Epic Story of China's Century-Old Relationship with
    Australia*, St Lucia: University of Queensland Press.
Walker, David (1999), *Anxious Nation: Australia and the Rise of Asia 1850–1939*, St Lucia:
    University of Queensland Press.
Walker, David (ed.) (1990), 'Australian Perceptions of Asia' (special issue), *Australian
    Cultural History* 9, Canberra: Australian National University Press.

See also: **Boat People; Refugees; Yellow Peril**.

Aung San Suu Kyi

Daw Aung San Suu Kyi is the co-founder and leader of the National League for Democracy,
an organisation that, since 1988, has worked towards establishing democracy in Burma
(Myanmar) through non-violent means. In 1991 she was awarded the Nobel Peace Prize,
bringing international attention to the struggle for human rights in Burma. Suu Kyi was
born in 1945, two years before her father, Aung San, an anti-imperialist insurgent who
emerged as Burma's leading political figure after World War II, was assassinated. Her
mother, Daw Khin Kyi, who was appointed Burma's first director of social welfare, remained
in Rangoon until 1960, when she became ambassador to India. Suu Kyi accompanied her
mother to New Delhi, where she completed her secondary education. In 1964 she left India
to study philosophy, politics, and economics at Oxford University.

   After earning her degree, Suu Kyi went to New York, where she worked for the
Advisory Committee on Administrative and Budgetary Questions at the United Nations.
In 1972 she married an Englishman, Michael Aris, and moved to the newly-established
nation of Bhutan, working for the Foreign Ministry. The next year, she and Aris moved
to Great Britain, where their two sons were born. There she began to research her father's
life and study Japanese, moving to Japan in 1985 to continue her work as a visiting scholar
at the University of Kyoto. In 1987 she joined Aris in Simla, receiving a fellowship from
the Indian Institute of Advanced Studies, and in the following year she returned with her
family to Great Britain, entering the London School of Oriental and African Studies.

Suu Kyi's political activities began in 1988 while visiting Burma to care for her dying mother. After Ne Win, Burma's military dictator since 1962, resigned, Suu Kyi co-founded the National League for Democracy (NLD), a political organisation dedicated to re-establishing civilian rule in Burma. Despite efforts by the military government to suppress the democratic movement, she continued to campaign nationally, advocating civil disobedience but not revolutionary violence. In July 1989 she was placed under house arrest and prevented from running for public office.

Although the NLD won more than 80 per cent of the seats in the elections of the following year, the military refused to relinquish power and Suu Kyi remained in detention until 1995. In the years that followed, the government continued to restrict her activities, and she was again detained from 2000 to 2002. Her political activities have not ceased, however, and she continues to be the leader of Burma's democracy movement.

Tom Henthorne

Literary Works

Kyi May Kaung (1993), *Pelted with Petals: Burmese Poems*, Anchorage: Intertext.
Khoo Thwe, Pascal (2002), *From the Land of the Green Ghosts*, London: HarperCollins.
Law-Yone, Wendy (1993), *Irawaddy Tango*, New York: Knopf.

Histories

Aung San Suu Kyi (1995), *Freedom from Fear*, New York: Penguin.
Aung San Suu Kyi (1997), *Letters from Burma*, New York: Penguin.
Fink, Christina (2001), *Living Silence: Burma under Military Rule*, New York: Zed Books.
Victor, Barbara (1998), *The Lady: Aung San Suu Kyi, Nobel Laureate and Burma's Prisoner*, Boston: Faber and Faber.

See also: **Anglo-Burmese Wars; Historiography: South-east Asia**.

B

'Back-to-Africa' Movement

A blanket term used to describe varied efforts and variously interconnected movements rather than a single organised endeavour, the 'Back-to-Africa' movement refers to emigration (voluntary and forced) by blacks from the USA (and a lesser extent Britain) to Africa. The concept can be traced to the eighteenth century. In 1787, the 'British

Committee for the Black Poor' sent a group of roughly 400 black volunteers and depor-
tees, as well as white prostitutes, to Sierra Leone. On the other side of the Atlantic, blacks
fighting for Britain during the Revolutionary War were sent to Sierra Leone in 1792 after
having been resettled in Nova Scotia for a time. While in America the Revolutionary
War, and the political climate before it, germinated ideas of sending blacks to Africa, the
nineteenth century was especially marked by burgeoning American interest in 'repatriation'. Thomas Jefferson (d. 1826) wrote in favour of sending free blacks, freed slaves, and
their descendants to Africa, and in 1816 the Virginia legislature proposed obtaining land
in coastal West Africa for this purpose. The embodiment of this project was the 'American
Colonization Society', which sent 18,858 black Americans to Liberia and Sierra Leone
between 1822 and 1867.

In the twentieth century Marcus Garvey (d. 1940) came to be synonymous with the
'Back-to-Africa' movement, and with 'Back-to-Africa' ideologies flourishing particularly
during the 1920s. For Garvey, however, the benefits of American connections to Africa
were as much economic as historical and cultural, and were not dependent on resettling
Americans in Africa. Indeed, much of his rhetoric was overblown by the popular media of
the time. For him, the merits of returning to a metaphorical homeland were simply embedded in a larger Pan-Africanist philosophy. The Pan-Africanism of the early and mid-
twentieth century was in a sense reborn in the Black Power and Afrocentrism movements'
calls of 'Back to Africa' during the 1960s. The fact that a historiography of 'Back-to-Africa'
ideas spans three centuries, from American to African independence, and does so against
the backdrop of sets of far-reaching political and social developments, demonstrates the
complexity of an idea that is often cast in singular terms.

Noah Butler

Literary Works

Garvey, Marcus (1983), *The Poetical Works of Marcus Garvey*, ed. Tony Martin, Dover, MA:
    Majority.
Haley, Alex (1976), *Roots: The Saga of an American Family*, New York: Random House.
Moses, Wilson Jeremiah (ed.) (1998), *Back-to-Africa Narratives from the 1850s*, University
    Park, PA: Pennsylvania State University.
Phillips, Caryl (1995), *Crossing the River*, New York: Vintage.

Histories

Campbell, Mavis (1993), *Back to Africa: George Ross and the Maroons: From Nova Scotia to
    Sierra Leone*, Trenton, NJ: Africa World Press.
Clarke, John Henrik (1986), 'The American Antecedents of Marcus Garvey', in Rupert
    Lewis and Maureen Warner-Lewis (eds), *Garvey: Africa, Europe, the Americas*,
    Trenton, NJ: Africa World Press.
Garvey, Amy Jacques (1963), *Garvey and Garveyism*, New York: Octagon.
Gershoni, Yekutiel (1985), *Black Colonialism: The Americo-Liberian Scramble for the
    Hinterland*, Boulder, CO: Westview.
Harris, Sheldon (1972), *Paul Cuffe: Black America and the African Return*, New York: Simon
    and Schuster.

Herskevits, Melville (1941), *The Myth of the Negro Past*, New York: Harper Bros.
Stein, Judith (1986), *The World of Marcus Garvey: Race and Class in Modern Society*, Baton Rouge, LA: Louisiana State University Press.

See also: **Garvey, Marcus Mosiah; Pan-Africanism; Slavery: Caribbean; United States of America**.

Balfour Declaration

One of three contradictory promises about the future of Palestine made by British authorities, the Balfour Declaration stands as one of the early Zionist movement's diplomatic achievements. However, it is also infamous as one of the first major betrayals of the Palestinian cause for self-determination.

During World War I, Britain pledged its support to three contradictory plans for a post-Ottoman Palestine. In the 1915 Sykes-Picot agreement, Britain and France secretly divided the Levant between their two empires in the event of the collapse of Ottoman authority. The 1916 McMahon-Husayn correspondence, however, promised British support for an independent Arab nation after the war, which included Palestinian territory. The Balfour Declaration devised yet another path for Palestine. In a letter written to prominent British Zionist Lord Rothschild, the British foreign secretary Arthur Balfour stated:

> His Majesty's Government view with favour the establishment in Palestine of a National Home for the Jewish people, and will use their best endeavours to facilitate the achievement of this object, it being clearly understood that nothing shall be done which may prejudice the civil and religious rights of existing non-Jewish communities in Palestine, or the rights and political status enjoyed by Jews in any other country.

Quickly taken up by Zionist leaders around the world as a legitimating force for their cause, the Balfour Declaration stemmed in part from a belief among members of the British cabinet that American and Russian Jewry could sway their governments to remain committed to the war effort against Germany. It also reflected Christian Zionist sympathies among some British officials. Moreover, British support for expanded Zionist settlement meant a stronger British presence in Palestine after the war, giving the British an excuse to keep the French away from the Suez Canal zone. However, the declaration was highly problematic. Not only did it contradict the McMahon-Husayn correspondence, but its vague language allowed for multiple interpretations. How could a 'Jewish national home' not infringe upon the rights of the majority non-Jewish population? What was the difference between a 'national home' and a nation-state? Controversial from the start, the Balfour Declaration became a diplomatic tool for the Zionist cause in post-World War I Palestine.

Nancy Stockdale

Literary Works

Soueif, Ahdaf (1999), *The Map of Love*, London: Bloomsbury.

Histories

Finkelstein, Norman G. (2003), *Image and Reality of the Israel-Palestine Conflict*, New York: Verso.
Laqueur, Walter (1989), *A History of Zionism*, New York: Schocken.
Said, Edward (1992), *The Question of Palestine*, New York: Vintage.
Sanders, Ronald (1983), *The High Walls of Jerusalem: A History of the Balfour Declaration and the Birth of the British Mandate for Palestine*, New York: Holt, Rinehart, and Winston.
Schalim, Avi (2001), *The Iron Wall: Israel and the Arab World*, New York: Norton.
Segev, Tom (2001), *One Palestine, Complete*, New York: Holt.

See also: **Levant Company; Nationalism(s): Arab; Palestinian Political Movements; Zionism.**

Banda, Ngwazi Hastings Kamazu

When he died in a Johannesburg clinic on 15 November 1997, Hastings Kamazu Banda, ruler of Malawi from 1966 to 1994, was officially said to be 91 years old, but the clinic gave his age as 99.

The son of peasants, Banda's early years were spent in Kasungu in what was then Nyasaland, a British protectorate that had been proclaimed in 1891. At the age of seventeen, Banda left for South Africa to pursue his education, which continued in the USA, where he qualified as a medical doctor in 1937. He then practised medicine and mixed with African anti-colonial leaders like Kwame Nkrumah in London; and in 1953 moved to Ghana.

Aside from the abortive uprising against British rule led by John Chilembwe in January 1915, there was little mass-based resistance to colonialism in Nyasaland in the first half of the twentieth century. The Nyasaland African Congress (NAC) was formed in 1944 by members of the educated African elite, and its pursuit of independence gathered momentum after 1953 when the British combined Nyasaland with Northern Rhodesia (Zambia after independence) and Southern Rhodesia (Zimbabwe after independence) to form the Federation of Rhodesia and Nyasaland.

Banda's return to Nyasaland in July 1958 is identified as a turning point in the independence struggle, as his leadership galvanised opposition. He was imprisoned in 1959, but released a year later to participate in constitutional conferences with the British over Nyasaland's future. These talks culminated in elections which Banda's Malawi Congress Party (MCP – the successor to the NAC) won comfortably, and in December 1963 the Federation of Rhodesia and Nyasaland was dissolved, with Banda becoming Malawi's first president six months later.

In 1966, Banda changed the constitution to make Malawi a one-party state, and in 1971 declared himself president for life. In the course of his rule, Banda eliminated all political opposition by the ruthless deployment of the police and the Young Pioneers (the youth wing of the MCP), and he encouraged foreign capital investment for export cash crops at the expense of subsistence peasant agriculture. His foreign policy was eccentric: he supported Zimbabwe's Patriotic Front in the 1970s, but he was also the first African leader to visit apartheid South Africa (in 1971), and his uncompromising anti-communism guided his tacit support for RENAMO in Mozambique.

Increasingly desperate levels of poverty and escalating human rights' abuses led to widespread popular opposition and the suspension of Western aid in 1992. A referendum in June 1993 overwhelmingly approved an end to the one-party state, and in multi-party elections a year later, Banda was voted out of power and replaced by Bakili Muluzi. Anti-Banda sentiment in Malawi persisted, and in 1996 Banda issued a statement under pressure acknowledging that he had been responsible for deaths and brutalities committed under his regime.

David Johnson

Literary Works

Chimombo, Steve (1994), *Napolo and the Python*, London: Heinemann.
Chipasula, Frank (1991), *Whispers in the Wings*, London: Heinemann.
Lwanda, John (1994), *The Second Harvest*, Glasgow: Dudu Nsomba Publications.
Mnthali, Felix (1998), *Yoranivyoto*, Glasgow: Dudu Nsomba Publications.
Mpanje, Jack (1993), *The Chattering Wagtails of Mikuyu Prison*, London: Heinemann.
Zeleza, Tiyambe (1992), *Smouldering Charcoal*, London: Heinemann.

Histories

Baker, Colin (2001), *Revolt of the Ministers. The Malawi Cabinet Crisis, 1964–1965*, London: I. B. Tauris.
Chimombo, Steve and Moira (1996), *The Culture of Democracy. Language, Literature, the Arts and Politics in Malawi, 1992–1994*, Zomba: WASI Publications.
Harrigan, Jane (2000), *From Dictatorship to Democracy. Economic Policy in Malawi 1964–2000*, Aldershot: Ashgate.
McCracken, John, Timothy J. Lovering and Fiona Johnson Chalamanda (eds) (2001), *Twentieth-Century Malawi. Perspectives on History and Culture*, Stirling: University of Stirling, Centre of Commonwealth Studies.
Short, Philip (1974), *Banda*, London and Boston: Routledge and Kegan Paul.
Sindima, Harvey J. (2002), *Malawi's First Republic: An Economic and Political Analysis*, Lanham, MD: University Press of America.
Williams, T. David (1978), *Malawi. The Politics of Despair*, Ithaca, NY: Cornell University Press.

See also: **Kaunda, Kenneth David**; **Migrancy: Southern Africa**.

Bangladesh: 1971

The emergence of Bangladesh in 1971 is often thematised under the '1971 Indo-Pakistan War' which peripheralises East and West Pakistan's relationship of 'internal' colonialism: West Pakistani Punjabis regarded Bangalis as non-martial, hence inferior; despite protests, Urdu, spoken only by 3.7 per cent, was declared the sole national language in 1948 (Bangla spoken by 55 per cent); Pakistani rulers considered Bangali Muslim culture to be Hinduised; East Pakistan was exploited for its raw material and cheap labour, and was a market for West Pakistani manufacturers; top governmental, commercial and industrial positions were monopolised by them, and big business interests were controlled either by West Pakistanis or Urdu-speaking Muslim refugees (ethnic Bihari/ Agha Khani), who had migrated at the time of partition.

After 1954, Pakistan's Cold War ally status helped strengthen colonising trends. The Awami League's (AL) Six Points programme of regional autonomy – the Bangali petty bourgeoisie's 'bill of rights' – threatened Pakistan's ruling interests. Popular upsurges against the military regime in 1968 and 1969 helped free AL leader Sheikh Mujibur Rahman and others from jail, led to President Ayub Khan's resignation, General Yahya Khan's declaration of martial law, and the promise of elections.

In the 1970 national elections, AL won a clear majority of the contested National Assembly seats. Military resistance to AL forming a government led to massive civil disobedience and escalated the Bangali–Bihari conflict. Military action began on the night of 25 March 1971 leading to the massacre of hundreds of thousands of men, women and children, the rape of an estimated 200,000 women (many of whom were housed in rape camps), 8–10 million refugees in West Bengal, and Sheikh Mujibar Rahman's re-imprisonment. AL leaders sought safety in Kolkata while Mukti Bahini (the liberation forces) and popular resistance steadily wore down the Pakistani army. Although nationality versus class issues prevented the formation of a national liberation front, most left-wing groups aided fleeing peoples, and fought the army at the local level. The nine-month military occupation was aided by Bangalis (Peace Committees and Al-Badr and Al-Shams death squads) as well as Biharis. The Indian army's intervention in December 1971 helped contain the armed struggle and dismember the arch-enemy, whilst allowing India to portray itself as a disinterested saviour.

Bangladesh became politically independent on 16 December 1971 (the nation was renamed on 17 April 1971) as the Pakistani army surrendered to its Indian counterpart, under the watchful eyes of the US Seventh Fleet, stationed in the Bay of Bengal. Recent feminist/pluralist history-writing has critiqued liberation struggle histories for being elitist, Bangali and male-centred. Alternative history-writing has forefronted the sufferings and continuing trauma caused by death, rape, and the dislocations experienced by poor peoples, women, Biharis and *adivasis* (indigenous peoples).

Rahnuma Ahmed

Literary Works

Ali, Monica (2003), *Brick Lane*, London: Doubleday.
Khan, Adib (1994), *Seasonal Adjustments*, St Leonards: Allen and Unwin.
Mistry, Rohinton (1992), *Such a Long Journey*, London: Vintage.
Rushdie, Salman (1981), *Midnight's Children*, London: Jonathan Cape.

Histories

ASK (2001), *Narir Ekattur O Juddhoporoborti Kotthokahini* (Women's 1971 and Postwar Oral Histories, English translation forthcoming), Dhaka: Ain O Salish Kendro.

Gough, Kathleen and Hari P. Sharma (eds) (1973), *Imperialism and Revolution in South Asia*, New York: Monthly Review Press.

Mookherjee, Nayanika (2002), '"A Lot of History": Sexual Violence, Public Memories and the Bangladesh Liberation War of 1971', D.Phil. thesis in social anthropology, SOAS, University of London.

See also: **Military Dictatorships: South Asia; Pakistan's Subaltern Struggles; Partition; Refugees; Religions: South Asia; Secessionism South Asia; Women's Histories: South Asia**.

Battle of the Plains of Abraham

Although its full significance continues to be debated by historians, the Battle of the Plains of Abraham remains one of the most important events in the history, and mythology, of Canada. The Seven Years' War was in many ways a global war, with one of its conflicts being that between the French and British in North America.

After the successful siege and capture of the French fortress at Louisbourg, Cape Breton, in 1758, the British army's attention shifted toward Quebec, the heart of New France. In June 1759, a powerful force under the command of Major-General James Wolfe and Vice-Admiral Charles Saunders headed up the St Lawrence River, arriving by the end of June. Although the French forces, under the command of the Marquis de Montcalm, outnumbered the British troops, a significant portion of them were poorly trained militia, and it was clear that the British would have a significant advantage if they were able to meet the French in open combat. The French, however, were safely entrenched, and thus Wolfe had to devise a means of forcing the French into the open. Montcalm, for his part, simply had to avoid being drawn into combat until the freezing of the St Lawrence would force the British navy and army to depart.

Afflicted by ill health and dissension from his subordinates, Wolfe unsuccessfully spent the summer trying various strategems to force the French into the open, including the destruction of outlying communities, the bombardment of Quebec, and a major attack to the east of the city on 31 July 1759 which resulted in the loss of over 200 British troops. Finally, in early September, Wolfe decided to attack from the west of the city. On the night of 12 September British troops made a surprise landing on the north shore of the St Lawrence upstream of the city and, meeting little resistance, successfully ascended the cliffs. By the morning of 13 September, Wolfe and his forces were in place on the Plains of Abraham, from which position they could threaten Montcalm's communications and supply lines. Forced into action, the French initiated an attack on the British lines and were quickly repulsed. Montcalm was mortally wounded and died the next day, while Wolfe was killed on the field of battle, a scene immortalised in Benjamin West's famous and iconic painting *The Death of Wolfe* (1771).

Although the British had won a decisive victory, it was not total, as the remains of the French army managed to escape and withdraw to Montreal. Quebec surrendered on 18 September, although it would not be until the next year that Montreal fell and the British had completed their conquest of New France.

Douglas Ivison

Literary Works

Cary, Thomas [1789] (1986), *Abram's Plains: A Poem*, London: Canadian Poetry Press.
Chudley, Ron (1980), *After Abraham: A Play*, Vancouver: Talonbooks.
Cockings, George (1766), *The Conquest of Canada, or, The Siege of Quebec: An Historical Tragedy of Five Acts*, London.

Histories

Connell, Brian (1959), *The Plains of Abraham*, London: Hodder and Stoughton.
Donaldson, Gordon (1973), *Battle for a Continent: Quebec 1759*, Toronto: Doubleday.
Frégault, Guy [1955] (1969), *Canada: The War of the Conquest*, trans. Margaret M. Cameron, Toronto: Oxford University Press.
Lapierre, Laurier L. (1990), *1759: The Battle for Canada*, Toronto: McClelland and Stewart.
Parkman, Francis [1884] (1984), *Montcalm and Wolfe*, Markham: Penguin.
Stacey, C. P. (1959), *Quebec, 1759: The Siege and the Battle*, Toronto: Macmillan.

See also: **Historiography: Canada; Quebec Independence Movement**.

Bengal Famine

Famine is generally perceived to be the result of a failure of food supplies, typically arising from the Malthusian notion of mismatch between population and natural resources. However, economists such as Amartya Sen (1984), argue that famine is less commonly caused by an absolute shortage of food than by the lack of 'entitlements' – that is, the existence of large numbers of people who do not possess the means either of producing food or of acquiring it through purchase or through transfer payments sanctioned by the state or by custom.

In Bengal, famine cannot be explained in terms of food shortage or failure of exchange entitlement alone. Polanyi blames 'cultural degeneration' (Polanyi 1944, p. 159) caused by British imperialism for famine in Bengal. Davis (2001, pp. 311–40) even argues that there is a serious flaw in famine historiography; and modern historians, including Hobsbawm and Landes, completely ignored 'mega-droughts' and famine that engulfed the so-called Third World during the colonial times. According to Davis, famines are wars over the right to existence, and the Fakir and Sannyasi Uprising, the Indian Mutiny, Faraizi movement, and Tebagha Andolan were all precipitated by colonial state repression. Further colonial policies, especially those related to land-tenure systems (permanent settlement), which directly affected the landless labourers who were subjected to over-extraction by various intermediary agents (*zamindars*) and moneylenders, destroyed the pre-colonial social fabric.

The colonial inroads into the economic base of Bengal, coupled with natural disaster and crop failure, resulted in the disastrous famine of 1770 to 1771 which wiped out almost one-third of the population of Bengal. The earliest recorded famine of Bengal (1770) resulted in the death of about 10 million people and in the great Bengal famine of 1943 between 1.5 and 3 million people perished.

Is language capable of a description of famine's horrors? In famine literature, questions about language's adequacy give way to a detailed attempt at representation. Nineteenth- and twentieth-century literary works – Bankimchandra's *Anandamath* (1992), which deals with Fakir and Sannyasi revolt of 1770, Bibuthibhusans *Ashani Sanket*, and Manikbando- padhay's short stories *Namuna* and his novel *Chintamani* – make the events of various Bengal famines imaginatively accessible for readers.

Suhail Islam

Literary Works

Chatterji, Bankimchandra [1896] (1992), *Anandamath*, Calcutta: Vision/Orient.

Histories

Bhattacharya, Mihir (2001), 'Realism and Syntax of Difference: Narratives of the Bengal Famine, in K. N. Panikkar and T. J. Byres (eds), *The Making of History: Essays Presented to Irfan Habib*, New Delhi: Tulika, pp. 478–99.
Davis, Mike (2001), *Late Victorian Holocausts*, London: Verso.
Mishra, H. K. (1991), *Famines and Poverty in India*, New Delhi: Ashish Publishing.
Polanyi, Karl (1944), *The Great Transformation*, Boston, MA: Beacon Hill.
Sen, Amartya, (1984), *Poverty and Famines: An Essay on Entitlement and Deprivation*, New Delhi: Oxford University Press.

Berlin Conference

The conference, called by German Prince Bismarck, convened in Berlin from 15 November 1884 through to 27 February 1885. At the European negotiating table, where the African continental prizes would be awarded, sat delegates from Germany, Britain, France, Portugal – major contestants – and Russia, Austro-Hungary, Denmark, Sweden, Belgium, Norway, and Holland. Present, too, were the United States and Leopold II's International Association of the Congo. All had designs on the map of Africa.

The General Act of the Conference of Berlin, signed on 26 February 1885, was divided into six chapters. Chapter I addressed 'freedom of trade in the Basin of the Congo'; Chapter II dealt expeditiously with the slave trade; Chapter III arbitrated neutrality in the region; Chapters IV and V adjudicated navigation rights for the Congo and Niger rivers; finally, Chapter VI laid out conditions to be observed by signatories for 'new occupations on the coasts of the African continent'.

Freedom of trade and navigation were prime motives in drafting the Berlin document's division and distribution of African resources to European predators, following British explorer David Livingstone's 'three C's' of imperial ambition: commerce, civilisation, and Christianity. There was the Suez Canal Company at the north-eastern tip of the continent, whose project was begun by Frenchman De Lesseps, finalised by British prime minister Disraeli's investments, and opened in 1869. On the western coast, Sir George Goldie, British colonial administrator, took advantage of the treaty's terms, and his Royal Niger Company was chartered by Britain in 1886. In 1889, mine magnate Cecil John Rhodes assured that his British South Africa Company would also have a charter. But it was

Belgium King Leopold II's concessions in the Congo Free State that most challenged – and abused – the treaty's terms on trade and territory, provoking both commercial and humanitarian objections.

The Berlin Conference brought rival European diplomats to the table for an orderly arrangement, but it was instead the occasion for the rather more disorderly 'scramble for Africa'. Already, German philosopher, G.W. F. Hegel, in *The Philosophy of History* (1822), had maintained that Africa was 'no historical part of the World; it has no movement or development to exhibit'. By the century's end, however, European contenders sought to appropriate African proceeds to their own historic purposes. The map of the 'dark continent' drawn in Berlin was a multi-coloured one, as Joseph Conrad's Marlow described it in 1898, 'There was a vast amount of red . . . a deuce of a lot of blue, a little green, smears of orange, and, on the East Coast, a purple patch, to show where the jolly pioneers drink the jolly lager beer.' Berlin: was it a conference or a scramble?

Barbara Harlow

Literary Works

Achebe, Chinua (1987), *Anthills of the Savannah*, London: Heinemann.
Conrad, Joseph (1898), *Heart of Darkness*, New York and London: Norton.
Foden, Giles (1998), *The Last King of Scotland*, London: Faber and Faber.

Histories

Davidson, Basil (1992), *The Black Man's Burden: Africa and the Curse of the Nation-State*, New York: Times Books.
Hegel, G.W. F. [1822] (1956), *The Philosophy of History*, trans. J. Sibree, New York: Dover.
Hochschild, Adam (1998), *King Leopold's Ghost: A Story of Greed, Terror, and Heroism in Colonial Africa*, Boston and New York: Houghton Mifflin.
Mamdani, Mahmood (1996), *Citizen and Subject: Contemporary Africa and the Legacy of Late Colonialism*, Princeton, NJ: Princeton University Press.
Pakenham, Thomas (1991), *The Scramble for Africa*, London: Weidenfeld and Nicolson.

See also: **British Imperialism**; **Historiography: British Empire**.

Biafran War

The Nigerian civil war (1967–70), also known as the Biafran War, was one of the first armed conflicts in postcolonial Africa, and one of the bloodiest. The background to the war lies in Nigeria's faltering struggles with nationhood, and a colonial legacy that fused politics with ethnicity.

At independence in 1960, Nigeria's federal constitution comprised three regions defined by the country's principal ethnic groups – Yoruba in the south-west, Igbo in the south-east, and the Hausa and Fulani in the north who held the balance of power. Regional tensions and a series of crises plagued the First Republic, and its prime minister, Sir Abubakar Tafawa Balewa, was assassinated in a military coup on 15 January 1966. Major General

Aguiyi-Ironsi, an Igbo, assumed control, heading a populist military government whose policies were interpreted as a threat to northern interests and an attempt to promote an Igbo political hegemony. Regional tensions increased and in May 1966 thousands of mainly Christian easterners living in the Muslim north were killed in pogroms. Massive internal displacement followed and in July 1966 Ironsi was killed in a counter-coup as Lt Col Gowon came to power. These moves, and further attacks on easterners, fuelled the prospect of secession by the predominantly Igbo Eastern Region. Reconciliation talks held in Ghana in January 1967 collapsed, and in March the decision of the Eastern Region to assume financial autonomy was met with an economic blockade. Decentralisation, with the creation of twelve federal states on 27 May, was perceived as an attempt to split the Igbo heartland and failed to deflect the secessionists' momentum. Three days later, on 30 May 1967, the charismatic military governor of Eastern Nigeria, Lt Col Ojukwu, declared Eastern Nigeria as the independent Republic of Biafra, taking its name from the inlet of the West African Atlantic coast.

Fighting between Nigeria and Biafra broke out in July 1967. For the Nigerian side the secession was an 'internal rebellion' and the war was fought to re-unite the country; from the Biafran side it was a struggle to escape insecurity and genocide. Initial Biafran advances into the Mid-Western Region and the Niger delta stalled, and Nigerian forces gradually reduced the territory under Biafra's control.

The economic blockade of Biafra had a devastating impact. Foreign involvement, of France in particular, and of relief organisations in the world's first major humanitarian aid operation, became critical to Biafra's survival and fuelled its resistance. In the face of sustained air attacks and overwhelming numbers of federal troops, however, Ojukwu fled to Cote d'Ivoire, and the breakaway republic surrendered on 12 January 1970.

An international observer mission found no evidence to support allegations of systematic genocide, but an estimated 1 million people died in Biafra as a result of food shortages and disease during the 30-month conflict. A further 3 million people were internally displaced. Though criticisms of political marginalisation of the Igbo remain, the federal government's post-war policy of national reconciliation is acknowledged as a remarkable act of political moderation.

David Pratten

Literary Works

Achebe, Chinua (1972), *Girls at War and Other Stories*, London: Heinemann.
Amadi, Elechi (1973), *Sunset in Biafra: A Civil War Diary*, London: Heinemann.
Emecheta, Buchi (1994), *Destination Biafra*, Oxford: Heinemann.
Ike, Chukwemeka (1976), *Sunset at Dawn: A Novel about Biafra*, London: Collins and Harvill Press.
Iroh, Eddie (1976), *Forty-Eight Guns for the General*, London: Heinemann.
Mazrui, A. A. (1971), *The Trial of Christopher Okigbo*, New York: The Third Press and Joseph Okpaku Publishing.
Saro-Wiwa, Ken (1989), *On a Darkling Plain: An Account of the Nigerian Civil War*, Lagos and London: Saros International Publishers.
Saro-Wiwa, Ken (1994), *Sozaboy: A Novel in Rotten English*, London: Longman African Writers.
Soyinka, Wole (1972), *The Man Died. Prison Notes of Wole Soyinka*, London: Rex Collings.

Histories

Akpan, N. U. (1972), *The Struggle for Secession, 1966–1970: A Personal Account of the Nigerian Civil War*, London: Cass.

Cronjé, S. (1972), *The World and Nigeria: The Diplomatic History of the Biafran War, 1967–1970*, London: Sidgwick and Jackson.

Kirk-Greene, A. H. M. (1971), *Crisis and Conflict in Nigeria: A Documentary Sourcebook*, 2 vols, London: Oxford University Press.

Nafziger, E. W. (1983), *The Economics of Political Instability: The Nigerian–Biafran War*, Epping: Bowker.

Ojukwu C. O. (1969), *Biafra. Selected Speeches and Random Thoughts of C. Odumegwu-Ojukwu, General of The People's Army*, 2 vols, New York and London: Harper & Row.

St Jorre, J. de (1972), *The Nigerian Civil War*, London: Hodder and Stoughton.

Tamuno, Tekena and Samson Ukpbabi (eds) (1989), *Nigeria Since Independence: The First Twenty-Five Years*, vol. 6, The Civil War Years, Ibadan: Heinemann.

See also: **Languages and Ethnicities: West Africa; Religions: West Africa**.

Big Bear

Big Bear was a Plains Cree chief who gained prominence through his opposition to treaty-making with the government of Canada. Born in 1825 on the shores of Jackfish Lake in what is now Saskatchewan, Big Bear, or Mistahimusqua, was the son of a chief of a small mixed band of Cree and Ojibwa. Known as a warrior and spiritual leader who possessed strong medicine, Big Bear ascended to the position of chief upon his father's death in the mid-1860s. He came to wider prominence in 1876, when he refused to sign Treaty 6, which had been negotiated between the Plains Cree chiefs and the government of Canada and which allotted land in central Alberta and Saskatchewan to sixteen Alberta First Nations.

The failure of the government to fulfil its treaty obligations led to increased dissatisfaction with the treaties, and many of those who objected joined Big Bear's band, which gained in strength to 2,000 people. By 1882, however, his band was destitute and near starvation, due to the disappearance of the buffalo, and tensions increased as the younger men became disenchanted with Big Bear's policy of delay. Finally, on 8 December 1882, Big Bear reluctantly agreed to sign Treaty 6. However, he would still not bend to the will of the Canadian authorities, refusing to settle on a reserve and working to bring together the Plains bands, particularly the Cree, in order to present a united front when negotiating with the Canadian government.

At the same time, however, Big Bear was losing control over his own band. The winter of 1884 to 1885 was extremely harsh, and his band endured great hardship. Under pressure from the younger men, Big Bear finally accepted a reserve and promised to move there in the spring. His hopes of negotiating a better deal for his and the other Plains bands were destroyed, however, by the outbreak of violence in 1885.

In March, the Métis began the uprising that became known as the North-West Rebellion, and, inspired and excited by the news, the younger men of Big Bear's band rose against the non-Native population of Frog Lake. On 2 April, they killed nine non-Natives, in what became known as the Frog Lake Massacre, and two weeks later, they captured and burned Fort Pitt, taking forty-four prisoners. Finally, after suffering a minor defeat at Loon Lake, the forces that the band's war chief, Wandering Spirit, had assembled began to break up, and Big Bear, who had accompanied the band but wielded little influence, eventually surrendered along with his youngest son, near Fort Carlton on 4 July.

Although Big Bear had played no active role in the uprising, and in fact had counselled restraint and peace, he was convicted of treason-felony and sentenced to three years in prison. He soon fell ill, and was released in February 1887. He went to the Little Pine reserve to live out his days, and died on 17 January 1888.

Justin Edwards

Literary Works

Wiebe, Rudy (1973), *The Temptations of Big Bear*, Toronto: McClelland and Stewart.

Histories

Dempsey, Hugh A. (1984), *Big Bear: The End of Freedom*, Vancouver: Douglas and McIntyre.
Jenish, D'Arcy (1999), *Indian Fall: The Last Days of the Plains Cree and the Blackfoot Confederacy*, Toronto: Penguin.
Miller, J. R. (1996), *Big Bear (Mistahimusqua)*, Toronto: ECW Press.

See also: **Historiography: Canada; Native Reservations**.

Black Britain

'Black Britain' and 'black British' are relatively recent yet continually contested terms which often have been mobilised to reveal the perpetual presence of black peoples in the British Isles. As Peter Fryer (1984) famously asserted, this presence can be traced back at least as far as the Roman Empire, and black peoples have been a significant British constituency since the sixteenth century. Yet it is only since the 1960s and 1970s that their seminal contribution to British history and culture has been properly acknowledged and, as Yasmin Alibhai-Brown (2001) has argued, even today too few British people outside of specialist areas of academic interest know much about the history of black Britain. The strategic articulation of terms such as 'black British' and 'black Britain' has frequently been part of the related activities of political contestation and historical reclamation on behalf of black Britons; yet many of those who use these terms, or find themselves labelled by them, remain uncomfortable with their validity.

The advocacy of a 'black Britain' emerged in the late 1960s as a response to the discriminatory social conditions of the time. Since the talismanic arrival of the SS *Empire Windrush* on 22 June 1948, carrying 492 Caribbean migrants, significant numbers of African, Asian and Caribbean newcomers have arrived in Britain, prompted by the promise of employment and economic affluence or, in some cases, in flight from oppressive or tyrannical regimes (such as Kenya's expulsion of its Asian community in 1968, many of whom held British passports). The welcome they received from the colonial 'motherland' was frequently cool and occasionally violent. A 'colour bar' operated in housing and employment, which restricted the securing of decent accommodation and the possibility of getting a job (or being promoted), while assaults of black peoples in Britain were not uncommon. Experiencing racial discrimination on a daily basis, and let down by working-class British political organisations such as the trade unions, which could be as prejudiced and bigoted as employers and landlords, in the 1960s black peoples in Britain began to organise their own district forms of protest.

An important source of inspiration was the Black Power movement in the United States, with radicals such as Martin Luther King and Malcolm X serving as role models for black British dissidence. In particular, Malcolm X's articulate, outspoken and uncompromising politics, which claimed dignity in being black and supported physical conflict as a necessary form of anti-racist resistance, motivated British-based attempts to mobilise 'black' as a radical notion around which black peoples in Britain might construct political solidarity. The visit to Britain in the 1960s of Martin Luther King, Stokely Carmichael and Malcolm X had an enormous impact on Britain's black peoples, as Mike Phillips and Trevor Phillips explain:

> Blackness, being black, suddenly began to be an idea which could define us all, reconnecting us to our former roots wherever we lived or wherever we were born. And the experience of the Americans gave the idea a shape, turned it into a programme of action which energised the migrants everywhere, no matter how passive or isolated they were. (Phillips and Phillips 1998, p. 233)

Yet there were important differences between American and British radical approaches to 'black'. As James Procter explains, '"Black" in the US has conventionally referred to a particular "racial" community (African-American)' (Procter 2003, p. 5), whereas in the British context 'black' was initially an homogenising political category which attempted to unite the different constituencies of black peoples with diverse ancestral connections to Africa, Asia and the Caribbean in a common cause.

Cross-hatched with the influence of Black Power in the advocacy of 'black Britain' were appropriations of Marxist and socialist political theory. In the work of figures such as A. Sivanandan (a migrant from Sri Lanka who arrived in Britain in 1958) and the activities of journals such as *Race and Class* and *Race Today*, new forms of radical thinking emerged which both drew upon and complicated conventional historical materialist models of social analysis. In a parallel development, the late 1960s and 1970s saw the creation of many black political organisations influenced by American Black Power and British working-class activism which attempted to address the particular concerns of black peoples in Britain. Examples of these are the Campaign Against Racial Discrimination (CARD) established in 1965; Michael X's Racial Action Adjustment Society (RAAS) created in the same year; the United Coloured People's Association (UCPA) formed in 1967 by Nigerian playwright Obi Egbuna; the Black Unity and Freedom Party (BUFP); the Organisation of Women of Asian and African Descent (OWAAD) created in 1978; and the Southall Black Sisters set up by women of Asian descent in 1979. Many of these groups were short-lived or, as with Michael X's controversial RAAS, ill-fated, yet their creation bears witness to the radical and uncompromising atmosphere of the time. During this period, 'black Britain' was a politicised and radical term that serviced anti-racist goals and defiantly declared the rights of tenure for black peoples in Britain.

Part of this uncompromising and organised challenge to British racism was the result of the presence and perspectives of Britain's black youth. By the 1970s two out of every five black Britons was British-born, while many others had arrived as small children and knew no other country. Their strong opposition to those Britons who would not accept them as legitimate and equal members of the nation's people fuelled much black radicalism of the time, and revealed a particular generational response to being black in Britain which, in A. Sivanandan's phrase, constituted the 'different hunger' (Sivanandan 1982, p. 49) of youth. 'They brought to [the black struggle] not only the traditions of their elders but an experience of their own' (Sivanandan 1982, p. 37). Black Britain was often portrayed as a youthful constituency, and the phrase could be (and occasionally still is) mobilised to differentiate between the migrant and British-born/raised generation of black peoples in Britain. In the wake of the Brixton riots of 1981, however, the figure, in the popular press, of riotous black youth became synonymous with delinquency and lawlessness, whose black Britishness was evidence of (more often than not) his inability to integrate into respectable British society. In the British media, rarely sensitive to the predicaments and needs of black peoples in Britain at the time, 'black Britain' took on threatening, sinister and negative associations.

From its very inception 'black Britain' was always problematic. On the one hand, its existence was voiced as part of a vital attempt to make visible and instal black peoples into the narrative of the British nationhood from which they had been expelled, and in opposition to those (such as the Conservative politician Enoch Powell) who declared that black peoples were inevitably exterior to British history, society and culture. On the other hand, the phrase always risked a potential contradiction between 'black' and 'Britain', suggesting that black peoples were fated to exist in a semi-detached relationship with Britain, not fully within but not entirely beyond its imagined borders. The novelist and poet Fred D'Aguiar complained that the prefix 'black' damagingly 'syphons off so-called blackness from the general drive of creativity in Britain' (D'Aguiar 1989, p. 106). In the 1980s some of the dangers and constraints of the term were foregrounded by black writers and thinkers who had become increasingly dissatisfied with its tendency to overlook the differences within and between black communities. Its efficacy and appropriateness as a unifying category for Britain's heterogeneous black communities was called into question.

In an influential essay, 'New Ethnicities' (1996), Stuart Hall distinguished between two moments of black representation which in many ways captured some of the seismic shifts impacting upon black Britain across the 1970s and 1980s. Hall pointed to an initial attempt in 1970s black British culture to contest negative stereotypes of black peoples by producing positive images. In such a strategy the black figure assumed a certain burden of representation, standing as a synecdoche for an idealised and homogeneous black British community. But in a second moment, the possibility of creating a representative black Briton was called into question, as the heterogeneous differences of gender, age, sexuality, race and ethnicity were asserted and explored. Just as many radical unifying black groups of the 1960s and 1970s broke down because the competing needs of their diverse membership could not be happily co-ordinated through an overarching notion of 'black', so too did the portrayal of black peoples in Britain (chiefly but not exclusively in the 1980s) eschew the political aim of portraying a typical black person in a wholly positive light. Hence, from the 1980s, 'black Britain' began to be replaced with phrases such as 'black and Asian Britain' to reflect the divergent constituencies often discriminated against in similar terms of race but which could not be homogenised into a common racialised group. 'Black British' could not account for, or meaningfully associate, the diverse conflicts, traditions, ethnicities and experiences of black peoples in Britain.

Today, most articulations of 'black Britain' or 'black British' remain guarded, and rarely occur without acknowledgment of the difficulty and dangers of separating out black Britain from the nation in general, or pointing out the heterogeneity of black Britons. Nonetheless, the valuing of black Britain has had a crucial impact on the ways in which Britain's history, society and culture are imagined and narrated, and its advocacy should not be underestimated despite the problems which complicate its use. As a consequence, a great deal of important work has been done in locating black peoples in Britain at the centre, not the periphery, of the nation's history, as testified by books such as Peter Fryer's groundbreaking study *Staying Power* (1984) and Ron Ramdin's *Reimagining Britain* (1999). Several historians and writers have also called attention to the existence of a black Britain which stretches back for centuries, and have focused upon key black cultural figures in Britain who have hitherto been neglected, such as the eighteenth-century writers Ignatius Sancho and Olaudah Equiano.

The republishing of works like *The Letters of the Late Ignatius Sancho, an African* (1782) and *The Interesting Narrative of the Life of Olaudah Equiano* (1789) also points to the attempt to articulate a tradition of black British literature, an initiative which attempts to recognise and critically explore the cultural achievements of black peoples in Britain. More often than not the identification of a distinctly black British literature focuses upon the remarkable proliferation of texts by black writers in Britain since the late 1940s, calling attention to such figures as Sam Selvon, George Lamming, V. S. Naipaul, Buchi Emecheta, Linton Kwesi Johnson, Kamala Markandaya, Hanif Kureishi, Salman Rushdie, Grace Nichols, David Dabydeen, Caryl Phillips, Ferdinand Dennis, Mike Phillips, Fred D'Aguiar, Bernardine Evaristo and many others. Yet the declaration in recent years of a canon of black British writing remains a fraught affair (McLeod 2002), especially amongst so-called black British writers. Many of the pressures which came to bear upon the political articulation of black Britain in the 1960s and 1970s – heterogeneity, cultural and ethnic differences – have also influenced attitudes towards black British literature, while the transnational travails of many contemporary writers considered black British (several of whom no longer live in Britain, although continue to write about it) have produced texts which, as in Caryl Phillips' *Crossing the River* (1993), actively challenge the exclusionary inflections of the categories of race and nation which 'black Britain' inevitably risks.

Despite the continuing experiences of racism and the statistically small but by-no-means insignificant support for right-wing racist political parties, Britain has been transformed in recent decades as a consequence of the occasion and legacy of migration from Africa, Asia, the Caribbean and elsewhere. At one moment during a game of football at the World Cup tournament of 2002, the England team consisted of a majority of black players for the first time in its history. Although such occasions can be misleading (black peoples in Britain have found it easier to access the professions of sport and entertainment than industry and government), they also bear witness to the fact that in contemporary Britain the presence of black peoples is neither remarkable nor marginal to the nation's past, present and future. 'Black Britain' is perhaps best approached today as an historical signifier which points specifically to a particular period in the history of anti-racism. The historical and political consequences of constructing and advocating a 'black Britain' must never be underestimated despite the problems with the term. But discontinuing its usage is also desirable and necessary, due to the problematic severance of black peoples from the nation which inevitably lurks in the seeming conjunction of 'black' and 'Britain'.

John McLeod

Literary Works

Emecheta, Buchi [1974] (1994), *Second-Class Citizen*, London: Heinemann.
Equiano, Olaudah [1789] (2001), *The Interesting Narrative of the Life of Olaudah Equiano*, ed. Werner Sollors, New York and London: Norton.
Evaristo, Bernadine (2001), *The Emperor's Babe*, London: Hamish Hamilton.
Johnson, Linton Kwesi (2002), *Mi Revalueshanary Fren: Selected Poems*, intro. Fred D'Aguiar, London: Penguin.
Kureishi, Hanif (1990), *The Buddha of Suburbia*, London: Faber and Faber.
Lamming, George (1954), *The Emigrants*, London: Michael Joseph.
Levy, Andrea (2003), *Small Island*, London: Review.
Phillips, Caryl (1991), *Cambridge*, London: Bloomsbury.
Phillips, Caryl (1993), *Crossing the River*, London: Bloomsbury.
Rushdie, Salman (1988), *The Satanic Verses*, London: Viking.
Sancho, Ignatius [1782] (1998), *The Letters of the Late Ignatius Sancho, an African*, ed. Vincent Carretta, London: Penguin.
Selvon, Sam [1956] (1985), *The Lonely Londoners*, Harlow: Longman.
Smith, Zadie (2000), *White Teeth*, London: Hamish Hamilton.

Histories

Alibhai-Brown, Yasmin (2001), *Imagining the New Britain*, New York: Routledge.
D'Aguiar, Fred (1989), 'Against Black British Literature', in Maggie Butcher (ed.), *Tibisiri: Caribbean Writers and Critics*, Coventry: Dangaroo Press, pp. 106–14.
Fryer, Peter (1984), *Staying Power: The History of Black People in Britain*, London: Pluto.
Gilroy, Paul (1987), *'There Ain't No Black in the Union Jack': The Cultural Politics of Race and Nation*, London: Routledge.
Gilroy, Paul (1993), *Small Acts: Thoughts on the Politics of Black Cultures*, London: Serpent's Tail.
Hall, Stuart (1996), 'New Ethnicities', in David Morley and Kuan-Hsing Chen (eds), *Stuart Hall: Critical Dialogues in Cultural Studies*, London: Routledge, pp. 441–9.
Innes, C. L. (2002), *A History of Black and Asian Writing in Britain, 1700–2000*, Cambridge: Cambridge University Press.
McLeod, John (2002), 'Some Problems with "British" in "a Black British Canon"', *Wasafiri* 36, pp. 56–9.
Nasta, Susheila (2002), *Home Truths: Fictions of the South Asian Diaspora in Britain*, Basingstoke: Palgrave.
Phillips, Mike and Trevor Phillips (1998), *Windrush: The Irresistible Rise of Multi-Racial Britain*, London: HarperCollins.
Procter, James (2003), *Dwelling Places: Postwar Black British Writing*, Manchester: Manchester University Press.
Procter, James (ed.) (2000), *Writing Black Britain 1948–1998: An Interdisciplinary Anthology*, Manchester: Manchester University Press.
Ramdin, Ron (1999), *Re-imagining Britain: 500 Years of Black and Asian History*, London: Pluto.
Sivanandan, A. (1982), *A Different Hunger: Writings on Black Resistance*, London: Pluto.

Sivanandan, A. (1990), *Communities of Resistance: Writings on Black Struggles for Socialism*, London: Verso.
Visram, Rozina (2003), *Asians in Britain: 400 Years of History*, London: Pluto.

See also: **Diaspora: Caribbean; Pan-Africanism; United States of America.**

Black Consciousness: Southern Africa

The Black Consciousness movement was the first organised black opposition to the South African government after the crackdown of the early 1960s which had banned and decimated existing anti-apartheid black political parties (such as the African National Congress (ANC) and Pan African Congress (PAC)), and resulted in the detention, jailing and exile of many of the most visible of their members as well as their liberal and communist sympathisers. Arising initially among intellectuals in the segregated black universities and theological colleges, this movement was (during the 1970s at least) easily the most prevalent and widespread expression of radical black discontent against apartheid and spread to many parts of the country, with the exception of rural KwaZulu.

There is evidence that the South African government initially hoped that Black Consciousness might be amenable to its own vision of racial separation. This was because it was organisationally and philosophically strongly separatist in thinking and practice, eschewing formal contact with sympathetic whites and with the ideology of white liberalism. Self-liberation was a constant watchword. However, in its refusal of forced ethnic separation and its belief in the need for a wider black unity of all those South Africans oppressed because of their skin colour – Africans, Indians and Coloureds – Black Consciousness was on a collision course with the state, and by 1973 a number of its prominent leaders had already been banned. Although arguably always dependent on educated urban intellectuals and 'the youth' for most of its active support (its first body was the South African Students Organisation (SASO), founded in 1969) from the beginning it was strongly populist, wishing to spread outwards from its epicentre further into the black community. This impetus can be seen in the formation of a number of community, development, women's and trade union organisations in the first half of the 1970s; including the Black People's Convention (founded 1972), the Black Community Programmes (1973), the Black and Allied Workers' Union (BAWU) (1973), and the Black Women's Federation (1975).

Initially more apparent on the philosophical and cultural fronts, the movement held from early on the seeds of more decisive political activity. The diffuse nature of its appeal proved more of a strength than a weakness: instead of formal membership of its organisations, any black person who accepted its philosophical tenets was regarded as an adherent. The relatively small membership of its organisations is thus perhaps less indicative than some later commentators have suggested. The strong emphasis on the need for psychological liberation, and the assumption that this would in turn lead the individual to wider social activism, allowed many black people to get to grips with feelings of inferiority consequent to centuries of white rule, and therefore to take part in action with others to end apartheid. Attitude of mind and behaviour were seen as interwoven, and the binary between 'false' and 'true' consciousness vigorously proclaimed – anyone black who in any way assisted the maintenance of apartheid structures (such as community councillors and policemen) was regarded as a 'sell-out' and effectively one of the enemy.

Black Consciousness made a strong division between the 'haves' and the 'have-nots' in society. In the formative years of the movement, class and race were viewed as overlapping almost completely. Capitalism was analysed as a foreign intrusion into the pre-colonial history of an (often romanticised) African communalism; and consumerism or acquisitiveness at the expense of the community were sharply condemned. While various forms of African socialism were cited as inspirational from the start (Nyerere and Kaunda in particular), and while the theories of Frantz Fanon were an underlying presence for many intellectuals, it was after the uprisings in Soweto and elsewhere during 1976 and 1977 that the discourse and conceptualisations of Black Consciousness significantly began to include a Marxist-Leninist element – including African and diasporic proponents; in Cabral, Machel and Rodney.

The highlighting of issues of black history, identity and experience in Black Consciousness thought meant that artistic and literary issues were conspicuous from the start. A revival of black art took place in the 1970s and 1980s which can largely be attributed to its influence – notably in literature, music and fine art. From the beginning oral forms of literature were prominent: writers and performers spurred on by Black Consciousness saw it as their role to use their forms as media for primarily a black audience, many of whom were not effectively literate. Thus, dramatic works and a poetry suited to the microphone were the earliest forms of literature that emerged; and both of these forms remained powerfully present until the end of apartheid rule. Oral poetry took on an increasingly sophisticated performative element, and often included musical accompaniment. Prose fiction was less generally noticeable until the latter half of the 1970s. In addition, the so-called 'Soweto' uprising of 1976–7 provided inspiration for a number of novels. In short, no period in twentieth-century South African history matches this time for the emergence of important black artists and writers whose inspiration can be traced back to Black Consciousness. In drama, figures such as Mthuli Shezi (murdered in 1972), Matsemela Manaka, Maishe Maponya and groups such as Workshop '71 stand out; in poetry, the influence of musicians-cum-poets such as Lefifi Tladi and Molefe Pheto in the early 1970s assisted a subsequent flowering of performance poetry, with Ingoapele Madingoane perhaps the most widely known and imitated poet by the end of the decade. Poets more inclined to the published page such as Mongane Serote, Mafika Gwala, Sipho Sepamla, Chris van Wyk, Mandlenkosi (later Mandla) Langa, James Matthews, Farouk Asvat and Mbuyiseni Mtshali (in his later work) are important and enduring figures. Highlights of contemporaneous prose influenced by Black Consciousness included works by Mtutuzeli Matshoba, Miriam Tlali, Mbulelo Mzamane, Serote and Sepamla. The national and international noteworthiness of Black Consciousness in its heyday was also assisted by the emergence of a number of 'alternative' publishers in South Africa prepared to spread their work – especially A. D. Donker, David Philip and Ravan Press. Any study of Black Consciousness must also pay careful attention to the role of its own journals and (often cyclostyled) magazines, such as the annual *Black Review* (which went through five editions) and *SASO Newsletter*; and literary magazines such as *S'ketsh'*, *New Classic* and *Wietie*. Careful scrutiny of other small alternative white-run literary magazines of the early 1970s, such as *Izwi*, *Ophir*, *Donga* and *Bolt*, will also reap dividends. However, easily the most apparent vehicle for expression was the journal *Staffrider*, founded in 1978.

Among the radical proclivities of the ideology was a desire to (re)discover a more 'authentic', black, self-defined history and culture; to delimit the constituents of a more humane, democratic 'African personality', and a predisposition to search for relevant critical tools in the assessment of black literature to offset prior 'Eurocentric' judgments made by white critics, who formed by far the majority within academic and media utterance at the time. In place of the sterile aestheticism Black Consciousness perceived most white South African academics to have fallen into, art and politics were seen as inseparable. Literature and other forms of artistic expression had the potential to play a major role in black liberation generally and the conscientisation of audiences and readers in particular, especially in a political climate where many other forms of expression were banned or curtailed. Emphasising social commitment, they placed their art in the service of social change. Many insisted that, talent or no, the black artist must rather be concerned with a humble and consistent service to the people than with adulation. They should teach, but at the same time be prepared to learn from ordinary black people; and take advice and change their work if criticism came from this quarter. In line with this, stress was placed on group work – work-shopped plays, and the ritual of oral performance were highly valued, as were cultural groups. In some quarters individual creative work was downgraded (relatively speaking) in importance. As examples, during the late 1970s some younger poets criticised anyone who published at all – a criticism which encompassed some of the older and more established Black Consciousness poets; and, for a period of three years after its inception, *Staffrider* had no policy of editorial selection, preferring the cultural groups in many townships to select the work sent in for publication.

Despite its populist inclinations and the ideological emphasis placed on notions of a 'black experience' and 'collective consciousness' by its purveyors, it is however apparent that Black Consciousness was, at least in its formative years, primarily the ideology and programme of a radical, predominantly middle-class and urbanised, intelligentsia seeking to distance itself from the quietist or assimilationist tendencies of the previous generation; and eager to align with the masses. This urge was carried out in very specific (and with the benefit of hindsight, occasionally rather contradictory) ways. Most debatable was a desire to use English rather than African languages in its proselytisation and cultural expression: the latter were viewed as being *inter alia* tainted with tribalism (and therefore apartheid) and unequal to the task of black political unification. Despite one or two exceptions, and despite the fact that an Africanised 'township' English had some advocacy, it was, generally speaking, only at the beginning of the 1980s that more than a few voices were raised demanding that the languages of the majority of black South African people required attention. Moreover, in its early trade union organisations black workers were organised first and foremost in terms of a perceived mutual racial solidarity with intellectuals and students; and it is clear that the movement was strongly masculinist in attitude and phallocentric in discourse throughout its years of hegemony.

Arguably, Black Consciousness reached its apotheosis with the 'Soweto' revolt. It also spawned a new generation of those ready to leave the country for military training and who, naturally, became foot soldiers and, in some cases, influential thinkers and actors within the revitalising black exile organisations. In October 1977, a number of Black Consciousness organisations were banned, including the most important student, community, writers and journalists' organisations. In 1978 the Azanian People's Organisation (AZAPO) was formed, but, within a year or two, there were signs that the non-racial ANC was increasingly taking over Black Consciousness' hegemony. By 1983, with the formation of the United Democratic Front (UDF), this displacement was unmistakable; indeed, during the early 1980s there was a certain amount of internecine conflict between 'non-racial' youth and those who remained faithful to Black Consciousness, who were disparaged as 'zim-zims' (the term refers to mythological cannibal figures in South African oral narratives) by their comrades-turned-opponents. Although Black Consciousness remained powerful in the early 1980s among some writers (such as Mothobi Mutloatse, Jaki wa Seroke, Asvat, Manaka and others), in time its influence waned in this arena as well.

There is no doubt, however, that Black Consciousness was of vital (and at present underrated) importance, both philosophically and artistically. Although its single remaining political party of consequence, AZAPO, is now of relatively minor significance, many of its core concepts live on in South Africa. However, for many of its early adherents, it is now dismissed as part of a teleological rite of passage young black activists went through on their way to non-racialism (for an example, see Gwala 1982). Worse, Black Consciousness art has been ill-served by its critics. The contemporary trend towards more conservative conceptions of literary function, aesthetics and the role of the artist in society in South Africa's media and academia has resulted in a tendency to downplay its achievements. For example, at least one recent collection of essays emerging from a reputable publishing house, purporting to cover issues of literature, apartheid and democracy in South Africa from 1970 onwards, comes close to ignoring it completely, except as a point of negative comparison with the promises of the post-liberation 'rainbow nation' and its ideologues. For serious scholars wishing to study this period in South Africa's literature, however, the situation is less watertight. Despite the contemporary aestheticisation of views about art, there are contemporary black South African writers and performers who still show its profound influence, both formally and politically. It is possible that, whilst remaining mindful of its shortcomings, artists and intellectuals will again turn to its example as the contradictions and unfulfilled promises of the 'new South Africa' burgeon.

Kelwyn Sole

Literary Works

Biko, Steve (1988), *I Write What I Like: A Selection of his Writings*, ed. A. Stubbs, London: Penguin.

Chapman, Michael (ed.) (1982), *Soweto Poetry*, Johannesburg: McGraw-Hill.

Gwala, Mafika (1982), *No More Lullabies*, Johannesburg: Ravan Press.

Manganyi, Chabani (1973), *Being-Black-In-The-World*, Johannesburg: Spro-Cas/ Ravan Press.

Matshoba, Mtutuzeli (1981), *Call Me Not a Man*, Harlow: Longman.

Matshoba, Mtutuzeli (1981), *Seeds of War*, Johannesburg: Ravan Press.

Mtshali, Mbuyiseni Oswald [1971] (1982), *Sounds of Cowhide Drum*, Johannesburg: A. D. Donker.

Mzamane, Mbulelo (1982), *The Children of Soweto*, Harlow: Longman.

Oliphant, Andries and Ivan Vladislavic (eds), *Ten Years of Staffrider, 1978–1988*, Johannesburg: Ravan Press.

Sepamla, Sipho (1981), *A Ride on the Whirlwind*, Johannesburg: A. D. Donker.

Sepamla, Sipho (1984), *Selected Poetry*, Johannesburg: A. D. Donker.

Serote, Mongane (1981), *To Every Birth its Blood*, Braamfontein: Ravan Press.

Serote, Mongane (1982), *Selected Poetry*, Johannesburg: A. D. Donker.

Tlali, Miriam (1989), *Soweto Stories*, London: Pandora.

Histories

Fatton, Robert (1986), *Black Consciousness in South Africa: The Dialectics of Ideological Resistance to White Supremacy*, Albany, NY: SUNY Press.
Gwala, Mafika (1988), 'Black Consciousness in South Africa', *Research in African Literatures* 19: 1, pp. 89–94.
Hirson, Baruch (1979), *Year of Fire, Year of Ash. The Soweto Revolt: Roots of a Revolution?*, London: Zed Press.
Kavanagh, Robert (1985), *Theatre and Cultural Struggle in South Africa*, London: Zed Press.
Lodge, Tom (1983), *Black Politics in South Africa since 1945*, Johannesburg: Ravan Press.
Molteno, Frank (1979), 'The Uprising of 16 June: A Review of the Literature on Events in South Africa 1976', *Social Dynamics* 5: 1, pp. 18–20.
Pityana, Barney and Mamphela Ramphele (eds) (1991), *Bounds of Possibility: The Legacy of Steve Biko and Black Consciousness*, Cape Town: David Philip.
Sole, Kelwyn (1983), 'Culture, Politics and the Black Writer: A Critical Look at Prevailing Assumptions', *English in Africa* 10: 1, pp. 37–84.
Sole, Kelwyn (1991), 'Authorship, Authenticity and the Black Community: The Novels of Soweto 1976', in S. Clingman (ed.), *Regions and Repertoires: Topics in South African Politics and Culture*, Johannesburg: Ravan Press, pp. 178–222.

See also: **Anti-colonialism and Resistance: Southern Africa; Nationalism(s): Southern Africa; Pan-Africanism.**

Black Hole

The narratives around the Black Hole of Calcutta originated in a letter written by John Zephaniah Holwell, a member of the East India Company's Bengal Council, to William Davis on 28 February 1757, as he returned to England aboard the *Syren-Sloop*. In this letter, published as a tract in 1758, Holwell claimed to have survived an incident in which 146 people were interned overnight, on Nawab Siraj-ud-Daula's orders, in a cell measuring about eighteen square feet – 123 had died of suffocation, thirst, fright and fatigue. The Nawab's forces had stormed the garrison and a number of company officials and soldiers had been taken prisoner and thrown into the Black Hole. Earlier, hostilities had broken out between the parties over the strengthening of the company's defences at Fort William.

Holwell's account was aimed at arousing populist British opinion against the Nawab at a time when the company was riven with differences concerning policy towards military intervention. The ploy paid off as Robert Clive and his coterie used the story to justify belligerent action against the Nawab at Plassey.

In the years that followed, the Black Hole of Calcutta provided the British with an enduring foundational myth for Empire in India – avenging imperial martyrs by rooting out Oriental despotism (for example, in Thomas Macaulay's essay on Clive (1843)). The incident was enshrined in history textbooks and the term entered Victorian phraseology as a pejorative denoting any cramped and disorderly physical space. In the English popular imagination the Black Hole stood as a metaphor for the condition of India – a hot, unhealthy, overcrowded subcontinent teeming with the dark racial Other, its superstitious lawless ways forever resisting enlightenment sponsored by colonialism.

Holwell built a monument in memory of the incident, which became a pilgrimage site for British visitors to Calcutta. Mass-produced photographs of the monument were consumed as relics in a period when an imperial martyrology was being drawn up by British demagogues in the aftermath of the 1857 revolt. Lord Curzon had the monument rebuilt in 1902. In the twentieth century, commentators very convincingly challenged the reliability of Holwell's account. Subhash Chandra Bose was arrested in 1940 for launching a public campaign to have the monument removed. It was finally dismantled after India's independence although the debate on the incident continues.

Kaushik Bhaumik

Literary Works

Barber, Noel (1966), *The Black Hole of Calcutta: A Reconstruction*, London: W. Collins.
Holwell, J. Z. (1758), *A Genuine Narrative of the Deplorable Deaths of the English Gentlemen and Others*, London: A. Millar.

Histories

De, A. (1971), 'A Note on the Black Hole Tragedy', pts 1 and 2, *The Quarterly Review of Historical Studies* 10: 3,4.
Little, J. H. (1915), 'The Black Hole – the Question of Holwell's Veracity', *Bengal: Past and Present*, July–September.
Macaulay, T. B. (1843), 'Lord Clive', *Critical and Historical Essays*, London: Longman, Brown, Green and Longmans.
Macfarlane, I. (1975), *The Black Hole: The Makings of a Legend*, London: Allen and Unwin.
Teltscher, K. (1996), '"The Fearful Name of the Black Hole": Fashioning an Imperial Myth', in Bart Moore-Gilbert (ed.), *Writing India, 1757–1990: The Literature of British India*, Manchester: Manchester University Press.

See also: **East India Company; Governors-General; Raj**.

Boat People

'Boat people' is a term that refers to those arriving in Australia by sea in search of asylum, and was first applied to those fleeing Vietnam in 1976. By 1982, more than 2,000 Indo-Chinese, mainly Vietnamese, had reached Australia's shores. The public reaction to these arrivals was mixed, with initial sympathy being dampened as numbers grew. The conservative government of Malcolm Fraser, nevertheless, granted refugee status and permanent residence to nearly all of them.

With many Indo-Chinese refugees housed in South-east Asian camps, Australia arranged with regional governments to hold refugee boats in exchange for the establishment of a generous refugee resettlement programme in Australia. This would allow the Australian government to avoid political damage over unannounced boat arrivals, whilst satisfying Asian neighbours that Australia was shouldering some of the responsibility. As a result, no further boats arrived in Australia between 1982 and 1989 when a second wave of mainly Indo-Chinese boat people began to arrive, this time prompted by the war in Cambodia; followed by several boatloads from China.

Legislation authorising mandatory detention for unauthorised arrivals has been in place since 1992, brought in by the Labor government of Paul Keating, with boat people being held in remote detention camps, often for many months or even years, resulting in frequent instances of violent protest and self-harm.

A new influx of boats from Indonesia began in 1999, carrying people fleeing mainly from the tyrannies in Iraq and Afghanistan. Over 8,000 boat people arrived between October 1999 and August 2001. Because of the increase in numbers, the growing involvement of people smugglers, and community concerns regarding security, the conservative government of John Howard toughened Australia's stance on asylum seekers. Even refugees who fulfilled official criteria were only given reviewable temporary visas; they were not permitted to have family members join them; and they were denied access to social security benefits. When a boatload of 433 predominantly Afghan refugees was rescued at sea in 2001 by the Norwegian merchant vessel *Tampa*, the ship was boarded by Australian troops and the asylum seekers sent to Nauru for detention and processing, a policy which became known as the Pacific Solution. Papua New Guinea was also used as a holding and processing centre. Other aspects of the 'solution' included the interdiction of boats suspected of carrying asylum seekers and the excision of some Australian islands from the migration zone. Asylum seekers arriving at these 'excised offshore places' were not entitled to make a protection claim. This policy, coming after September 11 and an alleged link between 'boat people' and Islamic 'terrorists', was popular, helping the Howard government win the 'fear election' of November 2001. While commentators and cartoonists noted that the first invaders/settlers had come with difficulty by boat in 1788 this point had little impact. Since the adoption of the Pacific Solution the Australian border has become virtually impenetrable to boat people.

Sharron Scott

Literary Works

D'Alpuget, Blanche (1981), *Turtle Beach*, Melbourne: Penguin Books.
Keneally, Thomas (2004), *The Tyrant's Novel*, Sydney: Doubleday.

Histories

Grant, Bruce (1979), *The Boat People*, Ringwood: Penguin Books.
McMaster, Don (2001), *Asylum Seekers: Australia's Response to Refugees*, Carlton: Melbourne University Press.
Mares, Peter (2001), *Borderline: Australia's Treatment of Refugees and Asylum Seekers*, Sydney: University of New South Wales Press.
Marr, David and Marian Wilkinson (2003), *Dark Victory*, Crows Nest: Allen and Unwin.
Viviani, Nancy (1984), *The Long Journey: Vietnamese Migration and Settlement in Australia*, Carlton: Melbourne University Press.

See also: **Asianisation: Australia; Detention Centres: Australia; Refugees; White Australia Policy**.

Border Disputes: South Asia

The national boundaries of South Asia were drawn in the moment of decolonisation in August 1947, and three colonial boundaries in particular continue to mark the landscape of the subcontinent. The Durand Line of 1893, which now separates the North-West Frontier Province of Pakistan from eastern Afghanistan; the MacMahon Line of 1914 between Tibet (now China's Tibet Autonomous Region) and India's Himalayan fringe on either side of Nepal; and finally the Radcliffe Line of 1947, drawn to separate India from East and West Pakistan (now Bangladesh and Pakistan). However, the most serious and chronic border dispute in the region is along the Line of Control (LoC) in Kashmir, a province whose status remained moot at the time of independence and partition.

This boundary emerged from an armed conflict between the nascent states of the subcontinent in 1948. A UN brokered ceasefire in 1949 left Pakistan with approximately one-third of the erstwhile kingdom of Kashmir, while India held the remainder. Two subsequent wars in 1965 and 1971 produced minor territorial changes along the ceasefire line but despite a peace agreement in 1972 (the Shimla Accord) the LoC has remained an area of constant friction, regular artillery duels, and minor engagements.

One particularly costly node of conflict has emerged from an omission in the LoC which was demarcated only as far north as a point known as NJ9842 with the understanding that the line would continue 'north to the glaciers' – then deemed to be at too extreme an altitude for survey or conflict. In 1984 the forces of both countries raced to establish posts on these heights (at elevations between 17,000 and 22,000 feet above sea level) and a running battle has persisted on the Siachen Glacier ever since. Tensions were further heightened with the start of a separatist insurgency in Indian Kashmir in 1989, fuelled by the infiltration of militants from Pakistani Kashmir. The conflict reached a new climax in 1999 (shortly after the two countries conducted a series of tests of nuclear devices), when separatist insurgents and regulars of the Pakistani Northern Light Infantry occupied a ridge overlooking the towns of Kargil and Dras in Ladakh. A ceasefire was declared in July after Indian forces reclaimed most of these heights.

South of Kashmir the India-Pakistan border follows the less fractious Radcliffe Line, now known as the 'IB' or 'International Boundary', but a persistent dispute remains over the southern terminus of this boundary in the changing topography of Sir Creek, a tidal marsh in Kutch. The eastern section of the Radcliffe Line which is now the India–Bangladesh border is notable for the Chitmahals of Tin Bigha, a land-locked archipelago of territorial exclaves – Indian territory surrounded by Bangladesh and vice versa – which remain a topic of bilateral discussion and are in ongoing process of territorial exchange. But the only serious incident of armed conflict between the border patrols of the two countries occurred on another stretch of the border, the Pyrduwah and Boraibari incidents of April 2001. A maritime boundary dispute between the two countries persists over claims to an estuarine island known variously as New Moore, or Purbasha in India and South Talpatty in Bangladesh.

While the conflicts described above have emerged from anomalies in, or the imprecision of, national boundaries, another set of disputes has emerged from the postcolonial repudiation by neighbouring states of the imperial boundaries. The western fringe of the Empire, facing Afghanistan, was marked, somewhat unusually, by a combination of a zonal frontier and a clearly demarcated boundary, a situation that persisted after independence. Although Pakistan summarily dismissed Afghan objections that the Durand Line was invalid as early as 1956, the frontier provinces remained a loosely administered zone.

However this situation has become more complex since 2001 with the forces of both countries engaged in pursuit of remnants of the Taleban and Al-Qaeda in the frontier zone. In July 2003 the Afghan government accused Pakistani forces of incursions prompting a US brokered agreement to resolve outstanding border disputes with the help of GPS technology. The MacMahon Line was somewhat disingenuously regarded by the British Empire as an agreed frontier with China, but it was only after the invasion of Tibet by the People's Liberation Army in 1950 that Chinese forces approached this frontier, now regarded by India as its national boundary. Chinese demands for negotiations on this border were not entertained by New Delhi, but Indian control of much of this boundary was notional. In the month-long border war of October–November 1962 Chinese forces defeated the Indian Army on two fronts, in Ladakh to the west and NEFA or the North East Frontier Agency – now the Indian state of Arunachal Pradesh – to the east, before unilaterally declaring a ceasefire. At the end of this conflict the PLA withdrew to the MacMahon Line in the east but retained control of a corner of Ladakh known as Aksai Chin, which is still claimed by India. Meanwhile China maintains its claim to parts of Arunachal Pradesh. But this border has not seen any serious armed conflict since 1962. A number of minor disputes mark the India–Nepal border but only one of these, over the Kalapani tract on the India–Nepal–China trijunction, has crossed the threshold to a 'border incident'. India holds the area but Nepal claims it, maintaining that Indian forces occupied Kalapani in the course of the 1962 war with China.

Kai Friese

Literary Works

Alter, Stephen (2000), *Amritsar to Lahore, Crossing the Border between India and Pakistan*, New Delhi: Penguin Books.
Friese, Kai (2001), 'Marginalia', *Transition* 90, pp. 4–29.
Manto, Saadat Hasan (1989), 'Toba Tek Singh'; 'The Dog of Titwal'; 'The Last Salute', in Saadat Hasan Manto, *Kingdom's End and Other Stories*, New Delhi: Penguin Books, pp. 11–34.

Histories

Dixit, J. N. (1995), *Anatomy of a Flawed Inheritance: Indo-Pakistani Relations 1970–1994*, New Delhi: Konark Publishers.
Embree, Ainsley (1989), 'From Frontier to Boundary', in Ainsley Embree, *Imagining India*, New Delhi: Oxford University Press, pp. 67–84.
Holdich, T. Hungerford (1996), *The Indian Borderland 1880–1900*, New Delhi: Asian Educational Services.
Maxwell, Neville (1972), *India's China War*, Harmondsworth: Pelican Books.
Noorani, A. G., 'Easing the Indo-Pakistani Dialogue on Kashmir: Confidence-Building Measures for the Siachen Glacier, Sir Creek and the Wular Barrage Disputes', The Henry L. Stimson Centre Occasional Paper 16, pp. 5–18.

See also: **Hill Stations; Historiography: South Asia; Kashmir Dispute; Partition; Secessionism South Asia.**

Botany Bay Convicts

Botany Bay is synonymous with Australia's convict past. It was named for the botanical specimens collected by Captain James Cook in 1770 and was subsequently chosen as the site of the convict settlement that would begin the British colonisation of Australia.

When the First Fleet of convicts arrived in 1788, Captain Arthur Philip preferred the harbour at Port Jackson a few miles north and it was here that the convicts landed. Nevertheless, Botany Bay became immortalised in song and popular memory as a place of banishment. The transportation of convicts to eastern Australia continued until 1852 and to western Australia until 1868, with more than 125,000 men and 25,000 women being sent to 'Botany Bay'.

Historians are divided over the purpose of the convict settlement, whether it was a place of punishment, providing a solution to England's overcrowded jails following the loss of the North American colonies, or whether the convicts were simply needed to develop a strategically-located base for British expansion in the Pacific. Another debate has taken place over the harshness of the system. Here historians have argued over the freedoms and legal rights convicts were allowed, the frequency of floggings, the ability of convicts to pursue economic benefits. Male convicts lived in barracks and worked on public works; female convicts were incarcerated in the 'female factories'. Both were assigned to employers and farmers as servants and shepherds. Their children were placed in an orphanage. Tickets of leave or pardons could be acquired through hard work or marriage, but convicts could also be subjected to flogging or further transportation to more isolated settlements. Much historical discussion about convicts has been about whether they were criminals or workers caught by the dislocation of England's industrialising economy. The answer has partly depended on gender differences. For male convicts, questions have revolved around the role of free waged versus convict labour in the development of colonial capitalism, the assignment system as an allocator of labour resources, and the representativeness of convicts as a cross-section of the British working-class. Women convicts were usually discussed as prostitutes until feminist historians found they were as literate and skilled as the female population of England. Women were also usually transported for lesser offences than men, suggesting that their role was to become wives and mothers in the foundation of a new society.

Diane Kirkby

Literary Works

Clarke, Marcus [1874] (1975), *For the Term of his Natural Life*, Sydney: Angus and Robertson.

Histories

Damousi, Joy (1997), *Depraved and Disorderly*, Cambridge: Cambridge University Press.
Daniels, Kay (1998), *Convict Women*, Sydney: Allen and Unwin.
Frost, Alan (1980), *Convicts and Empire*, Melbourne: Oxford University Press.
Hirst, John (1983), *Convict Society and its Enemies*, Sydney: Allen and Unwin.

Hughes, Robert (1987), *The Fatal Shore*, London: Collins Harvill.
Nicholas, Stephen (1988), *Convict Workers*, Cambridge: Cambridge University Press.
Press Neale, David (1991), *The Rule of Law in a Penal Colony*, Cambridge: Cambridge University Press.
Robinson, Portia (1988), *The Women of Botany Bay*, Sydney: Macquarie Library.

See also: **European Exploration and Settlement: Australia/New Zealand/Pacific; Historiography: Australia; Kelly, Ned**.

Britain's Postwar Foreign Policy

The standard view is that Britain's postwar foreign policy has aimed to promote democracy, peace, human rights and overseas development. If these supposed goals are not always explicitly outlined in mainstream analysis, they are invariably assumed. This is an extraordinary and false view. The evidence shows that Britain is a systematic violator of the noble virtues noted above as well as international law. It has traditionally been, and remains under the current New Labour government, a key ally of some of the world's most repressive regimes and acts as a consistent condoner of human rights abuses. The twin goals of British foreign policy are clearly revealed in the declassified planning files and continue today: to maintain British elites' political standing in the world, that is, some form of 'great power' status; and to ensure that key countries and regions, and the global economy, function to benefit Western businesses. Both are to be secured primarily in alliance with US foreign policy. From these goals have flowed a great number of policies which consign much of the population of the world to the status of 'unpeople' – victims of British policies. Let us briefly sketch out some of the most important episodes in postwar foreign policy, some of which have been buried in the mainstream.

In 1953, Britain and the USA collaborated to overthrow the nationalist Iranian government of Mohamed Musaddiq and replaced it with the Shah's regime. Musaddiq had challenged British interests by nationalising oil operations – then controlled by the Anglo-Iranian Oil Corporation (AIOC), the forerunner of British Petroleum. The Labour government under Clement Attlee immediately began covert plans to overthrow Musaddiq, which were continued under the Churchill government. Britain's aim was to instal 'a more reliable government', Foreign Secretary Eden explained. 'Our policy', a British official later recalled, 'was to get rid of Mossadeq [sic] as soon as possible' (quoted in Curtis 2003, p. 303). When the oil talks collapsed, the main British negotiator advised the Shah that the 'only solution' was 'a strong government under martial law and the bad boys in prison for two years or so'; British planners preferred 'a non-communist coup d'état preferably in the name of the Shah'(quoted in Curtis 2003, p. 308). It was clearly understood by the British embassy in Tehran that 'this would mean an authoritarian regime', and Britain's ambassador in Tehran preferred 'a dictator', who 'would carry out the necessary administrative and economic reforms and settle the oil question on reasonable terms' (quoted in Curtis 2003, pp. 308–9). The subsequent repression under the Shah was supported both by Britain and the USA. Britain trained some officers of SAVAK, the Shah's secret police, when it was set up in 1957, according to its former co-ordinator. MI6 was in close touch with leading SAVAK officials while the head of MI6, Maurice Oldfield, met the Shah regularly in the 1970s and 'had a close and intimate relationship with His Imperial Majesty' (quoted in Curtis 2003, p. 314), according to a former MI6 officer.

Britain's invasion of British Guiana in the same year, 1953, is long forgotten. Democratic elections had resulted in victory for a popular, leftist government under Cheddi Jagan, committed to reducing poverty. Its plans also threatened the British sugar multinational, Bookers, which pleaded with London to intervene. Britain dispatched warships and 700 troops to overthrow the government, and ruled out further elections since 'the same party [i.e. Jagan's party] would have been elected again' (quoted in Curtis 2003, p. 351), the colonial secretary stated.

Many myths surround the British wars in Kenya and Malaya in the 1950s. Former members of the Mau Mau movement in Kenya are currently trying to sue the British government for human rights' abuses committed by British forces who fought against them. They are calling for compensation 'on behalf of the 90,000 people imprisoned and tortured in detention camps, 10,000 people who had land confiscated and a further half a million who were forced into protected villages' (quoted in Curtis 2003, p. 316). The declassified files I have seen paint a frightening picture of terrible human rights' atrocities by the colonial authorities, especially in the Nazi-style detention camps and 'protected villages' they established. Around 150,000 Africans are thought to have died as a result of British policy. Britain used the war against Mau Mau as a cover for halting the rise of popular, nationalist forces that threatened control of its then colony. This was an early postwar example of wiping out the threat of independent development, a key concern of British, as well as US, planners.

In the war in Malaya, Britain resorted to very brutal measures, including widespread aerial bombing and the use of a forerunner to modern cluster bombs. Britain also set up a grotesque 'resettlement' programme similar to that in Kenya, that provided a model for similar US programmes in Vietnam. It also used chemical agents from which the USA may again have drawn lessons in its use of agent orange. Despite the standard portrayal of the war as one fought in a noble cause against 'communist terrorists', the secret files reveal the Foreign Office understood it 'very much as war in defence of [the] rubber industry' (quoted in Curtis 2003, p. 336), then mainly under British control.

Britain's invasion of Egypt in 1956 was followed the next year by an intervention in Oman, intended to counter a rebellion against a regime as repressive as any that has existed in the Middle East. There was no economic development to speak of, there were few schools, there was widespread disease and a barbaric justice system with torture endemic. The oil-rich Omani regime was in effect run by Britons, who served as commanders of the armed forces and as government ministers. British strategy in the Middle East was and is based on propping up repressive elites that support the West's economic and political interests. This strategy has tended to undermine the prospects for more popular, democratic governments and has fanned the flames of religious extremism that is often the only alternative available to those being repressed.

The declassified British files show that the Gulf sheikhdoms were largely created by Britain to 'retain our influence' in the region, and London pledged to defend them against external attack and to 'counter hostile influence and propaganda within the countries themselves', providing police and military training which would help in 'maintaining internal security' (quoted in Curtis 2003, p. 256). The chief threat to these regimes was never Soviet intervention but what the Foreign Office called 'ultra-nationalist maladies' (quoted in Curtis 2003, p. 256). In 1957, the Foreign Office identified the danger of the existing rulers 'losing their authority to reformist or revolutionary movements which might reject the connection with the United Kingdom' (quoted in Curtis 2003, p. 257). The fundamental Western interest in the region is of course oil, described by British planners in

1947 as 'a vital prize for any power interested in world influence or domination. . . . We must at all costs maintain control of this oil' (quoted in Curtis 2003, p. 16), Foreign Secretary Selwyn Lloyd noted in 1956. In 1961 British planners were desperate to find a pretext to deploy military forces to Kuwait. The fear was that this newly independent country, where Britain had major oil interests, would sever ties from London. Kuwait had signed an agreement for Britain to defend it if requested, but the solidity of this agreement was questionable. British fears were that:

> as the international personality of Kuwait grows, she will wish in various ways to show that she is no longer dependent upon us. But we must continue to use the opportunities which our protective role will afford to ensure so far as we can that Kuwait does not materially upset the existing financial arrangements or cease to be a good holder of sterling. (quoted in Curtis 2003, p. 272)

Iraqi leader Qasim publicly claimed Kuwait as part of Iraq in June 1961 but the files show that British planners did not take this threat seriously. Foreign Office officials in London, together with the British embassy in Baghdad, concocted a story that Iraq had ordered a tank regiment to speed south towards Kuwait. British officials in Basra, near the Kuwait border, according to the files, saw no such threat. However, a terrified Kuwait emir, told by British officials that Iraq was about to invade, permitted the landing of British troops. A Ministry of Defence report eleven days later finally admitted it was 'unlikely' that Iraq had ever posed a threat.

1965 witnessed one of the postwar world's worst bloodbaths when the Indonesian army under General Suharto set out to destroy the Indonesian Communist Party (PKI), which led to around a million deaths. Britain, like the USA, wanted the army to act against the PKI and encouraged it to do so. 'I have never concealed from you my belief that a little shooting in Indonesia would be an essential preliminary to effective change' (quoted in Curtis 2003, p. 387), Britain's ambassador in Jakarta, Sir Andrew Gilchrist, informed the Foreign Office. British policy was 'to encourage the emergence of a General's regime' (quoted in Curtis 2003, p. 390), one intelligence official later explained. One British memo referred to 'an operation carried out on a very large scale and often with appalling savagery'; another simply referred to the 'bloodbath' (quoted in Curtis 2003, p. 392). Britain directly connived with those engaged in slaughter. By 1965, thousands of British troops were in Borneo, defending Malaya against Indonesian encroachments following territorial claims by Jakarta. British planners secretly noted that they 'did not want to distract the Indonesian army by getting them engaged in fighting in Borneo and so discourage them from the attempts which they now seem to be making to deal with the PKI' (quoted in Curtis 2003, p. 392). So Gilchrist proposed that 'we should get word to the Generals that we shall not attack them whilst they are chasing the PKI'; in October a US contact passed to the Generals 'a carefully phrased oral message about not biting the Generals in the back for the present' (quoted in Curtis 2003, p. 393).

A decade later in 1975, Britain supported Indonesia's invasion of East Timor, which led to further hundreds of thousands of deaths. The British ambassador in Jakarta informed the Foreign Office a few months before the invasion that 'the people of Portuguese Timor are in no condition to exercise the right to self-determination' and that 'the arguments in favour of its integration into Indonesia are all the stronger' (quoted in Curtis 2003, p. 404). He suggested giving 'greater sympathy towards Indonesia' if it decided to 'take strong action' in East Timor. He added:

It is in Britain's interest that Indonesia should absorb the territory as soon and as unobtrusively as possible, and that if it should come to the crunch and there is a row in the United Nations, we should keep our heads down and avoid taking sides against the Indonesian government. (quoted in Curtis 2003, p. 404)

In the 1980s, with diminished means of unilateral intervention, Britain continued to act as the world's leading supporter of US belligerence, notably in aggression against Central America (after 1981), the bombing of Libya (1986) and the invasion of Panama (1989). 'We support the United States' aim to promote peaceful change, democracy and economic development' (quoted in Curtis 2003, p. 104) in Central America, Prime Minister Margaret Thatcher stated in January 1984; by this time the US aim of destroying the prospects for peaceful change and economic development – evidenced in US backing for the murderous regimes in El Salvador and Guatemala and in creating a terrorist army to operate against Nicaragua – was abundantly clear. British apologias sometimes reached astounding heights. A Foreign Office minister stated in 1985 – after years of devastation wrought by the Nicaraguan contras – that 'the American government have stated time and again that they are seeking a solution by peaceful means to the problems of Central America' (quoted in Curtis 2003, p. 108). With a probable nod and a wink from London, the British private 'security company', KMS, trained some of the contras. KMS also organised the destruction of the El Chipote arms depot in the centre of Managua, and KMS helicopter pilots flew with the contras in Honduras. The company also recruited soldiers for Oliver North's gun-running operation to the contras.

A further forgotten British role is that in the Rwanda genocide of 1994. The evidence shows that Britain used its diplomatic weight as a permanent member of the UN Security Council to help reduce the UN force in Rwanda that, according to military officers on the ground, could have prevented the killings. It then helped ensure the delay of other plans for intervention, which gave a green light to the murderers in Rwanda to continue; and also refused to provide the military capability for other states to intervene. Throughout, Britain helped ensure that the UN did not use the word 'genocide', which would have obliged the UN to act, and put diplomatic pressure on others to ensure this did not happen. British officials also rebuffed personal pleas to stop the killings from the UN secretary general and the commander of the UN force.

Entering the New Labour years, the illegal invasion of Iraq in March 2003 was nothing new, certainly historically, nor even compared to Blair's other foreign policies. By then, the Blair government had already indulged in six specific violations of international law: in conducting without UN authorisation the wars in Yugoslavia (1999) and Afghanistan (2001); in committing violations of international humanitarian law in the bombing of Yugoslavia; in the illegal bombing of Iraq in December 1998; in maintaining the illegal 'no fly zones' over Iraq, a permanent 'secret' war; and in maintaining sanctions against Iraq, which over the previous decade contributed to the deaths of hundreds of thousands of people. The principally Anglo-American war in Afghanistan was much more brutal than is conventionally believed, with apparently deliberate US attacks on civilians – clearly war crimes. The one dominating fact about the war is surely that more – probably far more – people were killed in the bombing than on September 11, which provided its supposed rationale. But this fact has not noticeably upset the view across the mainstream political culture that Britain and the US were justified in bombing the world's poorest country in retaliation.

Key allies of the Blair government with whom arms trade continues as normal are among the most repressive regimes in the world, such as Russia – guilty of gross human rights abuses and aggression in Chechnya; Turkey – responsible for atrocities against Kurds on a far greater scale than even the Saddam regime in recent years; and Saudi Arabia – where human rights organisations are banned, along with any political opposition. It is clear that the new 'war against terrorism' is being used by Britain, and the USA, as a cover for a new phase of global intervention, similar to the cover provided by the 'Soviet threat'. The British military is enhancing its 'power projection' capabilities and now has a 'new focus on expeditionary warfare', a process that was beginning before 11 September 2001 but which is now justified by it. The extraordinary new phase of British military intervention under Blair is intended largely to secure the same basic goals as have motivated British foreign policy throughout the postwar era and are thus, sadly, consistent with a long, dark recent history.

Mark Curtis

Literary Works

Burgess, Anthony (1964), *Malayan Trilogy*, London: Pan.
Greene, Graham [1955] (1962), *The Quiet American*, Harmondsworth: Penguin.
Harris, Wilson (1985), *The Guyana Quartet*, London: Faber and Faber.
Kariuki, Josiah Mwangi (1963), *Mau Mau Detainee*, London and Nairobi: Oxford University Press.
Kimura, Hisao (1990), *Japanese Agent in Tibet*, Chicago: Serindia.
Le Carré, John (2001), *The Constant Gardener*, London: Hodder and Stoughton.
Mo, Timothy (1991), *The Redundancy of Courage*, London: Chatto and Windus.
Ngugi wa Thiong'o (1967), *A Grain of Wheat*, London: Heinemann.

Histories

Bloch, Jonathan and Patrick Fitzgerald (1983), *British Intelligence and Covert Action*, London: Junction.
Curtis, Mark (2003), *Web of Deceit: Britain's Real Role in the World*, London: Vintage.
Dorril, Stephen (2000), *MI6: Fifty Years of Special Operations*, London: Fourth Estate.
Lapping, Brian (1989), *End of Empire*, London: Paladin.
Lashmar, Paul and James Oliver (1998), *Britain's Secret Propaganda Wars 1948–1977*, Stroud: Sutton Publishers.

See also: **Anti-colonialism and Resistance: East Africa; Genocide: Rwanda; Historiography: British Empire; Iranian Revolution; Suez Crisis; United States of America**.

British Imperialism

Definitions of 'British imperialism' have mutated in subtle ways. In early nineteenth-century Britain, the connotations of 'empire' and 'imperialism' were derived principally from the model of the Roman Empire, and referred to the direct military, economic, political and cultural authority exercised by an imperial power over its colonies. In the middle of the nineteenth century, 'imperialism' acquired a pejorative meaning, as it was used by critics in Britain to describe the despotism of Napoleon III's Second French Empire. Disraeli's opponents in Britain drew upon these negative (French) associations when they labelled him 'imperialist', but in the final quarter of the century, as Britain's overseas empire quadrupled, public opinion swung in favour of Disraeli and his successors.

The late nineteenth-century supporters of British imperialism included many of the intelligentsia, who distinguished British imperialism in the first instance from Persian, Roman and Ottoman precursors in that it did not require conquest and occupation; economic and political domination, with rule via proxies, was sufficient. A second distinction was drawn between India, which was governed autocratically by indirect rule, and settler colonies like Australia, which were ruled by limited forms of democracy. Early critical accounts of British imperialism, notably by J. A. Hobson, V. I. Lenin, and Rosa Luxemburg, emphasised the economic interests underlying the official justifications of the Empire. In Luxemburg's words, 'imperialism is the political expression of the accumulation of capital in its competitive struggle for what remains still open of the non-capitalist environment' (Luxemburg 2003, p. 426). Imperialism in this sense describes how the dynamic of capitalism demands expansion into non-capitalist spaces in search of the physical elements of production, cheap labour power and new markets, with the result that all economies are integrated in differentiated and uneven ways into a global capitalist economy.

Debates over British imperialism have continued to proliferate in the twentieth century, mostly in British journals and books, and this variety of work is competently summarised and extracted in recent collections (see Cain and Harrison 2001, for example). However, in the context of historicising postcolonial writings, it is necessary to note that the Lenin–Luxemburg emphasis on the economic dimension of British imperialism has been especially influential upon writers from the 'postcolonial world' like Kwame Nkrumah, C. L. R. James and Amilcar Cabral. The tendency in much of postcolonial studies to focus exclusively upon the literary or cultural dimensions of 'imperialism' – and in the process to sideline the economic, military and political histories – therefore runs counter to the spirit of the anti-imperialist writings from Britain's former colonies.

Benita Parry

Literary Works

Boehmer, Elleke (ed.) (1998), *Empire Writing. An Anthology of Colonial Literature, 1870–1918*, Oxford: Oxford University Press.
Conrad, Joseph [1902] (1973), *Heart of Darkness*, Harmondsworth: Penguin.
Haggard, Rider [1885] (1989), *King Solomon's Mines*, Oxford: Oxford University Press.
Kipling, Rudyard [1901] (2000), *Kim*, Harmondsworth: Penguin.
Schreiner, Olive [1897] (1974), *Trooper Peter Halket of Mashonaland*, Pretoria: A. D. Donker.

Histories

Brewer, Anthony (1990), *Marxist Theories of Imperialism: A Critical Survey*, 2nd edn, London: Routledge.

Cain, Peter J. and Mark Harrison (eds) (2001), *Imperialism. Critical Concepts in Historical Studies*, vols 1–3, London and New York: Routledge.

Carter, Mia and Barbara Harlow (1999), *Imperialism and Orientalism: A Documentary Sourcebook*, Oxford: Blackwell.

Chilcote, Ronald M. (ed.) (1999), *The Political Economy of Imperialism: Critical Appraisals*, Boston: Kluwer Academic Publishers.

Luxemburg, Rosa [1913] (2003), *The Accumulation of Capital*, trans. A. Schwarzschild, London and New York: Routledge.

See also: **Berlin Conference; Cromer, Lord; Historiography: British Empire**.

Bumiputra

Also spelled 'Bumiputera', the term literally means 'sons of the soil' and refers to, in political as well as administrative contexts, the indigenous peoples of Malaysia: the Peninsular Orang Asli ('original people' or 'aboriginals'), the indigenous peoples of Sabah and Sarawak, and Malays. In 2000, Malaysia's population (23,260,000) officially stood at: 61.9 per cent Bumiputera, 29.5 per cent Chinese, 8.6 per cent Indian (Hooker). Although the term was coined to avoid classifying the Bornean peoples and the Peninsular indigenes in the same category with the Malays – since most were clearly not Malay in language, religion and culture – it still remains typified by the same linguistic, cultural and religious complexity. For example, in Peninsular Malaysia, while the Malays are all Muslims and speak the same language, the Orang Asli group is largely non-Muslim and often divided into nineteen subgroups on the basis of ethno-linguistic and socio-cultural criteria. In Sarawak, many of the Iban, who outnumber the Malays, have adopted Christianity; the Bidayuh are also largely Christian, but the more diverse Melanau, who live in Bintulu and Miri, are approximately 65 per cent Muslim. In Sabah, of the three largest indigenous groups, the Kadazan tend to be Christian, while the Dusun and the Sama-Bajau are generally Muslim. Bumiputeras are a privileged group in Malaysia and eligible for special affirmative action policies, or what Mahathir Mohamad calls constructive protection. Although all Bumiputeras are constitutionally entitled to the same privileges, in practice, however, distinctions within the category persist: on the Peninsula, Malay Bumiputera are clearly preferred over Orang Asli Bumiputera; in Sabah and Sarawak, Bornean Bumiputera take priority over Bumiputera from the Peninsula (Andaya and Andaya 2001).

The policy of special Malay privileges was initiated by the British and incorporated in Malaya's first constitution in 1957. In *The Malay Dilemma*, Mahathir argues that the Malays and other Bumiputeras deserve positive discrimination for two reasons: first, they are the definitive people and rightful owners of the land and second, they are economically backward compared to the other races and therefore merit rehabilitation. In the aftermath of the interracial riots of 13 May 1969, this policy of Bumiputera patronage was pursued more aggressively through the introduction of the New Economic Policy (NEP) in 1970, which sought to redress racial economic disparities, through poverty eradication and social restructuring, so that race was no longer identified with economic function. In spite of the relative success of NEP in improving the economic condition of the Bumiputeras the policy has drawn much criticism from both Bumiputera and non-Bumiputera communities. In *As I Please* (1994), Salleh Ben Joned, a local writer, taunts himself as part of a protected species, and in *The Malay Dilemma Revisited* (1999), M. Bakri Musa challenges the preferential policies as counter productive and tantamount to racial handicapping; such dependency syndrome or subsidy mentality, Musa argues, once acquired is extremely difficult to eradicate. However, in an unpublished working paper entitled 'Malaysia: The Way Forward', Mahathir envisions that by the year 2020 the Malay/Bumiputera millstone around the nation's neck will be removed, through the creation of an economically resilient and fully competitive Bumiputera community, and the formation of a Bangsa Malaysia, in which all the races will live in equal partnership and collectively as *one* nation.

The majority of the Bumiputera writers in Malaysia write in the national language, Bahasa Malaysia. However, some have chosen to use English as their creative medium, and this tendency is on the rise with an overall increase in the acceptance of the language since the late 1980s. Some of the Bumiputera writers who write in English include Che Husna Azhari, Dina Zaman, Ghulam-Sarwar Yousof, Karim Raslan, Rehman Rashid and Salleh Ben Joned.

Mohammad Abdul Quayum

Literary Works

Joned, Salleh Ben (1994), *As I Please*, London: Skoob Books.
Kee Thuan Chye (2003), 'We Could **** You Mr Birch', in Mohammad A. Quayum et al. (eds), *Petals of Hibiscus: A Representative Anthology of Malaysian Literature in English*, Kuala Lumpur: Pearson Education, pp. 159–89.
Lim, Shirley Geok-lin (2001), *Joss and Gold*, Kuala Lumpur, Singapore: Times Books.
Mohamad, Mahathir Bin (1970) *The Malay Dilemma*, Singapore, Kuala Lumpur: Times Books.
Musa, M. Bakri (1999), *The Malay Dilemma Revisited*, Gilroy, CA: Merantau.

Histories

Andaya, Barbara Watson and Leonard Y. Andaya (2001), *A Short History of Malaysia*, London: Palgrave.
Baker, Jim (1999), *Crossroads: A Popular History of Malaysia and Singapore*, Singapore, Kuala Lumpur: Times Books.
Cheah Boon Kheng (2002), *Malaysia: The Making of a Nation*, Singapore: ISEAS.
Hooker, Virginia Matheson (2003), *A Short History of Malaysia*, St Leonards: Allen and Unwin.
Khoo Boo Teik (1995), *Paradoxes of Mahathirism: An Intellectual Biography of Mahathir Mohamad*, Malaysia: Oxford University Press.

See also: **Engmalchin; Historiography: South-east Asia; Merdeka; Women's Histories: South-east Asia**.

C

Cabral, Amílcar

Born in Bafatá, Guinea-Bissau, on 12 September 1924, Amílcar Lopes Cabral is considered one of the greatest figures in the history of national liberation movements and African socialism. He is usually compared to such anti-colonial revolutionaries as Aimé Césaire, Frantz Fanon, Che Guevara, and Kwame Nkrumah. However, Mao Tse-tung and Ho Chi Minh in particular directly influenced Cabral's work. A poet, agronomist, political economist, cultural theorist, and militant organiser, Cabral firmly grounded his work in the specific colonial conditions of Guinea-Bissau – a small country in West Africa – that, together with the Cape Verde Islands, came under Portugal's governance in 1836. In 1879 the two territories were separated and Guinea-Bissau became a direct Portuguese colony.

In 1957 Cabral, along with the Angolan Agostinho Neto, formed in Paris the Movimiento Anti-Colonista of Africans from the Portuguese colonies, and then formed in Angola the MLPA (Popular Movement for the Liberation of Angola). Such experiences strengthened Cabral's own movement in Guinea-Bissau – the PAIGC (African Party for the Independence of Guinea and Cape Verde) – that he founded in 1956. As its secretary general, Cabral led the people of Guinea-Bissau in the armed struggle against the Portuguese. Cabral did not live to see the independence of Guinea-Bissau and Cape Verde respectively in 1974 and 1975, as he was assassinated by a Portuguese hit squad on 20 January 1973. However, it was under his leadership that the PAIGC came to control at least two-thirds of his homeland by 1968.

Cabral's early work analyses in detail the concrete agricultural conditions and class structures obtaining in his homeland. Such work also underlines the need for asserting political and cultural rights against the forces of colonialism, while Cabral's later work theorises culture as a site of – and a weapon in – both anti-colonial struggle and the movement for reconstructing a country after independence. Like Fanon and Nkrumah, Cabral is interested not only in the questions of colonialism but also in those of neo-colonialism and imperialism from the perspectives of both political economy and culture, as is particularly exemplified in his works (his major three speeches) such as 'The Weapon of Theory' (1966), 'National Liberation and Culture' (1970), and 'Identity and Dignity in the Context of the National Liberation Struggle' (1972). In such works Cabral makes an important distinction between mere political independence and the total liberation of the people. As for the latter, Cabral advocates socialism – organically tempered by the deep specificities of a given geographical site – reckoning the peasant as the central revolutionary agent of change; while for political independence he considers nationalism as a necessary, strategic and transitional phase of struggle. In his formulation that imperialist practices entail the economy of the accumulation and production of knowledge in the interest of legitimising power, Cabral anticipates one of Edward Said's fundamental arguments in *Orientalism* (1978). Today Cabral continues to serve as an inspiration to revolutionaries and writers in Africa, Asia, and Latin America at a time when decolonisation still remains an unfinished project from Puerto Rico to Palestine to the Philippines.

Azfar Hussain

Literary Works

Ellen, Maria M. (ed.) (1988), *Across the Atlantic: An Anthology of Cape Verdean Literature*, North Dartmouth, NH: Centre for the Portugese-Speaking World.
Ferreira, Manuel (ed.) (1975), *No Reino de Caliban, I: Cabo Verde e Guiné-Bissau*, Lisbon: Seara Nova.

Histories

Cabral, Amílcar (1969), *Revolution in Guinea: Selected Texts by Amílcar Cabral*, trans. Richard Handyside, New York: Monthly Review Press.
Cabral, Amílcar (1973), *Return to the Source: Selected Speeches of Amílcar Cabral*, New York: Monthly Review Press.
Chabal, Patrick with Moeme Parrente Angel (1996), *The Post-Colonial Literature of Lusophone Africa*, London: Hurst and Company.
Chilcote, Ronald H. (1991), *Amílcar Cabral's Revolutionary Theory and Practice: A Critical Guide*, Boulder, CO: Lynne Rienner.
Said, Edward (1978), *Orientalism, Western Conceptions of the Orient*, London: Routledge and Kegan Paul.
Young, Robert J. C. (2001), 'Africa IV: Fanon/Cabral', in Robert J. C. Young, *Postcolonialism: An Historical Introduction*, Oxford: Blackwell Publishing, pp. 274–92.

See also: **Anti-colonialism and Resistance: West Africa; Fanon, Frantz; Nkrumah, Kwame**.

Castes: South Asia

Caste in India – *jâti* in most North Indian languages – is a category that has suffered much from a certain roughness of translation. It has often been read parallel to usages of 'caste' in European languages and 'guilds' in medieval Europe – imposing on it certain inaccuracies as well as an element of datedness that was/is in keeping with a common European bourgeois tendency to see other peoples as following in the pioneering trails of the European bourgeoisie. This tendency was pronounced not only in European scholarship but also in socialist-nationalist readings of the twentieth century. For instance, Jawaharlal Nehru, the first prime minister of India, compared the Indian caste system to 'the medieval trade *guilds* of Europe' in *The Discovery of India* (1959).

In another – more complex – way, contemporary understandings of the 'caste system' are deeply informed by European perceptions. It was largely in the nineteenth century that European Orientalists – and later, nationalists who agreed or disagreed with them – reinforced the Brahminical understanding of 'caste'. This simplified and partly distorted the wide variety of *jâti* divisions, by appending each *jâti* to one and only one of four 'castes' (or caste-groupings), ranked thus in order of decreasing purity: Brahmin, Kshatriya, Vaishya and Shudra. This is what is today meant by the 'caste system'. But not only did this version allot too much credence to Brahminical literature, it also implied that caste divisions could be traced back unproblematically to the Vedas and the ancient Arya (Aryans). The truth, however, was and is more complex – and contentious.

Caste has been understood by scholars at a predominantly symbolic level – as does Louis Dumont when he explains 'caste' with reference to a theoretical hierarchy of 'purity-pollution' – or within a materialist–Marxist tradition, as do D. D. Kosambi and Irfan Habib. There is some truth in Dumont's reading of the caste system as a structure based on something like a Hegelian master–slave dialectics of purity, with the Brahmins (self-)ranked as the most pure and the Shudras as the most impure. However, this is also largely an idealist and Brahminical (self-)understanding of caste. On the other hand, the caste system can also be (partly) understood as a system of social stratification growing out of the three recorded early 'Aryan classes' (*varna*): the Kshatriyas (warriors/rulers), the Brahminas (priests) and the Vis (masses). Kosambi and Habib have convincingly illustrated the creation of the Vaishya class (from the Vis) and its promotion up the social scale as a consequence of (and in opposition to) the creation of the fourth class/caste, the Shudras, whose ranks were made up of the 'slave/servants' (Dasas) and peoples subalterned by the Aryans.

Habib explains the later creation of the unmentioned 'fifth caste' – the untouchables or 'scheduled castes' – by the displacement and 'absorption' of the hunting tribes (mostly aboriginals) by Aryan and Aryanised peasant communities. Surviving 'tribes' – known by general terms like *adivasi* (aboriginal), *vanvasi* (forest people) and so on in 'non-tribal' India or by specific tribe names such as Santhal, Bhil, Gond and so on – continue to present a problem for the 'caste system', appended to it at the bottom in Brahminised accounts but capable of other self-perceptions. Sometimes labelled 'criminal castes and tribes' by the British, these tribes have both resisted and adopted Brahminical (and Islamic, Christian and so on) influences in the past. In postcolonial India, they have often provided a popular base for environmentalist movements. Recently, new states have been created in (North) India to accommodate the aspirations of some aboriginal peoples.

In general, the description 'upper caste' is applied to the first three castes of Brahmins, Kshatriyas and the promoted Vaishyas (the so-called 'Aryan' castes, into which other groups have been incorporated only at a high level of economic production and Sanskritisation/Brahminisation). However, all these broad designations are intricately dissected by lines of sub-caste identification, and perhaps no sub-caste has been fixed in the hierarchy of the caste system either in time or in space.

Historical-materialist definitions, combined with Dumont's 'idealist' one, help explain the genesis of the caste system and its ideological maintenance. But both groups of definitions remain conditioned by the primacy of Brahminical accounts as reproduced by nineteenth-century Orientalism. They imply that the caste system is finally rooted in the *varna* divisions of the Vedas and has been, as such, a distinctive feature of India for about three millennia. This implication has been contended by recent scholarship. Gail Omvedt (2003), for instance, stresses that the development of the caste system was vigorously contested and that:

> [for centuries . . . there was a concerted effort by Brahminism to impose a varna social order on society, which the Buddhists and others [Jains, Charavakas etc.] resisted. This battle was gradually won by Brahminism, but the power shown by *varnashrama dharma* [the religion of varna-divisions; that is, Hinduism] at certain periods and in certain regions should not be 'read' into all of India or projected unrealistically backward in time. (Omvedt 2003, p. 134)

Caste has a convoluted relationship with class as well as race. Historical-materialist scholars of caste have often been criticised for linking caste to class in a simplistic manner.

However, the best of them (Habib 1997, p. 164) have stressed the difficulties of a contemporary one-to-one identification of castes with classes, even when they have implicitly equated our understanding of class with Vedic *varna*. To conclude, the caste (*jâti*) system as we know it today seems to have developed through five broad phases: (1) an initial language-marked demarcation between the hegemonising classes of the (diverse) Aryan peoples and resisting (and diverse) non-Aryan ones (to become largely a ruler/ruled or farmer-owning classes/landless labour demarcation). In this context, it should be noted that while the Aryans might have spoken languages belonging to one family of languages (the Indo-European), they probably did not speak the same language. And the non-Aryan communities spoke languages that belonged to three other language-families: Dravidian (Tamil), Sino-Tibetan and Austro-Asiatic.

This phase was followed by (2) a three-fold class (*varna*) distinction within the circumference of the settling Aryan/ised peoples propounded largely by sections of the Brahmins. However, this division was not hegemonic in non-Brahminical circles and sometimes not even followed by Brahmins. The word 'Brahmin' itself – especially in Buddhist literature – continued to denote a learned or a noble person rather than any endogamic caste affiliation well into the fourth century AD. However, in due course, this contended Brahminical demarcation, expanded into (3) a four-fold class structure with the assimilation of other subalterned or conquered peoples into Aryan society. Once again, this structure was heavily contested outside Brahminical Hinduism and sometimes deviated from even inside Brahminism. But to the extent to which this four-fold structure came into being, it still left many non-Aryan tribes and groups outside the circumference of Aryan/ised settlement at a time when land was not in short supply, forests (all over the Gangetic plain, for instance) were probably difficult to clear for sustained (instead of slash-and-burn) agriculture given the lack/paucity of iron tools and early peasant communities probably had to depend on tribal hunting communities for survival (especially as the Aryans seem to have taken a few centuries to learn the art of making cotton which was known to the preceding Dravidians). (4) The growing power of concepts of purity/pollution, *ahimsa* (non-violence) and vegetarianism marked the incorporation (and erosion) of many of these non-Aryan hunting tribes into the Aryan peasant fold. This phase, most extensive around the time when (anti-caste) Buddhism was a factor in India, marked the consolidation of the earlier four-class structure into a structure of four endogamous castes, with the fifth unmentionable non-caste of untouchables appended to it at the bottom. It is towards the end of this period that *Manusmriti* – the most systematic exposition of the Brahminical concepts and justification of caste – was written, and Buddhism disappeared from India.

The caste structure that came into being in this period of Brahminic reaction remained largely stable in its broad and theoretical constitution for the next 1,200 years or so, though it was by no means fixed or unchanging in its parts. It afforded much mobility to groups and individuals at least in some regions of India and during certain periods: even as late as the nineteenth century, there were Shudra land-owning castes (like the Nairs of Travancore), who nevertheless paid symbolic homage to the Brahmins and exercised caste-based privileges over lower castes. The caste structure was also critiqued from within by traditions such as the Bhakti movement and new religions like Sikhism and, finally, in the late nineteenth and early twentieth century by Dalit leaders and thinkers like Jotirao Phule, Periyar, Pandit Iyothee Thass and Dr Ambedkar.

The Muslim-dominated phase (roughly 800 out of these 1,200 years) appears to have left the general framework of the caste system largely unaffected, probably because of the combination of the relative suppleness of individual and collective caste mobility within the larger caste structure and a lack of opposition to (or even criticism of) the Hindu caste system by Muslims. But the coming of the British marked the final phase (5) of the development of the caste system: positively by putting the broad structure under pressure from industrialisation and modernisation and negatively by rigidly codifying the system with reference to late Brahminical texts (such as *Manusmriti*) instead of the ground realities (which had been and were more complex in spite of the hegemonising Brahminical ideal). In recent years, a number of scholars have illustrated how – contrary to popular wisdom about the matter – the British presence in India actually made a relatively flexible caste system much more rigid with the help of census-taking and Orientalist documentation as well as, perhaps, a desire to understand India along lines of stratification that were familiar to many Englishmen from their studies and, in terms of class, also from experiences back home.

In contemporary discourse, caste (and 'scheduled tribes') also imbricates with versions of race or colour, especially when it is seen as arising from the Vedic *varnas*. However, ethnicity or race is by no means identical to *varna* as it was used in the Vedas. Kosambi (1958, pp. 50, 317–19, 343; 1965, p. 33) convincingly argues that the perception of *varna* was not 'racial' in the current sense of the term – a fact indicated by the possibility (more so during the early period) for dominant non-Aryan groups/individuals to move up the Aryan structure and through a process of Aryanisation/Sanskritisation come to occupy such high positions as those of priests and kings. Moreover, the earliest literature – Brahminical or Buddhist – contains extensive evidence of inter-caste relations (including those of marriage); such relations (especially marriage) start being effectively discouraged fairly late, perhaps even as late as the writing of *Manusmriti*. While the Aryans appear to have largely or only spoken languages belonging to one family (the Indo-European), all evidence suggests that there was no such thing as an Aryan 'race' or 'colour' even in the Vedic periods and that there was considerable creolisation in the centuries to follow. The word 'Arya' was used to mean 'noble' or 'free-born' and had a class connotation.

Today, the caste system in India continues to operate between the poles of religion/pseudo-ethnicity (endogamy and so on) and secularisation (a kind of class system). While the Indian constitution rigorously opposes caste prejudices and many low-caste individuals and groups have moved up the class ladder, there do remain areas of caste-based discrimination. As in the past, caste continues to be a site of contention and power-struggles, so much so that in some states some low–middle-caste groups may be more politically powerful than the highest castes of Brahmins and Kshatriyas. The words used to describe the lowest castes indicate this ongoing contention: the somewhat-patronising word 'Harijan' (Children of God) that Mahatma Gandhi had popularised to replace the pejorative 'untouchable' has been replaced by the supposedly more agential 'Dalit' ('downtrodden') and 'Bahujan' ('masses'). However, the position of the scheduled castes (16.5 per cent in 1991) and the scheduled tribes (8 per cent) remains often embattled, perhaps less so on older caste-based grounds these days than those of the related ones of class, education, inscription into the 'nation' and 'modernisation'. Finally, it is an index of the tenacity and adaptability of the system that caste affinities remain significant – sometimes oppressively so – not only in India but also in predominantly Muslim Pakistan and Bangladesh today.

As such, caste remains a problem for much of postcolonial literature – which, as framed and taught today, effectively means Indian English literature. Almost all Indian English writers are opposed to caste (or at least caste-based discrimination) but they come from social circles and educational institutions in which Dalits are at best a small minority. They also write in a language that is spoken even less in Dalit-Bahujan circles than in non-Dalit, non-Bahujan ones. Even though Indian English literature began quite early to voice its objections to caste, it does not have anything like the corpus of Dalit literature in Marathi (Namdeo Dhasal and so on) or Hindi (Omprakash Valmiki and so on), or someone of the stature of the (non-Dalit) Bangla author, Mahasweta Devi, who has written powerfully about Dalit characters. Its critical assumptions have not been jostled by the rise of Dalit writers yet. One may agree with Arun Mukherjee (Valmiki 2003, p. ix) that even major Indian English novels (by Mistry and Roy) have depicted the Dalit in 'an appropriative voice'. One can also argue that 'tribes' are less visible in post-independence English literature than they were in colonial English literature (for example, Kipling). While sympathetic towards the lower castes, Indian English literature often runs the danger of representing Dalit realities (in an alien language) or re-inscribing the vaguely colonial-Kiplingesque duality between the noble forest-tribal and the ignoble urban member of a lower (caste?) class.

Tabish Khair

Literary Works

Anand, Mulk Raj [1933] (1983), *Untouchable*, Delhi: Arnold-Heinemann.

Anand, Mulk Raj and Eleanor Zelliot (eds) (1992), *An Anthology of Dalit Literature*, Delhi: Gyan Publishing House.

Chatterjee, Upamanyu [1988] (1996), *English, August*, Delhi: Rupa and Company.

Markandaya, Kamala [1966] (1985), *A Handful of Rice*, Delhi: Orient.

Mistry, Rohinton (1996), *A Fine Balance*, London: Faber and Faber.

Rao, Raja [1938] (1984), *Kanthapura*, Madras: Oxford University Press.

Roy, Arundhati (1997), *The God of Small Things*, London: Flamingo.

Histories

Bailey, F. G. (1960), *Tribe, Caste and Nation*, Manchester: Manchester University Press.

Bayley, Susan (1999), *Caste, Society and Politics in India: From the Eighteenth Century to the Modern Age*, Cambridge: Cambridge University Press.

Cohn, Bernard S. (1996), *Colonialism and its Forms of Knowledge: The British in India*, Princeton, NJ: Princeton University Press.

Das, Arvind N. (1996), *Changel: The Biography of a Village*, Delhi: Penguin Books.

Dumont, Louis [1980] (1998), *Homo Hierarchicus: The Caste System and its Implications*, New Delhi: Oxford University Press.

Habib, Irfan (1997), *Essays in Indian History*, Delhi: Tulika.

Ilaiah, Kancha (1996), *Why I am not a Hindu: A Sudra Critique of Hindutva*, Calcutta: Samya.

Kosambi, D. D. [1958] (1998), *An Introduction to the Study of Indian History*, Bombay: Popular Prakashan.

Kosambi, D. D. (1965), *Ancient India: A History of its Culture and Civilisation*, New York: Pantheon Books.

Mendelsohn, Oliver and Marika Vicziany (1998), *The Untouchables: Subordination, Poverty and the State in Modern India*, Cambridge: Cambridge University Press.

Omvedt, Gail (2003), *Buddhism in India: Challenging Brahminism and Caste*, New Delhi and London: Sage Publications.

Srinivas, M. N. (ed.) (1996), *Caste: Its Twentieth Century Avatar*, New Delhi: Penguin.
Valmiki, Omprakash [1997] (2003), *Joothan: A Dalit's Life*, autobiography trans. Arun
        Mukherjee, Calcutta: Samya.

See also: **Historiography: South Asia; Languages and Ethnicities: South Asia; Pre-
        colonial Histories: South Asia; Religions: South Asia.**

Cattle-Killing

In the first half of the nineteenth century, the Xhosa and the British were engaged in protracted conflict on the Cape Colony's eastern frontier. When the British took control of
the Cape Colony in 1806, the balance of power between the Xhosa and mainly Dutch settlers on the Eastern Cape frontier was evenly poised. However, after the major British military incursion of 1811, and then the state-aided settlement of 4,000 British immigrants in
1820, the Xhosa experienced an inexorable decline as the frontier fell increasingly under
settler control.

In 1846, is the War of the Axe, the British military, under pressure from wool farmers,
attacked and claimed further Xhosa land in the Ciskei region. A counter-attack by the
Xhosa precipitated the War of Mlanjeni of 1850 to 1853, which resulted in heavy Xhosa
losses in lives, cattle and land. These were further exacerbated by the epidemic of lung-
sickness in 1854 which killed 100,000 cattle.

In 1856, a teenage Xhosa girl, Nongqawuse, prophesied that if the Xhosa were to kill all
their cattle and destroy all their crops, their ancestors would be resurrected, drive the colonists from their land, and restore Xhosa prosperity. Nongqawuse's uncle Mhlakaza conveyed the prophecy to the paramount chief Sarhili, who endorsed it, and approved the
widespread destruction of cattle and crops. The Cattle-killing of 1856 to 1857 itself was
devastating, but it was the strategic actions of Governor George Grey in its immediate
aftermath that guaranteed the final destruction of Xhosa power. Within two years of the
prophecy, 35,000–40,000 Xhosa had died of starvation, 150,000 more Xhosa had been displaced, and 600,000 acres of Xhosa land had passed into the hands of white farmers. The
failure of the prophecy also saw resentment and disillusionment with the chiefs loyal to the
old order, and the consequent collapse of a unified Xhosa polity.

David Johnson

Literary Works

Cronin, Jeremy (1997), *Even the Dead, Poems, Parables and a Jeremiad*, Cape Town: David
        Philip.
Dhlomo, H. I. E. [1935] (1985), *The Girl Who Killed to Save – Nongqause*, in T. Couzens
        and N. Visser (eds), *The Collected Works of H. I. E. Dhlomo*, Johannesburg: Ravan
        Press.
Dike, Fatima (1977), *The Sacrifice of Kreli*, Johannesburg: Theatre One A.D. Donker.
Jordan, A. C. [1940] (1980), *The Wrath of the Ancestors/Ingqumbo Yeminyanya*, trans. A. C.
        and P. P. Jordan, Alice: Lovedale Press.
Mda, Zakes (2000), *The Heart of Redness*, Cape Town: Oxford University Press.

Histories

Bradford, Helen (1996), 'Women, Gender and Colonialism. Re-thinking the History of the British Cape Colony and its Frontier Zones, c. 1806–1870', *Journal of African History* 27, pp. 251–70.

Crais, Clifton (1992), *The Making of the Colonial Order: White Supremacy and Black Resistance in the Eastern Cape, 1770–1865*, Johannesburg: Witwatersrand University Press.

Mostert, Noel (1992), *Frontiers: The Epic of South Africa's Creation and the Tragedy of the Xhosa People*, London: Cape.

Peires, Jeff (1989), *The Dead Will Arise. Nongqawuse and the Great Xhosa Cattle-Killing Movement of 1856–7*, Johannesburg: Ravan Press.

Switzer, Les (1993), *Power and Resistance in an African Society: The Ciskei Xhosa and the Making of South Africa*, Pietermaritzburg: University of Natal Press.

See also: **Frontier Wars: Southern Africa**.

The Chauri Chaura Incident

> The tragedy of *Chauri Chaura* is really the index finger. It shows the way India may easily go if drastic precautions be not taken. If we are not to evolve violence out of non-violence, it is quite clear that we must hastily retrace our steps and re-establish an atmosphere of peace, rearrange our programme, and not think of starting mass civil disobedience until we are sure of peace being retained in spite of much civil disobedience being started and inspite of Government provocation

wrote Mohandas Karamchand Gandhi on 16 February 1922 in *Young India*. While the authenticity of the details pertaining to the incident still remain controversial, the Chauri Chaura tragedy is a defining moment in M. K. Gandhi's adoption of civil disobedience as a means to win India's independence from the British.

In February 1922, the peasants of Bardoli Taluk were poised to launch mass civil disobedience under Gandhi's guidance. But a prohibitory order had to be passed by the working committee of Congress because of a gruesome incident that had happened at Chauri Chaura in Uttar Pradesh, then known as the United Province. At Mandera, the local bazaar, which was the scene of vigorous picketing against foreign goods, a zealous police officer named Gupteshwar Singh was said to have assaulted and threatened some of the non-co-operation volunteers engaged in peaceful picketing. In retaliation, about 500 volunteers assembled at the village of Dumri on Saturday, 4 February 1922, and along with a mob of 3,000–4,000 men, marched to the police station at Chauri Chaura where Gupteshwar Singh was employed, and demanded explanation for his highhandedness. After most of the people had left, a scuffle broke out between the policemen and the mob at the rear end of the procession. It was alleged that the police fired at the crowd for a while and then, having run out of ammunition, retreated to the station and locked themselves up for safety. Reportedly, only two rioters' bodies were found after the incident. The mob set fire to the police station and some of the twenty-two self-imprisoned policemen died of smoke inhalation. The others who tried to escape from the building were reportedly attacked by the mob, hacked to pieces and their mangled remains thrown back into the engulfing flames. Shocked and distressed by the incident, Gandhi returned from Bardoli, and called for suspension of all Congress activities until the principles of non-violent action were completely understood by the workers and volunteers. Sensing dissent within Congress and rising public opinion against Gandhi's decision, the British charged Gandhi with four articles of sedition and imprisoned him for six years. Shahid Amin's analysis of the incident (1995) argues that the Gandhian praxis of non-violence is in itself a mutated form of political violence, but that it must nonetheless still be read as an instance of mass peasant politics and not a criminal act.

Kokila Ravi

Literary Works

Rao, Raja [1938] (2000), *Kanthapura*, Delhi: Oxford University Press.

Histories

Amin, Shahid (1995), *Event, Metaphor, Memory: Chauri Chaura 1922–1992*, Berkeley, CA: University of California Press.
Chatterjee, Manini (1999), *Do and Die: The Chittagong Uprising: 1930–34*, New Delhi: Penguin Books.
Gill, S. S. (2002), *Gandhi – A Sublime Failure*, New Delhi: Rupa and Company.
Gopal, Ram (1967), *How India Struggled for Freedom*, Bombay: The Book Centre.
Moon, Penderel (1989), *The British Conquest and Dominion of India*, London: Duckworth.
Williams, Rushbrook (1985), *India in 1921–2: Political, Social, and Economic Developments*, Delhi: Amol Publications.

See also: **Anti-colonialism and Resistance: South Asia; Mutinies in India.**

Chimurengas

Chimurenga is a Shona word which means upheaval and which has come to mean rebellion or even revolution. The current Zimbabwe government, which is propagating 'patriotic history', refers to three Chimurengas – the first being the uprisings against early colonial rule in 1896, which constituted the most formidable challenge to white occupation anywhere in Africa; the second the guerrilla war of the late 1960s and 1970s, which forced the Rhodesian government to a stalemate and to negotiation; and the third the reoccupation of white-owned farm land in the early 2000s, which has led to Zimbabwe's withdrawal from the Commonwealth.

These three upheavals are seen as constituting a sequence of resistance and reclamation of birthright. Appeal to them now constitutes the main legitimation of Robert Mugabe's ruling ZANU/PF party. The national heroine of independent Zimbabwe is the medium of the great female spirit, Nehanda, who was hanged by the British in 1897 for her participation in the first Chimurenga. After 1980 the Heroes Acre in Harare was set up to receive the bodies of leading participants in the second Chimurenga: these are venerated at the annual Heroes Day. The youth militia, who have been trained as the storm-troopers of the recent land occupation and who are the main agents in the repression of the opposition MDC, wear shirts inscribed 'Third Chimurenga'. A government-sponsored research project, involving the National Archives, the National Museums and the History Department of the University of Zimbabwe, has been established to collect oral and archival data on the first and second Chimurengas. This data will be displayed in a museum situated at Heroes Acre.

Prior to the enunciation and elaboration of 'patriotic history' in the early twenty-first century the first two Chimurengas constituted the subject of much historical and imaginative writing. Historians, poets and novelists now have to decide where they stand in relation to the increasingly ideological and narrow version of revolutionary history proclaimed by the Zimbabwe government.

Terence Ranger's history of the 1896 risings – *Revolt in Southern Rhodesia* – was published in 1967. Although completed before the liberation war began it inspired guerrillas in the 1970s and copies of it were also issued to Rhodesian administrators as a guide to the challenge they were facing. The book has triggered much historiographical debate and has been criticised for exaggerating the unity of the 1896 rebels, the modernity of their aims, and the central role of spirit mediums and the priests of the High God, Mwali. From another direction it has been criticised for underplaying the whole sequence of Shona resistances in order to focus on the dramatic events of 1896. Nevertheless it has been very influential on nationalist literature. Stanlake Samkange's *The Year of the Uprising* (1976) draws very heavily on its text; Lawrence Vambe's *An Ill-Fated People* (1972) openly acknowledges *Revolt* as an authority. Despite the historiographical debate there has been no subsequent monograph on the first Chimurenga.

The most important fictional treatment of 1896–7 since Zimbabwean independence, Yvonne Vera's brilliant *Nehanda* (1993), is much less derivative. In fact it consciously sets out to ignore academic historical or anthropological writing and to reimagine events and symbols. In the novel events which in fact were compressed into two years extend to Nehanda's whole life-time, so that we witness her birth, maturity and death. Vera does not end her book with the Nehanda medium being executed by the colonialists. History, she has said, should be at the service of imagination and Zimbabweans imagine Nehanda as a living spirit rather than as a hanged old woman. Vera's book is far from the over-simplicities of 'patriotic history'. Nevertheless, it is a glorification of Shona 'tradition' and of the role of women as its custodians. Her later novels form a critique of the corruption of 'tradition' in the twentieth century and of its abuse by patriarchs.

The guerrilla war of the 1970s – the second Chimurenga – has stimulated much more writing, both scholarly and fictional. Historians, anthropologists and political scientists have written case studies of different areas of Zimbabwe during this period. The most influential of these academic studies has been David Lan's *Guns and Rain* (1985), which applied structural anthropology to an analysis of the war in the Dande Valley in Zimbabwe's north-east. Lan emphasised the role of the spirit mediums in legitimating the guerrillas and presenting them as ancestral heroes. He describes the influence of the Nehanda medium active in the 1970s but his book is mainly about male spirits and male mediums and it has been criticised for offering too patriarchal a picture of Shona religion. The book was hailed by many anthropologists, however, as a proof of the contemporary relevance of their discipline. Lan has since pursued a career as a director and playwright – one of his plays is a representation of the role of mediums during the guerrilla war. In retrospect what is striking about his book is its dramatic presentation and foreshortening of symbolic landscapes.

Other expatriate scholars have also produced district studies focusing on or climaxing in the war. There has again been much debate on the importance of religion; on the extent to which intimidation rather than peasant enthusiasm marked the rural war; on the central-ity of land to the guerrilla political agenda. A particularly influential study is Norma Kriger's *Zimbabawe's Guerrilla War* (1992), with its emphasis both on intimidation and on the frac-tured nature of peasant politics. Kriger's treatment of class, gender and generational divi-sions in African rural society, while preliminary in itself, has inspired subsequent scholars.

Zimbabwean historians have themselves published monographs on the guerrilla war. Two outstanding books are Ngwabi Bhebe's *ZAPU and ZANU Guerrilla Warfare* (1999) and Josephine Nhongo-Simbanegavi's *For Better or for Worse. Women and Zanla* (2000). Bhebe's book was the first to offer a balanced treatment of the contribution of both guerrilla armies, Joshua Nkomo's Zipra as well as Robert Mugabe's Zanla; it combined this overview and analysis with remarkable oral data on the interaction of the guerrillas with Lutheran mis-sions. Josephine Nhongo was the first academic to gain access to the Zanu/Zanla archives where she found material of extraordinary richness. Her book provides a realistic and often harrowing account of the experience of women during the war. It is very far from the heroic accounts required by 'patriotic history'. Nhongo's account fits with the picture presented by two remarkable collections of oral reminiscence, *Mothers of the Revolution* (Staunton 1990) and *Women of Resilience* (Zimbabwe Women Writers 2000).

There have been three main weaknesses in the academic literature on the liberation war. As the late David Beach complained (1986), the war itself – the actual fighting – is largely absent from it. Moreover, the history of the war in western Zimbabwe, in Matabeleland, has been until recently largely ignored. This has been a major impediment in creating a legitimate and inclusive patriotic history. Finally, there has been no single monograph pulling together all the area studies. The closest thing to this is the two volumes edited by Bhebe and Ranger on *Soldiers* and *Society* (1995, 1996) in Zimbabwe's liberation war. As for Matabeleland, two books appeared in the first years of the twenty-first century which depicted the rise of nationalism, the guerrilla war and the terrible events which followed independence in 1980 in western Zimbabwe. Terence Ranger's *Voices from the Rocks* (1999), which explores the history of the Matopos mountains, and Alexander, McGregor and Ranger's *Violence and Memory* (2000), which narrates the experience of two districts in northern Matabeleland, have gone far to enter Matabeleland into the Zimbabwean his-torical record.

The only novel to interact with this scholarly literature on western Zimbabwe, though a very remarkable one, is Yvonne Vera's *The Stone Virgins* (2002). Set in the Matopos mountains and in Kezi township to the south of them, Vera's book takes as its hero-villain an ex-Zipra guerrilla, who spent the war hiding out among the dead and in the caves of the Matopos; he becomes a 'dissident' after independence and, transformed by his experiences from the idealistic nationalist he once was, kills one woman in Kezi and maims another. Vera shows how the people of Kezi are caught between men like this and the brutal repres-sion of Zimbabwean government forces, who burn down stores and torture human beings. In its location in Matabeleland, its creation of Ndebele characters as protagonists, and its compassionate indignation with the abuses of nationalism, the novel is a long way from *Nehanda*.

All the rest of the abundant fictional literature on the second Chimurenga relates to Zanla and to eastern and central Zimbabwe. It is characterised by its rootedness in memory. Many of the novelists – for example, Alexander Kannengoni – were Zanla guerrillas them-selves; others lived in the Shona rural areas during the guerrilla war. Their novels are very different from the fiction on the first Chimurenga, which was so reliant on academic history. Except for Vera's novel, there has been very little interaction between the scholarly and the fictional treatments of the guerrilla war. (An exception to this is the novel, *Guerrilla Snuff*, by the anthropologist and missiologist Martinus Daneel, who has also written fascinating academic accounts of the involvement of spirit mediums in the second Chimurenga.) However, apart from some early triumphalist accounts, these novels of experience are very far from the heroics of 'patriotic history'. As its title suggests, Shimmer Chinodya's *Harvest of Thorns* (1989) is a disillusioned account of a guerrilla's life. Kannengoni's *Echoing Silences* (1997) begins with an educated guerrilla recruit being forced to beat an innocent woman and her child to death in order to prove his loyalty; he spends the rest of the war in dumbed trauma; and ends his life after 1980 after a dramatic purgation by a spirit medium. The poetess and dancer, Freedom Nyambuya, was a woman soldier in Zanla. She eloquently condemns the treatment of women during the war and the narrowness of patriarchal nationalism since independence.

These novelists and poets – and Zimbabwean academics – are now being compelled to choose between the triumphalism of 'patriotic history', with its emphasis on the glories of the three Chimurengas; a critical stance derived from the traumatic memories of the war; and a compassionate exploration of the suffering of ordinary people. Kannengoni has thrown his support behind the third Chimurenga; Chenjerai Hove, whose novels and poems express the perspective of a teacher resident in the rural areas during the war, has been a violent critic and has now gone into exile in France. No novelist has yet written about the third Chimurenga except the extraordinary Yvonne Vera, whose forthcoming novel *Obedience* is set in the year 2000, and deals among much else, with intimidation of the 'disloyal'.

Of course, Zimbabwean novelists and academics who have not written directly about any of the three Chimurengas are also now compelled to choose. One such is Tsitsi Dangarembga, whose only novel, *Nervous Conditions* (1988), was chosen as one of the twelve best books of the African twentieth century, and who is now a film-maker. Dangarembga, who lives in Berlin, takes the view that there is so much criticism of Zimbabwe in Europe and North America that it is the duty of a Zimbabwean artist to highlight anything positive. She could be called a film-maker of the third Chimurenga and one of her recent films documents a successful land resettlement.

In Zimbabwe there are many attempts to call for a fourth Chimurenga – to win justice for workers or to protect the environment. But it seems likely that the Mugabe government's definition of the three Chimurengas will dominate political, academic and literary debate for the foreseeable future.

Terence Ranger

Literary Works

Chinodya, Shimmer (1989), *Harvest of Thorns*, Harare: Baobab.
Chipamaunga, E. (1982), *A Fighter for Freedom*, Gweru: Mambo.
Daneel, Martinus, see Gumbo.
Dangarembga, Tsitsi (1988), *Nervous Conditions*, London: Women's Press.
Gumbo, Mafuranhunzi [Martinus Daneel] (1995), *Guerrilla Snuff*, Harare: Baobab.
Hove, Chenjerai (1988), *Bones*, Harare: Baobab.
Kannengoni, Alexander (1997), *Echoing Silences*, Harare: Baobab.

Nyamfukudza, Stanley (1980), *The Non-Believer's Journey*, London: Heinemann.
Staunton, Irene (ed.) (1990), *Mothers of the Revolution*, Harare: Baobab.
Vera, Yvonne (1993), *Nehanda*, Harare: Boabab.
Vera, Yvonne (2002), *The Stone Virgins*, Harare: Weaver.
Zimbabwe Women Writers (2000), *Women of Resilience. The Voices of Women Ex-combatants*, Harare: ZWW.

Histories

Alexander, Jocelyn, JoAnn MacGregor and Terence Ranger (2000), *Violence and Memory. One Hundred Years in the 'Dark Forest' of Matabeleland*, Oxford: James Currey.
Beach, David (1986), *War and Politics in Zimbabwe, 1840–1900*, Gweru: Mambo Press.
Bhebe, Ngwabe (1999), *The ZAPU and ZANU Guerrilla Warfare and the Evangelical Church in Zimbabwe*, Gweru: Mambo Press.
Bhebe, Ngwabe and Terence Ranger (eds) (1995 and 1996), *Soldiers and Society in Zimbabwe's Liberation War*, London: James Currey.
Kriger, Norma (1992), *Zimbabwe's Guerrilla War. Peasant Voices*, Cambridge: Cambridge University Press.
Lan, David (1985), *Guns and Rain. Guerrillas and Spirit Mediums in Zimbabwe*, London: James Currey.
Moorcraft, Paul and Peter McLaughlin (1982), *Chimurenga! The War in Rhodesia 1865–1980*, Marshalltown: Sygma/Collins.
Nhongo-Simbanegavi, J. (2000), *For Better or for Worse. Women and Zanla in Zimbabwe's Liberation Struggle*, Harare: Weaver.
Ranger, Terence (1967), *Revolt in Southern Rhodesia, 1896–7*, London: Heinemann.
Ranger, Terence (1985), *Peasant Consciousness and Guerrilla War in Zimbabwe*, London: James Currey.
Ranger, Terence (1999), *Voices from the Rocks. Nature, Culture and History in the Matopos Hills of Zimbabwe*, Oxford: James Currey.
Samkange, Stanlake (1978), *Year of the Uprising*, London: Heinemann.
Vambe, Lawrence (1972), *An Ill-Fated People*, London: Heinemann.

See also: **Anti-colonialism and Resistance: Southern Africa; Land: Southern Africa; Nationalism(s): Southern Africa.**

Chinese Gold-diggers

Chinese gold-diggers joined the rush for gold in the Pacific-rim white settler societies following the 1848 discovery of gold in California. The great majority came from the two southern provinces of Guandong (Kwantung) and Fujian (Fukien) and formed a significant proportion on the fields of California, Victoria, New South Wales, Queensland and the South Island of New Zealand. In the colony of Victoria, the site of the richest of the Australian alluvial gold deposits, the Chinese population peaked close to 35,000 in 1858; in New South Wales at 15,000 in 1862. In Victoria Chinese gold-diggers made up more than 20 per cent of the mining population, on the poorer New South Wales fields some 60 per cent. During the relatively small Queensland gold rush of the 1860s and 1870s, the

Chinese predominated on many fields. Thus in the far north, on the River Palmer, the Chinese population reached an estimated 17,000, heavily outnumbering the 1,500 Europeans.

The Chinese diggers formed a distinct element on the gold fields, distinguished by their appearance, customs, languages, separate camps, and working methods, and the almost total absence of women. Unlike the Europeans, the Chinese worked systematically in large groups. On some fields they had rich gold-bearing ground, but generally they worked the poorer areas, at times reworking soil already mined by Europeans. While they were accorded a large measure of equality in the first years of the Victorian and New South Wales fields, the Chinese miners faced mounting hostility. European miners harboured a sense of superiority and negative views of Chinese civilisation and of 'coolie' labour. The Chinese faced sporadic acts of violence and on occasion were the targets of mob hostility.

From 1855 onwards the colonial legislatures experimented with methods to control the Chinese populations. In Victoria special taxes were imposed on the Chinese, they were required by law to reside in separate camps on the major fields, and their entry to the colony was restricted by a poll tax and limitations on their numbers who could travel on each ship. Queensland sought to exclude Chinese miners from some gold fields. In eastern Australia the peak of the Chinese population was reached during the late 1850s; more than half the Chinese returned to their homeland. As the alluvial deposits were worked out, typically in less than ten years, the opposition of white miners kept the Chinese from the deep-lead quartz mines. Other forms of employment were also difficult for them to obtain in Victoria and New South Wales.

Andrew Markus

Literary Works

Castro, Brian (1983), *Birds of Passage*, Sydney: Allen and Unwin.
Jong Ah Sing (2000), *Difficult Case: An Autobiography of a Chinese Miner on the Central Victorian Goldfields*, Daylesford: Jim Crow Press.
Miller, Alex (1992), *The Ancestor Game*, Ringwood: Penguin.
Newton, Nerida (2003), *The Lambing Flat*, St Lucia: University of Queensland Press.

Histories

Chan, Henry (2001), 'Becoming Chinese but Remaining Australasian', in Henry Chan, Ann Curthoys and Nora Chiang (eds), *The Overseas Chinese in Australasia*, Taipei: Interdisciplinary Group for Australian Studies, National Taiwan University, pp. 1–15.
Cronin, Kathryn (1982), *Colonial Casualties: Chinese in Early Victoria*, Melbourne: Melbourne University Press.
Markus, Andrew (1979), *Fear and Hatred: Purifying Australia and California*, Sydney: Hale and Iremonger.
Price, Charles (1974), *The Great White Walls Are Built*, Canberra: Australian National University Press.
Rolls, Eric (1992), *Sojourners*, St Lucia: University of Queensland Press.

Wang Sing-wu (1978), *The Organization of Chinese Emigration 1848–1888*, San Francisco: Chinese Materials Centre.

See also: **Historiography: Australia; Multiculturalism: Australia**.

Colonial Cultural Cringe: Australia

Settler/invader colonies experienced dual colonialism: settler colonials perceived their superiority over the 'Natives' but were seen as inferior by the imperial centre. In elite Britain, Australians were looked down on as rough colonials, of convict stock; in Les Murray's words 'the poor who got away'. A lack of respect for Aboriginal culture and the land reinforced this internalised colonial 'Cultural Cringe': the idea that Australian culture and achievement is inferior. The left-wing nationalist literary critic Arthur (A. A.) Phillips coined the term in *The Australian Tradition: Studies in a Colonial Culture* (1958). Phillips defined the Cringe Direct as 'a tendency to make needless comparisons. The Australian reader, more or less consciously, hedges and hesitates, asking himself, "yes, but what would a cultivated Englishman think of this?"' Phillips located the Cringe in social behaviour, in crawling after and giving deference to the English: 'There is a certain type of Australian intellectual who is for ever sidling up to the cultivated Englishman, insinuating "I, of course, am not like these other crude Australians".' The Cringe Inverted, exaggerating self-confidence, stemmed from isolation and ignorance: a 'we're-the biggest and the best mentality', 'the attitude of the . . . God's Own-country and I'm a-better-man-than-you are, Australian Bore'.

The Cultural Cringe pervades popular media debate and is sometimes misused to suggest an 'uncultured' Australia, uninterested in culture, itself inaccurate. 'Tall poppies' are Australians getting above themselves. In Cultural Cringe terms, 'expatriates', like colonial elites, are drawn to cultural and economic centres. Later, like other metropolitan stars, welcomed back as keynote speakers, they are also excoriated as 'expatriots' (a common press spelling) who are 'out of touch' with Australia.

Patterns of hierarchy, metropolitan-provincial and centre-periphery, compound the coloniser–colonised experience. Like 'educated' Africans and Indians in the British Empire, and some US intellectuals, many Australians dreamed of the mystique of London. Frantz Fanon's (1970) theory of the 'colonised' has partial applicability to the settler colonials' relationship to Britain, explaining hesitant cultural development:

> Every colonised people . . . every people in whose soul an inferiority cultural complex has been created by the death and burial of its local cultural originality – finds itself face to face with the language of the civilising nation; that is, with the culture of the mother country. (Fanon 1970, p. 18)

Neither English derivation nor language denied that hierarchical separation, although it differed in nature as well as degree. Over time, however, Australia has acquired its own accent and voice. Imperial-colonial relations have merged into a metropolitan-provincial relationship. Globally centralised cultural power makes the Cringe now 'world class' (to fashionable ideas, the USA or global logos); arguably it pervades most peripheral nations, societies and regions.

Stephen Alomes

Literary Works

Carey, Peter (1985) *Illywhacker*, St Lucia: University of Queensland Press.
Stead, Christina (1990), *For Love Alone*, North Ryde: Angus and Robertson.

Histories

Alomes, Stephen (1998), *When London Calls: The Expatriation of Australian Creative Artists to London*, Cambridge: Cambridge University Press.
Fanon, Frantz (1970), *Black Skin, White Masks*, London: Paladin.
Phillips, A. A. (1958), *The Australian Tradition: Studies in a Colonial Culture*, Melbourne: Cheshire.

See also: **European Exploration and Settlement: Australia, New Zealand, Pacific; Historiography: Australia.**

Coloured: Southern Africa

The label 'Coloured' has been condemned by some as an imposed racial category, accepted by others as a self-identity, and remains contested. Coloured identity emerged in the British Cape Colony during the nineteenth century from a dialectical relationship between racialisation by 'whites' and self-definition. From the 1840s, after Khoi and slave emancipation, whites sometimes used the term Coloured to refer to all black Cape Colonists. But Coloured was also used to refer only to those who were not Bantu-speaking Africans, in other words to those of Khoi, slave or 'mixed race' descent, most of whom spoke Afrikaans. Coloured, in this narrower sense, became an acceptable self-identity at least in part because it closely correlated with historical and contemporary experience among many of the ex-bonded. Events and processes in the late Victorian period gave greater salience to such identity. In particular, the western migration of large numbers of Xhosa-speaking Africans helped produce an approximate three-tiered division of labour between whites, Coloureds and Africans. In addition, white racism spawned social segregation that led to members of Coloured elites forming parallel social institutions such as sporting clubs and temperance organisations. At much the same time, the white-settler dominated Cape government passed laws that discriminated specifically against Africans (initially in terms of liquor control and residential segregation), giving some practical advantages to those adhering to a Coloured identity. The latter was also promoted by elite ethnic mobilisation, through both political organisation and journalistic endeavour, initially prompted by the raising of the (non-racial) Cape franchise and the threat of educational segregation in the early 1890s.

Ethnic mobilisation gathered speed during the South African War, partly as an attempt to hold the British to their promise of equal rights for all civilized men south of the Zambezi in the event of imperial victory. But the Treaty of Vereeneging, which ended the war, allowed whites in the defeated Boer Republics to retain a whites-only franchise. In response to this betrayal, the African Political Organisation was established in 1902 to fight overtly for Coloured political and social rights. The Union of South Africa (1910), which enshrined white political supremacy, did not end such efforts. Yet hope was all but destroyed by the coming of apartheid. The Population Registration Act (1949) gave legal definition to Coloured identity, and was the lynchpin of much further legislation enforcing cradle to grave segregation between South Africa's 'race groups'. Laws extended to Coloureds the prohibition from sexual relations with whites that already applied to Africans. Coloureds were removed from the common voters roll in the Cape, and were the principal victims of a 'Group Areas Act' that sought comprehensive residential segregation in South African cities. The demolition of District Six, a predominantly Coloured area, was dubbed 'Cape Town's Hiroshima' by the novelist Richard Rive. South African writers like Rive have explored Coloured experience, with particular (and predictable) attention to themes such as life in District Six, (racial) identity, discrimination, politics, poverty, crime, love across the colour bar and miscegenation.

Vivian Bickford-Smith

Literary Works

Abrahams, Peter (1952), *The Path of Thunder*, London: Faber and Faber.
Abrahams, Peter (1954), *Tell Freedom*, London: Faber and Faber.
Brink, André (1974), *Looking on Darkness*, London: W. H. Allen and Co. Ltd.
Dangor, Achmat (1985), *Waiting for Leila*, Johannesburg: Ravan Press.
Fugard, Athol (1963), *The Blood Knot*, Johannesburg: Simondium Publishers.
Gool, Reshard (1990), *Cape Town Coolie*, Oxford: Heinemann International.
La Guma, Alex (1991), *The Stone Country*, Cape Town: David Philip.
La Guma, Alex (1991), *A Walk in the Night*, Cape Town: David Philip.
Rive, Richard (1987), *'Buckingham Palace', District Six*, Cape Town: David Philip.
Rive, Richard (1988), *Emergency*, Cape Town: David Philip.
Rive Richard (1990), *Emergency Continued*, Cape Town: David Philip.
Wicomb, Zoë (1996), *You Can't Get Lost in Cape Town*, London: Virago.

Histories

Bickford-Smith, Vivian (1995), 'Black Ethnicities, Communities and Political Expression in Late Victorian Cape Town', *Journal of African History* 36, pp. 443–65.
February, V. A. (1991), *Mind Your Colour: The 'Coloured' Stereotype in South African Literature*, Bognor Regis: John Wiley and Sons Ltd.
Field, Sean (ed.) (2001), *Lost Communities, Living Memories: Remembering Forced Removals in Cape Town*, Cape Town: David Philip.
Goldin, Ian (1987), *Making Race: The Politics and Economics of Coloured Identity in South Africa*, Cape Town: Masker Miller Longman.
Lewis, Gavin (1987), *Between the Wire and the Wall: A History of South African 'Coloured' Politics*, Cape Town: David Philip.
Spivak, Gayatri Chakravorty (1988), *In Other Worlds: Essays in Cultural Politics*, New York: Routledge.

See also: **Anti-colonialism and Resistance: Southern Africa; Apartheid and Segregation; Nationalism(s): Southern Africa.**

Commonwealth

The notion of Commonwealth emerged in the wake of the British Empire to redefine the relationship between Britain and its colonies, selected former colonies (now sovereign states) and their dependencies, and internally self-governing associated states whose external relations remained under the jurisdiction of Britain. The redefinition of the relationship between the Empire and its colonies in these terms was motivated by several factors, including the economic strain of the debt incurred from World War I, increasing growth of nationalist movements, and Britain going through a more liberal period of reform and change with, for example, the 1833 abolition of slavery, the 1832 Reform Act, the 1867 Reform Act, and the repeal of Corn Laws in 1846.

It was within such an atmosphere that the Commonwealth was born. As early as 1829, the idea of limited self-government for certain colonies was mooted, where a cabinet would be elected by the nationals of a colony to take care of internal affairs. This cabinet would work alongside a British governor-general who would maintain responsibility for foreign affairs and defence to ensure that the Empire could display a unified front when needed.

Self-governing dominion status was first given to Canada (1867), followed by Australia (1900), New Zealand (1907), and South Africa (1910) – the 'white nations' of the British Empire. This is why it has been suggested that the Commonwealth is synonymous with Empire as much as it has been suggested that it marks the process of decolonisation. It was this selective nation-group, including Britain, that was first informally known as the British Commonwealth and initially established in principle in 1926, with British acceptance of the dominions as freely associated members of a British Commonwealth. This principle was ratified in 1931 with the endorsement of the Statute of Westminster because of growing dissatisfaction with the operations of the Empire and rising nationalistic sentiments within colonies such as India and Iraq, which gained independence in 1947 and 1932 respectively.

The next major signpost in the history of the Commonwealth occurred in 1949, when it was decided, as part of the London Declaration, to revise the emphasis of the British Commonwealth and expand membership to include the newly independent colonies such as India. In the same year, however, the Republic of Ireland withdrew its membership of the Commonwealth. Furthermore, the declaration recommended the removal of the term 'British' and the new collectivity was renamed Commonwealth of Nations, to describe countries willing to be in alliance for mutual benefit and co-operation under a set of shared ideals, and not simply the imposed ideals of the British Empire. The consequence of this was the expansion of the Commonwealth and currently membership stands at fifty-four nations.

Commonwealth is indeed a slippery terms for various reasons: it signifies, simultaneously, colonisation, decolonisation, self-governance, and independence; it is difficult to date precisely; and it refers to a historical moment as well as to a process.

Vijay Devadas

Literary Works

Achebe, Chinua (1963), *No Longer at Ease*, London: Heinemann.
Bhabhani, Bhattacharya (1964), *So Many Hungers!*, Bombay: Jaico.
Kipling, Rudyard (1923), 'Our Lady of the Snows', in R. Kipling, *The Five Nations*, London: Methuen, pp. 87–9.

Naipaul, V. S. (1979), *A Bend in the River*, New York: Knopf.

Rushdie, Salman [1983] (1995), *Shame*, London: Vintage.

Rushdie, Salman (1991), '"Commonwealth Literature" Does Not Exist', in S. Rushdie, *Imaginary Homelands: Essays and Criticism 1981–1991*, London: Granta Books, pp. 61–70.

Said, Edward (1992), 'Figures, Configurations, Transfigurations,' in A. Rutherford (ed.), *From Commonwealth to Post-Colonial*, New South Wales: Dangaroo Press, pp. 3–17.

Histories

Hall, Duncan (1971), *Commonwealth: A History of the British Commonwealth of Nations*, London: Van Nostrand Reinhold Company.

McIntyre, David (1977), *The Commonwealth of Nations: Origins and Impact, 1869–1971*, Minneapolis, MN: University of Minnesota Press.

McIntyre, David (1999), 'Commonwealth Legacy', in J. Brown and W. M. R. Louis (eds), *The Oxford History of the British Empire: Volume IV The Twentieth Century*, Oxford and New York: Oxford University Press, pp. 693–702.

Naidis, Mark (1970), *The Second British Empire 1783–1965: A Short History*, Reading, MA: Addison-Wesley Publishing Company.

Walker, Eric [1943] (1944), *The British Empire: Its Structure and Spirit*, London: Oxford University Press.

See also: **Anglicisation; Britain's Postwar Foreign Policy; British Imperialism; Decolonisation; Historiography: British Empire; United Nations.**

Communism: South Asia

The Communist Party of India (CPI) was formed in the course of the 1920s, primarily under the leadership of the Marxist theorist and activist M. N. Roy (1887–1954). From the 1920s to early 1930s, a determination on the part of the CPI to distance itself from the Congress Party, which represented Indian aspirations under colonial rule most cogently, led to an uneasy location in the anti-colonial struggle (primarily in militant activities). From the mid-1930s the policy changed, and the formation of the Congress Socialist Party in 1936 allowed communists and Congress members with socialist sympathies to collaborate. From the mid-1930s the communists in India started mobilising and organising not only in urban centres but more significantly in the vast rural areas. Around the independence period, significant peasant uprisings were organised with communist support, especially in Telengana (1944–51), Tebhaga (1946–7), and Kakdwip (1946–50).

After independence in 1947 and the installation of Congress as the ruling party, the CPI adopted a policy of non-collaboration with Congress, and effectively pushed itself outside legislative politics. In 1951 a change of policy brought communists into the legislative process and the first CPI state election victory took place in Kerala in 1957. However in 1964 the party split, and CPI-Marxist (CPI-M or CPM) – members of which alleged that the CPI was increasingly taking a 'revisionist' position – emerged as the dominant communist alignment. CPI-M became the ruling party in Kerala in 1965, and a CPI-M-controlled coalition, People's United Front, came to power in West Bengal in 1967. In 1967, a further split in CPI-M saw the birth of the CPI-Marxist–Leninist or CPI-ML, which essentially incorporated communists who felt disenchanted with the progress of socialist transformation through legislative means and felt that more militant measures along Maoist lines were called for.

Armed Naxalite activism formed a significant element in communist politics through the 1970s and 1980s – especially in West Bengal, Bihar, and Andhra Pradesh – and to some extent still plays a role in the rural sector. The variously split radical to moderate communist and socialist parties have also continued to enjoy mixed success in the legislative process. In the course of the 1990s, however, at the national level the secular Congress Party has been seriously challenged by the Hindu communalist Bharatiya Janata Party (BJP) and its right-wing allies, which entered central government at the head of a coalition in 1998. As a result, a concerted effort is now afoot to write out and otherwise vilify the efforts and influence of communists in modern Indian social, cultural and political history.

The influence of communists in Indian intellectual production and culture (especially in the numerous Indian languages) – in literature, films, plays, music, academic writing – has been enormous. Insofar as postcolonial studies in the West have registered the political realities and complexities of communist influences, the results are patchy. In literature, for instance, this has been apprehended hazily primarily through writings in English and translations. V. S. Naipaul's ill-informed and hostile analysis of revolutionaries in India (especially in A *Wounded Civilization* (1997), on the one hand, and Gayatri Spivak's discourse-theory-based interventions vis-à-vis the work of subaltern historians and translations of Mahasveta Devi's novels (which often express Naxalite sympathies), on the other, represent the two poles here.

As in India, so too in Sri Lanka communism has roots in the 1920s. A small group of Sinhalese students influenced by Harold Laski while at university in London returned to promote communism. Their influence grew steadily: in 1931, A. S. Wickremasinghe was elected as an independent to the State Council on a left-wing platform; and in December 1935, the Lanka Sama Samaja Party (LSSP) was formed, and won two seats in the 1936 elections (Philip Gunawardena and N. M. Perera). The party adopted a consciously Trotskyist line, and in November 1940 Stalinist members left the LSSP to form the United Socialist Party. The anti-war politics of the LSSP led to the arrest of the LSSP leadership in June 1940, but they escaped to India in April 1942, where they forged links with the Bolshevik–Leninist Party of India (BPLI). There was a further split, but this did not hinder progress fundamentally, as in the 1947 elections, the two Communist parties – the Lanka Sama Samaja Party and the Bolshevik Samasamaja Party – gained ten and five seats respectively, while the governing United National Party gained forty-two. After the war, communist parties helped unionise over 300,000 workers, and were heavily involved in general strikes in 1946, 1947 and 1953. A Maoist communist faction broke away in 1962, but the next major turning point was the 1964 election, when the LSSP (by then the largest left party) decided to join the government of the Sri Lankan Freedom Party. This was viewed as a betrayal of Sri Lanka's poor, and the Janatha Vimukthi Peramuna (JVP) was formed in 1965 and quickly captured the support of the mainly Sinhalese workers and peasants of the south, whereas the Liberation Tigers of Tamil Eelam (LTTE) made similarly swift inroads in recruiting disaffected Tamil youth in the north. The LSSP was part of the 1970 coalition government which crushed the 1971 JVP uprising with such violence, and has since played a secondary role in Sri Lanka's communist politics, with the JVP still prominent despite violent state reprisals (it won ten seats in the 2000 elections).

Pakistani communism, of course, shares the same origins in 1920s Indian communism, and only took a distinctive route after the final undivided CPI congress in 1948, when communists of Muslim origin like Sajjad Zaheer and Sibte Hassan were dispatched to help organise the Communist Party of Pakistan (CPP), and a provincial committee of the Communist Party was established in East Pakistan under Khoka Roy. From 1948 to 1950, the communists in the eastern wing of Pakistan followed an ultra-left line, and echoing the Urdu poet Faiz Ahmad Faiz, raised the slogan *Lakho Insan Bhuka Hai, Ye Azadi Jhoota Hay* ('Millions of people are starving and we reject this independence'). This was soon replaced by a more cautious approach, as Stalin's two-stage theory of revolution (first national liberation, then socialism) was adopted, and a strategic alliance (as a very junior partner) with the Muslim League was pursued. The CPP's botched coup attempt in 1951 (known as the Rawalpindi Conspiracy) led to its banning, and the imprisonment of key leaders. The remaining CPP members formed the small Azad Pakistan Party, which merged a few years later in 1957 with liberal progressive groups to form the reformist National Awami Party (NAP).

The activism against Ayub Khan's military dictatorship in the late 1960s saw a resurgence of communist ideas, but Zulfiqar Ali Bhutto's Pakistan People's Party that came to power in 1972 quickly reneged on its socialist promises, and the communists in his coalition government were marginalised.

For the embattled communist left in Pakistan, the 1980s – the decade of Zia ul Haq's dictatorship – was characterised by a sequence of mergers followed by splits, and then more mergers, with no mass support base established at any time. The collapse of the Soviet Union saw a further reconfiguring of left-wing Pakistan politics, as Stalinist parties fell away, and new parties emerged.

The main communist parties now are the Labour Party of Pakistan (LPP), the National Workers Party (NWP), and the Communist Mazdoor Kissan Party (CMKP), which has had some success supporting the struggle for peasant rights in the regions bordering Afghanistan.

Suman Gupta

Literary Works

Devi, Mahasweta (1995), *Imaginary Maps: Three Stories*, trans. G. C. Spivak, London: Routledge.

Devi, Mahasweta (2003), *Chotti Munda and his Arrow*, trans. G. C. Spivak, Oxford: Blackwell.

Naipaul, V. S. (1977), *India: A Wounded Civilization*, London: André Deutsch.

Roy, Arundhati (1997), *The God of Small Things*, New Delhi: IndiaInk.

Sivanadan, A. (1997), *When Memory Dies*, London: Arcadia.

Histories

Alexander, Robert J. (1991), *International Trotskyism 1929–1985: A Documented Analysis of the Movement*, Durham, NC: Duke University Press.

Ali, Tariq (1982), *Can Pakistan Survive?*, London: New Left Books.

Gupta, A. K. (1996), *Agrarian Drama: Leftists and the Rural Poor in India 1934–1951*, New Delhi: Manohar.

Lerski, George (1968), *Origins of Trotskyism in Ceylon*, Stanford, CA: Hoover Institute.

Mallick, Ross (1994), *Indian Communism: Opposition, Collaboration and Institutionalization*, New Delhi: Oxford University Press.

Nossiter, T. J. (1988), *Marxist State Governments in India: Politics, Economics and Society*, London: Pinter.

Omvedt, Gail (1993), *Reinventing Revolution: New Socialist Movements and the Socialist Tradition in India*, New York: M. E. Sharpe.

Singh, Randhir (1990), *Of Marxism and Indian Politics*, New Delhi: South Asia Books.

See also: **Anti-colonialism and Resistance: South Asia; JVP Insurrection; Naxalites; Pakistan's Subaltern Struggles; Years of Terror.**

Communism: South-east Asia

The European colonisation of South-east Asia contributed to the low level of political involvement and education among the great majority of South-east Asia people. When the colonists withdrew, they left behind a political vacuum that was filled only by various forms of nationalism largely associated with traditional ruling elites. Communism emerged as an alternative political ideology to fill some part of this vacuum. The aspiration towards a communist state was inextricably bound to relations with mainland China, which had provided migrant labour and a mercantile class for South-east Asia for more than a thousand years. Chinese communism provided a model that many among the left in South-east Asia found more attractive than the Soviet alternative, with its large-scale collectivisation of open agricultural spaces. Yet the fear of domination by another state – a role that had been filled historically by China – meant that such a connection could never be sustainable.

The three states where communism won power – Vietnam, Laos and Cambodia – each adopted a regime very different from the other. In Vietnam, the rigidity of French colonial rule and its violent suppression of the struggle for independence meant that communism became identified with nationalism. The Lao People's Revolutionary Party has continually struggled to articulate a revolutionary stance that is distinctively Laotian in nature. However, because of its low population and proximity to Vietnam, Laotian communism seems forever destined to be linked to communism in Vietnam. Meanwhile, in Cambodia, the extraordinary level of radicalism reached by Pol Pot and the Communist Party of Kampuchea remain a mystifying phenomenon, making all attempts at accounting for the origins and nature of Cambodian communism a matter of conjecture, debate and controversy.

The nature and spread of communism in South-east Asia has varied according to the internal political situation in each country from the region. In Indonesia, communism flourished early: the Partai Komunis Indonesia was formed in 1920. Attempts to organise strikes and a revolution in 1925 proved disastrous: thousands were either exiled or imprisoned, and the remaining membership was left feeling betrayed. Indonesian independence was achieved under the charismatic and autocratic figure of Sukarno, who sought to integrate all opposition to colonialism into his brand of nationalism. In British-controlled Malaysia and Singapore, armed opposition held communist bands at bay. In the Philippines, Myanmar (Burma) and uncolonised Thailand, communism has remained a background threat of insurrection and revolution, to be suppressed wherever possible.

Through the Cold War period, American support for anti-communist forces and policies became a significant force in South-east Asia. In Singapore and Thailand, for example, the desire to root out communism and communist thought wherever it was believed to have taken root, took on an almost fanatical aspect.

South-east Asian literature traditionally focused on the actions of kings and courts, recounted ritualistically in chronicles. In the twentieth century, these forms were modernised under Western influences and, in Vietnam and Laos especially, revolutionary literature of varying quality has appeared.

John Walsh

Literary Works

Duong Thu Huong (2002), *Paradise of the Blind*, New York: Perennial.
José, Francisco Soinil (1984), *Mass*, New York: HarperCollins.
Suyin Han (1956), *. . . and the Rain My Drink*, New York: Vintage/Ebury.
Toer, Pramoedya Anant (1997), *House of Glass*, New York: Penguin.

Histories

Barlow, Tani E. (ed.) (2002), *New Asian Marxisms*, Durham, NC: Duke University Press.
Lee Ting Hui (1996), *The Open United Front: The Communist Struggle in Singapore, 1954–1966*, Singapore: South Seas Society.
Saulo, Alfredo B. (1990), *Communism in the Philippines: An introduction*, Manila: Ateneo de Manila University Press.
Smith, Charles B. Jr (1984), *The Burmese Communist Party in the 1980s*, Singapore: Institute of South-east Asian Studies.
Swift, Ann (1989), *The Road to Madiun: The Indonesian Communist Uprising of 1948*, Ithaca, NY: Cornell Modern Indonesia Project, South-east Asia Program, Cornell University.
Van der Kroef, Justus M. (1981), *Communism in South-east Asia*, London: Macmillan.

See also: **Britain's Postwar Foreign Policy; Historiography: South-east Asia; Vietnam War**.

Creolisation

'Creolisation' derives from 'creole', which is believed to originate from a combination of the Spanish words *criar* (create, imagine, establish, settle) and *colon* (founder, settler). The meaning of 'creole' has changed over time: in the early seventeenth century, 'Creole' referred to those Europeans 'born and bred' in the Caribbean, whereas arguably its primary meaning in the twenty-first century has come to be 'the language spoken in the Caribbean'. A very loose definition would nonetheless emphasise the process by which languages, identities and ideas deriving from different cultures combine in subversive (but not necessarily harmonising) ways to form new creole (linguistic, social, political) communities.

In recent postcolonial theory, the term 'creolisation' has on occasions been abstracted from Caribbean history, and assimilated to concepts like 'hybridity' and 'multiculturalism'. The major debates, however, remain located in the Caribbean, and broadly speaking, two views of creolisation can be identified.

Arguably the most influential understanding of creolisation is the one proposed by Edward Kamau Brathwaite, who has argued (1971) that the 'middle passage' from Africa to the Caribbean was not an entirely destructive journey; in the process of adapting to plantation society, slaves created new modes of living and new forms of cultural expression. Focusing on Jamaica, Brathwaite believed that the material, psychological and spiritual processes of slaves adapting both to their new environments and to each other were creative ones, and that communities of survival and resistance developed. One example of such creativity is of slaves developing Creole languages to create a communicative space impenetrable to the slave-owners.

With the abolition of slavery in 1834, new forms of creolisation developed, not only as a consequence of the immigration of Indian indentured labour, but also because of migration within the Caribbean itself. Creolisation continued from the 1850s to the 1880s, as there was significant migration from Jamaica to Panama, Costa Rica and Venezuela, where there were jobs on the first (unsuccessful) Panama canal project, the railways, and the gold mines.

Although not axiomatically oppositional, creolisation has often been associated with anti-slavery, anti-colonialism, worker struggles, and political resistance. Creolisation – in the broad sense of the coming together of oppressed but disparate Caribbean groups – has continued to be a defining characteristic of post-independence protests. For example, in Trinidad-Tobago, anger at deteriorating economic conditions was expressed in 1970 in massive demonstrations against the domination of the economy by foreign multinationals and indigenous white or fair-skinned elites, with the National Joint Action Committee (NJAC) leading demonstrations which included workers, the unemployed, students and teachers. The movement mobilised thousands, but retained grass-roots agency, as there 'was little organisation, and the cumulative and available ideological context was defined by flexibility, openness and the absence of hierarchy' (Meeks 1996, p. 67).

The second, alternative, view of creolisation in the Caribbean is that of Orlando Patterson (1967), who regards Brathwaite's reading of plantation society as too optimistic. For Patterson, the emergent creole societies in Jamaica were highly stratified, with hierarchy, domination and subordination rather than community and reciprocity their defining characteristics. Seeing little evidence of social cohesion in Jamaica's creole communities, Patterson concluded that 'Jamaica is best seen as a collection of autonomous plantations' (Patterson 1967, p. 70).

Quite how Caribbean creolisation is to be defined, both in eighteenth- and nineteenth-century histories, and in contemporary forms of Caribbean identity and community, is likely to continue to be keenly contested.

Heidi Bojsen

Literary works

Bennett, Louise (1982), *Selected Poems*, ed. M. Morris, Kingston: Sangsters.
Brathwaite, Edward Kamau (1968) *Rights of Passage*, London, New York and Toronto: Oxford University Press.
Chamoiseau, Patrick [1988] (1999), *Solibo Magnificent*, trans. R.-M. Réjouis and V. Vinokurov, London: Granta.

Harris, Wilson [1960] (1998), *The Palace of the Peacock*, London: Faber and Faber.
Selvon, Sam (1956), *The Lonely Londoners*, London: Longman.
Walcott, Derek (1986), *Collected Poems 1948–1984*, New York: Farrar, Straus and Giroux.

Histories

Balutansky, Kathleen M. and Marie-Agnes Sourieau (eds) (1998), *Caribbean Creolization: Reflections on the Cultural Dynamics of Language, Literature and Identity*, Gainesville, FL: University of Florida Press.
Benitez-Rojo, Antonio (1992), *The Repeating Island. The Caribbean and the Postmodern Perspective*, trans. J. Maraniss, Durham, NC: Duke University Press.
Brathwaite, Edward Kamau (1971). *The Development of Creole Society in Jamaica 1770–1820*, Oxford: Clarendon Press.
Brathwaite, Edward Kamau (1984), *History of the Voice*, London and Port of Spain: New Beacon Books.
Hennessy, Alistair (ed.) (1992), *Intellectuals in the Caribbean*, London: Macmillan.
King, Nicole (2001), *C.L.R. James and Creolization*, Jackson, MS: University Press of Mississippi.
Knight, Franklin W. and Colin A. Palmer (1989), 'The Caribbean. A Regional Overview', in Franklin W. Knight and Colin A. Palmer (eds), *Modern Caribbean*, Chapel Hill and London: The University of North Carolina Press, pp. 1–19.
Meeks, Brian (1996), *Radical Caribbean. From Black Power to Abu Bakr*, Barbados, Jamaica, Trinidad and Tobago: The Press University of the West Indies.
Patterson, Orlando (1967), *The Sociology of Slavery. An Analysis of the Origins, Development and Structure of Slave Society in Jamaica*, London: MacGibbon and Kee.
Sheller, Mimi (2003), *Consuming the Caribbean*, London: Routledge.

See also: **Anti-colonialism and Resistance: Caribbean; Historiography: Caribbean; Indentured Labour: Caribbean.**

Cromer, Lord

Evelyn Baring, better known as Cromer, came from the family of financiers who founded Barings Bank. Starting out as a self-proclaimed Liberal in politics, the young Baring began his career with the Indian Army, but in 1872 joined the Indian Civil Service under the patronage of his relative, the Viceroy Lord Northbrook. In 1877, his achievements and connections gained him a job in Egypt with the commissioner of the public debt, a position he shared with a Frenchmen under the dual control established over Egyptian finances installed as a result of Egypt's declaration of bankruptcy the previous year. Resigning from this post in 1879, after a brief spell back in India he returned to Egypt as the British controller of finance, following the deposition of the khedive Ismail (one of several Turkish viceroys ruling Egypt from 1867 to 1914).

Baring missed the Egyptian crisis of 1881–2 that ended with the British occupation, but returned once more to Egypt in 1883, this time in the position of consul-general. Within a short period, Baring established himself as effective ruler of Egypt behind what he himself termed the 'veiled protectorate' (Britain did not proclaim a formal protectorate over Egypt until the start of the Great War), a typically British colonial facade in which Egyptian ministers were shadowed by British 'advisers'. Under Baring's rule, Egypt's finances were gradually put in order and reforms were instituted, such as the abolition of the *corvee* (forced labour) imposed on peasants in order to maintain the system of Nile canals essential for irrigation, and corporal punishment by the *korbash* (whip).

Working on the self-declared principle 'If we are to stay here, we ought to try and make ourselves popular', Baring initiated improvements in irrigation by British engineers that were appreciated by the *fellahin*. However, he discouraged indigenous industrial projects started by Ismail, and held back the development of education beyond secondary level and rudimentary technical college.

More than anyone else, Baring oversaw the process whereby Britain's tentative hold on Egypt was translated, despite oft-repeated protestations to the contrary, into permanent occupation. The British presence was justified by pointing out the vital importance of reforms being undertaken (as argued by Milner in *England in Egypt* (1892)).

The role of the khedive, first under the accommodating khedive Tawfiq, then his son, the rebellious Abbas II, was emasculated. Puppet ministers continued, in the main, to be chosen from the traditional Turco-Circassian ruling elite rather than from native Egyptians. By the start of the new century, now styled Lord Cromer, the consul-general had become the all-knowing, pompous imperial pro-consul who penned the self-congratulatory account of his own reign, *Modern Egypt* (1908). Here, Cromer proclaims his sympathy for the *fellahin* against the despotic khedive and above the European bondholders. But he postpones to a distant future all prospects of Egyptian self-government, and generally disparages the 'oriental' in the 'Orientalist' mode argued by Edward Said (1978).

Cromer's contemptuous dismissal of the new generation of nationalists led by Mustafa Kamil, compounded by his endorsement of the vicious and vindictive punishments of the *fellahin* exacted in the Denshawai case (1906) in which two villagers were executed and others lashed for causing the death of an English officer who shot pigeons in their village, made him a liability by the time of his retirement in 1907.

Geoff Nash

Literary Works

Blunt, Wilfrid Scawen (1919–20), *My Diaries 1888–1914*, 2 vols, London: Martin Secker.
Soueif, Ahdaf (1999), *The Map of Love*, London: Bloomsbury.

Histories

Al-Sayyid, Afaf Lutfi (1968), *Egypt and Cromer*, London: Longman.
Cromer, Lord (1908), *Modern Egypt*, 2 vols, London: Macmillan.
Mansfield, Peter (1971), *The British in Egypt*, London: Weidenfeld and Nicolson.
Milner, Alfred (1892), *England in Egypt*, London: Edward Arnold.
Said, Edward (1978), *Orientalism, Western Conceptions of the Orient*, London: Routledge and Kegan Paul.

See also: **Balfour Declaration; Historiography: Middle East; Nasser, Abdel Gamal; Nationalism(s): Arab; Suez Crisis.**

Cuban Revolution

Cuba is a small country with a world power mentality. While many attribute this to Fidel Castro's (1927–) exalted socialist vision, what remains constant is his pragmatic world view, his foreign policy on 'internationalism' and the Cuban people's immutable solidarity with the Third World, which has consistently found the country supporting socialist causes abroad and thus ensuring the survival of the revolution for over five decades.

The Cuban journey has not been an easy one. Its culmination in revolution is best understood by an examination of the historical circumstances leading up to it. Independence from Spain came late and at a high price. The Ten Years War fought from 1868 to 1878 was the first incursion to liberation. After the unsuccessful revolt, José Martí (1853–95) founded the Partido Revolucionario Cubano (PRC) and unified islanders of all races in the thrust for independence. US intervention in April 1898 precipitated the Spanish American War. The war ended with the Treaty of Paris, signed on 10 December 1898, which transferred sovereignty to the USA.

Although Cuba was declared a republic in 1902, and America ended its military occupation of the island, the Platt Amendment was instituted. This American legislation established conditions for US intervention in Cuba and allowed the building of the US naval station at Guantánamo Bay, 80 km east of Santiago. Although the Amendment was repealed in 1934, the naval base remained and so too the American occupation of it.

The 1930s and 1940s saw mounting economic difficulty and political instability caused by complete US domination of Cuban agriculture, finance and industry. By 1958, Cuba was a country with one of the highest per capita incomes, but ordinary Cubans survived on the brink of social collapse.

It was against this backdrop of rampant hedonism, excess and poverty that the young lawyer Fidel Castro created the 'Movimiento 26 de Julio' [the 26 of July movement]. The group included the revolutionary Argentinian doctor Ernesto 'Che' Guevara (1928–67). The rebel army made steady gains throughout 1958 culminating with President Fulgencio Batista's flight from the country on 1 January 1959. This victory of 1959 marks the anniversary of the Cuban Revolution's triumph. Castro, who later became commander-in-chief of the armed forces and president of the republic, began to lead the nation down the path of socialism, a move that saw the country square up to the imperialistic might of the USA. In 1961 all political and economic relations were severed. Castro remained the unchallenged leader, and the masses – many of them poor and black and whose living conditions he had improved – rallied behind him. His success as well as that of the revolution is marked by fierce determination.

Finally, more than four decades later, Cuba directly inspires an anti-US sentiment in all of Latin America. In fact Castro and indeed the Cuban Revolution have become icons of Third World resistance, radicalism faced with US hegemony as well as Latin American and Caribbean solidarity and unity.

Nicole Roberts

Literary Works

Arenas, Reinaldo (1993), *Before Night Falls*, trans. D. M. Koch, New York: Viking.
Cabrera Infante, Guillermo (1994), *Mea Cuba*, trans. K. Hall, London: Faber and Faber.

Garcia, Cristina (1992), *Dreaming in Cuban*, New York: Ballantine Books.
Greene, Graham (1958), *Our Man in Havana: An Entertainment*, London: Heineman.

Histories

Miller, Nicola (1993), 'The Intellectual in the Cuban Revolution', in Alistair Hennessy
    (ed.), *Intellectuals in the Twentieth-Century Caribbean. Volume II Unity in Variety: The
    Hispanic and Francophone Caribbean*, London: Macmillan Press Ltd, pp. 83–98.
Montaner, Carlos Alberto (1989), *Fidel Castro and the Cuban Revolution: Age, Position,
    Character, Destiny, Personality and Ambition*, New Brunswick, NJ: Transaction
    Publishers.
Perez Jr, Louis A. (1988), *Cuba: Between Reform and Revolution*, New York: Oxford
    University Press.
Perez Sarduy, Pedro and Jen Stubbs (eds) (1993), *AfroCuba: An Anthology of Cuban Writing
    on Race, Politics and Culture*, Melbourne: Ocean Press; London: Latin American
    Bureau.
Perez-Stable, Marifeli (1993), *The Cuban Revolution: Origins, Course and Legacy*, New
    York: Oxford University Press.
Quirk, Robert E. (1993), *Fidel Castro*, New York: Norton.

See also: **Anti-colonialism and Resistance: Caribbean; Latin America**.

D

Decolonisation

Decolonisation is the process whereby an alien occupying power is expelled from or leaves
a colonised territory, which then becomes politically sovereign. While the term applies to
a variety of historical moments, it is especially apposite for the political transformation that
followed World War II.

At their height in 1919, the European empires ruled more than 72,000,000 square km
and more than 500 million people, that is, over half of the earth's land surface and a third
of its population. The imperial territories – colonies, dominions and protectorates – of
France, Britain, Belgium, the Netherlands, Portugal and Spain included much of Africa,
South Asia, South-east Asia, Australia, Canada, the Middle East and the Caribbean. By
1980, European rule in these areas had virtually ended. This rapid and extensive decolonisation can be understood in terms of the rise of anti-colonial resistance and national-
ism(s), changes in international economic relationships, and a questioning of priorities in
the imperial metropoles.

Colonialism created the structural and ideological conditions for nationalist movements, many of which gained mass support. These anti-colonial movements were frequently spearheaded by charismatic leaders and powerful political parties – Gandhi, Nehru and the Indian National Congress, Nasser in Egypt, Nkrumah in the Gold Coast, which became Ghana, Senghor in Senegal, Kenyatta and the Mau Mau in Kenya, the FLN in Algeria, Sukarno in Indonesia – that were key in precipitating decolonisation. On the international front, the USA and the USSR, which emerged as superpowers after World War II, by and large opposed European imperialism. The creation of the United Nations in 1945, and its recognition of the right of colonised territories to self-determination, also put pressure on the imperial powers to decolonise. In the metropolitan centres, the colonies came to be seen as a drain on financial resources that might otherwise be used by an emerging welfare state.

The actual process of decolonisation was often a violent one, and it was overwhelmingly the subject peoples in the colonies who bore the brunt of this carnage. Even when independence was supposedly achieved peacefully, violence was a direct repercussion of the process of decolonisation. For instance, in the case of India, the decision of the British abruptly to partition the country before they departed meant that organic communities where people of different religions had co-existed relatively peacefully were torn apart: over 1 million people died during the partition riots.

Many argue that decolonisation is itself incomplete. Ngugi (1986), for instance, points to the persistent cultural hegemony of the West and calls for a decolonising of the mind. Neo-colonialism – the continued financial and economic hegemony of the former colonial powers over the decolonised territories – has succeeded colonialism. In other words, the line between the 'colonial' and the 'postcolonial' remains blurred. Indeed, the argument has been made with reference to the Israeli occupation of the West Bank and the US occupation of Iraq that decolonisation in its fundamental geopolitical sense has far from ended, and that the forms of an older mode of colonial occupation persist.

Yumna Siddiqi

Literary Works

Ngugi wa Thiong'o [1963] (1985), *Weep Not, Child*, London: Heinemann.
Rao, Raja [1938] (2000), *Kanthapura*, Delhi: Oxford University Press.
Rushdie, Salman (1980), *Midnight's Children*, New York: A. A. Knopf.
Sidhwa, Bapsi (1991), *Cracking India*, Minneapolis, MN: Milkweed.

Histories

Ansprenger, Franz (1981), *The Dissolution of the Colonial Empires*, London and New York: Routledge.
Cain, P. J. and A. G. Hopkins (1993), *British Imperialism: Crisis and Deconstruction*, London and New York: Longman.
Duara, Prasenjit (ed.) (2004), *Decolonization*, London and New York: Routledge.
Hargreaves, J. D. (1988), *Decolonization in Africa*, London and New York: Longman.
Howe, Stephen (1993), *Anticolonialism in British Politics: The Left and the End of Empire, 1918–1964*, Oxford: Oxford University Press.

Louis, William Roger (1984), *The British Empire in the Middle East, 1945–1951: Arab Nationalism, the United States, and Postwar Imperialism*, Oxford: Oxford University Press.

Ngugi wa Thiong'o (1986), *Decolonising the Mind: The Politics of Language in African Literature*, London: Heinemann.

Porter, A. N. and A. J. Stockwell (1987), *British Imperial Policy and Decolonization, 1938–64*, 2 vols, New York: St Martin's Press.

Springhall, John (2001), *Decolonisation since 1945*, Basingstoke: Palgrave.

Tarling, Nicholas (1993), *The Fall of Imperial Britain in South-East Asia*, New York: Oxford University Press.

See also: **Anti-colonialism and Resistance (all regions); Historiography: British Empire; Partition.**

Detention Centres: Australia

Australian internment and detention policies have contributed significantly to national identity and citizenship debates. During both World Wars, those thought potentially disloyal or not fully committed to the 'cause' came under close surveillance. The government distinguished between citizens and non-citizens, constructing citizenship categories based on country of origin. The treatment of people under suspicion depended on their classification. They were subjected to registration, social control, loss of civil rights, internment, imprisonment or deportation. Many were voluntary internees, struggling because of discrimination and loss of employment.

State approaches to internment varied and the numbers interned bore little relation to the threat. Most of the 4,000 interned during World War I were immigrants (or their descendants) from enemy countries, classified as 'enemy subjects' or 'enemy aliens'. Those persecuted and/or interned in World War II included Nazi and Fascist party members, expatriate employees of German firms, German Jews, recent German and Italian immigrants, former Italian soldiers, Italian farmers from North Queensland, Japanese, European socialists, conscientious objectors, pacifists, communists, Jehovah's Witnesses and members of the Australia First Movement. Of approximately 7,000 internees, 66 per cent were Italians (indicative of pre-war prejudices), 16 per cent Germans and 8 per cent Japanese.

Since 1992, the Australian government has used mandatory detention as part of a broader policy to control and deter 'illegal' arrivals. All non-citizens without a valid visa are detained. Legislation in 1994 and 1999 allowed the removal of 'unauthorised' asylum seekers refused refugee status, and refugees able to access protection elsewhere. The increase in 'people smuggling', 'unauthorised' boat arrivals, and protection visa applications between 1999 and late 2001 prompted more punitive measures. Three-year temporary (rather than permanent) protection visas were adopted. While these policies achieved government objectives, they provoked widespread protest inside and outside the detention centres over alleged human rights violations, the time taken to process applications and the effect of prolonged detention, especially on children. Woomera, the most controversial of the centres, was closed in April 2003; at the same time eight others across Australia remained in operation.

Michele Langfield

Literary Works

Alcorso, Claudio (1993), *The Wind You Say*, Sydney: Angus and Robertson.
Bonutto, Oswald (1963), *A Migrant's Story*, Brisbane: H. Pole.

Histories

Bevege, Margaret (1993), *Behind Barbed Wire: Internment in Australia during World War II*, St Lucia: University of Queensland Press.
Bosworth, Richard and Romano Ugolini (eds) (1992), *War, Internment and Mass Migration: The Italo-Australian Experience 1940–1990*, Rome: Gruppo Editoriale Internazionale.
Crock, Mary and Ben Saul (2002), *Future Seekers, Refugees and the Law in Australia*, Sydney: Federation Press.
Fischer, Gerhard (1989), *Enemy Aliens, Internment and the Homefront Experience in Australia 1914–1920*, St Lucia: University of Queensland Press.
Human Rights and Equal Opportunity Commission (1998), *Those Who've Come across the Seas: Detention of Unauthorised Arrivals*, Commonwealth of Australia.
Mares, Peter (2002), *Borderline: Australia's Treatment of Refugees and Asylum Seekers*, Sydney: University of New South Wales Press.
Nagata, Yuriko (1996), *Unwanted Aliens: Japanese Internment in Australia*, St Lucia: University of Queensland Press.
Saunders, Kay and Roger Daniels (2000), *Alien Justice: Wartime Internment in Australia and North America*, St Lucia: University of Queensland Press.

See also: **Boat People; Pre-colonial Histories: Australia; Refugees.**

Diaspora: Caribbean

The roots of the Caribbean diaspora began when West Indian slaves settled in the New World and Europe along with their masters. Caribbean migration increased after the USA seized Cuba and Puerto Rico from Spain in 1898. The emergence of the USA as a major economic power in the early part of the twentieth century encouraged many West Indians to go there to seek employment. As the Panama Canal project got under way, many West Indians left their homeland to work there as early as 1903, when the USA took over the construction project from the French. World War I in Europe and the Great Depression in the USA affected the tide of Caribbean migration but American and, to a lesser extent, European employers continued to seek seasonal workers from the West Indies.

During World Wars I and II, inter-island migration in the Caribbean increased. After World War II, Caribbean migration continued until the passing of the McCarran-Walker Act in 1952, which restricted the immigration of West Indians into the United States. The trend of seeking employment continued nonetheless in the form of temporary employment visas (H-2).

During the 1950s, West Indians sought employment and better economic conditions by migrating to Great Britain, especially since until 1962 Britain's colonial subjects were also considered British subjects. As Britain began to tighten its immigration laws, with the passing of the Commonwealth Immigrants Act in 1962, West Indians started going to Canada, which also began changing its immigration system. The new Canadian immigration system required immigrants to pass a point test that was applied equally to all applicants. Double-lap migration was another method whereby West Indians went into diaspora. Such persons migrated first to Britain then to Canada, or to Canada then to the USA.

West Indian workers and migrants retained their culture and separate identity in the diaspora. Early Caribbean migrants were mainly single young men (labourers) and women (domestic servants); those who were married usually left their spouses and children back in the West Indies with the intention of sending for them at a later date. Middle-class and educated West Indians also migrated, looking for better opportunities in the West.

Suha Kudsieh

Literary Works

Giscombe, C. S. (2000), *Into and Out of Dislocation*, New York: North Point Press.
Hopkinson, Nalo (1998), *Brown Girl in the Ring*, New York: Warner Books.
Kincaid, Jamaica (1990), *Lucy*, New York: Plume.
Phillips, Caryl (1987), *The European Tribe*, London: Faber and Faber.
Winkler, Anthony C. (1995), *Going Home to Teach*, Kingston: Kingston Publishers.

Histories

Coniff, Michael L. and Thomas J. Davis (eds) (1994), *Africans in the Americas: A History of the Black Diaspora*, New York: St Martin's Press.
Henry, Frances (1994), *The Caribbean Diaspora in Toronto: Learning to Live with Racism*, Toronto: University of Toronto Press.
Palmer, Ransford W. (ed.) (1990), *In Search of a Better Life: Perspectives on Migration from the Caribbean*, New York: Praeger.
Winston, James and Clive Harris (1993), *Inside Babylon: The Caribbean Diaspora in Britain*, New York: Verso.

See also: **Black Britain**; **Slavery: Caribbean**; **United States of America**.

Diaspora: Pacific

Broadly speaking, the dispersal of peoples in the region known as Oceania may be divided into two significant temporal phases: before and after contact with the historical event known as (Western) modernity. The pre-contact phase goes back several thousand years when, it is supposed, waves of Austronesian emigrants sailed from South-east Asia to occupy parts of the central and, later, eastern Pacific. Sections of Melanesia, Micronesia and Polynesia were settled in this manner. These Asian mariners were the original ancestors of the indigenous populations of Oceania. Except for the miserly data thrown up by archaeological finds, we know very little about them. What is known is that they were travelling people in a very special sense, using ocean routes to barter, marry, wage wars and resettle. Whether they ever constituted a diasporic cluster is improbable. For, ideally, the term 'diaspora' refers to a community translocated to an inhabited territory towards which it displays ambivalence. This may be a direct consequence of its experience of the new context or because the home territory exercises a measure of imaginary, cultural or economic influence on its imagination. For genuine examples of groups that adhere to this definition, we have to turn to the post-contact moment, where modernity and its handmaidens (colonialism, industrial agriculture, and so on) deposited migrant clusters in already-peopled territories. While it is true that a scattering of adventurers, missionaries and castaways were already in the region in the early post-contact period, these could not be said to constitute cohesive diasporic fragments.

Not until the introduction of industrial (plantation) agriculture in the 1800s do we see the formation of identifiable diasporic groups from a diverse body of recruited or 'black-birded' labour. It is estimated that more than 100,000 'kanaks' (colonial shorthand for anyone from the Solomon Islands, New Hebrides, the Banks and Torres Strait Islands, the Gilbert Islands and Papua New Guinea) were recruited for sugar, cotton or coconut plantations of Queensland, Fiji, New Caledonia and Samoa. While most returned home, a significant proportion stayed behind in these host territories. For instance, Fiji has a visible community of Solomon islanders in a place called Wailoku. It is often forgotten that Suva's major roads were built on the back of 'kanak' labourers. Colonial forms of labour recruitment also gave rise to a notable Japanese community in Hawaii and a considerable Indian presence in Fiji. Of these older style diasporic communities, the case of the Banaban community is perhaps the most unfortunate. When Ocean Island was virtually mined away for its phosphate, the Banaban community 'resettled' in Rabi, an island in the Fiji group, where they have lived since 1945.

More recently, Pacific islanders have formed vibrant diasporas in the heartlands of modernity. The coups of 1987 and 2000 drove nearly one-fifth of Fiji's Indo-Fijian population to New Zealand, Australia, Canada and the USA, where they continue to experience the despairs and pleasures of a double displacement. There are significant Tongan and Samoan communities in Australia and the USA, and around 170,000 Samoans in New Zealand. According to recent statistics, there are more Niueans in New Zealand than in Niue itself. In fact, Auckland is a veritable cultural hub for Pacific islanders. One of the city's foremost artists is John Pule, a Niuean. The Samoan novelist, Albert Wendt, is based there, as is Raymond Pillai, the Indo-Fijian author.

Although coups, constraints of tradition, lifestyle and economic opportunities account for the migratory trend in most cases, another factor has come into play recently – that of rising sea levels due to global warming. The case of Tuvalu is exemplary. Although some monitoring bodies have found no evidence to support the complaint, Tuvaluan authorities maintain that a number of low-lying atolls are at risk of being completely submerged from tidal flooding. Whatever the truth, the people of the atolls continue to emigrate in substantial numbers. Some 16 per cent of the country's total population now reside permanently in New Zealand. Not too long ago, Tuvalu appealed to Australia to resettle a section of its population, but was turned down.

Sudesh Mishra

Literary Works

Figiel, Sia (1996), *Where We Once Belonged*, Auckland: Pasifika Press.
Figiel, Sia (1999), *They Who Do Not Grieve*, Auckland: Vintage.

Gaskell, Ian (ed.) (2001), *Beyond Ceremony: An Anthology of Drama from Fiji*, Suva: University of the South Pacific.

Mishra, Sudesh (1992), *Tandava*, Melbourne: Meanjin Press.

Mishra, Sudesh (2002), *Diaspora and the Difficult Art of Dying*, Dunedin: Otago University Press.

Nandan, Satendra (1991), *The Wounded Sea*, Sydney: Simon and Schuster.

Pillai, Raymond (1980), *The Celebration*, Suva: University of the South Pacific.

Pule, John (1992), *The Shark that Ate the Sun*, Auckland: Penguin.

Subramani (1988), *The Fantasy Eaters: Stories from Fiji*, Washington, DC: Three Continents.

Thomas, Larry (2002), *To Let You Know and Other Plays*, Suva: Pacific Writing Forum.

Wendt, Albert (1974), *Sons for the Return Home*, Auckland: Longman Paul.

Histories

Edmond, Rod and Vanessa Smith (eds) (2003), *Islands in History and Representation*, London and New York: Routledge.

Howe, K. R., Robert C. Kiste and Brij V. Lal (eds) (1994), *Tides of History. The Pacific Islands in the Twentieth Century*, Sydney: Allen and Unwin.

Lal, Brij V. and Kate Fortune (eds) (2000), *The Pacific Islands: An Encyclopedia*, Hawaii: University of Hawaii Press.

Subramani (1979), *The Indo-Fijian Experience*, St Lucia: University of Queensland Press.

Subramani (1992), *South Pacific Literature: From Myth to Fabulation*, Suva: University of the South Pacific.

Wendt, Albert (1995), *Nuanua: Pacific Writing in English since 1980*, Auckland: Auckland University Press.

See also: **Pacific Sub-imperialism; Pacific Way**.

Diaspora: South Asia

Numerous scholars provide evidence of trade and the movement of people in ancient times between Asia, the Middle East, and the east coast of Africa, and perhaps even further afield. Long before the better known passage of indentured labour from South Asia to various British colonies beginning in the nineteenth century, there is evidence of an earlier transfer of labour. In the semi-historical book, *In an Antique Land*, Amitav Ghosh tells of an Indian slave who had travelled to the Middle East in the twelfth century. How many more there were of his ilk is unknown but the account opens up intriguing possibilities for a study of the South Asian diaspora far back into the past. Buddhist missionary work may well have carried proselytisers beyond the shores of the Indian subcontinent as early as the third century BC, while commerce between India and Egypt could well have sent traders sailing during the Roman Empire, despite the vaunted proscription among Hindus against crossing the waters. Economic historian Richard Pankhurst (2003) suggests that commercial contacts between Ethiopia and India probably date back to pre-Christian times, with written evidence of trade links emerging around the first century AD. There is evidence of periodic and modest immigration of South Asians since then to the Horn of Africa, chiefly through the movement of merchants and craftsmen in the medieval and early modern periods. Exchanges along the Indian ocean routes and within different parts of Asia may thus have a long history that awaits fuller explanation.

In the absence of definitive historical records, accounts of the South Asian diaspora focus on its relatively recent history. Although scholars acknowledge the significance of Indian Ocean trading between 1400 and 1800, most histories of the South Asian diaspora commence in the nineteenth century when the number of migrants becomes noticeably large. As with most mass migrations, the movement of peoples from South Asia to other locations is tied to key developments in history. The abolition of slavery in the mid-nineteenth century in various parts of the West, for instance, created a demand for labour in the plantation economies of the Caribbean islands, British Guiana and Surinam. Indentured labourers from various parts of India signed agreements to work in the colonies, spawning the Hindi neologism 'girmitya' (one who has signed a 'girmit,' corruption of 'agreement'). In addition to exporting labour to the Caribbean, India also supplied a substantial labour force to Mauritius, Natal, and Fiji. While indentured labourers were migrating to plantations overseas, labour from south India was flowing into Sri Lanka even as Indians from other areas were seeking employment and opportunities in Myanmar and Malaya. In rubber plantations, migrants were recruited by headmen known as the 'Kangani'. Despite the abolition of the indenture system in 1920, migration to the Caribbean continued.

The search for jobs and business ventures also propelled many Indians to British East Africa. Although their numbers in the Horn of Africa are not significant today, Saeed Naqvi (2003) tells us that Gujarati businessmen settled in Asmara, the capital of Eritrea, at the turn of the twentieth century when Mussolini decided to make considerable investments in the colony. South Asians were thus taking the initiative to seek employment under systems far less coercive than those common to the indentured and Kangani contract systems.

The dawn of the twentieth century inaugurated waves of immigration into Europe, the USA, Canada and Australia, as well as countries in the Middle East. The colonial connection with Britain ensured a stream of immigration, including many Anglo-Indians who were unsure of their future in the subcontinent after the departure of the British in 1947. As early as the seventeenth century, British company officials would bring servants and nannies back from their sojourns in South Asia. The presence of South Asians, however, becomes numerically significant only after 1950 when a period of acute postwar labour shortage in the UK encouraged a relaxation in immigration policy. The earliest sizable wave of immigrants brought in a workforce of peasants and craftsmen without significant education or professional training. Subsequent generations have demonstrated considerable upward mobility and ingenuity regarding career choices and presence in the mainstream culture. Even though some of this group have moved on to Canada and the USA, numbers in the British South Asian community have grown steadily and are now thought to be in excess of 2 million. Today South Asians in Britain register a powerful economic and cultural presence. Writers such as Hanif Kureishi, Ayub Khan-Dhin, Meera Syal, Romesh Gunesekera, and Sunetra Gupta, and film-makers such as Gurinder Chadha now claim recognition on an international stage.

Across the Atlantic, the numbers of South Asians in USA and Canada may seem substantial today but the population has grown sporadically rather than steadily. Before the Johnson-Reed Immigration Act of 1924 stemmed the tide, no more than 6,400 Asian Indians had gone to America as opposed to about 430,000 Chinese, 380,000 Japanese, and

150,000 Filipinos (Takaki 1989, pp. 63, 65). South Asians were demographically insignif-icant in both countries till the 1960s President Johnson enacted a bill in 1965 that elimi-nated race, religion, and nationality as criteria for immigration, and the Canadian government removed racial and national immigration restrictions in 1967. The volume of South Asians rose dramatically in both countries in the post-1960s period. From 1966 to 1972, for instance, 'immigrants from India [to the United States] totaled 50,990, a number equivalent to more than seventy percent of all the East Indian immigration over the last one hundred and fifty years' (Hess 1976, p. 78). In Canada, approximately 200,000 South Asians arrived between 1971 and 1982, with their numbers growing to over 300,000 by the end of 1982. Idi Amin's expulsion of Ugandan Indians in the 1970s brought 'some 70,000 Indian refugees from business and professional classes . . . under a special clause' to the United States; moreover, 'many overseas Indians also immigrated from other countries, particularly the Caribbean Islands and the British Commonwealth countries' (Sheth 1995, p. 173). According to the 2000 census, the number of people of South Asian origin in the USA stands at a staggering 4 million while being just under a million in Canada, a nation with a total population of some 30 million. The first wave of South Asian immigrants to both countries consisted mostly of those from the uneducated labouring and farming class, although a small number of middle-class students, elites and political refugees were sprin-kled into the mix (Sheth 1995, p. 171). Newer immigrants are better-educated, more eco-nomically empowered, and a good bit more demanding of recognition on a global stage.

The quest for acknowledgment by immigrants comes in various forms. One face of it is represented by South Asian diasporic writers writing back to the centre with award-winning literature. Salman Rushdie and V. S. Naipaul may be the better-known of this stripe, but scores of other writers with origins in the subcontinent have been telling their tales to an appreciative global audience in the last fifty-odd years. Prominent writers resi-dent in Canada and the USA include Talat Abbasi, Meena Alexander, Anita Desai, Chitra Banerjee Divakaruni, Amitav Ghosh, Jhumpa Lahiri, Rohinton Mistry, Bharati Mukherjee, Suniti Namjoshi, Shyam Selvadurai, Bapsi Sidhwa, Shashi Tharoor, and M. G. Vassanji, while a chorus of South Asian voices echo from various parts of the world outside South Asia: Tasleema Nasreen, Farida Karodia, Yasmine Gooneratne, among many others. In the more demotic cultural forms, M. Night Shyamalan is a household name for films like *The Sixth Sense* while Apache Indian, Bally Sagoo, and Tjinder Singh of the group Cornershop, to name only a few, have become familiar names in music.

Another face of the sizeable South Asian diaspora's presence and clamour for recogni-tion is manifest in the growing links of this population with homeland business and poli-tics. Theories of hybridity and liminal identity, foundational concepts in postcolonial studies, often target for study the global dispersal of South Asians while populations in homeland locations remain under-theorised or seen as fundamentally sundered from their expatriate fellows in the diaspora. The rise of the novel phenomenon of a digital diaspora is now beginning to compel a reconceptualisation of the relationship between home and abroad.

The conjunction of media and migration, identified by Arjun Appadurai as the driver of postnational identities in globalisation, is certainly a vital one but not necessarily only for thinking postnationally. A new sort of diasporic formation has begun to take shape through the aid of new technologies, linking expatriate and homeland nationalisms, some-times with unexpected, and frightening consequences. The coming of age of South Asian communities settled abroad and the facilitation of spatial contiguity effected by computer electronics together reinflect issues of identity and nation in unprecedented ways. In the

USA and Canada, South Asian professionals have early taken a lead in the software field, ensuring that expatriate populations stay well acquainted with homeland culture, politics, and socio-historical developments. South Asian use of computers and the internet in these countries involves services and software that introduce Indian classics, languages, and history, provide high-tech job referral services, create a forum for discussions on sub-continental religions, and give recipes and sundry cultural particulars, thus manifestly linking the originary and diasporic worlds. Globalisation has famously expedited the flows of all that was capable of being mobile: labour, capital, culture, ideology. Along with the rapid exchange and international trade of cultural flows that allow books written by authors in India to become overnight bestsellers on the *New York Times* list, nationalisms and relig-ious fundamentalisms, too, are being circulated by the new technologies of our times as the numbers of domestic internet users climbs. South Asians abroad, however, are not only consumers of national culture but its producers as well, since their investment in its pres-ervation is a function of psychic needs fostered by the very condition of diaspora.

A network of electronic resources such as television serials, music and film cassettes and CDs, and websites not only keeps the diasporic population connected with the homeland culture, but can sometimes fuel a supernationalism in South Asians abroad. If anything, nationalism is not only alive and well but it may have found a new lease of life both through media and through migration. Although the possibilities for imagining transnational sodal-ities are certainly more available than ever before because of new communication technol-ogies, older ways of thinking based on bounded territorial and cultural forms of community continue to persist. If print capitalism, as Benedict Anderson so famously argued, was the engine of nationalist movements and thinking in modern times, a form of electronic cap-italism is today powering the continuum between diasporic and homeland nationalisms alongside a resurgence in religious identitarianism.

The 'South Asian' that has begun to emerge on the global socio-political scene more recently is the result of the intersection of past histories with present conditions, arising from the more pronounced South Asian presence in the West in general and Anglo-America in particular. Aware of the economic, psychic, and social benefits enjoyed by cit-izens of powerful nations like the United States and Canada, diasporic communities are no less desirous of promoting a strong national presence globally for their nations of origin. This digitally-enabled South Asian citizenry reflects a lifestyle filled with the rewards of modernity and a mindset saturated with its values; values which include instrumental rationality on the one hand and a commitment to a universalist end of history character-ised by economic and political liberalism on the other. At the same time, however, capi-talist modernity also entails a neo-Darwinist struggle for ascendancy in the global order of nations and immersion in ceaseless competition between various economic forces and interests. The junction between these two value-structures can be good for the home economy which benefits from the export of capital and job creation in the homeland through the off-shoring of production – a phenomenon that is becoming more common in globalisation. At the same time, however, investment in the idea of a strong state may stim-ulate expatriate promotion of totalitarian agendas in the homeland. There is evidence of religious or ethnic nationalism being directly funded and fuelled in many a South Asian state, by diasporic compatriots. The speed of the internet and its ability to collapse dis-tances make it a crucial ally in the dissemination of information, propaganda, petitions, and fund-raising campaigns.

It is not yet clear whether digital nationalism among South Asians will ever be over-taken by digital crusades for civil society, peace, democracy and the environment in the homeland. Such cyber-communities may teach us that the resources of the digital media are available not only for the promotion of exclusionary and totalitarian discourses but peaceable and democratic ones as well.

Deepika Petraglia-Bahri

Literary Works

Alexander, Meena (1996), *The Shock of Arrival: Reflections on Postcolonial Experience*, Boston, MA: South End Press.

Aziz, Nurjehan (ed.) (1994), *Her Mother's Ashes, and Other Stories by South Asian Women in Canada and the United States*, Toronto: TSAR Publications.

Desai, Anita (1980), *Clear Light of Day*, London: Heinemann.

Gunesekera, Romesh (1994), *Reef*, London: Granta.

Maira, Sunaina and Rajini Srikanth (eds) (1996), *Contours of the Heart: South Asians Map North America*, New York: Asian American Writers' Workshop.

Parmasad, Kenneth Vidia (ed.) (1984), *Indian Folk Tales of the Caribbean, a First Collection: Salt and Roti*, Chaguanas, Trinidad and Tobago: Sankh Productions.

Rustomji-Kerns, Roshni (ed.) (1995), *Living in America: Poetry and Fiction by South Asian American Writers*, Boulder, CO: Westview Press.

Selvadurai, Shyam (1994), *Funny Boy*, San Diego, CA: Harvest Books, Harcourt Brace and Company.

Syal, Meera (1997), *Anita and Me*, London: Flamingo.

Vassanji, M. G. (ed.) (1985), *A Meeting of Streams: South Asian Canadian Literature*, Toronto: TSAR Publications.

Women of South Asian Descent Collective (eds) (1993), *Our Feet Walk the Sky: Women of the South Asian Diaspora*, San Francisco: Aunt Lute Books.

Histories

Anderson, Benedict (1983), *Imagined Communities*, London: Verso.

Appadurai, Arjun (1996), *Modernity at Large: Cultural Dimensions of Globalization*, Minneapolis, MN: University of Minnesota Press.

Coward, Harold, John R. Hinnells, and Raymond Brady Williams (eds) (2000), *The South Asian Religious Diaspora in Britain, Canada, and the United States*, Albany, NY: SUNY Press.

Ghosh, Amhitav (1992), *In an Antique Land*, New Delhi: Ravi Dayal Publisher.

Hess, Gary R. (1976), 'The Forgotten Asian Americans: The East Indian Community in the United States', in Norris Hundley (ed.), *The Asian American: The Historical Experience*, Santa Barbara, CA: Clio, pp. 157–77.

Mishra, Pramod Kumar and Urmila Mohapatra (2001), *South Asian Diaspora in UK: A bibliographical study*, Delhi: Kalinga Publications.

Mishra, Pramod Kumar and Urmila Mohapatra (2002), *South Asian Diaspora in North America: an Annotated Bibliography*, Delhi: Kalinga Publications.

Naqvi, Saeed (2003), 'Someone Else's Peace: Two Warring Nations and an Indian Contingent in Africa', 20 August. Available at http://www.indianexpress.com/columnists/saee/20010615.html

Nasta, Susheila (2002), *Home Truths: Fictions of the South Asian Diaspora in Britain*, Basingstoke: Hampshire; New York: Palgrave.

Pankhurst, Richard (2003), 'Ethiopian-Indian Relations in Ancient and Early Medieval Times', 29 August. Available at http://www.civicwebs.com/cwvlib/africa/ethiopia/pankhurst/ethiopia_across_red_sea_&_indian_ocean.htm#1.2

Puwar, Nirmal and Parvati Raghuram (eds), (2003), *South Asian Women in the Diaspora*, Oxford: Berg.

Sheth, Manju (1995), 'Asian Indian Americans', in Pyong Gap Min (ed.), *Asian Americans: Contemporary Trends and Issues*, Thousand Oaks, CA: Sage, pp. 169–98.

Sugunasiri, Suwanda H. J. (1987), *The Literature of Canadians of South Asian Origins: An Overview and Preliminary Bibliography*, Toronto: Multicultural History Society of Ontario.

Takaki, Ronald (1989), *Strangers from a Different Shore: A History of Asian Americans*, New York: Penguin.

Van der Veer, Peter (ed.) (1995), *Nation and Migration: The Politics of Space in the South Asian Diaspora*, Philadelphia: University of Philadelphia Press.

Visram, Rozina (2002), *Asians in Britain: 400 Years of History*, London: Pluto Press.

See also: **Diaspora: Caribbean; Historiography: South Asia; Indentured Labour: Caribbean; Indians: Southern Africa; Kala Pani; World Wars I and II: South Asian Soldiers.**

Dutch East India Company (VOC)

Dutch interest in South-east Asia began in earnest with Jan Huyghen van Linschoten who served under the Portuguese Archbishop of Goa (1583–9). Linschoten published a record of his travels (*Reysgeschrift* (1595) and *Itinerario* (1596) after his return to Europe, which gave away Portuguese secrets concerning the important trade routes to the Far East. The book was immediately translated into other European languages and played an important role in the foundation of the Dutch and English East India Companies. The Dutch quickly established a foothold in Indonesia, exploiting the negative reputation which the Portuguese had earned with many locals. Contrary to other European powers at the time, the Dutch made it their policy not to mix trade and piracy, and since their ships were superior to the Portuguese, they were also more competitive.

At the time of the Dutch military victory in the Moluccas (Maluku), Jan Pieterszoon Coen was building up a trade imperium with Batavia (Jakarta) as its headquarters. The Batavian Empire spread its reign throughout the archipelago and the British traders in Ambon were arrested and executed in 1623. From then on the British concentrated their efforts on India, while the Dutch controlled trade in much of the Indonesian archipelago.

Further wars under Governor-General van Diemen against the Portuguese, led to the Portuguese displacement from Malacca and Ceylon, and the establishment of factories in India, Cambodia, and Taiwan. Finally, the Netherlands was the only European nation with access to Japan. Exploration by Dutch merchant ships led to the 'discovery' of Australia, New Zealand and numerous islands, most famously during Abel Tasman's expeditions. Economically, however, these expeditions failed to deliver what the company wanted, and the expansionist period of the VOC ended with Tasman's unsuccessful expeditions and the Dutch capture of Malacca.

The Netherlands power was overthrown by France and Britain in the 1700s, and from then on it merely sought to hold onto its possessions in South-east Asia. Without the military might to support their trading posts the Dutch lost ground and the company itself became gradually immersed in heavy debts, and finally dissolved at the end of 1799. However, the Dutch colonial empire replaced the VOC, which the Dutch government had subsidised since 1781.

Lars Jensen

Literary Works

Dekker, Edouard Douwes [1860] (1982), *Max Havelaar*, Amherst, MA: University of Massachusetts Press.

Histories

Beekman, E. M. (1996), *Dutch Colonial Literature from the East Indies 1600–1950*, Oxford: Clarendon Press.
Boxer, C. R. (1965), *The Dutch Seaborne Empire 1600–1800*, New York: Knopf.
Bruijn, J. R. and F. Gaastra (eds) (1993), *Ships, Sailors and Spices: East India Companies and their Shipping in the 16th, 17th and 18th Centuries*, Amsterdam: International Institute of Social History.
Landwehr, John P. and P. J. van der Krogt (eds) (1991), *VOC: A Bibliography of Publications Relating to the Dutch East India Company, 1602–1825*, Utrecht: Hes Publishers.
Meilink-Roelofsz, M. A. P. (1992), *The Archives of the Dutch East India Company (1602–1795)*, Gravenhage: Sdu Uitgeverij.
Zandvliet, Keet (1998), *Mapping for Money: Maps, Plans and Topographic Paintings and their Role in Dutch Overseas Expansion during the 16th and 17th Centuries*, Amsterdam: Batavian Lion International.

See also: **East India Company; Free Trade; Hudson's Bay Company; Levant Company.**

E

East Asia

East Asia, traditionally including China, Taiwan, Japan and Korea, presents complex histories and theoretical frameworks for postcolonial studies. Unlike the African, South American, Australian, Indian, and other South Asian colonial and postcolonial histories, which are defined primarily via the Western/European powers in which the 'oppressive other' is unambiguously the West, in East Asia, one of the chief colonising forces that shaped much of its recent history is its own: Japan.

In the name of anti-colonialism against the West, in the nationalist language of unifying Asia in order to protect itself from the Western Imperial expansion, Japan had become a dominant colonising force against Korea, Manchuria, areas of China, Philippines, Indonesia, and other parts of South-east Asia from the late 1800s to the end of World War II in 1945. However, the postcolonial reactions against Japan and the degrees to which the Japanese colonial experiences mark and shape the recent histories differ considerably among these colonised or partially-colonised nations. Korea, for example, has a clear and fairly unanimous stance against the history of Japanese occupation and colonisation, while Taiwan presents a different case because of the co-presence of the Japanese Imperial Army and the Chinese National Army both trying to conquer it. Hong Kong's history is shaped by Great Britain (thus resembling the more standard post-European postcolonial history) as much as the Japanese occupation. Thus, the analysis of the postcolonial histories of East Asia must involve not only the traditional postcolonial discourse via the European forms of colonialism adopted by the Japanese in its process of modernisation/Westernisation, but also its application in the Asian context against other Asian nations. Postcolonial histories must also take on board the complex identities of the colonised cultures within Asia against one of their own, mediated as their stances often were toward the West.

First, a brief history of Japanese colonialism. With the arrival of the American 'Black Ships' led by Commodore Perry in 1853, Japan ended its 250 years of isolation from the rest of the world; and with the establishment of the new imperial government in 1868, Japan began its process of rapid modernisation. It quickly adopted Western-style industrialisation and expansionist trade policies, and with the Sino-Japanese war of 1894–5, Japan battled against China over the Korean peninsula, acquiring territory in the north as well as Taiwan (then known as Formosa). With the Russo-Japanese war of 1904–5, it defeated Russia over Manchuria.

Through World War I and the 1929 Great Depression, the leading Western nations were forming trade and economic 'blocs' and continued to expand their colonial presence in South and South-east Asia. In order to resist Western colonial expansion and to pursue a vision of an 'Asian bloc', Japan aggressively began its own colonial expansion in Asia in an attempt to secure resources and geographical consolidation. In 1931 Japan invaded Manchuria (known as the Manchurian Incident) and took control of the South Manchuria Railway Company. After this Japan also extended its colonial policies to Korea and solidified its activities there. In 1937 Japan began its brutal invasion of China (The Rape of Nanking Incident in which more than 300,000 civilians were killed), and continued to move south to the territories of French Indo-China.

With the attack of Pearl Harbor in 1941, Japan entered the Pacific war, continuing its expansion into other parts of China, Formosa, and the Philippines. During the Pacific war years, the Japanese imperial army exploited more than 4 million Korean and Chinese citizens, primarily for labour, who were transferred to various locations throughout the Japanese Empire. By 1942 the Japanese military effort to establish the Greater East-Asian Co-Prosperity Sphere (*dai to-a kyo-ei ken*) was in place, which was its vision of the 'Asian bloc' led by the Japanese imperial house. Its borders included not only Korea, China, Formosa, and Manchuria but extended as far as the Philippines, Thailand and Burma. Some leading Japanese intellectuals, including the philosophers from the Kyoto School, were participating in a series of roundtable discussions that were published in national intellectual journals, in order to discuss the role and philosophy of Japanese leadership in Asia. This series of discussions during 1942 and 1943, called the 'Overcoming of (European) Modernity' (*kindai no chokoku*) debates, focused on the possibility of creating an alternative, 'non-Western' form of modernity arising out of Japanese culture, and spreading across East Asia under Japanese imperialism. By late 1944 and early 1945, the Japanese navy was losing much of its power. After the atomic bombings of Hiroshima and Nagasaki during August 1945, Japan finally submitted to an unconditional surrender to America. (For an overview and chronological developments, see Beasley 1991.)

The postcolonial period in East Asia after the Japanese surrender was complex. On the one hand, some historians argue that as Japan established numerous industries in the colonies, the infrastructure (railroads, factories, urban planning, schools) helped modernise the respective nations. The acceptance of Japanese presence, for example, was higher in Indonesia, where the Japanese occupation helped the Dutch to withdraw. The current anti-Japanese sentiments are relatively low in Taiwan in comparison to Korea and China. Taiwanese in China experienced worse conditions under the occupation by the Chinese National Army. On the other hand, the terrible legacy of Japanese violence and terror have left permanent and deep scars among the people. Koreans, Chinese and Manchurians were forced to adopt Japanese names and learn Japanese 'in order to become more civilised', their sacred lands were occupied and confiscated, their centuries-old traditions eradicated, their men shipped out to labour camps and their young women taken away to be 'comfort women', a government-sanctioned prostitution network run by the Japanese imperial army. Families were broken up, people were dislocated, their dignity and national/cultural identities were stripped away, and countless lives were sacrificed in labour camps and medical experiments (for example, the infamous case known as the Medical Unit 731 in China, where Japanese doctors conducted a number of experiments on humans including work on germ warfare and vivisection).

It is therefore not surprising that today's postcolonial literature of East Asia focuses not only on the standard postcolonial trope of personal testimonies, memory narratives and dislocated identities, but also offers complex critiques of multi-layered power. It analyses the structures of double or triple levels of colonial oppression (against the West and Japan, or the West, Japan, and men; or in Taiwanese women's case, a quadruple layering: the West, Japan, the Chinese, and men). The layers are, moreover, mediated by Japan, a force 'from within' which nevertheless adopted a Western modernisation discourse (including expansionism and colonialism), but presented itself as a sympathetic liberator of Asia from the threats of Western colonialism, arguing that it offered a radically different model of governance and theories of national identities. The Kyoto School philosophers (the students of Kitaro Nishida – Nishitani, Kosaka, Koyama), for example, theorised that the spiritual roots of East Asia – specifically Buddhism – guaranteed that Japan could not simply be another aggressor, like the Western powers, since the metaphysics of 'nothingness' or 'emptiness' made the Japanese identity 'empty' and its presence should be considered more like a 'place' or a 'field' in which all other Asian nations could express their national identities and thrive according to their own cultural traditions (see Nishida 1996).

In the light of what was actually happening in Asia under brutal Japanese expansion, such theorising should have been condemned as justifying imperial policies, but in the sweeping nationalism of the day, such ideas became not only accepted but welcomed. During the postwar period, however, most of these Kyoto School thinkers were charged with complicity with the ultranationalist government (Nishitani, for example was expelled from his teaching post) and Japanese philosophy in general came to be regarded as belonging to the darkest period of recent Japanese history (and therefore to be forgotten). However, the legacy continues. Today, the students of Nishitani, now in their second generation, continue to defend the theoretical efforts made by their predecessors, claiming that Japanese philosophy may indeed be able to offer an alternative model of national identities, and that its historical and philosophical contribution cannot be ignored. This was one of the earliest forms of anti-Eurocentric theory-making which was based on resources other than Western theories.

Among the critical works, Tani Barlow's 450-page edited volume, *Formations of Colonial Modernity in East Asia* (1997), is an excellent collection that gathers postcolonial reflections in China, Okinawa, Hong Kong, Korea, as well as Japan's assimilation of the 'imagined' West. Many of the essays are reprints from the inaugural volume of *Positions*, a journal dedicated to contemporary literary critiques focusing on East Asia. Leo Ching's *Becoming 'Japanese'* (2001) focuses specifically on the complex Taiwanese identities formed at the intersection of the Japanese occupation, the Chinese occupation, and negotiations with its own indigenous history. It is an excellent study of how a colonial and postcolonial discourse can go well beyond the standard model of the oppressor and the oppressed. Lisa Yoneyama's *Hiroshima Traces* (1999) is also an extremely valuable study of memory-construction in postwar Japan. Although Japan was never colonised by the USA, the postwar occupation and subsequent influence of America had a tremendous impact on how Japan constructed its own postwar narrative, and no such account is complete without a careful analysis of the representation of Hiroshima – the first city ever to be a victim of atomic bombing. In particular, the book offers an insightful analysis of the feminised 'peace discourse' as well as 'Japan as victim' in the nationally-constructed Hiroshima narrative. It also makes a contribution in its inclusion of the often-erased voices of the Korean minority in Hiroshima at that time, while Japan was still a colonial power in Korea.

Among the historical studies, by far the most controversial is Iris Chang's *The Rape of Nanking* (1997). The book contains numerous historical facts regarding the incident that are bitterly contested by some Japanese historians and other public intellectuals. In particular, the Chinese and American historians of East Asia were quite unprepared for the level of Japanese defensiveness and aggressiveness in the attempts to discredit the book. In conjunction with the controversies surrounding Japan's inability to take responsibility for the issue of Korean comfort women, the reception of Chang's book painfully highlights the fact that bitter postcolonial legacies are still very much alive and contentious between China and Japan as well as Korea and Japan.

Ramon Myers and Mark Peattie's 500-page anthology, *The Japanese Colonial Empire, 1895–1945* (1984), is perhaps the most comprehensive collection of essays on the nature of Japanese colonialism and its legacies. It contains fourteen excellent essays by the leading historians of East Asia, focusing on topics such as the meaning of the Japanese colonial empire, its management, the economic dynamics, historical contexts, and global contexts. Stefan Tanaka's *Japan's Orient* (1995) is a good example of literary postcolonial historiography, following Edward Said's seminal work, *Orientalism*. Tanaka's reconstruction offers an interesting analysis of how Japan created its discourse of national identity vis-à-vis the West as well as China during the post-Meiji Restoration period (after 1853). It problematises historical representation and presents an ideological critique of how Japan came to have its own self-consciousness as a 'modern nation', situating itself to be a unified power against China.

In comparison to the vast and well-developed South Asian literature on postcolonialism, the material on East Asia is much sparser. Given the complexity of the subject, further analyses as well as reconstructions of East Asian postcolonial histories are much needed and should continue.

Yoko Arisaka

Literary Works

Keller, Nora Okja (1997), *Comfort Woman*, New York: Viking.
Kimura, Hisao (1990), *Japanese Agent in Tibet*, Chicago: Serindia.
Tanizaki, Junichiro [1924] (2001), *Naomi*, New York: Random House.
Teo Hsu-Ming (2001), *Love and Vertigo*, Sydney: Allen and Unwin.

Histories

Barlow, Tani (ed.) (1997), *Formations of Colonial Modernity in East Asia*, Durham, NC and London: Duke University Press.
Beasley, William (1991), *Japanese Imperialism 1894–1945*, Oxford: Clarendon Press.
Chang, Iris (1997), *The Rape of Nanking: The Forgotten Holocaust of World War II*, New York: Penguin Books.
Chang, Sung-sheng Yvonne (1997), 'Beyond Cultural and National Identities: Current Reevaluation of the *Kominka* Literature from Taiwan's Japanese Period', *Journal of Modern Literature in Chinese* 1:1, pp. 75–107.
Ching, Leo (2001), *Becoming 'Japanese': Colonial Taiwan and the Politics of Identity Formation*, Berkeley, CA: University of California Press.
Positions: East Asia Cultures Critique, Durham, NC: Duke University Press.
Duus, Peter (1998), *The Abacus and the Sword: The Japanese Penetration of Korea, 1895–1910*, Berkeley, CA: University of California Press.
Gold, Hal (1996), *Unit 731 Testimony*, Boston and Tokyo: Charles E. Tuttle Publishing.
Hicks, George (1997), *The Comfort Women: Japan's Brutal Regime of Enforced Prostitution in the Second World War*, New York: Norton and Company.
Mendel, Douglas (1970), *The Politics of Formosan Nationalism*, Berkeley, CA: University of California Press.
Myers, Ramon and Mark Peattie (eds) (1984), *The Japanese Colonial Empire, 1895–1945*, Princeton, NJ: Princeton University Press.
Nishida, Kitaro (1996), 'The Principle of the New World Order', trans. in Y. Arisaka, 'Nishida Enigma', *Monumenta Nipponica* 51:1, pp. 81–99.
Sakai, Naoki (1997), *Translation and Subjectivity: On Japan and Cultural Nationalism*, Minneapolis, MN: University of Minnesota Press.
Schmid, Andre (2002), *Korea Between Empires*, New York: Columbia University Press.
Shin, Gi-Wook and Michael Robinson (eds) (2001), *Colonial Modernity in Korea*, Cambridge, MA: Harvard University Press.
Tanaka, Stefan (1995), *Japan's Orient: Rendering Pasts in History*, Berkeley, CA: University of California Press.
Yoneyama, Lisa (1999), *Hiroshima Traces: Time, Space, and the Dialectics of Memory*, Berkeley, CA: University of California Press.
Young, Louise (1998), *Japan's Total Empire: Manchuria and the Culture of Wartime Imperialism*, Berkeley, CA: University of California Press.

See also: **Historiography: South-east Asia; Women's Histories: South-east Asia; Yellow Peril**.

East India Company

On 31 December 1600, Queen Elizabeth I granted the East India Company a trade monopoly in the East Indies. Initially, the company established factories along the coastlines to compete with rival European firms. How this company of traders became a ruling government is a subject of ongoing debate. Earlier scholarship suggests that the British conquered India in a fit of absent-mindedness. More recent work, however, divides those who emphasise historical continuity and Indian collaboration from those who define the 'transition to colonialism' as a historical rupture enabled by military conquest and resulting in the transformation of Indian culture and society.

A decisive moment in the company's history was the Battle of Plassey (1757), when Robert Clive defeated the Nawab of Bengal. Shortly after Clive's victory, the Mughal emperor granted the company the right to collect revenue and administer justice in Bengal. This not only made the company servants 'trader-sovereigns', it also had crucial implications for economic relations. Land revenues allowed the company to buy Indian goods with Indian money. Taxes (rather than trade) were increasingly used to satisfy shareholders in Britain and to fund military expansionism in India. The plunder of eastern India had a devastating impact on indigenous land-holding patterns and on the Bengali people, one-third of whom died during the famine of 1769–70. Economic historians have described 'company Raj' (1757–1857) as a period of deindustrialisation in which little was done to promote Indian economic development. Early company rule was guided by the policy of non-intervention, which held that existing social, political and economic institutions should provide the basis for British governance. The company financed Orientalist institutions to produce written digests of Indian languages, laws, and religions. Working with elite interpreters, the knowledge produced by scholars such as William Jones resulted in the textualisation and reinvention of the traditions they aimed to preserve.

In 1813, the company's monopoly was broken and missionaries were permitted entry into India. The Christian concept of the civilising mission and the rise of liberalism contributed to important shifts in colonial ideology and practice. Hailing the promise of modernity and self-governance, company officials during the Age of Reform (1828–56) sought to transform Indian society by introducing free trade, English education, and legal reforms. As a result of territorial annexation and economic oppression, in 1857, large segments of Indian society revolted. Fourteen months later, the rebellion was brutally suppressed and the Crown took direct control of India.

Elizabeth Kolsky

Literary Works

Hyder, Qurratulain (2003), *River of Fire*, New York: New Directions.
Ray, Satyajit (1977), *The Chess Players* (film adaptation of Munshi Premchand's story, *Shatranj ke Khiladi*).
Saraogi, Alka (2002), *Kalikatha: Via Bypass*, Calcutta: Rupa and Company.
Sealy, Allan (1988), *The Trotter-Nama*, New York: Knopf.

Histories

Bayly, C. A. (1988), *Indian Society and the Making of the British Empire*, Cambridge: Cambridge University Press.
Cohn, Bernard (1996), *Colonialism and its Forms of Knowledge*, Princeton, NJ: Princeton University Press.
Dalrymple, William (2003), *White Mughals*, New York: Viking.
Guha, Ranajit (1981), *A Rule of Property for Bengal*, London: Mouton.
Teltscher, Kate (1995), *India Inscribed: European and British Writing on India 1600–1800*, Delhi: Oxford University Press.

See also: **Free Trade; Governors-General and Viceroys; Historiography: South Asia; Mutinies in India; Raj.**

East Timor

On 30 August 1999, the people of East Timor voted overwhelmingly in favour of independence from Indonesia after twenty-five years of brutal occupation, preceded by almost 400 years of Portuguese colonisation. The tiny nation was subsequently granted formal independence on 20 May 2002 following two years of United Nations administration supported by a multinational peace-keeping force.

From the early 1970s educated East Timorese elites, many of whom had studied in Portugal, were discussing their dissatisfaction with colonial rule. Following the collapse of Portugal's Caetano regime in 1974, an immediate policy of decolonisation was embarked upon. Portugal sanctioned political associations in East Timor, out of which emerged the left-wing FRETILIN party and the conservative pro-Portugal UDT. However, the Indonesians launched a clandestine destabilisation campaign resulting in a bloody civil war between UDT and FRETILIN in August 1975. With East Timor by now virtually abandoned by the Portuguese, FRETILIN declared independence in November fearing invasion was imminent. Indonesia's illegal invasion took place in December 1975 and led to twenty-five years of violent occupation. It is estimated more than 200,000 East Timorese died during that time.

Timorese resistance was met by sustained bombing campaigns, mass starvation, cultural genocide and relocations of non-compliant villagers. A strong campaign was advanced internally by FRETILIN's guerrilla army, known as FALINTIL, and externally by exiles in Australia and Portugal. Following the death of leader Nicolau Lobato, new commander, Xanana Gusmão, broke FALINTIL into mobile guerrilla units in 1981, supported by a sophisticated clandestine network across East Timor.

Despite his capture and imprisonment by the Indonesians in 1992, Xanana managed to facilitate a coalition between former enemies, UDT and FRETILIN, under what became known as the CNRT (National Council of Timorese Resistance) which was a significant achievement. Meanwhile, José Ramos-Horta, among others, helped to advance East Timor's cause in exile from bases in Australia, Portugal and New York, working closely with the UN and significant Timorese and non-Timorese solidarity networks. He and East Timor's Bishop Belo jointly won the 1996 Nobel Peace Prize for their efforts. Along with the publicity surrounding the 1991 Dili massacre, the Nobel Prize was seen as instrumental in harnessing international support for the Timorese cause. The downfall of Indonesia's President Soeharto in 1998 signalled the beginning of the end of the occupation.

Amanda Wise

Literary Works

Cardoso, Luis (2000), *The Crossing: A Story of East Timor*, London: Granta.
Da Costa, Francisco Borja (1976), *Revolutionary Poems in the Struggle against Colonialism: Timorese Nationalist Verse*, Sydney: Wild and Woolley.
Mo, Timothy (1991), *The Redundancy of Courage*, London: Chatto and Windus.
Sylvan, Fernando (1999), *Timor Livro, A Lenda De Timor*, Aveiro: Universidade de Aveiro.

Histories

Gunn, Geoffrey (1999), *Timor Loro Sae: 500 years*, Lisbon: Livros do Oriente.
Gusmao, Xanana (2000), *To Resist is to Win!: The Autobiography of Xanana Gusmao*, ed. Sarah Niner, Melbourne: Aurora.
Ramos-Horta, Jose (1987), *Funu*, New York: Red Sea Press.
Taylor, John G. (1999), *East Timor: The Price of Freedom*, Sydney: Pluto Press.
Turner, Michelle (1992), *Telling: East Timor, Personal Testimonies 1942–1992*, Sydney: New South Wales University Press.

See also: **Asianisation: Australia; Britain's Postwar Foreign Policy**.

Emergency: India

The state of emergency in India (1975–7) was an eighteen-month hiatus in the nation's normal democratic processes. A range of forces brought Prime Minister Indira Gandhi from the pinnacle of national admiration as victor of the 1971 war with Pakistan, to an isolated and paranoid despotism in three and a half short years. Perhaps most important were a series of economic crises in the early 1970s. At the same time there was an increased radicalisation of certain sections of the population. The Naxalite peasant insurgency spread to other parts of the country, while the ranks of the disaffected were swelled by large numbers of unemployed from the educated, professional classes. Forms of direct action included a series of strikes, most famously the all-India rail strike of 1974. The same period saw Indira Gandhi isolated, and coming to rely on an ever-smaller band of close confidants, centralising more and more power in her own hands. The atmosphere of embattled authoritarianism was ripe for abuses, and the early 1970s were marked by a rise in peremptory arrests, the fettering of prisoners, torture and 'disappearances'.

The immediate constitutional precursor to the emergency was a decision of the Allahabad High Court, early in June 1975, that Indira Gandhi had been guilty of electoral malpractices in relation to the 1971 general election. The court decreed that she should be debarred from holding public office for six years. However, citing the growing tide of 'internal disturbances' threatening India, Mrs Gandhi instructed the president of India to announce a state of emergency just before midnight on 25 June. Opposition leaders, and even suspect members of Mrs Gandhi's own Congress Party, were taken from their beds and interned: the right to trial was effectively suspended; public meetings were banned; newspapers were subject to strict controls; and even the writings on freedom by Indira's father Jawaharlal Nehru, and Mahatma Gandhi were censored (Ali 1985, p. 185). Indira even introduced constitutional amendments conferring on herself retrospective immunity from prosecution in respect of past or future criminal offences. However, perhaps the most sinister elements of the emergency were initiated by Indira's son and heir-apparent, Sanjay, who, despite having no electoral mandate, used his power base in Youth Congress to add some ideas of his own to his mother's 'Twenty Point Programme' for national rejuvenation – including slum clearance and family planning. The former often meant clearing the poor away from areas which they had improved and made habitable themselves, so they could be utilised by property developers; while the latter turned into what has been described as 'a grotesque carnival of abduction, mutilation and disease' (Adams and Whitehead 1997, p. 261), as people were forced and tricked into being sterilised. With the situation apparently stabilised, Indira called a general election early in 1977, but the ill feeling created by the emergency ensured her wing of the Congress Party was soundly beaten.

Peter Morey

Literary Works

Mistry, Rohinton (1996), *A Fine Balance*, London: Faber and Faber.
Rushdie, Salman (1981), *Midnight's Children*, London: Picador.
Sahgal, Nayantara (1987), *Rich Like Us*, London: Sceptre.
Tharoor, Shashi (1989), *The Great Indian Novel*, London: Viking.

Histories

Adams, Jad and Phillip Whitehead (1997), *The Dynasty: The Nehru–Gandhi Story*, Harmondsworth: Penguin.
Ali, Tariq (1985), *The Nehrus and the Gandhis: An Indian Dynasty*, London: Picador.
Dhar, P. N. (2000), *Indira Gandhi, the 'Emergency' and Indian Democracy*, New Delhi: Oxford University Press.
Sahgal, Nayantara (1983), *Indira Gandhi: Her Road to Power*, London: Macdonald and Company.
Selbourne, David (1977), *An Eye to India: The Unmasking of a Tyranny*, London: Pelican.

See also: **Nehru, Jawaharlal**.

English in India: Eighteenth and Nineteenth Centuries

In 1769, the 11-year-old Dean Mahomet (1759–1851), resident of Patna, attached himself to the company of the teenage Anglo-Irish Ensign, Godfrey Evan Baker. This decision not only took Mahomet across much of India and, finally, to a prosperous existence in Brighton and Bath, but it also led, in 1794, to the publication of the first extant book in English by an Indian. Mahomet justified the writing of this book, an account of his travels in India framed as an epistolary narrative addressed to a fictional patron, in these words, 'I felt some timid inclination, even in the consciousness of incapacity, to describe the manners of my countrymen, who, I am proud to think, have still more the innocence of our ancestors, than some of the boasting philosophers of Europe.'

It is significant that Mahomet chose to join the East India Company and work for the British. Surely, the first texts written in English by Indians must have been administrative and bureaucratic texts. We see a vast profusion of them – some verging on the socio-historical – in the nineteenth century. M. K. Naik lists the twenty-eight-page essay 'Account of the Jains' by C. V. Boriah as the earliest extant work in English by an Indian in this genre. The essay was included in *Asiatic Researches or Translations of the Society Instituted in Bengal for Inquiring into the History and Antiquities, the Art, Sciences and Literature of Asia* (1776–1803), but, as Mahomet's book suggests, South Asians working for the British would have been capable of writing in English from the 1750s. The question of what the choice of English implied is too intricate to be settled here, but it is revealing to refer to other travel accounts of the period: for example, Abu Taleb Khan's Farsi (Persian) travel book, written less than a decade after Mahomet's book. Khan, who learnt English on the ships that took him, via Africa, to Ireland and England, had a different excuse to commit his experiences to paper. He wished 'to describe the curiosities and wonders' which he saw in Europe, which he hoped 'would afford a gratifying banquet to his countrymen'.

About four years after Khan wrote his account in Persian, a boy was born to a Portuguese-Indian family in Bengal. Henry Derozio (1809–31), belonged to a generation of young men in Calcutta who were inspired by the iconoclasm of the reformer Raja Rammohun Roy (1772–1835). It has become common to see Roy as an 'anglophone reformer' – partly because those of his texts that historians refer to were written in English or included translations into English. These include attempts to revive the 'true' Vedic traditions by translating the obscure Sanskrit texts of the Upanishads (*Translation of an Abridgement of the Vedanta*, 1816–17) as well as polemical-political tracts calling for the end of widow burning (1818), and so on. In actual fact, Roy wrote his first (reformist) work in Persian and Arabic in 1801 and continued to edit a Persian journal (and write in that language) until 1823, by which time he had switched (starting in 1816) to English and Bangla for largely pragmatic reasons.

Derozio was to have a short and controversial life as a free thinker at the Hindu College, Calcutta, from which he was finally fired for his intellectual iconoclasm. His radical friends and followers constituted the so-called Young Bengal Group, and some of them – like K. M. Banerji and Ram Gopal Ghose – also wrote in English. Today Derozio is known to us as the first Indian English poet. His well-known poem, *The Fakeer of Jungheera*, was published in 1828. Derozio was by no means the only Indian writing poems in English in the 1820s: Kashiprasad Ghosh's *Shair and Other Poems* came out in 1830, and K. M. Banerjee, one of Derozio's students, was the author of *The Persecuted* (1831), the earliest extant play in English by an Indian (also a critique of orthodoxy).

As well as Derozio, there were many others who wrote poetry in English in the nineteenth century, who were accused – often in retrospect – of merely following in the wake of the waning romantic star and of selling out to the British. The first accusation seems superfluous at least in the case of Derozio if we recall that he wrote at a time when Wordsworth and Byron were still alive. As for the second accusation, not only did Derozio urge the Eurasians to identify with India (and not with the colonising British), his poems lend themselves to explicitly patriotic interpretations. In the sonnet, 'The Harp of India',

Derozio sees the harp silenced by contemporary conditions and prays, 'but if thy notes divine/ May be by mortal wakened once again,/ Harp of my country, let me strike the strain!' Of course, the 'harp of India' was by no means silent in the 1820s and 1830s. Urdu poetry, for instance, was going through its greatest flowering – and, having absolved Derozio of the blame of mindless imitativeness, one has to add that his choice of language might have rendered him partly deaf to the music of other harps in India. Actually, perhaps the greatest of all Urdu poets and a significant Persian writer, Asadullah Khan Ghalib, was a contemporary of Derozio (though based in Delhi) and, if the letters that he wrote to the British are any evidence, reasonably fluent in English.

In general, though, Indians who wrote in English also wrote – like Rammohun Roy – in other Indian languages. While Derozio and Toru Dutt (1856–77), often considered the most significant nineteenth-century Indian English poet, do not seem to have written in any language other than European ones, there were also writers – like Michael Madhusudhan Dutt and Bankimchandra Chatterjee – who started off writing in English and then switched to Bangla. Madhusudhan Dutt wrote his early poetry – in a derivative romantic mode but with Indian settings – in English and Bankimchandra is credited with writing the first Indian English novel, *Rajmohan's Wife* (1864), though he achieved his canonical status in Bengal only after switching to Bangla.

The trajectory of Indians who wrote in English has been recorded, but often in a way that separates them from those Indians – usually of a similar background – who wrote in Indian languages but knew English. Why is it that between 1750 and 1850 an entire class of Indians grew up with reasonable knowledge of English? This was the consequence of a series of events set in motion by the constitution of the East India Company in 1600, but was also prepared, perhaps, by the cosmopolitan character of urban life in pre-colonial India. Indians, as C. A. Bayly (1996, pp. 10–56) has remarked, were used to receiving information from other parts of the world – and the language of culture over most of India, namely Persian, was itself (like English) a language that had come to India from abroad. However, in some ways, the reasons for the rise of English in the late eighteenth and early nineteenth century can be located within the brackets to two dates: 1813, when the East India Company's charter was renewed, and 1857. If the renewal of the charter, by urging the company to educate the natives, provided an impetus to English education, the Ghaddar/Mutiny/First War of Independence of 1857 (decisively defeated by 1858) marked the last consolidated challenge of the traditional orders to British colonialism. It is just as significant that in 1857 the first three company universities were set up at Calcutta, Bombay and Madras. Other universities or colleges were to follow in Poona, Agra, Delhi, and an entire network of missionary schools and colleges was to provide English education to at least some of the privileged natives.

Perhaps the most significant event of the 1813–57 period – and the one highlighted most often by historians – was the governor-general's adoption of Thomas Babington Macaulay's *Minute on Education* in 1835, which settled the Orientalist-Anglicist controversy of the past four decades in favour of the Anglicist position. Other significant events in the period included the rise of missionary schools, as mentioned, and publications and the effective use of English (along with some vernaculars at times) as the medium of administration in the company's India. The 1853 opening up of the Indian Civil Service to Indian applicants probably provided a major fillip to English education in India as well. Macaulay, who sincerely believed that a single shelf of a European library was worth all the literatures of Arabia and India, has become almost an emblematic figure: the villain or hero of 'modern education' in India and the consequent cleft between those educated in English and those who continued – and continue – to receive education in other Indian languages. While Macaulay's *Minute* and other administrative acts played a part in the spread of English, it should be noted that Indians were learning English – and writing in the language – even before 1835. The controversy between the Orientalists who wanted Indians to be taught in their own (pre-colonial) languages and the Anglicists who preferred European education in English for the natives presents only one side of the picture.

The other side is presented by people like Rammohun Roy, who called for education in English but continued to write in traditional Indian languages and translated Sanskrit texts: evidently, the extreme binarism that the Orientalist-Anglicist opposition suggests in English discourse might not have existed for many Indians. After all, there were Indians like Dean Mahomet, who adopted English willingly, and Abu Taleb and (perhaps) Ghalib, who learnt English even though they might not have 'written' extensively in it. It is also significant that Mahomet, writing in English, should have sought to defend Indians against the 'boasting philosophers' of Europe and Taleb, writing in Persian, should have simply turned the occidental gaze around and found Europe 'exotic' enough to be narrated. Mahomet's defence of Indians – as well as Rammohun Roy's translations and various other texts in the nineteenth century – highlights that Indians who wrote in English very often wrote within a discursive world framed by other European texts: the writings of people as varied (and, at times, contradictory in their approach to Indians) as Sir William Jones, James Scurry, Charles ('Hindoo') Stuart, Macaulay and P. M. Taylor.

Missionaries played a prominent role in the spread of European education, though not always in English. Gauri Viswanathan (1989) has shown that English literature as a subject of curriculum was established in India well before its institutionalisation in England in the nineteenth century. This was partly due to the exigencies of British colonisation and partly the result of a compromise between bureaucratic pragmatism and missionary demands: to teach English literature was to propagate Christian and European values without evangelising directly.

This might be one of the factors that explains the emergence of various literary genres – and magazines – in English in the first half of the nineteenth century. Following the rise of the administrative-survey genres of writing and the travel book in the eighteenth century, Derozio's poetry, K. M. Banerji's play, K. C. Dutt's 'science fiction' novella (1835) and, finally, Bankimchandra Chatterjee's novel (1864) more or less rounded up the major genres of Indian English writing. Apart from poetry, which attracted a number of anglophone Indians throughout the nineteenth century – even Sarojini Naidu (1879–1950); arguably the most significant of early twentieth-century Indian English poets, Sri Aurobindo and Manmohan Ghose started writing poetry in that century – travel books and novels appear to have been the dominant genres.

Indian English fiction in the nineteenth century consisted mostly of historical romances (for example, K. K. Lahiri's *Roshinara* (1881) and K. Chakravarti's *Sarata and Hingana* (1895)) and social realist novels (for example, R. Debi's *The Hindu Wife* (1876)). Of the latter, Krupabai Sathianadhan's *Saguna* (1895), first serialised in 1887, is remarkable for its depth and also because it is probably the first autobiographical novel by an Indian woman. It is relevant to note that significant Indian English texts were being published not only from Calcutta and London but also Madras, Bombay, Lahore and even small places like Dinapur in the second half of the nineteenth century.

While travel texts were also written in Bangla, Hindi, Marathi and so on, the number of travel books in English by South Asians in the nineteenth century is astounding. These include J. Nowrojee and H. Merwanjee's *Journal of a Residence of Two Years and a Half in*

Great Britain (1841), Ishuree Dass's account of a voyage to England and America (1851), Bholanath Chanda's *Travels of a Hindoo to Various Parts of Bengal and Upper India* (1869) and Nandalal Dasa's *Reminiscences – English and Australasian* (1893). The Parsi B. M. Malabari's *The Indian Eye on English Life or Rambles of a Pilgrim Reformer* (1893) illustrates, among other things, how the British attempt to create a buffer class of anglophone Indians had proved a mixed blessing for the colonisers. This Bombay journalist was not only an anglophile, but also a democrat and socialist who remained sceptical of European pretensions to civilisation. Unapologetic about the English of his class, he asked:

> Talking of 'Babu English', I should like to know how many Englishmen speak Bengali half so well as Bengalis speak English. How many are the English scholars who handle the language more effectively than, for instance, Sambhu Chunder Mookerji, or Rajendralal Mitra, Kristodas Pal, or Keshub Chunder Sen?

Tabish Khair

Literary Works

Chatterji, Bankimchandra [1864] (1996), *Rajmohan's Wife. A Novel*, ed. M. Mukherjee, Delhi: Ravi Dayal.

Debi, Rajlakshmi (1878), *The Hindu Wife or The Enchanted Fruit*, Calcutta: The author.

Derozio, Henry Louis Vivian (1928), *The Fakeer of Jungheera: A Metrical Tale*, Calcutta: Samuel Smith.

Dutt, K. C. (1835), *A Journal of Forty Eight Hours of the Year 1945*, Calcutta Literary Gazette, June.

Dutt, S. C. (1883), *The Young Zamindar*, London: The author.

Dutt, Toru (1878), *A Sheaf Gleaned in French Fields*, Calcutta: Saptahik Sambad Press.

Dutt, Toru (1885), *Ancient Ballads and Legends of Hindustan*, London: Kegan Paul.

Ghose, Man Mohan (1926), *Songs of Love and Death*, Oxford: Basil Blackwell.

Mahomet, S. D. (1794), *The Travels of Dean Mahomet, a Native of Patna in Bengal, Through Several Parts of India, while in the Service of The Honourable The East India Company, Written by Himself, In a Series of Letters to a Friend*, Cork: J. Connor and the author.

Malabari, B. M. (1893), *The Indian Eye on English Life or Rambles of a Pilgrim Reformer*, London: Archibald Constable.

Sathianadhan, K. (1895), *Saguna: A Story of Native Christian Life*, Madras: Srinivasa, Varadachari and Co.

Satthianadhan, S. (1893), *Four Years in an English University*, Madras: Srinivasa, Varadachari and Co.

Sinha, K. K. (1893), *The Star of Sikri*, Dinapur: The author.

Histories

Bayly, C. A. (1996), *Empire and Information: Intelligence Gathering and Social Communication in India, 1780–1870*, Cambridge: Cambridge University Press.

Blackburn, Stuart and Vasudha Dalmia (eds) (2003), *India's Literary History: Essays on the Nineteenth Century*, Delhi: Permanent Black.

Das, Sisir Kumar (1991), *A History of Indian Literature: 1800–1910*, vol. 8, Delhi: Sahitya Akademi.

Das, Sisir Kumar (2001), *Indian Ode to the West Wind: Studies in Literary Encounters*, Delhi: Pencraft.

Fisher, Michael H. (1996), *The First Indian Author in English*, Delhi: Oxford University Press.

Mehrotra, A. K. (ed.) (2003), *A History of Indian Literature in English*, London: Hurst and Company; New Delhi: Permanent Black.

Mukherjee, Meenakshi (2000), *The Perishable Empire*, Delhi: Oxford University Press.

Naik, M. K. (1989), *A History of Indian English Literature*, Delhi: Sahitya Akademi.

Trivedi, Harish (1993), *Colonial Transactions: English Literature and India*, Manchester and New York: Manchester University Press.

Viswanathan, Gauri (1989), *Masks of Conquest: Literary Study and British Rule in India*, New York: Columbia University Press.

See also: **East India Company; Historiography: South Asia; Language and Ethnicities: South Asia; Raj.**

Engmalchin

Engmalchin is a portmanteau word derived from the initial syllables of three major languages in postwar Malaya: English, Malay, and Chinese. It was used in the early 1950s to describe an artificial interlanguage devised largely for poetic expression by undergraduates at the University of Malaya in Singapore. At a time of growing national consciousness, these undergraduates represented an anglophone elite which wished to build a national culture on the model of those of Europe. Essayists in the student journals *The Cauldron* and *The New Cauldron* thus called not for writing in Malay but rather for the development of a new national language, 'a Malayan language' evolving from the 'linguistic melting pot' of the new nation. In practice, Engmalchin proved much more modest in scope. Of its progenitors, only the Indonesian-born Chinese Wang Gungwu was fluent in all three languages and could draw upon the literary resources of three traditions. The majority of his fellow correspondents in *The New Cauldron*, as Anne Brewster has noted (1989), were Straits Chinese, and Engmalchin, in its inclusion of colloquial Malay and Hokkien words, mimicked the linguistic competences of that community.

Wang published poems in Chinese in the journal, but his Engmalchin poems at the most incorporate brief transliterated phrases from so-called Chinese 'dialects'. Engmalchin's engagement with Malay, the future national language of both Malaysia and Singapore, was more thoroughgoing. Poems such as the pseudonymous Chu Chin Chow's 'Enigma Variations' are written in a combination of Malay and English, with a smattering of Hokkien. Engmalchin was never, however, simply an attempt to represent directly the hybrid, code-shifting linguistic expression of Singapore streets; rather it was a response to a multilingual environment through the creation of an artificial language.

Its pretence to be representative was further undercut by its exclusion of Tamil, a language that would be an important component of multiculturalism in both Singapore and Malaysia. In an essay written in 1958, Wang noted that he and the group of poets to which he belonged had been in too much of a hurry to produce a distinctively Malayan poetry, taking on a political, cultural, and poetic project at the same time. Noting that 'our moral and political attitudes to Malaya distracted us from the poetry' (Wang 1958, p. 6), Wang felt that Malayan cultural expression should follow political change: until then, he noted, 'good poetry is all we need' (Wang 1958, p. 8). If Engmalchin's life was short, however, the issues to which it responded persist to this day. The indigenisation of English, and the representation of regional forms of English and multilingual cultural realities in poetry, prose, drama, and film continue to be central questions in cultural expression and criticism in both Malaysia and Singapore.

Philip Holden

Literary Works

The New Cauldron (1949–50 and 1950–1), Singapore: Raffles Society, University of Malaya.
Wang Gungwu (1951), *Pulse*, Singapore: Beda Lim.

Histories

Brewster, Anne (1989), *Towards a Semiotic of Post-Colonial Discourse: University Writing in Singapore and Malaya, 1949–1965*, CAS Occasional Paper 4, Singapore: Heinemann Asia/Centre for Advanced Studies.
Lim Beda (1949–50), 'Talking of Verse by Malayan Students', *Magazine of the University of Malaya Student's Union*, pp. 1–6.
Lim Beda (1953), 'Preface', in Lim Thean Soo, *Poems 1951–53*, Singapore: S. Sim at the University of Malaya.
'The Way to Nationhood' (1949–50), *The New Cauldron*, Hilary Term, pp. 3–6.
Wang Gungwu (1958), 'Trial and Error in Malayan Poetry', *Malayan Undergrad.* 9:5 (July), pp. 1–9.

See also: **Anglicisation; Bumiputra; Historiography: South-east Asia; Lee Kuan Yew.**

European Exploration and Settlement: Australia, New Zealand, Pacific

Pacific exploration probably began with the arrival of Aborigines in Australia by boat at least 60,000 years ago, although the most extensive exploration took place when Polynesians set out in ocean-going canoes around 3,500 years ago. Contrary to the predominant historiographical representation, the European exploration, which began in the early 1500s in the wake of Vasco da Gama's and Columbus' expeditions to India and the Caribbean, was not a first. However, the particular methods of European exploration as well as the pattern of colonialism which followed in its wake were unique and applied throughout the Pacific. Exploration here was governed by intense rivalry between the major European powers, which all sought to take over the lucrative Portuguese trade. The Pacific expeditions can be divided roughly into the following periods: Spanish and Portuguese expeditions from the early 1500s to the early 1600s; Dutch expeditions from the early 1600s to the 1640s; British expeditions from the mid-1700s to the early 1800s; French expeditions from the mid-1700s to the early 1800s. In Australia, there were expeditions both by sea and land, but by 1850 sea expeditions, or rather coastal boat expeditions, had ceased, whereas overland expeditions began almost as early as British settlement (1788) and had finished as a major activity by the 1870s.

Much information concerning early Spanish and Portuguese expeditions has been lost, partly due to the secrecy with which discoveries were jealously guarded. The Treaty of Tordesillas (1494) divided the world into a Spanish and a Portuguese half, but because of the inability to determine accurately longitude, the location of the dividing line on the other side of the globe was open to interpretation and political opportunism. Because it was in their interest, Portuguese maps showed a much wider Pacific Ocean than did the Spanish. The contentious issue of the dividing line owed less to the Pacific *per se* than to the fabled riches of the Spice Islands, which both countries sought to place inside their own global half.

In terms of European beginnings, the Portuguese probably came first, with a fleet of three caravels disappearing on a journey beyond Timor in 1522. Later French copies of secret Portuguese maps indicate that they may have sailed down the east coast of Australia. Much evidence from the Portuguese expeditions perished in the fires caused by the Lisbon earthquake of 1755. Portugal's political power based on the riches gathered from the Indian and South-east Asian trade soon began to decline, and Spanish expeditions took over the exploration from the eastern side. Most famous of them all was that of the Portuguese captain, Fernão de Magalhães, one of whose ships became the first to circumnavigate the globe in 1522, although Magalhães himself was killed in the Philippines in 1521.

Much of the European exploration in the Pacific focused on the fabled Great South Land whose assumed existence owed much to a mixture of European myth-making condoned both by map makers and expedition sponsors. Two examples are the Solomon Islands which Mendana de Neira named after he discovered gold on them; while the Portuguese captain Quirós named one of the islands of Vanuatu, Austrialia del Espiritu Santo, thinking he had struck the outskirts of a continent.

Dutch exploration in the Pacific began with the establishment of a Dutch colony in Batavia (1619). A Dutch ship had reached Cape York in 1606, and over the next fifty years a number of expeditions mapped two-thirds of the Australian coastline. Two mutineers from the ship *Batavia*, which was shipwrecked off the Australian west coast, became the first two known white settlers when they were left there as punishment. The most well-known Dutch expeditions in the Pacific were undertaken by Abel Tasman, who discovered Tasmania in 1642 and went on to map the coastline of what he thought was a great continent. It was, in fact, New Zealand, and here Tasman had a violent encounter with the Maori inhabitants. Tasman was also the first European to visit Tonga and Fiji. Although the Dutch mapped much of the Australian coastline, they seldom went ashore, were generally hostile towards the Aborigines and unimpressed with what they saw. The first British visitor who followed in their wake was the pirate William Dampier, who visited the northwest coast in 1688 and 1699 and was equally dismissive.

In the 1760s a new type of much more carefully planned scientific exploration practice began with the French and British expeditions, helped also by the invention of the sextant and chronometer. These expeditions led to the European discovery of most remaining archipelagos in the Pacific as well as the rediscovery of many islands visited earlier by Spanish, Dutch or Portuguese explorers. Best known of the French explorers is Louis Antoine de Bougainville, whose long expedition (1766–9) brought him to the Solomon Islands and the islands off Papua New Guinea. The most famous of all the Enlightenment explorers is James Cook who undertook three long expeditions to the Pacific. The first expedition was sent to observe the transit of Venus from Tahiti, an island that had enthralled both Bougainville and Captain Wallis during their visits. The infatuation with Tahitians as reincarnations of a lost Greek idealised civilisation grew into a cult in Europe. The Tahitian, Tupaia, was brought back as the first of a number of Pacific islanders, Maoris and Aborigines taken to Europe.

Contrary to the Enlightenment obsession with rationality and *tabulae rasae*, Cook was also sent out to look for the Great South Land and the North-west Passage. The end of Pacific exploration came with George Vancouver's four-year-long expedition, most of which the frustrated explorer spent among the innumerable islands and islets off the Canadian west coast, searching for a passage either to the large Canadian lakes or the North-west Passage to the Pacific, which Cook had suggested he might have located in what subsequently became known as Cook's Inlet. Much debate concerning the Enlightenment expeditions has focused on the territory between 'disinterested' scientific curiosity and 'interested' first steps towards colonisation. One of the foci for this debate has been Cook's personification as either a 'disinterested' Enlightenment figure, an acute ethnographic observer, or even a Romantic figure given to metaphorical namedropping; or an 'interested' coloniser putting pigs on shore to pave the way for later colonisation, a patriarchal white father figure using gunboat diplomacy and kidnapping to bend the indigenes to his will, and whose image represents a genealogy of patriarchal governors in Australia, as he is shown in Aboriginal artist Gordon Bennett's painting *Australian Icon* (1989). A particularly interesting manifestation of this schizophrenic image has been the anthropological argument over the significance of Cook's arrival and death in Hawaii between Marshall Sahlins and Gananeth Obeyesekere (see Edmonds 1997) which became a battleground over the right to speak scientifically on behalf of the indigene. The debate has petered out, but remains unresolved.

The early phase of the British exploration of Australia was dominated by sea expeditions after small parties sent into the bush from the penal settlement at Sydney found that penetrating the hinterland was extremely arduous, and that it was impossible to cross the nearby Blue Mountains even with the Aboriginal guides that were widely used by Australian inland expeditions. The most significant sea explorer was Matthew Flinders, who circumnavigated the continent in order to search for suitable sites for settlements to ward off European rivals. Expeditions by French explorers such as Nicholas Baudin and Bruny d'Entrecastreux showed much interest in the southern parts of the continent, which prompted British flag-raising and settlement in these areas. Flinders' other mission was to look for navigable passages from the continent's coastline to its interior, an early illustration of an obstinate obsession with finding an inland sea or a large river which could open the interior to large-scale settlement, as the Mississippi had done for North America. Indeed, a large river flowing from the mountains west of Sydney into the Indian Ocean off north-west Australia was considered so desirable that a map was actually produced showing such a river, aptly named 'The Desired Blessing'. The British interest in such a river, and in Australia generally, was related to its interest in its growing empire in South and Southeast Asia. However, although several other sea expeditions were undertaken, their inability to locate suitable entries to the continent's interior meant that overland expeditions soon became the dominant method of exploration.

The discovery by Blaxland, Lawson and Wentworth of a way across the Blue Mountains in 1813 was quickly followed by the construction of a road that eased the access into the interior. A string of expeditions was sent to look for new grasslands for the sheep and cattle of the land-hungry squatters and to attract more migrants. Inevitably these expeditions ran into larger problems the further west they went. Lack of water and feed for their cattle, horses and sheep became a favourite topic in the long narratives produced by explorers who felt the injustice of searching a continent that lacked dramatic mountain peaks and large rivers and which only reluctantly surrendered new swathes of monotonous bush to their gaze. The narratives focused on the ordeal and sacrifices made by explorers: the land as protagonist and quite often antagonist became an established theme that has subsequently been explored in Australian literature and art. Notable exceptions to such ordeals of non-discovery were Major Mitchell who quickly realised the lack of potential of the interior and instead veered off to the south-east corner where he knew greener pastures were to be 'discovered'; and Charles Sturt's second expedition down the Murray River. Even so, the Murray did not lead Sturt to the inland sea, but veered off into Lake Alexandrina on the coast south-east of Adelaide. Moreover, its value as a navigable part of Australia's largest river system was partly negated by its shallow mouth, with the river sometimes being cut off from the sea by a sand barrier.

After the settlement of Melbourne (1835) and Adelaide (1836), Sydney ceased to be the base for exploration activity. The expeditions of Edward John Eyre (1840–1) and Charles Sturt's third expedition (1844–6) were sent out from Adelaide with specific instructions to locate suitable pastures (and, of course, the inland sea), because of fears that the infant settlement might otherwise have to be abandoned. In spite of the failure by these expeditions in both respects, the colony survived. After dragging his boat through the deserts of outback Australia, Sturt finally had to give up and return to Adelaide, convinced that the inland sea had eluded him. Edward John Eyre, protector of Aborigines and subsequently to become infamous as governor of Jamaica, quickly surrendered any hope of finding an inland sea as he made his way north from Adelaide. Turning back after naming the hill he was standing on Mount Hopeless, Eyre set off instead on an epic trek along the Great Australian Bight until he reached Albany in the south-west corner of Western Australia with his overseer and three Aborigines. Eyre's narrative reaches its dramatic peak when the overseer is killed by two of his Aboriginal guides, although what exactly happened is never satisfactorily explained. Instead, with the two 'perpetrators' having fled, Eyre concentrates on painting a picture of the white explorer left in the company of the remaining Aborigine, who he fears might have been in league with the others.

Eyre had learned that in order to survive in such an arid and treeless environment, explorers had to travel, like the Aborigines, in small groups with minimal reliance on domesticated animals. Yet Eyre's method of exploration was not the norm, and certainly not for the heavily-sponsored official expeditions, which culminated with the disastrous Burke and Wills expedition (1860–1). Burdened by the mid-Victorian belief in their own superiority, and obsessed with the search for fame through conquering the land, Burke and Wills' expedition wanted to be the first to cross Australia from south to north. After an extravagant farewell in Melbourne, lack of patience with the expedition's slow progress, caused by carrying twenty-one tons of equipment, soon made Burke decide to leave most of the group at Cooper's Creek, halfway to the Gulf of Carpentaria. Although Burke and Wills and their two companions managed to reach their objective, they arrived back at Cooper's Creek on the day when the main expedition had given up waiting for them. Too exhausted to pursue them, Burke and Wills starved to death at a place where hundreds of Aborigines thrived on native foods.

Wherever they went, the European explorers crossed Aboriginal territories. Although not fenced or signposted, each territory had boundaries that were understood and respected by the indigenous inhabitants who lived on its resources. The areas which provided the best and most reliable sources of food for Aborigines were also the most sought-after regions for the European pastoralists, while in the more marginal areas of Aboriginal settlement even a short visit by an exploring expedition, with its complement of sheep, cattle and horses, could upset the local ecological balance. The European-Australian explorers used Aboriginal trackers, and these would at times send people ahead to warn about the white people penetrating into territory without observing any of the ritual exchanges established for intertribal relationships. In the exploration narratives the Aboriginal trackers often disappear at moments when the explorer makes an important discovery. At other points they are dismissed by the expedition leader, although it is clear from the unfortunately few competing accounts from the same expeditions that they simply refuse to put up with their ill-treatment and leave. Other diaries tend to show a very different explorer from the official narrative, which often places the explorer as the valiant protagonist engaged in an epic struggle against a hostile environment.

There were also clashes between the exploration parties and local Aboriginal groups. Thomas Mitchell's expedition party's vicious attack (mid-nineteenth century) on a group of Aborigines in the continent's south-east was one example of this. More famous, because they involved the killing and disappearance of white men, were the expeditions (1848) of Edmund Kennedy and Ludwig Leichhardt. After the Burke and Wills expedition, however, exploration ceased to be a major activity, although it has continued to influence the Australian imagination.

Lars Jensen

Literary Works

Johnson, Colin (1983), *Dr. Wooreddy's Prescription for Enduring the Ending of the World*, Melbourne: Hyland House.
Melville, Herman [1846] (1972), *Typee*, Harmondsworth: Penguin.
Simons, Margaret (1992), *The Ruthless Garden*, Port Melbourne: Minerva.
Toohey, John (2002), *Quiros*, Sydney: Duffy and Snellgrove.
White, Patrick (1960), *Voss*, Ringwood: Penguin.

Histories

Beaglehole, J. C. (1955–67), *The Journals of Captain James Cook on His Voyages of Discovery*, vols I–III, Cambridge: Cambridge University Press.
Carter, Paul (1987), *The Road to Botany Bay: An Essay in Spatial History*, London: Faber and Faber.
Edmond, Rod (1997), *Representing the South Pacific: Colonial Discourse from Cook to Gauguin*, Cambridge: Cambridge University Press.
Haynes, Roslynn (1998), *Seeking the Centre: The Australian Desert in Literature, Art and Film*, Melbourne: Cambridge University Press.
Smith, Bernard (1960), *European Vision and the South Pacific 1768–1850*, London: Oxford University Press.

See also: **Diaspora: Pacific; Dutch East India Company; Historiography: Australia; Precolonial Histories: Australia.**

European Exploration and Settlement: Canada

England and France exploited familiar northern fishing routes in their approaches to the New World in the fifteenth century, challenging Spain and Portugal's claims to the hemi-sphere and hoping to duplicate their successes. En route to Asia John Cabot, a Venetian in England's service, made landfall at or near Newfoundland in 1497. European states drew on scriptural precedent, agriculturalist ideology, or doctrines of *vacuum domicilius* and *terra nullius* to justify conquest, Cabot's letters patent baldly granting licence to 'subdue, occupy, and possess' any 'village, town, castle, isle or mainland newly found'. Those who followed plied the rich fishery from which European-aboriginal fur trade partnerships grew. Meanwhile, Peter Martyr's writings (1516; 1555 in English) leant credence to a North-west Passage to the Orient, on whose discovery Britain would expend three centuries of explor-atory energies. Richard Hakluyt Jr proposed colonisation to relieve excess population and buttress declining markets at home, his *Principal Voyages* – which Froude called 'the Prose Epic of the modern English nation' – appearing in 1589. Gaining momentum only in the mid-eighteenth century, colonisation of British North America would entail the manage-ment, dispersal, or destruction of Native communities as well as French settlements in Acadia, Newfoundland, and the St Lawrence River valley, ceded in 1713 and 1763. Aboriginal settlement had begun millennia earlier. Crossing a land bridge in the Bering Strait between 75,000 and 14,000 years ago, Asian migrants established settlements inside the present boundaries of Canada between 9,000 and 15,000 years ago. Of the estimated 18 million inhabitants of North America at the time of contact, 500,000–2 million inhab-ited Canada, concentrated in fertile and resource-rich southern Ontario and coastal British Columbia.

The Mi'kmaq of Nova Scotia, numbering some 12,000 in 1500 CE, along with the Innu of Labrador, the Beothuk of Newfoundland, and Maliseet of Nova Scotia, comprised the main hunting-gathering groups of the north-east. Native confrontations discouraged Norse settlement in Newfoundland about 1000 CE. Jacques Cartier of France explored much of the region (1534, 1535–6), encountering Natives eager to trade, among them the agriculturalist Iroquoians of the St Lawrence River. Samuel de Champlain continued French exploration of the coast and the St Lawrence system in the early seventeenth century. Small, often temporary settlements were established, then changed hands as France and Britain vied for control of the area. A French trading post was established at Tadoussac (1600). Favourable conditions and Mi'kmaq friendship saw French agricultural settlement at Port-Royal (1605) on the Bay of Fundy, while Plaisance (1624) on the Avalon peninsula of Newfoundland administered the French fishery. At Cupid's Cove, Newfoundland (1610), the London and Bristol Company traded furs and harvested fish. British, French, and New England pressures bore especially on Acadia. While claims to a 'New Scotland' inside the colony were dashed in 1632, between 1654 and 1668, Acadia was in British hands. New England influence halted French settlement and brought the colony into the commerical orbit of Boston. France resumed control until 1710, the year of its capture by New England troops. The Treaty of Utrecht (1713) transferred Acadia to Britain while the French continued to exert pressure from Louisbourg on Cape Breton Island. The founding of Halifax (1749) confirmed Britain's imperial ambitions in the region and spurred Mi'kmaq resistance, their territory annexed without consultation. Some 13,000 Acadians were deported in 1755, Louisbourg fell in 1758, New France fol-lowed in 1760. Displaced Acadians returning to the region after 1763 found their lands occupied by foreign settlers, some of them New England planters who had arrived in Nova Scotia between 1758 and 1781. Thirty thousand of the 50,000 Loyalist refugees of the American Revolution arrived in 1783, bringing about the partitioning of the colony to form New Brunswick in 1784.

British and New England merchants, who would come to dominate Canadian trade, followed the capitulation of New France, which placed nearly 70,000 French settlers under British rule. Under a proclamation of 1763, lands were offered to demobilised soldiers and sailors, and British law was guaranteed to British immigrants to Quebec. Forbidding private land sales, the proclamation also sought to assuage Native anger over territory ceded to the British. Yet while colonial administrators assured Natives to the contrary, transfers proceeded apace and occupation by settlers was rarely prevented. Between 6,000 and 10,000 Loyalists opted for Canada, followed by American settlers seeking cheap land. The British surrender of the Ohio Valley with the Peace of Paris (1783) without the consultation of Amerindian allies administered another shock to deteriorating Native-British relations. The war of 1812–14 stemmed the tide of American settlers; demobilised soldiers as well as groups of Scots and Irish were assisted in settlement, although until the famine migrations of the 1840s most of the settlers were independent. The conclusion of the Napoleonic Wars, the elimination of restrictions on emigration, and the Irish famine brought a dramatic rise in British immigration after 1815. Between 1825 and 1846, about 600,000 settlers arrived via the St Lawrence; by 1851 Upper Canada's population stood at 900,000. Government dominated land speculation, while settlers established basic infrastructure.

French *coureurs de bois* Radisson and Des Grosseilliers mounted a British expedition to Hudson Bay in 1668. By 1670, the Hudson's Bay Company (HBC) had begun operations linking the western interior with the European fur market. Five groups of hunting and gathering peoples, migrating seasonally within traditional territories – the Chipewyan, the Cree, Ojibwa, Assiniboine, and the Blackfoot confederacy of Peigan, Blood and Siksikaw – inhabited the region. In 1690, HBC explorer Henry Kelsey and twenty-three Natives journeyed up the Hayes River from York Factory to encourage trade. Relinquishing claims to Hudson Bay in 1713, the French pushed overland as far as the Saskatchewan River, intersecting HBC routes. Meanwhile, the European presence intensified inter-tribal conflicts, pushing some off their lands; others, such as the Cree and Assiniboine, migrated to take advantage of the expanding trade. In 1754, explorer Anthony Henday was dispatched in response to French expansion, penetrating as far as present-day Alberta. From 1774, the HBC established interior posts, many close to North West Company (NWC) rivals. In 1811 Lord Selkirk started a centre of agriculture and supply for the HBC on the Red and Assiniboine Rivers. British, Swiss and French-Canadian settlers arrived between 1812 and 1848. But French-speaking Métis and English-speaking 'country born', the legacy of 150 years of Native-European partnership in the fur trade, dominated. The NWC encouraged Métis harassment of the colony, which intersected NWC trade routes. Missionaries aiming to assimilate Native and mixed bloods began to arrive in the 1820s, while Canadian expansionists advocated acquisition of Rupert's Land from the 1850s. The arrival of a territorial governor and survey team, a sure threat to the customary land-holding system, prompted Métis resistance in 1869 under Louis Riel. In 1870, provincial autonomy was granted to Manitoba, yet land provisions would be inadequate to local needs, and Crown lands and resources remained under Ottawa's control. Land was again at stake in the 'rebellion' of 1885 for the Métis who had migrated into Saskatchewan. The survey expeditions of Pallisher and Hind (1857) prepared the way for agricultural settlement. The newly confederated Canada formulated its vision of the west in the 1870s: an agricultural hinterland integrated with the manufacturing centres of the east. Policies and settlement schemes followed US models. Facing diminishing resources and white incursion, western Natives negotiated seven treaties between 1871 and 1877, surrendering lands in exchange for economic aid, reserves, and education. Although white settlement experienced stalls, by 1921, the wheat economy supported 1.9 million residents and over 228,000 farms in Manitoba and the provinces of Saskatchewan and Alberta (established 1905). Immigration policy limited or excluded non-whites, except for such labour-hungry projects as the transcontinental railway. English-speaking Protestants dominated prairie society, non-British European immigrants assimilating to varying degrees.

The Pacific coast was explored by James Cook in the late 1770s, George Vancouver in the 1790s, its river systems by fur traders Alexander Mackenzie in 1793 and Simon Fraser in 1808. The area was home to the highest concentration of aboriginals – some 60,000 in coastal areas; between 30,000 and 40,000 inland – among them the Coast and Interior Salish, Haida, Tsimshian, Nootka, and Kootenay. The region's political and cultural diversity hampered the expanding fur trade. Consequently, NWC traders employed eastern Natives in trapping, causing friction with local groups. Fort Victoria was established in 1843, anticipating extension of the 49th parallel boundary. Hitherto a territory of the Hudson's Bay Company, the mainland joined the Crown colony Vancouver Island (1849) on the discovery of gold. Two short-lived gold rushes began an upsurge of white incursion after 1850. While those of 1858 and 1863 around the Fraser River brought comparatively small numbers of transient prospectors and settlers – largely male of individualistic, competitive cast – white settlements emerged along mining supply routes. A great number of the miners were Californians, whose growing presence prompted British concerns over sovereignty and the rule of law. Their presence also precipitated Native–white conflict and coincided with a 50 per cent decline in the Native population in the 1860s. The Interior Salish, long engaged in trading gold with the HBC, confronted incoming miners in what Victoria newspapers falsely reported as a massacre of whites. Little was done to curb the miners' predations on Native life. Moreover, colonial and provincial governments denied aboriginal title to lands in British Columbia (BC), and reductions of allotments to Natives began in 1865. The only province to retain title to Crown lands upon entry into confederation in 1871, British Columbia suffered federal disallowal of its 1874 Crown Lands Act for not creating Native reserves.

The last of Canada's regions, the Arctic – settled by Asian migrants, the Inuit, arriving from Siberia by sea 4,000 years ago – saw Leif Ericsson's visit to Baffin Island around 1000 AD, from Norse Greenland settlements. The voyages of Martin Frobisher (1576), John Davis (1585–7) and Henry Hudson (1610) sought the North-west Passage. Though early encounters with inhabitants were sometimes violent, penetration of the north was generally peaceful, as explorers sought native assistance and had few designs on lands or resources. The Hudson's Bay Company played a role in Arctic exploration, grudgingly undertaken to fend off challenges to the company's monopoly charter. Samuel Hearne's overland expeditions to the Arctic coast (1770–2) sought to discredit the idea of the North-west Passage. An idle post-Napoleonic British Royal Navy countered Russian territorial claims, John Franklin's scientific expedition mapping the northern coast to Hudson's Bay in 1819. Inuit diplomacy averted the massacre of Franklin's 1826 expedition. Expeditions led by George Back (1834), Thomas Simpson and Warren Dease (1836–9), and Dr John Rae (1845–6) mapped the Arctic interior and coastline. Meanwhile, explorations by sea under Edward Parry (1819, 1821) and John Ross (1829) pushed further north. More than thirty searches for Franklin's lost third expedition (1846) greatly enlarged knowledge of northern geography. By 1918, a basic map of the Arctic archipelago had been completed with the Canadian Arctic Expedition under Vilhjalmur Stefansson. Meanwhile, whalers, traders, missionaries, agents of law, and government bureaucrats increasingly dominated the lives of Inuit and Natives. White–Inuit relations centred on whaling at Cumberland Sound and Pond Inlet as well as Hudson's Bay; operations here and in the western Arctic drew the Inuit into dependent, destructive relations. Missionaries and HBC traders introduced further disruptions even as they assumed paternal care of those affected. The North West Mounted Police arrived in 1903, partly to ensure Canadian sovereignty. Government gradually assumed provision of Native welfare from the sporadic efforts of the HBC or the meagrely funded Christian missions.

Although penned by foreign hands according to foreign aesthetic norms, the writings of explorers, missionaries, soldiers, and fur traders are seen to constitute an imaginative record in English-Canadian literature. Fiction, history, and poetry of the nineteenth and early twentieth centuries largely celebrate exploration as a triumph of British civilisation and nation-building. Parallel with the scholarly editing and contextualisation of exploration writings by Barbara Belyea, Richard Davis, I. S. MacLaren, and Germaine Warkentin, the late twentieth-century fiction of Bowering, Richler, Steffler, Thomas, and Wiebe questions the image of the heroic masculine adventurer; interrogates the textual journey from field notes to narrative; and restores women, Native, and Inuit peoples to their historical place. The English-language literature of settlement includes the captivity narrative, statistical and promotional tracts, natural history, emigrants' guides, narrative long poems (Sinclair), settler life writing (including the hybrid account-book diary examined by Carter), and sentimental and realist fiction (Connor, Grove). Settler life writing (Beavan, Moodie, Traill) locates aboriginal struggles in a distant past, sentimentalises encounters in the present, and concerns itself with 'going a-head,' articulating an ethos of independence, instituting British paternalism in a diverse bush community, and embracing white communalism and Native knowledges when survival requires it. Much like the explorer's renunciation of literary polish, the settler's recording 'I' emerges as 'naked subjectivity' guaranteeing 'truth and authenticity' and furthering 'the expansion of empire without appearing to do so' (John Thurston 1995, pp. 185–6).

Christopher J. Armstrong

Literary Works

Atwood, Margaret (1970), *The Journals of Susanna Moodie: Poems*, Toronto: Oxford University Press.

Beavan, Frances [1845] (1980), *Life in the Backwoods of New Brunswick*, St Stephen: Print'N'Press.

Bowering, George (1980), *Burning Water*, Don Mills: General Publishing.

Connor, Ralph [1901] (1993), *The Man from Glengarry: A Tale of the Ottawa*, Toronto: McClelland and Stewart.

Grove, F. P. [1925] (1989), *Settlers of the Marsh*, Toronto: McClelland and Stewart.

Moodie, Susanna [1852] (1989), *Roughing It in the Bush*, Toronto: McClelland and Stewart.

Richler, Mordecai (1989), *Solomon Gursky Was Here*, Markham: Viking.

Sinclair, David (ed.) (1972), *Nineteenth-Century Narrative Poems*, Toronto: McClelland and Stewart.

Steffler, John (1992), *The Afterlife of George Cartwright*, Toronto: McClelland and Stewart.

Traill, Catherine Parr [1836] (1989), *The Backwoods of Canada*, Toronto: McClelland and
    Stewart.
Warkentin, Germaine (ed.) (1993), *Canadian Exploration Literature: An Anthology*,
    Toronto: Oxford University Press.
Wiebe, Rudy (1994), *A Discovery of Strangers*, Toronto: McClelland and Stewart.

Histories

Bumsted, J. M. (1992), *The Peoples of Canada: A Pre-Confederation History*, Toronto:
    Oxford University Press.
Carter, Kathryn (1999), 'An Economy of Words: Emma Chadwick Stretch's Account Book
    Diary, 1859–60', *Acadiensis* 1, pp. 43–56.
Dickason, Olive Patricia (2002), *Canada's First Nations: A History of Founding Peoples from
    Earliest Times*, Toronto: Oxford University Press.
Harris, R. Cole (ed.) (1987), *Historical Atlas of Canada*, 3 vols, Toronto: University of
    Toronto Press.
Harris, R. Cole and John Warkentin (1974), *Canada before Confederation: A Study in
    Historical Geography*, New York: Oxford University Press.
Levere, Trevor Harvey (1993), *Science and the Canadian Arctic: A Century of Exploration,
    1818–1918*, Cambridge: Cambridge University Press.
Miller, J. R. (1991), *Skyscrapers Hide the Heavens: A History of Native–White Relations in
    Canada*, Toronto: University of Toronto Press.
Quinn, David B. (1977), *North America from Earliest Discovery to First Settlements: The
    Norse Voyages to 1612*, New York: Harper and Row.
Thurston, John (1995), '"Remember, My Dear Friend": Ideology and Genre in Upper
    Canadian Travel and Settlement Narratives', *Essays on Canadian Writing* 56, pp.
    183–97.

See also: **Genocide: Canada; Hudson's Bay Company; Inuit; Native Reservations**.

F

Fanon, Frantz

Fanon was born in Fort-de-France, Martinique on 20 July 1925, son of Eléanore Fanon, a
successful retailer, and Casimir Fanon, a customs official. He studied at the Lycée
Schoelcher, where he was briefly taught by Aimé Césaire, soon to become the island's
leading politician and poetic mouthpiece. After war-time experience fighting alongside the
Free French in North Africa and Toulon, he studied medicine at the University of Lyon,

where research in psychiatry formed the basis for his first book *Peau Noire, Masques Blanches* (*Black Skin, White Masks*), an existentialist-influenced study of racial alienation published in 1952.

After marrying the French classicist Marie-Josephe Dublé, and appointments as a psychiatrist in various French hospitals, he took up an appointment in Blida, Algeria during the early years of the War of Liberation. Case studies of patients there traumatised by French colonialism convinced him that violence possessed its own therapeutic value, a view that in a series of partly diagnostic, partly polemical works he transferred from the individual to the collective plane. In these works the very nation becomes a patient lying on an analyst's couch. The most urgent and incisive is probably *L'An V de la Révolution Africaine* (1959, translated as *Studies in a Dying Colonialism* 1970), a series of essays on Arab society remarkable for its portrayal of the role of women in the ongoing struggle.

Fanon's growing commitment to the cause of liberation then led him to work for the FLN, the Algerian government in waiting, first at their offices in Tunis, later in Accra, Ghana, ultimately as a roving ambassador. With the help of Claude Lanzmann, deputy editor of *Les Temps Modernes* and later a film director, he met Jean-Paul Sartre in Rome in July 1961; their guarded friendship was to lead Sartre to write his celebrated preface to *Les Damnés de la Terre*, a collection of speeches and essays published after Fanon's death. It was Constance Farrington's English translation of this book under the title *The Wretched of the Earth* in 1965 that launched Fanon on the international scene. Its author had, however, died of leukaemia in New York on 6 December 1961.

During the late 1960s and the 1970s Fanon's writing would attain an iconic status on the international left. His passionately worded interventions had given the cause of Algerian independence intellectual coherence, and his example was to inspire theorists, novelists, poets and revolutionaries all over the Third World. Though his star is no longer in the ascendant, Fanon's literary legacy is permanent. Nonetheless, two large questions hover over his life and work. Fanon's account of the Algerian situation assumes homogeneity of the political will, though it concentrates on Arab identity whilst ignoring the complicating factor of Israel, and throughout subsumes a Berber element that has for long considered itself a victim of oppression within North Africa. Fanon's doctrine of the cathartic effects of insurgence, moreover, seemed apposite at a time of burgeoning nationalist movements worldwide. In an age of global freelance terror, it appears far less attractive.

Robert Fraser

Literary Works

Armah, Ayi Kwei (1969), *Fragments*, London: Heinemann.
Ngugi wa Thiong'o (1977), *Petals of Blood*, London: Heinemann.

Histories

Caute, David (1970), *Fanon*, London: Collins.
Fanon, Frantz (1965), *Studies in a Dying Colonialism, or A Dying Colonialism*, New York: Monthly Press.

Fanon, Frantz (1967), *The Wretched of the Earth*, pref. J.-P. Sartre, Harmondsworth: Penguin.
Fanon, Frantz (1986), *Black Skin, White Masks*, London: Pluto.
Gibson, Nigel (2003), *Fanon: The Postcolonial Imagination*, Cambridge: Polity.
Gordon, Lewis, T. Denean Sharpley-Whiting and René Ranée (eds) (1995), *A Critical Reader*, Oxford: Blackwell.
Macey, David (2000), *Frantz Fanon: A Life*, London: Granta.

See also: **Algerian War of Independence; Anti-colonialism and Resistance (all regions)**.

Free Trade

The doctrine of free trade is based on the idea that government interference with trade inevitably reduces economic efficiency and lowers the standard of living. The mercantilist system, based upon the granting of trade charters to the likes of the East India Company, the Levant Company and the Dutch East India Company, saw the purpose of foreign trade as the enrichment of the nation as a whole, rather than of private individuals, and thus imposed tariffs on imports.

Adam Smith's *The Wealth of Nations* (1776) proposed an economic model based on free markets which has been enormously influential ever since. Smith thought the gains from specialisation and trade should not be confined within national borders; indeed the larger the market, the greater the benefits. He argued that market forces would drive the economy to efficient outcomes as if by an 'invisible hand', and that state-led regulation of commerce would necessarily reduce the economic well-being of a nation. Smith was critical of colonialism but did not entirely repudiate it: on the one hand, he praised the stimulating effect the opening up of American and Asian trade had had on the British economy, despite the inherently mercantilist nature of colonial trade. On the other hand, he supported the independence of the colonies in order to promote the free-trading system. His argument, which would be repeated by liberal economists and anti-colonialists over the following centuries, was that the benefit from monopoly relations with colonies was more apparent than real, because of the cost of protecting such monopolies. Smith's mistake was to assume that the market would self-regulate to the best possible advantage of all the parties involved, whereas since his time the economic and political balance of power has tilted decisively towards the wealthier and more powerful trading partners. Indeed Britain, unlike the other European empires, adopted a free trade economic policy throughout the nineteenth century which privileged commercial growth, minimal government control, and military dominance. During the 1880s Britain shifted to a more protectionist policy in its metropolitan-colonial relations, as its competitors Germany, France and the USA expanded their economies at Britain's expense. This shift in policy prompted a wave of liberal criticism by many authors back home, with J. A. Hobson, for example, arguing that imperialism repudiates free trade. By and large, however, governments still broadly approved *laissez-faire* economic policies in the USA and Western Europe, but the Wall Street Crash of 1929 drove these nations to adopt strongly protectionist policies.

In the post World War II period, however, arguments were repeated that trade was vital to restore struggling Western economies. GATT (General Agreement on Tariffs and Trade) was created in 1948, in which a number of nations came together to lower customs tariffs. In 1995, the WTO (World Trade Organization) came into being, a forum where trade negotiations between countries take place. Today, there is an increasingly outspoken (and politically varied) opposition to the neo-liberal policies that prevail in international financial institutions like the International Monetary Fund and the World Bank. According to Joseph Stiglitz, the imposition of what he calls 'free market fundamentalism' on developing nations is hypocritical. 'The Western countries have pushed poor countries to eliminate trade barriers, but kept up their own barriers, preventing developing countries from exporting their agricultural products and so depriving them of desperately needed export income' (Stiglitz 2002, p. 6). In other words, what passes for 'free trade' nowadays is actually a form of neo-mercantilism on the part of richer nations. The failure of the 2003 Cancun summit on world trade was also due to the unwillingness of the USA and the EU to reduce their agricultural tariffs in favour of imports from developing countries. Much criticism of free trade as it is practised now does not advocate its abolition, but a more equitable distribution of resources that will enable developing nations to compete more fairly with their far richer trading partners.

Neelam Srivastava

Literary Works

Crosthwaite, Luis Humberto (1997), *The Moon Will Forever Be a Distant Love*, trans. Debbie Nathan and Willivaldo Delgadillo, El Paso, TX: Cinco Puntos Press.
Iyer, Pico (1994), *Falling Off the Map: Some Lonely Places of the World*, London: Black Swan.
Kincaid, Jamaica (1988), *A Small Place*, London: Virago.

Histories

Friedman, Thomas L. (1999), *The Lexus and the Olive Tree*, London: HarperCollins.
Irwin, Douglas A. (1996), *Against the Tide: An Intellectual History of Free Trade*, Princeton, NJ: Princeton University Press.
Semmel, Bernard (1993), *The Liberal Ideal and the Demons of Empire: Theories of Imperialism from Adam Smith to Lenin*, Baltimore, ML: Johns Hopkins University Press.
Stiglitz, Joseph (2002), *Globalization and its Discontents*, London: Penguin.

See also: **Anti-globalisation Movements; Dutch East India Company; East India Company; International Monetary Fund; Levant Company; World Bank**.

Frontier Wars: Southern Africa

Over the course of the eighteenth century, the extensive scale of settler farming combined with a rapidly increasing white population led the boundaries of the Cape to be extended to the north and east. At the forefront of this expansion were the escaped slaves, deserting soldiers and sailors, and criminals fleeing the harsh laws of the colony. Though these fugitives had a largely destructive influence on the societies of the interior, many were sheltered by the Khoikhoi, San or Xhosa, and contributed to the emergence of hybrid cultural groups such as the Griqua and Kora of the Orange River area. Also preceding the arrival of frontier farming were the hunting and trading parties that journeyed into the interior. In 1738 an illegal expedition to barter cattle in the Namaqualand turned brutal when the colonists plundered the kraals of the Khoi. Khoi resistance, often led by former servants of the colonists, intensified in the following year, and the conflict assumed the proportions of a war. The government's initial attempts to return the stolen cattle to the Khoi sparked a settler rebellion led by Estienne Barbier, causing colonial policy to become increasingly focused on placating the farmers by supporting them in repelling Khoisan attacks. Khoi numbers had been decimated by a smallpox epidemic in 1713; after 1740 they were increasingly subjugated and forced into destitution and near slavery on white farms.

As the frontier of the colony expanded eastwards, skirmishes between Boers and the Xhosa took place in 1779 and 1793. These constituted the first of what were to be nine so-called Frontier Wars. The conflict between settlers and the Xhosa became increasingly brutal after the British decided to retain control over the Cape Colony in 1806, ending only in 1878 after the infamous Cattle-killing had substantially weakened Xhosa resistance. Several other frontier encounters arose in the course of the nineteenth century as disaffected Boers migrated to the interior, and as the British clashed with the Zulu in Natal. British imperialism was fuelled by the discovery of gold and diamonds in the late nineteenth century, and colonists like Cecil John Rhodes expanded the Empire into what is now Zimbabwe.

Christopher Warnes

Literary Works

Brink, André (1976), *An Instant in the Wind*, London: W. H. Allen.
Coetzee, J. M. (1974), *Dusklands*, Johannesburg: Ravan Press.
Mda, Zakes (2000), *The Heart of Redness*, Cape Town: Oxford University Press.
Schreiner, Olive (1897), *Trooper Peter Halket of Mashonaland*, London: T. Fisher Unwin.

Histories

Coetzee, J. M. (1993), *On the Contrary*, London: Secker and Warburg.
Elphick, Richard and Hermann Giliomee (eds) (1979), *The Shaping of South African Society, 1652–1820*, Cape Town: Longman.
Peires, Jeff (1981), *The Dead will Arise. Nongqawuse and the Great Xhosa Cattle-Killing Movement of 1856–7*, Johannesburg: Ravan Press.
Peires, Jeff (1989), *The House of Phalo. A History of the Xhosa People in the Days of their Independence*, Johannesburg: Ravan Press.
Penn, Nigel (1999), *Rogues, Rebels and Runaways: Eighteenth-Century Cape Characters*, Cape Town: David Philip.
Wilson, Monica and Leonard Thompson (eds) (1969), *The Oxford History of South Africa*, Oxford: Oxford University Press.

See also: **Cattle-Killing; Missionaries: Southern Africa.**

G

Garvey, Marcus Mosiah

Marcus Mosiah Garvey was born in St Ann's Bay, Jamaica, in 1887. Following a career as a printer and pamphleteer, after a series of trips to Central America, he founded the Universal Negro Improvement Association (UNIA) in Kingston, Jamaica, in 1914. After his move to New York, the UNIA became one of the most famous black organisations of Harlem, and burgeoned throughout the black world with nearly a thousand divisions, and tens of thousands of members. The primary organ of the UNIA, the *Negro World*, propagated ideas of equal rights, economic independence, and a unified independent Africa. Linking the destinies of the black diaspora worldwide, Garvey emphasised the centrality of race. In order to transform blackness into a positive symbol of racial pride, he propagated various separatist plans, including emigration to Africa, the creation of a separate black economy, and a black nation within a nation formed with the co-operation of white supremacist organisations. His populist doctrine of collective self-help and racial independence appealed to urban workers as well as to impoverished peasants.

Declaring himself the provisional president of Africa, Garvey took on the role of a racial messiah or a prophet. The elaborate pageantry of the UNIA, with the flag of red, black and green, represented the symbolic plane of Afrocentric traditions, while the Black Star Shipping Line between New York and the Caribbean carried out the same ideas on a material plane. Garvey's decline matched his spectacular rise. Convicted on mail fraud charges in 1923, he was deported from the USA, and eventually died in England in obscurity in 1940.

Garvey met with fierce opposition from the US government, the full extent of which is just becoming known, from the National Association for the Advancement of Coloured People (NAACP) and W. E. B. Du Bois, from the Communist Party, and from European governments. Although Garvey is sometimes seen as a simple advocate for racial purity and a return to Africa, his life and writings offer a rich resource for the current interest in transnationalism. His version of black nationalism, while certainly reliant on nineteenth-century notions of race and nation, also draws from his numerous travels between Jamaica, England, Central America, and the USA. Garvey's vast influence spread as far as South Africa and Cuba, impacting on such future nationalist leaders as Kwame Nkrumah and Nnamdi Azikiwe. Afterlives of Garvey continue to manifest themselves in cultural phenomena as varied as Rastafarianism, reggae, Black Power ideologies, and Pan-Africanist programmes. The phenomenon of Garveyism helps us rethink the relationship of nationalism to racial essentialism, feminism, and black Atlanticism.

Yogita Goyal

Literary Works

Du Bois, W. E. B. [1928] (1995), *Dark Princess: A Romance*, Jackson, MS: Banner Books, University Press of Mississippi.
Griggs, Sutton [1899] (1969), *Imperium in Imperio*, New York: Arno Press.

Histories

Hill, Robert and Barbara Bair (1988), *Marcus Garvey: Life and Lessons*, Los Angeles: University of California Press.
Lewis, Rupert (1987), *Marcus Garvey: Anti-Colonial Champion*, London: Karia Press.
Martin, Tony (1986), *Race First: The Ideological and Organizational Struggles of Marcus Garvey and the Universal Negro Improvement Association*, Dover, MA: Majority Press.

See also: **Anti-colonialism and Resistance: Caribbean; 'Back to Africa' Movement; Pan-Africanism**.

Genocide: Canada

The history of the genocide of Canada's First Peoples dates back to the British policies of colonial administration and the battles over the territory of British North America. As early as 1763, at a peace delegation at Fort Pitt the British gave the Native leaders smallpox in blankets and little silver boxes that were presented to them as gifts to take back to their communities. Tens of thousands of Natives were murdered in this manner, and the practice of disseminating smallpox became widely used by the British military as a way of saving the lives of their soldiers.

Another example of genocide during the colonisation of Canada is found in the history of the Beothuk, once a large group of hunters and gatherers who lived on Newfoundland Island. The extinction of the Beothuk in the early nineteenth century was, according to Jerry Wetzel (1995), a result of the encroachment of European settlers and the introduction of foreign diseases. At this time, the main territories of the Beothuk land around the Avalon Peninsula, Conception Bay, Mary's Bay, Bonavista Bay and Trinity Bay were taken over by Europeans who were hostile to Native presence. Although experts disagree on exactly who had the biggest part in the demise of the Beothuk, the controversy continuing today is overshadowed by the evaporation of Beothuk culture.

Another Native group facing extinction is the Abenaki nation, comprising several bands in the southern Maritimes, eastern Quebec and northern New England. Abenaki is a geographical and linguistic grouping of nations, rather than a political grouping, made up of separate bands such as the Penobscot, Odanak and Onondaga. The Abenaki nations banded together due to various wars in the eighteenth and nineteenth centuries with the English and the Iroquois. These wars were a contributing factor in the decrease of the Abenaki population, as was the spread of disease contracted from European settlers. Several separate outbreaks of smallpox combined with high rates of influenza, diphtheria, measles and other epidemics led to a 75 per cent mortality rate. Although they continue to exist today, the Abenaki population has diminished from over 40,000 people at the time of European contact to approximately 5,000 living in Canada today.

This history of genocide has inspired a non-governmental organisation, the Truth Commission into Genocide in Canada, to compile a report documenting the testimonies of nearly 200 aboriginal eyewitnesses to murder, torture, sterilisation and other crimes against humanity committed at church-run residential schools and hospitals across Canada. The Truth Commission reports that more than 50,000 Indian children died in these facilities between 1891 and 1984, according to government statistics which indicate a continual death rate of between 35 per cent and 60 per cent in these schools. This history of genocide is only now beginning to be recognised by non-Native historians and the Canadian government.

Justin Edwards

Literary Works

Assiniwi, Bernard and Wayne Grady (2002), *The Beothuk Saga*, New York: Thomas Dunne Books.
Bruchac, Joseph (1985), *The Wind Eagle and Other Abenaki Stories*, New York: Bowman Books.
Richardson, John (1991), *Wacousta*, Toronto: McClelland and Stewart.

Histories

Marshall, Ingeborg (1991), *The Beothuk of Newfoundland: A Vanished People*, St John's: Breakwater Books.
Marshall, Ingeborg (1998), A *History of Ethnography of the Beothuk*, Montreal: McGill-Queen's University Press.
Wetzel, Jerry (1995), 'Decolonizing Ktaqmkuk Mi'kmaq History', unpublished LL M thesis, Dalhousie University, Halifax, Nova Scotia.
Wiseman, Frederick Matthew (2001), *The Voice of the Dawn: An Autohistory of the Abenaki Nation*, Middlebury: Middlebury College Press.

See also: **European Exploration and Settlement: Canada; Inuit; Native Reservations**.

Genocide: Rwanda

On 6 April 1994, the plane carrying President Juvénal Habyarimana of Rwanda and President Cyprien Ntariyamira of Burundi was shot down as it approached Kigali airport in Rwanda. The next day, the Interahamwe (Hutu militias) in Kigali used Habyarimana's death as a pretext for commencing the systematic genocide of Tutsi and moderate Hutu, with the deputy prime minister Agathe Uwilingiyimina and ten Belgian peace-keepers among the first killed. Hard-line Hutu parliamentarian Théodore Sindikubwabo formed an interim government on 8 April, and in the next 100 days, over 800,000 Tutsis and moderate Hutus were killed in a government-orchestrated slaughter. The genocide ended when the opposition forces of the Rwandese Patriotic Front (RPF) under Paul Kagame defeated the final remnants of the Rwandan government army on 18 July 1994.

The roots of the genocide are to be located in Rwanda's history. Before European colonialism, the region of what was to become Rwanda was occupied by a Hutu majority who cultivated crops, a substantial Tutsi community who were cattle-herders, and the Twa who were hunter-gatherers and made up 1 per cent of the total population. All three groups spoke the same language (Kinyarwanda), shared the same religion, and inhabited a common cultural universe. The 1885 Berlin Conference allocated the region designated

Ruanda-Urundi to Germany, and in 1910 the borders were fixed in Brussels when the Belgian Congo, British Uganda and German East Africa (which included Ruanda-Urundi) were delineated. In 1916, Belgian troops drove out the German administration, and in 1923, Ruanda-Urundi became a mandated territory under Belgian supervision. The Belgian authorities presided over the introduction of cash crops like coffee, and pursued a policy of promoting the Tutsi within the colonial administration and economy. In 1933, identity cards were issued classifying everyone as Hutu, Tutsi or Twa, and legal and bureau-cratic barriers preventing Hutu upward mobility were cemented.

The struggle for independence was led from 1957 by Hutu rebels, and, accompanied by anti-Tutsi violence, Rwanda was declared independent in 1962 with Gregoire Kayibanda as president. Tension between Hutu and Tutsi persisted after decolonisation, with large numbers of Tutsis killed in 1963, 1967 and 1973, and the massacre of 200,000 Hutu in Burundi in 1972. Habyarimana promulgated a new constitution for a one-party state, and as leader of the National Republican Movement for Democracy (MRND) duly became president of a Hutu-dominated government in 1978, a post he held until his death in 1994.

The Rwandan economy suffered severely after the collapse of the world coffee price in 1989, and violence escalated steadily from 1990, with 3,000 Tutsi killed from 1990 to 1993 in four planned massacres, and over a million refugees displaced by fighting between MRND and RPF forces. The immediate precursor to the genocide was the Arusha Accords signed in August 1993 between the parties to the civil war. The Arusha Accords prescribed multi-party elections within twenty-two months, but were presented to the populace by Hutu extremists as returning Rwanda to Tutsi domination under the RPF. Genocide of the Tutsi was therefore a strategy adopted to derail the Arusha Accords.

If Rwanda's history explains the roots of the genocide, the reason for the sheer scale of the killings resides in the *realpolitik* of the West in 1994. The immediate United Nations response to the genocide was for the Security Council to accept on 21 April the British ambassador David Hannay's proposal to reduce the size of the peace-keeping force from 2,500 to 270, with the result that by 25 April General Romeo Dallaire, the head of the UN force, had lost over 2,000 of his peace-keepers. Fears of a repetition of Somalia, where eighteen US soldiers had been killed in October 1993, appear to have determined the UN decision. Following appeals from Dallaire, the Security Council voted on 17 May to send 5,500 peace-keepers, but their deployment was delayed by countervailing pressure from the USA and Britain. Dallaire's opinion, supported by human rights groups and academics, has been that prompt international intervention could have saved hundreds of thousands of lives. By the time Dallaire was replaced by General Guy Tousignant on 16 August, the death toll in Rwanda had risen beyond 800,000; the number of UN peace-keepers had risen to 1,624.

David Johnson

Literary Works

Dallaire, Romeo (2003), *Shake Hands with the Devil. The Failure of Humanity in Rwanda*, Toronto: Random House of Canada.

Diop, Boubacar Boris (2000), *Murambi, le Livre des Ossements* (*Murambi, the Book of Remains*), Paris: Stock.

Jennings, Christian (2000), *Across the Red River: Rwanda, Burundi and the Heart of Darkness*, 2nd edn, London: Phoenix.

Kyomuhendo, Goretti (1999), *Secrets No More*, Oxford: African Book Collective.

Monenembo, Tierno (2004), *The Oldest Orphan*, trans. M. F. Nagem, Lincoln, NE: University of Nebraska Press.

Mukagasana, Yolande (1997), *La Mort ne Veut pas de Moi* (Death Doesn't Want Me), Paris: Fixot.

Tadjo, Veronique (2001), *In the Shadow of Imana*, trans. V. Wakerley, London: Heinemann.

Umutesi, Marie Béatrice (2000), *Fuir ou Mourir au Zaire: Le Vécu d'une Réfugiée Rwandaise* (To Flee or to Die in Zaire: The Experiences of a Rwandan refugee), Paris: L'Harmattan.

Histories

Barnett, Michael (2002), *Eyewitness to a Genocide: The United Nations and Rwanda*, Ithaca, NY: Cornell University Press.

Des Forges, Alison (1999), *Leave None to Tell the Story. Genocide in Rwanda*, New York: Human Rights Watch. Available at http://hrw.org/reports/1999/rwanda/

Malvern, Linda (2000), *A People Betrayed. The Role of the West in Rwanda's Genocide*, London: Zed Books.

Malvern, Linda (2004), *Conspiracy to Murder. The Rwandan Genocide*, London: Verso.

Mamdani, Mahmood (2001), *When Victims Become Killers. Colonialism, Nativism and the Genocide in Rwanda*, Oxford: Currey.

Omaar, Rayiya (1995), *Rwanda. Death, Despair and Defiance*, 2nd edn, London: African Rights.

See also: **Britain's Postwar Foreign Policy; Refugees; United Nations**.

Governors-General and Viceroys

In the mid-eighteenth century, the amount of Indian territory under the East India Company's control expanded dramatically. Apprehension at such vast obligations as well as the immense revenues it promised prompted almost a century of parliamentary intervention in the company's administrative and political affairs. One of the first of these so-called reforms was Lord North's Regulating Act (1773), which among other things elevated the company's governor of Fort William in Bengal, Warren Hastings at the time, to the position of governor-general (renamed, in 1833, governor-general of India).

The office was made the head of British affairs in India, responsible not only for the company's jurisdiction in eastern India but for superintending the previously independent company presidencies at Madras, Bombay, and Bencoolen. With Pitt's India Act (1784), the Regulating Act also centralised the expanding British presence in India by institutionalising state authority and oversight over the governor-general. In India, he was in fact a governor-general-in-council, statutorily bound to the majority vote of four councillors (more in later years), who could pose significant obstacles to his authority. In Britain, though the governor-general was still in theory appointed by the company, after 1784 his selection and dismissal became the prerogative of the Crown and the newly created Board of Control. This persisted until after the rebellion of 1857–8, when control over Indian affairs was formally transferred from the company to the Crown.

At this point, the governor-general became a viceroy – head of the government of India and the direct representative of the Queen, particularly important on diplomatic and ceremonial occasions. The viceroy, generally an aristocrat, lived regally and exercised his office with great pomp. This reinforced a British political ideal of hierarchy and status, which many Britons at home and in India felt essential for keeping order and obedience amongst their Indian subjects and the nominally independent princely states. The Indian viceroyalty became one of the most prized in the British imperial service and served as a model for its analogues throughout the Empire. Conversely, many governors-general and viceroys cut their teeth not typically in India, but in Ireland, Canada, Australia, and as military commanders from the American Revolution to World War II. Indeed, these men were much more likely to have experience in Westminster or Whitehall than at Fort William. Yet despite these institutional and political ties to the 'home' government and the Empire more broadly, many governors-general and viceroys nonetheless struggled for autonomy for the government of India and greatly influenced its development. In fact, certain events in the British Empire in India have become almost synonymous with particular administrations: for example, the revenue collection scheme known as the Permanent Settlement (1793) with Cornwallis (1786–93, 1805); company social interventionism, particularly marked by obsessions with eradicating *sati* and *thugi* with Bentick (1828–35); the consolidation of the British Indian Empire both through technological expansion and the gradual annexation of Indian states via the 'doctrine of lapse' and 'doctrine of paramountcy' with Dalhousie (1848–56); the partition of Bengal with Curzon (1898–1904, 1905); and, perhaps most famously, the independence and partition of India itself with Mountbatten (1947).

Philip Stern

Literary Works

Anonymous [1789] (1989), *Hartly House, Calcutta. A Novel of the Days of Warren Hastings*, introd. and notes Monica Clough, London: Pluto Press.
Ghosha, Nava-Krishna (1919), 'On Lord Northbrook, the Governor-General of India', ed. with a short memoir by Debendra Chandra Mullick in *The Poetical Works of Ram Sharma*, Calcutta: P. N. Mallick.
Kipling, Rudyard (1928), 'One Viceroy Resigns', *The Works of Rudyard Kipling*, New York: Walter J. Black.
Ray, Satayjit (1978), dir., *Shatranj Ke Khilari* (*The Chess Players*), Devki Chitra Productions (Suresh Jindal), based upon Premchand [1924] (2001), 'Shatranj ke Khilari', in Amit Chaudhuri (ed.), *The Picador Book of Modern Indian Literature*, London: Picador.
Sheridan, Richard Brinsley (1799), *Pizarro: A Tragedy in Five Acts* (taken from the German drama of Kotzebue), London: printed for James Ridgway.

Histories

Cohn, Bernard (1990), 'Representing Authority in Victorian India', in B. Cohn (ed.), *An Anthropologist among the Historians and Other Essays*, Delhi: Oxford University Press, pp. 632–82.
Curzon, George Nathaniel Curzon, Marquis of (1925), *British Government in India: The Story of Viceroys and Government Houses*, London: Cassell and Company Ltd.

Ghosh, Suresh Chandra (1975), *Dalhousie in India, 1848–56: A Study of his Social Policy as Governor-General*, New Delhi: Munshiram Manoharlal.

Goradia, Nayana (1993), *Lord Curzon: The Last of the British Moghuls*, Delhi: Oxford University Press.

Marshall, P. J. (1988), *Bengal: The British Bridgehead, Eastern India, 1740–1828*, Cambridge: Cambridge University Press.

Mersey, Charles Clive Bingham (1949), *The Viceroys and Governors-General of India, 1757–1947*, London: John Murray.

Misra, B. B. (1970), *The Administrative History of India, 1834–1947*, Bombay: Oxford University Press.

Teignmouth, John Shore, Baron (1933), *The Private Record of an Indian Governor-Generalship*, ed. Holden Furber, Cambridge, MA: Harvard University Press.

Tinker, Hugh (1997), *Viceroy: Curzon to Mountbatten*, Karachi: Oxford University Press.

Woodruff [Mason], Philip (1954), *The Men who Ruled India*, 2 vols, New York: St Martin's Press.

See also: **East India Company; Raj.**

H

Haitian Revolution

In 1789 San Domingue was the most valuable colony in the world. Powered by slave labour and blessed with fertile soil and an ideal climate, its cane estates produced 40 per cent of the world's sugar. Inhabitants of the island were divided by law into three racial castes: 465,000 black slaves (two-thirds of whom were born in Africa), 30,000 whites, and 27,000 mulattos (free people of colour).

At the time of the slave uprising, each of these groups was engaged in its own revolutionary movement, and all three movements were influenced by the French Revolution. The white planters were moving toward independence because they chaffed at trade regulations that prohibited trading with any country other than France. The mulattos, who owned a third of the colony's plantation property and a fourth of its slaves, resented their second-class status and agitated for the same 'Rights of Man' afforded to the whites. The slaves, hearing talk of human equality and suffering under inhuman conditions, revolted to improve their lot.

The revolution began on 22 August 1791, when the slaves on the Northern Plain rose up. Returning in kind the barbaric treatment to which they had been subjected, the insurgents destroyed plantations and murdered their masters. Shortly after the initial uprising, Toussaint L'Ouverture (1743–1803), a former coachman, joined the fight. A brilliant tactician, Toussaint quickly rose to the position of general, making agreements with Spain and

Britain to receive arms and assistance in fighting the French forces sent to quell the rebellion. Faced with imminent defeat, France abolished slavery in San Domingue. The remaining white planters were outraged; and in 1793 when British forces landed on the island, they were welcomed by white property owners who wanted the colony to become a British possession in exchange for the reinstatement of slavery. Toussaint then returned to the French side, and by 1798 he had driven the British from San Domingue, overseen the retreat of the Spanish to Santo Domingo (the Spanish half of the island, now the Dominican Republic), displaced all genuine French authority and become governor-general and commander-in-chief of the island.

In 1802 Napoleon sent 20,000 men to win San Domingue back for France and restore slavery. Although Napoleon captured Toussaint, who was transported to France where he died in a fortress in the Jura Mountains, the invasion ultimately failed due to the fierce resistance of Toussaint's generals Jean Jacques Dessalines (1758–1806) and Henri Christophe (1767–1820), and to the effects of yellow fever, which decimated the French troops. On 1 January 1804, Dessalines proclaimed himself emperor of the independent nation of Haiti.

Jennifer Sparrow

Literary Works

Carpentier, Alejo [1957] (1989), *Kingdom of this World*, trans. H. de Onís, New York: Noonday Press.
Césaire, Aimé (1969), *The Tragedy of King Christophe*, trans. R. Manheim, New York: Grove Press.
Smartt Bell, Madison (1995), *All Souls' Rising*, New York: Pantheon Books.
Smartt Bell, Madison (2000), *Master of the Crossroads*, New York: Pantheon Books.
Walcott, Derek (2002), *The Haitian Trilogy*, New York: Farrar, Straus and Giroux.

Histories

Fick, Carolyn E. (1990), *The Making of Haiti: The Saint Domingue Revolution From Below*, Knoxville, TN: University of Tennessee Press.
Heinl, Robert Debs and Nancy Gordon; updated by Michael Heinl (1996), *Written in Blood: The Story of the Haitian People 1492–1995*, Lanham, MD: University Press of America.
James, C. L. R. [1938] (1963), *The Black Jacobins: Toussaint L'Ouverture and the San Domingo Revolution*, New York: Vintage Books.

See also: **Anti-colonialism and Resistance: Caribbean**; **Slavery: Caribbean**.

Hill Stations

Indian hill stations were created to meet a number of requirements of the British colonial government, especially after the mutiny ending in 1858. Of these, three were of paramount importance, providing: refuge to the British during summer months; military surveillance;

and health retreats. The hills allowed the British to maintain racial exclusivity more easily than on the plains. From 1864, the hill station of Simla served as the summer capital of British India. In addition, under British patronage, hill stations became centres of missionary activity, and trade and commerce in natural resources. Over time, the hill station came to embody for the British a contradictory utopian vision of a home away from home. While the climate and vegetation of the hills reminded them of Britain and Europe, a tendency strongly coloured by Victorian Romantic valorisations of nature, the imperial defence of the hills against local insurgents and foreign powers allowed colonials to test out codes of masculine violence learnt in British public schools and military academies. In Rudyard Kipling's work, the hill station emerges as an ambiguous geopolitical entity where the romance of the hills is perpetually haunted by suspicion of the nomadic racial other and the unknown, and vitiated by colonial violence and greed.

Hill stations gradually became popular haunts for ever-increasing numbers of British and European travellers. From very early on, European tourism ensured that hill stations were home to modern amenities like cinemas, hotels and commodity goods unavailable in many larger towns on the plains. Domestic and international tourism boomed in the 1970s. Upper-class Indians started visiting and living in hill stations, and their children began studying in hill station boarding schools. A slew of Indian films in the 1960s glorified the beauty of the hills, especially of Kashmir, and their role as an Edenic retreat where the hero discovers romance and adventure. Others such as Satyajit Ray's *Kanchanjanga* persist in and perpetuate the vision of the hill station as a resort created for the enjoyment of the Europeans/wealthy plainsmen. Offsetting this romantic vision was the military presence in hill stations, a reminder of their geopolitical significance in military surveillance, and the impoverishment of these regions resulting from a callous and intense exploitation of natural resources.

The 1980s saw tensions escalating across India's mountainous international borders and the rise of separatist demands in regions dominated by hill stations in many parts of India. In Mani Ratnam's film *Roja* (1992), the hills emerge as a paradise that has failed to deliver its promise of peace and romance, compromised by the complexities of their topography, their natural wealth, and human greed and ruthlessness.

Kaushik Bhaumik

Literary Works

Bond, Ruskin (1989), *The Night Train at Deoli and Other Stories*, New Delhi: Penguin.
Farrell, J. G. (1987), *The Hill Station*, London: Flamingo.
Godden, Rumer (1939), *Black Narcissus*, London: P. Davies.
Kipling, Rudyard (1889), *Plain Tales from the Hills*, Calcutta: Thacker, Spink and Company.
Kipling, Rudyard (1901), *Kim*, London: Macmillan.
Sealy, Allan (1998), *The Everest Hotel*, Delhi: IndiaInk.

Histories

Hopkirk, Peter (1990), *The Great Game: On Secret Service in High Asia*, London: John Murray.
Kanwar, P. (1999), *Imperial Simla: The Political Culture of the Raj*, New Delhi: Oxford University Press.

King, A. D. (1976), *Colonial Urban Development: Culture, Social Power, and Environment*, London: Routledge and Kegan Paul.
Kennedy, Dale (1996), *The Magic Mountains: Hill Stations and the British Raj*, Berkeley, CA: University of California Press.

See also: **English in India: Eighteenth and Nineteenth Centuries; Raj**.

Historiography: Australia

Written histories of Australia began with the publication of the journals of British and French voyagers and colonisers from the 1770s onwards. The journals of Captain James Cook and Joseph Banks recording their 1770 visit to the east coast of the Australian continent, together with the journals from 1788 of the officers on the First Fleet, such as the observant Watkin Tench, inaugurated a long historiographical tradition. For these voyagers and settlers, Australia was an unknown land with unknown people to be discovered and claimed for the British Crown. For the next two centuries, many histories about Australia had hidden within them these originary motifs.

The first academic historians like George Arnold Wood, Stephen Roberts, and Ernest Scott, in the early twentieth century, followed in the tradition of the journal writers, and wrote of voyaging, exploration, and land settlement. Yet as settlement expanded, with its bloody skirmishes, frontier violence, and devastating effects on the indigenous population, a new and different historical consciousness seemed necessary. With settlement, most Australian incomers now believed, a new civilisation was introduced to an already inhabited country, though the legal doctrine of *terra nullius* (land belonging to no-one) helped many to disregard the claims and even the existence of these indigenous peoples. During the nineteenth century, histories of frontier violence were written during or soon after the events they depicted. Some took the settler point of view, seeing the indigenous people as having no claim to the land because they did not use it productively and because they were treacherous, savage, and contemptible, while others expressed shame that indigenous peoples had been treated brutally or with callous disregard, so endangering Britain's and British people's moral reputation in history (see Melville 1835, West 1852, Rusden 1883). From the 1890s through to the 1970s, a third historical narrative appeared: one of widespread indifference and denial. As memories of the frontier faded, settlers came to believe that colonisation had proceeded peacefully and smoothly, and that Aboriginal people had somehow simply faded away.

With the constitution of the nation in 1901 in formal terms, and the consolidation of the nation with Australian fighting forces in World War I in emotional terms, the way was open for yet another new national narrative. Historians not only charted histories of discovery and settlement, but also of the emergence of a proud independent nation. One of the earliest to do so was Ernest Scott, who wrote a widely-used general text, *A Short History of Australia* (1916), which in its first edition began with Australia as 'a blank space on the map', and ended with the early years of World War I, placing on record 'a new name on the map, that of Anzac'. After World War II, the rapid expansion in secondary and university education stimulated a substantial growth in the writing and reading of Australian history. From the mid-1950s, a growing number of general histories (see Crawford 1952, Greenwood 1955, Douglas Pike 1962, Shaw 1995, Barnard 1962, Clark 1962–87, and Russel Ward 1958, 1965) and detailed historical monographs appeared on a range of topics, from the history of transportation and colonial administration to federation, Australian involvement in war, and the history of class and labour relations.

Most of these histories conceptualised their subject firmly within the framework of British colonisation, the British Empire, and later the British Commonwealth (see J. M. Ward 1958). Familial metaphors abounded, telling a story of birth, youth, separation from the mother country, and finally adulthood, connected by continuing threads of kinship and feelings of attachment. Yet there was already evident by the late 1950s a growing desire for a more Australia-focused historiography, placing the experience of Australian immigrants and their descendants – rather than British officialdom and governing institutions – at the centre of the analysis. In *The Australian Legend* (1958), Russel Ward used folk songs and literary material to help investigate male rural working-class consciousness and character, which he admired as egalitarian, unpretentious, irreverent, laconic, collectivist, and nomadic. In his six-volume *History of Australia* (1962–87), Manning Clark showed how some of the greatest conflicts in Western Europe – between the Enlightenment and religion, and between Protestant and Catholic sensibilities – were played out on the Australian continent.

While these histories varied enormously in style and argument, nearly all confined the discussion of Aboriginal people – if they dealt with them at all – to a single chapter placed early in the story. These scant references to indigenous experience contributed to a popular collective imagination that largely erased prior indigenous occupation from consciousness. Instead of a story of Indigenous suffering as a result of colonisation, dispossession, loss of liberty, health, and very often life itself, popular Australian understandings of the past stressed the sufferings, defeats and heroism of white Australians as they colonised the country. Australian popular culture, indeed, continues to emphasise loss and defeat, and the status of Australians as victims in history. This narrative of victimology begins with stories of convict history, of men exiled from their British homeland and treated inhumanely. It continues with 'pioneer' narratives which emphasise the struggle to survive in a hostile land marked by fire, flood, and drought, where British farming know-how was either absent or inadequate to the task of developing agriculture and pastoralism in a different environment. A particularly well-developed form of this historiography is that of Australian involvement in war. Historians and the Australian public have been especially interested in experiences of World War I, especially of the Australian soldiers who participated in the unsuccessful Gallipoli campaign in the Dardanelles in 1915 (see Bean 1921–, Gammage 1974), and they have also been interested in how this wartime experience is embedded in national memory (see Inglis 1998). Other wars have also attracted historians' attention, especially World War II, and to a lesser extent the Vietnam conflict (see McKernan 1983).

The desire for a national history with Australia at the centre of the story accelerated from the 1970s. A new generation of Australian historians emerged who were products of an enhanced Australian education system. Events in Africa, Vietnam, and the USA all led to new thinking about questions of race, culture, and equality, and many historians were influenced by involvement in the new social movements. They shared, too, a new sense of national identity, which was marked by a declining interest in Australia's British inheritance and a desire to create a vibrant cosmopolitan culture in Australia itself. Historians from the 1970s onward were also influenced by the work of other disciplines, especially anthropology and literary studies. For all these reasons, a fast-growing and lively national historiography rapidly emerged, which tackled questions of colonialism and postcolonialism in a critical spirit.

In particular, as the indigenous political movement strengthened, a thorough reconsideration of Aboriginal history was undertaken, and specialist histories based on archival and sometimes oral history research began to detail the processes of culture contact, violence, employment, institutionalisation, and attempted assimilation of indigenous peoples (see Rowley 1970, Barwick 1998, Reece 1974, Reynolds 1981, 1987, 2001, Ryan 1981, Goodall 1996, Read 1984). This work was synthesised into a general text by Richard Broome, *The Aboriginal Australians* (1982). Sympathetic recognition of Aboriginal experience was difficult in a culture which had traditionally cast white Australians as victims. By the 1980s, however, the roles had been reversed, and Aboriginal Australians were increasingly seen as defeated but heroic victims. These new histories were in the form of Aboriginal testimony – as autobiography, biography, family story, and oral histories (see Morgan 1987, Perkins 1975, Tucker 1977, Huggins 1994 and Read 1984). Aboriginal histories were also recounted by non-Aboriginal historians and anthropologists anxious to recover and develop empathetic accounts of what Henry Reynolds in his 1981 book termed 'the other side of the frontier'. Feminist historians played a significant role in the new critical historiography: Ann McGrath (1987) undertook a gendered analysis of the lives of Aboriginal workers in the Northern Territory pastoral industry, and Fiona Paisley (2000) and Marilyn Lake (1999) investigated feminist activists' concern with Aboriginal issues. Historians responded and contributed to public debates on these matters, with two events particularly prominent. The first was the bicentennial celebration of the British settlement of the Australian continent, which provided an opportunity to build white public awareness that 1788 had been a disaster for Aboriginal people. The second was the *Mabo* case in 1992, which (influenced by Reynolds' scholarship) overturned the fiction of *terra nullius*, and recognised original prior occupation and native title rights.

The *Mabo* decision led white Australians to feel the legitimacy of their occupation of the country was under question, and many dubbed the new histories 'black armband histories'. Some argued that history was losing popularity in schools because of a steady diet of unpalatable and uninspiring stories of white wrongdoing. Public debate over truth and history continued with the publication in 1997 of *Bringing them Home*, a government-commissioned report on the removal of children from Aboriginal parents under earlier Church and government policies. Based largely on the testimony of those who had been removed, the human suffering recorded was uncomfortable for many Australians. Outraged conservatives rejected the veracity of the report, which described the child removal as 'genocide' as defined by the United Nations in 1948. More public questioning of Aboriginal history came with the publication of Keith Windschuttle's *The Fabrication of Aboriginal History* (2002), which questioned the accuracy of those histories which emphasised settler violence and the loss of Aboriginal life on the frontiers. The huge public debate and historical response to this book have been dubbed the 'History Wars', and it is clear that they are far from over (see Manne 2003).

If the history of colonisation is being contested and re-examined, the history of decolonisation is also attracting new attention. In the Australian context, 'decolonisation' has two very distinct facets. One is the 'decolonising' of Australia itself and its emergence as an independent nation state. This involves political histories investigating federation, Australia's role in international arenas like the British Commonwealth and United Nations, and the development of its own defence, immigration and foreign policies, particularly in relation to the USA (see Irving 1997). The second aspect of decolonisation refers to the 'decolonising' of indigenous peoples, and the emergence of political and cultural movements which recognise prior indigenous occupation. These histories focus on cultural resistance and protest politics (see Attwood 2003, Curthoys 2000a, 2002 and Goodall 1996), and may also include the study of the new institutions which arise to manage Aboriginal claims.

Histories of migration, one of the key features of Australian life since 1788, have also been transformed in recent years. The earliest study of Australia's racially based immigration policies, Myra Willard's well-researched A History of the White Australia Policy (1923), had been sympathetic to the policy it investigated. The Labor historians of the 1960s saw working-class support for the policy as driven by economic rather than racial ideas (see Nairn 1989). Most studies from the 1970s, however, assumed that racial policies were undesirable, and set out to explain why they had been so widely supported in Australia for so long (see Markus 1983, Curthoys and Markus 1978, Evans et al. 1975). The arrival of large numbers of immigrants from continental Europe, the Middle East and later Asia stimulated the development of histories of particular immigrant groups, tracing their motivations for migration, and their difficulties in the face of Anglo-Celtic resistance, as well as their successes. Despite a shared concern to investigate the place of racism in Australian culture, however, Aboriginal and migration histories have usually been studied separately (see Curthoys 2000b), but this separation is now slowly dissolving, as historians explore relations between Aboriginal people and non-British immigrants, and more generally the development of mixed-race people and hybrid identities (see Govor 2000, Shen 2001, Edwards and Shen 2003).

Cultural history has also been a significant area of growth within Australian historiography, and has been influenced by the development of cultural studies (see Teo and White 2002). Cultural historians have investigated Australian literature and popular culture as expressed in journalism, theatre, film, broadcasting, sport, music, and folklore, and in leisure pursuits like picnicking or going to the beach (see Adair and Vamplew 1997, Spearritt and Walker 1979, Pike 1962, Bertrand 1989, Collins 1987, Sturma 1991, Johnson 1988). Some scholars considered the wider cosmopolitan connections developed within Australian culture from the early nineteenth century until today, investigating, for example, the intense sympathetic interest by Anglo-Celtic Australians in continental European cultures and in the Orient (see Docker 1991 and Walker 1999).

Finally, three further new departures in Australian history-writing need to be noted. The first has been a shift away from national histories towards more transnational forms of history, forms of history that trace events, themes, and people beyond national boundaries, often in surprising ways. The second has been the growing attention to environmental history, in which scientists and historians combine to trace histories of fire, water, forests, farming practices and landscapes. Underlying their work is an examination of the impacts of empires and colonisation on the movement of plants, animals, and diseases around the world (see Dovers 1994, Griffiths and Robin 1997, Grove 1997). The third new departure has been a reconsideration of the British imperial context in order to understand better Australian historical processes (see Woollacott 2001). In the spirit of Catherine Hall's Civilising Subjects (2002), these histories have stressed the ways in which the colonies constituted Britain as much as Britain constituted them. An interesting example of such an approach is Cassandra Pybus and Hamish Maxwell-Stewart's history of freed and loyalist African Americans after the American War of Independence, who were eventually transported as convicts to the Australian colonies (see Pybus and Maxwell-Stewart 2002, Frost and Maxwell-Stewart 2001).

Australian historiography is therefore witnessing major changes. In the last five years, imperial history has been transformed from old-fashioned and reserved to adventurous, transnational, comparative and cutting-edge; national history, once seen as radical and committed, now appears a trifle conservative and enclosed. As a society still in the throes of decolonisation, Australia finds its own histories challenging, even threatening, yet all the more necessary for that.

Ann Curthoys

Literary Works

Flanagan, Richard (1997), *The Sound of One Hand Clapping*, Sydney: Picador.
Flanagan, Richard (2001), *Gould's Book of Fish*, Sydney: Picador.
Lucashenko, Melissa (1998), *Steam Pigs*, St Lucia: University of Queensland Press.
Mahood, Kim (2000), *Craft for a Dry Lake*, Sydney: Anchor.
Malouf, David (1982), *Fly Away Peter*, London: Vintage.
Malouf, David (1993), *Remembering Babylon*, New York: Random House.
Martin, Catherine [1923] (1987), *An Incredible Journey*, London: Pandora.
Morgan, Sally (1987), *My Place*, Fremantle: Arts Centre Press.
Scott, Kim (1999), *Benang: From the Heart*, Fremantle: Arts Centre Press.
Teo Hsu-ming (2000), *Love and Vertigo*, St Leonards: Allen and Unwin.

Histories

Adair, Daryl and Wray Vamplew (1997), *Sport in Australian History*, Melbourne, New York: Oxford University Press.
Attwood, Bain (2003), *Rights for Aborigines*, Sydney: Allen and Unwin.
Barnard, Marjorie (1962), *A History of Australia*, Sydney: Angus and Robertson.
Barwick, Diane (1998), *Rebellion at Coranderrk*, Canberra: Aboriginal History Inc.
Beaglehole, J. C. (1999), *The Journals of Captain Cook*, London: Penguin.
Bean, Charles (1921–), *The Official History of Australia in the War of 1914–1918*, Sydney: Angus and Robertson.
Bertrand, Ina (ed.) (1989), *Cinema in Australia: A Documentary History*, Kensington: New South Wales University Press.
Broome, Richard [1982] (2001), *Aboriginal Australians*, Sydney: Allen and Unwin.
Clark, Manning (1962–87), *A History of Australia*, 6 vols, Carlton: Melbourne University Press.
Collins, Diane (1987), *Hollywood Down Under: Australians at the Movies, 1896 to the present day*, North Ryde: Angus and Robertson.
Crawford, Max (1952), *Australia*, London: Hutchinson.
Curthoys, Ann (2000), 'An Uneasy Conversation: The Indigenous and the Multicultural', in John Docker and Gerhard Fischer (eds), *Race, Colour and Identity in Australia and New Zealand*, Sydney: New South Wales University Press.
Curthoys, Ann (2000), 'Mythologies', in Richard Nile (ed.), *The Australian Legend and its Discontents*, St Lucia: University of Queensland Press.
Curthoys, Ann (2002), *Freedom Ride: A Freedomrider Remembers*, Sydney: Allen and Unwin.
Curthoys, Ann and Andrew Markus (eds) (1978), *Who Are Our Enemies?* Sydney: Hale and Iremonger.

Davison, Graeme, John Hirst and Stuart Macintyre (eds) (1998), *The Oxford Companion to Australian History*, Melbourne: Oxford University Press.

Docker, John (1991), *The Nervous Nineties*, Melbourne: Melbourne University Press.

Dovers, S. (ed.) (1994), *Australian Environmental History: Essays and Cases*, Melbourne: Oxford University Press.

Edwards, Penny and Yuanfang Shen (eds) (2003), *Lost in the Whitewash: Aboriginal-Asian Encounters in Australia, 1901–2001*, Canberra: Humanities Research Centre.

Evans, Ray, Kathryn Cronin, Kathryn Saunders and Kay Saunders [1975] (1988), *Race Relations in Colonial Queensland. Extermination, Exploitation, and Exclusion*, St Lucia: University of Queensland Press.

Frost, Lucy and Hamish Maxwell-Stewart (eds) (2001), *Chain Letters. Narrating Convict Lives*, Carlton South: Melbourne University Press.

Gammage, Bill (1974), *The Broken Years: Australian Soldiers in the Great War*, Canberra: Australian National University Press.

Goodall, Heather (1996), *Invasion to Embassy*, Sydney: Allen and Unwin.

Govor, Elena (2000), *My Dark Brother: The Story of the Illins, A Russian-Aboriginal Family*, Sydney: University of New South Wales Press.

Greenwood, Gordon [1955] (1974), *Australia: A Social and Political History*, London: Angus and Robertson.

Griffiths, Tom and Libby Robin (eds) (1997), *Ecology and Empire: Environmental History of Settler Societies*, Edinburgh: Keele University Press.

Grove, Richard (1997), *Ecology, Climate and Empire: Colonialism and Global Environmental History, 1400–1940*, Cambridge: Cambridge University Press.

Hall, Catherine (2002), *Civilising Subjects: Colony and Metropole in the English Imagination, 1830–1867*, Chicago: University of Chicago Press.

Huggins, Jackie and Rita Huggins (1994), *Auntie Rita*, Canberra: Aboriginal Studies Press.

Inglis, K. S. with Jan Brazier (1998), *Sacred Places: War Memorials in the Australian Landscape*, Carlton: Miegunyah Press.

Irving, Helen (1997), *To Constitute a Nation: A Cultural History of Australia's Constitution*, Cambridge: Cambridge University Press.

Johnson, Lesley (1988), *The Unseen Voice: A Cultural Study of Early Australian Radio*, London: Routledge.

Lake, Marilyn (1999), *Getting Equal: The History of Australian Feminism*, St Leonards: Allen and Unwin.

Manne, Robert (2003), *Whitewash: On Keith Windschuttle's Fabrication of Aboriginal History*, Melbourne: Black Inc.

Markus, Andrew (1983), *Fear and Hatred: Purifying Australia and California, 1850–1901*, Sydney: Hale and Iremonger.

McGrath, Ann (1987), *Born in the Cattle*, Sydney: Allen and Unwin.

McKernan, Michael (1983), *All In!: Australia During the Second World War*, Melbourne: Nelson.

Melville, Henry (1835), *The History of the Island of Van Dieman's Land*, London: Smith and Elder.

Morgan, Sally (1987), *My Place*, Fremantle: Arts Centre Press.

Nairn, Bede (1989), *Civilising Capitalism. The Beginnings of the Australian Labor Party*, Carlton: Melbourne University Press.

Paisley, Fiona (2000), *Loving Protection? Australian Feminism and Aboriginal Women's Rights, 1919–1939*, Carlton: Melbourne University Press.

Perkins, Charles (1975), *A Bastard Like Me*, Sydney: Ure Smith.

Pike, Andrew, and Ross Cooper, (1980), *Australian Film, 1900–1977: A Guide to Feature Film*, Melbourne: Oxford University Press and Australian Film Institute.

Pike, Douglas (1962), *Australia: The Quiet Continent*, Cambridge: Cambridge University Press.

Pybus, Cassandra and Hamish Maxwell-Stewart (2002), *American Citizens, British Slaves: Yankee Political Prisoners in an Australian Penal Colony 1839–1850*, Carlton South: Melbourne University Press.

Read, Peter (1984), *Down There with Me on the Cowra Mission*, Sydney: Pergamon Press.

Reece, R. H. W. (1974), *Aborigines and Colonists: Aborigines and Colonial Society in the 1830s and 1840s*, Sydney: Sydney University Press.

Reynolds, Henry (1981), *The Other Side of the Frontier*, Ringwood: Penguin.

Reynolds, Henry (1987), *Law of the Land*, Ringwood: Penguin.

Reynolds, Henry (2001), *An Indelible Stain: The Question of Genocide in Australia's History*, Ringwood: Viking.

Roberts, Stephen (1924), *History of Australian Land Settlement, 1788–1920*, Melbourne: Macmillan.

Rose, Deborah Bird (1991), *Hidden Histories: Black Stories from Victoria River Downs and Wave Hill Stations*, Canberra: Aboriginal Studies Press.

Rowley, C. D. (1970), *The Destruction of Aboriginal Society*, Ringwood: Penguin.

Rusden, G. W. (1883), *History of Australia*, London: Chapman and Hall.

Ryan, Lyndall (1981), *The Aboriginal Tasmanians*, Sydney: Allen and Unwin.

Scott, Ernest (1916) *A Short History of Australia*, Melbourne: Oxford University Press.

Shaw, A. G. L. [1955] (1983), *The Story of Australia*, London: Faber and Faber.

Shen Yuanfang (2001), *Dragonseed in the Antipodes*, Melbourne: Melbourne University Press.

Souter, Gavin (1976), *Lion and Kangaroo: The Initiation of Australia, 1901–1919*, Sydney: Collins.

Spearritt, Peter and David Walker (eds) (1979), *Australian Popular Culture*, Sydney: Allen and Unwin.

Sturma, Michael (1991), *Australian Rock 'n Roll: The First Wave*, Sydney: Kangaroo Press.

Tench, Watkin (1996), *1788: Comprising a Narrative of the Expedition to Botany Bay and a Complete Account of the Settlement at Port Jackson*, ed. and intro. Tim Flannery, Melbourne: Text Publishing.

Teo Hsu-ming and Richard White (eds) (2002), *Cultural History in Australia*, Sydney: New South Wales University Press.

Tucker, Margaret (1977), *If Everyone Cared: Autobiography of Margaret Tucker*, Sydney: Ure Smith.

Walker, David (1999), *Anxious Nation: Australia and the Rise of Asia 1850–1939*, St Lucia: University of Queensland Press.

Ward, J. M. (1958), *Earl Grey and the Australian Colonies, 1846–1857: A Study of Self-Government and Self-Interest*, Carlton: Melbourne University Press.

Ward, Russel (1958), *The Australian Legend*, Melbourne: Oxford University Press.

Ward, Russel [1965] (1977), *Australia*, Sydney: Ure Smith.

West, John [1852] (1971), *History of Tasmania*, Sydney: Angus and Robertson.

Willard, Myra [1923] (1967), *A History of the White Australia Policy*, London: Cass.

Windschuttle, Keith (2002), *The Fabrication of Aboriginal History*, Sydney: Macleay Press.

Wood, George Arnold (1922), *The Discovery of Australia*, Melbourne: Macmillan.

Woollacott, Angela (2001), *To Try Her Fortune in London: Australian Women, Colonialism, and Modernity*, Oxford: Oxford University Press.

See also: **Land: Australia; Pre-colonial Histories: Australia; Women's Histories: Australia, New Zealand, and the Pacific; World Wars I and II: Anzac.**

Historiography: British Empire

The historians who have written about the British Empire in the last 140 years bear some resemblance to a large, dysfunctional Victorian family (the metaphor is from Orwell's description of England in 1940, in his essay 'The Lion and the Unicorn'). Until very recently, all family members were male, which might in part account for the intensity of the Oedipal conflicts, the fratricidal rivalries, the fraternal bonding, and the subtly managed hierarchies of favourite sons, neglected uncles, and foreign cousins. All of which adds to the fascination of reading this rich and varied body of historical work.

The first histories of the British Empire were written in the late nineteenth century by John Seeley (1883), J. A. Froude and Charles Dilke, and focused upon the deeds of Britain's explorers, military and political leaders, and colonial administrators. They were in broad sympathy with the ideals of the Empire, discussed in detail Britain's imperial competitors past and present, and paid relatively little attention to the indigenous populations incorporated under British rule. Seeley was the most influential, and summed up the widely held view of the Empire as 'a natural growth, a mere normal extension of the English race into other lands, which for the most part were so thinly peopled that our settlers took possession of them without conquest' (Seeley 1883, p. 296). Another feature of British Empire historiography of this era is that significant political actors in the colonies themselves wrote self-serving histories, notably Alfred Milner's *England in Egypt* (1893), George N. Curzon's *Problems in the Far East* (1894), and Lord Cromer's two-volume *Modern Egypt* (1908). The assumptions, concerns and methods of Seeley's generation were shared by Britain's professional historians in the next half-century, and were given their fullest expression in the eight-volume *Cambridge History of the British Empire*, published between 1929 and 1936 (Holland Rose et al.). The first three volumes cover the general history of overseas expansion and imperial policy, volumes 4 and 5 British India, volume 6 Canada and Newfoundland, volume 7 Australia and New Zealand, and volume 8 South Africa. The tenor of the *Cambridge History* is set in the Preface to volume 1:

> Out of the ambitions of that adventurous age [of the Tudors], when men dreamed great dreams for England and set out to realise them, grew the maritime State which, shaped amid the successive conflicts of modern history, has developed in the twentieth century into the British Commonwealth of Nations. (p. v)

Optimistic and teleological, fascinated with the heroic men (and occasionally women) who made Britain great, and alternately uninterested or patronising about the Empire's subject peoples, the *Cambridge History* represents a culmination of this tradition of history-writing. (See Wormell 1980, Louis 1976 and Winks 1999.)

Roughly contemporaneous with the Seeley-to-*Cambridge* histories of the British Empire were two further traditions of history-writing: British liberal anti-imperialism, and continental Marxism. Whereas Seeley's tradition stressed professional scholarship, the rigorous scrutiny of primary sources, and the strict separation of history and politics, both these alternative traditions were characterised by a greater reliance (often enforced) on secondary sources, and an explicit polemical purpose. The political sentiments driving the liberal anti-imperialists are vividly expressed in the speeches of John Bright and Richard Cobden in the 1860s. Convinced that Britain's best interests were betrayed by imperial expansion, Bright and Cobden argued that the Empire favoured *only* Britain's aristocracy, and that the settler colonies should enjoy self-government. This stance is modified, and supplemented by historical analysis, in J. A. Hobson's influential *Imperialism: A Study* (1902), which argues that:

> [a]gressive imperialism, which costs the taxpayer so dear, which is of so little value to the manufacturer and trader, which is fraught with such grave incalculable peril to the citizen, is a source of great gain to the investor who cannot find at home the profitable use he seeks for his capital. (p. 62)

Further varieties of this argument are expressed in political tracts like H. M. Hyndman's *England for All: A Textbook of Democracy* (1881) and George Bernard Shaw's *Fabianism and the Empire: A Manifesto of the Fabian Society* (1900), as well as in historically inflected studies like Norman Angell's *The Great Illusion* (1910), H. N. Brailsford's *The War of Steel and Gold* (1914), and Leonard Woolf's *Empire and Commerce in Africa* (1920) and *Imperialism and Civilisation* (1928). The Woolfs' Hogarth Press was especially significant in the post-World War I period, as it brought out a number of histories critical of imperialism that disputed the conclusions of Seeley's successors published in the traditional university presses. It is worth adding that this tradition has subsequently shown great vitality, with Hobson's work in particular continuing to excite vigorous attacks (see Hyam and Martin 1975) and stout defences (see Freeden 1990, and more generally, Porter 1996, Howe 1993 and Louis 1976).

The continental Marxist tradition is extrapolated from Marx's own scattered writings and observations on colonialism and imperialism. Marx echoed the moral outrage of the liberal anti-imperialists, but went further in anchoring his understanding of the British Empire in an economic analysis of capitalism, which saw Western capitalism's global expansion in pursuit of profit simultaneously destroying non-capitalist modes of production and creating the material conditions for the dialectical progression to communism. In his essays and letters on India, China, Ireland and Russia, Marx applied his economic theory of capitalism to these different contexts in cryptic form, leaving it up to his successors – Nikolai Bukharin, Rudolf Hilferding, V. I. Lenin, Karl Kautsky and Rosa Luxemburg – to develop substantial Marxist histories of imperialism in general, and of the British Empire in particular. The most influential study was Lenin's *Imperialism. The Highest Stage of Capitalism* (1917), which drew heavily not only on earlier Marxists, but also on Hobson, in order to argue that after the 1870s, the transition of capitalism based on free competition 'to the stage of monopoly capital, to finance capital, *is connected* with the intensification of the struggle for the partitioning of the world' (p. 75). A more historically textured version of this argument is provided in Luxemburg's *The Accumulation of Capital*, which has a long chapter on British imperialism in Egypt in the nineteenth century. An influential variation on Lenin's interpretation of imperial history is provided by Kautsky's *Socialism and Colonial Policy* (1907). Whereas Lenin emphasised competition between the imperial powers, and how transitions in European capitalist economies determine social change beyond Europe, Kautsky defined imperialism as primarily the unequal conflict between the capitalist West and the non-capitalist world, or in the terms of André Gunder Frank, between developed and underdeveloped economies. As in the case of liberal anti-imperialism, so too Continental Marxism has continued to draw adherents, as numerous histories of imperialism and of the British Empire have used Marx's economic problematic as their frame of reference, or point of departure: Hannah Arendt's *The Origins of Totalitarianism* (1951), Immanuel Wallerstein's *The Modern World System*. Three volumes (1974–89), Angus Calder's *Revolutionary Empire* (1981), V. G. Keirnan's *European Empires from Conquest to Collapse, 1815–1960* (1982), and Eric Hobsbawm's *The Age of Empire, 1875–1914* (1987). (See Barone 1985, Brewer 1990, and Owen and Sutcliffe 1972.)

Major shifts have occurred in the historiography of the British Empire since World War II. These shifts are nicely captured by Bernard Porter in the Preface to the third edition of his highly-regarded textbook *The Lion's Share. A Short History of British Imperialism, 1850–1995* (1996). According to Porter, 'When I first taught [the British Empire] . . . people assumed I must be an "imperialist" by that fact alone. That may have been partly because up to that time most imperial historians had been' (p. xiv). Moving forward, Porter recalls that 'In 1975 [capitalism] was a touchy issue. Historians debated hotly over whether Britain's imperial expansion was mainly economically motivated, or driven by other [more noble] causes' (p. xv). And he concludes with his impressions of British Empire historiography in the 1990s, observing that 'No one any more seriously doubts that capitalist pressures were the primary reason for Britain's imperial expansion in the nineteenth century' (p. xv).

Each of these overlapping phases was accompanied by exceptions and by fierce debate. By the 1950s, the dominant tradition, epitomised by Eric Walker's *The British Empire: Its Structure and Spirit* (1943), was already being challenged by histories that favoured area studies over Empire history, and that also were in sympathy with anti-imperial nationalist movements. Examples of this emergent form of history included W. M. Macmillan's *Bantu, Boer and Briton: The Making of the South African Native Problem* (1929), Edward Thompson and G. T. Garratt's *Rise and Fulfilment of British Rule in India* (1934), Rupert Emerson's *Malaysia: A Study of Direct and Indirect Rule* (1937), George Antoninus' *The Arab Awakening: The Story of the Arab National Movement* (1938), and Eric Williams' *Capitalism and Slavery* (1944). The rise of area studies was resisted after the war by powerful figures like Vincent T. Harlow at Oxford, whose *The Founding of the Second British Empire, 1763–1793* (1952) was based squarely on official documents at the Colonial Office. Harlow argued that the end of the American War of Independence in 1783 marked a fundamental transition from the first British Empire, which started in the seventeenth century and was based in the Americas, to the second British Empire, which saw a swing to the East as Britain established itself as the major power in India. The efforts of Harlow and his ilk were in vain, however, as area studies proliferated dramatically (see the other Historiography entries below), and Harlow's own 'Second Empire' thesis was called into question, as historians like Hyam and Martin (1975) showed that the continuities in the late eighteenth-century Empire were more significant than the impact of the American War of Independence.

The next phase was dominated by what has come to be known as 'The Robinson-Gallagher Controversy'. Ronald Robinson and John Gallagher were committed British socialists suspicious of both Cold War power blocs, and in their influential essay 'The Imperialism of Free Trade' (1952) and book *Africa and the Victorians* (1961), they laid out three major themes that were to engage their peers in prolonged debate. Firstly, they argued that in the nineteenth century Britain's economic empire extended way beyond the red parts of the map; to assume otherwise, they suggested, 'is rather like judging the size and character of an iceberg solely from the parts above the water-line' (Gallagher 1982, p. 1). This view of Britain's 'informal empire' in the nineteenth century was influenced by their sense of how US imperialism in Gallagher and Robinson's own century was in the process of securing economic dominance by 'informal' means. Secondly, they emphasised the continuity of the economic forces framing Britain's interests throughout the period of Empire (including after decolonisation), rejecting chronological demarcations based on formal political events. Thirdly, in *Africa and the Victorians*, they exposed the inadequacy of Anglocentric histories of the Empire by demonstrating the agency of Africans in shaping nineteenth-century colonial encounters. Again, the present – they were writing in the context of decolonisation – would appear to have marked their interpretation of this aspect of the imperial past. (See Gallagher 1982, Louis 1976 and Platt 1968).

British Empire history-writing in the 1980s was given new momentum by the Manchester University Press Studies in Imperialism series and Greenwood Press' Contributions in Comparative Colonial Studies. Both presses introduced new scholars and themes into the writing of Empire history: the Manchester series, for example, published J. A. Mangan's edited collection '*Benefits Bestowed'? Education and British Imperialism* (1988) and Ronald Hyam's *Empire and Sexuality: The British Experience* (1990); and Greenwood Press published both major reference works (James S. Olsen's *Historical Dictionary of the British Empire* and Frederick Madden and David Fieldhouse's *Select Documents on the Constitutional History of the British Empire and Commonwealth* (1985–7)) and monographs like Caroline Oliver's *Western Women in Colonial Africa* (1983). Another major contribution to British Empire historiography in the 1980s was the work of P. J. Cain and A. G. Hopkins, which introduced and subsequently expanded the thesis of 'gentlemanly capitalism'. As the Robinson-Gallagher Controversy functioned as a focus in the 1960s and 1970s, so the Cain-Hopkins thesis played a similar role in the final decades of the twentieth century. Acknowledging an intellectual debt to V. I. Lenin, Joseph Schumpeter, J. A. Hobson and Thorstein Veblen, Cain and Hopkins at the same time orientated their research in relation to the reconfiguring of the British economy during the post-Thatcher years, with a particular eye to the decline of British industry. They argued that in the nineteenth century 'non-industrial forms of capitalist enterprise, particularly those in finance and commercial services, have not received the historical recognition they deserve' (Cain and Hopkins 2002, p. 35). Heroic conceptions of British industrialisation have skewed historical accounts of the relation between metropolitan and colonial economies, and the nature and extent of the influence exerted by London-based 'gentlemanly capitalism' under-estimated. One consequence of this view is a different periodisation of imperial expansion. Prior accounts had stressed the 'Scramble for Africa' in the 1880s, but Cain and Hopkins regard 'the rapid growth of services after 1850 [as] the key to a better understanding of the peculiar nature of British overseas expansion and imperialism' (p. 30). (See also Dumett 1999 and Long 1995).

In conclusion, writing about the historiography of the British Empire has itself become a minor industry, with selective and partial surveys (like this one!) on the shifting preoccupations of British Empire historians by Dumett 1999, Hyam and Martin 1975, Long 1995, Louis 1976, Schlatter (1984), and Winks (1999). The fact that the final volume of the formidable five-volume *Oxford History of the British Empire* (edited by Winks) is dedicated to historiography attests to the catholicity of current approaches, as well as to an increased self-consciousness on the part of those writing imperial histories. There are also any number of popular histories of British Empire, which are (as the genre requires) anecdotal, Anglocentric and derivative (James Morris' three-volume history (1973–8) remains the most compelling). The literature of the British Empire, too, has received increasing attention, with critical anthologies and surveys by Boehmer (1998), Brantlinger (1988), Darby (1998), Mackenzie (1986) and Said (1993); the short list of literary works below represents but a short selection of those most frequently studied.

David Johnson

Literary Works

Arden, John [1960] (1989), *Sergeant Musgrave's Dance*, London: Heinemann.
Boehmer, Elleke (ed.) (1998), *Empire Writing. An Anthology of Colonial Literature 1870–1914*, Oxford: Oxford University Press.
Buchan, John [1910] (1994), *Prester John*, Oxford: Oxford University Press.
Conrad, Joseph [1899] (1996), *Heart of Darkness*, Basingstoke: Macmillan.
Forster, E. M. [1924] (1991), *A Passage to India*, London: Hodder and Stoughton.
Lawrence, T. E. *Seven Pillars of Wisdom* [1922] (1997), Fordingbridge: Castle Hill.
Haggard, Rider [1885] (1989), *King Solomon's Mines*, Oxford: Oxford University Press.
Kipling, Rudyard [1901] (2000), *Kim*, Harmondsworth: Penguin.
Mason, A. E. W. [1902] (1986), *The Four Feathers*, London: Dent.
Orwell, George [1935] (1985), *Burmese Days*, London: Secker and Warburg.
Rhys, Jean [1966] (2000), *Wide Sargasso Sea*, London: Penguin.
Samkange, Stanlake (1966), *On Trial for My Country*, London: Heinemann.
Shaw, George Bernard [1907] (1984), *John Bull's Other Island*, Harmondsworth: Penguin.

Histories

Barone, Charles A. (1985), *Marxist Thought on Imperialism: Survey and Critique*, Basingstoke: Macmillan.
Brantlinger, Patrick (1988), *British Literature and Imperialism, 1830–1914*, Ithaca, NY and London: Cornell University Press.
Brewer, Anthony (1990), *Marxist Theories of Imperialism: A Critical Survey*, 2nd edn, London: Routledge.
Cain, Peter J. and A. G. Hopkins (2002), *British Imperialism, 1688–2000*, London, Harlow: Longman.
Darby, Phillip (1998), *The Fiction of Imperialism. Reading between International Relations and Postcolonialism*, London: Cassell.
Dumett, Raymond E. (ed.) (1999), *Gentlemanly Capitalism and British Imperialism: The New Debate on Empire*, Harlow: Longman.
Frank, André Gunder (1978), *Dependent Accumulation and Underdevelopment*, Basingstoke: Macmillan.
Freeden, Michael (ed.) (1990), *Reappraising J. A. Hobson: Humanism and Welfare*, London: Unwin Hyman.
Gallagher, John, with Ronald Robinson (1982), *The Decline, Revival and Fall of the British Empire*, Cambridge: Cambridge University Press.
Hobson, J. A. [1902] (1998), *Imperialism. A Study*, London: Routledge.
Holland Rose, J., A. P. Newton and E. A. Benians (eds) (1929–36), *The Cambridge History*

of the British Empire. The Old Empire. From the Beginnings to 1783, vols 1–5, Cambridge: Cambridge University Press.

Howe, Stephen (1993), *Anti-Colonialism in British Politics: The Left and the End of Empire, 1918–1964*, Oxford: Oxford University Press.

Hyam, Ronald and Ged Martin (1975), *Reappraisals in British Imperial History*, London: Macmillan.

Kautsky, Karl [1907] (1975), *Socialism and Colonial Policy*, trans. A. Clifford, London: Athol Books.

Lenin, V. I. [1917] (1986), *Imperialism, the Highest Stage of Capitalism*, Moscow: Progress Publishers.

Long, Roger D. (ed.) (1995), *The Man on the Spot. Essays on British Empire History*, Westport, CT and London: Greenwood Press.

Louis, W. Roger (ed.) (1976), *Imperialism. The Robinson and Gallagher Controversy*, New York: New Viewpoints.

Luxemburg, Rosa [1913] (2003), *The Accumulation of Capital*, trans. A. Schwarzschild, London and New York: Routledge.

MacKenzie, John M. (ed.) (1986), *Imperialism and Popular Culture*, Manchester: Manchester University Press.

Morris, James [1973–8] (1992), *The Pax Britannica Trilogy*, London: The Folio Society.

Owen, Roger and Bob Sutcliffe (eds) (1972), *Studies in the Theory of Imperialism*, London: Longman.

Platt, D. C. M. (1968), *Finance, Trade and Politics in British Foreign Policy, 1815–1914*, Oxford: Oxford University Press.

Porter, Bernard (1968), *Critics of Empire. British Radical Attitudes to Colonialism in Africa, 1895–1914*, London: Macmillan.

Porter, Bernard (1996), *The Lion's Share. A Short History of British Imperialism, 1850–1995*, 3rd edn, London and New York: Longman.

Said, Edward (1993), *Culture and Imperialism*, London: Chatto and Windus.

Schlatter, Richard (ed.) (1984), *Recent Views of British History: Essays on Historical Writing since 1966*, New Brunswick, NJ: Rutgers University Press.

Seeley, John (1883), *The Expansion of England*, London: Macmillan and Company.

Winks, Robin W. (ed.) (1999), *The Oxford History of the British Empire, Volume V: Historiography*, Oxford: Oxford University Press.

Wormell, Deborah (1980), *Sir John Seeley and the Uses of History*, Cambridge: Cambridge University Press.

See also: **British Imperialism; Britain's Postwar Foreign Policy; Cromer, Lord; Decolonisation; Historiography (all regions)**.

Historiography: Canada

Canadian historiography and Canadian literature share a tellingly uneven relationship with postcolonial theory and practice, one that reflects that country's layered and polyvocal experience of imperialism and its aftermaths. In Canada, the most obvious form of colonialism has been the dispossession and alienation of indigenous peoples and the dominance of European imperial states from the sixteenth century until the present. As in other settler colonies, the colonised/coloniser dichotomy is complicated by the colonisation of settlers from France and then from Britain, the latter an imperial power to whom Canada remains officially and unofficially tied. Since the eighteenth century this colonial relationship has been further refracted by British Canada's dominance over French Canada and, especially in the twentieth century, Québécois demands for national independence. The inequality of northern and western Canada and the marginalisation of the eastern provinces within the Canadian nation-state formed in 1867 has constituted another kind of colonialism. Added to this mix is Canada's geographical proximity to the USA and its place within the flows of global capital and culture, all of which render American ideas, money, and culture omnipresent. And, since early settlement but with increasing significance since World War II, this chorus of overlapping positions has been joined by the postcolonial diaspora. Canadians with origins in South Asia, East Asia, Africa, the Caribbean and the Middle East have called new and sharp attention to the histories of dispossession, loss and exploitation that have shaped their various departures from colonial and postcolonial societies and their arrivals in Canada.

Given this fragmented experience it is no surprise that postcolonial perspectives have had uneven reception and application in Canadian historiography and literature. Exploration, travel and missionary literature, including particularly Canadian genres like fur-traders' narratives, constituted Canada's first form of colonial literature, and have continued to be served as literary models, historical sources, and objects of postcolonial criticism into the twenty-first century. Central works of nineteenth-century Canadian women's literature can easily be interpreted within the broad framework of imperialist travel writing. Themes of settler Canada's relationship to empire persisted well into the twentieth century, something that the title of Sara Jeanette Duncan's *The Imperialist* (1904) makes clear enough.

For the last decades of the nineteenth century and the first of the twentieth, English-Canadian historical scholarship wore its faith in British imperialism proudly, as did much of Canadian literature. The development of professionalised history departments in the early years of the twentieth century shifted historical practice but did not sever it from an imperialist impulse and from both French and English Canadian nationalisms. In English Canada, a disproportionate number of history faculties boasted Oxbridge Ph.D.s. They tended to imagine English Canadians not as colonised subjects but as colonisers par excellence, as proud members of an imperial community who were destined to take their place at the table of nations burdened with the responsibilities of civilisation and superiority. Scholars like Harold Innis who were willing to acknowledge the presence and contribution of indigenous peoples to the Canadian past were a scarce commodity. When they did appear in mainstream historiography, aboriginal peoples were stock characters in an imperial melodrama where the uncivilised would necessarily give way to the worldwide onslaught of British superiority, as George Stanley argued in his 1936 analyses of the Métis anti-colonial struggles of the late nineteenth century.

Analyses of colonialism, celebratory or otherwise, fell out of fashion in the mid-twentieth century as English Canadians increasingly looked to continental and national frameworks to explain their past. Carl Berger's influential 1970 study of English Canada and imperialism's ironic and telling argument was that imperialism was of only peripheral relevance. It would be the flowering of aboriginal protest, Québécois sovereignty movements and English-Canadian nationalism in the 1960s and 1970s that would put colonialism back on historians' and writers' maps. Historians of French-Canada charted the long history of French-Canadian nationalism and launched intense debates about the viability of pre-conquest French Canada and, by implication, of the viability of an independent Quebec. At the same time Québécois literature produced a vibrant body of work that not only explored the specificity of French Canada but did so in the distinctive language of *joual* represented in the works of authors like playwright Michel Tremblay.

The resurgence of English-Canadian cultural nationalism in the 1960s and 1970s would have a different but nonetheless significant imprint on Canadian literature and historiography. Out of it would emerge a discernible canon of 'Can lit' anchored by authors like Margaret Lawrence, Margaret Atwood, Alice Munro, and Timothy Findlay. This cultural revival was mirrored by a substantial flowering of Canadian history, which emerged as a major teaching area of Canadian universities during these years. Just as authors and painters argued for the need for Canadians to tell 'their stories', so historians set about producing work that would explain Canada on its own terms and to its own people. Canada as a colonised subject vis-à-vis the United States was an increasingly discussed topic, as were regional and national or linguistic tensions between French and English Canada. Questions of indigenous dispossessions animated the work of Lawrence, but for the most part took second place to concerns about settler Canada's distinctive experience and the need to articulate it.

Indigenous issues would put colonialism on the agenda in a newly insistent way in the years that followed. Aboriginal peoples who had rarely been the topic of historical inquiry took on an unprecedented prominence as Native history developed as a viable sub-field in the 1970s and bloomed in the 1980s and 1990s. By 2002, it was reasonable to estimate that more was published on Canadian aboriginal history in the preceding decade than in the five that went before it. Authors like Jennifer S. H. Brown, Sylvia Van Kirk, J. R. Miller, Robin Fisher, A. R Ray, and Bruce Trigger took on new prominence. Cumulatively, this new scholarship pressed two points. First, it used the examples of the early European exploration and settlement, the fur trade and the 'treaty era' of the prairie West to argue that aboriginal peoples and cultures were active agents that had critically shaped Canadian history. Secondly, it suggested that the full incorporation of Native peoples into Canadian history was dependent on methodological innovation, and more particularly on the adaptation of a practice of ethnohistory. Works like *Life Lived like a Story: Life Stories of Three Yukon Native Elders* by Julie Cruikshank in collaboration with Angela Sidney, Kitty Smith and Annie Ned (1990) and *Reading beyond Words: Contexts for Native History* edited by Jennifer S. H. Brown and Elizabeth Vibert (1996) made clear the possibilities of the aboriginal oral archive and alternative readings of written texts.

The publication of three survey texts of aboriginal history – Miller's *Skyscrapers Hide the Heavens*, Ray's *We have Been Here since the World Began*, and Olive Dickason's especially comprehensive *Canada's First Nations* in the late 1980s and 1990s represent a significant maturation of this scholarship. These histories remained overwhelmingly written by historians who are not themselves aboriginal. Métis scholars like Dickason and aboriginal historians like Georges Sioui, whose *Towards an Amerindian Auto-history* (1992) call for a substantially new perspective of the North American past, remain the exception rather than the rule.

This telling emergence of the aboriginal Canadian as a frequent subject of, but a rare author of, history played out differently in literature. In the 1970s and 1980s the Canadian aboriginal person became a frequent figure of mainstream Canadian literature in works by authors like Rudy Wiebe and W. P. Kinsella. The body of work would be explicitly challenged by indigenous authors arguing for the importance of aboriginal self-representation. This critique was supported by a developing body of indigenous literature by writers like Maria Campbell, Bernice Culleton, Jeanette Armstrong and, more recently, Thomas King, Tomson Highway, and Eden Robinson.

Canadian historians and authors have negotiated the legacies of colonialism and the possibilities of postcolonialism around questions of diaspora as well as around those of dispossession. John Marlyn's *Under the Ribs of Death* (1957) uses the story of a migrant Hungarian in urban Winnipeg to reflect on the migrant experience. Immigration and migration was less often a topic of scholarly history until the 1970s when, alongside women's history and working-class history, the history of immigration and ethnicity took on a new significance. Historians documented the extent of racism and prejudice directed against migrants from Eastern, Central and Southern Europe and, more especially, from East and South Asia. At the same time historians emphasised migrants' resistance, creating narratives that Franca Iacovetta described in 1995 as stories of 'manly militants, cohesive communities, and defiant domestics'. Novels by Nino Ricci, Mordecai Richler, and Michael Ondaatje provided the literary counterpart to this exegesis of the European migrant experience.

The particular patterns of postwar migration would tie Canada into the politics of postcolonialism in new ways. Revisions to Canada's immigration policy in 1962 and 1967, combined with the shifts in world economy and geopolitics, were to shift radically patterns of migration to Canada. Immigrants who had once come mainly from Britain, the USA and Western Europe now increasingly came from Southern Europe, East Asia, South Asia, the Caribbean, the Middle East, Latin America, and Africa. By the 1980s some historians were working to produce scholarship that explicitly addressed the history of these groups and in doing so, legitimated their claims to membership within the Canadian nation. Works like *'We're Rooted Here and They Can't Pull Us Up': Essays in African Canadian Women's History* (1994) worked to insert the histories of marginalised peoples of colour into mainstream Canadian historiography and in doing so challenge their erasure from social memory. At the same time work like Constance Backhouse's *Colour-Coded: A Legal History of Racism in Canada* (1999) worked to expose the centrality of racial hierarchy, identity, and exclusion to the Canadian past and to challenge hegemonic conceptions of Canada as an egalitarian and equitable counterpart to the racist USA.

The imprint of postcolonial politics is even clearer in a growing body of critical scholarship that traces the processes that work to constitute and maintain Canada as a 'white' nation and consign both indigenous and non-white migrants to the social and ideological periphery. In *The Dark Side of the Nation: Essays on Multiculturalism, Nationalism and Gender* (2000), sociologist and poet Himani Bannerji utilises the terrain and claims of Canadian history to mount an explicit challenge to national gate-keeping in Canada, one that owes much to the migrant experience read through the particular lens of postcolonial theory and politics. Questions of indigenous dispossession and, to a lesser extent, Québécois nationalism are reinterpreted within a global and distinctly postcolonial, Marxist and feminist framework. Similarly the essays collected in Sherene Razack's *Race, Space, and the Law: Unmapping a White Settler Society* (2002) reinterpret the terrain of Canadian history in a way that positions Canada within a larger postcolonial framework which highlights the connectedness of local and global dispossessions, colonialisms, and postcolonialisms.

In the past decade disciplinary historians have most thoroughly explored Canadian colonialism within the particular context of the eighteenth and nineteenth centuries, especially in Western Canada. Cole Harris, Daniel Clayton, Adele Perry and Elizabeth Vibert have each reread British Columbia's past through different threads in the international, postcolonial historiography. Sarah Carter's *Capturing Women: The Manipulation of Cultural Imagery in the Prairie West* (1997) similarly revisits the late nineteenth-century West through the recent literature on gender and colonialism. Colin Coates and Cecilia Morgan's *Heroines and History: Representations of Madeline de Vercheres and Laura Secord* (2001) take these insights eastward to discuss the relationship between national heroines and Canadian colonialisms.

The global imprint that animates these historiographies is articulated more loudly in literature that both straddles and complicates the usual definitions of 'Canadian literature' and 'postcolonial literature'. Rohinton Mistry, Shyam Selvadurai, Anita Rau Badami, and M. G. Vassanji each, in different ways, refract the South Asian experience via Canada, as does Ondaatje's recent work. Austin Clarke, Dionne Brand and Shani Mootoo negotiate the Caribbean and Canada simultaneously. Now canonical work like Joy Kogawa's *Obasan* (1981) has been joined by works from, for example, Fred Wah and Sky Lee who read Canada – and Canadian history – through the Asian-Canadian experience.

That this literature has taken so many major prizes in the past decade speaks to the importance of the postcolonial for contemporary Canada. Historical scholarship has not entirely kept step with this explosion of literary voices that are simultaneously postcolonial and Canadian. Nonetheless, the postcolonial, like the colonial, has had, and will likely continue to have, many meanings in Canada.

Adele Perry

Literary Works

Armstrong, Jeanette (1988), *Slash*, Penticton: Theytus.
Brand, Dionne (1997), *In Another Place, Not Here*, Toronto: Vintage.
Cruikshank, Julie, Angela Sidney, Kitty Smith and Annie Ned (1991), *Life Lived like a Story: Life Stories of Three Yukon Elders*, Vancouver: University of British Columbia Press.
Highway, Tomson (1989), *Dry Lips Oughta Move to Kapuskasing: A Play*, Saskatoon: Fifth House.
Lawrence, Margaret (1974), *The Diviners*, New York: Knopf.
Lee, Sky (1990), *Disappearing Moon Café*, Vancouver: Douglas and McIntyre.
Marlyn, John [1957] (1990), *Under the Ribs of Death*, Toronto: McClelland and Stewart.
Ondaatje, Michael (1987), *In the Skin of a Lion*, Toronto: Vintage.
Ricci, Nino (1990), *Lives of the Saints*, Dunvegan: Cormorant.
Robinson, Eden (2001), *Monkey Beach*, Toronto: Vintage.
Tremblay, Michel (1968), *Les Belles-Soeurs*, Montreal: Holt, Rinehart and Winston.

Histories

Backhouse, Constance (1999), *Colour-Coded: A Legal History of Racism in Canada, 1900–1950*, Toronto: Osgoode Society for Canadian Legal History and University of Toronto Press.
Bannerji, Himani (2000), *Dark Side of the Nation: Essays on Multiculturalism, Nationalism and Gender*, Toronto: Canadian Scholars' Press.
Berger, Carl (1986), *The Writing of Canadian History: Aspects of English-Canadian Historical Writing since 1900*, 2nd edn, Toronto: University of Toronto Press.
Bristow, Peggy, Dionne Brand, Linda Carty, Afua P. Cooper, Sylvia Hamilton and

Adrienne Shadd (eds) (1994), 'We're Rooted Here and They Can't Pull Us Up': Essays in African Canadian Women's History, Toronto: University of Toronto Press.

Brown, Jennifer S. H. and Elizabeth Vibert (1996), Reading Beyond Words: Contexts for Native History, Ontario: Broadview Press.

Carlson, K. T., M. M. Jetté and K. Matsui (2002), 'An Annotated Bibliography of Major Writings in Aboriginal History, 1990–99', Canadian Historical Review 82: 1, pp. 122–71.

Carter, Sarah (1997), Capturing Women: The Manipulation of Cultural Imagery in Canada's Prairie West, Montreal: McGill-Queen's University Press.

Coates, Colin and Cecilia Morgan (2001), Heroines and History. Representations of Madeleine de Verchères and Laura Secord, Toronto: University of Toronto Press.

Dickason, Olive P. (1992), Canada's First Nations: A History of Founding Peoples from Earliest Times, Norman, OK: University of Oklahoma Press.

Diskason, Olive P. (ed.) (1995), The Native Imprint. The Contribution of First Peoples to Canada's Character, Athabasca: Athabasca University.

Duncan, Sara Jeannette [1904] (1996), The Imperialist, a critical edition ed. Thomas E. Tausky, Ottawa: Tecumseh.

Gagnon, Serge (1982), Quebec and its Historians, trans. Y. Brunelle, Montreal: Harvest House.

Iacovetta, Franca (1995), 'Manly Militants, Cohesive Communities, and Defiant Domestics: Writing about Immigrants in Canadian Historical Scholarship', Labour/Le Travail 36, pp. 217–52.

Miller, J. R. (1989), Skyscrapers Hide the Heavens: A History of Indian-White Relations in Canada, Toronto: University of Toronto Press.

Razack, Sherene H. (ed.) (2002), Race, Space, and the Law: Unmapping a White Settler Society, Toronto: Garamound.

Shore, M. (1995), '"Remember the Future": The Canadian Historical Review and the Discipline of History', Canadian Historical Review 76: 3, pp. 410–63.

Sioui, Georges E. (1992), For an Amerindian Auto-History: An Essay on the Foundations of a Social Ethic, trans., S. Fischman, Montreal: McGill-Queen's University Press.

Vibert, E. (1997), Traders' Tales: Narratives of Cultural Encounters in the Columbia Plateau, 1807–1846, Norman, OK and London: University of Oklahoma Press.

See also: **Diaspora: South Asia; European Exploration and Settlement: Canada; Genocide: Canada; Inuit; Nationalism(s): Canada; United States of America; Women's Histories: Canada.**

Historiography: Caribbean

The first text written on the region known as 'the Caribbean' is Christoforo Colón's (Columbus') diary of his first voyage in 1492–3 to the 'sea of isles', which for him was part of 'India', and for other travellers the mythical 'Antilia'. Columbus' writings, together with those of Pedro Mártir (Peter Martyr), are the main sources for the period, and they generated myths that have assumed iconic status over the centuries. The most important of these myths is that of the 'cannibal', which was disseminated in both colonial oral testimonies and in Pedro Mártir de Anglería's Décadas (1516), the first written history of the Antilles. All ideological forms of legitimisation of colonial domination for almost 500 years draw on this figure of the 'cannibal', embellishing elements of barbarism, unnatural cruelty and sexual behaviour. The first descriptions of the religious culture of the Taínos were by the Catalan monk Ramón Pané in his *Relación Acerca de las Antigüedades de los Indios*, which describes the religions of La Española (Haiti and the Dominican Republic), and was included in the biography of Columbus written by his son Hernando Colón.

The first major corpus of Caribbean histories was produced in the course of the Spanish Crown's efforts to dominate the native peoples and administer their newly conquered territories. These texts include the letters, memoirs and biographies of explorers and conquistadors (Hernán Cortés, Bartolomé Díaz del Castillo, Hernando Colón), and the polemics of theologians over the treatment of the indigenes (most famously, between Bartolomé de Las Casas and Juan Ginés de Sepúlveda) which represent important sources for the historiography of the first phase of the colonial encounter. A third category of sources is the cartography, the 'visual historiography' of the Caribbean. Fourthly, there are the first written histories of the region by Las Casas (*Breve Relación de la Destruyción de Las Indias* (1532) and *Historia General de las Indias* (1552–61)); and Gonzalo Fernández de Oviedo y Valdés (*Sumario de la Natural y General Historia de las Indias* (1526) and *Historia General y Natural de las Indias* (1535)). These two also wrote the first descriptions of the new Spanish colonies – La Española and Fernandina (Cuba) – as well as the coastal parts of the new continent, which today may be called Greater Caribbean: the coasts of Venezuela, Colombia, Panamá, Central America, Yucatán and Mexico, and the southern coast of North America. Las Casas and Oviedo were followed by historians, many of them functionaries of the Spanish Crown, like Francisco López de Gómara, Martín Fernández de Enciso, Juan López de Velasco, Antonio de Herrera y Tordesillas, José de Acosta and Girolamo Benzoni, who were known collectively as the 'Historiadores de las Indias' or 'Occidentales'. In their writings, indigenes are mostly represented as colonial servants, victims, or objects; if the texts do treat them as subjects, they are mostly represented overwhelmingly as strange warriors and cruel man-eaters, with only Las Casas and some Franciscan missionaries presenting them as possible good Christians. Finally, official colonial papers like the *Visitas*, the *Relaciones Geográficas de las Indias*, and the main codices of legislation like *Cedularios Indianos* and the *Recopilación de las Leyes de los Reinos de las Indias* (1680) have much historical detail, and also shed light on the first century of European settlement.

With the intrusion of North-west-European pirates, corsairs, buccaneers and filibusterers, an 'unofficial' historiography of the Caribbean emerged, made up of innumerable oral stories about hidden treasures, competitions and alliances forged in pursuit of wealth, and struggles by indigenes and ex-slaves against Spanish Catholic dominance. The region came to be known as *mar del norte* by the Spanish and *mer des caraïbes* by the French. Several of the most significant works in this filibuster history of the Caribbean were written in English, and include Walter Raleigh's *Large, Rich and Beautiful Empire of Guiana* (1595) and William Dampier's *New Voyage Around the World* (1697), and because of the appeal of the genre, others like Alexandre O. Exquemeling's *De Americaeneche Zee Roovers* (1678) (*Buccaneers of America* (1684)) were swiftly translated into English. During this period, there were many narratives of exploration and missionary endeavour that focused both on the islands and on the hinterlands of the Greater Caribbean. The majority were in Spanish, and include the writings of Pedro Simón, Antonio de Berrío, Lucas Fernández de Piedrahita, José de Oviedo y Baños, José Luis de Cisneros, Juan Rivero, Felipe Salvador Gilij, Alonso Zamora, Antonio Caulín, José Gumilla, Hernando de Soto, Alvar Núñez Cabeza de Vaca and Vázquez Coronado, but there were a number of published works by English explorers like Francis Sparre and Lawrence Keymis.

The succeeding category of Caribbean historiography is made up of works that focus on single European colonies, both islands and parts of the mainland. These include Du Tertre's *Histoire Generale des Antilles* (1667–71), Jean-Baptiste Labat's *Memoirs, 1693–1705* (1931) and Christian G. A. Oldendorp's *Historie der Karibischen Inseln Sanct Thomas, Sanct Crux und Sanct Jan* (1693–1705). Many of these histories describe the African slave trade in the Caribbean and the customs of the slaves in the expanding plantation societies there. Continuing the focus on single colonies, in the eighteenth century a body of 'proto-national' histories emerged, with studies of the most economically important colonies in the Caribbean: Cuba, with histories by Joseph de Urrutia y Matos, José Martín Félix de Arrate y Acosta, Nicolás Joseph de Ribera and Francisco de Arango y Parreño; Saint-Domingue, with histories by Wimpffen and Moreau de Saint Méry; and Jamaica, with histories by Edward Long and Bryan Edwards. Detailed travel narratives – J. G. Stedman's *Narrative of a Five Years Expedition against the Revolted Negroes of Surinam* (1765), Philippe Fermin's *Histoire Naturelle de la Hollande Équinoxiale* (1765) and Robert Hermann Schomburgk's descriptions of Dutch Suriname and British Guiana – supplemented these histories. Major works on the Caribbean appeared from France, Spain and Britain in the second half of the eighteenth century: from France, Abbé Raynal's *Histoire Philosophique* (1770), which included a denunciation of slavery; from Spain, Juan Bautista Muñoz's lengthy riposte to Raynal, *Historia del Nuevo Mundo* (1793); and from Britain, William Robertson's *History of America* (1777), as well as the works of Bryan Edwards (1793–1801) and Marcus Rainsford (1805). The revolution in Saint-Domingue/Haiti (1791–1804) spurred interest in the region, and profoundly informed the subsequent works.

The most important general work about the Caribbean in the nineteenth century was Humboldt's *Essay on the Island of Cuba*, first published as part of his *Relation Historique* (*Personal Narrative* (1814–29)), and later as a monograph (1826–31). This was the first modern statistical and scientific text about the Caribbean, in which Humboldt condemned slavery, and considered the possibility of the Caribbean being governed by a 'reign of Ethiopians' centred in the new state of Haiti. Humboldt's work was followed by many statistical, demographic, cartographic, economic and political works, starting in Cuba, and extending to histories of slavery, and geographical and historical descriptions of Puerto Rico, Jamaica, Haiti, the islands of the Lesser Antilles, Venezuela and Nueva-Granada/Colombia. Haiti was the first new nation in the Caribbean to have an elaborated version of its own territorial and 'national' history, followed by Colombia and Venezuela. These histories do not represent a strictly 'Caribbean' historiography because they simply reinvent European nationalistic discourses by narrating the histories of different islands (or groups of islands) as 'nations', 'proto-nations', or economic systems. From 1780 to 1960, the term 'Caribbean' was absent from histories of the region, and if it was used, 'Caribbean' was associated with rebellion and unrest, as in Raymond Buell's 'The Caribbean Situation. Cuba and Haiti' (1933). Both the bigger republican states with Caribbean coastlines (Mexico, Colombia and Venezuela) and the smaller Central American republics (Panamá, Nicaragua, Costa Rica, Honduras and Guatemala) concentrated on their interior and Pacific histories, and neglected their Caribbean regions in the process of nation-building, dismissing them as 'non-European', 'insane', 'unscientific' and 'unproductive'. European historians writing about the region through the same period focused less on nationalism, and more on the imperial relationship or the economic structures of slavery and trade, from Lucien Peytraud's *L'Esclavage aux Antilles Françaises avant 1789* (1897), to Goslinga's monumental three-volume-history, *The Dutch in the Caribbean* (1971) and Kenneth Andrews' *The Spanish Caribbean* (1978).

The postcolonial historiography of the Caribbean starts with the works of Fernando Ortiz in *Cuban Counterpoint* (1940), and the Marxists C. L. R. James in *The Black Jacobins* (1938) and Eric Williams in *Capitalism and Slavery* (1944). The Cuban revolution of 1959 and the beginnings of European mass tourism to the region (from 1980) parallel this new research in Caribbean history, archaeology, prehistory, languages and culture. Several themes can be identified in this recent work. Firstly, archaeologists and ethno-historians have developed new perspectives on pre-colonial histories of the Caribbean; fresh interpretations of the first moments of contact between Europeans and Caribbean peoples, including trans-cultural and hybrid cultures of Caribbean native peoples (like the Caribes of Guyana and the Lesser Antilles), and of 'colonial' ethnic groups (like Garifunas, Llaneros, Kuna, Seminoles and Guajiros-Wajúu); and finally, histories of postcolonial identities that have accompanied Caribbean nationalisms (see for example, Franklin Knight's *The Caribbean: Genesis of a Fragmented Nationalism* (1978)). Secondly, histories of slavery have continued to proliferate, and Williams' argument that slavery was abolished because it was no longer profitable has been subjected to searching questions by scholars like Roger Anstey, Seymour Drescher and David Eltis. Thirdly, women's histories have emerged as a dynamic field of inquiry as a result of the efforts of historians like Barbara Bush, Marietta Morrissey and Deborah Gray White. Institutions such as the University of the West Indies and the Casa del Caribe in Santiago de Cuba that were founded in the 1960s, and scholarly journals such as the *New West Indian Guide/Nieuwe West-Indische Gids*, *Journal of Caribbean Studies*, *Revista Mexicana del Caribe* and *Del Caribe*, have supported and disseminated this new work. Since the 1990s, all nations within the region (Mexico, Venezuela and Colombia, and more recently, the US states of Louisiana, Florida and Texas) have turned to 'their' Caribbean regions, and produced new research; and in Europe and North America, good surveys of recent scholarship are contained in the UNESCO six-volume *General History of the Caribbean* (1997–2003), and in the many chapters on the Caribbean in the five-volume *Oxford History of the British Empire* (1998–9) edited by William Roger Louis.

Looking at the broader context, all this fresh scholarly interest is part of a general cultural endeavour seeking to reconstruct the histories and contemporary meanings of 'the Caribbean', and as such constitutes a corollary of the political and economic struggles for control of sea-territories, ecologies, and economic resources (fishery, oil, tourism) in the region.

Michael Zeuske

Literary Works

Behn, Aphra (1988), *Oroonoko and Other Writings*, ed. P. Salzman, Oxford: Oxford University Press.

Belgrave, Valerie (1988), *Ti Marie*, London: Heinemann.

Carpentier, Alejo (2001), *Explosion in a Cathedral*, trans. J. Sturrock, Minneapolis: University of Minnesota Press.

Colón, Cristóbal (1992), *The Voyage of Christopher Columbus. Columbus's Own Journal of Discovery*, trans. J. Cummings, London: Weidenfeld and Nicolson.

Gilroy, Beryl (1991), *Stedman and Joanna. A Love in Bondage*, New York: Vintage.

Harris, Wilson (1960), *The Palace of the Peacock*, London: Faber and Faber.

Hollar, Constance (1932), *Songs of Empire*, Kingston: Gleaner.

Naipaul, V. S. (2001), *The Loss of El Dorado: A Colonial History*, London: Picador.

Robertson, James (2003), *Joseph Knight*, London and New York: Fourth Estate.

Scott, Lawrence (1995), *Ballad for the New World*, London: Heinemann.

Sealey, Carl (1960), 'My Fathers before Me' (short story), in A. Salky (ed.), *West Indian Stories*, London: Faber and Faber.

Walcott, Derek (1974), 'The Muse of History', in O. Coombs (ed.), *Is Massa Day Dead?*, New York: Doubleday/Anchor Press.

Walcott, Derek (1990), *Collected Poems*, Trinidad: Noonday.

Histories

Andrews, Kenneth A. (1978), *The Spanish Caribbean: Trade and Plunder, 1536–1630*, New Haven, CT: Yale University Press.

Anghiera, Pietro Martire d'/Peter Martyr [1516] (1970), *De Orbe Novo, the Eight Decades of Peter Martyr d'Anghiera*, trans. F. A. MacNutt, New York: B. Franklin.

Anghiero, Pietro Martire d' [1516] (1998), *De Orbe Novo*, English and Latin Selections, ed. G. Eatough, *Repertorium Columbianum* 5.

Buell, Raymond Leslie (1933), 'The Caribbean Situation. Cuba and Haiti', *Foreign Policy Reports* IX: 8, pp. 82–92.

Coronil, Fernando (1995), 'Transculturation and the Politics of Theory. Countering the Center, Cuban Counterpoint' in F. Ortiz (ed.), *Cuban Counterpoint. Tobacco and Sugar*, Durham, NC: Duke University Press, pp. ix–lvi.

Covinton, Paula H. (ed) (1992), *Latin America and the Caribbean. A Critical Guide to Research Sources*, New York, Westport, CT and London: Greenwood Press.

Dampier, William [1697] (1998), *A New Voyage Round the World: The Journal of an English Buccaneer*, foreword G. Milton, London: Hummingbird Press.

Dunn, Oliver and James E. Kelly Jr. (eds) (1989), *The Diary of Christopher Columbus's First Voyage to America, 1492–1493*, Norman, OK: University of Oklahoma Press.

Edwards, Bryan [1793] (1901), *The History, Civil and Commercial, of the British Colonies in the West Indies*, 3 vols, London: John Stockdale.

Fuson, Robert H. (1983), 'The Diario de Colón: A Legacy of Poor Transcription, Translation and Interpretation', *Terrae Incognitae* 15, pp. 51–75.

Hennessy, Alistair (ed.) (1992), *Intellectuals in the Twentieth-Century Caribbean*, 2 vols, London: Macmillan.

Hulme, Peter (1992), *Colonial Encounters. Europe and the Native Caribbean 1492–1797*, London: Routledge.

Humboldt, Alexander von [1814] (1971), *Personal Narrative of Travels to the Equinoctial Regions of the New Continent, During the Years 1799–1804*, 7 vols, trans. H. M. Williams, Amsterdam: Theatrum Orbis Terrarum.

Humboldt, Alexander von [1826] (2000), *The Island of Cuba*, trans. J. S. Thrasher, ed. L. Martínez-Fernández, Princeton, NJ: Marcus Wiener Publishers.

James, C. L. R. [1938] (1963), *The Black Jacobins: A Study of Toussaint L'Ouverture and the San Domingo Revolution*, 2nd edn, New York: Random House.

James, C. L. R (1992), *The C. L. R. James Reader*, ed. A. Grimshaw, Oxford and New York: Blackwell.

Keegan, William F. (1992), *The People who Discovered Columbus: Prehistory of the Bahamas*, Gainesville, FL: University Press of Florida.

Knight, Franklin W. (1978), *The Caribbean: Genesis of a Fragmented Nationalism*, New York: Oxford University Press.

Labat, Jean Baptiste (1931), *The memoirs of Père Labat, 1693–1705*, trans. and abr. J. Eaden, intro. P. Gosse, London: Constable and Company.

Las Casas, Bartolomé de [1552–61] (1971), *History of the Indies*, ed. Andrée Collrad, New York: Harper and Row.

Las Casas, Bartolomé de [1532] (2003), *An Account, Much Abbreviated, of the Destruction of the Indies*, ed. F. W. Knight, trans. A. Hurley, Indianapolis, IN: Hackett.

Long, Edward (1774), *The History of Jamaica: or General Survey of the Ancient and Modern State of that Island; with Reflections on its Situation, Settlements, Inhabitants, Climate, Products, Commerce, Laws, and Government*, 3 vols, London: T. Lowndes.

Louis, W. Roger (general editor) (1998–9), *The Oxford History of the British Empire*, 5 vols, Oxford: Oxford University Press.

Mintz, Sidney W. (1966), 'The Caribbean as a Socio-Cultural Area', *Journal of World History* 9: 4, pp. 912–37.

Ortiz, Fernando [1940] (1994), *Cuban Counterpoint*, Durham, NC: University of North Carolina Press.

Paquette, Robert L. and Stanley Engerman (1996), *The Lesser Antilles in the Age of European Expansion*, Gainesville, FL: University of Florida Press.

Rainsford, Marcus (1805), *An Historical Account of the Black Empire of Hayti: Comprehending a View of the Principal Transactions in the Revolution of Saint Domingo; with its Ancient and Modern State*, London: James Cundee.

Raleigh, Sir Walter [1595] (1997), *The Discoverie of the Large, Rich and Bewtiful Empyre of Guiana*, ed. N. Whitehead, Manchester: Manchester University Press.

Raynal, Guillaume-Thomas François [1776] (1788), *A Philosophical and Political History of the Settlements and Trade of the Europeans in the East and West Indies*, 10 vols, trans. J. O. Justamond, London: A. Strahan; and T. Cadell.

Robertson, William (1996), *The Works of William Robertson*, 12 vols, London: Routledge.

Rogozinski, Jan (1994), *A Brief History of the Caribbean. From the Arawak and the Carib to the Present*, New York: Penguin Books.

Stedman, John Gabriel [1765] (1988), *Narrative of a Five Years Expedition against the Revolted Negroes of Surinam*, eds R. Price and S. Price, Baltimore and London: Johns Hopkins University Press.

Stevens-Arroyo, Antonio M. (1988), *The Cave of the Jagua*, Albuquerque, NM: University of New Mexico Press.

Trouillot, Michael-Rolph (1992), 'The Caribbean Region. An Open Frontier in Anthropological Theory', *Annual Review of Anthropology* 21, pp. 19–42.

UNESCO (1997–2003), *General History of the Caribbean*, 6 vols, Paris: UNESCO Publishing.

Williams, Eric [1944] (1994), *Capitalism and Slavery*, Chapel Hill, NC: University of North Carolina Press.

See also: **Anti-colonialism and Resistance: Caribbean; Indentured Labour: Caribbean; Slavery: Caribbean; Women's Histories: Caribbean.**

Historiography: East Africa

It is important to register the importance of orality in the historiography of East Africa. East Africans in the pre-colonial era produced oral narratives in literary, historical, and anthropological forms in their own languages. In the colonial era, from 1915, the Christian Bible was translated into African languages, circulated in both oral and literary forms, and was appropriated to inspire (among other things) resistance to colonialism. In the postcolonial era, a pivotal aspect of the long conversation concerning the relation between tradition and modernity was the debate over mother-tongue or English-language usage (carried on by Okot p'Bitek and Ngugi wa Thiong'o). These overlapping processes are all anchored in the fact of orality, for the peoples of East Africa continue to produce primarily oral accounts of their experiences with colonialism and the postcolonial dispensations.

The first written histories by East Africans followed the Christian revolution in Buganda (1875–1900), when a tradition emerged in most communities of writing up histories, folktales, sayings and proverbs as a record for posterity. The pioneer author in this field was Apolo Kagwa, the leading Protestant chief in Buganda, who initiated the canon with his *Basekabaka be Buganda* (*The Kings of Buganda* (1902)), followed by *Empisa za Baganda* (*Customs of the Baganda* (1905)). Kagwa was emulated by the prime minister of Bunyoro, Petero Bikunya, who wrote a dynastic history of his kingdom, *Ky'Abakama ba Bunyoro* (1927). Bikunya's work was superceded in turn by the work of the *Omukama* (king) of Bunyoro, Kabalega Winyi, in the 1930s. Publishing in the *Uganda Journal* in the 1935–7 period, Winyi set down the genealogy of the kings of Bunyoro, from the fourteenth century to his own reign, linking his Babito dynasty to the earlier semi-mythical Batembuzi and Bachwezi dynasties that preceded the Babito accession. John Nyakatura used these histories as the basis for *Abakama ba Bunyoro-Kitara* (*The Kings of Bunyoro-Kitara* (1947)). This early work was facilitated by the launching of the East African Literature Bureau in 1948. The motivation for all these histories is fundamentally tied up with the quest for identity, and is eloquently expressed by Francis Xavier Lwamgira, *Katikiro* (prime minister) of the kingdom of Kiziba in western Tanzania in the preface to his *Amakuru ga Kiziba N'Abakama Bamu* (*The History of Kiziba and its Rulers* (1949)):

> It saddens us to see that many people in our country fail to understand how the ancients used to record [their history] . . . [A]sk those who guard the burial of the former kings and they will tell you the history; inquire about the types of trees planted around them and you will find that each tree has its significance; inquire about the buildings in the royal enclosure . . . and you will be told their origins. I am saying that a person should look at them as important documents in our country and anyone who destroys them destroys our history. (quoted in Rowe 1977, p. 24)

The first professional East African historians built their academic reputations by asserting the value of oral traditions as legitimate sources for the recovery of the African past. Bethwell Ogot made the further claim that it was possible to discover the histories of the many non-kingdom societies in East Africa, and in the same spirit Semakula Kiwanuka built his historical narrative on the edifice constructed by Apolo Kagwa. Following the publication of Ogot's *History of the Southern Luo* (1967), this region saw local historians seize the initiative with a number of important works: Gideon Were's *History of the Abaluyia* (1967), Isaria Kimambo's *A Political History of the Pare of Tanzania, c. 1500–1900* (1969), Kiwanuka's *A History of Buganda: From the Origins of the Kingdom to 1900* (1971), Ahmed I. Salim's *The Swahili-Speaking Peoples of Kenya's Coast, 1895–1965* (1973), Godfrey Muriuki's *History of the Kikuyu: 1500–1900* (1974), and William Ochieng's *A Pre-Colonial History of the Gusii of Western Kenya from c. A.D. 1500 to 1914* (1974). The value of this scholarship has been reaffirmed by the recent research of historians like James de Vere Allen (1993) and Chapurukha Kusimba (1999), who have argued that the internal dynamic of African society is central, thus rejecting the orthodox view that Swahili civilisation was fundamentally outward-looking and 'Arab' in its origins, as scholars like Chauncy Stigand in *The Land of Zinj* (1913) and Hubert Chittick in *Kilwa – An Islamic City on the East African Trading Coast* (1974) had proposed. Randall Pouwels sums up the shift in historical consensus in recent decades as follows:

> Africans [must be placed] at the beginnings of Swahili civilisation late in the first millennium as well as at the core of its subsequent development. Recent work has emphasised the African background and environment in which coastal culture developed . . . [and] the vitality this essentially African civilisation has shown in controlling exogenous influences. (Pouwels 2002, p. 424)

The literary works of Grace Ogot (*The Promised Land* (1966) and *Land Without Thunder* (1968)) and Taban Lo Liyong's *Eating Chiefs* (1970) capture the mood of this historiography.

The work of B. A. Ogot and his contemporaries in the late 1960s and early 1970s was challenged by John Lonsdale's review of Ochieng's work 'When Did the Gusii (or Any Other Group) Become a Tribe?' (1977). Lonsdale's question was taken up in Eric Hobsbawm and Terence Ranger's *The Invention of Tradition* (1983), as historians and anthropologists explored the nuances behind the 'invention of tradition,' the 'creation of tribalism' and the 'making of customary law'. The previously sacrosanct Ur-texts of elders like Jomo Kenyatta's *Facing Mount Kenya* (1938) and Paulo Mboya's *Luo Kitgi Gi Timbegi* (*Luo Customs and Practices* (1938)) – collectively described as *Desturi na Mila* (Customs and (Traditional) Laws) – were now seen as having been legitimised by indirect rule, particularly in Uganda and Tanganyika between the wars. For Lonsdale and his successors, African politics and history under colonial rule had with the tutelage of British pro-consuls assumed the mantle of neo-traditionalism. Lonsdale stressed how ethnicity was a malleable entity in the hands of both the colonial authorities, the elders and the African elites:

> 'customary law', the main field in which the British sought to hitch local culture to ruling hegemony, rested on a legal delusion. District Commissioners and senior African men together tried to limit the new liberties with allegedly 'customary' rules that were equally novel. Chiefly influence in the African courts made the position worse. Repeated efforts failed to separate 'custom' from the corruptions of office. (Lonsdale 2000, p. 201)

A number of carefully focused studies into the complex interplay of identities and ethnicities under colonial rule followed this intellectual lead. Charles Ambler explored the local pressures influencing so-called ethnic boundaries in *Kenyan Communities in the Age of Imperialism* (1988). In the same spirit, Jeff Fadiman examined the Meru, Embu and Mbeere in *When we began, there were Witchmen* (1993). Cohen and Atieno Odhiambo in *Siaya* (1989) argued that Luo ethnicity may have been promoted by colonial officials and the educated elite, but it was also domesticated and spread by Luo teachers, Maseno alumni and cattle traders, and in the process:

> a common Luo ethnicity took root in extended genealogies and ideologies, myths of common origins, folk tales and legends, and emotionally charged ideas of 'home' propagated in Luo bars, football clubs and political organizations throughout the Luo diaspora. (Spear 2003, p. 23)

In *Burying SM* (1992), Cohen and Atieno Odhiambo demonstrated that history and tradition may be social facts and fabrications invented as they happen, suspended as they are between the high politics of the state and the deep politics of the clan. Bill Bravman's study of Taita ethnicity, *Making Ethnic Ways* (1998) also elucidated how designated ethnic groups make their histories, and Justin Willis demonstrates the porous boundaries of ethnicity in his *Mombasa, the Swahili and the Making of the Mijikenda* (1993). The most nuanced discussion came from Lonsdale in *Unhappy Valley* (1992, co-authored with Bruce Berman), and his subsequent essays. Lonsdale distinguished between on the one hand, 'moral ethnicity', which denotes the historic sense of self-regarding collective selfhood, 'the rights and duties that make us "we"'(Lonsdale 2000, p. 207), the identity that makes social behaviour possible within communities, and on the other hand, 'political tribalism', which serves as the core of peoples' collective consciousness in struggles for power, meaning and resources within the turbulent African state. Spear and Waller in *Being Maasai* (1993) argue that the being, becoming and transforming of individual and corporate identity constitute a continual historical process, well beyond the control capacity of the state, and Dorothy Hodgson in *Once Intrepid Warriors* (2001) extends their argument to assess the impact of developmentalism. In addition to all these case studies of African responses to colonial rule, there have also been a number of studies focused more on the colonial state itself. Mungeam (1968), Sorrenson (1968), Steinhart (1977) and Twaddle (1993) all in different ways emphasised the colonial state's constant search for new alliances, and its strategic discarding of erstwhile allies (like the Maasai). Mamdani (1976), Bunker (1987), Berman (1990) and Berman and Lonsdale (1992) reflect upon the colonial state's responses to class formation in the inter-war years in different East African contexts.

Another major theme in East African historiography has been anti-colonial resistance and nationalism. By the end of World War II, it was considered important to give each state its narrative of struggle and explanation of how the nation-state came into existence. Colonial conquest generated substantial literature on the tradition of resistance, and the refrain was that although the East Africans were defeated, they were not cowed. Rather, combatants retained memories of the primary resistances of the period up to 1914, and these formed the bedrock of nationalist resistances of the 1950s. More problematic was the need to plot a nationalist narrative for each state-in-waiting, and the historiographical challenge lay in creating a narrative that connected (1) the primary resistances of the late nineteenth century, (2) the era of modernisation, (3) the accommodation in the 1930s, and (4) the mass nationalisms of the 1950s. The most successful synthesis remains John Iliffe's *Modern History of Tanganyika* (1979), and for useful surveys of this work, see the articles by Lonsdale (1968) and Ranger (1968).

For each of the East African nations, the exigencies of their respective colonial social formations led to different periods of the struggle towards nationhood being emphasised. For Tanzania, the formative years of the nation were seen as anchored in the Maji Maji war of resistance against the Germans in 1905–7. This was the period when the various acephalous groups of south-eastern Tanzania like the Zaramo, the Ngindo, the Hehe, the Mwera, the Makonde and, the Waluguru all stood up and bore arms against the imperial might of Germany, fortified by the Maji water that was given out by the Bokero religious cult under the prophetic leadership of Kinjekitile. The nation as an imagined community was seen to have been formed then. The literary works narrating this resistance were Ebrahim Hussein's play, *Kinjekitile* (1974), the long poem by Jamaliddini *Utenzi wa Vita vya Maji Maji* (1957), and Gabriel Ruhumbika's novel *Village in Uhuru* (1969). The most recent histories of this resistance are by James Giblin and Marcia Wright (1995), who emphasise the centrality of local memories in motivating resistance in Njombe, Masasi and Mwera.

For Kenya, the turning moment was the Mau Mau War waged against the British some fifty years later (1952–6). The historiography of Mau Mau has gone through at least five sequences, the first four being listed by Lonsdale as: (1) the nationalist phase (see Rosberg and Nottingham 1966 and Spencer 1985); (2) the revolution betrayed (Maina wa Kinyatti 1991 and Furedi 1989); (3) the postwar crisis and rural household history phase (Kanogo 1987, Throup 1987 and Kershaw 1997); and (4) the Mau Mau as discourse phase (Atieno Odhiambo 1987, Sabar-Friedman 1995, Wamue 2001). Most recently (5) the return to history phase (Lonsdale and Odhiambo (2003)) has been added. The perennial questions haunting the legacy of Mau Mau include: Who were the Mau Mau? Did they win or lose the war? Who has benefited from their sacrifice? How does the nation sanctify their memory? Above all, what was Jomo Kenyatta's relationship to the Mau Mau? Did he as Kenya's founding president betray the Mau Mau guerrillas? Kenya emerged from the colonial experience as a strong state but not a nation. The key literary explorations of the Mau Mau War have been the novels of Ngugi wa Thiong'o: *Weep Not Child* (1964), *The River Between* (1965), *A Grain of Wheat* (1967), *Petals of Blood* (1977) and *Matigari* (1987). Ngugi's views shift in these novels, as he vividly dramatises a range of attitudes towards the Mau Mau War. Uniquely for this region, Kenyan historians have written histories of the postcolonial state: the collection edited by B. A. Ogot and W. R. Ochieng', *Decolonization and Independence* (1995) reflects upon the meaning of independence and the challenges of creating a nation out of a multicultural state. The literary works on post-colonial Kenya depict failure and decadence, markedly in Charles Mangua's *Son of A Woman* (1973), Meja Mwangi's *Going Down River Road* (1976) and Thomas Akare's *The Slums* (1981).

Uganda never had a pivotal unifying experience of the colonial moment, nor has its postcolonial experience served to galvanise resistance to the state, in spite of Idi Amin's murderous excesses. The most consistent theme of historiographical concern remains the position of Buganda within Uganda. The Buganda Agreement of 1900 would appear to be the fulcrum around which this troubled nation-state refuses to move forward or even back-ward. 'The Buganda Agreement is the lifeblood of our nation,' intoned the Baganda Protestant patricians to the Joint Select Committee of the British parliament in 1931. Much of the best historical writing on Uganda covers the period from the Kabaka crisis of 1953 to the attainment of independence in 1962 (see, for example, Low 1971a and b) and Ingham 1994). The most influential literary works from Uganda remain Okot p'Bitek's reflections on modernity in *Song of Lawino* (1966) and *Song of Ocol* (1967).

In conclusion, three vigorous areas of recent East African history-writing need to be noted. First, histories of women and gender have proliferated, but as there is a separate entry on East African women's histories, I simply list here some of the most influential studies: Margaret Strobel's *Muslim Women in Mombasa, 1890–1975* (1979), Luise White's *The Comforts of Home* (1990), Steven Feierman's *Peasant Intellectuals* (1990), Sandra Wallman's *Kampala Women Getting By* (1996), Susan Geiger's *TANU Women* (1997), Greet Kershaw's *Mau Mau from Below* (1997), Claire Robertson's *Trouble Showed the Way* (1997), Fiona MacKenzie's *Land, Ecology and Resistance in Kenya* (1998), and Heike Behrend's *Alice Lakwena and the Holy Spirits* (1999). In terms of literary works, Margaret Ogola's *The River and the Source* (1994) is an admonitory novel about AIDS and Margaret Oludhe Macgoye's *The Present Moment* (1987) a historical sweep of twentieth-century Kenyan society. The second emerging area of East African history-writing is that of environmental history, which has incubated in a series of distinguished essays by David Anderson, Richard Waller, Gregory Maddox and James Gilbin since the 1980s, and has now come of age with Anderson's *Eroding the Commons* (2002). Finally, cultural history, initiated by Terence

Ranger in *Dance and Society* (1975), has regained momentum with innovative studies like Geiger's *TANU Women* (1997), Laura Fair's *Pastimes and Politics* (2001), Justin Willis' *Potent Brews* (2002), and Kelly Askew's *Performing The Nation* (2002).

E. S. Atieno Odhiambo

Literary Works

Akare, Thomas (1981), *The Slums*, London: Heinemann.
Liyong, Taban Lo (1970), *Eating Chiefs*, Nairobi: East Africa Publishing House.
Macgoye, Marjorie Oludhe (1987), *The Present Moment*, Nairobi: Heinemann.
Mangua, Charles (1973), *Son of a Woman*, Nairobi: East Africa Publishing House.
Mwangi, Meja (1976), *Going Down River Road*, London: Heinemann.
Ngugi wa Thiong'o (1964), *Weep Not, Child*, London: Heinemann.
Ngugi wa Thiong'o (1965), *The River Between*, London: Heinemann.
Ngugi wa Thiong'o (1967), *A Grain of Wheat*, London: Heinemann.
Ngugi wa Thiong'o (1977), *Petals of Blood*, London: Heinemann.
Ngugi wa Thiong'o (1987), *Matigari*, London: Heinemann.
Ogola, Margaret (1994), *The River and the Source*, Nairobi: Focus Books.
Ogot, Grace [1966] (1990), *The Promised Land*, London: Heinemann.
Ogot, Grace (1968), *Land Without Thunder*, Nairobi: East Africa Publishing House.
p'Bitek, Okot (1966), *Song of Lawino*, Nairobi: East Africa Publishing House.
p'Bitek, Okot (1967), *Song of Ocol*, Nairobi: East Africa Publishing House.
Ruhumbika, Gabriel (1969), *Village in Uhuru*, London: Longmans.

Histories

Allen, James de Vere (1993), *Swahili Origins*, London: James Currey.
Ambler, Charles (1988), *Kenyan Communities in the Age of Imperialism*, New Haven, CT: Yale University Press.
Anderson, David (2002), *Eroding the Commons. The Politics of Ecology in Baringo, Kenya, 1890s–1963*, Oxford: James Currey.
Askew, Kelly (2002), *Performing the Nation. Swahili Music and Cultural Politics in Tanzania*, London and Chicago: Chicago University Press.
Atieno Odhiambo, E. S. (1987), 'Democracy and the Ideology of Order in Kenya', in M. G. Schatzberg (ed.), *The Political Economy of Kenya*, New York: Praeger, pp.177–201.
Atieno Odhiambo, E. S. and John Lonsdale (2003), *Mau Mau and Nationhood*, Oxford: James Currey.
Berman, Bruce (1990), *Control and Crisis*, London: James Currey.
Berman, Bruce and John Lonsdale (1992), *Unhappy Valley*, 2 vols, London: James Currey.
Bunker, Steven (1987), *Peasants Against the State*, Urbana, IL: University of Illinois Press.
Cohen, D. W. and E. S. Atieno Odhiambo (1989), *Siaya. The Historical Anthropology of an African Landscape*, London: James Currey.
Cohen, D. W. and E. S. Atieno Odhiambo (1992), *Burying SM. The Politics of Knowledge and the Sociology of Power*, Portsmouth, NH and London: Heinemann.
Fadiman, Jeffrey (1993), *When we began, there were Witchmen*, Berkeley, CA: University of California Press.

Fair, Laura (2001), *Pastimes and Politics, Culture, Community and Identity in Post-Abolition Urban Zanzibar, 1890–1945*, Athens, OH: Ohio University Press.

Feierman, Steven (1990), *Peasant Intellectuals*, Madison, WI: University of Wisconsin Press.

Furedi, Frank (1989), *The Mau Mau War in Perspective*, London: James Currey.

Geiger, Susan (1997), *TANU Women. Gender and Culture in the Making of Tanganyikan Nationalism, 1955–1965*, Portsmouth, NH: Heinemann.

Giblin, James (1992), *The Politics of Environmental Control in Northeastern Kenya, 1840–1940*, Philadelphia: University of Pennsylvania Press.

Gunner, Liz (2002), 'Dislocation, Memory and Modernity', in Jan-Georg Deutsch, Heike Schmidt and Peter Probst (eds), *African Modernities*, Oxford: James Currey, pp. 67–84.

Iliffe, John (1979), *A Modern History of Tangankiya*, Cambridge: Cambridge University Press.

Ingham, Kenneth (1994), *Obote*, London: Routledge.

Kabwegyere, Tarsus (1974), *The Politics of State Formation in Uganda*, Nairobi: East African Literature Bureau.

Kanogo, Tabitha (1987), *Squatters and the Roots of Mau Mau*, London: James Currey.

Kershaw, Greet (1997), *Mau Mau from Below*, Oxford: James Currey.

Kusimba, Chapurukha (1999), *The Rise and Fall of Swahili States*, Walnut Creek, CA: Altamira Press.

Lonsdale, John (1968), 'Some Origins of Nationalism in East Africa', *Journal of African History* 9, pp. 119–46.

Lonsdale, John (1977), 'When Did the Gusii (or any other Group) Become a Tribe?', *Kenya Historical Review* 5: 1, pp. 123–33.

Lonsdale, John (2000), 'Kenyatta's Trials: The Breaking and Making of an African Nationalist,' in P. Coss (ed.), *The Moral World of the Law*, Cambridge: Cambridge University Press, pp. 196–239.

Lonsdale, John (2002), 'Jomo Kenyatta, God and the Modern World,' in Jan-Georg. Deutsch, Heike Schmidt and Peter Probst (eds), *African Modernities*, London: James Currey, pp. 31–66.

Low, D. A. (1971a), *Buganda in Modern History*, Berkeley, CA: University of California Press.

Low, D. A. (1971b), *The Mind of Buganda*, Berkeley, CA: University of California Press.

Mackenzie, Fiona (1998), *Land, Ecology and Resistance in Kenya*, Edinburgh: Edinburgh University Press.

Maina wa Kinyatti (1980), *Thunder from the Mountains*, London: Zed Books.

Maina wa Kinyatti (1991), *Mau Mau. A Revolution Betrayed*, Jamaica, NY: Mau Mau Research Centre.

Mamdani, Mahmood (1976), *Politics and Class Formation in Uganda*, New York: Monthly Review Press.

Mungeam, Gordon (1968), *British Rule in Kenya, 1895–1912*, Oxford: Oxford University Press.

Ogot, B. A. and W. R. Ochieng (eds) (1995), *Decolonization and Independence in Kenya*, London: James Currey.

Pouwels, Randall (2002), 'Eastern Africa and the Indian Ocean to 1800: Reviewing Relations in Historical Perspective', *International Journal of African Historical Studies* 35: 2–3, pp. 385–424.

Ranger, Terence (1968), 'Connections Between the "Primary Resistance" Movement and Modern Mass Nationalism in East and Central Africa', *Journal of African History* 9, pp. 437–53, 631–41.

Ranger, Terence (1975), *Dance and Society in Eastern Africa 1890–1970: Beni Ngoma*, London: Heinemann.

Ranger, Terence (1983), 'The Invention of Tradition in Colonial Africa', in E. J. Hobsbawm and T. O. Ranger (eds), *The Invention of Tradition*, Cambridge: Cambridge University Press, pp. 211–62.

Ranger, Terence (1993), 'The Invention of Tradition Revisited', in T. O. Ranger and Olufemi Vaughn (eds), *Legitimacy and the State in Africa*, London: Macmillan, pp. 62–111.

Rosberg, C. G. and John Nottingham (1966), *The Myth of Mau Mau*, New York: Praeger.

Rowe, John (1977), 'Progress and a Sense of Identity: African Historiography in East Africa', *Kenya Historical Review* 5: 1, pp. 23–34.

Rowe, John (2002), 'Mutesa and the Missionaries: Church and State in Pre-colonial Buganda', in H. B. Hansen and M .Twaddle (eds), *Christian Missionaries and the State in the Third World*, Oxford: James Currey, pp. 52–65.

Sabar-Friedman, Galia (1995), 'The Mau Mau Myth: Kenyan Political Discourse in Search of Democracy', *Cahiers d'Etudes Africaines* 35, pp. 101–31.

Sorrenson, M. P. K. (1968), *Origins of White Settlement in Kenya*, Oxford: Oxford University Press.

Spear, Thomas (2003), 'Neo-Traditionalism and the Limits of Invention in British Colonial Africa', *Journal of African History* 44, pp. 3–27.

Spencer, John (1985), *The Kenya African Union*, Boston, MA: KPI.

Steinhart, E. I. (1977), *Conflict and Collaboration*, Princeton, NJ: Princeton University Press.

Strobel, Margaret (1979), *Muslim Women in Mombasa, 1890–1975*, New Haven, CT: Yale University Press.

Throup, David (1987), *Economic and Social Origins of Mau Mau*, London: James Currey.

Twaddle, Michael (1993), *Kakungulu and the Creation of Uganda*, London: James Currey.

Wamue, Grace N. (2001), 'Revisiting our Indigenous Shrines through Mungiki', *African Affairs* 100, pp. 453–67.

Willis, J. (2002), *Potent Brews. A Social History of Alcohol in East Africa, 1850–1999*, Oxford: British Institute in Eastern Africa, with James Currey.

Wright, Marcia [1984] (1993), *Strategies of Slaves and Women. Life Stories from East/Central Africa*, New York: L. Barber Press.

Wright, Marcia (1995), 'Maji Maji: Prophesy and Historiography', in D. M. Anderson and D. Johnson (eds), *Revealing Prophets*, London: James Currey, pp. 124–42.

See also: **Anti-colonialism and Resistance: East Africa; Kenya African National Union; Nyerere, Julius and Ujamaa; Pre-colonial histories: East Africa; Women's Histories: East Africa**.

Historiography: Middle East

An overview of the ways in which any history has been penned must immediately enter into complex ideological territory, for the writing of history has been shown to be built through asymmetrical power relations. The case of Middle East history, especially as written in the English language, is a prime example. For centuries, the modern West has been interested in the land extending east from the Mediterranean, from Napoleon Bonaparte's missions to Egypt in 1798, to Richard Burton's 1885 translations of the *Thousand and One Arabian Nights*, and T. E. Lawrence's *Seven Pillars of Wisdom* of 1935 (written as a British spy). Britain's 1917 Balfour Declaration assured the Jewish character of Palestine, and American-led initiatives, like the 1993 Oslo Accords, the 2002 Road Map for Peace, and the 2003 war in Iraq, have attempted to secure so-called 'peace in the Middle East'. Such prolonged interest by the West has given shape to a particular oeuvre of history whose differences have sparked deeply-embedded debates about ideology and the position of the historian. The following overview thus traces several theoretical paradigms and scholarly traditions that have grappled with the Middle East in the context of a history of colonialism and imperialism.

Any discussion of the region must start with a question whose answer is still disputed: What exactly *is* the Middle East, and whose history is being narrated through its representation? For example, the centuries-old traditions of 'Arab' or 'Islamic' history – often thought of as synonymous – are themselves distinct. The former emphasises ethnic and cultural similarities while the latter addresses religious commonalities. Both have geographical bounds that vary widely depending on the era being studied. The 'Orient' as a field of study covers a wide range of disciplines, including philology, linguistics, archaeology, art history and religious studies, and the 'Orient's' geographic bounds sometimes overlap those used in Arab and Islamic histories, and sometimes, especially in the early twentieth century, have extended as far as India, China and Japan. By contrast, so-called 'Middle East' studies grows out of Cold War-era interest in national military and economic strategy, covering territory extending east from Libya, Turkey and Egypt to Iran and Afghanistan. Even today's most established historians cannot agree on the etymology of the term 'Middle East history'. Albert Hourani (1991) argues that the term grows out of a creation of nineteenth-century British imperial policy built to rival the more locally-established Islamic and Arab histories; Martin Kramer (2001), on the other hand, claims the term was coined by an American naval strategist at the turn of the twentieth century. Regardless, to resolve the dispute over what constitutes Middle East studies is itself a political move that rests on assumptions of interest.

Middle East historiography, then, can most accurately be described as the writing of histories about Arab, Islamic, and other territories by the West, in the tradition of other Western histories. It is an essentially modern project, often imbued with French, German, British, and American Enlightenment ideals of national self-determination, freedom, individuality, and social progress. The 'Middle East' – unlike the Arab and Islamic worlds – was invented by the West in order to further the acquisition of economic, political, and cultural capital throughout a broad swathe of Africa and Asia. As Melani McAlister emphasises in her description of the all-encompassing nature of Middle East historiography, 'the attempt to tell a "total story" of culture and society that would tie together the diversity of the region was itself something of an imperializing ambition' (McAlister 2001, p. 36).

The United Kingdom, and later the United States, have both studied the Middle East with imperial and colonial interests in mind. For the British, from the time of the vast colonial expansion of the nineteenth century, the land on the eastern shores of the Mediterranean marked a stopping point on the way to the riches of British holdings in China, India, and other locations in the Far East. As D. A. Farnie (1969) and other historians have described, the development and administration of the Suez Canal during the mid-century, for example, point precisely to the degree of investment Britain was putting forth in developing a trade route through the Middle East, as well the extent of competition between Britain and other imperial powers towards colonial expansion. For the United States, the Middle East has held a wealth of interests suitable for fuelling the American economic boom from the late nineteenth century into the present. The complex and far-reaching diplomatic and military relationships the United States has pursued to maintain access to the Middle East include supporting the founding of the state of Israel in 1948, the coaxing of a coup d'état to overthrow the democratically-elected Mohammed Mossadegh in Iran in 1953, and the overthrow of Saddam Hussein's Ba'athist regime in Iraq in 2003. The conventional paradigm that sees 'imperialising ambition' as purely economic, though, overlooks the other American interests in the region, including a Manifest Destiny-era conception of responsibility for the 'holy' places of Western religious faiths, and a moral responsibility, in the wake of the Holocaust before and during World War II, to support the state of Israel as a safe haven for the world's Jews.

Such imperialising ambition, whether overtly or not, has led to at least three theoretical paradigms for framing Middle East history. The first paradigm examines various aspects of the region's culture. This type of history often emphasises the importance of religion generally and Islam specifically on the development of culture – often, as Maxime Rodinson (1987) and others have argued, to paint a mystique of essential difference around the devout Muslim. The second paradigm examines the political and institutional arrangements of a given mode of governance. Histories of this sort address the development of the Ottoman Empire's decline in the 1800s and collapse after World War I, the British colonial administration of Egypt, Jordan, Palestine, and Iraq in the inter-war period, the post-World War II burst of national self-determination, and contemporary diplomatic, military, and economic relations with governments in Israel/Palestine, Iran, Afghanistan, and Iraq. The third paradigm explores the interaction between the cultural and the political/institutional – what is often termed 'social history'. This is arguably the most common paradigm for history-writing today. Social histories generally take as their starting point a specific community (Aref Abu-Rabia's study of Bedouins living in the Negev (1994), for example) or practice (Fadwa El-Guindi's study of veiling by Egyptian university students (1999)), and explicate the ways in which cultural and religious influences combine with involvement by the state to shape the given subject. Unlike the other two paradigms, which attempt to represent the historian as an objective reporter of fact, social histories often make clear the ideological position of the researcher.

Each of these paradigms is located in institutional traditions that support research on the Middle East. The ample library of Middle East history can be broken down into at least three traditions, each of which overlaps the other. The first, Islamic studies, comes from research done in the Arab world by scholars at academic institutions in Egypt, Israel, Palestine, Lebanon, Jordan, and elsewhere. (To a lesser degree, this work also takes place in institutions in the West.) Generally speaking, this scholarship places Islamic doctrine at the centre of its inquiry, and addresses the manner in which Islamic legal, religious, and cultural practices are forces in the development of regional history. Work of this nature has flourished in the last fifty years, and as regional governments have loosened restrictions on communication with the West, some of this work has been translated and become more accessible to English-speaking historians. Several prominent scholars in this tradition have themselves migrated to British and American universities and are conducting intensive studies of the region beyond the political borders of the Arab world.

The second scholarly tradition, Oriental studies, has roots in nineteenth-century Britain and extends to France, Germany and Italy, as well as to the United States. This tradition takes as its starting point the Western discovery of a foreign, other, eastern, way of life, and attempts to compare it to Western conceptions of race, sexuality, religion, world image, and other aspects of selfhood. Focus has been primarily on linguistics, archaeology and art history, and universities such as Oxford and Cambridge maintain long-standing departments engaging in these studies. This tradition has been shown to have a complex and specific relationship to the development of Western, and especially British, colonial power over many parts of the Arab world.

The third scholarly tradition, area studies of the 'Middle East', is primarily an American invention of the last fifty years. While the first institutions in the USA to study the Middle East were founded in the 1920s and 1930s as counterparts to Europe's Oriental studies centres, the onset of the Cold War changed the priorities of US research. Like France and Britain in the 1800s, after 1945 the US intelligence establishment saw it as necessary to develop a wide-ranging knowledge of 'areas' of the world. Instead of forming knowledge in order better to administer new territorial holdings, as the French and British had done, the American interest in world knowledge during this period revolved around positioning itself in relation to the Soviet Union and the newly-formed nation-states formerly under colonial occupation. Thus the focus shifted to more pragmatic and strategic theses, examining modes of governance, economics, foreign relations, and diplomacy. In 1958, the US government began funding universities to house Middle East studies centres, of which there are still fifteen receiving funds today. (The success of these area studies centres in turn influenced Britain to open institutions whose interests were primarily pragmatic and strategic.) Persistent questions, though – almost since the inception of these centres – have been how closely scholarship in the humanities and the social sciences should be connected to state interests, and whether foreign policy should dictate academic pursuits.

In the late 1970s, a profoundly influential line of critique was developed to address these questions of scholarly interest and imperialising ambition. Edward Said, a literature professor, argued in his work entitled *Orientalism* (1979)that production of historical knowledge about the so-called 'Orient' was intimately related to maintaining power over colonial holdings in the East. The discourse about the Orient produced by a wide range of nineteenth-century writers constructed a coherent – albeit skewed – representation of the Middle East and its people: this discussion invented the Orient. And in the process, it invented the West. Not only did Westerners construct the image of the East as they saw fit, but, according to Said:

> [t]he Orient [was] an integral part of European *material* civilisation and culture. Orientalism expresses and represents that part culturally and even ideologically as a mode of discourse with supporting institutions, vocabulary, scholarship, imagery, doctrines, even colonial bureaucracies and colonial styles. (Said 1979, p. 2)

In short, from Napoleon's missions east, to T. E. Lawrence and his work as a spy, and into the present, the discourse that shaped the West's view of the Orient was seen at its core as an invention built to buttress the development of a notion of Western selfhood in opposition to an Eastern other.

Said's argument has become ubiquitous in studies of cultural otherness. While countless theorists (and indeed Said himself) have revised the Orientalism thesis, the text has become a useful entry-point in developing analyses of Western modes of representation. There have been at least two sustained critiques of *Orientalism*, one of which addresses the relative theoretical simplicity of its structure, and the other which is concerned with its application in contemporary scholarship. The theoretical simplicity critiques revolves around the inflexibility of Said's structure of binary opposition that pits East against West, Self against Other, Male against Female. Scholars have shown that relations between Europe and the Middle East in the nineteenth century, and the USA and the Middle East in the twentieth century, have been far more complex. The other concern, voiced mostly by those in the Oriental studies tradition, questions whether Said's personal political ideology hinders his theory.

Since the 1980s, and especially since the fall of the Berlin Wall in 1989, the area studies tradition of American scholarship on the Middle East (and other regions of the world) has gone through significant and unresolved upheavals, distancing itself from defence- and diplomacy-related inquiries and incorporating the Orientalism thesis. A look at the programme for a recent annual meeting of the Middle East Studies Association of North America shows how wide-ranging research on the Middle East has become. For example, far more histories are now investigating the social aspects of Middle Eastern life; a wide array of research is being pursued on the discursive, political, economic, and cultural ramifications of the colonial encounter; and the relationship between the cultural, the religious, and the political are being put in more of a global context, tracing the movement of people, capital, and ideas between and beyond the framework of the nation-state.

The recent US-led War on Terror, responding to the 2001 attacks by an Islamic fundamentalist group in New York City and Washington, DC, however, has brought back a focus on American strategic interventions in the Middle East. Military actions in Afghanistan and Iraq have used a segment of Middle East scholarship intimately tied to interest not in the formation of knowledge, but rather in the defence of American hegemony. Critiques of this scholarship often compare it to the nineteenth-century studies utilised by Britain and France to support colonial administration. Needless to say, the far-reaching American intervention into the Middle East at the beginning of the twentieth century will have significant, unseen, and long-term ramifications for the writing of Middle East history.

Keith Feldman

Literary Works

Adnan, Etel (1982), *Sitt Marie Rose: A Novel*, trans. Georgina Kleege, Sausalito, CA: Post-Apollo Press.

Burton, Richard [1885] (2001), *The Arabian Nights: Tales from a Thousand and One Nights*, London: Modern Library.

Cavafy, C. P. (1992), *Collected Poems*, trans. E. Keeley and P. Sherrard, Princeton, NJ: Princeton University Press.

Durrell, Lawrence (1962), *The Alexandria Quartet*, London: Faber and Faber.

El Saadawi, Nawal (1988), *The Fall of the Imam*, trans. S. Hetata, London: Methuen.

Lawrence, T. E. [1935] (1991), *Seven Pillars of Wisdom: A Triumph*, London: Anchor.

Mahfouz, Naguib (2001), *The Cairo Trilogy*, London: Everyman's Library.

Newby, P. H. (1969), *Something to Answer For*, Philadelphia: Lippincott.

Munif, Abdelrahman (1989), *Cities of Salt/Mudan al-milh*, trans. P. Theroux, New York: Vintage.

Salih, Tayeb (1989), *Season of Migration to the North*, trans. D. Johnson-Davies, New York: Michael Kesend Publishers.
Soueif, Ahdaf (1999), *The Map of Love*, London: Bloomsbury.

History

Abu-Rabia, Aref (1994), *The Negev Bedouin and Livestock Rearing, Social, Economic and Political Aspects*, Oxford: Berg.
El-Guindi, Fadwa (1991), *Veil: Modesty, Privacy and Resistance*, New York: Berg.
Fanmie, D. A. (1969), *East and West of Suez. The Suez Canal in History 1854–1956*, Oxford: Clarendon Press.
Fromkin, David (1990), *A Peace to End All Peace: The Fall of the Ottoman Empire and the Creation of the Modern Middle East*, New York: Avon Books.
Hitti, Phillip K. (1966), *A Short History of the Near East*, Princeton, NJ: D. Van Nostrand.
Hourani, Albert (1991), *A History of Arab Peoples*, Cambridge, MA: The Belknap Press of Harvard University Press.
Karsh, Ephram and Enari Karsh (2001), *Empires of the Sand: The Struggle for Mastery in the Middle East*, Cambridge, MA: Harvard University Press.
Kramer, Martin (2001), *Ivory Towers on Sand. The Failure of Middle Eastern Studies*, Washington, DC: Washington Institute for Near East Policy.
Lewis, Bernard (1995), *The Middle East: A Brief History of the Last 2,000 Years*, New York: Simon and Schuster.
McAlister, Melani (2001), *Epic Encounters: Culture, Media, and U.S. Interests in the Middle East, 1945–2000*, Berkeley, CA: University of California Press.
Rodinson, Maxime (1987), *Europe and the Mystique of Islam*, trans. R. Veinus, Seattle, WA: University of Washington Press.
Said, Edward W. (1979), *Orientalism*, New York: Vintage Books.

See also: **Balfour Declaration; Islam; Nationalism(s): Arab; Oil: Middle East; Ottoman Empire; Zionism.**

Historiography: South Asia

The genealogy of the historiography of South Asia can be traced back to the moment of the colonial encounter (see Chatterjee 1992, Sarkar 1997, Breckenridge and van der Veer 1994, and Spencer 1990). The consensus is that history-writing, both as a modern academic discipline and as a form of power, is the result of the profound rupture that British colonialism produced in native conceptions of temporality. Despite having a venerable written culture (with its family genealogies, dynastic chronicles, histories of castes and religious sects, biographies of holy men), Indian ways of narrating the past were discounted by British historians (see Rao et al. 2001). The only text that passed by the standards of the European Enlightenment as an authentic history of pre-colonial India was Kalhana's *Rajatarangini*, a twelfth-century text of Kashmiri history (see Thapar 2002); other Indian writings describing the past simply did not qualify as 'history'. This 'absence of history' was explained, or more accurately, explained away, by the argument that 'the concept of time in early India was cyclic . . . This was inimical to a historical perspective that required each event to be seen as unique' (Thapar 2002, p. 2).

Knowledge of the colonies and their pasts was essential to the project of colonial domination (see Guha 1988, pp. 1–26). Histories of India by Europeans in the late eighteenth and early nineteenth centuries mainly took two forms: liberal and Orientalist. Whereas liberal historiography elevated the modern West and denigrated the Indian past, the emphasis in Orientalist scholarship was to recover India's ancient greatness and glory (see Bhattacharya 2003, pp. 12–13). Although imperialism and Orientalism went hand in hand, once the codification of Orientalist knowledge had been achieved 'its veracity escaped the political nexus' (Ludden in Breckenridge and van der Veer 1994, p. 259). Initially pursued in an empirical-pragmatic mode, Western knowledge production about South Asia shifted to a more sociological discourse during the last third of the nineteenth century that tended simply to confirm existing Western assumptions about 'the East'. James Mill's *History of British India* was by far the most influential work written in this spirit (see Sarkar 1997, pp. 1–49; Guha 1988). However, the labours of Colin Mackenzie in collecting manuscripts on pre-colonial history suggest that even by the middle of the nineteenth century, 'India's lack of history – and of a sense of history – had not yet become colonial orthodoxy' (Dirks in Breckenridge and van der Veer 1994, p. 303).

'Indian' historiography begins as a reaction against foreign, particularly the liberal, interpreters of Indian past, yet the discursive forms adopted by this anti-colonial historiography were never entirely free of the methodological assumptions of colonial interpretations. Reviewing the historiography of nineteenth-century Bengal, Partha Chatterjee argues that modern forms of historiography are 'necessarily constructed around the complex identity of a people-nation-state' (Arnold and Hardiman 1994, p. 2). The 'gods and kings' approach (where the historical, the mythical, and the contemporary were presented in such a way that they fused into one single chronology) of Mrityunjay Vidyalankar's *Rajabali* (1808), the 'secular' *Bharatbarsher Itihas* (1858) by Tarinicharan Chattopadhyaya, and Bankim Chandra's writings all contribute to the historical constitution of a Hindu national past. The schema sanctioned by European scholarship of a dark age of medievalism falling between the periods of classical glory and modern renaissance was in congruence with the nationalist agenda. Invested both with a historical agency and a mission – the project of modernity – the Indian nation could then look to ancient India as a classical source of modernity while at the same time banishing the 'Muslim Period' (with the help of British historians) to medieval gloom.

Towards the end of the nineteenth century the influence of Western notions of secular and linear time on Indian historiography becomes clearer. History came to be understood as a secular process, uncontrolled by divine providence. Colonial history and education, European social philosophy and statecraft, and modern forms of politics led the educated literati to accept the basic methodology of modernist historiography, but not the version of Indian history served up by British scholars. An open contestation with colonialist interpretations started taking place when the nation as an autonomous subject of history was both imagined, and ready to take up the project of liberation from colonial rule (see Chatterjee 1992, pp. 109–13). The struggle for independent historiography started to become a part of the struggle for independent nationhood (see Kaviraj 1992, pp. 10–19).

In contrast to this unitary history of India, Chatterjee gestures toward a future of alternative histories for different regions, a confederal notion that delegitimises the sovereignty of a single state. Because the 'fragments' that constitute Indian society are centralised under the rubric of the colonial and postcolonial state, the investigation, he has argued, must be widened to include a critique of Enlightenment rationalism and secularism. Taking issue with Benedict Anderson's argument in *Imagined Communities* (1983) that emergent nationalism in European colonies was derived from European modular forms, Chatterjee presents a powerful alternative case: 'The most creative results of the nationalist imagination in Asia and Africa are posited not on an identity but rather on a *difference* with 'modular' forms of the national society propagated by the modern West' (Chatterjee 1992, p. 5). Anderson's later retraction that the immediate genealogy should instead be traced to the imaginings of the colonial state resonates with the ironic angst of the postcolonial intellectual: 'Here lies the root of our postcolonial misery: not in our inability to think out new forms of modern community but in our surrender to the old forms of the modern state' (Chatterjee 1992, p. 11).

The bourgeois fabrication of the nation-state and its attempts to frame communities has led Gyan Pandey (1991) to consider 'the prose of otherness', the historiography of partition which, although the single most significant event in twentieth-century South Asia, has been relegated to a minor motif in the denouement of independence. Pandey sees this historiography as lying within one of three modes: (1) as a chronicle of British administration in India, (as in Ian Talbot's *Punjab and the Raj, 1849–1947* (1988)); (2) as a catalogue of actions by Jinnah and other 'rational' political leaders (as in Ayesha Jalal 1985, *The Sole Spokesman: Jinnah, the Muslim League and the Demand for Pakistan*); and (3) as a narrative of deepening class contradictions and growing anti-imperialist movement (as in Sumit Sarkar's *Critique of Colonial India* (1985)). According to Pandey, these imperialist, nationalist, and Marxist historiographies respectively banish 'communal violence' to the realm of 'an Other history', that of Primitive India threatening Civilisation. To support his argument, Pandey draws upon Anees Qidwai's recollections as a volunteer among refugees, *Azadi ki Chhaon Mein* (1990), and Saadat Hasan Manto's story *Toba Tek Singh* (1948) (where the refusal of the supposedly insane to be repatriated is the only sane response to the project of partition, with the central protagonist dying in the borderless no-man's land).

Where history becomes indistinguishable from the legitimisation of the nation, the two independent states of India and Pakistan lay claim to wholly different versions of the past. Pakistani nationalist historians (such as I. H. Qureshi, A. H. Dani and Hafeez Malik) exhibit a profound suspicion of the secular claims made by the Congress leadership, and uphold instead the two-nation theory that the Muslim League had propagated at the beginning of the twentieth century. In his study of school history textbooks in India and Pakistan, Krishna Kumar concludes that:

> the Pakistan master narrative denies that India's independence struggle was secular. At the heart of this narrative lies the two-nation theory which claims that the urge to create Pakistan arose out of certain irreconcilable differences between Hindus and Muslims. The Indian narrative, of course, denies the validity of this theory, and by doing so, it disapproves of Pakistan, imbuing its existence – as the signifier of a regressive, divisive tendency – with suspicion. (Kumar 2001, p. 48; see also Aziz 1993 and Ali 1999)

The question of separate national identity reared its head yet again when the demand for provincial autonomy by the people of East Pakistan, now Bangladesh, was transformed into a demand for full independence. Whereas a supposedly common sub-continental Muslim identity provided the basis for partition in 1947, it was a cultural and linguistic Bengali nationalism which was decisive in the 1960s (see Ahmed 2004).

In the case of Sri Lanka, too, history is deeply implicated in the politics of nationalism and ethnic identity. Historiography in Sri Lanka has traditionally derived from a Pali text called *Mahavamsa* (*Great Dynasty*) written by Buddhist priests under the editorship of monk Mahanama in about the fifth century CE. The *Mahavamsa* is an account of kings, beginning with the arrival of Prince Vijaya from the north of India to the island, and ending with the death of King Mahasena in 352 CE. Its sequel, the account of later kings, called *Culavamsa* (*Lesser Dynasty*), was continued by Buddhist monks at various times after the thirteenth century. The *Culavamsa* continues the chronicle of kings until the last of the Kandyan rulers, Sri Wickrama Rajasinha, was deposed by the British in 1815. These texts mix historical facts with mythological and miraculous events, and glorify Buddhism. Colonial historians considered the *Mahavamsa* as the central text for the understanding of Sri Lankan past and established a link between Sri Lankan history and Sinhalese ethnic identity. The colonial interpretation of *Mahavamsa* became a vital ingredient in nurturing Sinhala-Buddhist cultural nationalism (see Spencer 1990, pp. 5–6). This understanding of history give the Sinhalese-Buddhist people a monopoly over Sri Lanka's past, and is responsible for the formation of majoritarian and exclusivist nationalism with little space for non-Buddhist identities. The question of how the past has been appropriated (as in the Indian subcontinent) has had a direct bearing on the current conflict in Sri Lanka. 'The war which has been fought between the armed Tamil separatists and the Simhala-dominated government has been accompanied by rhetorical wars fought over archaeological sites, place name etymologies and the interpretation of ancient inscriptions' (Spencer 1990, p. 3).

Marxist historians in the 1960s and 1970s shifted attention to questions of social formation, feudalism, the (thwarted) possibilities of indigenous capitalist development in pre-colonial times, political economy, technological changes, agrarian relations and peasant resistance. Their work was challenged in the 1970s by the Subaltern Studies collective of historians (including Chatterjee and Pandey), who launched their alternative version of 'history from below'. Their relationship to Marxist (as opposed to nationalist) historiography is less confrontational, and a tactical silence is usually maintained. However, some members have been more outspoken: Dipesh Chakrabarty concedes that Marxist historiography did turn to popular movements, but objects that it was largely economistic insofar as it erased subaltern agency from history, and more seriously, that it was marked by elitist prejudices 'in the garb of scientism, enlightened consciousness or historical inevitability' (Chakrabarty 2002, pp. 3–19). Rejecting the view that Europe is the subject of history, and that all national histories are no more than footnotes to this European meta-narrative, the subaltern project was therefore concerned with producing histories from the standpoint of Europe's other, the dispossessed in the peripheries. In pursuing its aims, the collective has insisted on a rigorous self-reflexivity – interrogating both the problems involved in accessing subaltern histories, and at the same time, maintaining a critical self-consciousness of its own class and national locations in relation to the subjects of research. Ranajit Guha's valedictory statement in the Preface to the sixth volume of *Subaltern Studies* (1982–9) indicts the 'bad faith' and neo-colonialism of the Cambridge school of historiography. According to Guha, the historical establishment had fundamentally misread Indian history by characterising British rule as based on the collaboration of its subjects, by discerning continuities between the pre-colonial and the postcolonial periods, and by concluding that contemporary problems in India are a function of incomplete modernisation.

In attempting to recover the neglected voices of history, subaltern historians have produced studies of many different instances of peasant consciousness in riots, forms of tribal solidarity in forest uprisings, communal disturbances, and insurgencies. This subaltern consciousness has generally been located in religiosity, rumour and myth, rather than in hegemonic cultural forms. In the later volumes, where colonial power is understood in Michel Foucault's terms as a diffuse force-field circulating through the entire body politic, the subaltern is no longer seen as an autonomous entity and but as one implicated in elite discourses. The subalternist project sees postcoloniality as a strategy, which demands, in Gayatri Spivak's terms not only the erection of local narratives to Europe's long story, but also a 'tampering with the authority of storylines'(Spivak 1990, p. 229). These themes resonate in historical research carried out from the perspective of feminism and ecology (see Women's Histories: South Asia below and Rangarajan 2002, for example). Another recent history that introduces a fresh understanding of agency is Sanjay Subrahminyam's *Penumbral Visions* (2001), which draws on an impressive array of sources in metropolitan and vernacular languages in order to dislodge the standard models of conquest that have been applied to South Indian polities between 1500 and 1800. For a decolonised historiography, the recuperation of undocumented voices remains 'a crucial utopian aspiration' even as its pursuit will always 'stretch the bounds of "acceptable" history' (Schwarz 1997, p. 143). While it might be argued that almost all postcolonial writing from South Asia can be seen as exploring the tension between the discourses of nationhood and subaltern consciousness, the works cited below are examples of more sustained attempts to imagine the lives and worlds of South Asia's non-literate classes.

In considering the relation between subaltern or post-Orientalist history-writing and South Asian literature of the same period, an important distinction between the vast body of writing in vernacular languages like Marathi, Gujarati, Kannada, Urdu, Sinhalese, Tamil and Hindi, and literature written in English must be observed. Distinctive examples of the former category include the stories of Maheswata Devi's as well as Dalit (the downtrodden) writers like Namdeo Dhasal, Daya Pawar, Baburao Bagul and Kusum Meghval.

Mohinder Singh and Prem Poddar

Literary Works

Anand, Mulk Raj [1935] (1990), *Untouchable*, Harmondsworth: Penguin.

Anand, Mulk Raj and Eleanor Zelliot (eds) (1992), *An Anthology of Dalit Literature*, New Delhi: Gyan Publishing House.

Bhalla, Alok (ed.) (1994), *Stories about the Partition of India*, 3 vols, Indus: HarperCollins.

Dangle, Arjun (1992), *Poisoned Bread: Translations from Modern Marathi Dalit Literature*, Bombay: Orient Longman.

Ghosh, Amitav (1995), *The Shadow Lines*, New Delhi: Oxford University Press.

Hossian, Attia (1961), *Sunlight on a Broken Column*, London: Chatto and Windus.

Kunzru, Hari (2002), *The Impressionist*, London: Hamish Hamilton.

Manto, Saadat Hasan (1991), *Partition: Sketches and Stories*, trans. K. Hasan, New Delhi: Viking.

Muller, Carl (1997), *Children of the Lion*, New Delhi: Penguin.

Nasreen, Taslima (1994), *Lajja (Shame)*, trans. T. Gupta, New Delhi: Penguin.

Rao, Raja [1938] (1989), *Kanthapura*, Delhi: Oxford University Press.

Roy, Arundhati (1998), *The God of Small Things*, New York: HarperCollins.

Rushdie, Salman (1984), *Midnight's Children*, London: Jonathan Cape.

Rushdie, Salman (1997), *The Moor's Last Sigh*, London: Vintage.

Sahni, Bhisham (1988), *Tamas (Darkness)*, trans. J. Ratan, New Delhi: Penguin.

Saraogi, Alka (2002), *Kalikatha: Via Bypass*, trans. by the author, Calcutta: Rupa and Company.

Sealy, Alan (1988), *Trotter-Nama*, London: Viking Press.

Shamsie, Muneeza (ed.) (1997), *A Dragonfly in the Sun: An Anthology of Pakistani Writing in English*, Karachi: Oxford University Press.

Sivanandan, A. (1998), *When Memory Dies*, New Delhi: Penguin.

Tagore, Rabindranath (1999), *Home and the World*, trans. S. Tagore, New Delhi: Penguin.

Histories

Ahmed, Salahuddin (2004), *Bangladesh: Past and Present*, New Delhi: APH Publishing Company.

Ali, Mubarak (1999), *History on Trial*, Lahore: Fiction House.

Arnold, David and David Hardiman (eds) (1994), *Subaltern Studies, Volume 8*, Delhi: Oxford University Press.

Aziz, K. K. (1993), *The Murder of History in Pakistan*, Lahore: Vanguard.

Bhabha, Homi (1994), *The Location of Culture*, London and New York: Routledge.

Bhadra, Gautam, Gyan Prakash and Susie Tharu (eds) (1999), *Subaltern Studies*, Delhi: Oxford University Press.

Bhattacharya, Neeladri (2003), 'The Problem', *Seminar*, special issue on Rewriting History, 522. Available at http://www.india-seminar.com/2003/522.htm

Breckenridge, Carol A. and Peter van der Veer (eds) (1994), *Orientalism and the Postcolonial Predicament: Perspective on South Asia*, New Delhi: Oxford University Press.

Chakrabarty, Dipesh (2002), *Habitations of Modernity: Essays in the Wake of Subaltern Studies*, Chicago: University of Chicago Press.

Chakravarty, Uma (1988), 'In Search of the Past: A Review of the Limitations and Possibilities of the Historiography of Women in Early India', *Economic and Political Weekly* 23, pp. WS2–WS10.

Chatterjee, Partha (1992), *Nation and its Fragments: Colonial and Postcolonial Histories*, New Delhi: Oxford University Press.

Guha, Ramachandra (2000), *Environmentalism: A Global History*, Oxford and Delhi: Oxford University Press.

Guha, Ranajit (1988), *An Indian Historiography of India: A Nineteenth Century Agenda and its Implications*, Calcutta: Centre for the Study of Social Sciences.

Guha, Ranajit (ed.) (1982–1989), *Subaltern Studies*, vols I–VI, New Delhi: Oxford University Press.

Ilaih, Kancha (1996), 'Productive Labour, Consciousness and History: The Dalitbahujan Alternative', in S. Amin and D. Chakrabarty (eds), *Subaltern Studies*, vol. 9, New Delhi: Oxford University Press, pp. 165–200.

Inden, Ronald (1990), *Imagining India*, Oxford: Blackwell.

Ismail, Qadri (2000), 'Constituting Nation, Contesting Nationalism: The Southern Tamil (Woman) and Separatist Tamil Nationalism in Sri Lanka', in Partha Chatterjee and Pradeep Jaganthan (eds), *Subaltern Studies*, vol. 11, New Delhi: Permanent Black, Ravi Dayal Publishers, pp. 212–83.

Jahan, Rounaq (ed.) (2001), *Bangladesh: Promise and Performance*, London: Zed Books.

Jalal, Ayesha (1985), *The Sole Spokesman: Jinnah, the Muslim League and the Demand for Pakistan*, Cambridge: Cambridge University Press.

Kaviraj, Sudipta (1992), 'The Imaginary Institution of India', in Partha Chatterjee and Gyan Pandey (eds) *Subaltern Studies*, vol. 7, New Delhi: Oxford University Press, pp. 1–39.

Kumar, Krishna (2001), *Prejudice and Pride*, New Delhi: Viking.

Kumar, Krishna (2003), 'Peace with the Past', *Seminar*, special issue on Rewriting History, 522. Available at http://www.india-seminar.com/2003/522.htm

Nandy, Ashish (1995), 'History's Forgotten Doubles', *History and Theory* 34, pp. 44–66.

Pandey, Gyanendra (1991), 'In Defence of Fragment: Writing about Hindu-Muslim Riot in India Today', *Economic and Political Weekly*, Annual Number, pp. 559–72.

Philips, C. H. (ed.) (1961), *Historians of India, Pakistan, and Ceylon*, London: Oxford University Press.

Qureshi, I. H. (1997), *Muslim Community of the Indo-Pakistan Subcontinent: 610–1947 – A Brief Historical Analysis*, Karachi: Ma'aref.

Qureshi, I. H., A. H. Dani, M. Kabir, A. Rashid, M. A. Rahim, M. D. Chugtai, W. Zaman and A. Hamid (1967), *A Short History of Pakistan*, Karachi: University of Karachi Press.

Rangarajan, Mahesh (2002), 'Polity, Ecology and Landscape: New Writings on South Asia's Past', *Studies in History* 18: 1, pp. 135–47.

Rao, Velcheru Narain, David Shulman and Sanjay Subramaniam (eds) (2001), *Textures of Time: Writing History in South India, 1600–1800*, New Delhi: Permanent Black, Ravi Dayal Publishers.

Sangari, Kumkum and Sudesh Vaid (eds) (1989), *Recasting Women: Essays in Colonial History*, New Delhi: Kali for Women.

Sarkar, Sumit (1985), *A Critique of Colonial India*, Calcutta: Papyrus.

Sarkar, Sumit (1997), *Writing Social History*, New Delhi: Oxford University Press.

Schwarz, Henry (1997), *Writing Cultural History in Colonial and Postcolonial India*, Philadelphia: University of Pennsylvania Press.

Spencer, Jonathan (ed.) (1990), *Sri Lanka: History and the Roots of Conflict*, London and New York: Routledge.

Spivak, Gayatri Chakravarty (1990), 'Poststructuralism, Marginality, Postcoloniality, and Value', in P. Collier and H. Geyer-Ryan (eds), *Literary Theory Today*, New York: Cornell University Press.

Subrahmanyam, Sanjay (2001), *Penumbral Visions*, Ann Arbor, MI: University of Michigan Press.

Talbot, Ian (1988), *Punjab and the Raj*, Delhi: Manohar Publications.

Thapar, Romila (2002), *Early India: From the Origins to AD 1300*, London: Penguin/Allen Lane.

See also: **Anti-colonialism and Resistance: South Asia; Castes: South Asia; Communism: South Asia; Naxalites; Partition; Pre-colonial Histories: South Asia; Women's Histories: South Asia.**

Historiography: South-east Asia

An enormous diversity of narratives concerning peoples, cultures, institutions, ideologies, and processes is contained within the notion of 'South-east Asia'. Benedict Anderson points out that the 'imagined reality' (Anderson 1998, p. 6) of this geographical entity has a provenance no older than the early 1940s. Since then, it has served the function of bracketing geo-political issues affecting the region from those concerning South or East Asia, regardless of whether the peoples thus designated might ever call themselves 'South-east

Asians'. The region shares with South Asia a history of modern nationhood shaped by the struggle against European colonialisms (which excludes Thailand). Contemporary scholars from D. G. E. Hall (1995, *A History of Southeast Asia*) to Nicholas Tarling (2001, *Southeast Asia: A Modern History*) have done much to establish it as a unit of historical study. It comprises three broad periods: the large time-span prior to European historical records about the region, colonialism, and postcolonial nationhood in an era of asymmetrical globalisation. The 1960s also heard a call for 'autonomous' histories. The notion was borrowed from the Dutch historian J. C. van Leur, and used by John Smail (1961) to urge historians to foreground South-east Asia as the subject of history, instead of treating it in terms of its connections with colonial, Chinese, or Indian history. The notion has exercised an influence on most historical writing since the 1970s, while the question of whether it provides sufficient bases for new methods, and what these might be, remain debated issues (see, for example, Chutintaranond and Baker 2002).

In terms of orientation, the diversity of South-east Asian historical writing tends to adopt one of two approaches, of which the first treats an area or a topic as its unit of study. Area studies focus on a region associated with a form of territorial or ethnic nationalism. Such studies are the inevitable outcome of practical considerations in respect of the historian's profession and of the themes favoured by the postcolonial nation. However, as noted by Paul Kratoska (in Ahmad and Tan 2003, pp. 104–20), a preoccupation with reading the past through the retrospective projections of the modern nation-state is prone to ignore or marginalise other issues, such as minority histories. Reynaldo Ileto's call for alternative, non-linear approaches describes the nationalist agenda as afflicted by selective amnesia, 'remembering/furthering that which it deems meaningful for its concept of development, and forgetting/suppressing the dissonant, disorderly, irrational, archaic, and subversive' (Ileto 1997, p. 125).

The second approach selects a discursive topic, and lets the questions generated from that perspective determine the nature of the investigation. The topics covered by such trans-national history include imperialism, nationalism, migration, ethnicity, gender studies, minorities, popular movements, trade and commerce, the impact of religion on social formations, regional developments in science and technology, and the insertion of the local in the global. A contemporary environment characterised by political turbulence, rapid social change, and numerous changes of government brought about through the use of force in several South-east Asian countries reinforces the need for historiography to revision the past from the perspective of a continually shifting present.

The incredible proliferation of historical writing during the last five decades is the result of an increased access to archival materials, and a new impetus to local and overseas investment in academic scholarship. The need to retell histories from local perspectives complements a new respect for the interpretive challenges and opportunities provided by previously untapped indigenous materials. The result is a more variegated sense of how histories can be written. This transformation has been accompanied by a growing awareness that South-east Asian historical study needs to be connected to larger trends throughout the world (see, for example, Victor Leiberman 1999), and that it needs to learn from the methods of related disciplines such as sociology, political science, and literary studies (for example, Oliver Wolters' (1982) use of Vietnamese poetry).

The practice of modern historical writing bases its professional authority on modes of constructing knowledge derived from an Enlightenment ideal of rationality and scientific method. This empowered a historian like D. G. E. Hall to claim that 'none of the languages of South East Asia possessed a word capable of expressing correctly the western concept of history' (Hall 1961, p. 2). Some of the major pitfalls underlying such hubris have been underlined by work such as Edward Said's *Orientalism* (1978). The historian's commitment to an ideal of objectivity does not automatically ensure that historical writing becomes innocent of ideological conditioning, or immune to complicity with unacknowledged agendas. The historian is not free to repress or disguise the subjective nature of the narrative enterprise, and historiography based on Western methods need not ignore or underestimate modes of oral or written transmission that do not conform to its expectations.

Anderson points out that virtually all the major historians of the colonial era were civil servants, whose attachment to their subject was more or less complicit with the colonial enterprise. In his 1992 survey of regional historiography, John Legge reinforces this perception:

> Some, who became deeply attached to the societies in which they worked, were attracted by the romanticism of the exotic. Others displayed a paternalistic conviction that their duty was to achieve the uplift of those they had come to rule . . . [and] an unquestioned assumption that the ultimate outcome would be the transformation of that society by Western civilisation. (Legge 1992, p. 14)

Such tendencies led to yet another bias:

> The intellectual climate in which colonial scholars constructed the first modern national histories . . . determined that the more remote past would attract most of the attention, and the immediate pre-colonial past be seen in terms of failure and missed opportunities. (Reid 1999, pp. 238–9)

The period since World War II has been marked by an intensive political and economic American involvement in the region, accompanied by a huge increase in financial and academic investment from universities and foundations, starting with the Southeast Asia Program at Cornell University. Here, during the 1960s and 1970s, many subsequently influential historians received their training under Oliver Wolters, a student of Collingwood, who emphasised the need to 'walk around in the shoes of those you write about'. The American investment soon grew to proportions unmatched by the European nations, despite their colonial nostalgias and archives. Since the 1970s, the discipline has seen the founding of many similar programmes in Australia and the ASEAN region, along with the inception of scholarly journals, and regular international symposia. Anderson's claim that the American involvement in South-east Asian studies is relatively free from the 'bureaucratically beholden' (Anderson 1998, p. 9) has not gone unchallenged. In *Writing Diaspora* (1993), Rey Chow notes that the US interest in South-east Asian area studies is 'fully in keeping with U.S. foreign policy in the post-Second World War period' (Chow 1993, p. 7). Current debate within the American academic community focuses quizzically on the assumptions and predilections that subsidise such studies (for example, Watson Andaya).

Meanwhile, South-east Asian historiography since the end of colonialism continues to expand on models associated with metropolitan scholarship outside Asia. A large part of the most influential work on the region continues to emanate from scholars trained in the West, or in Australia and New Zealand, and from publishing houses associated with Western institutions. Notable contributions from the Asia-Pacific region have slowly begun to redress the imbalance. The division between local and overseas scholarship has been blurred by increased opportunities for local scholars to acquire overseas training. This development has been reinforced by numerous collaborative projects, and the extended attachment of overseas scholars to South-east Asian institutions of learning. These changes have coincided with a new self-awareness concerning the materials of the discipline. In 1979, the Singapore scholar Wang Gungwu acknowledged a new trend that 'forced a radical rethinking of the questions that have been asked of the indigenous writings and led historians . . . to reconsider the nature of their materials' (in Reid and Marr 1979, p. 5). These factors have alleviated some of the tension raised by the issue of whether the writing of historical narratives should take place from a perspective outside, or within, the concerns of the region. In a recent overview, Lysa Hong (1996, pp. 56–8) divides contemporary historians of the region into two groups: disciples fighting a rearguard action on behalf of von Ranke's tenet that 'truth can be but one', and historians influenced by the Annales school, who produce trans-national histories, such as Reid's *Southeast Asia in the Age of Commerce 1450–1600* (1988–93). It moves, like Braudel's approach, from physical geography through demography and the economics of production to issues of culture and the social framework governing resources and expressions of material culture, 'with one eye always open for comparable developments in other parts of the world' (Reid 1988–93, vol I, p. xv).

The conviction that the subjects of history should draw upon local materials or perspectives to write alternative histories has opened up the field of scholarship to a negotiation between nationalist or indigenising agendas and Western models of historiography. Those who support the latter argue that such models retain their claim to a form of consensual validity, while those who challenge them argue that the so-called universals within a discipline are little more than hegemonic assumptions or predilections. For an example of alternative history that uses indigenous materials to produce fresh insights one can turn to Ileto's *Pasyon and Revolution: Popular Movements in the Philippines, 1840–1910* (1979). Ileto examines the link between subaltern resistance and the indigenous popular Catholic poetic form of the *Pasyon*, to show how its representation of suffering and resurrection 'flowed into the language of nationalism and revolution at the turn of the century' (in Reid and Marr 1979, p. 380). In rare cases, such as the work in Thai from Nidhi Aeusrivongse, indigenous historiography also works as history written primarily for a local audience in the local language. Such work takes the risk of being ignored by Eurocentric historiography. It also requires the discipline to broaden or shed its linguistic Eurocentrism.

Meanwhile, some of the most compelling literary writing from South-east Asia continues to use the resources of local languages and English to engage historical experience by blurring the line separating historical from fictional narrative. The Vietnamese novels of Bao Ninh, Le Luu, and Duong Thu Huong, for example, immerse character, plot and setting in a vivid sense of lived historical experience to produce narratives of great conviction and power from the perspective of those who suffered the devastations of war in their personal lives. A spirit of subjective participation has also brought several national leaders (for example, Lee Kuan Yew, who equates his own history with that of Singapore) to the authoring of political autobiographies from the unique perspective of their involvement in the life of their times, transforming *petits récits* into grand narratives of the nation.

In contrast, a writer like Pramoedya Ananta Toer provides a view of history in which the relations between agency, power, and victimisation are more complicated. His *Buru Quartet* presents an ambitious analysis of the experience of Dutch colonialism during the early decades of the twentieth century. It uses the life and eventual downfall of a potentially heroic figure, Minke (based partly on a historical person), as the lens through which to refract an absorbing representation of the sociological, intellectual, cultural, and political processes involved in colonial experience. Material that a historian might address in neutral and omniscient terms is dramatised through narrative personas who are deeply implicated in their dual role as the agents and patients of history. Pramoedya's narrative also makes room for sustained reflections on the nature of Dutch and Javanese cultures, the factors that enabled colonialism, the issues at stake in rivalries among European colonialists, the factors that produced anti-colonial resistance, the role of women and individual leadership in nationalist movements, and the effects of an idea of modernity assimilated by the colonised from the West. Pramoedya links his fictional survey of the colonial past to a diagnostic analysis of the failure of the postcolonial nation to live up to the promises of modernity. His narrative gives voice to historical experience with a tonal range rarely accessed by professional historians, ranging from the admonitory to the optative.

On a smaller scale, Philip Jeyaretnam's *Abraham's Promise* (1995) provides an ironic, but equally deflating perspective on a failure whose analysis equivocates between Singapore as a modern nation whose success is bought at the price of human curtailment and a protagonist whose idealism fails to extricate itself from the depredations of historical change at the personal and the collective levels. If a colonised people find themselves the subjects of history, the outcome as narrative can hardly fail to include the colonisers as alter-subjects of the same bipartite historiography. The human implications of that involvement are evoked with great sensitivity and nuance in Mary Morgan's *The House at the Edge of the Jungle* (1999), confirming the symbiotic relation between imaginative history and the historical imagination in South-east Asia.

Rajeev Patke

Literary Works

Bao Ninh (1994), *The Sorrow of War*, New York: Minerva.
Duong Thu Huong (1996), *Novel without a Name*, New York: Penguin.
Fernando, Lloyd (1992), *Scorpion Orchid*, Singapore: Times Books.
Jeyaretnam, Philip (1995), *Abraham's Promise*, Singapore: Times Books.
José, Francisco Sionil (1979), *My Brother, My Executioner*, Quezon City: New Day Publishers.
Kampoon Boontawee (1991), *A Child of the Northeast*, Bangkok: Editions Duang Kamol.
Le Luu (1997), *A Time Far Past*, Amherst, MA: University of Massachusetts Press.
Ma Ma Lay (1991), *Not out of Hate*, Athens, OH: Ohio University Press.
Morgan, Mary (1999), *The House at the Edge of the Jungle*, New York: Thomas Dunne Books.
Toer, Pramodeya Ananta (1990–3), *The Buru Quartet*, 4 vols, Harmondsworth: Penguin.

Histories

Ahmad, Abu Talib and Liok Ee Tan (eds) (2003), *New Terrains in Southeast Asian History*, Athens, OH: Ohio University Press.
Anderson, Benedict (1998), *The Spectre of Comparisons: Nationalism, Southeast Asia and the World*, London and New York: Verso.
Benda, Harry J. (1962), 'The Structure of Southeast Asian History: Some Preliminary Observations', *Journal of Southeast Asian History* 3, pp. 103–38.
Chow, Rey (1993), *Writing Diaspora: Tactics of Intervention in Contemporary Cultural Studies*, Bloomington, IN: Indiana University Press.

Chutintaranond, Sunait and Chris Baker (eds) (2002), *Recalling Local Pasts: Autonomous History in Southeast Asia*, Bangkok: Silkworm Books.

Hale, D. G. E. (1955), *A History of South-East Asia*, New York: St Martin's Press.

Hall, D. G. E. (ed.) (1961), *Historians of South East Asia*, Oxford: Oxford University Press.

Hong, Lysa (1996), 'History', in Mohammed Halib and Tim Huxley (eds), *An Introduction to Southeast Asian Studies*, New York: I. B. Tauris, pp. 46–70.

Ileto, Reynaldo C. (1997), 'Outlines of a Nonlinear Emplotment of Philippine History', in Lisa Lowe and David Lloyd (eds), *The Politics of Culture in the Shadow of Capital*, Durham, NC and London: Duke University Press, pp. 98–131.

Legge, J. D. [1992] (1999), 'The Writing of Southeast Asian History', in Nicholas Tarling (ed.), *The Cambridge History of Southeast Asia: Volume 1*, Cambridge: Cambridge University Press, pp. 1–50.

Leiberman, Victor (ed.) (1999), *Beyond Binary Histories*, Ann Arbor, MI: University of Michigan Press.

Reid, Anthony (1988–93), *Southeast Asia in the Age of Commerce 1450–1600*, London and New Haven, CT: Yale University Press.

Reid, Anthony (1999), *Charting the Shape of Early Modern Southeast Asia*, Chiang Mai: Silkworm Books.

Reid, Anthony and Anthony Marr (eds) (1979), *Perceptions of the Past in Southeast Asia*, Singapore: Heinemann.

Smail, John R. W. (1961), 'On the Possibility of an Autonomous History of Modern Southeast Asia', *Journal of Southeast Asian History* 2: 2, pp. 72–102.

Tarling, Nicholas (1999), 'The British Empire in South-East Asia', in Robin W. Winks (ed.), *The Oxford History of the British Empire, Volume 5. Historiography*, Oxford: Oxford University Press, pp. 403–15.

Tarling, Nicholas (2001), *Southeast Asia: A Modern History*, South Melbourne and Oxford: Oxford University Press.

Watson, Andaya Barbara (1997), 'The Unity of Southeast Asia: Historical Approaches and Questions', *Journal of Southeast Asian Studies* 28: 1, pp. 161–71.

Wolters, O. W. [1982] (1999), *History, Culture and Region in Southeast Asian Perspectives*, Ithaca, NY: Cornell University Press.

See also: **Bumiputra**; **Communism: South-east Asia**; **Engmalchin**; **Lee Kuan Yew**; **Vietnam War**; **Women's Histories: South-east Asia**.

Historiography: Southern Africa

South African historiography in the latter half of the twentieth century was characterised by a long-running ideological feud of exceptional viciousness between 'liberal' and 'revisionist' (or, broadly, Marxist) historians. The strength of this polarisation reflected the intensity of feeling that surrounded the epochal political struggle against apartheid. Although both liberals and revisionists were hostile to the South African racial order, each accused the other of failing to understand its origins, and thus of wrongly estimating the conditions for its demise. Retrospectively, though, it might be said that the passion of the polemics deflected attention from the important divisions within both camps and the variable quality of the scholarship on both sides.

Early twentieth-century historiography was dominated by the work of G. M. Theal and

G. E. Cory, whose chronicles of conquest were deeply sympathetic to the colonial project. Popular historical writings espousing the causes of Afrikaner and African nationalism also emerged in the same era. Gustav Preller played an important role in codifying Afrikaner nationalism's official version of the Great Trek and other major events. Literary works that engaged with these histories include Sarah Gertrude Millin's novels *King of the Bastards* (1950) and *The Burning Man* (1950), and (more critically) C. Louis Leipoldt's posthumously published *The Valley* (2001). The writings of Mangena Fuze, Silas Molema and Sol Plaatje articulated African elite perspectives on historical events, and Plaatje in *Mhudi* (1930) also produced in novel form his interpretation of the Southern African past.

Academic historical scholarship in the region can fairly be said to start with the work of W. M. Macmillan. The Scots-born, Cape-raised Macmillan began his seminal contribution to southern African historiography while employed at the University of the Witwatersrand ('Wits'), immediately after World War I. The Oxford-trained historian set a new standard of textual scholarship and for the first time placed the experience of black South Africans at the centre of academic enquiry. Although retrospectively often seen as a 'liberal', Macmillan was in fact strongly influenced by the British socialist scholar R. H. Tawney, and was pivotal in turning the attention of historians to social and economic questions. Macmillan's seminal work was his *Bantu, Boer and Briton* (1927), a study based on the papers of the early nineteenth-century missionary, John Philip. This book centrally challenged the account of colonial conquest given by settler-apologist historians. In terms of publication dates, the southern African literary work closest to Macmillan's history is William Plomer's youthful effort *Turbott Wolfe* (1925), which shocked its first readers with its liberal and sexual content.

From the 1940s through to the 1960s, a substantial body of 'liberal' scholarship was produced by historians who were strongly opposed to the emerging apartheid policy, but who also rejected the claims of Marxism. Amongst these historians perhaps the outstanding figures were C. W. De Kiewit and Leonard Thompson. But a great deal of historically informed work was produced by liberal anthropologists, notably Monica Wilson, Leo Kuper and Eileen J. Krige, and by the social psychologist I. D. MacCrone. All of this writing was markedly hostile to Afrikaner nationalism. It tended to see the origins of apartheid in a 'frontier' racist mentality, developing amongst whites in general, but Afrikaners in particular, during the historical experience of colonial conquest in the eighteenth and nineteenth centuries. In this perspective, apartheid was an anachronistic resistance to the forces of modernity. Given free rein, capitalist development would gradually foster racial egalitarianism. The high point of the liberal scholarship was the *Oxford History of South Africa*, edited by Wilson and Thompson (1969, 1971). These volumes were the subsequent focus of particular ideological dispute, some of which unfairly has obscured the importance of much material of permanent value which they contain. Literary works contemporaneous with, and loosely in the same spirit as, these histories include Alan Paton's *Cry, the Beloved Country* (1948), Nadine Gordimer's *The Lying Days* (1953) and Dan Jacobson's *A Dance in the Sun* (1956).

Roughly contemporaneous with these academic histories was a small but significant body of popular Marxist history-writing. These included works by activist historians aligned with the African National Congress and the South African Communist Party, like H. J. and R. E. Simons' *Class and Colour in South Africa* (1969) and Eddie Roux's *Time Longer than a Rope* (1948), as well as histories by anti-Stalinist activist historians associated with the Non-European Unity Movement, like Dora Taylor's *The Role of the Missionaries in Conquest* (1952) and Hosea Jaffe's *Three Hundred Years: A History of South Africa* (1952).

SACP member Alex la Guma's novels *A Walk in the Night* (1962) and *In the Fog of the Season's End* (1972) are fictional accounts of anti-apartheid political struggles, and Baruch Hirson's autobiography *Revolutions in My Life* (1995) sheds further light on the non-Stalinist South African left of this period.

By the beginning of the 1970s, exile South African scholars at the School of Oriental and African Studies, Warwick University and Sussex University in Britain were launching a full-scale ideological attack on the liberals. An obvious defect of the liberal position was that its view of apartheid as atavistic failed to explain the historically unprecedented industrialisation and economic growth that South Africa attained in the 1960s, at the high point of the implementation of the policy of racial separation. The Marxist-oriented scholarship which now emerged saw racial domination and capitalism in South Africa as being in a complementary relationship. Consequently, these 'revisionists' were keen to insist on the complicity of white Anglophone dominated capitalists in the maintenance of the racial order, and of British imperialism in its creation; Afrikaner nationalists were no longer the sole villains of the story. Liberal historians were therefore portrayed as apologists for capital, who neglected the material dimension of apartheid.

A particular role in the development of this strand of historiography was played by scholars influenced by the structuralist Marxism of Louis Althusser. Most important of these writers was the exiled communist lawyer-turned-academic, Harold Wolpe. Wolpe argued that apartheid constituted a system for the reproduction of cheap labour power. In this argument, mining capital had, historically, been able to avoid paying a living wage to its work force by displacing its costs onto rural households and their economy of subsistence agriculture. Apartheid, by denying urban residential rights to black workers perpetuated this system even though the agricultural productivity of the rural areas was in decline. A similar (although less structuralist and better historically informed) version of this approach was articulated in the work of another exile, Martin Legassick. Nicos Poulantzas' development of Althusserianism into an analysis of political divisions in the state as based on 'fractions of capital' was also enthusiastically taken up in the 1970s by a group of South African scholars including Rob Davies, Mike Morris and Dan O'Meara. This approach seemed to offer the benefits of accounting for splits within white South Africa over racial policy as reflecting divergent capitalist interests, while still asserting the essentially capitalist nature of the state. Influential in its time, much of this Poulantzian work appears in retrospect as mechanistic and economistic. However, O'Meara did move beyond the limits of his paradigm to produce two superb books (1983, 1996) on Afrikaner nationalism, which rank, with the work of the Weberian-inclined historian, Herman Giliomee, as the most important on their subject. Another aspect of the Marxist historiography was Legassick's critique of the liberal's 'frontier' thesis (See his 1980 essay). If the origins of apartheid were, as the Marxists claimed, to be found in the industrial era, then the importance of earlier events in explaining racial division was correspondingly reduced. Contrary to the liberal picture of an adamantine racial hostility rooted in the frontier, Legassick portrayed the frontier as a liminal zone in which Boers, Africans and Griquas moved as competing but relatively similar groups of pastoralists.

Another strand of Marxist influenced historical writing on southern Africa emerged out of the broader Africanist historiography which had developed in the UK and to a lesser extent in the USA in the 1960s. An important role in bringing the influence of this historiography to southern African studies was played by Terence Ranger, the foremost historian of Zimbabwe. But the central role was undoubtedly played by Shula Marks, a South African historian at the University of London. Although sharing some of the concerns of the structuralist scholars, Marks explored these in a manner which was much more historically sensitive and knowledgeable. Marks' seminar at the Institute of Commonwealth Studies became the main forum in which a new generation of southern African scholars developed their work. Marks' contributions to the scholarship are so numerous as to defy categorisation, but they include substantively, a detailed account of the role of British imperialism in establishing the industrial and racial orders of late nineteenth and early twentieth-century southern Africa and major contributions to feminist history, the history of ethnicity and medical history. Methodologically, Marks played a key role in introducing into southern African studies both the approach of the new Africanist historians and that of the new British social historians of the 1970s. Marks provided magisterial overviews of southern African history in introductions to a number of edited volumes (see Marks and Atmore 1980, Marks and Rathbone 1982, and Marks and Trapido 1987). Amongst the important works produced by her students were key monographs on the era of colonial conquest, notably those of Peter Delius on the Pedi, Jeff Guy on the Zulus, and Philip Bonner on the Swazis.

In the late 1970s and through the 1980s, the impact of the new political insurgency against the South African regime and the intellectual developments in the UK combined to generate dynamic new social history literature in South Africa itself. The dominant individual in this development was Charles van Onselen, whose studies of mine labour in Zimbabwe in the 1970s, of the early history of Johannesburg in the 1980s, and of black sharecroppers in the western Transvaal in the 1990s represent scholarship of the highest calibre. The development of this new body of literature was characterised by strength in two key areas: region- and community-focused studies (or what later came to be called micro-history), and biography. The micro-history strand is well represented in the work of the Wits History Workshop in Johannesburg, which is reflected in the collections of papers edited by Belinda Bozzoli. In these studies questions of 'experience' and of communal and class identity were given central attention. This era also saw a rich crop of biographical studies, notably those by Bill Nasson, Tim Couzens, Paul La Hausse and Richard Mendelson. Much of this work centred on 'marginal' historical figures. All of the new work was written from positions hostile to the apartheid regime; but the historians were politically divided. Some, like Van Onselen, were politically sceptical; others, especially the Johannesburg historians, tended to be sympathetic to independent trade unions; still other historians like Jeff Peires aligned themselves strongly with the ANC. In much the same way that historians were defined and animated by the political exigencies of the 1970s and 1980s, so too were novelists like Gordimer in *Burger's Daughter* (1979), André Brink in *A Dry White Season* (1979), J. M. Coetzee in *The Age of Iron* (1990), and Mongane Serote in *To Every Birth its Blood* (1981), playwright Athol Fugard in *Sizwe Banzi is Dead* (1972) and *The Island* (1973), and poets like Dennis Brutus in *Letters from Martha* (1968) and Jeremy Cronin in *Inside* (1983).

It was only with the beginning of the transition to democracy in 1990, and the consequent global reintegration of South Africa that historians began to engage with postcolonial theory. In many cases this engagement did not go very far, with historians retreating into an empiricist laager. A notable exception to this determined empiricism has been the work of US-based or US-educated historians like Jean and John Comaroff, Clifton Crais and Carolyn Hamilton. Hamilton's work, for example, is on the representation of the Zulu king Shaka, and shows how 'black' and 'white' images of the king had interacted with each other; her edited collection on the nineteenth-century *Mfecane* migrations (1995) focused on the historicity of this 'event'; and her more recent work has problematised the idea of the archive in South Africa.

In the post-apartheid era, South African history continues to be rewritten, with the consolidation and extension of existing themes, and the emergence of new fields like environmental history. In addition to monographs, a number of journals publish Southern African history: *The Journal of Southern African Studies* (JSAS), the *Journal of African History* (JAH), *Kronos*, the *South African Historical Journal* (SAHJ) and the *Journal of Natal and Zulu History* (JNZH). Although not as consistently combative as in the 1970s and 1980s, the book review sections of these journals still display frequent signs of rancorous debate. Since 1994, there has also been a concern with public histories in the forms of both the Truth and Reconciliation Commission, and of museums, monuments and commemorative festivals. Finally, Southern African historiography itself has been subjected to ongoing scrutiny by, amongst others, Ken Smith, Christopher Saunders, Martin Legassick and Gary Minkley, and the editors and contributors to the special issue of *SAHJ* on 'The Future of the Past'.

These developments notwithstanding, the democratic era in South Africa has in general seen a marked decline in levels of popular and academic interest in history. In a sense this is the outcome of a series of disillusionments. The liberal hope that apartheid would peacefully fade away under the pressures of modernity was illusory; it took two decades of near-civil war to remove the system. But contrary to some Marxist expectations, apartheid and capitalism proved all too separable; the latter has flourished after the demise of the former. In the demobilised civil society of the early 2000s, the social historians' romanticisation of past struggle, or the rigours of contemporary theory have little attraction for consumerist-orientated youth. It seems as if, for the moment, South Africans have had more history than they can bear.

Jonathan Hyslop

Literary Works

Brink, André (1979), *A Dry White Season*, London: W. H. Allen.

Brutus, Dennis (1968), *Letters from Martha*, London: Heinemann.

Coetzee, J. M. (1990), *The Age of Iron*, London: Secker and Warburg.

Cronin, Jeremy (1983), *Inside*, Johannesburg: Ravan Press.

Fugard, Athol (1993), *The Township Plays*, Oxford: Oxford University Press.

Gordimer, Nadine [1953] (2002), *The Lying Days*, London: Bloomsbury.

Gordimer, Nadine [1979] (2000), *Burger's Daughter*, London: Bloomsbury.

Hirson, Baruch (1995), *Revolutions in My Life*, Johannesburg: Witwatersrand University Press.

Jacobson, Dan (1956), *A Dance in the Sun*, Oxford: Oxford University Press.

La Guma, Alex (1962), *A Walk in the Night*, London: Heinemann.

La Guma, Alex (1972), *In the Fog of the Season's End*, London: Heinemann.

Leipoldt, C. Louis (2001), *The Valley*, Cape Town: Stormberg.

Millin, Sarah Gertrude (1950), *King of the Bastards*, London: Heinemann.

Paton, Alan [1948] (1958), *Cry, the Beloved Country*, Harmondsworth: Penguin.

Plaatje, Sol [1930] (1989), *Mhudi. An Epic of South African Life*, London: Heinemann.

Plomer, William [1925] (1993), *Turbott Wolfe*, Johannesburg: A. D. Donker.

Serote, Mongane (1981), *To Every Birth its Blood*, Johannesburg: Ravan Press.

Histories

Bozzoli, Belinda (ed.) (1983), *Town and Countryside in the Transvaal: Capitalist Penetration and Popular Response*, Johannesburg: Ravan Press.

Bozzoli, Belinda (ed.) (1987), *Class, Community and Conflict: South African Perspectives*, Johannesburg: Ravan Press.

Giliomee, Herman (2003), *The Afrikaners: Biography of a People*, Charlottesville, VA: University of Virginia Press.

Hamilton, Carolyn (ed.) (1995), *The Mfecane Aftermath: Reconstructive Debates in Southern African History*, Johannesburg: Witwatersrand University Press.

Hamilton, Carolyn (ed.) (1998), *Terrific Majesty: The Powers of Shaka Zulu and the Limits of Historical Invention*, Cape Town: David Philip.

Hamilton, Carolyn, Verne Harris, Jane Taylor, Michele Pickover, Graeme Reid and Razia Saleh (eds) (2002), *Refiguring the Archive*, Cape Town: David Philip.

Legassick, Martin (1974), 'South Africa: Capital Accumulation and Violence', *Economy and Society* 3: 3, pp. 253–91.

Legassick, Martin (1980), 'The Frontier Tradition in South African Historiography', in S. Marks and A. Atmore (eds), *Economy and Society in Pre-Industrial South Africa*, London: Longman, pp. 44–79.

Legassick, Martin (1989), 'The Northern Frontier to c. 1840: The Rise and Decline of the Griqua People', in Richard Elphick and Herman Giliomee (eds), *The Shaping of South African Society*, Cape Town: Maskew Miller Longman, pp. 340–58.

Legassick, Martin and Gary Minkley (1998), 'Current Trends in the Production of South African History', *Alternation* 5: 1, pp. 98–129.

Macmillan, W. M. (1927), *Bantu, Boer and Briton: The Making of the South African Native Problem*, London: Faber and Gwyer.

Marks, Shula and Anthony Atmore (eds) (1980), *Economy and Society in Pre-Industrial South Africa*, London: Longman.

Marks, Shula and Richard Rathbone (eds) (1982), *Industrialisation and Social Change in South Africa: African Class Formation, Culture and Consciousness, 1870–1930*, London: Longman.

Marks, Shula and Stanley Trapido (eds) (1987), *The Politics of Race, Class and Nationalism in Twentieth Century South Africa*, London: Longman.

O'Meara, Dan (1983), *Volkskapitalisme: Class, Capital and Ideology in the Development of Afrikaner Nationalism, 1934–1948*, Johannesburg: Ravan Press.

O'Meara, Dan (1996), *Forty Lost Years: The Apartheid State and the Politics of the National Party 1948–1994*, Johannesburg: Ravan Press.

Saunders, Christopher (1988), *The Making of the South African Past*, Cape Town: David Philip.

Smith, Ken (1988), *The Changing Past. Trends in South African Historical Writing*, Johannesburg: Southern Book Publishers.

South African Historical Journal (1996), 35: special issue on 'The Future of the Past'.

Van Onselen, Charles (1976) *Chibaro: African Mine Labour in Southern Rhodesia 1900–1933*, London: Pluto.

Van Onselen, Charles (1982), *Studies in the Social and Economic History of the Witwatersrand*, 2 vols, Johannesburg: Ravan Press.

Van Onselen, Charles (1996), *The Seed is Mine: The Life of Kas Maine, A South African Sharecropper 1894–1985*, Cape Town: David Philip.

Wilson, Monica and Leonard Thompson (1969, 1971), *The Oxford History of South Africa*, 2 vols, Oxford: Oxford University Press.

Wolpe, Harold (1972), 'Capitalism and Cheap Labour Power in South Africa: From Segregation to Apartheid', *Economy and Society* 1: 4, pp. 425–56.

See also: **Apartheid and Segregation; Labour Histories: Southern Africa; Nationalism(s): Southern Africa; Post-apartheid; Women's Histories: Southern Africa**.

Historiography: West Africa

Until the close of World War II, African history was not recognised as an academic discipline, and Africa's contribution to world history in general was neglected by scholars. When West Africa was mentioned, it was in the context of European expansion, and many positivist historians – proceeding on the assumption that historical methods require written documents – overlooked the wealth of knowledge available from oral traditions, literary *griots*, and local historians.

Prior to the 1940s, three approaches were taken in recording the West African past. The first approach was expressed in European histories, which propagated the misconceptions that African societies were static, and that they represented earlier stages in human development. Africa was depicted as having no history before the coming of Europeans, and evidence of centralised states or complex societies was explained away as the results of external agency. To facilitate the administration of British colonies, a minimal understanding of African institutions and societies was necessary, and to this end, colonial agents and missionaries compiled ethnographic and demographic surveys. Their reports championed the contributions of the British Empire and denied indigenous development. Nevertheless, these documents became accepted versions of history and saturated curricula in schools across the continent, thus playing a role in the colonisation of the African mind. An example of this phenomenon was the lionising of colonial administrators at the expense of African intellectuals and past heroes, although there was limited disagreement and dialogue over Africa's past within institutions such as the Royal African Society and the International African Institute. Closely associated with this first category of African history-writing was anthropology, which promoted the analysis of unwritten records and expanded the range of historical evidence, but ultimately did little besides justifying colonial rule and validating the supposed cultural superiority of the West. One especially resilient assumption, which continues to obfuscate academic and political debate, is the notion of the African 'tribe' as the only permanent and powerful collective identity in Africa. The second approach to West African historiography was pursued by West Africans themselves. Arabic travelogues and local histories were the most common expression of this research. These endeavours retained the styles of antecedent traditions, and often highlighted less attractive realities of British rule. These historians disagreed over the nature and impact of colonial rule, with some angry at the devastation of indigenous institutions, and others anticipating progress and modernisation from new colonial institutions. The third approach to West African history was pursued in the USA, and advocated by W. E. B. Du Bois and his Pan-Africanist contemporaries. By 1916, *The Journal of Negro History* linked the realities of Africans to those of the African diaspora.

West Africa was thus incorporated into 'black history', but did not as yet stand alone as a field of inquiry.

The post-World War II period saw the emergence of African history as an academic field, as well as an increase in the number of West African universities. As a more coherent and objective approach became the academic norm, many Africans also assumed responsibility for correcting past misrepresentations, and social and economic histories on migration, agriculture, urbanisation, and race relations were published. At the same time, in Britain and in the USA, colonial history received fresh attention, and the failures and injustices of colonialism were acknowledged. Early Africanists from this period were aligned to one of three camps. The first and largest group comprised those with the fewest grievances against colonial rule, who believed Africa had benefited from the colonial experience. The second group for the most ignored the colonial era altogether – often because of internal political disagreements within universities, and the continuing clout of imperial historians – and preferred to study the pre-colonial period, leaving more contemporary issues to other disciplines. The third group were the radical anti-colonialists, who were influenced by the British Labour Party and nationalist sentiment. All three groups, despite their disagreements, believed the time had come for Africans to control their own affairs, and this included African histories.

During the decade leading up to independence, any remaining Eurocentric myths were dispelled by the publication of John Fage's *An Introduction to the History of West Africa* (1995), and the *Cambridge History of Africa* (1978). Increasing numbers of African students received higher education, an Africanised curriculum was adopted, societies and journals were established, and an interdisciplinary approach to African history embraced. Equally important was the recognition of oral sources as valuable historical evidence, and archives were created using an array of sources. In the 1960s, newly trained scholars – many schooled in West Africa – contributed to the rise in popularity of the study of African history. Further, the civil rights movement in the USA influenced new Africanists, who supported anti-imperialist struggles. Various works appeared to proclaim the African past, with strong emphasis on internally generated historical changes, and the survival of great civilisations. As independence dawned, histories and literary works celebrating Africa, and condemning British colonial rule increased, and history in particular was employed to authenticate conditions of independence.

With decolonisation, African historians sought to rectify the inaccuracies of the past, to condemn British rule, and to dictate the internal politics of their universities. In many cases, an 'African perspective' – identified as nationalist historiography – took hold. Nationalist historiographers emphasised the pre-colonial social and environmental equilibrium of Africa, and argued that colonial intrusion had interrupted a period of unparalleled African achievement, and had undermined the foundations of African societies. Nationalist historians were criticised for manipulating the past – especially colonial history – in sympathy with nationalist sentiment, in the process promoting neo-colonial elitism, misrepresenting the problems of African societies, and incapacitating the study of the colonial period. Disillusionment with nationalist historiography was closely related to the wider post-independence disillusionment with what were increasingly seen as neo-colonial oligarchies. Yesterday's heroes of independence struggles had become corrupt politicians fleecing stagnant economies, and scholars started questioning nationalist truisms – for example, had the pre-colonial past really been such a model of perfection? – and even turned from history to the social sciences in their efforts to address pressing contemporary social concerns. By the 1970s, this nationalist phase of history-writing had been succeeded by a Marxist historiography that was concerned to return once again to studying the colonial era. Themes in Marxist historiography that were explored included: capitalist penetration of pre-capitalist West African economies; the role of indigenous and Atlantic forms of slavery in reconfiguring West African societies; the impact of British colonial policy; the transitions in the forms of labour; and the relation between class, gender, ethnic and national social formations. Marxist scholars understood the colonial era as a major disruption in the evolution of West African societies, and questioned any simplistic connection between the pre-colonial past and postcolonial present.

After about 1980, British West African historiography can be divided into four broad themes: Anglo-African relations, British administration, nationalism and independence, and the assessment of British rule. The first theme, Anglo-African relations, has inspired studies of the first European contacts in West Africa, the 'scramble for Africa' in the late nineteenth century, and the expansion of British missionary and commercial activities. The motivation for British involvement in West Africa has been a topic of debate, but most West African scholars now reject the arguments suggesting that missionary or 'civilising' motives predominated in favour of the arguments of those theorists and historians (like J. A. Hobson and Emmanuel Wallerstein) who have stressed the economic motivations. Another general pattern in histories of Anglo-African relations is that there is a tendency for British histories to focus on African dependency and complicity, whereas African histories have focused on anti-colonial resistance and opposition. The second theme, British administration, has inspired research into the period 1900–60 particularly, with studies on topics like the evolution and nature of the colonial civil service, the relation between indigenous and British legal systems, policing and education, and the similarities and differences between British and French colonial policies. The overall impact of the British administration continues to be debated, with historians disagreeing over the negative and positive aspects. Interpretations of the third theme, independence and nationalism, have changed significantly over time, with the initial emphasis on a vanguard of activists leading the masses to independence increasingly superceded by explanations that acknowledge a multitude of both internal and external factors in bringing about independence. The fourth theme, the assessment of British rule, has taken a number of forms, with historians for the most part critical of Britain's role in laying the foundations for ongoing problems that have dogged postcolonial West Africa, like the politicisation of ethnicity, and the proliferation of political dictatorships.

In conclusion, certain challenges and prospects facing West African historiography can be identified. Of the challenges, the first is one of resources: despite increasing student numbers, African universities are severely under-funded, and US and British universities have the accessibility and material advantages to dominate the study of African historiography. The results have been contradictory: on the one hand, historical knowledge is produced and circulates in the north, and audiences in Africa are frequently denied ready access to such material; on the other hand, historians of West Africa at Western universities have invigorated the discipline by introducing new approaches and perspectives. A second challenge for historians, and one they have taken up with great zeal, is to relate studies of colonial and pre-colonial West Africa to contemporary economic, political and social problems – the dominance of cash crop economies; the lack of political participation; and the erosion of traditional politico-religious institutions. One certain prospect is that the debate over the appropriate place of Western values and institutions in West Africa is likely to continue: should corrosive Western influences be excised in the search for an 'authentic Africa'? Or should Africa take advantage of universal knowledge and continue the process of Western modernisation? The latter appears more likely because as the penetration of Western capitalism in West Africa accelerates, so the reclaiming of African institutions of the past becomes increasingly difficult.

Toyin Falola with Ashley Rothrock

Literary Works

Achebe, Chinua [1958] (1992), *Things Fall Apart*, London: Heinemann.
Armah, Ayi Kwei [1968] (1988), *The Beautiful Ones Are Not Yet Born*, Oxford: Heinemann.
Falola, Toyin (2004), *A Mouth Sweeter than Salt: An African Memoir*, Ann Arbor, MI: Michigan University Press.
Kane, Hamidou (1972), *Ambiguous Adventure*, trans. K. Woods, London: Heinemann.
Soyinka, Wole [1981] (1994), *Ake. The Years of Childhood*, London: Vintage.

Histories

Ajayi, J. F. Ade and Michael Crowder (eds) (1972), *History of West Africa*, 2 vols, New York: Columbia University Press.
Ake, Claude (ed.) (1985), *The Political Economy of Nigeria*, Basingstoke: Macmillan.
Fage, John (1955), *An Introduction to the History of West Africa*, Cambridge: Cambridge University Press.
Fage, John (1978), *Cambridge History of Africa, Volume 2: From 500 BC to AD 1050*, Cambridge: Cambridge University Press.
Falola, Toyin (ed.) (1991), *Yoruba Historiography*, Madison, WI: African Studies Program, University of Wisconsin-Madison.
Falola, Toyin (ed.) (1993), *African Historiography*, London: Longman.
Falola, Toyin (ed.) (2000), *Tradition and Change in Africa: The Essays of J. F. Ade Ajayi*, Trenton: Africa World Press.
Falola, Toyin (2001), *Nationalism and African Intellectuals*, Rochester, NY: Rochester University Press.
Falola, Toyin and Christian Jennings (eds) (2002a), *Sources and Methods in African History: Spoken, Written, Unearthed*, Rochester, NY: University of Rochester Press.
Falola, Toyin and Christian Jennings (eds) (2002b), *Africanizing Knowledge: African Studies across the Disciplines*, New Brunswick and London: Transaction.
Falola, Toyin and Atieno Odhiambo (eds) (2002), *The Challenges of History and Leadership in Africa: The Essays of Bethwell Allan Ogot*, Trenton, NJ: Africa World Press.
Fitch, Bob and Mary Oppenheimer (1966), *Ghana: End of an Illusion*, New York: Monthly Review Press.
Graf, William (1988), *The Nigerian State*, Oxford: James Currey.
O'Brien, Donal B. Cruise, John Dunn and Richard Rathbone (eds) (1989), *Contemporary West African States*, Cambridge: Cambridge University Press.
Olukoshi, A. O. (1993), *The Politics of Structural Adjustment in Nigeria*, Oxford: James Currey.
Osaghae, Eghosa (1998), *Crippled Giant: Nigeria since Independence*, London: Hurst.
Phillips, Anne (1989), *The Enigma of Colonialism: British Policy in West Africa*, Oxford: James Currey.

See also: **Religions: West Africa; Slavery: West Africa; Universities: West Africa; Women's Histories: West Africa**.

HIV/AIDS

The pandemic of the human immunodeficiency virus/acquired immune deficiency syndrome (HIV/AIDS) is the biggest global public health crisis today. HIV and AIDS have a number of characteristics that make the disease peculiarly difficult to control, especially in countries marked by poverty and poor infrastructure. HIV is transmitted through bodily fluids (blood, semen or vaginal secretions, from mother to child *in utero* or breastmilk), with the most common route sexual intercourse. Like other sexually-transmitted infections, AIDS is surrounded by stigma, including shame, secretiveness and denial. Moreover, it is an unusually easy infection to deny or conceal, because for adults the length of time between infection with HIV and the development of full-blown AIDS is seven to ten years. In the meantime, the infected individual appears to be healthy, and therefore has plenty of opportunities for infecting others. The slow, secret onset of HIV has meant that only when people fall sick and die in large numbers have governments acknowledged the need for action, as in South Africa where HIV prevalence grew from near zero in 1990 to 25 per cent of the adult population in 2003. The virus itself is an extraordinarily difficult microbial adversary: it readily mutates and develops resistance to treatment. Twenty years after the HIV was first isolated, the first vaccine trials are under way, but the prospects for an effective vaccine remain remote. In the meantime, anti-retroviral treatment has become effective at slowing down the progression of the virus, transforming it from a death sentence to a chronic condition. Until 2003, the cost of these treatments put them far beyond the reach of the great majority in poor countries. As the cost has come down, other challenges for reaching the majority of the world's 42 million people living with HIV and AIDS are becoming apparent: treatment can only be effective if the person is well-nourished, and treatment can be provided in a well-controlled health setting. These factors have conspired to turn a few isolated cases of a hard-to-catch infection into a global pandemic that by 2003 has killed over 30 million people, with death rates rising.

AIDS is barely a generation old. The first diagnosis of a new syndrome was reported in June 1981 in the United States. Within three months, more than 100 cases of the new disease had been reported, most of them marked by a collapse of the patient's immune system and the advent of a rare cancer called Kaposi's sarcoma, along with other opportunistic infections. Most of the early patients were homosexual men. Rarely in medical history has there been such an accelerated scientific search for the cause of a syndrome. Within a few years, the culprit was found to be a lentivirus, a class of slow-acting viruses only recently identified. Scientific progress was marred by acrimonious competition over credit for the discovery. Dr Roberto Gallo of the National Cancer Institute in the USA, Dr Luc Montagnier at the Pasteur Institute in Paris, and Dr Jan Levy at the University of California all separately identified the virus responsible for AIDS, though each gave it a different name. The clash of egos and institutional interests slowed progress in developing a test (essential for the effective screening of blood supplies) and further research into possible treatment. Only in 1987 did the president of the USA and the prime minister of France announce a joint agreement on the name HIV. It was an ominous augur that a scientific dispute should eventually need resolution at such a high political level. The fact that the epidemic first occurred among gay men in the USA has had a lasting imprint on the way in which the world has responded. The US gay community was relatively affluent and educated, and already actively involved in supporting medical research. AIDS activism was, from the outset, scientifically sophisticated and outspoken. As the gay community was already subjected to discrimination and stigma by the Reagan administration, activists were fearful that the presence of a new incurable disease in their ranks could lead to systematic ostracism, and hence they stressed the right to privacy and confidentiality of those living with HIV. In the 1980s, the epidemic cut a swathe through the US and European gay communities, killing among others leading actors, musicians and writers. The experience was reflected in writing and artistic output on themes of love, sex, death, and society's stigmatisation of gay men (see, for example, Toibin 1999, and White and Mars-Jones 1987).

Africa rapidly emerged as the epicentre of the world's pandemic. AIDS was diagnosed in Uganda in the early 1980s, where the first national epidemic occurred, but earlier cases have been retrospectively traced to the Congo as far back as 1959. Most scientists believe that HIV is a variant of simian immunodeficiency virus, endemic in some monkey species in central Africa, which has crossed the species barrier. The AIDS pandemic is thus ultimately traceable to Africa, where early cases had gone undiagnosed because of the poor medical facilities and the confounding presence of so many other causes of illness and death. The apparent African origin of AIDS has, in turn, added a racial dimension to the politics of the pandemic. Today, more than 20 million Africans have died and about 30 million are infected with HIV, with numbers growing. It is a heterosexual epidemic entrenched in the general population, with secondary infection through mother-to-child transmission. Adult HIV prevalence rates have passed 20 per cent in seven southern African countries and in Swaziland and Botswana are pushing 40 per cent. This means that teenagers in Southern Africa have a more than 50 per cent lifetime chance of contracting HIV, while in Swaziland and Botswana it is up to 90 per cent. Life expectancy has fallen from over 60 years to the mid-30s in the worst-hit countries. In contrast to the developed world, there are more infections among women than men, and women and girls are on average infected six to eight years younger than men. It is the greatest crisis afflicting the continent, with Botswana's president declaring that the epidemic may destroy his country.

The epidemic is also growing in the Caribbean, South Asia (India is estimated to have the world's second largest number of people living with HIV and AIDS, after South Africa), China and the former Soviet Union. Each of these has a distinct epidemic: in Russia, Eastern Europe and parts of South-east Asia it is centred upon injecting drug users (IDUs); in China a major cause has been contaminated blood supplies; in India it is a combination of IDUs, men who have sex with men and heterosexual intercourse. Once a certain level of infection reaches the general population, there are worries that generalised epidemics will ensue. Fears about the impact of the epidemic on the economies and national security of Russia and Asian countries prompted the USA to recognise AIDS as a threat to national security in 2000, followed by a resolution to similar effect at the UN Security Council. In general, however, governments have been slow and ineffectual in responding. The pattern started with the US government in the early 1980s, which was notably uninterested in a disease that appeared mainly to affect gay men. Both national and international organisations are ill-suited to addressing such a complex and intimate issue, so that few responses have been commensurate with the scale of the problem. The United Nations agencies tasked with tackling HIV/AIDS, namely UNAIDS (established in 1996) and the Global Fund for AIDS, TB and malaria (created in 2001), are seriously under-funded.

In Europe and North America, preventive measures – 'safe sex' – very largely brought the AIDS epidemic under control by the late 1980s, although there are recent signs of an upsurge. However, in Africa, the Caribbean and Asia, for the most part, efforts to control HIV transmission have been remarkably ineffective. Information about the dangers of AIDS and how HIV is transmitted appears to have only marginally affected sexual behaviour. In many cultures, men continue with risky sexual behaviour because the prospect of dying of a mysterious disease in a decade's time is so remote from day-to-day risks and hardships, for example as a miner or soldier. In Africa, where about 95 per cent of those living with HIV have not been tested, there is often sheer fatalism: a belief either that one already has the virus, or that contracting it is inevitable. Many women simply have no alternative but to submit to unsafe sex, either from their husbands or partners because to demand a condom would amount to an admission or accusation of unfaithfulness, or (in the case of sex workers) from clients, because skin-on-skin sex earns more money. Women in many countries are virtually powerless when it comes to negotiating sexual encounters. Add to this persisting confusion and denial about this new and often inexplicable disease, and the obstacles to the kinds of sustained changes in sexual behaviour are immense. At the end of 2002, fewer than one in 500 Africans living with HIV and AIDS were on a prescribed course of anti-retroviral treatment, though there are hopes that the numbers will increase with a rapid reduction in the price of drugs and increasing funds being made available for treatment programmes. Several countries have marked important successes in controlling the pandemic, for example Senegal (which has kept rates very low) and Uganda (where HIV prevalence has come down markedly). In most countries, however, a combination of denial, stigmatisation and the lack of capacity to design and implement programmes means that the epidemic has remained essentially unchecked. Outside Africa, Thailand succeeded in containing the pandemic through strict regulation of commercial sex; Brazil launched early and vigorous public education campaigns; while Cuba took the draconian measure of screening its population and all immigrants. The consensus among international AIDS organisations, however, is that all testing should be voluntary and that AIDS programming should be founded on scrupulous respect for the individual rights of the person living with HIV.

The HIV/AIDS epidemic is bringing major social and economic problems in its wake. Although its impact on national economies has thus far been modest (in the range of a shackle of 0.4 per cent to 1.5 per cent on annual growth), it is jeopardising programmes to reduce poverty and increase employment. In Africa, many rural communities have been accustomed to living close to the margin of survival. The stress of an adult falling sick and dying of AIDS may plunge a farming household into destitution: the family loses a bread-winner, spends money on treatment, diverts family labour into caring for the ill person, and then has to cover the costs of a funeral. Moreover, if one adult is infected, often her or his partner will be too, and young children may also be HIV positive. Neighbours and relatives may absorb some of the burden by helping to care for the sick and children orphaned by AIDS, but with very high rates of HIV across the population, this informal safety net quickly becomes saturated. Africa currently has more than 12 million children orphaned by AIDS, and the numbers are growing. The disease is also contributing to social crises across southern and eastern Africa, with women bearing the brunt: they are not only infected more frequently and younger than men, but also have to bear most of the burdens of supporting the stricken family. The HIV/AIDS pandemic has meant that key institutions such as schools, health departments and national armies are increasingly unable to fulfil their functions, and labour forces are shrinking. For example, in Zambia and Malawi, teachers are dying much faster than they can be trained, and soldiers and policemen tend to have higher rates of HIV than the general population, with levels of professionalism and experience declining as a consequence. The simultaneous erosion of capacities across so many sectors, combined with impoverishment and food crises, poses an immense threat to the stability of states and the cohesion of societies. Historically, major demographic disasters such as wars, famines or epidemics commonly give rise to knock-on calamities that are comparably severe. The AIDS-related food crisis that unfolded across southern Africa during 2002 may be the first such augur of grave and intractable secondary impacts. Globally, HIV/AIDS may prove to be the most significant global demographic shock since the Black Death six centuries ago, a Darwinian episode in human history.

Finally, as regards literary works, by contrast to the many works on AIDS from the USA and Europe in the 1980s and 1990s, AIDS has generated relatively little literary output in developing countries. There have in more recent times, however, been several novelists who have addressed the impact of AIDS in their work, namely Margaret Ogola and Meja Mwangi on Kenya, Neshani Andreas on Namibia, Phaswane Mpe on South Africa, Unity Dow on Botswana, and Henning Mankell on Mozambique, and Louise Bourgault has surveyed dramatic performances confronting AIDS in Mali and South Africa. The South African play *Sarafina 2*, commissioned in 1998, achieved fame more for allegations of financial profligacy than its content, which focused upon AIDS. Satirist Pieter Dirk-Uys, formerly best known for making fun of the absurdities of apartheid, has achieved the unique distinction of successfully satirising AIDS: 'In the old South Africa we killed people, now we are just letting them die.'

Alex de Waal

Literary Works

Andreas, Neshani (2001), *The Purple Violet of Oshaantu*, London: Heinemann.

Dow, Unity (2000), *Far and Beyon'*, San Francisco: Aunt Lute Books.

Mankell, Henning (2002), *Playing with Fire*, trans. A. Petersen, London: Allen and Unwin.

Mpe, Phaswane (2001), *Welcome to our Hillbrow*, Pietermaritzburg: University of Natal Press.

Mwangi, Meja (2001), *The Last Plague*, Nairobi: Kenya East African Educational Publications.

Ogola, Margaret (1994), *The River and the Source*, Nairobi: Focus.

Tóibín, Colm (1999), *The Blackwater Lightship*, London: Picador.

White, Edmund and Adam Mars-Jones (1987), *The Darker Proof: Stories from a Crisis*, London: Faber and Faber.

Histories

Barnett, Tony and Alan Whiteside (2002), *AIDS in the 21st Century: Disease and Globalization*, London: Macmillan Palgrave.

Bourgault, Louise M. (2003), *Performance in Africa in the Age of AIDS*, Durham, NC: Carolina Academic Press.

Campbell, Catherine (2003), *Letting them Die: Why HIV/AIDS Prevention Programmes Fail*, London: International African Institute in association with James Currey.

D'Adesky, Anne-Christine (2004), *Moving Mountains. Dispatches from the Frontline of Global AIDS*, London: Verso.

Farmer, Paul (2001), *Infections and Inequalities: The Modern Plagues*, Berkeley, CA: University of California Press.

Hooper, Ed (1990), *Slim: One Man's Journey through the AIDS Zone of East Africa*, Oxford: Bodley Head.

Shilts, Randy (1987), *And the Band Played On: Politics, People and the AIDS Epidemic*, New York: St Martin's Press.

Van der Vliet, Virginia (1996), *The Politics of AIDS*, London: Bowerdean.

See also: **Migrancy: Southern Africa; United Nations**.

Hong Kong Handover

Hong Kong's handover to the People's Republic of China on 30 June 1997 after over 150 years of British rule signalled, rarely, a voluntary return of territory (Hong Kong island and adjoining Kowloon and New Territories) by one colonial master to the nation from which it had been forcibly taken. The handover marked an end to Britain's history as an imperial power decades after other Asian colonies – India, Malaysia and Singapore, for example – had achieved independence. When the British governor, Chris Patten, stepped down, in a historical ceremony televised to millions all over the world, Tung Chee-hwa became nominated chief executive of Hong Kong, now China's first Special Administrative Region (SAR). China's premier Deng Xiaoping had supported the establishment of post-handover Hong Kong's complicated constitution, founded on basic law and an understanding of 'one country, two systems' that maintains for fifty years the Hong Kong people's economic and political rights, which are ideologically capitalist and radically different from those in the People's Republic, ruled by the communist government in Beijing.

Negotiated through a joint declaration between the People's Republic of China and the United Kingdom in 1984, the handover must be viewed in the context of nineteenth-century Western expansionism in the East. British desire for Chinese tea, beginning in the eighteenth century, by the early nineteenth century had resulted in a dangerous trade imbalance, until British traders were able to exploit segments of the Chinese population's addiction to opium, produced with enormous profits from plantations in British India. The Ching court, alarmed by the deleterious effects of opium on the nation, criminalised its consumption and trade. Weakened by corruption and excess, the Chinese government suffered military defeats in a series of Opium Wars (1839–42 and 1855–8); exorbitant indemnities were placed on its treasure and territory, and treaty ports such as Canton and Shanghai were forced open to Western mercantile interests. Such military and diplomatic humiliations led eventually to the fall of the Ching dynasty and the beginning of a revolutionary people's republic in China.

Hong Kong island, a small fishing village in the south-east corner of mainland China, possessing a splendid harbour, was ceded in perpetuity to Britain in the Treaty of Nanking after the first Opium War. Kowloon was ceded after the second Opium War, and the New Territories were leased to Britain on a ninety-nine-year contract in 1898. Serving as a portal for Western trade in China, Hong Kong was occupied by Japanese forces between

1941 and 1945. Returned to the United Kingdom, it attracted millions of refugees fleeing the communist regime from 1949 onwards, and grew in population and wealth as laissez faire policies encouraged robust commercial and international interests. The run-up to 1997 saw a panicked exodus of people from Hong Kong, many emigrating to Canada, Australia, the UK, the USA, and other Asian countries. The 1980s–1990s emigration out of Hong Kong led to fears of brain drain and capital flight and repercussions both for Hong Kong society and for the host countries welcoming this exodus of émigrés. But by 1997 the emigration rate had slowed down and many migrants in fact returned to participate in the transition.

Shirley Geok-Lin Lim

Literary Works

Ho, Louise (1994), *Local Habitation*, Hong Kong: Twilight Books.
Ho, Louise (1997), *New Ends, Old Beginnings*, Hong Kong: Asia 2000.
Lam, Agnes (2001), *Water Wood Pure Splendour*, Hong Kong: Asia 2000.
Leung Ping-Kwan (1992), *City at the End of Time*, trans. Gordon Osing, Hong Kong: Twilight Books.
New, Christopher (2002), *A Change of Flag*, New York: Soho Press.
OutLoud: An Anthology of Poetry from OutLoud Readings, Hong Kong (2002), Hong Kong: XtraLoud Press.
Parkin, Andrew (1995), *From the Bluest Part of the Harbour*, New York: Oxford University Press.
Parkin, Andrew and Lawrence Wong (eds) (1997), *Hong Kong Poems in English and Chinese*, Hong Kong: Ronsdale Press.
Theroux, Paul (1997), *Kowloon Tong*, London: Penguin.
Xu Xi (1996), *Hong Kong Rose*, Hong Kong: Asia 2000.
Xu Xi (2001), *The Unwalled City*, Hong Kong: Chameleon Press.
Xu Xi (2001), *History's Fiction*, Hong Kong: Chameleon Press.
Xu Xi (ed.) (2002), 'Valediction' in *Daughters of Hui*, 2nd edn, Hong Kong: Chameleon Press.
Xu Xi and Mike Ingham (eds) (2003), *City Voices: Hong Kong Writing in English, 1945 to the Present*, Hong Kong: Hong Kong University Press.

Histories

Bolton, Kingsley (2001), *Hong Kong English: Autonomy and Creativity*, Hong Kong: Hong Kong University Press.
Courtauld, Caroline (1997), *The Hong Kong Story*, Hong Kong and New York: Oxford University Press.
Fok, K. C. (1990), *Lectures on Hong Kong History: Hong Kong's Role in Modern Chinese History*, Quarry Bay: Commercial Press.
Hsu, Immanuel Cheung-yueh (1995), *The Rise of Modern China*, New York: Oxford University Press.
Lane, Kevin P. (1990), *Sovereignty and the Status Quo: The Historical Roots of China's Hong Kong Policy*, Boulder, CO: Westview Press.

Lim, Shirley Geok-Lin (2002), '"Traveling Transnationalism": Locating Hong Kong Literature in English', *Sun Yat-sen Journal of Humanities*, April, pp. 53–66.

Morikawa, Makio (1998), 'Migration from Hong Kong and Asian Modernity', in Sydney C. H. Cheng (ed.), *On the South China Track: Perspectives on Anthropological Research and Teaching*, Hong Kong: Chinese University of Hong Kong, pp. 71–80.

Murphy, Cait (1991), 'Hong Kong: A Culture of Emigration', *The Atlantic Monthly*, 267: 4, pp. 20–6.

Skeldon, Ronald (1996), 'Migration from China', *Journal of International Affairs*, 49: 2, pp. 434–57.

See also: **Britain's Postwar Foreign Policy; Historiography: South-east Asia**.

Hudson's Bay Company

Chartered as a joint-stock company in 1670, overseen by governors and committee in London, the Hudson's Bay Company (HBC) assumed monopoly fur-trading rights in Rupert's Land, 7.7 million square kilometres centred on the drainage basin of Hudson Bay. After 1821, the company extended control to Alaska and the Arctic, Oregon, and Labrador with mixed success. Trade was conducted from shore posts, to which Natives brought furs, trading upon the company's standard of exchange, the Made Beaver. In 1774, inland posts appeared in response to overland competition from the Montreal-based North West Company (NWC), which took over the French trade after 1763. Rivalry was fierce, at times violent, the Red River settlement becoming a flashpoint of Métis resistance and NWC harassment.

In 1821 the HBC absorbed its rival. The ensuing restructuring included conservation and deliberate overtrapping, the reorganisation and expansion of trading districts, revision of ranks and incentives, and retrenchment of 60 per cent of the workforce. Officers sought to eliminate the alcohol trade, and curb credit and other aid to Native partners. With growing pressures for western settlement in the 1850s, the company's interest shifted to land speculation and economic development. Rupert's Land was transferred to Canada in 1870 for a price of £300,000, the HBC retaining 21 million acres of designated settlement lands. Both Natives and Métis – especially the wives of white traders – played an essential and active role in the trade, although at the bottom of a hierarchical system reflecting the prejudices of its British officers. 'Gentlemen', mostly Scots, occupied the upper strata of chief factors and chief traders; 'men, or servants' were divided into as many as twenty different grades. Recruitment and management of British and Canadian employees exploited regional and ethnic identities in the maintenance of hierarchy.

Christopher J. Armstrong

Literary Works

Stenson, Fred (2001), *The Trade*, Vancouver: Douglas and McIntyre.

Thomas, Audrey (1999), *Isobel Gunn*, Toronto: Viking.

Wiebe, Rudy (1977), *The Scorched-Wood People*, Toronto: McClelland and Stewart.

Histories

Binnema, Theodore, Gerhard J. Ens and R. C. Macleod (eds) (2001), *From Rupert's Land to Canada: Essays in Honour of John E. Foster*, Edmonton: University of Alberta Press.

Brown, Jennifer (1980), *Strangers in Blood: Fur Trade Company Families in Indian Country*, Vancouver: University of British Columbia Press.

Bumstead, J. M. (1999), *Fur Trade Wars: The Founding of Western Canada*, Winnipeg: Great Plains Publications.

Burley, Edith (1997), *Servants of the Honourable Company: Work, Discipline, and Conflict in the Hudson's Bay Company, 1770–1870*, Toronto: Oxford University Press.

Payne, Michael (1989), *The Most Respectable Place in the Territory: Everyday Life in Hudson's Bay Company Service, 1788 to 1870*, Ottawa: Environment Canada.

Ray, Arthur J. (1974), *Indians in the Fur Trade: Their Role as Trappers, Hunters, and Middlemen in the Lands Southwest of Hudson Bay, 1660–1870*, Toronto: University of Toronto Press.

Rich, E. E. (1958–9), *The History of the Hudson's Bay Company, 1670–1870*, 2 vols, London: Hudson's Bay Record Society.

Van Kirk, Sylvia (1980), *'Many Tender Ties': Women in Fur Trade Society in Western Canada, 1670–1870*, Winnipeg: Watson and Dwyer.

See also: **Historiography: Canada**; **Inuit**; **Riel's Métis Rebellion**.

I

Indentured Labour: Caribbean

The date that marked the arrival of the first group of Indian indentured labourers, variously called East Indians and coolies, to the Caribbean is acknowledged as 5 May 1838. The initial batch of 396 disembarked in British Guiana. Indentureship, which lasted from 1838 to 1917, saw the introduction of 519,483 Indians to the Caribbean (see Seecharan 1997, p. 3). This forced population transfer could be seen as part of the imperial project to shift surplus labour from India to where there was a need for a cheap and reliable workforce. The distribution of Indian indentured immigration by colony for the period 1834 to 1917 was as follows:

Colony	Period	Number
Mauritius	1834–1912	453,309
British Guiana	1838–1917	238,909
Trinidad	1845–1917	143,939

Jamaica	1845–1915	36,412
Grenada	1856–1885	3,200
St Lucia	1858–1895	4,354
Natal (South Africa)	1860–1911	152,184
St Kitts	1860–1861	300
St Vincent	1860–1880	2,472
Réunion	1861–1883	26,507
Dutch Guiana (Surinam)	1873–1916	34,304
Fiji	1879–1916	60,965
East Africa (Kenya/Uganda)	1895–1901	39,771
Seychelles	1899–1916	6,315
Martinique	1854–1889	25,509
Guadeloupe	1854–1885	42,326
French Guiana	?	19,296

(Source: Seecharan 1997, p. 4)

A further set of statistics also worth noting is the different origins of indentured labour in the Caribbean. The majority were from India, but significant minorities were drawn from other countries, as the figures for indentured workers in British Guiana in the period 1834 to 1917 indicate:

Source	Period	Number
India	1838–1917	238,909
Madeira	1835–1881	32,216
Africa	1834–1867	14,060
China	1852–1884	13,533
Europe	1834–1845	381
Other	1835–1867	1,868
Total		**300,967**

(Source: Seecharan 1997, p. 3)

Indentureship called forth several responses. For the plantocracy, Indian labour saved the sugar plantations, and by extension the colonies, from ruin. Reflecting this view Anthony Trollope quoted a planter as saying, 'Give me my heart's desire in coolies and I will make you a million hogshead in sugar' (Trollope 1860, p. 172). By contrast, the newly freed African slaves saw the indentureship system as inimical to their struggle for better wages and working conditions. Further, since their taxes served to assist in covering the costs for the importation of their replacements, they were doubly aggrieved. Therefore, while their initial response to the indentured workers was sympathetic, by 1848 more antagonistic relations had developed. The indentured workers were seen as interlopers undercutting their wages and taking away their work. The extremely harsh work and living conditions led to Indian indentureship being labelled 'a new system of slavery' (Dabydeen and Samaroo 1987, p. 25). The anti-slavery society and other humanitarians in Britain and in the colonies joined in the struggle to abolish indentureship. Poor diet, poor housing, tropical diseases like malaria, inadequate medical facilities, and a shortage of Indian women meant that the Indian population during indentureship increased principally through further immigration. These harsh conditions called forth resistance against the plantation system, and these as acts of self-emancipation are well documented by scholars like Kusha

Haraksingh for Trinidad and Tyran Ramnarine for British Guiana. In countries where the Indians were in a minority, like Martinique, Guadeloupe and St Kitts, they were assimilated into the larger Creole society, although recognisable cultural habits have persisted (see Ramdin 2000, p. 265). However, in British Guiana, Dutch Guiana and Trinidad, due mainly to their larger numbers, indentured labourers were able to affirm group solidarity and resist the surrender of their ancestral culture. Whether they came from eastern Uttar Pradesh, western Behar, Bengal or Madras, whether they were lower caste Chamars or upper castes Brahmans, whether they were Hindus, Muslims or Christians, the Indian indentured labourers overcame many hardships and made many contributions to their new homes in the Caribbean.

Kampta Karran

Literary Works

Dabydeen, David (1988), *Coolie Odyssey*, London: Hansib.
Dabydeen, David (1996), *The Counting House*, London: Jonathan Cape.
Das, Mahadai (1977), *I Want to Be a Poetess of my People*, Georgetown: Guyana National Service Publishing Centre.
Das, Mahadai (1988), *Bones*, Leeds: Peepal Tree Books.
Itwaru, Arnold (1982), *Scattered Songs*, Toronto: Aya.
Monar, Rooplall (1987), *Backdam People*, Leeds: Peepal Tree Books.
Naipaul, V. S. [1961] (1969), *A House for Mr Biswas*, Harmondsworth: Penguin.
Persaud, Lakshmi (1993), *Sastra*, Leeds: Peepal Tree Books.
Singh, Rajkumari (1971), *Days of the Sahib Are Over*, Georgetown: The author.
Webber, A. R. F. [1917] (1988), *Those That Be in Bondage – A Tale of Indian Indentures and Sunlit Western Waters*, Wellesley, MA: Calaloux Publications.

Histories

Dabydeen, David and Brinsley Samaroo (eds) (1987), *India in the Caribbean*, London: Hansib/University of Warwick CCS Publication.
La Guerre, John (ed.) (1974), *Calcutta to Caroni. The East Indians of Trinidad*, St Andrews: Longman Caribbean.
Nath, Dwarka (1970), *A History of Indians in Guyana*, London: The author.
Poynting, Jeremy (2003), *The Second Shipwreck. A Study of Indo-Caribbean Literature*, London: Hansib.
Ramdin, Ron (2000), *Arising from Bondage: A History of the Indo-Caribbean People*, London: I. B. Tauris.
Seecharan, Clem (1997), *Tiger in the Stars: The Anatomy of Indian Achievement in British Guiana 1919–1929*, London: Macmillan Education.
Tinker, Hugh (1974), *A New System of Slavery. The Export of Indian Labour Overseas, 1830–1920*, Oxford: Oxford University Press.
Trollope, Anthony (1860), *The West Indies and the Spanish Main*, London: Chapman and Hall.

See also: **Diaspora: Caribbean; Historiography: Caribbean; Indians: Southern Africa; Slavery: Caribbean.**

Indian National Army

The Indian National Army (INA) was inspired and led by the revolutionary zeal of Netaji Subhas Chandra Bose in its attempt to free the Indian subcontinent during the final years of British colonial rule. Rash Behari Bose, another exiled Indian revolutionary, inspired officers of the British Indian army stationed in South-east Asia to break away and form the Azad Hind Fauj – the Indian National Army – in December 1941. Encouraged by the Japanese, Captain Mohan Singh assumed leadership of the fledgling INA and more than 30,000 Indian soldiers volunteered. However, this initial effort faced a number of practical difficulties and the INA virtually collapsed within a year. In July 1943, Netaji Subhas Bose formally took over the leadership of the exiled Indian independence movement in South-east Asia. The reorganised INA had as its motto 'Unity, Faith, Sacrifice', and was inspired by Bose's battle cry '*Chalo* Delhi!' ('To Delhi!').

Erstwhile officers of the British Indian army as well as a huge number of patriotic young Indian civilians from Malaysia and Singapore joined the INA. A women's wing of the army, the Rani of Jhansi regiment, was constituted under the leadership of Dr Lakshmi Swaminathan. At a historic gathering in Singapore on 21 October 1943, Bose declared the birth of a provisional government of free India. In January 1944 headquarters were shifted to Rangoon, Burma, which meant that now only one border separated India from the liberation army.

The INA first successfully attacked the Arakan front on 4 February 1944. On 18 March, the INA crossed the border into India and fighting ensued in Imphal and Kohima. On 14 April, INA soldiers planted the Indian flag at Moirang, Manipur. However, the INA's campaign was beset by trouble: provisions and ammunition were depleted, training was inadequate, communication and supply routes were flooded by monsoons, and the siege on Imphal had to be lifted. While remnants of the army battled on for over a year, the British advanced on Rangoon and in August 1945 Japan surrendered to Russia. In Subhas Bose's last message to the INA before he left Singapore for Japan en route to Russian-occupied Manchuria, he said, 'The roads to Delhi are many, and Delhi still remains our goal.'

It was reported that Bose died in a plane crash during that journey. The INA's military challenge collapsed and when the Anglo-American forces reoccupied East Asia, about 17,000 INA soldiers were taken to India by the British as prisoners of war, and three officers were brought to a historic trial in the Red Fort of Delhi at the end of 1945. The role of the INA in the subcontinent's freedom struggle fired the imagination of patriotic Indians despite its eventual retreat and failure.

Brinda Bose

Literary Works

Ghosh, Amitav (2000), *The Glass Palace*, New Delhi: Permanent Black, Ravi Dayal Publishers.

Histories

Ayer, S. A. (1972), *The Story of the INA*, New Delhi: National Book Trust.
Bose, Sisir K. and Sugata Bose (eds) (1997), *Subhas Chandra Bose: The Indian Struggle 1920–42*, New Delhi: Oxford University Press.

Fay, Peter Ward (1994), *The Forgotten Army: India's Armed Struggle for Independence 1942–45*, New Delhi: Rupa and Co.

Gordon, Leonard A. (1990), *Brothers Against the Raj*, Delhi: Penguin India.

Safrani, Abid Hasan and J. A. Thivy (1995), *The Men from Imphal and Indian Independence Movement in East Asia*, 2nd edn, Calcutta: Netaji Research Bureau.

See also: **Japanese Occupation South-east Asia; World Wars I and II: South Asian Soldiers**.

Indians: Southern Africa

For much of the twentieth century the community of Indian origin in South Africa was the largest of any such grouping outside South Asia. Though now overtaken by migration to Britain and the USA, the statistic remains valid in a narrow sense in that the 1 million Indians in South Africa have their roots in India as opposed to what later became Pakistan and Bangladesh.

Several subgroups within South Africa can be discerned. A primary distinction can be drawn between those who descend from the 150,000 indentured labourers brought by the British to start the sugar, coffee and tea plantations of Natal in the period 1860 to 1911, and those who arrived as traders (or passenger Indians) from 1875 onwards. Within the indentured grouping two strands continue to maintain some sense of regional identity: people emanating from North India (speaking eastern dialects of Hindi and Urdu), and those from South India (speaking mainly Tamil and Telugu). The trading class Indians spoke Gujarati, Meman (Sindhi) and Konkani (Marathi). The history of the community thus parallels that of similar communities in Mauritius, British Guiana/Guyana, Trinidad, Suriname and Fiji.

The indentured diaspora elsewhere produced a Nobel Laureate in literature in V. S. Naipaul. Though no writer of such stature has yet emerged in the South African Indian community, it can boast of a more widely known statesman and writer as the place that 'made' the Mahatma. M. K. Gandhi arrived in South Africa as a barrister and stayed on for twenty years (1893–1913) as a community leader against British and Afrikaner racism. Gandhi's record of his South African years, *Satyagraha in South Africa*, was written in Gujarati (as a conscious anti-colonial choice when he could have written in English), and published in Ahmedabad in 1928. It is a classic of the colonial period; indeed the very notion of post-colonialism may be said to have originated in the South African Indian community, via Gandhi.

Indian languages in South Africa have survived against great odds for over 100 years, but are today giving way to English, which is the main language of the community. However, the culture of the community is a synthesis of many strands, and still looks to India as one of its mainstays. The literary output of Indians in South Africa has been, until recently, modest, but there are signs of considerable activity in the present generation. Since the 1960s there has been a lively tradition of plays dwelling on working-class and anti-apartheid issues. The best-known is Ronnie Govender's *The Lahnee's Pleasure* (1980), but also of interest are the plays combining social commentary and political satire by Kessie Govender, Strini Moodley, Dinesh Narandas, Mohammed Ali, Essop Khan, Kriben Pillay, Aldrin Naidu, Charles Pillai, Rajesh Gopi and the female playwrights, Muthal Naidoo and Krijay Govender. Significant poets include Shabbir Banoobhai, Deena Padayachee, Essop Patel, Farouk Asvat and Kriben Pillay, and there have been fine collections of short stories by Ahmed Essop (1978) and

Agnes Sam (1989). Novels, too, have recently started to proliferate, the first being Ansuya Singh's *Behold the Earth Mourns* (1960) set in South Africa and India in the era of passive resistance. Other novels of interest include Ahmed Essop's *The Visitation* (1980) and *The Emperor* (1984), Brenda Kali's *Kismet* (1984), Mewa Ramgobin's *Waiting to Live* (1986), Resham Gool's *Cape Town Coolie* (1990), Farida Karodia's *Daughters of the Twilight* (1986) and *Other Secrets* (2000), Imraan Coovadia's justly acclaimed *The Wedding* (2001), Aziz Hassim's *The Lotus People* (2002), Prabashini Moodley's 'sugar cane romance' *The Heart Knows No Colour* (2003), and Pat Poovalingam's more realist work *Anand* (2003).

Given Indians' prominent role in the anti-apartheid movement and the new freedom to write, it is not surprising that the political memoir as a genre is flourishing. These include: reminiscences of life before forced removals of Indians in the 1950s and 1960s like Jay Naidoo's *Coolie Location* (1990) and Ronnie Govender's *At the Edge* (1996); autobiographies by activist female figures like those of medical doctor Kesavaloo Goonam (*Coolie Doctor* (1991)), Zuleikha Mayat (*A Treasure Trove of Memories* (1996)), sociologist Fatima Meer (*Prison Diary* (2001)), and Sita Gandhi, grand-daughter of the Mahatma (*Sita* (2003)); and memoirs by prominent male political veterans of struggle like Indres Naidoo (*Island in Chains* (1982)), Natoo Babenia (*Memoirs of a Saboteur* (1995)), Ahmed Kathrada (*Letters from Robben Island* (2000)), and Ismail Meer (*A Fortunate Man* (2002)). A useful collection of prose, plays, interviews and short biographies is contained in Rajendra Chetty's *South African Indian Writings in English* (2002).

Rajend Mesthrie

Literary Works

Chetty, Rajendra (ed.) (2002), *South African Indian Writings in English*, Johannesburg: Madiba.
Coovadia, Imraan (2001), *The Wedding*, New York: Picador.
Essop, Ahmed (1978), *The Haji and Other Stories*, Johannesburg: Ravan Press.
Essop, Ahmed (1980), *The Visitation*, Johannesburg: Ravan Press.
Essop, Ahmed [1984] (1995), *The Emperor*, Johannesburg: Ravan Press.
Gool, Reshard (1990), *Cape Town Coolie*, Oxford: Heinemann.
Govender, Ronnie (1980), *The Lahnee's Pleasure*, Johannesburg: Ravan Press.
Hassim, Aziz (2002), *The Lotus People*, Johannesburg: STE Publications.
Kali, Brenda (1984), *Kismet*, Johannesburg: Advent.
Karodia, Farida (1986), *Daughters of the Twilight*, London: Women's Press.
Karodia, Farida (2000), *Other Secrets*, Sandton: Penguin.
Moodley, Prabashini (2003), *The Heart Knows No Colour*, Cape Town: Kwela.
Poovalingam, Pat (2003), *Anand*, Johannesburg: Madiba.
Ramgobin, Mewa (1986), *Waiting to Live*, Cape Town: David Philip.
Sam, Agnes (1989), *Jesus is Indian*, London: Women's Press.
Singh, Ansuyah (1960), *Behold the Earth Mourns*, Johannesburg: Central News Agency.

Histories

Bhana, Surendra and Joy Brain (1990), *Setting Down Roots: Indian Migrants in South Africa, 1860–1911*, Johannesburg: Witwatersrand University Press.

Dhupelia-Mesthrie, Uma (2000), *From Canefields to Freedom: A Chronicle of Indian South African Life*, Cape Town: Kwela Books.

Freund, William (1995), *Insiders and Outsiders: The Indian Working Class of Durban 1910–1990*, Pietermaritzburg: University of Natal Press.

Meer, Fatima (ed.) (1996), *The South African Gandhi: An Abstract of the Speeches and Writing of M. K. Gandhi*, 2nd edn, Durban: Institute for Black Research/ Madiba Publishers.

Swann, Maureen (1985), *Gandhi: The South African Experience*, Johannesburg: Ravan Press.

See also: **Anti-colonialism and Resistance: Southern Africa; Diaspora: South Asia; Indentured Labour: Caribbean**.

Indigo Rebellion

The emergence of Britain's modern textile industry greatly increased the demand for the indigo plant, which yields the dye used for blueing cotton textiles. The East India Company was persuaded to revive the indigo trade in Bengal after events in other colonies: British planters in the West Indies had abandoned indigo for sugar and coffee and the American Revolution had placed all sources of dye in the hands of Britain's enemy. It soon became a rich source of profit. From the very beginning, *ryots* (tenant cultivators) were forced to grow indigo at low prices. Methods of coercion ranged from looting, burning houses and destroying crops to flogging, imprisonment in factory godowns, rape, and murder. Individual European planters and their private armies of *lathials* terrorised *ryots* into accepting advances, planting indigo, and signing contracts; local-level members of law-enforcement agencies (magistrates, police) generally colluded in these acts of terror.

Before 1829 all cultivation was theoretically *be-ilaka*: on land controlled by Indian land-holders. After 1837, when legal restraints on the acquisition of property were removed, planters acquired vast *ilaka* (proprietary) estates throughout the indigo districts, leading to planter–zamindar clashes of interests. Gradual improvements in Bengal's administration changed the planter-*ryot* relationship as less violent and more subtle methods of coercion were adopted, reducing the peasants' possibilities of escape.

In autumn 1859, the indigo revolt began in Barasat as peasants refused to take advances for spring sowing. In the following spring, contracts were made criminally enforceable (Act XI of 1860) and peasant revolt flared up again. Peaceful demonstrations of earlier periods gave way to armed violence and often any symbol of the British presence (all whites, native military/civilian officials, jails, courts, indigo factories, bungalows) became susceptible to attack. Peasants resisted planters' attacks by mobilising and rallying through traditional night cries and drumbeats. By the summer, the rebellion had engulfed all indigo districts and masses of armed angry peasants vowed to end indigo cultivation. Landed magnates active in the rebellion were quick to disassociate themselves from militant peasants as the struggle turned into a rent strike. Solidarity among poorer sections of villagers cut across ethnic divisions of local and 'tribal'. Ethnic distinctions were over-ridden at the other end, too, as common proprietary interests of Bangali zamindars and white planters surfaced. Kulin Mandal, a Kangrapore peasant, who testified before the Indigo Commission (appointed in May 1860), summed up the intensity of peasant feelings: 'I would sow indigo for nobody, not even for my father and mother' (Desai 1979, p.

155). The rebellion forced indigo cultivation out of Bengal districts. Its cultivation was relocated to Bihar and Uttar Pradesh.

Rahnuma Ahmed

Literary Works

Mitra, Dinabandhu (1860), *Neel Darpan*. English translation available in Amiya Rao and G. B. Rao (1993), *The Blue Devil: Indigo and Colonial Bengal*, New Delhi: Oxford University Press.

Histories

Desai, A. R. (ed.) (1979), *Peasant Struggles in India*, Delhi: Oxford University Press.
Guha, Ranajit (1974), 'Neel-Darpan: The Image of a Peasant Revolt in a Liberal Mirror', *The Journal of Peasant Studies* 2: 1, pp. 1–46.
Kling, Blair B. (1966), *The Blue Mutiny. The Indigo Disturbances in Bengal, 1859–1862*, Philadelphia: University of Pennsylvania Press.

See also: **Anti-colonialism and Resistance: South Asia; East India Company**.

Indirect Rule

Indirect rule, or indirect administration, was the administrative structure through which the majority of Africans encountered colonialism. The British colonial policy of indirect rule was first applied in India. Indirect rule in Africa was first practised in the late nineteenth century in Natal by Theophilus Shepstone. The British devised indirect rule as a practical system to control the Empire. Indirect rule in British West Africa was adopted and developed by Frederick Lugard, after he observed its practice in Uganda and the Sudan. Lugard believed that the policy of indirect rule was appropriate to the requirements of traditional rule in West Africa. He based this opinion on the traditionally hierarchical and Islamic structure of the emirates of northern Nigeria. Under the authority of Native Administration, the peoples of Nigeria were divided into tribes, which were deemed to possess distinctive characteristics. Indirect rule relied on cultural essentialism through which subject peoples identified themselves as belonging to sub-nationalities. Missionaries and ethnologists encouraged this perception of tribal uniqueness. To belong to a tribe implied paradoxically that one was a 'modern' and at the same time an 'authentic' African. The idea was that due to their different characteristics, each tribe would enter into Western modernity at its own pace. Tribes would incorporate their indigenous practices into modernity and discover their own routes to progress. Benevolent though this system seems in theory, in practice indirect rule was very much a means of controlling Africans through their own institutions. Where such institutions did not cater for indirect rule, chiefs and tribes were invented and propped up by colonial authority.

Indirect rule was based on four principles: Native Administration, taxation, rule-making and chiefly rule. Tribes fell under chiefly rule. Chiefs were given powers that under pre-colonial rule they never possessed. Tribes that had a decentralised administration were subsumed under tribes that possessed centralised authority. In areas that were republican in nature such as the Igbo of southern Nigeria, warrant chiefs were appointed and traditions invented to secure their authority. Indirect rule was interventionist and regulatory. Africans could not be part of civil society, which could ensure individual liberties, for this would mean that they were equal to their British colonists. Rather, they fell under regimes of tribal law and order, under the institution of chiefly authority. The chief was directly under the district officer, who passed on laws to be communicated to the people. It was difficult to remove a corrupt chief, for to do so was to challenge colonial authority. Lugard and the chiefs sidelined educated Africans, who were in a position to mediate between tradition and modernity.

Lugard saw educated Africans as aberrations, pale imitators aping a superior culture. The educated Africans rejected chiefly authority, leading them to create cultural identities of their own that were influenced by their indigenous cultures and by Pan-Africanism. Africans of all classes challenged chiefly authority when their interests were threatened, where the chiefs abused their power, or where these imposed rulers were considered illegitimate. The legacy of indirect rule is directly implicated in the ethnic antagonisms plaguing several parts of English-speaking Africa today.

Oladipo Agboluaje

Literary Works

Achebe, Chinua (1958), *Things Fall Apart*, London: Heinemann.
Soyinka, Wole (1975), *Death and the King's Horseman*, London: Eyre Methuen.

Histories

Kirk-Greene, A. H. M. (1965), *The Principles of Native Administration in Nigeria: 1900–1947*, Oxford: Oxford University Press.
Lugard, Frederick (1922), *The Dual Mandate in British Tropical Africa*, London: Frank Cass.
Mamdani, Mahmood (1996), *Citizen and Subject: Contemporary Africa and the Legacy of Late Colonialism*, Kampala, Cape Town, London: Fountain, David Philip, James Currey.

See also: **Anti-colonialism and Resistance: West Africa; Pan-Africanism; Universities: West Africa.**

International Monetary Fund

The International Monetary Fund, also known as the 'IMF' or the 'Fund', is an international organisation that was established at a conference held at Bretton Woods, New Hampshire, USA, in July 1944. The twenty-four represented governments at that time sought to develop a plan for economic co-operation between its members in order to avoid disastrous economic policies such as those that caused the Great Depression in the 1930s. The organisation now has 184 member countries. Its mandate is to promote international monetary co-operation, foster expansion and balanced economic growth of international trade, promote exchange stability, and provide temporary financial assistance to member countries experiencing payment difficulties. To meet those objectives the IMF assumes three functions: surveillance, technical assistance and lending. At the top of the organisation is its board of governors, consisting of one governor from each of the member countries. All governors meet annually at the IMF and World Bank Annual Meetings. Twenty-four governors sit on the International Monetary and Finance Committee (IMFC), meeting biannually. The IMF's daily operations are run from its Washington DC headquarters by its twenty-four member executive board with the guidance of the IMFC.

A declared goal of the IMF is to reduce global poverty by implementing independent projects in collaboration with the World Bank and other organisations. The IMF provides financial support through its concessional lending facility. Despite its global efforts, the IMF's policies have been widely criticised, especially by the anti-globalisation movement (see Chomsky (1997), Klein and Levy 2002, Monbiot 2003, Pilger 2002, and Stiglitz 2002). The Fund is seen to give out massive loans to developing countries in order to open up their markets for foreign investment while at the same time reducing public expenditure on social services. Its policies, therefore, are construed to be advantageous for industrial countries who are able to invest globally, while they weaken local and traditional industries in developing countries. Moreover, the USA, a major IMF monetary donor, is seen to dictate the IMF's loan-related decisions. Finally, the IMF has been criticised because it has not been able to predict or stop several economic crises, such as the Mexican crisis in 1994 and the Asian crisis in 1997.

Suha Kudsieh

Literary Works

Kincaid, Jamaica (1988), *A Small Place*, New York: Plume Books.

Histories

Bird, Graham R. (2003), *IMF and the Future: Issues and Options Facing the International Monetary Fund*, New York: Routledge.
Chomsky, Noam (1997), *World Orders, Old and New*, London: Pluto.
Darrow, Mac (2003), *Between Light and Shadow: The World Bank, the International Monetary Fund and International Human Rights Law*, Portland, OR: Hart Publishing.
Fox, Jeremy (2001), *Chomsky and Globalisation*, Duxford: Icon.
Klein, Naomi and Debora Ann Levy (eds) (2002), *Fences and Windows*, Toronto: Vintage Canada.
Monbiot, George (2003), *The Age of Consent*, London: Flamingo.
Pilger, John (2002), *The New Rulers of the World*, London: Verso.
Polak, Jacques J. (1994), *The World Bank and the International Monetary Fund: A Changing Relationship*, Washington, DC: Brookings Institution.
Stiglitz, Joseph E. (2002), *Globalization and its Discontents*, New York: W. W. Norton.
'The IMF at a Glance'. Available at http://www.imf.org/external/np/exr/facts/glance.htm

See also: **Anti-globalisation Movements**; **Free Trade**; **World Bank**.

Inuit

Until recently the public school system in Canada taught that the Arctic lands remained undiscovered until Europeans arrived and drew their own maps and created a new cultural landscape defined by English place names. Students learned that prior to European settlement and exploration, the Arctic was terra incognita – an unknown land. Recent historical reflection, however, has become more sensitive to the aboriginal peoples of the Arctic region and now students are given a different historical perspective; one that begins 4,500 years earlier, with the Inuit. This shift in historical narrative has worked to replace a European calendar of events with one made up of Inuit histories, as well as to replace the gazetteer of the north, by getting Inuktitut names on the official maps of Canada.

Although there are still many important questions to be answered, the available evidence indicates that within the vast geographic regions of the Arctic, the Inuit carved out a homeland and established a way of life under extremely harsh conditions. What is remarkable is that even under these difficult conditions (or perhaps because of them) much of the Inuit cultural identity, social coherence and territorial integrity has been retained; in fact, many Inuit suggest that no other living culture has maintained such a continuous and consistent way of life for such a long period of time over such a large territory.

When we think about the origins and history of Inuit culture we must recognise that the Inuit have never divided the past from the present. As a result, European concepts like 'pre-history' are, strictly speaking, part of a foreign discourse and a non-Inuit understanding of time. Inuit groups have recently begun stressing this point and thus taking more control over determining how their culture is conceived and how it should be interpreted. The Inuit past is, like all oral societies, preserved and explained through the telling of stories and the passing of information from one generation to another. Today the Inuit recognise the importance of maintaining this oral tradition as a part of their culture and as a way of learning. At the same time, though, many Inuit groups have embraced other ways of unearthing the past through activities such as archaeology and the study of historical documents.

Nevertheless, many Inuit story-tellers, archaeologists and historians are interested in the European voyages of exploration. This is in part because the European encounters with Inuit and with the Arctic environment set the stage for a process of contact that would eventually have an impact on the Inuit way of life. These encounters began in the late 1500s when the first explorers sailed into the waters of the Davis Strait, Hudson Strait and Hudson Bay. Although these first meetings were limited in number and duration, as well as geographically dispersed, they did mark a transition to what might be called the 'period of contact'. Between the arrival of Martin Frobisher in 1576 and the famous disappearance of Franklin in 1848, about twenty-two explorers entered Inuit territory. Not all of these had a direct impact on the course of recent Inuit history. Nevertheless, with each trip, the map of the Arctic became more European and then Inuit land itself started to be claimed by settlers.

The early period of contact saw Europeans introducing new materials and technology. However, unlike in other histories of contact, these materials did not have a deep impact on the lives of the Inuit. During the eighteenth century when Europeans started to enter the Arctic, first as whalers and then as fur traders, Europeans brought in wood as a building material to replace the bone which the Inuit had previously used. Iron and copper were also introduced to replace stone, and trade developed so that the Inuit were exposed to nails, needles, cloth, glass, tools and weapons. Today Inuit leaders and educators have been engaged in the process of measuring the significance of these changes. Were the Inuit giving up stone for iron, or simply replacing one useful material with an even more useful material? How did this process work with respect to traditions and values? What were the losses and what did the Inuit gain in return? Some Inuit argue that these changes had a negative effect upon their culture, distancing them from their traditions and setting the stage for colonisation. Others suggest that what has been remarkable about Inuit culture is the way it has incorporated change to create new adaptations and ways of living, enabling the Inuit to transform rather than abandon their traditions.

What is certain is that European whaling had a devastating impact on the Inuit. The economic benefits of whaling in Europe meant that during the eighteenth and nineteenth centuries many Europeans began harvesting the most valuable of the Inuit's natural resources. Inuit communities such as the Taissumanialungmiut (or Thule Inuit) had exploited the large whale stocks for centuries; this stock would have been sustained but the explorers of Davis Strait and Hudson Bay reported huge schools of whales. This was, of course, an incentive for commercial whalers to enter the Arctic whaling grounds and devastate the stocks which were a vital part of Inuit life.

Whaling began to have a direct impact on Inuit life during the early 1700s. The whaling historian William Scoresby Jr, who was writing in 1820, described its initial intensity, recording that between 1719 and 1778, a total of 3,161 Dutch ships had carried out whaling activity in Davis Strait. A single season could see as many as thirty-five ships in Davis Strait alone. At this time, the whalers would arrive as the ice broke up and leave when the new ice began to form.

After 1850, the patterns of whaling changed. Year-round shore stations were established in some areas like Cumberland Sound, thus creating a permanent presence of Europeans in the Arctic. It was the constant presence of the whalers that brought about a new level of impact on trade, on the pattern of seasonal land use and perhaps most significantly, on Inuit health. During his stay in the Frobisher Bay area from 1861 to 1862, the explorer Charles Francis Hall wrote that European contact would eventually lead to the destruction of the Inuit: 'The days of the Inuit are numbered. There are very few of them left now. Fifty years may find them all passed away, without leaving one to tell that such a people ever lived' (Przybylak 2003, p. 132). While Hall's prediction was exaggerated and premature, sickness and the introduction of new diseases did wipe out a large percentage of the Inuit population.

During the last half of the nineteenth century over-harvesting of whales by Europeans finally went beyond the limit of sustainability. The decline in the harvest made this activity no longer profitable for the commercial whalers, but it also meant that one of the Inuit's important sources of food was endangered. This problem was made worse by the fact that towards the end of the whaling period the whalers turned to smaller marine mammals such as beluga whales, walrus and even the larger seals. At the same time, the market for whale oil and other products was declining. Some whaling captains and crews started trapping Arctic fox, marking the beginning of the fur trading era for the Inuit. The whalers supplied various Inuit communities with steel traps and taught them to trap the fox and then trade the fur to obtain guns, ammunition and other goods. The transition to the fur economy occurred over a period of about twenty-five years so the economy and culture of fox trapping did not fully develop much before the 1920s. Thus, the first two decades of the twentieth century began a major transition in the type of economic adaptation that would define Inuit way of life into the 1990s.

The first missionaries to enter the Arctic along the Labrador coast were Moravians, who established a mission station at Nain in 1771. The Moravian Church still operates in this region. For most other areas, however, active contact with missionaries did not get under way until the early nineteenth century and missionaries only expanded their influence in the eastern and other parts of the Arctic late that century. The majority of missionaries had no direct ties with the government, except for their role in education and, in places, in medical services.

The Royal Canadian Mounted Police (RCMP) began to establish their own type of influence on Inuit communities when they entered the eastern Arctic in the early twentieth century. The mandates of the missions and the police created different types of impact on the Inuit, one based on ideology and the other on law. The services of the RCMP began with concerns about 'law and order' in the north, the protection of northern biological resources, and the question of territorial sovereignty. The first posts were created in 1903 in the western Arctic with the mandate to demonstrate Canada's sovereignty throughout the region. A few years later, the RCMP established posts in the eastern Arctic. The location of these posts had certain strategic significance since they controlled access to the Arctic lands and waters.

For decades, the Inuit of the central and eastern Arctic have been calling for the creation of a new territory. This effort took on added impetus in 1976 when the Inuit Tapirisat of Canada submitted a proposal to the federal government requesting the creation of 'Nunavut' ('our land' in the Inuktitut dialect of the region). A 1982 plebiscite and several years of negotiations followed. A key provision of the Tungavik Federation of Nunavut land claim agreement, which was finalised in 1991, was the formation of a new territory. The final agreement committed Canada, the government of the Northwest Territories, and the Tungavik Federation of Nunavut to negotiate a political accord to deal with powers, financing and timing for the establishment of the Nunavut government. This political accord was formally signed in 1992. Inuit control through public government is premised upon the existence of an Inuit majority in Nunavut. Currently, 85 per cent of the population of the region is Inuit.

On 15 February 1999, residents of Nunavut held their first election for members of their legislative assembly. Paul Okalik was selected as the territory's first premier. The Nunavut territory and government was established on 1 April 1999. It has jurisdictional powers and institutions similar to those of the government of the Northwest Territories.

Justin Edwards

Literary Works

Moses, Daniel David and Terry Goldie (eds) (1997), *An Anthology of Native Canadian Literature in English*, Toronto: Oxford University Press.
Petrone, Penny (ed.) (1992), *Northern Voices: Inuit Writing in English*, Toronto: University of Toronto Press.
Thérieult, Yves (1997), *Agaguk*, Montreal: Hexagone.
Wiebe, Rudy (1995), *A Discovery of Strangers*, Toronto: Vintage.

Histories

Crowe, Keith J. (1991), *A History of the Original Peoples of Northern Canada*, Montreal: McGill-Queen's University Press.
Duffy, R. Quinn (1988), *The Road to Nunavut: The Progress of the Eastern Arctic Inuit since the Second World War*, Montreal: McGill-Queen's University Press.

Eber, Dorothy (2000), *When the Whalers were up North: Inuit Memories from the Eastern Arctic*, Montreal: McGill-Queen's University Press.

Grygier, Pat Sandiford (1997), *A Long Way from Home: The Tuberculosis Epidemic Among the Inuit*, Montreal: McGill-Queen's University Press.

Hulan, Renée (2002), *Northern Experience and the Myths of Canadian Culture*, Montreal: McGill-Queen's University Press.

Przybylak, Rajmund (2003), *The Climate of the Arctic*, New York: Kluwer.

See also: **Big Bear; European Exploration and Settlement: Canada; Genocide: Canada; Historiography: Canada; Land: Canada; Native Reservations**.

Iranian Revolution

One of the most dramatic and influential revolutions of the twentieth century, the Iran Revolution of 1978 to 1979 destroyed the secular regime of the Pahlavi Shahs. After his reinstatement into power following the CIA-backed coup that deposed Muhammad Mossadiq in 1953, Shah Muhammad Reza Pahlavi was viewed by millions of Iranians as a puppet for Western nations. His regime promoted Westernisation, secularity and foreign investments, and brutally oppressed dissent. Although a small percentage of Iranians benefited from his free-market policies, the majority remained in dire poverty, while the regime flaunted its extreme wealth. Furthermore, Islamic expression was heavily regulated, and Shi'a clerics who were critical of the regime were often jailed, banned, and exiled.

One leading cleric exiled for opposing the Shah was Ayatollah Ruhollah Khomeini (1902–89). From his base abroad, Khomeini urged his followers to oppose the Shah and struggle for an Islamic government. At the same time, leftists were outraged at the regime's pro-Western capitalist economy that privileged a small minority at the expense of an impoverished majority. Both clerics and leftist activists viewed Shi'a Islam as an Iranian national expression that could serve as a force for change, and in 1978 they joined forces to overthrow the Shah. In January, supporters of Khomeini took to the streets of Qum to protest against the government. The regime responded by attacking the protesters, killing many. In accordance with Shi'a custom, another march was scheduled after the forty-day mourning period. The government again used troops against the demonstrators. This led to a cycle of protest which followed the Islamic calendar of mourning, giving a religious hue to the demonstrations, which quickly spread throughout the country. Merchants, workers, students, clerics, and other opponents of the Shah took to the streets to protest against the regime, and were met with brutality by the army.

By January 1979, millions of Iranians were on the streets calling for the end of the Pahlavi regime. Ill with cancer, the Shah fled the country, and Khomeini returned from exile, ready to lead the nation. He found the economic, military, and bureaucratic infrastructure in a state of collapse. From 1979 until 1982, Khomeini and his cleric allies battled opposition from secularists, finally consolidating power as direct rulers over the newly declared Islamic Republic of Iran. Crushing opposition and rigorously instituting their interpretations of Islam over the whole of the population, the Council of the Islamic Republic, led by Khomeini, became a symbol throughout the world of Islamic revivalism, anti-Westernism, and cross-class social and political revolution.

Nancy Stockdale

Literary Works

Parsipur, Shahrnush (1998), *Women without Men*, Syracuse, NY: Syracuse University.
Sullivan, Soraya Paknazar (trans.) (1991), *Stories by Iranian Women since the Revolution*, Austin, TX: University of Texas.

Histories

Bakhash, Shaul (1986), *The Reign of the Ayatollahs*, New York: Basic Books.
Esposito, John L. (ed.) (2001), *The Iranian Revolution: Its Global Impact*, Miami: Florida International University.
Keddie, Nikki R. (2003), *Modern Iran: Roots and Results of Revolution*, New Haven, CT: Yale University.
Mottahedeh, Roy (1985), The Mantle of the Prophet, New York: Oneworld Publications.

See also: **Britain's Postwar Foreign Policy.**

Ireland

Ireland is regarded by many commentators as England's oldest colony. The history of major political relations between the two islands began with the commissioning in 1155 by Pope Adrian IV, in the form of a 'bull', of Henry II of England to reform the Irish Church and people. This proposal was not acted upon, but it provided a retrospective justification for events that later transpired. In 1166, the Gaelic king of Leinster, Dermot MacMurrough, invited Richard FitzGilbert, the earl of Pembroke, to assist him in his war with his Irish enemies and rivals. FitzGilbert, known in Ireland as 'Strongbow', was promised Dermot's daughter, Eva, the Leinster succession, and handsome fiefs for his lieutenants. After small incursions and expeditions, Strongbow arrived in Waterford, in the south-east of Ireland, in 1170, took the city by force, and married Eva in its cathedral. Within a couple of months, Dermot and Strongbow had taken Dublin. In 1171, Dermot died, destined to be remembered scornfully as 'Diarmaid na nGall' (Dermot of the Foreigners), and Strongbow, faster than he could ever have hoped, became king of Leinster. Faced, however, with Irish forces rallying against him, he had already sent his submission to Henry II in London. Henry arrived in Waterford on 17 October 1171. He came with an army but without the intention of conquest, wishing to ensure that the gains of the adventurers under Strongbow should depend on the Crown of England, and to secure a voluntary submission of the Irish Church and princes. He did not proclaim the donation of Adrian IV, as, due to the murder of Thomas à Becket, his relations with the papacy were very poor; but his stay of only six months in Ireland was enough to establish the basis of English sovereignty there.

It was Henry II who received the homage of the Irish chieftains, princes, kings, who appear to have believed, on the basis of Henry's show of peace and his rights under a papal concession, that he would be content to be an absentee supreme ruler, leaving them undisturbed in their provincial kingdoms. Yet Henry's first action had been to confirm to Strongbow the land of Leinster as an appanage of the earldom of Pembroke: already he was extending English sovereignty over Ireland. Henry called a synod of the Irish bishops, in

Cashel. This resulted in various internal church reforms, but also submission to the English king. Nothing was said of the claims of Canterbury over the Irish Church, and the supremacy of Rome was accepted by a Church long recalcitrant to the papacy, but at the behest of the English sovereign. Henry meanwhile gave to Dublin its first charter of municipal liberties, and in this way it was incorporated into the expanding network of the English merchant traders. Finally Henry provided for the royal government of Ireland. He appointed a viceroy, and placed garrisons in Dublin, Wexford and Waterford. He annexed much of the east coast as Crown demesne, and began the process of imposing feudal law on the previously Gaelic dispensation.

At the conclusion of the Cashel synod, Henry sent envoys to Pope Alexander III, asking for a papal privilege for Ireland. In May 1172, he was reconciled with the papacy, and Alexander published three letters on the Irish question. These criticised the evil customs of the Irish and enjoined the Irish bishops to assist Henry in keeping possession of Ireland; urged Henry to continue his good work in reforming these same evil customs; and commended the lay princes of Ireland for receiving the English sovereign as their king of their own free will. The pope also, finally, sent a privilege which conferred on Henry the dominion over the Irish. Thus, whatever about the 'bull' of Adrian IV, the letters and privilege of Alexander conferred the lordship of Ireland on Henry II of England.

These events constitute the beginning of English rule in Ireland. The ensuing history was long, complex and often violent. It altered in significant ways, however, in the early modern period, under the Tudors. Up to the rule of Henry VIII of England, a form of 'home rule' had obtained, whereby most of the senior officials of English governance in Ireland were themselves Irish; the viceroy was appointed from among the great Irish lords; and a measure of separation stood between England and Ireland. But with the accession of the absolutist Henry VIII, this situation changed rapidly. The new king aimed to turn the English lordship of Ireland into a kingdom, to secure assent among the Catholic Irish for his breach with Rome and his takeover of the English Church, and to win over the Irish aristocracy.

The main policy in this line was that of 'surrender and regrant'. According to English feudal theory, all land-titles depended on the Crown, while in Ireland the greater part of the island was owned by Gaelic chieftains whose titles came from Irish law. In 1541, parliament was convened in Dublin, and Henry was there confirmed king of Ireland. The kingdom of Ireland was to last until the Act of Union of 1801. With this behind him, Henry undertook the most far-reaching set of policies in Ireland since the arrival of Strongbow: (1) he imposed Church reform on Ireland in the same manner he had in England; (2) he instituted a system of government in which the royal will was supreme, and in place of native lords English deputies ruled the country; (3) following the acceptance of his monarchy in Church and state, he tried to establish it in treaties with the Irish lords, whom he left unmolested in their lands if they would accept tenure under the Crown; (4) Henry's policy also included anti-measures in favour of English speech and 'civility', and the Irish language and culture, as expressed by the bards, poets and others, were forbidden and their use even punishable. Ireland, in effect, was to be made a second England through the hegemony of the amenable bishops and nobility, and no provision was made for the recognition or legitimacy of Irish and Gaelic tradition.

It was under Henry's Catholic daughter, Mary, that the policy of plantation was first tried in Ireland. In the midland counties of Laois and Offaly, lived Gaelic families and septs that had long harried the Pale, the centre of English rule around Dublin. Their lands were declared forfeit following the crime of treason, the local landowners attainted, and in 1556, grants were made for the first time to English settlers. Their estates were to be limited in size and were to descend to the eldest son by the English law of primogeniture; the grant-ees were compelled to take only English servants, and to build stone houses; lastly, they were obliged to serve the viceroy with a stated number of troops and to pay a head-rent to the Crown. These confiscated territories were made into shires, as King's and Queen's counties. Native resistance to this scheme lasted fifty years. The next scheme of planta-tion, in the southern province of Munster, in 1586, was no more conclusive. But after the long war fought in the north of the country, by the greatest of the Gaelic families, the O'Neills, in the last years of the sixteenth century, the most thorough, long-lasting and careful plantation scheme was undertaken in Ulster, the results of which are still shaping contemporary Ireland. The end of that war at the Battle of Kinsale in 1603, and the sym-bolic departure from Ireland for Rome in 1607 of Hugh O'Neill and over sixty other Irish aristocrats – the 'Flight of the Earls' – heralded the defeat of the Gaelic order in Ireland, and the end of real independence for the next 300 years.

Depictions of colonial Ireland in this early modern period are not difficult to find. The most well-known is Edmund Spenser's *View of the Present Condition of Ireland*, written near Cork, where he also wrote *The Faerie Queen*, in 1596. The *View* is infamous for its analysis of the Irish resistance to English civil law and modes of sociality, and for its advocacy of war and famine as methods to reduce the Irish to obedience. Very broadly speaking, the image of the Irish purveyed by Spenser – that of a 'barbarous' people, lacking a proper relationship to the land, given to primitive customs of dress and behaviour, wedded blindly to Catholicism – is one that is in keeping with portrayals of the 'native' by the metropolitan polity and culture in other colonised regions of the world, including those of the peoples of North America, also experiencing penetration by England at this time. It is an image that began to put in place the discursive framework within which Irish culture, Irish literature in particular, was to understand itself and to be understood by others down to the present day.

The next major change in the constitutional position of Ireland came with the rise of 'Protestant patriot' politics towards the end of the eighteenth century. This was essentially an Anglo-Irish liberal reformism, that sought to have a true parliament in Dublin, Irish control over the army, and to give Ireland a constitution akin to that which England won for itself after 1689. The most famous figure of this movement was Henry Grattan; the most famous literary and intellectual figure of this period was Edmund Burke, with the figure of Jonathan Swift looming behind him. Grattan and his colleagues learned from the lessons of the American Revolution. They contributed to the formation of the Volunteers, a largely Protestant militia ostensibly designed to protect Ireland at a time when the army was largely embroiled in wars overseas, but also used the Volunteers as a lever in domestic politics. This activity issued eventually in 'Grattan's parliament' of 1782, a reformed assem-bly that gave Ireland a degree of legislative independence. This was not enough to stave off the influence of Enlightenment and French revolutionary ideas, which led to the for-mation in Belfast in 1791 of the United Irishmen, a Jacobin revolutionary society, led by Wolfe Tone. Enunciating a republican liberalism, seeking to unite Catholic, Protestant and dissenter, and confident that breaking the tie with England was the essential prerequisite to Irish advancement, Tone and his confederates launched their great rebellion in 1798. Denied by storm and confusion of the French support which was key to their success, the rebellion was crushed with great violence. The British government, under Pitt, through the Act of Union of 1800, united the Irish and British parliaments, and Ireland lost its status as a separate kingdom, becoming instead part of the United Kingdom.

Irish history through the nineteenth century was marked by various conflicts and struggles, but behind them all lay the rise of Irish nationalism, first articulated by Tone, given a true mass constituency by Daniel O'Connell and the campaign for Catholic emancipation (a contest for abolition of law prejudicial to Catholics brought in after William III in the early eighteenth century; finally won in 1829), implicit in the Tithe Wars of the early nineteenth century, openly articulated again by the Romantic Young Ireland movement of the 1840s, and even perversely developed by the catastrophic Great Famine of 1845–51. All of these factors contributed to the rise of Irish national consciousness, mediated through the English language, and buttressed by romantic interest in Irish antiquities and culture. The 1860s saw the creation of the Irish Republican Brotherhood (IRB) by Irish exiles in America, which eventually contributed to the 1916 Easter Rising. In the 1870s and 1880s, the Land War was led by Michael Davitt and Charles Stewart Parnell – the definitive modern Irish struggle for land reform, issuing in a series of Land Acts from 1860 up to 1903 which bought out the great Protestant estates and landlords and produced the Irish rural middle class which has dominated the country ever since.

In the 1890s, the second Irish cultural revival began, famously prosecuted by great figures such as W. B. Yeats, Lady Augusta Gregory, J. M. Synge, George Russell, and critiqued by James Joyce and Samuel Beckett in the early twentieth century. All of this writing, in multifarious ways, seized on the issue of national identity, even if only (as in the case of Beckett) to reject it. This identity politics of high culture found its mass correlatives in institutions such as the Gaelic League (formed in 1893 to preserve the Irish Gaelic language), and the Gaelic Athletic Association (founded in 1884 to preserve, promote and codify Irish field games).

All of these cultural initiatives inevitably overlapped with political and revolutionary developments, of which the main landmarks were the successive failures, in 1886, 1892 and 1912 of Home Rule Bills in the Westminster parliament, and the military uprising organised by the IRB at Easter 1916, which was arguably a result of that failure of constitutional politics. The rebellion was crushed in a week, and was initially unpopular with the mass of the population, but the long litany of executions enacted under martial law served considerably to sway a significant portion of opinion in favour of Patrick Pearse, James Connolly and their colleagues. Out of the ashes of the rising, the Irish Republican Army was formed, and in the period 1919 to 1921, it fought an increasingly bloody guerrilla war with the British army and the Royal Irish Constabulary. Meanwhile, the old constitutional nationalist parties had lost all political credibility and were replaced by the hugely successful Sinn Fein ('Ourselves') party, which won a sizable majority of Irish seats in the 1918 general election. Sinn Fein in this period developed a state and government-in-waiting, which operated a cabinet and law courts while on the run from British forces. Eventually, David Lloyd George and his government enacted the Government of Ireland Act of 1920, which legislated for separate parliaments in Northern Ireland and in the south, in Belfast and Dublin respectively. In 1922, the Anglo-Irish Treaty was negotiated with Lloyd George by Michael Collins, Arthur Griffith and others in London, setting up the Free State in the twenty-six southern counties of Ireland, while leaving a self-governing northern statelet in the remaining six counties. The creation of the Free State, a dominion of the British Commonwealth, was accompanied by a bitter civil war, fought between those in Sinn Fein and the IRA who accepted the treaty and its provisions, and those who did not. The fate of the 'six counties' of Ulster was not the major issue behind this war, though partition did leave a substantial nationalist and Catholic minority in a state that refused to accept their national identity and regarded them with suspicion, and that was to prove unsustainable by the late 1960s.

The Free State declared itself a republic and removed itself from the Commonwealth in 1949. It joined the United Nations in 1955, and the European Economic Community in 1973. The constitutional status of Northern Ireland has been considerably adjusted by the Good Friday Agreement, negotiated between the British and Irish governments, and most of the political parties in Northern Ireland, including paramilitary-related parties, in 1998. The political institutions thereby created have yet to work consistently and in a stable manner, but Northern Ireland has enjoyed since 1993, when the IRA declared a ceasefire, its longest period of relative peace for over three decades.

In conclusion, a strong argument can be made for looking at all Irish anglophone cultural production through a colonial or postcolonial lens. The literary works listed below include but a small selection of works that have been analysed from a postcolonial perspective. Listed under Histories, the works by Deane, Cairns and Richards, Kiberd and Lloyd provide useful critical surveys of Irish literature from a postcolonial perspective, and the studies by Cleary, Graham, Innes, Nolan and Howes provide more focused analyses.

Conor McCarthy

Literary Works

Friel, Brian (1984), *Selected Plays*, London: Faber and Faber.
Heaney, Seamus (1980), *Selected Poems 1965–1975*, London: Faber and Faber.
Joyce, James (1993a), *A Portrait of the Artist as a Young Man*, London: Penguin.
Joyce, James (1993b), *Ulysses*, London: Penguin.
Synge, J. M. (1958), *Plays, Poems and Prose*, London: Dent.
Yeats, W. B. (1984), *W. B. Yeats: The Poems*, ed. Richard Finneran, Dublin: Gill and Macmillan.

Histories

Cairns, David and Shaun Richards (1988), *Writing Ireland: Colonialism, Nationalism and Culture*, Manchester: Manchester University Press.
Canny, Nicholas (2001), *Making Ireland British 1580–1650*, Oxford: Oxford University Press.
Cleary, Joe (2002a), 'Misplaced Ideas? Locating and Dislocating Ireland in Colonial and Postcolonial Studies', in Crystal Bartolovich and Neil Lazarus (eds), *Marxism, Modernity and Postcolonial Studies*, Cambridge: Cambridge University Press, pp. 101–24.
Cleary, Joe (2002b), *Literature, Partition and the Nation-State: Conflict and Culture in Ireland, Israel and Palestine*, Cambridge: Cambridge University Press.
Deane, Seamus (1985), *Celtic Revivals: Essays in Modern Irish Literature 1880–1980*, London: Faber and Faber.
Deane, Seamus (1997), *Strange Country: Modernity and Nationhood in Irish Writing Since 1790*, Oxford: Clarendon.
Deane, Seamus (ed.) (1991), *The Field Day Anthology of Irish Writing*, 3 vols, Derry: Field Day.
Eagleton, Terry (1995), *Heathcliff and the Great Hunger*, London: Verso.
Foster, R. F. (1988), *Modern Ireland 1600–1972*, London: Allen and Unwin.

Lydon, James (1998), *The Making of Ireland: From Ancient Times to the Present*, London: Routledge.

Graham, Colin (2001), *Deconstructing Ireland: Identity, Theory, Culture*, Edinburgh: Edinburgh University Press.

Howe, Stephen (2000), *Ireland and Empire: Colonial Legacies in Irish History and Culture*, Oxford: Oxford University Press.

Howes, Marjorie (1996), *Yeats's Nations: Gender, Class and Irishness*, Cambridge: Cambridge University Press.

Innes, C. L. (1993), *Woman and Nation in Irish Literature and Society 1880–1935*, Athens, GA: University of Georgia Press.

Kiberd, Declan (1995), *Inventing Ireland: The Literature of the Modern Nation*, London: Jonathan Cape.

Lloyd, David (1993), *Anomalous States: Irish Writing and the Post-colonial Condition*, Dublin: Lilliput Press.

McCarthy, Conor (2000), *Modernisation, Crisis and Culture in Ireland 1969–1992*, Dublin: Four Courts Press.

Nolan, Emer (1995), *James Joyce and Nationalism*, London: Routledge.

See also: **British Imperialism**.

Islam

Islam ('submission') is a monotheism with a holy book, the Koran, revealed in the early seventh century to its historical founder, Muhammad ibn Abdallah of the Quraysh tribe, (born 570 at Mecca in the Arabian Peninsula). From its inception, Islam has been a complex cultural synthesis and religious faith set in a political framework, characteristics that have been heightened through its development over the centuries and across a vast geographic space.

Muhammad's socio-political religious message drew on, in dialogue and in antagonism, diverse Near Eastern cultural traditions: Judaism, Christianity, Manicheism, Zoroastrianism, Greek philosophy, Arab polytheism; formative political influences were inter-Arab tribal rivalries, Byzantine administrative structures and Sasanian monarchism. The worldwide community of Muslims (*umma*) was first established in 622 when Muhammad and his earliest followers took refuge in Medina (the 'city' [of Islam], hitherto known as Yathrib), escaping the hostility of the still largely polytheistic Arabs of Mecca; their flight, the *hijra*, begins the Muslim calendar. These early years of Islam, its relationship to the personality of Muhammad, and its self-definition against the pre-Islamic Arab period of ignorance (*jahiliyya*) have found detailed, if controversial exploration in Salman Rushdie's *Satanic Verses* (1988). Through mercantilism, conquest, land-clearing and popular appeal, Islam spread rapidly to Iran, Central, South and Southeast Asia, and trans-Saharan Africa – a motility manifested today in Islam's resurgence in the West. A juridical orthopraxy binds together the now diverse *umma*, but competes with equally long-standing sectarian, localised and mystic tendencies sustained by that very diversity.

During the eighth century, doctrinal and political controversies, especially surrounding the question of leadership following Muhammad's sudden death, predicated Islam's major sectarian divide between Sunnis and Shi'as. Under the Umayyad dynasty, Muhammad was developed into the seal on the inherited Abrahamic prophetic lineage and the ultimate figure of emulation. Authority became increasingly invested in a juridical understanding of textual traditions – the Koran, the *hadith* (orally transmitted sayings of Muhammad that took written form by the ninth century) and the *sharia* (Islamic law) – and were relocated in the body of *ulama* (religious and legal scholars). The Sunnis were those who, accordingly, came to consider Muhammad's life (*sunna*) as exemplary, the *ulama* as the authoritative interpreters of the *sharia*, and Muhammad's friend, Abu Bakr, as the first Caliph and Muhammad's legitimate successor. This long and rooted historical tradition behind Sunni Muslim attitudes towards the prophet and the Koran helps explicate some of the outrage surrounding Rushdie's attempts in *Satanic Verses* to deconstruct the prophetic and the revelatory through the tools of fiction and magic realism.

Rushdie's achievement was arguably to evoke both Sunni and Shi'a outrage against his alternative narrative of the key events of early Islam. From the eighth century itself, divergent memorialisations of those events circulated in the form of Shi'ism, that emerged to contest Sunni understanding of the relationship between political and religious authority. Shi'as situate legitimate leadership not in the Caliph but in the charismatic figure of the Imam, descended from Muhammad through his cousin and son-in-law Ali, and continuing through Ali's son Husain, killed by the Umayyads at Karbala in 680. The Imam, appointed by his predecessor, is imbued with complete political, religious and juridical sovereignty over the community and the world. Constructed as supremely innocent, he is invested with quasi-prophetic authority and a mystic, cosmological character heightened by a belief in his occultation and messianic return. Differences concerning the precise moment of the Imam's occlusion led to further cleavages. Among the several Shi'a subsects the most prominent are the Twelver Shi'as (the state religion of Iran) and the Ismailis, associated with the notorious Assassins, and with the powerful Fatimid dynasty of Egypt. Precolonial and colonial migratory patterns have also created a distinct East African Gujarati Ismaili culture, that has been best captured in the novels of M. G. Vassanji, such as *The Gunny Sack* (1990).

Shi'a Islam is, in other words, far from monolithic; nevertheless, a distinctive Shi'a identity has crystallised around persistent dissatisfaction with the ruling house, divergent understanding of the legal tool of interpretation (*ijtehad*), intense emotional investment in the memory of martyrdom and the practice of dissimulation (*takiyya*). Shi'a understanding of the Imamate thus constitutes a multiple break – doctrinal, historiographic, politico-juridical, and, crucially, emotional – with the rest of the umma. Paradoxically, however, its affective reservoir can function as a general Muslim idiom for loss, mourning and nostalgia. For instance, Aamer Husain's collection of short stories, *Turquoise* (2002), especially 'Cactus Town', evokes the mood of Karachi, and postcolonial Pakistan, through Shi'a rituals surrounding *muharram* or the month of mourning. Likewise, in his poetry collection, *Rooms are Never Finished* (2001), Agha Shahid Ali uses those same rituals within a searing commentary on the political conflict and violence in Kashmir. The 'ecumenical' appeal of this Shi'a idiom has been enhanced by the considerable, if confusing, overlap between Shi'a esoterism, anti-establishmentarianism and dissimulation and the conglomeration of mystic, ascetic and individualistic movements known as Sufism.

Sufism emerged along the non-metropolitan frontiers which, encouraged by the mercantile character of early Islam, have been crucial to Islam's dynamics of expansion. This affiliation of Sufism with the marginal offered alternative para-orthodox spaces for working out syncretistic Islamic identities more amenable to local non-Islamic religious practices and cultural expressions. From the Maghreb to Central Asia and to Bengal, Sufism has thus regularly merged with 'popular' Islam at local levels. This portrayal of Sufism has been invoked by authors such as Qurratulain Hyder, in *The River of Fire* (1998), to offer paradigms of Islam's expansion that are alternative to theories of civilisational clash and rapacious Muslim armies. Of course, such narratives of Sufi-driven syncretism run the danger of eliding how much Sufism colluded with as much as critiqued the prescriptive and juridical dimensions of orthodox Islam. In the later medieval Near Eastern urban landscape, the Sufi became as much a fixture as the merchant or the judge. Sufi orders such as the Naqshbandis, the Chistis and the Suhrawardis exerted enormous influence over different political houses; while groups such as the Janissaries and the Kizilbashes powerfully combined and deployed mystic, military and bureaucratic subjectivities.

Politically and culturally, the high noon of Islam corresponds to Western historiography's pre-modern periods. Throughout the European Middle Ages, Islamicate empires, including those of the Ottomans and the Mughals, flourished across Africa and Asia. Those empires based within the boundaries of modern Europe, such as in Andalusia and Sicily, were rich contact zones between what today we would demarcate as 'Europe' and 'the Orient'. The civilisational refinement and military might of these Islamicate empires provoked European wonder, and, from the early modern period onwards, European colonial expansionisms that gradually eroded their political power. Several postcolonial writers engage with these historical processes as a way of recuperating a richly complex prehistory of the binaries of Saidean 'Orientalism'. In Tariq Ali's *Shadows of the Pomegranate Tree* (1996), Al-Andalus on the eve of the emergence of Catholic Spain becomes an emblem of a pre-modern cosmopolitan Islamic culture that invites the creation of a contemporary pan-Islamic identity grounded on the very memory of its loss. Through the parallel stories of an Indian anthropologist in modern Egypt and a Jewish Egyptian slave in medieval South India, Amitav Ghosh's *In an Antique Land* (1992) laments the destruction of the Arab-controlled Indian Ocean trade under the pressures of Portuguese exploration. By imagining the intertwined cultures and economies within Islamicate empires, both authors counter the violence of colonialism as well as the political and cultural nationalisms that are its postcolonial afterlife.

The memory and history of pre-colonial Islam thus rearticulates the individual as a cultural entity, functioning within a paradigm grounded on a reflective rather than a reactive and competitive interaction of ideas, goods and peoples. This rearticulation asks us to consider how the colonial encounter precipitated by trade-induced expansion had long-term consequences not merely on the cultural structures and systems of the Islamicate empires, but also on the psyche of the colonial subject who was Muslim by faith and cultural orientation. French and British colonial administrations introduced, although differently, Western-style education into the regions they took control over. Such modernising processes catalysed in the Muslim colonial subject responses of mimicry and introspection, including, from the eighteenth century onwards, powerful reformist Islamist or Wahabi movements and nascent, often socialist nationalisms. Ahdaf Soueif's *In the Eye of the Sun* (2000) poignantly conveys how such competing ideologies exerted conflicting demands on the educated Muslim colonial and postcolonial subject. The influence of Nasserite socialism, the pan-Arabism generated through the Palestinian question, Western-style modernity symbolised by English literature, and the magnetic music of the Arab singer Umm Kulthoum are equally potent influences on the heroine, a modern, urban(e), Egyptian woman, whose fraught emergence into adulthood charts the fractured birth of decolonised Egypt and, by extension, the decolonised Muslim nation.

It is no coincidence that several Muslim authors who have traced the splitting of the colonial and postcolonial Muslim subject are female, narrating the coming of age of women who echo their own subject-positions. In consonance with general colonial and anti-colonial constructions of the female subject, the construction of the modern Muslim woman sought to suture the fractures on the level of nation, family and individual that resulted from the struggles between 'tradition' and 'modernity' set in motion by colonialism. For the protagonist Laila in Attia Hosain's *Sunlight on a Broken Column* (1961), class and religion cohere as the composite legacy of North Indian feudal Muslim culture, against which are pitted incipient socialism, feminism and secular nationalism; nevertheless, the divisions induced in Laila's extended family through the negotiation of this complex terrain embody unresolved and unbearable tensions. Through Laila and her familial ties, Hosain demonstrates how, like other anti-colonial ideologies, alternative Muslim cosmopolitanisms that could have emerged from the encounter between 'tradition' and 'modernity' did not fully materialise in the course of the twentieth century.

This trajectory of decolonisation is exemplified by the partition of British India in 1947. The ultimately split family in *Sunlight on a Broken Column* mirrors two initial paths of decolonisation taken by South Asian Islam through partition: on the one hand, the Muslim nation of Pakistan, self-professed guardian of South Asian Muslim culture and interests; and on the other, secular India, offering an alternative narrative of Islam's place within a decolonised pluralist nation, a classic account of the latter being Hyder's *River of Fire*. Several Pakistani authors have struggled to accommodate a sense of a separate political destiny from India within a fidelity to the transnational contours of South Asian Islam. This struggle is memorialised through shared cultural practices: the preparation of food, as in *Meatless Days* (1989), Sara Suleri's memoir of a Pakistani childhood, or an English style redolent of Urdu, the language of high culture in late Mughal India, as in Hussain's *Turquoise*. Pakistani attempts to write a South Asian Islamic nation into being have, however, been conducted in the shadow of the secession, in 1972, of Pakistan's Eastern Wing as Bangladesh. The demand for, and achievement of, an independent nation on the basis of a specific intersection of ethnicity (Bengali) and Islam enact yet another set of coordinates for the decolonised Muslim state, one that has now begun to find fictional articulation in English, as for instance, in Monica Ali's recent *Brick Lane* (2003).

Although rooted in the regional specificities of South Asian history and politics, the consequences of the partition for South Asian Muslim cultures gesture towards cultural and political choices that have had to be made on individual and collective levels across the world of decolonised Islam. By focusing on the parallel yet intersecting lives of two sisters, one in London's East End and the other in Dhaka, *Brick Lane* accurately captures the reformation of contemporary Bangladeshi identity as forged through frameworks of economic deprivation, cultural deracination, and pan-Islamic reformism that impact in tandem on populations both at home and in the diaspora. From the late twentieth century onwards, in nation-states with large Muslim populations (apart from India, where resurgent Hindu nationalism has muzzled its substantial Muslim minority), postcolonial disillusionment with secular elite leadership has converged with the re-emergence of purportedly grassroots reformist movements. These dovetail with radical, often bellicose, identity politics articulated by youthful diasporic Muslim populations in the 'First World'. Its most visible locus is a neo-traditional feminism, which perpetuates colonial and anti-colonial investments in the Muslim woman's subjectivity as the privileged site for enacting the relationship between religion, politics and the law.

Writers from an array of postcolonial backgrounds have attempted to contest the implications of such pan-Islamism. For instance, Leila Aboulela's *The Translator* (2001) explores, through a female protagonist's memories of a Sudanese Muslim upbringing, the possible alignments between academic study of Islamic culture and the affective dimensions of particular heritages. Yet such intellectual and writerly voices claiming liberal or 'moderate' Muslim positions are crowded out by the cyber-savvy, political Islam, far from atavistic but usually claiming anti-modern status. The former attempts to reclaim populistic, local 'syncretic' Islams for ideological and emotional support, but, from the *Satanic Verses* controversy to the events of September 11, the latter has captured the global public sphere as its most spectacular theatre.

Ananya Jahanara Kabir

Literary Works

Aboulela, Leila (2001), *The Translator*, Edinburgh: Polygon.
Ali, Agha Shahid (2001), *Rooms are Never Finished*, New York: Norton.
Ali, Monica (2003), *Brick Lane*, London: Doubleday.
Ali, Tariq (1996), *Shadows of the Pomegranate Tree*, London: Verso.
Ghosh, Amitav (1992), *In an Antique Land*, London: Granta.
Hossain, Attia (1961), *Sunlight on a Broken Column*, London: Chatto and Windus.
Hussein, Aamer (2002), *Turquoise*, London: Saqi.
Hyder, Qurratulain (1998), *River of Fire*, Delhi: Kali for Women.
Rushdie, Salman (1988), *The Satanic Verses*, London: Viking.
Soueif, Ahdaf (2000), *In the Eye of the Sun*, London: Anchor.
Suleri, Sara (1989), *Meatless Days*, Chicago: University of Chicago Press.
Vassanji, M. G. (1990), *The Gunny Sack*, London: Heinemann.

Histories

Abu-Lughod, Lila (ed.) (1998), *Remaking Women: Feminism and Modernity in the Middle East*, Princeton, NJ: Princeton University Press.
Berkey, Jonathan P. (2003), *The Formation of Islam: Religion and Society in the Near East, 600–1800*, Cambridge: Cambridge University Press.
Daftary, Farhad (1990), *The Isma'ilis: Their History and Doctrines*, Cambridge: Cambridge University Press.
Eaton, Richard M. (1993), *The Rise of Islam and the Bengal Frontier, 1204–1760*, Berkeley, CA; London: University of California Press.
Esposito, John (1992), *Islam: The Straight Path*, New York: Oxford University Press.
Ewing, Katherine Pratt (1997), *Arguing Sainthood: Modernity, Psychoanalysis and Islam*, Durham, NC and London: Duke University Press.
Gilsenan, Michael (1990), *Recognizing Islam: Religion and Society in the Modern Middle East*, London: Tauris.
Holt, P. M., Ann K. S. Lambton and Bernard Lewis (eds) (1977), *The Cambridge History of Islam*, 4 vols, Cambridge: Cambridge University Press.
Jalal, Ayesha (2001), *Self and Sovereignty: Individual and Community in South Asian Islam since 1850*, Oxford: Oxford University Press.
Hasan, Mushirul (1997), *Legacy of a Divided Nation: India's Muslims since Independence*, London: Hurst.

Nasr, Seyyed Vali Reza (2001), *Islamic Leviathan: Islam and the Making of State Power*, Oxford: Oxford University Press.
Schimmel, Annemarie (1975), *The Mystical Dimensions of Islam*, Chapel Hill, NC: University of North Carolina Press.

See also: **Religions: East Africa**; **Religions: South Asia**; **Religions: West Africa**; **Slave Trade: East Africa**; **Slavery: West Africa**; **Sudanese Civil War**.

J

Jallianwala Bagh Massacre

On 13 April 1919, General Reginald Dyer of the British Indian Army ordered troops to open fire on an unarmed crowd of Indian civilians who had gathered for a local fair, the Baisakhi Mela, in an enclosed plot of land known as the Jallianwala Bagh in the city of Amritsar. His actions resulted in the deaths of approximately 400 people and injuries to 1,200, making this the worst massacre in the history of British colonial rule in India. Dyer's actions served to galvanise further organised Indian opposition to colonial rule, which had already gained great impetus after the passing of the Rowlatt Acts in early 1919.

The Rowlatt Acts, referred to by nationalists as 'the Black Act', extended wartime provisions of search and seizure without warrants, detention without trial, and trials without juries or appeals into post-armistice India. Nationalist agitation in response to the Rowlatt Acts had been widespread, and the colonial government reacted swiftly; martial law was declared in many areas. Under the dictates of martial law, the gathering at Jallianwala Bagh on the day of the massacre was unlawful. Despite the peaceful – and apolitical – nature of the Indian gathering, Dyer was unrepentant for his actions, arguing that he had helped quell what many colonial officers viewed as an indigenous uprising of potentially uncontrollable proportions through the 'moral effect' of his armed response. The massacre hardened opinions in both colonialist and nationalist camps. The nationalists, in particular Mohandas Gandhi, responded with a call for non-violent non-cooperation with the colonial state, which responded with ever more repressive ordinances to retain its control over Indian society. The 'crawling order', for example, promulgated in response to an attack on a British woman in Amritsar, made every Indian passing through the lane where the attack was perpetrated crawl along on all fours.

The non-co-operation movement started by Gandhi largely in response to the Rowlatt Acts and the Jallianwala Bagh massacre was the first mass movement of the Indian nationalist struggle. Dyer was officially censured for his actions, but received a hero's welcome in London. Many Britons felt that he had acted dutifully and that his had been the required response to the agitation extant in the Indian province of Punjab at the time. Chief among his defenders was Michael O'Dwyer, who had been lieutenant-governor of the Punjab at the time of the massacre. Some held O'Dwyer equally responsible for the atrocity. Udham Singh, a survivor of the massacre, assassinated him in London in 1940. Singh was tried in London and executed. His remains were returned to India in 1974, where he is revered as a nationalist hero and his portrait is prominently displayed in the memorial hall at Jallianwala Bagh.

Farina Mir

Literary Works

Hussein, Abdullah [1963 (Urdu)] (1999), *The Weary Generations*, London: Peter Owen.
Manto, Saadat Hasan [1951 (Urdu)] (1989), 'It Happened in 1919', in Jai Rattan (ed. and trans.), *The Best of Manto*, trans. Jai Rattan, Delhi: Sterling Publishers.
Rushdie, Salman (1980), *Midnight's Children*, London: Cape.
Scott, Paul (1976), *The Raj Quartet*, New York: Morrow.
Wolpert, Stanley (1970), *An Error of Judgment*, Boston, MA: Little, Brown and Company.

Histories

Draper, Alfred (1981), *Amritsar: The Massacre that Ended the Raj*, London: Cassell.
Furneaux, Rupert (1963), *Massacre at Amritsar*, London: Allen and Unwin.
Punjab Disturbances 1919–20 [1920] (1976), 2 vols, Report of the Commissioners, New Delhi: Deep Publications.

See also: **Anti-colonialism and Resistance: South Asia**.

James, C. L. R.

Cyril Lionel Robert James, historian, political theorist, and novelist, was born in Tunapuna, Trinidad in 1901. His father was a schoolteacher; his mother was, as he described in *Beyond a Boundary* (1963), 'a reader, one of the most tireless I have ever met'. The opening pages of this book reveal the major influences at work in James' early life: cricket, literature, and the British school code. As a young man, James was a central figure in the Beacon Group, a set of young intellectuals who published the small magazines, *Trinidad* and *The Beacon*. He migrated to England in 1932, where he was a cricket correspondent for the *Manchester Guardian* and active in Marxist and Pan-African political organisations.

He was an early advocate of decolonisation in Africa and the Caribbean, and his 1933 publication *The Life of Captain Cipriani: An Account of British Government in the West Indies* became a founding document in the cause of West Indian independence. In 1936 he published his only novel, *Minty Alley*, which expands on themes raised in his earlier short stories, 'La Divina Pastora' (1927) and 'Triumph' (1929): life struggles in the lower-class poverty of the barrack yard and the resiliency of the 'folk,' the common people of Trinidad. He did not forget those common people when he published his best-known work, *The Black Jacobins: Toussaint L'Ouverture and the San Domingo Revolution* (1938).

Although his Marxist account of L'Ouverture and the Haitian revolution was the first major historical study to popularise a black hero, his work affirms foremost that the masses, the anonymous enslaved men and women who resisted and prevailed, were indeed the makers of history.

In 1938 James travelled to the USA on a lecture tour; he remained in the USA, active in the Trotskyist movement until 1953 when he was interned at Ellis Island. He was later deported because of his political views. From 1958 to 1960 he travelled throughout the Caribbean lecturing on behalf of the West Indian Federation. In 1963 James published *Beyond a Boundary*, a combination of autobiography, cricket memoir, and cultural critique that narrates the story of Trinidadian cultural emergence within the context of its thoroughly British national sport. Although he never earned a university degree, James was a mentor to politicians, a role model for social historians, and a tireless activist for grass-roots political movements. James died in 1989.

Jennifer Sparrow

Literary Works

All works by C. L. R. James:

(1933), *The Life of Captain Cipriani: An Account of British Government in the West Indies*, Nelson: Coulton.

[1936] (1997), *Minty Alley*, Jackson, MS: University Press of Mississippi.

[1938] (1963), *The Black Jacobins: Toussaint L'Ouverture and the San Domingo Revolution*, New York: Vintage Books.

[1952] (1978), *Mariners, Renegades and Castaways: The Story of Herman Melville and the World We Live In*, Detroit, MI: Bewick Editions.

[1963] (1994), *Beyond a Boundary*, London: Serpent's Tail.

(1977), *The Future in the Present, Selected Writings, Volume 1*, Westport, CT: L. Hill.

(1980), *Spheres of Existence, Selected Writings, Volume 2*, Westport, CT: L. Hill.

(1984), *At the Rendezvous of Victory, Selected Writings, Volume 3*, London: Allison and Busby.

Histories

Buhle, Paul (1988), *C. L. R. James: The Artist as Revolutionary*, New York and London: Verso.

Buhle, Paul (ed.) (1986), *C. L. R. James: His Life and Work*, London: Allison and Busby.

Dhondy, Farrukh (2001), *C. L. R. James: A Life*, New York: Pantheon.

Farred, Grant (1996), *Rethinking C. L. R. James*, Oxford: Blackwell.

See also: **Anti-colonialism and Resistance: Caribbean; Black Britain; Pan-Africanism; Slavery: Caribbean.**

Japanese Internment: Canada

From their first arrival in Canada, particularly British Columbia, in the late nineteenth century, Japanese Canadians faced a racist environment in which they were seen as unassimilable. As a result, as World War II loomed, they quickly came to be seen as a threat to national security. Following the attack on Pearl Harbor, antagonism toward, and fear of, Japanese Canadians escalated and led to their eventual evacuation, internment, resettlement, and deportation. Regardless of age, sex, national status, or place of birth, 20,881 men, women and children of Japanese ancestry were required to register with the authorities and were then interned. The Canadian government designated a 100-mile wide protected area along the west coast which persons of Japanese origin were forced to evacuate. Fishing boats, licences and cars were impounded and confiscated, properties and chattels placed under the custody of a government agency, and all activity policed. Those detained were herded into a camp in Vancouver, where they awaited further removal to the British Columbia interior. The government should have provided housing, food, care and protection for the evacuees, but the Japanese Canadians' property was eventually liquidated and the funds from the sale used to finance their own internment.

Beginning in the spring of 1942, the evacuees were dispersed to ghost towns, isolated road camps and sugar beet farms, and had to cope with dreadful, overcrowded living conditions. Housing was scarce and ill-equipped to withstand the winter, and in some areas there was no electricity or running water. In the sugar beet farms, the backbreaking labour yielded only low wages. In addition, the camp residents suffered from inadequate health care and provision for education. In 1944, Prime Minister Mackenzie King announced his postwar reconstruction policy, which called for the permanent dispersal of the Japanese. Following Japan's surrender in 1945, the camp residents were given a choice between repatriating to Japan (and thus, in the cases of the naturalised and Canadian-born, relinquishing their British nationality) or relocating east of the Rockies. The camps were scheduled to be closed in November 1946, but the government continued to impose restrictions on Japanese Canadians until well after the war, with the last removed on 1 April 1949.

In the decades that followed, groups representing Japanese Canadians lobbied for the re-entry of Japanese Canadians who had been stranded in Japan at the outbreak of war in the Pacific, as well as the re-entry of repatriated people who had voluntarily complied with the deportation scheme. By the early 1980s, redress was being demanded, and, finally, in 1988 a settlement with the Canadian government was reached, providing a formal apology and $21,000 in direct cash payments to individuals who had been interned.

Batia Boe Stollar

Literary Works

Kogawa, Joy (1981), *Obasan*, Toronto: Lester and Orpen Dennys.
Kogawa, Joy (1992), *Itsuka*, Toronto: Viking Penguin.
Sakamoto, Kerri (1998), *The Electrical Field*, Toronto: Knopf.

Histories

Adachi, Ken (1991), *The Enemy That Never Was: A History of the Japanese Canadians*, Toronto: McClelland and Stewart.
Omatsu, Maryka (1992), *Bittersweet Passage: Redress and the Japanese Canadian Experience*, Toronto: Between the Lines.
Roy, Patricia, E. J. L. Granatstein, Musako Iino and Hiroko Takamura (1990), *Mutual*

Hostages: Canadians and Japanese during the Second World War, Toronto: University of Toronto Press.

Takata, Toyo (1983), *Nikkei Legacy: The Story of Japanese Canadians from Settlement to Today*, Toronto: N. C. Press.

See also: **Multiculturalism: Canada**.

Japanese Occupation: South-east Asia

For a three-and-a-half-year period (1942–5) of the Pacific War, following the British surrender to Japan in Singapore on 15 February 1942, Japan occupied most of South-east Asia (excepting Thailand), from Burma and Indochina to Malaya, Singapore, Borneo, Indonesia and the Philippines. The ostensible reasons for the Japanese invasion of South-east Asia were to free Asia from colonialism, and to establish the 'Greater East Asia Co-Prosperity Sphere'. The truth lay in Japan's need for raw materials which were abundant in these countries.

The war began with the Japanese attack on Pearl Harbor (Hawaii) on 7 December 1941. Japanese troops landed at Kota Bahru on the north-eastern coast of peninsular Malaya in the early hours of 8 December 1941. In what became known as the Seventy-Day War, the Japanese advance down Malaya was so swift that by 31 January 1942, they had reached Johore Bahru, just across the narrow Straits of Johore from Singapore. The actual onslaught on Britain's 'impregnable fortress' began on 9 February with the amphibious Japanese landing on the north-western part of Singapore. Despite being outnumbered and poorly equipped, the troops launched a fierce offensive; and within a week, the British under Lieutenant General A. E. Percival had surrendered to General Yamashita Tomoyuki, Commander of the 25th Army.

On 15 August 1945, shortly after atomic bombs were dropped on Hiroshima and Nagasaki, Japan announced an unconditional surrender. The Japanese occupation came to an official end on 12 September 1945 when General Itagaki Seishiro surrendered to Lord Louis Mountbatten, Supreme Allied Commander in South-east Asia, in Singapore. Despite Japan's eventual defeat, the Pacific War disproved ideas about the superiority of the white man and initiated the sequence of events which led to political independence for British colonies like Burma, Malaya/Malaysia, Singapore, as well as (French) Indo-China, (Dutch) Indonesia and the (American) Philippines. Arguably, in the diverse literature catalysed by this war may be found the beginnings of a 'national' literature (in English) for Malaysia and Singapore.

Leong Liew Geok

Literary Works

Barber, Noel (1981), *Tanamera: A Novel of Singapore*, London: Hodder and Stoughton.

Braddon, Russell (1951), *The Naked Island, with Drawings Made in Changi Prison Camp by Ronald Searle*, London: D. Laurie.

Chin Kee Onn [1952] (1981), *The Silent Army*, Singapore: Eastern Universities Press.

Choy, Elizabeth (1974), 'My Autobiography' [as told to Shirle' Gordon], *Intisari* IV: 1, pp. 12–65.

Farrell, J. G. [1978] (1984), *The Singapore Grip*, London: Flamingo.

Fusuyama, Takao (1997), *Memoir of Takao Fusuyama: A Japanese Soldier in Malaya and Sumatera*, Bangi: University Kebangsaan Malaysia.

Hammond, Robert (1984), *A Fearful Freedom: The Story of One Man's Survival Behind the Lines in Japanese Occupied Malaya, 1942–45*, London: L. Cooper, in assoc. with Secker and Warburg.

Hastain, Ronald (1947), *White Coolie*, London: Hodder and Stoughton.

Kathigasu, Sybil [1954] (1983), *No Dram of Mercy*, Singapore: Oxford University Press.

Mohd, Tajuddin Samsuddin (1984), *The Price has been High*, Kuala Lumpur: Arenabuku.

Sebastian, James (2000), *Man of the Rising Sun*, Singapore: Landmark.

Shelley, Rex (1993), *People of the Pear Tree*, Singapore: Times Books.

Takeyama, Michio [1966] (1992), *Harp of Burma*, trans. Howard Hibbett, Rutland, VT and Tokyo: Charles E. Tuttle.

Histories

Ban, Kah Choon and Hong Kuan Yap (2002), *Rehearsal for War: Resistance and the Underground War against the Japanese and the Kempeitai, 1942–1945*, Singapore: Horizon Books.

Cheah, Boon Kheng (1987), *Red Star over Malaya: Resistance and Social Conflict During and After the Japanese Occupation of Malaya, 1941–1946*, Singapore: Singapore University Press.

Farrell, Brian and Sandy Hunter (eds) (2002), *Sixty Years On: The Fall of Singapore Revisited*, Singapore: Eastern Universities Press.

Hayashi, Saburo, in collaboration with Alvin D. Cox [1959] (1978), *Kogun: The Japanese Army in the Pacific War*, Westport, CT: Greenwood.

Kratoska, Paul (1998), *The Japanese Occupation of Malaya: A Social and Economic History*, London: C. Hurst; Honolulu: University of Hawaii Press.

Lim, P. Pui Huen and Diana Wong (eds) (2000), *War and Memory in Malaysia and Singapore*, Singapore: Institute of South-east Asian Studies.

Ong, Chit Chung (1997), *Operation Matador: Britain's War Plans against the Japanese, 1918–1941*, Singapore: Times Academic Press.

Shinozaki, Mamoru (1975), *Syonan – My Story: The Japanese Occupation of Singapore*, Singapore: Asia-Pacific Press.

Silver, Lynette Ramsay (2000), *Sandakan: A Conspiracy of Silence*, Bowral: Sally Milner Publishing.

Tsuji, Masanobu [1960] (1988), *Singapore 1941–1942. The Japanese Version of the Malayan Campaign of World War II*, trans. Margaret E. Lake, Singapore: Oxford University Press.

Warren, Alan (2002), *Singapore 1942: Britain's Greatest Defeat*, Singapore: Talisman; London: Hambledon.

See also: **Anglo-Burmese Wars**; **Historiography: South-east Asia**; **East Asia**; **Women's Histories: South-east Asia**.

Jinnah, Mohammed Ali

Mohammed Ali Jinnah, the first governor-general of Pakistan and president of the Constituent Assembly, is remembered in Pakistan as the 'The Great Leader' and founder of the new state. Born in Karachi in 1876, he was a lawyer by profession. After his admission to the bar in England, he returned to India as an advocate at the Bombay High Court. Jinnah was actively involved in the freedom movement and for some time was a member of both the All India Congress (1906–20) and the All India Muslim League (which he joined in 1913). He was instrumental in negotiating the Lucknow Pact between Congress and League in 1916, an agreement critical for its concession of a separate communal electorate for Muslims. Jinnah felt the Nehru Report of 1927, an attempt to draft an independent Indian constitution, reneged on this principle. His opposition was outvoted and he withdrew from the Indian political scene, spending 1932 in London. On returning, he committed himself to the Muslim League. He was leader of the organisation from 1919 to 1947, turning it into a significant political force in the late 1930s and early 1940s.

Jinnah figures prominently in the heavily debated history of the partition of India and Pakistan. Jinnah and the Muslim League advocated a state that acknowledged their distinctive political and social identity as a group. In March 1940, the Muslim League passed a landmark resolution demanding the creation of autonomous regions demarcated by the majority religious affiliation. Historians are divided in their reading of this definitive moment. In recent years, the most convincing argument has favoured reading Jinnah's action as a strategy to gain legitimacy for group representation (see Jalal 1985). Supporters of this position emphasise the fact that Jinnah and the Muslim League approved of the 1946 Cabinet Mission Plan that would see a united India with three autonomous provinces and a centre with limited federal powers, but other historians argue the 1940 resolution was the first attempt to establish a separate state. The latter offer as evidence the Muslim League plan to withdraw support for the 1946 plan even before Jawaharlal Nehru stated that Congress would enter the Constituent Assembly without an agreement (see Sayeed 1960, p. 158). This plan marks the final attempt to formulate a single post-colonial state. Jinnah and the Muslim League agreed to a scheme to partition the subcontinent and to transfer power to the two successor states of India and Pakistan on 15 August 1947. Jinnah died in 1948.

Sukeshi Kamra

Literary Works

Rushdie, Salman (1981), *Midnight's Children*, Toronto: Vintage Canada.
Sidhwa, Bapsi (1991), *Cracking India: A Novel*, Minneapolis, MN: Milkweed Editions.
Tharoor, Shashi (1989), *The Great Indian Novel*, New York: Arcade.

Histories

Ahmad, Jamil-Ud-Din (ed.) (1960–4), *Speeches and Writing of Mr. Jinnah*, Lahore: Shaikh Muhammad Ashraf.
Ahmed, Akbar S. (1997), *Jinnah, Pakistan and Islamic Identity: The Search for Saladin*, London: Routledge.

Bolitho, Hector (1956), *Jinnah, Creator of Pakistan*, London: John Murray.
Jalal, Ayesha (1985), *The Sole Spokesman: Jinnah, the Muslim League and the Demand for Pakistan*, Cambridge: Cambridge University Press.
Jinnah, Mohammed Ali (1943), *Nationalism in Conflict*, Bombay: Home Study Circle.
Khairi, Saad (1995), *Jinnah Reinterpreted*, Karachi: Oxford University Press.
Sayeed, Khalid Bin (1960), *Pakistan: The Formative Phase*, Karachi: Pakistan Publishing House.
Wolpert, Stanley (1984), *Jinnah of Pakistan*, New York: Oxford University Press.

See also: **Historiography: South Asia; Partition**.

JVP Insurrection

The insurrection of 1971 is regarded as the first armed rebellion in modern Sri Lanka since independence. The JVP (Janatha Vimukthi Peramuna – People's Liberation Front) emerged from a group of dissidents within the Ceylon Communist Party in the mid-1960s under the leadership of Rohana Wijeweera. Initially it began as an underground political group, recruiting members from universities, trade unions and among the rural educated youth, with the aim of capturing state power. The leaders of the JVP were from the poorer strata of rural society and attracted considerable support from the rural masses. Led by Wijeweera, they disassociated themselves from traditional Marxist groups and built up an organisation and strategy which was in operation underground for almost six years, and indoctrinated large numbers of youths.

By the time of the 1970 parliamentary elections, the JVP had secured a significant support base. Its campaign in the post-election period pivoted around anti-government propaganda, and the acquisition of money and arms through violence and crime. On 16 March 1971, Wijeweera was arrested and the government declared a state of emergency, giving extraordinary powers to the armed forces. Beginning on the night of 5 April, attacks were launched on police stations throughout the country – ninety-three were attacked in the space of a few days. The civil administration in many areas collapsed almost completely and by 14 April all areas except Colombo had come under JVP control. The attacks on the police stations were designed to yield firearms and cripple government control over the rural areas, thus facilitating the capture of the cities. The JVP also anticipated a crossover of the lower ranks of the police and the army which would bolster public support.

On 6 April, the government proscribed the JVP and began its military counter-offensive. Thousands of youths were arrested, tortured, and killed or imprisoned. By the end of April there was only small and sporadic resistance. The estimated death toll was around 4,000–5,000; the official figure was 1,200 while the opposition claimed 5,000–10,000 had been killed and thousands were in custody.

This insurrection is considered the biggest by young people in any part of the world, hinging on a class revolt. Economic inequalities originating in unemployment and frustration were the key factors. Although the insurrection failed, and most of its leaders were imprisoned or killed, the JVP continued to have an ideological support base in the university student movement, and its radical character continued to attract large sections of youth, leading to a second, more pronounced insurrection in 1987–8.

Neluka Silva

Literary Works

Ondaatje, Michael (1982), *Running in the Family*, London: Picador.
Sarachchandra, Ediriweera (1978), *Curfew and a Full Moon*, Singapore: Heinemann.

Histories

Alles, A. C. (1990), *The JVP 1969–1989*, Colombo: Lake House Investments.
De Silva, K. M. (1981), *A History of Sri Lanka*, London: C. Hurst and Company.
Keerawella, G. B. (1980), 'The Janatha Vimukthi Peramuna and the 1971 Uprising', *Social Science Review* 2, pp. 1–55.
Uyangoda, Jayadeva (2003), 'Social Conflict, Radical Resistance and Projects of State Power in Southern Sri Lanka: The Case of the JVP', in Markus Mayer, Darini Rajasingham-Senanayake and Yuvi Thangarajah (eds), *Building Local Capacities for Peace: Rethinking Conflict and Development in Sri Lanka*, Delhi: Macmillan, pp. 37–64.

See also: **Sinhala Only Bill; Sri Lankan Civil War; Years of Terror.**

K

Kala Pani

The term *Kala Pani*, Sanskrit for 'dark waters', refers to the Vedic interdict against overseas travel for high-caste Hindus. The first explicit ban against travel by sea was articulated in the 500–300 BC *Dharmasutras*, which described it as a 'grave ritual impurity' and outlined a three-year penance period for the contaminated voyager (Basham 1964, p. 162). Over the next sixteen hundred years, Hindu texts reiterate the ban on transoceanic travel but limit this to Brahmins of the 'twice-born' caste. Basham suggests that Muslim migration to India and the opening of Islamic trade routes shifted Hindu trading practices away from the ocean and thus contributed to a religiously-sanctified 'antipathy' towards mariners and non-Hindus (Basham 1964, p. 165).

Although the term has religious roots, writers have adopted it as a metaphor for the 'dark waters' encountered by over a million indentured Indians who migrated to British plantation colonies in the nineteenth and early twentieth century. Recruits reflected the broad demographics of (North) Indian diversity, so it remains questionable to what extent Muslim, Christian, and Dalit migrants were concerned about losing caste. While Indians were enslaved in Mauritius and recruited to labour in the coffee, tea, and rubber plantations of Ceylon and Malaya, the production of Kala Pani narratives largely has arisen from the former sugar colonies of the Caribbean and Fiji. This can be traced to the centennial of Fiji-Indian indenture when Subramani and Vijay Mishra's edited collections drew from African diaspora studies and framed Indian migrations in terms of crossing Kala Pani (De Loughrey forthcoming). After the Fiji coups of 1987 and 2000, a secondary diaspora of Indo-Fijians to Australia and New Zealand gave rise to a body of poetry that framed Kala Pani in terms of the 'twice-banished' in writers such as Satendra Nandan. The most sustained literary engagement with the experience of crossing 'dark waters' remains J. S. Kanwal's historical novel, *The Morning* (1992). The rise of ethnic nationalism in the Caribbean, particularly Guyana and Trinidad, has also contributed to a secondary Indian diaspora and a deeper examination of what Ron Ramdin (1994) calls 'the other middle passage'. While Mauritian writers have explored 'coolitude', Indo-Caribbean authors have foregrounded migratory triangulations across the Atlantic. A growing body of work has concentrated on Indo-Caribbean women migrants, including the works of Ramabai Espinet, Verene Shepherd and Brinda Mehta.

Elizabeth De Loughrey

Literary Works

Birbalsingh, Frank (ed.) (1988), *Jahaji Bhai: An Anthology of Indo-Caribbean Literature*, Toronto: TSAR.
Dabydeen, David (1988), *Coolie Odyssey*, Coventry: Dangaroo Press.
Espinet, Ramabai (2003), *The Swinging Bridge*, Toronto: HarperCollins.
Kanwal, J. S. (1992), *The Morning (Savera)*, New Delhi: Diamond Publications.
Nandan, Satendra (1997), *Lines across Black Waters*, Adelaide: CRNLE.

Histories

Basham, A. L. (ed.) (1964), *Studies in Indian History and Culture*, Calcutta: Sambodhi Publications.
Carter, Marina and Khal Torabully (eds) (2002), *Coolitude: An Anthology of the Indian Labour Diaspora*, London: Anthem South Asian Studies.
De Loughrey, Elizabeth (forthcoming), *Routes and Roots: Navigating Caribbean and Pacific Island Literatures*, Ithaca, NY: Cornell University Press.
Lal, Brij (1999), *Crossing the Kala Pani: A Documentary History of Indian Indenture in Fiji*, Canberra: Division of Asian and Pacific History.
Mehta, Brinda (2004), *Diasporic (Dis)locations: Indo-Caribbean Women Writers Negotiate the 'Kala Pani'*, Kingston: University of West Indies Press.
Mishra, Vijay (ed.) (1979), *Rama's Banishment: A Centenary Tribute to the Fiji Indians 1879–1979*, Auckland: Heinemann Educational Books.
Ramdin, Ron (ed.) (1994), *The Other Middle Passage: Journal of a Voyage from Calcutta to Trinidad, 1858*, London: Hansib Publications.
Shepherd, Verene A. (2002), *Maharani's Misery: Narratives of a Passage from India to the Caribbean*, Mona: University of West Indies Press.
Subramani (ed.) (1979), *The Indo-Fijian Experience*, Queensland: University of Queensland Press.
Tinker, Hugh (1974), *A New System of Slavery: The Export of Indian Labour Overseas 1830–1920*, London: Oxford University Press.

See also: **Castes: South Asia; Diaspora: Caribbean; Diaspora: Pacific; Diaspora: South Asia; Indentured Labour: Caribbean; Religions: South Asia; Slavery: Caribbean.**

Kama Sutra

The *Kama Sutra* is a collection of writings about sexuality and the pursuit of pleasure, compiled by the celibate monk Vatsayana Mallanaga in the fourth century. Very little is known about him, other than what can be gleaned from the text itself. The *Kama Sutra* was first produced in Sanskrit, the literary language of ancient India. The text presents a practical guide to love and sex for the well-to-do urban man. Topics include the pursuit of a wife, the keeping of a courtesan, and lists of often-acrobatic sexual positions, among other matters. Subsequent erotic texts, including the twelfth-century *Ratirahasya* by Kokkoka, and the fifteenth-century *Ananga Ranga* by Kalyanamalla, drew upon the *Kama Sutra* as the authoritative text in literary representations of Indian eroticism.

Illustrated editions of the *Kama Sutra* began to appear by the fifteenth century, and seventeenth- and eighteenth-century Persian illustrated erotic literature borrowed from this. The nineteenth-century British explorer Richard F. Burton is frequently credited as the translator of the *Kama Sutra* for English readers in 1883. More precisely, Burton commissioned a sanitised translation through his collaborator, F. F. Arbuthnot, with the actual work of translation done by Indian scholars Bhagavanlal Indrajit and Shivaram Parashuram Bhide. Burton's edition has served as the basis of many early twentieth-century publications in the West. German Orientalist Richard Schmidt published a translation of the *Kama Sutra* in 1897, and Schmidt's scholarship on Indian erotica had a formative effect on the work of Alex Comfort, particularly the *Joy of Sex* (1972).

Throughout the twentieth century Indian scholars published their own translations of the *Kama Sutra*, in English and vernacular languages, sometimes editing out parts concerning prostitution and homosexuality. The mid-twentieth-century relaxation of literary obscenity laws globally and the advent of the sexual revolution of the 1960s began a publishing frenzy of dozens of reprints of Burton's *Kama Sutra* around the world, a trend continuing to the present. The *Kama Sutra* has become a household term for sexual knowledge when published as erotica or used as a brand name for consumer products including condoms, tonics and sex kits. In this way, it is an important part of contemporary global sexual consumer culture.

Anne Hardgrove

Literary Works

Siegel, Lee (1999), *Love in a Dead Language*, Chicago: University of Chicago Press.
Vatsyayana (2002), *Kamasutra*, trans. W. Doniger and S. Kakar, New York: Oxford University Press.

Histories

Brodie, Fawn (1967), *The Devil Drives: A Life of Sir Richard Burton*, New York: Ballantine.
Peterson, Valerie (2002), 'The Text as Cultural Antagonist: The *Kama Sutra* of Vatsyayana', *Journal of Communication Inquiry* 26: 2, pp. 133–54.
Puri, Jyoti (2002), 'Concerning Kamasutras: Challenging Narratives of History and Sexuality', *Signs* 27: 3, pp. 603–39.

Roy, Kumkum (1998), 'Unravelling the Kamasutra' in M. E. John and J. Nair (eds), *A Question of Silence? The Sexual Economies of Modern India*, London: Zed Books, pp. 11–34.

Zysk, Kenneth (2002), *Conjugal Love in India: Ratisastra and Ratiramana. Text, Translation, and Notes*, Leiden: Brill Academic Publishers.

See also: **Women's Histories: South Asia**.

Kashmir Dispute

The Kashmir Dispute is rooted in the period of flux which marked the end of British colonial rule and the partition of India in August 1947. The division was on religious lines with Muslim majority areas of eastern and western British India forming the new state of Pakistan. Over 600 'princely states', ruled by independent monarchs, hitherto suzerainties of the British Empire, were required to join either of the two new dominions. Until the mid-nineteenth century, when the Dogra chieftains consolidated their kingdom, the state of Jammu and Kashmir simply did not exist. Its constituent regions of Jammu, Kashmir, Ladakh, Mirpur, Muzzafarabad, Gilgit and Baltistan were divided demographically by separate histories, ethnicities, languages, religions, cultures and politics. Although its monarch, Maharaja Hari Singh, was Hindu, the idea of joining an India which was to be secular, socialist and democratic, and where his hereditary rights were to be forfeited, was anathema. An Islamic Pakistan that was guaranteeing these was more attractive, but still problematic. His dilemma was further complicated by the politics of the time with the Muslims, a numerical majority, fractured along class lines.

In 1939, the Muslim Conference led by the charismatic Sheikh Abdullah of the Kashmir valley, became the National Conference (NC) to reflect its nationalist, secular and socialist values. Abdullah, greatly influenced by the leftist intellectuals of Punjab and Kashmir had led the popular Quit Kashmir agitation against the monarchy, and later launched the New Kashmir movement which called for land reforms favouring the tiller over the feudal owner. Ideologically, Abdullah and the NC tilted towards the idea of a secular, democratic India rather than an Islamic Pakistan. These developments greatly disturbed the Muslim elite who, reviving the Muslim Conference favouring accession to Pakistan, were popular in Mirpur and Muzzafarabad, but found only limited support in the Kashmir valley. Thus, by August 1947 when most of the princely states had acceded to either India or Pakistan, Kashmir still remained undecided. Events were precipitated by a revolt of the Maharaja's Muslim troops in Poonch, an economic blockade by Pakistan, and subsequent raids in mid-October 1947 by armed tribesman from the North-west Frontier Province of Pakistan, backed by Pakistani irregulars. The Maharaja released the incarcerated Abdullah who raised 15,000 Kashmiri volunteers to fight the invaders, and sought military assistance from India. India agreed only after the Maharaja had signed the instrument of accession in its favour, and on 27 October 1947, dispatched airborne troops to the valley. Fierce fighting ensued with Pakistani regulars joining the fray until the UN-brokered ceasefire of 1 January 1949. A ceasefire line was drawn with India holding Jammu, the Kashmir valley and Ladakh, and Pakistan controlling the areas of Mirpur and Muzzafarabad, Gilgit and Baltistan.

India had complained of Pakistani aggression to the UN in December 1947 under Article 35 of the UN Charter, which requires the UN to undertake investigations into situations 'likely to endanger . . . international peace and security', and to issue its findings as an advisory brief. Under Article 35 the UN could not impose a solution. The issue of a plebiscite, which was to sour Indo-Pakistan relations over Kashmir for decades, was a verbal assurance Indian Prime Minister Nehru made to the Kashmiri people in an emotional speech of 2 November 1947. The UN resolution of 13 August 1948 recommended that following a withdrawal of Pakistani tribesmen and troops under UN supervision, India would agree to maintain minimum strength of its forces, and once peace was restored India and Pakistan would determine 'the future status of the State of Jammu and Kashmir . . . in accordance with the will of the people . . .' Pakistan refused to withdraw its troops and India refused to hold a plebiscite until Pakistan did so. Although the scope of the UN resolutions included the entire state of Jammu and Kashmir, following the armed separatist movement in the Kashmir valley in 1989, any discussion of the 'Kashmir Dispute' became confined to the status of the areas which are part of the Indian Union, particularly the valley, a small swathe of land measuring seventy-five by twenty-five miles, with a Muslim majority.

India maintains that Jammu and Kashmir is an integral part of India, that the instrument of accession is the legal basis of its claim to and control of the state, and that its army is stationed there as a right of nation states to defend their territories. It regards the numerous elections held in the state since 1947, the presence of the state assembly, the constitution of Kashmir (drafted by Kashmiris and separate from the Indian constitution), and the special provisions of Article 370 of the Indian constitution as acts which have more than compensated for the absence of the plebiscite. It views political disturbances in Kashmir since the 1950s as an 'internal matter'. Pakistan is regarded as having no *locus standi* with its presence in Jammu and Kashmir illegal (though India is willing to relinquish claim over those territories if Pakistan were amenable to give up its claim on India's, and to convert the line of control into an international border). Lastly, India describes the insurgency as a 'proxy war' conducted by Pakistan on its soil, particularly since the mid-1990s when terrorist strikes, hitherto confined to the valley, have become commonplace in Indian metropolises.

Pakistan's position is that by the logic of the partition of India, Jammu and Kashmir ought to have naturally gone over to it; that the accession itself was illegal since the Maharaja had no authority to execute the instrument of accession when the people had revolted against him; and that it considered itself a party to the dispute. Pakistan renamed the region of Mirpur and Muzzafarabad as Azad (free) Kashmir, which though it has its own prime minister and president, is administered by the Ministry of Kashmir Affairs in Islamabad. Prospective candidates for the forty-two-seat legislative assembly have to sign an affidavit declaring that they support the accession of Azad Jammu and Kashmir to Pakistan. In 1949 Pakistan issued a proclamation separating Gilgit and Baltistan from Azad Kashmir and placing them under the administration of the federal government under the name of Northern Areas of Pakistan. However, there is no adult franchise, no constitution guaranteeing fundamental rights, and no democratic representation. On India's charge of fomenting terrorism in Kashmir, Pakistan claims to provide only moral support to the seccessionists.

The Kashmiris are also divided on the issue of accession. Initially, the armed struggle for an independent Kashmir was launched by the Jammu and Kashmir Liberation Front (JKLF) which was soon decimated and hijacked by numerous Pakistan-based armed groups fighting for Kashmir's merger with Pakistan. India responded with strong military force, provoking censure from human rights groups around the world when civilians were mercilessly targeted. Apart from Jammu and Ladakh, both pro-India, all Kashmir is not with the separatists. The NC (pro-India) has a large support base in the valley, which was eaten into by the People's Democratic Party, presently in power after the 2002 assembly elections. Also involved in Kashmir's electoral politics and fairly popular are mainstream Indian parties like the Congress and Communist Party of India. However, since the early 1990s any vocal opposition to the separatists, whether by Kashmiri Hindus or Muslims has been brutally repressed by the militants.

Sonia Jabber

Literary Works

Ali, Agha Shahid (1998), *The Country without a Post Office*, New York: Norton.
Jabber, Sonia (2002), 'Blood Soil', in Urvashi Butalia (ed.), *Speaking Peace: Women's Voices from Kashmir*, New Delhi: Kali for Women, pp. 226–40.
Jabber, Sonia (2003), 'Spirit of Place', in Kalpana Sharma, Ammu Joseph (eds) *Terror, Counter-Terror*, London: Zed Books, pp. 184–211.
Koul, Sudha (2002), *The Tiger Ladies: A Memoir of Kashmir*, London: Review/Headline Book Publishing.
Rushdie, Salman (1981), *Midnight's Children*, London: Jonathan Cape.

Histories

Abdullah, Sheikh (1993), *Flames of the Chinar*, New Delhi: Viking.
Ali, Tariq (2002), *The Clash of Fundamentalisms: Crusades, Jihads and Modernity*, London: Verso.
Behera, Navnita Chadha (2000), *State, Identity and Violence: Jammu, Kashmir and Ladakh*, New Delhi: Manohar.
Hewitt, Vernon (1995), *Reclaiming the Past: The Search for Political and Cultural Unity in Contemporary Jammu and Kashmir*, London: Portland Books.
Jha, Prem Shankar (1998), *1947: Rival Versions of History*, New Delhi: Oxford University Press.
Puri, Balraj (1993), *Kashmir: Towards Insurgency*, New Delhi: Orient Longman.

See also: **Border disputes: South Asia; Partition.**

Kaunda, Kenneth David

Born in Lubwa in Northern Rhodesia (Zambia) in 1924 to parents who were both teachers, Kenneth Kaunda also worked, in his early years, as a teacher in Tanganyika (Tanzania) and Zambia. In 1948, he started working as a welfare officer at Chingoal copper mine, and also served as an interpreter for the Northern Rhodesian Legislative Council.

Kaunda became involved in politics in the early 1950s, working as organiser and later secretary-general in the African National Congress (ANC) in the campaign against the Federation of Northern Rhodesia, Southern Rhodesia and Nyasaland. Frustrated with ANC leader Harry Nkumbula's cautious style, Kaunda left the party in 1958. Dedicating his efforts to organising mass actions in the copper-belt, Kaunda was imprisoned in 1959–60, and upon his release formed the more radical United National Independence

Party (UNIP). In 1962, UNIP was at the centre of a large-scale civil disobedience campaign, a year later the federation was abolished, and in 1964 UNIP won fifty-five of the sixty-five seats in the first elections, with Kaunda installed as Zambia's first president on 24 October of the same year.

Espousing his inclusive nationalist ideology of 'Zambian Humanism' (see Kaunda 1973; Kandeke 1977), Kaunda contained ethnic differences within the new nation, and in the first years of his rule enjoyed economic growth. However, two factors interrupted the steady progress: (Southern) Rhodesia's unilateral declaration of independence (UDI) in 1965, and the collapse of the world copper market in the 1970s. Concerning UDI, Zambia joined the rest of the world in imposing sanctions on Rhodesia, but suffered more than others as a result because it lost a major trading partner, and access to key transport routes to the sea. The effects of the plummeting world copper prices were even more damaging, as Zambia's economy had been fundamentally restructured to service copper exports. Zambians endured even greater economic hardship in the 1980s when the IMF imposed structural adjustment policies. Although never repressive in the brutal fashion of Banda in Malawi, Kaunda did also introduce one-party rule in 1973, and became more authoritarian as criticism of the state's economic and bureaucratic mismanagement mounted in the 1980s. Kaunda acquiesced to this pressure by authorising elections in 1991, which he lost to the former trade unionist Frederick Chiluba.

During his period in office, Kaunda had played a prominent role in African politics, supporting anti-colonial and anti-apartheid struggles in south-west Africa (Namibia), South Africa, and Zimbabwe, and also chairing the Organisation of African Unity (1970–1, 1988–9), the Frontline States (1985), and the Non-Aligned Movement (1970–3). Since losing power, he has continued to have an international profile as an AIDS campaigner and as an advocate of debt relief for African countries.

David Johnson

Literary Works

Chipeta, Dominic (1986), *The Pregnant Clouds*, Lusaka: Kenneth Kaunda Foundation.
Ellison, Gabriel (1998), *Chisi: A Woman of Courage*, Lusaka: Bookworld.
Kaunda, Kenneth (1973), *Letter to my Children*, Harlow: Longman.
Liswaniso, Mufalo (ed.) (1971), *Voices of Zambia: Short Stories*, Lusaka: Neczam.
Mulaisho, Dominic (1971), *The Tongue of the Dumb*, London: Heinemann.
Simushi, Lucy Siyumbwa (2000), *I Nearly Killed a President*, Lusaka: Multimedia.
Sinyangwe, Binwell (2000), *A Cowrie of Hope*, London: Heinemann.

Histories

Anglin, Douglas George (1994), *Zambian Crisis Behaviour: Confronting Rhodesia's Unilateral Declaration of Independence, 1965–1966*, Montreal: McGill-Queen's University Press.
Chan, Stephen (1992), *Kaunda and Southern Africa: Image and Reality in Foreign Policy*, London: British Academic Press.
Esomba, Stephen Nangoh (1996), *Zambia under Kaunda's Presidency: The Conditions, Experiment with Socialism, and the Final Lap to Democracy*, Hamburg: Hochschulschriften.

Gertzel, Cherry J. (ed.) (1984), *The Dynamics of the One-Party State in Zambia*, Manchester: Manchester University Press.

Hamalengwa, Munyonzwe (1992), *Class Struggles in Zambia, 1889–1989 and the Fall of Kenneth Kaunda, 1990–1991*, Lanham, MD: University Press of America.

Hansen, Karen Tranberg (1997), *Keeping House in Lusaka*, New York: Columbia University Press.

Kandeke, Timothy K. (1977), *Fundamentals of Zambian Humanism*, Lusaka: National Education Company of Zambia.

See also: **Anti-colonialism and Resistance: Southern Africa; Banda, Ngwazi Hastings Kamazu; Migrancy: Southern Africa.**

Kelly, Ned

Bushranging was an integral part of European colonial Australia's rural history. The Kelly outbreak, led by Ned Kelly, is generally seen as the last significant outbreak of bushranging in Australia and took place in north-eastern Victoria between 1878 and 1880.

Ned Kelly was born in December 1854. His father was an Irish ex-convict, John Kelly. His mother, Ellen Quinn, was the daughter of free immigrant parents from Ireland. By the 1860s, the Quinn clan had gained a reputation for criminal activity, especially when it came to stock theft, and Ned Kelly came early to the attention of the police. He first saw the inside of Victoria's prisons at the age of sixteen.

The Kelly outbreak was triggered by an attempt to arrest Dan Kelly, Ned's brother, on a charge of stock theft by Trooper Alexander Fitzpatrick in April 1878. Fitzpatrick claimed that the Kellys had tried to murder him. The police arrested Mrs Kelly and she was sentenced to three years' hard labour. They declined an offer by the brothers to surrender themselves if their mother was released. Instead, they sent two heavily armed parties into the bush to find them. In a gun battle at Stringybark Creek in October 1878, three policemen were shot dead. The Kelly brothers and their companions, Steve Hart and Joe Byrne, were declared outlaws and a reward was put on their heads. A massive police hunt for the four outlaws followed but came up with nothing. In December 1878, the Kelly gang emerged from hiding and held up the bank at Euroa. The reward jumped. In February 1879, the gang appeared in Jerilderie in New South Wales, robbing another bank. The reward was raised to £8,000; and black trackers from Queensland were brought into the hunt. But again, the gang seemed to have vanished.

The Kellys did not reappear until June 1880 at Glenrowan, where Ned Kelly was captured and his three companions were killed. Kelly was hanged on 11 November 1880 for the murder of one of the policemen at Stringybark Creek. Ned Kelly always maintained that he had been driven to outlawry by police persecution and he set out his claims in the 'Jerilderie Letter'. His claim was not as self-serving as it sounds. More importantly, Ned Kelly seemed to touch a chord with many ordinary Australians. He and his gang remained at large because of the support or sympathy they commanded from most of the population of the north-east between 1878 and 1880. After his sentence, a massive agitation for a reprieve drew over 30,000 signatures in Melbourne. The outbreak itself was as much a social protest as a personal one. Some argue Glenrowan was planned as the start of an insurrection with a republican aim. Ned Kelly was a legendary figure even before his execution and, since 1880, his legend has been explored through novels, plays,

films, opera, folk songs and paintings. Something in this man's story is still relevant to
Australians today.

John McQuilton

Literary Works

Balcarek, Dagmar (1984), *Ellen Kelly*, Glenrowan: The author.
Bedford, Jean (1982), *Sister Kate: A Novel*, Ringwood: Penguin.
Carey, Peter (2000), *True History of the Kelly Gang*, St Lucia: University of Queensland
    Press.
Chandler, A. Bertram (1983), *Kelly Country*, Ringwood: Penguin.
Drewe, Robert (1992), *Our Sunshine*, Ringwood: Penguin.
Langford, Garry (1980), *The Adventures of Dreaded Ned*, Beecroft: Randolph Press.
Stewart, Douglas [1943] (1969), *Ned Kelly*, Sydney: Angus and Robertson.

Histories

Jones, Ian [1995] (2003), *Ned Kelly: A Short Life*, Port Melbourne: Lothian Books.
McDermott, Alex (ed.) (2001), *The Jerilderie Letter by Ned Kelly*, Melbourne: Text
    Publishing.
McQuilton, John [1979] (2004), *The Kelly Outbreak 1878–1880: The Geographical
    Dimension of Social Banditry*, Carlton: University of Melbourne Press.
Moloney, John [1981] (2001), *Ned Kelly*, Carlton: Melbourne University Press.
Morgan, Wendy (1994), *Ned Kelly Reconstructed*, Melbourne: Cambridge University Press.
Phillips, John Harber (1987), *The Trial of Ned Kelly*, North Ryde: Law Book Company.
Seal, Graham (2002), *'Tell 'Em I Died Game': The Legend of Ned Kelly*, Flemington: Hyland
    House.

See also: **Historiography: Australia; Rebellions: Australia.**

Kemalism

The Ottoman Empire, which ruled over most of North Africa and the Middle East from the
early sixteenth century, was defeated in World War I. By the end of the war, a national resistance movement under Mustafa Kemal Paşa, a general in the army, kept European imperial
interests at bay, defeated a short-lived Armenian Republic and overcame a Greek invasion
in 1922. The modern Turkish republic was proclaimed in October 1923 with its capital in
Ankara. Mustafa Kemal ruled the new republic until his death in 1938. His Republican
People's Party (RPP) had support in the army, and among civil servants and the urban elite.
It had much less support among peasants and in small towns. The RPP implemented an
aggressive programme of Westernisation. Among the changes imposed were: the Arabic
alphabet was replaced by the Latin alphabet; the fez and other symbols of Ottoman Islamic
life were banned; the remaining vestiges of Islamic law were replaced by the Swiss Civil
Code; Sufi brotherhoods such as the Mevlevi ('whirling dervishes') based in Konya were
proscribed, and a series of other regulations were imposed fully to 'modernise' Turkey.
    Over time the modern nation-state of Turkey was represented as being wholly European,

having cast aside the spell of retrogressive religion. Mustafa Kemal was the master architect of these secularising policies still very much pursued as an ideal today. They are conveniently captured in the term Kemalism. He took the surname of 'Ataturk' ('father of the Turks') when he made surnames obligatory. His official Turkish nationalism and republicanism has been highly secularist and modernist and is embodied in the constitution and state policies. A rigid secularism is cast against 'Islamism', and distinctive ethnic aspirations, such as those of the Kurds.

No opposition was tolerated from the outset of the republican period. The Kurdish language was banned and only through underground and guerrilla struggle have the Kurds been able to advance their cause. The first really free elections were held in 1950, which the RPP lost, and there followed a decade of parliamentary politics under the Democratic Party until a military coup in 1960. Since then the military has never been genuinely kept outside of politics. Ataturk still looms very large more than sixty years after his death. Various images of him – from larger-than-life paintings to miniature statues – can be seen throughout Turkish public space. It is against Turkish law to criticise him; even Islamist political parties have had to avoid appearing to criticise him and his legacy.

Shamil Jeppie

Literary Works

Gun, Guneli (1979), *A Book of Trances*, London: Friedmann.
Kemal, Yashar [1974] (1997), *Iron Earth, Copper Sky*, trans. T. Kemal, London: Harvill.
Pamuk, Orhan (2002), *My Name is Red*, trans. E. M. Golinar, London: Faber and Faber.

Histories

Kazancigil, Ali and Ergun Özbundun (1981), *Atatürk: Founder of a Modern State*, London: C. Hurst and Co.
Navarro, Yael (2002), *Faces of the State: Secularism and Public Life in Turkey*, Princeton, NJ: Princeton University Press.
Yavuz, Hakan M. (2003), *Islamic Political Identity in Turkey*, New York: Oxford University Press.

See also: **Islam; Levant Company; Nationalism(s): Arab; Ottoman Empire**.

Kenya African National Union

The KANU (Kenya African National Union), Kenya's first national party, was formed in May 1960 with the aim of uniting the African representatives in the legislative council into one political party. Oginga Odinga writes that each member of the legislative council was to bring sixteen representatives, and the district associations up and down the country were to be converted into branches of KANU, thereby providing it with some grassroots base (Odinga 1967, p. 193). Although there was determination that Jomo Kenyatta would be the president of KANU, this was not possible because the colonial government had threatened not to register the new party if Kenyatta was made its president. James Gichuru was elected KANU president, on the understanding that he would be holding the seat for

Kenyatta. Oginga Odinga was elected vice-president; Tom Mboya, general secretary; and Ochwada, assistant secretary-general.

Right from the moment of its inception, KANU was racked with internal rivalry and suspicion. The major source of fear, partly fuelled by the settler minority, was that the minority ethnic communities in Kenya would be dominated by the Kikuyu and Luo alliance. It was feared that the minority groups would have their interests and welfare subordinated to majority dictatorship in an independent Kenya. It was these fears that led to the formation of KADU (Kenya African Democratic Union) on 25 June 1960, whose remit was the care of minority interests. KADU's fears were rooted in the belief that KANU would appropriate the lands historically owned by minority ethnic groups. KANU, which had positioned itself as the heir to the Kenyan African Union (KAU), attracted huge followings in Central Province, the home ground of KAU before its proscription under the state of emergency in October 1952. KANU continued to gain ground, and in the 1961 general elections it improved its national mandate, emerging victorious over KADU and gaining the legitimacy to press for Kenyatta's release. The 1962 Lancaster House conference led to a coalition government, in which KANU entered government for the first time. In 1963, KANU won the elections and formed the government. Overall KANU emerged looking like a true nationalist party with seats in every region and two-thirds of the vote. With this widespread strength, Kenyatta had the confidence to form a broad-based national government thereby placing KANU in a position that would see it dominate Kenya's political scene for the next thirty-nine years. When KADU was dissolved in 1964 and joined KANU, Kenyatta's national power was beyond challenge. Over the years KANU grew into a *de jure* one-party state in which presidential authority and that of the party were virtually collapsed into one, both under Kenyatta and Moi leadership, until KANU's massive electoral defeat by the National Rainbow Coalition (NARC) under the leadership of Mwai Kibaki in December 2002.

James Ogude

Literary Works

Ngugi wa Thiong'o (1967), *A Grain of Wheat*, London: Heinemann.
Ngugi wa Thiong'o (1977), *Petals of Blood*, London: Heinemann.

Histories

Bennett, George and Carl G. Rosberg (1961), *The Kenyatta Election: Kenya, 1960–1961*, London: Oxford University Press.
Kenyatta, Jomo (1968), *Suffering without Bitterness*, Nairobi: East Africa Publishing House.
Kyle, Keith (1999), *The Politics of the Independence of Kenya*, London: Macmillan Press.
Odinga, Oginga (1967), *Not Yet Uhuru*, London: Heinemann.
Ogot, B. A. and W. R. Ochieng' (1995), *Decolonisation and Independence in Kenya 1940–93*, London: James Currey.
Ogot, Bethwell (1981), *Historical Dictionary of Kenya*, London: The Scarecrow Press.
The KANU Manifesto for Independence, Social Democracy and Stability (1960), Nairobi: Press and Publicity Department, Kenya African National Union.

See also: **Anti-colonialism and Resistance: East Africa; Historiography: East Africa.**

Khama, Seretse

Postcolonial literary works on Botswana often invoke the good governance associated with the name of Seretse Khama as the country's first president, or make reference to other members of the Khama family. Seretse Khama was born in 1921 to be the hereditary leader of the BaNgwato people, the largest pre-colonial kingdom enclosed by the British protectorate of Bechuanaland (Botswana). He was the grandson of Khama III (c. 1835–1923), who achieved world fame as a Christian temperance king and for saving the country from white settlement and becoming part of Rhodesia or South Africa.

While a student in London in 1948, Seretse Khama married an Englishwoman, Ruth Williams, and thus offended his uncle Tshekedi Khama, who was acting as regent for him. After vigorous protests in South African and Rhodesian governing circles, Seretse was barred from chieftainship in 1950 and exiled to London with his wife by the British government. There was considerable political controversy and media attention as British authorities refused to admit bowing before white racism. In 1956 Seretse and his wife were permitted to return home as ordinary citizens. He founded a political party, which was voted into power in 1965.

At independence in 1966, Botswana was possibly the poorest state in Africa, and was seen as a helpless hostage of white neighbours that almost entirely surrounded it. Over the next few years Seretse Khama, as president, quietly oversaw the construction of effective and uncorrupt government, the achievement of national unity among diverse peoples, and the beginnings of rapid economic growth that was to continue for decades. As a prosperous and stable non-racial democracy, Botswana was ready to challenge the credibility of unstable, white-ruled neighbouring states in the 1970s and 1980s. President Khama took Botswana into the 1970s alliance known as the Front-Line States, collaborating closely with Presidents Nyerere of Tanzania and Kaunda of Zambia, and by 1979 was seen as the leading figure in the alliance – in converting it into an economic community, and in its facilitating the independence of Zimbabwe just before his death in 1980. Ruth Khama lived on near the Botswana capital, Gaborone, and died there in 2002. Their son Ian Khama became the country's vice-president.

As a love story and as a tale of moral courage, the tale of Seretse and his wife Ruth inspired a play banned from the London stage at the time of the marriage controversy, and since then a number of biographies, television documentaries, and one feature film (ultimately much changed by Hollywood) *Guess Who's Coming to Dinner?* Seretse Khama and other members of the Khama family are major reference points in the literary works of Bessie Head, who lived in their home town of Serowe, and for the fictional characters of the Gaborone-based novels of Norman Rush and Alexander McCall Smith.

Neil Parsons

Literary Works

Head, Bessie (1972a), *When Rain Clouds Gather*, London: Heinemann.
Head, Bessie (1972b), *Maru*, London: Heinemann.
Head, Bessie (1981), *Serowe: Village of the Rain Wind*, London: Heinemann.
McCall Smith, Alexander (1998), *The No. 1 Ladies' Detective Agency*, Edinburgh: Polygon.
McCall Smith, Alexander (2000), *Tears of the Giraffe*, Edinburgh: Polygon.

Rush, Norman (1986), *Whites*, London: Heinemann.
Rush, Norman (1992), *Mating*, London: Jonathan Cape.

Histories

Parsons, Neil (1998), *King Khama, Emperor Joe, and the Great White Queen: Victorian Britain
    through African Eyes*, Chicago and London: University of Chicago Press.
Tlou, Thomas, Neil Parsons and Willie Henderson (1995), *Seretse Khama, 1921–1980*,
    Gaborone: Botswana Society; Johannesburg: Macmillan Boleswa.

See also: **Migrancy: Southern Africa; Nationalism(s): Southern Africa.**

L

Labour Histories: Southern Africa

Labour organisation in South Africa originated in the 1880s and 1890s with the formation
of unions and small socialist groups amongst migrant British, Australian and German
workers in Cape Town, Kimberley and Johannesburg. In the post-Boer War period, these
organisations developed into a substantial labour movement, centred on the goldmines of
the Witwatersrand, which was extremely militant but exclusively white and determined to
exclude black workers from skilled jobs. This movement was involved in major, violent
confrontations with employers and the state in 1907, 1913, 1914, and above all in the 1922
Rand revolt, when several hundred people were killed in fighting between armed strikers
and government forces.

   Black trade unionism originated during World War I with the Industrial Workers of
Africa, who organised significant strikes on the Rand in 1917 and 1918. The Industrial and
Commercial Workers' Union (ICU), formed in 1919 and led by a charismatic Malawian,
Clements Kadalie, made a greater impact with strikes and protests by rural workers across
the country before collapsing at the end of the 1920s largely because of internal leadership
conflicts.

   The political organisation of labour in the first half of the twentieth century was dominated by the South African Labour Party (founded in 1909), which represented white
labour's interests; and the Communist Party of South Africa (CPSA – formed in 1921),
which briefly supported the white workers in the 1922 revolt, but then reoriented to organising black labour. Although the communists attained some success in initiating unions
and in influencing the ICU, they were decimated by the self-destructive policies pursued
by the Comintern in the early 1930s, which led to the expulsion of all the party's most able
leaders. The 1930s saw the emergence of small unions, some under Trotskyist leadership,

as well as a bold attempt by the ex-communist Solly Sachs, leader of the Garment Workers' Union, to organise white and black women in a single militant union. In the 1940s, both the unions and the CPSA revived, and their activities culminated in a massive strike of black mine workers in 1946. The Communist Party dissolved itself under threat of government banning in 1950, but later re-emerged in clandestine form as the South African Communist Party (SACP). The SACP controlled the South African Congress of Trade Unions (SACTU), a union federation aligned with the African National Congress which was prominent in the 1950s.

When SACTU and the ANC were driven underground by the state in 1960, a decade of labour quiescence began. Labour organisation continued in the very restrained form of the segregated black and white unions grouped around the Trades Union Congress of South Africa (TUCSA). By the early 1970s, old ANC and SACTU activists, some TUCSA organisers, and groupings of white students influenced by the ideas of the European New Left, were working to encourage more militant forms of unionism. In early 1973, their work contributed to a wave of strikes in the Durban area, which opened a new period of trade union militancy. By the end of the 1970s, the impact of militant new unions had forced the apartheid government to concede significant labour and organisational rights to urban black workers. The 1980s were to see the all-time high point of South African labour militancy, as ever-increasing numbers of workers were unionised (most significantly black mineworkers by the National Union of Mineworkers led by Cyril Ramaphosa), and unions combined with the political movements to oppose apartheid by organising political strikes and stayaways. There were important ideological divisions amongst the trade unionists of the 1980s: the 'workerist' faction of the unions, grouped around the Federation of South African Trade Unions (FOSATU), stressed strong workplace organisation and working-class independence from political leaders, whereas the 'populist' unions were ideologically aligned with the underground ANC. In 1985, the workerist and populist strands came together in the Congress of South African Trade Unions (COSATU), but COSATU has remained internally divided along nationalist versus working-class/socialist lines. Since the 1994 transition to democracy, COSATU has had an ambiguous relationship with the ANC government: on the one hand, COSATU leaders have generally been personally supportive of Presidents Mandela and Mbeki, but on the other, have been opposed to the ANC's acceptance of privatisation policies and other free-market forms of globalisation embraced by the ANC.

The labour movement of the period from the 1890s to the 1920s had an extensive press, producing many pamphlets and newspapers, such as the *Johannesburg Witness* (1898–9), the *Cape Socialist*, *The Worker*, the *Voice of Labour* (1908–12), and the *Eastern Record* (1914–15) which contain much important political and literary material. Sadly, the lack of adequate library curatorship in South Africa has led to the complete disappearance of many editions of these publications. The first book-length study of unions in South Africa was by Gitsham and Trembath in 1926, and reflects the views of the white labourists. R. K. Cope's 1944 biography of CPSA founder Bill Andrews provides a lively version of the first half-century of labour organisation, as do Eddie Roux's 1944 biography of the CPSA's expelled leader, S. P. Bunting and Walker and Weinbren's invaluable discussion of the early unions (1961). The most substantial work in CPSA tradition of 'official party history' is that of Jack and Ray Simons (1969), which contains a wealth of information, but is marred by its manipulation of historical issues to provide a rationale for party policy. Of the more scholarly literature, the studies by E. Katz (1976) and S. Johns (1995) of the early left are useful, and the heyday of Marxist scholarship in South Africa in the 1980s generated a number of significant works on labour: Helen Bradford's work on the ICU (1987), Jon Lewis' work on unions from the 1920s to 1950s (1984), and Phil Bonner's key chapter on the 1918–19 strike wave (1982). Since the 1990s, most South African writing on labour has been influenced by Eddie Webster, who follows the 'labour process theory' elaborated by the American, Harry Braverman in *Labour and Monopoly Capital* (1975). This approach has tended to lead to a rather economistic analysis, which 'reads off' political phenomena from features of production in an excessively direct way. However, the better products of the Webster stable, like the work of Karl von Holdt, do attain a greater degree of analytical subtlety in handling issues of race and culture. Another notable contribution in the 1990s of a different temper is the biography of the early communist leader David Ivon Jones by the South African Trotskyist Baruch Hirson and Gwyn A. Williams (1995). Very little South African literature has reflected directly on labour issues, in part perhaps because the ideological power of nationalism in the anti-apartheid struggle has closed down space for the assertion of a specifically labour-focused point of view. Some exceptions include the early novels by Blackburn and Lewis (who has a protagonist in *Wild Deer* (1933) based loosely on Clements Kadalie), the worker poetry of the 1980s collected by Ari Sitas (1986), and the autobiographies by Kadalie (1970) and Emma Mashinini (1989).

Jonathan Hyslop

Literary Works

Blackburn, Douglas [1908] (1991), *Leaven: A Black and White Story*, Pietermaritzburg: University of Natal Press.
Kadalie, Clements (1970), *My Life and the ICU: The Autobiography of a Black Trade Unionist in South Africa*, ed. S. Trapido, London: Cass.
Lewis, Ethelreda [1933] (1984), *Wild Deer*, Cape Town: David Philip.
Mashinini, Emma (1989), *Strikes Have Followed Me All My Life: A South African Autobiography*, London: Women's Press.
Sitas, Ari (ed.) (1986), *Black Mamba Rising. South African Worker Poets in Struggle*, Durban: Worker Resistance and Culture Publications.

Histories

Bonner, Philip (1982), 'The Transvaal Native Congress 1917–1920: The Radicalization of the Black Petty Bourgeoisie on the Rand', in S. Marks and R. Rathbone (eds), *Industrialisation and Social Change in South Africa: African Class Formation, Culture and Consciousness, 1870–1930*, London: Longman, pp. 270–313.
Bradford, Helen (1987), *A Taste of Freedom: The ICU in Rural South Africa, 1924–1930*, New Haven, CT: Yale University Press.
Cope, R. K. (1944), *Comrade Bill: The Life and Times of W. H. Andrews, Workers' Leader*, Cape Town: Stewart Printing Company.
Gitsham, E. and Trembath, J. F. (1926), *A First Account of Labour Organisation in South Africa*, Durban: E. P. and Commercial.
Hirson, Baruch and Gwyn A. Williams (1995), *The Delegate for Africa: David Ivon Jones 1883–1924*, London: Core.

Johns, Sheridan (1995), *Raising the Red Flag: The International Socialist League and the Communist Party of South Africa 1914–1932*, Bellville: Mayibuye.

Katz, Elaine N. (1976), *A Trade Union Aristocracy: A History of White Workers in the Transvaal and the General Strike of 1913*, Johannesburg: African Studies Institute, University of the Witwatersrand.

Lewis, Jon (1984), *Industrialisation and Trade Union Organisation in South Africa, 1924–1955*, Cambridge: Cambridge University Press.

Roux, Edward (1944), *S. P. Bunting: A Political Biography*, Cape Town: African Bookman.

Simons, H. J. and R. E. (1969), *Class and Colour in South Africa 1850–1950*, Harmondsworth: Penguin.

Von Holdt, Karl (2003), *Transition from Below: Forging Trade Unionism and Workplace Change in South Africa*, Pietermaritzburg: Natal University Press.

Walker, Ivan L. and Ben Weinbren (1961), *2000 Casualties: A History of the Trade Union and Labour Movement in South Africa*, Johannesburg: South African Trades Union Congress.

Webster, Eddie (1985), *Cast in a Racial Mould: Labour Process and Trade Unionism in the Foundries*, Johannesburg: Ravan Press.

See also: **Anti-colonialism and Resistance: Southern Africa; Historiography: Southern Africa; Post-apartheid**.

Land: Australia

The struggle for indigenous land rights in Australia have been dominated by the case of *Mabo and Others* vs *Queensland*. Eddie Mabo was born in 1936 on Mer, a Torres Strait island, and from 1981 until he died in January 1992, he fought for indigenous land rights. The case was decided on 3 June 1992, when the High Court of Australia ruled that indigenous customs provide a basis for traditional ownership that does not depend on government recognition. The court implied that such native title might exist over lands in Australia and not only granted by governments to settlers. By a 4–3 majority it rejected compensation for those whose traditional lands were stolen. It also renounced the colonial fiction of *terra nullius*, that Australia had no original owners, but affirmed the colonial power of governments to extinguish native title. In 1993, after negotiating with Aboriginal land councils from remote areas with least destruction of such title, the federal government created a Native Title Act. That validated any past alienation of indigenous land, and established procedures for future alienation and judicial determinations of native title. In 1996 the High Court decided that pastoral leases could coexist with native title, but leaseholders' rights would have priority. In 1999 a new government amended the Act so that such leases destroy native title, and made it harder for traditional owners to get customary links to their lands recognised. In 2002, a different High Court denied an Aboriginal claim to traditional lands by refusing to accept that indigenous traditions developed autonomously after 1788, when the colonial invasion of Australia began. The spectre of *terra nullius* was replaced by a new historical fiction of law-making as exclusive to settlers, denying the reality of changing indigenous customs. The broader implications of the *Mabo* case for acknowledging the coexistence of indigenous and settler cultures have still to be resolved through negotiations for a political agreement or treaty such as exists in other settler societies. Consequently the hopes raised by the *Mabo* case, which Aboriginal poet

Kevin Gilbert called the turning point for justice, remain unfulfilled, and indigenous people doubt that Australia is yet postcolonial.

Roderic Pitty

Literary Works

Douglas, Josie (ed.) (2001), *Untreated: Poems by Black Writers*, Alice Springs: Jukurrpa.
Gilbert, Kevin [1993] (1995), '*Mabo* is the Turning Point for Justice', in Irene Moores (ed.), *Voices of Aboriginal Australia: Past, Present, Future*, Springwood: Butterfly, pp. 158–9.
Gilbert, Kevin (1994), *Black from the Edge*, Melbourne: Hyland House, pp. 158–9.
Winter, Joan (ed.) (2002), *Native Title Business: Contemporary Indigenous Art*, Southport: Keeaira Press.

Histories

Bartlett, Richard (1999), 'Native Title in Australia', in P. Havemann (ed.), *Indigenous Peoples' Rights in Australia, Canada and New Zealand*, Auckland: Oxford University Press, pp. 408–27.
Huggins, Jackie, Rita Huggins and Jane Jacobs (1995), 'Kooramindanjie: Place and the Postcolonial', *History Workshop Journal*, 39, pp. 164–81.
Langton, Marcia (2001), 'Dominion and Dishonour: A Treaty between our Nations?', *Postcolonial Studies* 4: 1, pp. 13–26.
Pearson, Noel (1995), 'From Remnant Title to Social Justice', *Australian Journal of Anthropology* 6: 1 and 2, pp. 95–100.
Sharp, Nonie (1996), *No Ordinary Judgment*, Canberra: Aboriginal Studies Press.
Watson, Irene (2001), 'One Indigenous Perspective on Human Rights', in S. Garkawe, L. Kelly and W. Fisher (eds), *Indigenous Human Rights*, Sydney: Institute of Criminology, pp. 21–40.

See also: **Historiography: Australia; Pre-colonial Histories: Australia**.

Land: Canada

Prior to confederation on 20 July 1871, treaties and land claims with First Nations were the responsibility of regional governments. Following confederation and the creation of the Dominion of Canada, the federal government became responsible for 'Indian affairs' in all provinces. But the British colonial administration had begun to shift responsibility for Native land issues to a centralised government as early as 1864 through section 91, sub-section 24 of the British North America Act. The federal government claimed that it had a responsibility, as representative of the British Crown, to 'protect' the interests of First Nations peoples from exploitation by European settlers. As a result, the federal government created a 'special status' legislation known as the 'Indian Act'. However, the 'Indian Act' singled out a segment of society – largely on the basis of race and ethnicity – and removed much of its land and property from the commercial mainstream, giving the minister of Indian affairs, and other government officials, a degree of discretion that was not only intrusive but frequently offensive. Part of this 'special status' was to maintain areas deemed to be Native land under the many treaties signed between First Nations and European settlers. But there have been land claims disputes about the regions constituting Native territories in Canada since the first French and British settlements and the status of much of this land is still disputed.

Today the Department of Indian and Northern Affairs manages the negotiations, settlement and implementation of comprehensive and specific land claims agreements, as well as special claims settlements and self-government arrangements. Negotiations are between Aboriginal groups, the federal government and, in areas affecting its jurisdiction and interests, the relevant province or territory. In these negotiations, the Canadian government maintains that the interests of Aboriginal and non-Aboriginal people are respected, and, if affected, are dealt with fairly. However, the Mohawk defence of Kanasetake (aka Oka, in Quebec) has exposed the unjust practices of the Canadian government regarding land claims.

The period between 11 March and 26 September 1990 was marked by the confrontation between Mohawk Indians, the Quebec provincial police, and the Canadian armed forces near Oka. The first barricades were in place in March, and the last torn down in September, with considerable cost and damage to both sides, in what is referred to as 'a standoff'. The problem started when the courts allowed a controversial and publicly challenged Oka Town Council plan to develop a nine-hole golf course into an eighteen-hole golf course, insensitively located on one of the last small parcels of sacred grounds, including a Mohawk meeting place and a centuries-old cemetery. Despite police brutality and sweeping arrests, as well as being outnumbered by the massive fire power of thousands of army troops, the Mohawks emerged triumphant though trodden, and the land was protected.

Justin Edwards

Literary Works

Campbell, Maria (1973), *Halfbreed*, Lincoln, NB: University of Nebraska Press.
Wiebe, Rudy (1973), *The Temptations of Big Bear*, Toronto: Vintage.

Histories

Cairns, Alan C. (2001), *Citizens Plus: Aboriginal Peoples and the Canadian State*, Vancouver: University of British Columbia Press.
Clark, Bruce (1999), *Justice in Paradise*, Montreal: McGill-Queen's University Press.
Daniels, Harry W. (ed.) (1979), *The Forgotten People: Métis and Non-Status Indian Land Claims*, Ottawa: Native Council of Canada.
Frideres, James S. (1988), *Native Peoples in Canada: Contemporary Conflicts*, Scarborough: Prentice-Hall.
MacLaine, Craig (1990), *This Land is Our Land: Mohawk Revolt at Oka*, Maxville: Optimum Publishing.
Mores, Bradford W. (1989), *Aboriginal Peoples and the Law: Indian, Métis and Inuit Rights in Canada*, Ottawa: Carleton University Press.
Purich, Donald (1986), *Our Land: Native Rights in Canada*, Toronto: James Lorimer.

See also: **European Exploration and Settlement: Canada; Historiography: Canada; Inuit.**

Land: South Asia

In India, land reform emerged from peasant politics in the 1930s, which forced it onto the political agenda of democratic party politics. Beginning in 1938, the Kisan Sabha (the main peasant organisation) gave its support to the Indian National Congress, which in turn had to address peasants' demands. In north India, a main issue was 'Abolition of Zamindari,' that is, the elimination of intermediaries, such as landlords, between peasant cultivators and the government. However, the power and financial influence of landlords in the government made the implementation of land reform an ongoing challenge. Bihar state took the initiative, passing the Zamindari Abolition Act in 1949 and amendments 1 and 4 of the constitution assured the constitutionality of such laws, but also regulated the process.

Over the next decades, states began implementing, with various degrees of enthusiasm and resistance, land ceilings. Land above the ceiling was redistributed to the rural poor in a process that continues today, each state following a plan based on the different kinds of land tenures prevalent in the region: *raiyatwari* – peasant settlement in the west; *janman* rights – land grants in the south.

There were several important and sometimes contradictory consequences of Indian efforts to implement land reform. For example, Operation Barga in West Bengal registered land rights for 1.2 million peasants (1978–81), lending great popularity to the Communist Party, which led the Left Front government. Land reform in Bengal was accompanied by a reinvigoration of the *panchayat* system of local self-government, giving peasants even more control over local development and anticipating similar policies instituted by the federal government in the 1990s. Some communities benefited especially: OBCs (Other Backward Classes), many of whom were among the larger tenant farmers, who were the first to gain lands from upper caste landlords, translated their new economic strength into political successes.

Major issues remained and remain to be addressed in the continuing process of instituting effective land reform in India, especially guarantees of land rights for women, who have been almost completely overlooked. N. T. Rama Rao in Andhra Pradesh, after his ousting from the position of chief minister, called women's land rights a main, but unfulfilled, goal of his administration. In Sri Lanka, land reform was high on the agenda of the SLFP (Sri Lanka Freedom Party) governments (1956–60, 1960–5). The Paddy Lands Act of 1948 assured security of tenure and the maximum of how much landlords could be charged for rent. In 1972 the SLFP, as part of a coalition, introduced effective land ceilings, collecting surplus lands and redistributing them. This policy was reinforced in 1975 when foreign-owned estates were nationalised. However, land reform had restricted results. As reported by the 1990 Land Commission, increased landlessness, smaller holdings per family, increased control by those who could afford new technology, and evidence that recipients of distributed land were often associates of the government rendered land reform inadequate at best. Plus, two significant policies, the introduction of dry paddy agriculture and *chena* – planting crops within forest tracts – were rendered ineffective by ongoing civil war. Pakistan inherited a mixed land tenure situation, with some peasant proprietors, but also strong and influential landlords. Ayub Khan (1958–69) enacted land reform regulation in 1959, characterised by land ceilings and security for peasants, including share-croppers (*hari*). However, given the political power of the landlords, the ceilings were high (500 acres of irrigated land and 1,000 of unirrigated) and the law contained many exemptions. Still some land was redistributed. Under Zulfikar Ali Bhutto (1971–7) the reforms were extended and tightened. Ceilings, for example, were cut to 150 acres of irrigated land; but the programme remained incomplete. By the time Bhutto was overthrown, about 3 million acres of land had been redistributed by the government. Nevertheless, landed interests still remain an important force in the Pakistani government.

Wendy Singer

Literary Works

Ali, Monica (2003), *Brick Lane*, New York: Scribner.
Devi, Mahasweta (1990), *Of Women, Outcasts, Peasants, and Rebels*, trans. K. Bardhan, Berkeley, CA: University of California Press.
Mistry, Rohinton (1996), *A Fine Balance*, New York: Knopf.
Ondaatje, Michael (2000), *Anil's Ghost*, New York: Knopf.
Premchand, Munshi (1968), *Godaan (The Gift of a Cow)*, trans. G. Roadarmel, Bloomington, IN: Indiana University Press.
Seth, Vikram (1993), *A Suitable Boy*, NewYork: HarperCollins.

Histories

Agarwal, B. (1994), *A Field of One's Own: Gender and Land Rights in South Asia*, Cambridge: Cambridge University Press.
Bandyopadhyay, D. (2001), 'Tebhaga Movement in Bengal: A Retrospect', *Economic and Political Weekly of India*, 13 October, pp. 3,901–7.
Chattopadhyay, Raghebendra and Esther Duflo (2001), 'Women as Policy Makers: Evidence from an India-Wide Randomized Policy Experiment', National Bureau of Economic Research Working Paper Series.
Das, Arvind (1983), *Agrarian Unrest and Socio-Economic Change in Bihar, 1900–1980*, Delhi: Manohar Publications.
Farmer, B. H. (1993), *An Introduction to S. Asia*, London: Routledge.
Government of India (2003), Department of Land Resources, 'Land Reforms Policy'. Available at http://rural.nic.in.lr.htm
Nathan, Dev (2002), 'Breaking the Deadlock: Land Reform Revisited', *Economic and Political Weekly of India*, 29 June, pp. 2,545–39.
Nieuwenhuys, Olga (1991), 'Emancipation for Survival: Access to Land and Labour of Thandans in Kerala', *Modern Asian Studies* 25: 3, pp. 599–619.
Talbot, Ian (2000), *Inventing the Nation: India and Pakistan*, London: Arnold.

See also: **Historiography: South Asia; Naxalites; Sri Lankan Civil War; Women's Histories: South Asia.**

Land: Southern Africa

The dispossession of Africans from their land in Southern Africa started in the seventeenth century with the arrival of European settlers, continued gradually through the eighteenth century, and accelerated rapidly in the final third of the nineteenth century, with the discovery of minerals in the interior. Since the end of colonial or settler rule in Southern Africa, faltering efforts have been made to redress the racially skewed ownership of land.

The most extensive postcolonial redistribution of land to date in Southern Africa has taken place in Zimbabwe, where the colonial land grab sanctioned by Rhodesia's Land Apportionment Act of 1930 was to a limited extent reversed in the immediate aftermath of independence: 3 million hectares of land were transferred to African owners, with results beneficial in terms of social stability and increased agricultural production. However, the basic imbalance in ownership remained, and twenty years after independence 70 per cent of Zimbabwe's most fertile land was concentrated in 4,500 white-owned farms. Frustration at the state's failure to redress this imbalance led to escalating protests from 1997 onwards. The regime of Robert Mugabe's responses – to give pensions and one-off payments to protesting war veterans, and to legislate the transfer of 3.4 million hectares of land to 71,000 black families – stalled because of large-scale corruption: the first million hectares of land taken from 270 white farms went not to the rural poor, but to 400 wealthy urban acolytes of the regime. The failure to administer meaningful land reform provoked heightened opposition within the country and the withdrawal of foreign aid to fund land reform, precipitating a rapid economic collapse.

In 1999 Mugabe sought to change the constitution by referendum in order to be able to confiscate white farms without compensation. Defeated in the referendum, Mugabe's ZANU party has nonetheless retained power by a combination of the severe intimidation of political opposition and promises of land to rural supporters. Opposition critics argue that the state-orchestrated violence and extensive human rights abuses committed in the name of land reform in Zimbabwe are driven not by any sudden desire to redistribute land, but rather by Mugabe's strategic efforts to retain power.

As in Zimbabwe, so too in South Africa the distribution of land was dramatically skewed in favour of white farmers at the moment when white minority rule ended. The 1913 Land Act, extended by subsequent racist legislation, ensured that in 1994 when the African National Congress (ANC) assumed power after South Africa's first democratic elections, a white minority (13 per cent of the population) owned 87 per cent of the land. The ANC government has committed itself to redressing this legacy, and they have attempted to do so by a combination of (1) restitution of land appropriated under racist legislation; (2) reform of insecure forms of land tenure; and (3) redistribution by land reform. Regarding restitution, the statistics are updated regularly on the government website (http://dla.pwv.gov.za/), but they tell of slow progress (500,000 hectares by the beginning of 2003), and extra-parliamentary opposition led by the Landless People's Movement has applied pressure on the ANC to move more quickly. (In 2004, for example, their slogan in the build-up to the national elections has been 'no land, no vote'.) One important development has been the legal recognition of pre-colonial land rights in the 2003 case of *Richersveld* vs *Alexkor*: as in the *Mabo* case in Australia, the court rejected the doctrine of *terra nullius*, and found in favour of the dispossessed community. Regarding tenure reform, new legislation gives legal recognition in certain cases to customary, pre-colonial, communal forms of ownership. However, the quantity of communally-owned land is unlikely to increase significantly because the ANC government ultimately favours individual private ownership as the exclusive form of land tenure, and land use dedicated to cash crops for export markets, rather than the forms of subsistence farming associated with communal land ownership. Lastly, redistribution by land reform has been framed by the World Bank. Sensitive to the uncertainties and fresh opportunities of post-1990 South Africa, the World Bank presented itself as an intermediary between the new government, international donors, NGOs and rural development projects, and the landless masses. The organising principle for land reform in South Africa, according to the World Bank, is that all reforms should be market-driven (see van Zyl et al., 1996), with the only concession low-interest loans to those seeking to acquire land.

Public debate about land reform in South Africa polarises along racial lines, with white farmers arguing that the break-up of large commercial farms will lead to a dramatic fall in productivity, and landless black farm workers arguing that they should not have to pay for land originally stolen from their forefathers; rather, the state should confiscate white-owned farms. Critics of the World Bank have argued that the vast majority of the rural poor will remain impoverished, as they simply will not be able to raise the credit necessary to buy land, and that the only beneficiaries of such reform are likely to be a small elite of black commercial farmers.

David Johnson

Literary Works

Berold, Rob (ed.) (2002), *It All Begins. Poems from Postliberation South Africa*, Pietermaritzburg: Gecko.
Bila, Vonani (2001), *In the Name of Amandla*, Elim: Timbila Poetry Project.
Chinodya, Shimmer (1990), *Harvest of Thorns*, London: Heinemann.
Coetzee, J. M. [1977] (1982), *In the Heart of the Country*, Harmondsworth: Penguin.
Schoeman, Karel [1978] (1987), *Promised Land*, trans. M. V. Friedmann, New York: Simon and Schuster.
Steinberg, Jonny (2002), *Midlands*, Johannesburg: Jonathan Ball.
Vladislavic, Ivan (1994), *The Folly*, London: Serif.

Histories

Baker, Colin (1993), *Seeds of Trouble: Government Policy and Land Rights in Nyasaland, 1946–1964*, London: British Academic Publishers.
Beinart, William, Peter Delius and Stanley Trapido (1986), *Putting a Plough to the Ground. Accumulation and Dispossession in Rural South Africa, 1850–1930*, Johannesburg: Ravan Press.
Bennett, T. W. (1996), 'African Land – A History of Dispossession', in R. Zimmerman and D. Visser (eds), *Southern Cross. Civil Law and Common Law in South Africa*, Oxford: Clarendon Press, pp. 65–94.
Bowyer-Bower, T. A. S. and C. Stoneman (eds) (2000), *Land Reform in Zimbabwe: Constraints and Prospects*, Aldershot: Ashgate.
Cliffe, Lionel (2000), 'Land Reform in South Africa', *Review of African Political Economy* 84, pp. 273–86.
Human Rights Watch (2002), 'Fast Track Land Reform in Zimbabwe', 14, 1 March, New York. Available at http://www.hrw.org
Moyo, S., B. Rutherford and D. Amanor-Wilks (2000), 'Land Reform and Changing Social Relations for Farm Workers in Zimbabwe', *Review of African Political Economy* 84, pp. 181–202.
Plaatje, Solomon T. [1916] (1987), *Native Life in South Africa*, Harlow: Longman.

Van Zyl, J., J. Kirsten and H. P. Binswanger (eds) (1996), *Agricultural Land Reform in South Africa*, Cape Town: Oxford University Press.
Walker, Cheryl (2000), 'Relocating Restitution', *Transformation* 44, pp. 1–16.

See also: **Maaori; Post-apartheid; World Bank**.

Languages and Ethnicities: South Asia

The complex array of overlapping identities on the subcontinent does not necessarily lend itself nicely to the rubric of ethnicity, however, the term underlines the political potency that shared identities of language, caste and religion have customarily carried in South Asia. Historically, these identities have shaped access to opportunities, audiences and participation in cultural and political arenas, determining who could speak with whom, or which groups were equipped to play mediating roles. The linguistic mapping of South Asia through Orientalism, the discipline of colonial philology, and its shared assumptions with European race theory acquired a wider currency through educational policy and other institutional arenas such as the Royal Asiatic Society, and eventually influenced the rhetorical ground upon which collective identities and claims were being forged in the nineteenth century. Further, this has fed into the foregrounding of ethnic tensions under the imperatives of the processes of political representation in the colonial and postcolonial periods. Significantly, literary production has been an important aspect of the making and contesting of such claims.

In keeping with the linguistic fluidity of the South Asian social world, traditional cultural elites characteristically displayed an astonishing propensity towards multilingualism that sustained a distinctive cosmopolitan culture. A significant outcome of the introduction of English and print under colonial rule and the concomitant processes of linguistic standardisation was to discipline such linguistic promiscuity. However, since the early twentieth century, political modernisation has only spurred mobilisation under categories of caste and religion. These contrary pulls have posed challenging dilemmas to the contemporary South Asian creative writer, who is increasingly likely to be monolingual in his or her literary tastes and proficiency. With the gradual erosion of multilingual capabilities during the colonial and postcolonial periods, these shifts can only be partially reflected in the emerging literatures. Clearly, then, the literary mapping of ethnic identities and their changing trajectories resists any easy recuperation. However, inspired by postcolonial critiques and insights provided by the work of the subaltern studies collective, literary scholars have recently begun to redefine their field by asking new questions about the links between evolving linguistic communities, literary practices and structures of political authority in South Asia (Pollock 2003).

The entry of English in the eighteenth century and its subsequent dissemination, first through missionary and trading agents, and then helped by official policy and the press, enabled it to displace the pre-existing 'high' textual traditions of Sanskrit, Persian and Arabic. As the oldest literary culture in South Asia, Sanskrit was also the most regionally extensive of these; on the other hand, English became the only literary language in India without a prior oral textual tradition. Less than five centuries after writing was applied to the Indic languages from around the middle of the third century BC, Sanskrit became the vehicle for intellectual and public functions beyond the liturgical, developing distinctive uses such as *kavya* (literature), *sastra* (philosophy), *itihaas* (historical narrative), besides also being employed for worldly-political practices such as coinage and inscriptions. There were two other learned languages with which Sanskrit partially shared these domains, namely, Prakrit and Apabramsha, and these textual languages essentially represented non-localised cultivated registers that transcended specific ethnic groups. Further, although the distribution of literate skills was ideologically controlled through social categories such as *varna* and *jati* (caste), till around the late medieval period, none of these languages was entirely tied to any specific religious community. At its height, the circulatory universe of Sanskrit manuscripts extended impressively from parts of Central Asia to South-east Asia; further, the composition of Sanskrit texts continued to attract royal patronage well beyond the beginning of the second millennium when its pre-eminent public status on the subcontinent began to be challenged by the emergence of vernacular textual traditions. These changes were stimulated by cultural influences including the poetry of the Sufi orders entering South Asia along with the new Turkish ruler lineages at this time. Beginning as a surreptitious defiance of the authority of Sanskrit, these processes of cultural and political vernacularisation gradually forced it to relinquish its exclusive claims as the language of literary composition and royal public communication through most of the subcontinent by the middle of the second millennium. Claiming to augment the prestige of classical traditions by recreating some of its devotional texts and narratives in the emerging vernacular *bhakti* (i.e. devotional) repertoires from Tamil to Kashmiri, these 'translations' gradually produced alternative literatures, often telling the same stories with different emphases to different audiences.

The Turkish rulers also brought Persian. As north India became part of the Perso-Islamic world first under the Ghaznavids (977–1186) and later under the Delhi Sultanate (1206–1526), Persian established a significant presence through court patronage and the popular following for Sufi centres, and reached its first mature efflorescence in India during Amir Khusrau Dihlavi's time in the late thirteenth and early fourteenth centuries. Absorbing local ideas, phrases and expressions, particularly from Hindvi, Indian Persian acquired its own distinctive identity. Muhammad Tughalq's shifting of the sultanate's headquarters to Daulatabad between 1327 and 1335 occasioned an influx of elite families to the Deccan, making for sustained literary contact between Hindvi/Persian and regional varieties such as Gujri, Marathi and Dakhani. These conditions added an interesting dimension to concurrent trends towards political vernacularisation throughout India: for example, early sixteenth-century rulers in Deccan such as Sultan Adil Shah of Bijapur and Ibrahim Qutb Shah of Golconda continued to promote Persian, but additionally, proclaimed Hindvi and Telugu as the languages of their respective governments. Partly in response, the Mughal period saw a renewed enthusiasm in affirming Persian as the language of court culture. Especially under Akbar's kingship (1556–1605), with the employment of Iranian functionaries and Hindu literate castes (mainly *kayasthas* and *khatris*) at all levels of the administration, Persian, as *sabk-i-hind* (language of India), acquired a trans-continental reach as the language of politics, courtly literature and imperial record-keeping. The intermixing between the languages of Delhi and Deccan gave rise to Urdu, which produced its own rich repertoire of courtly poetry and its first great poet Vali (1665–1707) by the late seventeenth century. The rise of British power and the capture of Delhi after the Great Rebellion of 1857 eventually sapped the foundations of these Indo-Islamic literary cultures.

The title of the first published English text by an Indian writer partly tells its own story: *The Travels of Dean Mahomet, A Native of Patina in Bengal, Through Several Parts of India, while in the Service of the Honourable East India Company, written by Himself, In a Series of Letters to a Friend* was published in 1794 in Cork, Ireland, to where its author, Din Muhammad, had emigrated a decade earlier. English arrived in India through European traders and missionaries from the late sixteenth century. It grew roots, however, from around 1660 when literate Indians began to be employed as middle-men, brokers, personal agents (*banias*), translators and interpreters (*dubashis*) to help with the business of the East India Company. The study of major regional languages was attractive to missionary groups and early colonial officials. This led to the compilation of the first printed primers, lexicons, philological treatises, dictionaries and other elementary texts at centres such as Fort William College, Calcutta, founded in 1800. These early bi/multilingual agents who worked with British officials and missionaries were the predecessors of the English-educated colonial middle class that emerged as a result of policies pursued by the British from around 1818, and in a more concerted fashion, after Macaulay's recommendations in 1835 were accepted. These measures disavowed the earlier support for the study of Oriental languages and instead made English the normative centre of education policy and the sole language of higher learning. In 1837, English replaced Persian in higher administration, but needed to be supplemented by the regional languages at the lower levels.

Along with print, the entry of the new 'high' language, English, initiated several conceptual shifts that included the introduction of new meanings and standards of learning, literacy and literature. Existing classical and vernacular literary traditions were now measured against these new norms, and were to be 'improved' by absorbing ideas, models and practices through translations of exemplary European texts. Thus, colonial education introduced the principles of a laicised literate order to the subcontinent. Remaining as it did, however, an elitist project, it also established hierarchies between 'newly-educated' and 'illiterate'; 'English-knowing' and 'vernacular-speaking'. As regional intellectuals sought to create distinctive modern traditions of vernacular writing through borrowings in equal measure from Sanskrit and English, the fields of literature and journalism became the primary arenas through which dominant regional identities were forged. However, South Asian bilingualism denoting equal fluency in two regional languages was quite unusual among the educated elite, rather, since at least 1835, South Asian bilingualism has denoted the asymmetrical linking of the regional languages with the normative presence of English. English grew in importance, not simply as the language of modernity, but also as the only medium of pan-Indian exchange, and the vehicle of communication/contestation with the colonial state. Even if they did not have a clear choice, colonial-modern Indian writers have been aware that the medium of expression carries implicit questions about notions of readership, community and nation; further, that whatever the chosen option, their creative and intellectual lives remain inescapably built around the colonial bilingual relation. For example, even while consciously choosing to write fiction or poetry in their mother tongue, writers such as Bankimchandra (1838–94), Michael Madhusudan Dutt (1824–73), and Govardhan Tripathi (1855–1907) continued to use English for their introspective personal correspondence.

Significantly, the rise of anti-colonial nationalism coincided with a strong impetus towards the creation of subnational linguistic identities. In this setting, the bilingual capabilities of regional intelligentsias represented a unique political capital; interestingly, however, there was also reluctance to reflect upon these linguistic divisions in a sustained or open way. The spectacular rise of Hindi within a hundred years of its history to being the largest linguistic zone in post-independence India, and its recognition as official language is, perhaps, the best example of how linguistic identities served to foreground and contest political rivalries. Beginning with a modest demand in 1867 for Hindi-Devnagiri to be recognised as an official language alongside Persian in the lower courts and administrative levels, the Hindi movement pitted itself against its cultural other, Urdu, by identifying itself squarely with majority Hindu interests. It had a rapid and enormous impact in shaping consciousness, identities and territorial boundaries in north India, contributing in significant ways towards support for the 'two-nation' theory that led to partition in 1947. It is interesting to note in this context that Premchand (1880–1936), acclaimed as the greatest writer of fiction in either Hindi or Urdu, wrote his first five novels and several short stories in Urdu, but after 1915, moved gradually to writing almost exclusively in Hindi.

Independence from colonial rule saw three nation-states emerge in South Asia between 1947 and 1948. The question of a national language has posed a vexing challenge in each case: often, political conflicts rooted in demographics of caste and/or religious groupings have congealed along linguistic lines. In 1950, the lack of a consensus forced India's constituent assembly to grant Hindi and English joint official status, under the assumption that the former would gradually replace English. Across the border in Pakistan, the supposed marker of Muslim identity, Urdu, became Pakistan's official language, although spoken by less than 5 per cent of the population. Yet, in India, actual practice diverged substantially from policy: the adoption of Hindi as the primary administrative language had to be deferred, and the introduction of economic planning and the related emphasis on science, technology and other forms of standardised information actually saw the importance of English only increase at the national level in subsequent years. Simultaneously, in the late 1950s and 1960s, governments came under pressure from regional groups: in India, this took the form of pressure for the reorganisation of states along linguistic lines. In Sri Lanka, eight years after independence, the Sinhala Only Bill was passed in June 1956, declaring Sinhala the sole national language. Under these opposing pressures, the bilingualism that had held the national movement together has tended to fall apart: in India and Pakistan, a largely monolingual group of English-speaking managerial globalising elites find themselves increasingly divorced from the lower slices of the pyramid of society that use the vernaculars. Even as the power of English remains undiminished, its influence has been exploited as the object of resentment by regional monolingual-vernacular aspirant groups. Particularly, in Sri Lanka, the cultural protectionism of the Sinhala Only Act impelled many highly-educated professionals, for whom English was a first language, to migrate to Europe and North America.

This history has made it common for the South Asian writer in English to be routinely confronted with questions regarding his or her 'authenticity' in a way that the *bhasha* (vernacular) writer does not face. So even as the writer in English is more likely to be anxious to prove his or her authenticity, their location in the national imaginary renders it challenging to write in a minutely local way that records the stresses and strains of intricately woven identities in the way that the Hindi or the Malayalam or the Kannada writer might be equipped to do. As Meenakshi Mukherjee empathetically notes, for India, English texts may reflect 'a greater pull towards homogenization of reality, an essentialising of India, a certain flattening out of complicated and conflictual contours, the ambiguous and shifting relations that exist between individuals and groups in a plural community' (Mukherjee 2002, p. 172). And yet, even as regional language literatures evolve their own postcolonial trajectories, the great visibility that South Asian writers in English have gained internationally since the 1980s is tied to their relationship with the subcontinent and ability to represent it for the multiculturally oriented global audience that exists in English. Simultaneously, the expanding size of the market is making available an increasing (but still selective) number of translations from regional literatures to these sizeable English reading audiences in South Asia and abroad.

Veena Naregal

Literary Works

Dangle, Arjun (ed.) (1992), *Poisoned Bread: Translations from Modern Marathi Dalit Literature*, Bombay: Orient Longman.
Ghosh, Amitav (1992), *In an Antique Land*, Delhi: Ravi Dayal.
Nagarkar, Kiran (1995), *Ravan and Eddie*, New Delhi: Penguin.
Ondaatje, Michael (2000), *Anil's Ghost*, Toronto: Vintage Press.
Ravikant and Tarun Saint (eds) (2001), *Translating Partition*, Katha: New Delhi.
Roy, Arundhati (1998), *The God of Small Things*, New York: HarperCollins.
Rushdie, Salman (1991), *Midnight's Children*, New York: Penguin.
Sahni, Bhisham (1974), *Tamas*, New Delhi: Penguin.

Histories

Ahamed, Aijaz (1992), *In Theory: Classes, Nations, Literatures*, Delhi: Oxford University Press.
Breckenridge, Carol and Peter van der Veer (eds) (1991), *Orientalism and the Post-Colonial Predicament*, Philadelphia: University of Pennsylvania Press.
Chandra, Sudhir (1992), *The Oppressive Present: Literature and Social Consciousness in Colonial India*, Delhi: Oxford University Press.
Chatterjee, Partha (1999), 'Talking About our Modernity in Two Languages', in Partha Chatterjee, *The Partha Chatterjee Omnibus*, New Delhi: Oxford University Press, pp. 263–85.
Dalmia, Vasudha (1997), *The Nationalization of Hindu Traditions: Bharatendu Harischandra and Nineteenth-Century Banaras*, New Delhi: Oxford University Press.
Das, Sisir Kumar (1991), *A History of Indian Literature, 1800–1910. Western Impact: Indian Response*, New Delhi: Sahitya Akademi.
Kaviraj, Sudipta (1992), 'Writing, Speaking, Being: Language and the Historical Formation of Identities in India', in D. Helmman-Rajanayagam and Deitmar Rothermund (eds), *Nationalstaat und Sprachkonklifte in Sud und Sudostatesein*, Stuttgart: Steiner, pp. 25–65.
King, Robert (1997), *Nehru and the Language Politics of India*, Delhi: Oxford University Press.
Mehrotra, Arvind (ed.) (2003), *A History of Indian Literature in English*, London: Hurst and Co.
Mukherjee, Meenakshi (2002), *The Perishable Empire: Essays on Indian Writing in English*, New Delhi: Oxford University Press.
Naregal, Veena (2002), *Language, Politics, Elites, and the Public Sphere: Western India under Colonialism*, London: Anthem Press.
Orsini, Francesca (2002), *The Hindi Public Sphere 1920–1940: Language and Literature in the Age of Nationalism*, New Delhi: Oxford University Press.
Pollock, Sheldon (2003), *Literary Cultures in History: Reconstructions from South Asia*, Berkeley, CA: University of California Press.
Ramanujan, A. K. (1999), *The Collected Essays of A. K. Ramanujan*, New Delhi: Oxford University Press.
Ramaswamy, Sumathi (1997), *Passions of the Tongue: Language Devotion in Tamil India, 1891–1970*, Berkeley, CA: University of California Press.

Tambiah, Stanley (1996), *Leveling Crowds: Ethnonationalist Conflicts and Collective Violence in South Asia*, Berkeley, CA: University of California Press.
Tharu, Susie (1991), *Women Writing in India: 600 B.C. to the Present*, New Delhi: Oxford University Press.

See also: **Bangladesh: 1971; Castes: South Asia; Historiography: South Asia; Islam; Religions: South Asia; Sinhala Only Bill.**

Languages and Ethnicities: West Africa

Africa is the most multilingual and multiethnic of all the world's continents. According to Crystal (1997), some 2,000 languages are spoken as first languages by about 480 million people. In Nigeria alone there are 400 languages and 250 ethnic groups, and three of the main languages, Hausa (25 million), Yoruba (20 million) and Igbo (12 million) place respectively second, third and fourth on the African list. Language and ethnic pluralism support a vast cultural repertoire, and potentially feed a rich literary heritage.

In sub-Saharan Africa, the second half of the twentieth century began with a wave of independence struggles and the births of new nations, closely followed by civil wars, most of which have been fought along ethno-linguistic lines – in the Sudan, Nigeria, Sierra Leone, and Liberia to name but a few. Governments, therefore, have focused on nation-building and the promotion of harmony among groups divided along ethnic, linguistic and religious lines within the nation-states. It is understandable that much of the literature from this period is dominated by themes of group and national identity and survival. Literary figures like Wole Soyinka, Chinua Achebe, Ayi Kwei Armah, Léopold Senghor and Ferdinand Oyono have been intimately involved in wrestling with these tensions. As Peter Young noted:

> the African writer has his place in a modern society; he is not a resurrection of the dim past, a colourful, conjured ghost to be smiled on by the connoisseurs of the quaint. First of all he is Africa's 'new voice'; but, in quite another way, he is also the voice of a language in the process of adaptation and change. (Young 1971, p. 171)

Ethnicity is subsumed in language and literature in that it provides a context for the production and appreciation of both. Language and literature impact on each other in significant ways and in the process mark ethnicity. Most African literatures exist in oral form. Preservation is thus an obvious concern as inter-generational wear-and-tear undermines the sanctity of community values and identity. Literary traditions are subject to the same processes of attrition as the world's languages. So, what factors determine which languages and literatures die and which survive? There are indications that the survival of languages is tied to external political and socio-economic factors, as well as to the internal relationships between ethnic native speakers and other groups within the nation. There are four aspects to the survival of languages and ethnicities (and their literatures) within the Anglophone West Africa states to consider: (1) the relationship between the majority group and minorities; (2) the opposition between English literature and literature in English; (3) the access to publishing and the production of public knowledge; and (4) the choice of language for writing literature. Each of these aspects is considered in turn.

Within each of the multiethnic and multilingual polities of sub-Saharan Africa, there are numerous literatures, and their status depends on the numerical strength and political status of the ethnic group that produces and owns it. The majority ethnicities tend to produce the 'main' national literature, while those produced by minority ethnicities are accorded token recognition as part of the national heritage. The point is best illustrated by reference to Nigeria. In most published references to Nigerian literature, there is the acknowledgment of a vast body of works from multiple ethnic backgrounds, but invariably attention narrows to those produced in the major national languages: Hausa, Yoruba and Igbo. The national school curriculum reflects the imbalance between the statuses of ethnic languages and literatures in many subtle ways, as this example from the primary school reading texts demonstrates. The stories included are dominated by characters whose names derive from the major ethnic language groups, as in the following extract from Module 11 of Book 4 of the *Macmillan Primary English Course*:

> *The story of Alake*
> Alake was a beautiful woman, and her husband, Olu was a prince. They had a son, whom they named Dele. In a nearby village there lived a wicked magician, named Ali. Ali already had many wives but he was not contented. When he heard about Alake, he wanted her to be his wife, too. He dressed himself like a holy man and went to her house. He told her to follow him. Alake was afraid to disobey a holy man so she went with him. Ali quickly changed her into a dog and carried her away to his village. (Taiwo et al. 1983, p. 53)

The first three italicised names (Alake, Olu and Dele) derive from Yoruba ethnicity, and the wicked magician's name suggests a northern Nigerian, probably Hausa ethnicity. At the level of social psychology, pupils of minority ethnic groups are thus excluded in this assumed (Yoruba/Hausa) bilingualism, and they are at the same time directed subtly to internalise certain linguistic and ethnic hierarchies within the nation-state. At the level of national language policy, two forms of majoritarianism need to be distinguished: number and/or political dominance. Kiswahili in Tanzania is an example of the former, and Afrikaans in apartheid South Africa an example of the latter. Finally, local oral literatures specific to each ethnic area may or may not 'travel' across ethnic boundaries, depending on the power, status and mobility its users enjoy within the nation.

The second aspect influencing the survival of languages, ethnicities and their literatures within the West African nation-state is the relation between 'English literature' and 'literatures in English'. Although 'English literature' on even the most cursory inspection turns out to be less than 'English', and in fact heavily populated by Irish, Scots and Welsh writing (see Talib 2002), in the West African context it is nonetheless erected as a point of reference much superior to indigenous African literatures. Indeed, African literatures are routinely ranked behind not only 'Christian/Western' literatures, but also behind Arabic/Middle Eastern literatures. The acclaim in recent years accorded West African writers like Wole Soyinka, Chinua Achebe, Christopher Okigbo, Niyi Osundare and Ben Okri has substantially undermined this hierarchy, but further insidious hierarchies remain to be contested. Within the broad category of 'Other Literatures in English' (OLE), a descending order of greatness anchored to a tradition of Englishness is observed, with the works of an elite of creative writers writing in English elevated above both African folk tales such as the Ananse stories from Ghana, and pamphlets in 'broken English' produced for mass consumption for a 'less discerning' readership (see, for example, Ogali 1977 and the Onitsha Market Literature discussed by Obiechina (1973)). The hierarchies between

'English literature' and West African 'literatures in English' roughly parallel the opposition between first and third-world economies.

The third aspect influencing language survival in West Africa is access to publishing. As Canagarajah (1996) and others have argued, publishing is at the centre of knowledge production and dissemination, and is a major determinant of what and how socio-cultural forces influence society. Literatures in indigenous West African languages have by and large failed to attract publishers because low literacy rates mean modest local consumption and limited profits. Further, in Bourdieu's terms (1991), indigenous languages lack the necessary 'linguistic capital' to attract the major publishing houses, which are based in Europe and maintain but a low-key presence in Africa. The two main educational publishers are Macmillan and Heinemann, which enjoy funding from UNESCO as part of the 'education for all' programme; and they continue to play a major role in textbook publishing for primary schools in West Africa. Regarding literary publishing, Heinemann with its African Writers Series and Longman with its Drumbeat Series have been the major names in the region, and Methuen, Nelson and Faber have operated on a smaller scale. However, none of these publishers has published a literary series in an indigenous language, a clear indication of the unacknowledged split between English and West African languages. Also of significance since independence have been the publications of Ibadan-based offices of Oxford University Press and University Press Limited, which include titles like *Essentials of Yoruba Grammar* (Awobuluyi 1979) and *Elements of Modern Igbo Grammar* (Emenanjo 1978). These have had the effect of standardising these languages for literary purposes. Finally, there are several small West African presses whose impact is limited from a global perspective, an indication of their confinement to the margins. Some Nigerian examples of these include: Fourth Dimension Publishers, Concept Publications, Malthouse, Kraft Books and African Cultural Institute. Especially in the cities, there are increasing numbers of one-person publishing businesses, along with rampant self-publishing facilitated by computer and information technology. More books, therefore, are being published, but arguably less stringent controls are placed on their standards.

The final factor influencing the survival of languages in West Africa is the choice of literary language. Most of Africa's literatures exist in oral form and are thus preserved as integral parts of their cultures. Kenyan writer Ngugi wa Thiong'o's bold experiment in switching from English in his early novels (*A Grain of Wheat* (1967), *Petals of Blood* (1977) and *The River Between* (1965)) to Gikuyu in his novel *Matigari* (1989) was closely followed by writers in West Africa. Ngugi's political ambitions in switching to an indigenous language should, of course, be distinguished from market-driven motives governing choice of literary language, and they struck a chord with West African writers trapped in the same neo-colonial linguistic binary. The most distinctive West African example of using translation to negotiate this binary is Wole Soyinka's retelling of Daniel Fagunwa's Yoruba story *Ogboju Ode Ninu Igbo Irunmole* in English as *Forest of a Thousand Demons: A Hunter's Saga* (1968). Soyinka's translation has made the story accessible to a wider world, and has established both authors' reputations as literary giants of the twentieth century. Fagunwa's story was already a classic in its Yoruba version, but its subsequent global success in translated form attests to the symbolic power of English, and indeed the asymmetry in power between English (language and identity) on the one hand, and Yoruba (language and identity) on the other.

To conclude, there are many examples in postcolonial West Africa of indigenous literatures enriching and affirming minority ethnic groups, preserving their local languages, and contributing to mass literacy programmes (see Clark 1980 for examples). In every instance, however, they have been obliged to function within a contradictory complex of national, regional, ethnic, linguistic and religious tensions that are unique to West Africa.

Tope Omoniyi

Literary Works

Achebe, Chinua (1964), *Arrow of God*, London: Heinemann.
Armah, Ayi Kwei [1968] (1988), *The Beautiful Ones Are Not Yet Born*, London: Heinemann.
Ekwensi, Cyprian [1962] (1990), *Burning Grass. A Story of the Fulani of Northern Nigeria*, Oxford: Heinemann.
Ngugi wa Thiong'o (1965), *The River Between*. London: Heinemann.
Ngugi wa Thiong'o (1967), *A Grain of Wheat*, London: Heinemann.
Ngugi wa Thiong'o (1977), *Petals of Blood*, London: Heinemann.
Ogali, Ogali A. (1977), *Veronica My Daughter (A Drama)*, Onitsha: Appolos Brothers.
Okri, Ben (1991), *The Famished Road*, London: Jonathan Cape.
Osundare, Niyi (1983), *Songs of the Marketplace*, Ibadan: New Horn Press.
Oyono, Ferdinand (1968), *The Old Man and the Medal*, London: Heinemann.
Soyinka, Wole and Daniel Fagunwa (1968), *Forest of a Thousand Demons: A Hunter's Saga*, (*Ogboju Ode Ninu Igbo Irunmole*), London: Nelson.
Taiwo, O., L. Longe and W. Ijioma (1983), *Macmillan Primary English Course: Pupils' Book 4*, Ibadan: Macmillan Nigeria Publishers Ltd.
Tutuola, Amos (1952), *The Palmwine Drinkard and his Dead Palm-Wine Tapster in the Deads Town*, London: Faber and Faber.

Histories

Achebe, Chinua (1975), *Morning Yet on Creation Day*, New York: Doubleday.
Awobuluyi, Oladele (1979), *Essentials of Yoruba Grammar*, Ibadan: Ibadan University Press.
Bamgbose, Ayo (1991), *Language and Nation*, London: Longman.
Bourdieu, Pierre (1991), *Language and Symbolic Power*, Cambridge: Polity Press.
Canagarajah, Suresh A. (1996), 'Non-Discursive Requirements in Academic Publishing, Material Resources of Periphery Scholars, and the Politics of Knowledge Production', *Written Communication* 13, pp. 435–72.
Clark, Ebun (1980), *Hubert Ogunde: The Making of Nigerian Theatre*, Oxford: Oxford University Press.
Crystal, David (1997), *The Cambridge Encyclopaedia of Language*, 2nd edn, Cambridge: Cambridge University Press.
Emenanjo, Nolue E. (1978), *Elements of Modern Igbo Grammar*, Ibadan: Oxford University Press.
Ngugi wa Thiong'o (1986), *Decolonizing the Mind: The Politics of Language in African Literature*, London: Heinemann.
Obiechina, Emmanuel Nwanonye (ed.) (1973), *An African Popular Literature. A Study of Onitsha Market Pamphlets*, London: Cambridge University Press.
Omoniyi, Tope (2003), 'Local Policies, Global Forces: Multiliteracy and Africa's Indigenous Languages', *Language Policy* 2, pp. 133–52.

Pennycook, Alistair (1998), *English and the Discourses of Colonialism*, London: Routledge.

Senghor, Léopold Sédar (1976), *Prose and Poetry*, trans. J. Reed and C. Wake, London: Heinemann.

Senghor, Léopold Sédar (1991), *The Collected Poetry*, Charlottesville, VA: University Press of Virginia.

Talib, Ismail S. (2002), *The Language of Post-Colonial Literatures: An Introduction*, London: Routledge.

Young, Peter (1971), 'The Language of West African Literature in English', in J. Spencer (ed.), *The English Language in West Africa*, London: Longman, pp. 165–84.

See also: **Historiography: West Africa; Religions: West Africa; Universities: West Africa**.

Latin America

The historical literature on Latin America has grown exponentially over the past four decades. A prime characteristic of this output is its empirical richness, a reflection of better archival organisation within the region. The impact of postcolonial theory on the historiography of Latin America has been somewhat muted. However, rather than being an implicit critique of postcolonial studies or denoting some innate intellectual sclerosis among historians, this reflects the fact that the colonial history of Latin America, subsequent internal colonialism, and large racially and ethnically diverse subaltern groups, above all its indigenous and 'caste' peoples, have long been studied from inherently postcolonial perspectives. For the same reason, the rise of subaltern studies has had relatively small impact, explicable by the existence of numerous studies of protest, rebellion and revolution (see Knight 1997 and Thomson 2002). Broadly speaking, Latin American history-writing since the 1960s has reacted against a long tradition of metropolitan-centred analysis in favour of a counter-hegemonic view, a tendency that anticipated much of subaltern studies' focus, methods, freshness and potency. Nonetheless, some historians revel in the use of terminology drawn from postcolonialism and postmodernism (see Mallon 1994 and van Young 2001), a trend becoming more widespread with a new generation of historians influenced by interdisciplinary research. While the major impetus to postcolonial studies may be traced to the post-World War II dissolution of empire and the literature spawned by that process, Latin America's period of colonial rule began with conquest in 1492, and the 'postcolonial' strictly speaking began in 1830 with emancipation from Spanish rule.

This schema admits of exceptions: apart from Brazil's separate process of installing Portugal's refugee emperor as its first independent head of state in 1822, Cuba and Puerto Rico had to wait until 1898 for their independence, when the USA chose to inaugurate its own empire by appropriating Spain's imperial remnants. However, from a Latin American perspective, the origins of the US 'empire' are more properly located in its mid-nineteenth century invasion of Mexico, when it expropriated the old Spanish borderlands, stripping the Mexican republic of California, Arizona, Texas and New Mexico (see Weber 1992). Against that background, present-day Mexican mass immigration to the USA and the emergence there of distinct Latino and Chicano cultures takes on the appearance – ironically but with much justice – of a Mexican reconquest of its former territories from the northern colossus. There were some maverick cases in the independence scenario: Haiti's spectacularly successful slave rebellion of 1791 brought eventual emancipation from France in 1804. Out of fragmented empire came twenty postcolonial republics, supplemented with the ostensibly 'self-governing' Commonwealth of Puerto Rico.

The extraordinary diversity of local, regional and national histories of the macro-region has produced an enormous historical literature, each year witnessing an avalanche of new scholarly work. Indeed, in the USA alone, the field of Latin American studies is industrial in scale. Latin Americans themselves are now driving much of the agenda, and an earlier nationalistic and *belletrist* stamp to their historical writing has long given way to theoretically sophisticated and empirically informed studies by local avatars, often with North American or European Ph.D.s. This daunting bibliography is, in the first instance, best accessed through the several Cambridge University Press compendia, which contain extensive bibliographical essays, and the annual *Handbook of Latin American Studies*, a valuable bibliographical launch pad (*CHLA, CHLAL, CHNPA, HAHR, Handbook*). Alan Knight's short historiographical essay (1997), delivered in crackling prose, is compulsory reading, for all that it makes few allowances for postcolonial approaches. The origins of the historical record are located in the early accounts of the Spanish conquerors and subsequent chroniclers (often friars) – frequently based on the oral testimonies of native elites – and the native chronicles and codices of pre-lapsarian and early conquest decades, but above all in the almost infinite documentation produced by erstwhile Spanish and Portuguese colonial administrations and the inexhaustible material subsequently produced by the republican states (see Salomon 1999).

The hallmark of the region's modern historiography is its unsurpassed empirical richness, with ethno-history, otherwise known as historical anthropology or anthropological history, above all the history of the native peoples of the great civilisations of Mesoamerica and the Andes especially impressive (see Prem 1989). Almost by definition, many of its practitioners are anthropologists, but there have also been signal contributions from historians, linguists, geographers and literary specialists. This interdisciplinary focus has long been in evidence because the difficulties of teasing out indigenous histories from often abundant, though always intractable, original sources are manifold, requiring a plurality of approaches and methodologies. Less praiseworthy is the fact that few historians have attempted to incorporate the archaeological record in their analyses of colonial or even pre-Columbian ethno-history. The methodological challenges posed by this strand of historical writing are various, but a common denominator is the awkward circumstance that most available primary sources are non-native. The codices and indigenous histories of Mexico are, however, much more abundant than native Andean or even Mayan texts. The key problem, of course, is the familiar one of who is to represent the colonised and marginalised: who speaks for the subaltern? Detecting indigenous voices through the palimpsest of centuries of Spanish chronicles and legal documents, with their incompetently rendered official Spanish translations of indigenous testimonies, must always be tentative (see Barber and Berdan 1998). In the case of the peoples of the Aztec and Maya civilisations, the current generation of scholars has broken new ground with its evaluation of accessible, and previously little explored, colonial Nahuatl and Maya language documents. Under the aegis of James Lockhart, these pathfinders have radically revised our understanding of the experience of the indigenous peoples of Mesoamerica.

Overall, then, the predominant theoretical influence on this sub-field has been the several branches of anthropology. Indeed, *pace* many postcolonialist interpretations, the origins of anthropology lay not in nineteenth-century British practitioners but in the ethnologically rich and often nuanced writings of the Spanish chroniclers (see Pagden 1982).

The difficulties and dangers of this kind of history have always been obvious, and have been handled with varying degrees of success. An awareness of Orientalism *avant la lettre* has always been built into ethno-historical research; navigating it, surmounting it, is an exercise fraught with cultural misunderstandings. In this sense, ethno-historical research belongs to a continuum of colonial encounter literature, beginning with the awed if patronising reports of conquistadores, chroniclers, friars, and the European literature of the early modern era with its fabulous accounts of the 'marvellous possessions' of the Indies. Their interest was often instrumentalist, concerned as they were to reach understandings of native cultures and praxis, the better to evangelise, subdue and extract surplus product from indigenous peoples, in the interest of an imperial hegemony.

The notion of hybridity is a corollary of First Nations research and for long has been a part of the research agenda. It is a recent neologism much favoured by literary scholars, joining a plethora of older, cognate notions, including acculturation, syncretism, transculturation (the historians' current favourite), cultural transmission and, above all, the all-embracing *mestizaje*. The indigenous peoples and languages encountered by the conquistadores were numerous, such that ethnicity in Latin America was and remains a subdivision of race. Epidemic-led demographic disaster, European settlement, and the introduction of millions of African slaves made Latin America the first great 'melting pot' – all these processes contributed to widespread miscegenation (see Cook 1998). These went hand-in-hand with European appropriation of indigenous lands, labour, and liquid capital through the European real property laws and notably burdensome taxation; the subsequent proceeds, with mining revenue, provided the specie for the development of an internal market and international mercantilist trade during the colonial era. In Brazil, Cuba and elsewhere, the imperatives of slavery lent a different texture, parsed by region, endowing their loci with a rich cultural heritage (see Klein 1999). The cities, especially, were propitious sites for miscegenation, not least because urban slavery and manumission resulted in an ethnic mosaic to a degree different from that of the rural districts. At various junctures, the several streams of *mestizaje* merged. Research on the cultural and social results of slavery has recently caught up with its study as an economic and legal institution.

The chronicles of the conquistadores, friars and bureaucrats who ruled and evangelised the Americas in the sixteenth and seventeenth centuries are a perennial site of scholarly concern (see Brading 1991). It is one to which postcolonialist scholars are increasingly drawn. New editions have been discovered in dusty private libraries, better editions prepared, and there is a growing awareness of the extent to which these key sources are inscribed within the classical tradition (see MacCormack 1991) and of the alterity embodied in their production and subsequent interpretation. Native chronicles and codices are major sites of close textual readings, particularly useful for exploring counter-hegemonic critiques. Memorials, diaries and political testimonies – the most salient written by women, including nuns and beguines (*beatas*) – have been grist to the mill of *testimonio* studies (see Myers 2003). Anthropologists especially have interested themselves in this genre, with varying degrees of scholarship and partisanship (see Arturo Arias 2001).

From the 1960s, historians have increasingly employed a regional focus in their research, a more encompassing view than that from the presidential palace. National history tended to downgrade or reify subaltern groups, all too often cast as mere spear-carriers to populist military or political leaders and political parties. Above all, taking the analysis down to regional and even micro-regional or village level brings subaltern groups into sharp focus, disaggregating them from generalised anonymity (see Guardino 1996 and Thomson 2002). The regional focus has been especially fruitful for the study of mass political movements.

In particular, a Marxist approach, owing much to Gramsci and E. P. Thompson, has been revelatory in this regard, a sophisticated forerunner of subaltern studies, which some of the leading avatars of post-Marxism have incorporated into their analysis (see Mallon 1995). Postcolonialist approaches have perhaps encouraged the study of those subaltern political projects that failed, though 'history from below' has had a strong presence in Latin American ethno-history, peasant studies, and rebellions. What appears to be novel is an enhanced emphasis on the exegesis of subaltern ideologies. While the Marxist approach continues to be popular, indeed revelatory when accompanied with empirical detail, its best practitioners have long left behind its once innate determinism. An inherent assumption of much regionalist research is that the history of the provinces can be sewn together, more or less seamlessly, to make a national whole. This has never been the case, though, even allowing for internal cultural differentiation. In historical writing on the colonial era, the problem of harmonising the several levels of analysis is exacerbated, with the local, regional and national having to be knitted into the imperial.

Following independence in the early nineteenth century, the economies of the nascent republics were, for the most part, moribund, but from the 1850s, and increasingly from the 1880s, major export economies and modernised regional economies developed apace, fuelled by vigorous international demand, internal capital accumulation, technological advance and infrastructural development (not least the railways and their multiplier effects), and widespread European (notably Italian) immigration, especially to Argentina, Uruguay and Brazil. In the postcolonial era, national and regional histories necessarily have been interpreted in an international and now globalised context, above all in terms of international economic disparities and terms of trade. The once popular dependency theory was found wanting in explaining local and regional case studies, and not least because its economistic arguments were simplistic. Moreover, it frequently gave short shrift to such key internal issues as internal capital accumulation, social conflict, political culture, technical education, and cultural ideology in influencing large-scale regional change and international economic disparities (see Rory Miller 1993). Economic history generally has lost popularity with researchers, partly due to changing academic fashion, partly because its arguments are often seen as overly deterministic, elite-centred, and dismissive of social and cultural factors in explaining causation, change, and even economic growth. Its present unpopularity within academe has drawn forth recriminations from its practitioners, though demographic history, especially as regards the devastating decline of indigenous populations following the conquest, remains a much-tilled field. For both colonial and national histories the familiar socio-economic explanations of collective violence have been, from the 1980s, downgraded in favour of culturalist explanations, a trend that has generated a sometimes bitter debate (see, for example, *HAHR* 1999). At the national level, state formation, nationalism, revolutions and party politics are not only studied with many methodologies, but are often seen to be shorthand for multiple phenomena. Studies on military authoritarianism and dictatorships begin in the independence era, though the colonial origins of the over-mighty Latin American military are disputed.

More traditional approaches to many central issues are sometimes cloaked in postmodernist terminology, without adding much to substance, but these have greatly benefited from a renewed emphasis on discourse. Benedict Anderson and James Scott are favoured guiding lights. Discourse analysis has, most markedly, reinvigorated the history of gender and sexuality. Foucault's influence is felt here, sometimes in path-breaking ways, above all in writing the history of women in cloisters and other gendered spaces; the great importance of the female religious orders in the colonial era, especially their functioning as financial institutions, has long attracted historians, not least for its abundant extant documentation. Questions of power, discourse and prescriptive gendered space and behaviour figure hugely in the study of these cloistered women: laity, servants and 'fallen women' as well as nuns. Foucault's 'critical theory on space' and 'heterotopias' are employed to join historical and literary to geographical research, with a particular focus on colonial conceptions of space, spatial configurations of alterity, and 'imagined geographies' (see Arias and Meléndez 2002). The research on the history of women is growing exponentially, while the history of sexuality is emerging as a new focus of interest (see Twinem 1999). Historians continue to locate new primary sources for the study of the economic, social and political roles of women of the under-classes, and this topic looks set to attract many future researchers. In a similar vein, the artisans and their guilds are gradually coming into focus, sometimes connected with the study of urban religious confraternities.

Historical writing on Latin America has become truly interdisciplinary and thematically all-embracing. The grand narratives have not gone away, but are incomparably more complex in content and nuance than a generation ago. The concerns of historical writing reach into all areas of postcolonial interest, and its published and unpublished primary sources – historical documents, fictional and travel literature, chronicles, memoirs and *testimonios* – provide unsurpassed materials for research on the postcolonial era. Many of the chronicles are available in English translations. The most revealing of these sources are written overwhelmingly in Spanish and Portuguese, but the corpus of historical materials in native American languages, most importantly Nahuatl, Maya and Quechua, allow a depth of understanding of the First Nations only rarely encountered in other culture regions. Above all, the present agenda for historical writing on Latin America is being set there: intellectual dialogue between metropolis and colony has reached parity.

Latin American history has until recently attracted the attention of postcolonial literary scholars only as a broad context for the study of the region's fictional production. The terms 'modernism' and 'postmodernism' were both originally coined by Latin American intellectuals, Rubén Darío and Federico de Onís, respectively. The recent three-volume *Cambridge History of Latin American Literature* (CHLAL) is an indispensable resource for postcolonial studies. Similarly useful is Jean Franco's 2002 survey of several generations of scholarship, in which she address *inter alia* the notion of 'borders'. Besides Franco's guide, there are key studies (of variable perceptiveness) by Gerald Martin (1989), Doris Sommer (1991), Nestor García Canclini (1992), Djelal Kadir (1993), Neil Larson (1995), Nicola Miller (1999) and John Beverley (1999). I have listed these under 'Literary Works' below, as they themselves provide extensive guides to Latin American writers – including Gabriel García Marquez, Mario Vargas Llosa, Carlos Fuentes, Isabel Allende, Octavio Paz and Jorge Luis Borges – who have been read through 'postcolonial' lenses.

David Cahill

Literary Works

Beverley, John (1999), *Subalternity and Representation: Arguments in Cultural Theory*, Durham, NC: Duke University Press.

Borges, Jorge Luis (1962), *Labyrinths: Selected Stories and Other Writing*, D. A. Yates and J. Irby (eds), New York: New Directions.

Echevarría Roberto González, and Enrique Pupo-Walker (eds) (1996), *Cambridge History of Latin American Literature*, 3 vols (CHLAL), Cambridge: Cambridge University Press.

Franco, Jean (2002), *The Decline and Fall of the Lettered City: Latin America in the Cold War*, Cambridge, MA: Harvard University Press.

García Canclini, Nestor [1982] (1993), *Transforming Modernity: Popular Culture in Mexico*, trans. Lidia Lozano, Austin, TX: University of Texas Press.

Kadir, Djelal (1993), *The Other Writing: Postcolonial Essays in Latin America's Writing Culture*, West Lafayette, IN: Purdue University Press.

Larson, Neil (1995), *Reading North by South: On Latin American Literature, Culture and Politics*, Minneapolis, MN: University of Minnesota Press.

Martin, Gerald (1989), *Journeys through the Labyrinth: Latin American Fiction in the Twentieth Century*, London: Verso.

Miller, Nicola (1999), *In the Shadow of the State: Intellectuals and the Quest for National Identity in Twentieth Century Spanish America*, London: Verso.

Sommer, Doris (1991), *The National Romances of Latin America*, Berkeley, CA: University of California Press.

Histories

Adams, R. E. W. and M. MacLeod (eds) (2000), *The Cambridge History of the Native Peoples of the Americas, Volume II, Parts 1–2*, Cambridge: Cambridge University Press.

Arias, Arturo (ed.) (2001), *The Rigoberta Menchú Controversy*, Minneapolis: Minnesota University Press.

Arias, Santa, and Mariselle Meléndez (eds) (2002), *Mapping Colonial Spanish America: Places and Commonplaces of Identity, Culture and Experience*, Lewisburg, PA: Bucknell University Press.

Barber, Russell J. and Frances F. Berdan (1998), *The Emperor's Mirror: Understanding Cultures through Primary Sources*, Tucson, AZ: Arizona University Press.

Bethell, L. (ed.) (1984–90), *The Cambridge History of Latin America*, 11 vols (CHLA), Cambridge: Cambridge University Press.

Brading, D. A. (1991), *The First America: The Spanish Monarchy, Creole Patriots, and the Liberal State 1492–1867*, Cambridge: Cambridge University Press.

Cook, Noble David (1998), *Born to Die: Disease and New World Conquest, 1492–1650*, Cambridge: Cambridge University Press.

Guardino, Peter F. (1996), *Peasants, Politics, and the Formation of Mexico's National State: Guerrero, 1800–1857*, Stanford, CA: Stanford University Press.

Handbook of Latin American Studies (1935–Present), 67 vols, Hispanic Division, Library of Congress, Austin, TX: University of Texas Press.

Hispanic American Historical Review (HAHR) (1999), Special Issue: 'Mexico's New Cultural History: *Una Lucha Libre*', 79: 2.

Klein, Herbert (1999), *The Atlantic Slave Trade*, Cambridge: Cambridge University Press.

Knight, Alan (1997), 'Latin America', in M. Bentley (ed.), *Companion to Historiography*, London: Routledge, pp. 728–58.

Lockhart, James (1992), *The Nahuas after the Conquest: A Social and Cultural History of the Indians of Central Mexico, Sixteenth through Eighteenth Centuries*, Stanford, CA: Stanford University Press.

MacCormack, Sabine (1991), *Religion in the Andes: Vision and Imagination in Early Colonial Peru*, Princeton, NJ: Princeton University Press.

Mallon, Florencia E. (1994), 'The Promise and Dilemma of Subaltern Studies: Perspectives from Latin American History', *American Historical Review* 99, pp. 1,491–515.

Mallon, Florencia E. (1995), *Peasant and Nation: The Making of Postcolonial Mexico and Peru*, Berkeley, CA: University of California Press.

Miller, Rory (1993), *Britain and Latin America in the Nineteenth and Twentieth Centuries*, London: Longman.

Myers, Kathleen Ann (2003), *Neither Saints nor Sinners: Writing the Lives of Women in Spanish America*, Oxford: Oxford University Press.

Pagden, Anthony (1982), *The Fall of Natural Man: The American Indian and the Origins of Comparative Ethnology*, Cambridge: Cambridge University Press.

Prem, Hanns J. (1989), *The Ancient Americas: A Brief History and Guide to Research*, Salt Lake City, UT: University of Utah Press.

Salomon, F. and S. Schwartz (eds) (1999), *The Cambridge History of the Native Peoples of the Americas, Volume III, Parts 1–2*, Cambridge: Cambridge University Press.

Salomon, Frank (1999), 'Testimonios: The Making and Reading of Native South American Historical Sources', in Frank Salomon and Stuart Schwartz (eds), *The Cambridge History of the Native Peoples of the Americas Volume III, Part 1*, Cambridge: Cambridge University Press, pp. 19–95.

Thomson, Sinclair (2002), *We Alone Will Rule: Native Andean Politics in the Age of Insurgency*, Madison, WI: The University of Wisconsin Press.

Trigger, B. and W. E. Washburn (eds) (1996), *The Cambridge History of the Native Peoples of the Americas, Volume I, Parts 1–2* (CHNPA), Cambridge: Cambridge University Press.

Twinam, Ann (1999), *Public Lives, Private Secrets: Gender, Honor, Sexuality, and Illegitimacy in Colonial Spanish America*, Stanford, CA: Stanford University Press.

Van Young, Eric (2001), *The Other Rebellion: Popular Violence, Ideology, and the Mexican Struggle for Independence, 1810–1821*, Stanford, CA: Stanford University Press.

Weber, David J. (1992), *The Spanish Frontier in North America*, New Haven, CT: Yale University Press.

See also: **Historiography: Caribbean; Pre-colonial Histories: Caribbean; Slavery: Caribbean.**

Lee Kuan Yew

Lee Kuan Yew is undoubtedly the most influential figure in Singaporean politics over the last half century. Born in 1923 into a wealthy Straits Chinese family, Lee received an Anglophone education and was admitted to Raffles College. His studies were cut short by the Japanese occupation of Singapore. He survived by learning Japanese, and later working for the occupying forces transcribing Allied radio broadcasts.

After World War II Lee studied law at Cambridge, and then returned to Singapore. His initial involvement in politics was with the liberal Progressive Party, but it was his participation as a lawyer in cases representing workers' grievances that led him to hope for more radical social change. Lee was instrumental in forming the People's Action Party in 1954, leading it to victory in the 1959 elections. Over the next few years, Lee survived a split in his party and the departure of its radical largely Chinese-speaking wing, and led Singapore into and then out of federation with Malaysia. Lee served as prime minister of an independent Singapore from 1965 to 1990 before stepping down to take the position of senior minister, a title which he holds to this day.

Lee is a controversial figure both within Asia and in the wider world. Singapore certainly achieved political stability and phenomenal economic growth under his leadership; a feat made all the more impressive considering its geographical vulnerability and lack of natural resources. Lee himself has attributed this to a non-ideological policy of pragmatism pursued by his successive governments. As a small city state, Singapore is uniquely reliant on international markets, and has consciously made itself a low tariff, low tax environment in a bid to lure multinational corporations. In contrast to this stress on market-driven liberalism, however, the government has embarked on ambitious projects of social engineering, transforming the living environment of most Singaporeans through huge public housing projects and retirement saving schemes, eliminating so-called Chinese 'dialects' and managing ethnicity.

From the 1980s onwards, Lee became a vocal spokesperson for 'Asian Values', proclaiming the compatibility of Confucianism and capitalism, and chastising the West for social indiscipline which he claimed led it to fall away from the project of modernity. Western descriptions of Lee have frequently taken his Confucianism or Chineseness at face value, neglecting the hybrid background from which he emerged: he speaks English and Malay with much greater fluency than he does Mandarin Chinese. Similarly, while Lee's politics have often been represented as simplistically authoritarian, he has paid careful attention to achieving legitimacy: his party has won regular elections since it first came to power. If anything, Lee's rule increasingly emphasised governmentality – the production of docile citizens through self-discipline – rather than the overt repression of sovereignty. As Singapore trims itself once more, 'reinventing' itself to catch the winds of the global marketplace, there is increasing debate about the nature of Lee's legacy.

Philip Holden

Literary Works

De Souza, Dudley (1985), 'The Convert' in Edwin Thumboo, Y. W. Wong, T. P. Lee, Masuri Salikum and V. T. Arasund (eds), *The Poetry of Singapore*, Singapore: ASEAN Committee on Culture and Information.
Lau Siew Mei (2000), *Playing Madame Mao*, Rose Bay: Brandl and Schlesinger.
Tan Tarn How (1995), 'Undercover' in *Dirty Laundry, Mergers and Undercover: Plays from Theatreworks' Writers' Lab*, Singapore: Theatreworks and Singapore Press Holdings.

Histories

Barr, Michael (2000), *Lee Kuan Yew: The Beliefs behind the Man*, Richmond: Curzon Press.
Han Fook Kwang, Warren Fernandez and Sumiko Tan (1998), *Lee Kuan Yew: The Man and his Ideas*, Singapore: Times Editions.
Lee Kuan Yew (2000), *From Third World to First: The Singapore Story: 1965–2000: Memoirs of Lee Kuan Yew*, Singapore: Times Editions.

Minchin, James (1990), *No Man Is An Island: A Portrait of Singapore's Lee Kuan Yew*, 2nd edn, North Sydney: Allen and Unwin.

See also: **Japanese Occupation: South-east Asia**.

Levant Company

The Levant Company, which operated between 1592 and 1825, was a joint stock company of London merchants established for the purpose of trading with the Levant. In 1578, William Harborne obtained a letter from the sultan of the Ottoman Empire, Murad III, addressed to Queen Elizabeth I, offering to open up the Turkish dominions to English traders. In 1581, the Turkey Company was set up following the establishment of a commercial treaty with Turkey. Two years later, an English (later British) embassy was established in Turkey, accredited by the queen but financed by the Turkey Company, which in 1592 united with the Venice Company to form the Levant Company. The right to select the ambassadorial candidate was held by the Levant Company until 1691, but it continued to finance the post until 1803.

The Levant Company's vessels travelled to Constantinople and the Near East exchanging English woollens, tin and lead for cotton, silk, mohair, carpets, glass, spices and drugs. In 1660, the company was granted a charter by King Charles II and there followed a period of prosperity.

Its decline began in 1718, hastened by competition from its rivals (French and Dutch companies, the East India Company and the English Muscovy Company), by the effects of Britain's wars with the Dutch and the French and by opposition to its monopoly on the home front. In 1767, the company was forced to apply to the government for aid and in 1825 its charter was given up.

The Levant Company was one of the tributaries which fed the main stream of English economic development in the seventeenth and eighteenth centuries, helping to transform the narrow commercial culture of pre-Tudor England into the great mercantile community it was to become. With the prices of eastern commodities reduced, former luxuries became widely available and at the same time a powerful boost was given to the trade in domestic products, especially English cloth and tin. The Levant Company was the first to introduce coffee to England, and the first to import raw cotton wool, laying the foundations of the English textile industry. The company's work was, in a political sense, complementary to that of its great rival, the East India Company. While the latter was laying the foundation of an Anglo-Indian empire, the former was establishing a connection with Turkey which was to become indispensable to the strategic interests of maintaining English power in India. The work of the Levant Company did not plant the seeds of empire, apart from possibly in Egypt, but it handed on to the English government a tradition of over two centuries of intercourse with Turkey and representation at the sultan's court. It employed scholars, writers and other collectors whose work constructed images of Eastern life and thought in the minds of the educated classes in England. It disappeared in 1825 because the days when such a commercial monopoly was justified had passed away, and because its functions could then be more efficiently administered by the government.

Priscilla Ringrose

Literary Works

Montagu, Lady Mary Wortley (1994), *The Turkish Embassy Letters*, London: Virago.
Parker, Kenneth (ed.) (1999), *Early Modern Tales of Orient*, London: Routledge.
Unsworth, Barry (1980), *Pascali's Island*, London: Michael Joseph.

Histories

Epstein, M. [1908] (1969), *Early History of the Levant Company*, New York: Augustus M. Kelley Publishers.
Lewis, Bernard (1997), 'The West and the Middle East', *Foreign Affairs* 76: 1, pp. 114–32.
Wood, Alfred Cecil [1935] (1964), *A History of the Levant Company*, London: Frank Cass Publishers.

See also: **Dutch East India Company; East India Company; Ottoman Empire**.

Liberalism: Southern Africa

The antecedents of twentieth-century South African liberalism can be traced back to the nineteenth-century Cape Colony. Cape liberalism was underpinned by a qualified non-racial franchise, enshrined in the constitution of 1853, which allowed for the inclusion of a small class of black peasant farmers based mainly in the Eastern Cape. Their interests were closely allied to those of British mercantile capitalists, who in turn exercised a significant influence on the colonial administration. The alliance prospered during the 1860s and 1870s, but subsequently came to be undermined by the mineral discoveries of the late nineteenth century. As diamond mining in Kimberley and gold mining on the Witwatersrand became more labour-intensive in the 1880s, a steady and expanding supply of black migrant labour was required. In turn, peasant production gave way to larger capital interests. This process dovetailed with an increasing racialisation of politico-legal discourse, such that the power of Cape liberalism was severely depleted by the time of white political unification in 1910.

Although the Act of Union maintained the non-racial franchise in the Cape, Cape representatives did not actively attempt to extend the colour-blind franchise to the other provinces. Nevertheless, during the twentieth century, South African liberalism continued to be articulated by a small band of (predominantly Anglophone) white educators, philanthropists, missionaries and social workers. They were concerned to temper the socio-economic ills wrought by industrialisation and urbanisation in a racially polarised society. As such, their energies were geared towards welfare work in the urban townships. Contemporary liberal intellectuals cultivated a philosophy of race relations premised on inter-racial mediation, and espoused their views from within the Joint Council movement (founded in 1921) and the South African Institute of Race Relations (founded in 1929). Throughout the late 1920s and 1930s several prominent liberal thinkers supported territorial segregation as a pragmatic solution to the so-called 'native problem'. The fight against fascism in World War II, coupled with internal developments in black South African politics, gave a democratic impetus to South African liberalism in the 1940s. However, certain political limitations, which had always bedevilled the South African incarnation of liberal ideology, were brought into sharp relief by the victory of the National Party in the 1948 election. Nevertheless, liberals continued to hold the middle ground between rival African and Afrikaner nationalisms during the apartheid era, and conscientiously attacked the policies of the Nationalist regime.

Michael Cardo

Literary Works

Butler, Guy (1975), *Selected Poems*, Johannesburg: A. D. Donker.
Paton, Alan [1948] (1987), *Cry, the Beloved Country*, London: Penguin.

Histories

Butler, J., R. Elphick and D. Welsh (eds) (1987), *Democratic Liberalism in South Africa: Its History and Prospect*, Cape Town: David Phillip.
Kirkwood, Mike (1976), 'The Colonizer: A Critique of the English South African Culture Theory', in P. Wilhelm and J. Polley (eds), *Poetry 74*, Johannesburg: A. D. Donker, pp. 102–33.
Rich, Paul (1984), *White Power and the Liberal Conscience: Racial Segregation and South African Liberalism, 1921–1960*, Johannesburg: Ravan Press.
Trapido, S. (1980), '"The Friends of the Natives": Merchants, Peasants and the Political and Ideological Structure of Liberalism at the Cape', in S. Marks and A. Atmore (eds), *Economy and Society in Pre-Industrial South Africa*, London: Longman, pp. 247–74.
Vigne, Randolph (1997), *Liberals against Apartheid: A History of the Liberal Party of South Africa, 1953–1968*, London: Macmillan.

See also: **Anti-colonialism and Resistance: Southern Africa; Historiography: Southern Africa**.

M

Maaori

New Zealand/Aotearoa's 'First People' or *tangata whenua* ('people of the land') arrived in c. 800 from the mythical homeland of Hawaiki (possibly Tahiti) in Eastern Polynesia by sailing across the Pacific in double outrigger vessels. Although archaeological evidence now rules out the traditional belief that migration culminated in a Great Fleet in c. 1350, nevertheless the names and landing-sites of the seven *waka* remain important regional sources of Maaori kinship organisation, and provide names for the largest groupings. The Maaori (also Maori) was a hunter-gatherer tribal society with a complex hierarchical structure when the navigators, Abel Tasman (1642) and Captain Cook (1769) first 'discovered' New Zealand. Identity in this pre-contact world was conferred by *hapuu* (sub-tribe) or *whaanau* (family group). The term 'Maaori', meaning 'normal', was only applied from 1801, after a decade of contact with Europeans.

Initial contact with British, French and American whalers, sealers and traders occurred mainly round the coasts of both islands. In the 1820s, the importation of flax and kauri to Australia flourished alongside the whaling industry. Between 1800 and 1830, when New Zealand was virtually a frontier of Australia, the Maaori population, estimated at about 200,000 at the time of Cook's arrival, diminished by 40 per cent, partly because of European diseases, but also because muskets started to be used in inter-tribal fighting. Evangelical missions – Samuel Marsden's Anglican mission; Wesleyan and Methodist missions – sought to convert souls and encourage literacy, but weakened the tribal structure by undermining the Polynesian gods, Maaori customs, and the sacred values of *tapu* (taboo) and *mana* (prestige). The Maaori began to turn to the missionaries for guidance in a new and bewildering world.

New Zealand's annexation as a British colony in 1840, however, had the greatest consequences for the Maaori as *tangata whenua* and for the development of the New Zealand state in general. When Edward Gibbon Wakefield introduced systematic colonisation with the New Zealand Company, he promoted the utopian ideal of a 'better Britain' by offering inducements of land and employment. However, the proposed settlement coincided with a land grab activated by expansion from Australia and increasing lawlessness. The British Crown, responding to the humanitarian ethos of the evangelical movement, somewhat reluctantly intervened to enforce law and order, to control purchase of Maaori land by Europeans, and eventually to prevent unrestricted settlement by the New Zealand Company. The Treaty of Waitangi was signed by 500 Maaori chiefs and the British Crown on 6 February 1840.

This foundational document has since been used by Maaori as confirmation of Crown protection of their rights. These rights were indeed guaranteed, but some radical Maaori now claim that sovereignty had never been ceded to the British Crown in the first place. Less controversial today is the view that reinterpretations of the treaty enabled successive governments to betray the trust implied in it, and the treaty produced deep divisions, as it could not satisfy all parties. Governor Hobson and his successor Robert Fitzroy envisaged a bi-racial community, whereas the company settlers, underestimating the importance of inter-racial relations to their enterprise, saw New Zealand purely as a home for British migrants. Governor George Grey (who had presided over the Cattle-killing in the Cape Colony in 1856 to 1857) was governor of New Zealand from 1845 to 1853 and 1861 to 1868, and shared his predecessors' view of the state as an impartial arbiter of conflicting racial interests.

The succeeding decades saw vastly different concepts of land ownership come into conflict. Increased immigration in the 1850s coincided with shortages of land, and this undermined the government's land purchase policy and led to breaches of the treaty. There was fighting and there were threats of war over disputed land purchases, particularly in South Taranaki, where the Wakefield Company's title was deemed defective by the Crown. The Bay of Islands and the far north were ravaged by fighting from 1845 to 1847, but the Maaori were ultimately suppressed by Grey's forces. Maaori unease over the Waikato area sale of land to the government led to the rise of Maaori nationalism: the pan-tribal Kotahitanga or 'unity' movement consisted of a loose federation of North Island tribes united in their refusal to sell land. It culminated in the election of a king in 1858: Te Wherowhero, who reigned as Potatau I with his own flag, council of state, code of laws, and a police system.

The three New Zealand wars which followed between 1860 and 1872 stemmed from conflicts over sovereignty in relation to land ownership. Threats to Maaori land possession led them to defy the authority of the Crown, while the settlers, believing that the Maaori would either be assimilated or die out, expected to rule New Zealand. The Taranaki War (1860–1) broke out when a minor Te Atiawa chief sold Waitara land to the Crown without the consent of his tribe, and Governor Browne endorsed the sale. The British troops besieged Maaori *paas* (fortified villages) with modest successes, but the Maaori also won minor victories, including at Puketakuere paa on 27 June 1860. The war ended in a truce with the surrender of Te Arei paa, and Maaori seizure of British-owned land at Tataraimaka. The Waikato War began in 1863 when Governor Grey drove the Taranaki Maaori from Tataraimaka; it spread to the Waikato River region, which then became the British target. Grey's general, Duncan Cameron, commanded a powerfully equipped army of up to 14,000 troops and used gunboats and heavy artillery. But the Maaori used guerrilla tactics, and despite several victories, Cameron failed to make the 'decisive blow'. In the third war (1864 to 1872), hostilities spread throughout the North Island. What was notable was the appearance of the new millennial religion, Pai Mariri (Good and Peaceful) or Hauhau, founded by the Taranaki prophet Te Ua Haumene, who led passive resistance and to whose creed the nationalist King movement, partly converted. From 1868 to 1872, the Kingites were reinforced by the Ringatu warrior cult, led by the great prophet-general, Te Kooti Arikirangi, who had escaped imprisonment in the Chatham Islands; and by Riwha Titokowaru, a successor of Te Ua. Te Kooti, after a defeat at Ngatapa in 1869, evaded capture before taking refuge in the King Country. Titokowaru, who defeated two large colonial forces near Wanganui, lost momentum due to an internal dispute in 1869, and escaped to refuge in central Taranaki. It was only by recruiting some 500 soldier farmers (to whom Grey, by now prime minister, apportioned the best of Maaori confiscated land), and supporting Maaori forces (*kuupapa*), that an end was brought to Maaori resistance in 1872. The British had greatly weakened the King movement and with it Maaori autonomy through a combination of 'creeping confiscation' and military force. Their supporters retreated to the King Country in the west-central North Island, which survived as a diminished independent state until the 1890s. Massive confiscations of the best land followed, the Native Land Court was formed to deal with Native affairs, and Maaori society was permanently disrupted.

In the aftermath of the wars, the Maaori suffered demoralisation, a breakdown of their leadership system, and continued land loss, while increased urbanisation further weakened tribal structures. They survived colonial rule with subsistence agriculture, casual or seasonal work, and manual labour in the forest service. In the 1918 flu pandemic, the death toll was 2,160, seven times higher than the Paakehaa (Pakeha), with poor housing and inadequate nutrition exacerbating the losses. Nevertheless, the population doubled to 82,000 between 1896 and 1936, and since 1940 there has been a marked decline in Maaori mortality rates. The prevailing ethos was one of assimilation, as epitomised by the Hunn Report (1961), which addressed problems of Maaori social disadvantage and envisaged state aid rather than Maaori aid.

The traditions of indigenous protest and prophecy which evolved in the wars of the

1860s continued. The tribes that backed the Paakehaa or were neutral re-formed the Kotahitanga or Maaori unity movement in the years 1892 to 1902. The pantribal Kingite movement also revived under the leadership of Te Puea, the daughter of King Tawhaiao, who advocated passive resistance to Waikato Maaori conscription in World War I, and rallied support during the 1918 flu epidemic. The most significant contributor to Maaori recovery was the Young Maaori movement, whose founding father in the 1890s was James Carroll, but whose greatest leader was Sir Apirana Ngata. Ngata's exceptional achievement was to persuade Paakehaa governments to produce funds for improving Maaori livelihood: his land development scheme allowed Maaori to group their landholdings into economical farms, and to run them co-operatively. From 1935, Ngata established dairy farms for 12,000 Maaori, organised funds for research, revived interest in the Maaori language, collected and translated hundreds of songs, encouraged Maaori wood carving, and sponsored Maaori education. The benignly segregationist Young Maaori movement played an important role on the national stage, and co-operated with the religious and spiritual movements that developed. The Ringatu religion was led by Te Kooti's successor, the prophet Rua Kenana, from the 1900s until his death in 1937, and continues to this day. Another Maaori Christian religion, the Ratana movement, was founded by Tahupotiki Wiremu Ratana in 1918. It grew rapidly, and by 1936 when Ratana made an alliance with the Labour Party, up to 50 per cent of Maaori had converted to this faith. By 1943, Ratana Labour members of parliament held all four Maaori seats in parliament. Both Ratana and the Kotahitanga used the treaty as a political credo and stressed Paakehaa breaches.

In the 1970s, Maaori history converged once more with New Zealand history. Land issues were again central, causing the treaty to be resurrected as a new foundation of the state. The mood of political and cultural assertiveness was expressed through radical demonstration embodied by the activist protest group, Nga Tamatoa. In the Maaori Land March of 1975, 30,000–40,000 people marched from Cape Reina to parliament in Wellington. This was followed by the occupation of Bastion Point in Orakei in 1977 and 1978 in protest against the government selling off Maaori land. Ethnic politicisation encouraged the reinvestigation of colonial race relations. An advisory tribunal was appointed to determine the treaty's meaning and effect and to decide issues raised by disagreements between the different English and Maaori versions, and by 1985, the concept of 'the principles of the treaty' became the basis of government attempts to remedy Maaori disadvantage. The ideology of biculturalism – that Maaori should have a unique place alongside the Paakehaa by the latter acknowledging past injustices and indicating willingness to remedy them – led to initiatives to provide greater opportunity to Maaori, particularly in education, administration, and politics. These have met with varying degrees of success: the Maaori language was rescued from threatened extinction in 1981 by pre-school immersion programmes, *kohanga reo* (language nests), and *te kura kaupapa Maaori* (Maaori language schools), and as a result is now spoken by 4 per cent of Maaori (10,000–20,000), as opposed to 70,000 in 1970. The number of Maaori at universities doubled between 1986 and 1993, and the number of Maaori leaving school with no qualifications halved between 1979 and 1993.

The 'Maaori Renaissance' began in the early 1970s with Witi Ihimaera's pastoral narratives, *Whanau* (1974) and *Tangi* (1973), which were about the effects of urbanisation, and Patricia Grace's short stories, *Waiariki* (1975), and novel, *Mutuwhenua: The Moon Sleeps* (1978), which treat miscegenation from a Maaori point of view. Although not overtly political, the English forms used encode a linguistically inflected treatment of racial and social issues. In the 1980s, when the Maaori began to demand sovereignty, three key texts appeared: Ihimaera's *The Matriarch* (1986), Grace's *Potiki* (1986) and Keri Hulme's *The Bone People* (1983). All refocus contemporary debates by engaging with the legacy of the colonial and pre-colonial pasts and blending Polynesian mythology and legend with European forms. By switching between languages and introducing Maaori phrases, syntactic patterns and grammatical structures, the writers convey ethnic specificity as well as cultural critique of the Paakehaa.

Ethnic politicisation provided new incentives to recuperate *Maaoritanga* (Maaori culture). However, recent writing has been considered mainstream because of the mastery of rhetorical traditions and the introduction of issues affecting the nation's identity. The commitment to Maaoridom in Grace and Ihimaera's work involves recentring its concerns within the wider Paakehaa sphere. Grace tackles problems like Paakehaa land theft; cultural and economic impoverishment such as loss of language, partly due to prohibitions against speaking Maaori at school during the Native School System (1867–1969); racial discrimination through stereotyping; and in *Baby No-Eyes* (1998) genetic experimentation with ethnicity. Ihimaera's fiction tells the saga of a single Maaori family, the Mahana, over several generations, and his political novels rewrite colonial history and Paakehaa settlement from the Maaori point of view. Inter-textual threads link stories of the Mahana family to those of European culture in *The Matriarch* whose narrator, Tama, rediscovers ancestors like Te Kooti, and traces the pattern of dispossession under colonialism to the present. In *The Matriarch*'s sequel, *The Dream Swimmer* (1997), Tama returns to New Zealand to petition parliament for the return of Maaori land confiscated during the Land Wars. In *The Whale Rider* (1987) Ihimaera draws on a Polynesian myth of discovery to develop the story of a new leader whose relationship with a whale will save her village. Hulme, by contrast, writing out of the gulf between the races in her short stories in *Te Kaihau: The Windeater* (1986) and *The Bone People*, is celebrated for imagining the new bicultural nationalism of the 1980s. Reconciliation appears in *The Bone People* in the unity based on *aroha* (love) of her three protagonists, in the epilogue's vision of commensualism, and suggestion of 'transformative hope' for a divided nation. Bicultural paradigms also appear in the undermining of gender stereotypes, hybrid representations of ethnic identity, and fluent switching between languages. All three writers draw on the perspectives and lessons of pre-contact and colonial histories in representing contemporary Maaori and Paakehaa society, and all stress the connection to the land as a vital source of Maaori identity and spiritual renewal. In Ihimaera's work, in particular, the return to the past is energised with fabulous, mythological figures, blending the magical, the fantastic and the supernatural. All use Maaori prophecy and belief to reflect upon the destiny of the race, and the visionary language of the spiritually enlightened, the *kaumatua* (elder) or *tohunga* (priest) is a crucial element in overturning the legacy of defeat.

Of more questionable relevance to the Maaori Renaissance, but often read as a coda to its concerns, is Alan Duff's writing. Duff exploits the register and lexicon of the working-class male rather than the Maaori, and his right-wing philosophy which advocates Maaori self-help in escaping the poverty-trap has distanced him from the other writers. The perceived assimilation to Paakehaa values in his fiction has made him controversial with both cultures. Nevertheless, the social realism of his famous novel, *Once Were Warriors* (1990), the first of a trilogy, has drawn attention to the violence which occurs in Maaori working-class domestic life, and which is endemic among gangsters such as the Mongrel Mob and the Black Power Gang.

Janet Wilson

Literary Works

Duff, Alan [1990] (1994), *Once Were Warriors*, Auckland: Tandem Press.
Duff, Alan (1996), *What Becomes of the Broken-Hearted?*, Auckland: Vintage.
Duff, Alan (2003), *Jake's Long Shadow*, Auckland: Vintage.
Grace, Patricia [1975] (1986), *Waiariki*, Auckland: Penguin.
Grace, Patricia [1978] (1986), *Mutuwhenua: The Moon Sleeps*, Auckland: Penguin.
Grace, Patricia (1986), *Potiki*, Auckland: Penguin.
Grace, Patricia [1998] (1999), *Baby No-Eyes*, London: Women's Press.
Hulme, Keri [1983] (1985), *The Bone People*, Auckland: Spiral, and Hodder and Stoughton.
Hulme, Keri (1986), *Te Kaihau: The Windeater*, Wellington: Victoria University Press.
Ihimaera, Witi (1973), *Tangi*, Auckland: Heinemann.
Ihimaera, Witi (1974), *Whanau*, Auckland: Heinemann.
Ihimaera, Witi (1986), *The Matriarch*, Auckland: Heinemann.
Ihimaera, Witi (1987), *The Whale Rider*, Auckland: Heinemann.
Ihimaera, Witi (1994), *Bulibasha: King of the Gypsies*, Auckland: Penguin.
Ihimaera, Witi (1997), *The Dream Swimmer*, Auckland: Penguin.
Ihimaera, Witi and Dan Long (eds) (1982), *Into the World of Light: An Anthology of Maaori Writing*, Auckland: Heinemann.
Ihimaera, Witi, Haare Williams, Irihapeti Ramsden and D. S. Long (eds) (1992–96), *Te Ao Marama: Contemporary Maaori Writing*, 5 vols, Auckland: Heinemann.

Histories

Adams, Peter (1977), *Fatal Necessity: British Intervention in New Zealand, 1830–1847*, Auckland: Auckland University Press; Oxford: Oxford University Press.
Belich, James (1986), *The New Zealand Wars and the Victorian Interpretation of Racial Conflict*, Auckland: Auckland University Press.
Belich, James (1989), *'I Shall Not Die': Titokowarau's War*, Wellington: Allen and Unwin/Port Nicholson Press.
Belich, James (1996), *Making Peoples: A History of the New Zealanders. From Polynesian Settlement to the End of the Nineteenth Century*, Auckland: Allen Lane, Penguin.
Belich, James (2001), *Paradise Reforged: A History of the New Zealanders from the 1880s to the Year 2000*, Auckland: Allen Lane, Penguin.
Binney, Judith (1995), *Redemption Songs: A Life of Te Kooti Arikirangi Te Turuki*, Auckland: Auckland University Press.
Kawharu, I. H. (ed.) (1989), *Waitangi: Maaori and Paakehaa Perspectives of the Treaty of Waitangi*, Auckland: Auckland University Press.
Rice, G. W. (ed.) (1992), *The Oxford History of New Zealand*, Auckland: Oxford University Press.
Robinson, Roger and Nelson Wattie (eds) (1998), *The Oxford Companion to New Zealand Literature*, Oxford: Oxford University Press.
Rutherford, J. (1961), *Sir George Grey, K.C.B., 1812–1898: A Study in Colonial Government*, London: Cassell.
Salmond, Anne (1991), *Two Worlds: First Meetings between the Maaori and Europeans 1642–1772*, Auckland: Penguin.

Sharp, Andrew and Paul McHugh (eds) (2001), *Histories of Power and Loss: Uses of the Past – A New Zealand Commentary*, Wellington: Bridget Williams Books.

Sinclair, Keith [1959] (2000), *A History of New Zealand*, Auckland: Penguin.

Sinclair, Keith (ed.) [1993] (1996), *The Oxford Illustrated History of New Zealand*, Auckland: Oxford University Press.

Spoonley, Paul, David Pearson and Cluny McPherson (eds) (1996), *Nga Patai: Racism and Ethnic Relations in Aotearoa/New Zealand*, Dunmore Press: Palmerston North.

Sturm, Terry (ed.) [1991] (1998), *The Oxford History of New Zealand Literature in English*, Auckland: Oxford University Press.

Temple, Philip (2003), *A Sort of Conscience – the Wakefields*, Auckland: Auckland University Press.

See also: **European Exploration and Settlement: Australia, New Zealand, Pacific; Pakeha; Waitangi Treaty**.

Maghrebine Resistance: Algeria

The ailing Bourbon monarchy's decision to attack Algiers in 1830 on the pretext of an insult by the Dey to a French official resulted in 132 years of conflict as the French army of Africa attempted to conquer an always resistant Algeria. Between 1830 and 1870, over half of the French army marshals earned their promotions from fighting in the Algerian wars, amongst them Thomas-Robert Bugeaud who struggled for eleven years to defeat the best-known of Algeria's resisters – the emir Abd al-Qadir. Despite the emir's defeat at the battle of Isly in 1844 his fight continued until a final surrender in 1848. He and his extended family were exiled to France. Other resisters were also deported including seventy-one members of the family of the former khalifa of Médéa.

The endemic violence of the French conquest is illustrated by the asphyxiation of the Oulad Riah in a cave in 1845 by Generals Pélissier and Saint-Arnaud. After Abd al-Qadir's defeat, an uneasy peace reigned in the western region until 1870 when a further ten years of conflict ensued between the Oulad Sidi Cheikh and the French army. Meanwhile, the conquest of Kabylia had begun in the 1850s under the governor-generalship of Marshal Randon. The exigencies of the conquest devastated the region and led to famine and starvation in the 1870s. With a simmering conflict in the west, a second conflict was opened in the east in 1871, by al-Muqrani. Armed resistance did not end with their defeats but was supplanted by political resistance as reform movements throughout the Middle East came into being inspired by the Young Turks.

While the Young Algerians sought a secular political reform and in particular, access to citizenship, a different movement began in the 1930s located around the Constantine religious figure, Sheikh Ben Badis (died 1941). Known as the Association of Reformist Ulama, it left a long-term legacy as its ideas were recycled in the writings of Malek Bennabi and Ben Badis' co-founder, Tawfik al-Madani became, post-independence, Minister for Religiously Endowed Property as well as an influential arabiser. In the period leading up to the founding of the Front de Libération Nationale in 1954, it was the secularist movements that were most influential, and an important place is held by the Mouvement pour le Triomphe des Libertés Démocratiques of Messali Hadj whose founding of the *Etoile Nord Africaine* amongst Algerian migrant workers in Paris in the 1920s politically radicalised many young Algerians.

Kay Adamson

Literary Works

Dib, Mohammed (1985) [1962], *Who Remembers the Sea? (Qui se Souvient la Mer?)*, trans. L. Tremaine, New York: Three Continents Press.
Djebar, Assia [1985] (1993), *Fantasia. An Algerian Cavalcade*, London: Heinemann.
Moore, Brian (1998), *The Magician's Wife*, London: Flamingo.

Histories

Adamson, Kay (2002), *Political and Economic Thought and Practice in Nineteenth-Century France and the Colonization of Algeria*, Lewiston, NY: The Edwin Mellen Press.
Ageron, Charles-Robert (1991), *Modern Algeria – A History from 1830 to the Present*, trans. and ed. Michael Brett, London: Hurst and Company.
Bennoune, M. (1988), *The Making of Contemporary Algeria, 1830–1987*, Cambridge: Cambridge University Press.
Berque, Jacques (1967), *French North Africa: The Maghrib between Two World Wars*, trans. Jean Stewart, London: Faber and Faber.

See also: **Algerian War of Independence; Islam; Nationalism(s): Arab**.

Maghrebine Resistance: Morocco and Tunisia

Algeria's independence struggle has overshadowed resistance to colonisation in France's other two North African colonies or 'protectorates' – Tunisia and Morocco. Although Tunisia was declared an official French protectorate in 1881, France had been increasing her presence and her political control there for many years. Colonial ideologues like Paul Leroy-Beaulieu might declare that colonisation would be different from Algeria but they failed to take account of the political awakening in the Middle East in the last quarter of the nineteenth century.

Opposition emerged in two forms, the largely secular Young Tunisians and a more traditional opposition centred on Tunisia's great mosque, the Zituna. By 1920, the Destour (Constitutional) Party had been formed and opposition intensified aided by a growing industrial workforce organised in a trade union movement led by Ferhat Hached, who was assassinated in 1952. In 1934, the Destour Party, under pressure from the Bourguiba brothers, Habib and M'hamed, split to form the Neo-Destour Party which became the party of independence. Meanwhile, in Morocco, France officially became a colonial power in March 1912, and in the process restricted a long-standing Spanish colonial interest to two areas of influence, the Rif in the north and Tarfaya and Ifni in the south. However, in July 1921, Spanish troops in the Rif were annihilated at Anoual by 'Abdulkrim al-Khattabi whose continued success pushed the Spanish back to the coastal areas. Now also a threat to French Morocco, an army of 160,000 commanded by Marshal Pétain was deployed. Al-Khattabi surrendered in May 1926 and was deported to Réunion until 1947.

Under General Lyautey, France followed a policy of indirect rule based on the idea that there existed two separate ethnicities – Berbers and Arabs – for whom distinct institutional arrangemments were required. The first Moroccan nationalist movement led by Allal el-

Fassi, founded in December 1934, contested this division but the decisive move came when Sultan Sidi Mohammed ben Moulay Arafa (Mohammed V) joined with the nationalists in 1943 to create under Ahmed Balafredj the Istiqlal (Independence) Party. Mohammed V's deportation to Madagascar by the French authorities in 1953 was brief and his return in November 1955 was followed by independence in 1956 when Tunisia also became independent.

Kay Adamson

Literary Works

Abouzeid, Leila [1993] (1999), *Return to Childhood: The Memoir of a Modern Moroccan Woman*, trans. the author and Heather Logan Taylor, Austin, TX: University of Texas Press.

Chraibi, Driss (1998), *Muhammad. A Novel*, trans. N. Benabid, Boulder, CO: Lynne Rienner.

Khatibi, Abdelkebir [1983] (1990), *Love in Two Languages*, Minneapolis, MN: University of Minnesota Press.

Maghraoui, Driss (2002), 'Nos Goumiers Berbères': The Ambiguities of Colonial Representations in French Military Novels', *The Journal of North African Studies* 7: 3, pp. 79–100.

Memmi, Albert [1957] (1990), *The Colonizer and the Colonized*, intro. Jean-Paul Sartre, new one Liam O'Dowd, London: Earthscan Publications.

Histories

Berque, Jacques [1962] (1967), *French North Africa. The Maghrib between Two World Wars*, London: Faber and Faber.

Findlay, Allan, Anne Findlay and Richard Lawless (1982), *Tunisia*, Oxford: Clio.

Larqui, Abdallah [1970] (1977), *The History of the Maghrib: An Interpretative Essay*, Princeton, NJ: Princeton University Press.

Maxell, Gavin (1966), *Lords of the Atlas*, London: Longmans.

Waterbury, John (1970), *The Commander of the Faithful*, London: Weidenfeld and Nicolson.

Ziadeh, Nicola A. (1969), *Origins of Nationalism in Tunisia*, Beirut: Lebanon Bookshop.

See also: **Algerian War of Independence; Islam; Nationalism(s): Arab**.

Mahdism

The Sudanese Mahdi was announced in June 1881 when Muhammad Ahmad ibn 'Abdallah began to dispatch letters to local leaders proclaiming himself the expected Mahdi. He had been a member of an Islamic mystical order in the north and moved to the Nile River island of Aba, south of Khartoum, where he established himself with a small band of followers. The Sudan was then an Ottoman-Egyptian colony. By the 1870s the colonial state was thoroughly neglected by the rulers based in Egypt, creating opportunities

for revolt. The administration and significant sectors of the colonial economy had substantial European participation right up to the level of governor. A few Sudanese were part of
the government but most of the indigenous peoples resented their foreign rulers. Much
support for the Mahdi was based on the belief that he was a divinely inspired figure.
Important towns such as El-Obeid, the main city of Kordofan, fell to the Mahdi's forces in
January 1883, and the defeat of the expedition of Colonel William Hicks in September of
the same year at Shaykan tremendously bolstered the movement.

The already weak government in Cairo was unable to do much to stem the tide of the
Mahdi's success, and the British, who had recently occupied Egypt (in 1882) were hesitant
to act. When General Charles Gordon was dispatched to the Sudan he was sent with
contradictory instructions: to restore 'good government' and to evacuate the colony. When
he reached Khartoum he wrote to the Mahdi offering him the sultanship of Kordofan,
which he rejected. The Mahdi had much bigger ambitions that transcended political
authority especially in an isolated province.

In January 1885 Khartoum fell to the Mahdists. But instead of installing himself there
the Mahdi established a new capital called Omdurman, opposite the old one. There he died
in June 1885, was buried, and a tomb was built for him. But the Mahdi's tomb was
destroyed, and his body disinterred, in the reconquest of the Sudan by Sir Herbert
Kitchener in 1898. The Mahdi's successor in 1885, Khalifa Abdullahi, sent his armies onto
multiple fronts: in the West to pacify the state of Dar Fur, onto the Ethiopian marches, and
onto the Egyptian border. Internal schisms surfaced between various layers of supporters
who were dissatisfied with the khalifa's policies. By the early 1890s the khalifa's armies had
been easily beaten in numerous engagements. Their final defeat came at the hands of
Kitchener, beginning in August 1897 until the last battle at Karari, outside Omdurman, in
September 1898. Thousands of Sudanese fighters were killed and wounded while the
Anglo-Egyptian losses numbered fewer than fifty.

Shamil Jeppie

Literary Works

Mahjoub, Jamal (1996), *In the Hour of Signs*, Oxford: Heinemann.

Histories

Holt, P. M. (1958), *The Mahdist State in the Sudan 1881–1898: A Study of its Origins,
    Development and Overthrow*, Oxford: Clarendon Press.
Holt, P. M. and M. W. Daly (2000), *A History of the Sudan: From the Coming of Islam to the
    Present Day*, 5th edn, Harlow: Longman.

See also: **Sudanese Civil War**.

Marcos, Ferdinand and Imelda

Ferdinand E. Marcos was elected president of the Philippines in 1965 and was re-elected
in 1972, the year martial law was declared. After this, Marcos and his wife, Imelda
Fomualdez Marcos, began to obliterate the legal, congressional, and constitutional struc-

tures that comprised the Philippine government, and replace them with what he called 'constitutional authoritarianism'. His justification for imposing martial law was a precipitous increase in crime and the threat of insurrection by communist and Muslim guerrilla groups. However, he deemed its continuation until 1981 essential to create what he called the 'New Society', which included major land reform, extensive infrastructure projects, and reorganisation of the political process. Initially, martial law did provide some relief to the people, giving the government a stronger hand against the insurgent groups and organised crime. However, the ultimate effect of concentrating power in so few hands, in stripping the judiciary of its independence, and of curtailing the media's freedom of speech led to a corrupt government that operated with ruthless brutality. Opposition to government policies was considered sedition and led to tactics typical of a dictatorial regime: random arrests, intimidation, torture and assassination.

This style of government was Marcos's undoing. In 1981, his most prominent opponent, Ninoy Aquino, was murdered upon his return to the Philippines after many years of exile in America. The popular mandate that Marcos had enjoyed began to disintegrate in the incredible wave of sympathy for Aquino and his family. Marcos occasionally called elections to give a democratic veneer to his autocratic government. These elections were fraught with corruption and no real opposition was allowed to participate. However, in the election of 7 February 1986, Corazon Aquino, the widow of Ninoy Aquino, was permitted to run, and she garnered massive popular support. It was clear to the general population that she had won, but Marcos declared victory for himself. The peaceful public demonstrations protesting this victory grew steadily, and ultimately the army refused to retaliate against the demonstrators, who were from all walks of Philippine life. Eventually, the minister of defence, Jose Enrile, and the head of the Philippine constabulary, Fidel Ramos, put their support behind Aquino, and Marcos was forced to flee to Hawaii. The EDSA (Epifanio de los Santos Avenue) revolution is named after the road where the demonstrations took place, and the revolution's success has been credited to the strength of 'people power'.

Jennifer McMahon

Literary Works

Dalisay, Jose Y., Jr. (1992), *Killing Time in a Warm Place*, Pasig: Anvil Press.
Hagedorn, Jessica (1991), *Dogeaters*, New York: Penguin.
José, Francisco Sionil (1983), *Mass*, Manila: Solidaridad.
Rosca, Ninotchka (1988), *State of War*, New York: Norton.
Ty-Casper, Linda (1986), *Wings of Stone*, New York: Readers International.

Histories

Aquino, Belinda (1987), *The Politics of Plunder: The Philippines under Marcos*, Quezon City: Great Books Trading.
Celoza, Albert F. (1997), *Ferdinand Marcos and the Philippines: the Political Economy of Authoritarianism*, Westport, CT: Praeger.
Rosenberg, David A. (ed.) (1979), *Marcos and Martial Law in the Philippines*, Ithaca, NY: Cornell University Press.

See also: **Historiography: South-east Asia; Spanish-American War; Thomasites.**

Merdeka

The Malay word *merdeka* is associated with the phrase *orang merdeka* or 'free men'. As a rallying cry for independence from British colonial rule, it had the historical resonance of the ancient Malacca laws which differentiated between *orang merdeka* and *orang hamba* (slaves). For many Malaysians, the popular iconographic image of independence, reproduced recurrently in the mass-media, is that of the first prime minister, Tengku Abdul Rahman shouting the word *merdeka* three times to proclaim the country's new status on 31 August 1957, in the packed Merdeka Stadium. As the leader of the Alliance, a combination of the UMNO (United Malay National Organisation) and the other major ethnic parties representing the Chinese and the Indians, the tengku is the elite, conservative nationalist voice.

The anti-colonial struggle in Malaya (as Malaysia was then called) was most clearly militant in the case of the Malayan Communist Party whose members took up armed struggle when the party was banned and the 1948 emergency declared. The more conservative elements in the negotiations for self-rule were negotiating for gradual political changes and were careful not to evince an anti-Western tone. The British were more prepared to deliberate with political leaders who would ensure that on independence Malaya would not embark on a course of nationalist development that would jeopardise British economic and military influence.

Besides the communist insurgency, the other stumbling block to independence was communalism. A multicultural Malayan nationalism that transcended ethnicity was almost totally absent. In early 1952, the colonial secretary, Lyttleton, issued a statement that Malaya was to be given independence only when the various races were united. In the 1940s and 1950s political parties in Malaya were communal in nature with the Malays being concerned about special privileges and the non-Malays concerned about citizenship rights. The MCA (Malayan Chinese Association) founded by Tan Cheng Lock, wanted citizenship legislation to be revised and non-Malays to be given more opportunities to work in the civil service. Attempts to form non-racial political parties, for example, the Independence of Malaya Party (IMP) by Onn Jaafar in September 1951 were unproductive. An alliance of convenience between the UMNO and the MCA (17 March 1953) and later the MIC (Malayan Indian Congress) was eventually formed. The MCA and the UMNO pushed for federal elections in 1954 and party members threatened to resign from the legislation council should the proposal be rejected by the British. Elections were called on 27 July 1955 and the alliance (comprising the UMNO, the MCA and the MIC) won fifty-one of the fifty-two elected seats. As an overwhelming majority of the registered voters were Malay, the problem of communalism remained. Nonetheless a kind of 'consociationalism' among the parties in the alliance was evident as a strategy to push for self-rule. The tengku also used the failure of the talks with the communists (in Baling, December 1955), who refused the conditions of amnesty as they did not include the recognition of the Malayan Communist Party as a legal organisation, to pressure the British government to grant independence. From 18 January 1956 onwards, talks were held in London between the tengku and the Malay princes and the colonial secretary, Alan Lennox-Boyd. An agreement was reached that independence within the Commonwealth was to be proclaimed by 31 August 1957. Lord Reid was appointed to draft the details of a constitution. In the constitution, Malay special privileges were to be maintained but subject to revision after fifteen years.

In the gradual progress toward *merdeka* or independence, Malayan anti-colonialism may be said to have given rise to an elite bourgeois nationalism and a more popular, socialist nationalism. The radicalisation of the masses in the 1940s and 1950s surfaced in labour organisations and among the urban proletariat. The roles of more socialist-leaning nationalist figures such as Lim Chin Siong and Ahmad Boestamam have been given new scholarly attention with the publication of their own writings and historical accounts from their contemporaries. This 'revisioning' adds to the complex historiography of Malaya's anti-colonial struggle and reveals that the road to *merdeka* did have different signposts for different groups.

Wong Saokoon

Literary Works

Ee Tiang Hong (1976), *Myths for a Wilderness*, Singapore: Heinemann.
Fernando, Lloyd (1974), *Twenty-Two Malaysian Stories*, Singapore: Heinemann.
Fernando, Lloyd (1976), *Scorpion Orchid*, Singapore: Heinemann.
Lee Kok Liang (1964), *The Mutes in the Sun*, Hong Kong: Heinemann.
Usman Awang (1998), 'Pak Utih' (Father Utih), trans. A. Amin, in Usman Awang, *Malaysian Literary Laureates: Selected Works*, trans. by S. Isyak et al., Kuala Lumpur: Dewan Bahasa and Pustaka.

Histories

Ahmad Boestamam (1979), *Carving the Path to the Summit*, trans. W. R. Roff, Athens, OH: Ohio University Press.
Pluvier, J. M. (1977), *South-East Asia from Colonialism to Independence*, Kuala Lumpur: Oxford University Press.
Ratnam, K. J. (1965), *Communalism and the Political Process in Malaya*, Singapore: University of Malaya Press.
Roff, William R. (1974), *The Origins of Malay Nationalism*, Kuala Lumpur: University of Malaya Press.
Tan Jing Quee and K. S. Jomo (eds) (2001), *Comet in our Sky: Lim Chin Siong in History*, Kuala Lumpur: Insan.
Tregonning, K. G. (1964), *A History of Modern Malaya*, London: University of London Press.

See also: **Communism: South-east Asia; Engmalchin; Historiography: South-east Asia.**

Mfecane

Early nineteenth-century Southern African societies went through great social convulsions that have fascinated and divided historians ever since. 'Mfecane' is the historical term used to described these convulsions which culminated in the rise between 1790 and 1830 of major polities such as the Zulu, Swati, Sotho, Pedi, Khumalo, and the Ngoni near Lake Victoria. The sequence of historical explanations for the Mfecane is as follows. The colonial/settler historians like G. M. Theal and G. E. Cory argued that the interior of southern Africa had been empty until the arrival from the north of African communities at roughly the same time that Afrikaners from the Cape started their trek inland. Accordingly, any legal rights to African land were up for grabs: 'What more right has the Fingo to privileges in South Africa than any member of the European family?' (quoted in Saunders 1988, p. 38), asked Theal in 1906. The next explanation of the Mfecane was put forward by the Africanist historian John Omer-Cooper, who proposed in *The Zulu Aftermath* (1966) that the Mfecane was a process of social, political and military change internal to African society that had taken place with explosive rapidity, and had seen the epic rise of new African states under charismatic leaders like Shaka of the Zulu, Mzilikazi of the Ndebele, and Moshoeshoe of the Sotho. These polities came into being by raiding and absorbing weaker states into their fold, and provided security for their expanding numbers of followers and livestock. The third, and in many ways most hotly-disputed, phase of the Mfecane debate was initiated by Julian Cobbing in 1983. According to Cobbing, Shaka was not the centre of an internal revolution (as Omer-Copper had argued), but rather the cause of the violence and upheavals of the Mfecane lay in the slave trade centred in Delagoa Bay, which had depopulated the interior. Another important element in Cobbing's argument is that the violence in the interior was not Zulu-inspired, but came from armed bands such as the Griquas. For example, Cobbing argues that during the Battle of Dithakong on 26 June 1823 in the Northern Cape, missionary officials and Griqua mercenaries colluded in order to acquire prisoners for the Cape Colony's labour market, and he also locates the cause of the Ndebele migrations of 1827, 1832 and 1837 not with the Zulu expansionism, as most writers have assumed, but with Griqua and later Boer attacks from the south. The fourth phase of the Mfecane debate is ongoing, and comprises both formidable contributions in support of Cobbing's thesis (like Norman Etherington's recent *The Great Treks* (2001)), and bitter attacks on Cobbing (see the chapters by Peires, Kinsman and Hartley in Hamilton (1995), and Legassick's review of Etherington (2002)). At present, the weight of scholarly opinion appears to be slightly against Cobbing's thesis, but there is no doubt that the arguments about the Mfecane are far from settled. Literary scholars have also taken up the themes of the Mfecane and particularly Shaka, with both eyewitness accounts and historical fiction.

Rachidi Molapo

Literary Works

Kunene, Mazisi (1979), *Emperor Shaka the Great: A Zulu Epic*, London: Heinemann.
Mofolo, Thomas (1989), *Chaka*, trans. D. P. Kunene, London: Heinemann.
Opperman, D. J. (1947), 'Shaka', in D. J. Opperman, *Heilige Beeste*, Cape Town: Nasionale Boekhandel, pp. 53–67.
Plaatje, Sol T. (1978), *Mhudi*, London: Heinemann.
Van Coller, P. P. R. (1946), *Die Swart Atilla*, Johannesburg: Dagbreek-pers.

Histories

Cobbing, Julian (1983), 'The Case against the *Mfecane*', Cape Town: African Studies Centre seminar paper, University of Cape Town.

Cobbing, Julian (1988), 'The Mfecane as Alibi: Thoughts on Dithakong and Mbholompo', *Journal of African History* 29, pp. 487–519.

Cory, G. E. (1926), *The Rise of South Africa*, London: Longmans, Green.

Etherington, Norman (2001), *The Great Treks. The Transformation of Southern Africa, 1815–1854*, London: Longman Pearson.

Hamilton, Carolyn (ed.) (1995), *The 'Mfecane' Aftermath. Reconstructive Debates in Southern African History*, Johannesburg: Witwatersrand University Press.

Harries, Patrick (1981), 'Slavery, Social Incorporation and Surplus Extraction: The Nature of Free and Unfree Labour in South-East Africa', *Journal of African History* 22, pp. 309–30.

Legassick, Martin (2002), 'The Great Treks', *South African Historical Journal* 46, pp. 283–99.

Mashingaidze, E. K. (1989), 'The Impact of the Mfecane on the Cape Colony', in J. F. Ade Ajayi (ed.), *The General History of Africa, Volume 1. Africa in the Nineteenth Century until the 1880s*, Berkeley, CA: University of California Press.

Omer-Cooper, J. D. (1966), *The Zulu Aftermath: A Nineteenth-Century Revolution in Bantu Africa*, London: Longmans.

Saunders, Christopher (1988), *The Making of the South African Past*, Cape Town: David Philip.

Theal, G. M. (1908), *History of South Africa from 1795 to 1872*, London: George Allen and Unwin.

See also: **Frontier wars: Southern Africa; Historiography: Southern Africa; Pre-colonial Histories: Southern Africa**.

Migrancy: Southern Africa

Central to the moral panic over immigration which gripped South Africa after 1994 is the notion that the country is being swamped by a 'black tide' from the north. The number of non-citizens in the country at any one time has certainly increased substantially since South Africa reconnected to the rest of the world, but it is highly misleading to assume that everyone is actually an immigrant who wants to stay.

Unfortunately, South Africa's long history of cross-border migration seems to have faded from public view and myopia is everywhere evident. This is understandable, perhaps, in public discourse. But when a scholarly work includes a chapter entitled 'Illegals in South Africa: Historical Overview' which appears to assume that cross-border migration did not begin until the first Mozambican crawled under the electrified fence in 1985, there is clearly a major problem of historical amnesia that needs to be addressed (see Minnaar and Hough 1996).

Cross-border migration has taken various forms. At one end of the spectrum is the highly formalised and regulated contract system to the South African mines, which was put in place in the period between 1890 and 1920. At the other are various kinds of informal, unregulated or clandestine movements across borders. South Africa has been receiving and returning both kinds of migrants for decades. Cross-border migration between South Africa and its neighbours is therefore nothing new. In its modern form, labour migration to South Africa from the region dates back over 150 years. Indeed, long-distance migration for employment pre-dates the drawing of international borders by the colonial powers in the latter half of the nineteenth century.

Migrants from present-day Mozambique, Malawi, Lesotho and Zimbabwe came to work in the sugar-cane fields of Natal and the diamond mines of Kimberley from the 1840s onwards, long before South Africa itself came into existence (see Worger 1987 and Harries 1994). They came primarily to earn money to buy guns to defend themselves against colonial encroachment and to buy agricultural implements to expand agriculture at home. The migrants came and went virtually as they pleased until pass laws and compounds were introduced to curtail and control their movements. Borders existed on colonial maps, not on the ground. Crossing borders was the least of migrants' worries on the long and dangerous journey south.

The history of mine migrancy, and its role in the development of economic and racial oppression within South Africa, has been well-documented (see Jeeves 1985, Crush, Jeeves and Yudelman 1992, and James 1992). So, too, have the negative health and social impacts of working in the mines for communities and countries of the Southern African region (see Packard 1989). This material can easily be consulted by interested readers, who will notice a historiographic shift over the last twenty years from studies of the political economy of the migrant labour system towards studies of the actual experience of migration and mine-work by the migrants themselves (see Moodie 1994 and Coplan 1994).

With the discovery of gold in the 1880s, the Witwatersrand came into existence. Within twenty years, Johannesburg had grown into a city of over 200,000 people. Many were temporary residents from areas as far away as Tanganyika (Tanzania). The mines had a voracious appetite for cheap, male labour and the rural areas of the subcontinent began to supply it. Colonial taxation, land dispossession and the destruction of peasant agriculture explain some of the movement. But migrants had their own reasons for going too – to earn money, to invest in agriculture back home, and to purchase consumer goods. Recruiting stations were established throughout the region and modern transport systems (road, rail, ferry and eventually air) speeded migrants to the mines. Neighbouring colonies did not want to lose the migrants permanently, so agreements were reached between governments to make sure that miners were recruited on fixed contracts and that they went home afterwards. Fearful that they might stay in South Africa if their families accompanied them, everyone agreed that only the migrants themselves could go.

During the expansionary phase that followed, the numbers of migrants in the mines grew rapidly as new regions were bundled into the system. Between 1920 and 1940, the number of foreign miners in South Africa doubled from 100,000 to 200,000. At the peak, in the early 1970s, the number rose close to 300,000. The largest supplier was Malawi (at 120,000 in 1973), followed by Mozambique, Lesotho, Botswana and Swaziland. Even Zambians, Angolans and Tanzanians came in their thousands before their newly independent governments told them not to. The only country where the numbers were small was Zimbabwe, which had its own mining industry and employment opportunities. The contract migration system was consistently expansionist for most of its history. Few rural areas of the subcontinent were inaccessible to the sophisticated recruiting apparatus of the South African mining industry. Although the migrant flow from particular zones fluctuated over time, few rural areas were untouched. Some, such as Lesotho and southern Mozambique, became highly integrated into and deeply marked by the system.

Malawi was thrown out of the system after a dispute over AIDS testing in the late 1980s. But migrants continued to come from the traditional sources of Mozambique, Lesotho, Swaziland and Botswana. In the late 1980s and early 1990s, the mines suffered massive retrenchments. The companies laid off three South Africans to every one foreign miner. In proportional terms, the mine workforce is over 50 per cent foreign once again. Almost a quarter of the mine workforce is now from Mozambique. Minework is physically and psychologically debilitating. Many migrants prefer to avoid the mines altogether. This is nothing new. When the mines experienced periodic labour shortage 'crises', it was usually because migrants could find work in other sectors. For much of the twentieth century, clandestine migration referred not to the 'illegal' crossing of borders per se but to the process of going to South Africa without documentation (travelling passes in the early days, identity documents and passports more recently). However, since colonial governments were generally more interested in monitoring the movement than controlling it, passes were relatively easy to get. There were no border posts and people crossed where they wanted.

Outside the contract system, the journey south for migrants was a fairly hazardous undertaking. Migrants had to pay for their own transport or travel on foot, and often stopped to work en route to their final destination. An elaborate word-of-mouth information network told migrants where to look for work and whom to avoid. Most migrants headed for the towns and cities and found work in construction, services and secondary industry. There they were subject, like black South Africans, to pass laws and constant police harassment. Many were arrested and shipped off to work on the farms under apartheid's notorious prison labour system. But the farmers were still desperate for labourers. They organised private recruiting companies and intercepted migrants at the borders, dragooning them into farmwork. South Africa's rich agricultural farmland was developed with the labour of migrants from the east and north.

The history of informal cross-border migration in Southern Africa also reveals an intense moral panic attached to one particular group of migrants – women. Women migrants from the region, like their South African counterparts, were always marginalised and pushed to the back of the queue in local labour markets (see Miles 1991 and Cockerton 1995). The only paid work that many could get was domestic service in white households. Others turned to professions that at least ensured a livelihood – informal trading, liquor production and sex work. All were 'illegal' and in constant conflict with the law. From very early in the century, therefore, black women in town were depicted as moral polluters. Their mere presence in town was seen to signify the disintegration of rural society (see Bozzoli 1991). These images were, of course, highly misleading. In the supplier areas, colonial governments, chiefs and male elders collaborated to keep women in the rural areas. This 'patriarchal coalition' checked women's migration, though some escaped its chains. Studies of women migrants from Lesotho, Swaziland and Botswana show that as the decades passed, more and more women spent time in South Africa. Initially, they accompanied spouses and partners. Later, they went on their own as young, single women.

After 1960 (with the political independence of black Africa), the apartheid government espied a new *swaart gevar* (black peril) from the north. Migrants, once welcomed for economic reasons, were now seen as a political threat. Border posts were established between South Africa and its immediate neighbours for the first time in the early 1960s. Foreign women coming now had to carry passes. This, taken with increased harassment by the police, made life very uncomfortable. Many returned home during this period of heightened oppression and the numbers of foreign-born African women shrank. One of the great imponderables of the history of migration in Southern Africa is whether more people from the region would have made South Africa their permanent home if they had been allowed to. It is generally assumed that the reason why black people continued to migrate, rather than immigrate, to South Africa was because they had no choice. The policies of the day ensured that they remained migrants. Others would argue that the impact of the policies has been exaggerated; that even if immigration had been allowed, most would have continued to migrate. Certainly, black people from the region could never aspire to be legal immigrants under apartheid. Legislation specified that all immigrants had to be 'assimilable' by the white population. That restriction was on the statute books until as recently as 1986.

Unsurprisingly, the apartheid government's hostile attitude to black immigrants contrasts sharply with the attitude taken towards white immigrants. The racist underpinnings of South African immigration policy became particularly transparent in the 1970s and 1980s when whites threatened by political independence in neighbouring states were welcomed with open arms in South Africa. The drift south of whites from the region began in Zambia, Kenya and Malawi in the 1960s with political independence from Britain. White flight accelerated dramatically when Angola and Mozambique won their independence in the mid-1970s. The haven of white South Africa was even more attractive to whites who deserted newly-independent Zimbabwe in the 1980s.

At the same time, South African destabilisation wrought havoc on the landscape and peoples of Mozambique. The South African-sponsored civil war had a calamitous impact on that country and, as a result, Southern Africa faced its first ever mass refugee migration. Surrounding countries such as Malawi, Zimbabwe and Swaziland took the refugees in while South Africa did its utmost to keep them out, electrifying the Mozambican border and arresting and deporting asylum seekers. The South African government's callous failure to afford protection to the refugees caused by its own policies was apartheid at its most cynical. Nevertheless, the government found it impossible to keep out desperate people and by 1990, an estimated 350,000 refugees had crossed the border. Rights and privileges normally accorded to refugees under international conventions were denied as South Africa had never signed these protocols. But as long as these Mozambicans remained in border villages they were not harassed. If they left those areas they were arrested and deported as 'illegal aliens'.

South Africans have had to contend, since 1994, with a deluge of misinformation and several competing visions of the implications of migration and immigration for their country. The natural tendency has been to assume the worst and to pull up the drawbridge. Post-1994 public policy on migration and immigration in South Africa has been based on two main sources of information. One is the extravagant claims and simplistic imagery of xenophobia in the popular press. Migrants rarely 'enter' or 'come' to South Africa. Rather, they 'flood', 'deluge' and 'swarm'. The other is the appeal to 'science'. Rarely does an opportunity go by without official reference to the 'scientific basis' of policies to garner more resources for border controls and policing. The history of migration is of little interest to this agenda. On the contrary, cross-border migration in the Southern African region is nothing new. Borders have always been exceedingly porous. The truth is that if people really want to come they will find a way to do so. Logically, there was no reason why 1994 should have brought an epochal change in longstanding patterns and modes of migrant behaviour. That, indeed, has proved to be the case.

Jonathan Crush

Literary Works

Abrahams, Peter [1946] (1963), *Mine Boy*, London: Heinemann.
Diescho, Joseph (1988), *Born of the Sun. A Namibian Novel*, New York: Friendship Press.
Gordimer, Nadine (1992), *Jump and Other Stories*, Penguin: London.

Gunn, S. and M-M. Tal (eds) (2003), *Torn Apart. Thirteen Refugees Tell their Stories*, Cape Town: Human Rights Media Watch.

Head, Bessie (1973), *A Question of Power*, London: Heinemann.

Mda, Zakes (1990), 'The Hill', in A. Horn (ed.), *The Plays of Zakes Mda*, Johannesburg: Ravan Press, pp. 67–115.

Mda, Zakes (1995), *She Plays with Darkness*, Johannesburg: Vivlia.

Mpe, Phaswane (2001), *Welcome to our Hillbrow*, Pietermaritzburg: University of Natal Press.

Mungoshi, Charles [1972] (1989), *The Setting Sun and the Rolling World*, Boston, MA: Beacon.

Histories

Bozzoli, B. (1991), *Women of Phokeng: Consciousness, Life Strategy and Migrancy in South Africa, 1900–1983*, Portsmouth, NH: Heinemann.

Cockerton, C. (1995), 'Running away from the Land of the Desert: Women's Migration from Colonial Botswana to South Africa, c. 1895–1966', Kingston: Queen's University unpublished Ph.D.

Coplan, D. (1994), *In the Time of the Cannibals: The Word Music of South Africa's Basotho Migrants*, Chicago: University of Chicago Press.

Crush, J. (1995), 'Vulcan's Brood. Spatial Narratives of Migration on Southern Africa', in R. King, J. Connell and P. White (eds), *Writing across Worlds. Literature and Migration*, London and New York: Routledge, pp. 229–47.

Crush, J. and W. James (1995), *Crossing Boundaries: Mine Migrancy in a Democratic South Africa*, Cape Town: Idasa; IDRC.

Crush, J., A. Jeeves and D. Yudelman (1992), *South Africa's Labor Empire: A History of Black Migrancy to the Gold Mines*, Boulder, CO: Westview Press.

Harries, P. (1994), *Work, Culture and Identity: Migrant Labourers in Mozambique and South Africa, c. 1860–1910*, Portsmouth, NH: Heinemann.

James, W. (1992), *Our Precious Metal: African Labour in South Africa's Gold Industry, 1970–1990*, Cape Town: David Philip Publishers.

Jeeves, A. (1985), *Migrant Labour in South Africa's Mining Economy: The Struggle for the Gold Mines' Labour Supply, 1890–1920*, Montreal and Kingston: McGill-Queen's University Press.

Jeeves, A. and J. Crush (eds) (1997), *White Farms, Black Labour: The State and Agrarian Change in Southern Africa, 1910–1950*, Portsmouth, NH: Heinemann.

Miles, M. (1991), 'Missing Women: A Study of Female Swazi Migration to the Witwatersrand, 1920–1970', Kingston: Queen's University unpublished MA thesis.

Minnaar, A. and M. Hough (1996), *Who Goes There? Perspectives on Migration and Illegal Aliens in Southern Africa*, Pretoria: Human Science Research Council.

Moodie, D. (1994), *Going for Gold: Men, Mines and Migration*, Berkeley, CA: University of California Press.

Nixon, R. (1996), 'Rural Transnationalism. Bessie Head's Southern Spaces', in K. Darian-Smith, L. Gunner and S. Nuttall (eds), *Text, Theory, Space: Land, Literature and History in South Africa and Australia*, London: Routledge, pp. 243–54.

Packard, R. (1989), *White Plague, Black Labour: Tuberculosis and the Political Economy of Health and Disease in South Africa*, Berkeley, CA: University of California Press.

Southern African Migration Project. Available at http://www.queensu.ca/samp/

Stotesbury, John A. (1990), 'The Function of Borders in the Popular Novel on South Africa', *English in Africa* 17: 2, pp. 71–89.

Worger, W. (1987), *South Africa's City of Diamonds: Mine Workers and Monopoly Capitalism in Kimberley, 1867–1895*, New Haven, CT: Yale University Press.

See also: **Historiography: Southern Africa; Labour Histories: Southern Africa; Mineral Revolution: Southern Africa; Refugees.**

Military Dictatorships: South Asia

When the British partitioned India, they left behind a robust constitutional administrative structure. But where India moved rapidly to democratise its polity by writing a new constitution and breaking the hold of the landed elites, Pakistan fumbled with vague ideas of democracy based on Islam. It survived its first coup attempt at the hands of the army led by messianic Major-General Akbar Khan in 1951. Within two years of the constitution coming into being in 1956, political chaos led to the imposition of martial law, on 7 October 1958, called for by President Iskander Mirza, himself a former army major-general. But the real power was with Gen Ayub Khan, the chief of army staff who, as the chief martial law administrator soon removed Mirza from the scene and exiled him. Ayub survived until March 1969 when he allowed army chief General Yahya Khan to take power as the martial law administrator. Yahya called for elections in 1971, but he also proclaimed a Legal Framework Order (LFO) to give the army a veto on all the national assembly deliberations. This was used to curb the demands of the Awami League (one of the oldest and major political parties in Bangladesh) and led to the civil war that ended with the creation of Bangladesh.

After a spell of civilian rule under Z. A. Bhutto, Pakistan again faced political turmoil leading to the military coup of 4 July 1977 by the army chief General Zia ul Haq who declared himself chief martial law administrator. Bhutto was interned, imprisoned and later hanged, in April 1979.

Zia was not just another dictator, he was a devout Muslim and worked to Islamise the Pakistani state. On 17 August 1988 Zia died in an as yet unsolved plane crash. Free and fair elections were held and Benazir Bhutto came to power as prime minister. After a decade of ups and downs in which civilian governments managed the affairs of Pakistan, the army, under its chief General Pervez Musharraf, struck once again, on 12 October 1999 to take the reins of power directly into its hands. The coup was somewhat accidental, but Musharraf has used all the devices of past dictators – the LFO and referendums – to legitimise his power.

On 15 August 1975, President Mujib-ur-Rehman of Bangladesh was assassinated in a coup, led by some army officers. After a brief period of instability, Major General Zia-ur-Rehman, the army chief, took over. Rehman legitimised his rule through the June 1978 elections that elected him president of Bangladesh. On 30 May 1981, he was assassinated and political instability returned, until Lieutenant-General H. M. Ershad took over on 24 March 1982 and declared martial law. On 15 October 1986, Ershad was elected as president and martial law was repealed the following month. In December 1990, he was deposed and arrested after a popular uprising. Bangladesh has been a democracy since the 1991 general election in which the Bangladesh National Party, led by Begum Khaleda Zia-ur-Rehman, came to power.

Manoj Joshi

Literary Works

Hussein, Aamer (2002), *Turquoise*, London: Saqi Books.
Khan, Adib (1994), *Seasonal Adjustments*, St Leonards: Allen and Unwin.
Naqvi, Maniza (1998), *Mass Transit*, Karachi: Oxford University Press.
Rushdie, Salman (1983), *Shame*, New York: Holt.
Suleri, Sara (1991), *Meatless Days*, Chicago: Chicago University Press.

Histories

Arif, K. M. (2001), *Khaki Shadows: Pakistan 1947–1997*, Karachi: Oxford University Press.
Gauhar, Altaf (1996), *Ayub Khan Pakistan's First Military Ruler*, Karachi: Oxford University Press.
Hasan Zaheer, Hasan (1998), *The Times and Trial of the Rawalpindi Conspiracy 1951: The First Coup Attempt in Pakistan*, Karachi: Oxford University Press.
Imam, Jahanara (1998), *Of Blood and Fire: The Untold Story of Bangladesh's War of Independence*, trans. M. Rahman, Dhaka: Dhaka University Press.
Jalal, Ayesha (1990), *The State of Martial Rule: The Origins of Pakistan's Political Economy of Defence*, Cambridge: Cambridge University Press.
Lifschultz, Lawrence (1979), *Bangladesh: The Unfinished Revolution*, London: Zed Books.

See also: **Bangladesh: 1971; Pakistan's Subaltern Struggles; Partition; Secessionism: South Asia; Terrorism: South Asia.**

Mineral Revolutions: Southern Africa

Mining was practised in Southern Africa before European contact, but the discovery of diamonds at the Orange-Vaal River confluence in 1867, and of gold on the Witwatersrand in 1886, had unprecedented socio-political effects on the region. Speculators thronged to what soon became the site of the world's largest diamond diggings, by 1910 producing 95 per cent of the world's diamonds. In 1871, British arbitration settled disputes over the area's control in favour of Waterboer's Griqua people; Griqualand West immediately became a Crown colony, joining the Cape Colony in 1880. Unskilled labourers, recruited from Bapedi, Basotho, Shona, Ndebele, Tswana and Zulu areas, were housed in often unsanitary compounds. By 1889 De Beers, Cecil Rhodes' company, had secured complete control of the industry. De Beers Consolidated and Anglo American continue to monopolise the international diamond trade.

The capitalisation of the region continued with the discovery of gold, and Johannesburg quickly grew on the site of the main gold-bearing reef. By 1898 South Africa was the world's largest gold producer. Tensions between foreign miners and the Transvaal republic's government contributed to the Anglo-Boer War. The Chamber of Mines (est. 1887) ensured uniform wages across the industry, recruiting cheap labour throughout Southern Africa. Between 1904 and 1907, 70,000 indentured Chinese labourers were imported to alleviate labour shortages. Most early black labourers in the gold mines were Mozambican, but in the 1930s recruitment extended to Malawi, Zambia, Botswana, Namibia, Lesotho and Swaziland. Even by the 1970s, 80 per cent of workers were non-South Africans. Male miners were forced to leave their families in impoverished rural areas. Repeated strikes for improved pay and conditions yielded little; the National Union of Mineworkers, only recognised in 1982, became a key member of COSATU, the powerful trade union congress.

The industry has been expanding to exploit Southern Africa's many significant mineral reserves. Though credited with funding infrastructure, it has also created huge wealth disparities, exploited migrant labour, and was a significant source of tax revenue for the apartheid government. The influence of the most powerful industry in the region has been profound, and pervasive.

Andrew van der Vlies

Literary Works

Abrahams, Peter (1946), *Mine Boy*, London: Dorothy Crisp and Company.
Blackburn, Douglas (1908), *Leaven: A Black and White Story*, London: Alston Rivers.
Couzens, Tim and Essop Patel (1982), *The Return of the Amasi Bird: Black South African Poetry, 1891–1981*, Johannesburg: Ravan Press.
Gordimer, Nadine (1974), *The Conservationist*, London: Jonathan Cape.
Paton, Alan (1948), *Cry, the Beloved Country*, New York: Scribner.

Histories

Crush, Jonathan, Alan Jeeves and David Yudelman (1991), *South Africa's Labor Empire: A History of Back Migrancy to the Gold Mines*, Boulder, CO: Westview; Cape Town: David Philip.
Davenport, Rodney and Christopher Saunders (2000), *South Africa: A Modern History*, 5th edn, London: Macmillan.
Gray, Stephen (1985), 'Third World Meets First World: The Theme of "Jim Comes to Jo'burg" in South African English Fiction', *Kunapipi* 7: 1, pp. 61–80.
Innes, Duncan (1984), *Anglo American and the Rise of Modern South Africa*, London: Heinemann Educational Books.
Moodie, T. Dunbar (1994), *Going for Gold: Men, Mines, and Migration*, Berkeley, CA: University of California Press.

See also: **Historiography: Southern Africa; Labour Histories: Southern Africa**.

Missionaries: Southern Africa

In terms of Christianity, Southern Africa represents the most intensively missionised part of the continent. Catholic missionaries were present in the Portuguese enclaves of Angola and Mozambique from the sixteenth century. Serious inland proselytisation began in the late eighteenth century as Protestant missions and converts moved into the interior. By the late nineteenth century, and in many instances assisted by colonial conquest, innumerable mission societies had established themselves and had made considerable advances.

As with missions in the rest of the continent, the historiography of these missions can be divided into three phases. The first emanated from the missions themselves and portrayed a master narrative of ever-growing conversion and 'civilisation'. The second phase of historiography is associated with anti-colonial nationalism which portrayed missionaries as colonial agents who denigrated African culture and history, dampened resistance, and spread forms of capitalism by introducing converts to the world of Western commodities. More recently thinking on missions has shifted. This last view maintains that the nationalist interpretation attributes too great a power to missions to shape, control and direct African societies. Missionaries were often few and far between and the bulk of proselytising was done by African catechists, evangelists and itinerant preachers. Christianity in Africa was, in effect, spread by Africans. It was they who made the religion accessible and assimilable to African intellectual traditions. The work of these foot soldiers resulted in a strong strand of popular forms of African Christianity, particularly African Initiated Churches.

In terms of literary history, missions were central. They established orthographies, set up printing presses, undertook translation and dominated black education. Most late nineteenth- and early twentieth-century writers and intellectuals, like for example Sol Plaatje, H. I. E. Dhlomo and R. R. R. Dhlomo were mission school graduates. The cultural and linguistic work undertaken by missions was the site of intense disagreement between mission and convert, particularly over language. Disputes over the grammar and orthography of African languages form an ongoing theme of much Southern African cultural history. Elsewhere in the continent there has been interesting work on how such contested processes of translation and vernacularisation have affected the meanings and trajectories of African Christianity.

Isabel Hofmeyr

Literary Works

Dangarembga, Tsitsi (1988), *Nervous Conditions*, Harare: Zimbabwe Publishing House.
Head, Bessie (1981), *Serowe: Village of the Rain Wind*, London: Heinemann.
Jordan, A. C. (1980), *The Wrath of the Ancestors/Ingqumbo Yeminyama*, trans. A. C. Jordan and P. Jordan, Lovedale: Lovedale Press.
Soga, Tiyo (1983), *The Journals and Selected Writings of the Reverend Tiyo Soga*, ed. Donovan Williams, Cape Town: A. A. Balkema.

Histories

Elbourne, Elizabeth (2002), *Blood Ground: Colonialism, Missions, and the Contest for Christianity in the Cape Colony and Britain, 1799–1853*, Montreal: McGill-Queen's University Press.
Elphick, Richard and Rodney Davenport (eds) (1997), *Christianity in South Africa: A Political, Social and Cultural History*, Berkeley, CA: University of California Press.

See also: **Frontier wars: Southern Africa; Historiography: Southern Africa; Religions: Southern Africa**.

Morant Bay Uprising

Slavery was abolished in Jamaica in 1834, but the government remained firmly in the hands of whites, who resisted the enfranchisement of the emancipated Afro-Jamaican people. Political conflict grew over the following decades, as restrictions on voting rights, high taxes and unpopular laws were implemented. On 11 October 1865, following a series of local political conflicts, several hundred black people marched into the town of Morant Bay, the capital of the predominantly sugar-growing parish of St Thomas, in the east. They attacked the police station, took weapons, confronted the local militia, and forced local vestry members to retreat into the court house, which was then set alight. By the end of the day the crowd had killed eighteen people and wounded thirty-one others. The 'rebellion', said to be led by a Native Baptist deacon Paul Bogle (d. 1865), spread across the district, with more whites killed or threatened. Governor Edward John Eyre (1815–1901) mobilised troops from the British army, local Jamaican forces and the Maroons to suppress the rebels. Under martial law, nearly 500 people were killed and many more seriously wounded; houses were burnt down, and hundreds of men and women were imprisoned and flogged. An outspoken member of the House of Assembly for the parish, George William Gordon (d. 1865) (a 'free person of colour' and associate of Bogle) was executed after court martial, along with other political dissidents.

   When news of these events reached London controversy erupted. The Eyre Defence Committee including Charles Kingsley, Thomas Carlyle and Charles Dickens, supported the governor. The Jamaican Committee, which included Charles Buxton, John Stuart Mill, John Bright and other radical non-conformists, tried unsuccessfully to prosecute him for unleashing his vengeance on innocent people. These events led to a royal commission of investigation, Eyre's recall to England, and the eventual abolition of Jamaica's 200-year old House of Assembly.

   The change to Crown colony rule brought reforms in local government policy, but also ended any possibility for Afro-Jamaican electoral participation in government until well into the twentieth century. Reminiscent of the Indian Mutiny eight years earlier, these two events are said to have contributed to the hardening racism of nineteenth-century British imperialism.

                                                                                  Mimi Sheller

Literary Works

Berry, Francis (1961), 'Morant Bay', *Morant Bay and Other Poems*, London: Routledge and
        Kegan Paul.
Mais, Roger [1945–9] (1996), *George William Gordon: A Historical Play in 14 Scenes*, in Errol
        Hill (ed.), *A Time and a Season: Eight Caribbean Plays*, 2nd edn, revised, Trinidad and
        Tobago: School of Continuing Studies, University of the West Indies.
McKay, Claude (1912), 'Gordon to the Oppressed', *Jamaica Journal*; reprinted in Cobham-
        Sander, Rhonda, (2000), 'Fictions of Gender, Fictions of Race: Retelling Morant Bay
        in Jamaican Literature', *Small Axe* 4, pp. 1–30.
Reid, Vic (1949), *New Day*, New York: Alfred Knopf.
Reid, Vic (1960), *Sixty-Five*, London: Longmans, Green.

Histories

Curtin, Philip D. (1955), *Two Jamaicas: The Role of Ideas in a Tropical Colony, 1830–1865*, Cambridge, MA: Harvard University Press.

Hall, Catherine (1992), *White, Male and Middle Class: Explorations in Feminism and History*, Cambridge: Polity Press.

Heuman, Gad (1994), *'The Killing Time': The Morant Bay Rebellion in Jamaica*, London and Basingstoke: Macmillan Caribbean.

Holt, Thomas (1992), *The Problem of Freedom: Race, Labor and Politics in Jamaica and Britain, 1832–1938*, Baltimore, MD: Johns Hopkins University Press.

Semmel, Bernard (1962), *The Governor Eyre Controversy*, London: McKibbon and Kee.

Sheller, Mimi (2000), *Democracy after Slavery: Black Publics and Peasant Radicalism in Haiti and Jamaica*, London and Basingstoke: Macmillan Caribbean.

See also: **Anti-colonialism and Resistance: Caribbean; Historiography: Caribbean; Mutinies in India**.

Multiculturalism: Australia

Multiculturalism has emerged as an official policy and a major political discourse in Australia since the 1960s. It repudiated nearly two centuries of asserting the monocultural British character of the Australian colonies which had achieved self-government between 1855 and 1861, and had then united into federation in 1901. Multiculturalism as an official policy was inspired by the Canadian model, and became a policy for the gradual and cautious inclusion of other cultures in a nation founded on a notion of a British-derived national identity. As political discourse, however, multiculturalism claimed to challenge the naturalisation of British-Australian values. Multiculturalism was a response to the increased variety in the mass intake of immigrants following World War II. Australia initially only accepted immigrants from the British Isles, but as increasing the population was regarded as the key to large-scale development, gradually migrants from other parts of the world were invited. Yet they were expected to assimilate, to work hard and remain invisible.

Australia formally abandoned its racially-based 'White Australia' immigration policy in 1973, as by then it had substantial Asian, and particularly Chinese, populations, and the Aboriginal population had also developed its own political agendas vis-à-vis multiculturalism. Australian multiculturalism has been contentious with conservatives because it rejects the strongly-held view that Australians are a uniform people of British origin. In practice, the Australian approach has not been particularly progressive, especially in Aboriginal affairs, as it has resisted granting political autonomy and self-government. Australian policy on multiculturalism has been under the control of the Department of Immigration. Consequently, multiculturalism at the level of central government has been concerned less with cultural issues than with regulating immigration. The Department of Immigration has been in charge of the much-criticised detention centres which, under the right-wing government of John Howard, have enforced increasingly restrictive policies towards refugees. At the level of state government, multicultural policies in relation to education and language policy have been given nominal support in national agendas in the 1980s and 1990s.

James Jupp

Literary Works

Castro, Brian (1989), *Birds of Passage*, Sydney: Sirius.
Dutton, Geoffrey (1985), *Snow on the Saltbush*, Ringwood: Penguin Books.
Gunew, Sneja and Kateryna Longley (1992), *Striking Chords: Multicultural Literary Interpretations*, Sydney: Allen and Unwin.
Khan, Adib (1994), *Seasonal Adjustments*, Sydney: Allen and Unwin.
Morgan, Sally (1988), *My Place*, Fremantle: Fremantle Arts Centre.

Histories

Castles, Stephen, Mary Kalantzis, Bill Cope and Michael Morrissey (1988), *Mistaken Identity: Multiculturalism and the Demise of Nationalism in Australia*, Sydney: Pluto Press.
Jupp, James (2002), *From White Australia to Woomera*, Melbourne: Cambridge University Press.
Jupp, James (ed.) (2001), *The Australian People*, Melbourne: Cambridge University Press.
Kymlicka, Will (1995), *Multicultural Citizenship*, Oxford: Clarendon Press.
Lopez, Mark (2000), *The Origins of Multiculturalism in Australian Politics*, Melbourne: Melbourne University Press.

See also: **Asianisation: Australia; Chinese Gold-diggers; Historiography: Australia; Land: Australia; White Australia Policy.**

Multiculturalism: Canada

In 1971, Canada's federal government adopted an official multiculturalism policy placed Canadian multiculturalism on the agenda in national and international debates focused on the production and management of cultural diversity. With the 1988 ratification of the Canadian Multiculturalism Act, this policy was transformed into an Act of Parliament that, in the government's words, would provide for 'the preservation and enhancement of multiculturalism in Canada', effectively elevating multiculturalism to the level of government institution and dramatically increasing its role in the nation's cultural and social programming. Closely linked with Canada's Charter of Rights and Freedoms (1982), the Citizenship Act (1985), the Canadian Human Rights Act (1985), and the International Convention on the Elimination of All Forms of Racial Discrimination (1965), the Multiculturalism Act (1988) has been crucial to Canadian domestic and foreign policy, and instrumental in government dealings with immigration and minority rights.

Rooted ideologically in cultural pluralism and cultural nationalism, the Multiculturalism Act provides for economic incentives and legislation that bridge rights-based questions of social justice and the material production of Canadian culture, art and literature. Formulated around the notion that Canada is a 'cultural mosaic,' the Multiculturalism Act moves Canada beyond an earlier bilingual or bicultural model of society, while providing an alternative to the USA's assimilationist 'melting pot.' External impetus for the Act came, in part, from a series of postwar International Conventions on Human Rights

(1948), the Elimination of Racial Discrimination (1965), and Economic, Social, and Cultural Rights (1966); thus, the Act has been vital to Canada's international relations, particularly with Asia.

Historically, within Canada there has been support for official multiculturalism. In recent years, however, it has been criticised by various, often opposed groups: fiscal and social conservatives, racial minorities, and First Nations. For conservatives, Multiculturalism is too expensive and challenges Canada's national identity. Progressive critics perceive it as failing to meet initial promises, particularly around anti-racism and equity issues. As the Act grew out of a crisis between Canada's 'two founding cultures' (French and English), critics suggest that, contrary to the liberal rhetoric, the Act was conceived to control dissent. They argue that it does not deal effectively with issues of race and see the lack of discussion around First Nations treaty rights, land claims or sovereignty as a problem. Others suggest the Act gives too much weight to culture. Despite limitations, official multiculturalism has had tremendous impact on the Canadian public, and it is still seen by critics as a positive step. Canada's attempt to recognise diversity constitutionally remains vital to rights-based discussions of culture, particularly in an increasingly diverse or globalised society.

Glen Lowry

Literary Works

Bissoondath, Neil (2002), *A Casual Brutality*, Montreal: Cormorant.
Kamboureli, Smaro (ed.) (1996), *Making a Difference: Canadian Multicultural Literature*, Toronto: Oxford University Press.
Ondaatje, Michael (1988), *In the Skin of a Lion*, Toronto: Vintage.
Vassanji, M. G. (1996), *No New Land*, Toronto: McClelland and Stewart.

Histories

Bannerji, Himani (2000), *The Dark Side of the Nation: Essays on Multiculturalism, Nationalism, and Gender*, Toronto: Canadian Scholars' Press.
Day, Richard (2000), *Multiculturalism and the History of Canadian Diversity*, Toronto: University of Toronto Press.
Kymlicka, Will (2001), *Politics in the Vernacular: Nationalism, Multiculturalism, and Citizenship*, Oxford: Oxford University Press.
Mackey, Eva (2002), *The House of Difference Cultural Politics and National Identity in Canada*, Toronto: University of Toronto Press.
Taylor, Charles (1994), *Multiculturalism: Examining the Politics of Recognition*, Princeton, NJ: Princeton University Press.

See also: **Genocide: Canada; Inuit; Nationalism(s): Canada.**

Multinationals

The multinational corporation (MNC) is a large parent company, usually situated in the developed world, that engages in direct foreign investment, and conducts other business through its affiliates located in several countries. A defining characteristic of the MNC is that it exhibits no loyalty to the country in which it is incorporated, since it often repatriates profits back to the home country. Moreover, the decision-making processes of MNCs tend to be centralised, though their business strategies usually have a global vision. The development of communications technologies and innovative organisational techniques have been important factors in the success of MNCs. They tend to open branches in countries most favourable to their business operations, which offer low taxation or cheap labour. Their mobile nature gives them significant bargaining power with the host country, which is even more accentuated in the case of developing nations.

The economic clout of some MNCs on a global level exceeds that of many states. For example, General Motors' 1992 sales ($134 billion) were larger than the gross domestic product of most national economies. MNCs are controversial. Their proponents argue that MNCs have contributed to the economic growth of developing countries by bringing in foreign investment and technology that can be transferred to the local economy, and that they create jobs. Their critics, however, accuse them of exploiting the countries they operate in, with little regard to environmental and labour standards which they would be required to meet in their home countries. For example, they often ban labour unions in their factories in nations where labour laws are not enforced, or government officials can be corrupted. An outstanding example of how MNCs have been allowed to operate with impunity in developing countries is the Union Carbide case. In 1984, the Union Carbide plant in Bhopal, India leaked forty-two tons of the deadly gas methyl isocyanate into an impoverished community, killing more than 2,500 people in the first night of the disaster, and injuring up to 200,000 others. No criminal verdicts were issued against Union Carbide, and it refused to clean up the extensive pollution of water and soil caused by the gas leakage. Some MNCs have even intervened in the internal affairs of their host countries, both legally and illegally, in order to protect their business operations.

The left's critiques of MNCs stem from the feeling that globalisation in its current form is overly corporate-led, thus reducing decision-making capabilities of peoples and governments, and handing over more influence to corporations. Given the controversies surrounding the role of MNCs, the United Nations has been working on establishing codes of conduct for them. It is clear that rechannelling the enormous resources of MNCs could close the gap between the developed and developing world, but the implementation of more ethical business practices will depend in large part on the pressures brought to bear upon MNCs by the international community.

Neelam Srivastava

Literary Works

Burstyn, Varda (2004), *Water, Inc.*, London: Verso.
Chamoiseau, Patrick (1998), *Texaco*, trans. Rose-Myriam Réjouis and Val Vinokurov, London: Granta.
Lapierre, Dominique and Javier Moro (2001), *Five Past Midnight in Bhopal*, trans. K. Spink, Delhi: Full Circle.
Malladi, Amulya (2003), *A Breath of Fresh Air*, New Delhi: Penguin.
Saro-wiwa, Ken (1995), *A Forest of Flowers: Short Stories*, Harlow: Longman.

Histories

Jones, G. G. (ed.) (1993), *Transnational Corporations: A Historical Perspective*, New York: Routledge.
Klein, Naomi (2001), *No Logo: No Space, No Choice, No Jobs*, London: Flamingo.
Teichova, Alice, Maurice Lévy-Leboyer and Helga Nussbaum (eds) (1986), *Multinational Enterprise in Historical Perspective*, New York: Cambridge University Press.

See also: **Anti-globalisation Movements; International Monetary Fund; World Bank**.

Music: Caribbean

The history of Caribbean music is rooted in the process of cultural borrowing, transfer and socio-political confrontation. Calypso music is widely considered to have originated in the Caribbean, from the music of slaves shipped to the region from Africa. This cultural art form evolved on slave plantations throughout the Caribbean and came to be titled kaiso/calypso in the early twentieth century. Calypso song is characterised by its commentary on social, political and cultural issues. The calypsonian has tended to voice the concerns of the under-privileged. Although the nation state of Trinidad and Tobago has the most celebrated, vibrant and structured calypso tradition, the art form has grown in prominence in other islands of the region, aided by annual carnivals, festivities and calypso competitions.

In the 1970s a dance-oriented variant called soca emerged. Soca was less concerned with making 'serious' social comments and more concerned with celebration, and commercial imperatives. In the post-1980s period newer fusions of calypso with reggae and other popular musics gave rise to even more hardcore styles. Such hybrid and technologised styles are chutney soca, ragga soca and ringbang. In Trinidad and Tobago the tamboo bamboo band was the forerunner of the steel band. When drums were banned in the early twentieth century, musicians used the locally growing bamboo as instruments. In the 1940s left-over oil cans/drums were used to produce sound. Eventually skilled persons and musicians started to treat the instrument with heat in order to produce cleaner, clearer melodic notes. In the following decades bands spread throughout the islands and abroad to places like New York, London and Toronto.

Reggae music proper evolved in Jamaica through firstly ska in the late 1950s/early 1960s, and rocksteady in the mid-to-late 1960s. By the late 1960s and early 1970s reggae was coming into its own as a dedicated category of music. Reggae grew in popularity through-out the 1970s, and served multiple functions. It was used for protest and rebellion, for cel-ebration, and also for national and partisan political ends. The art form was supported by sound systems. Dub poets employed reggae sound tracks to accompany their lyrical perfor-mances. The Rastafarian movement also contributed to reggae's lyrical philosophy. The Rastafarian message of repatriation, spiritual renewal and liberation pervaded the music in the 1970s and 1980s. Within this period Bob Marley, along with the group The Wailers, came to international attention through signing with Island Records. In the 1980s reggae evolved into dancehall. Dancehall music was characterised by its heavier employing of music technology, synthesisers, drum machines, and by a greater lyrical emphasis on gun play, sexual themes and posturing. In the post-1990s period a substantial number of artists were signed to large independent and major labels.

Other musical styles have been less widely successful, but have nonetheless helped to shape the regional sound of Caribbean music. Spouge music was popular in the 1960s and 1970s, especially in the eastern Caribbean. Chutney soca music achieved growing popularity in the late 1980s. The several islands of the region have nurtured their own folk and/or national music. For instance, Belizean punta rock, Barbadian tuk, and Bahamian goombay. Many of these musics have their origins in plantation society and the process of encounter that forged regional variations on quite similar musical phenomena. These folk-derived forms are often percussive in sound and make-up. They evolved maintaining some use of acoustic instruments, but in many cases have been embellished, appropriating modern musical equipment. Anglophone islands have also been influenced by francophone musical styles like cadence, bouyon and zouk. Latin rhythms have also had an impact on the region.

Curwen Best

Literary Works

Brathwaite, Edward Kamau (1973), *The Arrivants*, Oxford: Oxford University Press.
Dawes, Kwame (1998), *Wheel and Come Again*, Leeds: Peepal Tree.
Gibbons, Rawle (1999), *A Calypso Trilogy*, Kingston: Ian Randle Publishers.
Lovelace, Earl (1982), *The Wine of Astonishment*, Oxford: Heinemann.
Mais, Roger (1954), *Brother Man*, London: Jonathan Cape.
Trellwell, Michael (1980), *The Harder they Come*, London: The X Press.
Walcott, Derek (1980), *Pantomime*, New York: Farrar Strauss and Giroux.

Histories

Best, Curwen (1999), *Barbadian Popular Music*, Rochester, VT: Schenkman Books.
Chang, Kevin O'Brien and Wayne Chen (1998), *Reggae Routes*, Kingston: Ian Randle Publishers.
Cooper, Carolyn (1993), *Noises in the Blood*, London: Macmillan.
Davis, Stephen (1990), *Bob Marley*, Rochester, VT: Schenkman Books.
Hebdige, Dick (1987), *Cut and Mix*, London: Methuen.
Hill, Errol [1972] (1997), *The Trinidad Carnival*, London: New Beacon Books.
Larkin, Colin (ed.) (1994), *The Guinness Who's Who of Reggae*, London: Guinness Publishing Ltd.
Quevedo, Raymond (1983), *Atilla's Kaiso*, Port of Spain: Superservice Printing.
Rohlehr, Gordon (1990), *Calypso and Society*, Tunapuna: Hem Printers.
Stolzoff, Norman (2000), *Wake the Town, Tell the People*, Durham, NC: Duke University Press.
Stuempfle, Stephen (1995), *The Steelband Movement*, Barbados: University Press of the West Indies.
Warner, Keith (1982), *The Trinidad Calypso*, London: Heinemann.

See also: **Anti-colonialism and Resistance: Caribbean.**

Music: East Africa

The three East African countries – Kenya, Uganda and Tanzania – are bound by their shared experience of British colonialism, as well as by their somewhat intermittent post-colonial design of an economic alliance termed the East African Community. In all three countries officially subsidised national troupes and choirs have kept traditional music alive, even as popular music of the dancehall variety has gradually dominated the scene. This popular music resonates with evidence of the region's encounters with modernity. Its central defining feature is precisely its sheer capacity to accommodate, absorb and adapt musical styles and trends from cultures as varied as Anglo-European, Cuban, Arab, African-American, Congolese, Southern African, and West African, while at the same time significantly retaining the modes, rhythms, instruments and languages of the various indigenous East African peoples.

Popular music of the independence era featured modern instruments such as the acoustic and the electric guitar, played after the fashion of Congolese musicians, such as Jean Bosco Mwenda. But the work of Daudi Kabaka, John Mwale and D. O. Misiani reveals that this modern music was also modelled on the rhythms of lute-playing communities such as the Abaluhya and Luo of Western Kenya. Significantly, so-called ethnic musicians such as Joseph Kamaru borrowed much from Western icons like Jim Reeves. The songs of this era amounted to social commentaries on subjects as varied as the pressures of urban existence, anxieties over traditional mores and the joys and pains of romantic love. Even more importantly, popular songs of the era were a studied response to unfolding political events, usefully providing new idioms to confront the moment. They celebrated *uhuru* (freedom) with a peculiarly nationalist discourse that placed emphasis on East African unity, which was often metaphorically mirrored through the companionship of the leaders – Nyerere, Kenyatta and Obote. In Tanzania, the changed consciousness of independence led to a dramatic shift in cultural allegiance at the official level. The new government instituted fairly radical cultural policies aimed at promoting local artistes and indigenous musical practices in the Swahili language. In the absence of international recording companies, the state-owned Radio Tanzania recorded and popularised emerging artists. After the Arusha Declaration of 1967, there was an outburst of music thriving on the newly created sense of patriotism and national engineering. It is worth noting that, by contrast, political events in Uganda, particularly the violent upheaval of the Amin years, sent cultural activity underground, deeply affecting musical development in that country. In Kenya, songs that lingered on disenchantment with independence marked the 1970s. Some were so openly critical of political intrigues such as the assassination of first Tom Mboya and then J. M. Kariuki, that the authorities arrested the composers and banned the songs. Kenyan popular music has indeed continued to provide counter-hegemonic discourse. In the general election of December 2002 the spirit of resilience and the radical assertion of new nationalist leaders carried in Gidi Gidi Maji Maji's 'Unbwogable' (Unbeatable) became the banner of the opposition party, National Rainbow Coalition, and significantly contributed to its defeat of the ruling party, KANU.

Joyce Nyairo

Literary Works

Kasigwa, Barnabas (ed.) (1991), *An Anthology of East African Plays*, Nairobi: Longman.
Mwangi, Meja (1989), *Weapon for Hunger*, Harlow: Longman.

Ngugi wa Thiong'o (1977), *Petals of Blood*, Nairobi: Heinemann.

Ogot, Grace (1968), *Land Without Thunder*, Nairobi: East African Educational Publishers.

P'Bitek, Okot [1966] (1984), *Song of Lawino and Song of Ocol*, intro. by G. A. Heron, London: Heinemann.

Tejani, Bahadur (1971), *Day after Tomorrow*, Nairobi: East African Educational Publishers.

Wainaina, Binyavanga (2003), *Discovering Home*, Nairobi: The author.

Histories

Bender, Wolfgang (1991), *Sweet Mother: Modern African Music*, Chicago: Chicago University Press.

Graebner, Werbner (1997), 'Whose Music? The Songs of Remmy Ongala and the Orchestra Super Matimila', in Karin Barber (ed.), *Readings in African Popular Culture*, Oxford: James Currey, pp. 110–17.

Kubik, Gerhard (1981), 'Neo-Traditional Popular Music in East Africa since 1945', *Popular Music 1*, pp. 83–104.

Nyairo, Joyce and James Ogude (2003), 'Popular Music and the Negotiation of Contemporary Kenyan Identity: The Example of *Nairobi City Ensemble*', *Social Identities 9: 3*, pp. 383–400.

Odhiambo, Atieno (2002), '*Kula Raha*: Gendered Discourses and the Contours of Leisure in Nairobi, 1946–1963', in Andrew Burton (ed.), *The Urban Experience in East Africa*, Nairobi: British Institute.

Stapleton C. and Chris May (1990), *African All-Stars: The Pop Music of a Continent*, New York: Obelisk/Dutton.

Wallis R. and K. Malm (1984), *Big Sounds from Small Peoples: The Music Industry in Small Countries*, New York: Pendragon Press.

See also: **Anti-colonialism and Resistance: East Africa**.

Music: West Africa

Music from West Africa by the late 1980s was a major symbol of 'world music', a large amorphous category that lumps together music from outside the West. The modern music of this vast region, which is so successful among cosmopolitan youth, in the north and south, is rooted in a centuries-old tradition of the *griots* or praise-singers (also genealogists/historians/advisors) of the region. The words *jali* in Manding and *guewel* in Wolf have the same meaning as *griot*. In the widespread Manding societies of the region certain craft groups (*nyamakala*) such as blacksmiths, and *griots*, to a large extent are endogamous and have particular social functions.

The *griots* (feminine: *griottes*) have often had an ambiguous status, being both despised for being entertainers and respected for having the ear of the powerful. The *Sunjata* epic, named after the warrior prince, Sunjata Keita, who founded the Mali empire, is still a widely sung epic of *griot* musicians. Songs are often formulaic with a measure of improvisation on a set pattern. But lyrics about contemporary affairs and politics are in no short supply among the singers from the *griot* tradition. Indeed, commentary on society and politics is a customary part of their repertoire.

Music was transformed with independence in the 1960s. Official radio and television broadcasters used musicians to broadcast nationalist and 'developmental' messages. The presidents of Mali and Guinea, in particular, vigorously supported music and the arts to promote their respective political causes. Bands established then lasted through the late 1970s. The economic hardship of the 1980s and 1990s forced many people, including musicians, to migrate to the European metropoles. In Paris and London musicians found more than the single basic recording studio they had at home. Mande musicians not only got audiences among expatriates but also began to be played on mainstream airwaves and found contracts from established labels in the West.

A range of instruments is played by West African musicians. The kora, balafon, ngoni lute, and various drums are widely used, with the twenty-one-stringed kora the icon of sudanic West African music. From World War II the guitar became part of the instrumentation in 'traditional' music. Cuban dance music was a major influence in francophone West Africa in the 1960s. Nigeria has had a relatively well-developed music industry and large market for its three major kinds of contemporary music, juju, highlife and fuji. The country's two most famous musicians are King Sunny Ade and Fela Kuti, both from the south-western Yoruba-speaking region. Kuti, from a family of musicians and himself trained in London, called his fusion of sounds 'Afro-beat' music. Kuti has used his music and his fame to take up politics, even running for president in the 1970s. His out-spoken politics, exemplified in provocative album titles such as *Coffin for Head of State*, led to exile and imprisonment.

Shamil Jeppie

Literary Works

Niane, D. T. (1960), *Sundiata: An Epic of Old Mali*, London: Longman.

Histories

Hale, Thomas A. (1998), *Griots and Griottes*, Bloomington, IN: Indiana University Press.
Pfeiffer, Katrin (ed.) (1997), *Mandinka Spoken Art, Folk-Tales, Griot Accounts, and Songs*, Koln: R. Koppeverlag.
Tunde, Jegede (1994), *African Classical Music and the Griot Tradition*, London: Diabaté Arts.

See also: **Religions: West Africa**.

Mutinies in India

The revolt of 1857 to 1858 was not a unique event, though it was more massive, more widespread, and in the beginning more overwhelming in its implications for colonial authorities than any uprising the British had previously faced in India. Armed revolt frequently occurred in all parts of British India during the early phase, and it did not cease to occur after the brutal squashing of the 1857–8 uprising. Most revolts before and after that major conflagration were in some ways caused by the policies of colonial rule and the conditions produced by those policies.

The eighteenth century was marked in particular by the great revolts of Sikhs, Jats, and

Marathas that occurred mostly in the countryside, against colonial revenue policies. The counter-insurgency measures by the British included first pacification of the countryside, followed by forfeiture of a family's zamindari land when that family failed to pay revenue. Under colonial rule, in contrast with pre-colonial rule, revenue rates were higher, the policies and procedures for exacting them were more uncompromising, and relief for drought or flood-ravaged areas non-existent. The result was a disgruntled and resentful populace in rural India. Thus when, in the Sivaganga revolt of 1799 to 1801, the poligars in the south put up fierce resistance to the colonial forces, they received considerable support from the villagers resentful of the British attempt to control and tax territories that had relative autonomy from pre-British rulers. Thus at least some of the revolts were supported, perhaps even fuelled, by deep-seated negative sentiment among the natives.

Many of the major mutinies and revolts before the events of 1857 to 1858 sprang from the native refusal of the East India Company's claim to total dominance over the territories they ruled. The company sought not simply to increase its revenues but also to have complete control over all sources and means of political authority throughout India, and this seems to have caused innumerable revolts against the British in the eighteenth and nineteenth centuries. The British often claimed that various local tyrants seeking to avoid payment of revenue fomented rebellion. This, however, was questionable since, in the 1844–6 revolt in the countryside near Goa and in the revolts in Tamilnadu and Kerala, village headmen provided recruits and resources for the rebels, making the revolts far more general and popularly based than isolated incidents of outrage by disgruntled local tyrants.

British interference in the succession among the Marathas in the 1770s, in Awadh in 1797, and in several Rajput states in the 1820s and 1830s led to serious resistance from zamindars and their followers, who were generally supporters of the spurned claimants. The whole army in the south had been in a state of agitation, and occurred in mutiny at least three times in the pre-mutiny period, for instance, at Vellore (1806), at Nagpur (1820), and at Bengalore (1832). The riots in Bengal between 1857 and 1860 occurred when indigo cultivators rose up against European planters who they thought discouraged indigo cultivation in order to favour more valuable cash crops, like jute. There were literally scores of places where the Native populace was in a state of agitation and frequently took recourse to violent uprising. The poligar uprisings in south India from 1800 to 1806; the rebellion at Mysore from 1830 to 1831; the uprising of the Bhils from 1818 to 1831; the disturbances at Cutch from 1815 to 1832; the uprising of the Gujjars in 1824; the upheavals in Assam from 1830 to 1850; the rebellion of the Santals from 1855 to 1856; and the disturbances at Bareilly in 1816 – these are only a few instances of resistance that British rule encountered throughout the period before the revolt of 1857 to 1858.

The mutiny at Vellore resembled in some ways the events of that later revolt. At 2 a.m. on 10 July 1806, Native soldiers rose up and attacked their officers and the European soldiers and officials of the garrison. The rebels were subdued only after a fierce battle resulting in the deaths of several hundred men. An interesting feature that the Vellore mutiny shares with the events of 1857 to 1858 is that the mutineers in 1806 took the introduction of European headgear as a form of assault on their religion. The new order sought to deprive Muslims of their beards and earrings and Hindus of their caste marks; and it stoked their fears that the sepoys were to be made Christians. As in 1857, rumours of an imminent end to British rule and the dawn of a new era were in the air. Although there were religious, political, and racial overtones to this mutiny, it was basically a military event, perhaps a desperate and calculated act of violence against the policies imposed by European officers. More striking, however, than the brutality of the soldiers was the enormity of the British response, which foreshadowed the harshness with which the colonial authorities squashed the later uprisings.

On 10 May 1857 a regiment of native cavalry at Meerut mutinied. Cutting down their officers and setting their houses on fire, the mutineers marched to Delhi, where a similar situation occurred. Many from the Delhi cantonments joined the mutineers. Seizing a major cache of arms stored outside the city, they entered the city triumphantly, and declared the titular Mughal emperor, Bahadur Shah, their leader. Before long, the mutiny spread to many areas of north and central India, covering the major centres of Agra, Lucknow, Bareilly, Allahabad, Kanpur, and Gwalior. Almost the entire northern and central regions of India was soon engulfed by the revolt. In Kanpur the mutineers promised the surviving British soldiers, women and children a safe passage, but then set their boats on fire and attacked them from the shore. Those who survived that were taken prisoner. On the news of a British advance on the river, Nana Saheb is believed to have ordered the survivors killed. When General Henry Havelock entered the city two days later, he punished the rebels by forcing them to lick the bloodstains of the murdered Europeans before having them hanged. Meanwhile, Colonel James Neill, in charge of a force at Benares and Allahabad, pursued a policy of revenge by a veritable reign of terror throughout the neighbouring countryside. Under Neill's orders, British troops burned whole villages, killed natives indiscriminately, and hanged great numbers of men, women and children. Many sepoys were blown from the mouths of cannons. As William Howard Russell (1860) points out, however, such atrocities were committed even before the rebels had carried out the massacre in Kanpur.

In Awadh, discontent had been growing since the British annexation in 1856. The British revenue settlement, generally known as the Summary Settlement of 1856 to 1857, dispossessed many talukdars and exposed the peasants to overassessment, making them vulnerable to loss of their tenancy and disrupting severely the traditional fabric of life in this rural society. As a result, the nobility, urban populace, village proprietors, and farmers were all united in their resentment of foreign rule. So, here, more than in any other region of India, the revolt was popular in character, and not just an uprising of the soldiers. Civil rebellion and the mutiny reinforced each other almost immediately in the garrison towns, as artisans, day-labourers, and impoverished farmers joined the fray. In spite of the tremendous military and tactical superiority of the British, the revolt in Awadh was maintained for nearly a whole year, almost every village putting up fierce resistance and inflicting heavy losses on British troops. The strength of the resistance and its duration sprang from the interdependence in Awadh of the talukdars and peasants. When the British did finally succeed in quashing it there, they did so in part by breaking up the insurgent groups with promises of land to the talukdars, thus making them allies of the Raj collaborating in a new politics of order and loyalty. The systematic neglect of the central provinces by the British Rule after the mutiny was the punishment meted out to those regions, and that largely explains the underdevelopment there even today. The impact of these policies of state terror are still with us today and can be noticed, for instance, in the disparities between the poor state of Bihar and the affluence of regions like Punjab.

The events of 1857 to 1858 were motivated in part by the grievances of native soldiers that had been mounting since the early 1850s. The General Service Enlistment Act of 1856 that required soldiers to agree to serve abroad meant for Hindu soldiers a transgression of their religion's injunction against going overseas, exposing them to the risk of losing their caste-purity. The rumour that the greased (that is, with pig or cow fat) cartridges for the new Enfield rifle would pollute Hindus and Muslims alike, forcing them to become Christians, worsened the already mounting tensions in native soldiery. Although the revolt was unique in scale and exceptionally successful in its early phase, in substance it resembled scores of other rebellions that opposed colonial rule and its policies. However tenacious and forceful, nearly all of them seem to have been quite fragmentary and unco-ordinated, and that fact accounts in large part for the success of the colonial authorities in quashing them.

The events that began unfolding on 10 May 1857 are described variously as the Sepoy Mutiny, the Sepoy Rebellion, the Sepoy Revolt, the Indian Mutiny, and the First War of Independence. These different labels illustrate the different ways in which the events have been interpreted, and the huge body of administrative, historiographical, and literary writing attests to the conflicting emotions and attitudes these events have provoked. Because it was restricted largely to the northern regions of India, some question its characterisation as an Indian mutiny. Many contemporary Britons called it mutiny by the Bengal sepoys, refusing to acknowledge that it was not confined to the soldiers. And while it was not a planned war of independence, it drew upon feelings that eventually came to be articulated in the struggle for independence that began to gather force in the late nineteenth century. It clearly made Indians more fully conscious of the gulf between their rulers and themselves, and it gave them a definite impetus to become involved in the affairs of their country. The social and racial distinctions that existed before this mutiny were intensified by distrust and disaffection. Its brutal suppression tore apart the style and structure of East India Company rule. Every aspect of British rule came to be thoroughly examined in London, and company rule was replaced by Crown.

The revolt has been the object of an enormous amount of writing, both historical and literary. Military historians constitute the biggest single group of British historians who wrote on the mutiny and saw it as strictly a military event. Major nineteenth-century British historical writings on the events of that period, especially those by J. W. Kaye (1864–80), G. B. Malleson (1901), G. O. Trevelyan (1865), and Charles Ball (n.d.), are in essence narratives about the triumph of British character and courage over the cruelty and cowardice of the Indians. The events are treated in ways that develop profiles of fortitude and heroism displayed by the British commanders in charge of their forces at Delhi, Lucknow, Allahabad, Kanpur and elsewhere. Insisting that Indians were lacking in any longing for freedom from British rule, most of these historians characterise the mutiny as a battle between civilisation and barbarism. Imperialist historiography portrays the rebellion as a crime, and insists that the rebels perpetrated atrocities that required bold and swift measures by the British forces. Historians like Ball take popular rumours of Indian atrocities, including those about violation of British women, as historical fact in order to produce narratives of Indian savagery and inferiority and of British fortitude, courage and triumph. These constitute classic examples of representations of the Other as a lesser and hopelessly inferior being. Although imperialist historians lay great stress on the massacres at Meerut, Kanpur and Lucknow, later historians, British as well as Indian, agree that violent reprisals occurred on both sides.

Indians in the twentieth century have produced historical accounts that seek to provide a native perspective on the mutiny. Like their British counterparts, Indian historians also depend on the documents and sources produced by the military officers, the courts and other governmental agencies. Committed to democracy, non-violence and modernity, most of the Indian historians write in a nationalist spirit and condemn the excesses of rebel violence, and in that sense they seem to replicate the overall narrative structure and purpose of imperialist historiography. S. B. Chaudhuri (1957), however, has given an account of the civil rebellion that accompanied the mutiny from its earliest stages, one that is in effect an alternative account which presents the native perspective and challenges imperialist British histories. During the last two decades, subaltern historians like Ranajit Guha and Gautam Bhadra, and postcolonial theorists like Homi Bhabha have undertaken careful studies of the colonial archives to articulate the strategies and practices of the rebels and the causes and contexts of the mutiny.

That troubled episode was arguably the event in the nineteenth century that most fascinated the popular imagination in Britain, inspiring many novels in the late nineteenth and early twentieth centuries. Many of the writers – civil servants and soldiers in India, or their wives – and their outlooks, marked by outrage or sentimentality, had nothing objective or sophisticated about them, and so their novels dramatise views that are generally lacking in any serious grasp of the workings of colonial rule and the natives' understandable resentment toward it. The novels are often romantic adventure stories in which the mutiny serves at best as a colourful background, and they create little sense of the history or the country in which their characters are placed. Even postcolonial mutiny novels such as those by John Masters and M. M. Kaye draw on the heroes celebrated in imperialist historiography; these novels evoke an India already presented in the myths of the Raj. J. G. Farrell's novel *The Siege of Krishnapur* (1973), however, is an exception to this. Farrell brings historical accuracy and critical sensitivity to his portrayal of the mutiny and its historical and cultural contexts. Manohar Malgonkar's *The Devil's Wind: Nana Saheb's Story* (1972) is the only novel written from an Indian perspective, or rather from Nana Saheb's perspective, one that attempts to question and undermine those myths and the negative portrayals given of him in conventional British histories.

Suresh Raval

Literary Works

Collins, Wilkie [1868] (1994), *The Moonstone*, Harmondsworth: Penguin.
Fanthorne, J. F. (1896), *Mariam: A Story of the Indian Mutiny of 1857*, Benares: Chandraprabha Press.
Farrell, J. G. [1973] (1979), *The Siege of Krishnapur*, Harmondsworth: Penguin.
Kaye, M. M. [1959] (1980), *Shadow of the Moon*, Harmondsworth: Penguin.
Malgonkar, Manohar (1972), *The Devil's Wind, Nana Saheb's Story*, New York: Viking.
Masters, John (1951), *Nightrunners of Bengal*, New York: Viking.
Muddock, J. E. (1895), *The Star of Fortune, A Story of the Indian Mutiny*, London: Hutchinson and Company.
Muddock, J. E. (1896), *The Great White Hand or The Tiger of Cawnpore*, London: Hutchinson and Company.
Rees, Ruutz, L. E. (1858), *The Siege of Lucknow*, London: Longman.
Steel, Flora Annie (1896), *On the Face of the Waters, A Tale of the Mutiny*, London: William Heinemann.
Taylor, P. J. O. (1996), *The Companion to the Indian Mutiny*, New Delhi: Oxford University Press.

Histories

Ball, Charles (n. d.), *The History of the Indian Mutiny*, 2 vols, London: The London Printing and Publishing Company.

Brantlinger, Patrick (1988), 'The Well at Cawnpore: Literary Representations of the Indian Mutiny of 1857', in Patrick Brantlinger, *Rule of Darkness: British Literature and Imperialism 1830–1914*, London: Cornell University Press, pp. 199–224.

Chaudhuri, S. B. (1957), *Civil Rebellions in the Indian Mutinies (1857–59)*, Calcutta: World Press.

Guha, Ranajit (1983), *Elementary Aspects of Peasant Insurgency in Colonial India*, Delhi: Oxford University Press.

Kaye, J. W. (1864–80), *History of the Sepoy War*, 3 vols, London: W. H. Allen.

Majumdar, R. C. (1957), *The Sepoy Mutiny and the Revolt of 1857*, Calcutta: Firma K. L. Mukhopadhyay.

Malleson, G. B., Colonel (1901), *The Indian Mutiny of 1857*, London: Seeley and Company.

Mukherjee, R. (1984), *Awadh in Revolt: 1857–58*, Delhi: Oxford University Press.

Russell, William Howard (1860), *My Indian Mutiny Diary*, London: Cassell and Company Ltd.

Sen, S. N. (1957), *Eighteen Fifty-Seven*, Delhi: Ministry of Information, Government of India.

Stokes, Eric (1986), *The Peasant Armed: The Indian Rebellion of 1857*, Oxford: Clarendon Press.

Thompson, Edward [1926] (1989), *The Other Side of the Medal*, ed. Mulk Raj Anand, New Delhi: Sterling Publishers.

Trevelyan, G. O. [1899] (1865), *Cawnpore*, London: Macmillan.

See also: **Anti-colonialism and Resistance: South Asia; Black Hole; East India Company; English in India: Eighteenth and Nineteenth Centuries; Historiography: South Asia; Raj; World Wars I and II: South Asian Soldiers.**

N

Nasser, Gamal Abdel

Gamal Abdel Nasser, leader of Egypt from 1952 to 1970, was born in Assiyut in 1918. He was educated mainly in Cairo and Alexandria, and in 1937 enrolled in the military academy. His command of a battalion during the 1948 war in Palestine earned him the status of military hero. The defeat the Egyptian army experienced there at the hands of Israeli forces was viewed by Nasser and many of his fellow officers as a symbol of the corruption of the nation's political and social system. He used his position as a lecturer at the military academy to recruit support for the 'Free Officers' movement, a group of young, disenchanted army officers whose mission it was to succeed where Egypt's nationalist movement – a coalition of disparate groups and ideologies – had failed, by effecting the overthrow of the existing monarchical regime. The Free Officers movement successfully executed a coup and forced King Farouk to abdicate, establishing the Revolutionary Command Council led by General Mohammed Naguib.

In 1954, Nasser ousted Neguib and consolidated his hold over the government establishing a succession of single-party organisations in place of the pre-revolutionary multi-party system. In the international arena, Nasser placed Egypt in the forefront of resistance to Western imperialism. Nasser's participation in the 1955 Bandung conference, his refusal to join the US-sponsored 'Baghdad Pact' and his increasingly close ties with the former Soviet bloc caused the USA and Britain to withdraw funding for the Aswan Dam. In response, Nasser nationalised the Suez Canal in 1956. Invading Israeli, British and French forces were forced to withdraw after pressure from the USA and the USSR, and Nasser emerged overnight from the 'Suez Canal Crisis' as an international hero and an undisputed leader of the non-aligned movement.

In the late 1950s and early 1960s, Nasser adopted a more unified programme of national development than the piecemeal reforms (such as the 1952 land reform, which limited agricultural holdings) carried out in the years immediately after the revolution. Under the rubric of 'Arab Socialism' Nasser nationalised public utilities and foreign-owned companies, implemented a state plan for economic development and attempted to mobilise previously marginalised groups such as workers, peasants and women through the creation of bureaucratic, corporatist institutions such as the Arab Socialist Union. In spite of the regime's authoritarian tendencies and curtailing of political dissent, Nasser enjoyed genuine popular support from a people who, for the first time, were addressed as citizens with an investment in the project of state- and nation-building.

His attempts to bring other progressive Arab regimes together under the aegis of Arab nationalism drove much of Egypt's foreign policy during this period, including its 1958 unification with Syria (which collapsed in 1963) and its involvement in the civil war in Yemen (1962–7) on the side of the republicans. In May 1967, in response to Syrian criticism that he had failed to respond adequately to Israeli attacks on Syria and Jordan, Nasser ordered the Egyptian army to occupy the Straits of Tiran. Israel responded with a pre-emptive strike which destroyed the combined Egyptian, Syrian and Jordanian armies. The devastating defeat prompted Nasser to resign, but popular protest convinced him to remain in power. He died in 1970.

Laura Bier

Literary Works

'Abd al-Quddus, Ihsan (1978), *I am Free and Other Stories*, trans. T. Le Gassick, Cairo: General Egyptian Book Organization.

Ghali, Wagdi (1964), *Beer in the Snooker Club*, New York: Knopf.

Mahfuz, Najib (1978), *Miramar*, trans. F. M. Mahmoud, Cairo: American University in Cairo Press.

Soueif, Ahdaf (1993), *In the Eye of the Sun*, New York: Pantheon Books.

Zayyat, Latifa (2000), *The Open Door*, trans. M. Booth, Cairo: American University in Cairo Press.

Histories

Beattie, Kirk (1994), *Egypt during the Nasser Years*, Boulder, CO: Westview Press.
Dekmenjian, Hrair (1971), *Egypt under Nasser*, Albany, NY: SUNY Press.
Gordon, Joel (1992), *Nasser's Blessed Movement: Egypt's Free Officers and the July Revolution*, Oxford: Oxford University Press.
Gordon, Joel (2002), *Revolutionary Melodrama: Popular Film and Civic Identity in Nasser's Egypt*, Chicago: Middle East Documentation Center.
Jankowski, James (2001), *Nasser's Egypt, Arab Nationalism and the United Arab Republic*, Boulder, CO: Lynne Riener.
Vatikiotis, P. J. (1978), *Nasser and his Generation*, London: Croom Helm.

See also: **Historiography: Middle East; Nationalism(s): Arab; Suez Crisis**.

Nationalism(s): Arab

Arab nationalism (*al-qawmia al-Arabia*) – as a political movement uniting the Arabs on the basis of a shared language, culture and history – was generally a phenomenon of the twentieth century. It evolved out of its encounters with Ottoman, European and US imperialisms, and with Zionist settler colonialism, in the context of an unequal development of global capitalism. But the 'Arab world' – encompassing as many as twenty-one countries plus Palestine, and thus stretching from the Atlantic shores of Morocco in North Africa to the Persian Gulf in Asia; from the Mediterranean to the centre of the Sahara and the Upper Nile Valley – unevenly took part in the Arab nationalist movement. Indeed, the path of Arab nationalism – like other nationalisms in Asia, Africa, and Latin America – never did run smooth. The substantial presence of linguistic, ethnic and religious minorities in countries ranging from Morocco and Algeria, through Egypt and Sudan, to Jordan, Lebanon, Syria and Iraq complicated and even unsettled any postulation of a unitary discourse of Arab nationalism as such. Also, conflicts between different Arab nation states and nationalist organisations – accompanied by the increasing alienation of the national ruling classes from the Arab masses on the one hand and the rise of Islamic fundamentalism on the other – undermined a secular Arab nationalism from within. Thus it remained simultaneously consequential and contested throughout the twentieth century – a century that witnessed both the ascent and decline, if not the death, of Arab nationalism.

The twentieth century, however, did not suddenly inaugurate Arab nationalism. Its genealogy can be traced from the nineteenth century or even before. Certain discourses envisaging the possible cultural cohesiveness of the Arabs can be traced from Ibn al-Muqaffa of the eighth century, through Ibn Qutayba of the ninth century, to the exemplary Arab historian Ibn Khaldun of the fourteenth century. Indeed, Arab nationalists later drew upon Ibn Khaldun's famous notion of '*asabiya* which was taken to mean a range of categories from esprit de corps to solidarity to nationality. But the encounter of the Arabs with European colonialism from the nineteenth century onward began to forge the dialectics of Arab nationalism in decisive ways: such nationalism appropriated European discourses to confront and combat not only Ottoman domination but also European colonialism and imperialism.

Despite many earlier commercial and cultural contacts between Europe and the Arab world, it was Napoleon's invasion of Egypt in 1798 that first brought at least part of the Arab world into an active intellectual encounter with modern Europe. Napoleon invaded Egypt not only with his army but also with scientists from different disciplines, a scientific laboratory, a library of modern European literature, and a printing press. Napoleon also founded the Institut d'Égypte – the first Western academic institution in the Arab world – one that attracted a host of Arab intellectuals. It was partly against this background that the early nationalist thinkers emerged during the nineteenth century: the Egyptian writer Rifaa Rafi al-Tahtawi and Islamic scholars such as Jamal al-Din al-Afghani and Muhammad Abdu. Other figures associated with the Arab literary renaissance – known as the Nahda – played a role in forging a discourse of Arab nationalism in the nineteenth century: Nasif al-Yazji, Faris al-Shidyaq, Ibrahim al-Yaziji, and, most significantly, the Syrian scholar Butrus al-Bustani who founded – along with Yasif al-Yaziji – a nationalist Syrian scientific society in 1857.

The Arab nationalist revolt of 1916 against Ottoman domination (1516–18) is the first case in point. In 1916, Sharif Hussein of Mecca, backed by Britain, led the Arab nationalists against the Ottomans. The sharif, however, understood that Britain would allow the Arabs to form an independent, unified state after the war. But barely a month before the sharif led the revolt, the British, French and Russians had secretly made the Sykes-Picot agreement to divide the Arab world under their separate spheres of influence. It was V. I. Lenin who first divulged and withdrew from this secret agreement in 1917. The same year also saw the (in)famous Balfour Declaration: Arthur James Balfour, British secretary of state for foreign affairs, openly promised a national home for the Jews in Palestine where the Palestinians continued to constitute the overwhelming majority, owning nearly 90 per cent of the land.

Palestine thus remained at the centre of Arab nationalist consciousness and practices. The 1936 to 1939 Arab revolt in Palestine defined Zionism as an 'illegitimate offspring of imperialism' at a time when sixty-four more Zionist colonies were founded in Palestine. The revolt developed into widespread demonstrations and popular protests not only in Palestine but also in Iraq, Syria and Egypt, on a massive scale. From it emerged a popular conviction among Arabs, regardless of their location, that Zionism and imperialism were their common foes. The first Arab-Israeli war in 1948 marked yet another critical point for Arab nationalism. In 1948, when the British left Palestine enabling David Ben-Gurion and other Jewish leaders to declare the birth of the state of Israel on the land under their control, the Arab League countries such as Egypt, Syria, Lebanon, Transjordan and Iraq entered Palestine to fight in the spirit of an Arab nationalist solidarity. But the war was a military debacle and a political disaster for the Arabs. It led to the proclamation of an independent Jewish state at Tel Aviv and the uprooting of nearly one million Palestinians from their homeland. It also destabilised the old nationalism and elites who had taken over from western colonialism.

The birth of Israel called forth a new, radicalised Arab nationalism. The Syrian educationist Sati al-Husri had been the foremost theoretician of Arab nationalism in the 1930s. He continued to develop his theory of nationalism, propagating it with full force in different Arab countries. Al-Husri fashioned a version of cultural nationalism that imagined an Arab community unified by three different yet interconnected factors such as shared language, culture and history. Islam alone, despite its important role, could not be reckoned as the singularly shaping principle of Arab nationalism. The Syrian scholar Constantine Zurayk and the Iraqi scholar Abdul Rahman al-Bazzaz also advanced a liberal version of

Arab cultural nationalism with its accents falling primarily on language and history. At the same time, the Ba'th Party activists such as Munif al-Razzaz, Salah al-Din Bitar, and particularly Michel Aflaq, theorised an Arab nationalism foregrounding the struggle against imperialism, while pointing it in a totalitarian direction.

Arab nationalism became deeply pronounced and politicised by at least three revolutions – the Egyptian revolution of 1952, the Iraqi revolution of 1958, and the Algerian revolution of 1954 to 1962. They were each directed against both the monarchical regimes that had failed the Arabs in 1948, and European colonialism. This was the context in which the most influential nationalist movements of the next two decades – Nasserism and Ba'thism – arose. The movement initiated by the Egyptian president Gamal Abdel Nasser was by far the greater force. He began land reforms in the 1950s and nationalised the Anglo-French owned Suez Canal Company in 1956. Some of Nasser's initiatives – undertaken in the name of Arab nationalism – energised the Algerian National Movement and, later, the Palestinian Liberation Organisation (PLO), founded in 1964. The Arab Nationalists' Movement (ANM), formed by the Palestinians in 1951, also followed Nasser's lead throughout the 1960s, while the merger of the nationalist Ba'th Party with the Arab Socialist Party in 1953 created conditions for the phenomenal rise of Nasserism itself. In the same year, Nasser published his pamphlet *The Philosophy of the Revolution*, spelling out the three major strengths of the Arab world: its achievements in civilisation, its strategic location at the crossroads of three continents, and its oil resources; at the same time mobilising the nationalist unity of the Arab world against Western imperialism and Zionism. Under Nasser's leadership, the United Arab Republic (UAR) was formed in 1958 through the union of Egypt and Syria, although this union was shortlived. During the 1950s and the early 1960s, Nasser steered Egypt into closer association with the Soviet Union and the Warsaw Pact, at a time when his radical nationalism was perceived as a potential threat to the US oil and strategic interests in the Middle East. The USA for its part drew even closer to Israel as a strategic ally, continuing to lend her massive military and financial support.

The conflicts between the Ba'thists and Nasser's own political party, the Arab Socialist Union, began to weaken Arab nationalism. Then the Six Day War of June 1967 with Israel dealt a deadly blow to Nasserism and by extension Arab nationalism itself. Israel occupied Sinai, the Gaza Strip, the West Bank, the whole of Jerusalem, and the Golan Heights. The war aggravated the plight of the Palestinians: more than 350,000 Palestinians fled the West Bank across Jordan, while 100,000 Syrians left the Golan Heights. By the time of Nasser's death in 1970, the PLO, under the increasingly militant leadership of Yasser Arafat, was developing a line independent of the Arab states, whose practical interest in the Palestine issue was on the wane.

The chain of subsequent events, including the 1970 civil war in Jordan, the Lebanese civil war beginning in 1975, the Iraq–Iran war throughout the 1980s, and the 1982 Israeli invasion of Lebanon, further undermined Arab nationalism. The cause of the suffering, stateless, exiled and occupied Palestinians seemed without a helper as the Palestinian leadership moved from one location of exile to another. The popular Intifada (uprising) in 1987 began independently and constituted the most concerted revolt of the Palestinians since 1936. Despite Israeli repression, the Intifada turned out to be a consequential force as it prompted King Hussein of Jordan to give up his claim to the West Bank in 1988, opening the way for the PLO to form a Palestinian state in the West Bank and Gaza. In bringing into being a Palestinian National Authority, headed by Arafat, the Oslo accords of 1993 not only split Palestinian nationalism, they threw up a potential Islamist opposition to

Arafat, swinging radical opposition to Zionism away from secular nationalism into a new Islamist phase. The trend was shadowed elsewhere in the Arab world as Islamic parties attracted varying degrees of popular support against the residue of Ba'thism, installed in deeply unpopular dictatorships in Syria and Iraq, and the Western-leaning oligarchies in control in Egypt and Jordan. The renewed Intifada beginning in 2000, coupled with the events of 11 September, 2001, has accentuated the movement away from secular nationalism toward militant Islamism in the Arab world.

The relationship between Arab nationalism and Arabic literature in the twentieth century remains both explicit and troubled. Arab creative writers generally prefer to communicate in their mother tongue (be it Arabic or not), although some writers use English. The Arab world has a very long and rich tradition of poetry. In the twentieth century, Arabic poetry adopted a modern vocabulary that was often politically engaged, as seen in the work of the Iraqi poet, Al-Bayati. The Arabic novel is a relatively recent phenomenon growing out of its encounters with European colonialism. But the novel also captures, mediates and reproduces the turbulent political and social realities of the Arab world, both reinforcing and challenging Arab nationalism. Indeed, the Arab world has produced a rich body of the literatures of occupation, exile, diaspora, dispossession, disillusionment and resistance. At least three poets – the Syrians Adunis and Nizar Qabbani as well as the Palestinian national poet Mahmoud Darwish – stand out both for their anti-colonial resistance variously inflected by an Arab nationalist stance and for their trenchant critiques of bourgeois Arab nationalism.

Feminist poets such as the Palestinian Fadwa Tuqan and the Jordanian-Lebanese-Palestinian Salma Khadra Jayyusi, as well as the Egyptian novelist Nawal el Sa'adawi – among many others – deal with the question of national liberation as it relates to women's struggles for freedom. They might be said all to focus particularly on four sites of oppression and opposition: land, labour, language and the body, which they see under both colonial and patriarchal occupation. The work of Naguib Mahfouz – the leading Arab novelist from Egypt – directly and critically engages with Nasserism and Arab nationalism. Mahfouz's early work looks at different phases of both Egyptian and Arab nationalism, while his later work offers a scathing critique of Nasser's nationalist government and its corruptions. Other Arab novelists, differentially tracking the trajectories of Arab nationalism in the Palestinian context, include the foremost Palestinian writers Emile Habibi and Ghassan Kanafani. The experimental Lebanese novelist Elias Khoury also approaches the issues of Nasserism and Arab nationalism in a world torn by war. Arab writers using English yet asserting an Arab identity were the *mahjar* (emigrant) Arab-American poets Ameen Rihani and Kahlil Gibran, while those writing in English today include the poet Fawaz Turki and the prose writers Ahdaf Soueif and Fadia Faqir. Soueif's *In the Eye of the Sun* (1992) is an ambitious, if flawed evocation of the atmosphere of later twentieth-century Arab nationalist politics, particularly in the Egyptian context. Finally, among the critics writing in English about Arabic literature, Edward Said was most notable for producing worldly and oppositional work.

Azfar Hussain

Literary Works

Barakat, Halim (1983), *Days of Dust*, trans. T. Le Gassick, Boulder, CO: Lynne Rienner.
Faqir, Fadia (1989), *Nisanit*, Harmondsworth: Penguin.

Habibi, Emile [1974] (2001), *The Secret Life of Saeed, the Ill-fated Pessoptimist: A Palestinian who became a Citizen of Israel*, trans. S. K. Jayyusi and T. Le Gassick, New York: Interlink Books.

Handal, Nathalie (ed.) (2001), *The Poetry of Arab Women: A Contemporary Anthology*, New York: Northampton.

Jayyusi, Salma Khadra (1992), *Anthology of Modern Palestinian Literature*, New York: Columbia University Press.

Jayyusi, Salma Khadra (ed.) (1987), *Modern Arabic Poetry: An Anthology*, New York: Columbia University Press.

Kanafani, Ghassan [1963] (1978), *Men in the Sun*, trans. H. Kilpatrick, Washington, DC: Three Continents.

Khalid, Leila (1973), *My People Shall Live: The Autobiography of a Revolutionary*, ed. George Hajjar, London: Hodder and Stoughton.

Khoury, Elias (1989), *Little Mountain*, Minneapolis, MN: University of Minnesota Press.

Mahfouz, Naguib [1967] (1978), *Miramar*, trans. F. Moussa-Mahmoud, Cairo: American University in Cairo Press.

Soueif, Ahdaf (1992), *In the Eye of the Sun*, London: Bloomsbury.

Histories

Al-Musawi, Muhsin Jassim (2003), *The Postcolonial Arabic Novel: Debating Ambivalence*, Leiden: Brill.

Amin, Samir (1978), *The Arab Nation*, trans. M. Pallis, London: Zed Books.

Antonius, George (1938), *The Arab Awakening: The Story of the Arab National Movement*, Beirut: Khayat's.

Dawisha, Adeed (2003), *Arab Nationalism in the Twentieth Century: From Triumph to Despair*, Princeton, NJ: Princeton University Press.

Duri, A. A. (1987), *The Historical Formation of the Arab Nation: A Study in Identity and Consciousness*, trans. L. I. Conrad, London: Croom Helm.

Nash, Geoffrey (1998), *The Arab Writer in English: Arab Themes in a Metropolitan Language, 1908–1958*, Brighton: Sussex Academic Press.

Nasser, Abdel Gamal (1959), *The Philosophy of the Revolution*, trans. D. Al-Maaref, Buffalo, NY: Smith, Keynes and Marshall.

Said, Edward W. (1979), *The Question of Palestine*, New York: Times Books.

Tibi, Bassam (1997), *Arab Nationalism: Between Islam and the Nation-State*, New York: St Martin's Press.

See also: **Algerian War of Independence; Fanon, Frantz; Historiography: Middle East; Islam; Palestinian Political Movements; Zionism.**

Nationalism(s): Canada

Canada's history is one of contested and contradictory nationalisms. At the moment of confederation (1867), Canadian nationalist discourse was torn between civic and ethnic nationalisms, that is, between (1) the project of bringing together, in a political union, communities that might otherwise have formed independent nations, and (2) the nineteenth-century European ideal of a nation unified by a single language and culture (epitomised in French Canada by the journalism of Abbé Louis Leflèche and in English Canada by the Anglo-Saxon Protestant 'Canada First' movement). Native peoples have consistently refused the very terms on which the Canadian nation was founded. Their self-identification as 'First Nations' is, as Arun Mukherjee has observed, intended 'to counteract the racist nationalist discourse of "two founding races" which undergirds the Canadian state and all its social and cultural hierarchies' (Mukherjee 1999, p. 156).

At the turn of the twentieth century, Canada, still very much rooted in the British Empire, debated various possible futures for itself, including federation on a Commonwealth model among members of the British Empire (imperialism); annexation with the United States (continentalism); and identification as an independent nation (nationalism). In the early decades of the century, the success of the Canadian Corps in World War I combined with many other factors to produce a sense of independence from Britain. The work of the Group of Seven painters and of poets such as F. R. Scott and E. J. Pratt illustrates this break. Their turn away from European models toward the land and especially toward the north inspired the anti-colonialist narratives of Canadian identity presented by cultural nationalists such as Margaret Atwood in the 1960s and 1970s. In the mid-century, Canada shifted from worrying about its relationship with Britain to worrying about its relationship with the United States. In 1948, Harold Innis remarked that Canada had 'moved from colony to nation to colony' (cited in Cook 1995, p. 191). The wave of Canadian nationalism of the 1960s and 1970s was thus a celebration of the centenary, a form of resistance to American domination of Canadian affairs, and an expression of the desire to make Canada cohere in spite of its cultural and linguistic heterogeneity. However, in its preoccupation with the relationship with the United States and Britain, Canadian nationalism has often overlooked the uneven relations of power within the nation. As numerous historians and cultural critics have observed, the civic idealism which structured confederation and which subtends official policies of 'bilingualism' and 'multiculturalism', actually conceals the privilege of white Anglo-Saxon Protestants. This privilege has provoked various forms of resistance including Quebec nationalism which, associated first with the Church and, after 1960, with the state, has worked actively to assure the future of French-language culture and to secure political sovereignty for Quebec.

Lianne Moyes

Literary Works

Brand, Dionne (1999), *At the Full and Change of the Moon*, Toronto: Knopf Canada.
Campbell, Maria (1973), *Halfbreed*, Toronto: McClelland and Stewart.
Duncan, Sara Jeannette [1904] (1996), *The Imperialist*, ed. Thomas E. Tausky, Ottawa: Tecumseh.
Ferretti, Andrée and Gaston Miron (1992), *Les Grands Textes Indépendantistes: Écrits, Discours et Manifestes Québécois, 1774–1992*, Montreal: l'Hexagone.
Findley, Timothy [1977] (1986), *The Wars*, Toronto: Penguin.
Kogawa, Joy [1981] (1983), *Obasan*, Toronto: Penguin.
MacLennan, Hugh [1945] (1991), *Two Solitudes*, Toronto: General.

Histories

Mukherjee, Arun Prabha (1995), 'Canadian Nationalism, Canadian Literature and Racial
    Minority Women', in Makeda Silvera (ed.), *The Other Woman: Women of Colour in
    Contemporary Canadian Literature*, Toronto: Sister Vision Press, pp. 421–45.
Cook, Ramsay (1995), *Canada, Québec and the Uses of Nationalism*, 2nd edn, Toronto:
    McLelland and Stewart.
Davey, Frank (1993), *Post-National Arguments: The Politics of the Anglophone-Canadian
    Novel since 1967*, Toronto: University of Toronto Press.
Dickenson, Peter (1999), *Here is Queer: Nationalisms, Sexualities and the Literatures of
    Canada*, Toronto: University of Toronto Press.
Godard, Barbara (2000), 'Notes from the Cultural Field: Canadian Literature from Identity
    to Hybridity', *Essays on Canadian Writing* 72, pp. 209–47.
Kamboureli, Smaro (2000), *Scandalous Bodies: Diasporic Literature in English Canada*,
    Toronto: Oxford.

See also: **Historiography: Canada**; **Inuit**; **Multiculturalism: Canada**; **Quebec Independence Movement**.

Nationalism(s): Southern Africa

The nationalisms of southern Africa, Robert Ross has argued, were shaped by the British model introduced to the Cape Colony in 1795. Applying to southern Africa Benedict Anderson's well-known argument that late eighteenth-century European and US models of nationhood have functioned as models or blueprints for all subsequent nationalisms, Ross argues that British nationalism 'was the prime nationalism of South Africa, against which all the subsequent ones, whether Afrikaner or African, reacted, either directly or at a remove' (Ross 1999, p. 43). The particularities of social conditions in southern Africa – substantial European settler populations, the resilience of pre-colonial social systems, and the widespread practice of indirect rule – have complicated profoundly the nature and form of the competing nationalisms that have emerged.

Turning first to settler nationalism, the most significant form is Afrikaner nationalism. An ethnic nationalist ideology forged in response to military defeat in the South African War (1899–1902) and forced anglicisation by Britain thereafter, it gained added impetus and urgency from accelerated white urbanisation during the inter-war decades, culminating in its infamous electoral victory in 1948, which initiated what Dan O'Meara (1996) has called the 'forty lost years' of apartheid. Although laying formal claim through massive civil festivals to direct descent from the participants in the so-called Groot Trek (Great Migration) of 1838 (see Grundlingh and Sapire 1989) and the arrival of the Dutch East India Company in 1652 (see Rassool and Witz 1993), Afrikaner nationalism's rise can more plausibly be dated to the so-called Tweede Taal Beweging (Second Language Movement) beginning in 1902, which sought to rehabilitate the Dutch patois *kombuis taal* into 'Afrikaans' by equipping it with a modern lexicon and literature (see Giliomee 2003 and Hofmeyr 1987).

Afrikaner nationalism has always been deeply fissured along regional and class lines, despite the insistence of its ideologues and enemies on its essentially undifferentiated nature. The accommodationist patrician leadership of the rural gentry in the prosperous wine and wheat farming south-western Cape was always contested by a more radically republican motley crew of *backveld* Dutch Reform Church *dominees* (ministers), teachers and small businessmen who spearheaded the movement in the northern Boer republics-cum-provinces of the new nation state (see O'Meara 1983). Similarly, the leadership fought long and hard battles to wean the nascent Afrikaner urban underclass from its class affiliations and securely attach it to a programme of racial exclusivism (see O'Meara 1983, Brink 1987 and Du Toit 1996). The unifying idea of *volkskapitalisme* (people's capitalism) neatly encapsulated Afrikaner nationalism's inherent ambiguities by suggesting the possibility of elite accumulation alongside Afrikaner underclass advancement. This was achieved only at the expense of the institutional immiseration of the majority black population under apartheid and sustainable only during the long postwar boom in the international economy. With the onset of global recession in the mid-1970s, the disintegration of the *cordon sanitaire* provided by the Portuguese colonies (1974–5) and Ian Smith's Rhodesia (1980), the resurgence in the black labour movement and the Soweto revolt (see Saul and Gelb 1986), Afrikaner nationalism fragmented along its regional and class faultlines. In the 1980s, a more secure Afrikaner bourgeoisie made common cause with once-reviled British capitalism in order to pursue a 'total strategy' aimed at the incorporation of suitably 'moderate' black allies into the political process, albeit as perpetual minors, while crushing radical black nationalism with military force both at home and abroad (see O'Meara 1983). The jettisoned Afrikaner petty-bourgeoisie and working class in turn espoused an increasingly uncompromising racism and rediscovered its fascist tendencies as represented by the formation of the Afrikaner Weerstands Beweging (1981) and Conservative Party (1982) among others to oppose the new accommodationist policies of the National Party (see Furlong 1991 and O'Meara 1983).

The end of the Cold War, by robbing militarised Afrikaner nationalism of American patronage, forced it belatedly to compromise with black nationalism in the subcontinent. The long military occupation of southern Angola and the Namibian colony was thus swiftly ended (1990) and the attempt to divide and destroy black nationalism in South Africa was gradually abandoned in favour of a new democratic dispensation (1994) (see Marais 2001). The disavowal of racial exclusivism for a new minority politics has led to the propagation of a culturally-based Afrikaner 'imagined community' that has tried with little success to include previously ignored black elements (see Giliomee 2003). The Afrikaner petty bourgeoisie and underclass meanwhile have remained true to the old ideals of white racial exclusivity now pursued partially through parliamentary politics, but most energetically via intermittent campaigns of terrorism and the embracing of both indigenous and internationalist millenarian white supremacist doctrines.

In the twentieth century, other variants of settler nationalism in the British colonies of southern Africa defined themselves in opposition to Afrikaner nationalism. Thus the anglophone minority in South Africa espoused a liberalism founded on fidelity to the British connection via the Commonwealth and friendliness to the natives who were believed to be assimilable through a process of anglicisation (see Merrington 2002 and Hyam and Henshaw 2003). Strongest in the Cape, where a qualified franchise was instituted in the nineteenth century, liberalism's purchase on either Afrikaner or African nationalism was always more imagined than real and its willingness to compromise with both according to circumstance, provided private property and free trade were sacrosanct, its abiding characteristic (see Trapido 1980 and Ross 1999).

Settler nationalism in Zimbabwe was also initially defined both by its opposition to

British South Africa Company rule, but also Afrikaner nationalism. In refusing incorporation as the fifth province of South Africa in 1923, the anglophone settler population con-
jured an alternative imagined community under the British imperial aegis. The liberal
strain within Rhodesian nationalism accepted the inevitability of compromise with black
nationalism as embodied in the ill-fated federation experiment with Zambia (Northern
Rhodesia) and Malawi (Nyasaland) (1953–62). The more radical and racially exclusive
element saw no need for compromise and advocated independence under white minority
rule and the suppression of radical black nationalism, as in South Africa. The unilateral
declaration of independence in 1965 under Ian Smith initiated a protracted fifteen-year
guerrilla war with insurgent black nationalists, before the white minority accepted majority government in 1980. The white diaspora to South Africa in the aftermath of independence sustained a Rhodesian nationalism in exile, which waned perceptibly during the
1980s as the anticipated socialist revolution in Zimbabwe failed to materialise.

No comparable settler nationalisms emerged in the Portuguese colonies of Angola and
Mozambique where the Portuguese fascist dictatorship maintained control over the administration and settlers continued to exercise political rights in Portugal. Dependent on cheap
land and black labour and so overtly hostile to black nationalism, with the collapse of the
dictatorship in the 1974 coup and subsequent abandonment of the African colonies, the
vast majority of settlers relocated back to Portugal or to South Africa. Similarly in
Namibia, the original German and post-1918 Afrikaner settler populations were very small
and retained loyalties to their original national imagined communities. Implacable foes of
black nationalism, they have survived its ultimate triumph as small ethnic minorities exercising disproportionate economic power, and thus perpetually anxious that their wealth
might be expropriated in the interests of the national black majority.

The trajectory of the black nationalisms in southern Africa closely followed the contours of Christian missionary activity, flourishing in areas where the latter established stations and their associated schools and failing to appear where these were absent (see Vail
1989 and Odendaal 1984). The mission schools, by providing literacy in both indigenous
vernaculars and the language and history of the colonisers in pursuit of souls, inadvertently
produced a native intelligentsia. The rise of a national consciousness was forestalled,
however, because the various versions of indirect rule instituted in southern Africa under
European colonialism insisted on the quintessentially tribal nature of Africans, and
encouraged the mission school intelligentsia to address themselves to an ethnic rather than
a national audience. The migrant nature of the proletarian armies mobilised by the region's
mineral revolution – retaining access to land in the countryside and looking to the pliant
chiefly authority authorised by indirect rule to keep a watchful eye over women, children
and cattle during their long absences from home – further reinforced this trend (see Vail
1989, Marks 1986 and Cope 1993). The emergence of an urban audience of free labourers
for black nationalism was also actively thwarted by the ubiquitous segregationist policies
implemented across the region designed to preserve urban space for the more or less exclusive permanent abode of whites. Therefore although the oldest black nationalist organisation, the South African Native National Congress, forerunner of the African National
Congress, was founded in Bloemfontein in 1912, two years before the political vehicle of
Afrikaner nationalism, the National Party, it engaged in a futile 'toy telephone' petition
politics with the white government until the mid-twentieth century (see Walshe 1970 and
Odendaal 1984).

World War II kick-started a secondary industrial revolution in the region centred on
South Africa, and led to accelerated black urbanisation coincident with the coming of age

of a new generation of mission-educated youth disdainful of their elders' accommodations with settler racism. This generation was encouraged by the postwar international discourse of anti-colonialism and self-determination, and sought to fashion a popular audience in a national rather than ethnic mould (see Lodge 1983). Like Afrikaner nationalism before it, black nationalism did not have the field to itself, for in addition to the pull of ethnic loyalties, the black urban under-class had already been significantly wooed and won to ideologies of class during the war (see Alexander 2000). Facing increasing repression from white minority governments, black nationalism sought and secured alliances with trade union and other class-based organisations with the argument that national liberation was a necessary precursor to socialist transformation (see Lodge 1983). Such alliances and those with sympathetic elements among the white and other settler minorities remained a contentious issue, and ultimately split the nationalist movement in South Africa in 1959 and have continued to dog it ever since (see Pogrund 1990, Biko 1978, Fatton 1986 and Lewis 1987).

The majority settler populations across the region, however, refused all compromise with black nationalism for fear of jeopardising their continued access to land and cheap labour. Instead, they adopted a dual strategy of crushing nationalism and seeking moderate black allies, particularly from among the so-called native authorities (see O'Meara 1983). The effect of repression was to force the nationalist movements into armed insurrections against settler minorities and their comprador black allies. Armed struggle radicalised nationalism, particularly in the cases of the Portuguese colonies and Zimbabwe, where nationalists were forced into a dependence on the peasantry for the conduct of guerrilla war. The central place of the land question in settler southern Africa led radical nationalism to espouse variants of more or less scientific socialism intended to redress the massive imbalances in ownership of land and other productive resources. The liberation wars also took on the character of civil wars through the widespread mobilisation and use of loyal black auxiliaries to fight the nationalist insurgents on the settlers' behalf (see Lodge 1983).

In South Africa, the apartheid policy of separate development led to an efflorescence in black ethnic nationalisms each organised around its own embryonic nation state. Several of these so-called Bantustans were given their 'independence' from the mid-1970s onwards, replete with all the trappings of nationhood (Transkei, Ciskei, Venda, Bophuthatswana), while the Zulu nationalist organisation, Inkatha in KwaZulu, declined this option in favour of a federal alternative with settler minorities in the Natal province in the 1980s (Mare and Hamilton 1987).

While black nationalism in the Portuguese colonies and Rhodesia was able to break the Portuguese army and Smith's UDI regime by the mid-1970s, settlers in South Africa beat off the challenge of radical nationalism at home and across the region by dint of the strength of their military power and alliances with the United States abroad and black clients at home. The South African Defence Force either directly (Namibia and Angola) or indirectly (Mozambique and Zimbabwe) attacked black nationalism along its borders and conducted a policy of 'destabilisation' throughout the region during the late Cold War, with American blessing (Hanlon 1986).

Black nationalism's ultimate 'victory' in South Africa itself owed far more to shifts within the international arena than any successes on the battlefield. With the end of the Cold War, the shelf life of white South Africa as a bastion of Christianity and civilisation guarding the mineral wealth and sea routes of southern Africa against communism expired. Almost overnight, after a half-century of attempting to destroy the black nationalist movements in Namibia and South Africa, the apartheid regime belatedly granted

Namibia independence (1990) and reincorporated the Bantustans into a unitary South African state with a system of universal rather than ethnic suffrage (1994) (see Marais 2001). The jury is still out on South Africa's new 'rainbow nationalism', which represents a crude attempt to confect an inclusive imagined community out of the myriad ethnic fragments generated by the long and bitter history of racial and ethnic strife in the country, and has little real purchase on the popular imagination beyond the urban middle class. The neighbouring examples of Namibia and Zimbabwe suggest that the prognosis for this 'new' South Africa is not good. The failure to address adequately either the land issue or the legacy of the decades-long dirty war suggests that the new South African nationalism is merely sowing dragons' seeds for the future (see Marais 2001).

The literary works below provide but a preliminary guide to imaginative works that have engaged with the many southern African nationalisms: on Afrikaner nationalism, see Louw, Leipoldt and van Heerden; on Zimbabwean nationalisms before and after independence, see Samkange and Chinodya respectively; on nationalism in Angola, see Pepetela; and on post-apartheid 'rainbow nationalism', see Coetzee, Gordimer, Mda and Berold.

Lance van Sittert

Literary Works

Berold, Robert (2002), *It All Begins. Poems from Post-Liberation South Africa*, Pietermaritzburg: University of Natal/Gecko.

Chinodya, Shimmer (1989), *Harvest of Thorns*, London: Heinemann.

Coetzee, J. M. (2002), *Youth*, London: Secker and Warburg.

Gordimer, Nadine (1998), *The House Gun*, New York: Farrar, Straus and Giroux.

Leipoldt, C. Louis (2001), *The Valley*, Cape Town: Stormberg.

Louw, N. P. van Wyk (1975), *Oh Wide and Sad Land*, trans. A. Small, Cape Town: Maskew Miller.

Mda, Zakes (2000), *The Heart of Redness*, Cape Town: Oxford University Press.

Pepetela [1984] (1996), *Yaka*, trans. M. Holness, London: Heinemann.

Samkange, Stanlake (1966), *On Trial for My Country*, London: Heinemann.

Van Heerden, Etienne [1993] (1997), *Leap Year: A Novel*, trans. M. Hacksley, London and Sandton: Penguin.

Histories

Alexander, Peter (2000), *Workers, War and the Origins of Apartheid: Labour and Politics in South Africa 1939–1948*, Oxford: James Currey.

Anderson, Benedict (1991), *Imagined Communities: Reflections on the Origins and Spread of Nationalism*, 2nd edn, New York: Verso.

Biko, Steve (1978), *I Write what I Like: A Selection of his Writings*, London: Bowerdean Press.

Brink, E. (1987), 'Maar 'n Klomp 'Factory Meide: Afrikaner Family and Community on the Witwatersrand during the 1920s', in B. Bozzoli (ed.), *Class, Community and Conflict*, Johannesburg, Ravan Press, pp. 177–208.

Cope, N. (1993), *To Bind the Nation: Solomon kaDinuzulu and Zulu Nationalism 1913–1933*, Pietermaritzburg: University of Natal Press.

Du Toit, M. (1996), 'Women, Welfare and the Nurturing of Afrikaner Nationalism: A Social History of the Afrikaanse Christelike Vroue Vereniging c. 1870–1939', Cape Town: unpublished Ph.D. thesis, University of Cape Town.

Fatton, R. (1986), *Black Consciousness in South Africa: The Dialectics of Ideological Resistance to White Supremacy*, Albany, NY: SUNY Press.

Furlong, P. J. (1991), *Between Crown and Swastika: The Impact of the Radical Right on the Afrikaner Nationalist Movement in the Fascist Era*, Johannesburg: Witwatersrand University Press.

Giliomee, Herman (2003), *The Afrikaners: Biography of a People*, London: C. Hurst.

Grundlingh, A. M. and H. Sapire (1989), 'From Feverish Festival to Repetitive Ritual?: The Changing Fortunes of Great Trek Mythology in an Industrialising South Africa 1938–1988', *South African Historical Journal* 21, pp. 19–37.

Hanlon, James (1986), *Beggar Your Neighbours: Apartheid Power in Southern Africa*, London: James Currey.

Hofmeyr, Isabel (1987), 'Building a Nation from Words: Afrikaans Language, Literature and Ethnic Identity, 1902–1924', in S. Marks and S. Trapido (eds), *The Politics of Race, Class and Nationalism in Twentieth Century South Africa*, Harlow: Longman, pp. 95–123.

Hyam, R. and P. Henshaw (2003), *The Lion and the Springbok: Britain and South Africa since the Boer War*, Cambridge, Cambridge University Press.

Lewis, G. (1987), *Between the Wire and the Wall: A History of South African 'Coloured' Politics*, Cape Town: David Philip.

Lodge, Tom (1983), *Black Politics in South Africa since 1945*, Harlow: Longman.

Marais, Hein (2001), *South Africa Limits to Change: The Political Economy of Transition*, Cape Town: University of Cape Town Press.

Mare, Gerry and Georgina Hamilton (1987), *An Appetite for Power: Buthelezi's Inkatha and the Politics of Loyal Resistance*, Johannesburg: Ravan Press.

Marks, Shula (1986), *The Ambiguities of Dependence: Class, Nationalism and the State in Twentieth Century Natal*, Johannesburg: Ravan Press.

Merrington, Peter (2002), 'Heritage, Letters and Public History: Dorothea Fairbridge and Loyal Unionist Cultural Initiatives c. 1890–1930', Cape Town: unpublished Ph.D. thesis, University of Cape Town.

Odendaal, Andre (1984), *Vukani Bantu: The Beginnings of Black Protest Politics in South Africa to 1912*, Cape Town: David Philip.

O'Meara, Dan (1983), *Volkskapitalisme: Class, Capital and Ideology in the Development of Afrikaner Nationalism 1934–1948*, Cambridge: Cambridge University Press.

O'Meara, Dan (1996), *Forty Lost Years: The Apartheid State and the Politics of the National Party 1948–1994*, Johannesburg: Ravan Press.

Pogrund, Benjamin (1990), *Sobukwe and Apartheid*, Johannesburg: Jonathan Ball.

Ross, R. (1999), *Status and Respectability in the Cape Colony, 1750–1870. A Tragedy of Manners*, Cambridge: Cambridge University Press.

Rassool, Ciraj and Lesley Witz (1993), 'The 152 Jan van Riebeeck Tercentenary Festival: Constructing and Contesting Public National History in South Africa', *Journal of African History* 34, pp. 447–68.

Saul, John and Stephen Gelb (1986), *The Crisis in South Africa*, London: Zed Books.

Trapido, Stan (1980), 'The Friends of the Natives: Merchants, Peasants and the Political and Ideological Structure of Liberalism in the Cape', in S. Marks and A. Atmore (eds), *Economy and Society in Pre-Industrial South Africa*, Harlow: Longman, pp. 247–74.

Vail, Leroy (ed.) (1989), *The Creation of Tribalism in Southern Africa*, London: James Currey.
Walshe, Peter (1970), *The Rise of African Nationalism in South Africa: The African National Congress 1912–1952*, London: C. Hurst.

See also: **Anti-colonialism and Resistance: Southern Africa; Historiography: Southern Africa; Post-apartheid.**

Native Reservations

Native reservations in Canada developed out of the Indian Act (1876), which was said to 'protect' the small share of Canada's land base allotted to people of First Nations. Statutes dating back to the middle of the nineteenth century created the concept of 'status' to separate those who were entitled to reside on Indian lands and use their resources from those who were forbidden to do so. In this respect, the early legislation was an expression of the concepts set forth in the royal proclamation of 1763. The exemption of reserve lands from municipal taxation and seizure under legal process were other measures said to 'secure' those lands for First Nations.

Critics of Canada's reserve system state that the government is practising a form of apartheid. First Nations in Canada are, like indigenous peoples around the world, segregated from the legal and administrative structures of society based on their race or ethnic identity. Many people on the reserves, according to statistics published by the UN, suffer from much more poverty, unemployment and housing shortage than non-native Canadians. This has led to questions about potential human rights violations being directed toward the Canadian government. The government's response to such criticism has been to develop the existing reserve system into Native self-government. The Cree and Naskapi First Nations of northern Quebec were the first aboriginal groups to negotiate self-government as part of their land claim agreements (the James Bay and Northern Quebec Agreement and North-eastern Quebec Agreement) in 1975 and 1978. Provisions for local government were implemented in 1984 by the Cree-Naskapi (of Quebec) Act, which replaced the Indian Act for the Cree and Naskapi, and limited the responsibilities of the federal government in the day-to-day administration of band affairs and lands. All the Cree and Naskapi bands were incorporated and some of their lands constitute municipalities or villages under the Quebec Cities and Towns Act. Band corporations have by-law powers similar to those possessed by local governments under provincial legislation.

The council for Yukon First Nations, the government of the Yukon and the federal government signed an umbrella final agreement (UFA) on 29 May 1993. The UFA established the basis for the negotiation of final land claim settlements and self-government agreements with each of the fourteen Yukon First Nations. It provides land, cash compensation, wildlife harvesting rights, land and resource co-management, and protection for the culture and heritage of Yukon Indians. It also sets out the framework for individual Yukon First Nations Final Agreements, which will address the specific circumstances of each First Nation. Some aboriginal groups have criticised these policies as municipal-type arrangements, governed by provincial legislation and not far-reaching enough to move toward a large-scale policy of Native self-government.

Justin Edwards

Literary Works

Armstrong, Jeanette (2001), *Slash*, Penticton: Theyus Books.
Highway, Tomson (1988), *The Rez Sisters*, Saskatoon: Fifth House.
King, Thomas (1993), *Green Grass, Running Water*, Toronto: HarperCollins.

Histories

Harris, Cole (2002), *Making Native Space: Colonialism, Resistance, and Reserves in British Columbia*, Seattle, WA: University of Washington Press.
Lithman, Yngve Georg (1984), *The Community Apart: A Case Study of a Canadian Reserve Community*, Winnipeg: University of Manitoba.

See also: **European Exploration and Settlement: Canada; Genocide: Canada; Historiography: Canada; Inuit; Multiculturalism: Canada**.

Naxalites

In May 1967, there was a peasant uprising in Naxalbari, an impoverished area in the north-eastern tip of West Bengal. Led by communist revolutionaries belonging to a breakaway faction of the country's largest Marxist party, the Communist Party of India, the uprising drew upon Maoist revolutionary strategy – armed rebellion by landless and poor peasants to seize power from the rulers and establish liberated zones in the countryside. It also drew upon the legacy of earlier peasant struggles, notably Tebhaga – a movement demanding that the landlords' share of the produce was reduced to a third, and Telengana – an armed insurrection in the southern state of Andhra Pradesh in the late 1940s and early 1950s which challenged India's independence.

Failing to spread with the rapidity assumed by its leaders and ideological mentors, the Naxalite movement was soon crushed. Nevertheless, attracting and involving some of the country's brightest intellectuals and students, it did capture the worldwide revolutionary imagination of the 1960s. As the movement petered out in the countryside, it shifted locus to the city. From 1967 to 1972 there were many violent clashes between rebellious youth and the symbols of state power, which engendered a violent state response and the loss of many lives. The term 'Naxalites' thus came to occupy an ambiguous and contradictory space in the Indian imagination. At one level it came to symbolise any assault upon the assumptions and institutions that hold up the social and political order. It also contributed significantly to a growth in peasant militancy against iniquitous economic and extra-economic relations, including bonded labour and sexual servitude, which marked India's semi-feudal countryside. This even involved the development of armed squads and a military wing which directly challenged the legitimacy of the Indian state.

Many critics aver that the Naxalites and their movements, in their fascination with armed rebellion, only strengthened the authoritarian tendencies of the state and helped weaken the 'regime of law'. Worse, many groups slipped into brigandage and extortion, some over time becoming mercenaries on behalf of various groups contending for power. Whilst hailed as uncompromising activists, their 'infantile adventurism' only increased the level of violence in society and the suffering of the 'innocents' caught in the cross-fire. But it is undeniable that they irreversibly altered the lexicon of Indian politics, not just in the rise of militancy and confrontation across the economic and social terrain, but by loosening the self-limiting shackles inhibiting the struggle for rights. By directly increasing the agency and self-worth of *all* oppressed strata – peasants, tribals, workers, women and Dalits – they helped provide an edge to many movements and struggles – feminist, ecological, civil rights and so on. This multi-faceted challenge to India's ideological superstructure helped expose the upper caste class and patriarchal bias of the country's formally liberal democratic order, and forced the passage of new laws and regulations that have helped enlarge the space for freedom.

Harsh Sethi

Literary Works

CPI(M-L) (1986), *Report from the Flaming Fields of Bihar: A CPI(M-L) Document*, Calcutta: Prabodh Bhattacharya.
Devi, Mahashweta (1997), *Mother of 1984*, trans. and intro. by Samik Bandyopadhyay, Calcutta: Seagull Books.
Roy, Bhaskar (2002), *An Escape into Silence*, Delhi: New Century.

Histories

Bannerji, Sumanta (1980), *In the Wake of Naxalbari: A History of the Naxalite Movement in India*, Calcutta: Subarnarekha.
Mukherji, Partha N. (1983), *From Left Extremism to Electoral Politics: Naxalite Participation in Elections*, Delhi: Manohar.
Sen, Samar, Debabrata Panda and Ashish Lahiri (eds) (1978), *Naxalbari and After: A Frontier Anthology*, Volumes I and II, Calcutta: Kathashilpa.
Shah, Ghanshyam (1990), *Social Movements in India: A Review of Literature*, Delhi: Sage Publications.

See also: **Communism: South Asia; Historiography: South Asia; Terrorism.**

Negritude

Coined by the Martinican poet, Aimé Césaire, the term Negritude was first used in his 1939 poem *Cahier d'un Retour au Pays Natal* (translated as *Return to my Native Land*). Developed in association with Leopold Sedar Senghor and Leon Damas in Paris in the 1930s, Negritude soon became a philosophical affirmation of African and diasporic cultures and a major literary and cultural movement focused on the celebration of the virtues and values of African civilisations and black identity. The description of the characteristics of different races and the theories of race that began with the Enlightenment philosophers had, by the nineteenth century, created an intellectual tradition that basically stigmatised blackness by constructing negative stereotypes of the nature and abilities of black people. Negritude represented an attempt to reverse this stigmatisation by revaluing these images of black identity and reconstructing the terms of the discourse of Blackness.

The historical antecedents of Negritude can be found in the Harlem Renaissance and the various strands of Pan-African thought from Edward Wilmot Blyden's concept of the 'African personality' to Marcus Garvey's Back to Africa movement, and W. E. B. Du Bois' *The Souls of Black Folk* (1903), to name a few influences. As the concept was being developed in the 1940s, Negritude received the endorsement of the intellectual and artistic establishment in France. André Breton had written a preface to Cesaire's *Cahier* and Jean-Paul Sartre's preface to Senghor's *Anthologie de Nouvelle Poésie Nègre et Malgache de Langue Française* helped secure international attention for the new concept and movement. When Alioune Diop started *Présence Africaine* in 1947, the journal provided the Negritude movement with an intellectual organ for disseminating its ideas. Apart from the publication itself, *Présence Africaine* sponsored conferences in the Sorbonne in 1956, Rome in 1959, and the First World Festival of Negro Arts in Dakar in 1966, brought African and diasporic intellectuals and artists together, and provided an important forum for the exchange of ideas.

In the exponents' elaboration of the concept, there appeared to have developed two identifiable tendencies within the Negritude movement. One is usually associated with Césaire who is generally credited with a more objective, historical conception of Negritude while the other, identified with Senghor, is more ontological and essentialist. Senghorian Negritude was passionately criticised by English-speaking African writers because it claimed a set of essential characteristics such as emotion, intuition, rhythm and so on for black peoples, and opposed these to what he termed 'Hellenic Reason'. Though Senghor ascribed positive value to 'intuition', 'emotion' and so on, and even celebrated them, this essentialisation of race and the construction of racial characteristics in binary opposition to others was seen as merely subscribing to long discredited notions of racial biologism.

Despite these critiques and Frantz Fanon's denunciation of it, there can be little doubt Negritude will always be counted as one of the major philosophical and literary movements of African and diasporic nationalism of the twentieth century.

                                                                                        Harry Garuba

Literary Works

Césaire, Aimé [1938] (1995), *Notebook of a Return to my Native Land*, trans. M. Rosello with A. Pritchard, Newcastle-upon-Tyne: Bloodaxe.
Du Bois, W. E. B. [1903] (1999), *The Souls of Black Folk*, ed. H. L. Gates Jr and T. H. Oliver, New York and London: W. W. Norton.
Eshleman, Clayton and Annette Smith (1983), *Aimé Césaire: The Collected Poetry*, Berkeley, CA: University of California Press.
Senghor, Léopold Séder (1991), *The Collected Poetry*, trans. M. Dixon, Charlottesville, VA: University of Virginia Press.

Histories

Asante, Molefi Kete (1987), *The Afrocentric Idea*, Philadelphia: Temple University Press.
Hountondji, Paulin J. (ed.) (1983), *African Philosophy, Myth and Reality*, trans. H. Evans, London: Hutchinson.

Howe, Stephen (1998), *Afrocentrism. Mythical Pasts and Imagined Homes*, London and New York: Verso.
Mudimbe, V. Y. (ed. and intro.) (1992), *The Surreptitious Speech. 'Présence Africaine' and the Politics of Otherness, 1947–1987*, Chicago: University of Chicago Press.

See also: **Anti-colonialism and Resistance: West Africa; Fanon, Frantz; Pan-Africanism; Senghor, Léopold Sédar.**

Nehru, Jawaharlal

Nehru was one of the most charismatic leaders of the Indian nationalist movement and the first prime minister of India. He represented the left-leaning faction of the nationalist Congress Party that had led India to independence in 1947. His political praxis tried to reconcile socialism and the interests of the agrarian and business classes that backed Congress. Therefore, the transition from colonial to postcolonial state under Nehru was characterised by a 'passive revolution': the transformative role of the new national state was limited to reformist and molecular changes, so that the coming of independence acquired the dual character of revolution/restoration, consolidating the Indian middle class while eliminating the possibility of a complete social revolution and redistribution of resources, though significant land reforms were carried out throughout the 1950s and 1960s.

Nehru was born in 1889 in Allahabad, India, of an extremely wealthy Brahmin family, originally from Kashmir. His father, Motilal Nehru, who was also a nationalist, sent his son to Harrow and Cambridge, where Jawaharlal read natural sciences. These studies influenced his rationalist and scientific intellectual outlook. In the 1920s, he joined the Non-Cooperation movement led by Mahatma Gandhi, and in a short while became Gandhi's closest ally, which enabled him to assume an enduring legitimacy in an all-India political role. A nationalist leader with a very wide-ranging political and intellectual perspective, Nehru's nationalism differed significantly from Gandhi's because it was strongly influenced by Western political thought, especially Marxism. Moreover, Nehru, being an agnostic, was troubled by the religious dimension to Gandhi's politics.

In 1929, he was elected president of the All-India Congress Committee, the party that led India to independence. Throughout the 1920s and 1930s, because of his political activity, he spent long periods in prison, during which he wrote two of his books. Towards the end of the 1930s, his political influence within Congress began to outweigh that of Gandhi. Nehru became the chief negotiator on behalf of Congress for the transfer of power from the Raj to the independent nation, and was thus implicated in the partition of India into two independent states, India and Pakistan. As prime minister, Nehru formulated India's 'non-alignment' policy towards the world power blocs, while maintaining friendly relations with both the USA and the USSR. His economic plans promoted the growth of heavy industry and the building of dams, policies that were subsequently criticised in view of India's predominantly agrarian economy. One of Nehru's primary political goals was to make India into an important world player. He formulated the secular and multicultural principles underlying the Indian constitution, which guaranteed state protection for India's many minorities and effectively stabilised communal tensions for many decades after partition.

Neelam Srivastava

Literary Works

Advani, Rukun (1994), *Beethoven among the Cows*, New Delhi: Ravi Dayal.
Nehru, Jawaharlal (1936), *An Autobiography*, London: John Lane.
Nehru, Jawaharlal [1946] (1956), *The Discovery of India*, London: Meridian Books.
Sahgal, Nayantara (1954), *Prison and Chocolate Cake*, London: Victor Gollancz.
Seth, Vikram (1993), *A Suitable Boy*, New York: HarperCollins.

Histories

Brown, Judith M. (1999), *Nehru*, Harlow: Longman.
Chatterjee, Partha (1986), *Nationalist Thought and the Colonial World: A Derivative Discourse?*, London: Zed Books.
Gopal, Sarvepalli (1989), *Jawaharlal Nehru: A Biography*, New Delhi: Oxford University Press.
Khilnani, Sunil (1997), *The Idea of India*, London: Penguin.

See also: **Anti-colonialism and Resistance: South Asia; Historiography: South Asia**.

Nkrumah, Kwame

Kwame Nkrumah, first president of independent Ghana and one of the father figures of Pan-Africanism, was born 21 September 1909 in the village of Nkroful in the south-western part of the British colony of the Gold Coast. His father was a traditional goldsmith and his mother a petty retail trader. His formal education began in Roman Catholic mission schools from where he proceeded to the famous Achimota College in Accra and then to the USA, where he obtained degrees from Lincoln University and the University of Pennsylvania.

At Achimota, he was strongly influenced by the vice-principal Dr Kwegyr Aggrey. The nationalist sentiments Aggrey had wakened in him were strengthened by the activities of the other early West African nationalist leaders such as Nnamdi Azikiwe whose articles in the *African Morning Post* were a further inspiration. However, it was later that his political ideas began to take shape, when he read nationalist thinkers such as Marcus Garvey and Mohandas Gandhi; European radicals like Hegel, Marx and Lenin; and met with leading activist-philosophers of Pan-Africanism such as C. L. R. James, George Padmore and W. E. B. Du Bois.

In 1945, Nkrumah moved to England to register for a doctorate at the London School of Economics and simultaneously to pursue a law degree. Instead, he was caught up in the activities of the West African Students Union to which George Padmore had introduced him as soon as he arrived. In his position as secretary of the union, he helped organise the fifth Pan-African congress in Manchester, and together with Du Bois drafted the declarations adopted by the congress. During his London years, he was to meet other future African leaders such as Jomo Kenyatta of Kenya and Hastings Banda of Malawi, and he developed the organisational and mobilisational skills that were later to become invaluable on his return to Ghana.

In 1947, he was persuaded by the leaders of the United Gold Coast Convention (UGCC) to return to Ghana to become secretary general of the party. In this position,

Nkrumah toured the various regions of the country calling for unity and vastly increasing the party's membership. His grassroots approach transformed the UGCC from an elite middle-class party into a mass movement, and it was not long before he came into conflict with the party bosses who favoured a conservative gradualist approach to Nkrumah's call for mass action. In 1949, he left the UGCC and formed the Convention Peoples Party (CPP) where he finally had a free hand to put his strategy of civil disobedience, boycotts and strikes into full use, in the struggle against the British colonial authorities. In 1951, while Nkrumah was in prison on charges of 'sedition' and 'subversion', the CPP won thirty-four of the thirty-eight contested seats in the legislative assembly. The colonial governor Charles Arden-Clarke then released him and asked him to form a government as part of a phased programme of limited self-rule to independence. Nkrumah thus became prime minister and held office through a series of elections until independence on 6 March 1957.

In 1960, Ghana became a republic with Nkrumah as its first president. He held office till 1966 when he was overthrown in a military coup, and went into exile in Guinea where he devoted his energies to writing. He died of cancer in 1972 in a hospital in Rumania. Nkrumah is best remembered for his strong advocacy of Pan-Africanism, the major role he played in the establishment of the Organisation of African Unity and his bold and visionary political, social and economic programmes. Even though, for a variety of reasons, some were not always successfully implemented, his ideas have remained major sources of inspiration in Africa and the African diaspora.

Harry Garuba

Literary Works

Armah, Ayi Kwei (1968), *The Beautiful Ones Are Not Yet Born*, London: Heinemann.
Nkrumah, Kwame (1957), *The Autobiography of Kwame Nkrumah*, Edinburgh: Thomas Nelson.

Histories

Birmingham, David (1998), *Kwame Nkrumah: The Father of African Nationalism*, Athens, OH: Ohio University Press.
Hadjor, Kofi Buenor (1988), *Nkrumah and Ghana: The Dilemma of Post-Colonial Power*, London and New York: Kegan Paul International.
Poe, Daryl Zizwe (2004), *Kwame Nkrumah's Contribution to Pan-African Agency: An Afrocentric Analysis*, London and New York: Routledge.

See also: **Anti-colonialism and Resistance: West Africa; Negritude; Pan-Africanism**.

Nyerere, Julius and Ujamaa

Apart from the title, Mwalimu (meaning teacher), the idea most closely associated with the name of Julius Nyerere is summed up in the word *ujamaa*. Ujamaa (Swahili for 'family-hood') was the specific version of African socialism conceived and implemented by Nyerere during his years in power in Tanzania. Many African leaders of the post-independence period of the 1960s, even the most capitalist oriented, regularly claimed socialism (invariably always conjoined with the significant qualifier 'African') as their guiding ideology. But none of them attempted as extensive a 'philosophical' exposition of their notions of African socialism *and* then tried with such honesty and vigour systematically to implement it at the political, economic and social spheres of national life as did Julius Nyerere.

Nyerere was born in March 1922 in Butiama in colonial Tanganyika. He studied at the only secondary school then in the colony, in Tabora, and obtained a scholarship to Makerere University in Uganda, from where he graduated with a teacher's degree in 1945. After teaching for a period, he left for the University of Edinburgh in 1949, where he studied for a degree in economics and history. On his return to Tanganyika, he become president of the Tanganyikan African Association in 1953. One year later, he had transformed this civic group into the Tanganyika African National Union (TANU), an organisation with the more clearly articulated political goal of gaining self-governance for Tanganyika. After elections in 1960 in which TANU candidates won a majority, Nyerere was appointed chief minister and guided the country to independence on 9 December 1961. Barely a month after assuming office as prime minister, Nyerere resigned to concentrate on rebuilding the party. Less than a year later, he was re-elected president and remained in office till 1985 when he retired.

Before the official adoption of ujamaa as party ideology and guiding principle of government in the Arusha Declaration of 5 February 1967, Nyerere had shown a commitment to rural development and to the building of a socialist society. In the paper 'Ujamaa – The basis of African Socialism', published as a TANU pamphlet in April 1962, he had sketched the outlines of his idea that socialism in Tanzania had to be built on the foundations of traditional African society in the extended family system. He lauded the affective ties of kinship and reciprocity and the organisation of work and reward within the extended family unit, because these provided every individual with a sense of belonging, sharing and security within the traditional heritage. This 'tribal socialism' needed to be recovered and reconstituted so that the new nation could be seen as an extension of the traditional family unit. The result was the philosophy of ujamaa which became the national ideology. This perspective, which avoided the classical Marxian dictum of class struggle, has been criticised for its idealism and for trying to sidestep history. However, it is the villagisation process that resulted from the attempts to implement ujamaa as government policy that has drawn the greatest attention.

The creation of ujamaa villages and the initial efforts to persuade peasants to resettle in them, which began in the late 1960s, had by the 1970s become a major party-and-government driven objective that inevitably led to huge bureaucratic bungles. Many analysts now believe that the villagisation programme was an economic failure. In this respect it is no different from many of the centrally planned modernist social engineering projects of the twentieth century. However, very few doubt the honesty and integrity of Nyerere's vision and the human and social development which his government brought to the people of Tanzania.

Harry Garuba

Literary Works

Hussein, Ebrahim (1970), *Kinjeketile*, Dar es Salaam: Oxford University Press.
Kagwema, Prince (Osija Mwambungu) (1984), *Society in the Dock*, Dar es Salaam: Three Stars Publication.

Mbise, Ismael R. (1974), *Blood on our Land*, Dar es Salaam: Tanzania Publishing House.
Palangyo, Peter (1968), *Dying in the Sun*, London: Heinemann Educational.
Ruhumbika, Gabriel (1969), *Village in Uhuru*, London: Longman.

Histories

Blommaert, Jan (1997), 'The Impact of State Ideology on Langauge: Ujamaa and Swahili
    Literature in Tanzania', in B. Smieja and M. Tasch (eds), *Human Contact through
    Language and Linguistics*, Frankfurt: Peter Lang, pp. 353–70.
Hold, Michael (ed.) (1988), *Tanzania after Nyerere*, London: Pinter Publishers.
Hyden, Goran (1980), *Beyond Ujamaa in Tanzania*, London: Heinemann.
Nyerere, Julius (1968), *Ujamaa: Essays on Socialism*, Dar es Salaam: Oxford University
    Press.
Scott, James C. (1998), 'Compulsory Villagisation in Tanzania: Aesthetics and
    Miniaturization', in J. C. Scott, *Seeing Like a State*, New Haven, CT: Yale University
    Press, pp. 223–61.

See also **Anti-colonialism and Resistance: East Africa; Wabenzi.**

O

Oil: Middle East

Industrial production of oil first developed in Baku at the end of the nineteenth century.
Seepages were noticed in Persia in the 1890s and oil was made part of Julius de Reuter's
package of concessions, which, however, were rescinded in 1899. William Knox D'Arcy
gained the concession for the whole of Persia except the northern provinces, and drillings
began near Qasr-i-Shirin in 1905. Backers were on the point of pulling out when oil was
discovered at Masjid-i-Suliman in 1908. In the following year, D'Arcy's syndicate was
absorbed into the newly formed Anglo-Persian Oil Company, 51 per cent of whose shares
belonged to the British government. Between 1910 and 1913 a refinery was constructed at
Abadan. But even by 1920 Middle East oil production 'barely exceeded 1 per cent of world
output' (Longrigg 1968).

Oil was a factor in the British advance to Mosul in Iraq in the latter part of World War I.
France demanded a share in Iraqi oil as a condition of giving up her claim to Mosul as did
America, jealous of British control of Middle East oil. Oil revenues were considered important for the viability of the new Iraqi state. When the Iraqi Petroleum Company was
founded Anglo-Persian and Shell held major interests. In 1922, a New Zealander, Major

Holmes, gained a concession for oil exploration from the sultan of Najd and future king of Saudi Arabia, Abdul Aziz ibn Saud, despite pressure from the British government. However, when the concession became available once more in 1931, the British government let the opportunity pass and exploration rights were picked up by Standard Oil of California. The discovery of oil in Bahrain at around this time disclosed the vast potential of the much larger fields of Saudi Arabia, henceforth under the influence of the United States.

Oil revenues really only began to impact on the economies of Middle East states in the 1950s, when the issue of oil nationalisation merged with struggle for decolonisation. In 1951, when the Iranian premier Mossadeq came out in favour of nationalising Iranian oil, the British tried to destabilise his government. A battle ensued between the nationalist Mossadeq and conservative forces around the Shah. The Shah was briefly forced into exile, but in 1953 a CIA-engineered, British-supported coup removed Mossadeq from power and facilitated the return of the monarch.

Mossadeq's legacy was not only important for Iranian opposition politics, it was seen by some as a dress rehearsal for Nasser's nationalisation of the Suez Canal in 1956. Ironically, the sign that control of Middle East oil had been wrested from the Western oil companies was the OPEC price rises of the mid-1970s, led by the West's 'policemen' in the region, the Shah's Iran. The oil weapon became a double-edged sword indeed as wielded by conservative and radical regime alike.

Geoff Nash

Literary Works

Daneshvar, Simin [1969] (2002), *A Persian Requiem (Savushun)*, trans. Roxane Zand, London: Peter Halban.
Munif, Abdelrahman (1987) *Cities of Salt (Mudun al-milh)*, trans. Peter Theroux, New York: Vintage.

Histories

Brill, J. A. and William Roger Louis (eds) (1988), *Musssadiq, Iranian Nationalism, and Oil*, London: I. B. Tauris.
Longrigg, S. H. (1968), *Oil in the Middle East*, Oxford: Clarendon Press.
Mosley, Leonard (1974), *Power-Play, Oil in the Middle East*, Harmondsworth: Penguin.
Philby, H. St John (1948), *Arabian Days: An Autobiography*, London: R. Hale.
Rihani, Amin (1928), *Ibn Saoud, His People and His Land*, London: Constable.

See also: **Britain's Postwar Foreign Policy; Iranian Revolution.**

Ottoman Empire

The Ottoman Empire was labelled by nineteenth-century European diplomacy, 'the sick man of Europe'. The accounts of life in the palaces of Istanbul by writers such as Mary Wortley Montagu inspired a genre of painting exemplified by John Frederick Lewis'

'Harem life – Constantinople' (c. 1857), and latterly, T. E. Lawrence's autobiography (1926), and served to create an image of an exotic, corrupt and corrupting polity and society.

The beginnings of the Ottoman Empire date back to 1280, and at the height of its power included in the west, the Balkans and most of North Africa, and in the east the Caspian Sea, thus incorporating modern-day Iran, Iraq and Syria. It was sufficiently powerful to threaten the West militarily, besieging Vienna in 1525 and 1683, and attempting to curb Venetian naval power in the Mediterranean at the Battle of Lepanto in 1571. Its power, despite the Crimean War of 1853 to 1856, was not finally broken until World War I when its alliance with Germany led to its subsequent dismemberment, finalised in the 1920 Treaty of Sèvres. This makes it one of the longest continuous political entities in Europe. Accounting for why such an enormously significant political and cultural entity is known through such a distorted lens is in effect also an exploration of the development of knowledge in Western Europe during the eighteenth and nineteenth centuries.

The Ottoman Empire was the classical territory of 'Orientalism' as is illustrated by Condorcet's *Esquisse d'un Tableau Historique des Progrès de l'Esprit Humain* (1792). Condorcet, like many of the other Enlightenment philosophers, deployed a series of oppositions that contrasted the Orient and the Occident, as a means to explore the failings of his own state. The Ottoman Empire was the Muslim power that occupied the perimeter of European space and interpreting its history is made more difficult by the role played by the victorious powers in 1918 and the subsequent carving-up of its territories, as well as the claims of nineteenth-century Balkan nationalists. The question of the interpretation of the nature and origins of the Ottoman polity has come increasingly under scrutiny as some of the seminal assumptions appear less tenable (see Lowry 2003). However, studying the Ottoman Empire illustrates the political nature of history and the distorting mirror of Orientalist assumptions.

Kay Adamson

Literary Works

Pamuk, Orhan [1979] (2001), *The White Castle*, trans. V. Holbrook, London: Faber and Faber.
Pamuk, Orhan [1998] (2001), *My Name is Red*, trans. E. M. Göknar, London: Faber and Faber.

Histories

Hourani, Albert (1991), *A History of the Arab Peoples*, London: Faber and Faber.
Inalcik, Halil with Donald Quataert (eds) (1994), *An Economic and Social History of the Ottoman Empire, 1300–1914*, Cambridge: Cambridge University Press.
Lowry, Heath W. (2003), *The Nature of the Early Ottoman State*, New York: SUNY Press.
Melman, Billie (1992), *Women's Orients – English Women and the Middle East, 1718–1918 (Sexuality, Religion and Work)*, London: Macmillan.

See also: **Historiography: Middle East; Kemalism; Levant Company.**

P

Pacific Sub-imperialism

When we attach the prefix 'sub' to 'imperialism,' we get a peculiar formation. 'Imperialism' we know means the creation of subsidiary nations by a more powerful nation-state, which then exercises control over its resources and peoples, either territorially or through economic and military threats. 'Sub', of course, alludes to that which is 'under' or 'below' something else, as in subaltern or subordinate. So sub-imperialism would, it seems, refer to those nation-states that act as willing lieutenants of a hyper-imperial power. It is their role to keep recalcitrant nations, or territories that do not fit into some predetermined economic or ideological scheme, in some kind of bondage. In other words, sub-imperial nations are overseer states that profit in one way or another from being the watchdogs of a truly global power. A current example of such an overseer state in the Pacific region is Australia. Having no economic or military clout of its own and nervous of non-white neighbours, it habitually aligns itself with Britain or North America, even at the expense of its own export markets and national concerns.

When the Howard government joined the US-led assault on Iraq in 2003, it compromised – albeit, as it turned out, only in the short-term – its lucrative wheat trade to that country. Now that the United States is keen to intervene in the affairs of so-called 'failed' states, treating them as potential breeding grounds for all manner of 'terrorists', Australia, as befits an exemplary deputy, has found it necessary to revise its usual lackadaisical approach to regional micro-states. In recent times it has intervened decisively in the Solomon Islands, although several years after that country's slide into anarchy and financial ruin, and for the first time taken serious notice of the Pacific Islands Forum to the extent of lobbying for an Australian appointment to the position of secretary general. Furthermore, a recent Senate report has floated the idea of 'a South Pacific economic and political community with a common currency and labour market' (*The Australian*, 13 August 2003). To be led by Australia, this community would keep an eye on money launderers and terrorist financiers in the South Pacific.

Of course, Australia is not the only sub-imperial entity in the region. Not too long ago, Indonesia acted the part when, with 'US diplomatic support and arms – used illegally, but with secret authorization' (Chomsky 2000, p. 51), it brutally invaded and annexed East Timor in December 1975. The American support of Suharto was tied to the perverse logic of the Cold War, whereby unpalatable regimes were routinely shored up against the domino effect of communism. More than 200,000 East Timorese lost their lives during the twenty-four years of occupation, and many remain displaced. That East Timor's independence came shortly after the fall of Suharto and the end of the Cold War may be a coincidence, but it is clearly a telling one.

Sudesh Mishra

Literary Works

Mo, Timothy (1991), *The Redundancy of Courage*, London: Chatto and Windus.
Pascoe, Bruce (1996), *Ruby-Eyed Coucal*, Broome: Magabala.
Stow, Randolph (1981), *Visitants*, London: Picador.

Histories

Chomsky, Noam (2000), *Rogue States: The Rule of Force in World Affairs*, Cambridge, MA: South End Press.
Cristalis, Irena (2002), *Bitter Dawn: East Timor – A People's Story*, London: Zed Books.
Niner, Sarah (ed.) (2000), *To Resist is to Win: The Autobiography of Xanana Gusmão*, Australia: Aurora Books.
Ramos-Horta, Jose (1987), *Funu: The Unfinished Saga of East Timor*, Trenton, NJ: Red Sea Press.

See also: **Asianisation: Australia; Britain's Postwar Foreign Policy; East Timor; Historiography: Australia.**

Pacific Way

There is something mildly disturbing about a cultural category whose origins may be traced back to an address given by an Oxford-educated prime minister of chiefly rank to the United Nations General Assembly in 1970. Moreover, when this category assumes the status of a forceful – albeit murkily defined – regional discourse through a system of scholarly mediation, the creeping sense of unease is heightened. According to Ron Crocombe, a non-islander academic who wrote the definitive pamphlet on the subject, the concept 'was launched on the international stage by Fiji's Prime Minister' (Crocombe 1976, p. 1) in the year of his country's independence from colonial rule. Somewhat oddly, Crocombe declines to cite any part of Ratu Sir Kamisese Mara's speech to back up his assertion. Nor does he, for that matter, dwell on the prime minister's understanding of the expression he is credited as having introduced to the international community.

There are a couple of explanations for the oversight. The first concerns Crocombe's sense of the Pacific Way as a clutch of partially articulated, free-floating concepts and practices unifying the diverse peoples of Oceania but lacking in any real definitional shape or substance. The second pertains to the still emergent discourse of 'group identification' (Crocombe 1976, p. 2) his essay is about to describe and which must, in the meantime, remain suspended, unarticulated, a culture-specific secret to be uncovered through academic intervention. Once the task of attributing the phrase to an indigenous leader is done, the burden of an ongoing critical exposition falls on the expert in the field. Nothing is made of the expert's own subject position, background, knowledge systems, emphases, informants, his methodological grid, the nature of his archives, and so on. The issue of representation is silently and perhaps knowingly bypassed. There is an excellent reason for this manoeuvre. Crocombe's essay, it turns out, does not intend to perform a second-order commentary on some extant indigenous practice; rather, it is itself a first-order knowledge system that draws on certain floating anecdotes and impressions to engender an intellectual object. That Crocombe's essay has played a vital role in delimiting and popularising an indigenous-style of response to late modernity testifies to its massive impact on regional consciousness in general, and on political elites in particular.

So what is this thing called the Pacific Way? In a sub-section entitled 'A Living, Growing Field of Meaning', Crocombe maintains that, 'the Pacific Way has no single precise meaning, but it carries a core of basic ideas and emotional responses plus a range of other meanings which can be attached to it according to context' (Crocombe 1976, p. 2). He continues, 'Like other terms which are loaded with meaning, it means somewhat different things to different people or at different times – think of "The American way of life", "love", "God", "development" or "freedom". The very fact that they are not precise, that they cover a field of meaning which allows each person to respond and interpret in relation to his own needs and feelings, makes them so full of meaning. So it is with the Pacific Way' (Crocombe 1976, pp. 2–3). Then comes a most revealing observation: 'Once the term was there, and everyone liked the ring of it, the search was on for meanings to attach to it' (Crocombe 1976, p. 3).

Having established both the permissiveness and emptiness of the Pacific Way, the expert Crocombe sets out to chart the broader field and to isolate those occasions when the term reifies into cultural, political or economic significance. However, the meaning of the term 'the Pacific Way' refuses to settle and commit itself to any singular meaning, and in this manner, is gradually defined without becoming in any way definite. Even more crucially, the Western expert may disclaim any responsibility for the alleged quirkiness of the phrase, because 'only islanders can ascribe new meanings to it. For others to do so would be regarded as presumptuous or illegitimate' (Crocombe 1976, p. 4). Crocombe does not acknowledge that his own enterprise is complicit in this kind of presumption and illegitimacy. If the Pacific Way is, as he maintains, semantically portable as well as malleable, then this fact is delineated and defined in the meaningful discourse of his own project, which seeks to, as Crocombe puts it, pin down both its 'theology' and 'technology' – disciplinary tactics hardly derived from indigenous knowledge systems. The point is that the Pacific Way in fact did not exist prior to Crocombe's mediation of it; in fact, the signal – and doubtless egregious – achievement of the essay is that it actually inaugurates an islander way of knowing, performing and being. To get any kind of purchase on the term, we have to pass through Crocombe's hall of mirrors.

Crocombe's Pacific Way has a theological as well as a technological component. The theological component comprises those aspects of the term that may be classified as 'beliefs, values, political and psychological responses', whereas the technological component relates to 'the actual behaviour and activity which seems identified with it' (Crocombe 1976, p. 3). Having established this dichotomy, Crocombe then sets about isolating those ideas and practices that best define 'the Pacific Way', identifying 'brotherhood' as a key idea:

> It is based on an assumption, usually unspoken, that all islanders are, for certain ideological purposes, brothers . . . The realities of brotherhood, anywhere, include squabbling, jealousy, conflict and competition. But the ideology is of mutual help, and common interests and origins. This implies common ancestry and common heritage as well as present common concern. Here the facts need shoring up by myths. (Crocombe 1976, pp. 4–5)

The 'unspoken' assumption of islander brotherhood (as spoken through and by Crocombe) is one in a series of grand unifying concepts linking the diverse communities of the region.

To what effect it is not made clear, but like all such concepts, however, 'brotherhood' betrays a certain unavoidable strain of racism, since it excludes those male islanders who are either European or Asian. Of course, it also betrays a certain strain of sexism by excluding women, whether Asian, European or Polynesian. In addition to specifying a gender- as well as 'race'-specific collective identity (male Melanesians, Micronesians and Polynesians qualify, but not women and Indo-Fijians), Crocombe also excludes people from isolated villages from the Pacific Way:

> [Their] . . . world is not a Pacific world, for most purposes it is one village or one island, and at the very outside one nation or territory. The Pacific Way concept is of the most value to the mobile elite of the Pacific Islands: the politicians, the senior officers of government, leading churchmen, the few leading islands businessmen and so on. (Crocombe 1976, p. 7)

In other words, for Crocombe the legitimate speakers of the Pacific Way are elite islanders, who employ it as a 'symbol of Pacific unity' (Crocombe 1976, p. 8) by actively excluding Europeans, Asians, women and subaltern villagers, that is to say, the vast majority of the inhabitants of the terrain encompassed by the term 'Pacific' – shorthand, it seems, for Oceania.

Having established the Pacific Way as a brotherhood of the elite, and exclusively articulated by them, Crocombe says that the concept, despite the massive differences between Melanesian and Polynesian social structures, one egalitarian and the other aristocratic, is bound to 'the idea of chieftainship' which he warns may turn out to be its Achilles heel. Immediately after this passage, he extends his discursive field by citing one such chieftain's call for islanders to return to 'the [pre-colonial] ways and friendships of our forefathers' (Crocombe 1976, p. 12). While maintaining that this sense of the past is based on a remarkable degree of historical forgetting, he concedes that it affords 'a much-needed rationale for linkage, unity and cooperation' (Crocombe 1976, p. 13) among the diverse communities. A brotherhood of the elite, the Pacific Way clearly strives to bring together the hegemonic groups of the various islands against all those who fall outside the category. It is therefore first and foremost a discourse of exclusion that uses ideas of unity, consensus and inclusiveness to fabricate consent. 'Talking things over rather than taking rigid stands, preparedness to negotiate, flexibility, adaptation and compromise are frequently spoken of as key features of the Pacific Way' (Crocombe 1976, p. 15). Clearly such an approach is possible, even inevitable, when the conversation takes place among subjects already unified by a common sense of feudal status, economic privilege and political hegemony. In some measure this accounts for Crocombe's overwhelming, albeit erratic, reliance on informants who are chiefs, big men or political leaders.

In the second part of his essay, Crocombe targets those daily practices that ground the Pacific Way in a less abstract cultural realm. For example, he lists the practice of sharing food, goods and resources, considered the social obligation of the chieftains, to be another sign of the Pacific Way, as is the general ability to 'accommodate, feed and look after large numbers at short notice, to re-orient one's whole time-schedule to suit the convenience of others, and to go broke if necessary' (Crocombe 1976, p. 18). Crocombe concedes that the burden of such extraordinary largesse 'falls disproportionately on women' (Crocombe 1976, p. 20), but this in no way disrupts his enthusiasm for the Pacific Way in general. Further characteristics of the Pacific Way include that 'more bodily contact [is involved] than the English or Australian way' (Crocombe 1976, p. 22), and that with reference to time, it lags 'at least half an hour behind clock time and has considerable range of flexibility'

(Crocombe 1976, p. 22). Further, despite the statistics on anxiety syndromes and suicide rates, laughter and good fellowship are also part and parcel of the discourse. Even sartorial habits qualify. Although a prototype of the garment may have been introduced by evangelising missionaries in the nineteenth century, 'the truest emblem of The Pacific Way is the lavalava or rami or pareu or sulu or laplap or vala' (Crocombe 1976, p. 27). In fact, the exchange and wearing of leis, the respect for protocol, the preference for bare feet, the celebration of pidgin and dialect, the revival of culture-specific songs and dances, the ritual of kava consumption, the fondness for local root crops, indigenised Christianity – everything but the kitchen sink qualifies as the Pacific Way. The troubling aspect to the increasing capaciousness of Crocombe's Pacific Way is that it manifestly conceals the hierarchical (social, gender, economic, ethnic and so on) relations underpinning it.

Since the publication of Crocombe's essay nearly three decades ago, much has happened through and to the discourse of the Pacific Way. While Crocombe has recently reiterated his earlier understanding of the term, others have departed considerably from his view that it stands for 'some common [feudal, patriarchal] values, practices and sentiments in the region which differed from those of Europeans and Asians' (Crocombe 2001, p. 159). In fact, what redeems the Pacific Way is its radical reconfiguration by those excluded constituencies who negatively constituted the discourse in first instance. Of those excluded, local NGOs (usually multi-ethnic in composition), commoner islanders, and women have had the most impact. In 1998, for instance, the Fourth NGO Parallel Forum issued a communiqué that pulled the rug from under official regional representatives by pressing for a revival of the Pacific Way. To its credit, the NGO Forum approached the Pacific Way in terms markedly different from the so-called elites, for whom it was always a cynical consent-manufacturing concept unifying the already-empowered against other competitors in the general pursuit of profit, development and modernity. Instead of employing it as a defensive cultural smokescreen, the NGO communiqué invoked the Pacific Way in order to address urgent regional issues and problems. These included the neglect of non-market based economies, the danger posed to customary systems of land tenure, the establishment of regional trade networks, the spectre of nuclear waste dumping, the creation of regional human rights bodies, the protection of indigenous intellectual property rights and the development of an effective gender policy.

A few years previously, Atu Emberson-Bain, a feminist scholar based in Fiji, anticipated this rethinking of the term in her assessment of an environmental impact report:

> In fact, the greater involvement of the region's own human resources – its local communities, NGOs and women – would seem to be where the real (perhaps the only) hope lies for more sustainable and self-reliant forms of development. Part of this task would be to integrate traditional knowledge systems, but not for their instrumental value in advancing macroeconomic growth and strengthening the prevailing free market development model. Traditional knowledge and development ethics can and should be incorporated as fundamental guiding principles of a genuinely 'Pacific Way' model for development. This would provide a sound basis for safeguarding and enhancing long-term supply of food, (traditional) medicines, craft materials and other resources necessary for the reproduction of sustainable livelihoods. (Emberson-Bain 1994, p. 49)

Such substantive counter-hegemonic accounts of the Pacific Way, if implemented as clear-headed policy, may give the discourse a productive agency it presently lacks and a materiality it so sorely needs.

Sudesh Mishra

Literary Works

Gaskell, Ian (2001), *Beyond Ceremony: An Anthology of Drama from Fiji*, Suva: University
    of the South Pacific.
Hau'ofa, Epeli (1993), *Tales of the Tikongs*, Suva: Beake House.
Hau'ofa, Epeli (1995), *Kisses in the Nederends*, Hawaii: University of Hawaii Press.
Wendt, Albert (1981), *Leaves of the Banyan Tree*, Auckland: Penguin.
Wendt, Albert (1987), *Pouliuli*, Auckland: Penguin.

Histories

Crocombe, Ron (1976), *The Pacific Way: An Emerging Identity*, Suva: Lotu Pasifica
    Productions.
Crocombe, Ron (2001), *The South Pacific*, Suva: University of the South Pacific.
Emberson-Bain, Atu (1994), *Sustainable Development or Malignant Growth?*, Suva: Marama
    Publications.

See also: **Diaspora: Pacific; Pacific Sub-imperialism; Women's Histories: Australia, New
    Zealand, Pacific.**

Pakeha

'Pakeha' (also spelt Paakeha) is an indigenous term of New Zealand's First People, *Ngai Iwi
Maori*, to denote white-skinned visitors or Europeans in general, as distinct from Maori
(also spelt Maaori), the *tangata whenua* (original indigenes). As such, Pakeha was for the
most part a neutral oppositional categorisation used to describe the British founders of what
eventually became a supra-tribal, bi-ethnic polity and settler colony after the signing of the
Treaty of Waitangi in 1840. Today the term means either New Zealanders of European
descent lines and/or non-Maori citizens who collectively comprise the second (and historically dominant) treaty partner.

Lexically, the word has a contested history. In some contexts it meant an enemy in a
fight, one who belonged to a different race or one with a pale skin. Some have suggested
that Pakeha may have been derived from the Maori expression for ghost (*kehua*) or for lime-
stone or white clay (*pakeho*) or from *pakepakeha* or *patupaiarehe*, the spectral people of the
mists with pale skins. Its use for a European was first recorded by the French voyager
Dumont d'Urville in 1824. Williams (1844) offers the nuanced definition, 'A person of predominantly European descent' and/or 'foreign'.

Pakeha quickly came to signify both formal representatives of the British Crown and,
more proximately, French and British settlers: strangers to the shores of the New Zealand
archipelago when it was exclusively inhabited by Polynesian people (the first human
migrants). These Pakeha were the 'sky-piercers' who introduced literacy, Christianity and
firearms into 'Maoriland' (*Nu Tireni*). The word early became a floating, revisable and flexible signifier of attachment, co-operation and ethno-political sharing: in the nineteenth
century the label Pakeha embraced European runaways and ex-convicts who lived as Maori
(Pakeha-Maori), as imaged by George Baines in Jane Campion's 1992 film *The Piano*. It

even denoted some Maori who avidly adopted *Pakehatanga*: the practices of European modernity. There is no evidence that Pakeha is or was pejorative (as some white New Zealanders fear) and there is merit in the argument that a term which signified British colonists has now migrated to connote all non-Maori citizens who make a home and a lasting commitment to New Zealand and that *te taha Pakeha* constitutes a secondary tier of indigenous culture to that of the Maori in Aotearoa/New Zealand. This conceptualisation is a vast improvement on the twentieth-century notions of assimilation-integration: the colonialist regime which confined Maori to a subordinate constitutional and citizenship status under the 'We are one people' doctrine.

Bruce Harding

Literary Works

Duff, Alan (1990), *Once Were Warriors*, Auckland: Tandem Press.
Finlayson, Roderick (1938), *Brown Man's Burden*, Auckland: Unicorn Press.
Hulme, Keri (1984), *The Bone People*, London: Spiral in assoc. with Hodder and Stoughton.
Mason, Bruce (1960), *The Pohutukawa Tree*, Wellington: Price Milburn.

Histories

King, Michael (ed.) (1991), *Pakeha: The Quest for Identity in New Zealand*, Auckland: Penguin Books NZ.
Pearson, David and Jeffrey Sissons (1997), 'Pakeha and Never Pakeha', *Sites* 35, pp. 64–80.
Sturm, Terry (ed.) [1991] (1998), *The Oxford History of New Zealand Literature in English*, Auckland: Oxford University Press.
Williams, Herbert W. [1844] (1985), *A Dictionary of the Maori Language*, Wellington: Government Printer.

See also: **European Exploration and Settlement: Australia, New Zealand, Pacific; Maaori; Waitangi Treaty**.

Pakistan's Subaltern Struggles

Pakistan's national identity was defined in religious terms when it was carved out of the Muslim-majority areas of India in 1947. From its inception, Pakistan's route to survival was, 'to become a Cold War patient under the permanent supervision of Western imperialism' (Ali 2002, p. 166), with the USA quickly superseding Britain as the dominant influence. With Pakistan's military and political elites only too happy to play this role, all peasant and worker insurgencies ever since have been suppressed in the name of national security.

By the early 1950s, Pakistan's leaders espoused a pro-Western Islamic ideology that functioned as a bulwark against communism and radical nationalism. This did not, however, succeed in containing all subaltern resistance. In 1958, workers in Lahore took to the streets, and peasant opposition spearheaded by the All Pakistan Peasants Association made swift organisational advances. Their momentum was violently checked, however, by

General Ayub Khan seizing power in October 1958, and a decade of military rule followed. This period ended in November 1968 when a student revolt against the military spread rapidly, with workers joining the movement in January 1969, and many other disaffected sectors adding their support. In March 1969, the military backed down, and following elections in December 1970, Zulfiqar Ali Bhutto's Pakistan People's Party assumed power. Despite co-opting communists into his government, Bhutto's extravagant election promises of social reform came to nothing, and the wave of popular support for his party mutated first into a violent ethnic nationalism directed against Bengali Muslims in East Pakistan in 1971, and then dissipated into cynicism and disappointment.

In 1978, Bhutto was removed from office and killed following a military coup led by General Zia ul Haq. In the 1980s, subaltern struggles in Pakistan suffered extreme repression under Zia's military dictatorship, particularly in Sindh, North-West Frontier Province and Baluchistan, as Zia subordinated the interests of Pakistan's people to serving strategic US interests in Afghanistan and lining his own pockets. Following Zia's death in an air-crash in 1989, there have been civilian governments under Benazir Bhutto and Nawaz Sharif, with a return to military rule under Musharraf in 1999.

Although the 1990s were dominated by even greater levels of state corruption, further impoverishment for the majority as a consequence of IMF and World Bank neo-liberalism, and the rise of Islamic fundamentalism, it was also a decade of intensified subaltern struggle. The biggest civil disobedience campaign has involved over a million peasant-tenants in the Punjab, especially in the Okara and Sargodha districts, who have raised the slogan *Malkiyat ya Maut* (Ownership or Death') as they have resisted attempts on the part of the military and land-owners to seize their land and turn them into wage-slaves. There are also 2 million workers in about 200 trade unions engaged in an ongoing struggle for a minimum wage; women's groups are actively challenging the draconian *hudood* laws; and groups representing a variety of constituencies – fishing communities, religious minorities, students, regionalists and secularists – are protesting on single-issue campaigns.

Anadi P. Chhetri

Literary Works

Ahmed, Rukshana (ed. and trans.) (1990), *Contemporary Feminist Urdu Poetry*, Lahore: ASR Publications.
Durrani, Tehmina (1994), *My Feudal Lord*, Bantam: London.
Faiz, Faiz Ahmad (1971), *Poems by Faiz*, trans. V. G. Kiernan, London: George Allen and Unwin.

Histories

Ali, Tariq (2002), *The Clash of Fundamentalisms*, London: Verso.
Alavi, Hamza (1979), 'The State in Post-Colonial Societies', in Harry Goulbourne (ed.), *Politics and the State in the Third World*, London: Macmillan, pp. 38–69.
Gilmartin, David (1998), 'Partition, Pakistan, and South Asian History: In Search of a Narrative', *Journal of Asian Studies* 57: 4, pp. 1068–95. Available at http://www.ptudc.org/
Jalal, Ayesha (1995), 'Conjuring Pakistan: History as Official Imagining', *International Journal of Middle East Studies* 27: 1, pp. 73–89.

See also: **Bangladesh: 1971; Historiography: South Asia; Land: South Asia; Military Dictatorships: South Asia; Partition; Progressive Writers' Movement.**

Palestinian Political Movements

At the turn of the nineteenth century, Palestinians viewed themselves principally in confessional terms, as Muslims, and then, secondarily, as citizens of the Ottoman Empire, in addition to possessing a strong attachment to their local clans. These self-definitions existed alongside, and to a degree were incorporated by, a rising sense of national consciousness, sharpened by the conflict with Zionism. This, however, was obscured in the mandate years by the tactical appeal to Britain to be included in a Syrian state, and by the tendency in the West only to recognise national groups and cultures that conformed to Eurocentric definitions. The mandate, however, did give Palestine a territorial sense, and Palestinian parties and institutions were formed during this period. However, they never had the organisational flair or coherence of their Zionist rivals. Palestinian Arab conferences and conventions were held from 1919 onwards, and in 1920 they formed the Arab Executive, under the presidency of Musa Qassem al-Husseini.

The Istiqlal (Independence) Party, a pan-Arab group, formed a Palestinian branch in 1932. In 1934, the National Defence Party was set up by Ragheb Nashashibi. In 1935, the Palestine Arab Party was formed under the leadership of Jamal Husseini, the brother of Haj Amin al-Husseini, the mayor of Jerusalem. These were the main Palestinian parties of the 1930s, but their activities were marred by squabbling and a tendency to try to play off the mandate authorities against rivals. Overall, during the mandate, Palestinians failed to organise anything like the state-in-waiting that Zionism managed to assemble. As the 1930s progressed, Palestinians began to realise that Britain was, in spite of the Balfour Declaration, the principal guarantor of Zionist colonisation of the land, and violent action eventually exploded in the Great Revolt of 1936 to 1939. This was a rebellion against both Jewish colonisation and against Britain. It cost 5,000 Palestinian lives, as against only hundreds of Jewish and British casualties, but its historical effect was equally important. The organs of Zionism emerged from the revolt strengthened; Palestinian movements were severely damaged, losing manpower and leadership cadres. This left the Palestinian population largely vulnerable and unprepared for the ensuing war of 1948, following the withdrawal of Britain, and the partition of Palestine under the auspices of the United Nations.

Palestinian politics, severely hampered after 1948 by the scattering of Palestinian refugees, did not start a serious recovery until the creation of the Arab National Movement, a pan-Arab organisation influenced by Nasserism and in which Palestinians, including George Habash, were prominent. After the 1967 Six Day War, the Palestinians in the ANM formed the Popular Front for the Liberation of Palestine. Al-Fatah, a broadly nationalist movement, had already emerged at the end of the 1950s, under the leadership of Yasser Arafat. The importance of *Fatah* has lain in its stress on Palestinian self-reliance, rather than on waiting for a pan-Arab defeat of Israel. The Palestine Liberation Organisation, formed by the Arab League in 1964, is an umbrella organisation not only of Palestinian parties and factions but also all the elements of civil society, in exile and in the occupied territories. The Palestinian national movement has for most of its history been secular in orientation, but since the 1980s, a number of Islamist movements, Hamas and Islamic Jihad notably, have emerged in the territories to challenge the hegemony of the PLO.

Conor McCarthy

Literary Works

Barghouti, Mourid (2003), *I Saw Ramallah*, London: Bloomsbury.
Darwish, Mahmoud (2003), *Unfortunately, it was Paradise: Selected Poems*, trans. and ed. Munir Akash and Carolyn Forche, Berkeley, CA and London: University of California Press.
Faqir, Fadia (1989), *Nisanit*, Harmondsworth: Penguin.
Kanafani, Ghassan [1863] (1978), *Men in the Sun and other Palestinian Stories*, (*Rajal fil Shams*), trans. Hilary Kilpatrick, Washington, DC: Three Continents.
Shammas, Anton [1986] (1990), *Arabesques*, trans. V. Eden and A. Shammas, London: Penguin.

Histories

Ashrawi, Hanan Mikhail (1976), *Contemporary Palestinian Literature under Occupation*, Bir Zeit: Bir Zeit University Press.
Kimmerling, Baruch and Joel S. Migdal (1993), *Palestinians: The Making of a People*, New York: The Free Press.
Pappe, Ilan (2004), *A History of Modern Palestine: One Land, Two Peoples*, Cambridge: Cambridge University Press.
Sayigh, Yezid (1997), *Armed Struggle and the Search for State: The Palestinian National Movement, 1949–1993*, Oxford: Oxford University Press.

See also: **Balfour Declaration; Historiography: Middle East; Nationalism(s): Arab; Zionism.**

Pan-Africanism

'Pan-Africanism' is the term that describes the diverse reactions of the African elite and Africans in the diaspora to racism, slavery, colonialism and exploitation. As a whole, Pan-Africanism became a series of movements that sought to redefine the identity and relationship of Africans and Africa with the modern world. Like Negritude, it went through several phases and is amorphous in its ideologies and politics. The major aim was similar: to create an idea of Africa and African personality based on a progressive and positive notion of history that had been blighted by slavery and colonialism. Pan-Africanism brought together Africans and Africans in the diaspora, with the political aim of fostering continental and racial unity for the cultural and economic benefit of Africa and Africans. Africans were defined by race and geography. Geographical definition signified the importance of the diaspora, the forceful dislocation and dispersal of Africans and the centrality of Africa as a metaphorical, spiritual and physical homeland of the black race. Shaped by its cosmopolitan roots, Pan-Africanism was antagonistic of the divisive and parochial nature of indirect rule. This attitude served as a precursor to nationalism, in which different ethnic groups would form a larger polity.

Henry Sylvester Williams convened the first Pan-African Congress in London in 1900. William Du Bois convened and presided over conferences in 1919 and 1945. The 1945 conference in Manchester, the fifth in the series, was significant in that it advocated a militant anti-colonial ideology. For the first time, Africans and Africans in the diaspora came together and designed a programme for Africa's decolonisation. Several future leaders of African states like Kwame Nkrumah and Hastings Banda attended the conference. Independent Ghana under Nkrumah played a pivotal role as the political reality of Pan-African idealism. The 1958 Accra conference was attended by nine independent countries, most of which were Arab Islamic nations. National liberation efforts made Africans realise that they faced similar problems, which could only be properly addressed by coming together. Political organisation has manifested from the competing groups that formed the Organisation of African Unity in 1963, to its successor, the African Union (2002).

Pan-Africanist thought predates the formal organisational activities that tried to give it coherence. It can be found in the imaginings of Africa in slave narratives and in the works of liberated slaves like Olaudah Equiano. The liberal bent of early Pan-Africanism, typified by writers such as Du Bois and Edward Wilmot Blyden, sought both to carve out a space of cultural authenticity, while at the same time incorporate Africa into Western-style modernity. Pan-Africanism was not simply a call to return to the past. It was a reinventive response of the interactions of Africans from within and outside the continent, people united through racial oppression and colonial exploitation. Fundamental to it was an understanding of Africa as potential. Despite its taking of Africa as a whole, Pan-Africanism was the ground on which nationalism grew. Pan-Africanism affirmed an imaginative, cultural unity of Africa that expressed itself through the different histories and cultures of its various peoples.

Oladipo Agboluaje

Literary Works

Armah, Ayi Kwei (1973), *Two Thousand Seasons*, Nairobi: East Africa Publishing House.
Armah, Ayi Kwei (1995), *Osiris Rising: A Novel of Africa, Past, Present and Future*, Propenguine: Per Ankh.
Casely Hayford, J. E. [1911] (1969), *Ethiopia Unbound: Studies in Race Emancipation*, 2nd edn, London: Frank Cass.
Gates, Henry Louis, Jr (1988), *Six Women's Slave Narratives*, New York: Oxford University Press.
Ngugi wa Thiong'o [1977] (1988), *Petals of Blood*, Portsmouth, NH: Heinemann.
Soyinka, Wole [1965] (1987), *The Interpreters*, London: Heinemann.

Histories

Ackah, William B. (1999), *Pan-Africanism: Exploring the Contradictions: Politics, Identity and Development in Africa and the African Diaspora*, Aldershot: Ashgate.
Bernal, Martin (1987), *Black Athena. The Afroasiatic Roots of Classical Civilisation*, London: Vintage.
Esedebe, P. Olisanwuche (1994), *Pan-Africanism: The Idea and Movement, 1776–1991*, Washington, DC: Howard University Press.
Gilroy, Paul (1993), *The Black Atlantic. Modernity and Double Consciousness*, London: Verso.

Kanneh, Kadiatu (1998), *African Identities: Race, Nation and Culture in Ethnography, Pan-Africanism and Black Literatures*, London: Routledge.
Langley, J. Ayodele (1973), *Pan-Africanism and Nationalism in West Africa 1900–1945: A Study in Ideology and Social Classes*, Oxford: Clarendon Press.
Nkrumah, Kwame (1963), *Africa Must Unite*, London: Heinemann.

See also: **Anti-colonialism and Resistance: Caribbean; Anti-colonialism and Resistance: West Africa; Nkrumah, Kwame; United States of America**.

Partition

In 1947, after a long, protracted movement for freedom, India became independent of British rule. Independence, however, came simultaneously with the political division of the country into two, India and Pakistan, the latter a country conceived as a homeland for Muslims. The political decision to partition the country caused one of the great convulsions of human history. As new boundaries were drawn and familiar territories became alien, fear of the 'Other' drove millions of people to cross long distances to places where they felt they would be safer with their 'own kind'. Within the space of a few months, some 12 million people moved between the new, truncated India and the two wings, east and west, of the newly-created Pakistan. This great migration, made up of vast columns of people travelling on foot, by road, rail and smaller numbers by air, was accompanied by terrible violence. Millions of homes were destroyed, villages abandoned, crops left to rot, as neighbour turned upon neighbour, friends became foes, and loot, arson, rape and destruction became the order of the day.

More than a half-century after the event, historians on both sides of the border continue to debate the possible causes of partition. Much responsibility has been laid at the door of the British, whose divide and rule policy is often seen as being at the heart of the decision to divide the country. It is also believed that the last viceroy of India, Mountbatten, anxious to be done with the business of India's independence, gave in to partition as its cost because he was 'a man in a hurry'. Where Indian historians are concerned, blame has, by and large, been laid at the door of the Muslim League and Muhammad Ali Jinnah, who led the demand for a homeland for the Muslims. Similarly, much history written in Pakistan projects the Indian leaders as having agreed to partition because they were anxious to seize the opportunity to assume the reins of power.

The plan to partition the country, known as the Partition Plan, was announced on 3 June 1947. But the idea of a separate homeland for the Muslims, which came to be called Pakistan, is believed to have been in circulation many years earlier. The birth of an idea is, of course, always difficult to trace and partition is no exception. Writings on the subject attribute it variously to Chaudhry Rahmat Ali, a Punjabi who lived in Cambridge and who is said to have put forward the idea as early as 1933, the poet Muhammad Iqbal, and the politician Lala Lajpat Rai, both of whom apparently suggested something similar a few years earlier. The idea itself was said to reflect the growing tension on the ground between the two major Indian communities, the Hindus and the Muslims. While there is ample evidence of such tension in much of the north in the years preceding partition, historians have also shown that religious differences were not so rigid as partisan histories would have us believe. Indeed, the period leading up to the partition was marked by two seemingly contradictory processes, a number of protest movements in which Hindu-Muslim unity was a notable feature; and a series of processes at the broader political level in which the Congress and the Muslim League, the two parties which saw themselves as representing the two 'sides', played a complicated game of alliance and separation.

The idea of partition acquired substance in 1940 with the passing of the Lahore Resolution, also known as the Pakistan Resolution. Previous to this, the history of division between the two communities is usually traced to the Morely-Minto reforms of 1909 which introduced separate electorates into the Indian polity and created a further barrier between the communities. Following this, employment in government, entry into educational institutions and so on were fixed on a communal basis (that is, on the basis of religious identity). The 1941 census – the last before partition – showed a total population of 389 million, with Muslims making up 92 million, Hindus (including scheduled castes, those outside the caste system, also known as untouchables, or later, Dalits) making up 255 million, and Christians and Sikhs standing at 6.3 million and 5.5 million respectively. Although at a national level the Muslims were clearly in a minority, at the local level this was sometimes different. In Punjab, which was one of the provinces to be partitioned, the Muslims had a slight numerical lead over the Hindus. The Communal Award of 1932 further exacerbated tensions by giving the Muslims in Punjab a permanent edge over the Hindus in the legislature although theoretically, because they were not a minority in the state, they did not qualify for this. The argument, which the colonial power accepted, was that although greater in numbers, Muslims in Punjab were economically backward when compared with Hindus and Sikhs and therefore needed the protection promised by the Communal Award.

The focus on Hindus and Muslims and their leaders as the main actors in the drama of partition has helped to obscure what this event meant for many others. In Punjab, the Sikhs were anxious about their future and when, in 1942, Sir Stafford Cripps announced that any province in the state would have the right to secede from the centre if it wished, the Sikhs began to worry about their fate if the Punjab, where the Muslims were in a majority, were to secede. It was at this point that they made their demand for a homeland of their own. Similarly, the Dalits, a powerful organised group under the leadership of B. R. Ambedkar, countered the instrumentalist attempts to appropriate them in the game of numbers being played by the Congress and the Muslim League by placing their own demand for a homeland before the British.

While this was the picture in Punjab, on the eastern side, in Bengal, the movement towards partition took a somewhat different trajectory. There was considerable opposition in some quarters to the idea of partition along communal lines, with people emphasising the idea of Bengali unity, even as terrible Hindu-Muslim riots in Noakhali, Bihar and other places, complicated this picture. The Bengali identity, as opposed to a Hindu or Muslim identity, expressed in language, also became a rallying point for people across the border in the language movement that took place after partition, in 1950. Indeed, one of the things that marked the Bengal partition was that it was not a sudden, onetime affair, as it had been in the west. Instead, it was long and drawn out, with migrations taking place over a much longer period, and with the borders remaining comparatively more porous for many years to come.

Although partition has formed the subject of much history writing on both sides of the border, the focus of such writing has, until recently, remained fairly limited. Much of it is preoccupied with the broader political patterns: the growing differences between the major political parties and their leaders, the complicated negotiations that took place with the British, and the question of assigning blame or responsibility. Relatively little attention has been paid to the human dimensions of this major historical event, and to the huge human cost it entailed. By contrast, these aspects – the violence of dislocation, the anguish of losing home, family, country, the terrible violence that was unleashed, the stories of courage and friendship across borders – have formed the stuff of much literary writing, particularly in north and east India. The creative writing of many of the first generation of writers on partition (for example, Sadat Hasan Manto, Meher Nigar Masroor, Intizar Hussain, Altaf Fatima, Rajinder Singh Bedi, Khushwant Singh, Amrita Pritam, Krishna Sobti, Bhisham Sahni, Quratulain Hyder, Ismat Chugtai, Sabitri Roy, Bapsi Sidhwa, Ashoka Gupta) is imbued with and informed by the direct experience of division and dislocation, an experience that lives on also inside families on both sides where tales of enmity, courage, friendship and loss are told and retold. Apart from this important corpus of work, a number of film makers, such as Ritwik Ghatak, Govind Nihalani, M. S. Sathyu, Deepa Mehta and Pankaj Butalia, have tried to capture the experience of partition.

More than 12 million people are said to have moved across the two new borders created by partition in 1947. Almost immediately they came into existence, the two new states, one separated by thousands of miles from its 'other' (eastern) part, were faced with the problem of dealing with millions of displaced people. Not only did the state in both countries have to respond to the need for new homes, but the refugees needed money, jobs, food, clothing and most of all, security. The massive relief and rehabilitation efforts that took place have virtually no parallel anywhere in the world, and the need for state intervention did not end once people were located within the four walls of a home, for there was also the very delicate task of mental, psycho-social rehabilitation which both states had to address. One of the striking things about this effort on both sides of the border was how much support it received, despite some opposition, from the large refugee community as well as from those who received them and made space for them in their lives.

As with all political violence, during partition too, women suffered in very specific ways: they were raped, abducted, sold into sexual slavery, forcibly married, bartered for freedom, paraded naked in the streets. Many had their breasts cut off while others had symbols of the 'Other' religion tattooed on their bodies. Because of the disruption of everyday life, and the dislocation caused by forced migration, many women were unable to marry, and by the time things had returned to some semblance of normality, they were past the marriageable age; while at the other end of the scale, thousands of women lost their husbands and were widowed as a result of partition violence. The fate of women – particularly those who had been raped and/or abducted – became a major cause of concern for both governments as families began to file reports of missing/abducted women (the number was said to be as high as 100,000). In an attempt to address the problem, both India and Pakistan set up committees made up of police and women social workers, whose mandate it was to go into each other's territories to seek out abducted women and bring them back to their families. Ironically, when they were found – which was often many years after the event – some women did not wish to return, while others, at least on the Indian side, were not accepted by their families because they were seen as having been polluted by sexual contact with the 'Other'. In Pakistan, what accounts there are (and in both places historians have only just begun the difficult task of unearthing these hidden histories) seem to indicate that families were not so reluctant to take abducted women back into the fold, and the state and women's organisations played a role in helping them to reintegrate into society.

Indeed, the issue of women's sexuality became a crucial one during partition, with both states seeing the failure of their men to protect their women as somehow a failure of the nation, and an indication of weakness or effeminacy. Within India, there was considerable preoccupation with the 'virility' and 'rapaciousness' of the Muslim man, and on both sides there seemed to be a fear of what could result from an unleashing of women's sexuality through sexual contact with the 'Other'.

However, the women also displayed agency. In the end, the Central Recovery Operation to seek out abducted women had to be abandoned because of the resistance of women to being recovered, and also because of the problem posed by children of mixed unions. While many families in India were willing to take women back, they were not prepared to accept children who had been born of mixed unions, and partition history has been reluctant to address this particular silence about the fate of the many children who were thus abandoned. Interestingly, within India, while the problem of the rape and abduction of women existed both in the east and the west, the state saw no necessity of either setting up search committees or legislating about recovering women in the east as they did in the west. There is considerable speculation on why this was so, and whether it had anything to do with the more gradual nature of the separation in Bengal.

In recent years there has been a fair amount of discussion in India, Pakistan and Bangladesh (erstwhile East Pakistan, which became an independent country in 1971 after a fierce battle with Pakistan) about why these aspects of partition history – that is, how ordinary people lived through the violence, why so many turned against each other, how friendships endured across borders, and whether the project of making two nations out of one – have not received the attention they deserve. Partly, this interest has been generated with the entry, into the world of history writing, of a younger generation of historians who are questioning the whole process of how canons are made. The opening up of partition historiography to feminist tools of exploring history has helped to make these histories much more nuanced, and has also enabled oral narratives to enter and inflect existing histories. In addition, the growing polarisation of identities along religious lines, as well as the huge increase in sectarian violence in the subcontinent, has forced people to return to partition narratives in order to learn from them. Interestingly, activists and researchers in the three countries are offering very different ways of looking at partition history from the vantage point of the present: for Pakistanis, for example, partition is often seen as the gain of a country; for Indians, it is generally seen as a loss, not only of territory, but also of national pride and honour; and for Bangladeshis, any exploration of partition inevitably becomes tied in with the history of 1971. A half-century later, we have barely begun to scratch the surface in our understanding of these complex histories.

Urvashi Butalia

Literary Works

Cowasjee, S. and K. S. Duggal (eds) (1995), *Orphans of the Storm: Stories on the Partition of India*, New Delhi: UBS Publishers.

Hasan, Mushirul (ed.) (1995), *India Partitioned: The Other Face of Freedom*, Volumes 1 and 2, Delhi: Roli Books.

Kidwai, Anis (1990), *In the Shadow of Freedom (Azadi ki Chaon Mein*, Hindi), trans. Jai Ratan, Delhi: National Book Trust.

Manto, Saadat Hasan (1991), *Partition: Sketches and Stories*, New Delhi: Viking.

Memon, M. U.(1998), *An Epic Unwritten: The Penguin Book of Partition Stories*, New Delhi: Penguin.

Ravikant and Tarun Saint (eds) (2001), *Translating Partition*, New Delhi: Katha.
Rushdie, Salman (1981), *Midnight's Children*, London: Jonathan Cape.
Sahni, Bhisham (1988), *Tamas*, trans. Jai Ratan, New Delhi: Penguin.
Shah Nawaz, Mumtaz [1957] (1990), *The Heart Divided*, Lahore: ASR.
Sidhwa, Bapsi (1991), *Cracking India*, Minneapolis, MN: Milkweed Publications.
Singh, Khushwant (1956), *Train to Pakistan*, New York: Grove Weidenfeld.

Histories

Butalia, Urvashi (1998), *The Other Side of Silence: Voices from the Partition of India*, New
    Delhi: Viking Penguin.
Chatterji, Joya (1999), 'The Fashioning of a Frontier: The Radcliffe Line and Bengal's
    Border Landscape, 1947–52', *Modern Asian Studies* 33: 1, pp. 185–242.
Das, Veena and Ashis Nandy (1985), 'Violence, Victimhood and the Language of Silence',
    Contributions to Indian Sociology 9:1, pp. 177–95.
Hasan, Mushirul (ed.) (2000), *Inventing Boundaries: Gender, Politics and the Partition of
    India*, Delhi: Oxford University Press.
Jalal, Ayesha (1996), 'Secularists, Subalterns, and the Stigma of "Communalism":
    Partition Historiography Revisted', *Modern Asian Studies* 30: 3, pp. 681–737.
Menon, Ritu (ed.) (1999), 'The Partition of the Indian Sub-Continent', *Interventions:
    International Journal of Postcolonial Studies*, Special Topic, 1: 2.
Panday, Gyanendra (2001), *Remembering Partition: Violence, Nationalism and History in
    India*, Cambridge: Cambridge University Press.
Philips, C. H. and M. D. Wainwright (eds) (1970), *The Partition of India: Policies and
    Perspectives 1935–47*, London: Allen and Unwin.
Rai, Alok (2000), 'The Trauma of Independence: Some Aspects of Progressive Hindi
    Literature', in Mushirul Hasan (ed.), *Inventing Boundaries: Gender, Politics and the
    Partition of India*, Oxford: Oxford University Press, pp. 351–70.
Sarkar, Sumit (1983), *Modern India 1885–1947*, Madras: Macmillan India.
Singh, Kirpal (1991), *Select Documents on Partition of Punjab, 1947 – India and Pakistan:
    Punjab, Haryana and Himachal – India and Punjab – Pakistan*, New Delhi: National
    Bookshop.
Talbot, Ian and Gurharpal Singh (eds) (1999), *Region and Partition: Bengal, Punjab and the
    Partition of the Subcontinent*, Karachi: Oxford University Press.
Talib, G. S. (ed.) [1950] (1991), *Muslim League Attack on Sikhs and Hindus in the Punjab
    1947*, New Delhi: Shiromani Gurdwara Parbandhak Committee.
The Partition of Punjab: A Compilation of Official Documents (1993), Lahore: Sang-e-
    Meel.

See also: **Anti-colonialism and Resistance: South Asia; Historiography: South Asia;
    Jinnah, Mohammed Ali; Nehru Jawaharlal; Refugees; Religions: South Asia.**

Post-apartheid

Indian author Arundhati Roy has written about the denouement to the anti-apartheid
struggle as follows:

And what of Mandela's South Africa? Otherwise known as the Small Miracle, the Rainbow Nation of God? South Africans say that the only miracle they know of is how quickly the rainbow has been privatised, sectioned off and auctioned to the highest bidders. Within two years of taking office in 1994, the African National Congress genuflected with hardly a caveat to the Market God. In its rush to replace Argentina as neo-liberalism's poster boy, it has instituted a massive programme of privatisation and structural adjustment. The government's promise to re-distribute agricultural land to 26 million landless people has remained in the realm of dark humour. While 60 per cent of the population remains landless, almost all agricultural land is owned by 60,000 white farmers. Post-apartheid, the income of 40 per cent of the poorest black families has diminished by about 20 per cent. Two million have been evicted from their homes. Six hundred die of AIDS every day. Forty per cent of the population is unemployed and that number is rising sharply. The corporatisation of basic services has meant that millions have been disconnected from water and electricity. (Roy 2003, Znet)

The positive side of post-apartheid is undeniable, of course. In South Africa, the 1990s witnessed the transition from a system of racially-driven authoritarian rule towards an outcome far more peacefully defined and democratically realised than most observers would have predicted at the end of the previous decade. Given the difficulties of such a transition, the consolidation of a functioning liberal-democratic system must be deemed a considerable achievement, one that has spawned celebratory literatures particularly in the fields of politics and international relations. Yet the dramatic transition to a democratic dispensation has been twinned with a simultaneous transition towards ever more sweeping neo-liberalism (free-market policies). Both components of 'post-apartheid' require consideration.

Looking first at the political transformation, during the 1994 election and its aftermath, South Africa stabilised the shift to a constitutionally premised and safely institutionalised democratic order – 'making peace' without suffering the potentially crippling backlash from the right wing, both black and white, that many had predicted, and without suffering the collapse into chaos or dictatorship that some had anticipated with the establishment of majority rule. Moreover, this political stability was sustained through the five years of Mandela's presidency, reconfirmed in the mundane 1999 election, and carried unscathed into the Thabo Mbeki presidency. This remains cause for a certain kind of admiration, on a continent where apparently lesser contradictions have proven far more difficult to resolve.

It was evident by the late 1980s to both dominant business circles and sufficient numbers within the ruling political elite that a stalemate had been reached, and that some steps would have to be taken to incorporate the African National Congress (ANC) into the circle of legitimate political players. In spite of the release from a twenty-seven-year prison sentence of Nelson Mandela in February 1990 and the unbanning of the ANC, President F. W. de Klerk and his associates had still not reconciled themselves to the notion of the ultimate establishment of an ANC government. Well into the transition period (1990–4), they continued to harbour hopes of safeguarding various attributes of the existing racial order within any new constitutional/political dispensation that would eventually emerge from negotiations.

There was also a significant threat to a peaceful transition from further to the right within the white polity, from groups such as the Afrikaner Weerstands Beweging. However, General Constand Viljoen concluded that the Afrikaners' best hope lay in separatism, not apartheid overlordship. When the ANC skilfully allowed some space in the negotiations for the separatist notion of a Volkstaat to remain a possibility, the general chose, late in the day but fatefully, to commit himself to the electoral process. Despite a spate of bombings on the eve of the elections, the White Right was thus largely corralled into the fold of peaceful transition.

The ANC was equally adept in dealing with Chief Gatsha Buthelezi and the Inkatha Freedom Party (IFP). The IFP brought to the table a bloody record of harassment of the ANC, often carried out hand in glove with the apartheid state. But it had also developed a significant base amongst some Zulu-speakers in the rural areas and squatter settlements of the KwaZulu Bantustan and in workers' hostels, especially in Johannesburg. Despite Inkatha's eleventh-hour conversion to participation in the 1994 polls, fraud, violence and considerable chaos marked the electoral process in the province. The poll result was diplomatically brokered in the IFP's favour, as the ANC drew Buthelezi further into the tent of compromise. The IFP formed the government in the province of KwaZulu-Natal, one of nine such provincial units established within the new federal system affirmed in the constitutional guidelines produced by the inter-party negotiations that preceded the elections.

The vote in the Western Cape province broke along racial ones, producing a unity government of the white-dominated Democratic Party (DP) and apartheid-era National Party (NP). The two parties merged into a 'Democratic Alliance' but subsequently split, with the NP deciding to work in a provincial unity government with the ANC. In 1999, the DP became the official national opposition (albeit with only 11 per cent of the vote compared to the ANC's near two-thirds poll). The DP cleaved to a particularly business-friendly, neo-liberal line as regards socio-economic policy during the election, but this did not much distinguish the party from the ANC itself in policy terms.

The so-called 'sunset clauses' safeguarded for a period the positions of whites in public employment, the agreement on a 'government of national unity' in May 1994 meant cabinet positions for both NP and IFP politicians (including both de Klerk and Buthelezi), and an amnesty offered some protection to those who had committed various gross abuses of power in defence of apartheid. The amnesty was, however, sufficiently qualified to prepare the ground for the subsequent establishment of the Truth and Reconciliation Commission.

Thanks to legislation and a strong female presence in the ANC's parliamentary ranks, gender relations record some improvements, especially in reproductive rights, albeit with extremely uneven access. But structurally, contemporary South Africa retains apartheid's patriarchal modes of surplus extraction, due to both residual sex discrimination and the migrant (rural–urban) labour system, which is subsidised by women stuck in the former Bantustan homelands. These women are not paid for their role in social reproduction, which in a normal labour market would be handled by state schooling, health insurance and pensions. This structured super-exploitation is exacerbated by an apparent increase in domestic sexual violence associated with rising male unemployment and the feminisation of poverty.

Women also bear the main burden of a public healthcare service in decline due to under-funding and the increasing penetration of private providers. Infectious diseases such as tuberculosis, cholera, malaria, and AIDS are rife. Most of the 5 million South Africans with HIV in 2004 have little prospect of receiving anti-retroviral medicines to extend their lives, thanks to the 'denialist' policies of Mbeki and his health minister, which senior health professionals and researchers regularly label genocide. Although a roll-out of medicines was finally promised by the cabinet in September 2003, Mbeki immediately denied (in a *New York Times* interview of 25 September 2003) that he knew anyone who had died of AIDS or was even HIV positive.

On another topic of local grievances, Mbeki repulsed opposition from human rights and arms-control groups to the $6 billion purchase of sophisticated weaponry from European corporations. Notwithstanding peace deals in Central Africa and Liberia, concerns remain over how durable the Mbeki government's interventions can ever be when they fail to grapple with underlying structural causes of failed states and inter-ethnic conflict. One indication of bully-boy diplomacy was Pretoria's 1998 military invasion of neighbouring Lesotho to prop up an unpopular government. Moreover, the widespread influence-peddling scandals associated with the arms deal suggest that then-President Mandela was correct when he warned that this would be a cancer in the ANC government.

However, even added to the fiasco over Mbeki's nurturing of Robert Mugabe's repressive rule in Zimbabwe, these are somewhat peripheral problems for South African society. There can be little doubt that, in the end, the relative ease of the political transition was principally guaranteed by the ANC's withdrawal from any form of genuine class struggle in the socio-economic realm and the abandonment of an economic strategy that might have been expected directly to service the immediate material requirements of the vast mass of desperately impoverished South Africans.

Turning now to the economy, even as racist laws were tumbling and the dignity of the majority black population was soaring, 1 December 1993 was the point at which the struggle for socio-economic justice in South Africa was conclusively lost, at least in the short term. The very first act of the interim ANC–National Party government was to accept an $850 million loan from the International Monetary Fund (IMF). The loan's secret conditions – leaked to the South African press in March 1994 – included the usual items from the classical structural adjustment menu: lower import tariffs, cuts in state spending, and large cuts in public sector wages. In addition, then IMF managing director Michel Camdessus put informal but intense pressure on incoming president Mandela to reappoint the two main stalwarts of apartheid-era neo-liberalism, the finance minister and the central bank governor, both from the National Party.

In January 1995, privatisation began in earnest. Financial liberalisation in the form of exchange control abolition occurred in March 1995. Pretoria's chosen protection from capital flight was to raise interest rates to a record high (often double-digit after inflation is discounted), where they have remained ever since. Later, from 1998 to 2001, the government granted permission to South Africa's biggest white-owned companies to move their financial headquarters and primary stock market listings to London.

Another crucial milestone was reached in June 1996, when the top echelon of ANC policymakers imposed a 'non-negotiable' wide-ranging economic strategy without bothering to consult 'Alliance' partners in the union movement and SA Communist Party, much less its own constituents. The World Bank contributed two economists and its model for the exercise, known as 'Growth, Employment and Redistribution' (GEAR). Introduced in the wake of a currency crash to promote investor confidence, GEAR allowed the government to distance itself psychologically from the somewhat more Keynesian 'Reconstruction and Development Programme', which in 1994 had served as the ANC's campaign platform. Of all GEAR's targets, the only ones successfully reached were those most crucial to big business: inflation (down from 9 per cent to 5.5 per cent) and the fiscal deficit (below 2 per cent of GDP, instead of the projected 3 per cent). The success of the business agenda was reflected in a soaring (pre-tax) profit share during the late 1990s, reaching 1960s-era levels associated with apartheid's heyday. The ANC also cut primary corporate taxes dramatically (from 48 per cent in 1994 to 30 per cent in 1999).

The working class, in contrast, found job loss to be the most damaging aspect of South Africa's neo-liberalism. The official measure of unemployment rose from 16 per cent in 1995 to 30 per cent in 2002. However, reliable unofficial sources suggest the figure is closer to 43 percent. As a result, according even to the government's own statistics, average black African household income fell 19 per cent from 1995 to 2000 (to $3,714 per year), while white household income rose 15 per cent (to $22,600 per year). The proportion of house-holds earning less than $90 of real income per month increased from 20 per cent of the population in 1995 to 28 per cent in 2000.

If not succeeding at home, the ANC leadership could at least claim to be tackling 'global apartheid' (as Mbeki has called it) at the international level. Pretoria's officials began the post-apartheid era by presiding over the Non-Aligned Movement, the UN Conference on Trade and Development, the Commonwealth, the Organisation of African Unity, the African Union, the Southern African Development Community, the board of governors of the IMF and World Bank and other important international bodies. The pace for Mbeki and his leading colleagues then picked up in the momentous month of September 2001: hosting the World Conference Against Racism in Durban; playing the central role in the New Partnership for Africa's Development (NEPAD) launch in Abuja, Nigeria (October 2001); leadership at the Doha, Qatar ministerial summit of the World Trade Organisation (WTO) (November 2001); co-chairing the UN's Financing for Development conference in Monterrey, Mexico (March 2002); a high profile at the G8 summit in Kananaskis, Canada (June 2002); hosting the launch of the African Union in Durban (July 2002); hosting the World Summit on Sustainable Development in Johannesburg (August–September 2002); promoting NEPAD at a UN heads of state summit (September 2002); and leadership at other key meetings, including the Cancun WTO ministerial summit (September 2003), the World Bank/IMF annual meeting in Dubai (September 2003), and the Socialist International in Sao Paolo (October 2003).

Still, the international stage is slippery, for not only could scant progress be claimed from these initiatives (most facets of global inequality in power/income increased), but hypoc-risy also emerged in the geo-political sphere. The ANC deployed strident anti-imperialist rhetoric against the 2003 US/UK war on Iraq, while critics in the Anti-War Coalition pointed out that South Africa's state arms agency, Denel, had sold $250 million-worth of high-tech munitions to Bush and Blair; warships docked in Durban on their way to the Gulf; and Bush enjoyed an extremely warm reception by Mbeki in July 2003 when they discussed future military and economic co-operation. Bush responded in kind, calling Mbeki his 'point man' on the Zimbabwe crisis. Bush's Africa hand, Walter Kansteiner, termed NEPAD 'philosophically spot-on'.

Under these conditions, South Africa's independent left – called the 'ultraleft' by Mbeki – will continue growing and making powerful international solidarity links. Organisations repeatedly challenging the ANC and capital from the late 1990s include social movement and community activist coalitions such as the national Social Movements Indaba, the Johannesburg Anti-Privatization Forum, the eThekwini (Durban) Social Forum, and the Western Cape Anti-Evictions Campaign, as well as a variety of sector-specific groups: the Education Rights Project, Environmental Justice Networking Forum, Jubilee SA, Keep-Left, Khulumani (apartheid victims support group), Landless Peoples Movement, Palestine Solidarity Committee, Soweto Electricity Crisis Committee, Treatment Action Campaign, Youth for Work, and sometimes the SA Non-Governmental Organisations Coalition. For them, 'post-apartheid' means worsening class apartheid, with more challenging gender, public health and environmental problems. A critical post-apartheid scholarly literature, not to mention numerous websites (for example http://www.ukzn.ac .za/ccs and http://southafrica.indymedia.org), provides background information for understanding South Africa's post-apartheid, postcolonial literary output.

Of the main genres of literature, poetry has arguably produced the greatest variety of new work, with poems innovative in both form and content much in evidence. The anthologies edited by Berold (2003) and Hirson (1997) provide useful selections, and there have been significant single-authored collections by Tatamkhulu Afrika, Vonani Bila, Jeremy Cronin, Ingrid de Kok, Mzi Mahola, Joan Metelerkamp, Mxolisi Nyezwa, Karen Press, Lesego Rampolokeng, Mongane Serote, Ari Sitas, Kelwyn Sole and Stephen Watson. Magazines that regularly publish new poetry include *Botsotso*, *Carapace*, *New Coin*, *New Contrast*, and *Timbila*. Sole (2002) provides a detailed overview of this new work and its relation to post-apartheid South African society. As regards drama, works by established playwrights like Zakes Mda and Athol Fugard have continued to enjoy centre stage. The most controversial play of the 1990s was Mbongeni Ngema's state-commissioned anti-AIDS *Sarafina*, and the most critically-acclaimed new work *Ubu and the Truth Commission* by William Kentridge and Jane Taylor. Useful overviews of post-apartheid theatre are provided in Blumberg and Walder (1999) and Banham et al. (2003). Concerning South African fiction, the major writers of the apartheid era, like André Brink, Nadine Gordimer, J. M. Coetzee and Njabulo Ndebele have continued to produce new works and to win awards (Gordimer, the Nobel Prize in 1991, Coetzee, the Booker in 1999 and the Nobel in 2003), and at the popular end of the market, Wilbur Smith continues to sell. Other novelists to have enjoyed critical attention include Zakes Mda, Achmat Dangor, Zoë Wicomb and Ivan Vladislavic, as have Afrikaans writers like Elsa Joubert, Karel Schoeman, Marlene Van Niekerk and Etienne Van Heerden, all of whom have been translated into English.

Patrick Bond and John Saul

Literary Works

Berold, R. (ed.) (2002), *It All Begins. Poems from Postliberation South Africa*, Durban: Gecko.
Coetzee, J. M. (1999), *Disgrace*, London: Secker and Warburg.
Dangor, Achmat (2001), *Bitter Fruit*, Cape Town: Kwela.
Galgut, Damon (2003), *The Good Doctor*, London: Viking.
Gordimer, Nadine (1998), *The House Gun*, London: Penguin.
Hirson, Denis (ed.) (1997), *The Lava of the Land. South African Poetry 1960–1996*, Evanston: Triquarterly Books.
Krog, Antje (1998), *Country of my Skull*, Parktown: Random.
Mda, Zakes (2002), *The Madonna of Excelsior*, Cape Town: Oxford University Press.
Ndebele, Njabulo (2003), *The Cry of Winnie Mandela*, Cape Town: David Philip.
Van Heerden, Etienne [1993] (1997), *Leap Year: A Novel*, trans. M. Hacksley, Sandton and London: Penguin.
Van Niekerk, Marlene [1994] (2000), *Triomf*, trans. L. de Kock, London: Abacus.
Wicomb, Zoë (2001), *David's Story*, New York: Feminist Press.

Histories

Alexander, N. (2002), *An Ordinary Country*, Pietermaritzburg: University of Natal Press.

Banham, M., J. Gibbs, Osofisan and D. Kerr (eds) (2003), *African Theatre: Southern Africa*, London: James Currey.

Barchiesi, F. and T. Bramble (eds) (2003), *Rethinking the Labour Movement in the 'New South Africa'*, London: Macmillan.

Bell, T. and D. Ntsebeza (2001), *Unfinished Business*, London: Verso; Cape Town: Red Works.

Blumberg, M. and D. Walder (eds) (1999), *South African Theatre as/and Intervention*, Amsterdam: Rodopi.

Bond, P. (2000), *Elite Transition. From Apartheid to Neoliberalism in South Africa*, Pietermaritzburg: University of Natal Press; London: Pluto.

Desai, A. (2002), *We are the Poors*, New York: Monthly Review Press.

Hart, G. (2002), *Disabling Globalization*, Pietermaritzburg: University of Natal Press; Berkeley, CA: University of California Press.

Jacobs, S. and R. Calland (eds) (2002), *Thabo Mbeki's World*, London: Zed Books; Pietermaritzburg: University of Natal Press.

Kimani, S. (ed.) (2003), *The Right to Dissent*, Johannesburg: Freedom of Expression Institute.

Marais, H. (2000), *South Africa Limits to Change*, London: Zed Books; Cape Town: University of Cape Town Press.

McDonald, D. (ed.) (2002), *Environmental Justice in South Africa*, Cape Town: University of Cape Town Press; Columbus, OH: Ohio University Press.

Roy, A. (2003), 'When the Saints Go Marching Out', Znet 2 September. Available at www.zmag.org.

Sole, K. (2002), 'The Witness of Poetry: Economic Calculation, Civil Society and the Limits of Everyday Experience in Liberated South Africa', *New Formations* 45, pp. 24–53.

See also: **Apartheid and Segregation; Historiography: Southern Africa; Labour Histories: Southern Africa; Land: Southern Africa.**

Pre-colonial Histories: Australia

For most of the twentieth century, mainstream Australia forgot or deliberately neglected the presence of Aboriginal Australians in the constructed historical landscape. Imperial conquerors, administrators, explorers, discoverers and settlers were glorified, and Aboriginal people were largely ignored. If historians mentioned Aboriginal Australians at all, they did so from pre-conceived positions of imagined and enforced superiority. Aboriginal people were categorised within the confines of the 'noble savage' myth, as relics of the Stone Age, a dying race which had not utilised the country or its resources, and had failed to defend its way of life. Traditional Aboriginal stories and songs with deep spiritual, social and environmental significance were reshaped by European colonisers into fairytales, myths and legends (examples of such writing still litter the libraries and education facilities of Australia today).

Since the 1960s, Aboriginal and non-Aboriginal writers have attempted to correct the biases of the past, and to sweep away the inaccuracies of Australian historical understanding. It is now accepted that Aboriginal culture holds the oldest collective memory, and that prior to 1788 the continent was home to a diverse range of over 300 differing language or tribal groups. Western archaeology dates the presence of Aboriginal culture on the Australian continent at 60,000 years; the Aboriginal conception of the past is that Aboriginal people have been a part of the Australian continent 'since the time before time began'.

Aboriginal belief systems assume the existence of a deep religious and spiritual connection to the natural world and the land of their ancestors. The Dreaming is the core of Aboriginal life and spirituality. It is a religious doctrine that promotes harmony and unity; and celebrates life, nature and the environment. The Dreaming is expressed through stories, ceremonies and rituals which enshrine Aboriginal beliefs, and have been passed from generation to generation for tens of thousands of years. The anthropologist W. E. H. Stanner (1979) explains that the Dreaming conjures up the notion of a sacred, heroic time of the indefinitely remote past. Such a time is also still part of the present so that the Dreaming cannot be fixed *in* time: it was, and is, 'everywhen'. According to the Dreaming, the Creation Ancestors rose up from their slumber beneath the plain or descended from the sky to invoke the Creation period. They moved across the landscape, hunting, loving, fighting and caressing the landscape to life. Every geographical feature and living thing on the land bore the mark of the Creative Ancestors. From these originary moments, kinship has always been central to the egalitarian Aboriginal extended family system, with no chiefs, kings or headmen, and all Aboriginal adults bound by ongoing commitments to one another.

Aboriginal people lived in diverse areas ranging from the coast, to rainforests, wetlands, woodland, riverbanks, deserts and the cold areas in the Snowy Mountains and Tasmania. Accordingly, Aboriginal technology was complex and differed significantly from area to area. All Aboriginal groups were hunters and gatherers, and used many similar weapons, tools and utensils such as stone hammers, knives, scrapers and axe heads. Many beautifully designed wooden implements were produced to be functional in everyday life, such as coolamons, spear-throwers, boomerangs, shields and clubs. The Western desert spear-thrower could be compared to a Swiss army knife for versatility, as it incorporated an edge used as a fire saw, a stone attached to the handle used as a knife and a curved body used as a mixing bowl. Trade and gift exchange were very important elements of Aboriginal economic, social and ritual life, and trade routes crisscrossed Australia. Goods traded included shells, wood, gums, ochre and a variety of manufactured items such as tools, ornaments and sacred objects.

Colonisation after 1788 brought the systematic stripping of the land, culture and resources of indigenous peoples. The European colonisers put down Aboriginal resistance violently, and in their greed for land inflicted horrific losses on the Aboriginal population. They also introduced diseases like smallpox, influenza, measles and venereal disease, which had a catastrophic effect on people who had no immunities. Some studies estimate that disease was responsible for killing 60 to 90 per cent of the indigenous population (see Butlin 1983 and Grimshaw et al. 1994).

European interpretations and recordings were heavily tainted by their own preconceived sense of superiority. The sociologist C. D. Rowley (1978) reflected that European culture held the belief that Native cultures were moral evils which should be destroyed. To explain the modern problems of Aboriginal poverty, unemployment, incarceration, health and education, one need look no further than the violent historical process of colonisation. In the wake of European settlement, Europeans had differing opinions about whether Aborigines should be integrated within or excluded from white society. Segregation in the nineteenth century saw several generations of Aboriginal people forced to live in captivity under intolerable conditions, on closed reserves set up on land that was worthless. State-controlled Aborigines 'Protection' Boards eventually took complete control over every aspect of Aboriginal life. Such bodies did not make decisions with long-term goals in mind, as they were guided by social Darwinist thinking. For example, the New South Wales (NSW) parliament decreed in 1883 that there was no need to increase the funding for Aborigines as they were dying out anyway! Reserve managers had the right to search Aborigines, their dwellings, and belongings at any time; they could confiscate property, read their mail, order medical inspections, confine children to dormitories, exert control over mobility; they had power over food, clothing, education, employment, and even the right of people to marry; and they could expel Aborigines from particular reserves and break up families. Aboriginal children were taken from their families, and placed into protective custody until they forgot Aboriginal ways. They were to be absorbed, at whatever the personal cost, into the dominant society, and were taught to reject their Aboriginal identity and culture. They received little education, with the girls trained as domestic servants and the boys as labourers. The effects on Aboriginal family life, where children were taken and in most instances never returned, were devastating and still have an impact today. The most lasting legacy of these mission 'prisons' and the practice of taking children away is the bitterness etched into Aboriginal consciousness.

In response to this thinly camouflaged attempt at cultural genocide, Aboriginal people, during the late nineteenth and early twentieth centuries, began to write and speak out more vehemently against the inequality of Aboriginal existence. These protests were isolated to individual or community campaigns. This changed with the rise in 1924 of the first united politically organised all-Aboriginal group, the Australian Aboriginal Progressive Association (AAPA), in Sydney. The AAPA demands centred on Aboriginal rights to land, stopping the practice of taking Aboriginal children, acquiring citizenship rights, and defending Aboriginal cultural identity. They drew their inspiration from international black influences, including Marcus Garvey. Other groups with similar platforms and varying degrees of non-Aboriginal influence were established in South Australia, Victoria and Western Australia in the 1920s and 1930s.

In 1938 Aboriginal political agitation burst into the public spotlight with the highly symbolic 'Day of Mourning' protest held to coincide with the sesquicentenary celebration of the raising of the British flag on the continent. The onset of World War II saw Aboriginal political activism forced into hibernation, but there was a fresh resurgence in the 1960s. Aboriginal protest was galvanised by the political struggles against the war in Vietnam and the civil rights movement in the USA. Charles Perkins imitated Martin Luther King and his Freedom Ride campaign in the USA by taking a group of students across New South Wales, drawing media attention to the horrific nature of Aboriginal living conditions. The key moments of the period included the Gurindji stockmen and -women walk-off at Wave Hill in 1966. Their protest was in response to inequality, poor working conditions; and included a demand for the return of their traditional land. A referendum held in 1967 was responsible for changes to the discriminatory federal constitution, and Aboriginal people were finally recognised as Australian citizens. The establishment of an Aboriginal tent embassy on the lawn of Parliament House in 1972 was a powerful symbol in the fight for social and political change. The most significant advance of the 1990s has been the far-reaching High Court Mabo decision recognising that Aboriginal Native Title was not extinguished by British colonisation, that Australia was not *terra nullius* or empty land on the establishment of British settlement. The decision influenced subsequent federal parliament legislation, including the Native Title Act and the Wik decision. The Native Title Act (1993) allowed Aboriginal people who could prove unbroken links with their traditional land the opportunity to lodge claims. The Wik decision, handed down in 1996, ruled that a pastoral lease could co-exist with Native Title. This decision represented a giant leap forward in indigenous land rights, but was met with furious opposition. The federal government pressed for legislation known as the 'ten-point plan' to resolve the confusion and deadlock following the judgment. Its plan became law in 1998, and extinguished many of the indigenous gains made through Native Title. Attempts at reconciling the wrongs of the Australian past have thus been bogged down in bureaucratic and political bickering.

The place of Aboriginal people within the construction of Australian identity, culture and history has been shaped by many literary contributions. From the late nineteenth and early twentieth century, the perception of Aboriginal people was to a great extent constructed by anthropologists, both professional and amateur. Studies by B. Spencer and F. J. Gillen, A. W. Howitt, A. R. Radcliff-Browne, A. P. Elkin, Daisy Bates, A. Montagu and others had a very negative impact on Aboriginal people in more settled areas of the continent, through their misinformed construction of the 'real Aborigine'. More popular works by writers and artists began to challenge entrenched stereotypes and drew a more sympathetic understanding of Aboriginal issues. The powerful and tragic story of an Aboriginal woman *Coonardoo* (1929) by Katharine Prichard and *Capricornia* (1938) by Xavier Herbert, which focused on racial prejudice in Northern Australia and won the Commonwealth Sesquicentenary Literary prize, were works that altered general understanding. The period also witnessed the first published Aboriginal writer David Unaipon *Legendary Tales of the Australian Aborigines*, 1924–5). Ion L. Idriess and Arthur Upfield went against the trend by conforming to classic and misleading stereotypes in their highly popular works. The Jindyworobak movement of the 1930s and 1940s saw a group of non-indigenous poets attempt to attach white Australia to the rich Aboriginal cultural identity of the continent. During and after the 1960s the works of Aboriginal writers and poets became more visible and accessible to the wider public, with Oodgeroo Noonuccal, Jack Davis, Mudrooroo, Kevin Gilbert, Eric Willmot and Archie Weller playing a significant role in presenting Aboriginal culture and history to the wider populace. Non-indigenous academics like W. E. H. Stanner, C. D. Rowley and Henry Reynolds were instrumental in establishing a new understanding of Australian history, which recognised dispossession and resistance: Stanner was particularly polemical in his writings, and highlighted the neglect of Aborigines in Australian history. Life histories by Aboriginal people like Ella Simon and Margaret Tucker led the way for popular works like Ruby Langford's *Don't Take Your Love to Town* (1988) and Sally Morgan's *My Place* (1989). In general Aboriginal literature to date has been dominated by autobiography. Controversial issues of appropriation and identity fraud have dogged more recent writings by and on Aborigines, and sadly, there has been a marked return to older attitudes, as the decolonising histories of the past thirty years have been questioned.

John Maynard

Literary Works

Barker, Jimmie (1982), *The Two Worlds of Jimmie Barker*, Sydney: Australian Institute of Aboriginal Studies.
Davis, Jack (1982), *Kulkark and the Dreamers*, Sydney: Currency Press.

Gilbert, Kevin (1973), *Because a White Man'll Never Do It*, Sydney: Angus and Robertson.
Herbert, Xavier (1938), *Capricornia*, Sydney: Angus and Robertson.
Idriess, Ion (1931), *Lasseter's Last Ride: An Epic of Central Australian Gold Discovery*, Sydney: Angus and Robertson.
Langford, Ruby (1988), *Don't Take Your Love to Town*, Ringwood: Penguin.
Morgan, Sally (1989), *My Place*, Fremantle: Fremantle Arts Centre Press.
Mudrooroo (1992), *Wildcat Screaming*, Sydney: Angus and Robertson.
Noonuccal, Oodgeroo (1964), *We Are Going*, Brisbane: Jacaranda Press.
Prichard, Katharine (1929), *Coonardoo*, London: Macdonald.
Scott, Kim (1999), *Benang: From the Heart*, Fremantle: Fremantle Arts Centre Press.
Simon, Ella (1978), *Through My Eyes*, Adelaide: Rigby.
Tucker, Margaret (1984), *If Everyone Cared*, Melbourne: Grosvenor.
Unaipon, David (2001), *Legendary Tales of the Australian Aborigines*, Melbourne: Melbourne University Press.
Upfield, Arthur (1938), *The Bone is Pointed*, Sydney: Angus and Robertson.
Weller, Archie (1986), *Going Home*, Sydney: Allen and Unwin.
Willmot, Eric (1994), *Pemulwuy – The Rainbow Warrior*, Sydney: Bantam Books.

Histories

Broome, Richard (2001), *Aboriginal Australians*, Sydney: Allen and Unwin.
Butlin, N. G. (1983), *Our Original Aggression*, Sydney: Allen and Unwin.
Grimshaw, P., M. Lake, A. McGrath and M. Quartly (1994), *Creating a Nation 1788–1990*, Sydney: McPhee Gribble Publishers.
Huggins, Jackie (1998), *Sister Girl*, Brisbane: University of Queensland Press.
Miller, James (1986), *Koori: A Will To Win*, Sydney: Angus and Robertson.
Reynolds, Henry (1990), *The Other Side of the Frontier*, Ringwood: Penguin.
Rowley, C. D. (1978), *The Destruction of Aboriginal Society*, Ringwood: Penguin.
Shoemaker, Adam (1988), *Black Words, White Page: Aboriginal Literature 1929–1988*, St Lucia: University of Queensland Press.
Stanner, W. E. H. (1979), *White Man Got No Dreaming Essays 1938–1973*, Canberra: Australian National University Press.

See also: **European Exploration and Settlement: Australia, New Zealand, Pacific; Historiography: Australia; Land: Australia; Multiculturalism: Australia; Stolen Generations; Women's Histories: Australia, New Zealand, and the Pacific.**

Pre-colonial Histories: Caribbean

Every island of the Caribbean has its own history, and the 'Caribbean' as an entity is itself an invention of the late nineteenth century. The history of the Caribbean as an area or region has tended either to focus on the Greater Caribbean (all the islands and the surrounding coasts and their hinterlands as well as the Guyanas), or only on the islands themselves (Greater Antilles, Lesser Antilles, Bahamas). Postcolonial historians of the Caribbean have tended to emphasise the continuities in pre-colonial culture, and have argued that binary division between peaceful Indians (like the Taínos) and warlike Caribs have been exaggerated by earlier historians, as all Caribbean communities shared certain characteristics – notably their organisation into groups (or peoples) under the rule of *caciques* (chiefdoms).

There are two main schools of thought that try to explain the development of the pre-colonial Caribbean culture. The older school – including the first liberal histories of the nineteenth century, as well as nationalist and Marxist histories of the twentieth century – argues that there were three main cultures: (1) pre-Taíno or sub-Taíno and some other 'tribes', like the Siboney or the Guanahatabeyes; (2) the Taíno; and (3) the Caribs. These three cultures arrived in approximate sequence on the islands from 1000 BC, starting from the Guyanas and the Orinoco. The argument is that from their centre in Bohio (Haiti/Dominican Republic), the Taíno assimilated the earlier groups of the Greater Antilles in a process of 'Taínification'. Following this stage, and coinciding with Columbus' arrival, the dominant Taíno culture was in conflict with the new, warlike culture of the Caribs at Borinquen (Puerto Rico) and the Lesser Antilles. Note that all the names of peoples (Taíno and Carib, or even Siboney) are based on Spanish sources, and embellished in the first liberal national histories in the nineteenth century. The second and newer school of thought refuses methodologically to start with the colonial words, names, concepts and icons. This is complicated because there is very little written evidence of the pre-colonial peoples (Ramón Pané is one exception). However, archaeological, religious, linguistic, climatic and other evidences have shown a very much older history, which some archaeologists and historians date to 8,000–10,000 years ago. This school argues that there were three or four waves of immigration, with peoples mixing in the islands to produce a pan-Caribbean culture under the dominance of what has been termed the 'Taíno-culture'. Rather than being seen as a distinct group (as had been assumed before), the so-called 'Caribs' were part of this culture, sharing the same Aruak-language and a similar religion.

Michael Zeuske

Literary Works

Brathwaite, Edward Kamau (1973), *The Arrivants, A New World Triology: Rights of Passage, Islands and Masks*, Oxford: Oxford University Press.

Colón, Cristóbal (1992), *The Voyage of Christopher Columbus. Columbus's Own Journal of Discovery*, trans. J. Cummings, London: Weidenfeld and Nicolson.

Harris, Wilson (1963), *The Whole Armour and the Secret Ladder*, London: Faber and Faber.

Las Casas, Bartolomé de (2003), *An Account, Much Abbreviated, of the Destruction of the Indies*, ed. F. W. Knight, trans. A. Hurley, Indianapolis, IN: Hackett.

Melville, Pauline (1997), *The Ventriloquist's Tale*, London: Bloomsbury.

Mittelholzer, Edward [1958] (1986), *Kaywana Blood*, London: Grafton.

Histories

Allaire, Louis (1980), 'On the Historicity of Carib Migrations to the Lesser Antilles', *American Antiquity* 45: 2, pp. 238–45.

Keegan, William F. (1992), *The People who Discovered Columbus: Prehistory of the Bahamas*, Gainesville, FL: University of Florida Press.

Paquette, Robert L. and Stanley Engerman (eds) (1996), *The Lesser Antilles in the Age of European Expansion*, Gainesville, FL: University of Florida Press.

Rouse, Irving (1992), *The Taínos: Rise and Decline of the People who Greeted Columbus*, New Haven, CT: Yale University Press.

Stevens-Arroyo, Antonio M. (1988), *Cave of the Jaguar: The Mythological World of the Taínos*, Albuquerque, NM: University of New Mexico Press.

Watts, David (1999), 'Introduction: The Natural Environment and the First Settlers', in P. C. Emmer and G. C. Damas (eds), *General History of the Caribbean, Volume II. New Societies: The Caribbean in the Long Sixteenth Century*, London and Hong Kong: UNESCO Publishing, pp. 29–42.

Whitehead, Neil L. (1999), 'Native Society and the European Occupation of the Caribbean Islands and Coastal Tierra Firme, 1492–1650', in P. C. Emmer and G. C. Damas (eds), *General History of the Caribbean, Volume II. New Societies: The Caribbean in the Long Sixteenth Century*, London and Hong Kong: UNESCO Publishing, pp. 180–200.

See also: **Historiography: Caribbean**.

Pre-colonial Histories: East Africa

The primary sources for the pre-colonial histories of East Africa are mainly oral for the vast majority of the hinterland communities, supplemented by written sources in chronicle and verse for the some of the coastal cities. Oral tradition has been refined into a recognised methodology for the study of East African societies since B. A. Ogot legitimised it as a valid source in the 1960s. Resulting from his efforts, publications including his own *History of the Southern Luo* (1967), Gideon Were's *History of the Abaluyia* (1967), Godfrey Muriuki's *History of the Kikuyu* (1974), Semakula Kiwanaku's *History of Buganda* (1971), Samwiri Karugire's *A History of the Kingdom of Nkore in Western Uganda to 1896* (1971), J. B. Webster's *The Iteso during the Asonya* (1973), Steven Feierman's *The Shambaa Kingdom* (1973), and William Ochieng's *History of the Gusii* (1974) are regular fare in university classes. All these works pay due obeisance to the many organic intellectuals that preceded the authors in the respective societies studied. These founding fathers include Apolo Kagwa, John Nyakatura, Paulo Mbuya and Francis Lwamgira.

The establishment of the East African Literature Bureau in 1947 also provided the opportunity for many Africans to author their histories, folklore and customs in their various vernaculars and in the Kiswahili lingua franca. These include titles such as Justin Lemenye's *Maisha ya Ole Kivasis*, J. D. Otiende's *Desturi za Abaluyia*, Samuel Ayany's *Kar Chakruok Mar Luo*, and Lacito Okech's *Acholi Macon*. The Swahili coastal input includes texts such as the *Kilwa Chronicle*, the *Pate Chronicle*, *The Mombassa Chronicle*, political 'gungu' narratives like 'Muyaka', and such literary verses as the epics of Fumo Liyongo, Utendi ya Mwana Kupona, and Al Inkishafi. The colonial period also witnessed works in English that gave history to the colonised, most prominently Jomo Kenyatta's *Facing Mount Kenya*.

As a result of these efforts, the history of the East African hinterland over the past five centuries is fairly evenly covered. The themes covered by the historians include the migration and settlement of the various groups into their present habitats, the formation of the various cultures obtaining within the boundaries, ethnic interaction among the communities, and the events immediately preceding British and German conquest. The role of prophets, forth-tellers, medicine men and famous warriors are encapsulated as important topics for study. This region is also richly endowed in folk tales depicting the relationship between men and animals, especially valorising the cunning rabbit, the tolerant elephant, and the totemic birds such as the dove.

E. S. Atieno Odhiambo

Literary Works

p' Bitek, Okot (1974), *Horn of my Love*, London: Heinemann.
p' Bitek, Okot (1978), *Hare and Hornbill*, London: Heinemann.
Whiteley, J. (ed.) (1969), *Four Centuries of Swahili Verse*, Oxford: Oxford University Press.

Histories

Kenyatta, Jomo [1953] (1965), *Facing Mount Kenya. The Tribal Life of the Gikuyu*, London: Mercury Books.
Kimambo, I. (1969), *History of the Pare*, Nairobi: East Africa Publishing House.
Kiwanuka, S. M. (1970), *The Kings of Buganda*, Nairobi: East Africa Publishing House.
Ogot, B. A. (1967), *History of the Southern Luo, Volume 1*, Nairobi: East Africa Publishing House.

See also: **Historiography: East Africa**.

Pre-colonial Histories: South Asia

Imagine one fine day being told that the discarded mounds and ruins of your village are thousands of years old. This is how Indian history was pushed back by more than 5,000 years in 1924 when archaeologist John Marshall reported the discovery of Harappan civilisation. Preceding him in 1826 was Charles Masson who visited Harappa village (in Western Punjab, now in Pakistan) and thought that the high mounds were remnants of Alexander the Great. A few years later in 1872 archaeologist Alexander Cunningham concurred with the villagers' view that the ruins were thousands of years old, and left. Marshall's conclusion, which gave Harappa a 5,000-year pre-history, was based on sound archaeological principles. He found that the seals, written scripts and works of art found there were unique. Secondly, in Mohenjodaro in Sind he came upon similar finds, except that here the settlement was underneath a Buddhist monastery of the Kushan period. This was a clear indication that the structure below belonged to an earlier period. Thirdly, Marshall found that people in these areas did not know the use of iron. Since iron came into use during the second millennium BCE, Harappan civilisation clearly dated to an earlier period. Finally, the discovery of objects similar to those at Harappa and Mohenjodaro in Mesopotamia made it clear that the newly found civilisation also existed there at the same time. Since the period ascribed to Mesopotamia is the third millennium BCE, Harappa and Mohenjodaro were therefore dated as belonging to the same period. Marshall's conclusions have been confirmed by the latest methods of radio carbon dating.

With Harappan script yet to be deciphered, debate over the period is far from settled. Some historians argue that Harappans spoke Sanskrit and that they were also the authors of the later text of *Rig Veda*. Others, like Romila Thapar (2002), hold that the essential characteristics of Harappan urbanism is absent in *Rig Veda*. This text, Thapar affirms, lacks a sense of the civic life found in the functioning of planned and fortified cities. It does not refer to non-kin labour or even slave labour being organised for construction works, or the performance of rituals at permanent locations such as water tanks or buildings.

The progressive stage of Indus Valley civilisation was succeeded by what is known as the Vedic Age. It boasted a long written tradition and produced numerous texts of recognisable historical intent or value. Though the efficacy of oral histories – since they are not records of actual happenings – has been questioned, there is little doubt that anthropologists and historians have successfully used them to understand myths and kinship patterns by prising out of the social assumptions implicit in them some reconstruction of history. While the epics – *Ramayana* and *Mahabharata* – are based on oral traditions and command popularity and respect, religious literature which has been handed down from ancient times reflects the concerns of the elite providing little insight into the life and religion of ordinary people.

The linguistic diversity found in India was registered during this period. Thapar believes that this diversity is partly responsible for the problem of deciphering the Indus script. While archaeology still holds the key to Indus Valley civilisation, literary sources of diverse nature explain the Vedic Age. German Indologist Max Mueller believed that Aryans came from Central Asia, one branch migrating to Europe, another settling in Iran, and a section of the Iranian family coming to India. According to him, the earliest possible composition of *Rig Veda* was in 1,200 BCE. Aryans, he said, invaded India and enslaved the local population and imposed their superior culture on the conquered. Mueller's thesis has lead to various interpretations. For example, Dalit writer and intellectual Jyotiba Phule in the nineteenth century wrote that Brahmins descended from Aryans and were the rightful inheritors of the land. But the right-wing Hindutva ideologues now deny the Aryan invasion theory, claiming instead that the Aryans were indigenous people who spoke Sanskrit.

The *Mantra* (saying, song, formula) constitutes the oldest division of Vedic literature and is divided into four *samhitas* – Rig, Sama, Yajur and Atharva. Another group of Vedic literature are the *Brahmanas* or texts dealing with observations on sacrifice. The *Aranyakas*, appendices to *Brahmanas*, deal with instructions meant for forest dwelling hermits. *Upanishads*, supplements to *Aranyakas*, are considered to be the fountainhead of Indian philosophy.

Revolutionary changes occurred in the sixth century BCE, with massive urbanisation and the rise of the new religions of Buddhism and Jainism. The economy had a major role to play in this transformation since the use of iron in agriculture led to surplus in food production. Thapar lists *Gana-Sanghas* (or people groups) as an important feature of this period. Since power was diffused, *Gana-Sanghas* were less authoritarian than kingdoms. The Buddhist text *Anguttara Nikaya*, a part of *Sutta Pitaka*, gives a list of sixteen *Mahajanapadas* (or great realms) while the Jaina text *Bhagavati Sutra* lists a slightly different sixteen *Mahajanapadas*. Urbanisation and the emergence of a strong merchant class is seen by historians as having relaxed the Brahminical stranglehold, with the associated cumbersome rituals.

Buddha's teachings come to us codified in *Sutta Pitaka*, *Vinaya Pitaka* and *Abhidhamma Pitaka*. Information on Magadha, considered to be the first empire in Indian history spreading during Asoka's time, mainly comes from Buddhist and Jain texts like *Tripitaka*, *Jatakas*,

Acarangasutra and *Sutrakritanga*. Later Buddhist chronicles like *Mahavamsa* and *Dipavamsa* provide an insight into Asoka's reign. For the first time foreign sources, mainly accounts of travellers, make an appearance. Foremost among them were the works of Megasthenes, who visited the court of Chandragupta Maurya, who established the Mauryan empire. Megasthenes' piece *Indica* has been lost, but his work finds mention indirectly in the Greek accounts left by Strabo and Diodorus of the first century BCE and Arrian of the second century CE. Herodotus details the spell of foreign rule in north-western India by Achaemenians and Alexander. Kautilya's *Arthasastra*, a treatise on statecraft and economics discovered in 1905, is considered to be one of the most important indigenous sources of the Mauryan period.

The decline of the Mauryan dynasty began during Asoka's later years, finally ending some fifty years later, in 180 BCE. Historians have suggested various reasons for the decline of Mauryas, like resentment of Brahmins (Haraprasad Shastri), military inactivity (H. C. Raychaudhuri) and economic pressure (D. D. Kosambi), but Thapar is not convinced and feels it was due to the top-heavy administration where authority was entirely in the hands of a few persons, and an absence of any national consciousness. Shungas, a Brahmin family that had worked for Mauryas, succeeded them. Literary sources give contrary views of Shungas. While the Buddhist text *Divyavadana* says that Buddhists were persecuted, a claim proved by archaeological evidence, Kalidasa's *Malavika-agnimitram* does not even mention it.

By the second century BCE, the decline of the Seleucid empire saw rulers of Bactria and Parthia breaking away and annexing parts of north-western India. Menander, an Indo-Greek ruler, was one of the best-known of the breakaway kings. Bactrian power ended with attacks from nomadic tribes of Scythians (referred to as Shakas in Indian sources), Parthians, Kshatraps and Kushanas.

The Gupta period is often called the classical age for its all-round development. It also sees the idealisation of women in literature, and the composition of *Dharmashastras* by Yajnavalkya, Brihaspati, Narada and Katyayana. In terms of a knowledge system there is now the emergence of astronomy, astrology and mathematics. Six philosophical systems – *Nyaya* (analysis), *Vaisheshika* (particular characteristics), *Sankhya* (enumeration), *Yoga* (application) and *Mimansa* (inquiry) – developed. Literature like Kalidasa's *Meghaduta*, *Abijnana-shakuntala*, Bharavi's *Kiratarjuniya*, Magha's *Sisupalavadha* and Bhavabhuti's *Malati-Madhava* also belong to this time. *Kamasutra*, the book of love, discourses about the life of the elite.

Another classical period flourished in south India under the Cholas, during the late first millennium CE. Thapar (2002) argues that it was based less on political authority and more on institutions established at this time, together with the articulation of cultural forms. From the mid-sixth century CE, Chalukyas of Badami, Pallavas of Kanchi and Pandyas of Madurai dominate the political scene in the Deccan and south India. North Indian society was witnessing other changes between the eighth and thirteenth centuries, like the emergence of a new caste of scribes called kayasthas and the inclusion of new castes among the untouchables. The realm of religion saw the growth of the Bhakti cult, an attempt by Brahminism to assimilate gods like Siva and Vishnu, and Tantrism which gave higher status to women and sexual rituals.

The tenth century is marked by the invasion by Mahmud of Ghazni followed a century later by Mahmud of Ghori, leading to the establishment of a Delhi sultanate by Turks in the thirteenth century. They ruled from Delhi over a large area of north India and developed new institutions. In the sixteenth century, the sultanate was succeeded by the Mughal empire, which in turn transformed India's political and economic system. The distinctive features of the Mughal period (described by the historians Irfan Habib and Tapan Raychaudhuri) include: military authority over a large territory; a ruling class controlling shares of the produce directly; proliferating urban centres along lines favoured by immigrant rulers; the growth of small-scale industries such as paper and lime mortar producers; and finally, the introduction of new technology.

It is ironic that despite the long tradition of written culture from ancient times, when the British at the beginning of colonial era began searching for an authentic history of pre-colonial India, the only text that satisfied the Enlightenment-inspired European view of history was Kalhana's *Rajatarangini*, a history of twelfth-century Kashmir (Thapar 2002, p. 1). All the other genealogies of prominent families, dynastic chronicles, histories of castes and religious sects, and biographies of holy men were treated as non-history, as fiction. Historian Sumit Sarkar notes, 'There were evident links between the quantum of such texts or documents and levels of organised, bureaucratic power' (Sarkar 1997, p. 6). Sarkar contrasts ancient India with China in this regard, and concludes that 'ancient Indian historiography, not surprisingly, never attained the stature of that of China with its unique bureaucratic continuity, and historical accounts became much more numerous under the Delhi Sultanate and Mughal Empire' (Sarkar 1997, p. 6). Another feature of pre-colonial histories was its didactic nature, with exploration of the historical past less important than teaching obedience through moral tales and exemplary archetypes. According to the historian Majumdar (1961), even Kalhana felt that *Rajatarangini* would be useful for kings as a stimulant or a sedative.

One reason why many pre-colonial works did not stand up to the British measurement of history was that they, as Romila Thapar points out, discounted Indian ways of looking at the past. She writes:

> Absence of history was explained by [Britishers] arguing that the concept of time in early India was cyclic. Therefore, all human activities were continually repeated in each cycle. This was inimical to a historical perspective that required each event to be seen as unique, a view endorsed by a linear concept where time moves not in a circle but in a straight line, from a given beginning to a stipulated end. (Thapar 2002, p. 2)

An example of this British disdain for Indian forms of history-writing is the story of the patronage of Mrityunjoy Vidyalankar's *Rajabali* (*Chronicle of Kings*), published in 1808. Sarkar describes how Mrityunjoy was asked by the British to write the first overall historical survey in Bengali prose to serve as a language text for company officials being trained at Fort William College. Sarkar explains how:

> The text begins by expounding in an unself-conscious manner the standard Brahmanical concept of time as cyclical, with Satya, Treta, Dwapar and Kaliyuga endlessly succeeding each other. The moral trajectory across the four-Yuga cycle was always imagined as inevitably retrogressive and the present (kaliyuga) was the worst of times, characterized by mighty shudras and insubordinate women.

Sarkar concludes that:

> Time . . . was never an abstract, empty duration: it was relevant primarily for moral qualities assumed to be inseparable from its cyclical phases. The principal role of the yuga-cycle in

Brahmanical discourses from the Mahabharata down to Mrityunjoy was to suggest dystopia and the indispensability of high caste and gender hierarchy. (Sarkar 1997, p. 7)

Accordingly, Sarkar suggests that a complex appreciation of notions of temporality in pre-colonial societies is vital:

> It is important to resist bland, homogenized presentations, both of pre-colonial notions of time and history as well as of the colonial rupture. It is now generally recognised that the cyclical/linear binary is not absolute, for duration or sequentiality is common to both. High-Hindu cyclical time, for instance, encompassed an element of linearity, for within a mahayuga, the successive downward movement of satya through Treat and Dwapar to Kali were taken to be irreversible. (Sarkar 1997, p. 9)

The author of *Rajatarangini* was the son of Canpaka, a hereditary Brahmin court official writing under King Jayasimha. The eight books of the text were translated by M. A. Stein and published in 1900 as Kalhana's *Rajatarangini, a Chronicle of the Kings of the Kasmir*. Although the text was written in the *vamshavali* tradition (history of a dynasty, a region or a monastery), *Rajatarangini* is exceptional for this genre in many ways:

> Kalhana did search for reliable evidence on the past from a variety of sources, so his narrative is infused with events and their explanations, many of which are historically insightful. It is undoubtedly an exceptional text, and his extraordinary sense of history may have evolved from a familiarity with Buddhist writing. (Thapar 2002, p. 468)

One of the great historical insights gleaned from *Rajatarangini* by modern historians concerns the origins of feudalism in Kashmir. Using Kalhana's work, D. D. Kosambi analyses Kashmir's history and finds that 'it shows the true force of Indian feudalism, the need to increase commodity production by local concentration of surplus, whose extraction was heightened by force in the hands of the nobles' (Kosambi 1956–7, p. 120). Kosambi's work covered Kashmir's caste and class; land grants and investment foundations for Brahmins and religious institutions; the government's initiative in controlling floods and promoting irrigation; the role of *damaras* (originally agriculturists who through surplus accumulated military power); and the expropriation of accumulated wealth by the kings to pay for the struggle against local chiefs. Kalhana's famous boast about Kashmir, 'That country may be conquered by the force of spiritual merits but not by forces of soldiers' (Kalhana 1900, Book 1, Verse 39, p. 9) was not without foundation, as his text talks of how foreigners came there as merchants, teachers and officials. Kosambi notes that the main influences that were cultivated or imported deliberately from outside the valley were Indian, first Buddhist, and then Brahmin. In the eight books of *Rajatarangini*, Kalhana recorded donations by name, including the first *agrahara* (land grant) given to Brahmins by King Lava. Kalhana even commented on the greed of Brahmins, who accepted grants from the Hun rulers, which for Kosambi 'indicates that Brahmins were the main support of class division, king, and state' (Kosambi 1956–7, p. 110).

Warren Hastings, William Jones and their Orientalist heirs were concerned with the culture and languages of India, and their ambitious explorations of the cultural legacy of the East produced an assembly of scholarship grounded in what was considered unprejudiced knowledge. If there was rediscovery as a result of Orientalism's inquiry into classical Indian history, a cultural past was also fashioned. As Thapar argues, whatever we know of

Indian history is thus entrapped in a 'major contradiction' in that our 'understanding of the entire India past' is 'derived from the interpretation of Indian history made in the last two hundred years' (Thapar 1966, p. 3).

Akshaya Mukul

Literary Works

Abul Fazl, Allami (1988), *Ain-i-Akbari*, ed. Jadunath Sarkar, trans. H. S. Jarrett, New Delhi: Crown Publications.

Babur, Zahiruddin (1922), *Babur-Nama*, trans. A. S. Beveridge, London: Sang-E-Meel Publications.

Dharwadker, Vinay (2003), *Kabir: The Weaver's Song*, New Delhi: Penguin.

Kalidasa (1901), *Works of Kalidasa*, trans. W. Jones and H. H. Wilson, Calcutta: Society for the Resuscitation of Indian Literature.

Kanda, K. C. (ed. and trans.) (1992), *Masterpieces of Urdu Ghazal*, New Delhi: Sterling.

Mahabharata (2004), trans. J. L. Fitzerald, Chicago: University of Chicago Press.

Nagarjuna (1995), *The Fundamental Wisdom of the Middle Way. Nagarjuna's Mulamadhyamakakarika.*, trans. J. L. Garfield, Oxford: Oxford University Press.

Ramayana (2000), told by William Buck, intro. B. A. van Nooten, New Delhi: Motilal Benarsidass.

Rig Veda, Van Nooten, B. A. and G. B. Holland (eds and intro.) (1994), Cambridge, MA and London: Department of Sanskrit and Indian Studies.

Sealy, Alan (1999), *The Trotter-Nama: A Chronicle*, New Delhi: IndiaInk.

Somadeva (1994), *Tales from the Kathasaritsagara*, trans. Wendy Doniger, New Delhi: Penguin.

Tharu, Susie and K. Lalita (eds) (1993), *Women Writing in India: 600 B.C. to the Early Twentieth Century*, London: Pandora.

Tiruvalluvar (1991), *The Kural*, Harmondsworth: Penguin.

The Jataka or Stories of the Buddha's Former Birth (2000), ed. E. B. Cowell, San Diego, CA: Blue Dove.

Upanishads (1998), trans. P. Olivelle, Oxford: Oxford University Press.

Histories

Agrawal, D. P. (1984), *The Archaeology of India*, Delhi: Select Book Service.

Alam, Muzaffar and Sanjay Subrahmanyam (eds) (1999), *The Moghul State 1526–1750*, New Delhi: Oxford University Press.

Allchin, Bridget and Raymond Allchin (1997), *Origins of a Civilisation: The Prehistory and Early Archaeology of South Asia*, London: Penguin/Viking.

Altekar, A. S. (1972), *State and Government in Ancient India*, New Delhi: Motilal Banarsidas.

Basham, A. L. (1985), *The Wonder that was India*, London: Sidgwick and Jackson.

Chakrabarti, Dilip K. (1997), *India: An Archaeological History*, Delhi: Oxford University Press.

Erdosy, G. (1988), *Urbanisation in Early Historic India*, Delhi: Oxford University Press.

Habib, Irfan and Tapan Raychaudhuri (1982), *The Cambridge Economic History of India, Volume 1*, New Delhi: Orient Longman; Cambridge: Cambridge University Press.

Kalhana (1900), *Rajatarangini, a Chronicle of the Kings of Kasmir*, 8 vols, trans. M. A. Stein, Westminster: Archibald Constable and Company.

Kosambi, D. D. (1956–7), *Journal of the Bombay Branch of the Royal Asiatic Society* 31: 2.

Majumdar, R. C. (1961), 'Ideas of History in Sanskrit Literature', in C. H. Philips (ed), *Historians of India, Pakistan and Ceylon*, London: Oxford University Press, pp. 13–28.

Marshall, John (1973), *Mohenjodaro and the Indus Civilisation, Volumes 1–3*, London: Probsthain.

Mueller, F. Max (1869), *Rig-Veda Samhita*, trans. and explan. F. M. Mueller, London: Trubner and Company.

Sarkar, Sumit (1997), *Writing Social History*, Delhi: Oxford University Press.

Sastri, K. A. Nilkanta (1974), *A History of South India*, Delhi: Oxford University Press.

Sharma, R. S. (1965), *Indian Feudalism*, Calcutta: University of Calcutta Press.

Sharma, R. S. (1968), *Aspects of Political Ideas and Institutions in Ancient India*, New Delhi: Motilal Banarsidas.

Thapar, Romila (1966), *A History of India, Volume 1*, Harmondsworth: Penguin.

Thapar, Romila (2002), *Early India: From the Origins to AD 1300*, Harmondsworth: Penguin/Allen Lane.

Upreti, Kalpana (1995), *India as Reflected in the Divyavadana*, New Delhi: Munshiram Manoharlal.

Vidyalankar, Mrityunjoy (1808), *Rajabali, Chronicle of Kings*, Serampur: The author.

See also: **Historiography: South Asia**; **Languages and Ethnicities: South Asia**; **Religions: South Asia**; **Women's Histories: South Asia**.

Pre-Colonial Histories: Southern Africa

Any review of the pre-colonial histories of southern Africa needs to take account of three things. The first is the extraordinary time depth of human occupation, making for a complex and crowded field that switches in and out of various intellectual modes and genres. These include a biological narrative of human evolution, an anthropological narrative of cultural development, and a historical narrative of more contemporary processes and events. The second is the comparatively early date of colonial settlement and the shifting nature of the colonial frontier (and its associated histories). While European settlement at the Cape dates to the mid-seventeenth century, some regions remained outside the colonial state until the close of the nineteenth century. The third is the contested nature of knowledge production within the field, whose own historiography has been deeply marked by both colonialism and apartheid. This has tended to determine the shape and structure of our conception of the past (including notions of the 'colonial' and the 'pre-colonial'), as much as the nature of the various academic disciplines involved, mainly archaeology and history.

There existed (and exists) a substantial, varied and under-acknowledged body of indigenous conceptions of past-times, including narratives of creation, indigenous cosmologies, and narratives of the creation of place and culture. Examples are the Venda narrative of the ancestors who left their footprints in molten lava, thereby marking the landscape as theirs, and the many San or Bushman narratives of origin. Beginning in the early eighteenth century these were replaced by European world views organised around various modes of writing and projects of collecting. Partly because of their materiality and their accessibility on the landscape, archaeological artefacts have provided a common route to reflecting on the pre-colonial past. Descriptions of rock art and stone tool types occurred in the accounts of early travellers in the interior. However, it was not until the 1870s that we find a substantial published record on prehistory.

Three events in the 1920s served to transform a loosely organised and dilettante field, and set in place a framework for subsequent conceptions of the pre-colonial past. The first was Raymond Dart's description of the Taung fossil of *Australopithecus africanus* in *Nature* in 1925. Dart's paper was criticised heavily in Britain, and it was not until Le Gros Clark examined the material from Taung, Sterkfontein and Swartkrans in 1947 in the run-up to the first Pan African Congress on Prehistory that the genus gained more general acceptance. Now known from a range of sites on the southern African highveld, the East African Rift Valley and elsewhere, it has established itself as the foundation of a progressively unfolding narrative of human evolution. Small-bodied and fully bipedal, *Australopithecus* had a dentition similar to our own, indicating similarities in diet. The cranial capacity of *Australopithecus*, at around 600 cubic centimetres, is approximately one half that of anatomically modern *Homo sapiens*, on a par with modern chimpanzees.

From this point around 3 million years ago through to the present, the story of human evolution is the story of gradually increasing cranial capacity. A compelling argument has linked cognitive ability to an increasingly complex material culture, in the form of a feedback loop. The fossil hominid *Homo habilis* is thought to have been the first hominid to base a toolkit on flaked stone. *Homo erectus* is associated with the commonly occurring hand-axes, and was the first hominid to move out of continental Africa, settling in large parts of what are today Asia and Europe between 1 and 2 million years ago. Recent developments in archaeology have suggested that anatomically modern *Homo sapiens sapiens* may have first evolved in southern Africa. A number of sites have yielded material of apparently modern morphology from around 100,000 years ago. With the re-emergence of South Africa post-1994 human origins research has played an important role in the discourse of the African Renaissance. In September 2002 President Thabo Mbeki and United Nations secretary general Kofi Annan imprinted their bare feet in a tray of wet cement at the 'Cradle of Humankind' World Heritage Site outside Johannesburg, as part of the ceremonies associated with the World Summit on Sustainable Development.

The second event to transform conceptions of pre-colonial history was John Goodwin's establishment of a local chronology and typology for the stone ages, published through the mid- to late 1920s. Goodwin established a tri-partite division of Early, Middle and Later Stone Ages, based on changes in stone tool morphology and provenance. This had two side effects. The first was to unshackle the southern African sequence from the European Paleolithic, previously thought to be the type sequence for cultural development around the world. The second was to introduce the notion of stages in prehistory, previously conceptualised as an undifferentiated entity associated with a contemporary 'ethnic' group, the Bushmen.

The gradual elaboration of material cultural forms described by Goodwin's schema was associated with a way of life, gathering and hunting, which has sustained humanity through the vast majority of our existence. Ethnographic study of contemporary gathering and hunting groups has combined with the results of archaeological research to paint a picture of small, mobile bands organised along kin lines, responding to the seasonal availability of resources over vast home ranges. Perhaps the most vivid image of hunter-gatherer life comes from the rock paintings and engravings found through large parts of southern Africa. A fertile strand of enquiry linking rock art to the ethnographies gathered by Wilhelm Bleek and Lucy Lloyd in the late nineteenth century has resulted in a richly nuanced reading of the art in terms of altered states of consciousness and the practices of healing, rain-making and social magic.

This image of a peopled landscape was transformed by the arrival of new groups of people, new forms of production and new technologies just under 2,000 years ago. The first of two roughly contemporaneous developments was the advent in the western and central parts of southern Africa of nomadic pastoralism, based on the keeping of sheep and goats, and later of increasing numbers of cattle. Debates exist as to whether this new subsistence economy was the result of a movement of people, or of a technology (in the form of the movement of an idea). By the time European mariners rounding the Cape encountered these nomadic pastoralists more than a millennium later, they referred to themselves as Khoikhoi and were organised into a number of clans, each of which controlled vast herds and territories. The story of the dispossession and destruction of the Cape Khoikhoi and Bushman groups forms a violently genocidal passage in the history of the colonial frontier. Disease, the unequal balance of arms, and a shrinking resource base all played a role, so that by the early nineteenth century there were no independent Khoikhoi polities at the Cape.

The second development involved the arrival of farming groups in the eastern parts of southern Africa, corresponding with the zone of summer rainfall. They brought with them domesticated plants and animals, and new technologies in the form of iron smelting and working. Initially tentative in their incursion, they went on to establish settled villages along the length of the eastern seaboard and its interior. This movement of people and ideas represents the southernmost extent of the migration of Bantu-speaking people from a probable point of origin in Central or West Africa, one of the dramatic events of pre-colonial African history.

Through the course of the first millennium CE the practices of cattle keeping and cereal cropping fundamentally transformed modes of subsistence production in southern Africa. The origins of domestic stock in Africa can be traced back to paleoclimatic events in North Africa around 8,000 years ago. In that period the region of what is today the Sahara desert was a comparatively well-watered zone, with lakes and grasslands and abundant opportunities for gathering, hunting and fishing. With the onset of profound climatic change, gathering and hunting groups experimented with the domestication of a range of animal species, including the wild progenitors of today's domestic cattle. The distribution of dated archaeological sites with the remains of domestic stock suggests a gradual southward movement of a pastoral way of life. The timing of the advent of Bantu-speaking farmers in southern Africa was long a matter of historical controversy. Colonial and apartheid ideologies were concerned to establish the lateness of this arrival, placing it contemporaneous with (or later than) European settlement in the south, as a way of minimising indigenous claims to the land. Their substantially earlier arrival was established in the early 1970s, as part of the burgeoning archaeology of the southern African Iron Age, as it was termed. However, this revisionist account, largely uncommunicated by archaeologists, failed to find its way into either public histories or anti-apartheid discourses.

The third event to transform subsequent conceptions of pre-colonial history was Gertrude Caton-Thompson's excavations at the site of Great Zimbabwe in the late 1920s, and the resultant public controversy. Ever since its 'discovery' in the 1870s (as part of a more general rediscovery of Africa which had been in progress since mid-century) the ruins of Great Zimbabwe had been a site of speculation and interest. Partly because of their size and sophistication – they are the largest pre-colonial built structures in Africa south of the

Pyramids – it had become a commonplace of settler discourse to ascribe a non-African origin to the ruins. Caton-Thompson was able to produce strong evidence for the idea that the ruins represented an indigenous development. Rather than that settling the matter things simmered for decades, and re-emerged in the Rhodesian Front era when the ruins were commonly interpreted as evidence of prior white civilisation.

Great Zimbabwe was the centre of a vast trading empire, run by the descendants of Shona-speaking people in the area today. It is one of more than fifty *madzimbahwe*, stone-built settlements that acted as way stations in the movement of cattle and goods. At its height between the twelfth and fourteenth centuries CE it had trading connections via the Swahili city states on the East African coast with south-western Asia and the Indian sub-continent. The principle item of external trade was gold, evidence of a substantial pre-colonial gold mining industry on the Zimbabwe plateau. To find the roots of pre-colonial state formation in southern Africa one needs to go back to developments in the Limpopo River valley as early as the tenth century CE. The substantial town that arose around the site of Mapungubwe Hill shows some of the earliest evidence for a class stratified society, including an area of elite residence and grave goods made of gold.

If the sites of Mapungubwe and Great Zimbabwe represent one model of state formation and urbanisation in pre-colonial southern Africa, then the Tswana towns that developed in the central interior in the eighteenth century give an intriguing glimpse of a different model. The sites of Molokwane and Kaditshwene are cases in point. These urban sites were loosely agglomerated, decentralised and extensive. We see them today as vast networks of low stone walls, most clearly visible from aerial photographs. Flexibly organised into wards under local headmen, such towns are thought to be a unique response to conditions at this furthest point of the colonial frontier. In 1820 the population of Kaditshwene is estimated to have been in the region of 20,000 people, about the same size as contemporary Cape Town.

The notion of a 'pre-colonial' history is a shifting one, which gives way to various 'frontier' histories of contact and interaction. In addition, a feature of the development of the discipline of archaeology in southern Africa has been its relative lack of articulation with other disciplines given to the study of African history and society, in particular the disciplines of history and social anthropology. Partly for these reasons, archaeologists have had relatively little to contribute to the Mfecane debate, and to other debates in the field. Recent developments in the discipline have seen archaeologists attempting to come to grips with other sources and epistemologies, including oral histories and local and indigenous accounts of the deep past. The result has been a developing sense of the pre-colonial past in southern Africa as one of enormous antiquity, and of social and cultural complexity and dynamism. Such a picture stands in stark contrast to colonial discourse, both with respect to the myth of Africa as empty land, and the myth of African societies as static and ahistorical.

Nick Shepherd

Literary Works

Bleek, W. H. I. and L. Lloyd (1911), *Specimens of Bushmen Folklore*, London: George Allen and Company.
Brink, André (1983), *An Instant in the Wind*, London: Fontana.
Coetzee, J. M. (1974), *Dusklands*, Johannesburg: Ravan Press.

Mutswairo, S. M. (1974), *Zimbabwe*, Washington, DC: Three Continents.
Opland, Jeff (ed.) (1992), *Words that Circle Words: A Choice of South African Oral Poetry*, Johannesburg: A. D. Donker.

Histories

Deacon, H. J. and J. Deacon (1999), *Human Beginnings in South Africa; Uncovering the Secrets of the Stone Age*, Cape Town: David Philip.
Finnegan, R. (1970), *Oral Literature in Africa*, Oxford: Oxford University Press.
Hall, M. (1987), *The Changing Past: Farmers, Kings and Traders in Southern Africa, 200–1860*, Cape Town: David Philip.
Hall, M. (1996), *Archaeology Africa*, Cape Town: David Philip.
Mitchell, P. J. (2002), *The Archaeology of Southern Africa*, Cambridge: Cambridge University Press.
Shepherd, N. (2003), 'State of the Discipline: Science, Culture and Identity in South African Archaeology, 1870–2003', *Journal of Southern African Studies* 29: 4, pp. 823–44.

See also: **Mfecane; Nationalism(s): Southern Africa; San.**

Pre-colonial Histories: West Africa

Pre-colonial West African societies have long histories of political, economic, cultural and religious wealth. The fertility of the upper Niger area and modern northern Nigeria encouraged the growth of a relatively large agricultural population which was well-placed to trade with both the forest region to the south and with North Africa. The region was home over the centuries to many empires.

The empire of Ghana flourished from the eighth century CE until at least late into the eleventh century CE and probably well into the twelfth. By the beginning of the thirteenth century, Ghana had been marginalised and was replaced as the major power in the region by Mali. Under this empire, towns like Timbuktu and Jenne became important centres of Islamic learning and scholarship. It was also Mali's king, Mansa Musa (1312–37) who made such an impression along the pilgrimage route to Mecca, especially in Cairo, with his immense wealth, lavish retinue and large gifts of gold – displaying the power of Mali. Mali disintegrated in the fifteenth century because of internal disputes that allowed it to be attacked from the north and the south. It was replaced by the Songhai empire, the largest of the West African Sudanic empires. Songhai was centred on the easternmost province of Mali. It was also a great Islamic centre and had a wide-ranging influence, especially on the Hausa of modern-day Nigeria. It was destroyed, but not conquered, by Morocco in the sixteenth century, in an attempt to capture and control the gold mines. A new Islamic state failed to replace Songhai and instead, in the western Sudan, a series of non-Islamic states formed such as the Bambara states of Segu and Kaarta. It was not until the jihadist movement of the nineteenth century that Islamic-based government returned to the western Sudan as a true force.

The forest region also produced strong states. Under the cultural and political influence of its ancient centre Ife, the Yoruba of modern western Nigeria formed a series of city-states from the forest regions and from the north. During the fourteenth century, Oyo achieved supremacy and extended its influence into the modern state of Benin. The history of Dahomey is closely tied to Yoruba history, especially to Oyo. Centred on Abomey, Dahomey became a powerful state in the eighteenth century when Agaja Trudo conquered the small Aja city-states and brought them under a single government. Dahomey was able to free itself from Oyo domination because of the economic strength it derived from the trans-Atlantic slave trade.

To the west of Dahomey, the kingdom of Asante was founded in the seventeenth century by Osei Tutu when he formed a federation of a number of small Akan states. Asante was originally created as a federation for self-defence and was held together by the religious symbol of the Golden Stool, which stood for Asante unity. However, Asante soon became the dominant power in modern Ghana and was at its height early in the nineteenth century. There were in addition a number of smaller states such as the Fante states along the coast of modern Ghana and the city-states of the Niger delta area.

West African people also organised themselves in so-called stateless societies which were organised along kinship and lineage relationships. The Igbo in modern-day eastern Nigeria is one of the better known pre-colonial stateless societies. The people organised themselves around a kinship system, with a village head and a council of elders governing a community of homesteads. While no centralised political organisation existed, age grades provided community-wide relationships, and the younger age grades were used to enforce the orders of their elders.

Jennifer Lofkrantz

Literary Works

Achebe, Chinua [1958] (1978), *Things Fall Apart*, London: Heinemann.
Amadi, Elechi (1976), *The Great Ponds*, London: Heinemann.
Equiano, Olaudah [1789] (1995), *The Interesting Narrative and Other Writings*, ed. V. Carretta, Harmondsworth: Penguin.
Laye, Camara [1954] (1959), *The African Child*, trans. J. Kirkup, London: Fontana.

Histories

Ajayi, J. F. and Michael Crowder (1985), *History of West Africa*, 2 vols, 3rd edn, London: Longman.
Bovill, Edward William (1995), *The Golden Trade of the Moors. West African Kingdoms in the Fourteenth Century*, 2nd edn, Princeton, NJ: Markus Weiner Publishers.
Connah, Graham (ed.) (1998), *Transformations in Africa. Essays on Africa's Later Past*, London and Washington: Leicester University Press.
McCaskie, T. C. (1995), *State and Society in Pre-Colonial Asante*, Cambridge: Cambridge University Press.
Northrup, David (1978), *Trade without Rulers: Precolonial Economic Developments in Southeastern Nigeria*, Oxford: Clarendon Press.

See also: **Asante Wars; Historiography: West Africa; Islam; Pre-colonial Histories: Southern Africa; Slavery: West Africa.**

Progressive Writers' Movement

The Progressives were anti-establishment, radical anti-colonialists who brought a new spirit of rebellion to the literatures of India in the 1930s. The movement they pioneered created a forum for the rejection of colonial values and a shift toward a literary social revolution marked by Freudian and Marxist influences. The Progressives cited the publication and immediate ban by the British authorities of the Urdu collection of short stories entitled, *Angare* (*Embers*) in 1932 as their formative moment. It was authored by Sajjad Zaheer (1905–73), Rashid Jahan (1905–52), Mahmuduzzafar (1908–56), and Ahmed Ali (b. 1910). The public outrage caused by the book led Mahmuduzzafar and Ali to make a public appeal for the formation of a league of progressive authors. The actual establishment of the Progressive Writers Association (PWA) took place in London during 1934. Sajjad Zaheer was a founder member of the London coterie which included the Indian English novelist Mulk Raj Anand (b. 1905).

Their first meeting laid the foundations for a progressive proposal which supported Indian independence. This progressive manifesto heralded change with an express desire to cleanse Indian literature of its pre-modern sensibilities. It reiterated an urgent need for the modernising influences of realism and reality. Other aims included: Hindustani as the national language for India along with a shared Indo-Roman script; the production and translation of progressive literature; the establishment of writers' groups across the multi-lingual provinces of India; the formation of a network of writers; and contact and communication with other Indian literary organisations sympathetic to their cause. Different versions of the manifesto prepared by the PWA committee were published in the Hindi literary journal *Hans* in 1935, and the London *Left Review* in February 1936. Ahmed Ali and Sajjad Zaheer organised the first meeting in Lucknow of the All India PWA on 9–10 April 1936.

The most significant change triggered by the Progressives was the transgression of social boundaries of class, caste and gender in literary representations. Progressive liberalism emancipated women prose writers from their separate existence and placed them on an equal footing with their male contemporaries. Eventually, partition and its aftermath displaced the original progressive struggle for a united Indian nation and writers, disillusioned with the independent postcolonial state, looked toward their regional locations for a new sense of identity.

Amina Yaquin

Literary Works

Ali, Ahmed (ed.) (1989), *Selected Short Stories from Pakistan: Urdu*, Delhi: Uppal Publishing House, pp. 5–19.
Anand, Mulk Raj (1940), *Untouchable*, Harmondsworth: Allen Lane, Penguin.
Chander, Krishan (1990), 'Kalu Bhangi' and 'The Mahalakshmi Bridge', in G. C. Narang (ed.), *Selected Short Stories*, trans. J. Ratan, Delhi: Sahitya Akademi, pp. 34–47.

Histories

Ali, Ahmed (1977–8), 'The Progressive Writers' Movement in its Historical Perspective', *Journal of South Asian Literature* 13: 1–4, pp. 91–7.

Coppola, Carlo (ed.), [1974] (1988), *Marxist Influences and South Asian Literature, Volume 1*, Delhi: Chanakya.

Dryland, Estelle (1993), *Faiz Ahmad Faiz 1911–1984: Urdu Poet of Social Realism*, Lahore: Vanguard.

Malik, Hafeez (1967), 'The Marxist Literary Movement in India and Pakistan, *Journal of Asian Studies* 26: 4, pp. 649–64.

See also: **Anti-colonialism and Resistance: South Asia**; **Communism: South Asia**; **Historiography: South Asia**; **Pakistan's Subaltern Struggles**.

Q

Quebec Independence Movement

According to separatist rhetoric of the mid-1990s, the Quebec independence movement has deep roots 'in the fields of history . . . sown for us by four hundred years of men and women and courage, rooted in the soil'. In reality, the separatist agenda in Canada is of a more recent lineage, dating back no further than the so-called 'Quiet Revolution' of the 1950s and 1960s. In 1963 the Front de Libération du Québec (FLQ) was formed, committed to overthrowing the symbols and institutions of colonialism and anglophone domination through revolution. At the same time, more moderate separatist leaders such as René Lévesque emerged through the ranks of the Liberal Party, and later broke away with other groups to form the Parti Québécois in 1968. The movement received official encouragement from General de Gaulle's (in)famous 'Vive le Québec libre' speech in Montreal in 1967, and philosophical ballast with the publication of Pierre Vallières' *White Niggers of America* in 1971.

The more revolutionary face of Quebec separatism suffered a terminal setback during the 'October crisis' of 1970, when a British consular official and a provincial government minister were kidnapped (the latter was subsequently murdered) by the FLQ. Public sentiment proved to be anything but in tune with this kind of revolutionary strategy, and the independence movement has been confined to the ballot box ever since.

In 1976, Lévesque's Parti Québécois gained power in Quebec, and in 1980 a referendum was held on the issue of 'Sovereignty Association' – a formula whereby Quebec would acquire exclusive authority over legislation, taxation, and external relations, while maintaining an economic association with Canada including a common currency. The campaign was opposed by anglophone and other non-French Quebeckers, but more significantly by a vocal minority of French-Canadian federalists, championed by Prime Minister Pierre Trudeau. The referendum was rejected by a comfortable majority of 59.6 per cent of voters, and the Parti Québécois was defeated at the polls in 1985. Here the independence movement might have dissolved completely, but it received fresh impetus with the formation of the Bloc Québécois as a federal party under Lucien Bouchard in 1991, and the electoral success of the Parti Québécois under Jacques Parizeau in the provincial elections of 1994. This led to a further sovereignty referendum in 1995, where the result was far closer. Of the unprecedented 93.5 per cent of the electorate who cast a vote, 49.4 per cent voted 'yes', with the 'no' vote winning by the slimmest of margins: a mere 50.6 per cent of voters. The closeness of the referendum prompted the federal government of Jean Chrétien to adopt the 'clarity law' in 2000, subjecting provincial referenda to federal scrutiny as a means of containing further moves towards unilateral secession.

Stuart Ward

Literary Works

Aquin, Hubert (1965), *Next Episode*, trans. Sheila Fischman, Toronto: McClelland and Stewart.
MacLennan, Hugh (1945), *Two Solitudes*, Toronto: Macmillan.
Scott, Gail (1988), *Heroine*, Toronto: Coach House Press.

Histories

Coleman, William D. (1984), *The Independence Movement in Quebec, 1945–1980*, Toronto: University of Toronto Press.
Mathews, George (1990), *Quiet Revolution: Quebec's Challenge to Canada*, Toronto: Summerhill Press.
Vallières, Pierre (1971), *White Niggers of America*, Toronto: McClelland and Stuart.
Young, Robert (1998), *The Secession of Quebec and the Future of Canada*, Montreal and Kingston: McGill-Queen's University Press.

See also: **Historiography: Canada**; **Multiculturalism: Canada**; **Nationalism(s): Canada**.

R

Racial Discrimination Act: Australia

The 1975 Racial Discrimination Act (RDA) of the Whitlam Labour government was a milestone in multiculturalism and in relations between settlers/invaders and indigenous Australians. Passed two years after the 1973 implementation of a universal migration policy, it also stands with the 1992 *Mabo* and 1996 *Wik* land rights decisions as a belated landmark in enacting progressive change. The RDA enacted the International Convention on All Forms of Racial Discrimination prohibiting direct discrimination on the grounds of race, colour, descent, ethnic or national origin. Further change came slowly: an amended RDA (1990) made indirect discrimination unlawful.

Whether because of the period, place or character of settlement, or its political culture, Australia has been tardy in developing a culture of human rights. It has no Bill of Rights (unlike Canada) and has state but not federal age discrimination laws. Lawyers and the white public had limited interest in philosophical questions until the Whitlam government law reforms, the law reform commissions and the Human Rights and Equal Opportunity Commission (HREOC). The other gap, between principle and practice, was documented by HREOC's National Inquiry into Racist Violence (1990). The 1994 Keating Labour government's Racial Hatred Act amended the RDA, prohibiting all forms of racist violence and incitement to racial hatred. Similarly, the amended NSW Anti-Discrimination Act (1977) specified racial vilification, including civil and criminal sanctions.

Was the law effective in diminishing racist behaviour? Two other transitions changed public attitudes and practices. First, Aboriginal achievement was recognised in the arts (painters such as Ginger Riley, writer Sally Morgan, the Banjarra dance company), music (Yothu Yindi, Rita Hunter), in Aboriginal leadership (Manduwuy Yunupingu, Lowitja O'Donoghue, Noel Pearson), in the media and in sport (the runner Cathy Freeman, rugby representative Mark Ella, and Michael Long and over fifty leading Aboriginal Australian footballers). Second was a development in the major sport, Australian Rules Football. When St Kilda player Nicky Winmar bared his skin to defeated opposition fans in April 1993, the Australian Football League (AFL) selected Aboriginal cultural themes for the 1993 Grand Final in the Year of Indigenous People. In 1995, the AFL codified Rule 30, against racial and religious vilification on the field. After initial education and reconciliation and mediation meetings, it implemented penalties in the form of fines and suspension. Racial vilification, once regulated by the vernacular sports law that 'what happens on the field stays on the field', has almost completely disappeared. Local leagues also implemented the policy, beginning grass-roots progress. However, Phillip Gwynne's 1999 novel, *Deadly, Unna?* (filmed as *Australian Rules* in 2002), exposed country town prejudice in sport, suggesting that the stroke of a legal pen cannot eliminate racism.

Stephen Alomes

Literary Works

Gwynne, Phillip (1999), *Deadly, Unna?*, Camberwell: Penguin.
Sykes, Roberta (1997), *Snake Cradle*, St Leonards: Allen and Unwin.
West, Ida (1987), *Pride against Prejudice: Reminiscences of a Tasmanian Aborigine*, Canberra: Australian Institute of Aboriginal Studies.

Histories

Attwood, Bain (2003), *Rights for Aborigines*, Crows Nest: Allen and Unwin,
McNamara, Luke (2002), *Regulating Racism: Racial Vilification Laws in Australia*, Sydney: Sydney University Law School.
Tiddy, Josephine (2001), *It's Just Not Fair: Overcoming Discrimination in Australia*, Sydney: ABC Books.
HREOC, http://www.hreoc.gov.au/

See also: **Historiography: Australia; Land: Australia; Multiculturalism: Australia.**

Raj

British rule in India effectively began with the activities of the East India Company at the end of the reign of Elizabeth I. The company gradually acquired trading bases in Madras (1639), Bombay (1664) and Calcutta (1696), and saw off competition from commercial rivals. In the eighteenth century the company's control spread over much of India, filling the space vacated by the disintegrating Mughal empires: a process assisted by the activities of military adventurers like Robert Clive and administrators such as the controversial governor-general of Bengal, Warren Hastings.

During this early phase Britons and Indians fraternised freely and there was a degree of cultural exchange. However, this more liberal view of India and its cultures gave way, in the nineteenth century, to a more utilitarian and at times evangelical attitude. The distance between ruler and ruled grew to such a degree that the British were completely unprepared for the mutiny of 1857. Triggered by objections to the introduction of cartridges greased with pig fat, the rebellion then took on a proto-nationalist colouring, with an attempt to restore the last of the Mughals to the long-defunct throne of Delhi. Although mercilessly suppressed, the Mutiny severely affected the psyche of the Raj in its subsequent formation, evident in a latent sense of vulnerability; and resulted in the introduction of direct political rule from London.

The tendency to play off Indian communities (Hindu, Muslim and Sikh) against one another became a longstanding tactic. The second half of the nineteenth century also saw increased surveillance and the categorisation of knowledge about India and Indians became a widespread tool of imperial rule. An unchanging, fully knowable 'India of the imagination' was created, open to the white man's panoptic gaze. Those who did question British rule – as did many urban, educated Indians – could be treated as aberrations, unrepresentative of the 'real India' of the princes and the rural peasantry. However, such voices became harder to ignore as the Indian National Congress, formed in 1886, became the spearhead of the independence movement.

Opposition to the Raj gathered momentum: in the cross-communal opposition to the proposal to partition Bengal in 1905; the Home Rule Movement during World War I; the rise of Gandhi and his doctrine of passive resistance; the Non-Co-operation Movement of the 1920s; and the cry to 'Quit India' in the 1940s. Setbacks in World War II, the mounting cost of empire, and pressure from Britain's wartime allies meant that by 1947 Indian independence was inevitable: even if its hurried nature – and the longer legacy of communal mistrust – meant that the fruits of freedom were somewhat bitter.

Peter Morey

Literary Works

Farrell, J. G. (1973), *The Siege of Krishnapur*, London: Weidenfeld and Nicolson.
Forster, E. M. [1924] (1985), *A Passage to India*, Harmondsworth: Penguin.
Kipling, Rudyard [1901] (1987), *Kim*, Harmondsworth: Penguin.
Kunzru, Hari (2003), *The Impressionist*, Harmondsworth: Penguin.
Masters, John [1954] (1960), *Bhowani Junction*, Harmondsworth: Penguin.
Rushdie, Salman (1981), *Midnight's Children*, London: Picador.
Scott, Paul [1966] (1988), *The Jewel in the Crown*, London: Pan.
Tharoor, Shashi (1989), *The Great Indian Novel*, New Delhi: Penguin/Viking.

Histories

Chandra, Bipan (1989), *India's Struggle for Independence*, New Delhi: Penguin.
Chatterjee, Partha (1986), *Nationalist Thought and the Colonial World: A Derivative Discourse?*, London: Zed Books.
Hutchins, Francis G. (1967), *The Illusion of Permanence: British Imperialism in India*, Princeton, NJ: Princeton University Press.
James, Lawrence (1997), *Raj: the Making and Unmaking of British India*, London: Little, Brown and Co.
Kiernan, Victor (1969), *'The Lords of Humankind': European Attitudes towards the Outside World in the Imperial Age*, London: Weidenfeld and Nicolson.

See also: **Anti-colonialism and Resistance: South Asia; East India Company; English in India: Eighteenth and Nineteenth Centuries; Governors-General and Viceroys; Hill Stations**.

Rebellions: Australia

Traditional histories of Australia have usually claimed that the country's foundation in 1788, and its achievement of independence over the subsequent two centuries, occurred with remarkably little conflict or violence. And they are mostly right, particularly if the sporadic conflict with the Aborigines is excluded from consideration. However, there were other significant outbreaks of armed conflict and popular rebellion. One of the most dramatic was a rebellion in 1804 by about 200 mainly Irish convicts who seized arms from farmhouses outside Sydney with the aim of mounting a general rising of the small British gulag. However, the rebel leaders were divided and the authorities, who were forewarned, pre-empted the attacks by confronting the ragtag rebellion head-on as the convicts with their pikes and pitchforks assembled on Vinegar Hill. Twenty-four were killed in the fighting, while the leaders were hanged and their captured supporters sent to Newcastle or Norfolk Island.

Along with Europeans influenced by the failed revolutions of 1848 and rebellious Americans, the Irish also comprised a large number of the gold miners who took up arms in 1854 to protest at a government tax on gold mining and the vigorous way in which it was collected. Setting up a fortified stockade on the Eureka goldfield near Ballarat, and flying a Southern Cross flag, the miners widened their protest to call for universal suffrage and even for a republic if their demands were ignored. The British governor sent in police and troops who attacked the camp in the early morning, killing about thirty of the miners for the cost of five soldiers. A group of miners, including their nominal leader, Peter Lalor, were tried for sedition but acquitted by the jury, while their demands concerning the iniquitous tax were conceded by a subsequent Royal Commission.

The Eureka rebellion had elicited wide public support and ensured that the granting of democratic government went further than it might otherwise have done. Lalor, who had lost an arm in the fighting, was elected to the Victorian parliament. The example of Eureka was an important inspiration for labour strikes during the early 1890s and beyond. Today, the Southern Cross flag is still used occasionally as a flag of protest and can often be seen flying at construction sites after being adopted as an emblem by a building union.

The rebellion itself is not widely commemorated outside of a tourist attraction in Ballarat.

David Day

Literary Works

Cook, Kenneth (1975), *Stockade: A Musical Play of the Eureka Stockade*, Melbourne: Penguin.
Haylen, Leslie (1948), *Blood on the Wattle: A Play of the Eureka Stockade*, Sydney: Angus and Robertson.
Lambert, Eric (1954), *The Five Bright Stars*, Melbourne: Australasian Book Society.
Richardson, Henry Handel (1930), *The Fortunes of Richard Mahoney*, London: Heinemann.

Histories

Carboni, Raffaello [1855] (1993), *The Eureka Stockade*, Melbourne: Melbourne University Press.
Molony, John (1984), *Eureka*, Melbourne: Viking.
Silver, Lynette (1989), *The Battle of Vinegar Hill*, Sydney: Doubleday.
Whitaker, Anne-Maree (1994), *Unfinished Revolution: United Irishmen in New South Wales, 1800–1810*, Sydney: Crossing Press.

See also: **Historiography: Australia**.

Refugees

'Refugee' derives from French term *réfugié* which is traceable to the high medieval period. The first recorded English usage in 1685 refers to the expulsion and flight of some 200,000 Huguenots from France as a result of Louis XIV's revocation of the Edict of Nantes that held together a frail religious and political compromise between French Catholics and the Protestant French Huguenots. Little is known about non-Western histories of statecraft and refugee development but in general since the seventeenth century statecraft is shaped by displaced populations and the modern nation-state as polity is defined by the perceived threat of the foreigner-alien, and increasingly in the twentieth century by the figure of the refugee (see Soguk 1999). Indeed, Liisa Malkki has argued that '[i]n the national order of things, refugeeness is itself an aberration of categories' (Malkki 1995, p. 4).

Since the end of World War II, there have been successive waves of refugees fleeing political, economic, military and ecological hardship: the Indian subcontinent in 1947; Palestine in 1948; Vietnam in the early 1960s; Somalia in 1993; Yugoslavia in the 1990s; and Afghanistan in 2002, to name but a few instances. Unsettled, undifferentiated, unaccommodated, undocumented, these tens of millions of refugees testify to Hannah Arendt's observation that 'the abstract nakedness of being nothing but human [becomes] their greatest danger' (Arendt 1951, p. 300).

Central to the narrative of modern political life is the privileging of the citizen/nation/state ensemble over the refugee-citizen, a destructive binary produced and reinforced over centuries, and still at the very core of colonial, neo-colonial and national histories. The colonial habit of literally drawing lines on maps to carve out territories, and the legal-institutional mechanism of the colonial state that set in motion particular political identities and produced subject races as virtual citizens limits the scope of postcolonial citizenship in many parts of the world. For example, the Tutsi are seen as racial strangers in Rwanda, and ethnic strangers in Uganda and Congo. There continue to be civil wars involving nationalism, marginalised minorities under threat, disputed borders, and neo-imperial interventions, all of which have produced refugees: there are currently 23 million refugees, and the vast majority are in the Third World, where 97 per cent of them are homeless. Instances of the human rights for refugees as prescribed by the 1951 Geneva Refugee Convention being observed have been the exception rather than the rule. According to Aleinikoff, 'persons forced to flee their homes [do so] because of conditions that make life there unbearable' (Aleinikoff 1995, p. 258), and those refugees who do make it through increasingly tightened borders of the West therefore come from poor countries. Once in the West, they are hastily designated as 'new asylum seekers', or even 'illegals', and they find themselves in a liminal zone of 'inclusionary exclusion', at the mercy of the laws of the host country and deprived of basic human rights during their internment.

Prem Poddar

Literary Works

Flutter, Naomi and Carl Solomon (eds) (1995), *Tilting Cages: An Anthology of Refugee Writings*, Sydney: The authors.
Gurnah, Abdulrazak (2001), *By the Sea*, London: Bloomsbury.
Langer, Jennifer (ed.) (2002), *Crossing the Border: Voices of Refugee and Exiled Women*, Nottingham: Five Leaves.
Phillips, Caryl (2003), *A Distant Shore*, London: Secker and Warburg.
Zephaniah, Benjamin (2001), *Refugee Boy*, London: Bloomsbury.

Histories

Aleinikoff, T. A. (1995), 'State-Centred Refugee Law: From Re-settlement to Containment', in V. E. Daniel and J. C. Knudsen (eds), *Mistrusting Refugees*, Berkeley, CA: University of California Press, pp. 257–78.
Arendt, Hannah [1951] (1973), *Origins of Totalitarianism*, New York and London: Harcourt Brace Jovanovich.
Malkki, Liisa (1995), *Purity and Exile*, London and Chicago: University of Chicago Press.
Soguk, Nevzat (1999), *States and Strangers: Refugees and Displacements of Statecraft*, Minneapolis, MN: University of Minnesota Press.
UNHCR (2000), *The State of the World's Refugees 2000: Fifty Years of Humanitarian Action*, Oxford: Oxford University Press.

See also: **Border Disputes: South Asia; Detention Centres: Australia; Migrancy: Southern Africa; Partition.**

Religions: East Africa

Religion in East Africa cannot be conceived of as a distinct sphere of social life, as is often assumed in Western contexts, separated or clearly distinct from other, supposedly non-religious ones, like 'politics' or 'art'. Rather, spread out over the whole East African region, there is a multiplicity of ways in which social action in everyday life is commonly directed at, or seen to be influenced by, a spiritual world beyond human experience. This world, which local actors see as an integral part of their reality, is central to a variety of local practices and expressions of self-understanding. When discussing religion in East Africa it is therefore important to consider the relevance of spirits (divinities, ancestors, djinns) and human interaction with them, as well as the relations between ritual performance and power, authority, and morality.

Thus 'religion' is closely related to, and intertwined with, political, moral and aesthetic concerns, as well as power interests and local cosmologies. This was already well documented in some classic ethnographies of the region (see Evans-Pritchard 1937, Middleton 1960 and Lienhardt 1961). Earlier 'research' had often been conducted by missionaries or colonial administrators with clear vested interests. In response, local critics rejected the Eurocentric bias in the research on African religions, and demanded that they should be approached and made understood from an internal perspective (see p'Bitek 1970). From then on, scholarship has largely tried to work along this guideline.

The diversity of religions in East Africa is inadequately reflected in the common but simple distinctions between Islam, Christianity, and 'African traditional religion'. Each strand has its own complex history and internal dynamics. Christianity has become the clearly dominant faith, having grown throughout the colonial and postcolonial era. It came to East Africa in the late fifteenth century with Portuguese seafarers who soon confronted the local Muslim population and destabilised the region. Islam arrived at the Swahili coast at around 800 CE. With its long history in the area, it must be seen as a local religion. The same applies to Christianity: both are locally rooted and contextualised, while at the same time part of global networks.

Islam in East Africa exists alongside and yet in tension with other indigenous cosmologies, cults and ritual practices. Sunni Islam (of the Shafi school) has historically been dominant, due to centuries-old trade and family links with the Hadramaut. It spread inland through marriage alliances with local communities, and by Arab and Swahili traders who ventured up country. Various Sufi networks were locally developed and adapted. Incoming Muslim traders from the Persian Gulf and the Indian subcontinent who were Shi'ite established their own religious communities separately within the towns (for example, Shi'a Ithnashari, Ismaili, Bohora). Through Omani channels, an East African Ibadhi tradition was initiated and re-affirmed during the nineteenth century, after the creation of the Zanzibari sultanate. By now, however, much of it has been absorbed into Shafi tradition. (See Brenner 1993, Levtzion and Pouwels 2000, Oded 2000, Parkin and Headley 2000, Pouwels 1987 and Westerlund and Rosander 1997; see too the literary works by Farah, Gurnah, Vassanji, and Salih, as well as the critical studies by Harrow.)

In the latter half of the twentieth century, a surge of reformist influence from the Middle East entered the region through global Islamic networks, as happened all around the Muslim world. A particular case is the radical Sunni Salafiyya movement, locally denounced as *Wahhabi* by its adversaries. Through its sustained attacks on Sufism and common festive and ritual practices of local Muslims this became a major reformist force.

Their sharp ideological critique was brought forward by local scholars who were educated and financed from countries like Saudi Arabia or Pakistan. For many Muslims in the region, this new dominance of the exterior led to a 'double self-alienation'. Next to the Islamic attack on their historically evolved Muslim identity, the postcolonial governments, dominated by Christians, were seen to threaten and dismantle many of the existing channels of political self-determination for Muslims.

Christianity too has in many ways adopted elements of existing local customs and rituals. However, it also still represents a 'Western' way of life. In this latter sense, Christians may see themselves as 'progressive' within a modernising world. In contrast, independent African churches were founded by local visionaries or 'prophets' against the threat of Western colonial dominance. They created a peculiar blend of biblical traditions and indigenous practice and cosmology, a 'vernacular Christianity' (see James and Johnson 1988). For some ethnic groups, such processes of 'christening' belief systems and ritual practices have been documented (Hutchinson 1996 and James 1989). Furthermore, in many African churches and sects spirit possession and local cultural idioms continue to play a significant role in establishing authority and mediating ethical demands to the community. This applies also to independent churches in the Kongo area, built up in resistance to the Belgian colonial empire, and led by self-declared prophets whose visions attracted large numbers of supporters, thus creating a significant political counter-force (see MacGaffey 1986). And in new evangelist churches, the experience of being 'saved' or 'reborn' is often seen to be connected to states of trance and spirit possession.

Christianity has been rejected and denounced as the white man's religion and as an ally to colonial doctrine. In postcolonial literature, it has been depicted as a colonial or neo-colonial force liaising closely with Western capitalism to suppress Africans and their cultural traditions and political aspirations. Particularly well-known examples of this are found in the novels of Ngugi wa Thiong'o (for example, *The River Between* (1965), *Devil on the Cross* (1990), *Matigari* (1989)), and also in the poetry of Okot p'Bitek, especially his two famous pieces *Song of Lawino* and *Song of Ocol* (1984).

Despite being the dominant faith, in public discourse Christianity is still sometimes ideologically defined in opposition to African 'tradition', both by supporters and critics of its supposed counterpart, Western 'modernity'. An example of this is the dispute concerning a prominent Luo lawyer, S. M. Otieno, which took place in Nairobi during the late 1980s. Conflicting views about the manner and place of his burial by his Christian Gikuyu widow and his Luo clan representatives led to a year-long legal battle in which the High Court of Kenya had to cast final judgment. It decided in favour of 'customary law' and against the widow's claims, presenting a case of 'traditionalisation' in Kenyan society. Ethnic blood-ties and traditions were in the last instance given preference over marital bonds. (See Cohen and Odhiambo 1992, Otieno 1998 and Ojwang and Mugambi 1989)

Some healing cults, as dynamic historical institutions with ongoing social relevance, are locally presented in Christian or Islamic or wholly indigenous idioms (depending on regional context), while maintaining the same core features of basic ritual activity. For instance, *ngoma* healing cults have been investigated comparatively in Central and southeast Africa as an underlying unifying cultural phenomenon (see Janzen 1992). This indigenous institution combines performative features of religious, political, medical, educational and musical character. To understand *ngoma* fully in its own terms, their complex inter-relationships have to be investigated. The unifying element of such phenomena, despite their different idiomatic surfaces (Christian, Islamic, or indigenous), is the ritual communication between humans and spirits. For the coastal Muslim region, a

detailed account of such interaction exists (see Lambek 1993). The forms of such communication – trance, spirit possession, spirit mediums, and divination – are widely distributed
in the whole East African area, but in each case distinct in relation to cultural context.

'Prophets' and spirit-mediums have been instrumental political leaders during colonial
and postcolonial times (see Anderson and Johnson 1995). For the Nuer, significant prophets of the last century have been carefully documented (see Johnson 1994). Nuer prophets
are recognised when possessed (chosen) by 'divinities', who also supply their mediums with
special powers. The British colonial government watched closely the prophets and their
followers, taking measures to guard its authority. Nowadays prophets may be influential
figures in the civil war in Sudan. A second example, the 'Holy Spirit' movement, was
formed in Uganda in the 1980s, and led by a spirit called Lakwena and its medium Alice,
a young Acholi woman (see Behrend 1999). This movement started a process of ritual
'cleansing' within Acholi society after the end of the big civil war, when returning soldiers
had to be reintegrated into the community. Casting itself as a Christian liberation movement (with a radical code of conduct), it gained followers and soon became engaged in an
armed struggle against the new government of Museveni. A third example further to the
west is of Zimbabwe during the liberation war in the 1970s, when guerrilla rebels made it
part of their strategy to secure the support of local spirits and their mediums for their struggle against the Rhodesian government (see Lan 1985 and Hove 1989). The spirits, the
ghosts of the royal ancestors ruling the land, were believed to be pleased by the guerrillas'
consideration and respect, and therefore supported their ultimately successful endeavours.

'Witchcraft', finally, has been a popular notion in studies of East African societies, but also
within social discourse itself. It denotes the instrumental use of, and reference to, occult forces
in social interaction. As a negative marker for the limits of morality in social discourse, it
points at rivalries and tensions within a given community. Guarding mechanisms like oracles
and divination are often put in place to control or trace it. Since Evans-Pritchard (1937),
'witchcraft' has been described and contextualised in relation to the particular framework of
the community in which it occurs (its cultural logic, cosmology, standards of reasoning).
Foreign and with specific historical connotations, 'witchcraft' is a very problematic term
when used analytically. Yet its use is inevitable as this term is nowadays frequently used in
Africa itself (see for example, Geschiere 1997 and Moore and Sanders 2002). Killings blamed
on 'witchcraft' or occurring in response to witchcraft accusations continue to happen in social
life, and are widely reported in the newspapers. The discourse on 'witchcraft' can be documented, but cannot be fully explained in general terms. This also applies to other issues we
encounter when dealing with the complex relationships between spirits and human beings.

Kai Kresse

Literary Works

Farah, Nuruddin (1985), *Maps*, London: Heinemann.
Gurnah, Abdulrazak (1995), *Paradise*, London: Penguin.
Gurnah, Abdulrazak (1997), *Admiring Silence*, London: Heinemann.
Hove, Chenjerai (1989), *Bones*, London: Heinemann.
Kenyatta, Jomo [1953] (1965), *Facing Mount Kenya*, London: Mercury Books.
Mwangi, Meja (1973), *Kill Me Quick*, London: Heinemann.
Mwangi, Meja (1976), *Going Down River Road*, London: Heinemann.
Mwangi, Meja (1987), *Carcase for Hounds*, London: Heinemann.

Ngugi wa Thiong'o (1965), *The River Between*, London: Heinemann.
Ngugi wa Thiong'o (1989), *Matigari*, London: Heinemann.
Ngugi wa Thiong'o (1990), *Devil on the Cross*, London: Heinemann.
p'Bitek, Okot (1984), *Song of Lawino* and *Song of Ocol*, London: Heinemann.
p'Bitek, Okot (1989), *White Teeth*, Nairobi: Heinemann.
Saleh, Tayib (1976), *Season of Migration to the North*, London: Heinemann.
Vassanji, M. G. (1989), *The Gunny Sack*, London: Heinemann.
Vassanji, M. G. (1991), *Uhuru Street*, London: Heinemann.

Histories

Anderson, D. and D. H. Johnson (eds) (1995), *Revealing Prophets: Prophets in Eastern African History*, London: James Currey.
Behrend, H. (1999), *Alice and the Spirits: War in Northern Uganda 1985–97*, London: James Currey.
Behrend, H. and U. Luig (eds) (1999), *Spirit Possession, Modernity and Power in Africa*, London: James Currey.
Brenner, L. (ed.) (1993), *Muslim Identity and Social Change in Sub-Saharan Africa*, London: Hurst.
Cohen, D. and E. S. Atieno Odhiambo (1992), *Burying SM: the Politics of Knowledge and the Sociology of Power in Africa*, London: James Currey.
Evans-Pritchard, E. E. (1937), *Witchcraft, Oracles, and Magic among the Azande*, Oxford: Clarendon Press.
Geschiere, P. (1997), 'Witchcraft and Sorcery', in J. Middleton (ed.), *Encyclopedia of Africa South of the Sahara*, vol. 4, London: Simon and Schuster, pp. 376–81.
Harrow, K. W. (ed.) (1991), *Faces of Islam in African Literature*, London: James Currey.
Harrow, K. W. (ed.) (1996), *The Marabout and the Muse: New Approaches to Islam in African Literature*, London: James Currey.
Hutchinson, S. E. (1996), *Nuer Dilemmas*, Berkeley, CA: University of California Press.
James, W. (1989), *The Listening Ebony: Moral Knowledge, Religion and Power among the Uduk of Sudan*, Oxford: Clarendon Press.
James, W. and D. H. Johnson (eds) (1988), *Vernacular Christianity: Essays in the Social Anthropology of Religion*, Oxford: Jaso.
Janzen, J. (1992), *Ngoma. Discourses of Healing in Central and Southern Africa*, Berkeley, CA: University of California Press.
Johnson, D. H. (1994), *Nuer Prophets*, Oxford: Clarendon Press.
Lambek, M. (1993), *Knowledge and Practice in Mayotte*, Toronto: Toronto University Press.
Lan, David (1985), *Guns and Rain*, London: James Currey.
Levtzion, N. and R. L. Pouwels (eds) (2000), *The History of Islam in Africa*, London: James Currey.
Lienhardt, G. (1961), *Divinity and Experience*, Oxford: Clarendon Press.
MacGaffey, W. (1986), *Religion and Society in Central Africa*, Chicago: Chicago University Press.
Middleton, J. [1960] (1999), *Lugbara Religion: Ritual and Authority among an East African People*, Hamburg: Lit-Verlag; Oxford: James Currey.
Moore, H. L. and T. Sanders (eds) (2002), *Magical Interpretations, Material Realities. Modernity, Witchcraft and the Occult in Postcolonial Africa*, London: Routledge.

Oded, A. (2000), *Islam and Politics in Kenya*, Boulder, CO and London: Lynne Rienner.

Ojwang, J. B. and J. N. K. Mugambi (eds) (1989), *The S. M. Otieno Case. Death and Burial in Modern Kenya*, Nairobi: Nairobi University Press.

Otieno, W. W. (1998), *Mau Mau's Daughter: A Life History*, ed. C. A. Presley, London: Lynne Rienner.

Parkin, D. and S. Headley (eds) (2000), *Islamic Prayer across the Indian Ocean*, Richmond: Curzon.

p'Bitek, Okot (1970), *African Religions in Western Scholarship*, Nairobi: Kenya Literature Bureau.

Pouwels, R. L. (1987), *Horn and Crescent: Cultural Change and Traditional Islam on the East African Coast, 800–1900*, Cambridge: Cambridge University Press.

Westerlund, D. and E. E. Rosander (eds) (1997), *African Islam and Islam in Africa*, London: Hurst.

See also: **Anti-colonialism and Resistance: East Africa; Chimurengas; Islam; Precolonial Histories: East Africa; Slave Trade: East Africa.**

Religions: South Asia

The intensification of religious nationalisms in South Asia in the twenty-first century has refocused attention both on the use of religion in the construction of national identity and the basis of such strategy in colonialism. The construction of 'the Other' as religiously different from 'the Self' marked the nationalist ideology in the same way it marked the colonial strategy of rule. In India, for example, the colonial representation of the Muslim as 'fanatic' in nineteenth-century government reports is reflected in the Hindu right's construction of its own identity and definitions of the nation in the current context. So in the colonial representation of religions, as an exercise in creating a self and its other(s), we can locate clues as to why modern nationalisms are premised on religion as the marker of difference.

Colonial governmentality in India eschewed the religious zeal of the Christian missionaries to reform native religions, even as it borrowed from their strategy to mark the native population as 'majority Hindu' and transform it through the production of knowledge about its religious beliefs and practices. At the close of the eighteenth century the Christian clergy of the Established Church of England 'recognized their responsibility for spreading the knowledge of Christianity more widely throughout the world' (Ingham 1956, p. 2). To them India looked most suitable for missionary work especially as the East India Company was becoming a dominant political force in the region. Yet fears of insubordination made the company hesitant to endorse missionary activities in India for a long while. In 1807 Lord Minto, for example, clearly articulated the company's policy 'to maintain perfect toleration of the various religious systems which prevailed in them; to protect the followers of each in the undisturbed enjoyment of their particular beliefs' (Muir 1915, p. 251). The point of conflict between the government and the missionaries also lay in the missionary zeal to undermine caste, considered by now to be the 'product of Hinduism and its chief support', and the government's need to build strategic alliances with upper-caste Hindus to govern the majority more effectively (Ingham 1956, p. 20). But both agreed that the religion of India was Hinduism, 'perverted' by Islam, the religion of the 'foreigners', or the Muslims (Ingham 1956, p. 2).

In colonial India, the marking of communities on the basis of religion was consistently highlighted in debates over the issue of 'native' education. In his note, dated 17 July 1823, Mr Holt Mackenzie (from the Territorial Department, Revenue Collections, Government of India) favoured the gradual introduction of English language and literature into existing native institutions. He felt sure that in publications of 'useful native works,' there might be ones of common interest between the Mohammedans and the Hindus, but at first 'these must necessarily constitute two great divisions, requiring distinct consideration' (Sharp 1920, p. 62).

In his ethnographies of the schooling systems of districts in Bengal, Bihar, and the Rajshahi (1836–8), William Adam, a government servant, makes observations that simultaneously homogenise and heterogenise the populations he is studying. Adam's work shows that, contrary to the common belief that Brahmins predominated in the Sanskrit academies, in the district of Murshidabad, Kayasthas and even lower castes were teaching (Di Bona pp. 2–3). In fact, Hindi schools had different curricula from Sanskrit academies thereby showing the diversity within Hindu education. Similarly, Bengali schools taught in both Bengali and Persian and boasted of a mix of Hindu and Muslim students (Di Bona 1983, p. 18).

The manifestation of cultural complexities in the diversity of the schools in the districts that Adam documented was not always reflected in his own reading of what constituted 'indigenous' vis-à-vis education in 'pre-colonial' India. His reports are peppered with references to the 'two great divisions of the population, Musalmans and Hindus . . . one exclusively trained in Mohammedan literature and the other in Hindu literature . . .' (Di Bona 1983, pp. 61–2). It did not reflect in Macaulay's Minute on Education (1835) which was adopted as official policy on education as soon as it was published and without waiting for the completion of Adam's research (Sharp 1920, p. 13). Even when Adam's reports were completed and compiled, their impact was evident nowhere in policy. The Hunter Commission Report (1882), another definitive statement by the government of India on the status of public education, echoed Hunter's historical reports on the 'Indian Musalmans' whom he represents as 'fanatics,' the Koran as the basis of their fanaticism (Hunter 1871, pp. 176–9). The Hunter reports influenced the turn-of-the-century change in policy that favoured the Hindu upper castes as the government's consultative group regarding the new majority and saw the formal characterisation of the Muslim as anti-Hindu and as the 'greatest threat to the British empire' (Hunter 1871, p. 11).

The nineteenth century, therefore, witnessed a new spurt in research that eulogised everything Hindu and marginalised anything Muslim. Warren Hastings' example of equal appeasement of the two communities of India through translations of their 'primary' religious texts (*Gita* and *Hedaya*) into English in the eighteenth century was abandoned in the nineteenth century (Muir 1915, p. 152). Orientalist scholars followed the example of Christian missionaries by documenting and translating Sanskrit curriculums and texts into English.

John Duncan, a resident of Benares, petitioned the Earl of Cornwallis to set up 'an institution of Hindoo college or academy for the preservation and cultivation of laws, literature, and religion of that nation, at this centre of their faith (Benares) and the common resort of all tribes' (Nicholls 1907, p. 1). The academy, he felt, would endear 'our government' to the Hindus while becoming a site for the systematic compilation of 'Hindoo religion, laws, arts, or sciences . . . create a precious library of the most ancient and valuable general learning and tradition' (Nicholls 1907, pp. 1–2). His petition echoes the sentiments of many Orientalists and their favouring of Hindu 'civilisation' and religion.

The Brahmins on their account did not hesitate to request the indulgence and interference of the colonial government in matters of learning and wrote to them frequently. The 'Humble petition of the students of the government Sanskrit college of Calcutta to the right hon'ble Lord George Auckland, Governor-general, dated 9 August 1836,' read:

> Impressed with the importance of cultivating the Sanskrit language owing to its being a vehicle to the sacred writings of the Hindoos and containing all works which represent their manners and customs, the ancient kings of Hindoostan endowed grants of lands to those Brahmins and Pandits . . . since the accession of Mohammedan power, though the progress of Sanskrit language was a little retarded; yet the Mohammedan kings not withstanding their tyrannical measures encouraged its cultivation not only by allowing the undisturbed possession of former grants of the Hindoos; but also presenting new ones to those who most deserved it. (Sharp 1920, p. 145)

Conversely, when Lord William Bentick, governor-general to the Empire in 1828, wanted to abolish 'inhuman practices' like Sati and female infanticide, he enlisted the advice of Horace Wilson, secretary to the Hindu college of Calcutta, and an 'enlightened native', Raja Ram Mohan Roy. Both were considered knowledgeable of the opinions of the cross-sections of the Hindu community. Roy was particularly apprehensive of the public enactment of the law banning both practices lest it create deep distrust amongst the natives regarding the British avowed policy of universal tolerance and 'make them no better than the Mohammedan conquerors', who 'said the same but were trying to improve their own religion' (Muir 1915, p. 295). Roy's presentation of himself as a representative of the Hindu community, demanding, on its behalf, accountability of the new rulers to reform Hinduism, and his use of the image of the Mohammedan conqueror as a separator between the latter and the British, is made possible only through the terms of discourse set by the British. In other words, the Hindu elite's representation of the Self, and as different from the Other, the 'Musalman', embodied the religion-based communal distinction embedded in colonial discourse.

Orientalism, or a body of knowledge about the 'Orient' based on the colonial and Brahminical reading of 'Indian pasts' as essentially Hindu, was not without critical commentaries. Shahpurshah Hormasji Hodivala and Romila Thapar in contemporary India have argued for the reading of 'Indian pasts', especially in court chronicles, within their context rather than through the lens of prevalent ideologies and political agendas. Hodivala wrote a two-volume *Critical Commentary on Elliott and Dowson's History of India as Told by its Historians* (1939). In response to the historians' criticism of the chronicler Zia-ud-din-Barni (*Tarikh-e-Firozshahi*) as being 'sparing and inaccurate in his dates' regarding the Tughlaq dynasty, Hodivala cited pages from Barni's text to strike the charge (Elliott and Dowson 1871, pp. 2–3, Hodivala 1939, p. 81). He also used his knowledge of Urdu and Persian to 'correct' meanings of words in translation (see Hodivala 1939, p. 97).

Romila Thapar has echoed Hodivala in her own work but more to inform the communally charged political contexts in post-colonial India. She suggests that marking people on the basis of religion may be the work specifically of the colonial political project to define the 'Other'. But that is not necessarily the reality of all pasts. For example, the 'Hindus', in the court chronicles of the sultans, were sometimes referred to as 'indigenous population', sometimes as 'followers of non-Islamic religions', and sometimes as a 'geographical entity' (Thapar 2000, p. 979). However, religion became the basis of classification with James Mill's periodisation of Indian history as the rule of three different religious civilisations (Hindu, Muslim, and British) (Mill 1975, p. 5). Since then nationalist and colonial histories have consistently used the past to justify the present or to justify the Empire in the nineteenth century and The Hinduising of the Indian polity in the twenty-first century. The Hindu nationalist narratives now make constant references to Indian Muslims as 'pro-Pakistan', and as 'children of Muslim invaders', while translating these into pogroms against the Muslims and in erasing monuments/historical moments that signify the 'Islamic past' of a 'Hindu India' (see Basu 1993, Mazumdar and Kasturi 1994, Tambiah 1996 and Ghosh and Hussain 2002).

The colonial representation of the Self and the Other in terms of religion also contributed to the violence in the island of Ceylon, now Sri Lanka. The axes along which violence was performed here was both similar and different from the Indian context. The violence was similar in its colonial origins but different in terms of its ethno-religious nature.

Territories of Ceylon, formerly controlled by the Portuguese and the Dutch, was a British Crown colony by 1802 (see Perera 1998, p. 37). This laid the foundation for socio-cultural projects of reform. The fear that conversions to Christianity would upset a religiously diverse population had determined the separation between government and missionary work in India till 1813. But in Ceylon, at the advent of British rule, it was assumed that the Dutch had Christianised the population sufficiently to not warrant an India policy. Nevertheless, the British now encouraged missionaries to proselytise those who were 'found' to be 'nominal Christians' (non-Protestants) and also to ensure their education in English (see Peebles 1995, p. 97). This served the purpose of recruiting the 'natives' into government jobs and administering the island with local co-operation. In Ceylon, therefore, the representation/conversion of the Other also helped mark the Self (government) as Christian, without fear or favour. This meant that education was not an issue and was never raised to the level of intense debate within and outside the government in the nineteenth century as it was in India.

For the purpose of administration the British preferred the Mudaliyars as they did the Brahmins in India. The Mudaliyars were considered the 'higher grade' of the Goyigama caste, who had also monopolised religious and secular administration in a feudalistic set-up of the Kandyan kingdom. They knew English, moreover, through their membership of the Dutch Christian Society (see Peebles 1995, p. 9). The importance of the collaboration was acutely felt by the British when, in 1796, a rebellion broke out to protest the replacement of the Mudaliyars with subordinates from India (the Amildars). Thereafter, the British way of maintaining social and economic control in the island was through 'securing the loyalty and co-operation of the Mudaliyars, by placating them with land-grants, honors, and privileges' (Peebles 1995, pp. 58–9). But over time, political supremacy and technical expertise, while also diversifying governmental functions (into legislative, judicial, and police), allowed the government more social control and made it less dependent on the Mudaliyars to 'prevent' social unrest on the island (Peebles 1995, p. 120).

The brazenness of British policy first to allow Christian missionaries a monopoly over English institutions of education and then to promote the Mudaliyars as the elites in the administration, produced reactions in the form of movements towards homogenising communities along ethno-religious lines. Sinhalese Buddhists, Tamil Hindus, and the coastal Muslims engaged in projects of religious reform and cultural revivalism but within self-defined boundaries of community, while also engaging in violence as part of the process (Tambiah 1996, p. 38).The Sinhala Buddhists and Sinhala Roman Catholics clashed in 1883; the Sinhala Buddhists and Muslims collided in 1915; and in Ceylon's post-independence years, especially from 1956, the Sinhala and Tamils have been engaged in a war that has claimed innumerable lives on the island (see Tambiah 1996, p. 39).

Shubhra Sharma

Literary Works

Ali, Ahmed (1984), *Twilight in Delhi*, Karachi and London: Oxford University Press.
Kesavan, Mukul (1995), *Looking through Glass*, New York: Farrar, Straus, and Giroux.
Rushdie, Salman (1997), *The Moor's Last Sigh*, New York: Vintage International.
Sidhwa, Bapsi (1988), *Ice Candy Man*, London: Heinemann.
Singh, Khushwant (1990), *Train to Pakistan*, New York: Grove Press.
Tharoor, Shashi (2002), *Riot: A Love Story*, New York: Arcade Publishing.

Histories

Ahmed, N. (1991), *Muslim Separatism in British India: A Retrospective Study*, Rawalpindi: Firozsons Private Ltd.
Bandarage, Asoka (1983), *Colonialism in Sri Lanka: The Political Economy of the Kandyan Highlands, 1833–1886*, Berlin, New York and Amsterdam: Mouton Publishers.
Basu, Tapan (1993), *Khaki Shorts and Saffron Flags: A Critique of the Hindu Right*, New Delhi: Orient Longman.
Di Bona, Joseph (ed.) (1983), *One Teacher, One School: The Adam Reports on Indigenous Education in Nineteenth-Century India*, New Delhi: Biblia Impex Private Ltd.
Elliott, H. M. (1966), The *History of India as Told by its Own Historians (The Muhammedan Period)*, New York: AMS Press.
Elliott, H. M. and John Dowson [1871] (1974), *Tarikh-i-Firozshahi by Zia-Ud-Barni*, Lahore: Sind Sagar Academy.
Ghosh, Lipi and Monirul Hussain (2002), *Religious Minorities in South Asia*, New Delhi: Manak.
Hodivala, Shahpurshah (1939), *A Critical Commentary on Elliott and Dowson's History of India as Told by its Historians, Volumes 1 and 2*, Lahore: Islamic Book Service.
Holden, Edward S. [1893] (1975), *The Mughal Emperors of Hindustan (1398 AD to 1707)*, Delhi: Metropolitan Book Company.
Holt, P. M., Ann K. S. Lambton and Bernard Lewis (1970, 1978), *The Cambridge History of Islam*, New York and Cambridge: Cambridge University Press.
Hunter, W. (1871), *Indian Musalmans, Are they Bound in Conscience to Rebel Against the Queen?*, London: Trubner and Company.
Hunter, W. W. (1969), *The Indian Musalmans*, Delhi: Indological Book House.
Ingham, Kenneth (1956), *Reformers in India (1793–1833)*, Cambridge: Cambridge University Press.
Kaye, J. W. (1859), *Christianity in India: A Historical Narrative*, London: Smith, Elder and Co.
Keene, H. G. (1972), *A Sketch of the History of Hindustan: From the First Muslim Conquest to the fall of the Mughal Empire*, Delhi: Idarah-I-Adabiyat.
Long, J. (Rev.) (1868), *Adam's Reports on Vernacular Education in Bengal and Bihar, Submitted to Government in 1835, 1836, and 1838*, Calcutta: Home Secretariat Press.

Mazumdar, Vina and Leela Kasturi (eds) (1994), *Women and Indian Nationalism*, New Delhi: Vikas Publishing House.

Mill, James (1975), *The History of British India*, Chicago: University of Chicago Press.

Muir, Ramsay (1915), *Making of British India (1756–1858)*, London: Longman Green and Co; New York: Manchester University Press.

Nicholls, G. (1907), *The Rise and Progress of the Benares Patshalla or Sanskrit College*, Allahabad: Government Press.

Peebles, Patrick (1995), *Social Change in Nineteenth Century Ceylon*, New Delhi: Navrang Booksellers and Publishers.

Perera, Nihal (1998), *Society and Space. Colonialism, Nationalism and Postcolonial Identity in Sri Lanka*, Boulder, CO: Westview Press.

Sharp, H. (1920), *Selections from Educational Records, Part 1 (1781–1839)*, Calcutta: Superintendent Government Printing, India.

Tambiah, Stanley J. (1996), *Leveling Crowds: Ethnonationalist Conflicts and Collective Violence in South Asia*, Berkeley, Los Angeles and London: University of California Press.

Thapar, Romila (1978), *Ancient Indian Social History: Some Interpretations*, New Delhi: Orient Longman.

Thapar, Romila (2000), *Cultural Pasts: Essays in Early Indian History*, New York, Oxford: Oxford University Press.

Thapar, Romila, Harbans Mukhia, and Bipin Chandra (1969), *Communalism and the Writing of the Indian History*, Delhi, Ahemdabad, Bombay: People's Publishing House.

See also: **Historiography: South Asia**; **Pre-colonial Histories: South Asia**; **Women's Histories: South Asia**.

Religions: Southern Africa

The use of religions as a category of analysis has opened Southern Africa studies to the themes of culture, power, and the role of the subject. It is not surprising that African traditional religion, Christianities and the African independent churches have received critical attention from scholars of historical anthropology, social history, and the history of religion. Sundkler's history of Zulu Zionists (1961), Muller's ethnography of the *amaNazaretha* women (1999), and Maxwell's social history of competing rural Catholic and pentecostal Christianities in Zimbabwe (1997), have highlighted how local contexts influence the use of beliefs and religious rituals by Africans in giving meaning to everyday life. Similarly, Ranger (1986) and Comaroff (1985) have pioneered studies of colonialism, nationalism and democratisation that bring to the fore the use of religious practices among oppressed Africans. Life histories – such as Van Onselen's study of a South African sharecropper Kas Maine and Ranger's narrative of the Samkange family in Zimbabwe (1995) – add to this approach by focusing on the everyday role of religion.

Thematic studies demonstrate how consciousness and agency are structured by religion. For example, how social entrapment of whites in the Western Cape influenced the turn to an apocalyptic Christianity during apartheid (Crapanzano 1985); how Hinduism and evangelical and pentecostal Christianities gave social order to the Indian working class in Durban (Freund 1995); and how witchcraft killings in the Sekhukhuneland rural revolt of 1986 were expressions of resistance and generational struggle by African youth against apartheid and chiefly authority (Delius 1996). These themes have been woven together in Elphick and Davenport's collection *Christianity in South Africa* (1997), which also marks the entry of religion into mainstream southern African historiography.

More recent studies influenced by post-structuralism focus on the role of beliefs in ordering political representations. For example, Crais (2002) traces folk religious narratives in the Eastern Cape to posit a view of apartheid as a politics of evil. In the religious studies tradition, scholars see religions as a historically pervasive and dynamic force in society. These studies cover a range of themes: the global circulation of politico-religious ideas (see Gifford (1991) on the new religious right); the hegemony of Christianities and syncretism of religions in the region (Chidester 1992); the resilience of African traditional religions (Kiernan 1990); the place of religions and theologies from below in resistance and liberation (Hope and Young 1981); and the role of religions in fostering national identity or healing the past – as in the Truth and Reconciliation Commission (Villa-Vicencio and Verwoerd 2000). While much of the literature focuses on Christianities, comparative perspectives on world faiths are crucial to understanding the varying roles of religions in Southern Africa (see Prozesky and De Gruchy 1995).

Glen Thompson

Literary Works

Dangarembga, Tsitsi (1988), *Nervous Conditions*, Harare: Zimbabwe Publishing House.
Dangor, Achmat (1991), *Z Town Trilogy*, Johannesburg: Ravan Press.
Du Plessis, Menán (1983), *State of Fear*, London: Pandora.
Jacobs, Rayda (1997), *Eyes of the Sky*, Oxford: Heinemann.
Sam, Agnes (1989), *Jesus is Indian*, London: Women's Press.

Histories

Chidester, David (1992), *Religions in Southern Africa*, London: Routledge.
Comaroff, Jean (1985), *Body of Power, Spirit of Resistance. The Culture and History of a South African People*, Chicago: University of Chicago Press.
Crais, Clifton (2002), *Magic, State Power, and the Political Imagination in South Africa*, Cambridge: Cambridge University Press.
Crapanzano, Vincent (1985), *Waiting. The Whites of South Africa*, London: Granada.
Delius, Peter (1996), *A Lion amongst the Cattle. Reconstruction and Resistance in the Northern Transvaal*, Johannesburg: Ravan Press.
Elphick, Richard and Rodney Davenport (eds) (1997), *Christianity in South Africa. A Political, Social and Cultural History*, Cape Town: David Philip.
Freund, Bill (1995), *Insiders and Outsiders. The Indian Working Class of Durban, 1910–1990*, Pietermaritzburg: University of Natal Press.
Gifford, Paul (1991), *The New Crusaders. Christianity and the New Right in Southern Africa*, London: Pluto.
Hope, Marjorie and James Young (1981), *The South African Churches in a Revolutionary Situation*, New York: Orbis.
Kiernan, Jim (1990), *The Production and Management of Therapeutic Power in Zionist Churches within a Zulu City*, Lewiston: Edwin Mellen Press.
Maxwell, David (1997), 'The Spirit and the Scapular: Pentecostal and Catholic

Interactions in Northern Nyanga District, Zimbabwe in the 1950s and early 1960s',
Journal of Southern African Studies 23: 2, pp. 283–300.

Muller, Carol (1999), *Rituals of Fertility and the Sacrifice of Desire. Nazarite Women's Performance in South Africa*, Chicago: Chicago University Press.

Prozesky, Martin and John de Gruchy (1995), *Living Faiths in South Africa*, Cape Town: David Philip.

Ranger, Terence (1986), 'Religious Movements and Politics in Sub-Saharan Africa', *African Studies Review* 29: 2, pp. 1–69.

Ranger, Terence (1995), *Are We Not Men? The Samkange Family and African Politics in Zimbabwe, 1920–1964*, London: James Currey.

Sundkler, Bengt (1961), *Bantu Prophets in South Africa*; 2nd edn, Oxford: Oxford University Press.

Villa-Vicencio, Charles and Wilhelm Verwoerd (2000), *Looking Back Reaching Forward: Reflections on the Truth and Reconciliation Commission of South Africa*, London: Zed Books.

See also: **Historiography: Southern Africa; Missionaries: Southern Africa; Pre-colonial Histories: Southern Africa**.

Religions: West Africa

To address West African religions, we must speak of three forms: indigenous heritages, Islam and Christianity. The indigenous heritages of West African people include what Western researchers have labelled 'religious', but religion as a distinct entity within West African societies has never existed. To speak of religion in this sense is to speak of an invented and imposed cultural element. In West Africa, religion and everyday life are inextricable from each other. Within the numerous regional, ethnic and language varieties, West African heritages conceive of political and social bonds as both spiritual and mundane, visible and invisible, human and divine, all intricately interweaving unseen beings, gods and ancestors with descendants and the natural world. Historically these heritages have shifted and adapted with the movement and the interaction of people throughout this region (see Adegbola 1983, Idowu 1973, Mbiti 1975 and Brenner 1989).

There are certain distinctive features of West African religious heritages. Instead of dogmatic hierarchical cosmologies, there generally exist complexes of shifting, interactive and competing spiritual powers: gods, ancestors, antagonistic or benevolent spirits, and forces of nature. These spiritual powers or entities characteristically are not omniscient, omnipotent, infinite 'gods' – as in Christian or Islamic notions – but have rather particular realms of influence and manifestation. Worshippers are more concerned with this life than with salvation in an afterlife, and they actively constitute the existence of spiritual entities through their own agency. Human action and power are vital to the life of the gods as well as to that of communities: if a god fails to fulfil one's needs, one tries a more promising one. As a result of individual and group experiences, new gods emerge to be popular and powerful, while others fade into obscurity. Therefore, conceptions of the universe are varied, and differ between individuals, groups of worshippers and regions. The presence of the gods becomes tangible through sophisticated cultural products such as oral texts, carvings, woven cloths, masquerades, drumming, songs, ritual festivals and architecture.

The close interaction of the physical and spiritual worlds is expressed in views of personhood itself. Each person, whether reincarnated or new, arrives on Earth with his/her own destiny, forgotten at birth, and remembered through a series of lifelong experiences including initiations, divinations, personal and communal rituals, and commensurate social roles and responsibilities. Humans are the loci of communication with gods and spirits, and they don masquerades and embody the spirits of departed ancestors. Initiated people become the vehicles for gods to possess and act in the physical world. Some people are explicitly seen as dual – equally spirit and human. Spirit children torment their parents by dying young only to be reincarnated and to die once more. The widespread, entrenched conceptions of 'witches' perceive certain people as (sometimes unintentional) containers of a pernicious spirit that foments chaos in the community. Sometimes their power must be destroyed; at other times it is appealed to for its supernatural capabilities (for examples, see Hallen 1986 and Parrinder 1963).

Divination is a form of communication between spiritual entities and humans that is necessary to fulfil individual destinies, maintain communal harmony, and convey the needs of both gods and worshippers. Utilising, for instance, cowry shells, kola nuts, palm nuts, bones, water and spirit possession, diviners engage in a dialogue with the invisible for information and solutions to problems in the everyday life of communities and their members. Frequently, divination must take place for chiefs or kings to legitimise their position, for the founding of new settlements, to determine festival dates, and before wars can be fought. Divination acts as a nexus around which multiple other actions occur, including sacrifices, rituals, initiations, healing ceremonies and the making of medicines. Also, divination frequently utilises bodies of oratures (oral texts) where textual performances, in the form of an embedded discourse, provide the answer or explanation to a problem (see Bascom 1969 and Peek 1991).

Indigenous West African heritages have predominantly been oral. As a result, many of the existing historical and contemporary written works on indigenous 'religions' in Africa were produced either by non-Africans or by African adherents of Islam or Christianity, each with a tradition of writing founded on a holy book. Thus, African religious practices have frequently been described in terms of an epistemology derived from the Judaic/Christian/Islamic tradition. This often includes a lack of appreciation or oversight of the historicity of cultural practices and a prejudice in favour of its own epistemic forms to the disadvantage of the indigenous. However, the presence in West Africa of Islam and Christianity since the seventh and the fifteenth century respectively has also contributed substantially to the recording of local religious belief and practice. For example, the earliest surviving travellers' descriptions of West African societies and their beliefs and religious practices were produced by Islamic scholars like Al-Bakri (1068) and Ibn Battuta (1352) (see Hopkins and Levtzion 1981). Al-Bakri, for example, described in sympathetic detail Gana burial rites, and also recorded the hospitality accorded Muslim travellers and caravan traders from North Africa, who conducted business and prayed in the twelve mosques in the Gana capital of Kumbi.

In Gana and Kanem-Bornu from the ninth century onwards, Islam became established in many of the West African cities connected to the trans-Saharan trade. Later, Islamic reform movements contributed to a further southward expansion and a strengthening of Muslim influence in Gana's successor empires of Mali (from the thirteenth to the fifteenth century) and Songhai (from the fifteenth to the seventeenth century). Other city-states and central Sudanese trading empires like Kanem-Bornu and the Hausa states experienced a similar – at least nominal – Islamisation of their elites and practices from the eleventh century onwards. Islam also linked West Africa to the wider world. When Musa Mansah, the emperor of Mali, went on a pilgrimage to Mecca from 1324 to 1326, he established diplomatic and trade relations in North Africa, Arabia and even southern Europe. Important Islamic centres of learning were established in Timbuktu and elsewhere in the fourteenth century, and Islamic scholars contributed to contemporary discourses in the world of science, law, poetry and philosophy.

For many centuries, West African Islam coexisted with local forms of worship and was influenced by existing religious practice. First established as a religion of the cities, Islam began to penetrate rural areas more strongly in the sixteenth century, where it was often further syncretised with traditional practices. In the eighteenth century, local oppositions to such syncretism led to a number of reform movements, which often combined their attempts to purge Islam with military actions against the local establishment. Scholars and warriors inspired religious wars (*jihads*) which led to a reorganisation of states from Futa Jallon in the western Sudan (1725) to Sokoto in the east (1804). Often these revolutions led to political expansion and the further southward movement of Islam into the forest zones of West Africa (see Levtzion and Pouwels 2000).

Meanwhile, the transatlantic slave trade, which began with the arrival of Portuguese and Spanish traders in the fifteenth century, facilitated the export of West African religions. As slaves, Africans brought their beliefs to the New World, adapting them to enforced Christianity and their new surroundings. New African-derived religions retained their social and political importance by subverting and enriching Christian discourse and identifying Catholic saints with West African deities. Also, synthesised practices and beliefs from Africa were often instrumental in the organisation of maroon communities, and even in slave rebellions and revolutions (see Fernandez Olmos and Paravisini-Gebert 2003 and Fick 1990).

Few West Africans converted to Christianity during the period of transatlantic slave trade, though the end of this commerce opened West Africa to Christianity. Sierra Leone played a major role in the making of an indigenous West African Christian elite. In its capital Freetown, a group, consisting of settlers from the USA and Great Britain as well as slaves liberated at sea, lived as educated, Christian Victorian gentlemen and -women. Like Bishop Ajayi Crowther (1807–91), the head of the Niger Mission and the first African bishop in the Anglican Church, many of them became successful proselytisers. Conversion to Christianity and Islam expanded even further under colonial rule. However, in the early decades of the twentieth century, many African Christian communities rejected Western interpretations of the Bible as well as racist policies within their churches and founded 'Ethiopian' or African Initiated Churches (AICs), which often reconciled important social and spiritual concerns such as polygamy and local burial practices with Christianity (see Isichei 1995 and Peel 1968).

Under colonial rule, the study of African societies expanded in the emerging academic discipline of anthropology. It has provided the most prolific literature to study, translate, systematise, and interpret local and 'traditional' religions. However, where anthropologists simply reproduced Western epistemologies, they were in danger of transforming African cultures into Western cultural models (see Mudimbe 1988). Often anthropological research focused on hegemonic practices that explained social structures and hierarchies with the explicit or implicit aim of aiding the integration of local societies into the colonial project. In practice, such interest integrated and embedded some religious practices into the colonial state, often encouraging what Hobsbawm and Ranger have characterised as 'invented traditions', while other practices were ignored or marginalised. For example, the European focus on male leadership often overlooked practices more usually associated with women, such as spirit possession or the existence of women's spiritual-cum-political roles and offices in pre-colonial West African societies (see Oyewumi 1997 and Amadiume

1987). European attempts to centralise the colonial administration of religious and linguistic groups often encouraged or furthered the making of religious and ethnic identities, and in areas where mission education played an important role, the production of new 'traditional' identities was furthered by the translation of the Bible and the reduction of African languages to writing (see Peel 2000). Literate Africans contributed to this emergent cultural nationalism in their contributions in books and newspapers.

Despite the growth of the world religions, indigenous religious heritages have continued to be the interpretive horizon for many local forms of Islam and Christianity. For example, the protection against bad luck, evil and witchcraft, the ritual performance of oral texts, the offering of sacrifices, and the belief in spirit possession are all important elements of indigenous West African heritages, and local Muslims and Christians often incorporate these aspects into their practices (see Brenner 1993 and Corten and Marshall-Fratani 2001). There has been reciprocal influence, as Christianity and Islam have also informed local practice. For example, Yoruba neo-traditionalists have produced a *Holy Book of Odu* which transforms the history and praxes of Ifa orature and divination into an 'African bible,' to compete with the Bible and Koran (see Barber 1990).

In dialogue with and in opposition to such trends, many West African countries have also witnessed a radicalisation of monotheistic groups. Since independence in the late 1950s and 1960s, reformist Islamic brotherhoods in northern Nigeria have become increasingly popular, as have pentecostal and charismatic churches in southern Nigeria and Ghana. Often the appeal of these movements is tied to political and economic struggles within the postcolonial state or in African trans-national communities (see Gifford 1998 and Corten and Marshall-Fratani 2001). This development has encouraged the production of Islamic and Christian videos as well as books, tracts and magazines. Popular Christian media, for example, explore contemporary spiritual attitudes towards wealth, sexuality and family obligations: local religious publications such as Stephen Adu-Boahen's *How to be Sure that You will Go to Heaven* (Ghana) (1999) and Matthias Ogudu's *The Master Key(s) to Prosperity* (Nigeria) (2001) examine the spiritual tools individuals can use to protect themselves from the confusion, poverty and exploitation unleashed by Satan and his followers. Similarly, popular video dramas narrate the rise and fall of those who have harnessed Satanic powers – often through vampiric methods – and the tribulations and triumphs of born-again converts (see Meyer 1995 and Haynes 2000).

In order to avoid the unintentional elevation of literacy over orality, indigenous oratures – the ceremonies, stories and rituals of daily life – should be considered together with written literature. For example, Gelede, a ritual masquerade and artistic festival popular in many parts of coastal Benin and Nigeria, is adapted in this 1920s Gelede song to lampoon the French colonial administration for compelling taxpayers to wear their tax receipts round their necks like a pendant: 'We have accepted the paying of tax./ Look at the bead I bought for a pound from Dadi Oku./ It is a Kange bead./ For you cannot move freely in Ketu/ Except and unless you put on the frightening bead' (Lawal 1996, pp. 134–5). French colonial taxation is thus mocked as tax receipts are likened to Kange beads, and the Gelede song is modified from the original to express resistance and a sense of spiritual power.

Oral genres of ritual, praise and worship have strongly influenced West African literature, and proverbs and quotations frequently punctuate written narratives. This applies to literary works in English and African languages, and to works directed at both local and international audiences. Many popular novels explore religious themes through the juxtaposition of (modern) city life and village practices, with wealth, family, gender relations, and women's sexuality as recurring concerns. To date scholarly attention has focused mainly on the textual, social and political implications of West African popular literature (see Barber 1987 and Newell 2000), but these prominent religious and spiritual dimensions warrant close attention too. Novels such as Kwabena Antwi-Boasiako's *No Way Back* (Ghana) (2000) and the conservative Christian videos condemn all un-Christian practices, whereas the Nigerian novels by Augustus Adebayo (*My Village Captured Hitler*, 1993) and Benson Ezenwa (*The Last Order*, 1993) revel in the comic celebration of occult practices.

The polyphony of dialogues between oral, popular and internationally read texts forbids the reading of postcolonial West African literature in isolation from its vital heritages. To appreciate social change in this literature, it is vital to note that in nearly all storylines, the religious plays a significant role. Culture and religion are represented as inextricable, as are the spirit world and the physical world. To conclude with a number of well-known examples: Ben Okri's *The Famished Road* (1991) and Debo Kotun's *Abiku* (1998) draw heavily upon West African oral genres, beliefs, practices about spirit children (including Gelede) and divination texts; Chinua Achebe's *Things Fall Apart* (1958) narrates how the activities of Okonkwo and the town Umuofia negotiate the symbiotic mix of life's pragmatics and spiritual matters; Ama Ata Aidoo's *Anowa* (1965) relies on the concepts of gods, priestesses, charms, oracles and witches; and Wole Soyinka's *Ake: The Years of Childhood* (1981) presents youthful images and experiences of Yoruba religious life under colonial rule. A wonderful moment occurs early on when the young Soyinka looks upwards at the stained-glass church window and, in a humorous misunderstanding, conflates three Christian saints with the Yoruba *egungun*, ancestral masquerades. The entire memoir swims with incidents involving matters of indigenous practices, Christianity and Islam, all bumping into one another in the youthful adventures of a child trying to make sense of it all.

Insa Nolte and K. Noel Amherd

Literary Works

Achebe, Chinua (1958), *Things Fall Apart*, London: Heinemann.
Adebayo, A. (1993), *My Village Captured Hitler*, Ibadan: Spectrum Books.
Adu-Boahen, S. (1999), *How to be Sure that You will Go to Heaven*, Kumasi: UGC.
Aidoo, Ama Ata [1965] (1987), *The Dilemma of a Ghost and Anowa*, Harlow: Longman.
Antwi-Boasiako, K. (2000), *No Way Back*, Agona: Anima Publications.
Ezenwa, B. (1993), *The Last Order*, Abuja: Totan Publishers.
Kotun, D. (1998), *Abiku*, Pasadena, CA: Nepotist Books.
Lawal, Babatunde (1996), *The Gelede Spectacle*, Seattle, WA: University of Washington Press.
Newell, S. (2000), *Ghanaian Popular Fiction. 'Thrilling Discoveries in Conjugal Life' and Other Tales*, Oxford: James Currey.
Ogudu, M. (2001), *The Master Key(s) to Prosperity*, Lagos: Rowfuns Printers.
Okri, Ben (1991), *The Famished Road*, London: Jonathan Cape.
Soyinka, Wole (1981), *Ake: The Years of Childhood*, New York: Vintage Books.

Histories

Adegbola, E. A. A. (ed.) (1983), *Traditional Religion in West Africa*, Ibadan: Daystar Press; Accra: Asempa Publishers.
Amadiume, I. (1987), *Male Daughters, Female Husbands: Gender and Sex in an African*

Society, London: Zed Books.

Barber, K. (1987), 'Popular Arts in Africa' in *African Studies Review* 30: 3, pp. 1–78.

Barber, K. (1990), 'Discursive Strategies in the texts of Ifá and in the 'Holy Book of Odù' of the African Church of Òrúnmìlà', in K. Barber and P. de Moraes Farias (eds), *Self-Assertion and Brokerage. Early Cultural Nationalism in West Africa*, Birmingham: Birmingham University African Studies Series, pp. 196–224.

Bascom, W. (1969), *Ifa Divination: Communication between Gods and Men in West Africa*, Bloomington, IN: Indiana University Press.

Brenner, L. (1989), '"Religious" Discourses in and about Africa', in K. Barber and P. F. de Moraes Farias (eds), *Discourse and its Disguises: The Interpretation of African Oral Texts*, Birmingham: Centre of West African Studies, pp. 87–102.

Brenner, L. (1993), *Muslim Identity and Social Change in Sub-Saharan Africa*, London: Hurst.

Corten, A. and R. Marshall-Fratani (eds) (2001), *Between Babel and Pentecost*, London: Hurst.

Fernandez Olmos, M. and L. Paravisini-Gebert (2003), *Creole Religions of the Caribbean: An Introduction from Vodou and Santeria to Obeah and Espiritismo*, New York: New York University Press.

Fick, C. (1990), *The Making of Haiti: The Saint Domingue Revolution from Below*, Knoxville, TN: University of Tennessee Press.

Gifford, P. (1998), *African Christianity. Its Public Role*, London: Hurst.

Hallen, B. (1986), *Knowledge, Belief, and Witchcraft*, Stanford, CA: Stanford University Press.

Hallen, B. (2000), *The Good, the Bad, and the Beautiful: Discourse about Values in Yoruba Culture*, Bloomington, IN: Indiana University Press.

Haynes. J. (ed.; revised edition 2000), *Nigerian Video*, Athens, OH: Ohio University Center for International Studies.

Hobsbawm, E. and T. Ranger (eds) [1983] (1992), *The Invention of Tradition*, Cambridge: Cambridge University Press.

Hopkins, J. F. P. and N. Levtzion (eds) [1981] (2000), *Corpus of Early Arabic Sources for West African History*, Cambridge: Cambridge University Press.

Idowu, E. B. (1973), *African Traditional Religion. A Definition*, London: SCM Press.

Isichei, E. (1995), *A History of Christianity in Africa: From Antiquity to the Present*, London: SPCK.

Levtzion, N. and R. L. Pouwels (eds) (2000), *The History of Islam in Africa*, Athens, OH: Ohio University Press.

Mbiti, J. S. [1975] (1991), *Introduction to African Religion*, Oxford: Heinemann.

Meyer, B. (1995), '"Delivered from the Powers of Darkness". Confessions of Satanic Riches in Christian Ghana', *Africa* 65: 2, pp. 236–55.

Mudimbe, V. Y. (1988), *The Invention of Africa: Gnosis, Philosophy, and the Order of Knowledge*, Bloomington, IN: Indiana University Press.

Newell, S. (ed.) (2002), *Readings in African Popular Fiction*, Bloomington, IN: Indiana University Press; London: James Currey.

Oyewumi, O. (1997), *The Invention of Women: Making an African Sense of Western Gender Discourse*, Minneapolis, MN: University of Minnesota Press.

Parrinder, G. (1963), *Witchcraft: European and African*, London: Faber and Faber.

Peek, P. M. (ed.) (1991), *African Divination Systems*, Bloomington, IN: Indiana University Press.

Peel, J. D. Y. (1968), *Aladura: A Religious Movement among the Yoruba*, London: Oxford
    University Press.
Peel, J. D. Y. (2000), *Religious Encounter and the Making of the Yoruba*, Bloomington, IN:
    Indiana University Press.

See also: **Anti-colonialism and Resistance: West Africa; Islam; Pre-colonial Histories:
West Africa; Slavery: West Africa.**

Riel's Métis Rebellion

Following Canada's confederation in 1867, Prime Minister John A. MacDonald sought
westward expansion into the lands held by the Hudson's Bay Company so as to assure economic prosperity and political vitality in the face of American expansionism. This put him
into direct conflict with the Métis, a group of mixed French and Native ancestry which
had occupied Rupert's land (present-day Manitoba) for generations. Faced with unscrupu-
lous land speculators, increasing white settlement, administrative delays, and indifference
from Ottawa, the Métis feared that union with Canada would undermine their land settlement claims, their traditional buffalo-hunting lifestyles, and their attempts at self-governance. In 1869 an alliance of Métis and Native leaders attacked and seized control over Fort
Garry (present-day Winnipeg) and set up a provisional government. Non-Métis refusal to
recognise Louis Riel's authority exacerbated tensions which culminated in the execution
of Thomas Scott, a Canadian settler, for insubordination in 1870. While this was received
in Ontario as an act of treason demanding swift retribution, considerable sympathy
emerged from Quebec for the Catholic, French-speaking insurgents. By the time Prime
Minister MacDonald sent federal troops to control the Red River Rebellion, Riel had fled
to Dakota and the resistance movement had dissipated.

Manitoba entered confederation in July 1870, with certain provisions being made for
the Métis, including land grants, protections for the French language, and Catholic
instruction. Riel remained in exile in the United States until 1885, when he returned to
Canada and petitioned Ottawa for adequate Métis representation in the Canadian parliament, their control over natural resources, and a fairer allocation of lands. Prime Minister
MacDonald's unwillingness to meet these demands escalated tensions and Riel proclaimed
a provisional government in March of 1885. Métis attacks at Duck Lake, Battleford, and
Frog Lake incited the federal government to send 5,000 militia, via a still-incomplete
Canadian Pacific Railway, who eventually captured Métis headquarters at Batoche after a
four-day siege. Cree Chiefs Poundmaker and Big Bear were captured and served prison
terms, while Riel was found guilty of treason and hanged in Regina on 16 November 1885.

Dominic Beneventi

Literary Works

Bowsfield, Hartwell (ed.) (1988), *Louis Riel: Selected Readings*, Toronto: Copp Clark Pitman.
Coulter, John (1962), *Riel: A Play in Two Parts*, Toronto: Ryerson Press.
Wiebe, Rudy (1973), *The Temptations of Big Bear*, Toronto: McClelland and Stewart.
Woodcock, George (1976), *Gabriel Dumont and the Northwest Rebellion*, Toronto:
    Playwrights Co-op.

Histories

Adams, Howard (1989), *Prison of Grass: Canada from a Native Point of View*, Saskatoon: Fifth House Publishers.
Beal, Bob and Rod MacLeod (eds) (1994), *Prairie Fire: The 1885 North-West Rebellion*, Toronto: McClelland and Stewart.
Bowsfield, Hartwell (1969), *Louis Riel: Rebel of the Western Frontier or Victim of Politics and Prejudice?*, Toronto: Copp Clark.
Bumsted, J. M. (1996), *The Red River Rebellion*, Watson and Dweyer Publishing.
Flanagan, Thomas (1996), *Louis 'David' Riel: 'Prophet of the New World'*, Toronto: University of Toronto Press.
Friesen, Gerald (1984), *The Canadian Prairies: A History*, Toronto: University of Toronto Press.
Stonechild, Blair and Bill Waiser (1997), *Loyal till Death: Indians and the North-West Rebellion*, Calgary: Fifth House Publishers.

See also: **Big Bear**; **Historiography: Canada**; **Land: Canada**; **Native Reservations**.

Rodney, Walter

Walter Rodney was born in Georgetown, the capital of British Guiana (now Guyana), on 23 March 1942. His mother was a seamstress and his father a tailor. The brilliance of this working-class youngster earned him scholarships, firstly to Queens College, British Guiana, then to the University of the West Indies (UWI) in Jamaica. In 1963, Rodney graduated with a first-class degree in history, and this earned him a scholarship to the School of Oriental and African Studies in London, where he obtained a Ph.D. on slavery on the Upper Guinea Coast. After graduation, Rodney proceeded to Tanzania to lecture until 1968, when he took up a lectureship at the UWI in Jamaica. There he worked on redefining the relationship between theory and practice by engaging in an activist-intellectual political practice he labelled 'groundings', an ideological discourse with grassroots groups such as the Rastafarians.

For Rodney, the role of intellectuals was to use their skills to assist the peoples' struggles. C. L. R. James observed that Rodney essentially used 'the revolutionary ideas, perspectives, and analysis of the Caribbean as something natural, normal, fixed, written, and beyond dispute' (Alpers and Fontane 1982, p. 133). One of the most significant events in Rodney's intellectual trajectory was the Black Writer Congress in Canada in 1968, where he established his reputation as a politically engaged historian.

The Black Power movement in the 1960s had been flourishing, and fearing Rodney's black consciousness-raising, the Jamaican government banned him from travelling after the Canada conference. There were violent protests on Rodney's behalf in Jamaica, led by UWI students in Kingston, who fought the police, destroyed property, blocked roads, and were tear-gassed by the police. The widespread reaction to his ban in Jamaica, London and Canada helped throw him into the vanguard of the pan-African and Caribbean liberation movement.

Rodney's ideas have had an influence on Caribbean literature and popular culture from around the late 1960s and early 1970s, when increasing numbers of songs of political protest emerged from Jamaica, celebrating African civilisation. Academics used the opportunity to demonstrate the need for further decolonization through the development of postcolonial literary texts and writings. Several new periodicals sprang up: *Tapia* and *Moko Jumbie* (Trinidad), and *Abeng* and *Savacou* (Jamaica). The names of these journals were drawn from the experiences of enslaved blacks in Caribbean. Unable to re-enter Jamaica, Rodney went briefly to Cuba, and then to Tanzania where he taught until 1974. Between 1969 and 1974 his work looked at issues such as race and class, theory and practice, history and revolution, political action and economic development, leadership, underdevelopment and development, colonisation and independence, and imperialism and freedom.

Another aspect of Rodney's legacy is his influence on the historiography of Africa. In the seminal work *How Europe Underdeveloped Africa*, he examines the patterns and impact of European activity in Africa. He attributes Africa's underdevelopment, which had been advanced as evidence of African 'racial' inferiority, to exploitation by European nations. In this process he provided a new theoretical launch pad for African scholars to counter racist, Eurocentric positions.

Rodney was primarily concerned with the condition of Africans in the Caribbean, and links with Africa. He also grappled with the class dynamics of African-Caribbean society; and interrogated the relationship between the African working class and the African political elite, and between the African and the East Indian working class. Thus, while he embraced Black Power ideology, he did so recognising that the Caribbean possessed a complex racial mix. As an avowed Pan-Africanist with a commitment to the working class, Rodney articulated the need for solidarity between Africans and Indians. Critiquing issues of empire and capitalism, his work also examined local political elites in Africa and the Caribbean. Rodney tried to understand why the decolonisation movement was in itself a recolonisation initiative. He acknowledged that the process of decolonisation would be incomplete if the fight focused solely on the colonial powers and imperialists but ignored 'their indigenous lackeys' (Rodney, Hill and Dodson 1990, p. 34). This Caribbean intellectual therefore believed that it was necessary to have the people develop an anti-neocolonial consciousness in addition to an anti-colonial consciousness.

In July 1979, Rodney was arrested and charged, along with several others in Guyana, for arson after two government offices were torched. Following continuous harassment by the Guyana state machinery, he was assassinated on 13 June 1980 on a Georgetown street when a bomb planted in a walkie talkie exploded.

                                                                        Cleve Scott

Literary Works

Huntley, Eric (ed.) (1980), '*And Finally They Killed Him*': *Speeches and Poems at a Memorial Rally for Walter Rodney, 1942–1980*, Ile-Ife: Positive Review Nigeria.
Huntley, Eric (ed.) (1992), *Walter Rodney: Poetic Tributes*, London: Bogle-L'Ouverture Press.

Histories

Alpers, Edward A. and Pierre-Michel Fontane (eds) (1982), *Walter Rodney: Revolutionary and Scholar: A Tribute*, Los Angeles: Centre for Afro-American Studies and African Studies Center, University of California.
Creighton, Al (2000), 'The Walter Rodney factor in West Indian Literature,' *Stabroek News*, 18 June 2000. Available at www. guyanacaribbeanpolitics.com

Hinds, David (2000), 'Review of Walter Rodney's *Intellectual and Political Thought* by Professor Rupert Lewis', 25 March. Available at DHinds6106@aol.com on brc-news list.

Kwayana, Eusi (1988), *Walter Rodney*, Georgetown: Working People's Alliance.

Lewis, Rupert Charles (1998), *Walter Rodney's Intellectual and Political Thought*, Kingston: University of the West Indies Press.

Rodney, Walter [1972] (1988), *How Europe Underdeveloped Africa*, London: Bogle L'Ouverture Publications.

Rodney, Walter, Robert Hill and Howard Dodson (1990), *Walter Rodney Speaks: The Making of an African Intellectual*, Trenton, NJ: Africa World Press.

See also **Anti-colonialism and Resistance: Caribbean**; **James, C. L. R.**; **Pan-Africanism**.

Rushdie Affair

On 26 September 1988, Salman Rushdie published his novel *The Satanic Verses*. In the months that followed, major demonstrations and riots, particularly in India, Pakistan, South Africa and Britain, were prompted by what was perceived as the novel's anti-Islamicism. On 14 February 1989, Ayatollah Khomeini of Iran proclaimed a *fatwa* (death sentence) on Rushdie. For the next decade, Rushdie lived under police protection. He was criticised for giving his novel the title of a contested Islamic text: there are real 'satanic verses' which Muhammad first included, and then excised from the Qu'ran because he believed them to be inspired by the Devil.

In the banned verses, as in Rushdie's fictionalisation of them, three pagan women (Al-lat, Uzza and Manat) seek and are granted Muhammad's admission of their status as goddesses. In addition to invoking these disputed verses, Rushdie jokingly renames Muhammad 'Mahound' (a name which implies devil rather than god), and Mecca 'Jahilia' (meaning 'ignorance'). He also describes a brothel in which the prostitutes take the names of Muhammad's wives. At issue was whether an author had the right to satirise faith, and whether Rushdie was joking or blaspheming Islam. Daniel Pipes observed that, 'Several aspects of the Rushdie incident were unprecedented. Never before had a government picked a fight with a private individual in a foreign country. Never had a book been the cause and the source of an international diplomatic crisis. Never before had censorship driven a conflict between states' (Pipes 1990, p. 1).

The *fatwa* against Rushdie reversed diplomatic negotiations between the West and Iran begun in the wake of the 1988 war with Iraq; it also caused the Western hostages in Lebanon to be held indefinitely, even though in the weeks preceding the *fatwa*, it seemed likely that they would be released. It deleteriously and dramatically affected international trade. Hitoshi Igarishi, the Japanese translator of *The Satanic Verses*, was one of twenty-two people who died as a result of the novel's publication. The novel and the *fatwa* provoked a storm of response amongst both writers and political advocates of freedom of expression. Often debates were carried out in open letters in the press; often Rushdie was a participant. Among the literary authors who wrote letters in support of Rushdie were Harold Pinter, Günter Grass, Norman Mailer and Margaret Atwood. Among those who criticised him was John le Carré.

Rushdie's cause was taken up by Article 19 (an organisation formed in 1986 to support freedom from censorship in accordance with Article 19 of the International Covenant of

Civil and Political Rights); the result was the Rushdie Defence Campaign. In the 1990s, when Rushdie began to speak in the USA, Britain, Denmark, Germany, Canada and elsewhere, he became a de facto ambassador for the freedom of speech. What the affair brought out was the urgent need to move beyond the easy polarities of fundamentalism and liberalism. On 24 September 1998, the United Kingdom and Iran issued a joint statement bringing the *fatwa* to an end. As Rushdie himself notes, the effect of this statement was gradual: 'As they say in the movies: *(slow fade)*' (Rushdie 2002, p. 258).

Antje M. Rauwerda

Literary Works

Caute, David (1998), *Fatima's Scarf*, London: Totterdown.
Kureishi, Hanif (1995), *The Black Album*, London: Faber and Faber.
Rushdie, Salman (1988), *The Satanic Verses*, London: Jonathan Cape.
Smith, Zadie (2000), *White Teeth*, London: Penguin.

Histories

Appignanesi, Lisa and Sara Maitland (1989), *The Rushdie File*, London: Fourth Estate.
Pipes, Daniel (1990), *The Rushdie Affair: The Novel, the Ayatollah, and the West*, New York: Birch Lane. Available at wysiwyg://10/http://danielpipes.org/books/rushdiechap.php
Rushdie, Salman (1991), *Imaginary Homelands: Essays and Criticism 1981–1991*, London: Granta.
Rushdie, Salman (2002), *Step Across this Line: Collected Nonfiction 1991–2002*, Toronto: Knopf.
Ruthven, Malise (1991), *A Satanic Affair: Salman Rushdie and the Wrath of Islam*, London: Hogarth.

See also: **Black Britain; Islam; Religions: South Asia.**

S

San

The San, or 'Bushmen', have the status of indigenes and thrived throughout southern Africa before the advent of European settlers (from 1652) or the encroachment on their hunting fields by African tribes (from about 500 AD). Before the arrival of Europeans there were thought to be some 150,000 to 300,000 San living throughout southern Africa.

Historians and anthropologists have debated the distinctness of the San from the Khoikhoi. The hunter-gathers were called 'San (Saan)' by the Khoikhoi or 'Hottentot' pastoralists. 'San' and 'Khoi' derive from 'Khoisan', the Nama 'Khoi' meaning 'man' and 'san' meaning 'men' in the language of the hunter-gatherers. Alternative names include /Kham-Ka-!k'e, /Kamka!e, /Xam-Ka-!k'e. This nomenclature is often unstable and contested, and the term 'Bushmen' ('Bossiesmans', 'Bosjesaman') has a pejorative connotation. Subject to competition by Nguni-speaking tribes and colonial settlers, a bitter war of extermination was waged against the San whose nomadic life-style was seen a threat to conventional modes of agriculture and stock rearing. During the eighteenth century expansion of numbers of Dutch settlers at the Cape, armed *trekboers* fought the San for water and grazing. The end of the rule of the Dutch East India Company in 1795 and the assumption of power by the British in 1806 saw commandos being replaced by a policy of 'pacification'. Those San who had survived were to be incorporated into a labouring class, and by the early 1870s their communities were impoverished and depleted.

One of the best documented of the Northern Cape San groups was the /Xam, six of whom were released from prison to be interviewed and recorded by German philologist W. H. I. Bleek (1827–75), librarian to Sir George Grey, and friend of William Colenso and his sister-in-law Lucy Lloyd (1834–1914). The Bleek and Lloyd archive, consolidated and extended by Dorothea Bleek (1873–1948), represents what survives of the /Xam language.

It is estimated that today about 50,000 San remain, some of whom are involved in asserting their land rights and contesting their commodification by academics, museums and the tourist industry. Many San who were used as trackers by the South African National Defence Force fighting anti-apartheid forces in Angola in the 1970s and 1980s are still waiting for the jobs and housing they were promised.

Shane Moran

Literary Works

Head, Bessie (1971), *Maru*, London: Heinemann.
Kendall, Edward (1834), *The English Boy at the Cape: An Anglo-African Story*, 3 vols, London: Whittaker.
La Guma, Alex (1972), *In the Fog of the Season's End*, London: Heinemann.
Pringle, Thomas (1834), *African Sketches*, London: E. Moxton.
Van der Post, Laurens (1972), *A Story like the Wind*, London: The Hogarth Press.
Watson, Stephen (1991), *Return of the Moon. Versions from the /Xam*, Cape Town: Carrefour Press.

Histories

Bank, Andrew (1997), 'The Great Debate and the Origins of South African Historiography', *Journal of African History* 38, pp. 261–81.
Gordon, Robert J. (1992), *The Bushman Myth: The Making of a Namibian Underclass*, Oxford: Westville Press.
South African Historical Journal (1996), Special Issue on the Khoisan in South African History, 35.
Stow, George W. (1905), *The Native Races of South Africa: A History of the Intrusion of the

Hottentots and Bantu into the Hunting Grounds of the Bushmen, the Aborigines of the Country, ed. George McCall Theal, London: Sonnenschein.

Wilson, Monica and Leonard Thompson (eds) (1969), *The Oxford History of South Africa, Volume 1*, Oxford: Oxford University Press.

See also: **Coloured Southern Africa; Pre-colonial Histories: Southern Africa; Slavery: Southern Africa**.

Secessionism: South Asia

With the possible exception of Pakistan's separation from a united India in 1947, the history of secessionism in South Asia can also be read as the history of the centralisation of the postcolonial state and of the triumph of a majoritarian approach to the task of nation-building. The creation of Pakistan, too, might not be an exception if one accepts the thesis of some historians that it was the refusal of Jawaharlal Nehru to accept a confederal, but united, India that made the Partition of the country inevitable. In postcolonial India, the newly independent state was almost immediately confronted with secessionist demands from regions and groups which had historically been outside the reach of Indian pre-colonial state formations and had been incorporated into the British Raj through a combination of military force and blandishment. Prime among these groups were the Nagas, Manipuris and Mizos. Armed insurgencies occurred, which the Indian state sought to crush through tough military means, thereby exacerbating the sense of alienation and distance. In Kashmir, popular resentment among Muslims over their Hindu king's decision to accede to India led to a latent secessionism that would be fanned later by the Indian government's attempts to strangle the region's constitutionally-guaranteed autonomy, by its repression, and by Pakistan's efforts in the 1990s to arm and train insurgent groups. The autonomous nature of the secessionist movement has been disputed by India, which claims Pakistan alone is responsible for its sustenance; however, the near total boycott of elections organised by the Indian state in the Kashmir valley in 1996 and 1999 suggests alienation and resentment were indeed very widespread.

In the 1990s, the Indian state was confronted by a new secessionist movement in the oil-rich province of Assam; however, this period also coincided with a weakening of militant movements elsewhere in the north-eastern region, thanks in part to the muscular use of the army and paramilitaries, as well as the initiation of a dialogue process with the principal Naga group. In Punjab, the Indian state used overwhelming force, including manufacturing disappearances and custodial killings, to crush a poorly organised but deadly movement among a section of Sikhs. They were driven as much by the remembrance of an earlier promise of a Sikh homeland as by brutal repression, including the massacre of 3,000 coreligionists in Delhi in November 1984, into demanding an independent 'Khalistan'.

India was not the only South Asian country to be confronted with secessionism. In 1971, Pakistan lost its eastern province, now Bangladesh, when Bengali nationalists, with the armed backing of India, liberated themselves in the teeth of brutal military suppression. The region was once the mainstay of the pro-Pakistani Muslim League; but the refusal of West Pakistan's political and military elites to share power with the East made its secession inevitable. In Sri Lanka, the officially sponsored ethnic assertiveness of the majority Sinhala community throughout the 1980s – which manifested itself, inter alia, in the 1983 massacre of Tamils in Colombo – spawned what was easily the subcontinent's most powerful secessionist movement among the country's Tamil population. Led by the Liberation Tigers of Tamil Eelam and supported initially by India, the struggle for a Tamil homeland, or 'Eelam' unleashed a civil war that took the lives of thousands, combatants and civilians alike.

Siddharth Varadarajan

Literary Works

Ali, Agha Shahid (1998), *The Country without a Post Office*, New York: W. W. Norton.
Mistry, Rohinton (1992), *Such a Long Journey*, New York: Random House.
Ondaatje, Michael (2001), *Anil's Ghost*, London: Picador.
Osman, Shaukat (1996), *God's Adversary and Other Stories*, trans. Osman Jamal, New Delhi: Penguin.
Sivanandan, A. (1997), *When Memory Dies*, London: Arcadia Books.

Histories

Baruah, Sanjib (1999), *India against Itself: Assam and the Politics of Nationality*, Philadelphia, PA: University of Pennsylvania Press.
Ganguly, Rajat and Ian Macduff (eds) (2003), *Ethnic Conflict and Secessionism in South and Southeast Asia*, New Delhi: Sage Publications.
Joshi, Manoj (1999), *Lost Rebellion: Kashmir in the 1990s*, New Delhi: Penguin Books.
Kumar, Ram Narayan and Laxmi Murthy (2002), *Four Years of the Ceasefire Agreement between the Government of India and the National Socialist Council of Nagalim: Promises and Pitfalls*, New Delhi: Civil Society Initiative on the Naga Peace Process.
Nag, Sajal (1999), *Nationalism, Separatism and Secessionism*, New Delhi: Manohar.
Sisson, Richard and Leo E. Rose (1990), *War and Secession: Pakistan, India and the Creation of Bangladesh*, Berkeley, CA: University of California Press.

See also: **Bangladesh: 1971; Border Disputes: South Asia; Jinnah, Mohammed Ali; Kashmir Dispute; Nehru, Jawaharlal; Sri Lankan Civil War**.

Senghor, Léopold Sédar

Léopold Sédar Senghor was born in Joal, Senegal in 1906, and died in France in 2001. In his youth, Senghor learned about his indigenous culture, which he later celebrated in poems. This early teaching probably accounts for his strong sense of a pre-colonial African civilisation, a certitude that neither his education in local French schools nor at the Libermann Seminary in Dakar altered. He ultimately joined a secular school. Senghor excelled in his studies, and was granted a scholarship to study literature –a select field – in France, a privilege bestowed for the first time on a black African pupil. In Paris, Senghor attended the prestigious Lycée Louis-Le-Grand, where he studied alongside political and literary personalities to be. In 1935 Senghor passed the *agrégation*, the highly competitive examination for professors, becoming the first African to achieve this.

In Paris, along with Aimé Césaire (Martinique) and Léon-Gontran Damas (Guyana),

Senghor founded the Negritude movement. His discovery of works by the Harlem Renaissance writers (Claude McKay and Langston Hughes) and of ethnographic works (by Leo Frobenius, Maurice Delafosse and Robert Delavignette) provided him with the credibility he needed to expose and defend his conviction that, far from being a *tabula rasa*, Africa had a civilisation of its own, and the black man his own soul. Along with essays, Senghor published poetry and engaged in politics, becoming deputy to the National Assembly.

Influenced by Mahatma Gandhi, Senghor was an advocate for the peaceful way. The French saw him as a convenient interlocutor prone to conciliation rather than conflict. He obtained independence for Senegal in 1960, became its first president and was re-elected several times until his resignation in 1980. He was the first African leader to leave of his own volition, avoiding bloodshed. In 1984, Senghor was elected to the Académie Française in recognition of his literary work.

Senghor's legacy is a controversial one; his intention to prove the black man's worthiness translated into an acceptance of Western clichés which characterise blacks as more emotional than rational. Rather than challenge preconceptions, he turned them into positive traits. Criticisms of his conception of Negritude, and his maintaining Senegal under French influence are many. Senghor's life and work are cornerstones and landmarks; he trod where no black man had before in the French system. The negative consequence of this is that he is perceived as too well-assimilated. Anglophone postcolonial writers like Wole Soyinka and Ezekiel Mphahlele criticised the abstract nature of his ideology arguing that it did not provide any concrete policy to free Africans from colonial oppression. However, as an erudite and articulate African, he instilled a sense of pride into many adherents.

Marie Hélène K. Tessio

Literary Works

Senghor, Léopold Sédar [1964] (1976), *Selected Poems of L. S. Senghor*, trans. J. Reed and C. Wake, London: Heinemann.
Senghor, Léopold Sédar (1965), *Prose and Poetry*, trans. J. Reed and C. Wake, London: Oxford University Press.
Senghor, Léopold Sédar (1991), *The Collected Poetry*, trans. M. Dixon, Charlottesville, VA: University Press of Virginia.

Histories

Hymans, Jacques Louis (1971), *Léopold Sédar Senghor: An Intellectual Biography*, Edinburgh: Edinburgh University Press.
Moore, Gerald (1980), *Twelve African Writers*, Bloomington, IN: Indiana University Press.
Mphahlele, Ezekiel (1974), *The African Image*, New York: Praeger Publishers Inc.
Ogede, Ode (1992), 'Negritude and the African Writer of English Expression: Ayi Kwei Armah', *Kunapipi* 14: 1, pp. 128–41.
Soyinka, Wole (1976), *Myth, Literature and the African World*, Cambridge: Cambridge University Press.
Spleth, Janice (1985), *Léopold Sédar Senghor*, Boston, MA: Twaine Publishers.

Vaillant, Janet G. (1990), *Black, French, and African: A Life of Léopold Sédar Senghor*, Cambridge, MA: Harvard University Press.

See also: **Anti-colonialism and Resistance: West Africa; Negritude; Pan-Africanism**.

Sinhala Only Bill

On 15 June 1956, eight years after independence, the Sinhala Only Bill was passed, declaring Sinhala the sole national language of Sri Lanka (then Ceylon). It was the culmination of a massive campaign that drew upon socialist and populist sentiment to unite the Sinhalese-speaking majority who were excluded from senior political and administrative positions that required fluency in English. It also served as a platform for those who wished to dismantle the pre-independence settlement that provided parity of status for Sinhala and Tamil after independence. The campaign was championed by S. W. R. D. Bandaranaike – an Oxford-educated, Sinhalese Catholic belonging to the incumbent United National Party (UNP). Bandaranaike left the UNP, converted to Buddhism, donned national dress, and – under the banner of the newly formed Sri Lanka Freedom Party (SLFP) – promised to deliver 'Sinhala Only' in twenty-four hours.

The SLFP and its allies gained a massive victory in the April 1956 general election when Bandaranaike became prime minister, ousting Sir John Kotelawala who had promised parity of status for Sinhala and Tamil – although he too had changed his party's language policy to 'Sinhala Only' prior to the elections. Upon election, Bandaranaike recognised the need to acknowledge the rights of the significant Tamil minority and sought to introduce legislation allowing for reasonable use of Tamil in the north and east. This provoked a *satyagraha* (peaceful protest) led by Professor F. R. Jayasuriya against giving concessions to the Tamils. On 5 June 1956, the Tamil Federal Party led by S. J. V. Chelvanayagam staged a *satyagraha* against 'Sinhala Only' which was disrupted by Buddhist clergy from the Eksath Bhikku Peramuna (United Bhikku Front) opposed to the 'reasonable use of Tamil' clause. The Federal Party also campaigned to remove the Sinhala word 'Sri' on motor vehicles, which led to a counter-campaign in the south to tar Tamil letters on signposts. Bandaranaike initiated talks with the Federal Party, producing the Bandaranaike-Chelvanayagam (B-C) Pact on 26 July 1957. They agreed to make Tamil the language of administration in the north and east, to review the 1948–9 disenfranchisement of Estate Tamils, and to create regional councils for the north and east. In response, J. R. Jayawardene – the leader of the UNP – organised a protest march to Kandy. The Buddhist clergy also launched a *satyagraha* opposite the prime minister's residence on 9 April 1958, refusing to move till he tore up the pact. The following month saw the first major riots between Sinhalese and Tamils in which over 1,000 Tamils were killed; and the country was put under emergency rule.

On 26 September 1959 Bandaranaike was assassinated by Somarama Thero, an aggrieved Buddhist monk, and his widow, Sirimavo Bandaranaike, became the world's first woman prime minister after two elections in March and July 1960. In 1972 the SLFP under the premiership of Mrs Bandaranaike presented a republican constitution that entrenched the edicts of 'Sinhala Only' with enactments that made Buddhism the state religion and Sinhala the official language. It was not until 1987, under a UNP government led by J. R. Jayawardene, that Tamil too was made a national language – a policy implemented by his successor Ranasinghe Premadasa.

The Sinhala Only Bill is retrospectively read as the prime piece of political legislation that triggered the call for a separate state by Tamils.

Minoli Salgado

Literary Works

Goonewardene, James (1995), *A Tribal Hangover*, New Delhi: Penguin India.
Proctor, Raja (1981), *Waiting for Surabiel*, Queensland: University of Queensland Press.
Selvadurai, Shyam (1994), *Funny Boy*, London: Jonathan Cape.
Sivanandan, A. (1997), *When Memory Dies*, London: Arcadia.

Histories

De Silva, K. M. (1981), *A History of Sri Lanka*, London: Hurst.
Jeyaratnam Wilson, A. (1994), *S. J. V. Chelvanayagam and the Crisis of Sri Lankan Tamil Nationalism 1947–1977*, London: Hurst.
Spencer, Jonathan (ed.) (1990), *Sri Lanka: History and the Roots of Conflict*, London: Routledge.
Wriggins, Howard [1960] (1990), *Ceylon: Dilemmas of a New Nation*, Princeton, NJ: Princeton University Press.

See also: **Communism: South Asia; Religions: South Asia; Secessionism: South Asia; Sri Lankan Civil War; Years of Terror.**

Slave Trade: East Africa

Like West Africa, East Africa experienced its own much older slave trade which sent slaves to the Arabian peninsula and the Persian Gulf region, where they served as sailors, soldiers and workers in the salt marshes of Iraq. The vast majority of them, however, ended up as domestic slaves who provided various forms of services in rich households. The East African Indian Ocean slave traffic was much smaller in volume in contrast to the transatlantic slave trade of West Africa. For one thing there was a local abundance of slaves in Asia and hence the demand (for instance, in India) remained rather low. More importantly, however, trade in East Africa was very much focused on ivory and gold. By the latter part of the eighteenth century and certainly by the beginning of the nineteenth century, the East African trade (which had been driven by the demand for ivory) shifted to slaves to satisfy growing French and Arab demand. The slave suppliers were drawn from among the upcountry Africans and Arabs and coastal Swahili. One of the most well-known of these Swahili Arab slave traders was Hamed Muhammad, nicknamed Tippu Tip, who established an important base west of Lake Tanganyika.

Three factors led to the expansion of the East African slave trade. The first had to do with Brazilian traders (in order to avoid the activities of the anti-slavery squadron in West Africa) turning to the Zambezi valley and the Portuguese colony of Mozambique for slaves. The second reason was related to the high death rates on the sugar planta-tions in Mauritius and Réunion which led the French to seek slaves from Mozambique as well as Zanzibar and Kilwa. The final reason which transformed the volume of this trade had to do with the establishment of clove plantations on Zanzibar and Pemba islands. Sultan Sayyid Said was responsible for making Zanzibar the centre of a commercial empire which was integrated into the international trade network. By the end of the nineteenth century European nations launched their colonial enterprises under the pretext of undermining the slave trade and abolishing slavery. Yet, the irony was that slavery when in fact it was ended (as late as 1914 in some colonies) was replaced by forced labour and other forms of colonial subjugation with far-reaching economic and political consequences.

Abdin Chande

Literary Works

El Zein, Abdul Hamid (1974), *The Sacred Meadows*, Evanston, IL: Northwestern University Press.
Gurnah, Abdulrazak (1994), *Paradise*, Harmondsworth: Penguin.

Histories

Alpers, Edward (1975), *Ivory and Slaves: Changing Pattern of International Trade in East-Central Africa to the Later Nineteenth Century*, Berkeley, CA: University of California Press.
Cooper, Frederick (1977), *Plantation Slavery on the East Coast of Africa*, New Haven, CT: Yale University Press.
Salim, A. T. (1992), 'East Africa: The Coast', in B. A. Ogot (ed.), *General History of Africa Volume V: Africa from the Sixteenth to the Eighteenth Century*, Berkeley, CA: University of California Press.
Sheriff, Abdul (1987), *Slaves, Spices and Ivory in Zanzibar*, Athens, OH: Ohio University Press.

See also: **Historiography: East Africa; Islam.**

Slavery: Caribbean

There is no single history of slavery for the whole Caribbean. If we define slavery simply as 'labour enforced by violence', then at the time of the first European intrusion into the Caribbean, we can identify three concepts of slavery that were in force. The first concept of slavery was the Indian concept of *naboría*, drawn from the Taíno culture, and describing a category of outcasts or war prisoners who were employed as labourers by the rulers (the *caciques*). The Spaniards converted this type of slavery into urban house-slavery, initially for women (who could not by law be sold). The second category of slavery was *repartimiento*, which was the distribution of the vanquished natives among the Spanish soldiers, the *conquistadores*. This type of personal service (initially as carriers) was transformed into the main source of unfree labour of the *conquista*, renamed *encomienda* (a legal form with a medieval tradition), which by law was not described as slavery, but rather as 'civilising by labour'. The third concept, familiar to Columbus himself, was a category of 'modern' slavery similar to the slavery used by the Portuguese in exploiting the labour of *negros de Guiné* in São Tomé or São

Jorge da Mina (West Africa). Columbus kidnapped Taínos from the Bahamas and from La Hispaniola and sent them to Spain to be sold at the slave-markets of Al-Andalus, the Algarves (Lisboa, Sevilla, Lagos, Córdoba, Granada) and Cataluña (Valencia, Barcelona). In Spain there was a well-defined and socially accepted form of slavery which was governed by the law code of the Siete Partidas. The Catholic monarchs, Isabella of Castile and Fernando of Aragón, however, forbade Columbus from pursuing the legal enslavement of Indians, except in cases of 'man-eating' Caribs and prisoners of the *guerra justa* (just war) after 1512. Indians were defined as vassals with minor rights, and had to pay tributes.

Despite these formal categories and proscriptions, descriptions of the first Spanish cities and mine-districts in the Caribbean abound with details of slaves and *naborías*. When the *indios nativos* began dying in increasing numbers, *baquianos* (slave traders) used the institution of *rescate* to supply the Spanish-dominated islands with slaves from the Lucayas (Bahamas), La Florida, the Lesser Antilles, the coast of Mexico, Honduras, Nicaragua and the Tierra Firme (Panama to the Guayanas). In turn many Indian peoples, like the so-called Caribs of the Guyanas and the Lesser Antilles, developed – under pressure and in response to the demand of European settlers and missionaries – their own forms of slavery and slave trade (*poitos*), as did other native peoples (Kuna, Wajúu, Misquito, Comanche, Seminoles and others).

The first African slaves arrived in the Caribbean from Europe as servants of the Spaniards. Obando, the governor of Santo Domingo after Columbus, rejected the *negros ladinos* in favour of African slaves for his first efforts in mining. In the wake of the genocide of the indigenous population of the Greater Antilles, larger groups of enslaved men and women from Guiné, São Tomé, the Senegal region and other parts of Africa were brought to Santo Domingo after 1518. In 1523, the king of Portugal gave permission to trade slaves directly from Guiné to America. Some of these were the so-called *esclavos blancos*, Moors from regions north of Senegal. Bartolomé de las Casas argued for the importation of Africans in two memoranda (1516 and 1518), praising the productivity of 'Negro' labour under Caribbean conditions, and bemoaning the negative impact of forced labour on the indigenous population, though he later repented this decision.

From 1493 to 1850, the Caribbean formed the core of Atlantic slavery, only surpassed in the nineteenth century by the continental slaveries of southern Brazil and the south of the United States. This long period is generally divided into three overlapping stages. The first stage stretches from 1440 to 1650. It starts with the identification of slavery and blackness (the *slavus nigrus* in Sicily in 1430, which meant 'black Slav'), and includes the beginning of the Atlantic slave trade in the 1440s, the establishment of mixed slavery in the Atlantic islands, and full introduction of African slave labour in plantations of the Americas. The first Caribbean centre of African and Indian slavery was the island of La Hispaniola (Santo Domingo), followed by Barbados, where British settlers and Dutch merchants introduced slavery on the Dutch model. The Atlantic slave triangle was cemented in about 1570 in Brazil; in about 1650 in the British, Dutch and Danish Caribbean; and slightly later in North America, the French Caribbean, and the Spanish Caribbean. The second stage stretches from about 1650 to about 1850. This was the 'high point' of Caribbean slavery, as about 40 per cent–50 per cent of the 10 to 12 million African slaves who arrived in America during this period alive were sold to work on the sugar, tobacco and coffee plantations of the Caribbean. Most slaves went to Jamaica and Saint-Domingue, but significant numbers also worked in Barbados, the Bahamas, the Antilles, Guiana, the western parts of Santo Domingo, Guadeloupe, Martinique and Cayenne. The North American colonies, like Louisiana, the Floridas, Virginia, Georgia and Carolina, were effectively peripheries of the Caribbean centres of slavery, and supplied wood, rice, tobacco, fish and other foods. An overlapping third stage of expanding slavery began with the Haitian revolution (1791–1804) and lasted until the final New World abolitions in the French colonies in 1848, the Dutch colonies (Curaçao and Suriname) in 1863, the southern United States in 1865, Cuba in 1886, and Brazil in 1888. Cuba was at the centre of this third stage, and by 1830 threatened Jamaica's pre-eminence as a sugar producer. Britain's abolition of slavery in 1834 confirmed Cuba's dominance, as it at the same time became increasingly tied into the US economy.

In the period immediately following abolition, there was an extended phase of so-called 'secondary slavery'. Secondary slavery did not prescribe any legal connection between race and slave status, but after several centuries of African enslavement, slavery had become a question of race, as most field workers on the plantations under slavery were black. Therefore, in the main 'secondary slavery' regions – the southern USA, Brazil and Cuba – free members of the population who were black always ran the risk of being attributed the status of a slave. As the nineteenth century progressed, however, the line between 'slave' and 'free' blurred further as new identities and cultures gradually emerged, like the post-emancipation Haitian national identity, the Jamaican folk culture and the Lucumí-culture, and the Cuban identity that combined a mix of slave Congo-culture and a national identity imposed from above (Cubanía).

The historiography of the Caribbean is dominated by studies of slavery, and the major debates – most notably between Eric Williams and Seymour Drescher over the relation between European capitalism and the abolition of slavery – are summarised elsewhere (see Historiography: Caribbean). However, one particular trend in the recent scholarship is worth emphasising, in conclusion. Since the period of decolonisation in the 1960s, historians of slavery have overwhelmingly turned from studying the planter class to studying the lives of the slaves themselves. The results of this research, a selection of which is listed below, has been what Gad Heuman has described in his recent overview 'an explosion of literature on slavery in the Empire' (Heuman 1999, p. 315). As regards the literary works, the selection here includes examples of early European travel narratives (Las Casas); late eighteenth- and early nineteenth-century English writings that bear the traces of Caribbean slavery (Austen, Defoe); slave narratives from the final decades of slavery (Prince, Wedderburn); and a variety of twentieth-century texts of different genres that have engaged at length with the histories of slavery (Brathwaite, Dabydeen, Nichols, Rhys and others).

Michael Zeuske

Literary Works

Austen, Jane [1814] (1966), Mansfield Park, Harmondsworth: Penguin.
Brand, Dionne (1999), At the Full and Change of the Moon, London: Granta.
Brathwaite, Edward Kamau (1973), The Arrivants, A New World Triology: Rights of Passage, Islands and Masks, Oxford: Oxford University Press.
Dabydeen, David (1986), Slave Song, Coventry: Dangaroo Press.
D'Aguiar, Fred (1994), The Longest Memory, London: Chatto and Windus.
Defoe, Daniel [1724] (1999), A General History of the Pyrates, Mineola, NY: Dover.
De Lisser, Herbert G. [1929] (1954), The White Witch of Rosehall, London: Ernest Benn.
Las Casas, Bartolomé de [1552] (1992), A Short Account of the Destruction of the Indies, trans. N. Griffin, Harmondsworth: Penguin.

Lovelace, Earl (1997), *Salt*, New York: Persea Books.

Marson, Una (1930), *Tropic Reveries*, Kingston: Gleaner.

Nichols, Grace [1983] (1990), *i is a long memoried woman*, London: Karnak House.

Prince, Mary [1831] (2000), *The History of Mary Prince*, ed. S. Salih, Harmondsworth: Penguin.

Reid, Vic [1958] (1980), *The Leopard*, London: Heinemann.

Rhys, Jean [1966] (1968), *Wide Sargasso Sea*, Harmondsworth: Penguin.

Schwarz-Bart, Simone [1974] (1982), *The Bridge of Beyond*, trans. B. Bray, London: Heinemann.

Toomer, Jean [1923] (1975), *Cane*, New York: Liveright.

Unsworth, Barry (1992), *Sacred Hunger*, London: Hamish Hamilton.

Wedderburn, Robert (1991), *The Horrors of Slavery and Other Writings*, ed. I. McCalman, Edinburgh: Edinburgh University Press.

Histories

Beckles, Hilary (1988), *Natural Rebels: A Social History of Enslaved Black Women in Barbados*, London: Zed Books.

Blackburn, Robin (1997), *The Making of New World Slavery. From the Baroque to the Modern, 1492–1800*, London and New York: Verso.

Bush, Barbara (1990), *Slave Women in Caribbean Society: 1650–1838*, Kingston: Heinemann.

Craton, Michael (1997), *Empire, Enslavement and Freedom in the Caribbean*, Kingston: Randle; Oxford: James Currey.

Edwards, Bryan (1807), *The History, Civil and Commercial, of the British Colonies in the West Indies*, London: Stockdale.

Engerman, Stanley L. and Barry W. Higman (1997), 'The Demographic Structure of the Caribbean Slave Societies in the Eighteenth and Nineteenth Centuries', in Franklin W. Knight (ed.), *General History of the Caribbean, Volume III: The Slave Societies of the Caribbean*, London: UNESCO, pp. 47–57.

Heuman, Gad (1999), 'Slavery, the Slave Trade, and Abolition', in R. W. Winks (ed.), *The Oxford History of the British Empire, Volume 5*, Oxford: Oxford University Press, pp. 315–26.

James, C. L. R. [1938] (1963), *The Black Jacobins: A Study of Toussaint L'Ouverture and the San Domingo Revolution*, 2nd edn, New York: Random House.

Kadish, Doris Y. (2000), *Slavery in the Caribbean Francophone World. Distant Voices, Forgotten Acts, Forged Identities*, Athens, GA and London: The University of Georgia Press.

Kiple, Kenneth (1984), *The Caribbean Slave: A Biological History*, Cambridge: Cambridge University Press.

Landers, Jane K. (1999), *Black Society in Spanish Florida*, Urbana, IL: University of Illinois Press.

Paquette, Robert L. and Stanley Engerman (1996), *The Lesser Antilles in the Age of European Expansion*, Gainesville, FL: University of Florida Press.

Scott, Rebecca J., Thomas Holt, Frederic Cooper and Aims McGuiness (2002), *Societies after Slavery. A Selected Annotated Bibliography of Printed Sources on Cuba, Brazil, British Colonial Africa, South Africa, and the British West Indies*, Pittsburgh, PA: University of Pittsburgh Press.

Shepherd, Verene and Hilary Beckles (eds) (2000), *Caribbean Slavery in the Atlantic World*, New Haven, CT: Yale University Press.

Tannenbaum, Frank (1946), *Slave and Citizen: The Negro in the Americas*, New York: Alfred A. Knopf.

Tomich, Dale W. (1988), '"The Second Slavery": Bonded Labor and the Transformations of the Nineteenth-Century World Economy', in F. O. Ramirez (ed.), *Rethinking the Nineteenth Century: Contradictions and Movement*, New York: Greenwood Press, pp. 103–17.

Williams, Eric (1944), *Capitalism and Slavery*, London: André Deutsch.

Zeuske, Michael (2002), 'Hidden Markers, Open Secrets: Race Marking and Race Making in Cuba', *New West Indian Guide/Nieuwe West-Indische Gids* 76: 3 and 4, pp. 235–66.

See also: **Anti-colonialism and Resistance: Caribbean**; **Historiography: Caribbean**.

Slavery: Southern Africa

Forms of internal servitude existed in pre-colonial Southern African societies, including hereditary bondage of prisoners of war, and voluntary, hereditary clientage. Harsher forms of servitude appear to have developed in the nineteenth century, in the context of 'new relations of production and exchange related to white frontier expansion from the 1840s' (Eldredge and Morton 1994, p. 104). Slavery was the main form of labour in the Cape Colony before its final abolition in 1838. Before the slave trade was abolished in 1807, approximately 63,000 slaves were imported into the Cape Colony. Refused permission to enslave Khoisan people, the Dutch imported slaves in three main ways: VOC (Dutch East India Company)-sponsored voyages to Madagascar and the East African coast, VOC return fleets en route from the East Indies to the Netherlands, and foreign slavers en route to the Americas. Cape slaves, therefore, were diverse in origin and cultural heritage. The labour required of them was also diverse, ranging from mostly domestic work for women, to farm labour or artisanship for men. Slave holdings were generally small: most slaves were in holdings of five slaves or less, on large, far-flung farms. This militated against slaves uniting in large-scale rebellion, although resistance was endemic, from arson to flight.

The British took over the Cape in 1806, and with the closure of the oceanic trade, increasing proportions of slaves were locally born. They worked closely with Khoisan labourers, who were not legally enslaved. In the 1820s, ameliorative regulations were introduced, which promised much but delivered little. Many slaves and their mostly Dutch slaveholders believed that the abolition of slavery was imminent. In 1825, the slave Galant van de Kaap led a rebellion of slave and Khoisan male workers in the north-western Cape. Having stolen horses and guns, they killed all the white men they could, before fleeing. They were later captured, and Galant and his second-in-command, Abel, were executed. This rebellion points to the gendered experience of subjection, and to the shared felt oppression of slave and Khoisan workers. Recently, historians have challenged the significance of purely legal definitions of slavery, arguing that slavery was endemic throughout the Cape Colony. Boer commandos captured indigenous people, often Khoisan women and children; they were surely enslaved. This new direction in historical studies has broadened understandings of the meaning of slavery.

Patricia van der Spuy

Literary Works

Brink, André (1982), *A Chain of Voices*, London: Faber and Faber.
Jacobs, Rayda (1997), *Eyes of the Sky*, Oxford: Heinemann.
Jacobs, Rayda (1998), *The Slave Book*, Cape Town: Kwela.

Histories

Armstrong, James and Nigel Worden (1988), 'The Slaves, 1652–1834', in R. Elphick and
    H. Giliomee (eds), *The Shaping of South African Society, 1652–1840*, Middletown,
    CT: Wesleyan University Press, pp. 109–83.
Eldredge, Elizabeth and Frank Morton (eds) (1994), *Slavery in South Africa: Captive Labor
    on the Dutch Frontier*, Boulder, CO: Westview Press.
Mason, John (2003), *Social Death and Resurrection: Slavery and Emancipation in South Africa*,
    Charlottesville, VA: University of Virginia Press.
Newton-King, Susan (1999), *Masters and Servants on the Cape Eastern Frontier, 1760–1803*,
    Cambridge: Cambridge University Press.
Ross, Robert (1983), *Cape of Torments: Slavery and Resistance in South Africa*, London:
    Routledge and Kegan Paul.
Shell, Robert C.-H. (1994), *Children of Bondage: A Social History of the Slave Society at the
    Cape of Good Hope, 1652–1838*, Hanover, NH: Wesleyan University Press.
Van der Spuy, Patricia (1996), '"Making himself Master": Galant's Rebellion Revisited',
    South African Historical Journal 34, pp. 1–28.
Worden, Nigel (1985), *Slavery in Dutch South Africa*, Cambridge: Cambridge University
    Press.

See also: **Coloured Southern Africa; Women's Histories: Southern Africa**.

Slavery: West Africa

Slavery existed in Africa from pre-colonial times and into the early colonial period. Africa
has served not only as an internal source of slaves, but also as a source for India, the Islamic
world, and the Americas. As Martin Klein and Paul Lovejoy have pointed out, there is a
huge difference between the theory of slavery and the practice of it. It is important to keep
in mind the double-nature of the slave in Africa, as a commodity that must be produced,
and as also a producer. Further, it is almost impossible to discuss the issue of slavery within
West Africa without also discussing the trans-Saharan and the transatlantic slave trades,
since as contact and trade with outsiders grew, the practice of slavery changed in West
African societies.

 Before discussing the issue of slavery in West Africa, however, it is important to distinguish four competing definitions of African slavery. First, for Orlando Patterson, a slave is
a dishonoured person, who has become alienated labour through permanent and violent
domination. Patterson (1982) attempts to construct a universal theory to explain the
process of enslavement and to define slavery for all time periods and societies. His key idea
is that of social death, which he defines as loss of community, family, status and name; and

having no social existence apart from the master. Second, for Suzanne Miers and Igor Kopytoff (1977), the distinctions between indigenous African and Western concepts of slavery are crucial. They argue that the first factor that distinguished Western from African slavery was that in the former, all rights in a slave were owned and could be transferred, whereas African forms of slavery allowed the fragmentation of this bundle of rights, which meant that one or a number of rights-in-persons could be transferred (for example, a master could control a slave's labour but not her/his sexuality). The second characteristic of Western slavery identified by Miers and Kopytoff is that newly-acquired slaves became 'non-persons', with no bonds to the new society (this is similar to Patterson's concept of a socially dead person). However, as slaves formed bonds with their masters over time, they became less marginalised and their descendants could be slowly incorporated into that society. Third, Claude Meillassoux concentrates on the 'mode of reproduction' of slaves, and argues that slavery is unique because it is the only mode of production that does not reproduce itself biologically, with new generations of slaves acquired either through political violence or through the transfer of individuals as commodities. Meillassoux (1986) differentiates further between 'aristocratic, warrior slavery', which is enslavement through the seizure of captives associated with the aristocracy; and warrior class, 'merchant slavery', which describes buying and selling of slaves-as-commodities. Finally, for Paul Lovejoy (1981, 2000), there are six defining characteristics of slavery: (1) slaves were property, and could be bought and sold at will; (2) slaves were either outsiders or people who were denied their heritage through judicial or other sanctions; (3) coercion could be used at will against a slave and at the owner's discretion; (4) slaves' labour power belonged to the master; (5) slaves did not have the right to their own sexuality or reproductive capacities; and (6) slave status was inherited unless special provisions were made to free descendants.

The existence of slavery in West Africa most likely pre-dated the trans-Saharan slave trade, and certainly existed before the beginning of the transatlantic trade. However, the number of enslaved individuals and the importance of slavery to the social structures of various societies varied over time and in different parts of West Africa. From the sixteenth century, the external demand for slaves combined with expanding insecurity to increase the spread of slavery in West Africa. West African merchants and rulers sought to acquire imported firearms, horses and textiles, and they financed such acquisitions by the sale of slaves whom they captured in large numbers in order to trade. In West Africa, in the seventeenth and the eighteenth centuries, societies in the northern savanna were affected differently by slavery and the slave trade from those along the coast. In the northern savanna, slavery continued to be an important element of production, whereas along the coast, the vast export market for slaves encouraged slave trading, and this resulted in an increased slave population. The sale of slaves was governed by the different demands of local and export markets: the local markets in the northern savanna and along the coast, as well as the Muslim slave-owning societies in North Africa, preferred women slaves and children, whereas the slave-owners in the Americas preferred male slaves to work their plantations. However, there were exceptions, as men still went across the Sahara, and as David Eltis has shown (2000), women and children in fact crossed the Atlantic in substantial numbers.

In all of West Africa there were three basic categories of slaves – captives, purchased slaves, and those born in the household. For the bulk of West Africa, most slaves were produced through warfare and raiding. The history of enslavement is closely tied to political history. Asante, Dahomey, and those operating under the Aro network, all relied either directly or indirectly upon raiding and warfare to acquire slaves. War captives and those newly enslaved had neither rights nor social identity. They had to be moved away from areas of easy escape or where they had ties. It was this group that fed the transatlantic and trans-Saharan slave trades.

In Islamic and non-Islamic African societies alike, a slave's integration into society was marked by marriage and parenthood. Usually those recently enslaved and unassimilated slaves had to wait for permission to marry by their masters, but the majority of slaves did eventually marry. In most societies, there were twice as many female slaves as male slaves, and so there were enough women to meet the demand for concubines, and to provide wives for slave men. Women and men belonging to different owners could marry, in which case the woman lived with her husband, but continued to work for her master, and her children belonged to her master. Usually with marriage and parenthood, slave couples became more autonomous. If they had been living in their owner's compound, they had the opportunity to move away, work their own fields in exchange for fixed dues, and if a man could afford it, to take another wife. Children born into slavery had the most security. They were the most assimilated into society, and even though it was possible to sell them, public opinion in most societies was heavily against it. Masters were usually able to put slave children to work either after they lost their baby teeth or after circumcision. In some areas, children worked on the slave father's plot, but his owner could have them do other activities. Slave children could also be moved away from their parents and onto their owner's compound.

Almost all societies provided avenues for manumission, although it is difficult to analyse the degree to which they were used. Islamic law emphasised the conversion and acculturation of slaves, and the conditions of slavery were supposed to ameliorate over time. It sanctioned manumission and self-purchase, and a concubine was freed upon the birth of a child by her master and the child was free. In the forest zone, kinship ideologies encouraged full assimilation, and over a generation or two, it was possible to move from the status of slave to that of a client or junior kinsman.

In West Africa, slaves were used for various purposes. They were used in the army, in government, in craft production, commerce, households, on plantations, and in mines. What made slaves important in the army and the government was their lack of kin or of any relationships apart from that of master–slave. Their lack of competing loyalties meant that they could be trusted by those in power. While there were elite slaves involved in warfare, government and commerce, the vast majority of slaves in Africa lived difficult lives. By the nineteenth century, plantation slavery was found all over West Africa. In the northern savanna, this was associated with the *jihads*, and along the coast with the final decades of the transatlantic slave trade.

The number of individuals enslaved in Muslim areas increased during the *jihads* of the nineteenth century. The *jihads* were a series of wars which started in 1804, encompassed a belt of territory from Senegambia east to the Red Sea, and resulted in the establishment of Islamic states such as the Sokoto Caliphate in Northern Nigeria. The *jihads* precipitated the enslavement of millions of people, some of whom were exported out of sub-Saharan Africa, but most of whom were settled in the new states. This expansion of the slave population, and the resulting intensification of slavery consolidated into a large-scale slave economy.

The largest of the Islamic states in West Africa formed through the jihadist movement was the Sokoto Caliphate. In many areas in the nineteenth century, slaves formed a large proportion of the population. According to Henrich Barth, who spent several years in the Sokoto Caliphate in the 1850s, slaves made up at least 50 per cent of the population of Kano, the largest and most prosperous emirate of the Sokoto Caliphate. Such figures were sustained into the early twentieth century. While some slaves in the Sokoto Caliphate were used in aristocratic households, merchant firms, the army and craft production, the vast majority of slaves worked in agriculture. Although many slave owners in the central areas of the Caliphate owned only a few slaves each, most agricultural slaves worked on the large plantations of the upper classes. The main crops produced were millet, sorghum, indigo, cotton, onions, tobacco and vegetables.

The onset of legitimate trade helped to promote the spread of plantation slavery to areas in West Africa not previously conquered by the jihadists, as slave labour was used for export crops, and furthermore, the closing of the Atlantic slave trade lowered the prices of slaves in Africa and made them more affordable. In Kumasi in Asante, slaves worked on plantations, in gold mines, kola gathering and processing, and in porterage. Slaves were used in Dahomey in palm plantations in order to produce palm oil and kernels for the export trade. In north-eastern Igboland, yam plantations run on slave labour were common, while in the Biafran hinterland, large numbers of slaves were used as porters and as canoe-men in order to transport products. In general, conditions for slaves were worst on large export-crop plantations where slave prices were low. Conversely, where there was a low master-to-slave ratio, the likelihood of assimilation increased and the egalitarian principles of Islam ameliorated the condition of slavery.

Historians continue to debate the nature and extent of the impact of slavery on West Africa, with scholars like Walter Rodney and Paul Lovejoy on the one hand arguing that African society was fundamentally transformed by the Atlantic slave trade, and others like J. D. Fage and David Eltis on the other insisting that internal wars and domestic slave-trading profoundly complicated the effects of Atlantic slavery. Whatever the general pattern, it is clear at least that at different times, and in different parts of West Africa, the effects of the Atlantic slave trade were registered in distinct ways. The literary works listed include eighteenth-century texts by European travellers to West Africa (Park 1799); slave narratives (Equiano 1794, Cugoano 1787); and a number of twentieth-century works that engage in fictional forms with the multiple legacies of slavery in West Africa (Amadi 1978, Aidoo Armah 1980, and others).

Jennifer Lofkrantz

Literary Works

Aidoo, Ama Ata (1980a), *The Dilemma of A Ghost*, London: Longman.
Aidoo, Ama Ata (1980b), *Anowa*, London: Longman.
Amadi, Elechi (1978), *The Slave*, London: Heinemann Educational.
Armah, Ayi Kwei (1979a), *Two Thousand Seasons*, London: Heinemann Educational.
Armah, Ayi Kwei (1979b), *The Healers*, London: Heinemann Educational.
Carretta, Vincent (ed.) (1996), *Unchained Voices: An Anthology of Black Authors in the English-Speaking World of the Eighteenth Century*, Lexington, KY: University of Kentucky Press.
Cugoano, Quobna Ottobah [1787] (1999), *Thoughts and Sentiments on the Evil of Slavery*, ed. V. Carretta, Harmondsworth: Penguin.
Easmon, R. Sarif (1981), *The Feud and Other Stories*, Harlow: Longman.
Emecheta, Buchi (1979), *The Slave Girl*, London: Fontana.
Equiano, Olaudah [1794] (1995), *The Interesting Narrative and Other Writings*, ed. V. Carretta, Harmondsworth: Penguin.

Park, Mungo [1799] (2002), *Travels in the Interior Districts of Africa*, ed. B. Waites, London: Wordsworth.
Tutuola, Amos (1978), *My Life in the Bush of Ghosts*, London: Faber and Faber.

Histories

Eltis, David (2000), *The Rise of African Slavery in the Americas*, Cambridge: Cambridge University Press.
Fage, J. D. (1980), 'Slaves and Society in Western Africa, 1440–c. 1770', *Journal of African History* 21, pp. 289–310.
Fisher, Humphrey J. (2001), *Slavery in the History of Muslim Black Africa*, New York: New York University Press.
Gemery, Henry A., and Jan S. Hogendorn (eds) (1979), *The Uncommon Market. Essays in the Economic History of the Atlantic Slave Trade*, New York: Academic Press.
Kitson, Peter and Deborah Lee (eds) (1999), *Slavery, Abolition and Emancipation: Writings in the British Romantic Period*, 8 vols, London: Pickering and Chatto.
Klein, Martin A. (2001), *A Historical Dictionary of Slavery and Abolition*, Lanham, MD and London: Scarecrow Press.
Lovejoy, Paul (2000), *Transformations in Slavery: A History of Slavery in Africa*, Cambridge: Cambridge University Press.
Lovejoy, Paul (ed.) (1981), *Ideology of Slavery in Africa*, Beverly Hills, CA: Sage Publications.
Manning, Patrick (1990), *Slavery and African Life: Occidental, Oriental and African Slave Trades* (African Studies Series, 67), Cambridge: Cambridge University Press,
Meillassoux, Claude [1986] (1991), *The Anthropology of Slavery. The Womb of Iron and Gold*, trans. A. Dasnois, London: Athlone Press.
Miers, Suzanne and Igor Kopytoff (eds) (1977), *Slavery in West Africa. Historical and Anthropological Perspectives*, Madison, WI: The University of Wisconsin Press.
Miers, Suzanne and Richard Roberts (eds) (1988), *The End of Slavery in Africa*, Madison, WI: The University of Wisconsin Press.
Northrup, David (1978), *Trade without Rulers: Precolonial Economic Developments in Southeastern Nigeria*, Oxford: Clarendon Press.
Patterson, Orlando (1982), *Slavery and Social Death: A Comparative Study*, Cambridge, MA: Harvard University Press.
Robertson, Claire C. and Martin A. Klein (eds) (1983), *Women and Slavery in Africa*, Madison, WI: The University of Wisconsin Press.
Rodney, Walter (1966), 'African Slavery and Other Forms of Social Oppression on the Upper Guinea Coast in the Context of the Atlantic Slave Trade', *Journal of African History* 7, pp. 431–43.
Segal, Ronald (2001), *Islam's Black Slaves. The History of Africa's Other Black Diaspora*, London: Atlantic Books.
UNESCO (1999), *The African Slave Trade from the 15th to the 19th Centuries Reports and Papers 2*, New York and London: UNESCO Publishing.
Walvin, James (1992), *Black Ivory. A History of British Slavery*, London: HarperCollins.

See also: **Historiography: West Africa; Islam; Pre-colonial Histories; Religions: West Africa**.

Spanish-American War

The Spanish-American War was fought in 1898 in two of Spain's colonies, Cuba and the Philippines. America claimed to be acting in the role of liberator, assisting the Cubans and the Filipinos in their quest for independence. For months before the war began, the press in the United States had been offering sensationalised coverage of the atrocities commit-ted by the Spanish in Cuba. On 15 February 1898, at the height of this media-induced frenzy, the American battleship, the *Maine*, was believed to have been blown up by the Spanish in the harbour of Havana. Though it was not clear whether this was a direct prov-ocation by the Spanish (who were busy conceding to nearly all of Washington's diplomatic demands regarding Cuba), it was interpreted as such by the press and the American people. America's President McKinley was under tremendous pressure to deal swiftly with the Spanish and retaliate in kind. The Teller Amendment, quickly passed in Congress, assured Americans that the United States was not interested in acquiring Cuba as a colony, but, instead, simply wanted to help the close neighbour in its fight for freedom.

The Philippines was initially of secondary concern; however, once the United States was officially at war, all of Spain's territories became vulnerable to attack. A fleet was sent to wait in Hong Kong just in case the hostilities escalated to an all-out war. American forces made contact with a group of Filipino rebels who had accepted exile in exchange for prom-ised reforms from the Spanish colonial government. The reforms were never enacted; this group, therefore, led by Manuel Aguinaldo, was eager to resume the revolution. The rebels predicted accurately that American naval power added to their own extensive revolution-ary army would be sufficient to topple the fragile Iberian hierarchy, and they believed that America's disinterest in colonial territory included the Philippines.

Spain was defeated in both Cuba and the Philippines. Under the Treaty of Paris, signed at the end of 1898, Cuba was granted independence (albeit with the United States exert-ing substantial indirect control) and the sovereignty of the Philippines was transferred to the United States. Its statements in the Teller Amendment notwithstanding, the United States had acquired foreign territory and began a colonial regime in the Philippines that lasted for decades.

Jennifer McMahon

Literary Works

Harper, Frank (ed.) (1991), *Just Outside Manila: Letters from Members of the First Colorado Regiment in the Spanish-American and Philippine-American Wars*, Denver, CO: Colorado Historical Society.
Kalaw, Maximo [1927] (1964), *The Philippine Rebel: A Romance of the American Occupation of the Philippines*, Manila: Filipiniana Book Guild.
Twain, Mark (1992), *Mark Twain's Weapons of Satire: Anti-Imperialist Writings on the Philippine-American War*, ed. Jim Zwick, Syracuse, NY: Syracuse University Press.

Histories

Brands, H. W. (1992), *Bound to Empire. The United States and the Philippines*, New York: Oxford University Press.

Gould, Lewis L. (1982), *The Spanish-American War and President McKinley*, Lawrence, KS: University Press of Kansas.
Green, Theodore P. (ed.) (1955), *American Imperialism in 1898*, Lexington, MA: D. C. Heath.

See also: **Cuban Revolution**; **Historiography: South-east Asia**; **Thomasites**; **United States of America**.

Sri Lankan Civil War

The political conflict in Sri Lanka between the Sinhalese and Tamils first took a violent turn in 1956, eight years after independence. For centuries Sinhalese and Tamils had lived alongside each other and had never viewed themselves as mutually opposed political groups. However, when a nationalist–populist coalition came to power in 1956, breaking with the Anglicised politics of the ruling elite and the Marxist politics of the main Trotskyist opposition on the promise to make Sinhala the only official language, Tamils became alienated. They shifted their allegiance to a Tamil nationalist party, which called for a federal political structure whereby Tamils could rule themselves. When the leaders of these two parties tried to resolve the tensions by negotiating an autonomy arrangement for Tamils one year later, more extreme nationalists opposed the pact, inciting anti-Tamil riots. This political dynamic, of the ruling party seeking to resolve the conflict through Tamil autonomy, and the opposition obstructing such an effort, has been a central obstacle to resolving the conflict.

During the 1970s, Tamil youth pushed the mainstream Tamil politicians to adopt a more narrowly Tamil nationalist position in favour of a separate state. They also began to organise an armed rebellion against the state. This rebellion initially began on a small scale with Tamil armed groups, ranging from leftist revolutionary to more narrowly nationalist ones. Following a major anti-Tamil pogrom organised by the ruling party in July 1983, armed groups of Tamil youth gathered considerable local Tamil and Indian support and mounted a campaign against the military forces.

Over time, the Tamil Tigers, a ruthlessly effective fighting force, came to dominate the military and political opposition to the Sri Lankan state within the Tamil community. They created a cult of martyrdom around suicide attacks and murdered political opponents – from leftist Tamils to mainstream politicians. They organised a sophisticated support network based on the Tamil diaspora that mobilised and moved money and arms from around the globe to keep the war going. This, along with the build-up of armed forces by the state increased the intensity of the civil war, from small skirmishes of a dozen guerrillas with light weapons, to large-scale battles involving thousands of fighters with heavy artillery. A major military intervention by India with 100,000 troops (1987–90) failed to force a solution. Repeated attempts by the Sri Lankan military to defeat the Tigers, and the Tamil Tigers to dislodge the Sri Lankan military from the Tamil dominated north-east region have not succeeded. In 1999, the Norwegian government became involved as a mediator in the conflict to seek a political solution with international backing. The Tamil Tiger intolerance of the Muslims, Sinhalese and other Tamil political groups living in the north-east, the rivalry between the two main Sinhala-dominated political parties, and the increased entanglement of the international community have all contributed to the current politico-military impasse in the civil war.

Ram Manikkalingam

Literary Works

Arasanayagam, Jean (1987), *Trial by Terror*, Hamilton: Rimu.

Arasanayagam, Jean (1991), *Reddened Water Flows Clear*, London and Boston: Forest Books.

Ranasinghe, Anne (1991), *At What Dark Point*, Colombo: English Writers Cooperative Sri Lanka.

Selvadurai, Shyam (1994), *Funny Boy*, London: Penguin.

Sivanandan, A. (1997), *When Memory Dies*, London: Arcadia Books.

Sivaramani (1991), Two Poems, *South Asia Bulletin* 9, p. 147.

Histories

Abeysekera, Charles and Newton Gunaratne (eds) (1985), *Ethnicity and Social Change in Sri Lanka*, Colombo: Social Scientists Association.

Abeysekera, Charles and Newton Gunaratne (eds) (1987), *Facets of Ethnicity*, Colombo: Social Scientists Association.

Hoole, Rajan, Daya Somasunderam, K. Sritharan and Rajani Thiranagama (1989), *Broken Palmyrah*, Jaffna: University Teachers for Human Rights. Available at http://uthr.org /BP/Content.htm

Jayawardena, Kumari (1985), *Ethnicity and Class Conflict in Sri Lanka: The Emergence of Sinhala-Buddhist Consciousness*, Colombo: Social Scientists Association.

Jeganathan, Pradeep and Qadri Ismail (eds) (1995), *Unmaking the Nation: The Politics of Identity and History in Modern Sri Lanka*, Colombo: Social Scientists Association.

Manor, James (1990), *The Expedient Utopian: Bandaranaike and Ceylon*, Cambridge: Cambridge University Press.

Silva, Neluka (ed.) (2002), *The Hybrid Island: Culture Crossings and the Invention of Identity in Sri Lanka*, Colombo: Social Scientists Association.

Swamy, Narayan M. R. (2002), *Tigers of Lanka: From Boys to Guerrillas*, Delhi: Konark.

Tambiah, S. J. (1986), *Sri Lanka: Ethnic Fratricide and the Dismantling of Democracy*, London: I. B. Tauris.

Wilson, A. J. (1994), *S. J. V. Chelvanayakam and the Crisis of Sri Lankan Tamil Nationalism 1947–1977: A Political Biography*, Honolulu: University of Hawaii Press.

See also: **Pre-colonial Histories: South Asia; Secessionism: South Asia; Sinhala Only Bill; Years of Terror.**

Stolen Generations

The term 'Stolen Generations' was coined by historian Peter Read in 1983 to describe those Aboriginal people who, as children, were forcibly removed from their families and culture by state and federal governments. By the time of federation (1901), there was already a long history of removing Aboriginal children for the purpose of enforced assimilation. Instead of the new Commonwealth government taking responsibility for Aboriginal people, the federal constitution invested it in the states, allowing their often heinous policies towards

Aboriginal people to continue without interference. Central to those policies was the idea of forced assimilation, which included the forcible 'relocation' of Aboriginal children, particularly those of mixed descent, to purpose-built institutions, or to white foster or adoptive parents so that, over time, their colour and their culture could be bred out of them. The NSW Aboriginal Welfare Board report of 1911 argued that it would be 'an injustice to the children themselves, and a positive menace to the State' (Read 1983, p. 7) if they were allowed to remain with their parents. Under state law, and supposedly in the interests of their protection, Aboriginal children automatically became wards of the state at birth. The Commonwealth government became involved with such policies in 1911 after it assumed administrative responsibility for the Northern Territory.

By the 1930s, when it was clear that Aboriginal numbers were increasing, the chief 'protector' of Aborigines in the Northern Territory pressed for the programme of taking children to be intensified in order to protect 'the purity of race' in tropical Australia. The destiny of mixed race children, in his view, lay in their 'ultimate absorption' by the people of the Commonwealth. Not until the federal constitutional referendum of 1967 were Aboriginal people recognised as citizens of Australia with rights and status equal to other Australians. Yet children continued to be taken from their Aboriginal parents. The Aboriginal Protection Act was not expunged from the statutes till 1973, so the state could still forcibly remove Aboriginal children until then.

The terrible cost to Aboriginal people of such policies included institutionalisation, unresolved trauma and grief, lack of parenting skills, behavioural issues and mental illness. The trans-generational effects are recorded in the *Bringing Them Home* report (1997), published after a damning inquiry by Australia's Human Rights and Equal Opportunity Commission. Continuing state intervention in Aboriginal family structures suggests a reluctance by governments and their officials to abandon those discredited practices. There is not one Aboriginal family who has not been affected by child removal policies. Tens of thousands of Aboriginal children fell victim to the racial policies of the states, leaving Australia with a legacy of deep and abiding shame.

Barbara Nicholson

Literary Works

Morgan, Sally (1987), *My Place*, Fremantle: Fremantle Arts Centre Press.
Pilkington, Doris (Nugi Garimara) (1996), *Follow the Rabbit-Proof Fence*, St Lucia: University of Queensland Press.
Scott, Kim (1999), *Benang: From the Heart*, Fremantle: Fremantle Arts Centre Press.
Ward, Glenyse (1987), *Wandering Girl*, Broome: Magabala Books.

Histories

Armitage, A. (1995), *Comparing the Policy of Aboriginal Assimilation: Australia, Canada, and New Zealand*, Vancouver: University of British Columbia.
Beresford, Q. and P. Omaji (1998), *Our State of Mind: Racial Planning and the Stolen Generations*, Fremantle: Fremantle Arts Centre Press.
Haebich, Anna (2000), *Broken Circles: Fragmenting Indigenous Families 1800–2000*, Fremantle: Fremantle Arts Centre Press.

Human Rights and Equal Opportunity Commission (1997), *Report: Bringing Them Home: National Inquiry into the Separation of Aboriginal and Torres Strait Islander Children from their Families*, Canberra: Commonwealth of Australia.

Read, Peter (1983), *The Stolen Generations: The Removal of Aboriginal Children in New South Wales, 1883 to 1969*, Canberra: Ministry of Aboriginal Affairs. Occasional Paper No. 1.

Read, Peter (1999), A *Rape of the Soul so Profound*, Sydney: Allen and Unwin.

See also: **Multiculturalism: Australia; Pre-colonial Histories: Australia**.

Straits Settlements

The Straits Settlements were a fluctuating number of littoral or island territories in contemporary Malaysia and Singapore, but the term is usually applied to the three major settlements: Penang (Pinang), Malacca (Melaka) and Singapore. In terms of European colonisation, the oldest was Malacca, occupied by the Portuguese in 1511, the Dutch in 1641, and finally ceded to the British East India Company in the early nineteenth century. The island of Penang, to the north, was established as the company's first outpost in Malaya in 1786, and control was later extended to a section of the mainland nearby. South of Malacca, the island of Singapore was first claimed by the company in 1819, but Singapore and Malacca also had lengthy pre-colonial histories as centres of power and commerce in the Malay world. The three territories were brought together administratively in 1826, and became a British Crown colony in 1867.

British control in the settlements was formal and direct, unlike the indirect rule in the Federated and Unfederated Malay States of the peninsula. The territories, however, saw the growth of several overlapping public spheres in which their inhabitants attempted to establish Asian modernities. Penang and Singapore's Chinese communities provided funds and support for the Chinese reformer Kang Youwei and later the revolutionary Sun Yatsen. Singapore of the early twentieth century provided a base for Malay reformers as diverse as the liberal Mohd. Eunos Abdullah and the Islamist editors of the journal *Al Imam* criticised traditional Malay rulers from an Islamic point of view and urged the application of *shari'ah* law in the peninsular states. Closer to colonial authority in all three major settlements was the Straits Chinese or Peranakan community; Chinese who had absorbed many elements of Malay culture, speaking various mixtures of Chinese dialects, Malay and English, and adopting Malay-influenced dress and cuisine. As a syncretic cultural community, the Straits Chinese challenged the taxonomies of colonial rule even as they attempted to align themselves with colonial power. The milieu of the Straits Settlement entrepôts also encompassed other communities from the Indian subcontinent and the archipelago which is now Indonesia.

The Straits Settlements ceased to function as a polity after the Japanese occupation of Singapore in 1942, and were formally dissolved in 1946. Singapore and its dependencies became a separate Crown colony, while Penang and Malacca were included in the Malayan Union, which became the Federation of Malaya in 1948. The territories were briefly rejoined in the early 1960s as elements of the Malaysian Federation before Singapore left to become an independent nation in 1965.

Philip Holden

Literary Works

Ee Tiang Hong (1985), *Tranquerah*, Singapore: National University of Singapore.
Kon, Stella [1983] (1989), *Emily of Emerald Hill*, London: Macmillan.
Kon, Stella (1986), *The Scholar and the Dragon*, Singapore: Federal Publications.
Lim Boon Keng and Song Ong Siang (eds) (1897–1907), *The Straits Chinese Magazine*, vols 1–11, Singapore.
Lim Suchen, Christine (2000), *A Bit of Earth*, Singapore: Times Books International.
Maugham, W. Somerset [1926] (2000), *More Far Eastern Tales*, London: Vintage.

Histories

Chew, Ernest and Edwin Lee (eds) (1991), *A History of Singapore*, Singapore: Oxford University Press.
Milner, Anthony (1995), *The Invention of Politics in Colonial Malaya. Contesting Nationalism and the Expansion of the Public Sphere*, Cambridge: Cambridge University Press.
Rudolph, Jürgen (1998), *Reconstructing Identities: A Social History of the Babas in Singapore*, Aldershot: Ashgate.

See also: **East India Company**; **Historiography: South-east Asia**; **Lee Kuan Yew**; **Women's Histories: South-east Asia**.

Sudanese Civil War

Sudan was at war from just before independence in 1955 until 1972, and again from 1983 to the present. The origins of this protracted conflict lie in the economic and political marginalisation of southern Sudan and the differing conceptions of what it is to be Sudanese held by the Arabised, Muslim leaders of the north and the 'African' southern Sudanese. This conflict over power and wealth has developed powerful religious and racial dimensions. The Sudan People's Liberation Army (SPLA), led from the outset by Colonel John Garang, has fought a guerrilla war. This sprang from a mutiny by southern army units against the increasingly dictatorial and Islamist-leaning government of President Jaafar Nimeiri, and contributed to the latter's overthrow in a peaceful uprising in 1985. The war continued under the elected but intolerant parliamentary regime headed by Prime Minister Sadiq el Mahdi, until he was in turn overthrown in a coup d'état, just as a peace process was making progress. The war then once again intensified under the military-Islamist regime headed by President Omer al Bashir. Originating in the south, the SPLA also gained support among non-Arab minorities in the north, notably the Nuba and people of southern Blue Nile, and briefly from groups in eastern Sudan. Its aim is a secular state, but it has compromised on its original ambition of self-determination for southern Sudan.

Successive governments in Khartoum have taken on an increasingly Islamist hue, culminating in an ambitious project of Islamist socio-political transformation and *jihad* under the leadership of Hassan al Turabi. Osama bin Laden was based in Sudan from 1991 to 1996, and the country exported *jihad* to its neighbours, provoking international isolation. In 1999 President Bashir removed Turabi in a palace coup, leading to a limited political relaxation, an end to UN sanctions, and ultimately to peace talks. The war has created immense human suffering, including repeated famines in the south. Since the launch of the United Nations Operation Lifeline Sudan in 1989, fighting has co-existed with an international relief programme. Subsequently, relief agencies including evangelical Christian organisations have become a major fixture in the south, helping to foster and shape an indigenous Christian revival. All sides have committed massacres and there has been a resurgence of enslavement. In late 2003, the peace process, led by Kenya and supported by a troika of the USA, Britain and Norway, appears poised to succeed, based on a formula of self-determination for the south, power and wealth sharing, and democratisation.

A number of fine poets have written about the war and associated abuses, but beyond a couple of writers living abroad, few have made their way into print. Mahjoub Sherif, 'the people's poet', who has been detained several times for his hostility to military governments, has written political and romantic poetry with humanistic imagery. In his 'Songs for Freedom' Sirr Anai Kulilang wrote from a southern perspective, challenging his 'cousin' Mohamed to see what unites him with his southern compatriots. SPLA leader Yousif Kuwa wrote a poem that became a famous rallying point for a Nuba cultural revival. All the above are in Arabic. Popular songs, such as the anonymous 'Deng and Mohamed in the land of Sudan' in the Dinka language, have gained currency across the south, capturing the intractability, the suffering, the humanity and the inhumanity of the war.

Alex de Waal

Literary Works

Lo Liyong, Taban (1999), *The Cows of Shambat: Sudanese Poems*, London: African Publishing.
Mahjoub, Jamal (1989), *Navigation of a Rainmaker*, London: Heinemann.

Histories

Daly, Martin and Awad Alsikainga (eds) (1994), *Civil War in Sudan*, London: I. B. Tauris.
Deng, Francis (1995), *War of Visions: Conflicts of Identities in Sudan*, Washington, DC: The Brookings Institution.
De Waal, Alex and Yoanes Ajawin (2002), *When Peace Comes: Civil Society and Development in Sudan*, Trenton, NJ: Red Sea Press.
El-Affendi, Abdelwahab (1991), *Turabi's Revolution: Islam and Power in Sudan*, London: Grey Seal.
Johnson, Douglas (2003), *The Root Causes of Sudan's Civil Wars*, London: International African Institute in association with James Currey.
Rahhal, Suleiman (2002), *The Right to be Nuba: The Story of a Sudanese People's Struggle for Survival*, Trenton, NJ: Red Sea Press.

See also: **Anti-colonialism and Resistance: East Africa; Mahdism**.

Suez Crisis

One of modern Egypt's most defining moments, the Suez Crisis, highlighted the newly-independent nation's ability to stand up to European might, as well as its burgeoning role as a leader of the Non-Alignment movement. Guided by Gamal Abdel Nasser, a group of Free Officers overthrew Egypt's puppet monarchy in 1952, destroying Britain's imperial claims to Egypt. Under Nasser, Egypt secured the withdrawal of British troops from the Suez Canal zone by April 1956, and Egyptians hoped they would see the end of Western interference in their political and economic affairs. However, the growing Cold War and Egypt's leading role in the Non-Alignment movement brought the country into conflict with Western powers, hastening the Suez Crisis of 1956.

In 1954, Nasser refused to commit Egypt to the Baghdad Pact, an alliance designed by the British to maintain influence in the Middle East. When Jordan and Syria were convinced not to join as well, Britain and the United States were alarmed by Egypt's independent stance. Meanwhile, Israel continued to decimate the army of Egypt in border skirmishes in Gaza, and the United States and Britain declined to give Egypt military aid to refurbish its army. Thus, Egypt traded cotton for arms with Czechoslovakia, a nation within the Soviet Union's sphere of influence. This move further outraged Western powers.

Finally, Egypt hoped to build a dam at Aswan to exploit further the Nile's waters, in an effort to increase agricultural output for its rapidly expanding population. As punishment for not aligning with the West, the United States revoked a proposed loan guarantee for the Aswan Dam through the World Bank. In response, Nasser dramatically nationalised the Suez Canal on 26 July 1956, hoping that the revenues from the canal would be enough to finance the dam project. This event was praised throughout the developing world; the Suez Canal stood as a stark reminder of European imperial success at the expense of thousands of Egyptians who died building and maintaining it. The British, French and Israelis, however, reacted by invading the country in October, in an effort to destroy Egypt's ability to govern the canal alone. Concerned about the impact of this illegal invasion on larger geopolitical affairs, both the Soviet Union and the United States condemned it, and by 6 November 1956, a ceasefire was accepted. The former imperial powers Britain and France, and the new nation of Israel, were thus humiliated by the new superpowers. Egypt was victorious, and Nasser became a hero throughout the Arab world and beyond. As a result of the move to nationalisation, the Suez Canal was finally under unchallenged Egyptian control.

Nancy Stockdale

Literary Works

Mahfouz, Naguib [1962] (1985), *Autumn Quail* (*Summan wa al-Kharif*), trans. R. Allen, New York: Doubleday.

Histories

Hopwood, Derek (1985), *Egypt: Politics and Society*, London: Routledge.
Kyle, Keith (1991), *Suez*, New York: I. B. Tauris.

Louis, William Roger and Roger Owens (eds) (1989), *Suez 1956: The Crisis and its Consequences*, Oxford: Oxford University Press.
Woodward, Peter (1992), *Nasser*, London: Addison-Wesley.

See also: **Britain's Postwar Foreign Policy**; **Historiography: Middle East**; **Nasser, Abdel Gamal**; **Nationalism(s): Arab**.

T

Terrorism: South Asia

Insofar as 'terrorism' is understood neutrally as the use of violence for anti-state political ends (that is, without the absolute moral opprobrium that the term increasingly attracts since 11 September 2001), its history and impact on modern Indian social/cultural life (indeed that of South Asia generally) has been enormous and complex. This incorporates the activities of more militant freedom fighters before independence in 1947 – Khudiram Bose (d. 1908), Bhagat Singh (d. 1931), Surjya Sen (d. 1934) and others were executed by the British India government as terrorists, and are remembered as martyrs in the struggle for India's freedom.

Terrorist activity in India since independence can be seen as belonging to several categories. Among these must be counted the acts of brutality that have been regularly perpetrated by landlords and politically aligned organisations against poor and landless peasants, and the equally violent reprisals directed by some leftist factions, who also oppose what they regard as a conservative and repressive state apparatus. These often overlap with caste interests and caste-based oppression. Another category includes the political violence of far-right religious organisations. M. K. Gandhi's assassination by the Hindu fanatic Nathuram Godse in 1948 is a famous instance, and the various deliberately provoked religious communal riots (incited primarily by fundamentalist Hindu and Muslim groups, more devastatingly the former). These categories sometimes, not always, merge into the third category, which has to do with separatist and secessionist movements. India has experienced and continues to experience a plethora of these: for example, Kashmiri separatists wishing either for an autonomously governed province or union with Pakistan, Sikh separatists hoping to create an independent Khalistan, tribals seeking the formation of the state of Jharkhand, north-eastern ethnic communities (the Nagas) wishing for self-determination, the xenophobic Shiv Sena in Maharashtra, and indirectly the Tamil separatists from Sri Lanka. Two Indian prime ministers have been assassinated by such alignments, Indira Gandhi in 1984 and Rajiv Gandhi in 1991; and numerous acts of violence against civilian populations and military targets can be placed in this category. These have sometimes been successful to a certain extent; for instance: substantial progress has been made in peace talks between Naga representatives and the Indian government in 2003; a separate state of Jharkhand was formed in 2000; the Shiv Sena has enjoyed electoral success in Maharashtra state; and in 2002 a ceasefire was agreed between the Sri Lankan government and the Tamil Tigers. Equally, the Nagas, and Sikh and Kashmiri separatists have faced (in some instances continue to face) the strong arm of state military repression. Some of the separatist impulses, in turn, merge into a fourth category (and one that has received the most media attention since the 1990s): terrorist activity that is allegedly aided and abetted by neighbouring states. Following a series of wars (1947–9, 1965, 1971), the traditional enmity between Pakistan and India is often sited as being at the heart of terrorism in India. Indian intelligence sources allege that a large number of terrorist acts committed by separatists and fundamentalist organisations in India were instigated with Pakistani support. An extraordinary terrorist attack on the Indian parliament in 2001 comes particularly to mind here. Similar allegations about India are made by the Pakistani government in the context of terrorist acts therein.

Terrorism in India, and more broadly in South Asia, has naturally affected the social and cultural lives – indeed the daily lives – of large populations. In the course of the 1990s terrorism has emerged as a particularly popular theme in Indian films (products of one of the largest film industries and markets in the world). From the downright populist to the more cerebral, such recent films include: *Roja* (dir. Mani Ratnam, 1992), *Maachis* (dir. Gulzar, 1996), *Sarfarosh* (dir. John Mathews, 1999), *Drohakaal* (dir. Govind Nihalani, 2001), *16th December* (dir. Mani Shankar, 2002), and *Bharat Bhagya Vidhata* (dir. Osho Raja, 2002). A growing interest within the West in Indian films as a cultural phenomenon, combined with the intensifying and ubiquitous interest in terrorism after 11 September 2001, ensures that terrorism in India is beginning to receive more attention from postcolonial theorists and researchers than used to be the case.

Suman Gupta

Literary Works

Hawksley, Humphrey (2003), *The Third World War*, London: Pan.
Ondaatje, Michael (2000), *Anil's Ghost*, London: Bloomsbury.

Histories

Basu, Amrita and Atul Kohli (eds) (1998), *Community Conflicts and the State in India*, Delhi: Oxford University Press.
Brasted, Howard V., Peter D. Reeves and J. McGuire (eds) (1996), *Politics of Violence: From Ayodhya to Behrampada*, New Delhi: Sage.
Chari, P. R. and Suba Chandra (eds) (2003), *Terrorism Post 9/11: An Indian Perspective*, New Delhi: Manohar.
Grover, Verinder and Ranjana Arora (eds) (1995), *Violence, Communalism and Terrorism in India*, New Delhi: Deep and Deep.
Gupta, Maya and A. K. Gupta (2001), *Defying Death: Struggles against Imperialism and Feudalism*, New Delhi: Tulika.
Karan, Vijay (1997), *War by Stealth*, New Delhi: Viking.
Marwah, Ved (1996), *Uncivil Wars: Pathology of Terrorism in India*, New Delhi: HarperCollins.

See also: **Communism: South Asia; JVP Insurrection; Kashmir Dispute; Naxalites; Sri Lankan Civil War; Years of Terror.**

Thomasites

After the Spanish-American War in 1898, the United States assumed control of the more than 7,000 islands that make up the Philippine archipelago. President McKinley coined the phrase 'benevolent assimilation' to describe American colonial policy. He referred to Filipinos as America's 'little brown brothers' and insisted on a relationship characterised by custodial tutelage in American manners and systems. The cornerstone of this effort was the establishment of a vast public school system, something that the Spanish, the previous colonisers of the Philippines, had never provided. The educational system was primarily designed to provide a basic grounding in literacy, arithmetic and civics.

Schoolhouses were built with amazing speed all over the Philippines and were considered the best venue to present an idealised America to a captive student audience and to shape Filipino culture according to that image. American soldiers were the first teachers. The fight for independence that the Filipinos had been waging against the Spanish did not abate simply because a new coloniser was in place. One of the American army's most effective tools in quelling resistance was the promise of education. As soon as an area was pacified, the soldiers would put down their arms and begin teaching. They were replaced by approximately 1,000 teachers who arrived from the United States on three ships, one named the *Thomas*. All of these teachers were later referred to as Thomasites, whether or not they arrived on that particular ship.

Many of those teachers believed the Filipinos were a backward and barbarous race and brought to their jobs a passionate zeal to 'civilise' their students. One important vehicle for imparting values associated with 'American ways' was the English language, which was considered to carry within it the traditions and ideals of the West. In spite of great hardships (cholera epidemics, very poor infrastructure, terrible communication systems), many of the teachers were successful in establishing school systems that continue to serve the Filipino public. This is in spite of an Orientalist perspective that pervaded the approach of American teachers and administrators who seemed never to lose sight of their own superiority and the perceived inferiority of their student body.

Jennifer McMahon

Literary Works

Fee, Mary Helen (1912), *A Woman's Impression of the Philippines*, Chicago: A. C. McClury and Company.
Freer, William B. (1906), *The Philippine Experiences of an American Teacher: A Narrative of Work and Travel in the Philippine Islands*, New York: Charles Scribner's Sons.
Pecson, Geronima and Maria Racehs (eds) (1959), *Tales of American Teachers in the Philippines*, Manila: Carmelo and Bauerman, Inc.

Histories

Alzona, Encarnacion (1932), *A History of Education in the Philippines, 1565–1930*, Manila: University of the Philippines Press.
Estioko, Leonardo R. (1994), *History of Education: A Filipino Perspective*, Manila: Logos Publications, Inc.

Pier, Arthur S. (1950), *American Apostles to the Philippines*, Boston, MA: The Beacon Press.
Usero, Alfonso B. (1935), *Teachers of the Philippines*, Manila: P. Vera and Sons.

See also: **Anglicisation; Historiography: South-east Asia; Spanish-American War; United States of America.**

Tourism: Caribbean

Tourism has become one of the key areas of critique within postcolonial thought in the Caribbean region because of the colonial legacies that inform it. Modern tourism began there in the late nineteenth century when journey times were cut by faster steam shipping lines developed for the fruit trade. New hotels were built to cater for the needs of wealthy Europeans and North Americans, along with a spate of travel books with titles such as *Down the Islands: A Voyage in the Caribbees* (William Agnew Paton, 1888) or *Through Jamaica with a Kodak* (Alfred Leader, 1907). Such travel writing was often condescending and racist, yet its depictions of Caribbean people and scenery set the tone for much that followed. After World War II, military 'rest and recreation' sites like Havana, Cuba and Kingston also attracted tourists and laid the foundations for contemporary sex tourism. Mass tourism took root in the 1960s with the development of long-distance air travel. Between 1970 and 1994 stay-over tourism arrivals in the Caribbean grew from 4.2 million to 14 million, and cruise ship arrivals from 4.2 million to 9.8 million, according to the Caribbean Tourism Organisation (CTO). Tourism became the strongest and fastest growing sector of the economy for many Caribbean countries, in several cases being the largest contributor to gross domestic product.

  Tourism 'density ratios' (the average daily number of tourists per square kilometre) and 'penetration ratios' (the average daily number of tourists per thousand local inhabitants) are generally very high. Although many Caribbean states promote tourism, the societies must negotiate the effects of unequal power relations of race, class and wealth that bring richer, often white tourists from powerful 'core' countries into contact with poorer, often black hosts in 'peripheral' locations and with little power. Caribbean postcolonial writers have pondered these issues in poems, novels and plays, while many diasporic writers have reflected on the tensions between locals and those 'from foreign' making return visits.

Mimi Sheller

Literary Works

Cliff, Michelle (1987), *No Telephone to Heaven*, New York: Dutton.
Conde, Maryse (1997), *The Last of the African Kings*, trans. Richard Philcox, Lincoln, NE: University of Nebraska Press.
Danticat, Edwidge (2002), *After the Dance: A Walk through Carnival in Jacmel, Haiti*, New York: Crown Publishing.
Kincaid, Jamaica (1988), *A Small Place*, London: Virago.
McMillan, Terry (1999), *How Stella Got Her Groove Back*, Penguin Books.
Naipaul, V. S. (1962), *The Middle Passage*, London: André Deutsch.
Phillips, Caryl (2000), *The Atlantic Sound*, London: Faber and Faber.

Rhone, Trevor (1981), *Smile Orange*, Harlow: Longman [a play and also a film].
Walcott, Derek (1980), *Pantomime*, New York: Farrar, Straus and Giroux [a play].
Winkler, Anthony C. (1987), *The Lunatic*, Kingston: Kingston Publishers [also a film].

Histories

Duval, David T. (2004), *Tourism in the Caribbean: Trends, Development, Prospects*, London and New York: Routledge.
Enloe, Cynthia (1989), *Bananas, Beaches and Bases: Making Feminist Sense of International Politics*, London and Sydney: Pandora.
Fonda Taylor, Frank (1993), *To Hell with Paradise: A History of the Jamaican Tourist Industry*, Pittsburgh, PA: University of Pittsburgh Press.
Gmelch, George (2003), *Behind the Smile: The Working Lives of Caribbean Tourism*, Bloomington, IN: Indiana University Press.
Pattullo, Polly (1996), *Last Resorts: The Cost of Tourism in the Caribbean*, London: Cassell/Latin America Bureau.
Sheller, Mimi (2003), *Consuming the Caribbean*, London: Routledge.
Strachan, Ian G. (2002), *Paradise and Plantation: Tourism and Culture in the Anglophone Caribbean*, Charlottesville, VA: University of Virginia Press.

See also: **Historiography: Caribbean; Women's Histories: Caribbean.**

U

Underground Railroad: Canada

Beginning in the early nineteenth century, a movement called the Underground Railroad helped enslaved people flee the Southern United States. Operating without formal organisation, participants in the Underground Railroad included both white and black abolitionists, enslaved African Americans, American Indians, and members of such religious groups as the Quakers, Methodists and Baptists.

Slaves passed information about methods of escape by word-of-mouth, in stories and through songs. No actual trains existed on the Underground Railroad, but guides were called conductors, and the hiding places that they used depots or stations. Runaways escaped to the free Northern States and Canada along a loosely connected series of routes that stretched through the southern border states. Guided north by the stars and sometimes singing traditional songs like 'Follow the Drinking Gourd', most runaways travelled at night on foot and took advantage of the natural protections offered by swamps, bayous, forests and waterways.

The Underground Railroad is directly linked to the history of blacks in Canada and the role of Canada in the movement to abolish slavery and emancipate enslaved Africans. As the Underground Railroad demonstrates, Canadian history has played an important role in the shaping of the African diaspora. In accepting fugitives who were oppressed by the injustices of slavery and racism in the United States, Canadian society demonstrated an early commitment to humanitarianism. An estimated 20,000 immigrants arrived in Ontario (known then as Upper Canada, and administratively as Canada West, after 1850) in the 1840s and 1850s, and as a result African Canadians contributed significantly to the settlement and development of the province, both at the time and continuing after the end of the American Civil War in 1865 and Canadian Confederation in 1867. The role of Canadians in the fight against slavery underscores the significance of resistance and struggle in the dispersal of Africans through enslavement, and highlights the vitality of a black Canadian identity.

Justin Edwards

Literary Works

Reed, Ishmael (1998), *Flight to Canada*, New York: Scribner.
Smucker, Barbara (1977), *Underground to Canada*, Toronto: Irwin Clarke.

Histories

Blockson, Charles L. (1987), *The Underground Railroad*, New York: Prentice-Hall Press.
Dorsey, Benjamin F. (1898), *Underground Railroad*, Toronto: s.n.
Johnson, H. U. (1996), *From Dixie to Canada: Romances and Realities of the Underground Railroad*, New York: Greenwood Publishing.
Mitchell, William M. (1860), *The Underground Railroad from Slavery to Freedom*, London: W. Tweedie.
Still, William (1872), *The Underground Railroad. A Record of Facts, Authentic Narratives, Letters, &c.*, Philadelphia: Porter and Coates.

See also: **Multiculturalism: Canada; Slavery (all regions); United States of America.**

United Nations

'That old UN girl,' Arundhati Roy (2003) lamented recently, 'it turns out she ain't what she was cracked up to be. She's been demoted (although she retains her high salary). Now she's the world's janitor . . . she's used and abused at will.' Roy conveys, characteristically, the palpable sense of crisis surrounding the United Nations, which is at once over-extended and under-funded, faced with countless demands, yet frequently brazenly ignored. The United Nations Organisation (UN) is the world's largest inter-governmental institution. It was established as a successor to the moribund League of Nations after a series of wartime allied meetings, culminating in the signing of the UN Charter in San Francisco in 1945 (see Schlesinger 2003 and Hilderbrand 1990).

The organisation's first responsibility was to maintain peace and collective security, but its many specialised agencies took on the role of international governance in fields such as health, agriculture, economic development, humanitarian assistance and education. In each of these guises, the UN has shaped the history of the postcolonial world. Critics have argued that the UN has been characterised by powerlessness and hypocrisy, intervening in conflicts to keep 'peace' only in the interests of one or another great power, most frequently the United States. Critics have noted further the countless violations of the UN Charter and General Assembly and Security Council resolutions when super-power interests are involved (see Gowan 2003 and Zolo 1997). Others have suggested that the UN's humanitarian missions have often created new forms of dependency, and have delayed or impeded sustainable political solutions to local conflicts.

The UN's crucial role in defining, planning and implementing schemes of international development have also come in for much critical comment, particularly when they have worked in tandem with the World Bank. Gayatri Spivak, for instance argues that:

> [t]he United Nations is based on the unacknowledged assumption that 'the rest of the world' is unable to govern itself. In fact, of course, no state is able to govern itself, in different ways. And, in the current conjuncture, the role of the state is less and less important. Therefore it is necessary to show, as lavishly as possible, global national unity. (Spivak 1996)

Rejecting the view that the UN is, more and more, but the political arm of the New World Order, other more sympathetic commentators have taken a more ambivalent view of the UN's history, highlighting occasions when it has been able to transcend super-power interests and serve as a forum for radical agendas. It has been suggested, for example, that the UN's universalistic principles, and its role as an arena of international debate, were crucial in lending legitimacy and international support to the Algerian revolution (see Connelly 2002), and there have also been brief periods when Third World governments have been able to advance their interests at the UN, particularly in the 1960s and 1970s. It is widely held that the end of the Cold War threw up unprecedented challenges: US hegemony, civil wars, and increasing economic inequality globally, to name but a few, have left the UN's future uncertain, and its capacity for creative renewal is at a premium.

Sunil Amrith

Literary Works

Farah, Nuruddin [1993] (2000), *Gifts*, New York: Penguin.
Gordimer, Nadine [1970] (2002), *A Guest of Honour*, London: Bloomsbury.
Gordimer, Nadine (2003), 'Mission Statement', in N. Gordimer, *Loot*, London: Bloomsbury, pp. 7–66.

Histories

Connelly, M. (2002), *A Diplomatic Revolution: Algeria's Fight for Independence and the Origins of the Post-Cold War Era*, New York: Oxford University Press.
Escobar, A. (1994), *Encountering Development: The Making and Unmaking of the Third World*, Princeton, NJ: Princeton University Press.
Ghosh, A. (1994), 'The Global Reservation: Notes towards an Ethnography of International Peacekeeping', *Cultural Anthropology* 9: 3, pp. 412–22.

Gowan, Peter (2003), 'US: UN', *New Left Review* 24, pp. 5–28.

Hilderbrand, Robert (1990), *Dumbarton Oaks. The Origins of the United Nations and the Search for Postwar Society*, Chapel Hill, NC: University of North Carolina Press.

Luard, E. [1982] (1989), *A History of the United Nations*, 2 vols, London: Macmillan.

Roy, Arundhati (2003), 'Mesopotamia, Babylon. The Tigris and Euphrates', *The Guardian*, 2 April. Available at http://www.guardian.co.uk/g2/story/

Schlesinger, Stephen (2003), *Act of Creation. The Founding of the United Nations*, Boulder, CO: University of Colorado Press.

Spivak, Gayatri C. (1996), '"Woman" as theatre: United Nations Conference on Women, Beijing 1995', *Radical Philosophy*, Jan/Feb. Available at http://www.radicalphilosophy.com/

Zolo, Danilo (1997), *Cosmopolis. Prospects of a World Government*, trans. D. McKie, Cambridge: Polity Press.

Zolo, Danilo (2002), *Invoking Humanity. War, Law, and Global Order*, trans. F. and G. Pool, London: Continuum.

See also: **Anti-globalisation Movements; Genocide: Rwanda; International Monetary Fund; United States of America; World Bank.**

United States of America

In their 1967 book *Black Power: The Politics of Liberation in America*, African-American activists Stokely Carmichael and Charles Hamilton linked civil rights movements in the United States to Third World movements for independence with the following claim: 'Black people are legal citizens of the United States with, for the most part, the same *legal* rights as other citizens. Yet they stand as colonial subjects in relation to the white society. Thus institutional racism has another name: colonialism. Obviously, the analogy is not perfect' (Carmichael and Hamilton 1967, pp. 5–6). In 1992, in an essay entitled 'American Literary Emergence as a Postcolonial Phenomenon', Harvard University Professor of English Lawrence Buell linked the post-1776 United States to the global South in the following terms:

> As the first colony to win independence, America has a history that Americans have liked to offer as a prototype for other new nations, yet which by the same token might profitably be studied by Americans themselves in light of later cases . . . This essay attempts precisely that: to imagine the extent to which the emergence of a flourishing national literature during the so-called Renaissance period of the mid-nineteenth century [United States] can be brought into focus through the lens of more recent post-colonial literatures. (Buell 1992, p. 411)

The question of what the United States has to do with postcoloniality resonates in the tension between these two claims.

In the case of *Black Power*, we see the now classic 'internal colonisation' argument that US minorities have been subjected to white rule in the USA in the same ways as Third World peoples have been subjected to colonial rule by the First World. By contrast, in his essay Buell claims that because US white settler colonials gained independence from British rule in the late eighteenth century, the United States in general was the first post-colony, and thus shares a historical and cultural form with, or perhaps even pioneered that form for, those Third World nation-states that gained independence in the nineteenth and twentieth centuries. The rhetorical difference between these two texts, and thus the tension I referred to above, lies in the use of analogy, a figure that comes from a Greek word meaning 'equality of ratios' which refers to making an argument by stressing the similarities between different cases. Since the figure of analogy stresses similarities, it necessarily 'de-emphasises dissimilarities, and so always runs the risk of producing arguments that are blind to, and thus falter on, the differences between its terms.

For Carmichael and Hamilton, the analogy between US minorities and the Third World is a political one between social movements. They are seeking to break the US civil rights movement out of its national framework, to show how that movement can be more successful by borrowing some of the analyses and tactics of Third World independence movements. Carmichael and Hamilton do not depict the United States as 'postcolonial'. Rather, they argue that the United States has long been an imperial power, at times colonial (occupying countries with military forces and permanent settlers), neo-colonial (occupying countries primarily with capital rather than people), and internally colonial (carving out de facto colonies for people of colour within its own territorial boundaries). They do, however, imagine a time when people of colour in the United States might decolonise themselves. Kindred arguments developed out of other minority social movements of the 1960s and 1970s, and were reflected in texts such as the 'El Plan Espiritual de Aztlán' (1972) and 'Alcatraz Reclaimed' (1971). A more traditionally sociological version of this line of thought can be found in Robert Blauner's 1972 text *Racial Oppression in America*.

This argument has important implications for the study of literature. It implies, for instance, that centuries-old networks of culture among black people taken to the Americas as slaves under colonialism are stronger than connections between black and white people in the United States. Logically, then, a US novel like Ishmael Reed's *Mumbo Jumbo* (1996) would share more historical and aesthetic concerns with a Caribbean play like Aimé Césaire's *A Tempest* (1969) than with Thomas Pynchon's *Crying of Lot 49* (1966), for example. In this, Carmichael and Hamilton's work is closely related to the work of black activists and intellectuals of the nineteenth century, such as Martin Delany, whose novel *Blake, or, the Huts of Africa* (1859–62) depicts a slave revolution arising in the Americas out of the activism of its title character. Carmichael and Hamilton's work also echoes the early twentieth-century black intellectual W. E. B. Du Bois, whose novel *Dark Princess* (1928) depicts a black American who learns, through activism and a melodramatic love affair with a South Asian princess, to connect his struggles with racism in the United States to the struggles of people of colour throughout the world.

It is crucial to notice, however, that immediately upon positing their analogy, Carmichael and Hamilton qualify it: 'Obviously, the analogy is not perfect.' The very moment they urge their readers to see the political potential of an analogy between US minorities struggling for civil rights and Third World peoples struggling for independence, they also warn those readers that there are important differences between these two struggles and thus that there are limits to this analogy and to the 'internal colonisation' argument based on it.

Ironically, the activists Carmichael and Hamilton here show themselves to be more precise in their use of analogy than the English Professor Buell. Though Buell makes a much more sweeping analogy, instead of acknowledging its limits he ends up turning it into a statement of historical fact, in effect suppressing the differences between its terms. One way to understand the 'achievement' of the American Renaissance, he argues, is 'to appropriate' the terms of 'Ashis Nandy's diagnosis of the intellectual climate of colonial India':

To transpose from the colonial to the postcolonial stage of the first half of the American nine-teenth century, we need only substitute cultural authority for political/military authority as the object of resistance. Although the 13 American colonies never experienced anything like the political/military domination colonial India did, the extent of cultural colonisation by the mother country, from epistemology to aesthetics to dietetics, was on the whole much more comprehensive – and partly because of the selfsame comparative benignity of the imperial regime. (Buell 1992, p. 415)

Similarly, Walt Whitman's *Leaves of Grass* is 'akin to modern West Indian inversions of the Prospero-Caliban trope' (Buell 1992, p. 420), the character of Natty Bumppo in James Fenimore Cooper's Leatherstocking novels, which modify the stylistics of the Scottish nov-elist Walter Scott, 'might be seen as a mark of the "colonized mind"' (Buell 1992, p. 422), and the use of vernacular English in Royall Tyler's play *The Contrast*, as well as much of Mark Twain's fiction, 'is the American equivalent of, say, the colloquial dramatic mono-logues of Indo-Anglian poet Nissim Ezekiel' (Buell 1992, p. 428).

Buell explicitly seeks to challenge the tradition in US literary and historical studies of American exceptionalism, which defined the United States as a singularly modern, liberal and democratic entity. While such exceptionalism may have its roots in the Puritan sep-aratists who first colonised North America, it achieved its greatest power over the study of US literature in the mid-twentieth century, in texts such as Perry Miller's *Errand into the Wilderness*. However, Buell's argument has important affinities with the very exceptional-ist tradition he seems to be challenging. That tradition has also consistently represented the singularity of the United States as not only exceptional, but also exemplary – to be fol-lowed by the rest of the world. By declaring the United States to be the first postcolony, and by seeing nineteenth-century Latin-American literature and twentieth-century liter-atures of the global South as extensions of the US's foundational postcoloniality, Buell resists Carmichael and Hamilton's distinctions between white settler colonials and US racial minorities. Carmichael and Hamilton, by contrast, suggest that this white settler US culture was itself a leading imperial force both internationally and domestically.

Buell's article also echoes the even more expansive argument-by-analogy that Bill Ashcroft, Gareth Griffiths, and Helen Tiffin made in their important 1989 text *The Empire Writes Back: Theory and Practice in Post-Colonial Literatures*. Ashcroft et al. claim that the literatures of all white settler colonies, including the USA, have more in common with the Third World than they have in contrast with it:

> So the literatures of African countries, Australia, Bangladesh, Canada, Caribbean countries, India, Malaysia, Malta, New Zealand, Pakistan, Singapore, South Pacific Island countries, and Sri Lanka are all post-colonial literatures. The literature of the USA should also be placed in this category. Perhaps because of its current position of power, and the neo-colonizing role it has played, its post-colonial nature has not been generally recognized. But its relationship with the metropolitan centre as it evolved over the last two centuries has been paradigmatic for post-colonial literatures everywhere. What each of these literatures has in common beyond their special and distinctive regional characteristics is that they emerged in their present form out of the experience of colonisation and asserted themselves by foregrounding the tension with the imperial power, and by emphasizing their differences from the assumptions of the imperial centre. It is this which makes them distinctively post-colonial. (Ashcroft et al. 1989, p. 2)

The problem with an argument like this is that certain 'special and distinctive regional characteristics' of the United States undermine the apparent similarities between it and the other countries Ashcroft et al. invoke. The white settlers of the American colonies used land grants from the European powers, the indentured labour of poor white convicts and children, and the indentured and slave labour of Native Americans and Africans to dispossess Native Americans of their lands and to incorporate North America into the capitalist world-system. As soon as independence from Britain was achieved, the United States continued these imperial practices, expanding its territory in the Americas and increasing its influence in North and West Africa. Throughout this period, many of these white settlers looked explicitly to the European powers as both models for, and rivals to, American cultural, historical and political development. Indeed, much of the country's foundational literature dramatises these imperial foundations of the United States. One could read a novel such as Charles Brockden Brown's *Edgar Huntly*, a play such as Susanna Rowson's *Slaves in Algiers*, or a polemical piece of children's literature such as the anonymously authored *Claims of the African* as allegories of a US imperialism that began the moment the United States gained political independence.

In recent years, many critics have developed the tension between the cautious analogy of Carmichael and Hamilton and the exuberant assertions of Buell, and Ashcroft, Griffiths and Tiffin. One of the most powerful lines of such development has been spurred by the work of Gayatri Chakravorty Spivak, who has criticised the conflation of white settlers and racialised minorities in the United States with either migrants from the global South to Europe, or postcolonial citizens of the South, or subalterns of South. At the most basic level, this argument draws from the Marxist notion of the international division of labour: even racialised minorities in the United States garner a certain degree of enfranchisement as citizens from the economic, political and ideological extraction of surplus value from the South. At the same time, by shifting the focus from analogies between nation-states (which produce arguments-by-analogy such as 'U.S. multiculturalism is the same as subalternity in India' (Spivak 1992, 1993)) to the framework of globality, Spivak has traced divergences and convergences across the international division of labour. Spivak's work on the United States and postcoloniality has been developed by Jenny Sharpe in her 1995 article 'Is the United States Postcolonial? Transnationalism, Immigration, and Race'.

We can discern two other, broadly construed lines of development of the tension between Carmichael and Hamilton, on the one hand; and Buell and Ashcroft et al., on the other. First, US scholars of African American Studies, Chicano Studies, Native American Studies, Asian American Studies, and Women's Studies have shown how the 'internal colonies' to which Carmichael and Hamilton referred do not have such coherently 'internal' borders, since racialised minorities in the United States have long been deeply and complexly connected to international dynamics. Such interdisciplinary literary critical work is exemplified by texts like Brent Hayes Edwards' *The Practice of Diaspora: Literature, Translation, and the Rise of Black Internationalism* (2003), Arnold Krupat's 'Postcoloniality and Native American Literature' (1994), Maria Josefina Saldaña-Portillo's *The Revolutionary Imagination in the Americas and the Age of Development* (2003), Colleen Lye's *America's Asia: The Making of Asiatic Racial Form, 1882–1945* (2004), and Shirley Hune's 'Asian American Studies and Asian Studies: Boundaries and Borderlands of Ethnic Studies and Area Studies' (2001).

The second line of development, which derives from the first, is 'new Americanist' or 'post-nationalist American Studies' scholarship. This work has generated analyses of US empire that are comparativist and international in scope, moving beyond critiques of US exceptionalism to expose the uneven specificities of US imperialism. The work of Amy Kaplan, Donald Pease and John Carlos Rowe exemplifies this line of development.

David Kazanjian

Literary Works

Anonymous (1832), *Claims of the Africans: or The History of the American Colonization Society*, Boston, MA: Massachusetts Sabbath School Union.
Brown, Charles Brockden [1799] (1984), *Edgar Huntly, or Memoirs of a Sleep-Walker*, Kent, OH: Kent State University Press.
Césaire, Aimé [1969] (1992), *A Tempest*, New York: Ubu Repertory Theater.
Delany, Martin R. [1859–62] (1970), *Blake, or, the Huts of Africa*, Boston, MA: Beacon Press.
Du Bois, W. E. B. [1928] (1995), *Dark Princess*, Jackson, MS: University Press of Mississippi.
Pynchon, Thomas [1966] (1996), *The Crying of Lot 49*, New York: Perennial Library.
Reed, Ishmael (1996), *Mumbo Jumbo*, New York: Simon and Schuster.
Rowson, Susanna (1794), *Slaves in Algiers; or, A Struggle for Freedom*, Philadelphia: Wrigley and Berriman.

Histories

'Alcatraz Reclaimed' (1971), *Newsletter of the Indian Tribes of All Nations* (January 1970). Reprinted in The Council on Interracial Books for Children (ed.), *Chronicles of American Indian Protest*, Greenwich, CT: Fawcett Publications, pp. 310–14.
Ashcroft, Bill, Gareth Griffiths and Helen Tiffin (1989), *The Empire Writes Back: Theory and Practice in Post-Colonial Literatures*, London: Routledge.
Blauner, Robert (1972), *Racial Oppression in America*, New York: Harper.
Buell, Lawrence (1992) 'American Literary Emergence as a Postcolonial Phenomenon', *American Literary History* 4: 3 (Fall), pp. 411–42.
Carmichael, Stokely and Charles Hamilton (1967), *Black Power: The Politics of Liberation in America*, New York: Vintage.
Edwards, Brent Hayes (2003), *The Practice of Diaspora: Literature, Translation, and the Rise of Black Internationalism*, Cambridge, MA: Harvard University Press.
'El Plan Espiritual de Aztlán' (1972), *El Grito del Norte*, 2: 9 (6 July 1969). Reprinted in Louis Valdez and Stan Steiner (eds), *Aztlan: An Anthology of Mexican American Literature*, New York: Vintage.
Hune, Shirley (2001), 'Asian American Studies and Asian Studies: Boundaries and Borderlands of Ethnic Studies and Area Studies', in Johnnella E. Butler (ed.), *Color-line to Borderlands: The Matrix of American Ethnic Studies*, Seattle, WA: University of Washington Press.
Kaplan, Amy (2002), *The Anarchy of Empire in the Making of U.S. Culture*, Cambridge, MA: Harvard University Press.
Krupat, Arnold (1994), 'Postcoloniality and Native American Literature', *Yale Journal of Criticism* 7: 1, pp. 163–80.
Lye, Colleen (2004), *America's Asia: The Making of Asiatic Racial Form, 1882–1945*, Princeton, NJ: Princeton University Press.
Miller, Perry (1956), *Errand into the Wilderness*, Cambridge, MA: Harvard University Press.
Pease, Donald E. and Amy Kaplan (eds) (1993), *Cultures of United States Imperialism*, Durham, NC: Duke University Press.
Rowe, John Carlos (2002), *The New American Studies*, Minneapolis, MN: University of Minnesota Press.

Rowe, John Carlos (ed.) (2000), *Post-Nationalist American Studies*, Berkeley, CA: University of California Press.

Saldana-Portillo, Maria Josefina (2003), *The Revolutionary Imagination in the Americas and the Age of Development*, Durham, NC: Duke University Press.

Sharpe, Jenny (1995), 'Is the United States Postcolonial? Transnationalism, Immigration, and Race', *Diaspora* 4: 2 (Fall), pp. 181–99.

Spivak, Gayatri Chakravorty (1992), 'Teaching for the Times', *MMLA* 25: 1, pp. 3–22.

Spivak, Gayatri Chakravorty (1993), 'Scattered Speculations on the Question of Cultural Studies', *Outside in the Teaching Machine*, New York: Routledge, pp. 255–84.

See also: **Anti-globalisation Movements**; **Black Britain**; **Britain's Postwar Foreign Policy**; **Diaspora: Caribbean**; **Diaspora: Pacific**; **Diaspora: South Asia**; **Spanish-American War**; **Vietnam War**.

Universities: East Africa

University education in East Africa began when Uganda Technical College was established in January 1922 at Kampala. It later became a university college offering courses and awarding general degrees of the University of London for Eastern Africa. The University of East Africa was established on 29 June 1963 to offer independent diploma and degree courses. In 1970 the University of East Africa split into three independent universities of Makerere, Nairobi and Dar es Salaam. Most of the staff in the universities of Nairobi and Dar es Salaam had studied at Makerere University. These scholars, notably Ngugi wa Thiong'o, Okot p'Bitek, Taban lo Liyong and Henry Anyumba, articulated a nationalist rhetoric and cultural decolonisation at Nairobi as a response to the literary curriculum at Makerere which privileged the English language, literature and culture. This group initiated a most significant historical moment in university education in East Africa when they successfully revolutionised the English syllabus at the University of Nairobi between 1968 and 1969 which led to the abolition of the English department and the establishment of the Department of Literature. Consequently, African literature and literatures from the rest of the world were taught alongside English literature in the new department. These changes in the literature syllabus were later reflected at Dar es Salaam and Makerere.

This was a definitive moment that at the same time established Ngugi wa Thiong'o as a leading crusader for cultural decolonisation in East Africa. Debates on culture, politics and economics in East Africa were carried out in university-published journals such as *Transition* and *Darlite* and in newspapers and magazines throughout the three countries. Prose, poetry and theatre provided other forums where these debates were conducted. Exchanges between university-based intellectuals and politicians, amongst others were quite lively from the 1960s into the mid-1970s when the Ugandan government under Idi Amin became repressive, which led to the departure of many academics from Makerere. The Kenyan government also started harassing intellectuals, notably Ngugi wa Thiong'o, who was involved in community theatre at Kamiriithu as part of the pursuit of the project of cultural decolonisation that he had initiated at the University of Nairobi. The literary and intellectual output from the three major public universities in East Africa declined from the 1980s onwards with many academics leaving for opportunities in Europe and the USA; but the intellectual marks that Ngugi wa Thiong'o and his colleagues established remain indelible.

Tom Odhiambo

Literary Works

Ngugi wa Thiong'o (1982), *Devil on the Cross*, Nairobi: Heinemann Educational Books.
Ngugi wa Thiong'o and Ngugi wa Mirii (1982), *I Will Marry When I Want*, Oxford: Heinemann Educational Books.

Histories

Ajayi, J. F. Ade, Lameck K. H. Goma and G. Ampah Johnson (eds) (1996), *The African Experience with Higher Education*, London: James Currey.
Ashby, Eric (1964), *African Universities and Western Tradition*, Cambridge, MA: Harvard University Press.
Killam, G. D. (ed.) (1984), *The Writing of East and Central Africa*, Nairobi: Heinemann East Africa.
Ngugi wa Thiong'o (1981), *Writers in Politics*, London: Heinemann Educational Books.
Ngugi wa Thiong'o (1993), *Moving the Centre: The Struggle for Cultural Freedoms*, Oxford: James Currey.
Taban lo Liyong (ed.) (1972), *Popular Culture in East Africa*, Nairobi: Longman Kenya.

See also: **Anglicisation**; **Anti-colonialism and Resistance: East Africa**; **Historiography: East Africa**.

Universities: West Africa

West African experience with universities pre-dated the region's contact with Europeans. Sankore, located in Timbuktu in the ancient Mali empire, was the first university to emerge in the region, in the fifteenth century. It was essentially Islamic in its academic and curriculum orientation. Recently, the Timbuktu Heritage Institute revealed that at Sankore there were well over 700,000 manuscripts, written by scholars, merchants and government officials between the twelfth and the nineteenth centuries. Sankore was a centre of higher learning unparalleled in West Africa prior to the advent of the European.

The history of modern (Western) universities in West Africa began with European colonisation. At first, much of the initiative for Western education came from European Christian missionaries for the propagation of Christianity. Fourah Bay College in Freetown, Sierra Leone, founded in 1826 by the Church Missionary Society (CMS), was the first modern university institution in West Africa. From the start, Fourah Bay was faced with crises – lack of funds, staff attrition, and temporary closure. Established for the training of African auxiliaries for the CMS, Fourah Bay College came under pressure from members of the West African educated elite, such as James Horton, Edward Blyden and James Johnson to provide a secular education. This demand was partially met in 1876 when Fourah Bay affiliated to the University of Durham, but the curriculum remained fundamentally ecclesiastical. The demand for full universities therefore continued, even as Fourah Bay College became the 'Athens of West Africa' and drew students from the entire region.

Until World War II, West Africans' demands for fully-fledged universities were ignored by European colonialists because of financial parsimony, the resistance of local chiefs empowered by indirect rule, and fears regarding the potential threat highly-educated Africans might pose. The impact of war on European colonial powers, the restive mood of the West African educated elite, the radicalising influence of overseas education on West Africans, and the prospect of colonial rule ending all coalesced to force European imperial powers to renegotiate deals with their colonial subjects in West Africa. The postwar era heralded a new attitude towards colonial peoples, and in 1948 Britain established two university colleges in West Africa – the University College of the Gold Coast and the University College at Ibadan, Nigeria – and reconstituted Fourah Bay College as a territorial college. These institutions were linked to the University of London.

The independence of most West African countries in 1960 provided the long-awaited opportunity for the expansion of universities. In Nigeria, the Ashby Commission was set up with members from Britain, the USA and Nigeria to report on the higher educational needs of the country, and its report led to the establishment of three new universities at Ife, Lagos and Zaria. In Ghana, Cold War and regional politics led Kwame Nkrumah to appoint an International Commission on Higher Education, with representatives from Britain, USA, Sierra Leone, USSR and Ghana. The commission recommended the establishment of two new universities in Kumasi and Cape Coast in 1961. From the 1970s, a combination of factors – increasing student demand, ethnic politics and regional development – have contributed to the continued push for more universities, especially in Nigeria, where there are now over fifty.

Since the 1980s, West African universities have grappled with inadequate resources, government meddling, decaying instructional and infrastructural facilities, student unrest and cultism. In Nigeria, for instance, intractable conflicts exist between the academic staff and government over university autonomy, non-payment of salaries and inadequate funding, resulting in incessant strikes, disruption of academic activities, and a brain drain. The academic staff unions have remained the major voice of opposition to government neglect of the higher educational sector. Despite these problems and in view of the richness and relevance of their academic curriculum, quality of faculty and graduates, West Africa universities have performed well in producing intellectuals and in meeting the manpower needs for national and regional development. Yet the process of intellectual decolonisation is far from complete as the universities struggle to adapt their curricula and focus to local needs rather than to meeting standards prescribed overseas.

Apollos O. Nwauwa

Literary Works

Armah, Ayi Kwei (1974), *Fragments*, Nairobi: East Africa Publishing House.
Diala, Isidore (1999), *The Lure of Ash: A Collection of Poems*, Owerri: Fasmen Publishers.
Ike, Chukwemeka (1999), *Our Children are Coming*, Lagos: Spectrum Publishers.
Ike, Chukwemeka (2001), *The Naked Gods*, Ibadan: Ibadan University Press.
Orji, Gabriel (1998), *Stirrings in Canaan*, Enugu: Fourth Dimension Publishers.
Osuafor, Chris (2003), *Tower of Glass*, Owerri: Global Publishers.
Soyinka, Wole [1965] (1987), *The Interpreters*, London: Heinemann.
Soyinka, Wole (1994), *Ibadan: The Penkelemes Years 1946–1965*, London: Methuen.

Histories

Ajayi, J. F. Ade, Lameck K. H. Goma and G. Ampah Johnson (eds) (1996), *The African Experience with Higher Education*, London: James Currey.
Ashby, Eric (1964), *African Universities and Western Tradition*, Cambridge, MA: Harvard University Press.
Davidson, Basil (1961), *Old Africa Rediscovered*, London: Gollancz.
Ezenwa-Ohaeto (1997), *Chinua Achebe. A Biography*, Oxford: James Currey.
Fafunwa, Babs and J. U. Aisiku (eds) (1982), *Education in Africa: A Comparative Study*, London: Allen and Unwin.
Nwauwa, Apollos O. (1997), *Imperialism, Academe and Nationalism: Britain and University Education for Africans, 1860–1960*, London: Frank Cass.

See also: **Anti-colonialism and Resistance: West Africa**; **Historiography: West Africa**; **Nkrumah, Kwame**.

Urabi Revolt

The Urabi Revolt takes its name from the army officer Colonel Ahmed Urabi who was the figurehead for the Egyptian national movement of 1881 to 1882. Urabi was both its catalyst and popular centre because of his *fellah* or native Egyptian origins. When, in January 1881, Urabi's opposition to a law hindering promotion of *fellah* officers from the ranks brought him to the forefront the Hizb i-Watani (National Party) formed around him. This was a coalition of constitutionalists mainly from the Turco-Circassian notable class, reformers including followers of the Muslim radical Jamal al-Din al-Afghani, and army officers, all united in their opposition to European control over Egypt.

The khedive Ismail had bankrupted Egypt in 1876 by running up huge debts on the bourses of Europe. He asked European controllers to oversee Egyptian finances but refused to yield to European financial control and in 1879 was deposed in favour of his son Tawfiq. In September 1881, Urabi and two other officers resisted arrest after refusing to obey orders sending their regiments to different parts of Egypt. They led a military demonstration to confront the khedive Tawfiq at the Abdin palace where their demands – an increase in the size of the army, a new government and a constituent assembly – were accepted. Weak and vacillating, Tawfiq had become reliant on the advice of the British consul-general, Edward Malet. Thus a triangle of Egyptian constitutionalists, the khedive, and diplomats representing European bondholders was set up. At first, Malet was not unsympathetic to the constitutionalists, but his hand was forced by politicians in Paris and London. French prime minister Gambetta was the instigator behind the Anglo-French Joint Note of January 1882 which in pledging support for the khedive, effectively threw down the gauntlet to the constitutionalists. Some of these, including the prime minister Sherif Pasha, went over to the khedive. Refusing to give up control of the national budget, the National Assembly formed a new ministry in which Urabi, as under-secretary for war, was the real leader. In the meantime Britain and France dispatched fleets as a demonstration of European power.

The sudden fall of Gambetta caused the French to turn away at the last moment, and the British fleet was left to bombard Alexandria after fake ultimatums in July. Two months later, a British expeditionary force crushed Urabi's *fellahin* army at Tel el-Kebir and Britain occupied Egypt. This action had ostensibly been taken to restore order and the power of the khedive. The British prime minister Gladstone was a declared opponent of imperial expansion, and was manoeuvred into the occupation by most of his cabinet, but many members of the English upper classes held Egyptian bonds. With a few notable exceptions without opposition in England, the occupation would later be seen by many as a key stage in the spread of European imperialism in Africa and Asia. For Egyptians, the action broke up a genuine constitutional movement bent on self-government and led to seventy years of British control of their affairs.

Geoff Nash

Literary Works

Mahfouz, Naguib (1990), *Palace Walk* (*Bayn al-Qasr*), New York: Vintage/Anchor.
Pickthall, Marmaduke (1908), *Children of the Nile*, London: John Murray.

Histories

Blunt, Wilfred Scawen (1907), *Secret History of the English Occupation of Egypt: Being a Personal Narrative of Events*, London: T. Fisher Unwin.
Broadley, A. M. (1884), *How we Defended Arabi and his Friends*, London: Chapman and Hall.
Cole, Juan Ricardo (1993), *Colonialism and Revolution in the Middle East. Social and Cultural Origins of the Urabi Movement*, Princeton, NJ: Princeton University Press.
Hopkins, A. G. (1986), 'The Victorians and Africa: A Reconsideration of the Occupation of Egypt, 1882', *Journal of African History* 27, pp. 363–91.
Owen, Roger (1981), 'Egypt and Europe: From French Expedition to English Occupation,' in R. Owen and B. Sutcliffe (eds), *Studies in the Theory of Imperialism*, London: Longman, pp. 195–209.

See also: **British Imperialism; Historiography: British Empire; Historiography: Middle East.**

V

Vietnam War

The war in Vietnam known in the USA as 'the Vietnam War' and in Vietnam as 'the anti-American resistance for national salvation' represents one of two occasions in which the Cold War between the USA and the Soviet Union turned into a 'hot' war in Asia (the other being the Korean War). This armed conflict can be understood, as it has been by many Vietnamese past and present, as part of a very long, ongoing struggle for Vietnamese independence from external domination. Beginning with the Chinese over 2,000 years ago, running through the explicit colonisation by France from 1858 to 1893, to the Japanese (along with the Vichy French control) during World War II, to the French again in the post World War II moment, to the USA beginning in the late 1940s, the Vietnamese people had faced periodic struggles for independence spanning two millennia. Thus, when the US military advisers first appeared in the nation as the French were pulling out, they were widely perceived as but the latest in a long line of external aggressors. Similarly for many colonised peoples throughout the world, the war waged in Vietnam by the USA was interpreted as an extension of explicit imperialist policies practised by the USA from the late 1890s onward, although the USA always claimed Vietnamese freedom and protection from communist tyranny as the reasons for its intervention. The colonial and neo-colonial dimensions of US involvement in Vietnam would haunt perceptions of the war within the USA and globally.

The Vietnam War proved exceptionally costly for all involved, with the US dead numbering 58,000 and over 300,000 wounded, and the Vietnamese losing almost 1 million lives, though this number is by no means certain. The US government spent more than $140 billion to wage a war it eventually lost, and in the process, its citizens also lost confidence in the government and military authorities. The USA also lost a great deal of credibility in the geopolitical sphere, not least because its declared intention to protect universal human values failed to disguise its imperialist desires. With only the most partisan exceptions, the perception of the USA as the defender of freedom disappeared during the years of conflict. The war left scars individually, collectively, nationally, and internationally. American military might and big money, it was painfully learned, could not always carry the day.

From the inception of US involvement, 'the domino theory' of potential communist influence held sway in policy decisions, and did so from Eisenhower, to Kennedy, to Johnson, to Nixon. The stated major threat to US security after World War II was communism, and each president felt that any change in the ideological landscape anywhere in the world held direct and explicit implications for the nation. 'The domino theory' asserted that any country with a communist regime perched on one of its borders was highly susceptible to communist influence, and hence political instability. The fall of one country to communism, the theory claimed, would inevitably lead to the fall of its neighbours throughout an entire region of the world, in this specific case, all the way to Australia and New Zealand. With China on Vietnam's border and supposedly exerting influence on nationalist aspirations within Vietnam, America became increasingly concerned about the entire South-east Asian (or 'Indo-Chinese') region, especially after the French pulled out of its former colony in 1954, leaving what the US considered a dangerous power vacuum in which Ho Chi Minh's Democratic Republic of Vietnam could emerge as the central authority, aided and abetted by the Chinese and Soviet governments. Ho, however, had earlier tried several times to build ties with America, and the lead-up to US involvement in the war is a paradigm of botched opportunities.

During World War II, Ho came back to Vietnam after living in France, Russia, and China, as well as travelling around the world organising Vietnamese exiles and nationalists. He intended to lead nationalist groups and form them into a single independence movement against French colonialism. During World War II, Ho and other Vietnamese nationalists had participated in anti-Japanese resistance, and had even helped Allied forces find downed pilots. With the Japanese surrender in 1945, Ho declared the independence of Vietnam, leading to the abdication of the Vietnamese emperor. The speech in which he named the nascent nation the Democratic Republic of Vietnam was modelled on the US Declaration of Independence, and he courted the USA as an ally in the struggle for freedom and autonomous statehood. However, his letters to the US president, Truman, asking for Vietnamese self-determination and official recognition of Vietnamese independence went unanswered. The postwar face of Vietnam had already been decided by Franklin Roosevelt, Joseph Stalin and Winston Churchill at the Potsdam conference.

The Chinese and British in the aftermath of the war divided control over Vietnam and the surrounding regions. Ho's government in the north held political power, while the Chinese held military power, a political fait accompli that was ignored. Following a deal with first the British and later the Chinese, France began reclaiming its former colony, starting almost immediately with the cessation of hostilities in the south and later in the north after reaching an agreement with the Chinese. The USA supported their claims and efforts, which were fuelled by France's national self-image after Nazi occupation during World War II. Further, US worries about the Cold War with Russia had already emerged in 1946, and as America wished to base nuclear weapons in France, placating French international desires seemed strategic.

The war between the Vietminh (Ho's army) and the French began in 1946, and ended with a French defeat in 1954 after a decisive battle at Dienbienphu, and the eventual acceptance of the Geneva Conference peace terms. All parties agreed at Geneva that Ho would rule the north of the country above the Seventeenth Parallel, and Ngo Dinh Diem, a strong anti-communist, would be prime minister for the south. There was to be two years of free travel between both halves of the country, and country-wide elections for a unified nation would be held at the end of that period.

The USA sent a team of military and intelligence officers to generate a propaganda campaign to convince the Vietnamese to vote against Ho and the Communist Party. This campaign charged Ho's government in the north of committing wide-scale murder and other atrocities. Their efforts to sway the election came to nothing when Diem refused to hold elections for a united Vietnam, and the USA backed his decision. Ho now turned to the Soviet Union for direct aid, feeling he could longer trust the USA, and as early as 1959 had begun to organise dissident groups in the south opposed to the Diem government, regardless of their ideological affiliation. The National Liberation Front (NLF), what the USA would call the Vietcong, thus came into being, and they promised free land to peasants if the front's campaign proved successful. This promise, after decades of colonial rule and in ongoing governmental exploitation and corruption, provided a powerful incentive for peasants to join the guerrilla force. Equally forceful in persuading peasants in the south to turn against the Diem government was the ill-conceived 'strategic hamlet' plan proffered by the Kennedy administration as means of countering NLF influence.

In the aftermath of the cancelled elections, Diem's regime grew increasingly repressive, with his brother as head of a secret police force feared for brutal methods that relied on fear and intimidation. Several coup attempts and many protests, especially from Buddhists, marred the regime's image at home and abroad. The Diem regime was fiercely Catholic, and as such contained more than a hint of French colonial power and privilege in a supposedly postcolonial moment. The number of Vietnamese Catholics had always been historically rather small, but their influence unduly large as the French rewarded those who converted to its official religion. The Catholic Church had been the largest property holder in colonial France, and the colonial government gave administration positions to Catholic

Vietnamese. The apparent and actual perpetuation of colonial power structures in a nation struggling to find unity and autonomy at a fragile postcolonial time created a substantial obstacle in the Diem government's attempt to find legitimacy, trust and influence. Nonetheless, Diem's anti-colonial pedigree remained strong. The biggest challenge to the legitimacy of his government came in the struggle between his anti-communist, as opposed to his anti-colonial, positions. When his administration cracked down on the anti-resistance forces, and when it incorporated personnel as well as policies from the days of French rule, he was perceived as capitulating to US interests, which coincided with feu-dalist disparities of the past.

Eventually the USA agreed to support a specific military coup, feeling Diem's govern-ment was no longer viable, and in 1963, Diem and his brother Nhu were overthrown and executed within hours of the regime change. The US president who gave tacit approval to the coup, John F. Kennedy, was himself assassinated just a few weeks later. His successor, Lyndon B. Johnson, held the same beliefs in the domino theory as his predecessors, and stated that if South Vietnam was not defended from the NLF, then the next battles would be waged in Hawaii and San Francisco.

From 1964 onward, direct US involvement slowly grew – widely called 'mission creep' – and the persistent term for the situation that emerged was the 'quagmire' that Vietnam became for US policy and military. The first US troops not designated merely 'military advisors' landed in 1965, although the military had been in the country since the late 1950s, and suffered its first combat death in 1959. President Johnson offered a development project plan to the North Vietnamese if they would stop the fighting, but the plan was rejected. US bombing raids escalated until the end of the year, when Johnson suspended them in the hope of negotiating a settlement. After attempts to secure such a settlement failed to produce results, the US resumed bombing the next year. Curtis LeMay, architect for allied bombing in the Pacific during World War II and again responsible for the massive bombing campaign in Vietnam, infamously asserted that superior US air power could bomb Vietnam 'back to the Stone Age'. Johnson preferred a strategy that would more precisely target military bases and infrastructure, but LeMay's heavier-handed approach was adopted later by the Nixon administration.

By end of 1966, US troop strength had reached 400,000, with the number rising to 500,000 the following year. American bombing intensified despite beliefs that it was not effective. In the face of such overwhelming force, the NLF relied on guerrilla tactics based on the type of warfare successfully deployed by Mao Zedong in his campaign in China. The NLF also educated peasants in economics and history, realising that if the peasants were not on its side, the NLF would fail. The NLF therefore 'liberated' land from the landown-ing minority and redistributed it to peasants when it could. Villagers in the south, believ-ing that land would be returned to the powerful minority if the US troops were successful, saw the NLF as friends and the US army as foes; in other words, whereas the USA was per-ceived as a defender of colonial and neo-colonial inequities, the NLF was a liberator from such tyrannies.

The NLF gained material and personnel support from the north along a supply line known as the Ho Chi Minh trail, which was based largely in Laos. The US military spent an enormous amount of firepower and money trying to destroy this line. As the LeMay view of air power began to gain sway in military planning, the US used B-52 bombers to attack from altitudes beyond air-to-ground retaliatory firepower. From 1965 to 1973, America dropped over 8 million tons of bombs on Vietnam, approximately three times the amount used in all of World War II. The horrific amount of bombing and the range of weaponry used during the Vietnam War entered the public imagination, along with the ubiquitous helicopters. Chemical weapons such as 'agent orange' and 'napalm' became part of public discourse. Originally developed as an incendiary device used in the firebombing raids of Tokyo during World War II, napalm attaches itself to the skin and often burns through to the bone, killing victims through pain as much as through actual wounds. Photographs of civilians burned by napalm and other fire attacks weakened US public support for the war.

Back in America, Johnson sought to stop the military escalation, and so sent no more troops in an effort to lay the ground for peace negotiations. Student unrest and massive protests against the war in America eventually led to Johnson's decision not to run again for president. In 1968, an unprecedented offensive assault by the North Vietnamese army and the NLF, now known as the 'Tet offensive', began, marking the most intense fighting of the war. The Tet offensive revealed that the most optimistic US military reports were at odds with the situation on the ground, and that the South Vietnamese and the US could not win the war. In the same year, Richard Nixon was elected, and peace talks began in Paris. These soon broke down, and US troop strength remained at record levels of approximately 540,000.

The years 1969 and 1970 proved pivotal for the war. Pressure for peace escalated at this moment for several reasons. Two incidents in 1970 were especially influential: the Kent State protest during which four unarmed students were killed by the US National Guard, and the trial of Lieutenant Calley for his involvement in the My Lai massacre, which resulted in the murder of over 100 innocent civilians. Additionally, the number of body bags with US soldiers continued to mount, despite Nixon simultaneously reducing troop numbers, and intensifying saturation bombing (including the secret bombing of Cambodia). All these factors – that the conflict had no apparent end in sight, that it had become public knowledge that the US had engaged in war crimes, and that US casualty lists continued to grow – combined to turn public opinion decisively against the war.

A breakthrough in negotiations in Paris prompted Nixon in 1972 to declare, 'Peace is at hand.' Political sceptics noted the timing of this announcement, just prior to the 1972 US presidential elections. Nixon was re-elected in a landslide, but the election would become infamous in US political history because of the Watergate scandal. In late 1972, when peace talks broke down again, Nixon ordered renewed bombing. During an eleven-day period, the cities of Hanoi and Haiphong had over 100,000 bombs dropped on them, containing the destructive power equivalent to five times that used on Hiroshima. Diplomatic processes continued at the same time, and an initial ceasefire agreement was signed by both sides on 23 January 1973. Later in that year, Vice-President Spiro Agnew resigned under a cloud, followed by Nixon the next year. The Watergate scandal became inextricably connected in the public imagination with the failures of the US military in Vietnam.

The war, however, continued to drag on, with communist forces eventually capturing Saigon in April 1975. The last US military, civilians, and embassy staff evacuated the city, and images of the helicopter lift from the American embassy resonated painfully throughout the USA. The combination of defeat in Vietnam and the anger and distrust generated by Watergate created what future US president, Jimmy Carter, would term a 'malaise'. The timing, too, of the North Vietnamese victory was significant: in 1976, the bicentennial year of the American Revolution, Vietnam was formally unified under communist rule, and the southern capital renamed Ho Chi Minh City.

With over a million and a half people killed, the Vietnam War cost the US its self-appointed role as a champion of freedom in global affairs. The end of the war marked a nadir for American power and ideological certainty. A dark night of the soul descended on the populace as the nation's explicit and implicit imperial presence in Asia drew to a close after nearly eighty years. At the same time, the cessation of hostilities created a long-awaited moment of peace for the Vietnamese nation and its people.

Ryan Bishop

Literary Works

Bao Ninh (1994), *The Sorrow of War*, London: Minerva.
Duong Thu Huong (1993), *Paradise of the Blind*, New York: Morrow.
Lan Cao (1997), *Monkey Bridge*, New York: Viking.
Mong-Lan (2001), *Song of the Cicadas*, Amherst, MA: University of Massachusetts Press.
Nguyen Qui Duc (1994), *Where the Ashes Are*, Reading, MA: Addison and Wesley.
Tran, Barbara, Monique T. D. Truong and Luu Truong Khoi (eds) (1998), *Watermark Vietnamese Poetry and Prose*, Philadelphia: Temple University Press.
Truong, Monique T. D. (2003), *The Book of Salt*, New York: Houghton Mifflin.
Truong Tran (2002), *Dust and Conscience*, Berkeley, CA: Apogee Press.

Histories

Anderson, David L. (2002), *The Columbia Guide to the Vietnam War*, New York: Columbia University Press.
Bui Diem (1987), *In the Jaws of History*, Bloomington, IN: Indiana University Press.
Clodfelter, Michael (1995), *Vietnam in Military Statistics: A History of the Indochina Wars, 1772–1991*, Jefferson, NC and London: McFarland and Company.
Duiker, William J. (1989), *Historical Dictionary of Vietnam*, Metuchen, NJ: Scarecrow Press.
Fitzgerald, Frances (1972), *Fire in the Lake*, Boston, MA: Little, Brown.
Halberstam, David (1972), *The Best and the Brightest*, New York: Random House.
Lehrack, Otto (1992), *No Shining Armor*, Lawrence, KS: University of Kansas Press.
Lewy, Guenter (1978), *America in Vietnam*, New York: Oxford University Press.
Karnow, Stanley (1983), *Vietnam: A History*, New York: Viking.
Komer, R. (1985), *Bureaucracy at War*, Boulder, CO: Westview Press.
Langguth, A. J. (2000), *Our Vietnam: The War, 1954–1975*, New York: Simon and Schuster.
Logevall, Fredrik (1999), *Choosing War: The Lost Chance for Peace and the Escalation of War in Vietnam*, Berkeley, CA: University of California Press.
Luong, Hy V. (ed.) (2003), *Postwar Vietnam: Dynamics of a Transforming Society*, Singapore: ISEAS Press; Lanham, MD: Rowman and Littlefield.
Plaster, J. L. (1997), *SOG: The Secret Wars of America's Commandos in Vietnam*, New York: Onyx Books.
Sheehan, Neil (1988), *A Bright Shining Lie*, New York: Picador.
Sorley, Lewis (1999), *A Better War: The Unexamined Victories and Final Tragedy of America's Last Years in Vietnam*, New York: Harcourt Brace.
Tucker, Spencer C. (ed.) (2000), *Encyclopedia of the Vietnam War: A Political, Social, and Military History*, New York: Oxford University Press.

See also: **Anti-war movements: Australia; Britain's Postwar Foreign Policy; Historiography: South-east Asia; United States of America.**

W

Wabenzi

Following the independence of Tanganyika on 9 December 1961, Julius Nyerere's government embarked on a policy of Africanisation through which posts previously held by
Europeans and Asians were offered to Africans. Inevitably, the officials were perceived as
political appointees who were being rewarded for their loyalty during the pre-independence struggle. The term, *wanaizi* (sing. *mnaizi*) was coined in Swahili during the early
1960s to refer to them, deriving it from the English '-nisation' of the process. *Wanaizi* were
stereotyped as individuals who were largely uneducated in the Western sense and unde-
serving of their positions on merit. They themselves firmly grasped the opportunities thrust
their way: they started businesses on the side which became more lucrative than their jobs.
Some left their posts to focus on their newer interests. Thus, between 1961 and 1967 –
when Nyerere declared *ujamaa*, socialism, as the official policy of Tanzania – the *wanaizi*
flourished as capitalistic entrepreneurs.

One of the success symbols of the time was the German car, Mercedes-Benz. Owning it
signified wealth, but also self-made success. The personal dimension was important.
Ordinary people were quick to categorise such individuals derisively as *wabenzi*, owners of
the Benz. The two categories – *wanaizi* and *wabenzi* – thus overlapped: their common goal
was to make money. They were proud of their status, despite the common man's attitude
towards them. Interestingly, Asians and other entrepreneurs were excluded from this category; the *wabenzi* were Africans whose success was perceived as derived from favours
received from the government. One such *mbenzi* is portrayed in Ebrahim Hussein's play in
Swahili, *Mashetani* (*The Devils*). He is Baba Kitaru, the father of one of the main characters. When Baba Kitaru first appears in the play, he is singing a ditty in English whose main
lines are: 'I like some money, I like some honey, a very good life, a very beautiful wife', in
that order. He tells his son, who seems not to share the views of his father, that this is the
time for the African to thrust forward and to achieve something for himself, otherwise he
will be left behind: 'and this is not the time to remain behind' (Hussein 1971, p. 24). He
shows off his brand new Mercedes-Benz which he calls 'my bird' (Hussein 1971, p. 22).

Nyerere's policy of *ujamaa*, embodied in the Arusha Declaration of February 1967,
attempted to stop such individuals from exploiting others (Nyerere 1968). It was initially
received well (Kamenju and Topan 1971), but economic stringencies, and responses from
the World Bank, forced its abandonment, especially after Nyerere's retirement in 1985.
Capitalism has once again returned to Tanzania, but one does not hear the term *wabenzi*
today. It too disappeared with the socialist policy of *ujamaa*.

Farouk Topan

Literary Works

Gurnah, Abdulrazak (2001), *By the Sea*, London: Bloomsbury.
Hussein, Ebrahim (1971), *Mashetani*, Dar es Salaam: Oxford University Press.

Histories

Hold, Michael (ed.) (1988), *Tanzania After Nyerere*, London: Pinter Publishers.
Nyerere, Julius K. (1968), *Ujamaa: Essays on Socialism*, Dar es Salaam: Oxford University
    Press.

See also: **Nyerere, Julius and Ujamaa**.

Waitangi Treaty

Lieutenant-Governor William Hobson, representing the British Crown, and forty-five
Maori chiefs signed the Treaty of Waitangi on 6 February 1840 in the Bay of Islands.
Another 500 chiefs signed during the following months. There are two versions of the
treaty, one in English and one in Maori. The drafters of the treaty seem to have deliberately mistranslated it into Maori. It contains a preamble, giving permission for British citizens to settle in New Zealand, and three articles. Article 1 of the English version ceded
sovereignty over New Zealand to the Crown; the Maori version only gave *kawanatanga* or
governorship to the Crown. The second article of the English version promised Maori the
'full, exclusive and undisturbed possession of their lands and estates, forests, fisheries and
other properties'; in the Maori version the Crown guaranteed the *tino-rangatiratanga* or
authority of Maori chiefs. The third article of both texts promised the Maori rights to
British citizenship. The differences between the texts have caused ongoing debate. The
Maori claim they did not cede sovereignty, but only *kawanatanga* or governorship, and that
by retaining their *tino-rangatiratanga*, which equates with *mana* (the highest form of authority), they in fact retained sovereignty. The historical evidence of the signings seems to
support this: British representatives denied the treaty was an attempt to seize sovereignty,
and claimed it was intended to protect the Maori. The treaty was internationally recognised as ceding sovereignty over New Zealand to the British but was never passed as an act
of domestic law. This allowed the British colonial government to ignore the promises they
made to protect Maori interests, land and culture.

   During subsequent decades wars were perpetrated against the Maori, and land acquired
through dubious means including confiscation and forced sale. Also, the Native/Maori
Land Court broke down communal ownership by establishing individual title to land.
Between 1840 and 1980 the Maori lost over 97 per cent of their lands. Maori language was
banned in schools.

   The Waitangi Tribunal was established to address these issues in 1975. In 1994, the
Office of Treaty Settlements was established to negotiate and settle outstanding grievances. The Maori have expressed concern that the settlements for lost lands and rights
are at best minimal. The treaty was also enacted into law to the extent that statutes recognised what are called the 'principles of the treaty', which are defined differently by the
Waitangi Tribunal, courts and the government. The Maori argue that the government
defines the principles in its own favour when it claims that the treaty ceded sovereignty
in 1840.

Rawiri Taonui

Literary Works

Duff, Alan (1990), *Once Were Warriors*, Auckland: Tandem Press.
Duff, Alan (1998), *Both Sides of the Moon*, Auckland: Vintage Books.
Finlayson, Roderick (1938), *Brown Man's Burden*, Auckland: Unicorn Press.
Hulme, Keri (1984), *The Bone People*, Wellington: Spiral Collective.
Ihimaera, Witi (1991 and 1993), *Te Aomarama: Regaining Aotearoa: Maori Writers Speak Out*, 2 vols, Auckland: Reed.
Mason, Bruce (1960), *The Pohutukawa Tree*, Wellington: Price Milburn.
Walker, Ranginui (1987), *Nga Tau Tohetohe: Years of Anger*, Auckland: Penguin.

Histories

Consedine, Robert and Joanna Consedine (2001), *Healing Our History: The Challenge of the Treaty of Waitangi*, Auckland: Penguin.
Durie, Mason (1993), *Te Mana, Te Kawanatanga: The Politics of Maori Self-Determination*, Auckland: Oxford University Press.
Kawharu, Ian H. (1989), *Waitangi: Maori and Pakeha Perspectives of the Treaty of Waitangi*, Auckland: Oxford University Press.
Oliver, William H. (1991), *Claims to the Waitangi Tribunal*, Wellington: Waitangi Tribunal Division.
Orange, Claudia (1987), *The Treaty of Waitangi*, Wellington: Allen and Unwin.
Sharp, A. (1997), *Justice and the Maori*, Auckland: Oxford University Press.
Walker, Ranginui J. (1990), *Ka Whawhai Tonu Matou: Struggle without End*, Auckland: Penguin.
Ward, Alan (1999), *An Unsettled History*, Wellington: Bridget Williams Books.

See also: **European Exploration and Settlement: Australia, New Zealand, Pacific; Maaori; Pakeha; Women's Histories: Australia, New Zealand, Pacific.**

War of 1812

The War of 1812 is generally seen as a defining event in Canadian history, providing Canadians with a heroic foundational myth underpinning a fragile sense of national distinctiveness and cohesiveness. Historians remain divided over the precise causes of the war, but three factors are generally cited. Firstly, US expansion into the mid-west brought to a head the three-way rivalry between American, Canadian and native American interests, and aroused American suspicions that the British were seeking to support tribal land rights in the Ohio country as a buffer to American expansion. An invasion of British North America was thus seen as a vital means of securing America's westward interests vis-à-vis the indigenous population.

More significant, however, were developments in the revolutionary wars in Europe, where American maritime and commercial interests had become unavoidably caught up in the Anglo-French conflict. In retaliation against Napoleon's continental blockade, the British had for several years taken to intercepting and harassing US commercial vessels, much to the outrage of Congress. In the absence of a strong American fleet to take retaliatory measures, a land invasion of Britain's northern colonies seemed the only practical way of striking back. Or as Secretary of State James Monroe put it, Canada was invaded 'not as an object of the war but as a means to bring to a satisfactory conclusion'. And finally there was a widespread American feeling that Canada would be easy pickings. Thomas Jefferson famously penned that an American victory over British North America would be a 'mere matter of marching', while the Speaker of the House, Henry Clay, implored Congress that 'the militia of Kentucky are alone competent to place Montreal and Upper Canada at your feet'. This was to prove a major miscalculation. The British quickly took the initiative when Brigadier General Isaac Brock, with the support of the Shawnee chief Tecumseh, captured the American fort at Detroit without firing a shot. This rallied the spirits of the local Upper Canadian community, many of whom had been equally convinced of the inevitability of a US victory.

There then ensued more than two years of sporadic battles and skirmishes, in which neither side was able to deliver a decisive blow. French militia entered the conflict to stave off an American advance on Montreal in October 1813. That same month, Tecumseh was killed at the Battle of the Thames, thereby putting paid to his ambitions to establish a continental confederacy of native peoples from the Great Lakes to the Gulf of Mexico. A year earlier, Isaac Brock too had been killed trying to defend the Niagara River from US attack, his martyrdom earning him the status of a national hero. But by far the best remembered event of the war is the British raid on Washington DC in August 1814, in which most of the city was burned including the Library of Congress and the White House. Usually depicted as an audacious 'Canadian' triumph, it provided Canadians with a long-since treasured tale of David and Goliath proportions. But in reality, the war petered out into a sordid stalemate, and was ultimately brought to a close in December 1814 by a peace settlement in which both sides reaffirmed the pre-existing borders.

Historians have questioned whether the scale and the significance of the military clashes really amounted to a 'war' in its own right, and the conflict is sometimes regarded as a mere appendage to the American war of independence, or alternatively, a sideshow to the revolutionary wars in Europe. But from a Canadian perspective it remains a significant event, which not only cemented the divisions between the loyalist and republican communities of North America, but also endeared British and French Canadians alike to monarchy and empire, in preference to the much-feared republican tyranny on the other side of the border.

Stuart Ward

Literary Works

Urquhart, Jane (1986), *The Whirlpool*, Toronto: McClelland and Stewart.

Histories

Benn, Carl (1998), *The Iroquois in the War of 1812*, Toronto: University of Toronto Press.
Hickey, Donald (1995), *The War of 1812: A Short History*, Champagne, IL: University of Illinois Press.
Mills, David (1988), *The Idea of Loyalty in Upper Canada, 1784–1850*, Montreal and Kingston: McGill-Queen's University Press.

Stagg, J. C. A. (1983), *Mr Madison's War: Politics, Diplomacy and Warfare in the Early American Republic*, Princeton, NJ: Princeton University Press.

See also: **European Exploration and Settlement: Canada; Nationalism(s): Canada; United States of America.**

West Indies Federation

One major continuity in British colonial policy in the West Indies (Caribbean) from the seventeenth to the twentieth century was the efforts aimed at amalgamating the West Indian colonies into some form of union. The earliest attempts at federation included an informal Leeward Islands Federation in 1674, a formal Leeward Islands Federation (1871–1956) and the Windward Islands Federation during the 1870s. From the nineteenth to the twentieth century royal commissions advanced ideas of federation. The desire to reduce the cost of administering the colonies prompted British colonial authorities to promote federation of the colonies up to the nineteenth century. During this period the white merchant/planter elite, who wanted no challenge to their power, convinced the masses that federation was an oppressive form of government.

The result of such propaganda was a negative public opinion and a fear of federation. Factions of West Indians came together to support federation as a way to speed up the independence process within their locale. These included the West Indian Standing Conference, which met annually from 1926 to 1929, and the Unofficial Conference in Dominica in 1932, which created the West Indian National League to propagate West Indian nationalism and the 1938 British Guiana and West Indian Labour Conference. The 1930s witnessed a series of labour rebellions and unrests in the region. The 1938 Moyne Commission which investigated the causes of these disturbances, reported a need for social and regional programmes as well as self-government; and convinced politicians self government was attainable through federation. The outbreak of World War II temporarily halted any articulation in this direction.

When the war ended the West Indian Labour Conference asked the British government for federation. The Montego Bay Conference was held in 1947 with this request in mind. The Standing Closer Association Committee met in 1949 to create a suitable constitution and it provided the 1949 Rance Report. Between 1953 and 1956 conferences were held in London to draft the federal constitution. Delegates worked out issues dealing with a customs union and freedom of movement between the islands. The Federation Act was passed on 2 August 1956 and the 1957 Standing Federation Committee meeting approved the final federation draft.

In 1958, the territories of the British West Indies became a federation. The members of the federation were Jamaica, Barbados, Trinidad and Tobago, Leeward Islands (Antigua, St Kitts-Nevis-Anguilla, and Montserrat) and the Windward Islands (Dominica, St Vincent, St Lucia and Grenada). The federal constitution allowed for a council of state, which included a governor-general (president), prime minister, ten ministers, nineteen members nominated to senate and forty-five elected members of a House of Representatives.

Author of *The Orchid House* (1953), Phyllis Shand Allfrey (1907–86), served in the federal parliament as one of Dominica's representatives. Elected in 1958, three years after establishing the Dominica Labour Party, Allfrey was minister of labour and social affairs during the period the federation lasted. The federal government had limited power, which included areas of auditing, borrowing, defence, exchange control, immigration and emigration, public service, and administering the funds of federal agencies. The lack of a firm political and ideological commitment, parochialism, division by the sea and competitive economies plagued the federation. Unit governments were committed to their individual territory rather than the federal body. A referendum held in Jamaica in 1961 gave the then government the necessary mandate to withdraw from the federation and withdraw it did. With the declaration 'One from ten leaves nought', the premier of Trinidad and Tobago, Dr Eric Williams, sealed the fate of the federation when he withdrew as well. The West Indies Federation was eventually dissolved in May 1962. Thereafter individual territories moved towards political independence.

Cleve Scott

Literary Works

Allfrey, Phyllis Shand (1953), *The Orchid House*, London: Constable.
Walcott, Derek [1958] (2002), *Drums and Colours*, in *The Haitian Trilogy: Plays: Henri Christophe, Drums and Colours, and The Haytian Earth*, New York: Farrar, Straus and Giroux.

Histories

Hector, L. T. (1997), 'The West Indies Federation – the End was in the Beginning'. *Fan The Flame*, 25 July. Available at http://www.candw.ag/%7Ejardinea/ffhtm/ff970725.htm
Mordecai, John (1968), *The West Indies: The Federal Negotiations*, London: Allen and Unwin.
Springer, Hugh W. (1962), *Reflections on the Failure of the First West Indian Federation*, Cambridge, MA: Center for International Affairs, Harvard University.

See also: **Anti-colonialism and Resistance: Caribbean**; **James, C. L. R.**; **Williams, Eric**.

White Australia Policy

From the late 1850s there was growing opposition in the Australian colonies to the presence of coloured labour in general and Chinese labour in particular. Most of the colonies penalised the entry of the Chinese through a range of taxes. A determination to ensure that the Australian continent should be preserved for European settlers, preferably British, was apparent in the debates leading up to federation in 1901. The passage of the Immigration Restriction Act (popularly known as the White Australia policy) in 1901 effectively barred the entry of non-Europeans into Australia and ensured the centrality of 'white Australia' to the new nation.

The policy had several motivations: a fear that cheap Asian labour would undercut European wages; concerns about the 'diseased' East; a belief that European civilisation in Australia was threatened by an influx from Asia; and fears that a mixed-race community would cause racial degeneration. The policy was largely unchallenged within Australia down to the 1930s. From the 1940s criticism of the policy as exclusionary, racist and internationally damaging, especially among the newly independent nations of Asia, grew more intense. From the late 1950s the policy was progressively modified and in 1973 was rescinded by the Labour government led by Gough Whitlam. In 1975 the Racial Discrimination Act made it unlawful to discriminate on the grounds of race, colour, descent, or national or ethnic origins.

While the White Australia policy was designed to keep non-Europeans out of Australia, it enforced assumptions about the inferiority of Aboriginal peoples and emboldened those who wanted Aboriginality to be bred out of the population. The exclusionary rhetoric of Pauline Hanson's One Nation party and recent policies of 'border protection' and the 'Pacific solution' have given rise to concerns that the racial logic and survivalist anxieties of White Australia have re-emerged.

David Walker

Literary Works

Castro, Brian (1983), *Birds of Passage*, Sydney: Allen and Unwin.
Castro, Brian (1992), *After China*, Sydney: Allen and Unwin.
Dark, Eleanor (1941), *The Timeless Land*, Sydney: Angus and Robertson.
Herbert, Xavier (1938), *Capricornia*, Sydney: Angus and Robertson
Lazaroo, Simone (1994), *The World Waiting to be Made*, Perth: Fremantle Arts Centre Press.
Yu Ouyang (2002), *The Eastern Slope Chronicle*, Sydney: Brandl and Schlesinger.

Histories

Ang, Ien, Sharon Chalmers, Lisa Law and Mandy Thomas (eds) (2000), *Alter/Asians: Asian – Australian Identities in Art, Media and Popular Culture*, Sydney: Pluto Press.
Brawley, Sean (1995), *The White Peril: Foreign Relations and Asian Immigration to Australasia and North America 1919–78*, Sydney: University of New South Wales Press.
Hage, Ghassan (1998), *White Nation: Fantasies of White Supremacy in a Multicultural Society*, Sydney: Pluto Press.
Jayasuriya, Laksiri, David Walker and Jan Gothard (eds), (2003), *The Legacies of White Australia: Race, Culture and Nation*, Perth: University of Western Australia Press.
Markus, Andrew (1979), *Fear and Hatred: Purifying Australia and California*, Sydney: Hale and Iremonger.
Walker, David (2002), 'Survivalist Anxieties: Australian Responses to Asia, 1890s to the Present', *Australian Historical Studies* 120, pp. 319–30.
Willard, Myra (1923), *History of the White Australia Policy to 1920*, Melbourne: Melbourne University Press.

See also: **Asianisation: Australia; Boat People; Chinese Gold-diggers; Historiography: Australia; Multiculturalism: Australia; Racial Discrimination Act: Australia; Yellow Peril.**

Williams, Eric

An innovative scholar, formidable politician, and versatile public intellectual, Eric Eustace Williams (1911–81) shaped his country, Trinidad and Tobago, like nobody else. Williams earned a doctorate in history from Oxford and taught at Howard University, but in 1956 he left academia (without ceasing to be a scholar) to organise the People's National Movement in his native Trinidad. He led his country to independence in 1962 and served as prime minister until his death.

Williams was a powerful orator who dominated the country's history as the 'father of the nation'. Though generally revered, his style of rule, charismatic to the point of authoritarianism, exposed him to criticism, often expressed in acerbically witty calypsos. While Williams the politician pursued a (largely successful) programme of 'pragmatic socialism', Williams the historian was a great deal more radical. A prolific writer, his reputation as a historian rests mainly on *Capitalism and Slavery* (1944), based on his doctoral thesis. In this groundbreaking study, Williams challenges the then dominant British humanitarianist reading of colonial history, which largely credited the 'saints' of the British abolitionist movement with ending slavery. Emphasising the economic aspect of slavery, Williams's major claims are that: slavery and the slave trade financed early British capitalism; and it was capitalism in its mature form that destroyed slavery.

While the impact of *Capitalism and Slavery* on Caribbean historiography can hardly be overestimated, its thesis (at least in its most extremely materialistic form) has since been questioned, and should be read in the context of Williams' struggle for national independence. However, this does not detract from the book's contribution to the study of slavery, and its author, a Trinidadian nationalist with a strong sense of West Indian identity, ranks with Walter Rodney and C. L. R. James (who portrayed Williams in his *Beyond a Boundary* (1963)), as one of the pioneers of the region's economic history. Other works by Williams include *From Columbus to Castro* (1970), a more comprehensive history of the Caribbean, and *Inward Hunger* (1969), a memoir.

Hans-Georg Erney

Literary Works

James, C. L. R. [1963] (2000), *Beyond a Boundary*, London: Serpent's Tail.
Lamming, George [1953] (1991), *In the Castle of my Skin*, Ann Arbor, MI: University of Michigan Press.
Lamming, George [1960] (1992), *The Pleasures of Exile*, Ann Arbor, MI: University of Michigan Press.
Lovelace, Earl [1979] (1998), *The Dragon Can't Dance*, London: Faber.
Naipaul, V. S. [1962] (2002), *The Middle Passage: The Caribbean Revisited*, New York: Vintage.

Histories

Paquet, Sandra Pouchet (ed.) (1997), *Eric Williams and the Postcolonial Caribbean*, special issue of *Callaloo* 20, pp. 702–912.

Solow, Barbara L. and Stanley L. Engerman (eds) (1987), *British Capitalism and Caribbean Slavery: The Legacy of Eric Williams*, New York: Cambridge University Press.

Williams, Eric [1944] (1994), *Capitalism and Slavery*, Chapel Hill, NC: University of North Carolina Press.

Williams, Eric [1969] (1971), *Inward Hunger: The Education of a Prime Minister*, Chicago, IL: University of Chicago Press.

Williams, Eric [1970] (1984), *From Columbus to Castro: The History of the Caribbean, 1492–1969*, New York: Vintage.

See also: **James, C. L. R.; Historiography: Caribbean; Slavery: Caribbean; West Indies Federation**.

Women's Histories: Australia, New Zealand, and the Pacific

Women's histories don't come neatly packaged in the discrete volumes of *The History of X* familiar to generations of school children. This is particularly true of the Pacific region that might of itself supply an apt metaphor for women's histories – scattered, disparate islands between which there may be few links, the expanse of water that separates them being so vast as to hinder effective communication. They are, however, connected by a history of European invasion and colonisation, and, until very recently, by the absence of any author-ised and authoritative form. These 'histories' are predominantly found in the form of per-sonal narrative – stories that when written are put into the 'literature' category and when spoken, reside either in the collective memory of their specific community of origin, or the sporadic collections of idiosyncratic anthropologists. Auto/biography then, whether spoken or written, is often the primary source of Pacific women's histories.

In 1959 Judith Wright published the biography of her Australian forebears, entitled *The Generations of Men*. This is the story of a settler family, and by extension a settler nation, and although much of the biography is a narrative of the 'generations of men' who 'settled' the land declared *terra nullius*, it is also a narrative of their wives and daughters that begins with a description of her grandmother's memory of her childhood home. The domestic sphere is given a place it would not have in a male-authored text, but the history of women is a story within the history of the men who led 'the great pastoral migrations' (Wright 1981, p. 3). This biography would be revised some twenty-two years later in order to 'do more justice to matters which I could not then include', and a narrative of 'great pastoral migrations' became a narrative of 'the great pastoral invasion' (Wright 1981, p. 3). *The Cry for the Dead* is a history that voices the silent desecration of land and the silenced suffering of Aboriginal people attendant on that invasion. Colonial women's histories are necessar-ily conflicted, entangled in the pillage of land and people that is so often imaged as the rape of woman. Wright's second history is an attempt to confront her own responsibility for and implication in this 'rape'. It is not until the publication of *Half a Lifetime* (1999) that she commits a more intimate history to print. What might best be described as a 'reluctant' autobiography depicts the restricted and stultifying world of Australian rural domesticity that is unrelentingly female, a world in which girls have few choices:

> Once the wedding was over, I began to understand my own feminine destiny. Girls, I now knew, had few choices. Their future lay Inside, while Outside was a male domain. Not even the Inside in which they had been born and reared would belong to them. (Wright 1999, p. 52)

However, whilst acknowledging the dispossession of birthright suffered by women under patriarchal rule, Judith Wright's political activism remained, until her death in 2000, centred upon indigenous rights and the imperative need for responsible custodianship of the land.

Focus on place of belonging and human relationship to natural environment is central to many Pacific women's histories. Lines from Wright's poem, 'Falls Country', are embroidered on the last section of the Parliament House Embroidery that now hangs in the Great Hall of Australia's new Parliament House in Canberra: 'There is/ there was/ a country/ that spoke in the language of leaves.' The fragility and the contingency of the natural environment is captured in the shift from present to past tense: 'There is/ there was'. This embroidery, designed and created in collaboration with the Embroiderers' Guilds of Australia, by Australian textile artist, Kay Lawrence, gives alternative form to the complexity of colonial women's histories as understood by Wright. The tapestry is in part a critique of the colonisation of the land, and like much of Lawrence's work, it acts as an intervention in white men's history and white men's government. Two of her other 'portrait' pieces hang in the House of Assembly in Adelaide, South Australia. These 'domestic' tapestries, commissioned by the Women's Suffrage Centenary Steering Committee in 1992, were a communal project, woven not by professionals but by ordinary members of the community during 1993 and 1994. Drawing on nineteenth- and twentieth-century South Australian legislation of women's rights, both the text and textile of these works represent black and white women's place in the nation (wittily encapsulated in the embroidered epigram 'A woman's place is in the house'). The tapestries sit uncomfortably with the classical framed photos of those generations of 'great men' who 'built the nation' – and unsettles the dominance of those men who still claim the largest space in the governance of the nation.

It is, however, only in the last twenty-five years that women's histories have been given a readily recognisable, coherent and articulate form in the documented histories of the Pacific. The writing of women's histories, initiated in large part by an activist cohort of predominantly white female academics in the 1970s, is part of the more general rise of subaltern history in which issues of class, race and gender are examined and given prominence. Journals dedicated to women's studies (like *Hecate* in Australia and New Zealand's *Women's Studies Journal*), and those dedicated to postcolonial studies (like *Kunapipi* and *New Literatures Review*) began to publish scholarly essays on women's histories; female journalists and editors not only infiltrated established publishing houses, but set up alternative houses that gave new space and place to women's writing about women's lives. Thus, in Australia for example, the history of the nation was revised from a (white) woman's point of view with the publication in 1975 and 1976 respectively, of Anne Summers' *Damned Whores and Gods Police: The Colonization of Women in Australia* and Miriam Dixson's *The Real Matilda: Women and Identity in Australia 1788–1975*; followed in the 1980s by Lucy Frost's *No Place for a Nervous Lady: Voices from the Australian Bush*, Kay Schaffer's *Women and the Bush: Forces of Desire in Australian Tradition*, and various collections of colonial women's writing like those compiled by Elizabeth Webby and Lydia Wevers, and Dale Spender (1987 and 1989, and 1988). Throughout the 1980s and 1990s Drusilla Modjeska's imaginative scholarship on Australian literary women and Australian women artists has made a significant contribution to the understanding and appreciation of women's contribution to cultural history (*Exiles at Home* (1981) and *Stravinsky's Lunch* (1999)). Additionally, the late 1980s' political discourse of multiculturalism was in part inspired by and inspired the retrieval of migrant women's stories that articulated a shared history of loss, struggle and achievement. These histories acknowledged and celebrated the postwar impact of 'Other' cultures on an Australia formerly (mis)represented as 'Anglo-Celtic' (see in particular the work of Sneja Gunew and Kateryna Longley 1992).

Similarly in New Zealand, the history of white women dominated the early revisionist period, with particular interest centring on women's suffrage and women's rights. Interest in feminism, colonialism and modernism has been generated by work on Katherine Mansfield, Robin Hyde and Janet Frame. Like Australia, the 1980s was a decade in which women writers were seen to 'come into their own' (Kedgley 1989, p. 9), as evidenced by the number of women interviewed in *Our Own Country* to have won national and international literary prizes, and the repertoire of stories by rural and urban, middle and working class, Maori and Pakeha women, published in Else and Roberts' *A Woman's Life* in 1989. Of particular significance, however, was the publication and the enormous popular appeal in New Zealand and Australia of the socio-historical fictions of Maori women, for instance, Keri Hulme's Booker Prize-winning novel, *The Bone People* (published by a women's collective press, Spiral, in association with Hodder and Stoughton in 1985) and Patricia Grace's *Potiki* (1986); and Aboriginal women's autobiographies, or 'life-writing', epitomised in the success of Sally Morgan's *My Place* (1987). All three narratives are in fact histories of 'my place', all speak a silence, and all explore the settler/indigenous relationship and the loss and restitution of home, land and identity that is founded upon a restored community of belonging. If there is one aspect that could be said to align indigenous women's histories in the Pacific it might be this need to restore self-respect and allegiance to communities that were fractured and fragmented by invasion and settlement of the Pacific nations, and are to some extent reconstituted by the creative act of writing. Keri Hulme writes, 'They were nothing more than people, by themselves . . . But all together, they have become the heart and muscles and mind of something perilous and new, something strange and growing and great. Together, all together, they are the instruments of change' (Hulme 1985, p. 4).

Perilous and new, community is not an easy thing to achieve, and for many women of the Pacific the negotiation of newly re-achieved and reconstituted sovereignty comes with a bitter sweetness, as the editors of *Bitter Sweet* (a recent volume of writing by indigenous women in the Pacific) observe: 'In the Pacific, families provide the heart and passion of life, as well as its limitations and sometimes maddening obligations. Colonisation has brought with it many technical benefits, but also the overwhelming bitterness of oppression and poverty. And the sweetness of indigenous gains in struggle for sovereignty and land rights have often been tinged for women with the sour inevitability of male privilege' (Jones et al. 2000, p. 11). This collection of essays written by and about the indigenous women of Aotearoa/New Zealand, Samoa, Fiji and Tonga, is a valuable source of women's histories that until relatively recently have been neither collected nor broadcast beyond closed communal borders. Often oral, fragmented and undervalued, the stories of women's lives are not generally or easily accessible. Sometimes they are carefully protected and silenced – for positive and negative, for personal and political, reasons. Gradually the silenced voices are speaking, and individuals hesitant or afraid to speak alone, are speaking as a collective. In 1994 Zohl dé Ishtar published a collection of women's stories gleaned from her extensive travel throughout the Pacific region in 1986 and 1987. *Daughters of the Pacific* brings together the histories of indigenous women in the Marshall Islands, Belau, the Northern Marianas, Guam, Hawaii, Fiji, Australia, Aotearoa, Tahiti-Polynesia and the west coast of North America. The stories of this volume had their origin in the network of Women Working for a Nuclear Free and Independent Pacific (co-founded with Bridget Roberts) that sponsored indigenous Pacific and Aboriginal women to tour the UK telling their own stories, 'stories of survival, of strength, determination and

compassion. . . of violence and of shame' (dé Ishtar 1994, xvii). Ishtar writes of the importance of retelling these stories in written form 'as they were told to me'.

Much publication of creative Pacific literature has been generated by the commitment of
Samoan scholar and author, Albert Wendt, whose anthologies, *Lali* (1980) and *Nua Nua*
(1995), included a number of women whose work is still little known beyond the Pacific
Islands. Yet it was a woman, Marjorie Tuainekore Crocombe, a Cook Islander and member
of the South Pacific Creative Arts Society, who founded *Mana*, the journal of South Pacific
creative writing, in 1973. Ten years later, *Mi Mere* (*I am Woman*) was published. This collection of poetry and prose by Solomon Islands' women writers was the result of two women's
writers' workshops held at the Solomon Islands Centre (University of the South Pacific) in
1980. The workshops gave these women of various backgrounds and levels of education the
opportunity to express themselves with confidence in ways they might not have considered
either possible or beneficial; and thus stories perhaps limited to a very small sphere make
their way into a larger world where connections are made in the unlikeliest of places:

> Mi Mere   I am a woman struggling to tell the world about my plight; educated, privileged,
> a lucky one – seen and not heard.
> Mi Mere   I am a woman who never went to school, destined to stay in the village for the
> rest of my life – seen and not heard.
> Mi Mere   A book of stories, poems and photographs about Solomon Islands women and
> their concerns.
> Mi Mere   A book by Solomon Islands women for men and women who want to under-
> stand. (Billy et al. 1983, p. 137)

The retrieval and publication of Pacific women's histories is integral to the furtherance
of our understanding of ourselves as a scattering of islands that although isolated and discrete are joined by ancient histories of migration and settlement, and the more recent histories of European colonialism, and of the progress toward a condition of postcolonialism
in which women played and continue to play a significant but often unrecognised role.
Whilst many groups of indigenous women are only beginning the work toward the
acknowledgment of their histories, Anne Summers, whose scholarly work was central to
the feminist revision of Australian history in the 1970s, reviews the gains and the losses of
twentieth-century affirmative action in a recently published report on 'work, babies and
women's choices'. Her history is based not only on the evidence of published sources, but
on the oral testimony of women 'whose views are not often reflected in books such as this
one' (Summers 2003, p. 12). Her conclusions are grim:

> Thirty years ago women had to reinvent the world and their place in it, to make the arguments
> for equality and to insist that the legislative and other apparatus was put in place to make it
> happen. We thought – or we hoped – we were on track to achieve this justice for women but
> we have been derailed. We now face the end of equality – unless we stand up again and refuse
> to allow it to happen. (Summers 2003, pp. 15–16)

Summers' history makes clear that despite the rhetoric of so-called 'liberal' governments,
women's battle to be recognised has not been won. This is a history that ends with a call
for action. 'If reading this book has made you stop and think, or even made you angry, don't
just sit there – do something! You *can* change the world' (Summers 2003, p. 268).

Anne Collett

Literary Works

Billy, Afu, Hazel Lulei and Jully Sipolo (eds) (1983), *Mi Mere: Poetry and Prose by Solomon Women Writers*, Honiara: University of the South Pacific, Solomon Islands Centre.

Frost, Lucy (1984), *No Place for a Nervous Lady: Voices from the Australian Bush*, Melbourne: McPhee Gribble.

Grace, Patricia (1986), *Potiki*, Auckland: Penguin.

Hulme, Keri (1985), *The Bone People*, Spiral, and Hodder and Stoughton.

Ishtar, Zohl Dé (1994), *Daughters of the Pacific*, Melbourne: Spinifex.

Kedgley, Sue (ed.) (1989), *Our Own Country: Leading New Zealand Women Writers Talk about their Writing and their Lives*, Auckland: Penguin.

Modjeska, Drusilla (1999), *Stravinsky's Lunch*, Sydney: Picador.

Morgan, Sally (1987), *My Place*, Fremantle: Fremantle Arts Centre.

Spender, Dale (ed.) (1988), *The Penguin Anthology of Australian Women's Writing*, Ringwood: Penguin.

The Parliament House Embroidery: A Work of Many Hands (1988), Canberra: Australian Government Publishing Service.

Webby, Elizabeth and Lydia Wevers (eds) (1987), *Happy Endings: Stories by Australian and New Zealand Women, 1850s–1930s*, Sydney: Allen and Unwin.

Webby, Elizabeth and Lydia Wevers (eds) (1989), *Goodbye to Romance: Stories by Australian and New Zealand Women, 1930s–1980s*, Wellington: Allen and Unwin.

Wendt, Albert (ed.) (1980), *Lali: A Pacific Anthology*, Auckland: Longman Paul.

Wendt, Albert (ed.) (1995), *Nua Nua: Pacific Writing in English since 1980*, Auckland: Auckland University Press.

Wright, Judith (1999), *Half a Lifetime*, Melbourne: Text Publishing.

Histories

Brewster, Anne (1996), *Reading Aboriginal Women's Autobiography*, Sydney: Sydney University Press.

Dixson, Miriam (1976), *The Real Matilda: Women and Identity in Australia 1788–1975*, Ringwood: Penguin

Else, Anne and Heather Roberts (eds) (1989), *A Woman's Life: Writing by Women about Female Experience in New Zealand*, Auckland: Penguin.

Gunew, Sneja and Jan Mahyuddin (eds) (1988), *Beyond the Echo: Multicultural Women's Writing*, St Lucia: University of Queensland Press.

Gunew, Sneja and Kateryna Longley (eds) (1992), *Striking Chords. Multicultural Literary Interpretations*, Sydney: Allen and Unwin.

Jones, Alison, Phyllis Herda and Tamasailau Suaalii (eds) (2000), *Bitter Sweet: Indigenous Women in the Pacific*, Dunedin: University of Otago.

Modjeska, Drusilla (1981), *Exiles at Home: Australian Women Writers 1925–1945*, Sydney: Sirius.

Schaffer, Kay (1988), *Women and the Bush: Forces of Desire in Australian Tradition*, Melbourne; Cambridge: Cambridge University Press.

Summers, Anne (1975), *Damned Whores and God's Police: The Colonization of Women in Australia*, Melbourne: Allen Lane.

Summers, Anne (2003), *The End of Equality: Work, Babies and Women's Choices in 21st Century Australia*, Sydney: Random House.
Wright, Judith (1959), *The Generations of Men*, Melbourne: Oxford University Press.
Wright, Judith (1981), *The Cry of the Dead*, Melbourne: Oxford University Press.

See also: **Diaspora: Pacific; European Exploration and Settlement: Australia, New Zealand, Pacific; Historiography: Australia; Pre-colonial Histories: Australia**.

Women's Histories: Canada

Recent historiography of women in Canada underlines the deep diversity of women's experience, which is also evident in postcolonial Canadian literature. Histories such as *Rethinking Canada* (Strong-Boag and Fellman 1997) and *We're Rooted Here and They Can't Pull Us Up* (Bristow et al. 1994) begin in the seventeenth century with European contact, well before Canada came into existence. Historians of women in Canada address the lives of people who were not Canadian but Mi'kmaq, Cree, Métis, Acadian, British, French, American or Newfoundlander, and so on.

Carol Devens (Strong-Boag and Fellman 1997, pp. 11–32) uses written records by Jesuit missionaries, traders and explorers to theorise pre-contact gender roles and to trace post-contact stress between women and men among the Montagnais-Naskapi, Huron, Algonquin and Ojibwa peoples, as First Nations women struggled to preserve traditional ways of life, 'which maximized female autonomy and authority' (Strong-Boag and Fellman 1997, p. 25). In the same collection, Sylvia van Kirk analyses the distinctive contributions of First Nations women in the fur trade, where they were indispensable as translators, guides and wives of the trappers and explorers (Strong-Boag and Fellman 1997, pp. 70–8). Drawing on First Nations' oral traditions, histories such as *Iroquian Women: The Gantowisas* (Mann 2000) reach back further to try to reconstruct women's lives generations before European contact and hundreds of years before Canada's 'founding fathers' signed the Act of Confederation in 1867.

Women of African origin also settled in Canada well before the nation existed as such. Sylvia Hamilton (Bristow et al. 1994, pp. 13–40) documents the arrival of enslaved, loyalist, maroon and refugee women and men from the mid-1600s on. In 1852, Mary Anne Shadd Cary, the first Canadian woman to edit and publish a newspaper, wrote *A Plea for Emigration, or Notes on Canada West* to inform others of African descent of the advantages of immigrating to the British colony. Adrienne Shadd writes (Bristow et al. 1994, pp. 41–68) that between 1815 and 1865, and particularly after 1850, when the passage of the Fugitive Slave Act put all African Americans at risk from bounty hunters, tens of thousands of women, men and children emigrated from the United States, seeking basic civil rights and freedom from slavery (Bristow et al. 1994, p. 41).

In the mid-eighteenth century, after many years of intermittent warfare, the British conquered the French North American colonies of Acadie and La Nouvelle France (now the Maritime Provinces and Quebec). Subsequently, colonial policies favoured immigration from the British Isles. The early nineteenth century saw the arrival of significant numbers of women and men from England, Scotland and Ireland, among whom were two well-known early Canadian writers, Catharine Parr Traill and her sister, Susanna Moodie, who arrived in Upper Canada with their husbands and children in 1832. They were typical of the relatively impoverished middle-class Britons who migrated to pre-confederation

Canada in search of better economic conditions, and who went on to form many of Upper Canada's elite families. Historians note that the more privileged women of this Victorian Canadian class were subject to the debilitating ideology of women's separate sphere, which severely limited their activities and education. Elizabeth Jane Errington (Strong-Boag and Fellman 1997, pp. 112–34) describes how women of 'respectable', British backgrounds were able to find work in the increasingly professional and class-conscious schools of the 1830s:

> It is somewhat ironic that the emergence of the cult of domesticity, which placed such a high premium on women being restricted to the private sphere and thus fulfilling 'natural' roles as teachers of their children, relied increasingly on wage-earning women to transmit these values and skills. (Strong-Boag and Fellman 1997, p. 126)

The gender ideology of separate spheres contrasts sharply with the social and economic power of women of New France a century before, as Jan Noel explains (Strong-Boag and Fellman 1997, pp. 33–56). Between 1663 and 1673, the French government sent over 900 women to New France to provide French spouses for the colonists. Les filles du roi, as they were known, were well-educated women from middle- or upper-class families, and they and their daughters played important roles within the essentially military culture of New France.

Historian Rusty Bitterman points out that, 'for the rural poor, of whom there were many, the notion of a distinct feminine sphere could not have much meaning' (Strong-Boag and Fellman 1997, p. 84). Bitterman argues that the dominant image of women's daily lives in the historical literature is biased towards the middle class:

> The existing literature emphasizes the long hours that women spent cleaning house, washing clothes, preparing meals and spinning and weaving. [But] it did not take long to clean a one-room dwelling, assuming that this was even an objective, nor did cooking and washing absorb a day's labour when household members ate boiled potatoes and oatmeal and possessed little clothing beyond what they were wearing. (Strong-Boag and Fellman 1997, p. 85)

By the end of the nineteenth century, women across the Dominion of Canada were organising for temperance, for women's rights, and moral reform. This period, known as the first wave of the women's movement, culminated in some important gains for women, including the right to vote, won between 1917 and 1922, with the exception of Quebec, where it was withheld until 1940; and, in October 1929, the right to be considered 'persons'. Strong-Boag argues that the 'persons' decision 'asserted . . . that women's right to equality in the public sphere was the cornerstone for any strategy for remedying injustice in private relationships' (Strong-Boag and Fellman 1997, p. 281). Canadian first-wave feminism is examined in Canadian Women: A History (Prentice et al. 1996) and The Age of Light, Soap and Water (Valverde 1991).

In one of the defining phrases of Canadian feminism's second wave, Quebec writer Nicole Brossard wrote, 'To write: I am a woman is full of consequences' (Brossard 1977, p. 45). In the following decades, feminists grappled with how those consequences differ for First Nations women, for women with disabilities, for lesbian women, and for women who are members of racialised minorities. Women of colour emerged as leaders of the women's movement, and First Nations women won a campaign to amend the Indian Act which, from 1876 until 1985, had decreed that women who married non-status men lost their rights as members of their First Nation. *Enough is Enough: Aboriginal Women Speak Out* (Tobique Women's Group 1987) documents women from the Tobique Reserve in New Brunswick who were leaders in that struggle. Important publications such as *Sharing our Experience* (Mukherjee 1993), *Telling It* (The Telling It Collective 1990), *Writing the Circle* (Perreault and Vance 1990), and *Sistahspeak* (Absinthe Collective 1995) zigzag over the boundary between historiography and literature as they work to represent the lives of marginalised women.

Women in Canada have been divided by race, nationality and class, even while their lives have been differently shaped by sexuality and gender. Ruth Haywood (Cook et al. 2001, pp. 124–8), depicts domestic workers who were sexually exploited by soldiers during the war. 'As in Canada, which Newfoundland joined in 1949, birth control 'was illegal until 1969' (Cook et al. 2001, p. 125). Midge Ayukawa (Strong-Boag and Fellman 1997, pp. 238–52) describes how, from 1908 to 1924, in a climate of hostility towards Asian immigration, 6,240 Japanese women arrived as 'picture brides'. Many of these well-educated pioneer women worked in harsh conditions in the mining camps and forests.

In the early years of the twentieth century, women's progress into sectors of the workforce other than domestic service and teaching was marked by the feminisation of clerical work, recreated as a rationalised series of tasks without hope of advancement (Strong-Boag and Fellman 1997, pp. 253–70). White working women were thus contained as a poorly paid labour pool, while First Nations and minority women were kept out of offices and factories altogether, or, if let in, given the hardest, most dangerous work (Bristow et al. 1994, pp. 171–91). Over the century, less racially restrictive immigration policies and legislation protecting cultural and linguistic rights has made Canada more multicultural, but not unproblematically, as Himani Bannerji makes clear in *The Dark Side of Nation* (2000). The Canadian Charter of Rights and Freedoms was passed in 1982, and the Supreme Court of Canada has delivered a series of landmark decisions supporting pay equity; yet, women are still paid less than men, and women with disabilities and lesbian women are still at risk from discrimination, as are racialised minority and immigrant women, who are also highly over-represented in the personal service sector (Bristow et al. 1994, pp. 193–229).

Canadian historiography has been transformed as the society has evolved:

> Self-consciousness of our own situated knowledge has been greatly assisted by the . . . revitalization of movements for social justice, many of which, including feminism and Native rights, also characterized the close of the last century

note the editors of *Rethinking Canada* (Strong-Boag and Fellman 1997, p. 5). An archives-based methodology has limitations, too, as the editors of *Framing Our Past* acknowledge:

> Most public archives in Canada, by their nature and mandates, reflect the figures and historical events of the dominant culture. As part of that culture, they have not acquired the same volume of representational material for non-dominant groups. (Strong-Boag and Fellman 1997, p. xxiii)

The six editors of *We're Rooted Here* (Bristow et al. 1994) state that they came together, at Peggy Bristow's suggestion, to address black women's history in Canada because the subject was neglected.

Postcolonial Canadian literature takes up the themes of women's histories, including immigration, hardship, and home-making as well as the intersection of forms of oppression, and the profound contributions of First Nations women to Canadian identity. Novels often begin elsewhere: Dionne Brand's *At the Full and Change of the Moon* (1999) opens in 1824 on the island of Trinidad, where Marie Ursule, the leader of a secret society of enslaved men and women, plans and carries out a mass suicide, which seems to be the only avenue open for revolt. Bernice Morgan's *Random Passage* (1992) begins with the story of a working-class family forced by company owners to leave England. In both novels, people struggle barely to survive.

Poverty and power are portrayed, too, in Margaret Atwood's *Alias Grace* (1996) when a young servant in Victorian Ontario is sexually exploited by her employer's son, and dies after an illegal abortion. Mavis Gallant's 'The Fenton Child' (1993) explores the bad faith of a man who fathers a child outside marriage, and the trauma and shame inflicted on the baby and young mother. The rape of an enslaved woman, and then of her daughter, make up the tale of George Elliott Clarke's *Beatrice Chancy* (1999), which replies to the cruelty of the slaver with the vengeance of the sexually exploited slave. One of the characters in Sky Lee's *Disappearing Moon Café* (1990) is a First Nations woman who helps Wong Gwei Chang when he is in need, and then is abandoned by him for a Chinese bride. Audrey Thomas' *Isobel Gunn* (1999) is a starving Orkney girl who cross-dresses to find work in the fur trade; raped, and thus discovered, the First Nations women who also make life possible for the European men emotionally rescue her. Lee Maracle's *Ravensong* (1993) interrogates the possibility of an emergent multicultural Canadian identity from the point of view of a well-educated woman who is a member of the Salish First Nation in the 1990s.

Joy Kogawa's 1981 novel *Obasan* was the focus of a dynamic dialectic between women's histories, social justice activism and literature. Based on her family history and on the letters of Muriel Kitigawa (1985), her novel depicts the evacuation of Japanese Canadians during World War II. *Obasan* helped to win the redress campaign that in 1988 obtained an apology and compensation for interned Japanese Canadians.

Susan Knutson

Literary Works

Atwood, Margaret (1996), *Alias Grace*, New York: Doubleday.
Brand, Dionne (1999), *At the Full and Change of the Moon*, Toronto: Alfred A. Knopf.
Brossard, Nicole (1983), *These Our Mothers, Or: The Disintegrating Chapter*, trans. Godard, Barbara, Toronto: Coach House Press.
Clarke, George Elliott (1999), *Beatrice Chancy*, Victoria: Polestar Books.
Gallant, Mavis (1993), 'The Fenton Child', in M. Gallant, *Across the Bridge: New Stories*, Toronto: McClelland and Stewart, pp. 163–98.
Kogawa, Joy (1981), *Obasan*, Toronto: Lester and Orpen Dennys.
Lee, Sky (1990), *Disappearing Moon Café*, Vancouver: Douglas and McIntyre.
Maracle, Lee (1993), *Ravensong*, Vancouver: Press Gang.
Morgan, Bernice (1992), *Random Passage*, St John's: Breakwater.
Shadd Cary, Mary Anne (1852), *A Plea for Emigration, or Notes on Canada West*, Detroit: G. W. Pattison.
Thomas, Audrey (1999), *Isobel Gunn*, Toronto: Penguin.

Histories

Absinthe Collective (1995), *Sistahspeak: Writings by Women of Colour and Aboriginal Women, absinthe* 8, pp. 1–2.

Backhouse, Constance (1999), *Colour-Coded: A Legal History of Racism in Canada, 1900–1950*, Toronto: University of Toronto Press.

Bannerji, Himani (2000), *The Dark Side of Nation: Essays on Multiculturalism, Nationalism and Gender*, Toronto: Canadian Scholars' Press.

Bristow, Peggy (co-ordinator), Dionne Brand, Lindy Carty, Afua P. Cooper, Sylvia Hamilton and Adrienne Shadd (eds) (1994), *'We're Rooted Here and They Can't Pull Us Up': Essays in African Canadian Women's History*, Toronto: University of Toronto Press.

Cook, Sharon Anne, Lorna McLean and Kate O'Rourke (eds) (2001), *Framing Our Past: Canadian Women's History in the Twentieth Century*, Montreal and Kingston: McGill-Queen's University Press.

Kitagawa, Muriel and Roy Miki (eds) (1985), *This Is My Own: Letters to Wes and Other Writings on Japanese Canadians*, Vancouver: Talonbooks.

Mann, Barbara Alice (2000), *Iroquian Women: The Gantowisas*, New York: Peter Lang.

Mukherjee, Arun (ed.) (1993), *Sharing Our Experience*, Ottawa: The Canadian Advisory Council on the Status of Women.

Perreault, Jeanne and Sylvia Vance (eds) (1990), *Writing the Circle: Native Women of Western Canada*, Edmonton: NeWest Publishers.

Prentice, Alison, Gail Cuthbert Brandt, Beth Light, Wendy Mitchinson and Naomi Black (1996), *Canadian Women: A History*, 2nd edn, Toronto: Harcourt, Brace, Jovanovich.

Strong-Boag, Veronica and Anita Clair Fellman (eds) (1997), *Rethinking Canada: The Promise of Women's History*, Toronto: Oxford University Press.

The Clio Collective (1987), *Quebec Women: A History*, trans. Roger Gagnon and Rosalind Quill, Toronto: Women's Press.

The Telling It Collective (1990), *Telling It: Women and Language across Cultures*, Vancouver: Press Gang.

Tobique Women's Group (1987), *Enough is Enough: Aboriginal Women Speak Out*, as told to Janet Silman, Toronto: Women's Press.

Valverde, Mariana (1991), *The Age of Light, Soap and Water: Moral Reform in English Canada, 1885–1925*, Toronto: McClelland and Stewart.

See also: **Historiography: Canada; Inuit; Nationalism(s): Canada**.

Women's Histories: Caribbean

In the main, anglophone Caribbean women's histories cluster around the central conflict out of which the present Caribbean was formed, that is, Atlantic slavery and the dynamics of the plantation system dating from the sixteenth century. More precisely, they are concerned with historical enquiry that makes accessible a fuller understanding of the part played by women in the region. That women were peripheral to or absent from textual accounts up to the early nineteenth century is one informing factor. The actual histories produced to date have, however, largely addressed the figure of the slave woman stereotypically presented in colonial history. In addition, a diversification of historical interest is emerging. Gender relations in the Caribbean and the power dynamics brought into play at key historical moments such as the period of post-emancipation indentureship introducing East Indians to the Caribbean following the abolition of slavery, have begun to be subjected to historical analysis. If a historical 'writing back' is suggested, this holds true also for late twentieth-century literary writing by women of the region who similarly engage with history and specifically with issues of slavery.

Scholarly attention to slavery is indicated in the following titles published in the postcolonial era: *Afro-Caribbean Women and Resistance to Slavery in Barbados* by Hilary Beckles (1988), *Slave Women in the New World: Gender Stratification in the Caribbean* by Marietta Morrisey (1989), *Natural Rebels: A Social History of Enslaved Black Women in Barbados*, by Hilary Beckles (1989), *Slave Women in Caribbean Society: 1650–1838*, by Barbara Bush (1990), and *More than Chattel: Black Women and Slavery in the Americas*, edited by David Barry Gaspar and Darlene Clark Hine (1996). The preoccupation with slavery also signals a profound questioning of the nature of historical explanation of the past, or historiography and the way in which history is written. In effect, the histories above, a more recent rewriting of colonial history, constitute a shared project evident also in the literary texts of the region.

If Atlantic slavery across the Caribbean basin divided the world into mainly masters and slaves, then colonial Caribbean history largely represented the dominant masters of the region. Women appeared to be of little interest historically whether in the Spanish, Dutch, French or English accounts. Yet, even the histories most sympathetic to the enslaved Africans within the region presented the slave or black woman as problematic. Significantly, the problem, notoriously interpreted in 1774 by the West Indian historian, Edward Long, was indicated as being located in the black woman's body. While it was, of course, the labouring body that was uniquely valuable to the Atlantic slave trade, the black woman's body became a site of multiple exploitation, sexually, reproductively as well as productively.

In order to appreciate subsequent postcolonial critique and the foci of the rewriting and reinterpretation project of the late twentieth century, a period in which four generations of African-heritage people were born following the abolition of slavery, it is useful to examine closely the example of Long's *History of Jamaica*. Long provides an important illustration of colonial interest in the Caribbean woman's body and a historical tradition against which writing of the twentieth century later stands. In Long's history, the black woman's body threatens the white family at its core. The juxtaposition of sexuality and history, interesting enough of itself, is further complicated by what appears to be a concern with biology. In a chapter entitled 'Of the Inhabitants', Long addresses the subject of 'Creole ladies', white women born locally in the region. Commenting upon the habits and customs of the 'Creoles', Long censures the mothers among them for a habit he highlights as particularly offensive. It is that the white mothers give their children to black wet nurses, without considering the possibility that the black woman's blood might be corrupted, or that her milk might affect the infant's health. Furthermore, he argues, most of the potential wet nurses, the black women who appear to be appropriate for the job, are indeed prostitutes. Thus, by Long's reasoning, the white women are gullible and the black women are immoral.

Postcolonial reinterpretation of plantation interrelationships necessarily undertakes an unenviable and a distinctive challenge. Since the mercantilism of the period was central to the complex historical forces in operation and readily justified a place for the forced transportation of Africans as slave labour; and since mercantile realities of colonial slavery depended on Britain's wealth produced by sugar and the labour of Africans, justification for this system also promoted as bestial the chattel identity of African-Caribbean women who came to be spoken for, or written about, well into the twentieth century.

Long's colonial history which, in elaborating further upon the nature of the health hazard posed by black woman, declares the group 'prostitutes', is also representative of the primary historical sources encountered by postcolonial writers and one which sheds light upon the legacy of plantation relationships. In other words, early historical preoccupation with the morality of the black woman would demand further enquiry and would become highly con- tested in a postcolonial era. Similarly, the portrayal of Long's phenotypical black woman, referred to as a *quasheba*, who is marked out for labour, ideally in the canefields, and for the procreation of additional labourers through her offspring would be viewed as one-dimen- sional. The fact that African-Caribbean people are no longer forced to function as chattels but instead properly lead their lives as nationals and citizens with rights and responsibilities belies the racist plantocratic assumptions of the earlier work. Interest in the sexual lives of the enslaved woman would be reinterpreted and the behaviour once regarded as indicators of race and type would begin to be understood as markers of resistance.

Lucille Mathurin's *The Rebel Woman in the British West Indies during Slavery* (1975) is to be acknowledged for its groundbreaking work in re-evaluating and representing the black woman during slavery. The history, published initially for young people, celebrates the remarkable resistance of black women under the traumatic conditions of slavery. The figure of Nanny of the Maroons, the single most acclaimed woman figure of slave resistance, is foregrounded. Nanny, a leader of the First Maroon War (1720–39) whose memory had sur- vived mainly through legend, song and poetry, has become emblematic of the rebel Jamaican woman and of a tradition of woman's resistance. Little contemporary historical documentation of Nanny's life in the eighteenth century has been unearthed partly because the British, against whom she fought, largely disregarded the role she played in the war.

Mathurin's work points also to ways in which Caribbean women's histories belong to a second wave of critique against colonialism. In a sense the earlier critique was concerned with a rewriting of the dominant historical discourse presenting the end of slavery as an achievement of abolitionists far removed from daily engagement with the realities and horror of plantation slavery. A counter-discourse presented the enslaved, principally men, as resisters and with them rare individual figures such as the maroon ancestral woman, Nanny.

Hilary Beckles' *Afro-Caribbean Women and Resistance to Slavery in Barbados* takes account of Mathurin's work and the criticism levelled against earlier historical accounts. Addressing this, he presents close analysis of the resistance culture of Barbadian women during slavery. The particular demographic position of Barbadian slaves lay in the greater population of women relative to men from 1673. The main implication for labour analy- sis is that black women formed the larger labour force on the plantations. This means that black women's labour was central to the wealth created by sugar production on the island. Moreover, using sources ranging from plantation records to letters from women slaves to their masters, Beckles contextualises women's resistance to slavery as a continuum, begin- ning with capture, intensifying during the middle passage and permeating life on the plan- tations. This is not to suggest a uniformly resistant enslaved black woman but rather, the ongoing existence of wide-ranging action including armed rebellion, collective bargaining, petitioning and maroonage.

Sharing a similar concern with enslaved women, Barbara Bush's *Slave Women in Caribbean Society: 1650–1838* begins by challenging the stereotype of the immoral black woman and her role on the plantation. That Bush found a dearth of documentation about slave women is indicative of the constraints and tensions within Caribbean women's histories. The 'invisibility' of the black woman coupled with plantocratic ideological investment in her body informed an important historical legacy. Since misrepresentation of the economic roles played by slave women on plantations constituted a key distortion produced by earlier accounts, Bush reappraises this important area to highlight the harsh conditions of the labour regimes for black women, including slave mothers across the region, and notably in Jamaica, Suriname and Trinidad. In addition, Bush writes of family history, culture and religion and argues for further enquiry showing the crucial role of the black woman in Caribbean history.

Hilary Beckles' *Natural Rebels* is first of all interesting for its framing or prefatory declaration that the book was 'conceived and shaped under intense intellectual pressure' (Beckles 1989, p. viii). By this gesture, Beckles renders visible the presence and the demands of his women students, who made up 81 per cent of the student total. Beckles' work at one level is therefore a response to the transformative action at the behest of a majority of women, and foregrounds the key issues of who speaks for the silenced black woman, and in particular who 'has spoken for' and who still 'speaks for' black women slaves.

Beckles analyses the demographic trends of slavery in Barbados to show that women were in the majority and that slave labour meant primarily women's labour as cultivators of sugar cane and producers of sugar. He examines the field slave/house slave dichotomy to argue that, 'fear of being relegated to the field . . . was sufficient to force many house women to conform to the requirements of white authority' (Beckles 1989, p. 65). Beckles' enquiry into the involvement of black women 'hucksters' in the slaves' marketing economy adds to the complexity he offers of slave life. The situation, moreover, of Barbados, self-sufficient in 1807 in the production of slaves, is rendered particularly illuminating in relation to the reproductive demands upon black women during slavery. Exploring family relations, including polygamy and Christian marriage, Beckles problematises the familial and argues that the majority of 'enslaved coloured children' were never freed (Beckles 1989, p. 135), and that those who were freed became actively pro-slavery. Furthermore, he underscores that 'most of those [black women] who mothered children for white men experienced no meaningful advancement in their social and material condition' (Beckles 1989, p. 138). Contextualising the figure of the 'prostitute' referred to above, Beckles shows that the 'sex market' out of which the prostitution claim arose was also integral to the system of Atlantic slavery and that organisational forms of resistance highlighted the centrality of enslaved black women as producers of anti-slavery ideologies.

Verene Shepherd et al.'s *Engendering History* (1995) builds upon the earlier research. The collection not only marks a key moment in Caribbean women's history, but also a departure from those works focusing singularly on the enslaved. While there is some redressing of the balance rendering the hitherto invisible African-heritage woman visible within Caribbean historiography, an aim is to move beyond the 'retrieval stage', and to apply gender analysis to that history while beginning to foreground the diversity of Caribbean historical experience (Shepherd et al. 1995, p. xvi). To this end, the collection offers a range of additional histories focusing upon women's part in the region's historical processes.

The collection makes important excursions into methods of presenting history that challenge the established canons. Mary Chamberlain, for example, argues for the use of oral sources in order to access 'a different set of historical evidence' (Shepherd et al. 1995, p. 108). Glory Robertson explores pictorial sources and particularly women's dress for a representation of nineteenth-century history. Slavery occupies a small section while the collection turns to (alter)native concerns such as street vendors, shop-owners, female lodging-house keepers, and girls' secondary schools for new sources of history. Importantly for the region's ethnic diversity, Verene Shepherd's 'Gender, Migration and Settlement' (1995, pp. 233–57) addresses the Indo-Caribbean presence in Jamaica and sets out specifically to demonstrate the impact of gender on migration, indentureship and settlement of the Indian female in nineteenth-century Jamaica.

An important historical source is usually the testimonies and autobiographical writing that survive. Within the reductivist categorising as slave, the denial of rights included the right to give voice. Since the practice of writing was at best circumscribed for black women very little autobiographical writing is to be found. Therein lies a significant methodological problem for historians of the Caribbean. Bridget Brereton in 'Text, Testimony and Gender' highlights the historians' difficulty when, as in the case of the Caribbean, the evidence concerning the majority of the region's population has been created mainly by a minority of European men. Examining nine autobiographical texts by women resident in the Caribbean from the 1770s to the 1920s, Brereton makes the case for similar reappraisal as a 'rich source of evidence about women's historical experience in the Caribbean' (Shepherd et al. 1995, p. 90).

African-Caribbean women had been largely refused a public voice, given the severity of the penalty for speech in the context of Caribbean slavery. Now, however, especially given the proliferation of writing from the 1970s and 1980s post-independence years, Caribbean women's writing constitutes a rich site of history. In other words, within the literature, history functions as a crucial dynamic. M. Nourbese Philip's (1993) 'Discourse on the Logic of Language', the fifth of nine poem cycles within the collection, offers a framing through the poetic lens of two slave edicts of crucial significance to the silencing of African-Caribbean women. The first edict enforced a Babel effect by ensuring that slaves 'belong to as many ethno-linguistic groups as possible', while the second edict threatened 'removal of the tongue'. Philip underscores the latter as ultimately the key to an understanding of African-Caribbean women's silence during Atlantic slavery. Thus, the search for textual evidence of women's presence leads, as poet and novelist, Merle Collins, indicates, to a point 'after the beginning' (Collins 1995, p. 17) when writers such as Grace Nichols (1990) rememories the slave woman's experience of slavery.

Jean Rhys' novel *Wide Sargasso Sea* (1968), set in 1830s Dominica, Jamaica and England, provides a unique critique of post-emancipation colonial relationships even as she rewrites the colonial text, Charlotte Bronte's *Jane Eyre*. The figure of the ex-slave woman, Christophene, 'a wedding present' (Rhys 1968, p. 18), and surrogate mother to the protagonist, Antoinette, challenges the slave woman stereotype in her role as articulate confidante and ally. Rhys' text may be considered alongside similar writing from the region which not only engages with history but links the theme to madness experienced by Caribbean women. Merle Collins' novel *The Colour of Forgetting* (1995) interrogates the region's history, its absences and omissions. The protagonist, Carib, who evokes the missing Amerindian past, also signifies madness. Most importantly, Collins foregrounds memory and Caribbean oral culture as keepers of the region's history. Erna Brodber's *Jane and Louisa Will Soon Come Home* (1980) is also thematically linked and offers a social history of a Jamaican community in which Nellie, the protagonist, traces her genealogy back to a white great-great-grandfather who does not acknowledge his 'khaki' offspring. By this means, Brodber rememories and re-presents plantation relationships in order to interrogate present-day social realities.

The starting point for Lakshmi Persaud's fictionalised autobiography, *Butterfly in the Wind* (1990), set in 1930s–40s Trinidad, is the childhood of the Hindu Kamla who is born into a wealthy Brahmin family. This may be compared to the childhood of Tee, Merle Hodge's protagonist in *Crick Crack Monkey* (1970), a novel which is also set in Trinidad, though a decade or two later. Zee Edgell's *Beka Lamb* (1982) in contrast offers a temporal setting portraying a pre-independence, 1950s British Honduras (later Belize). The eponymous Beka is a child whose awareness grows with the movement for independence in which her granny, Miss Ivy, is fully, if controversially, involved. Finally, Jamaica Kincaid's *A Small Place* (1988) contextualises many of the histories discussed, juxtaposing the region's colonial past against the postcolonial moment and its neo-colonial contradictions.

Joan Anim-Addo

Literary Works

Brodber, Erna (1980), *Jane and Louisa Will Soon Come Home*, London: New Beacon Books.
Collins, Merle (1995), *The Colour of Forgetting*, London: Virago Press.
Edgell, Zee (1982), *Beka Lamb*, London: Heinemann.
Hodge, Merle (1970), *Crick, Crack Monkey*, Oxford: Heinemann.
Kincaid, Jamaica (1988), *A Small Place*, London: Virago Press.
Nichols, Grace [1983] (1990), *i is a long memoried woman*, London: Karnak House.
Persaud, Lakshmi (1990), *Butterfly in the Wind*, Leeds: Peepal Tree Press.
Philip, M. Nourbese (1993), *She Tries Her Tongue, Her Silence Softly Breaks*, London: Women's Press.
Rhys, Jean (1968), *Wide Sargasso Sea*, London: Penguin Books.

Histories

Beckles, Hilary (1988), *Afro-Caribbean Women and Resistance to Slavery in Barbados*, London: Karnak House.
Beckles, Hilary (1989), *Natural Rebels: A Social History of Enslaved Black Women in Barbados*, London: Zed Books.
Beckles, Hilary (1993), 'White Women and Slavery in the Caribbean', *History Workshop* 36, pp. 66–82.
Brathwaite, Edward Kamau (1975), 'Submerged Mothers', *Jamaica Journal* 9: 2 and 3, pp. 48–9.
Bush, Barbara (1984), 'Towards Emancipation: Slave Women and Resistance to Coercive Labour Regimes in the British West Indian Colonies, 1790–1838', *Slavery and Abolition* 5: 3, pp. 222–43.
Bush, Barbara (1990), *Slave Women in Caribbean Society: 1650–1838*, Kingston: Heinemann Caribbean; Bloomington and Indianapolis: Indiana University Press; London: James Currey.
Ferguson, Moira (ed.) (1993), *The Hart Sisters: Early African Caribbean Writers, Evangelicals and Radicals*, Lincoln, NE: University of Nebraska Press.

French, Joan (1988), 'Colonial Policy towards Women after the 1938 Uprising: The Case of Jamaica', *Caribbean Quarterly*, 34 (3 & 4): pp. 38–61.

Gaspar, David Barry and Darlene Clark Hine (eds) (1996), *More than Chattel: Black Women and Slavery in the Americas*, Bloomington, IN: Indiana University Press.

Kossek, Brigette (1983), 'Racist and Patriarchal Aspects of Plantation Slavery in Grenada: "White Ladies", "Black Women Slaves", and "Rebels"', in W. Binder (ed.), *Slavery in the Americas*, Wurzburg: Konigshausen and Neumann, pp. 277–303.

Mathurin, Lucille (1975), *The Rebel Woman in the British West Indies during Slavery*, Kingston: Institute of Jamaica, for the African-Caribbean Institute of Jamaica.

Miller, Errol (1988), 'The Rise of Matriarchy in the Caribbean', *Caribbean Quarterly* 34 (3 & 4): pp. 1–21.

Morrisey, Marietta (1989), *Slave Women in the New World: Gender Stratification in the Caribbean*, Lawrence, KA: University Press of Kansas.

Shepherd, Verene, Bridget Brereton and Barbara Bailey (eds) (1995), *Engendering History: Caribbean Women in Historical Perspective*, Kingston: Ian Randle Publishers; London: James Currey.

See also: **Diaspora: Caribbean; Diaspora: South Asia; Historiography: Caribbean; Indentured Labour: Caribbean; Slavery: Caribbean.**

Women Histories: East Africa

There has been a tremendous growth in studies of women's histories in East Africa since the 1970s. Historians and literary scholars have life histories, oral sources and the colonial archive in order to recount the historical experience of East African women.

Researchers in their various disciplines have used individual testimonies to explain the aggregate human experiences of men and women in the cities and rural areas in East Africa. Even though the vast majority of historical research and creative works have focused on the accounts of men, the use of life stories in particular have demonstrated that women have always contributed to the socio-political and economic process (see Wright 1993, Otieno 1998, Ndambuki and Robertson 2000). Literary works, too, have registered the central historical role of women in East African society (see p' Bitek 1970, 1971, Said Ahmed Mohamed 1980 (*Utengo*, untranslated, published by Longman Kenya), Mohamed Suleiman Mohamed 1978 (*Nyota ya Rehena*, untranslated, published by Oxford University Press (East Africa)), Ngugi wa Thiong'o and Ngugi wa Mĩriĩ 1976). Despite these works, women are still not as visible as men in the historiography of East Africa.

Different perspectives have emerged in postcolonial studies on women in East Africa. These are the nationalist, the Marxist and the feminist social histories. The nationalist school of thought perceived and conducted research on women in terms of the roles they played in anti-colonial struggles and post-independence nation-building. The nationalists argued that African culture was not as backward as colonial literature had claimed. The Marxist historians were divided into two groups: the dependency school (derived from Andre Gunder Frank); and the class-based school (derived from classical Marxism). Marxist scholars assessed the experiences of women in terms of economic relations (see Fatton 1989). The final perspective is a feminist social history based heavily on the oral testimonies of East African women, routinely excluded from historical accounts of the region. This rather more eclectic approach gathered momentum in the 1990s, and has produced analyses of women's conditions in a variety of contexts (see Meena 1992).

It is interesting to elaborate on each of these schools. Firstly, the nationalist historians were influenced by post-independence priorities, and accordingly described how women had contributed – and have continued to contribute – to the efforts of nation-building (see Hafkin and Bay 1976, Ochwada 1995). They sought heroines in the African past to counter the portrayal of African females in colonial historiography as naturally inferior and as hapless, eternal victims of males with little agency in their own lives. These scholars eulogised queen mothers in Uganda as mothers and builders of the kingdom of Buganda (see Musisi), and also highlighted the efforts of women resistance leaders against colonial rule in Kenya, such as Wangu wa-Makeri and Meketilili wa Menza. In short, women were not only mothers and sisters of kings and other royalty, but also provided political balance and cemented social alliances. A major ambition in this school was to foreground the agency of East African women in pre-colonial, colonial and postcolonial societies of East Africa (see Geiger 1986, 1997; Fair 2002). One particular theme was that women were not oppressed or subordinated in pre-colonial institutions, as had been claimed by colonial anthropology; on the contrary, the contributors to the Hafkin and Bay volume argued that women had controlled their own destinies in Africa since the pre-colonial times. In recent years, however, these early feminist histories have been criticised for failing to interrogate with sufficient rigour closely-related issues of African masculinity (see Meena 1992).

Secondly, Marxist approaches to women's histories in East Africa emerged from the mid-1970s, as disillusionment with the economic performance of East African states escalated. There were various critiques of nationalist historiography from Marxist perspectives, as both creative writers and historians responded to the demands of the period with research on women in the materialist mould, which argued that it was useless to celebrate independence heroes and heroines when the economies and political systems were in crisis. The principal scholarly response was to focus on the roles women played within the political economy. Creative writers such as Ngugi wa Thiong'o and Ngugi wa Mīriī (1976), and Mohamed interrogated the roles of women in the neo-colonial economies of East Africa. They perceived global capitalism in connivance with the state as being behind the predicament of women. An influential example of historical research in this materialist spirit was Luise White's study of prostitution (1990) as an economic activity for women in Kenya.

The third historical approach to women's histories has been that of feminist social historians dedicated to recovering the life stories of East Africa's marginalised and impoverished women. This approach retains some of the influences of the earlier two schools, but places a much stronger emphasis on the life histories and testimonies of women. Susan Geiger (1986), for example, has argued that life histories reintroduce women into the postcolonial studies of Africa. According to Geiger, for too long women have been consigned to the fringes of historical studies in Africa largely because of their low literacy levels (she points out that 70 per cent of the world's illiterate women have mostly been ignored). Since the 1990s, there have been many examples of excellent research that has drawn upon life histories and oral testimony, and has been inspired by the aim of reversing stereotypes about women's invisibility and subordination: Wright (1993) has used life histories to analyse the participation of women in East and Central African slavery; Wallman (1996) has used oral testimony to explain how women in Kampala coped with the scourge of HIV/AIDS; Otieno (1998) has narrated the story of her role in the Mau Mau liberation struggle;

Hodgson and McCurdy (2001) have relied upon the accounts of women's experiences during the colonial and postcolonial period in Africa; Wanyoike (2002) has explored the life history of Wangu wa Makeri, an African woman leader under colonial rule; and Fair (2002) has used life histories to examine the relationship between the rural and urban aspects of women's lives.

Three examples of this kind of research warrant more detailed summary. Firstly, there is much of interest in Mirza and Strobel's (1991) record of the life stories of three women in the Kenyan city of Mombasa – Kaje wa Mwenye Matano, Mishi wa Abdala and Shamsa Muhamad Muhashamy. Their life narratives provide insights into the cultural changes for the Waswahili in Mombasa from slavery through colonialism to the independence period. The three narratives explain the roles of women in family life in rural as well as urban areas, with interesting contradictions laid bare: for instance, most affluent families resided in urban areas, but still owned farmlands in nearby rural areas, and the land-owning class also included women. The life story of Kaje wa Mwenye Matano discloses details about the lives of free-born and slave-born women in Mombasa. She claims that even after emancipation from slavery, those of slave ancestry were still tied to their former masters in specific ways. Former masters continued to use slave-born women as concubines, and in some instances, former slaves were sent on important commercial errands to the interior. Secondly, Susan Geiger (1997) investigates the political lives of women in their temporary migratory patterns from rural to urban areas. Using the life story of Bibi Titi Mohamed, a prominent politician, Geiger analyses the activities of women's involvement in Tanzanian politics. Acutely conscious that there are many women whose political lives have not been accounted for, Geiger attempts to use her study to recover the lost voices of African women. She argues that women migrated to cities in order to escape traditional male surveillance in the rural areas, and because there were more business opportunities in the city than there were in the rural areas. Women's involvement in businesses granted them autonomy to participate in the economy without restriction by fathers or husbands, and these economic advances in turn inspired struggles for political equality with men. The subject of Geiger's study, Bibi Titi, recruited women into politics via the *ngoma* (dance) groups or from beer shops, which both appear to have been important launching pads for women to enter political arenas. This pattern is confirmed in the life stories of other women interviewed by Geiger – Tatu Mzee, Halima Hamisi, Mwamvita Mnyamani, and Mashavu Binti Kibonge – all of whom overcame the highly gendered nature of political structures in order to further women's political interests. A third study is Claire Robertson's study of Berida Ndambuki entitled *We only Come Here to Struggle: Stories from Berida's Life* (also produced in video form as *The Second Face: Berida's Lives* (2000)). The book and video trace the life of Berida from her rural home of Kathonzweni to Gikomba market in Nairobi. Finally, it is worth noting that there have been contemporaneous literary works like Arthur Dobrin's *Malaika* (1998) and Marjorie Macgoye's *Chira* (1997), which have also explored the lives of impoverished women struggling to survive in the harsh socio-political and economic landscape of East Africa.

In conclusion, the writing of women's histories in East Africa has itself been influenced by the recent history of post-independence nationalist euphoria followed by neo-colonial disillusionment. Historians and literary scholars have responded creatively to these shifts by producing a rich, nuanced and diverse historiography of East African women.

Hannington Ochwada

Literary Works

Dobrin, Arthur (1998), *Malaika*, Nairobi: Jomo Kenyatta Foundation.
Likimani, Muthoni (1974), *What Does a Man Want?* Nairobi: Kenya Literature Bureau.
Macgoye, Marjorie Oludhe (1997), *Chira*, Nairobi: East African Educational Publishers.
Ngugi wa Thiong'o and Ngugi wa Mĩriĩ (1976), *I Will Marry When I Want*, Nairobi: East African Educational Publishers.
p'Bitek, Okot (1971), *Two Songs*, Nairobi: Heinemann.
p'Bitek, Okot (1972), *Song of Lawino and Song of Ocol*, Nairobi: East African Educational Publishers.

Histories

Allman, Jean, Susan Geiger and Nakanyike Musisi (eds) (2002), *Women in African Colonial Histories*, Bloomington, IN: Indiana University Press.
Fair, Laura (2002), *Pastime and Politics: Culture, Community, and Identity in Post-Abolition Urban Zanzibar*, Athens, OH: Ohio University Press.
Fatton Jr, Robert (1989), 'Gender, Class, and State in Africa', in Jan L. Parpart and Kathleen A. Staudt (eds) *Women and the State in Africa*, Boulder, CO: Lynne Rienner, pp. 47–66.
Geiger, Susan N. G. (1986), 'Women's Life Histories: Method and Content', in *Signs: Journal of Women in Culture and Society* 11: 2, pp. 334–51.
Geiger, Susan N. G. (1997), *TANU Women: Culture in the Making of Tanganyikan Nationalism, 1955–1965*, Portsmouth, NH: Heinemann.
Hafkin, Nancy J. and Edna G. Bay (eds) (1976), *Women in Africa: Studies in Social and Economic Change*, Stanford, CA: Stanford University Press.
Hodgson, Dorothy L. and Sheryl A. McCurdy (eds) (2001), *'Wicked' Women and the Reconfiguration of Gender in Africa*, Portsmouth, HA: Heinemann.
Meena, Ruth (1992), *Gender in Southern Africa: Conceptual and Theoretical Issues*, Harare: South Africa Political Economy Series.
Mirza, Sarah and Margaret Strobel (1991), *Three Swahili Women: Life Histories from Mombasa*, Bloomington, IN: Indiana University Press.
Nakanyike, B. Musisi (1992), 'Transformation of Baganda Women: From the Earliest Times to the Demise of the Kingdom in 1966', Toronto: Ph.D. thesis, University of Toronto.
Ndambuki, Berida and Claire C. Robertson (2000), *We Only Come Here to Struggle: Stories from Berida's Life*, Bloomington, IN: Indiana University Press.
Ochwada, Hannington (1995), 'Gender Analysis: The Stunted Discourse in Kenya's Historiography', *Africa Development* 20: 4, pp. 11–28.
Otieno, Wambui Waiyaki (1998), *Mau Mau's Daughter: A Life History*, Boulder, CO: Lynne Rienner.
Robertson, Claire (2000), *The Second Face: Berida's Lives* (video), Bloomington, IN: Indiana University Press.
Wallman, Sandra with Grace Bantebya-Kyomuhendo (1996), *Kampala Women Getting By. Wellbeing in the Time of AIDS*, London: James Currey.
Wanyoike, Mary W. (2002), *Wangu wa Makeri*, Nairobi: East African Educational Publishers.

White, Luise (1990), *The Comforts of Home: Women and Prostitution in Colonial Nairobi*, Chicago: Chicago University Press.

Wright, Marcia (1993), *Strategies of Slaves and Women: Life Stories from East/Central Africa*, New York: L. Barber Press.

See also: **Anti-colonialism and Resistance: East Africa; Historiography: East Africa; Pre-colonial Histories: East Africa.**

Women's Histories: Middle East

The colonial and postcolonial Middle East has been the site of historical contestation, particularly when women's historical participation and experiences are in question. Colonial histories featured prurient perspectives on women's sexuality, appearances and domestic spaces. Women were portrayed concurrently as victims of local patriarchal social structures and as sexually available and wanton creatures, devoid of agency or even intellect. Western writers, artists, historians and travellers were enamoured with images of Middle Eastern women living out idle existences in sensual harems, places where Westerners imagined the rampant sexuality of one man and countless women forced to do his erotic bidding. At the same time, colonial officials, missionaries and historians spoke of Westernisation as an antidote to perceived ills of Middle Eastern society: patriarchy, despotism and fanaticism. As a response to over a century of Western political and cultural domination, postcolonial histories of the Middle East have set out to revise assumptions about women devised in the colonial era.

Colonial histories were most fascinated with the common Middle Eastern practice of veiling. Although veiling was observed by Muslims, Jews and Christians in much of the region and in a variety of forms, Western scholars and media largely associated it with Islam, and the veil became a key symbol to Western eyes of Muslim women's 'victimisation' under indigenous rule. Colonial leaders, and even nationalist leaders inspired by Western feminism, called for the removal of the veil as a symbol of the 'emancipation' of Middle Eastern women that colonialism claimed to bring. The veil has continued to captivate the (often-lurid) imagination of the West, and continues to be popularly attributed to Islam and its perceived oppression of women.

Tremendously important historical examination of this issue has been conducted by scholars in the postcolonial era. One of the most influential writers in this area is Leila Ahmed (1992). Her work has shown the importance of Near Eastern practices of veiling and seclusion in pre-Islamic societies, demonstrating that the veil is neither an Islamic invention nor exclusive to Muslim history, but rather, a borrowed and adapted cultural production. Other historians, such as Fadwa el-Guindi (1999), have researched the multiple interpretations of the veil as experienced by women wearing it, both by choice as well as by social pressure. Some strains of postcolonial Islam have embraced *hijab*, or modest dress, as a marker of Islamic identity, as a vehicle for women's liberation, and as an anti-colonial political, religious and economic expression. Meanwhile, historians such as Malek Alloula (1986) and Sarah Graham-Brown (1988) have catalogued the ways colonial officials, institutions, and citizens fetishised the veil, making it a pornographic trope that revealed far more about the West than about Middle Eastern women's lived experiences.

Another issue that was exploited by colonial histories was the institution of the harem, particularly that of the Ottoman Empire. The popular Western imagination revelled in an image of the harem as debauched, but recent scholarship by Leslie Peirce (1993) has revealed a very different image of harem women from that of mere sexual slaves to a sexu-ally-insatiable, maniacal sultan. Whereas traditional scholarship has emphasised male hierarchical structures as working against a corrupt and meddling 'sultanate of women', Peirce argues that the dynasty was able to maintain control of the empire precisely *because* of female intervention in and regulation of the sexual and political structure of the 'family business'. She challenges the notion that the nature of Islamic society prevents women from exercising power within the household, and instead points out that sex-segregation allows for the development of parallel hierarchies of males and females to emerge, fully self-regulating and with their own rigid rules of sovereignty. In the Ottoman case, women's roles in maintaining the dynasty's control of the empire grew as the society moved from a dynamic, expanding empire led by a warrior sultan to a territorially-fixed empire led by a sultan stationed in one central locale. Scholarship such as this has given historians a much more nuanced understanding of the lives of privileged women in Middle Eastern societies, undermining the colonial assumption that they were entirely void of agency. That being said, it also reveals women's need to understand how to manipulate patriarchal rules without completely transgressing their imposed boundaries.

Many postcolonial histories of the Middle East have looked to the Islamic past to uncover women's positions in social and political life in an era before modern Western imperialism. The era of the Prophet Muhammad and the lives of his Companions have been rich terrain for feminist inspiration. Despite the common Western notion that women have never played a significant role in Islamic public life, histories of pre-modern Muslim women have provided fertile ground for Muslim women who are searching for politically and/or socially active role models. One of the most contested figures from early Islamic history is 'A'isha Bint Abi Bakr, wife of Mohammad. However, 'A'isha's legacy is complicated. She is considered by the Sunni the favourite of Mohammad's wives, and the inspiration of divine intervention when accused of adultery at age fourteen. She is also, however, a symbol of what can happen when women become too involved in politics: *fitna*, in the guise of the first civil war, broke out and irrevocably split the *umma* when 'A'isha challenged 'Ali at the Battle of the Camel. She is also defined by her genealogy and con-nections to her father's family, as well as her husband; this sets her up as a site of contest between the supporters of Abu Bakr and 'Ali. 'A'isha is also renowned for her *hadith* trans-mission, but only by the Sunni. The Shi'i use 'A'isha as a foil to construct their own iden-tity, making her very present but not authoritative in their accounts. As D. A. Spellberg reveals in her definitive study (1994), the battle between the Sunni and the Shi'i was/is often fought on the 'battleground' of 'A'isha's legacy. Because of this contestation, 'A'isha has become both heroine and villain, depending upon theological perspective, among Muslims, as woman to either emulate or defame.

For the modern period, a burgeoning location of primary sources that uncover histories of women in the Middle East is in the realm of memoirs. Many memoirs have been pub-lished in the postcolonial period by women from the region, revealing the divergences of life experience according to age, ethnicity and class. Many of the most poignant memoirs come from women whose early lives were in the harem, the private space reserved for women in middle class and elite homes. Many of these accounts reveal the ways in which seclusion provided women with an opportunity to develop rich homosocial knowledges and relationships despite the context of patriarchal control. For example, in the harem memoir of Moroccan scholar Fatima Mernissi (1993), readers are privy to the intense intergenera-tional relationships fostered between women and girls in the harem. Female knowledge about traditions was interspersed with encouragement for resistance against the effects of seclusion on the intellect. The harem memoirs of the Qajar princess Taj al-Saltana of Iran (1993) and Huda Shaarawi of Egypt (1986) are historic examples of how, for some women, the experience of the harem became a training ground for burgeoning feminism. Despite very different social, political and national circumstances, both of these women used their formative experiences in the harem to forge careers as feminists and anti-imperialist nationalists. At the same time, however, their harem memoirs reveal a life which could often be stifling and without the opportunities afforded to women with more mobility within the public sphere.

Memoirs have also given historians glimpses of the lived experiences of women who have survived traumas of war, displacement and political oppression in modern Middle Eastern history. For example, Nawal el-Saadawi's accounts of her life (1986) as a political prisoner in an Egyptian prison, Fay Afaf Kanafani's descriptions (1999) of living as a refugee from wars in both Palestine and Lebanon, and Nuha Radi's memoir (2003) detailing the impact of the 1991 Gulf War and subsequent sanctions on Iraq all point to the complexities women experience as both subordinate to local, often corrupt, patriarchies, and as members of societies that have still not recovered from the trauma of the colonial past. This similarity is apparent despite their diverse historical situations and locales.

Oral histories, too, have provided valuable evidence for historians seeking to understand the experiences of women in the Middle East. Many have focused on recording the memories and attitudes of illiterate women who have not produced written primary sources, or of women of all classes whose historical experiences have yet to be included in the traditional narratives. Anthropologists have been crucial in the historical understanding of women's lives in the Middle East, and have contributed a wealth of knowledge. For example, Lila Abu-Lughod's oral histories (1993) of women of the Awlad 'Ali Bedouin of Egypt in the 1970s and 1980s have revealed much about the historical and contemporary experiences of women living through tremendously complex social and economic changes. In the same vein, Erika Friedl (1989) has provided historians with great insights about the lives of women in the rural Iranian village of Deh Koh, presenting their traditions and beliefs about marriage, child rearing, work and family, as well as charting the impact of political, economic and social revolution on their lives.

Oral histories have been particularly relevant for understanding changes in women's lives as a result of the massive political and social upheavals that have occurred in the Middle East over the past century. A valuable example is the oral history work among Palestinian mother–daughter pairs conducted by Rafiqa Othman and Michael Gorkin in the 1990s (1996). By interviewing elderly women who have lived through the dramatic events of the loss of Palestine and the creation of Israel, as well as their daughters, historians have the opportunity to learn both the impact of political upheaval on these women, as well as their attitudes toward the patriarchal social structures governing them. Women's oral histories from the Middle East often grant historians key insights into social life-cycle regulation, relationships between women and governments, and the impact of modernity on Middle Eastern women's lives.

Female entertainers have also become the subjects of important postcolonial historical investigation. Biographies of twentieth-century stars such as Umm Kulthum and Asmahan have revealed these dynamic performers' abilities to transcend class and gender restrictions, as well as imperial and postcolonial political obstacles, to become potent actors in public life. Conversely, oral histories and field work among scholars such as Karin Van Nieuwkerk (1995) have demonstrated that more humble, anonymous entertainers, such as dancers and musicians, continue to struggle for acceptance in societies which enjoy their art forms, yet question their morality as women performers.

Although there are still tremendous gaps in the history of women in the Middle East, postcolonialism's call to hearing the voices kept outside of the imperial Metropole's houses of authority has led to a recent surge in interest. As the stories of women's lived experiences are pieced together through documentary evidence, as well as oral histories, anthropologies, and cultural productions, Middle Easterners and those from outside the region have much to gain; presenting a counter-narrative against the still-mainstream Western assumptions of women's complete lack of agency and social participation in Middle Eastern societies holds tremendous promise for understanding contemporary issues in Middle Eastern societies. It is also a crucial exercise for comparative histories of feminism, imperialism and nationalism throughout the world.

Nancy Stockdale

Literary Works

El Saadawi, Nawal (1983), *Women at Point Zero, and the Circling Story*, New Delhi: Kali for Women.

Faqir, Fadia (1966), *Pillars of Salt*, London: Quartet.

Parsipur, Shahrnush (1998), *Women without Men*, Syracuse, NY: Syracuse University.

Rifaat, Alifa (1987), *Distant View of a Minaret*, trans. D. Johnson-Davies, London: Heinemann.

Shaykh, Hanan (1998), *I Sweep the Sun off Rooftops*, New York: Doubleday.

Soueif, Ahdaf (1999), *The Map of Love*, London: Bloomsbury.

Sullivan, Soraya Paknazar (trans.) (1991), *Stories by Iranian Women since the Revolution*, Austin, TX: University of Texas.

Zahran, Yasmin (1995), *A Beggar at Damascus Gate*, Sausalito, CA: Post-Apollo Press.

Histories

Abu-Lughod, Lila (1993), *Writing Women's Worlds: Bedouin Stories*, Berkeley, CA: University of California Press.

Ahmed, Leila (1992), *Women and Gender in Islam: Historical Roots of a Modern Debate*, New Haven, CT: Yale University Press.

Al-Saltana, Taj (1993), *Crowning Anguish: Memoirs of a Persian Princess from the Harem to Modernity*, Washington, DC: Mage.

Al-Shaykh, Hanan (1988), *Women of Sand and Myrrh (Miskul Ghazal)*, trans. Catherine Cobham, New York: Doubleday.

Alloula, Malek (1986), *The Colonial Harem*, Minneapolis, MN: University of Minnesota Press.

Badran, Margot and Miriam Cooke (eds), (1990), *Opening the Gates: A Century of Arab Feminist Writing*, Bloomington, IN: Indiana University Press.

Danielson, Virginia (1997), *'The Voice of Egypt': Umm Kulthum, Arabic Song, and Egyptian Society in the Twentieth Century*, Chicago: University of Chicago Press.

El-Guindi, Fadwa (1999), *Veil: Modesty, Privacy and Resistance*, New York: Berg.

El-Saadawi, Nawal (1986), *Memoirs from the Women's Prison*, London: Women's Press.

Faqir, Fadia (ed.) (1998), *In the House of Silence. Autobiographical Essays by Arab Women Writers*, trans. F. Faqir and S. Eber, Reading: Garnet.

Friedl, Erika (1989), *Women of Deh Koh: Lives in an Iranian Village*, New York: Penguin.

Gorkin, Michael and Rafiqa Othman (1996), *Three Mothers, Three Daughters: Palestinian Women's Stories*, Berkeley, CA: University of California Press.

Graham-Brown, Sarah (1988), *Images of Women: The Portrayal of Women in Photography of the Middle East 1860–1950*, New York: Columbia University Press.

Kahf, Mohja (1999), *Western Representation of the Muslim Woman: From Termagant to Odalisque*, Austin, TX: University of Texas Press.

Kanafani, Fay Afaf (1999), *Nadia, Captive of Hope: Memoir of an Arab Woman*, Armonk: M. E. Sharpe.

Keddie, Nikki R. and Beth Baron (eds), (1991), *Women in Middle Eastern History: Shifting Boundaries in Sex and Gender*, New Haven, CT: Yale University Press.

Lazreg, Marnia (1994), *The Eloquence of Silence: Algerian Women in Question*, New York: Routledge.

Majaj, Lisa Suhair, Paula W. Sunderman and Therese Saliba (eds) (2003), *Intersections: Gender, Nation, and Community in Arab Women's Novels*, Syracuse, NY: Syracuse University Press.

Mernissi, Fatima (1993), *Dreams of Trespass: Tales of a Harem Girlhood*, Reading: Addison-Wesley.

Najjar, Orayb Aref (1992), *Portraits of Palestinian Women*, Salt Lake City, UT: University of Utah Press.

Peirce, Leslie (1993), *The Imperial Harem: Women and Sovereignty in the Ottoman Empire*, New York: Oxford University Press.

Peteet, Julie M. (1991), *Gender in Crisis: Women and the Palestinian Resistance Movement*, New York: Columbia University Press.

Radi, Nuha (2003), *Baghdad Diaries: A Woman's Chronicle of War and Exile*, New York: Vintage.

Shaarawi, Huda (1986), *Harem Years: The Memoirs of an Egyptian Feminist*, New York: The Feminist Press.

Sharoni, Simona (1995), *Gender and the Israeli-Palestinian Conflict: The Politics of Women's Resistance*, Syracuse, NY: Syracuse University Press.

Spellberg, D. A. (1994), *Politics, Gender, and the Islamic Past: The Legacy of 'A'isha Bint Abi Bakr*, New York: Columbia University Press.

Thompson, Elizabeth (2000), *Colonial Citizens: Republican Rights, Paternal Privilege, and Gender in French Syria and Lebanon*, New York: Columbia University Press.

Van Nieuwkerk, Karin (1995), *'A Trade Like any Other': Female Singers and Dancers in Egypt*, Austin, TX: University of Texas Press.

Zuhur, Sherifa (2001), *Asmahan's Secrets: Woman, War, and Song*, Austin, TX: University of Texas Press.

See also **Historiography: Middle East; Islam; Ottoman Empire**.

Women's Histories: South Asia

There have been two major developments in the writing of South Asian history in the post-colonial period – women's history and subaltern history. The emergence of a Dalit (literally 'oppressed': chosen term of self reference of the 'untouchables') public sphere and its intellectual output has been the other major development which has sharpened the sensitivity of feminist history to caste subordination.

Women's histories in South Asia took a more forceful and confident form with the emergence of the women's movements in this region in the 1970s, some thirty years after the end of colonial rule. Drawing upon contemporary leftist and democratic movements, women's movements provided the impetus for 'women's studies' as a specific aspect of the project of uncovering the histories of muted and marginalised groups, and viewing the past from their perspective. Feminist historians had to shift the focus from the dominant concerns of Indian history – the national movement, social reform, revenue systems, modes of production, economic underdevelopment and discrete cultural topics such as religion or architecture – to map historical experience in ways which acknowledged the place of gender in shaping hierarchy, power and identity.

The first venture was a sustained critique of history writing for leaving women out of the framework or subsuming them under men, often under the assumption that a particular theme really had nothing to do with gender. However, it was the historical treatment of the women's question in the nineteenth century which had to be challenged most forcefully, because it treated women as tropes for making cultural claims about the past. Women's histories in Europe and America sometimes began with the presumption that there was a lacuna that existed and women simply had to be inserted into the record of the past – referred to sometimes as the 'add women and stir' approach. In South Asia there was a swift awareness that the project would involve a challenge not only to the patriarchal structuring of the academy, but also to aspects of 'cultural nationalism', the nationalist project of challenging colonial constructions of Indian civilisation as degenerate by constructing a counter-version of a glorious Indian civilisation. The women's issue posed an insistent set of questions about the colonised present providing the context for the nationalist quest to retrieve imaginary golden ages in the ancient past where civilisational glory took the centre stage and internal contradictions, not only of gender but also of class and caste, could be excluded from the frame of historical research.

Early subaltern history sought to focus the historical searchlight on marginalised groups, their cultures, myths and mentalities, and their spontaneous resistance against the structures of power that oppressed them. However, these structures of power were sketched out in a rather static way. In addition, the rebellious agency which was valorised was most often an extremely masculinised phenomenon. The writing remained as male-centred as that of earlier nationalist or Marxist historians – women were subsumed under marginalised communities, whether peasant, tribal or artisanal.

In contrast, women's histories displayed an attentiveness to structures of power and hierarchy – for instance, the realm of law – because the complexity of their operations had to be grasped to understand the practices of gendered dominance. Further, in this project, the pre-colonial periods of history were as important as the transition to colonialism, which the subaltern authors usually focused on. Nor could this work restrict itself only to marginalised groups, because gendered forms of power extended to all women though in very different ways. Women's histories therefore did not seek to command attention as a 'school' of history writing, but developed in a variety of directions, some imaginatively, others rather mechanically, to insert gender as an analytical category into the writing of history. The effort to incorporate the distinctive experiences of women extended the historical scrutiny to the arena of reproduction – the household, the family, marriage, kinship and biological and social reproduction. This also began to bring other historical actors into the picture – slaves, domestic servants, children, migrants, the widow and the aged. Women's history writing in South Asia has been thus both self-conscious and not so. It has had no self-conscious originary moment, founder or a structured collective. The only thing common was that these women's histories were usually written by women historians. There are rarely any claims to being path-breaking. Instead there has been a slow and episodic but serious plotting of structures, institutions, and processes drawing from many schools of history and feminist theories.

While there has been almost no explicit engagement between core subalternists and 'feminist' historians, a tacit tension exists. Perhaps some subaltern historians believe that 'feminist' history represents a homogenising modernist drive while they need to rescue women who do not engage with some 'emancipatory' agenda. There is also a tendency to valorise the resources of 'tradition', (usually cast as Hindu tradition) through which Indian men manage to construct a form of nationalist modernity that is different from that which emerged in the West, a civilisation apparently bereft of similar conflictual legacies. From this resource male nationalists are described as finding the means to effect the smooth entry of respectable women into public life, without much of a focus on female agency, the anguish of women's struggles, or regard for the continuing barriers which assail women's quest for citizenship as such.

Accompanying the project of 'rewriting' history, considerable investment had to be made in the search for new sources from which the legacies of foremothers could be recovered. The two-volume *Women Writing in India* (Tharu and Lalitha 1993–5) has been an important landmark. The range of work collected in terms of region and social category has expanded over the last decade: for example, the Jadavpur Women's Studies Department has published many volumes of women's writing in Bengali from nineteenth-century journals and magazines. In the process, aspects of human activity found insignificant in existing archives, or in the scholarly interpretation of important historical texts, have been given their due. A larger and more diverse community of scholars has begun to engage with texts like the *Therigatha* from the Buddhist corpus and the writings of the medieval *bhakti* (devotional cults) poets, and many have brought a finely tuned feminist sensibility to their exploration of these works.

The problem of 'sources' has also led to the attempt to generate sources from the present. Women have participated in many movements but a textured account of their agency and outlook is absent even from mainstream leftist accounts of the Tebhaga share-croppers movement in Bengal and the communist-led peasant movement in Telengana just before and after independence. Women's histories have used oral history as a way of countering the biases or condescension of institutional records. In *We Were Making History* (Sanghatana 1989), a women's collective went back to women who had participated in the Telengana uprising some thirty years after it ended, and documented their account of issues that were suppressed or marginalised at the height of the movement, and the sense of betrayal that some of them felt. Oral history and the field study techniques of cultural anthropology are now also being used fairly effectively to gauge the historical experience of neglected groups such as Dalit women.

A fairly sustained critique of nationalism, especially cultural nationalism, marks a number of works in the field of women's history. There have also been critiques of the limitations of the positions of middle-class/upper-caste social reformers. Among the major areas of modern Indian history have been the focus on nineteenth-century social reform as a precursor of the national movement especially in Bengal, and the centrality of the women's question in the agendas of the social reformers. Feminist scholars have therefore had to engage with a pre-existing body of work that was centred on the male reformers and which paid little or no attention to women's voices. The narrowness of the social base of the reformers and their blinkered understanding of the women's question, drawn essentially from their own social class, has been part of the critique by feminist scholars. The debate on the social reformers' focus on women's education has also been analysed in terms of 'schooling' women into new norms of conjugality, dress and social conduct – aspects of a process of recasting patriarchal practices to suit an emerging *bhadralok* (gentlefolk). However, even while the critiques of nineteenth-century social reform by feminist scholars have been useful, the existing scripts are still almost obsessively focused on the upper caste, middle-class *bhadramahila* ('ladies') to the exclusion of other segments of society.

The dominance of Bengal in the writing of modern Indian history, which left its mark also on women's history, has been moderately redressed through histories of western and southern India. In these areas the more explicit political articulation of caste questions has had a fruitful impact in widening the social focus of women's histories and the range of legal regimes, work practices, sexual and marriage arrangements, and roles which are explored. These works have introduced caste into the debates in the nineteenth century, a factor normally missing in earlier studies on Bengal. Women's critiques of patriarchal agendas and lower-caste critiques of the continuing control of the upper castes in all sectors in Maharashtra had challenged the very conceptualisation of Indian nationalism in the nineteenth century but were erased from the public sphere, both then and well into the last few decades of the twentieth century.

A fairly solid body of women's histories has explored the law in terms of the changing structures and legal practice that shaped gender relations in important ways during colonial and postcolonial times. Feminist analyses have been wide-ranging and have suggested that processes of change were complex and uneven. The separation of the domains of civil, criminal and personal law, or family law, itself came to be constituted during the colonial period and has survived into postcolonial times as a complicated legacy. Nevertheless, the certainty with which some postmodernists (including some feminists) see pre-colonial structures and customary law as having given greater room for female agency is not shared by other feminist analyses. Pre-colonial India had a different, but not necessarily a milder or kinder patriarchy, and women could use emerging notions of rights and entitlements in the colonial period to manoeuvre themselves out of oppressive situations and expand the choices available to them.

Work on labouring women still requires much greater attention. The historical investment of nationalist leaders in 'rescuing' the female coolie caught up in indentured labour far away from home made her an early choice for historical investigation. There are now very important monographs on the female worker in the flow of intra-colonial migration. The female component of the industrial workforce has generated some substantial monographs, less so the diverse livelihoods which women take up as part of the urban underclass. Work on prostitution, entertainment and performance has generated some interesting contributions. In domestic labour, however, a huge field for exploring women's history, only a beginning has been made. The relationship between labour, sexuality, marriage, prostitution and slavery has recently been tied together in ways which open up women's history.

Feminist writers shone a light on a crucial dimension of history writing in their focus on the fate of women and children during the violent partition of the Indian subcontinent. This was a topic, veiled by notions of shame and dishonour, invoked to stoke communal passions rather than to recover the experience of the women affected. The work uncovered the double violence that women faced, first through abduction and rape, subsequently compounded by the violence of the forced retrieval agreed upon by the two countries. It drew attention to the ways in which the government of India and Pakistan sought to align Hindu and Muslim women to territorial boundaries drawn on communal lines and not on freely chosen rights as citizens. This writing provided a strong critique of a nationalism that presented itself as secular but accepted a community's right to own and possess its women based on religious lines.

Pioneering work in Sri Lanka by feminist scholars has examined the impact on the lives of women of militarisation and conflict between communities. Studies on the setting-up of the Mothers' Front to deal with disappearances of young people as part of repressive state actions by the government have movingly documented women's initiative in resisting the state. At another level the incorporation of many women into the Liberation Tigers of Tamil Eelam (LTTE) has led to major transformations in gender roles. Together, both these features of new writing by women scholars have complicated and enriched our understanding of nationalism, militarisation and gender.

To sum up, women's histories continue to be written in a variety of ways and from a range of positions. Since there is no structured collective against whose position one needs to define oneself very strongly, the controversies have fortunately not taken on a life of their own, thereby making women's histories one of the most open areas of research. And there is much to be done: histories of Dalit women, histories of the family and the domains of affect, of violence upon women, of communitarian authorities that sanction violence against women, amongst a host of other issues. Exploring these issues in all their complexities and contradictions without shutting off any possible lines of enquiry for a fuller understanding of women's histories remains a priority for feminist historians.

Uma Chakravarty

Literary Works

Bama (2002), *Karrukku*, trans. Lakshmi Holmstrom, Chennai: Macmillan.
Chugtai, Ismat (2003), *The Chugtai Collection*, New Delhi: Women Unlimited.
Devi, Mahasweta (1997), *The Breast Stories* (trans. with Introduction by Gayatri Chakravarty Spivak of three stories by Mahasweta Devi), Calcutta: Seagull Press.
Hossain, Attia (1961), *Sunlight on a Broken Column*, London: Chatto and Windus.
Hyder, Qurratulain (1998), *River of Fire*, New Delhi: Kali for Women.
Racine, Jean Luc and Jeanne Racine (1997), *Viramma: Life of an Untouchable*, London: Verso.
Shah Nawaz, Mumtaz (1990), *The Heart Divided*, Lahore: ASR.

Histories

Agrawal, Bina (1994), *A Field of One's Own: Gender and Land Rights in India*, Cambridge: Cambridge University Press.
Anandhi, S. (1998), 'Reproductive Bodies and Regulated Sexuality: Birth Control Debates in Early Twentieth-Century Tamilnadu', in Mary John and Janaki Nair (eds), *A Question of Silence: Sexual Economies of Modern India*, New Delhi: Kali for Women, pp. 185–202.
Arunima, G. (2003), *There Comes Papa: Colonialism and the Transformation of Matriliny in Kerala, Malabar c. 1850–1940*, New Delhi: Orient Longman.

Bannerji, Himani (2001), *Inventing Subjects: Studies in Hegemony, Patriarchy and Colonialism*, New Delhi: Tulika Press.

Butalia, Urvashi (1998), *The Other Side of Silence*, New Delhi: Penguin.

Caroll, Lucy (1989), 'Law, Custom and Statutory Social Reform: The Widow Remarriage Act of 1856', in J. Krishnamurti (ed.), *Women in Colonial India*, New Delhi: Oxford University Press, pp. 1–26.

Chakravarty, Uma (1998), *Rewriting History: The Life and Times of Pandita Ramabai*, New Delhi: Kali for Women.

Chatterjee, Indrani (1999), *Gender, Slavery and Law in Colonial India*, New Delhi: Oxford University Press.

Chowdhry, Prem (1994), *The Veiled Women: Shifting Gender Relations in Haryana, 1880–1990*, New Delhi: Oxford University Press.

De Alwiss Malathi (1998), 'Motherhood as a Space of Protest: Women's Political Participation in Contemporary Sri Lanka', in Patricia Jeffrey and Amrita Basu (eds), *Appropriating Gender: Women's Activism and Politicised Religion in South Asia*, New York and London: Routledge, pp. 185–202.

De Mel Neloufer (2001), *Women and the Nation's Narrative: Gender and Nationalism in Twentieth Century Sri Lanka*, Colombo: Social Scientists' Association.

Geetha, V. (1999), 'Gender and the Logic of Brahminism: Periyar and the Politics of the Female Body', in Kumkum Sangari and Uma Chakravarty (eds), *From Myths to Markets: Essays on Gender*, Shimla: Indian Institute of Advanced Study, pp. 198–236.

Jayawardena, Kumari (1986), *Feminism and Nationalism in the Third World*, London: Zed Books.

Mahapatra, P (1995), 'Restoring the Family: The Making of a Sexual Contract amongst Indian Immigrant Labour in the West Indies', *Studies in History* 11: 2, pp. 227–60.

Menon, Ritu and Kamla Bhasin (1998), *Borders and Boundaries*, New Delhi: Kali for Women.

Mody, Parveez (2002), 'Love and Law: Love Marriages in Delhi', *Modern Asian Studies* 36, pp. 223–56.

Nair, Janaki (1996), *Women and Law in Colonial India*, New Delhi: Kali for Women.

Rao, Anupama (ed.) (2003), *Gender and Caste*, New Delhi: Kali for Women.

Sangari, K. (2000), *Politics of the Possible*, New Delhi: Tulika.

Sangari, Kumkum and Sudesh Vaid (eds) (1989), *Recasting Women: Essays in Colonial India*, New Delhi: Kali for Women.

Sarkar, Tanika (2002), *Hindu Wife Hindu Nation*, New Delhi: Permanent Black, Ravi Dalal Publishers.

Sen, Samita (1992), 'Women Workers in the Bengal Jute Industry 1890–1940: Migration, Motherhood and Militancy', Ph.D. dissertation, Cambridge: University of Cambridge.

Singha, Radhika (1998), *A Despotism of Law*, New Delhi: Oxford University Press.

Stree Shakti Sanghatana (1989), *We Were Making History*, New Delhi: Kali For Women.

Tharu, Susie and K. Lalitha (1993–95), *Women Writing in India*, 2 vols, Oxford: Oxford University Press.

See also: **Anti-Colonialism and Resistance: South Asia; Castes: South Asia; Historiography: South Asia; Partition; Pre-colonial Histories: South Asia; Sri Lankan Civil War.**

Women's Histories: South-east Asia

The countries of South-east Asia are too diverse for their women to share a common history. Differences in culture, race, religion and language divide them. Many women continue to be raised for the domestic domain of marriage, childbearing, and housekeeping, but as more women receive Western educations, they attain an economic independence that makes marriage a choice rather than a necessity.

In the former colonies of Burma, Malaysia and Singapore, the English language continues – in ascending order of importance for the three countries – to be a medium of communication and written discourse. Although Malay is the national language of Malaysia and Singapore, English is the de facto national language of Singapore. In non-British former colonies like Indonesia, Indo-China (now Cambodia, Vietnam and Laos), English has replaced Dutch or French as the lingua franca. Outside of Malaysia, Singapore and the Philippines, there are few publications in English by women, principally because education continues in languages other than English, and there is little audience for writings in English. Under British rule, the works in English from Malaysia and Singapore shared a common history, but since decolonisation – independence for the Federation of Malaya in 1957, and the political separation of Malaysia and Singapore in 1965 – two distinct traditions of writing have developed.

The primary form of women's writing of historical interest is autobiography, and many have been published since the 1980s. As a genre, these women's autobiographies include the following chronology and thematic elements: childhood, adolescence, marriage, motherhood, widowhood, grandmotherhood, old age; and privation, education, aspiration, achievement. The self is thus constructed in traditional terms as filial daughter, loyal wife, loving mother, and strong and able woman. These writings are motivated by the desire to record the past for posterity, to inculcate a sense of rootedness and social history, and to record the trauma of the Japanese occupation of Malaya and Singapore between February 1942 and August 1945. In certain autobiographies, periods like the Japanese occupation or the Pacific war of 1941–5 are the primary focus. The selection of what the autobiographies recount varies widely: some tell of long and eventful lives; others end abruptly after a key event (the death of a father, the Japanese surrender); and others concentrate exclusively on the first fifteen or twenty-five years. These variations point to a certain arbitrariness in chronological selection, the presence of self-censorship, an element of authorial modesty, and a reluctance to give consideration to the demands of the literary or aesthetic. It may be argued that in their artlessness, these women place truth-telling over literary or artistic concerns.

Women's histories are reflected and refracted in autobiographies and biographies. For some, autobiography is the means for recording family history, as in Mangaleswary Ambiavagar's *Three Score Years and Twenty: Autobiography of an Eighty-Two Year Old Singaporean* (c. 1996), which also narrates her father and husband's stories. Ruth Ho's *Rainbow Round My Shoulder* (1975) and *Which I Have Loved* (1988) are family memoirs which begin with her grandmother's birth in 1870 in Malacca, and trace family history in the course of narrating her life and education. Ho is one of a number of *peranakan* women who have written about themselves and their families. *Peranakan* is Malay for native-born; it is a term used to refer to the locally-born Chinese who have assimilated Malay or Indonesian influences in their lives, most notably in language, attire and cuisine. The *nonya* or *nyonya* is the *peranakan* woman, the *baba*, the man. Regarding themselves in the early decades of the twentieth century as 'the King's Chinese', the *peranakans* benefited from British colonialism, worked for the British, and educated their children in English rather than Chinese schools.

In *A Nonya Mosaic: My Mother's Childhood* (1985), Gwee Thian Hock becomes surrogate autobiographer for his mother in her first fifteen years by adopting her persona. Queeny Chang's *Memories of a Nyonya* (1981) relates a privileged cosmopolitan life as the daughter of Tjong Ah Fie, her rich and powerful father, an immigrant to Sumatra. Chang's memoirs shuttle between a number of places – Malaya, Singapore, Sumatra, and China where she was married, but ends shortly after her father's death. In similar well-heeled vein, Betty Lim's *A Rose on my Pillow: Recollections of a Nyonya* (1994) is a casually undated account of an educated and well-married woman's life as wife, mother and hostess, beginning in the British colonial period, first in Singapore, then Malaya where her husband was a magistrate. But Lim San Neo's *My Life, My Memories, My Story: Recollections of a 75-Year Old Great-Grandmother* (n.d.) recounts a life of struggle: her formal education was terminated at twelve by the sudden death of her mother; she was married at seventeen and widowed at twenty-one when her husband was killed by the Japanese; and her second marriage created many tensions which further complicated her life. In comparison to these earlier women, both rich and poor, who were raised or educated for marriage, Shirley Geoklin Lim's *Among the White Moonfaces: Memoirs of a Nyonya Feminist* (1996) is an account of a life straddling Malaysia (where Lim was born and grew up) and the United States (where Lim became an academic, a poet, wife and mother, and an Asian-American).

Significantly, the biographies women have written, both about women and men, testify to the traditional division of gendered spheres of influence, with daughters often writing the life histories of notable fathers. Themes of fame, notoriety, wealth, power, and the struggle for respect from family and community are explored, but ultimately these biographies affirm patriarchal values. *The Patriarch* (1975) is Yeap Joo Kim's biography of her maternal grandfather, Khoo Sian Ewe, whose initialised name throughout the text is an acknowledgment of his status, fame and wealth in Penang in the 1940s and 1950s. Yeap's *Far from Rangoon* (1994) is the biography of Lee Chee San, her father-in-law, who married a daughter of one of the two Aw brothers, the legendary Tiger Balm Kings of Burma. Aung San Suu Kyi's *Aung San of Burma: A Biographical Portrait by his Daughter* (1991) is a slim work compared to Alice Scott-Ross' biography of her father, one of the leaders of Malayan independence, *Tun Dato Sir Cheng Lock Tan: A Personal Profile* (1990). In *Relatively Speaking* (1984), Joan Hon pays tribute to her father, Hon Sui Sen, who died in office as Singapore's finance minister. Eminent fathers like Dr Ong Chong Keng of Penang and Dato Panglima Kinta Eusoff of Perak are remembered by their daughters, Pamela Ong Siew Im in *Blood and the Soil: A Portrait of Dr Ong Chong Keng* (1995), and Ragayah Eusoff in *Lord of Kinta: The Biography of Dato Panglima Kinta Eusoff* (1995). Rose Ong's *A Journey with Uncle Yankee* (2001) is a biography of her artist father, Yan Kee Leong, the first Baha'i in Malaya and Singapore. An exception to the adulatory biographical narrative by the daughter or daughter-in-law is Lynn Pann's diasporic narrative of recovery, *Tracing it Home: A Chinese Journey* (1993). Pan's portrayal of her father's life in Shanghai, Sabah and Hong Kong is a sophisticated critique of family history and the turbulent history of China in the 1940s and 1950s.

Similar concerns with public life, service and recognition hold for biographies of women. Zhou Mei's *Elizabeth Choy: More than a War Heroine* (1995); *The Life of Family Planning Pioneer, Constance Goh* (1996), the slim biography of Malaysia's minister of finance, *Rafidah Aziz: Sans Malice* (1997); and Rose Ong's *Shirin Fozdar: Asia's Foremost Feminist* (2000) are portraits of women of influence in the public sphere. An exception is Maria Hertogh (Nadra bte Ma'arof) who, as a teenager, was at the centre of a legal battle between Aminah, her adoptive Malay mother and her Dutch (Catholic) parents. Her dramatic and tragic life is examined by a male biographer, Haja Maideen in *The Nadra Tragedy: The Maria Hertogh Controversy* (1989). The case highlighted the radical divide between Muslim law and British colonial law which returned Hertogh against her will to her Dutch parents, and even nullified her marriage to a Muslim. It so inflamed religious sentiments that eighteen people died in riots in Singapore in December 1950. The controversy inspired Leslie Netto's play, *Maria: Based on a True Story* (1998).

The Japanese occupation of Malaya and Singapore has produced numerous narratives. Among the earliest was Sybil Kathigasu's *No Dram of Mercy* (1954), a riveting recollection of her wartime life in Perak, Malaya, where she was captured, incarcerated, and tortured by the Japanese. Elizabeth Choy's 'My Autobiography' (1974) as told to Shirle' Gordon deals with her childhood in Sabah, her departure for Singapore to continue her education, her marriage, her torture by the Japanese, her imprisonment with more than twenty men for 200 days, and after the war a life of public service and teaching (Kim Ramakrishnan's play, *Not Afraid to Live [Not Afraid to Remember]* is based on Choy's captivity). Janet Lim's *Sold for Silver: An Autobiography* (1958) begins in China where her brother, sister and father died when she was a child; her mother remarried, and gave her away to a wealthy family who in turn sold her off as a bondmaid to be shipped to Singapore, where she was sold for $250 to a family. Rescued by a British woman, Lim was given an education and trained to be a nurse. Evacuated from Singapore just before it fell, Lim eventually made her way to Sumatra, where she spent three and a half years in and out of Japanese captivity. The narrative ends abruptly with her return to Singapore after the Japanese surrender. In *Aishabee at War: A Very Frank Memoir* (1990), Aisha Akbar focuses on a five-year period (1940–45) of childhood and adolescence, coinciding largely with the Pacific war. *Diary of a Girl in Changi: 1941–1945* (1994) is Sheila Allan's journal of internment, with a 1992 postscript about her trip to Singapore from Australia, her adoptive country, to visit the grave of her father who had died during internment. Autobiographical retrospection through a third party is exercised by Wong Moh Keed in *To My Heart, with Smiles . . . The Love Letters of Siew Fung Fong and Wan Kwai Pik (1920–1941)* (1988), an intimate portrait of Wong's maternal grandparents whose marriage ended with the untimely death of her grandfather during the Japanese occupation. Wong furnishes an introduction and commentary, but otherwise allows both the English translations of her subject's letters and her grandfather's diary to speak for their authors. Yeo Lai Cheng's *Because of Mama and Poh Poh* (2000) addresses the relationships between three generations of women: Yeo's maternal grandmother, her mother and herself, giving particular attention to the war. Beginning with her birth in 1928, the account, although written when the author was already a grandmother, ends early in her life with the Japanese surrender in 1945.

The confessional mode inherent in autobiography is particularly to the fore in more recent autobiographies, such as *'Excuse Me, Are you a Model?': The Bonny Hicks Story* (Hicks 1990) and *Escape from Paradise: (From Third World to First)* (2001) by John and May Chu Harding. The changing roles and greater opportunities for women today are redefining the autobiographical and biographical. Shelley Siu's *Barrier Breakers: Women in Singapore* (2000) is a compilation of the lives and times of fourteen successful contemporary women. Other than the centenarian Teresa Hsu, Siu's select company comprises professionals or entrepreneurs. Nick Aplin's *To the Finishing Line* (2002) is a biography of Singapore's pioneer female Olympians, Tang Pui Wah, Mary Klass and Janet Jesudason.

The diversification brings new dimensions to women's histories and stories. While auto-biography (and even biography) may be an invitation to self-fictionalisation, for the most part the authors discussed try to keep faith with the truth. The relative neglect of form in favour of 'truth', and the overall innocence of stylistic felicity, attest to the privileging of the historical impulse of retrieving or recovering the past over the aesthetic demands of craft.

Leong Liew Geok

Literary Works

Aisha, Akbar (1990), *Aishabee at War: A Very Frank Memoir*, Singapore: Landmark.

Allan, Sheila (1994), *Diary of a Girl in Changi: 1941–1945*, Kenthurst: Kangaroo Press.

Aplin, Nick (2002), *To the Finishing Line; Champions of Singapore: Tang Pui Wah, Mary Klass, Janet Jesudason*, Singapore: SNP Editions.

Aung San Suu Kyi (1991), *Aung San of Burma: A Biographical Portrait by his Daughter*, Edinburgh: Kiscadale.

Chang, Queeny (1981), *Memories of a Nyonya*, Singapore: Eastern Universities Press.

Choy, Elizabeth (1974), 'My Autobiography' [as told to Shirle' Gordon], *Intisari* IV: 1, pp. 12–65.

Gwee Thian Hock (1985), *A Nyonya Mosaic: My Mother's Childhood*, Singapore: Times Books International.

Haja Maideen [1989] (2000), *The Nadra Tragedy: The Maria Hertogh Controversy* [expanded edn], Subang Jaya: Pelanduk Publications.

Harding, John and May Chu Harding (2001), *Escape from Paradise (From Third World to First)*, Phoenix, AZ: IDK Press.

Hicks, Bonny (1990), *'Excuse Me, Are you a Model?': The Bonny Hicks Story*, Singapore: Flame of the Forest.

Ho, Ruth (1975), *Rainbow Round My Shoulder*, Singapore: Eastern Universities Press.

Ho, Ruth (1988), *Which I Have Loved*, Singapore: The author.

Hon, Joan (1984), *Relatively Speaking*, Singapore: Times Books International.

Kathigasu, Sybil [1954] (1983), *No Dram of Mercy*, Singapore: Oxford University Press.

Lim, Betty (1994), *A Rose on my Pillow: Recollections of a Nyonya*, Singapore: Armour.

Lim, Janet [1958] (1985), *Sold for Silver: An Autobiography*, Singapore: Oxford University Press.

Lim San Neo (n.d.), *My Life, My Memories, My Story: Recollections of a 75-Year-Old Great-Grandmother*, Singapore: Epic Management Services.

Lim, Shirley Geok-lin (1996), *Among the White Moonfaces: Memoirs of a Nyonya Feminist*, Singapore: Times Editions.

Mangalesvary, Ambiavagar (n.d., circa 1996), *Three Score Years and Twenty: Autobiography of an Eighty-Two Year Old Singaporean*, Singapore: Mangalesvary Ambiavagar.

Netto, Leslie (1998), *Maria: Based on a True Story*, London: Minerva.

Ong, Pamela Siew Im (1995), *Blood and Soil: A Portrait of Dr Ong Chong Keng*, Singapore: Times Books International.

Ong, Rose (2000), *Shirin Fozdar: Asia's Foremost Feminist*, Singapore: The author.

Ong, Rose (2001), *A Journey with Uncle Yankee*, Singapore: The author.

Pan, Lynn (1993), *Tracing it Home: A Chinese Journey*, New York: Kodansha.

Ragayah, Eusoff (1995), *Lord of Kinta: The Biography of Dato Panglima Kinta Eusoff*, Petaling Jaya: Pelanduk Publications.

Ramakrishnan, Kim (1986), *Not Afraid to Live [Not Afraid to Remember]*, Singapore: In the collection of the Central Library, National University of Singapore.

Scott-Ross, Alice (1990), *Tun Dato Sir Cheng Lock Tan: A Personal Profile by his Daughter*, Singapore: The author.

Siu, Shelley (2000), *Barrier Breakers: Women in Singapore*, Singapore: oneknowledge.com

Wong Moh Keed (1988), *To My Heart with Smiles: The Love Letters of Siew Fung Fong and Wan Kwai Pik (1920–1941)*, Singapore: Landmark.

Yeap Joo Kim [1975] (1984), *The Patriarch*, Singapore: Times Books International.

Yeap Joo Kim (1994), *Far from Rangoon*, Singapore: Lee Teng Lay.

Yeo Lai Cheng (2000), *Because of Mama and Poh Poh*, Singapore: Lam Lai Cheng.

Zhou Mei (1995), *Elizabeth Choy: More than a War Heroine; A Biography*, Singapore: Landmark.

Zhou Mei (1996), *The Life of Family Planning Pioneer, Constance Goh: A Point of Light*, Singapore: Graham Brash.

Zhou Mei (1997), *Rafidah Aziz: Sans Malice*, Singapore: Yuyue Enterprise.

Histories

Anchek, Herminia M., and Michaela Betran-Gonzalez (1984), *Filipino Women in Nation Building: A Compilation of Brief Biographies: Dedicated to the Decade of Women Proclaimed by UN, 1975–1985*, Quezon City: Phoenix Publishing House.

Blackburn, Susan (2001), *Love, Sex and Power: Women in Southeast Asia*, Clayton: Monash Asia Institute.

Bulbeck, Chilla (1998), *Re-Orienting Western Feminisms: Women's Diversity in a Postcolonial World*, New York: Cambridge University Press.

Chandler, Glen, Norma Sullivan and Jan Branson (eds) (1991), *Development and Displacement: Women in Southeast Asia*, Clayton: Centre of Southeast Asian Studies, Monash University [Monash Papers on Southeast Asia: No. 18].

Esterline, Mae Handy (1987), *They Changed their Worlds: Nine Women of Asia*, based on biographies, Lanham, MD and London: University Press of America.

Low Guat Tin (1993), *Successful Women in Singapore: Issues, Problems and Challenges*, Singapore: EPB Publishers.

Republic of Singapore (1981), Chapter 47, *The Women's Charter*, Singapore: Attorney General's Chambers.

Tan Joo Ean (1996), 'The Effect of Development on the Decline of Universal Marriage in Thailand, 1970–1990', *Southeast Asian Journal of Social Science* 24: 2, pp. 70–83.

Van Esterik, Penny (ed.) (1996), *Women of Southeast Asia*, De Kalb, IL: Northern Illinois University, Centre for Southeast Asian Studies.

Wazir, Jahan Karim (1995), *'Male' and 'Female' in Developing Southeast Asia*, Oxford and Washington, DC: Berg Books.

Wong, Aline K. and Leong Wai Kam (1993), *Singapore Women: Three Decades of Change*, Singapore: Times Academic Press.

See also: **Aung San Suu Kyi; East Asia; Historiography: South-east Asia; Japanese Occupation: South-east Asia.**

Women's Histories: Southern Africa

'Women's histories' in the Southern African context is a contested term, suggesting separate histories for women and for men; actually the two have always been interconnected and, indeed, interdependent. Nevertheless, the colonial, segregationist and apartheid contexts of Southern Africa have always been profoundly gendered, and women have often lived lives both contrasted and intersected with those of men. Much Southern African historiography is androcentric and does not recognise the significance of gender in the structuring of colonial and postcolonial contexts. At the same time, however, the blanket term 'women' needs to be disaggregated to take into account profound differences based on race, class, age, location and other factors. In order to contextualise postcolonial women writers, it is necessary to review the historiography which speaks to the impact of gender, race and class on the shaping of women's lives, and those of their 'foremothers', rather than merely depending on general histories. General histories of Southern Africa do, however, provide structural contexts and histories which focus on women and/or gender analyse the differential experiences or consciousness of women within these contexts. In other words, 'segregated' histories of, for example, black women can only provide a partial understanding of black women writers, as the wider interconnections of gender, class and race are central to understanding women's historical contexts. What follows is a survey firstly of scholarship that historicises the works of key women writers from Southern Africa, and secondly, of historical studies of women's histories and gender that do not explicitly refer to literary works by women, but nonetheless disclose necessary contexts for historicising women's literatures from Southern Africa.

Starting with literature-focused scholarship that provides historical contextualisation, the most extensive kind of work has been biographical research, which includes book-length biographies and critical studies of the major Southern African women writers. Olive Schreiner has attracted substantial scholarly attention, notably in historically textured biographies by Karel Schoeman (1991), and Ruth First and Ann Scott (1980), as well as the monographs by Liz Stanley, Joyce Avrech Berkman and Carolyn Burdett. Nadine Gordimer (the Nobel Prize winner for Literature in 1991) has also attracted considerable critical research, with significant studies by Stephen Clingman, Andries Oliphant and Brighton Uledi Kamanga. Clingman (1986) in particular analyses Gordimer's capacity to depict apartheid South Africa's historical consciousness. Bessie Head, who lived in both apartheid South Africa and Botswana, has been the subject of biographical studies by, inter alia, Craig MacKenzie (1999), Gillian Stead Eilersen and Virginia Uzoma Ola. Finally, Doris Lessing's life and contexts have been extensively researched, and there has been both biographical work (see Carole Klein 2000) and historically-inflected criticism (see Eve Bertelsen's edited collection, 1985), as well as significant scholarly research by critics including Anthony Beck, Carey Kaplan, Margaret Moan, Lorna Sage, Michael Thorpe and Ruth Whittaker. There have also been useful comparative studies with chapters on Lessing by Charlotte Bruner, Louise Yelin and Magali Cornier Michael. Biographical details and some historical contextualisation of Southern African women writers are also provided in the two edited collections by Cherry Clayton (1989) and Margaret Daymond (1995), and in Eva Hunter's collection of interviews with Nadine Gordimer, Menán du Plessis, Zoë Wicomb and Lauretta Ngcobo.

Turning now to historical studies that foreground Southern African women's histories and gender without explicit reference to literary works by women, there are two edited collections that provide a nice sense of the variety of such scholarship: Christine Qunta's

Women in Southern Africa (1987) and Cherryl Walker's Women and Gender in Southern Africa to 1945 (1990). The latter collection brings together important early work: Jeff Guy on gender oppression in pre-capitalist societies; Cherryl Walker and Phil Bonner on the gendered nature of the migrant labour system; Debbie Gaitskell on African women's relationship to Christianity; Elsabe Brink on the development of the volksmoeder ideology; Heather Hughes on women at the Inanda Seminary; Linda Chisholm on industrial schools and reformatories for girls; Jo Beall on Indian women's labour in colonial Natal; Walker on the white women's suffrage movement; Anne McClintock on how Rider Haggard's King Solomon's Mines reinvents patriarchy in colonial South Africa; and Sandra Burman on the changing legal status of women in Cape-ruled Basutholand.

Most historical research on women in Southern Africa is published in article form in a small number of academic journals, notably The Journal of Southern African Studies (JSAS), the Journal of African History (JAH), Kronos, the South African Historical Journal (SAHJ), and Agenda. In the last thirty years, many of the major issues in Southern African history-writing have been fundamentally influenced by contributions from historians attuned to the histories of women and of gender relations. What follows is a selection of the most significant instances of such work.

Recent work on eighteenth- and nineteenth-century Southern African history has included studies of women's lives under slavery. These studies have included monographs by Robert Shell and Pamela Scully; articles in SAHJ by Patricia van der Spuy and Yvette Abrahams (on the slavery of Khoisan people); and Elizabeth Eldredge's chapter on enslaved women on Eastern Cape Boer farms in Eldredge and Fred Morton's collection Slavery in South Africa (1994). Scholarship on a second major theme in early nineteenth-century Southern African history, the Mfecane, has tended to ignore women and gender. In Carolyn Hamilton's important collection, The Mfecane Aftermath: Reconstructive Debates in Southern African History (1995), women (and/or gender) are peripheral, but in more recent research by Sean Hanretta (JAH 1998) and Jennifer Weir (SAHJ 2000) this silence has been addressed, with the position of royal women in particular being explored. A third major theme, the Cattle-killing of 1856–7, has to date been interpreted as principally a conflict over land between white and black men (as in Jeff Peires' The Dead Will Arise: Nongqawuse and the Great Cattle-Killing Movement of 1856–7 (1990)), but Helen Bradford (1996) has responded in detail to this version of history by placing the young woman Nongqawuse at the centre of events. Fourthly, histories of different groups of settler women in the Cape Colony have been studied: Dutch-Afrikaner women by Yvonne Brink in Lynn Wadley's collection Our Gendered Past (1997) and Marijke du Toit (JSAS 2003); and middle-class British colonial women in Cape Town by Kirsten McKenzie and in the Eastern Cape by Natasha Erlanck. The South African War (1899–1902) has been explored in journal articles by Helen Bradford, Elizabeth van Heyningen, Liz Stanley and Helen Dampier, with particular attention to the experiences of white women, and the importance of gender in shaping the war.

Moving on to the twentieth century, there have been a number of important studies that examine the place of women in the racially differentiated economies and polities of Southern Africa. Shula Marks underlines how barriers of race have defined South African women's material existences in her study Not Either an Experimental Doll (1987), and Charles van Onselen's registers the crucial economic role of women in his two-volume social history of early Johannesburg (1982), with chapters on the domestic service sector ('The Witches of Suburbia: Domestic Service on the Witwatersrand, 1890–1914') and on the informal sector ('Prostitutes and Proletarians 1886–1914'). Jacklyn Cock has developed van Onselen's work in her monograph on the history of women in domestic service in South Africa up to the 1980s (1989). Women's histories under industrialisation have been recounted by Iris Berger in her monograph on women in South African industry in the twentieth century (1992), and there are important chapters that focus on particular histories of women and labour in the collections edited by Berger and E. Frances White (1999), Shula Marks and Stanley Trapido (1987), Belinda Bozzoli (1987), Joshua Brown (1991), Charles Ambler and Jonathan Crush (1992), and Paul Maylam and Iain Edwards (1996). South Africa's mining economy since the late nineteenth century has relied heavily on migrant labour, and the impact of the migrant labour system on women's lives has been the subject of monographs by Marc Epprecht (1996), Deborah James (1999) and Belinda Bozzoli with Mmantho Nkotsoe (1991), and of articles by Thsidiso Maloka (*JAH*, 1997) and Jock McCulloch (*JSAS*, 2003). Both in Bozzoli and Nkotsoe's study and in Isabel Hofmeyr's *We Spend our Lives as a Tale to be Told* (1994) impressive use is made of oral testimonies to access women's histories.

The role of women in anti-colonial and resistance struggles has also received scholarly attention. There have been a number of major studies on women's resistance in South Africa, starting with Hilda Bernstein's 1975 study of women's opposition to apartheid, and continuing with Richard Lapchick and Stephanie Urdang's examination of black women's lives under apartheid (1982), Lauren Platzky and Cherryl Walker's gender-sensitive history of forced removals (1985), Julie Frederikse's integrative survey of non-racialism in South Africa (1990), Kathryn Spink's study of white women's protests against apartheid (1991), Julia C. Wells' history of women's resistance to the pass laws in South Africa (1993), and Anne Mager's case study of women in the Ciskei Bantustan (1999). Beyond South Africa, the role of women in Namibian resistance struggles has been described by Tessa Cleaver and Marion Wallace (1990), Stephanie Urdang has recounted women's resistance in Mozambique (1989), and Norma Kriger's work on the Chimurangas in Zimbabwe foregrounds the experiences and contributions of women (1992). Of the Southern African nations other than South Africa, Zimbabwe has been the subject of the most extensive historical research into the histories of women, with substantial studies by inter alia Teresa Barnes (1999), Diana Jeater (1993), Elizabeth Schmidt (1992) and Christine Sylvester (2000).

Finally, there have been a number of influential interventions on the historiography of women's histories in the region by Belinda Bozzoli (1983), Penelope Hetherington (1993), Linzi Manicom (1992), Helen Bradford (1996), and Marc Epprecht (1996, 2000). These pieces collectively provide the most useful guide to further investigation of Southern African women's histories, and are accordingly listed below.

Patricia van der Spuy

Literary Works

Dangarembga, Tsitsi (1988), *Nervous Conditions*, Harare: Zimbabwe Publishing House.
Gordimer, Nadine (1966), *The Late Bourgeois World*, London: Gollancz.
Gordimer, Nadine (1980), *Burger's Daughter*, New York: Viking.
Gordimer, Nadine (1981), *July's People*, New York: Viking.
Gordimer, Nadine (1994), *None to Accompany Me*, New York: Farrar, Straus and Giroux.
Head, Bessie (1968), *When Rain Clouds Gather*, New York: Simon and Schuster.
Head, Bessie (1974), *A Question of Power*, London: Heinemann.
Head, Bessie (1995), *Maru*, Oxford: Heinemann.
Jacobs, Rayda (1997), *Eyes of the Sky*, Oxford: Heinemann.

Jacobs, Rayda (1998), *The Slave Book*, Cape Town: Kwela.
Kuzwayo, Ellen (1985), *Call Me Woman*, Johannesburg: Ravan Press.
Lessing, Doris (1950), *The Grass is Singing*, London: M. Joseph.
Lessing, Doris (2002), *The Sweetest Dream*, New York: HarperCollins.
Malan, Robin and Rochelle Kapp (eds) (1999), *'No Place Like' and other Short Stories by Southern African Women*, Cape Town: David Philip.
Schreiner, Olive (1883), *The Story of an African Farm*, New York: Mershon.
Vera, Yvonne (1993), *Nehanda*, Harare: Baobab.
Vera, Yvonne (2003), *The Stone Virgins*, New York: Farrar, Straus and Giroux.
Wicomb, Zoë (2000), *You Can't Get Lost in Cape Town*, New York: Feminist Press at the City University of New York.
Wicomb, Zoë (2001), *David's Story*. New York: Feminist Press at the City University of New York.

Histories

Ambler, Charles and Jonathan Crush (eds) (1992), *Liquor and Labor in Southern Africa*, Athens, OH: Ohio University Press.
Barnes, Teresa (1999), *'We Women Worked so Hard': Gender, Urbanization and Social Reproduction in Colonial Harare, 1930–1956*, Portsmouth, NH: Heinemann.
Berger, Iris (1992), *Threads of Solidarity: Women in South African Industry, 1900–1980*, Bloomington, IN: Indiana University Press.
Berger, Iris and E. Frances White (eds) (1999), *Women in Sub-Saharan Africa. Restoring Women to History*, Bloomington, IN: Indiana Press.
Bernstein, Hilda (1975), *For Their Triumphs and for Their Tears: Conditions and Resistance of Women in Apartheid South Africa*, London: International Defence and Aid Fund.
Bertelsen, Eve (ed.) (1985), *Doris Lessing*, Johannesburg: McGraw-Hill.
Bozzoli, Belinda (1983), 'Marxism, Feminism and South African Studies', *Journal of Southern African Studies* 9: 2, pp. 139–71.
Bozzoli, Belinda (ed.) (1987), *Class, Community and Conflict: South African Perspectives*, Johannesburg: Ravan Press.
Bozzoli, Belinda with Mmantho Nkotsoe (1991), *Women of Phokeng: Consciousness, Life Strategy, and Migrancy in South Africa, 1900–1983*, London: James Currey.
Bradford, Helen (1996), 'Women, Gender and Colonialism: Rethinking the British Cape Colony and its Frontier Zones, c. 1806–1870', *Journal of African History* 37: 3, pp. 351–70.
Brown, Joshua (ed.) (1991), *History from South Africa: Alternative Visions and Practices*, Philadelphia: Temple University Press.
Clayton, Cherry (ed.) (1989), *Women and Writing in South Africa. A Critical Anthology*, Marshalltown: Heinemann Southern Africa.
Cleaver, Tessa and Marion Wallace (1990), *Namibia: Women in War*, London: Zed Books.
Clingman, Stephen (1986), *The Novels of Nadine Gordimer. History from the Inside*, London: Allen and Unwin.
Cock, Jacklyn (1989), *Maids and Madams: Domestic Workers under Apartheid*, rev. edn, London: Women's Press.
Daymond, Margaret (ed.) (1995), *Feminists Reading South Africa: Writing, Theory and Criticism*, New York: Garland.

Eldredge, Elizabeth and Frank Morton (eds) (1994), *Slavery in South Africa: Captive Labor on the Dutch Frontier*, Boulder, CO: Westview Press.

Epprecht, Marc (1996), 'Gender and History in Southern Africa: A Lesotho "Metanarrative"', *Canadian Journal of African Studies* 30: 2, pp. 188–213.

Epprecht, Marc (2000), *'This Matter of Women is Getting Very Bad': Gender, Development and Politics in Colonial Lesotho*, Pietermaritzburg: University of Natal Press.

First, Ruth and Ann Scott [1980] (1989), *Olive Schreiner. A Biography*, London: Women's Press.

Frederikse, Julie (1990), *The Unbreakable Thread: Non-Racialism in South Africa*, London: Zed Books.

Hetherington, Penelope (1993), 'Women in South Africa: The Historiography in English', *International Journal of African Historical Studies* 26: 2, pp. 241–69.

Hofmeyr, Isabel (1994), *'We Spend our Lives as a Tale that is Told': Oral Historical Narrative in a South African Chiefdom*, London: James Currey.

James, Deborah (1999), *Songs of the Women Migrants: Performance and Identity in South Africa*, Edinburgh: Edinburgh University Press.

Jeater, Diane (1993), *Marriage, Perversion and Power: The Construction of Moral Discourse in Rhodesia, 1894–1930*, Oxford: Clarendon Press.

Klein, Carole (2000), *Doris Lessing. A Biography*, London: Duckworth.

Kriger, Norma (1992), *Zimbabwe's Guerrilla War. Peasant Voices*, Cambridge: Cambridge University Press.

Lapchick, Richard and Stephanie Urdang (1982), *Oppression and Resistance: The Struggle of Women in Southern Africa*, Westport, CT: Greenwood.

MacKenzie, Craig (1999), *Bessie Head*, New York: Twayne.

Mager, Anne (1999), *Gender and the Making of a South African Bantustan: A Social History of the Ciskei, 1945–1959*, Oxford: James Currey.

Manicom, Linzi (1992), 'Ruling Relations: Rethinking State and Gender in South African History', *Journal of African History* 33: 3, pp. 441–65.

Marks, Shula (1987), *Not Either an Experimental Doll*. London: Women's Press.

Marks, Shula and Stanley Trapido (eds) (1987), *The Politics of Race, Class and Nationalism in Twentieth-Century South Africa*, Harlow: Longman.

Maylam, Paul and Iain Edwards (eds) (1996), *The People's City: African Life in Twentieth-Century Durban*, Pietermaritzburg: University of Natal Press.

Ola, Virginia Uzoma (1994), *The Life and Works of Bessie Head*, Lewiston, NY: Edwin Mellen.

Platzky, Lauren and Cherryl Walker (1985), *The Surplus People: Forced Removals in South Africa*, Johannesburg: Ravan Press.

Qunta, Christine (ed.) (1987), *Women in Southern Africa*, London: Allen and Unwin.

Schmidt, Elizabeth (1992), *Peasants, Traders, and Wives: Shona Women in the History of Women in Zimbabwe*, Portsmouth, NH: Heinemann.

Schoeman, Karel (1991), *Olive Schreiner: A Woman in South Africa, 1855–1881*, Johannesburg: Jonathan Ball.

Scully, Pamela (1997), *Liberating the Family? Gender and British Slave Emancipation in the Rural Western Cape, South Africa, 1823–1853*, Portsmouth, NH: Heinemann.

Shell, Robert (1994), *Children of Bondage: A Social History of the Slave Society at the Cape of Good Hope, 1652–1838*, Johannesburg: Witwatersrand University Press.

Spink, Kathryn (1991), *Black Sash*, London: Methuen.

Stanley, Liz (2002), *Imperialism, Labour and the New Woman: Olive Schreiner's Social Theory*, Durham, NC: Sociology Press.

Sylvester, Christine (2000), *Producing Women and Progress in Zimbabwe: Narratives of Identity and Work from the 1980s*, Portsmouth, NH: Heinemann.

Urdang, Stephanie (1989), *And Still They Dance: Women, War and the Struggle for Change in Mozambique*, London: Earthscan.

Van Onselen, Charles (1982), *Studies in the Social and Economic History of the Witwatersrand 1886–1914*, 2 vols, Johannesburg: Ravan Press.

Wadley, Lynn (ed.) (1997), *Our Gendered Past: Archaeological Studies of Gender in Southern Africa*, Johannesburg: Witwatersrand University Press.

Walker, Cheryl (1990), *Women and Gender in Southern Africa to 1945*, London: James Currey.

Wells, Julia C. (1993), *We Now Demand! The History of Women's Resistance to Pass Laws in South Africa*, Johannesburg: Witwatersrand University Press.

See also: **Anti-colonialism and Resistance: Southern Africa; Cattle-Killing; Chimurengas; Historiography: Southern Africa; Mfecane; Migrancy: Southern Africa; Slavery: Southern Africa**.

Women's Histories: West Africa

The dominant history of West Africa has often been the story of men. Revisions of the history curriculum and the incorporation of women into the study of West Africa's history have grown in number with increasing rapidity, thanks to the explosion of African and non-African feminist scholarship since the 1970s. In the postcolonial era, historians and anthropologists have undertaken a major re-examination and expansion of material on West African women's lives, especially in the political and economic arenas.

Much of contemporary scholarship on West African women has looked to the past to uncover women's political and socio-economic power in an era before modern Western imperialism (see Coquery-Vidrovitch 1996; Berger and White 1999; and Callaway 1987). Some of these analyses represent the most provocative anthropological approaches to the study of contemporary sex-role differentiation from a historical perspective. For example, Amadiume in her ground-breaking work (1987) on female and male institutions among the Igbo of Nigeria argues that sex and gender did not necessarily coincide in pre-colonial society and shows how roles were not rigidly masculinised or feminised (a fact reflected in the absence of gender prefixes in the Igbo language).

Boserup (1970) and Oppong (1983) among others have categorically asserted that colonialism resulted in the deterioration of the status of women: the decline in significance of the stool of the Ashanti queen mother, the disappearance of ownership rights among Ga women and the decline of political power among the Igbo of south-eastern Nigeria represent just a few examples of women losing their culturally and economically acknowledged authority in dual-sex systems. Postcolonial historical investigation provides evidence that the traditional ways of doing things, especially in the political and economic arenas, were often less inimical to women's collective interests than the 'modernisation' that colonialism purported to export. Women leaders, such as the *iyalode* among the Yoruba and the *omu* among the Igbo, exercised considerable power and autonomy within society as a whole through all-female organisations (see Berger and White 1999, p. xlix).

Creative writers, such as Ama Ata Aidoo, share historians' idea that European imperialism and colonial rule have contributed to African women's exploitation and subordination. Both Emecheta in *Double Yoke* (1982) and Flora Nwapa in *Efuru* (1966) and *One is Enough* (1981)

have shown how women are caught in what Emecheta portrays as the 'double yoke' of traditional ideas and contemporary realities. Though both writers have emphasised the negative
effects of traditional constraints on women's lives, they are also critical of modern society:
society's expectations often work against women's interests, as postcolonial states have been
much more likely to support patriarchal control over women than to undermine it.

Since the 1990s, modern historiography has witnessed a proliferation of studies on
women's political movements and organisations during colonial and postcolonial times.
Modern researchers and feminists (see Mba 1982, Awe 1992, Callaway 1994, and Sweetman
1984) have embarked on more detailed analyses of women's political roles in West Africa
by rediscovering women's active resistance to their deterioration in status directly through
strikes and revolts aimed at creating a space outside of 'tradition'. Postcolonial historical
accounts of women's past and present ability to defend their own interests have attempted
to correct false ideologies and stereotypes of female passivity which worked against women's
willingness to make history on their own terms. The Aba women's revolt of 1929, no doubt,
provided an incredible stimulus to Igbo studies, comparable to the Nigeria–Biafran war of
the 1960s. The revolts across diverse territories in Nigeria (Owerri and Calabar Provinces
in the 1940s, Aba and Onitsha in 1956) contributed to the emergence of modern Igbo
women who are currently engaged in diverse occupations in postcolonial Nigeria.

In some cases, women's mobilisation accelerated the national project, like the Sierra
Leone women's movement in the 1950s which 'was a real crucible for the awakening of
Sierra Leonean national consciousness' (Coquery-Vidrovitch 1996, p. 176). The politicisation of women in the name of masculinist nationalism is a recurrent feature of early postcolonial male-authored fiction. Male writers interrogate the roles of women in the
neo-colonial economies of West Africa in a materialist fashion by portraying their female
characters as symbols of moral impoverishment and corruption (see Ekwensi 1966) or par-
asites and liberating prophetesses (see Armah 1979). In this dichotomic system of representation, the woman is removed from reality, and her predicament becomes an index of
the chaotic state of the nation in the early postcolonial era.

Histories of women's political and military roles have provided female counter-
narratives against male-centred nationalist historiographies by demonstrating that the fictional images of Igbo women, which portray women as marginalised and passive (as in
Amadi 1976 and Achebe 1958), do not reflect the historical reality. According to Parpart
et al. (1989), they have shown that whatever the regime's ideology, women's solidarity
organisations and movements have always attempted to advocate their interests in mainstream politics. Though recent studies highlight that today's women's organisations in
West Africa are becoming increasingly vocal about the need to enter politics, many scholars like Uchendu, Iweriebor, Mba and Awe are aware of problematic divisions among
women that inhibit effective political action. Mba has stressed the importance of bridging
the gap between grassroots and elite women in ways that defy postcolonial class and ethnic
stratifications of societies:

> At both levels, women remain marginal to the state, unless new organisations of women emerge
> that attempt to fuse the gender ideology of the female intelligentsia with the skills of the middle-
> class female aristocracy and the militancy of the mass female associations. (Mba 1982, pp. 86–7)

Robertson, Berger and White, Sudarkasa, Callaway, Ekechi and many other scholars
have explored women's limited access to the means of production as a result of increasing
class and gender stratification in postcolonial West Africa. As women's trading and farming
has a long history in West Africa, much of the literature on women sets their economic

role in a historical context. Recent studies have given greater nuance and historical depth to the study of women's position in pre-colonial, colonial and postcolonial economies in West Africa, and have emphasised the connection between the market and power in women's participation, control and management of economic spaces. Falola (1995) and Ekechi and House-Midamba (1995) respectively have demonstrated that the marketplace was a 'women's space' among the Yoruba and the Igbo, and as such represented both a political arena and one of the central institutions of those societies. They have shown how in Nigeria, many women acquired considerable property like their male counterparts thanks to their involvement in trade. After independence, because of their restricted access to credit and capital, as well as management problems and family obligations, few women have been able to develop large-scale businesses (see Hay and Stitcher 1984).

Most of postcolonial literature has begun to focus on a broader array of protest actions, such as market women's struggle against colonial rule to defend their economic interests as traders. Both the Lagos Market Women's Association led by Alimotu Pelewura, and the Abeokuta Women's Union funded by Ransome-Kuti, are good examples of women's organised resistance against taxation during and after World War II. The Women's Union in particular worked against indirect rule, clearly exhibiting both a nationalist bent and a concern for women's economic interests (see Johnson-Odim and Mba 1997). Emecheta's 1979 novel, *The Joys of Motherhood* gives a good sense of the difficulties that market women endured during the revolt in Lagos, where an active parallel market developed.

As scholars have increasingly recognised women's diverse strategies of survival across countries in West Africa and within the same country, recent studies have become more context-sensitive and massive research has been carried out on a regional scale. As a result, many postcolonial historical accounts have focused on the socio-economic status of groups of women in particular societies (see for example, Robertson 1984; Ekechi and House-Midamba 1995; and Callaway 1987). Robertson provides a historical analysis of the experiences of Ga women traders in Accra. Basing her analysis on archival and extensive interviews with market women traders in Accra, she demonstrates that 'women's trade was a cultural tradition. In one family five generations of women were engaged in the beads and cloth trade' (Robertson 1984, p. 111). Despite Ga, Igbo and Yoruba women's increasing participation in petty trading as a result of the mechanisation of the fishing, meat and cloth industry in the 1950s and 1960s, researchers seem to be particularly aware of the precarious situation of many ordinary women engaged in this kind of trading. Mami Korkor, in Amma Darko's 1998 novel *The Housemaid*, is an example of a fish-seller who is struggling to make ends meet in Accra. Like many other petty traders, she is at the mercy of the vagaries of the market economy and, as a result, she appears to subsist marginally. Postcolonial research has also been crucial in the historical understanding of the changing role of women in less-known and more secluded societies, like the Muslim Fulbe women of Yola in northern Nigeria, who have just recently engaged in trading due to constant economic pressures (see Callaway 1987; VerEecke 1988).

In general, the proliferation of historical studies on women in the economy of West Africa by scholars and development-studies researchers is the product of a renewed interest in women's position as agents and subjects in the ever-changing economic arena. Postcolonial scholars have brought to light historical and cultural truths about women's contribution to the economy, and have provided fertile ground for African women in search of socially and economically active role models. The Oriki, great eulogies that capture lives and experiences in grandiose ways, still testify to female power in the Yoruba communities as a result of women's socio-economic achievements. Barber (1991) has shown that men were only part of the story as this form of oral poetry is performed mainly by women, and nowadays some women have made a name for themselves by appearing on television or making records. Several researchers have found it important to look at women's oral production and some work is being done exclusively on women's oral literature. Several studies of the oral literature of specific groups include some discussion of women as creators, performers and subjects (see Arndt 1998; Hale). Hale argues that 'female wordsmiths' sing songs of praise and advice, serve as intermediaries in delicate interpersonal negotiations and articulate the values of society at major social events' (p. 71). Research in this area has also proved that significant socio-economic transformations have affected the context and frequency of oral storytelling. The advent of electronic mass communication media has created an entirely new situation for oral storytellers in Hausaland, with some of them able to step onto the airwaves with storytelling programmes (see Abba Aliyu 1997, p. 153). Though the field is expanding, researchers Davies and Graves (1986) affirm that there remains much more to be done to arrive at a balanced view of oral female artists and provide a clearer picture of their verbal art and social functions in West Africa.

Over the last ten years social historians have increasingly focused on individual life histories as a way to complement silences in the archives. A group of researchers, most influentially those with a feminist agenda focusing on women and women's struggle, created something of a genre, presenting African history through the collection and publication of life histories (see Strobel 1982, Romero 1988). Others have successfully explored the oral reconstruction of lives by supplementing them with archival records and careful interpretation (see Geiger et al. 2002 and Hoppe 1993). Oral history gained legitimacy not because of any methodological claims but because it was argued to be more authentic and thus more objective. Oral interviewing is largely becoming a way of recording the private, the personal and the political in dialogue with the present day. Here is a way for West African women to speak – to others and to one another – in ways that had never been included in more conventional histories with conventional sources (see Personal Narratives Group 1989).

Monica Bungaro

Literary Works

Achebe, Chinua (1958), *Things Fall Apart*, London: Heinemann.
Aidoo, Ama Ata (1977), *Our Sister Killjoy*, London: Longman.
Amadi, Elechi (1976), *The Concubine*, London: Heinemann.
Armah, Ayi Kwei (1979), *Two Thousand Seasons*, London: Heinemann.
Darko, Amma (1998), *The Housemaid*, London: Heinemann.
Ekwensi, Cyprian (1966), *Jagua Nana*, London: Heinemann.
Emecheta, Buchi (1979), *The Joys of Motherhood*, London: Heinemann.
Emecheta, Buchi (1982), *Double Yoke*, London: Longman.
Nwapa, Flora (1966), *Efuru*, Portsmouth: Heinemann
Nwapa, Flora (1981), *One Is Enough*, Enugu: Tana Press.

Histories

Abba Aliyu, Sani (1997), 'Hausa Women as Oral Storytellers in Northern Nigeria', in S. Newell (ed.), *Writing African Women: Gender, Popular Culture and Literatures in West Africa*, London: Zed Books, pp. 149–56.

Allman, Jean, Susan Geiger and Nalanyike Musisi (2002), *Women in African Colonial Histories*, Bloomington, IN: Indiana University Press.

Amadiume, Ifi (1987), *Male Husbands, Female Daughters: Gender and Sex in an African Society*, London: Zed Books.

Arndt, Susan (1998), *African Women's Literature, Orature and Intertextuality: Igbo Oral Narrative*, Bayreuth: Bayreuth University Press.

Awe, Bolanle (1992), *Nigerian Women in Historical Perspective*, Lagos: Sankore.

Barber, Karin (1991), *I Could Speak Until Tomorrow: Oriki, Women and the Past in a Yoruba Town*, Edinburgh: Edinburgh University Press.

Berger, Iris and Frances White (1999), *Women in Sub-Saharan Africa: Restoring Women to History*, Bloomington, IN: Indiana University Press.

Boserup, Ester (1970), *Women's Role in Economic Development*, London: Allen and Unwin.

Callaway, Barbara (1987), *Muslim Hausa Women in Nigeria*, Syracuse, NY: Syracuse University Press.

Callaway, Barbara (1994), *The Heritage of Islam: Women, Religion and Politics in West Africa*, Boulder, CO: Lynne Rienner.

Coquery-Vidrovitch, Catherine (1996), *African Women: A Modern History*, Oxford: Westview.

Davies, Carol Boyce and Anne Adams Graves (1986), *Ngambika: studies of Women in African Literature*, Trenton, NJ: Africa World Press.

Ekechi, Felix and Bessie House-Midamba (1995), *African Market Women and Economic Power*, Westport, CT: Greenwood Press.

Falola, Toyin (1995), 'Gender, Business and Space Control: Yoruba Market Women and Power', Felix Ekechi (ed.), *African Market Women*, Westport, CT: Greenwood Press, pp. 23–40.

Hay, Margaret Jane and Sharon Stitcher (1984), *African Women South of the Sahara*, London: Longman.

Hoppe, Kirk (1993), 'Whose Life Is It Anyway? Issues of Representation in Life Narrative Texts of African Women', *International Journal of African Historical Studies* 26: 3, pp. 623–36.

Iweriebor, Ifeyinwa (1997), 'Carrying the Baton: Personal Perspectives on the Modern Women's Movement in Nigeria', in O. Nnaemeka (ed.), *Sisterhood, Feminisms, and Power: From Africa to the Diaspora*, Trenton, NJ: Africa World Press.

Johnson-Odim, Cheryl and Nina Mba (1997), *For Women and the Nation: Funmilayo Ransome-Kuti of Nigeria*, Urbana and Chicago: University of Illinois Press.

Mba, Nina (1982), *Nigerian Women Mobilised: The Study of the Political Activity of African Women in Southern Nigeria 1900–1965*, Berkeley, CA: California University Press.

Mba, Nina (1989), 'Kba and Khaki: Women and the Militarised State in Nigeria', in Jane L. Parpart and Kathleen A. Staudt, *Women and the State in Africa*, Boulder, CO: Lynne Rienner, pp. 69–90.

Oppong, Christine (1983), *Female and Male in West Africa*, London: Allen and Unwin.

Parpart, Jane L. and Kathleen A. Staudt (1989), *Women and the State in Africa*, Boulder, CO: Lynne Rienner.

Personal Narratives Group (ed.) (1989), *Interpreting Women's Lives: Feminist Theory and Personal Narratives*, Bloomington, IN: Indiana University Press.

Robertson, Claire (1984), *Sharing the Same Bowl: A Socio-Economic History of Women and Class in Accra*, Bloomington, IN: Indiana University Press.

Romero, Patricia (1988), *Life Histories of African Women*, London: Ashfield.

Strobel, Margaret (1982), 'African Women', *Signs: Journal of Women in Culture and Society* 8: 1, pp. 109–31.

Sudarkasa, Niara (1973), *Where Women Work: A Study of Yoruba Women in the Marketplace and in the Home*, Ann Arbor, MI: University of Michigan Press.

Sweetman, David (1984), *Women Leaders in African History*, London: Heinemann.

Uchendu, P. K. (1993), *The Role of Nigerian Women in Politics: Past and Present*, Lagos: Eunugu.

VerEecke, Catherine (1988), *Cultural Constructions of Women's Economic Marginality: The Fulbe of Northeastern Nigeria*, East Lansing, MI: University of Michigan Press.

See also: **Anti-colonialism and Resistance: West Africa**; **Historiography: West Africa**; **Religions: West Africa**; **Slavery: West Africa**.

World Bank

The World Bank was formed at a meeting held at Bretton Woods, New Hampshire, USA, in July 1944. The bank's initial mandate was to rebuild Europe after the war. Nowadays, the bank's declared remit is to offer reconstruction loans and lend money to developing countries for development projects. Its headquarters are in Washington DC, and it also has centres in many other countries. Membership of the International Monetary Fund (IMF) is a prerequisite for any country before becoming a member of the World Bank. The bank funds development projects that are deemed to be profitable, or at least able to redeem their construction and development costs. The bank currently includes five institutions: the International Bank for Reconstruction and Development (IBRD), the International Development Association (IDA), the International Finance Corporation (IFC), the Multilateral Investment Guarantee Agency (MIGA), and the International Centre for Settlement of Investment Disputes (ICSID).

A key moment in World Bank history for the postcolonial world was its embrace in 1980 of structural adjustment, which required governments in developing countries (in order to secure loans) to adopt a range of austerity measures, including: currency devaluation, reduced public expenditure, reduced subsidies to consumers, reduction or elimination of price controls, revised trade policies to encourage exports, increased user charges for public services, and privatisation of enterprises and social services. The subject of hot debate at the time, the academic consensus by 2000 was that structural adjustment had singularly failed to alleviate poverty in the developing world. Arising from this failure, and other stringent criticisms, the World Bank commissioned the Wapenhans Report, which led to several reforms, including the establishment of an Inspection Panel.

In the 1990s, the bank has lent money for several emergency projects, such as: post-conflict work in Bosnia, Kosovo and East Timor, post-crisis assistance in East Asia, post-hurricane clean up in Central America, and post-earthquake support in Turkey. Nonetheless, it continues to be criticised because it is seen to impoverish citizens of poor countries that implement its policies of economic globalisation. Some critics stress that the bank's policies do not aim to help developing countries as much as enhance the economies of industrial countries and their rich corporations, who administer and draw profits from the majority of construction projects. Most recently, the World Bank and the IMF have been criticised for rejecting calls to provide debt relief by cancelling their claims against the poorest countries. Although there are not many literary works that depict the World Bank directly, a genre of popular journalism in sympathy with the anti-globalisation movement has emerged in recent years, and examples are listed below.

                                                                              Suha Kudsieh

Literary Works

Kincaid, Jamaica (1988), *A Small Place*, New York: Plume Books.
Kumar, Amitava (ed.) (2002), *World Bank Literature*, Minneapolis, MN: University of Minnesota Press.
Roy, Arundhati (1999), *The Cost of Living*, New York: Modern Library.

Histories

Caulfield, Catherine (1997), *Masters of Illusion. The World Bank and the Poverty of Nations*, London: Macmillan.
Chang Ha-Joon (ed.) (2001), *Joseph Stiglitz and the World Bank. The Rebel Within*, London: Anthem Press.
Danaher, Kevin (ed.) (2001), *Democratizing the Global Economy: The Battle against the World Bank and the International Monetary Fund*, Monroe, ME: Common Courage Press.
Fox, Jeremy (2001), *Chomsky and Globalisation*, Duxford: Icon.
Harriss, John (2001), *Depoliticizing Development: The World Bank and Social Capital*, New Delhi: Leftword Books.
Klein, Naomi (2002), *Fences and Windows: Dispatches from the Front Line of the Globalisation Debate*, London: Flamingo.
Monbiot, George (2003), *The Age of Consent: A Manifesto for a New World Order*, London: Flamingo.
Pilger, John (2002), *The New Rulers of the World*, London: Verso.
Pincus, Jonathan R. and Jeffrey A. Winters (eds) (2002), *Reinventing the World Bank*, Ithaca, NY: Cornell University Press.
Stiglitz, Joseph E. (2002), *Globalization and its Discontents*, New York: W. W. Norton and Co.
Weiss, Linda (1999), 'Managed Openness: Beyond Neoliberal Globalism', *New Left Review* 238, pp. 126–40.

See also: **Anti-globalisation Movements; Britain's Postwar Foreign Policy; Free Trade; International Monetary Fund; Land: Southern Africa; United States of America.**

World Wars I and II: African Soldiers

The role of colonial African soldiers in the World Wars underlines the common imperial context of these hostilities. Although Africa was of no relevance to the making of either war, with most of the continent under European control, mobilisation of African resources and people was inevitable. Incorporated into the demands of total war, huge numbers of Africans served in wars which were not their own, with few having more than the vaguest notion of what had precipitated 1914 or 1939, or the reasons for their risky service as volunteers or conscripts supplied by local chiefs. Approximately 70,000 British East and West African troops were raised from 1914 to 1918, while the World War II effort saw a massive expansion of colonial African regiments. By 1945, an estimated 500,000 belligerents had been enlisted from across British colonial Africa, well over three-quarters of these from East and West Africa. Africa was also a vital military labour pool for these mass war efforts, and most men toiled in labour corps or pioneer battalions as essentially non-combatant soldiering auxiliaries, service which still exposed them to severe and often deadly conditions.

Many hundreds of thousands of army carriers or porters were enlisted, mostly forcibly, in the World War I East African campaign, where disease, malnutrition and maltreatment produced high mortality rates. Thousands of labouring servicemen from Southern Africa were also used on the Western Front. This experience of arduous and dangerous work for little reward was repeated in 1939 to 1945, when African recruits were mustered as a massive labour contingent to maintain British forces in the Middle East, while others did duty as far afield as Burma. While African soldiers were obviously extraordinarily diverse in language and ethnicity, and in social and religious backgrounds, there were some significant similarities in experience. The scale, intensity, and European linguistic environment of industrialised warfare was completely new to most recruits, who came largely from fixed rural backgrounds. Involvement in hostilities meant the absorption of a range of radically new experiences of the imperial world. Only a small minority of soldiers were volunteers; the vast majority were pressed into the army by chiefs to fill recruitment quotas. Deployment, service conditions, and relationships with whites in both conflicts were regulated by segregationist assumptions and customary racial hierarchies, although more adventurous World War II soldiers did their bit for cross-colour social and sexual fraternisation. While servicemen were saddled with frustrations and punctured hopes of a better life at the end of the wars, historians no longer view a raised soldiering consciousness as a particular fillip to anti-colonial nationalist politics.

Bill Nasson

Literary Works

Beti, Mongo (1980), *Remember Ruben*, London: Heinemann.
Billany, Dan (1950), *The Trap*, London: Faber and Faber.
Blay, J. B. (1945), *After the Wedding*, Accra: Benibengor Books.
Boyd, William (1982), *An Ice-Cream War*, London: Hamish Hamilton.
Hanley, Gerald (1946), *Monsoon Victory*, London: Gollancz.

Histories

Jackson, Ashley (1999), *Botswana 1939–1945: An African Country at War*, Oxford: Clarendon Press.
Kiernan, V. G. (1995), 'Colonial Africa and its Armies', in Harvey J. Kaye (ed.), *Imperialism and its Contradictions*, London and New York: Routledge, pp. 77–96.
Killingray, David (1982), '"If I Fight for Them, Maybe then I can Go Back to the Village": African Soldiers in the Mediterranean and European Campaigns, 1939–45', in Paul Addison and Angus Calder (eds), *Time to Kill: The Soldier's Experience of War in the West 1939–45*, London: Pimlico, pp. 93–114.

Killingray, David (1998), 'The War in Africa', in Hew Strachan (ed.), *The Oxford Illustrated History of the First World War*, Oxford: Oxford University Press, pp. 92–103.

Killingray, David and Richard Rathbone (eds) (1986), *Africa and the Second World War*, London: Macmillan.

Page, Melvin E. (ed.) (1987), *Africa and the First World War*, London: Macmillan.

Waites, Bernard (2000), 'Black Men in White Men's Wars', in John Bourne, Peter Liddle and Ian Whitehead (eds), *The Great World War 1914–45, Volume 2*, London: Harper Collins, pp. 257–74.

See also: **British Imperialism; World Wars I and II: Anzac; World Wars I and II: South Asian Soldiers**.

World Wars I and II: Anzac

The term 'Anzac' was originally coined to describe the Australian and New Zealand Army Corps, which comprised part of the misguided British invasion of the Gallipoli peninsula in Turkey. The courageous feats of the Anzacs following their landing at Anzac Cove on 25 April 1915 imbued the term with an enduring significance for many Australians. Compared with their conscripted British counterparts, the volunteer Australians were reported to have fought magnificently, with a British officer declaring that they were 'not men, but gods'. As the first major battle for Australian troops, their reported valour expunged growing fears about the virility of the Australian 'race' and made Australians confident about their capacity to defend the lightly populated continent. Thus, the contribution to a British battle boosted the growing sense of Australian nationalism. Over time, Anzac came to have an almost sacred significance, with the word being protected by law against commercial exploitation and the anniversary of the landing being declared a public holiday. Every city and town soon had a memorial to the dead, often supplemented with tree-lined memorial avenues. During World War II, the potent imagery of Anzac was used to boost morale and maximise the war effort, with Prime Minister John Curtin calling on Australians to ensure that the continent remained 'the home of the Anzac people'.

Although soldiers were portrayed as upholders of the 'Anzac legend', their battles could not compete in the popular imagination with Gallipoli. A controversial play by Alan Seymour, *The One Day of the Year* (staged in 1960), was the first major attempt to question the place of Anzac in the Australian imagination. The subsequent Australian involvement in the Vietnam War caused many to spurn the Anzac legend as the central motif of Australian identity. At the same time, several Anzac Day marches saw protests by women wanting to remind participants about the female victims of war. In the face of these protests, and as the old diggers died off, it seemed that Anzac might fade from view. Although historians have questioned the extent to which the Anzac legend was an artificial creation of the official war historian, Charles Bean (writing in 1915), their work has done little to dent its image. Although the popular film *Gallipoli* (1981) pointed up the futility of the campaign, it combined with several books to provoke a resurgence of interest. Prime Minister Bob Hawke went to Anzac Cove for the 75th anniversary of the landing, with Anzac Cove becoming a site of pilgrimage for young Australians. More recently, with the last Gallipoli veteran being honoured with a state funeral, there have been calls for Anzac Day to be made Australia's national day.

David Day

Literary Works

Bennett, Jack (1981), *Gallipoli*, Sydney: Angus and Robertson.
McDonald, Roger (1979), *1915: A Novel*, Brisbane: University of Queensland Press.
Seymour, Alan (1962), *The One Day of the Year*, Sydney: Angus and Robertson.

Histories

Bean, C. E. W. [1915] (1993), *Anzac to Amiens*, Melbourne: Penguin.
Gammage, Bill (1980), *The Broken Years*, Melbourne: Penguin.
Inglis, Ken (1998), *Sacred Places*, Melbourne: Melbourne University Press.
Thomson, Alistair (1994), *Anzac Memories*, Melbourne: Oxford University Press.

See also: **Anti-war Movements: Australia; World Wars I and II: African Soldiers; World Wars I and II: South Asian Soldiers**.

World Wars I and II: South African Soldiers

South African historical experience of the two World Wars represents remarkable levels of similarities and continuities. In 1914 to 1918 and again in 1939 to 1945, the Union contribution to the British war effort was limited in comparison to that of Australia or New Zealand, despite its considerable strategic resources and industrial capacity. This was due to deep internal divisions over involvement in European wars in which much of the population had no obvious interest. Most Afrikaners, the dominant segment of the ruling white minority, were vociferously opposed to participation in what they regarded as British imperialist wars. Only a patriotic minority of British citizens and some Anglo-Afrikaner loyalists were ready to sacrifice for the Empire. Politically, in neither conflict could the state risk resorting to conscription to enlarge its war effort. As it was, South Africa's 1914 invasion of German South-West Africa triggered an armed republican Afrikaner rebellion, while by 1940 pro-Nazi Afrikaner paramilitary groups on the home front were committed to insurrectionary violence. War sentiment within the black majority was also mixed. Educated, middle-class African, Coloured and Indian political elites backed Union participation in both conflicts, if rather more guardedly in World War II than in World War I. Nationalist leadership clung to a belief in the liberal and moral capacity of British influence to persuade segregationist South Africa to improve black rights, and hoped that patriotic war service would produce some political or civic dividend. While resentful of the discriminatory 1912 Union Defence Act which barred Africans from armed service, in both wars they backed calls for volunteer enlistment as non-combatant military auxiliaries. On the other hand, the vast majority of black South Africans were deaf to an official war language of patriotic duty and imperial responsibility. Most of those recruited for war service were fleeing from peasant localities experiencing famine in World War I, or from extreme pockets of privation in World War II. In rural areas, a far-off white man's war meant nothing beyond domestic food shortages and rising inflation, and some labour recruiting campaigns faced considerable apathy and resistance. Urban industrial workers in both wars were more inclined to associate British power with labour exploitation than with democracy and human rights, and saw no gain from becoming involved in a dubious white man's war. Embittered mineworkers even celebrated German advances in East Africa in World War I and relished a German and Japanese threat to South Africa in World War II. Alienation from the imperial war effort was even sharper among impoverished peasant communities which became gripped by millenarian visions of the World Wars as a looming transcendence from colonial domination. In the Transkeian Territories in 1917, some coastal Xhosa chiefdoms imagined the coming of a seaborne German invasion which would drive out local whites and restore lost land and stock. Once again, in World War II, there were Zulu communities on the Natal coast in 1942 who looked to being liberated by a Japanese fleet to reclaim ancestral lands. Given such deep fissures in the wartime consciousness of both white Anglo-Afrikaner and black societies, in neither world conflict was South Africa able to mount a total war effort in support of the British Empire.

Predictably, the core of South African military campaigning was in support of British imperial interests on the African continent and in the Middle East. Moreover, as a dominion belligerent in both wars, the Union had its own sub-imperial ambitions for possible territorial gain or regional influence. Early in World War I, its troops captured German South-West Africa, while columns under General Smuts fought a prolonged offensive against the Germans in East Africa. In World War II, Union amphibious forces seized Madagascar from Vichy France, while other armoured brigades and air squadrons participated in the reconquest of Abyssinia (Ethiopia) and the invasion of Italian Somaliland. South African formations also fought hard in the North African campaigns and in the Central Mediterranean, taking part in the 1944–5 Italian campaign.

In both war efforts, Union governments found it difficult to attract sufficient white recruits for combat duty, especially for anything beyond home front defence. At the same time, they were saddled with the political handicap of a reluctance to arm black servicemen. For the 1914–18 war, South Africa raised some 145,000 white combatants and over 51,000 African and Coloured soldiers. Apart from several thousand Coloured Cape Corps infantrymen, black recruits were confined to non-combatant service in labour battalions and labour corps. Deployment in World War II closely mirrored the World War I picture. The Union mobilised around 132,000 white infantry volunteers and a further 54,000 men, spread between air and naval forces. Approximately 132,000 African and Coloured auxiliaries were placed in logistical or other support duties in a Non-European Army Services division. Given its comparatively low level of war sacrifice compared to Australia or New Zealand, mortality rates did not shock society with much of a sense of the horror and waste of disintegrative industrial warfare. Equally, the World Wars generated significant public cultures of commemoration of the dead. The drowning of almost 700 men of the South African Native Labour Contingent when the troopship Mendi sank in the English Channel in 1917 generated African nationalist representations of marginalised black sacrifice. A sombre Mendi vocabulary entered oral poetic traditions, and was also stimulated and appropriated by political forces, educational and cultural movements. The South African Infantry Brigade, whose soldiers died in droves in the Battle of Delville Wood during the 1916 Somme offensive, became recreated in historical memory through postwar cycles of Delville Day remembrance, and South African battlefield pilgrimages to northern France. By 1918, just over 12,000 South Africans had been killed, while the World War II death rate was close to 9,000.

Bill Nasson

Literary Works

Abrahams, Peter (1946), *Mine Boy*, London: Faber and Faber.
Butler, Guy (1952), *Stranger to Europe*, Cape Town: Balkema.
Campbell, Roy (1924), *The Flaming Terrapin*, London: Jonathan Cape.
Dikobe, Modikwe (1973), *The Marabi Dance*, London: Heinemann.
Mphahlele, Es'kia (1953), *Down Second Avenue*, London: Faber and Faber.
Paton, Alan (1948), *Cry, the Beloved Country*, London: Jonathan Cape.

Histories

Crwys-Williams, Jennifer (1992), *A Country at War, 1939–45: The Mood of a Nation*, Johannesburg: Ashanti.
Garson, N. G. (1979), 'South Africa and World War I', *Journal of Imperial and Commonwealth History* 8, pp. 76–94.
Gleeson, Ian (1994), *The Unknown Force: Black, Indian and Coloured Soldiers Through Two World Wars*, Johannesburg: Ashanti.
Grundlingh, Albert (1987), *Fighting Their Own War: South Africa Blacks and the First World War*, Johannesburg: Ravan Press.
Grundlingh, Albert (1999), 'The King's Afrikaners? Enlistment and Ethnic Identity in the Union of South Africa's Defence Force during the Second World War, 1939–45', *Journal of African History* 40, pp. 351–65.
Katzenellenbogen, Simon (1973), 'Southern Africa and the War of 1914–1918', in M. R. D. Foot (ed.), *War and Society*, London: Hurst, pp. 107–21.
Nasson, Bill (1994), 'A Great Divide: Popular Responses to the Great War in South Africa', *War and Society* 12, pp. 47–64.
Nasson, Bill (2001), 'South Africa', in John Bourne, Peter Liddle and Ian Whitehead (eds), *The Great World War 1914–45, Volume 2*, London: HarperCollins, pp. 243–56.
Phimister, Ian (1995), 'South Africa', in I. C. B. Dear and M. R. D. Foot (eds), *The Oxford Companion to the Second World War*, Oxford: Oxford University Press, pp. 1024–7.
Somerville, Christopher (1998), *Our War: How the British Commonwealth Fought the Second World War*, London: Weidenfeld and Nicolson.

See also: **Anti-colonialism and Resistance: Southern Africa; Historiography: Southern Africa; World Wars I and II: African Soldiers.**

World Wars I and II: South Asian Soldiers

Scholars in the service of empire developed a martial theory of races in order to recruit and deploy different ethnic and caste groups (Barua 1995). Ethnically organised regiments came in handy to quell rebellions in other parts of the subcontinent. After the Madras army was reorganised in 1796, traditional markers of the *sipahis'* (soldiers') appearance were effaced: turbans, earrings, caste-marks, beards. The *sipahi* became a *topiwallah* (synonymous with being a *feringhi*, or Christian, as far as his countrymen were concerned) dressed in a stiff round hat, like a 'pariah drummer's' with a flat top, a leather cockade and a standing feather (Kaye and Malleson 1888–93).

South Asian soldiers were used in the nineteenth century for colonial conquests in Africa, China and the Persian Gulf. They were also deployed for ceremonial purposes in Europe to foreground the power and glory of Britain. World War I marks the beginnings of their use in Europe's wars in Europe. More than 1.4 million fought on the fronts in Belgium, France, Gallipoli, Mesopotamia, Persia, and eastern Africa. More than 64,000 died, mostly in trench warfare. To this day they largely remain unnamed in memorials. Martial respect came in the wake of fierce trench warfare, dislodging European ideas of a weak and under-fed force: 'brown rascals not to be underrated', wrote a German soldier from the front (in Mason 1986, p. 413). Common was the prayer to 'release me from the climate of this country': their letters home complain bitterly about the climate: many suffered frostbite and yielded to pneumonia.

Nationalist sentiment and self-pride spread its roots as the myth of Asian barbarity was exploded and British self-conceptions of superiority destroyed. To generate favourable political effect in India, care was taken for those British Indian subjects wounded in the service of the king emperor to forestall any charges of differential treatment. After all, heg-emonic rule in India depended on the loyalty of the Indian army. Special arrangements were made lest the dietary and religious practices of soldiers were offended. Even sight-seeing tours in London were organised to instil in them the spectacle of *bilayati* (British) power. Despite the political expediency of treating them well, convalescing soldiers in Brighton were cordoned behind walls and barbed-wire fences with sentries on guard. A letter in *The Indiaman* reads:

> I have invariably found the manner [i.e., in which they are treated] of the sepoys exactly what it is in India. Moreover, the precaution taken to isolate the Indian from the indiscreet atten-tions of silly and ignorant women are all that the British prestige can require. (*India Office Records* 1915)

Amongst the most visible of South Asian soldiers, and certainly enjoying a privileged status in the British national imaginary – as opposed to the Sikhs, Pathans and Rajputs – were the Gurkhas, recruited from prisoners of war even as the Anglo-Nepal war of 1814–16 was going badly for the British. They were deployed by the Empire in the Anglo-Burmese War of 1824–26, in the theatres of World War I, Afghanistan in 1919, World War II, and more recently in the Falklands, Afghanistan and Iraq. Gurkhas were also used for the colonisation and consolidation of early nineteenth-century Assam by the British, having been attracted into service by the promise of land grants and settlements. Of them, Captain George Westmacott wrote, 'The Gorkhas are a noble set of fellows distinguished by some of the virtues and stained also by a few of the vices peculiar to Europeans.'

Two and a half million soldiers from all over India fought in the various theatres of World War II (over 24,000 killed and 65,000 wounded) while 8 million were engaged in auxiliary work and 5 million worked in Indian industries that had been turned into arsenals for the war effort. As POWs under the Japanese, they famously built the railway along the River Kwai; ironically they also fought other Indians who had joined the Japanese under the aus-pices of the Indian National Army. Today, as US hegemony morphs into empire, immense pressure has been applied on Pakistan, India and Bangladesh to supply troops in the name of keeping peace in the Gulf.

Prem Poddar

Literary Works

Anand, Mulk Raj [1940] (2000), *Across the Black Waters*, New Delhi: Vision/Orient
    Paperbacks.
Ghosh, Amitav (2000), *The Glass Palace*, London: HarperCollins.
Guleri, Chandradhar Sharma [1915] (1987), *Usne kaha tha aur anya kahaniyan* (in Hindi),
    Delhi: Manoharlal.
Ondaatje, Michael (1992), *The English Patient*, London: Bloomsbury.

Histories

Barua, Pradeep (1995), 'Inventing Race: The British and India's Martial Races', *Historian*
    58, pp. 107–16.
Caplan, Lionel (1995), *Warrior Gentlemen: 'Gurkhas' in the Western Imagination*,
    Providence and Oxford: Berghahn Books.
India Office Records (1915), MSS EUR F 143/96 *The Indiaman*, 30 April.
Kaye, Sir John William and G. B. Malleson (1888–93), *Kaye and Malleson's History of the
    Indian Mutiny of 1857–58*, London: W. H. Allen and Company.
Mason, Philip (1986), *A Matter of Honour*, London: Macmillan.
Omissi, David (1998), *The Sepoy and the Raj: The Indian Army, 1860–1940*, London: Palgrave.
Westmacott, George Edward (n.d.), 'Notes on the History of Assam', Ms. 2217, Special
    Collection, Aberdeen: King's College, University of Aberdeen.

See also: **Anglo-Burmese Wars; World Wars I and II: Anzac; Indian National Army;
    Mutinies in India; World Wars I and II: South African Soldiers.**

Y

Years of Terror

This refers to the violence experienced in the south of Sri Lanka from 1987 to 1989 during
the second uprising of the Janatha Vimukthi Peramuna (JVP or People's Liberation Front)
and its quelling by the United National Party (UNP) government under President
Ranasinghe Premadasa.

The JVP, founded in 1966 by Rohana Wijeweera as a revolutionary socialist movement,
drew its support from southern, educated, unemployed youth and first attempted to capture
state power in 1971. Its second uprising was based on a rejection of the liberalised 'open'
market economic policies launched by the UNP in 1977, and a Sinhala nationalist platform
as a response to the ongoing armed conflict between the Sri Lankan state and the Liberation

Tigers of Tamil Eelam (LTTE) fighting for a separate State of Tamil Eelam in the north and east of the island. Much of the latter activity was carried out by the JVP's wing Deshapremi Janatha Vyaparaya or Patriotic People's Movement.

The JVP targeted the military, police, politicians, activists and bureaucrats it classified as 'traitors to the nation'. Killing a number of those it identified as such, the JVP demanded the boycott of several elections. It campaigned against the 1987 provincial council elections held under the 13th amendment to parliament, adopted as a provision of the Indo-Lanka Accord, seeing it as a prelude to legitimising the separate Tamil State the LTTE was fighting for; the December 1988 presidential elections; and the general election of February 1989. The climate of intimidation and fear was widespread in the south of the country with an estimated 600 assassinations at the hands of both the JVP and the government taking place between the presidential elections of December 1988 and the beginning of the February 1989 general election.

The counter-offensive by the UNP government on the JVP was brutal. Those targeted by the government were not only JVPers (many youth were killed on mere suspicion of JVP sympathies), but also men who worked for the opposition Sri Lanka Freedom Party (SLFP). Amongst the murdered was renowned journalist and theatre actor-director Richard de Zoysa. Thousands 'disappeared'. The Presidential Commission into Involuntary Removal in the south of the country found evidence of 7,239 cases of 'disappearances' (4,858 at the hands of the state, 779 instigated by the JVP). However, journalists and scholars writing on the years of terror have placed the number of disappearances/deaths much higher, at around 40,000. A mass grave with the remains of some of the disappeared was subsequently discovered at Suriyakanda. Apart from the disappearances, bodies burnt on tyres, corpses floating down rivers and slumped bodies hung from lamp-posts became daily evidence of the violence of the times, and Sinhala words associated with terror like *bheeshanaya* (terror), *athurudahanwoowo* (the disappeared), *wadhakagaraya* (torture chamber) and *billa* (informant) entered the popular vocabulary. The violence subsided at the end of 1989 with the capture and killing of several JVP leaders, including Wijeweera.

Neloufer de Mel

Literary Works

Bandara, Sandaruwan Madduma (1999), *Just Another Bomb Blast*, Colombo: Midiro.
Gunesekera, Romesh (1992), *Monkfish Moon*, London: Granta and Penguin.
Halpe, Ashley (ed.) (1990), *An Anthology of Contemporary Sri Lankan Short Stories*, Colombo: The British Council.
Jayawardena, Sharmini (1998), *Wet Paint*, London: Minerva Press.
Obeysekere, Ranjini (1991), *A Grief Ago: Five Stories*, Colombo: International Centre for Ethnic Studies.
Ondaatje, Michael (2000), *Anil's Ghost*, London: Bloomsbury.
Ranasinghe, Anne (1989), *Not Even Shadows*, Colombo: The author.
Seneviratne, Maureen (1991), *Leaves from the Asvattha*, Colombo: Women's Education Research Centre.
Siriwardena, Regi (1993a), *Poems and Selected Translations*, Colombo: The author.
Siriwardena, Regi (1993b), *Poems and Selected Translations*, Colombo: The author.
Wijesinha, Rajiva (1989), *Days of Despair*, Colombo: English Writers Cooperative of Sri Lanka.

Wijesinha, Rajiva (1991), *The Lady Hippopotamus and Other Stories*, Colombo: English
    Writers Cooperative of Sri Lanka.
De Zoysa, Richard (1990), *This Other Eden: Collected Poems of Richard de Zoysa*, Colombo:
    The English Association of Sri Lanka.

Histories

Abeysekera, Charles and Newton Gunaratne (eds) (1985), *Ethnicity and Social Change in
    Sri Lanka*, Colombo: Social Scientists Association.
Abeysekera, Charles and Newton Gunaratne (eds) (1987), *Facets of Ethnicity*, Colombo:
    Social Scientists Association.
Jayawardena, Kumari (1985), *Ethnicity and Class Conflict in Sri Lanka: The Emergence of
    Sinhala-Buddhist consciousness*, Colombo: Social Scientists Association.
Jeganathan, Pradeep and Qadri Ismail (eds) (1995), *Unmaking the Nation; The Politics of
    Identity and History in Modern Sri Lanka*, Colombo: Social Scientists Association.
Silva, Neluka (ed.) (2002), *The Hybrid Island: Culture Crossings and the Invention of Identity
    in Sri Lanka*, Colombo: Social Scientists Association.
Tambiah, S. J. (1986), *Sri Lanka: Ethnic Fratricide and the Dismantling of Democracy* London:
    I. B. Tauris and Co. Ltd.

See also: **JVP Insurrection; Secessionism: South Asia; Sri Lankan Civil War; Terrorism:
    South Asia.**

Yellow Peril

Kaiser Wilhelm II, German emperor and king of Prussia, coined the term 'yellow peril' in
1895. *National Life and Character: A Forecast*, written by the Australian academic and political philosopher, Charles H. Pearson, may have quickened Wilhelm's apprehensions about
the threat posed by the East to the European world. Pearson's book was published in 1893
to great critical acclaim in Britain, North America and Europe. He warned of the rise of
China and the steady spread of Chinese influence throughout the world, not least in
Europe, but he had almost nothing to say about Japan.

Seized by the danger of the rising East, Kaiser Wilhelm drew a sketch of the confrontation between East and West, which Professor H. Knackfuss turned into an allegorical painting titled 'The Yellow Peril'. The painting caused a great sensation in Europe and all the
more so when Kaiser Wilhelm sent it to St Petersburg as a gift to the Tsar. The painting
depicts an Archangel leading a group of female personifications of the nations of Europe
(Germania to the fore, irresolute Britannia a little further back). The group gaze across a
river, possibly the Danube, where the threatening East is seen to be gathering its forces
amid fire and storm and the inevitable dragon. One of the paradoxical features of the painting is that the menacing East is represented by the tranquil figure of the seated Buddha.
The Japanese artist, Beisen Kubota, countered with another painting – 'The Real Yellow
Peril' showing the Chinese developing their skills as an efficient, industrialised power.

The 'yellow peril' quickly became a subject for popular novelists and was closely linked
to warnings about invasion. The threat was invoked to generate a greater sense of patriotism and a renewed commitment to the values of European civilisation. In Australia, the

'empty north' was considered a particularly tempting prize for the crowded nations of Asia well into the 1950s. However, from the 1960s the term was increasingly used to satirise exaggerated fears of Asian domination and is now largely employed in that context.

David Walker

Literary Works

Clancy, Tom (2000), *The Bear and The Dragon*, Melbourne: Penguin.
Mackay, Kenneth (1895), *The Yellow Wave: A Romance of the Asiatic Invasion of Australia*, London: Bentley.
Rohmer, Sax (1929), *The Emperor of America*, London: Cassell and Company.
Roydhouse, T. R. [Rata], *The Coloured Conquest*, Sydney: New South Wales Bookstall Company.
Shiel, M. P. [1898] (1999), *The Yellow Danger*, London: Routledge.

Histories

D'Cruz, J. V. and William Steele (2003), *Australia's Ambivalence towards Asia*, Melbourne: Monash Asia Institute.
Dijkstra, Bram (1996), *Evil Sisters: The Threat of Female Sexuality in Twentieth Century Culture*, New York: Henry Holt and Company.
Diosy, Arthur (1898), *The New Far East*, London: Cassell and Company.
Marchetti, Gina (1993), *Romance and the 'Yellow Peril': Race, Sex and Discursive Strategies in Hollywood Fiction*, Berkeley, CA: University of California Press.
Pearson, C. H. (1893), *National Life and Character: A Forecast*, London: Macmillan and Company.
Walker, David (1999), *Anxious Nation: Australia and the Rise of Asia*, Brisbane: University of Queensland Press.

See also: **Asianisation: Australia; Chinese Gold-diggers; Historiography: Australia; Multiculturalism: Australia; Racial Discrimination Act: Australia; White Australia Policy.**

Z

Zionism

Zionism is perhaps best understood as a Jewish ethnic nationalism. To this extent, it is not untypical of its late nineteenth-century origins in Europe, and bears some comparison with

European nationalisms of the same period. Crucial differences are: 1) the history of European anti-Semitism and persecution of the Jewish people; and 2) Zionism's success in attaching itself to the most powerful imperialist power of the day, Great Britain.

Theodor Herzl (1860–1904) was the first exponent of Zionism, in *The Jewish State* (1896) and its first institutional expression came with the Zionist World Congress in 1897. Zionism's origins lie in the link, according to its adherents, that connects Jews with the Holy Land. The final dispersal of the Jewish population came in 135 CE, with the breaking of the Bar Kokhba rebellion. At the opening of the nineteenth century, the Jewish population of Palestine was still only approximately 10,000, even after the influx of Jews expelled from Andalucia in the fifteenth century. The rest were scattered all over the world, forming the diaspora, the Hebrew word for 'dispersal'. The longing for the lost homeland was under these conditions preserved mostly by religion; hence the prayer, 'Next year in Jerusalem'. But in the nineteenth century, during his campaign in Egypt, Napoleon encouraged the Jews to flock to his flag and reconstruct Jerusalem. This cause gained such prominent supporters as Saint-Simon, Benjamin Disraeli and Lord Byron. More practical support came from thinkers such as Moses Hess and Leon Pinsker, and from financiers such as Baron Edmond de Rothschild. The work of Pinsker, such as *Self-Determination* (1882), inspired the Lovers of Zion, who promoted the first *aliya*, or migration of Jews to Palestine, bringing up to 30,000 Jews to the biblical lands between 1882 and 1903.

Herzl's immediate context was the Dreyfus Affair and East European pogroms from the early 1880s onwards. He supplied the movement with a theory, which rested on four main propositions: the existence of the Jewish people; the failure of their assimilation into other societies; their right to the Holy Land; and the non-existence of another people there with rights to the territory. This is, like other nationalisms, an ideology; its pretensions to scientificity are thus equally debatable. Zionism was a reaction to persecution of the Jews, and also to the failure of the hopes of emancipation promised in Europe by the Enlightenment and the French Revolution. But Zionism also profited by being perceived as a tool by the great powers of the time. Britain saw Zionism as a mechanism to consolidate its influence in the Middle East and to control the Suez Canal; Russia viewed Zionism as a way to get rid of potential revolutionary leaders; Germany's leaders wanted to weaken a large Jewish community; the tottering Ottoman Empire was looking for funds. Crucially, Zionism therefore came into being at the height of the European 'age of empire', and its status as a quasi-colonial project even today must be seen in that historical light.

Conor McCarthy

Literary Works

Ben Gurion, David (1970), *Memoirs*. Cleveland, OH: World Publishing Company.

Ben-Ezer, Ehud (1999), *Sleepwalkers and Other Stories: The Arab in Hebrew Fiction*, Boulder, CO: Lynne Rienner.

Castel-Bloom, Orly (2002), *Dolly City*, trans. D. Bilu, London: Loki.

Eliot, George [1876] (2000), *Daniel Deronda*, London: Wordsworth.

Grant, Linda (2000), *When I Lived in Modern Times*, London: Granta.

Grossman, David (1993), *Sleeping on a Wire. Conversations with Palestinians in Israel*, trans. H. Watzman, New York: Farrar, Straus and Giroux.

Shabtai, Aharon (2003), *J'accuse*, trans. P. Cole, New York: New Directions.

Yehoshua, A. B. (2003), *The Liberated Bride*, trans. H. Halkin, New York: Harcourt.

Histories

Avinieri, Shlomo (1981), *The Making of Modern Zionism: The Intellectual Origins of the Jewish State*, New York: Basic Books.
Simha Flapan, Flapan (1979), *Zionism and the Palestinians*, London: Croom Helm.
Sternhell, Ze'ev (1998), *The Founding Myths of Israel: Nationalism, Socialism and the Making of the Jewish State*, Princeton, NJ: Princeton University Press.

See also: **Balfour Declaration; Nationalism(s), Arab; Palestinian Political Movements.**

Contributors

Kay Adamson, Glasgow Caledonian University, UK
Oladipo Agboluaje, independent scholar, UK
Rahnuma Ahmed, DRIK, Dacca, Bangladesh
Stephen Alomes, Deakin University, Australia
K. Noel Amherd, Birmingham University, UK
Sunil Amrith, Birkbeck (University of London), UK
Joan Anim-Addo, Goldsmiths College, London University, UK
Yoko Arisaka, University of San Francisco, USA
Christopher J. Armstrong, Chukyo University, Japan
E. S. Atieno Odhiambo, Rice University, USA
Dominic Beneventi, University of Montreal, Canada
Curwen Best, University of West Indies, Barbados
Kaushik Bhaumik, University of Oxford, UK
Vivian Bickford-Smith, University of Cape Town, South Africa
Laura Bier, New York University, USA
Ryan Bishop, National University of Singapore
Heidi Bojsen, Roskilde University, Denmark
Patrick Bond, University of Kwazulu-Natal, South Africa
Brinda Bose, University of Delhi, India
Monica Bungaro, Birmingham University, UK
Urvashi Butalia, independent scholar, India
Noah Butler, Northwestern University, USA
David Cahill, University of New South Wales, Australia
Michael Cardo, Helen Suzman Foundation, South Africa
Uma Chakravarty, University of Delhi, India
Abdin Chande, Sidwell Friends School, USA
Anadi P. Chhetri, Kalimpong, independent scholar, India
Anne Collett, University of Wollongong, Australia
Jonathan Crush, Queen's University, Canada
Ann Curthoys, Australian National University
Mark Curtis, independent scholar, UK
David Day, La Trobe University, Australia
Vijay Devadas, University of Otago, New Zealand
Allison Drew, York University, UK
Justin Edwards, University of Bangor, Wales
Hans-Georg Erney, Armstrong Atlantic State University, USA
Toyin Falola, University of Texas, USA
Keith Feldman, University of Washington, USA
Robert Fraser, Open University, UK
Kai Friese, New Delhi, India

Harry Garuba, University of Cape Town, South Africa
Yogita Goyal, University of California, Los Angeles, USA
Suman Gupta, Open University, UK
Jeff Guy, University of Kwazulu-Natal, South Africa
Anne Hardgrove, University of Texas San Antonio, USA
Bruce Harding, Macmillan Brown Centre for Pacific Studies, New Zealand
Barbara Harlow, University of Texas, USA
Tom Henthorne, Pace University, USA
Tom Hickey, University of Brighton, UK
Isabel Hofmeyr, University of Witwatersrand, South Africa
Philip Holden, National University of Singapore
Azfar Hussain, Washington State University, USA
Jonathan Hyslop, University of Witwatersrand, South Africa
Emilia Ilieva, Egerton University, Kenya
Suhail Islam, Nazareth College of Rochester, USA
Douglas Ivison, Lakehead University, Canada
Sonia Jabber, Independent scholar, India
Pranav Jani, Ohio State University, USA
Lars Jensen, Roskilde University, Denmark
Shamil Jeppie, University of Cape Town, South Africa
David Johnson, Open University, UK
Stephanie Jones, Southampton University, UK
Manoj Joshi, *Times of India*, New Delhi, India
James Jupp, Australian National University
Ananya Jahanara Kabir, University of Leeds, UK
Sukeshi Kamra, Carleton University, Canada
Kampta Karran, Warwick University, UK
David Kazanjian, University of Pennsylvania, USA
Tabish Khair, Aarhus University, Denmark
Diane Kirkby, La Trobe University, Australia
Elizabeth Kolsky, Villanova University, USA
Susan Knutson, Université Sainte-Anne – Collège de l'Acadie, Canada
Kai Kresse, University of St Andrews, UK
Suha Kudsieh, Toronto University, Canada
Michele Langfield, Deakin University, Australia
Leong Liew Geok, National University of Singapore
Shirley Geok-Lin Lim, University of California, Santa Barbara, USA
Jennifer Lofkrantz, Furman University, USA
Elizabeth De Loughrey, Cornell University, USA
Glen Lowry, independent scholar, Canada
Conor McCarthy, University of Maynooth, Ireland
John McLeod, Leeds University, UK
Jennifer McMahon, New York University, USA
John McQuilton, University of Wollongong, Australia
Ram Manikkalingam, Rockefeller Foundation, USA
Andrew Markus, Monash University, Australia
John Maynard, Newcastle University, Australia
Cheralyn Mealor, Aarhus University, Denmark

Neloufer de Mel, Colombo University, Sri Lanka
Rajend Mesthrie, University of Cape Town, South Africa
Farina Mir, University of Virginia, USA
Sudesh Mishra, Deakin University, Australia
Rachidi Molapo, University of Venda, South Africa
Shane Moran, University of Kwazulu-Natal, South Africa
Peter Morey, University of East London, UK
Lianne Moyes, University of Montreal, Canada
Akshaya Mukul, *Times of India*, New Delhi, India
Veena Naregal, IEG, New Delhi, India
Geoff Nash, Sunderland University, UK
Bill Nasson, University of Cape Town, South Africa
Barbara Nicholson, University of Wollongong, Australia
Insa Nolte, Birmingham University, UK
Apollos O. Nwauwa, Bowling Green State University, USA
Joyce Nyairo, Moi University, Kenya
Hannington Ochwada, Marquette University, USA
Lennox Odiemo-Munra, Egerton University, Kenya
Tom Odhiambo, University of Witwatersrand, South Africa
James Ogude, University of Witwatersrand, South Africa
Tope Omoniyi, Surrey University, UK
Benita Parry, Warwick University, UK
Neil Parsons, University of Botswana
Rajeev Patke, National University of Singapore
Adele Perry, University of Manitoba, USA
Kirsten Holst Petersen, Roskilde University, Denmark
Deepika Petraglia-Bahri, Emory University, USA
Roderic Pitty, Deakin University, Australia
Prem Poddar, Southampton University, UK
David Pratten, University of Sussex, UK
Mohammad Abdul Quayum, International Islamic University, Malaysia
Terence Ranger, Oxford University, UK
Antje M. Rauwerda, Goucher College, USA
Suresh Raval, University of Arizona, USA
Kokila Ravi, Atlanta Metropolitan College, USA
Priscilla Ringrose, University of Trondheim, Norway
Nicole Roberts, University of West Indies, Trinidad
Ashley Rothrock, University of Texas, USA
Anita Rupprecht, University of Brighton, UK
Minoli Salgado, University of Sussex, UK
John Saul, York University, Canada
Cleve Scott, University of West Indies, Barbados
Sharron Scott, La Trobe University, Australia
Harsh Sethi, *Seminar*, New Delhi, India
Shubhra Sharma, University of Texas at Austin, USA
Mimi Sheller, Lancaster University, UK
Nick Shepherd, University of Cape Town, South Africa
Yumna Siddiqi, Middlebury College, USA

Neluka Silva, University of Colombo, Sri Lanka
Wendy Singer, Kenyon College, USA
Mohinder Singh, Delhi University, India
Lance van Sittert, University of Cape Town, South Africa
Kelwyn Sole, University of Cape Town, South Africa
Jennifer Sparrow, Medgar Evers College, CUNY, USA
Patricia van der Spuy, Emory University, USA
Mytheli Sreenivas, Ohio State University, USA
Neelam Srivastava, Newcastle University, UK
Philip Stern, Columbia University, USA
Nancy Stockdale, University of Central Florida, USA
Batia Boe Stolar, Memorial University of Newfoundland, Canada
Rawiri Taonui, University of Canterbury, New Zealand
Marie Helene K. Tessio, Bard College, USA
Glen Thompson, independent scholar, South Africa
Farouk Topan, SOAS, London University, UK
Siddharth Varadarajan, *Times of India*, New Delhi, India
Andrew van der Vlies, Sheffield University, UK
Alex de Waal, Justice Africa, UK
David Walker, Deakin University, Australia
John Walsh, Mahidol University, Thailand
Stuart Ward, University of Southern Denmark
Christopher Warnes, Cambridge University, UK
Janet Wilson, University of Northampton, UK
Amanda Wise, Macquarie University, Australia
Wong Saokoon, Kuala Lumpur, Malaysia
Amina Yaquin, SOAS, London University, UK
Alfred Zack-Williams, University of Liverpool, UK
Michael Zeuske, Cologne University, Germany

Index of Literary Works

Authors are in plain text.
Book titles are in italics and are followed by the author in parenthesis.
Single poems and short stories are in italics with single quotation marks and are followed by authors in parenthesis.

'Abd al-Quddus, Ihsan, *I am Free and Other Stories*, 339
Abeng (Michelle Cliff), 15
Abiku (D. Kotun), 426
Aboulela, Leila, *The Translator*, 251
Abouzeid, Leila, *Return to Childhood. The Memoir of a Modern Moroccan Woman*, 309
Abrahams, Peter, 49, 106, 318, 322, 537
  Mine Boy, 318, 322, 537
  Path of Thunder, The, 106
  Tell Freedom, 49, 106
Abraham's Promise (Philip Jeyaretnam), 210
Abram's Plains (Thomas Cary), 62
Abul Fazl, Allami, *Ain-i-Akbari*, 396
Abyssinian Chronicles (Moses Isegawa), 5
Account, Much Abbreviated, of the Destruction of the Indies, An (Bartolomé de Las Casas), 389
Achebe, Chinua, 7, 37, 42, 64, 65, 107, 220, 236, 290, 402, 426, 529
  Anthills of the Savannah, 42, 64
  Arrow of God, 37, 290
  Girls at War and Other Stories, 65
  No Longer at Ease, 37, 107
  Things Fall Apart, 7, 37, 220, 236, 402, 426, 529
Across the Atlantic. An Anthology of Cape Verdean Literature (ed. Maria M. Ellen), 91
Across the Black Waters (Mulk Raj Anand), 539
Across the Red River (Christian Jennings), 160
Adebayo, A., *My Village Captured Hitler*, 426
Admiring Silence (Abdulrazak Gurnah), 413
Adnan, Etel, *Sitt Marie Rose: A Novel*, 199
Adu-Boahen, S., *How to be Sure That You will Go to Heaven*, 426
Advani, Rukun, *Beethoven Among the Cows*, 357
Adventures of Dreaded Ned, The (Garry Langford), 268
African Child, The (Camara Laye), 402
African Sketches (Thomas Pringle), 433
After Abraham: A Play (Ron Chudley), 62
After China (Brian Castro), 485
After the Dance (Edwidge Danticat), 460
After the Wedding (J. B. Blay), 533
Afterlife of George Cartwright, The (John Steffler), 151
Agaguk (Yves Thérieult), 240
Age of Iron, The (J. M. Coetzee), 215
Ahmad, Rukhsana (ed.), *Contemporary Feminist Urdu Poetry*, 370
Aidoo, Ama Ata, 426, 447, 529
  The Dilemma of a Ghost and Anowa, 426, 447
  Our Sister Killjoy, 529

Ain-i-Akbari (Allami Abul Fazl), 396
Aishabee at War (Aisha Akbar), 519
Akare, Thomas, *The Slums*, 193
Akbar, Aisha, *Aishabee at War*, 519
Ake (Wole Soyinka), 220, 427
Al-Shaykh, Hanan, 42, 509
  Beirut Blues, 42
  I Sweep the Sun off Rooftops, 509
Alcorso, Claudio, *The Wind You Say*, 120
Alexander, Meena, *The Shock of Arrival*, 127
Alexandria Quartet, The (Lawrence Durrell), 199
Ali, Agha Shahid, 251, 265, 435
  The Country without a Post Office, 265, 435
  Rooms Are Never Finished, 265
Ali, Ahmed, 403, 419
  Selected Short Stories from Pakistan: Urdu (ed.), 403
  Twilight in Delhi, 419
Ali, Monica, *Brick Lane*, 60, 251, 279
Ali, Tariq, *Shadows of the Pomegranate Tree*, 251
Alias Grace (Margaret Atwood), 495
Alibhai-Brown, Yasmin, *No Place Like Home*, 52
All Souls' Rising (Madison Smartt Bell), 164
Allan, Sheila, *Diary of a Girl in Changi: 1941–1945*, 519
Allfrey, Phyllis Shand, *The Orchid House*, 484
Almanac of the Dead, The (Leslie Marmon Silko), 43
Alter, Stephen, *Amritsar to Lahore. Crossing the Border between India and Pakistan*, 80
Amadi, Elechi, 65, 402, 447, 529
  The Concubine, 529
  The Great Ponds, 402
  The Slave, 447
  Sunset in Biafra: A Civil War Diary, 65
Amazing Saga of Field Marshal Abdulla Salim Fisi (Or How the Hyena Got His!) (Alumidi Osinya), 5
Ambiguous Adventure (Hamidou Kane), 220
Among the White Moonfaces (Shirley Geok-lin Lim), 519
Amritsar to Lahore. Crossing the Border between India and Pakistan (Stephen Alter), 80
Anand (Pat Poovalingam), 233
Anand, Mulk Raj, 95, 204, 403, 539
  Across the Black Waters, 539
  An Anthology of Dalit Literature (ed. with Eleanor Zelliot), 95, 204
  Untouchable, 95, 204, 403
Anandamath (Bankimchandra Chatterji), 63
Ancestor Game, The (Alex Miller), 54, 103

Ancient Ballads and Legends of Hindustan (Toru Dutt), 141

'*And Finally They Killed Him*': *Speeches and Poems at a Memorial Rally for Walter Rodney* (ed. Eric Huntley), 430

... *and the Rain My Drink* (Suyin Han), 112

Andreas, Neshani, *The Purple Violet of Oshaantu*, 224

Angel (Merle Collins), 15

Anil's Ghost (Amitav Ghosh), 43, 279, 286, 435, 458, 540

Anita and Me (Meera Syal), 127

Annie John (Jamaica Kincaid), 15

Another Country (Karel Schoeman), 49

Anowa (Ama Ata Aidoo), 447

Anthills of the Savannah (Chinua Achebe), 42, 64

Anthology of Contemporary Sri Lankan Short Stories, An (ed. Ashley Halpe), 540

Anthology of Dalit Literature, An (ed. Mulk Raj Anand and Eleanor Zelliot), 95, 204

Anthology of East African Plays, An (ed. Barnabas Kasigwa), 331

Anthology of Modern Palestinian Literature (ed. Salma Khadra Jayyusi), 344

Anthology of Native Canadian Literature in English, An (eds Daniel David Moses and Terry Goldie), 240

Antwi-Boasiako, K., *No Way Back*, 426

Aplin, Nick, *To the Finishing Line: Champions of Singapore*, 519

Aquin, Hubert, *Next Episode*, 405

Arabesques (Anton Shammas), 372

Arabian Nights, The (Richard Burton), 199

Arasanayagam, Jean, 451
    Reddened Water Flows Clear, 451
    Trial by Terror, 451

Arden, John, *Sergeant Musgrave's Dance*, 177

Arenas, Reinaldo, *Before Night Falls*, 116

Armah, Ayi Kwei, 37, 51, 153, 220, 290, 358, 373, 447, 471, 529
    The Beautiful Ones Are Not Yet Born, 37, 220, 290, 358
    Fragments, 153, 471
    The Healers, 51, 447
    Osiris Rising: A Novel of Africa, Past, Present and Future, 373
    Two Thousand Seasons, 373, 447, 529
    Why Are We So Blest?, 37

Armstrong, Jeannette, *Slash*, 182, 353

Arrivants, The (Edward Kamau Brathwaite), 330, 389, 441

Arrow of God (Chinua Achebe), 37, 290

As I Please (Salleh Ben Joned), 89

Assiniwi, Bernard (and Wayne Grady), *The Beothuk Saga*, 159

At the Full and Change of the Moon (Dionne Brand), 345, 441, 495

At the Rendezvous of Victory (C. L. R. James), 255

At What Dark Point (Anne Ranasinghe), 451

Atlantic Sound, The (Caryl Phillips), 460

Atwood, Margaret, 151, 495
    Alias Grace, 495
    The Journals of Susanna Moodie: Poems, 151

Aung San of Burma: A Biographical Portrait by his Daughter (Aung San Suu Kyi), 519

Aung San Suu Kyi, *Aung San of Burma: A Biographical Portrait by his Daughter*, 519

Austen, Jane, *Mansfield Park*, 441

Autobiography, An (Jawaharlal Nehru), 357

Autobiography of Kwame Nkrumah, The, 358

Autumn Quail (Naguib Mahfouz), 456

Azadi (Chaman Nahal), 27

Aziz, Nurjehan (ed.), *Her Mother's Ashes and Other Stories by South Asian Women in Canada and the United States*, 127

Babur, Zahiruddin, *Babur-Nama*, 396

Babur-Nama (Zahiruddin Babur), 396

Baby No-Eyes (Patricia Grace), 306

Back-to-Africa Narratives from the 1850s (ed. Wilson Jeremiah Moses), 56

Backdam People (Rooplall Monar), 230

Backwoods of Canada, The (Catherine Parr Traill), 152

Ballad for the New World (Lawrence Scott), 187

Bama, *Karrukku*, 514

Bandara, Sandaruwan Madduma, *Just Another Bomb Blast*, 540

Bao Ninh, *The Sorrow of War*, 210, 478

Barakat, Halim, *Days of Dust*, 343

Barber, Noel, 77, 256
    The Black Hole of Calcutta: A Reconstruction, 77
    Tanamera: A Novel of Singapore, 256

Barghouti, Mourid, *I Saw Ramallah*, 372

Barker, Jimmie, *The Two Worlds of Jimmie Barker*, 387

Barrier Breakers: Women In Singapore (Shelley Siu), 520

Beach, The (Alex Garland), 42

Bear and the Dragon, The (Tom Clancy), 542

Beatrice Chancy (George Elliott Clarke), 495

Beautiful Ones Are Not Yet Born, The (Ayi Kwei Armah), 37, 220, 290, 358

Beavan, Frances, *Life in the Backwoods of New Brunswick*, 151

Because a White Man'll Never Do It (Kevin Gilbert), 388

Because of Mama and Poh Poh (Yeo Lai Cheng), 520

Bedford, Jean, *Sister Kate: A Novel*, 268

Beer in the Snooker Club (Wagdi Ghali), 339

Beethoven among the Cows (Rukun Advani), 357

Before Night Falls (Reinaldo Areinas), 116

Beggar at Damascus Gate, A (Yasmin Zahran), 509

Behn, Aphra, *Oroonoko and Other Writings*, 186

Behold the Earth Mourns (Ansuyah Singh), 233

Being-Black-In-The-World (Chabani Manganyi), 75

Beirut Blues (Hanan al-Shaykh), 42

Beka Lamb (Zee Edgell), 501

Belgrave, Valerie, *Ti Marie*, 186

Belles-Soeurs, Les (Michael Tremblay), 182

Ben-Ezer, Ehud, *Sleepwalkers and Other Stories*, 543

Ben Gurion, David, *Memoirs*, 543

Benang: From the Heart (Kim Scott), 170, 388, 452

Bend in the River, A (V. S. Naipaul), 108

Bennett, Jack, *Gallipoli*, 535

Bennett, Louise, *Selected Poems*, 113

Beothuk Saga, The (Bernard Assiniwi and Wayne Grady), 159

Berold, Robert (ed.), *It All Begins. Poems from Postliberation South Africa*, 281, 350, 383

Berry, Francis, '*Morant Bay*', 324

Beti, Mongo, *Remember Ruben*, 533
Beyond a Boundary (C. L. R. James), 15, 254, 486
Beyond Ceremony. An Anthology of Drama from Fiji (ed. Ian Gaskell), 123, 368
Bhalla, Alok (ed.), *Stories about the Partition of India*, 204
Bhattacharya, Bhabhani, 26, 107
   Shadow from Ladakh, 26
   So Many Hungers!, 107
Bhowani Junction (John Masters), 407
Biko, Steve, *I Write What I Like*, 75
Bila, Vonani, *In the Name of Amandla*, 281
Billany, Dan, *The Trap*, 533
Billy, Afu (ed. with Hazel Lulei and Jully Sipolo), *Mi Mere: Poetry and Prose by Solomon Women Writers*, 491
Birbalsingh, Frank (ed.), *Jahaji Bhai: An Anthology of Indo-Caribbean Literature*, 261
Birds of Passage (Brian Castro), 54, 103, 326, 485
Bissoondath, Neil, *A Casual Brutality*, 327
Bit of Earth, A (Christine Lim Suchen), 454
Bitter Fruit (Achmat Dangor), 383
Bitter Harvest (Grace Ibingira), 5
Black Album, The (Hanif Kureishi), 432
Black from the Edge (Kevin Gilbert), 276
Black Hole of Calcutta: A Reconstruction, The (Noel Barber), 77
Black Mamba Rising (ed. Ari Sitas), 50, 274
Black Narcissus (Rumer Godden), 165
Blackburn, Douglas, 8, 274, 322
   A Burger Quixote, 8
   Leaven: A Black and White Story, 274, 322
Blackwater Lightship, The (Colm Toibin), 224
Blake, or the Huts of Africa (Martin R. Delany), 468
Blame Me on History (William Bloke Modisane), 49
Blay, J. B., *After the Wedding*, 533
Bleek, W. H. I., *Specimens of Folklore*, 400
Blood and Soil (Pamela Siew Im Ong), 519
Blood Knot, The (Athol Fugard), 106
Blood on our Land (Ismael R. Mbise), 360
Blood on the Wattle (Leslie Haylen), 409
'Blood Soi' (Sonia Jabber), 265
Blood Vote, The (Jack Lindsay), 45
Blunt, Wilfrid Scawen, *My Diaries, 1888–1914*, 115
Boehmer, Elleke (ed.), *Empire Writing. An Anthology of Colonial literature 1870–1918*, 87, 177
Bond, Ruskin, *The Night Train at Deoli and Other Stories*, 165
Bone is Pointed, The (Arthur Upfield), 388
Bone People, The (Keri Hulme), 306, 369, 481, 491
Bones (Mahadai Das), 230
Bones (Chenjerai Hove), 32, 101, 413
Bonutto, Oswald, *A Migrant's Story*, 120
Book of Salt, The (Monique T. D. Truong), 478
Book of Trances, A (Guneli Gun), 269
Borges, Jorges Luis, *Labyrinths: Selected Stories and Other Writings*, 295
Born of the Sun. A Namibian Novel (Joseph Diescho), 318
Both Sides of the Moon (Alan Duff), 481
Bowering, George, *Burning Water*, 151
Bowsfield, Hartwell (ed.), *Louis Riel: Selected Readings*, 428
Boyd, William, *An Ice-Cream War*, 533
Braddon, Russell, *The Naked Island*, 256

Brand, Dionne, 182, 345, 441, 495
   At the Full and Change of the Moon, 345, 441, 495
   In Another Place, Not Here, 182
Brathwaite, Edward Kamau, 113, 330, 389, 441
   The Arrivants, 330, 389, 441
   Rights of Passage, 113
Breath, Eyes, Memory (Edwidge Danticat), 42
Breath of Fresh Air, A (Amulya Malladi), 328
Breytenbach, Breyten, *The True Confessions of an Albino Terrorist*, 49
Brick Lane (Monica Ali), 60, 251, 279
Bridge of Beyond, The (Simone Schwarz-Bart), 442
Brink, André, 49, 106, 156, 215, 400, 444
   A Chain of Voices, 444
   A Dry White Season, 215, 400
   An Instant in the Wind, 156
   Looking on Darkness, 49, 106
Brodber, Erna, *Jane and Louisa Will Soon Come Home*, 501
Brossard, Nicole, *These Our Mothers, Or: The Disintegrating Chapter*, 495
Brother Man (Roger Mais), 330
Brown, Charles Brockden, *Edgar Huntly, or Memoirs of a Sleep-Walker*, 468
Brown Girl in the Ring (Nalo Hopkinson), 121
Brown Man's Burden (Roderick Finlayson), 369, 481
Bruchac, Joseph, *The Wind Eagle and Other Abinaki Stories*, 159
Brutus, Dennis, *Letters from Martha*, 215
Buchan, John, *Prester John*, 177
'Buckingham Palace,' District Six (Richard Rive), 106
Buddha of Suburbia, The (Hanif Kureishi), 71
Bulcarek, Dagmar, *Ellen Kelly*, 268
Bulibasha (Witi Ihimaera), 306
Burger Quixote, A (Douglas Blackburn), 8
Burger's Daughter (Nadine Gordimer), 32, 215, 523
Burgess, Anthony, *Malayan Trilogy*, 86
Burmese Days (George Orwell), 177
Burmese Palace Tales (Henry Fielding-Hall), 9
Burning Grass (Cyprian Ekwensi), 290
Burning Water (George Bowering), 151
Burstyn, Varda, *Water, Inc.*, 328
Burton, Richard, *The Arabian Nights*, 199
Buru Quartet, The (Pramoedya Ananta Toer), 210
Butler, Guy, 301, 537
   Selected Poems, 301
   Stranger to Europe, 537
Butterfly in the Wind (Lakshmi Persaud), 501
By Sheer Pluck (G. A. Henty), 51
By the Sea (Abdulrazak Gurnah), 410, 479

Cabrere Infanta, Guillermo, Mea Cuba, 116
Cairo Trilogy, The (Naguib Mahfouz), 199
Call Me Not a Man (Mtutuzeli Matshoba), 75
Call Me Woman (Ellen Kuzwayo), 49, 524
Calling of Katie Makanya, The (Margaret McCord), 11
Calypso Trilogy, A (Rawle Gibbons), 330
Cambridge (Caryl Phillips), 71
Cambridge History of Latin American Literature (eds Roberto Gonzalez Echevarría and Enrique Pupo-Walker), 295
Campbell, Maria, *Halfbreed*, 277, 345
Campbell, Roy, *The Flaming Terrapin*, 537
Canadian Exploration Literature (ed. Germaine Warkentin), 152

Cane (Jean Toomer), 442
Cape Town Coolie (Reshard Gool), 106, 233
Capricornia (Xavier Herbert), 388, 485
Carcase for Hounds (Meja Mwangi), 19, 413
Cardoso, Luis, *The Crossing. A Story of East Timor*, 136
Carey, Peter, 105, 268
  Illywhacker, 105
  True History of the Kelly Gang, 268
Carpentier, Alejo, 164, 186
  Explosion in a Cathedral, 186
  Kingdom of this World, 164
Carretta, Vincent (ed.), *Unchained Voices*, 447
Cary, Thomas, *Abram's Plains: A Poem*, 62
Casely Hayford, J. E., *Ethiopia Unbound*, 373
Cass, Shirley (ed.), *We Took their Orders and are Dead*, 44
Castel-Bloom, Orly, *Dolly City*, 543
Castro, Brian, *Birds of Passage*, 54, 103, 326, 485
Casual Brutality, A (Neil Bissoondath), 327
Caute, David, *Fatima's Scarf*, 432
Cavafy, C. P., *Collected Poems*, 199
Celebration, The (Raymond Pillai), 123
Césaire, Aimé, 15, 164, 355, 468
  Notebook of a Return to my Native Land, 15, 355
  A Tempest, 468
  The Tragedy of King Christophe, 164
Césaire, Aimé (Clayton Eshleman and Annette Smith), 355
Cetshwayo and Battle of Isandlwana (H. I. E. Dhlomo), 11
Chain of Voices, A (André Brink), 444
Chaka (Thomas Mofolo), 314
Chamoiseau, Patrick, 113, 328
  Solibo Magnificent, 113
  Texaco, 328
Chander, Krishan, 'Kalu Bhangi', 'The Mahalakshmi Bridge', 403
Chandler, A. Bertram, *Kelly Country*, 268
Chang, Queeny, *Memories of a Nyonya*, 519
Change of Flag, A (Christopher New), 226
Chapman, Michael (ed.), 49, 75
  The Drum Decade, 49
  Soweto Poetry, 75
  Voice from Within: Black Poetry from Southern Africa (and Achmat Dangor), 49
Chattering Wagtails of Mikuyu Prison, The (Jack Mpanje), 59
Chatterjee, Upamanyu, *English, August*, 95
Chatterji, Bankimchandra, 63, 141
  Anandamath, 63
  Rajmohan's Wife. A Novel, 141
Chess Players, The/ Shatranj Ke Khilari (dir. Satyajit Ray), 134, 162
Chetty, Rajendra (ed.), *South African Indian Writings in English*, 233
Child of the Northeast, A (Kampoon Boontawee), 210
Children of Soweto, The (Mbulelo Mzamane), 75
Children of the Lion (Carl Muller), 204
Children of the Nile (Marmaduke Pickthall), 473
Chimombo, Steve, *Napolo and the Python*, 59
Chin Kee Onn, *The Silent Army*, 256
Chinodya, Shimmer, *Harvest of Thorns*, 101, 281, 350
Chipamaunga, E., *A Fighter for Freedom*, 101
Chipasula, Frank, *Whispers in the Wings*, 59

Chipeta, Dominic, *The Pregnant Clouds*, 266
Chira (Marjorie Oludhe Macgoye), 505
Chisi: A Woman of Courage (Gabriel Ellison), 266
Chotti Munda and his Arrow (Mahasweta Devi), 110
Choy, Elizabeth, 'My Autobiography', 256, 519
Chraibi, Driss, *Muhammad. A Novel*, 309
Chudley, Ron, *After Abraham: A Play*, 62
Chugtai, Ismat, *The Chugtai Collection*, 514
Chugtai Collection, The (Ismat Chugtai), 514
Cinnamon Gardens (Shyam Salvadurai), 27
Cities of Salt / Mudun al-milh (Abdelrahman Munif), 199, 361
City at the End of Time (Leung Ping-Kwan), 226
City Voices. Hong Kong Writing In English (eds Xu Xi and Mike Ingham), 226
Claims of the Africans (Anonymous), 468
Clancy, Tom, *The Bear and the Dragon*, 542
Clarke, George Elliott, *Beatrice Chancy*, 495
Clarke, Marcus, *For the Term of his Natural Life*, 81
Clear Light of Day (Anita Desai), 26, 127
Cliff, Michelle, 15, 460
  Abeng, 15
  No Telephone to Heaven, 460
Cockings, George, *The Conquest of Canada*, 62
Coetzee, J. M., 49, 156, 215, 281, 350, 383, 400
  The Age of Iron, 215
  Disgrace, 383
  Dusklands, 156, 400
  In the Heart of the Country, 281
  Life and Times of Michael K, 49
  Youth, 350
Coffer Dams, The (Kamala Markandaya), 26
Collected Poems 1948–1984 (Derek Walcott), 114
Collected Poems (C. P. Cavafy), 199
Collected Poems (Derek Walcott), 187
Collected Poetry, The (Léopold Sédar Senghor), 355, 436
Collected Works, H. I. E. Dhlomo, 49
Collins, Merle, 15, 501
  Angel, 15
  The Colour of Forgetting, 501
Collins, Wilkie, *The Moonstone*, 337
Colón, Cristóbal, *The Voyage of Christopher Columbus*, 186, 389
Colonizer and the Colonized, The (Albert Memmi), 309
Colour of Forgetting, The (Merle Collins), 501
Coloured Conquest, The (T. R. Roydhouse), 542
Comfort Woman (Nora Okja Keller), 133
Companion to the Indian Mutiny, The (P. J. O. Taylor), 337
Concubine, The (Elechi Amadi), 529
Conde, Maryse, *The Last of the African Kings*, 460
Connor, Ralph, *The Man from Glengarry*, 151
Conquest of Canada, The (George Cockings), 62
Conrad, Joseph, *Heart of Darkness*, 64, 87, 177
Conservationist, The (Nadine Gordimer), 322
Constant Gardener, The (John Le Carré), 86
Contemporary Feminist Urdu Poetry (ed. Rukhsana Ahmad), 370
Contours of the Heart (eds Sunaina Maira and Rajini Srikanth), 127
'Convert, The' (Dudley De Souza), 298
Cook, Kenneth, *Stockade*, 409
Coolie Odyssey (David Dabydeen), 230, 261

Coonardoo (Katharine Prichard), 388

Coovadia, Imraan, *The Wedding*, 233

Cost of Living, The (Arundhati Roy), 532

Coulter, John, *Riel: A Play in Two Parts*, 428

Counting House, The (David Dabydeen), 230

Country of my Skull (Antje Krog), 383

Country without a Post Office, The (Agha Shahid Ali), 265, 435

Couzens, Tim and Essop Patel (eds), *The Return of the Amasi Bird. Black South African Poetry*, 322

Cowasjee, S. and K. S. Duggal (eds), *Orphans of the Storm. Stories on the Partition of India*, 377

Cowrie of Hope, A (Binwell Sinyangwe), 266

Cows of Shambat, The (Taban Lo Liyong), 455

CPI(M-L), *Report from the Flaming Fields of Bihar*, 354

Cracking India (Bapsi Sidhwa), 27, 118, 258, 378

Craft for a Dry Lake (Kim Mahood), 170

Crick, Crack Monkey (Merle Hodge), 501

Cronin, Jeremy, 96, 215
 Even the Dead, 96
 Inside, 215

Crossing. A Story of East Timor, The (Luis Cardoso), 136

Crossing the Border (ed. Jennifer Langer), 410

Crossing the River (Caryl Phillips), 56, 71

Crosthwaite, Luis Humberto, *The Moon will Forever be a Distant Love*, 155

Cruikshank, Julie (ed.), *Life Lived like a Story. Life Stories of Three Yukon Elders*, 182

Cry, the Beloved Country (Alan Paton), 49, 215, 301, 322, 537

Cry of Winnie Mandela, The (Njabulo Ndebele), 383

Crying of Lot 49, The (Thomas Pynchon), 468

Cugoano, Quobna Ottobah, *Thoughts and Sentiments on the Evil of Slavery*, 447

Curfew and a Full Moon (Ediriweera Sarachchandra), 260

Da Costa, Francisco Borja, *Revolutionary Poems in the Struggle against Colonialism: Timorese Nationalist Verse*, 136

Dabydeen, David, 230, 261, 441
 Coolie Odyssey, 230, 261
 The Counting House, 230
 Slave Song, 441

D'Aguiar, Fred, *The Longest Memory*, 441

Dalisay, Jose Y., *Killing Time in a Warm Place*, 311

Dallaire, Romeo, *Shake Hands with the Devil. The Failure of Humanity in Rwanda*, 160

D'Alpuget, Blanche, *Turtle Beach*, 78

Dance in the Sun, A (Dan Jacobson), 49

Daneel, Martinus *see* Gumbo, Mafuranhunzi

Daneshvar, Simin, *A Persian Requiem*, 361

Dangarembga, Tsitsi, *Nervous Conditions*, 101, 323, 421, 523

Dangle, Arjun, *Poisoned Bread. Translations from Modern Marathi Dalit Literature*, 204, 286

Dangor, Achmat, 106, 383, 421
 Bitter Fruit, 383
 Waiting for Leila, 106
 Z Town Trilogy, 421

Daniel Deronda (George Eliot), 543

Daniel Venanda (William Scully), 49

Danticat, Edwidge, 42, 460
 After the Dance, 460
 Breath, Eyes, Memory, 42

Dark, Eleanor, *The Timeless Land*, 485

Dark Princess (W. E. B. Du Bois), 157, 468

Darker Proof, The (Edmund White and Adam Mars-Jones), 224

Darko, Amma, *The Housemaid*, 529

Darwish, Mahmoud, *Unfortunately, it was Paradise*, 372

Das, Mahadai, *Bones, I Want to be a Poetess of My People*, 230

Daughter of Mumbi (Charity Waciuma), 19

Daughters of the Pacific (Zohl Dé Ishtar), 491

Daughters of the Twilight (Farida Karodia), 233

David's Story (Zoë Wicomb), 32, 384, 524

Davis, Jack, *Kulkark and the Dreamers*, 387

Dawes, Kwame, *Wheel and Come Again*, 330

Dawood, Yusuf K., *Return to Paradise*, 52

Day after Tomorrow (Bahadur Tejani), 53, 332

Days of Despair (Rajiva Wijesinha), 540

Days of Dust (Halim Barakat), 343

Days of the Sahib Are Over (Rajkumari Singh), 230

De Lisser, Herbert G., *The White Witch of Rosehall*, 441

De Souza, Dudley, 'The Convert', 298

De Zoysa, Richard, *This Other Eden*, 541

Deadly, Unna? (Phillip Gwynne), 406

Death and the King's Horseman (Wole Soyinka), 236

Debi, Rajlakshmi, *The Hindu Wife or The Enchanted Fruit*, 141

Dedan Kimathi (Kenneth Watene), 19

Defoe, Daniel, *A General History of the Pyrates*, 441

Dekker, Edouard Dowes, *Max Havelaar*, 129

Delany, Martin R., *Blake, or the Huts of Africa*, 468

Derozio, Henry Louis Vivian, *The Fakeer of Jungheera*, 141

Desai, Anita, *Clear Light of Day*, 26, 127

Destination Biafra (Buchi Emecheta), 65

Devi, Mahasweta, 42, 110, 279, 354, 514
 The Breast Stories, 514
 Chotti Munda and his Arrow, 110
 Imaginary Maps: Three Stories, 42, 110
 Mother of 1984, 354
 Of Women, Outcasts, Peasants, and Rebels, 279

Devil on the Cross (Ngugi wa Thiong'o), 414, 470

Devil's Wind, The (Manohar Malgonkar), 337

Dharwadker, Vinay, *Kabir: the Weaver's Song*, 396

Dhlomo, H. I. E., 11, 49, 96
 Cetshwayo and Battle of Isandlwana, 11
 Collected Works, 49
 The Girl Who Killed to Save, 96

Diala, Isidore, *The Lure of Ash*, 471

Diary of a Girl in Changi, 1941–1945 (Sheila Allan), 519

Diaspora and the Difficult Art of Dying (Sudesh Mishra), 123

Dib, Mohammed, *Who Remembers the Sea? / Qui se Souvient la Mer?*, 308

Diescho, Joseph, *Born of the Sun. A Namibian Novel*, 318

Difficult Case (Jong Ah Sing), 103

Dike, Fatima, *The Sacrifice of Kreli*, 96

Dikobe, Modikwe, *The Marabi Dance*, 537

Dilemma of a Ghost, The (Ama Ata Aidoo), 447

Dilemma of a Ghost and Anowa, The (Ama Ata Aidoo), 426
Diop, Boubacar Boris, *Murambi, le Livres des Ossements / Murambi, the Book of Remains*, 160
Disappearing Moon Café (Sky Lee), 182, 495
Discovering Home (Binyavanga Wainaina), 332
Discovery of India, The (Jawaharlal Nehru), 357
Discovery of Strangers, A (Ruby Wiebe), 152, 240
Disgrace (J. M. Coetzee), 383
Distant Shore, A (Caryl Phillips), 410
Distant View of a Minaret (Alifa Rifaat), 509
Diviners, The (Margaret Lawrence), 182
Djebar, Assia, *Fantasia. An Algerian Cavalcade*, 3, 308
Dobrin, Arthur, *Malaika*, 505
Dogeaters (Jessica Hagedorn), 311
Dolly City (Orly Castell-Bloom), 543
Don't Take Your Love to Town (Ruby Langford), 388
Double Yoke (Buchi Emecheta), 529
Douglas, Josie (ed.), *Untreated: Poems by Black Writers*, 276
Dow, Unity, *Far and Beyon'*, 224
Down Second Avenue (Es'kia Mphahlele), 49, 537
Dr. Wooreddy's Prescription for Enduring the Ending of the World (Colin Johnson), 147
Dragon Can't Dance, The (Earl Lovelace), 486
Dragonfly in the Sun. An Anthology of Pakistani Writing In English, A (ed. Muneeza Shamsie), 27, 205
Dream Swimmer, The (Witi Ihimaera), 306
Dreaming in Cuban (Cristina Garcia), 117
Drewe, Robert, *Our Sunshine*, 268
Drum Decade, The (ed. Michael Chapman), 49
Dry Lips Oughta Move to Kapuskasing (Tomson Highway), 182
Dry White Season, A (André Brink), 215
Du Bois, W. E. B., 157, 355, 468
  Dark Princess, 157, 468
  The Souls of Black Folk, 355
Du Plessis, Menán, *State of Fear*, 421
Duff, Alan, 306, 369, 481
  Both Sides of the Moon, 481
  Jake's Long Shadow, 306
  Once Were Warriors, 306, 369, 481
  What Becomes of the Broken-Hearted?, 306
Duncan, Sara Jeannette, *The Imperialist*, 345
Duong Thu Huong, 110, 210, 478
  Novel without a Name, 210
  Paradise of the Blind, 112, 478
Durrani, Tehmina, *My Feudal Lord*, 370
Durrell, Lawrence, *The Alexandrian Quartet*, 199
Dusklands (J. M. Coetzee), 156, 400
Dust and Conscience (Truong Tran), 478
Dutt, K. C., *A Journal of Forty Eight Hours of the Year 1945*, 141
Dutt, S. C., *The Young Zamindar*, 141
Dutt, Toru, *A Sheaf Gleaned in French Fields*, 141
Dutton, Geoffrey, *Snow on the Saltbush*, 326
Dying in the Sun (Peter Palangyo), 360

Early Modern Tales of Orient (ed. Kenneth Parker), 300
Easmon, R. Sarif, *The Feud and Other Stories*, 447
Eastern Slope Chronicle, The (Yu Ouyang), 485
Eating Chiefs (Taban Lo Liyong), 193
Ebersohn, Wessel, *Store up the Anger*, 49

Echevarría, Roberto Gonzalez and Enrique Pupo-Walker (eds), *Cambridge Companion to Latin American Literature*, 295
Echoing Silences (Alexander Kannengoni), 101
Edgar Huntly, or Memoirs of a Sleep-Walker (Charles Brockden Brown), 468
Edgell, Zee, 15, 501
  Beka Lamb, 501
  In Times Like These, 15
Ee Tiang Hong, 313, 454
  Myths for a Wilderness, 313
  Tranquerah, 454
Efuru (Flora Nwapa), 529
Ekwensi, Cyprian, 290, 529
  Burning Grass, 290
  Jagua Nana, 529
El Saadawi, Nawal, 42, 200, 509
  The Fall of the Imam, 200
  Women at Point Zero, 42, 509
El Zein, Abdul Hamid, *The Sacred Meadows*, 439
Electrical Field, The (Kerri Sakamoto), 255
Eliot, George, *Daniel Deronda*, 543
Elizabeth Choy (Zhou Mei), 520
Ellen, Maria M. (ed.), *Across the Atlantic. An Anthology of Cape Verdean Literature*, 91
Ellen Kelly (Dagmar Balcarek), 268
Ellison, Gabriel, *Chisi: A Woman of Courage*, 266
Emecheta, Buchi, 65, 71, 447, 529
  Destination Biafra, 65
  Double Yoke, 529
  The Joys of Motherhood, 529
  Second-Class Citizen, 71
  The Slave Girl, 447
Emergency (Richard Rive), 106
Emergency Continued (Richard Rive), 106
Emigrants, The (George Lamming), 71
Emily of Emerald Hill (Stella Kon), 454
Emperor, The (Ahmed Essop), 233
Emperor of America, The (Sax Rohmer), 542
Emperor Shaka the Great (Mazisi Kunene), 314
Emperor's Babe, The (Bernadine Evaristo), 71
Empire Writing. An Anthology of Colonial Literature, 1870–1918 (ed. Elleke Boehmer), 87, 177
English, August (Upamanyu Chatterjee), 95
English Boy at the Cape, The (Edward Kendall), 433
English Patient, The (Michael Ondaatje), 539
Epic Unwritten, An (M. U. Memon), 377
Equiano, Olaudah, 71, 402, 447
  The Interesting Narrative and Other Writings, 402, 447
  The Interesting Narrative of the Life of Olaudah Equiano, 71
Error of Judgment, An (Stanley Wolpert), 253
Escape from Paradise (eds John Harding and May Chu Harding), 519
Escape into Silence, An (Bhaskar Roy), 354
Eshleman, Clayton and Annette Smith, *Aimé Césaire*, 355
Espinet, Ramabai, *The Swinging Bridge*, 261
Essop, Ahmed, *The Emperor, The Haji and Other Stories, The Visitation*, 233
Ethiopia Unbound (J. E. Casely Hayford), 373
European Tribe, The (Caryl Phillips), 121
Evaristo, Bernadine, *The Emperor's Babe*, 71
Even the Dead, Poems, Parables and a Jeremiad (Jeremy Cronin), 96

Everest Hotel, The (Allan Sealy), 165
'*Excuse Me, Are You a Model?*' (Bonny Hicks), 519
Explosion in a Cathedral (Alejo Carpentier), 186
Eyes of the Sky (Rayda Jacobs), 421, 444, 523
Ezenwa, B., *The Last Order*, 426

Facing Mount Kenya (Jomo Kenyatta), 413
Faiz, Faiz Ahmad, *Poems by Faiz*, 370
Fakeer, of Jungheera, The (Henry Louis Vivian
    Derozio), 141
Fall of the Imam, The (Nawal El Saadawi), 200
Falling Off the Map (Pico Iyer), 155
Falola, Toyin, *A Mouth Sweeter than Salt*, 220
Famished Road, The (Ben Okri), 290, 426
Fantasia. An Algerian Cavalcade (Assia Djebar), 3, 308
Fantasy Eaters: Stories from Fiji, The (Subramani), 123
Fanthorne, J. F., *Mariam: A Story of the Indian Mutiny
    of 1857*, 337
Faqir, Fadia, 343, 372, 509
    Nisanit, 343, 372
    Pillars of Salt, 509
Far and Beyon' (Unity Dow), 224
Far from Rangoon (Yeap Joo Kim), 520
Farah, Nuruddin, 413, 463
    Gifts, 463
    Maps, 413
Farrell, J. G., 165, 257, 337, 407
    The Hill Station, 165
    The Siege of Krishnapur, 337, 407
    The Singapore Grip, 257
Fatima's Scarf (David Caute), 432
Fearful Freedom, A (Robert Hammond), 257
Feast of the Nine Virgins, The (Jameela Siddiqi), 52
Fee, Mary Helen, *A Woman's Impression of the
    Philippines*, 459
'*Fenton Child, The*' (Mavis Gallant), 495
Feraoun, Mouloud, *Journal 1955–1962: Reflections on
    the French-Algerian War*, 3
Fernando, Lloyd, 210, 313
    Scorpion Orchid, 210, 313
    Twenty-two Malaysian Stories, 313
Ferreira, Manuel, *No Reino de Caliban, I*, 91
Ferretti, Andrée (and Gaston Miron), *Les Grands
    Textes Indépendantistes*, 345
Feud and Other Stories, The (R. Sarif Easmon), 447
Fielding-Hall, Henry, *Burmese Palace Tales*, 9
Fighter for Freedom, A (E. Chipamaunga), 101
Figiel, Sia, 122
    They Who Do Not Grieve, 122
    Where We Once Belonged, 122
Filter, H. and S. Bourquin (eds), *Paulina Dlamini:
    Servant of Two Kings*, 11
Findley, Timothy, *The Wars*, 345
Fine Balance, A (Rohinton Mistry), 26, 95, 137,
    279
Finlayson, Roderick, *Brown Man's Burden*, 369, 481
Five Bright Stars, The (Eric Lambert), 409
Five Past Midnight in Bhopal (Dominique Lapierre and
    Javier Moro), 328
Flaming Terrapin, The (Roy Campbell), 537
Flanagan, Richard, 170
    Gould's Book of Fish, 170
    The Sound of One Hand Clapping, 170
Flight to Canada (Ishmael Reed), 462
Floods (John Ruganda), 5

Flutter, Naomi and Carl Solomon (eds), *Tilting Cages:
    An Anthology of Refugee Writings*, 410
Fly Away Peter (David Malouf), 170
Foden, Giles, *The Last King of Scotland*, 64
Follow the Rabbit-Proof Fence (Doris Pilkington [Nugi
    Garimara]), 452
Folly, The (Ivan Vladislavic), 281
Fools and Other Stories (Njabulo Ndebele), 49
For Love Alone (Christina Stead), 105
For the Term of his Natural Life (Marcus Clarke), 81
Forest of a Thousand Demons (Wole Soyinka and
    Daniel Fagunwa), 290
Forest of Flowers, A (Ken Saro-Wiwa), 328
Forster, E. M., *A Passage to India*, 177, 407
Fortunes of Richard Mahoney, The (Henry Handel
    Richardson), 409
Forty-Eight Guns for the General (Eddie Iroh), 65
Fountain at the Centre of the World, The (Rob
    Newman), 43
Four Centuries of Swahili Verse (ed. J. Whiteley),
    391
Four Feathers, The (A. E. W. Mason), 177
Four Years in an English University (S. Satthianadhan),
    141
Fragments (Ayi Kwei Armah), 153, 471
Freedom Fighter (J. Wamweya), 19
Freer, William B., *The Philippine Experiences of an
    American Teacher*, 459
Friel, Brian, *Selected Plays*, 246
Friese, Kai, '*Marginalia*', 80
From the Bluest Part of the Harbour (Andrew Parkin),
    226
From the Land of the Green Ghosts (Pascal Khoo Thwe),
    55
Frost, Lucy, *No Place for a Nervous Lady*, 491
Fuentes, Carlos, *The Orange Tree*, 42
Fugard, Athol, 49, 106, 215
    The Blood Knot, 106
    Port Elizabeth Plays, 49
    The Township Plays, 215
Fuir ou Mourir au Zaire (Marie Béatrice Umutesi), 161
Fundamental Wisdom of the Middle Way, The
    (Nagarjuna), 396
Funny Boy (Shyam Selvadurai), 127, 438, 451
Fusuyama, Takao, *Memoir*, 257

Gabriel Dumont and the Northwest Rebellion (George
    Woodcock), 428
Gakwandi, Arthur, *Kosiya Kifefe*, 5
Galgut, Damon, *The Good Doctor*, 383
Gallant, Mavis, '*The Fenton Child*', 495
Gallipoli (Jack Bennett), 535
Garcia, Cristina, *Dreaming in Cuban*, 117
Garland, Alex, *The Beach*, 42
Garvey, Marcus, *The Poetical Works of Marcus Garvey*,
    56
Gaskell, Ian, *Beyond Ceremony. An Anthology of Drama
    from Fiji*, 123, 368
Gates, Henry Louis (ed.), *Six Women's Slave Narratives*,
    373
Gelede Spectacle, The (Babtunde Lawal), 426
General History of the Pyrates, A (Daniel Defoe), 441
General is Up, The (Peter Nazareth), 5, 52
*Genuine Narrative of the Deplorable Deaths of the English
    Gentlemen and Others, The* (J. Z. Holwell), 77

'*George William Gordon: A Historical Play*' (Roger Mais), 324
Ghali, Wagdi, *Beer in the Snooker Club*, 339
Ghanaian Popular Fiction (ed. Stephanie Newell), 426
Ghose, Man Mohan, *Songs of Love and Death*, 141
Ghosh, Amitav, 9, 26, 204, 231, 251, 286, 539
    The Glass Palace, 9, 231, 539
    In an Antique Land, 251, 286
    The Shadow Lines, 26, 204
Ghosha, Nava-Krishna, *On Lord Northbrook, the Governor General of India*, 162
Gibbons, Rawle, *A Calypso Trilogy*, 330
Gifts (Nuruddin Farah), 463
Gilbert, Kevin, 276, 388
    Because a White Man'll Never Do It, 388
    Black from the Edge, 276
    '*Mabo is the Turning Point for Justice*', 276
Gilroy, Beryl, *Stedman and Joanna*, 186
Girl Who Killed to Save – Nongqause, The (H. I. E. Dhlomo), 96
Girls at War and Other Stories (Chinua Achebe), 65
Giscombe, C. S., *Into and Out of Dislocation*, 121
Glass Palace, The (Amitav Ghosh), 9, 231, 539
Glissant, Edouard, *The Indies*, 15
God of Small Things, The (Arundhati Roy), 27, 43, 95, 110, 204, 286
Godaan (The Gift of a Cow) (Munshi Premchand), 279
Godden, Rumer, *Black Narcissus*, 165
God's Adversary and Other Stories (Shaukat Osman), 435
God's Bits of Wood (Sembene Ousmane), 37
God's Step-Children (Sarah Gertrude Millin), 49
Going Down River Road (Meja Mwangi), 19, 193, 413
Going Home (Archie Weller), 388
Going Home to Teach (Anthony C. Winkler), 121
Golden Miles (Katharine Prichard), 45
Good Doctor, The (Damon Galgut), 383
Goodbye to Romance. Stories by Australian and New Zealand Women, 1930s–1980s (eds Elizabeth Webby and Lydia Wevers), 491
Gool, Reshard, *Cape Town Coolie*, 106, 233
Goonewardene, James, *The Tribal Hangover*, 438
Gordimer, Nadine, 32, 49, 215, 318, 322, 350, 383, 463, 523
    Burger's Daughter, 32, 215, 523
    The Conservationist, 322
    A Guest of Honour, 463
    The House Gun, 350, 383
    July's People, 523
    Jump and Other Stories, 318
    Lying Days, 49
    None to Accompany Me, 523
    World of Strangers, 49, 215
'*Gordon to the Oppressed*' (Claude McKay), 324
Gould's Book of Fish (Richard Flanagan), 170
Govender, Ronnie, *The Lahnee's Pleasure*, 233
Grace, Patricia, 42, 306, 491
    Baby No-Eyes, 306
    Mutuwhenua: The Moon Sleeps, 306
    Potiki, 42, 306, 491
    Waiariki, 306
Grain of Wheat, A (Ngugi wa Thiong'o), 19, 86, 193, 270, 290

Grant, Linda, *When I Lived in Modern Times*, 543
Grass for My Feet (J. Vijayatunga), 27
Grass is Singing, The (Doris Lessing), 524
Great Indian Novel, The (Shashi Tharoor), 27, 137, 258, 407
Great Ponds, The (Elechi Amadi), 402
Great White Hand, The (J. E. Muddock), 337
Green Grass, Running Water (Thomas King), 353
Greene, Graham, 86, 117
    The Quiet American, 86
    Our Man in Havana, 117
Grief Ago, A (Ranjini Obeyesekere), 540
Griggs, Sutton, *Imperium in Imperio*, 157
Grossman, David, *Sleeping on a Wire*, 543
Grove, F. P., *Settlers of the Marsh*, 151
Guerrilla Snuff (Mafuranhunzi Gumbo [Martinus Daneel]), 101
Guest of Honour, A (Nadine Gordimer), 463
Guleri, Chandradhar Sharma, *Usne kaha tha aur anya kahaniyan*, 539
Gumbo, Mafuranhunzi [Martinus Daneel], *Guerrilla Snuff*, 101
Gun, Guneli, *A Book of Trances*, 269
Gunesekera, Romesh, 127, 540
    Reef, 127
    Monkfish Moon, 540
Gunew, Sneja and Kateryna Longley, *Striking Chords*, 326
Gunn, S. and M.-M. Tal (eds), *Torn Apart*, 319
Gunny Sack, The (M. G. Vassanji), 251, 414
Gurnah, Abdulrazak, 410, 413, 439, 479
    Admiring Silence, 413, 479
    By the Sea, 410
    Paradise, 413, 439
Guyana Quartet, The (Wilson Harris), 86
Gwala, Mafika, *No More Lullabies*, 75
Gwee Thian Hock, *A Nyonya Mosaic*, 519
Gwynne, Phillip, *Deadly, Unna*, 406

Habibi, Emile, *The Secret Life of Saeed*, 344
Hagedorn, Jessica, *Dogeaters*, 311
Haggard, Rider, *King Solomon' Mines*, 87, 177
Haitian Trilogy, The (Derek Walcott), 164, 484
Haja Maideen, *The Nadra Tragedy*, 519
Haji and Other Stories, The (Ahmed Essop), 233
Haley, Alex, *Roots*, 56
Half a Lifetime (Judith Wright), 491
Halfbreed (Maria Campbell), 277, 345
Halpe, Ashley (ed.), *An Anthology of Contemporary Sri Lankan Short Stories*, 540
Hammond, Robert, *A Fearful Freedom*, 257
Handal, Nathalie (ed.), *The Poetry of Arab Women*, 344
Handful of Rice, A (Kamala Markandaya), 95
Hanley, Gerald, *Monsoon Victory*, 533
Happy Endings. Stories by Australian and New Zealand Women, 1850s–1930s (eds Elizabeth Webby and Lydia Wevers), 491
Harder they Come, The (Michael Trellwell), 330
Harding, John and May Chu Harding (eds), *Escape from Paradise*, 519
Hare and Hornbill (Okot p'Bitek), 391
Harp of Burma (Michio Takeyama), 257
Harper, Frank (ed.), *Just Outside Manila*, 449

Harris, Wilson, 86, 114, 186, 389
   The Guyana Quartet, 86
   The Palace of the Peacock, 114, 186
   The Whole Armour and the Secret Ladder, 389
*Hartly House, Calcutta. A Novel of the Days of Warren
   Hatsings* (Anonymous), 162
Harvest (Manjula Padmanabhan), 43
Harvest of Thorns (Shimmer Chinodya), 101, 281, 350
Hasan, Mushirul (ed.), *India Partitioned*, 26, 377
Hassim, Aziz, *The Lotus People*, 233
Hastain, Ronald, *White Coolie*, 257
Hau'ofa, Epeli, 368
   Tales of the Tikongs, 368
   Kisses in the Nederends, 368
Hawksley, Humphrey, *The Third World War*, 458
Haylen, Leslie, *Blood on the Wattle*, 409
Head, Bessie, 271, 319, 323, 433, 523
   Maru, 271, 433, 523
   A Question of Power, 319, 523
   Serowe. Village of the Rain Wind, 271, 323
   When Rain Clouds Gather, 271, 523
Healers, The (Ayi Kwei Armah), 51, 447
Heaney, Seamus, *Selected Poems 1965–1975*, 246
Heart Divided, The (Mumtaz Shah Nawaz), 378,
   514
Heart Knows No Colour, The (Prabashini Moodley),
   233
Heart of Darkness (Joseph Conrad), 64, 87, 177
Heart of Redness, The (Zakes Mda), 96, 156, 350
Henty, G. A., *By Sheer Pluck*, 51
*Her Mother's Ashes, and Other Stories Stories by South
   Asian Women in Canada and the United States* (ed.
   Nurjehan Aziz), 127
Herbert, Xavier, *Capricornia*, 388, 485
Heroine (Gail Scott), 405
Hicks, Bonny, '*Excuse Me, Are You a Model?*', 519
Highway, Tomson, 182, 353
   Dry Lips Oughta Move to Kapuskasing, 182
   The Rez Sisters, 353
'*Hill, The*' (Zakes Mda), 319
Hill Station, The (J. G. Farrell), 165
Hindu Wife or The Enchanted Fruit, The (Rajlakshmi
   Debi), 141
Hirson, Baruch, *Revolutions in My Life*, 215
Hirson, Denis (ed.), *The Lava of the Land. South
   African Poetry 1960–1996*, 383
History of Mary Prince, The (Mary Prince), 442
History's Fiction (Xu Xi), 226
Ho, Louise, 226
   Local Habitation, 226
   New Ends, Old Beginnings, 226
Ho, Ruth, 519
   Rainbow Round My Shoulder, 519
   Which I Have Loved, 519
Hodge, Merle, *Crick, Crack Monkey*, 501
Hollar, Constance, *Songs of Empire*, 186
Holwell, J. Z., *The Genuine Narrative of the Deplorable
   Deaths of the English Gentlemen and Others*, 77
Home and the World (Rabindranath Tagore), 205
Hon, Joan, *Relatively Speaking*, 519
Hong Kong Poems in English and Chinese (eds Andrew
   Parkin and Lawrence Wong), 226
Hong Kong Rose (Xu Xi), 226
Hopkinson, Nalo, *Brown Girl in the Ring*, 121
Horn of my Love (Okot p'Bitek), 391

Horrors of Slavery and Other Writings, The (Robert
   Wedderburn), 442
Hossain, Attia, *Sunlight on a Broken Column*, 26, 204,
   251, 514
House at the Edge of the Jungle, The (Mary Morgan),
   210
House for Mr Biswas, A (V. S. Naipaul), 230
House Gun, The (Nadine Gordimer), 350, 383
House of Glass, The (Pramoedya Anant Toer), 112
Housemaid, The (Amma Darko), 529
Hove, Chenjerai, *Bones*, 32, 101, 413
How Stella Got Her Groove Back (Terry McMillan),
   460
How to be Sure that You will Go to Heaven (S. Adu-
   Boahen), 426
Hulme, Keri, 306, 369, 481, 491
   The Bone People, 306, 369, 481, 491
   Te Kaihau: The Windeater, 306
Huntley, Eric (ed.), 430
   '*And Finally They Killed Him*': *Speeches and Poems at
      a Memorial Rally for Walter Rodney*, 430
   Walter Rodney: Poetic Tributes, 430
Hussein, Aamer, *Turquoise*, 251, 321
Hussein, Abdullah, *The Weary Generations*, 253
Hussein, Ebrahim, 19, 359, 479
   Kinjeketile, 19, 359
   Mashetani, 479
Hutchinson, Garrie, *Not Going To Vietnam*, 44
Huxley, Elspeth, *A Thing to Love*, 19
Hyder, Qurratulain, *River of Fire*, 134, 251, 514

I am Free and Other Stories (Ihsan 'Abd al-Quddus),
   339
i is a long memoried woman (Grace Nichols), 442, 501
I Nearly Killed a President (Lucy Siyumbwa Simushi),
   266
I Saw Ramallah (Mourid Barghouti), 372
I Sweep the Sun off Rooftops (Hanan al-Shaykh), 509
I Want to be a Poetess of my People (Mahadai Das), 230
I Will Marry When I Want (Ngugi wa Thiong'o and
   Ngugi wa Mirii), 470, 505
I Write What I Like (Steve Biko), 75
Ibadan: The Penkelemes Years (Wole Soyinka), 471
Ibingira, Grace, *Bitter Harvest*, 5
Ice Candy Man (Bapsi Sidhwa), 419
Ice-Cream War, An (William Boyd), 533
Idriess, Ion, *Lasseter's Last Ride*, 388
If Everyone Cared (Margaret Tucker), 388
Ihimaera, Witi, 306, 481
   Ao Marama, 306
   Bulibasha, 306
   The Dream Swimmer, 306
   Into the World of Light, 306
   The Matriarch, 306
   Tangi, 306
   Te Ao Marama, 306, 481
   The Whale Rider, 306
   Whanau, 306
Ike, Chukwemeka, 65, 471
   Our Children are Coming, 471
   Sunset at Dawn: A Novel about Biafra, 65
   The Naked Gods, 471
Illywhacker (Peter Carey), 105
Imaginary Maps (Mahasweta Devi), 42, 110
Imperialist, The (Sara Jeannette Duncan), 345

Imperium in Imperio (Sutton Griggs), 157
Impressionist, The (Hari Kunzru), 7, 204, 407
In a Brown Mantle (Peter Nazareth), 5, 52
In an Antique Land (Amitav Ghosh), 251, 286
In Another Place, Not Here (Dionne Brand), 182
In Search of Tomorrow (Kirit Patel), 52
In the Castle of my Skin (George Lamming), 15, 486
In the Eye of the Sun (Ahdaf Soueif), 251, 339, 344
In the Fog of the Season's End (Alex La Guma), 49, 215, 433
In the Heart of the Country (J. M. Coetzee), 281
In the Hour of Signs (Jamal Mahjoub), 310
In the Name of Amandla (Vonani Bila), 281
In the Shadow of Freedom (Anis Kidwai), 377
In the Shadow of Imana (Veronique Tadjo), 161
In the Skin of a Lion (Michael Ondaatje), 43, 182, 327
In Times Like These (Zee Edgell), 15
Incredible Journey, An (Catherine Martin), 170
India: A Wounded Civilisation (V. S. Naipaul), 110
India Partitioned (ed. Mushirul Hasan), 26, 377
Indian Eye on English Life, The (B. M. Malabari), 141
Indian Folk Tales of the Caribbean, a First Collection (ed. Kenneth Vidia Parmasad), 127
Indies, The (Edouard Glissant), 15
Inside (Jeremy Cronin), 215
Instant in the Wind, An (André Brink), 156, 400
Interesting Narrative and Other Writings, The (Olaudah Equiano), 402, 447
Interesting Narrative of the Life of Olaudah Equiano, The (Olaudah Equiano), 71
Interpreters, The (Wole Soyinka), 373, 471
Into and Out of Dislocation (C. S. Giscombe), 121
Into the World of Light (Witi Ihimaera), 306
Invisible Weevil, The (Mary Karooroo Okurut), 5
Irawaddy Tango (Wendy Law-Yone), 55
Iroh, Eddie, *Forty Eight Guns for the General*, 65
Iron Earth, Copper Sky (Yashar Kemal), 269
Isegawa, Moses, *Abyssinian Chronicles*, 5
Ishtar, Zohl Dé, *Daughters of the Pacific*, 491
Isobel Gunn (Audrey Thomas), 227, 495
Isobelle's Journey (Elsa Joubert), 8
It All Begins. Poems from Postliberation South Africa (ed. Robert Berold), 281, 350, 383
'*It Happened in 1919*' (Saadat Hasan Manto), 253
Itsuka (Joy Kogawa), 255
Itwaru, Arnold, *Scattered Songs*, 230
Iyer, Pico, *Falling off the Map*, 155

Jabber, Sonia, '*Blood Soil*', '*Spirit of Place*', 265
J'accuse (Aharon Shabtai), 543
Jacobs, Rayda, 421, 444, 523
    Eyes of the Sky, 421, 444
    The Slave Book, 444, 523
Jacobson, Dan, *A Dance in the Sun*, 49, 215
Jagua Nana (Cyprian Ekwensi), 529
Jahaji Bhai: An Anthology of Indo-Caribbean Literature (ed. Frank Birbalsingh), 261
Jakata or Stories of the Buddha's Former Birth, The (ed. E. B. Cowell), 396
Jake's Long Shadow (Alan Duff), 306
James, C. L. R., 15, 254, 486
    Beyond a Boundary, 15, 254, 486
    Minty Alley, 254
Jane and Louisa Will Soon Come Home (Erna Brodber), 501

Japanese Agent in Tibet (Hisao Kimuru), 86, 133
Jayawardena, Sharmini, *Wet Paint*, 540
Jayyusi, Salma Khadra (ed.), *Modern Arabic Poetry*, 344
Jennings, Christian, *Across the Red River*, 160
Jesus is Indian (Agnes Sam), 233, 421
Jewel in the Crown, The (Paul Scott), 407
Jeyaretnam, Philip, *Abraham's Promise*, 210
John Bull's Other Island (George Bernard Shaw), 177
Johnson, Colin, *Dr. Wooreddy's Prescription for Enduring the Ending of the World*, 147
Johnson, Linton Kwesi, *Mi Revalueshanary Fren: Selected Poems*, 71
Joned, Salleh Ben, *As I Please*, 89
Jong Ah Sing, *Difficult Case*, 103
Jordan, A. C., *Wrath of the Ancestors, The / Ingqumbo Yeminyama*, 96, 323
José, Francisco Sionil, 112, 210, 311
    Mass, 112, 311
    My Brother, My Executioner, 210
Joseph Knight (James Robertson), 186
Joss and Gold (Shirley Geok-lin Lim), 89
Joubert, Elsa, *Isobelle's Journey*, 8
Journal 1955–1962: Reflections on the French-Algerian War (Mouloud Feraoun), 3
Journal of Forty Eight Hours of the Year 1945, A (K. C. Dutt), 141
Journals and Selected Writings of the Reverend Tiyo Soga, The (Tiyo Soga), 323
Journals of Susanna Moodie, The (Margaret Atwood), 151
Journey with Uncle Yankee, A (Rose Ong), 519
Joyce, James, 246
    A Portrait of the Artist as a Young Man, 246
    Ulysses, 246
Joys of Motherhood, The (Buchi Emecheta), 529
July's People (Nadine Gordimer), 523
Jump and Other Stories (Nadine Gordimer), 318
Just Another Bomb Blast (Sandaruwan Madduma Bandara), 540
Just Outside Manila (ed. Frank Harper), 449

Kabir: The Weaver's Song (Vinay Dharwadker), 396
Kadalie, Clements, *My Life and the ICU*, 274
Kaggia, Bildad, *Roots of Freedom*, 19
Kagwema, Prince (Osija Mwambungu), *Society in the Dock*, 359
Kalaw, Maximo, *The Philippine Rebel*, 449
Kali, Brenda, *Kismet*, 233
Kalidasa, Works of, 396
Kalikatha (Alka Saraogi), 134, 204
'*Kalu Bhangi*' (Krishan Chander), 403
Kamasutra (Vatsyayana), 262
Kamboureli, Smaro (ed.), *Making a Difference. Canadian Multicultural Literature*, 327
Kampoon Boontawee, *A Child of the Northeast*, 210
Kanafani, Ghassan, *Men in the Sun and other Palestinian Stories*, 344, 372
Kanda, K. C. (ed.), *Masterpieces of Urdu Ghazal*, 396
Kane, Hamidou, *Ambiguous Adventure*, 220
Kannengoni, Alexander, *Echoing Silences*, 101
Kanthapura (Raja Rao), 95, 96, 118, 204
Kanwal, J. S., *The Morning (Savera)*, 261
Kariuki, Josiah Mwangi, *Mau Mau Detainee*, 86
Karodia, Farida, *Daughters of the Twilight, Other Secrets*, 233

Karukku (Bama), 514
Kasiga, Barnabas (ed.), *An Anthology of East African Plays*, 331
Kathigasu, Sybil, *No Dram of Mercy*, 257, 519
Kaunda, Kenneth, *Letter to my Childern*, 266
Kaye, M. M., *Shadow of the Moon*, 337
Kaywana Blood (Edward Mittelholzer), 389
Kedgley, Sue (ed.), *Our Own Country: Leading New Zealand Women Writers*, 491
Kee Thuan Chye, *'We Could **** You Mr Birch'*, 89
Keller, Nora Okja, *Comfort Woman*, 133
Kelly Country (A. Bertram Chandler), 268
Kemal, Yashar, *Iron Earth, Copper Sky*, 269
Kendall, Edward, *The English Boy at the Cape*, 433
Keneally, Thomas, *The Tyrant's Novel*, 78
Kenyatta, Jomo, *Facing Mount Kenya*, 413
Kesavan, Mukul, *Looking through Glass*, 419
Khalid, Leila, *My People Shall Live*, 344
Khan, Adib, *Seasonal Adjustments*, 54, 60, 321, 326
Khan, Uzma Aslam, *Trespassing*, 26
Khatebi, Abdelkebir, *Love in Two Languages*, 309
Khoo Thwe, Pascal, *From the Land of the Green Ghosts*, 55
Khoury, Elias, *Little Mountain*, 344
Kidwai, Anis, *In the Shadow of Freedom*, 377
Kill Me Quick (Meja Mwangi), 19, 413
Killing of Idi Amin, The (Leslie Watkins), 5
Killing Time in a Warm Place (Jose Y. Dalisay), 311
Kim (Rudyard Kipling), 87, 165, 177, 407
Kimura, Hisao, *Japanese Agent in Tibet*, 86, 133
Kincaid, Jamaica, 15, 42, 121, 155, 237, 460, 501, 532
    Annie John, 15
    Lucy, 42, 121
    A Small Place, 42, 155, 237, 460, 501, 532
King, Thomas, *Green Grass, Running Water*, 353
King of the Bastards (Sarah Gertrude Millin), 215
King Solomon's Mines (Rider Haggard), 87, 177
Kingdom of this World (Alejo Carpentier), 164
Kingdom's End and Other Stories (Saadat Hasan Manto), 80
Kinjeketile (Ebrahim Hussein), 19, 359
Kipling, Rudyard, 87, 107, 162, 165, 177, 407
    Kim, 87, 165, 177, 407
    'One Viceroy Resigns', 165
    'Our Lady of the Snows', 107
    Plain Tales from the Hills, 165
Kismet (Brenda Kali), 233
Kisses in the Nederends (Epeli Hau'ofa), 368
Koch, Christopher, *The Year of Living Dangerously*, 54
Kogawa, Joy, 255, 345, 495
    Itsuka, 255
    Obasan, 255, 345, 495
Kon, Stella, 454
    Emily of Emerald Hill, 454
    The Scholar and the Dragon, 454
Konrad, James, *Target Amin*, 5
Kosiya Kifefe (Arthur Gakwandi), 5
Kotun, D., *Abiku*, 426
Koul, Sudha, *The Tiger Ladies*, 265
Kowloon Tong (Paul Theroux), 226
Krog, Antje, *Country of My Skull*, 383
Kulkark and the Dreamers (Jack Davis), 387
Kumar, Amitava (ed.), *World Bank Literature*, 532
Kunene, Mazisi, *Emperor Shaka the Great*, 314
Kunzru, Hari, *The Impressionist*, 7, 204, 407

Kural, The (Tiruvalluvar), 396
Kureishi, Hanif, 71, 432
    The Black Album, 432
    The Buddha of Suburbia, 71
Kuzwayo, Ellen, *Call Me Woman*, 49, 524
Kyi May Kaung, *Pelted with Petals: Burmese Poems*, 55
Kyomuhendo, Goretti, *Secrets No More*, 161

La Guma, Alex, 49, 106, 215, 433
    In the Fog of the Season's End, 49, 215, 433
    The Stone Country, 106
    A Walk in the Night, 106, 215
Labyrinths (Jorge Luis Borges), 295
Lady Hippotamus and Other Stories, The (Rajiva Wijesinha), 541
Lahnee's Pleasure, The (Ronnie Govender), 233
Lajja (Shame) (Taslima Nasreen), 204
Lali: A Pacific Anthology (ed. Albert Wendt), 491
Lam, Agnes, *Water Wood Pure Splendour*, 226
Lambert, Eric, *The Five Bright Stars*, 409
Lambing Flat, The (Nerida Newton), 103
Lamming, George, 15, 71, 486
    The Emigrants, 71
    In the Castle of my Skin, 17, 486
    The Pleasures of Exile, 486
Lan Cao, *Monkey Bridge*, 478
Land Without Thunder (Grace Ogot), 193, 332
Langa, Mandla, 32
    The Naked Song and Other Stories, 32
    Tenderness of Blood, 32
Langer, Jennifer (ed.), *Crossing the Border*, 410
Langford, Garry, *The Adventures of Dreaded Ned*, 268
Langford, Ruby, *Don't Take Your Love to Town*, 388
Lapierre, Dominique, *Five Past Midnight in Bhopal*, 328
Las Casas, Bartolomé de, 389, 441
    An Account, Much Abbreviated, of the Destruction of the Indies, 389
    A Short Account of the Destruction of the Indies, 441
Lasseter's Last Ride (Ion Idriess), 388
Last King of Scotland, The (Giles Foden), 64
Last of the African Kings, The (Maryse Conde), 460
Last Order, The (B. Ezenwa), 426
Last Plague, The (Meja Mwangi), 224
Late Bourgeois World, The (Nadine Gordimer), 523
Lau Siew Mei, *Playing Madame Mao*, 298
Lava of the Land. South African Poetry 1960–1996, The (ed. Denis Hirson), 383
Law-Yone, Wendy, *Irawaddy Tango*, 55
Lawal, Babatunde, *The Gelede Spectacle*, 426
Lawrence, Margaret, *The Diviners*, 182
Lawrence, T. E., *Seven Pillars of Wisdom*, 177, 199
Laye, Camara, *The African Child*, 402
Lazaroo, Simone, *The World Waiting to be Made*, 54, 485
Le Carré, John, *The Constant Gardener*, 86
Le Luu, *A Time Far Past*, 210
Le Roux, Etienne, 8, 49
    Magersfontein O Magersfontein, 8
    Seven Days at the Silbersteins, 49
Leap Year (Etienne Van Heerden), 350, 383
Leaven: A Black and White Story (Douglas Blackburn), 274, 322
Leaves from the Asvattha (Maureen Seneviratne), 540
Leaves of the Banyan Tree (Albert Wendt), 368
Lee, Sky, *Disappearing Moon Café*, 182, 495

Lee Kok Liang, *The Mutes in the Sun*, 313
Legendary Tales of the Australian Aborigines (David Unaipon), 388
Leipoldt, C. Louis, *The Valley*, 215, 350
Leopard, The (Vic Reid), 442
Les Grands Textes Indépendantistes (Andrée Ferretti and Gaston Miron), 345
Lessing, Doris, 524
  The Grass is Singing, 524
  The Sweetest Dream, 524
Letter to my Children (Kenneth Kaunda), 266
Letters from Martha (Dennis Brutus), 215
Letters of the Late Ignatius Sancho, an African, The (Ignatius Sancho), 71
Leung Ping-Kwan, *City at the End of Time*, 226
Levy, Andrea, *Small Island*, 71
Lewis, Ethelreda, *Wild Deer*, 49, 274
Liberated Bride, The (A. B. Yehoshua), 543
Life and Times of Michael K. (J. M. Coetzee), 49
Life in the Backwoods of New Brunswick (Frances Beavan), 151
Life Lived like a Story. Life Stories of Three Yukon Elders (eds Julie Cruikshank et al.), 182
Life of Family Planning Pioneer, Constance Goh, The (Zhou Mei), 520
Likimani, Muthoni, *What Does a Man Want?*, 505
Lim, Betty, *A Rose on my Pillow*, 519
Lim, Janet, *Sold for Silver*, 519
Lim, Shirley Geok-lin, 89, 519
  Among the white Moonfaces, 519
  Joss and Gold, 89
Lim Boon Keng and Song Ong Siang (eds), *The Straits Chinese Magazine, Vols 1–11*, 454
Lim San Neo, *My Life, My Memories, My Story*, 519
Lim Suchen, Christine, *A Bit of Earth*, 454
Lindsay, Jack, *The Blood Vote*, 45
Lines across Black Waters (Satendra Nandan), 261
Liswaniso, Mufalo, *Voices of Zambia: Short Stories*, 266
Little Mountain (Elias Khoury), 344
Lives of the Saints (Nino Ricci), 182
Living in America (ed. Roshni Rustomji-Kerns), 127
Liyong, Taban Lo, 193, 455
  The Cows of Shambat, 455
  Eating Chiefs, 193
Local Habitation (Louise Ho), 226
Lonely Londoners, The (Sam Selvon), 71, 114
Longest Memory, The (Fred D'Aguiar), 441
Looking on Darkness (André Brink), 49, 106
Looking through Glass (Mukul Kesavan), 419
Lord of Kinta (Eusoff Ragayah), 519
Loss of El Dorado, The (V. S. Naipaul), 186
Lotus People, The (Aziz Hassim), 233
Louis Riel: Selected Readings (ed. Hartwell Bowsfield), 428
Louw, N. P. Van Wyk, *Oh Wide and Sad Land*, 350
Love and Vertigo (Teo Hsu-Ming), 133, 170
Love in a Dead Language (Lee Siegel), 262
Love in Two Languages (Abdelkebir Khatebi), 309
Lovelace, Earl, 330, 442, 486
  The Dragon Can't Dance, 486
  Salt, 442
  The Wine of Astonishment, 330
Lucashenko, Melissa, *Steam Pigs*, 170
Lucy (Jamaica Kincaid), 42, 121
Lunatic, The (Anthony C. Winkler), 461

Lure of Ash, The (Isidore Diala), 471
Lwanda, John, *The Second Harvest*, 59
Lying Days, The (Nadine Gordimer), 49, 215

Ma Ma Lay, *Not out of Hate*, 9, 210
'*Mabo is the Turning Point for Justice*' (Kevin Gilbert), 276
McCall Smith, Alexander, 271
  The No. 1 Ladies Detective Agency, 271
  Tears of the Giraffe, 271
McCord, Margaret, *The Calling of Katie Makanya*, 11
McDonald, Roger, *1915: A Novel*, 535
Macgoye, Marjorie Oludhe, 193, 505
  Chira, 505
  The Present Moment, 193
McKay, Claude, '*Gordon to the Oppressed*', 324
Mackay, Kenneth, *The Yellow Wave*, 542
MacLennan, Hugh, *Two Solitudes*, 345, 405
McMillan, Terry, *How Stella Got Her Groove Back*, 460
Madonna of Excelsior, The (Zakes Mda), 383
Magala-Nyago, *The Rape of the Pearl*, 5
Magersfontein, O Magersfontein (Etienne Le Roux), 8
Magician's Wife, The (Brian Moore), 308
Magona, Sindiwe, *Mother to Mother*, 32
Mahabharata, 396
'*The Mahalakshmi Bridge*' (Krishan Chander), 403
Mahfouz, Naguib, 199, 339, 344, 456, 473
  Autumn Quail, 456
  The Cairo Trilogy, 199
  Miramar, 339, 344
  Palace Walk, 473
Mahjoub, Jamal, 310, 455
  In the Hour of Signs, 310
  Navigation of a Rainmaker, 455
Mahomet, S. D., *The Travels of Dean Mahomet*, 141
Mahood, Kim, *Craft for a Dry Lake*, 170
Maira, Sunaina and Rajini Srikanth (eds), *Contours of the Heart*, 127
Mais, Roger, 324, 330
  Brother Man, 330
  '*George William Gordon. A Historical Play*', 324
Making a Difference. Canadian Multicultural Literature (ed. Smaro Kamboureli), 327
Malabari, B. M., *The Indian Eye on English Life*, 141
Malaika (Arthur Dobrin), 505
Malan, Robin and Rochelle Kapp (eds), '*No Place Like*' *and Other Short Stories by Southern African Women*, 524
Malay Dilemma, The (Mahathir Bin Mohamad), 89
Malay Dilemma Revisited, The (M. Bakri Musa), 89
Malayan Trilogy (Anthony Burgess), 86
Malgonkar, Manohar, *The Devil's Wind*, 337
Malladi, Amulya, *A Breath of Fresh Air*, 328
Malouf, David, 70
  Fly Away Peter, 70
  Remembering Babylon, 70
Man Died: The Prison Years, The (Wole Soyinka), 65
Man from Glengarry, The (Ralph Connor), 151
Man of the Rising Sun (James Sebastian), 257
Mangalesvary, Ambiavagar, *Three Score Years and Twenty: Autobiography of an Eighty-Two Year Old Singaporean*, 519
Manganyi, Chabani, *Being-Black-In-The-World*, 75
Mangua, Charles, *Son of a Woman*, 193
Mankell, Henning, *Playing with Fire*, 224

Mansfield Park (Jane Austen), 441
Manto, Saadat Hasan, 80, 204, 253, 377
   'It Happened in 1919', 253
   Kingdom's End and Other Stories, 80
   Partition: Sketches and Stories, 204, 377
Map of Love, The (Ahdaf Soueif), 57, 115, 200, 509
Maps (Nuruddin Farah), 413
Marabi Dance, The (Modikwe Dikobe), 537
Maracle, Lee, *Ravensong*, 495
'Marginalia' (Kai Friese), 80
Maria (Leslie Netto), 519
Mariam: A Story of the Indian Mutiny of 1857 (J. F.
   Fanthorne), 337
Mark Twain's Weapons of Satire (Mark Twain), 449
Markandaya, Kamala, 26, 95
   The Coffer Dams, 26
   A Handful of Rice, 95
Markham, E. A. and Arnold Kingston (eds), *Merely a*
   Matter of Colour: The Uganda Asian Anthology, 52
Marlyn, John, *Under the Ribs of Death*, 182
Marson, Una, *Tropic Reveries*, 442
Martin, Catherine, *An Incredible Journey*, 170
Maru (Bessie Head), 271, 433, 523
Mashetani (Ebrahim Hussein), 479
Mashinini, Emma, *Strikes have Followed Me All My Life*,
   274
Mason, A. E. W., *The Four Feathers*, 177
Mason, Bruce, *The Pohutukawa Tree*, 369, 481
Mass (Francis Sionil José), 112, 311
Mass Transit (Maniza Naqvi), 321
Master Key(s) to Prosperity, The (M. Ogudu), 427
Master of the Crossroads (Madison Smartt Bell), 164
Master of the Ghost Dreaming (Mudrooroo), 43
Masterpieces of Urdu Ghazal (ed. K. C. Kanda), 396
Masters, John, 337, 407
   Bhowani Junction, 337
   Nightrunners of Bengal, 407
Matigari (Ngugi wa Thiong'o), 19, 193, 414
Mating (Norman Rush), 272
Matriarch, The (Witi Ihimaera), 306
Matshoba, Mtutuzeli, 75
   Call Me Not a Man, 75
   Seeds of War, 75
Mau Mau Detainee (Josiah Mwangi Kariuki), 86
Maugham, W. Somerset, *More Far Eastern Tales*, 454
Max Havelaar (Edouard Dowes Dekker), 129
Mayombe (Pepetela), 32
Mazrui, A. A., *The Trial of Christopher Okigbo*, 65
Mbise, Ismael R., *Blood on our Land*, 360
Mda, Zakes, 49, 96, 156, 319, 350, 383
   The Heart of Redness, 96, 156, 350
   'The Hill', 318
   The Madonna of Excelsior, 383
   The Plays of Zakes Mda, 49
   She Plays with Darkness, 318
Mea Cuba (Guillermo Cabrera Infante), 116
Meatless Days (Sara Suleri), 251, 321
Meeting of Streams: South Asian Canadian Literature, A
   (ed. M. G. Vassanji), 127
Melville, Herman, *Typee*, 147
Melville, Pauline, *The Ventriloquist's Tale*, 389
Memmi, Albert, *The Colonizer and the Colonized*,
   309
Memoir of Takao Fusuyama (Takao Fusuyama), 257
Memoirs (David Ben Gurion), 543

Memon, M. U., *An Epic Unwritten*, 377
Memories of a Nyonya (Queeny Chang), 519
Men in the Sun and other Palestinian Stories (Ghassan
   Kanafani), 344, 372
Merely a Matter of Colour: The Uganda Asian Anthology
   (eds E. A. Markham and Arnold Kingston), 52
Mhudi (Solomon T. Plaatje), 49, 215, 314
Mi Mere: Poetry and Prose from Solomon Women Writers
   (eds Afu Billy, Hazel Lulei and Jully Sipolo), 491
Mi Revalueshanary Fren (Linton Kwesi Johnson), 71
Middle Passage, The (V.S. Naipaul), 460, 486
Middlepost (Anthony Sher), 11
Midlands (Jonny Steinberg), 281
Midnight's Children (Salman Rushdie), 27, 60, 118, 137,
   204, 253, 258, 265, 286, 378, 407
Migrant's Story, A (Oswald Bonutto), 120
Miller, Alex, *The Ancestor Game*, 54, 103
Millin, Sarah Gertrude, 49, 215
   God's Step-Children, 49
   King of the Bastards, 215
Mimic Men, The (V. S. Naipaul), 7
Mine Boy (Peter Abrahams), 318, 322, 537
Minty Alley (C. L. R. James), 254
Miramar (Naguib Mahfouz), 339, 344
Mirrorwork: Fifty Years of Indian Writing, 1947–1997
   (eds Salman Rushdie and Elizabeth West), 27
Mishra, Sudesh, 123
   Diaspora and the Difficult Art of Dying, 123
   Tandava, 123
'Mission Statement' (Nadine Gordimer), 463
Mississippi Masala (dir. Mira Nair), 52
Mistry, Rohinton, 26, 60, 95, 137, 279, 435
   A Fine Balance, 26, 95, 137, 279
   Such a Long Journey, 60, 435
Mitra, Dinabandhu, *Neel Darpan*, 235
Mittelholzer, Edward, *Kaywana Blood*, 389
Mnthali, Felix, *Yoranivyoto*, 59
Mo, Timothy, 43, 86, 136, 364
   The Redundancy of Courage, 86, 136, 364
   Renegade or Halo², 43
Modern Arabic Poetry (ed. Salma Khadra Jayyusi), 344
Modisane, William Bloke, *Blame Me on History*, 49
Modjeska, Drusilla, *Stravinsky's Lunch*, 491
Mofolo, Thomas, *Chaka*, 314
Mohamad, Mahathir Bin, *The Malay Dilemma*, 89
Mohd, Tajuddin Samsuddin, *The Price has been High*,
   257
Monar, Rooplall, *Backdam People*, 230
Monenembo, Tierno, *The Oldest Orphan*, 161
Mong-Lan, *Song of the Cicadas*, 478
Monkey Beach (Eden Robinson), 182
Monkey Bridge (Lan Cao), 478
Monkfish Moon (Romesh Gunesekera), 540
Monsoon Victory (Gerald Hanley), 533
Montagu, Lady Mary Wortley, *The Turkish Embassy*
   Letters, 300
Moodley, Prabashini, *The Heart Knows No Colour*, 233
Moodie, Susanna, *Roughing It in the Bush*, 151
Moon Will Forever Be a Distant Love, The (Luis
   Humberto Crosthwaite), 155
Moonstone, The (Wilkie Collins), 337
Moore, Brian, *The Magician's Wife*, 308
Moor's Last Sigh, The (Salman Rushdie), 204, 419
'Morant Bay' (Francis Berry), 324
More Far Eastern Tales (W. Somerset Maugham), 454

Morgan, Bernice, *Random Passage*, 495
Morgan, Mary, *The House at the End of the Jungle*, 210
Morgan, Sally, *My Place*, 170, 326, 388, 452, 491
Morning (Savera), The (J. S. Kanwal), 261
Mort ne Veut pas de Moi, La (Yolande Mukagasana), 161
Moses, Daniel David and Terry Goldie (eds), *An Anthology of Native Canadian Literature in English*, 240
Moses, Wilson Jeremiah (ed.), *Back-to-Africa Narratives from the 1850s*, 56
Mother of 1984 (Mahasweta Devi), 354
Mother to Mother (Sindiwe Magona), 32
Mothers of the Revolution (ed. Irene Staunton), 102
Mouth Sweeter than Salt, A (Toyin Falola), 220
Mpanje, Jack, *The Chattering Wagtails of Mikuyu Prison*, 59
Mpe, Phaswane, *Welcome to our Hillbrow*, 224, 319
Mphahlele, Es'kia, *Down Second Avenue*, 49, 537
Mtshali, Mbuyiseni Oswald, *Sounds of a Cowhide Drum*, 75
Muddock, J. E., 337
    The Great White Hand, 337
    The Star of Fortune, 337
Mudrooroo, 43, 388
    Master of the Ghost Dreaming, 43
    Wildcat Screaming, 388
Muhammad. A Novel (Driss Chraibi), 309
Mukaddam, Sharf, *When Freedom Came*, 26
Mukagasana, Yolande, *La Mort ne Veut pas de Moi*, 161
Mukta, Parita, *Shards of Memory*, 52
Mukulu, Alex, *Thirty Years of Bananas*, 5
Mulaisho, Dominic, *The Tongue of the Dumb*, 266
Muller, Carl, *Children of the Lion*, 204
Mumbo Jumbo (Ishmael Reed), 468
Mungoshi, Charles, *The Setting Sun and the Rolling World*, 319
Munif, Abdelrahman, *Cites of Salt / Mudun al-milh*, 199, 361
Murambi, le Livres des Ossements / Murambi, the Book of Remains (Boubacar Boris Diop), 160
Musa, M. Bakri, *The Malay Dilemma Revisited*, 89
'Muse of History, The' (Derek Walcott), 187
Mutes in the Sun, The (Lee Kok Liang), 313
Mutswairo, S. M., *Zimbabwe*, 401
Mutuwhenua (Patricia Grace), 306
Mwangi, Meja, 19, 193, 224, 331, 413
    Carcase for Hounds, 19, 413
    Going Down River Road, 19, 193, 413
    Kill Me Quick, 19, 413
    The Last Plague, 224
    Taste of Death, 19
    Weapon for Hunger, 331
'My Autobiography' (Elizabeth Choy), 256, 519
My Brother, My Executioner (Francis Sionil José), 210
My Diaries 1888–1914 (Wilfrid Scawen Blunt), 115
'My Fathers Before Me' (Carl Sealey), 187
My Feudal Lord (Tehmina Durrani), 370
My Life, My Memories, My Story (Lim San Neo), 519
My Life and the ICU (Clements Kadalie), 274
My Life in the Bush of Ghosts (Amos Tutuola), 448
My Name is Red (Orhan Pamuk), 269, 362
My People Shall Live (Leila Khalid), 344
My Place (Sally Morgan), 170, 326, 388, 452, 491
My Village Captured Hitler (A. Adebayo), 426

Myths for a Wilderness (Ee Tiang Hong), 313
Mzamane, Mbulelo, *The Children of Soweto*, 75

Nadra Tragedy, The (Haja Maideen), 519
Nagarjuna, *The Fundamental Wisdom of the Middle Way*, 396
Nagarkar, Kiran, *Ravan and Eddie*, 286
Nagenda, John, *The Seasons of Thomas Tebo*, 5
Nahal, Chaman, *Azadi*, 27
Naipaul, Shiva, *North of South*, 52
Naipaul, V. S., 7, 108, 110, 186, 230, 460, 486
    A Bend in the River, 108
    A House for Mr Biswas, 230
    India: A Wounded Civilisation, 110
    The Loss of El Dorado, 186
    The Middle Passage, 460, 486
Nair, Mira (dir.), *Mississippi Masala*, 52
Naked Gods, The (Chukwemeka Ike), 471
Naked Island, The (Russell Braddon), 256
Naked Song, The and Other Stories (Mandla Langa), 32
Nandan, Satendra, 123, 261
    Lines across Black Waters, 261
    The Wounded Sea, 123
Naomi (Junichiro Tanizaki), 133
Napolo and the Python (Steve Chimombo), 59
Naqvi, Maniza, *Mass Transit*, 321
Narayan, R. K., *Waiting for the Mahatma*, 27
Nasreen, Taslima, *Lajja/ Shame*, 204
Native Title Business (ed. Joan Winter), 276
Navigation of a Rainmaker (Jamal Mahjoub), 455
Nazareth, Peter, 5, 52
    The General is Up, 5, 52
    In a Brown Mantle, 5, 52
Ndebele, Njabulo, 49, 383
    The Cry of Winnie Mandela, 383
    Fools and Other Stories, 49
Ned Kelly (Douglas Stewart), 268
Neel Darpan (Dinabandhu Mitra), 235
Nehanda (Yvonne Vera), 102, 524
Nehru, Jawaharlal, *An Autobiography*, *The Discovery of India*, 357
Nervous Conditions (Tsitsi Dangarembga), 101, 323, 421, 523
Netto, Leslie, *Maria*, 519
New, Christopher, *A Change of Flag*, 226
New Cauldron, The, 143
New Day (Vic Reid), 15, 324
New Ends, Old Beginnings (Louise Ho), 226
Newby, P. H., *Something to Answer For*, 199
Newell, Stephanie (ed.), *Ghanaian Popular Fiction*, 426
Newman, Rob, *The Fountain at the Centre of the World*, 43
Newton, Nerida, *The Lambing Flat*, 103
Next Episode (Hubert Aquin), 405
Nga Tau Tohetohe (Ranginui Walker), 481
Ngugi wa Thiong'o, 19, 86, 118, 153, 193, 270, 290, 332, 373, 414, 470, 505
    Devil on the Cross, 414, 470
    A Grain of Wheat, 19, 86, 193, 270
    (with Ngugi wa Mirii), *I Will Marry When I Want*, 470, 505
    Matigari, 19, 193, 414
    Petals of Blood, 19, 153, 193, 270, 332, 373
    The River Between, 19, 193, 414

(with Micere Mugo), *The Trial of Dedan Kimathi*, 19

Weep Not, Child, 19, 118, 193

Nguyen Qui Duc, *Where the Ashes Are*, 478

Niane, D. T., *Sundiata: An Epic of Old Mali*, 333

Nichols, Grace, *i is a long memoried woman*, 442, 501

Night Train at Deoli and Other Stories, The (Ruskin Bond), 165

Nightrunners of Bengal (John Masters), 337

1915: A Novel (Roger McDonald), 535

Nineteenth-Century Narrative Poems (ed. David Sinclair), 151

Nisanit (Fadia Faqir), 343, 372

Nkrumah, Kwame, *The Autobiography of Kwame Nkrumah*, 358

No Dram of Mercy (Sybil Kathigasu), 257, 519

No Longer at Ease (Chinua Achebe), 37, 107

No More Lullabies (Mafika Gwala), 75

No New Land (M. G. Vassanji), 327

No Place for a Nervous Lady (Lucy Frost), 491

'No Place Like' and Other Short Stories by Southern African Women (eds Robin Malan and Rochelle Kapp), 524

No Place Like Home (Yasmin Alibhai-Brown), 52

No Reino de Caliban, I (Manuel Ferreira), 91

No Telephone to Heaven (Michelle Cliff), 460

No Way Back (K. Antwi-Boasiako), 426

Non-Believer's Journey, The (Stanley Nyamfukudza), 102

None to Accompany Me (Nadine Gordimer), 523

Noonuccal, Oodgeroo, *We Are Going*, 388

North of South (Shiva Naipaul), 52

Northern Voices: Inuit Writing In English (ed. Penny Petrone), 240

Not Afraid to Live [Not Afraid to Remember] (Kim Ramakrishnan), 520

Not Even Shadows (Anne Ranasinghe), 540

Not Going to Vietnam (Garrie Hutchinson), 44

Not out of Hate (Ma Ma Lay), 9, 210

Notebook of a Return to my Native Land (Aimé Césaire), 15, 355

Novel without a Name (Duong Thu Huong), 210

Nua Nua: Pacific writing In English since 1980 (ed. Albert Wendt), 491

No. 1 Ladies' Detective Agency, The (Alexander McCall Smith), 271

Nwapa, Flora, 529

Efuru, 529

One is Enough, 529

Nwongo, D. I. (ed.), *West African Verse*, 37

Nyamfukudza, Stanley, *The Non-Believer's Journey*, 102

Nyonya Mosaic, A (Gwee Thian Hock), 519

Obasan (Joy Kogawa), 255, 345, 495

Obeysekere, Ranjini, *A Grief Ago*, 540

Of Women, Outcasts, Peasants and Rebels (Mahasweta Devi), 279

Ogali, Ogali A., *Veronica My Daughter*, 290

Ogola, Margaret, *The River and the Source*, 193, 224

Ogot, Grace, *Land Without Thunder*, 193, 332

Ogudu, M., *The Master Key(s) to Prosperity*, 426

Oh Wide and Sad Land (N. P. van Wyk Louw), 350

Okri, Ben, *The Famished Road*, 290, 426

Okurut, Mary Karooro, *The Invisible Weevil*, 5

Oldest Orphan, The (Tierno Monenembo), 161

Old Man and the Medal, The (Ferdinand Oyono), 290

Oliphant, Andries and Ivan Vladislavic (eds), *Ten Years of Staffrider, 1978–1988*, 75

Omowale, David, *A Season of Waiting*, 43

On a Darkling Plain (Ken Saro-Wiwa), 65

'On Lord Northbrook, the Governor-General of India' (Nava-Krishna Ghosha)162

On the Face of the Waters (Flora Annie Steel), 337

On Trial for My Country (Stanlake Samkange), 177, 350

Once Were Warriors (Alan Duff), 306, 369, 481

Ondaatje, Michael, 43, 182, 260, 279, 286, 327, 435, 458, 539, 540

Anil's Ghost, 43, 279, 286, 435, 458, 540

The English Patient, 539

In the Skin of a Lion, 43, 182, 327

Running in the Family, 260

One Day of the Year, The (Alan Seymour), 535

One is Enough (Flora Nwapa), 529

'One Viceroy Resigns' (Rudyard Kipling), 162

Ong, Pamela Siew Im, *Blood and Soil*, 519

Ong, Rose, 519

A Journey with Uncle Yankee, 519

Shirin Fozdar: Asia's Foremost Feminist, 519

Open Door, The (Latifa Zayyat), 339

Opland, Jeff (ed.), *Words that Circle Worlds*, 401

Opperman, D. J., *'Shaka'*, 314

Orange Tree, The (Carlos Fuentes), 42

Orchid House, The (Phyllis Shand Allfrey), 484

Ordeal in the Forest (G. Wachira), 19

Orji, Gabriel, *Stirrings in Canaan*, 471

Oroonoko and Other Writings (Aphra Behn), 186

Orphans of the Storm. Stories on the Partition of India (eds S. Cowasjee and K. S. Duggal), 377

Orwell, George, *Burmese Days*, 177

Osinya, Alumidi, *The Amazing Saga of Field Marshal Abdulla Salim Fisi (Or How the Hyena Got His!)*, 5

Osiris Rising (Ayi Kwei Armah), 373

Osman, Shaukat, *God's Adversary and Other Stories*, 435

Osuafor, Chris, *Tower of Glass*, 471

Osundare, Niyi, *Songs of the Marketplace*, 290

Other Secrets (Farida Karodia), 233

Our Children are Coming (Chukwemeka Ike), 471

Our Feet Walk the Sky (eds Women of South Asian Descent Collective), 127

'Our Lady of the Snows' (Rudyard Kipling), 107

Our Man in Havana (Graham Greene), 117

Our Own Country: Leading New Zealand Women Writers (ed. Sue Kedgley), 491

Our Sister Killjoy (Ama Ata Aidoo), 529

Our Sunshine (Robert Drewe), 268

Ousmane, Sembene, *God's Bits of Wood*, 37

OutLoud: An Anthology of Poetry from OutLoud Readings, Hong Kong, 226

Oyono, Ferdinand, *The Old Man and the Medal*, 290

Padmanabhan, Manjula, *Harvest*, 43

'Pak Utih' (Usman Awang), 313

Palace of the Peacock, The (Wilson Harris), 114, 186

Palace Walk (Naguib Mahfouz), 473

Palangyo, Peter, *Dying in the Sun*, 360

Palmwine Drinkard and his Dead Palm-Wine Tapster in the Deads-Town, The, 290

Pamuk, Orhan, 269, 362
  My Name is Red, 269, 362
  The White Castle, 362
Pan, Lynn, *Tracing it Home: A Chinese Journey*, 519
Pantomime (Derek Walcott), 330, 461
Paradise (Abdulrazak Gurnah), 413, 439
Paradise of the Blind (Duong Thu Huong), 112, 478
Park Mungo, *Travel in the Interior Districts of Africa*, 448
Parker, Kenneth (ed.), *Early Modern Tales of Orient*,
  300
Parkin, Andrew, 226
  From the Bluest Part of the Harbour, 226
  Hong Kong Poems in English (ed. with Lawrence
  Wong), 226
Parliament-House Embroidery: A Work of Many Hands,
  The, 491
Parmasad, Kenneth Vidia (ed.), *Indian Folk Tales of the
  Caribbean, a First Collection*, 127
Parsipur, Shahrnush, *Women without Men*, 242, 509
Partition: Sketches and Stories (Saadat Hasan Manto),
  204, 377
Pascali's Island (Barry Unsworth), 300
Pascoe, Bruce, *Ruby-Eyed Coucal*, 364
Passage to India, A (E. M. Forster), 177, 407
Patel, Kirit, *In Search of Tomorrow*, 52
Path of Thunder, The (Peter Abrahams), 106
Paton, Alan, *Cry, the Beloved Country*, 49, 215, 301,
  322, 537
Patriarch, The (Yeap Joo Kim), 520
Paulina Dlamini, Servant of Two Kings (eds H. Filter and
  S. Bourquin), 11
p'Bitek, Okot, 193, 332, 391, 414, 505
  Hare and Hornbill, 391
  Horn of my Love, 391
  Song of Lawino and Song of Ocol, 193, 332, 414, 505
  Two Songs, 505
  White Teeth, 414
p'Chong, Cliff-Lubwa, *Words of my Groaning*, 5
Pecson, Geronima and Maria Racehs (eds), *Tales of
  American Teachers in the Philippines*, 459
Pelted with Petals: Burmese Poems (Kyi May Kaung), 55
Pemulwuy – The Rainbow Warrior (Eric Willmot), 388
Penguin Anthology of Australian Women's Writing, The
  (ed. Dale Spender), 491
People of the Pear Tree (Rex Shelley), 257
Pepetela, 32, 350
  Mayombe, 32
  Yaka, 32, 350
Persaud, Lakshmi, 230, 501
  Butterfly in the Wind, 501
  Sastra, 230
Persian Requiem, A / Savushun (Simin Daneshvar), 361
Pestana, Artur Carlos Maurício *see* Pepetela
Petals of Blood (Ngugi wa Thiong'o), 19, 153, 193, 270,
  290, 332, 373
Petrone, Penny (ed.), *Northern Voices: Inuit Writing In
  English*, 240
Philip, M. Nourbese, *She Tries Her Tongue, Her silence
  Softly Breaks*, 501
Philippine Experiences of an American Teacher, The
  (William B. Freer), 459
Philippine Rebel, The (Maximo Kalaw), 449
Phillips, Caryl, 56, 71, 121, 410, 460
  The Atlantic Sound, 460
  Cambridge, 71

  Crossing the River, 56, 71
  A Distant Shore, 410
  The European Tribe, 121
Pickthall, Marmaduke, *Children of the Nile*, 473
Pilkington, Doris (Nugi Garimara), *Follow the Rabbit-
  Proof Fence*, 452
Pillai, Raymond, *The Celebration*, 123
Pillars of Salt (Fadia Faqir), 509
Pizarro (Richard Brinsley Sheridan), 162
Plaatje, Solomon T., *Mhudi*, 49, 215, 314
Plain Tales from the Hills (Rudyard Kipling), 165
Play of Zakes Mda, The (Zakes Mda), 49
Playing Madame Mao (Lau Siew Mei), 298
Playing with Fire (Henning Mankell), 224
Plays, Poems and Prose (J. M. Synge), 246
Plea for Emigration, A (Mary Anne Shadd Cary), 495
Pleasures of Exile, The (George Lamming), 15, 486
Plomer, William, *Turbott Wolfe*, 49, 215
Poems and Selected Translations (Regi Siriwardena), 540
Poems by Faiz (Faiz Ahmad Faiz), 370
Poetical Works of Marcus Garvey, The (Marcus Garvey),
  56
Poetry of Arab Women, The (ed. Nathalie Handal), 344
Pohutukawa Tree, The (Bruce Mason), 369, 481
*Poisoned Bread. Translations from Modern Marathi Dalit
  Literature* (Arjun Dangle), 204, 286
Poovalingam, Pat, *Anand*, 233
Port Elizabeth Plays (Athol Fugard), 49
Portrait of the Artist as a Young Man, A (James Joyce),
  246
Potiki (Patricia Grace), 42, 306, 491
Pouliuli (Albert Wendt), 368
Pregnant Clouds, The (Dominic Chipeta), 266
Premchand, Munshi, *Godaan (The Gift of a Cow)*, 279
Present Moment, The (Marjorie Oludhe Macgoye), 193
Prester John (John Buchan), 177
Price has been High, The (Tajuddin Samsuddin Mohd),
  257
Prichard, Katharine, 45, 388
  Coonardoo, 388
  Golden Miles, 45
*Pride against Prejudice: Reminiscences of a Tasmanian
  Aborigine* (Ida West), 406
Prince, Mary, *The History of Mary Prince*, 442
Pringle, Thomas, *African Sketches*, 433
Prison and Chocolate Cake (Nayantara Sahgal), 357
Proctor, Raja, *Waiting for Surabiel*, 438
Promised Land (Karel Schoeman), 281
Promised Land, The (Grace Ogot), 193
Prose and Poetry (Léopold Sédar Senghor), 436
Pule, John, *The Shark that Ate the Sun*, 123
Pulse (Wang Gungwu), 143
Purple Violet of Oshaantu, The (Neshani Andreas), 224
Pynchon, Thomas, *The Crying of Lot 49*, 468

Question of Power, A (Bessie Head), 319, 523
Quiet American, The (Graham Greene), 86
Quiros (John Toohey), 147

Racine, Jean Luc and Jeanne Racine, *Viramma: Life of
  an Untouchable*, 514
Rafidah Aziz: Sans Malice (Zhou Mei), 520
Ragayah, Eusoff, *Lord of Kinta*, 519
Rainbow Round My Shoulder (Ruth Ho), 519
Raj Quartet, The (Paul Scott), 253

Rajmohan's Wife (Bankimchandra Chatterji), 141
Ramakrishnan, Kim, Not Afraid to Live [Not Afraid to Remember], 520
Ramayana, 396
Ramgobin, Mewa, Waiting to Live, 233
Ranasinghe, Anne, 451, 540
    At What Dark Point, 451
    Not Even Shadows, 540
Random Passage (Bernice Morgan), 495
Rao, Raja, Kanthapura, 95, 98, 118, 204
Rape of the Pearl, The (Magala-Nyago), 5
Ravan and Eddie (Kiran Nagarkar), 286
Ravensong (Lee Maracle), 495
Ravikant and Tarun Saint (eds), Translating Partition, 286, 378
Ray, Satyajit (dir.), The Chess Players/ Shatranj Ke Khilari, 134, 162
Reddened Water Flows Clear (Jean Arasanayagam), 451
Redundancy of Courage, The (Timothy Mo), 86, 136, 364
Reed, Ishmael, 462, 468
    Flight to Canada, 462
    Mumbo Jumbo, 468
Reef (Romesh Gunesekera), 127
Rees, Ruutz, The Siege of Lucknow, 337
Refugee Boy (Benjamin Zephaniah), 410
Reid, Vic, 15, 324, 442
    The Leopard, 442
    New Day, 15, 324
    Sixty-Five, 324
Relatively Speaking (Joan Hon), 519
Remember Ruben (Mongo Beti), 533
Remembering Babylon (David Malouf), 170
Renegade or Halo² (Timothy Mo), 43
Report from the Flaming Fields of Bihar (CPI (M-L)), 354
Return of the Amasi Bird. Black South African Poetry, The (eds Tim Couzens and Essop Patel), 322
Return of the Moon (Stephen Watson), 433
Return to Childhood: The Memoir of a Modern Moroccan Woman (Leila Abouzeid), 309
Return to Paradise (Yusuf K. Dawood), 52
Revolutionary Poems in the Struggle against Colonialism: Timorese Nationalist Verse (Francisco Borja Da Costa), 136
Revolutions in My Life (Baruch Hirson), 215
Rez Sisters, The (Tomson Highway), 353
Rhone, Trevor, Smile Orange, 460
Rhys, Jean, Wide Sargasso Sea, 177, 442, 501
Ricci, Nino, Lives of the Saints, 182
Rich Like Us (Nayantara Sahgal), 27, 137
Richardson, Henry Handel, The Fortunes of Richard Mahoney, 409
Richardson, John, Wacousta, 159
Richler, Mordecai, Solomon Gursky Was Here, 151
Ride on the Whirlwind, A (Sipho Sepamla), 32, 49, 75
Riel: A Play In Two Parts (John Coulter), 428
Rifaat, Alifa, Distant View of a Minaret, 509
Rig Veda, 396
Rights of Passage (Edward Kamau Brathwaite), 113
Riot (Shashi Tharoor), 419
Rive, Richard, 'Buckingham Palace' District Six, Emergency, Emergency Continued, 106
River and the Source, The (Margaret Ogala), 193, 224

River Between, The (Ngugi wa Thiong'o), 19, 193, 290, 414
River of Fire (Qurratulain Hyder), 134, 251, 514
Robertson, James, Joseph Knight, 186
Robinson, Eden, Monkey Beach, 182
Rohmer, Sax, The Emperor of America, 542
Rooms are Never Finished (Agha Shahid Ali), 251
Roots (Alex Haley), 56
Roots of Freedom (Bildad Kaggia), 19
Rosca, Ninotchka, State of War, 311
Rose on my Pillow, A (Betty Lim), 519
Roughing It in the Bush (Susanna Moodie), 151
Rowson, Susanna, Slaves in Algiers, 468
Roy, Arundhati, 27, 43, 95, 110, 204, 286, 532
    The Cost of Living, 532
    The God of Small Things, 27, 43, 95, 110, 204, 286
Roy, Bhaskar, An Escape into Silence, 354
Roydhouse, T. R. (Rata), The Coloured Conquest, 542
Ruark, Robert, 19
    Something of Value, 19
    Uhuru, 19
Ruby-Eyed Coucal (Bruce Pascoe), 364
Ruganda, John, Floods, 5
Ruhumbika, Gabriel, Village in Uhuru, 193, 360
Running in the Family (Michael Ondaatje), 260
Rush, Norman, 272
    Mating, 272
    Whites, 272
Rushdie, Salman, 7, 27, 60, 71, 108, 118, 137, 204, 251, 253, 258, 265, 286, 321, 378, 407, 419, 432
    Midnight's Children, 27, 60, 118, 137, 204, 253, 258, 265, 286, 378, 407
    (ed. with Elizabeth West), Mirrorwork: Fifty Years of Indian Writing, 1947–1997, 27
    The Moor's Last Sigh, 204, 419
    The Satanic Verses, 7, 71, 251, 432
    Shame, 27, 108, 321
Rustomji-Kerns, Roshni, Living in America, 127
Ruthless Garden, The (Margaret Simons), 147

Sacred Hunger (Barry Unsworth), 442
Sacred Meadows, The (Abdul Hamid El Zein), 439
Sacrifice of Kreli, The (Fatima Dike), 96
Saguna (K. Sathianadhan), 141
Sahgal, Nayantara, 27, 137, 357
    Prison and Chocolate Cake, 357
    Rich Like Us, 27, 137
Sahni, Bhisham, Tamas, 204, 286, 378
Sakamoto, Kerri, The Electrical Field, 255
Saleh, Tayib, Season of Migration to the North, 7, 200, 414
Salt (Earl Lovelace), 442
Salt and Saffron (Kamila Shamsie), 27
Sam, Agnes, Jesus is Indian, 233, 421
Samkange, Stanlake, On Trial for My Country, 177, 350
Sancho, Ignatius, The Letters of the Late Ignatius Sancho, an African, 71
Sarachchandra, Ediriweera, Curfew and a Full Moon, 260
Saraogi, Alka, Kalikatha, 134, 204
Saro-Wiwa, Ken, 65, 328
    A Forest of Flowers, 328
    On a Darkling Plain, 65
    Sozaboy, 65

Sastra (Lakshmi Persaud), 230
Satanic Verses, The (Salman Rushdie), 7, 71, 251, 432
Sathianadhan, K., *Saguna*, 141
Satthianadhan, S., *Four Years in an English University*, 141
Scattered Songs (Arnold Itwaru), 230
Schoeman, Karel, 49, 281
    Another Country, 49
    Promised Land, 281
Scholar and the Dragon, The (Stella Kon), 454
Schreiner, Olive, 87, 156, 524
    The Story of an African Farm, 524
    Trooper Peter Halket of Mashonaland, 87, 156
Schwarz-Bart, Simone, *The Bridge of Beyond*, 442
Scorched-Wood People, The (Ruby Wiebe), 227
Scorpion Orchid (Lloyd Fernando), 210, 313
Scott, Gail, *Heroine*, 405
Scott, Kim, *Benang: From the Heart*, 170, 388, 452
Scott, Lawrence, *Ballad for the New World*, 187
Scott, Paul, 253, 407
    The Jewel in the Crown, 407
    The Raj Quartet, 253
Scott-Ross, Alice, *Tun Dato Sir Cheng Lock Tan: A Personal Profile by his Daughter*, 520
Scully, William, *Daniel Venanda*, 49
Sealey, Carl, 'My Fathers Before Me', 187
Sealy, Allan, 135, 165, 204, 396
    The Everest Hotel, 165
    The Trotter-Nama, 135, 204, 396
Season of Migration to the North (Tayib Saleh), 7, 200, 414
Season of Waiting, A (David Omowale), 43
Seasonal Adjustments (Adib Khan), 54, 60, 321, 326
Seasons of Thomas Tebo, The (John Nagenda), 5
Sebastian, James, *Man of the Rising Sun*, 257
Second-Class Citizen (Buchi Emecheta), 71
Second Harvest, The (John Lwanda), 59
Secret Life of Saeed, The (Emile Habibi), 344
Secrets No More (Goretti Kyomuhendo), 161
Seeds of War (Mtutuzeli Matshoba), 75
Selected Plays (Brian Friel), 246
Selected Poems 1965–1975 (Seamus Heaney), 246
Selected Poems (Louise Bennett), 113
Selected Poems (Guy Butler), 301
Selected Poems of L. S. Senghor, 436
Selected Poetry (Sipho Sepamla), 75
Selected Poetry (Mongane Serote), 75
Selected Short Stories from Pakistan: Urdu (ed. Ahmed Ali), 403
Selvadurai, Shyam, 27, 127, 438, 451
    Cinnamon Gardens, 27
    Funny Boy, 127, 438, 451
Selvon, Sam, *The Lonely Londoners*, 71, 114
Seneviratne, Maureen, *Leaves from the Asvattha*, 540
Senghor, Léopold Sédar, 355, 436
    The Collected Poetry, 355, 436
    Prose and Poetry, 436
    Selected Poems of L. S. Sénghor, 436
Sepamla, Sipho, 32, 49, 75
    A Ride on the Whirlwind, 32, 49, 75
    Selected Poetry, 75
Sergeant Musgrave's Dance (John Arden), 177
Serote, Mongane, 49, 75, 215
    Selected Poetry, 75
    To Every Birth its Blood, 49, 75, 215

Serowe (Bessie Head), 271, 323
Seth, Vikram, *A Suitable Boy*, 279, 357
Setting Sun and the Rolling World, The (Charles Mungoshi), 319
Settlers of the Marsh (F. P. Grove), 151
Seven Days at the Silbersteins (Etienne Le Roux), 49
Seven Pillars of Wisdom (T. E. Lawrence), 177, 199
Seymour, Alan, *One Day of the Year*, 535
Shabtai, Aharon, *J'accuse*, 543
Shadd Cary, Mary Anne, *A Plea for Emigration*, 495
Shadow from Ladakh (Bhabhani Bhattacharya), 26
Shadow Lines, The (Amitav Ghosh), 26, 204
Shadow of the Moon (M. M. Kaye), 337
Shadows of the Pomegranate Tree (Tariq Ali), 251
Shah Nawaz, Mumtaz, *The Heart Divided*, 378, 514
'Shaka' (D. J. Opperman), 314
Shake Hands with the Devil. The Failure of Humanity in Rwanda (Romeo Dallaire), 160
Shame (Salman Rushdie), 27, 108, 321
Shammas, Anton, *Arabesques*, 372
Shamsie, Kamila, *Salt and Saffron*, 27
Shamsie, Muneeza (ed.), *Dragonfly in the Sun. An Anthology of Pakistani Writing In English, A*, 27, 205
Shards of Memory (Parita Mukta), 52
Shark that Ate the Sun, The (John Pule), 123
Shaw, George Bernard, *John Bull's Other Island*, 177
She Plays with Darkness (Zakes Mda), 319
She Tries Her Tongue, Her Silence Softly Breaks (M. Nourbese Philip), 501
Sheaf Gleaned in French Fields, A (Toru Dutt), 141
Shelley, Rex, *People of the Pear Tree*, 257
Sher, Anthony, *Middlepost*, 11
Sheridan, Richard Brinsley, *Pizarro*, 162
Shiel, M. P., *The Yellow Danger*, 542
Shirin Fozdar: Asia's Foremost Feminist (Rose Ong), 519
Shock of Arrival, The (Meena Alexander), 127
Short Account of the Destruction of the Indies, A (Bartolomé de Las Casas), 441
Siddiqi, Jameela, *The Feast of the Nine Virgins*, 52
Sidhwa, Bapsi, 27, 118, 258, 378, 419
    Cracking India, 27, 118, 258, 378
    Ice Candy Man, 419
Siegel, Lee, *Love in a Dead Language*, 262
Siege of Krishnapur, The (J. G. Farrell), 337, 407
Siege of Lucknow, The (Ruutz Rees), 337
Silent Army, The (Chin Kee Onn), 256
Silko, Leslie Marmon, *The Almanac of the Dead*, 43
Simon, Ella, *Through My Eyes*, 388
Simons, Margaret, *The Ruthless Garden*, 147
Simushi, Lucy Siyumbwa, *I Nearly Killed a President*, 266
Sinclair, David (ed.), *Nineteenth-Century Narrative Poems*, 151
Singapore Grip, The (J. G. Farrell), 257
Singh, Ansuyah, *Behold the Earth Mourns*, 233
Singh, Khushwant, *Train to Pakistan*, 27, 378, 419
Singh, Rajkumari, *Days of the Sahib Are Over*, 230
Sinha, K. K., *The Star of Sikri*, 141
Sinyangwe, Binwell, *A Cowrie of Hope*, 266
Siriwardena, Regi, *Poems and Selected Translations*, 540
Sister Kate: A Novel (Jean Bedford), 268
Sitas, Ari (ed.), *Black Mamba Rising*, 50, 274
Sitt Marie Rose (Etel Adnan), 199
Siu, Shelley, *Barrier Breakers: Women In Singapore*, 520

Sivanandan, A., *When Memory Dies*, 27, 110, 205, 435, 438

Sivaramami, 'Two Poems', 451

Six Women's Slave Narratives (ed. Henry Louis Gates), 373

Sixty-Five (Vic Reid), 324

Slash (Jeanette Armstrong), 182, 353

Slave, The (Elechi Amadi), 447

Slave Book, The (Rayda Jacobs), 444, 524

Slave Girl, The (Buchi Emecheta), 447

Slave Song (David Dabydeen), 441

Slaves in Algiers (Susanna Rowson), 468

Sleeping on a Wire (David Grossman), 543

Sleepwalkers and Other Stories (Ehud Ben-Ezer), 543

Slums, The (Thomas Akare), 193

Small Island (Andrea Levy), 71

Small Place, A (Jamaica Kincaid), 42, 155, 237, 460, 501, 532

Smartt Bell, Madison, 164
  All Souls' Rising, 164
  Master of the Crossroads, 164

Smile Orange (Trevor Rhone), 460

Smith, Zadie, *White Teeth*, 71, 432

Smouldering Charcoal (Tiyambe Zeleza), 59

Smucker, Barbara, *Underground to Canada*, 462

Snake Cradle (Roberta Sykes), 406

Snow on the Saltbush (Geoffrey Dutton), 326

So Many Hungers! (Bhabhani Bhattacharya), 107

Society in the Dock (Prince Kagwema (Osija Mwambungu)), 359

Soga, Tiyo, *The Journals and Selected Writings of the Reverend Tiyo Soga*, 323

Sold for Silver (Janet Lim), 519

Solibo Magnificent (Patrick Chamoiseau), 113

Solomon Gursky Was Here (Mordecai Richler), 151

Somadeva, *Tales from the Kathasaritsagara*, 396

Something of Value (Robert Ruark), 19

Something to Answer For (P. H. Newby), 199

Son of a Woman (Charles Mangua), 193

Song of Lawino and Song of Ocol (Okot p'Bitek), 193, 332, 414, 505

Song of the Cicadas (Mong-Lan), 478

Songs of Empire (Constance Hollar), 186

Songs of Love and Death (Man Mohan Ghose), 141

Songs of the Marketplace (Niyi Osundare), 290

Sons for the Return Home (Albert Wendt), 123

Sorrow of War, The (Bao Ninh), 210, 478

Soueif, Ahdaf, 57, 115, 200, 251, 339, 344, 509
  In the Eye of the Sun, 251, 339, 344
  The Map of Love, 57, 115, 200, 509

Souls of Black Folk, The (W. E. B. Du Bois), 355

Sound of One Hand Clapping, The (Richard Flanagan), 170

Sounds of Cowhide Drum (Mbuyiseni Oswald Mtshali), 75

South African Indian Writings in English (ed. Rajendra Chetty), 233

Soweto Poetry (ed. Michael Chapman), 75

Soweto Stories (Miriam Tlali), 75

Soyinka, Wole, 65, 220, 236, 290, 373, 427, 471
  Ake. The Years of Childhood, 220, 426
  Death and the King's Horseman, 236
  Forest of a Thousand Demons (and Daniel Fagunwa), 290
  Ibadan: The Penkelemes Years, 471

The Interpreters, 373, 471
The Man Died. Prison Notes, 65

Sozaboy (Ken Saro-Wiwa), 65

Specimens of Bushmen Folklore (W. H. I. Bleek), 400

Spender, Dale (ed.), *The Penguin Anthology of Australian Women's Writing*, 491

'Spirit of Place' (Sonia Jabber), 265

Star of Fortune, The (J. E. Muddock), 337

Star of Sikri, The (K. K. Sinha), 141

State of Fear (Menán Du Plessis), 421

State of War (Ninotchka Rosca), 311

Staunton, Irene (ed.), *Mothers of the Revolution*, 102

Stead, Christina, *For Love Alone*, 105

Steam Pigs (Melissa Lucashenko), 170

Stedman and Joanna (Beryl Gilroy), 186

Steel, Flora Annie, *On the Face of the Waters*, 337

Steffler, John, *The Afterlife of George Cartwright*, 151

Steinberg, Jonny, *Midlands*, 281

Stenson, Fred, *The Trade*, 227

Stewart, Douglas, *Ned Kelly*, 268

Stirrings in Canaan (Gabriel Orji), 471

Stockade (Kenneth Cook), 409

Stone Country, The (Alex La Guma), 106

Stone Virgins, The (Yvonne Vera), 102, 524

Store up the Anger (Wessel Ebersohn), 49

Stories about the Partition of India (ed. Alok Bhalla), 204

Stories by Iranian Women since the Revolution (trans. Soraya Paknazar Sullivan), 242, 509

Story like the Wind, A (Laurens van der Post), 433

Story of an African Farm, The (Olive Schreiner), 524

Stow, Randolph, *Visitants*, 364

Straits Chinese Magazine, Vols 1–11, The (eds Lim Boon Keng and Song Ong Siang), 454

Stranger to Europe (Guy Butler), 537

Stravinsky's Lunch (Drusilla Modjeska), 491

Strikes Have Followed Me All My Life (Emma Mashinini), 274

Striking Chords (Sneja Gunew and Kateryna Longley), 326

Subramani, *The Fantasy Eaters: Stories from Fiji*, 123

Such a Long Journey (Rohinton Mistry), 60, 435

Suitable Boy, A (Vikram Seth), 279, 357

Suleri, Sara, *Meatless Days*, 251, 321

Sullivan, Soraya Paknazar (trans.), *Stories by Iranian Women since the Revolution*, 242, 509

Sundiata: An Epic of Old Mali (D. T. Niane), 333

Sunlight on a Broken Column (Attiah Hossain), 26, 204, 251, 514

Sunset at Dawn: A Novel about Biafra (Chukwumeka Ike), 65

Sunset in Biafra (Elechi Amadi), 65

Suyin Han, *… and the Rain My Drink*, 112

Swart Atilla, Die (P. P. R. Van Coller), 314

Sweetest Dream, The (Doris Lessing), 524

Swinging Bridge, The (Ramabai Espinet), 261

Swords of Kirinyaga, The (H. K. Wachanga), 19

Syal, Meera, *Anita and Me*, 127

Sykes, Roberta, *Snake Cradle*, 406

Sylvan, Fernando, *Timor Livo, A Lenda De Timor*, 136

Synge, J. M., *Plays, Poems and Prose*, 246

Tadjo, Veronique, *In the Shadow of Imana*, 161

Tagore, Rabindranath, *Home and the World*, 205

Takeyama, Michio, *Harp of Burma*, 257

Tales from the Kathasaritsagara (Somadeva), 396
Tales of American Teachers in the Philippines (eds
      Geronima Pecson and Maria Racehs), 459
Tales of the Tikongs (Epeli Hau'ofa), 368
Tamas (Bhisham Sahni), 204, 286, 378
Tan Tarn How, '*Undercover*', 298
Tanamera: A Novel of Singapore (Noel Barber), 256
Tandava (Sudesh Mishra), 123
Tangi (Witi Ihimaera), 306
Tanizaki, Junichiro, *Naomi*, 133
Target Amin (Konrad James), 5
Taste of Death (Meja Mwangi), 19
Taylor, P. J. O., *The Companion to the Indian Mutiny*,
      337
Te Ao Marama (Witi Ihimaera), 306, 481
Te Kaihau: The Windeater (Keri Hulme), 306
Tears of the Giraffe (Alexander McCall Smith), 271
Tejani, Bahadur, *Day After Tomorrow*, 53, 332
Tell Freedom (Peter Abrahams), 49, 106
Tempest, A (Aimé Césaire), 468
Temptations of Big Bear, The, 67, 277, 428
Ten Years of Staffrider, 1978–1988 (eds Andries
      Oliphant and Ivan Vladislavic), 75
Tenderness of Blood (Mandla Langa), 32
Teo Hsu-Ming, *Love and Vertigo*, 133, 170
Texaco (Patrick Chamoiseau), 328
Tharoor, Shashi, 27, 137, 258, 407, 419
      The Great Indian Novel, 27, 137, 258, 407
      Riot, 419
Tharu, Susie and K. Lalita (eds), *Women Writing in
      India*, 396
Thérieult, Yves, *Agaguk*, 240
Theroux, Paul, *Kowloon Tong*, 226
These Our Mothers, Or: The Disintegrating Chapter
      (Nicole Brossard), 495
They Who Do Not Grieve (Sia Figiel), 122
Thing to Love, A (Elspeth Huxley), 19
Things Fall Apart (Chinua Achebe), 7, 37, 220, 236,
      402, 426, 529
Third World War, The (Humphrey Hawksley), 458
Thirty Years of Bananas (Alex Mukulu), 5
This Other Eden (Richard De Zoysa), 541
Thomas, Audrey, *Isobel Gunn*, 227, 495
Thomas, Larry, *To Let You Know and Other Plays*, 123
Those That Be in Bondage (A. R. F. Webber), 230
Thoughts and Sentiments on the Evil of Slavery (Quobna
      Ottobah Cugoano), 447
*Three Score Years and Twenty: Autobiography of an
      Eighty-Two Year Old Singaporean* (Ambiavagar
      Mangalesvary), 519
Through My Eyes (Ella Simon), 388
Ti Marie (Valerie Belgrave), 186
Tiger Ladies, The (Sudha Koul), 265
Tilting Cages: An Anthology of Refugee Writings (eds
      Naomi Flutter and Carl Solomon), 410
Time Far Past, A (Le Luu), 210
Timeless Land, The (Eleanor Dark), 485
Timor Livro, A Lenda De Timor (Fernando Sylvan), 136
Tiruvalluvar, *The Kural*, 396
Tlali, Miriam, *Soweto Stories*, 75
To Every Birth its Blood (Mongane Serote), 49, 75, 215
To Let You Know and Other Plays (Larry Thomas), 123
To my Heart with Smiles (Wong Moh Keed), 520
To the Finishing Line: Champions of Singapore (Nick
      Aplin), 519

Toer, Pramoedya Anant, 112, 210
      The Buru Quartet, 210
      The House of Glass, 112
Toibin, Colm, *The Blackwater Lightship*, 224
Tongue of the Dumb, The (Dominic Mulaisho), 266
Toohey, John, *Quiros*, 147
Toomer, Jean, *Cane*, 442
Torn Apart (eds S. Gunn and M-M. Tal), 319
Tower of Glass (Chris Osuafor), 471
Township Plays, The (Athol Fugard), 215
Tracing it Home: A Chinese Journey (Lynn Pan), 519
Trade, The (Fred Stenson), 227
Tragedy of King Christophe, The (Aimé Césaire), 164
Traill, Catherine Parr, *The Backwoods of Canada*, 152
Train to Pakistan (Khushwant Singh), 27, 378, 419
Tran, Barbara *et al.* (eds), *Watermark Vietnamese Poetry
      and Prose*, 478
Tranquerah (Ee Tiang Hong), 454
Translating Partition (eds Ravikant and Tarun Saint),
      286, 378
Translator, The (Leila Aboulela), 251
Trap, The (Dan Billany), 533
Travels in the Interior Districts of Africa (Mungo Park),
      448
Travels of Dean Mahomet, The (S. D. Mahomet), 141
Trellwell, Michael, *The Harder they Come*, 330
Tremblay, Michel, *Les Belles-Soeurs*, 182
Trespassing (Uzma Aslam Khan), 26
Trial by Terror (Jean Arasanayagam), 451
Trial of Christopher Okigbo, The (A.mA. Mazrui), 65
Trial of Dedan Kimathi, The (Ngugi wa Thiong'o and
      Micere Mugo), 19
Tribal Hangover, A (James Goonewardene), 438
Triomf (Marlene Van Niekerk), 383
Trooper Peter Halket of Mashonaland, 87, 156
Tropic Reveries (Una Marson), 442
Trotter-Nama, The (Allan Sealy), 135, 204, 396
Truckful of Gold (S. Joshua L. Zake), 5
True Confessions of an Albino Terrorist, The (Breyten
      Breytenbach), 49
True History of the Kelly Gang (Peter Carey), 268
Truong, Monique T. D., *The Book of Salt*, 478
Truong Tran, *Dust and Conscience*, 478
Tucker, Margaret, *If Everyone Cared*, 388
*Tun Dato Sir Cheng Lock Tan: A Personal Profile by his
      Daughter* (Alice Scott-Ross), 520
Turbott Wolfe (William Plomer), 49, 215
Turkish Embassy Letters, The (Lady Mary Wortley
      Montagu), 300
Turquoise (Aamer Hussein), 251, 321
Turtle Beach (Blanche D'Alpuget), 77
Tutuola, Amos, 290, 448
      The Palmwine Drinkard, 290
      My Life in the Bush of Ghosts, 448
Twain, Mark, *Mark Twain's Weapons of Satire*, 449
Twenty-Two Malaysian Stories (Lloyd Fernando),
      313
Twilight in Delhi (Ahmed Ali), 419
Two Poems (Sivaramami), 451
Two Solitudes (Hugh MacLennan), 345, 405
Two Songs (Okot p'Bitek), 505
Two Thousand Seasons (Ayi Kwei Armah), 373, 447,
      529
Two Worlds of Jimmie Barker, The (Jimmie Barker), 387
Ty-Casper, Linda, *Wings of Stone*, 311

Typee (Herman Melville), 147
Tyrant's Novel, The (Thomas Keneally), 78

Uhuru (Robert Ruark), 19
Uhuru Street (M. G. Vassanji), 53, 414
Ulysses (James Joyce), 246
Umutesi, Marie Béatrice, *Fuir ou Mourir au Zaire*, 161
Unaipon, David, *Legendary Tales of the Australian Aborigines*, 388
Unchained Voices (ed. Vincent Carretta), 447
Under the Ribs of Death (John Marlyn), 182
'Undercover' (Tan Tarn How), 298
Underground to Canada (Barbara Smucker), 462
Unfortunately, it was Paradise (Mahmoud Darwish), 372
Unsworth, Barry, 300, 442
  Pascali's Island, 300
  Sacred Hunger, 442
Untouchable (Mulk Raj Anand), 95, 204, 403
Untreated: Poems by Black Writers (ed. Josie Douglas), 276
Unwalled City, The (Xu Xi), 226
Upanishads, 396
Upfield, Arthur, *The Bone is Pointed*, 388
Urquhart, Jane, *The Whirlpool*, 482
Usman Awang, 'Pak Utih', 313
Usne kaha tha aur amya kahaniyan (Chandradhar Sharma Guleri), 539

'Valediction' (Xu Xi), 226
Valley, The (C. Louis Leipoldt), 215, 350
Van Coller, P. P. R, *Die Swart Atilla*, 314
Van Der Merwe, Chris N. and Michael Rice (eds), *A Century of Anglo–Boer War Stories*, 8
Van der Post, Laurens, *A Story Like the Wind*, 433
Van Heerden, Etienne, *Leap Year*, 350, 383
Van Niekerk, Marlene, *Triomf*, 383
Vassanji, M. G., 53, 127, 251, 327, 414
  The Gunny Sack, 251, 414
  A Meeting of Streams: South Asian Canadian Literature (ed.), 127
  No New Land, 327
  Uhuru Street, 53, 414
Vatsyayana, *Kamasutra*, 262
Ventriloquist's Tale, The (Pauline Melville), 389
Vera, Yvonne, 102, 524
  Nehanda, 102, 524
  The Stone Virgins, 102, 524
Veronica My Daughter (Ogali A. Ogali), 290
Vijayatunga, J., *Grass for My Feet*, 27
Village in Uhuru (Gabriel Ruhumbika), 193, 360
Viramma: Life of an Untouchable (Jean Luc Racine and Jeanne Racine), 514
Visitants (Randolph Stow), 364
Visitation, The (Ahmed Essop), 233
Vladislavic, Ivan, *The Folly*, 281
Voices from Within Black Poetry from Southern Africa (eds Michael Chapman and Achmat Dangor), 49
Voices of Zambia: Short Stories (Mufalo Liswaniso), 266
Voss (Patrick White), 147
Voyage of Christopher Columbus, The (Cristóbal Colón), 186, 389

Wachanga, H. K., *The Swords of Kirinyaga*, 19
Wachira, G., *Ordeal in the Forest*, 19

Waciuma, Charity, *Daughter of Mumbi*, 19
Wacousta (John Richardson), 159
Waiariki (Patricia Grace), 306
Wainaina, Binyavanga, *Discovering Home*, 332
Waiting for Leila (Achmat Dangor), 106
Waiting for Surabiel (Raja Proctor), 438
Waiting for the Mahatma (R. K. Narayan), 27
Waiting to Live (Mewa Ramgobin), 233
Walcott, Derek, 114, 164, 187, 330, 461, 484
  Collected Poems, 114
  Collected Poems 1948–1984, 187
  The Haitian Trilogy, 164, 484
  'The Muse of History', 187
  Pantomime, 330, 461
Walk in the Night, A (Alex La Guma), 106, 215
Walker, Ranginui, *Nga Tau Tohetohe*, 481
Walter Rodney: Poetic Tributes (ed. Eric Huntley), 430
Wamweya, J., *Freedom Fighter*, 19
Wandering Girl (Glenyse Ward), 452
Wang Gungwu, *Pulse*, 143
Ward, Glenyse, *Wandering Girl*, 452
Warkentin, Germaine (ed.), *Canadian Exploration Literature*, 152
Wars, The (Timothy Findley), 345
Watene, Kenneth, *Dedan Kimathi*, 19
Water, Inc. (Varda Burstyn), 328
Water Wood Pure Splendour (Agnes Lam), 226
Watermark Vietnamese Poetry and Prose (eds Barbara Tran et al.), 478
Watkins, Leslie, *The Killing of Idi Amin*, 5
Watson, Stephen, *Return of the Moon*, 433
W. B. Yeats: The Poems, 246
We Are Going (Oodgeroo Noonuccal), 388
'We Could **** You Mr Birch' (Kee Thuan Chye), 89
We Took their Orders and are Dead (ed. Shirley Cass), 44
Weapon for Hunger (Meja Mwangi), 331
Weary Generations, The (Abdullah Hussein), 253
Webber, A. R. F., *Those That Be in Bondage*, 230
Webby, Elizabeth and Lydia Wevers (eds), 491
  Happy Endings. Stories by Australian and New Zealand Women, 1850s–1930s, 491
  Goodbye to Romance. Stories by Australian and New Zealand Women, 1930s–1980s, 491
Wedderburn, Robert, *The Horrors of Slavery and Other Writings*, 442
Wedding, The (Imraan Coovadia), 233
Weep Not, Child (Ngugi wa thiong'o), 19, 118, 193
Welcome to our Hillbrow (Phaswane Mpe), 224, 319
Weller, Archie, *Going Home*, 388
Wendt, Albert, 123, 368, 491
  Lali: A Pacific Anthology (ed.), 491
  Leaves of the Banyan Tree, 368
  Nua Nua: Pacific Writing In English since 1980 (ed.), 491
  Pouliuli, 368
  Sons for the Return Home, 123
West, Ida, *Pride against Prejudice: Reminiscences of a Tasmanian Aborigine*, 406
West African Verse (ed. D. I. Nwongo), 37
Wet Paint (Sharmini Jayawardena), 540
Whale Rider, The (Witi Ihimaera), 306
Whanau (Witi Ihimaera), 306
What Becomes of the Broken-Hearted?, 306

What Does a Man Want? (Muthoni Likimani), 505
Wheel and Come Again (Kwame Dawes), 330
When Freedom Came (Sharf Mukaddam), 26
When I Lived in Modern Times (Linda Grant), 543
When Memory Dies (A. Sivanandan), 27, 110, 205, 435, 438, 451
When Rain Clouds Gather (Bessie Head), 271, 523
Where the Ashes Are (Nguyen Qui Duc), 478
Where We Once Belonged (Sia Figiel), 122
Which I Have Loved (Ruth Ho), 519
Whirlpool, The (Jane Urquhart), 482
Whispers in the Wings (Frank Chipasula), 59
White, Edmund (with Adam Mars-Jones), *The Darker Proof*, 224
White, Patrick, *Voss*, 147
White Castle, The (Orhan Pamuk), 362
White Coolie (Ronald Hastain), 257
White Mughals (William Dalrymple), 134
White Teeth (Okot p'Bitek), 414
White Teeth (Zadie Smith), 71, 432
White Witch of Rosehall, The (Herbert G. De Lisser), 441
Whiteley, J. (ed.), *Four Centuries of Swahili Verse*, 391
Whites (Norman Rush), 272
Who Remembers the Sea? / Qui se Souvient la Mer? (Mohammed Dib), 308
Whole Armour and the Secret Ladder, The (Wilson Harris), 389
Why Are we so Blest? (Ayi Kwei Armah), 37
Wicomb, Zoë, 32, 50, 106, 384, 524
    David's Story, 32, 384, 524
    You Can't Get Lost in Cape Town, 50, 106, 524
Wide Sargasso Sea (Jean Rhys), 177, 442, 501
Wiebe, Rudy, 67, 152, 227, 240, 277, 428
    A Discovery of Strangers, 152, 240
    The Scorched-Wood People, 227
    The Temptations of Big Bear, 67, 277, 428
Wijesinha, Rajiva, 540, 541
    Days of Despair, 540
    The Lady Hippopotamus and Other Stories, 541
Wild Deer (Ethelrda Lewis), 49, 274
Wildcat Screaming (Mudrooroo), 388
Willmot, Eric, *Pemulwuy – The Rainbow Warrior*, 388
Wind Eagle and Other Abenaki Stories, The (Joseph Bruchac), 159
Wind You Say, The (Claudio Alcorso), 120
Wine of Astonishment, The (Earl Lovelace), 330
Wings of Stone (Linda Ty-Casper), 311
Winkler, Anthony C., 121, 461
    Going Home to Teach, 121
    The Lunatic, 461
Winter, Joan (ed.), *Native Title Business*, 276
Wolpert, Stanley, *An Error of Judgment*, 253
Woman' Impression of the Philippines, A (Mary Helen Fee), 459
Women at Point Zero (Nawal El Saadawi), 42, 509
Women of Resilience (Zimbabwe Women Writers), 102

Women of South Asian Descent Collective (eds), *Our Feet Walk the Sky*, 127
Women without Men (Shahrnush Parsipur), 242, 509
Women Writing in India (eds Susie Tharu and K. Lalita), 396
Wong Moh Keed, *To my Heart with Smiles*, 520
Woodcock, George, *Gabriel Dumont and the Northwest Rebellion*, 428
Words of my Groaning (Cliff-Lubwa p'Chong), 5
Words that Circle Words (ed. Jeff Opland), 401
Works of Kalidasa (Kalidasa), 396
World Bank Literature (ed. Amitava Kumar), 532
World of Strangers (Nadine Gordimer), 49
World Waiting to be Made, The (Simone Lazaroo), 54, 485
Wounded Sea, The (Satendra Nandan), 123
Wrath of the Ancestors, The / Ingqumbo Yeminyama (A. C. Jordan), 96, 323
Wright, Judith, *Half a Lifetime*, 491

Xu Xi, 226
    History's Fiction, 226
    Hong Kong Rose, 226
    The Unwalled City, 226
    'Valediction', 226
    City Voices. Hong Kong Writing in English (and Mike Ingham, eds), 226

Yaka (Pepetela), 32, 350
Yeap Joo Kim, 520
    Far From Rangoon, 520
    The Patriarch, 520
Year of Living Dangerously, The (Christopher Koch), 54
Yeats, W. B., *W. B. Yeats: The Poems*, 246
Yehoshua, A. B., *The Liberated Bride*, 543
Yellow Danger, The (M. P. Shiel), 542
Yellow Wave, The (Kenneth Mackay), 542
Yeo Lai Cheng, *Because of Mama and Poh Poh*, 520
Yoranivyoto (Felix Mnthali), 59
You Can't Get Lost in Cape Town (Zoë Wicomb), 50, 106, 524
Young Zamindar, The (S. C. Dutt), 141
Youth (J. M. Coetzee), 350
Yu Ouyang, *The Eastern Slope Chronicle*, 485

Z Town Trilogy (Achmat Dangor), 421
Zahran, Yasmin, *A Beggar at Damascus Gate*, 509
Zake, S. Joshua L., *Truckful of Gold*, 5
Zayyat, Latifa, *The Open Door*, 339
Zeleza, Tiyambe, *Smouldering Charcoal*, 59
Zephaniah, Benjamin, *Refugee Boy*, 410
Zhou Mei, 520
    Elizabeth Choy, 520
    The Life of Family Planning Pioneer, 520
    Constance Goh, 520
    Rafidah Aziz: Sans Malice, 520
Zimbabwe (S. M. Mutswairo), 401
Zimbabwe Women Writers, *Women of Resilience*, 102

Subject Index

This subject index includes only items that are NOT listed in the main List of Entries (pages xxii–xxvii).

Afghanistan, 85
African National Congress, 28–32, 72, 74, 214, 265, 273, 280, 379–82
Algeria, 3, 118, 153–4, 307–8, 340, 342, 463
Anglicist(s), 6, 139–40
Angola, 28, 29, 30, 31–2, 48, 90, 316, 318, 322, 347–50, 433
anthropology, 424–5
Arabic literature, 343
archaeology, 398, 399–400
Arctic, 150–1, 238–41
area studies, 198, 199, 207, 208
arms trade, 85–6
Arusha Declaration, 17
Asante, 402
asylum seekers, 77–8, 119–20, 318, 410
autobiographies, 516–19
Ava, Kingdom of see Burma

Bandung Conference, 339
Bangladesh, 24, 250, 320–1, 377
Barbados, 12–15, 114, 330, 440, 442, 483, 498–9, 501
Baring, Evelyn, 114–15
Belgium, 63–4, 117, 159–60, 412
Bengal, 234–5, 278, 353–4, 375, 512–13
Benin, 402, 425
Bhopal disaster, 328
Botswana, 29, 31, 222, 224, 271–2, 316–17, 319, 321, 521, 533
boundary disputes, 79–80
British Guiana, 83
Buddhism, 392–3
Burma, 9–10, 54–5, 111, 130, 231, 256–7, 516–17
bushranging, 267–8

Calcutta, 76–7
Cambodia, 109–11
capital(ism), 25, 39, 45, 73, 81, 87, 126, 174, 176, 212–13, 215, 219–20, 323, 340, 347, 412, 441, 467, 479, 486, 503
Castro, Fidel, 116–17
Ceylon National Congress, 25
Chatterjee, Partha, 200–3
chemical warfare, 83, 477
China, 130, 131, 132, 541–2
Christianity, 22–3, 24, 57, 63, 92, 134, 140, 288, 349, 367, 368, 411, 412, 415, 418, 424, 425, 426
citizen(ship), 34, 41, 48, 52, 119, 126, 268–9, 298, 307, 312, 315, 326, 371, 386, 409–10, 452, 464, 467, 480, 498, 512, 514, 535

Civil disobedience, 22, 23
Cold War, 28, 32
colonial subjects, 6, 120, 464, 471, 538
convicts, 81–2, 104
Cook, James, 144–5, 150
Corsica, 3
Crocombe, Ron, 364–8
Cuba, 11, 185–6, 449–50

Dahomey, 402
diamond mining, 321
digital nationalism, 126–7

East Africa, 16–20, 52–3, 188–95, 331–2, 390–1, 411–15, 438–9, 502–6
education
    in East Africa, 469–70
    in India, 139–40
    in Philippines, 459–60
    in West Africa, 470–2
Egypt, 83, 114–15, 174, 196–7, 248–9, 299, 309–10, 338–43, 456, 472–3, 508–10
emigration
    America to Africa, 55–6
    India to Caribbean, 228–30, 260–1
English language, 6, 89, 138–41, 282, 283–7
English literature, 6, 287–9
Enlightenment, 144–5, 167, 196, 200–1, 207, 244, 354, 362, 394, 543
ethnography, 398–9
Eurocentric, 74, 132, 209, 218, 371, 411, 430

famine, 62–3
Fanon, Frantz, 73, 90, 104, 152–3, 355
Flinders, Matthew, 145
France, 3, 9, 12, 39, 57, 63, 65, 117, 129, 148, 154, 163–4, 185, 198–9, 221, 307–8, 355, 360, 409, 435, 456, 472, 474–6
FRELIMO, 29, 30, 31, 32
Frontier Wars, 156
fur trade, 149–50, 179, 227, 238, 239, 492

G8, 38–9
Gambia, 33, 37, 446
Gandhi, Indira, 136–7
Gandhi, Mohandas K., 21–3, 97–8, 253–4
GATT, 154–5
Germany, 57, 63, 154, 160, 191, 198, 362, 543
Ghana, 33, 35, 36, 50–1, 58, 65, 118, 153, 220, 288, 357–8, 373, 401, 402, 425–7, 471, 556, 563
globalisation, 38–42, 125, 126, 207, 236–7, 273, 328, 379, 381–2, 531–2

gold mining, 102–4, 316–17, 321–2, 400
Guinea-Bissau, 90–1
Gupta period, 393

Harappa, 391–2
Hindi, 284–5
Hinduism, 92, 93, 415–18, 420
Hong Kong, 130
human rights, 32, 54, 59, 82, 83, 86, 119, 160, 264,
    280, 326, 352, 367, 381, 406, 410, 452
hybrid(ity), 7, 42, 113, 125, 169, 186, 293,
    305

immigration
    into Australia, 53, 77–8, 119–20, 169, 325–6,
        484
    into Britain, 52, 67–72, 120–1, 124–6
    into Canada, 121, 124–6, 149–50, 181, 462,
        492–5
    into Caribbean, 228–30, 389
    into New Zealand, 302
    into South Africa, 96, 315–18, 325
    into South America, 294
    into USA, 120, 124–6, 291
India, 6, 20–6, 59–60, 62–3, 76–7, 79–80, 91–5,
    97–8, 108–9, 118, 123–7, 134–41, 161–2,
    164–5, 200–4, 228–35, 248–50, 252–3, 263–5,
    278–9, 282–5, 333–7, 353–4, 356–7, 374–7,
    391–6, 407, 415–18, 431–2, 434–5, 457–8,
    511–14, 537–8
Indian National Congress, 21, 118, 278, 407
Indonesia, 84–5, 110, 128–9, 131, 135–6
intellectual(s)
    African, 36, 72–5, 270, 300, 323, 355, 390,
        469–71
    Arab, 341
    Caribbean, 13–14, 36, 253, 429–30, 486
    Indian, 109, 263, 284, 353
    Japanese, 130–2
    Latin American, 295
Iran, 82, 196–7, 241–2, 247–8, 283, 285, 342, 361–2,
    392, 431–2, 508–9
Iraq, 78, 84–5, 107, 118, 196–7, 199, 340–3, 360–1,
    362–3, 431, 438, 538
Iraq War, 44, 85, 118, 196–9, 363, 382, 538
Islamic studies, 197
Israel, 57, 118, 197, 338–9, 341–2, 371, 456, 508, 510,
    543

Jainism, 392
Jamaica, 12–14, 113–14, 146, 157, 185, 324–5, 329,
    429–30, 440–1, 460, 483–4, 497–501
Japan, 9, 23, 119, 122, 124, 128, 130–4, 225, 231,
    254–5, 256–7, 297, 474–5, 495, 516–18, 536, 538,
    541–2
    occupation by, 516, 518

kanaks, 122
Kenya, 7, 16, 17–19, 52, 83, 118, 189–93, 269–70,
    289, 318, 331–2, 357, 390, 412, 455, 469, 503,
    504
Khomeini, *Ayatollah* Ruhollah, 241, 431
Kinjekitile, 16, 17
Korea, 130, 131, 132
Kuwait, 84

Laos, 109–11
Lesotho, 29, 31, 316–17, 321, 381, 525
liberalism, 41, 45, 72, 110, 126, 134, 154, 173–5, 201,
    211, 212–15, 244, 298, 300–1, 347, 379, 389, 403,
    407, 432, 466, 535

Mabo, 168, 275–6, 280, 386, 405
Maji Maji Uprising, 16
Malawi, 29, 58–9, 224, 266, 272, 316, 318, 321, 348,
    357
Malaysia, 83, 84, 88–9, 142–3, 312–13, 453–4,
    516–18
Mali, 401
Mamdani, Mahmood, 34, 191
Manchuria, 130
Mandela, Nelson, 32, 379
Marx(ism), 14, 173, 212, 356, 502
Matabeleland, 100
Mau Mau War, 16, 17–19, 83, 191–2
Mbeki, Thabo, 379–82
memoirs, as genre, 507–8
Métis, 428–9
Middle East, 195–200, 360–1, 506–10
mining, gold, 102–4, 316–17, 321–2, 400
missionaries, 6, 122, 134, 139, 140, 149, 151, 165, 179,
    184, 212, 217, 219, 235, 239–40, 282, 284, 300,
    302, 314, 322–3, 348, 367, 411, 415, 416, 418,
    440, 470, 492, 506
modernity, 34, 121, 122, 126, 131, 134, 189, 192, 201,
    210, 212, 215, 235, 236, 249, 250, 284, 298, 331,
    336, 365, 367, 369, 373, 412, 508, 512
Morocco, 308–9, 340, 401
Mozambique, 14, 28, 29, 30, 31, 32, 59, 224, 316–18,
    348, 438, 523
MPLA, 29–32, 48
Muhammad ibn Abdallah, 247–8
Muslim League, 21, 24, 259–60, 374–5

Namibia, 29–32, 224, 321, 348, 349–50,
    523
nationalism, 191
    Afrikaner, 47–8, 212, 213, 346–7
    Arab, 339, 340–4
    digital, 126–7
    in Caribbean, 261
    in Ireland, 245
    in South-east Asia, 284–5
    Jewish ethnic, 532–4
    West African, 218–19
Negro World, 157
Nepal, 79–80, 538
New Zealand, 111, 301–7, 368–9, 480–1, 489
Nicaragua, 85
Nigeria, 33–4, 35–8, 64–6, 68, 235–6, 287–90, 333,
    401–2, 425, 464, 471, 526–8, 528
Non-Aligned Movement, 266, 339, 382
Non-Cooperation movement, 22–3
Nunavut, 240

Obote, Milton, 4, 5, 52
oil, 83–4
Oman, 83
Opium Wars, 225
oral history, 188–9, 218, 390, 500, 508–9,
    512

oral literature, 287, 289, 425–6, 528–9
Orientalism, 92, 94, 115, 134, 140, 198–9, 201, 282, 362, 395, 417
    Orientalist(s), 6, 91, 140, 262, 395, 416

Pacific exploration, 143–5
Pacific islanders, 121–3, 489–90
Pakistan, 24, 59–60, 108–9, 202, 250, 259–60, 263–4, 278–9, 320–1, 369–71, 374–8, 434; see also South Asia
Palestine, 57–8, 341, 342–3, 371–2, 508, 543
Pan-Africanism, 34–5, 372–4
Persian language, 283
Philippines, 310–11, 449–50, 459–60
plantations
    in Caribbean, 497–9
    in Ireland, 243–4
prophets, 413
publishing, 289

Quebec, 179–80, 345, 404–5
Quit India, 23–4

race, 47, 69, 70, 73, 88, 92, 94, 105–6, 125, 157, 167, 198, 218, 274, 276, 282, 293, 300, 304, 305, 327, 352, 354, 355, 366, 368, 372, 405, 410, 441, 452, 459, 460, 484–5, 488, 494, 498, 521–2, 534, 537
    and immigration, 125, 169, 325
    differentiation, 45, 46, 47, 88, 336
    domination, 28, 213, 316, 373, 379
    inter-racial marriage, 47
    inter-racial riots, 88
    race relations, 302
    racial pride, 157
    racialisation, 105, 300, 493–4
racial discrimination/racism, 21, 29, 30, 40, 169, 181, 212, 232, 254, 271, 280, 318, 324, 326, 345, 347, 349, 366, 372, 381, 387, 424, 430, 460, 462, 464, 465, 485, 498
    in Australia, 405–6
    in Britain, 68–70
    in South Africa, 105–6
Rastafarianism, 329
refugees, 60, 77–8, 119–20, 125, 149, 160–1, 202, 226, 318–20, 325, 371, 376, 409–10
RENAMO, 31–2, 59
Rhodesia, 29, 30–1
Rwanda, 85, 159–61

Said, Edward, 90, 115, 132, 198, 208, 343
San Domingue, 163–4
Sanskrit, 282–3
Seattle, 38–9
Senegal, 35–6, 118, 223, 435–6, 440
September 11, 39, 85, 86
sexuality, 262–3
Sharpeville Massacre, 28
Sierra Leone, 33, 35, 37, 56, 287, 424, 470–1, 527
Singapore, 210, 297–9, 453–4, 516–18
Smith, Adam, 154
social forums, 40–1
socialism, 3, 17, 68, 73, 90–1, 108–10, 116, 249, 263, 272–3, 313, 339, 348–9, 356, 358–9, 437, 479, 486, 539

soldiering, 534–9; see also Army, Indian National
South Africa, 7–10, 28–32, 45–50, 58–9, 72–6, 96–7, 105–6, 111, 156, 211–15, 221–2, 224, 232–3, 271–4, 280–1, 300–1, 314–18, 321–2, 346–50, 378–84, 398, 420–1, 432–4, 443–4, 521–3, 535–7
South Asia, 20–8, 79–80, 123–8, 200–6, 278–9, 282–7, 320–1, 391–7, 415–20, 434–5, 457–8, 510–15, 537–9
South-east Asia, 206–11, 256–7, 516–20
Southern Africa, 28–33, 155–6, 211–17, 232–4, 272–5, 279–82, 300–1, 313–15, 322–3, 346–52, 397–401, 420–2, 521–6
Soweto, 30, 74
Spenser, Edmund, 244
Spivak, Gayatri Chakravorty, 109, 204, 463, 467
Sri Lanka, 24–5, 26, 107–8, 202–3, 259–60, 278, 418, 434–5, 437–8, 514, 539–41; see also South Asia
Staffrider, 73–4
subaltern, 109, 203–4, 209, 282, 291–4, 337, 366, 369–71
Sudan, 35, 235, 251–2, 287, 309–10, 340, 401, 413, 423–4, 454–5
Swadeshi movement, 21
SWAPO, 29, 32
Swaziland, 29, 222, 316–18, 322

Taiwan, 130, 131
Tamils, 434–5, 437–8, 450–1, 514, 540
Tanzania, 5, 17, 29–30, 52, 189, 191, 265, 271, 288, 316, 331–2, 358–60, 429–30, 479–80, 504; see also East Africa
Tasman, Abel, 144
terror/terrorist, 78, 83, 85–6, 199, 264, 335, 347, 363, 457–8, 539–41
trade, 299–300, 448
    free, 154–5
    fur, 149–50
trade unions, 12, 31, 272–5, 322
Trinidad, 12–15, 113, 230, 253–4, 261, 329, 483–4, 486–7, 495, 499, 501
Tobago, 12, 14, 113, 329, 483–4, 486
Tunisia, 308–9
Turkey, 86, 196, 268–9, 299, 531, 534

Uganda, 4–6, 52, 125, 160, 190, 192, 222–3, 229, 235, 331–2, 390, 410, 413–14, 469, 503; see also East Africa
Union Carbide, 328
Universal Negro Improvement Association, 157
Urdu, 284–5

Vedic Age, 392
veiling, 506
Vietnam, 44, 109–11, 473–8, 534
    refugees, 77–8

West Africa, 33–8, 217–20, 287–91, 332–3, 401–2, 422–8, 444–8, 526–31
West Bank, 118
whaling, 238–9
witchcraft, 413
women, 26, 35, 192, 294–5, 317, 343, 366, 367, 376–7, 380, 487–531

World Trade Organisation (WTO), 38–9, 155
World War I, 21, 34, 130, 167, 532–9
World War II, 23, 28, 36, 117, 118, 130–1, 167,
    532–9

Xhosa, 96–7, 105, 155–6, 536

Zambia, 29–30, 58, 224, 265–7, 271, 316, 318, 321, 348
Zimbabwe, 28–9, 31, 58, 98–102, 156, 213–14, 266,
    271, 280, 316, 318, 347–8, 349, 350, 381–2,
    399–401, 413, 420, 523
Zulus, 10–11, 72, 156, 214–16, 313–14, 321, 349–50,
    380, 420–1, 536